DIETRICH BONHOEFFER WORKS, VOLUME 16

Conspiracy and Imprisonment: 1940–1945

This series is a translation of
DIETRICH BONHOEFFER WERKE
Edited by
Eberhard Bethge†, Ernst Feil,
Christian Gremmels, Wolfgang Huber,
Hans Pfeifer, Albrecht Schönherr,
Heinz Eduard Tödt†, Ilse Tödt

In memoriam
Timothy Lull
1943–2003

This volume has been made possible through the
generous support of the Lilly Endowment, Inc.; the
New England Synod, Evangelical Lutheran Church
in America; the Bowen H. and Janice Arthur McCoy
Charitable Foundation; the Lusk-Damen Charitable
Gift Fund; the Lutheran Theological Seminary at
Philadelphia; Pacific Lutheran Theological Seminary,
Berkeley; Trinity Lutheran Church, McMinnville,
Oregon; Trinity Lutheran Church, Tacoma, Wash-
ington; and numerous members and friends of the
International Bonhoeffer Society.

DIETRICH BONHOEFFER WORKS

General Editors
Victoria J. Barnett
Wayne Whitson Floyd Jr.
Barbara Wojhoski

DIETRICH BONHOEFFER

Conspiracy and Imprisonment

1940–1945

Translated from the German Edition
Edited by
Jørgen Glenthøj†, Ulrich Kabitz,
and Wolf Krötke

English Edition
Edited by
Mark S. Brocker

Translated by
Lisa E. Dahill

Supplementary material
Translated by
Douglas W. Stott

FORTRESS PRESS   MINNEAPOLIS

DIETRICH BONHOEFFER WORKS, Volume 16

Originally published in German as *Dietrich Bonhoeffer Werke*, edited by Eberhard Bethge et al., by Chr. Kaiser Verlag in 1996: Band 16, *Konspiration und Haft: 1940–1945*, edited by Jørgen Glenthøj, Ulrich Kabitz, and Wolf Krötke. First English-language edition of *Dietrich Bonhoeffer Works*, Volume 16, published by Fortress Press in 2006.

Jacket design: Cheryl Watson
Cover photo: Dietrich Bonhoeffer, 1944. © Chr. Kaiser/Gütersloher
    Verlagshaus, Gütersloh, Germany
Internal design: The HK Scirptorium, Inc.
Typesetting: Phoenix Type, Inc.

Library of Congress Cataloging-in-Publication Data

Bonhoeffer, Dietrich, 1906–1945. [Konspiration und Haft 1940–1945. English] Conspiracy and imprisonment, 1940–1945 / Dietrich Bonhoeffer ; translated from the German edition edited by Jørgen Glenthøj, Ulrich Kabitz, and Wolf Krötke ; English edition edited by Mark S. Brocker ; translated by Lisa E. Dahill with the assistance of Douglas W. Stott.
    p. cm. — (Dietrich Bonhoeffer works ; v. 16) Includes bibliographical references and index.
    ISBN-13: 978-0-8006-8316-0 (alk. paper)
    ISBN-10: 0-8006-8316-1 (alk. paper)
    1. Bonhoeffer, Dietrich, 1906–1945—Correspondence.   2. Theologians—Germany—Correspondence.   3. Political prisoners—Germany—Correspondence.   4. Bonhoeffer, Dietrich, 1906–1945—Imprisonment.
5. Church and state—Germany—History—1933–1945—Sources
6. Theology—Germany—History—20th century—Sources. I. Brocker, Mark S. II. Title. III. Series: Bonhoeffer, Dietrich, 1906–1945. Works. English. 1996 ; v.16.
    BR45 .B6513   1996 vol. 16
    [BX4827.B57 A4]
    230'.044 s—dc22   2006009218

The paper used in this publication meets the minimum requirements of American National Standard for Information Sciences—Permanence of Paper for Printed Library Materials, ANSI Z329.48-1984.

Manufactured in the U.S.A.

10   09   08   07   06   1   2   3   4   5   6   7   8   9   10

CONTENTS

Part 2
Essays and Notes

Part 3
Sermons and Meditations

General Editor's Foreword to Dietrich Bonhoeffer Works

SINCE THE TIME that the writings of Dietrich Bonhoeffer (1906–45) first began to be available in English after World War II, they have been eagerly read both by scholars and by a wide general audience. The story of his life is compelling, set in the midst of historic events that shaped a century.

Bonhoeffer's leadership in the anti-Nazi Confessing Church and his participation in the Abwehr resistance circle make his works a unique source for understanding the interaction of religion, politics, and culture among those few Christians who actively opposed National Socialism. His writings provide not only an example of intellectual preparation for the reconstruction of German culture after the war but also a rare insight into the vanishing world of the old social and academic elites. Because of his participation in the resistance against the Nazi regime, Dietrich Bonhoeffer was hanged in the concentration camp at Flossenbürg on April 9, 1945.

Yet Bonhoeffer's enduring contribution is not just his moral example but his theology as well. As a student in Tübingen, Berlin, and at Union Theological Seminary in New York—where he also was associated for a time with the Abyssinian Baptist Church in Harlem—and as a participant in the European ecumenical movement, Bonhoeffer became known as one of the few figures of the 1930s with a comprehensive and nuanced grasp of both German- and English-language theology. His thought resonates with a prescience, subtlety, and maturity that continually belies the youth of the thinker.

In 1986 the Chr. Kaiser Verlag, now part of Gütersloher Verlagshaus, marked the eightieth anniversary of Bonhoeffer's birth by issuing the first of the sixteen volumes of the definitive German edition of his writings, the *Dietrich Bonhoeffer Werke (DBW)*. The final volume of this monumental critical edition appeared in Berlin in the spring of 1998.

Preliminary discussions about an English-language edition *(DBWE)* began even as the German series was beginning to emerge. As a consequence, the International Bonhoeffer Society, English Language Section, formed an editorial board, initially chaired by Robin Lovin, assisted by Mark Brocker, to undertake this project. Since 1993 the *Dietrich Bonhoeffer Works,* English edition, has had its institutional home at the Lutheran Theological Seminary in Philadelphia. From 1993 through 2004 work on this series proceeded under the leadership of the general editor and project director, Wayne Whitson Floyd Jr., and its executive director, Clifford J. Green, with Victoria J. Barnett joining the staff in 2002 as associate general editor and then in 2004 as a second general editor for the English edition.

The *Dietrich Bonhoeffer Works* provides the English-speaking world with an entirely new, complete, and unabridged translation of the written legacy of one of the twentieth century's most notable theologians. The success of this edition is based foremost on the gifts and dedication of the translators producing these new volumes, upon which all the other contributions of this series depend.

The *DBWE* includes a large amount of material appearing in English for the first time. Key terms are now translated consistently throughout the corpus, with special attention being paid to accepted English equivalents of technical theological and philosophical concepts.

This authoritative English edition strives, above all, to be true to the language, the style, and—most importantly—the theology of Bonhoeffer's writings. Translators have sought, nonetheless, to present Bonhoeffer's words in a manner that is sensitive to issues of gender in the language they employ. The translators and editors of the present volume employed gender-inclusive language insofar as it was deemed possible without distorting Bonhoeffer's meaning or unjustifiably dissociating him from his own time.

At times Bonhoeffer's theology sounds fresh and modern, not because the translators have made it so, but because his language still speaks with a hardy contemporaneity even after more than half a century. In other instances, Bonhoeffer sounds more remote, a product of another era, not because of any lack of facility by the translators and editors, but because his concerns and rhetoric are in certain ways bound inextricably to a time that is past.

These volumes include introductions written by the editor(s) of each volume of the English edition, footnotes provided by Bonhoeffer, notes added by the editors of the German and the English editions, and afterwords composed by the editor(s) of the German edition. In addition, the volumes provide tables of abbreviations used in the editorial apparatus, as well as bibliographies that list sources used by Bonhoeffer, literature consulted by the editors, and other works related to each particular volume. Finally, the volumes contain pertinent chronologies, charts, and indexes of scriptural references, names, and subjects.

The layout of the English edition has retained Bonhoeffer's manner of organizing his publications, sometimes into chapters and at other times merely by sections or unnumbered manuscripts. The *DBWE* also reproduces Bonhoeffer's original paragraphing (exceptions are noted by a ¶ symbol to indicate any paragraph break added by the editors of the English edition or by conventions explained in the introductions written by the editor[s] of specific volumes). The pagination of the *DBW* German critical edition is indicated in the outer margins of the pages of the translated text. Text omitted in the German edition is indicated by three ellipsis points enclosed in square brackets, unless otherwise noted. At times, for the sake of precision and clarity of translation, a word or phrase that has been translated is provided in its original language, set within square brackets at the appropriate point in the text. Biblical citations come from the New Revised Standard Version (NRSV), unless otherwise noted.

Each volume in series B of the *DBWE*, numbered 9–16, contains collected writings from a particular period of Bonhoeffer's life. These volumes, which appear in chronological order, are each divided into three main parts, each of which also is arranged chronologically: (1) letters, journals, documents; (2) essays, seminar papers, papers, lectures, compositions; (3) sermons, meditations, catechetical writings, exegetical writings. Each item within each part—each separate letter, note, essay, sermon, and so on—is numbered consecutively from the start of each of the three major parts.

Bonhoeffer's own footnotes—which are indicated in the body of the text by plain, superscripted numbers—are reproduced in precisely the same numerical sequence as they appear in the German critical edition, complete with his idiosyncrasies of documentation. In these, as in the accompanying editorial notes, existing English translations of books and articles have been substituted for their counterparts in other languages whenever available. The edition of a work that was consulted by Bonhoeffer himself can be ascertained by consulting the bibliography at the end of each volume. When a non-English title is not listed individually in the bibliography (along with an English translation of the title), a translation of each title has been provided for the English reader within the footnote or editorial note in which it is cited.

The editorial notes, which are indicated in the body of the text by superscripted numbers in square brackets—except in *DBWE* 5, where they are indicated by plain, superscripted numbers—provide information on the intellectual, ecclesiastical, social, and political context of Bonhoeffer's pursuits during the first half of the twentieth century. These are based on the scholarship of the German critical edition; they have been supplemented by the contributions of the editors and translators of the English edition. In the present volume, all additions to or revisions of the German editors' notes are surrounded by square brackets and initialed by Mark Brocker, the editor of this volume. When any previously translated material is quoted within an

editorial note in altered form—indicated by the notation [trans. altered]—
such changes should be assumed to be the responsibility of the translator(s).
Page numbers in editorial note citations occur in the order of their relative
importance in the editor's judgment, sometimes leading to nonsequential
page references from a particular work.

Bibliographies at the end of each volume provide the complete information for each written source that Bonhoeffer or the various editors have
mentioned in the current volume. References to the papers and personal
library that had belonged to Bonhoeffer and that survived the war, as well
as pertinent correspondence and other documents still in private hands
and other archives, are cataloged in the *Nachlaß Dietrich Bonhoeffer* volume
edited by Eberhard Bethge and Dietrich Meyer. References to all such
material are indicated within the *Dietrich Bonhoeffer Works* by the abbreviation
NL, followed by the corresponding reference code within that published
index. The appendix "Unpublished Material from Bonhoeffer's Literary
Estate, 1940–1945" lists those documents that have not been included in
the *DBW* or the *DBWE* volume.

The production of any individual volume of the *Dietrich Bonhoeffer Works*
requires the financial assistance of numerous individuals and organizations,
whose support is duly noted on the verso of the half-title page. In addition,
the editor's introduction of each volume acknowledges those persons who
have assisted in a particular way with the production of the English edition
of that text. A special note of gratitude, however, is owed to all those prior
translators, editors, and publishers of various portions of Bonhoeffer's literary legacy who heretofore have made available to the English-speaking
world the writings of this remarkable theologian.

This English edition depends especially on the careful scholarship of all
those who labored to produce the critical German edition, completed in April
1998, from which these translations have been made. Their work has been
overseen by a board of general editors—responsible for both the concept
and the content of the German edition—composed of Eberhard Bethge†,
Ernst Feil, Christian Gremmels, Wolfgang Huber (spokesperson for the German editorial board), Hans Pfeifer (who still serves as the ongoing liaison
between the German and the English editorial board), Albrecht Schönherr,
Heinz Eduard Tödt†, and Ilse Tödt.

The ongoing work of the present English edition is overseen by the Edito-
rial Board of the *Dietrich Bonhoeffer Works* (Gaylon Barker, Victoria Barnett,
Mark Brocker, Keith Clements, John de Gruchy, Peter Frick, Clifford Green,
Barry Harvey, Geffrey B. Kelly, Reinhard Krauss, Michael Lukens, Larry Ras-
mussen, Martin Rumscheidt, and Barbara Wojhoski), with the support of its
Advisory Committee (Jim Burtness, Barbara Green, J. Patrick Kelley, Robin

Lovin, Nancy Lukens, Paul Matheny, and Mary Nebelsick). With the publication of *Conspiracy and Imprisonment: 1940–1945*, the general editorial work of Wayne Whitson Floyd comes to an end, as he assumes a new position as director of the Center for Christian Formation at the Cathedral College of Washington National Cathedral, Washington, D.C. Beginning in November 2004, Victoria J. Barnett and Barbara Wojhoski assumed the role of general editors of the English edition. Clifford J. Green continues in his role of executive director.

The deepest thanks for their support of this undertaking is owed, as well, to the various members, friends, and benefactors of the International Bonhoeffer Society, especially the Lilly Endowment, Inc. and the Thrivent Financial Foundation for Lutherans; to the National Endowment for the Humanities, which supported this project during its inception; to the Lutheran Theological Seminary at Philadelphia and its former Auxiliary who have provided space on the LTSP campus specifically for the purpose of facilitating these publications; and to our publisher, Fortress Press. The mutual respect and open collaboration required by a project such as this is fitting testimony to the spirit of Dietrich Bonhoeffer, who was himself always so attentive to the challenges and creative mystery of authentic community—and the ever-deepening collegiality that is engendered by our social nature as human beings.

Special mention must be made of the priceless contribution made to all Bonhoeffer scholarship, especially the *Dietrich Bonhoeffer Werke*, by Eberhard Bethge, who died on March 18, 2000. Eberhard was Dietrich's student, then friend and collaborator, later his editor and biographer—and also the husband of Bonhoeffer's niece Renate Schleicher. His impact on this English edition of the *Dietrich Bonhoeffer Works*—and on those persons whose labor has brought it about—is immeasurable. Everyone who meets Dietrich Bonhoeffer in the form of his printed words owes a never-ending debt of gratitude to this remarkable human being, Eberhard Bethge, who was almost single-handedly responsible for assuring that Bonhoeffer's legacy would endure for us and generations to come. With this volume we also especially recognize the contributions to our knowledge of Bonhoeffer, his family, and his times made by Renate Bethge, in honor of the celebration of her eightieth birthday.

Wayne Whitson Floyd Jr., General Editor and Project Director
January 27, 1995
The Fiftieth Anniversary of the Liberation of Auschwitz
Seventh revision on July 22, 2005

Abbreviations

BA	Bundesarchiv
CC	*Christ the Center*
DB-ER	*Dietrich Bonhoeffer: A Biography* (Fortress Press, rev. ed., 2000)
DBW	*Dietrich Bonhoeffer Werke,* German edition
DBWE	*Dietrich Bonhoeffer Works,* English edition
GS	*Gesammelte Schriften*
LKA	Landeskirchliches Archiv
LPL	Lambeth Palace Library
LPP	*Letters and Papers from Prison* (Simon & Schuster, 1997)
LW	*Luther's Works,* American edition
MW	*Die Mündige Welt*
NL	*Nachlaß Dietrich Bonhoeffer*
NL-Bibl.	Restbibliothek Bonhoeffers in *Nachlaß Dietrich Bonhoeffer* (supplement to the literary estate of Dietrich Bonhoeffer)
NRSV	New Revised Standard Version
SD	Sicherheitsdienst (Security Service)
SS	Schutzstaffel
WA	Weimar Ausgabe (Weimar edition), Martin Luther
WCC	World Council of Churches
ZE	*Zettelnotizen für eine "Ethik"*

MARK S. BROCKER

EDITOR'S INTRODUCTION
TO THE ENGLISH EDITION

Sharing Germany's Destiny

ON JUNE 20, 1939, Dietrich Bonhoeffer made his fateful decision to return to Germany from the United States. In a letter to Reinhold Niebuhr he explained his decision:

> I have made a mistake in coming to America. I must live through this difficult period of our national history with the Christian people of Germany. I will have no right to participate in the reconstruction of Christian life in Germany after the war if I do not share the trials of this time with my people. . . . Christians in Germany will face the terrible alternative of either willing the defeat of their nation in order that Christian civilization may survive, or willing the victory of their nation and thereby destroying civilization. I know which of these alternatives I must choose; but I cannot make this choice in security.[1]

Bonhoeffer returned to Nazi Germany with a sense of personal certainty and moral clarity, but it would be the surrender of France one year later, on June 17, 1940, that put him on his ultimate collision course with the Nazi regime and sealed his involvement in the conspiracy to overthrow Hitler. As his closest friend and colleague Eberhard Bethge narrates, on that day he and Bonhoeffer were in the Baltic village of Memel (now part of Lithuania),

---

[1.] *DB-ER*, 655.

1

conducting the first of three visitations by Bonhoeffer to eastern Prussia on behalf of the Confessing Church. That morning Bonhoeffer had attended a pastors' meeting. That evening he was scheduled to preach at a Confessing Church service.[2] In the afternoon Bonhoeffer and Bethge were relaxing in an open-air café when suddenly a special announcement came over the loudspeaker: "France has surrendered!" Bethge writes:

> The people around the tables could hardly contain themselves; they jumped up, and some even climbed on the chairs. With outstretched arms they sang "*Deutschland, Deutschland über alles*" and the Horst Wessel song.[3] We had stood up, too. Bonhoeffer raised his arm in the regulation Hitler salute, while I stood there dazed. "Raise your arm! Are you crazy?" he whispered to me, and later: "We shall have to run risks for very different things now, but not for that salute!"[4]

It was at this point, Bethge asserts, that Bonhoeffer's "double life" truly began. This Confessing Church pastor and theologian became deeply involved in the resistance movement against Hitler and the Nazis. While Bonhoeffer and his friends in the resistance continued to hope that military defeat or difficulties would bring down Hitler and the Nazis, it had become obvious that this would not happen soon. With Bonhoeffer's capacity to discern the reality of a given situation, he realized at the café in Memel that there would be no simple return to the way things had been prior to June 17.[5]

For the next three years, until his arrest on April 5, 1943, Bonhoeffer lived an unsettled life. He became a courier for the resistance group operating out of the Office of Military Intelligence (the Abwehr), even as he continued to teach and minister to the young seminarians and pastors of the Confessing Church. The restrictions placed on him by Nazi authorities prevented him from publishing, speaking in public, or traveling freely. He was constantly concerned about how he and Eberhard Bethge could evade military service. All these factors complicated his daily life and professional situation. Throughout this period his two primary vocational foci remained theological reflection and participation in the conspiracy. These two foci were inextricably connected and complemented each other.[6] The more

---

[2.] See 1/10 and *DB-ER*, 681.

[3.] Horst Wessel was a Nazi party member killed in a street scuffle in 1930; the "Horst Wessel song" became the Nazi party anthem.

[4.] See *DB-ER*, 681. In a June 21, 1940, letter to his parents, Bonhoeffer alluded to the surrender of France and to the way in which this event preoccupied his thoughts day and night, even into his dreams (1/12).

[5.] See *DB-ER*, 684.

[6.] Jørgen Glenthøj, Ulrich Kabitz, and Wolf Krötke stressed this point in their foreword to the German edition of this volume; see *DBW* 16:2.

deeply Bonhoeffer became involved in the conspiracy, the more deeply he became aware of the "profound this-worldliness of Christianity."[7]

On Behalf of the Confessing Church

By March 1940—the date of the first letter in this volume—the *Kirchenkampf*, or German Church Struggle, was largely over, yet its consequences within the German Evangelical Church would continue to be felt throughout the war years.[8] The Nazi policy of *Gleichschaltung* (literally, "switching into the same gear") of the churches had failed. Yet while the nationalist German Christian movement had failed in its goal of creating a nazified Reich church, it was represented in many of the regional church governments throughout Nazi Germany, and in several regions, such as Thuringia, it controlled the church. The Confessing Church—Bonhoeffer's church—was strongest in the provincial churches of the Evangelical Church of the Old Prussian Union. By the beginning of the war, the German church landscape consisted predominantly of thousands of parishes that sought to remain "neutral" with regard to church and national politics, with scattered German Christian parishes and a committed core of Confessing parishes.

The internal battles between these factions continued to divide the church and its leaders, and they provide the background for many of the documents in this volume, including Bonhoeffer's letters to his former Finkenwalde seminarians. Bonhoeffer remained an outspoken advocate of the Confessing Church, its founding document, the Barmen Declaration,[9] and the more radical position that the group had taken at the Dahlem synod in October 1934.[10] Throughout the 1930s, Bonhoeffer tried to persuade the

---

[7.] Bonhoeffer first used this phrase in his letter to Eberhard Bethge the day after the failure of the July 20 plot to assassinate Hitler, where he wrote that "during the last year or so I've come to know and understand more and more the profound this-worldliness of Christianity" (*LPP*, 369). He had spent that year in prison and had also undergone the severe trials of being interrogated. The experiences of imprisonment and interrogation had clarified for him in a powerful way the "this-worldliness of Christianity." In the documents in this volume written before his arrest, we can see the elements of this concept. See, for example, Bonhoeffer's discussion of the genuine worldliness of the worldly orders under the dominion of Christ in "'Personal' and 'Objective' Ethics" (2/13) or his critique of "two kingdoms" thinking in "Christ, Reality, and Good" (*DBWE* 6:55–68).

[8.] A review of the history of the Church Struggle goes beyond the scope of this volume. Works on this subject in English include Helmreich, *German Churches under Hitler*; Conway, *Nazi Persecution of the Churches*; Barnett, *For the Soul of the People*; and Bergen, *Twisted Cross*.

[9.] See "The Barmen Declaration (1934)," in *Creeds of the Churches*, 517–22.

[10.] See Matheson, *Third Reich and the Christian Churches*, 51.

European ecumenical movement to recognize the Confessing Church as the one true representative of German Protestantism,[11] and particularly through the community of seminarians he taught at Finkenwalde from 1935 through 1937,[12] he became a powerful influence on the young clergy who were just beginning their ministry during the Church Struggle.

The pressures on these young clergy were immense. At the 1934 Dahlem synod, the Confessing Church had decided to train, certify, and ordain its own clergy. Bonhoeffer's seminary at Finkenwalde was one of five Confessing seminaries.[13] In August 1937, however, Heinrich Himmler banned these seminaries, and the Gestapo closed Finkenwalde and the other seminaries one month later. The Confessing Church continued to examine and ordain its own candidates, but its examination commission in Berlin was arrested and tried in 1941.[14]

This made the young Confessing seminarians and clergy particularly vulnerable. Under the 1937 Himmler decree, they were "illegal" because they had not taken their ordination examinations within the official church, and they now came under new pressure to conform from official church leaders at the church chancellery in Berlin. The official church response to the Himmler decree was to offer "legalization" to these candidates. Legalization offered them greater financial security, particularly once the war began (only "legal" clergy were entitled to pensions; this became a crucial motive for those clergy who entered the military and feared that they might leave behind widows and families without pensions).[15]

Bonhoeffer bitterly opposed legalization, contending that it represented a theological compromise that would erode the very foundation of the Confessing Church.[16] And he continued, now illegally, to teach and supervise Confessing candidates for the ministry; the early documents in this volume cover the final period of his work for these "underground pastorates" until they, too, were shut down and the Gestapo bans on Bonhoeffer's activities effectively ended his ministry.[17]

By the beginning of the war, then, the Confessing Church movement had thwarted the German Christian goals of a pro-Nazi Reich church. Nevertheless, Bonhoeffer had become disillusioned with the Confessing Church

---

[11.] See, for example, *DB-ER*, 480–82.

[12.] *DBW* 14 contains the documentation of this period.

[13.] See *DB-ER*, 419–24.

[14.] See 1/141, ed. note 4, and 1/151.

[15.] See Barnett, *For the Soul of the People*, 94–98.

[16.] In this volume, see his comments to his former seminarians in 1/151; see also 1/10 and 1/72, ed. note 8.

[17.] *DBW* 15 covers most of the period of the "underground pastorates." In this volume, see the letters and documents 1/1 through 1/19.

and its moderate leadership. He believed that it had failed to resist the nazification of the life and governance of the church as well as the destructive Nazi political policies. The case could be made that Bonhoeffer's disillusionment with the Confessing Church contributed significantly to his decision to become engaged in the conspiracy to assassinate Hitler. According to Bethge, Bonhoeffer was ashamed that his own Old Prussian Union Confessing synod had yielded on the issue of an oath of allegiance that clergy were to swear to Hitler.[18] He was also particularly concerned that the Confessing Church issued no official statement against *Kristallnacht* ("night of broken glass"), the pogrom of November 9, 1938, that was carried out by the SS against Jewish synagogues and businesses throughout Germany. When, after watching the Köslin synagogue burn, some of Bonhoeffer's seminarians voiced the view that the suffering of the Jews was a curse on them, Bonhoeffer offered a different perspective: "When today the synagogues are set afire, tomorrow the churches will burn."[19]

With the beginning of the war, the pressures on Confessing clergy and on Bonhoeffer himself intensified in a new way. Bonhoeffer and Eberhard Bethge now desperately sought to avoid military service. In September 1939, shortly after Bonhoeffer returned from the United States, he applied for a position as an army chaplain. He received no reply to his application until February 1940. His application was denied because he did not have a record of active duty.[20]

Most Protestant clergy, however, as well as almost 98 percent of seminarians, were eventually conscripted for active duty.[21] Even though the draft severely reduced the number of Confessing Church ordinands, the Old Prussian Council of Brethren (the regional governing body of the Confessing Church) decided to have Bonhoeffer continue his work with the collective pastorate in Sigurdshof in eastern Pomerania. While working with these ordinands, Bonhoeffer found significant time to devote to theological work. His primary focus was a series of meditations on Psalm 119. In addition, he was asked by the Pomeranian Council of Brethren to write a theological reflection for their monthly newsletter to clergy. His March 1940 reflection on the resurrection[22] and his April 1940 reflection on the ascension[23] are included in part 2 of this volume.

[18.] *DB-ER*, 603.

[19.] Kenneth C. Barnes, "Dietrich Bonhoeffer and Hitler's Persecution of the Jews," in Ericksen and Heschel, *Betrayal,* 123.

[20.] *DB-ER*, 666.

[21.] Barnett, *For the Soul of the People,* 156.

[22.] See 2/1.

[23.] See 2/2.

We do not know what impact these theological reflections had on the pastors who read them. Nonetheless, we can surmise that they welcomed any support and encouragement during this very difficult time. State harassment of Confessing Church pastors was growing. Clergy struggled with the question of whether to enlist in the army. Very little discussion took place in the Confessing Church "about the legitimacy of becoming a soldier."[24] A number of pastors enlisted out of a sense of patriotic duty. Others simply did so out of fear of Nazi reprisal.[25] Those who enlisted voluntarily tended to draw a distinction between fighting for Germany and fighting for Adolf Hitler. The Confessing Church's illegal clergy were especially subject to Nazi pressures. At the onset of the war, the Gestapo began using a new tactic to force illegal pastors into military service; the illegals were registered as "unemployed" and sent directly into action on the front lines.[26] With so many pastors enlisting or being forced into military service, it became difficult for Confessing parishes to find replacements, and clergy who remained on the home front bore an increasing burden. In Bonhoeffer's May 1940 circular letter to his Finkenwalde seminarians, he counsels those serving in congregations not to let themselves "be worn out by scruples" when they run up against the limits of their ability to do ministry.[27]

The police dissolved the collective pastorates in March 1940.[28] With the dissolving of the collective pastorate in Sigurdshof, the Old Prussian Council of Brethren sought a new role for Bonhoeffer within the Confessing Church. From June through August of 1940, the council sent Bonhoeffer on a series of three visitations to churches in eastern Prussia. Eberhard Bethge, who was beginning to assume more of Bonhoeffer's church duties as Bonhoeffer became more involved in the resistance, accompanied him. Communication was not easy between the provincial churches of the Old Prussian Union, so this visitation work was vital to assessing the situation of the churches in eastern Prussia.[29] On these initial visitations Bonhoeffer was still able to travel without restriction and to preach and teach, but this was to change quickly.

On September 4, 1940, Bonhoeffer was informed that the Reich Central Security Office had banned him from public speaking on the grounds of "activity subverting the people."[30] A residency restriction was also imposed

---

[24.] Barnett, *For the Soul of the People,* 158.

[25.] Some who refused military duty, like Fellowship of Reconciliation secretary Hermann Stöhr, were shot (ibid., 159–60).

[26.] Ibid., 160.

[27.] See 1/6, p. 45.

[28.] See *DB-ER,* 589.

[29.] See *DB-ER,* 696.

[30.] See 1/18.

on Bonhoeffer, requiring him to report regularly to the police in Schlawe, his official place of residence.[31]

These restrictions severely complicated Bonhoeffer's professional situation and confronted the Old Prussian Council of Brethren with a dilemma. No longer was he allowed to preach or teach. Visitations on behalf of the Confessing Church were effectively precluded. Some council members, unaware of the full extent of his growing involvement in the conspiracy, proposed sending him to a small parish in a remote district, such as the village of Bismarck in Altmark.[32] Friedrich Justus Perels, a Confessing Church lawyer and fellow conspirator, spoke out against this proposal. Without divulging the full extent of Bonhoeffer's involvement in the conspiracy, he argued that Bonhoeffer should be freed to stay in Berlin and work on his *Ethics*. Eberhard Bethge also intervened with Council of Brethren chair Wolfgang Staemmler and explained Bonhoeffer's situation.[33]

The Old Prussian Council of Brethren decided to keep him on as the director of the Confessing Church pastoral training center and gave him a leave of absence. This arrangement freed Bonhoeffer to do theological work. He could focus on writing *Ethics*, but he would also be available to write occasional theological position papers on pressing issues facing the Confessing Church.[34]

Through circular letters Bonhoeffer also continued to correspond with his Finkenwalde seminarians, many of whom had been conscripted into the German military. The others were serving in a variety of contexts on behalf of the Confessing Church. These seven Finkenwalde circular letters are some of his most moving writings and a testimony to his pastoral sensitivity. Here we witness him caring for his seminary students in a profound way as they struggle with the challenges of living a faithful life during the war, whether on the front lines or at home. At the beginning of several of these letters, he lists the names of those who have fallen in battle and offers heartfelt reflections on their life and ministry. Although the brothers were scattered and unable to gather, it was almost as if Bonhoeffer were speaking at a memorial service for each fallen brother.

His letters from this period also reveal some of the key issues his seminarians raised in their correspondence with him: the difficulty of reconciling

---

[31.] See *DB-ER*, 698.

[32.] See *DB-ER*, 699. Altmark is a historic region, west of the Elbe River, in the district of Magdeburg in what is now Saxony-Anhalt.

[33.] See 1/27 and *DB-ER*, 699.

[34.] *DBWE* 16 includes three of these position papers: "State and Church" (2/10), "Co-report on the 'Reflection on the Question of Baptism' in Reference to the Question of Infant Baptism" (2/14), and "The Doctrine of the Primus Usus Legis according to the Confessional Writings and Their Critique" (2/18).

a daily order of Christian life with daily duties at the front;[35] what constitutes an authentic Christmas celebration;[36] the difficulty of comprehending God's purpose in the deaths of so many young pastors;[37] the significance of duty "behind the lines" in comparison to those doing their duty "on the front lines";[38] how to engage in meditation in unsettled circumstances;[39] whether it was permissible to accept legalization under the official church government;[40] and how to avoid becoming internally numb in the face of so much suffering.[41]

Legally these circular letters were not permitted. According to a July 12, 1940, decree, civilians were forbidden to send publications of any kind to members of the armed forces.[42] Thus Bonhoeffer and Bethge began producing all the Finkenwalde circular letters on the typewriter, circumventing the decree by sending them as personal letters. By using carbon copies, they were able to speed the process along. The name of each addressee was written by hand at the beginning, and Bonhoeffer signed each letter.

In the Conspiracy against Hitler

The title of this volume—*Conspiracy and Imprisonment: 1940–1945*—indicates the two primary contexts of Bonhoeffer's life and work during this time: his involvement in the conspiracy against Hitler, and his imprisonment following his arrest on April 5, 1943. *Conspiracy and Imprisonment* provides a case study of the effects of living and writing in a dictatorship in wartime, under the constant threat of surveillance and censorship. In Bonhoeffer's case these effects were even more pronounced because of the level of secrecy demanded by his active participation in the conspiracy.[43] Just how difficult it was to function under such circumstances becomes apparent in a letter Helmuth von Moltke wrote from Sweden to a friend in England:

[35.] See Bonhoeffer's Finkenwalde circular letter of May 1940, 1/6.

[36.] See Bonhoeffer's Finkenwalde circular letter of mid-December 1940, 1/47.

[37.] See Bonhoeffer's Finkenwalde circular letter of August 15, 1941, 1/119.

[38.] See Bonhoeffer's Finkenwalde circular letter of November 22, 1941, 1/137.

[39.] See Bonhoeffer's Finkenwalde circular letter of March 1, 1942, 1/144.

[40.] See Bonhoeffer's Finkenwalde circular letter, probably of April (although possibly of October) 1942, 1/151.

[41.] See Bonhoeffer's Finkenwalde circular letter of November 29, 1942, 1/212.

[42.] See Bonhoeffer's Finkenwalde circular letter of mid-December 1940, 1/47, ed. note 1.

[43.] Knowing that correspondence was being censored, Bonhoeffer and others had to use carefully coded language to communicate any information concerning resistance efforts. For example, "Uncle Rudy" referred to the current war situation; cf. *DBW* 16:3–4.

Can you imagine what it is like if you

a. cannot use the telephone,
b. cannot use the post,
c. cannot send a messenger, because you probably have no one to send, and if you have you cannot give him a written message as the police sometimes searches people in trains, trams, etc., for documents,
d. cannot even speak with those with whom you are completely *d'accord*, because the secret police have methods of questioning where they first break the will but leave the intelligence awake, thereby inducing the victim to speak out all he knows; therefore you must limit information to those who absolutely need it.[44]

In becoming actively involved in the conspiracy, Bonhoeffer took the ultimate step in resisting Hitler and the Nazis. Eberhard Bethge has identified five stages of resistance:

First, there was simple passive resistance. Then came the openly ideological stance that characterized the churches and men like Bishop von Galen, Martin Niemoeller, and Bishop Wurm, although they did not conceive of a new political future and work toward it. Third, there was the stage of being informed accessories to the preparations for the coup; some church officials such as Asmussen, Dibelius, Grüber, or Hanns Lilje belong in this category. Then came the fourth stage of active preparations for the post-revolt period; its most distinguished representative was Moltke, but Theodor Steltzer, Harald Poelchau, and Oskar Hammelsbeck were part of this as well. Finally there was the last stage: active conspiracy.[45]

There were few Protestants, even from the ranks of the Confessing Church, who took this final step into active conspiracy. From the Confessing Church, Bonhoeffer and Friedrich Justus Perels were active. Other Protestants included Eugen Gerstenmaier, a church lawyer in Bishop Theodor Heckel's Church Foreign Office, as well Hans Schönfeld, the German head of the academic department in the World Council of Churches in Geneva.[46] In

---

[44.] Moltke, *Letters to Freya*, 284. This passage is from Moltke's letter of March 25, 1943, written in English, to Lionel Curtis.

[45.] *DB-ER*, 792.

[46.] Bethge has noted that Bonhoeffer and Perels had numerous differences with Gerstenmaier and Schönfeld. Bonhoeffer viewed Gerstenmaier as too closely "associated with the Church Foreign Office that had collaborated theologically, ecclesiastically, and politically with the Third Reich" (*DB-ER*, 792). He was similarly suspicious of Schönfeld's close ties with Bishop Heckel and the Church Foreign Office. In turn, Gerstenmaier considered a radical "Dahlemite" such as Bonhoeffer to be too impractical. In the early years of the war, contacts between Bonhoeffer and Schönfeld served somewhat to ease the tension in their relationship (*DB-ER*, 792–93).

an evening conversation during Bonhoeffer's second trip to Switzerland, Willem Visser 't Hooft asked Bonhoeffer, "What do you really pray for in the present situation?" Visser 't Hooft reported that Bonhoeffer responded, "If you want to know, I pray for the defeat of my country, for I think that is the only possibility of paying for all the suffering that my country has caused the world."[47] Getting involved in the conspiracy was, in effect, a way of putting this prayer into action.

Bonhoeffer had to enter the final stage of active conspiracy without the blessing of his church. The secrecy required of the conspirators kept him from disclosing the extent of his involvement in resistance activities. Furthermore, there was no precedent for a Lutheran pastor in Germany to be involved in such conspiratorial activity.[48] Outwardly Bonhoeffer's involvement in the conspiracy looked more like collaboration to some. Even Karl Barth, for example, wondered how it was that a Confessing Church pastor, known to be an opponent of the National Socialist state, could be traveling so freely outside Germany at the height of the war.[49] Some of the correspondence between them in this volume sheds light on how Bonhoeffer addressed Barth's concerns. In a conversation in September 1941, during Bonhoeffer's second trip to Switzerland, Barth asked Bonhoeffer directly, "Why are you actually here in Switzerland?" Confiding in Barth, Bonhoeffer explained the plans to overthrow Hitler and establish a new government and clarified his own role in these resistance efforts.[50] Thinking he had resolved the matter with Barth, Bonhoeffer was surprised to hear a number of times during his third trip to Switzerland that Barth found his stay "unsettling as to its objectives."[51] He was concerned enough to write to Barth and once more clarify and remove any misunderstanding or mistrust between them. Bonhoeffer quickly received a response back from Charlotte von Kirschbaum, writing on behalf of Barth. She assured him of Barth's trust and desire to have him visit.[52]

[47.] See *DB-ER*, 744.

[48.] See *DB-ER*, 792.

[49.] Renate Wind, *Dietrich Bonhoeffer*, 142.

[50.] See Bonhoeffer's letter of May 17, 1942, to Karl Barth, 1/161, ed. note 3.

[51.] See Bonhoeffer's letter of May 17, 1942, to Karl Barth, 1/161.

[52.] See Charlotte von Kirschbaum's letter to Bonhoeffer, 1/162. This exchange, however, illustrates the distrust of the German resistance that existed even among people like Karl Barth, who believed that the conspirators were naive in their confidence in German military leaders. This distrust would effectively prevent any real foreign support for the resistance, as is evident in the correspondence between Bishop Bell and Anthony Eden and in the comments about Bell's efforts within the British Foreign Office, 1/187, 1/193, 1/194, and 1/195.

While Bonhoeffer was actively involved in the conspiracy during the war, the threat of military service continued to hang over his head until the time of his arrest. Eberhard Bethge would later write, "[T]he entire three years from 1940 to 1943 were really constantly accompanied by the struggle to renew the UK classifications."[53] Bonhoeffer's UK classification (declaring him *unabkömmlich*, or "indispensable," because he was engaged in a civilian occupation essential to the war effort) came only after he became a courier for military intelligence, assigned to engage in covert talks with foreign church leaders who would communicate with Allied leaders. With Hans von Dohnanyi's assistance, Bethge was able to use his position at the Gossner Mission to receive a UK classification as well,[54] although ultimately Bethge was unable to avoid active duty and was assigned to a military unit to Italy.

Bonhoeffer's UK military classification was a fiction, created to keep him out of active duty and provide a cover for his resistance activities, and this issue became a central focus of the Nazi investigations and interrogations of him, Dohnanyi, and Hans Oster.[55] His interrogators presumed that Bonhoeffer was considered fit for active service (*kriegsverwendungsfähig*),[56] and they claimed that the Office of Military Intelligence had acted illegally by issuing his UK classification.[57] The complete history, however, including the significance of certain statements found in this volume, remains unresolved to this day. Several documents in this volume mention *ein roter Zettel* or *ein roter Schein* (a red slip or a red certificate) that is clearly related to the issue of military classification for both Bonhoeffer and Bethge,[58] and Dohnanyi refers to it cryptically in the notes he smuggled from prison to his wife, Christine.[59] The context suggests that these "red slips" concerned the UK classification, yet this appears not to be the case.[60] This raises further questions about Bonhoeffer's actual status before he received the UK classification, since historians at the German Federal Archive note that an *Ausmusterungs-schein* (which declared someone permanently unfit for duty) was indeed red, and Winfried Meyer speculates that the "red slip" was "connected with

---

[53.] Bethge, "Drei Kriegsjahre bei Gossners: Erinnerungen an die Zeit bei der Gossner Mission," in Barteczko-Schwedler and Schwedler, *Wegmarken*, 81.

[54.] See 1/35.

[55.] See 1/229.1; 230.2, pp. 437, 440.

[56.] See 1/230.2, p. 434.

[57.] See 1/230.2, p. 437.

[58.] See 1/35 and 1/59.

[59.] 1/231, p. 447.

[60.] In a March 8, 2004, letter to the editors of this volume, Winfried Meyer wrote that the UK cards were gray; this was also confirmed by information received by Hans Pfeifer from the military history section at the German Federal Archive in Freiburg.

Bonhoeffer's status before the time of his UK classification in January 1941."[61] This would suggest that Bonhoeffer, contrary to the charges against him in the indictment,[62] was not eligible for duty. Moreover, contrary to his interrogators' charges, the Army High Command (which included Hans Oster) could indeed request UK classification for civilian personnel such as Bonhoeffer.[63] Despite the lack of definitive clarity here, it seems likely that Dohnanyi used an official military regulation and bent it somewhat to help both Bonhoeffer and Bethge evade active military duty. Once they were arrested, this became a serious charge against Dohnanyi, Bonhoeffer, and Oster.

In any case, Bonhoeffer's UK classification enabled him to travel abroad on behalf of the conspiracy. Eberhard Bethge has identified three stages in Bonhoeffer's active involvement in the conspiracy against Hitler.[64] The first stage began with the surrender of France on June 17, 1940, and continued until Hitler made his decision in June 1941 to invade the Soviet Union. In February 1941, Bonhoeffer made his first trip abroad for the conspiracy, traveling to Switzerland. The primary purpose of this trip was to reestablish lines of communication with the Allies. Bonhoeffer's previous ecumenical ties with people such as Bishop Bell and Visser 't Hooft made him well suited for such a task.

The second stage of Bonhoeffer's active involvement in the conspiracy began with the invasion of the Soviet Union. It ended with the defeat of the German Sixth Army at Stalingrad in the winter of 1941–42 and with Hitler's dismissal of Brauchitsch as commander in chief of the army on December 19, 1941. Bonhoeffer's primary purpose during this stage was to explore and help shape the peace aims of the Allies through his ecumenical contacts. Accordingly, he embarked on a second trip to Switzerland in September 1941. In Geneva he secured a copy of Bishop Bell's *Christianity and World Order*. Chapter 8 of Bell's book focused on "Christian and Peace Aims." From Visser 't Hooft he received a second book, William Paton's *The Church and the New Order*, in which peace aims are a central topic. Visser 't Hooft's and Bonhoeffer's reflections on Paton's book are included in *DBWE* 16.[65]

The third stage lasted until the failure of the March 1943 coup attempt,

---

[61.] Letter from Winfried Meyer to the editors, March 8, 2004.

[62.] See 1/230.2, p. 437.

[63.] Information received by Hans Pfeifer from the German Federal Archive, referring to a November 11, 1940, regulation on UK classifications of civilians (*Bestimmungen für Unabkömmlichstellung bei besonderem Einsatz [Eins.Uk.B] vom 11. November 1940, Berlin 1940, gedruckt im Oberkommando der Wehrmacht*).

[64.] See *DB-ER*, 724.

[65.] See 2/11 and 2/12.

which led to the obliteration of Hans Oster's resistance efforts. Oster was the chief of Department Z (Central Department) in the Military Intelligence Office;[66] Bonhoeffer's brother-in-law Hans von Dohnanyi worked under him. To a significant extent Dohnanyi was the mastermind of the conspiratorial work in Oster's office. Bonhoeffer's main task during this third stage was to convey information about the planned coup to Allied leaders through his ecumenical contacts. His travels included a trip to Norway, a third trip to Switzerland, a trip to Sweden to meet with Bishop Bell, and a trip with Dohnanyi to Italy.

Some of the most intriguing documents in *DBWE* 16 are the letters exchanged between Bishop Bell and Anthony Eden, the British secretary of state for foreign affairs, after Bell's conversations with Bonhoeffer and Hans Schönfeld in Sweden in late May and early June 1942.[67] Bell sought to convince British leaders to distinguish between the Nazi government and the conspirators and asked for Allied encouragement that he could pass on to the conspirators.[68] In January 1941, Winston Churchill had sent Eden a message stating clearly that "our attitude toward all such enquiries should be absolute silence."[69] Thus, Eden expressed sympathy to Bell for the dangers and difficulties faced by the opposition but noted that they had given little evidence of serious resistance.[70] Within the British Foreign Office considerable concern was expressed that the Nazi government was using the conspirators and Bishop Bell.[71] Another factor was the wartime climate in Britain, which was solidly anti-German; Bell, in fact, was taunted in the House of Lords as a sympathizer for his efforts on behalf of "good Germans."[72] After the January 1943 Casablanca conference, the viability of the conspiracy's peace feelers was effectively ended by the statement by Churchill and Roosevelt that only the unconditional surrender of Germany would be acceptable.[73]

On April 5, 1943, less than a month after the failure of the March 1943 coup attempt, Dohnanyi and Bonhoeffer were arrested. Ironically, they were not arrested for their involvement in this coup attempt or for their role in the conspiracy efforts; Nazi officials were not yet aware of the full extent of their conspiratorial activity. What led to their arrest was currency irregularities

---

[66.] See 1/225.1 and 1/229.2.

[67.] See 1/170, 1/172, 1/180, 1/186, 1/187, 1/191, 1/193, 1/194, and 1/195.

[68.] See George Bell's letter of July 25, 1942, to Anthony Eden, 1/193.

[69.] Von Klemperer, *German Resistance against Hitler,* 218.

[70.] See Anthony Eden's letter of August 4, 1942, to George Bell, 1/194.

[71.] See Foreign Office: Minutes of Proceedings, July 1–August 8, 1942, 1/187.

[72.] Von Klemperer, *German Resistance against Hitler,* 243.

[73.] Ibid., 237–44.

uncovered in the Munich Military Intelligence Office concerning Operation 7, the successful attempt to smuggle fourteen (originally it had been seven) "non-Aryans" into Switzerland. As Bonhoeffer wrote in his letter of August 26, 1942, Operation 7 lay very close to the hearts of the conspirators.[74]

During Dohnanyi's arrest, interrogator Manfred Roeder found notes that discussed plans for a journey on April 19, 1943, by Bonhoeffer and Josef Müller to Rome, where they would explain to church leaders why the assassination attempt on Hitler in March had failed.[75] Roeder's initial interrogations of Dohnanyi focused on these notes, which were evidence of highly treasonous behavior. Dohnanyi, Oster, and Canaris successfully argued that these papers were official coded Military Intelligence materials, and Roeder temporarily dropped this line of interrogation.[76]

Roeder's interrogations then turned to Operation 7. The fourteen "non-Aryans" in Operation 7 had been smuggled into Switzerland under the pretext that they were working for Military Intelligence. Dohnanyi was deeply involved in the planning and execution of Operation 7; Bonhoeffer's own role had been limited. He had requested that Charlotte Friedenthal, a "non-Aryan" who had worked faithfully for the Provisional Administration of the Confessing Church, be included in the group of those being rescued.[77] Bonhoeffer also introduced Wilhelm Schmidhuber of the Munich Military Intelligence Office to Alphons Koechlin, president of the Swiss Church Federation, who was able to facilitate the entry of the Operation 7 group into Switzerland. Roeder's interrogations of Bonhoeffer focused initially on his role in Operation 7, as indicated by several of Bonhoeffer's subsequent letters to Roeder that are included in *DBWE* 16.[78]

When this line of interrogation did not produce the needed results, Roeder turned to the issue of Bonhoeffer's UK classification. Bonhoeffer wrote a number of draft letters to Roeder, several of which are included in this volume, following up on the interrogations concerning his UK classification.[79] *DBWE* 16 also includes Bonhoeffer's "camouflage letter" *(Tarnbrief)*, which he wrote at Dohnanyi's request to disguise the true course of events.[80] In the indictment of Bonhoeffer nothing was mentioned about

---

[74.] See Bonhoeffer's letter of August 26, 1942, to Alphons Koechlin, 1/198.

[75.] See *DB-ER*, 786.

[76.] See *DB-ER*, 803–4; see also Christine von Dohnanyi's account in *DB-ER*, 786–87.

[77.] Friedenthal also worked for the Grüber office that helped Jews and "non-Aryan Christians." By the time of their rescue, those rescued in the Operation 7 attempt were under imminent danger of deportation; Friedenthal's parents, who stayed behind, perished in the concentration camps.

[78.] See 1/226 and 1/228.1.

[79.] See 1/228.2–6.

[80.] See 1/221.

his involvement in Operation 7; his UK classification and avoidance of military service were the primary concerns. In addition, he was indicted for helping Confessing Church pastors and students avoid military service.[81] The indictment also included a long list of his wartime activities for the Confessing Church, revealing the duration and extent of the Gestapo observation of both Bonhoeffer and Confessing Church circles.[82]

A Companion Volume to the *Ethics*

Conspiracy and Imprisonment: 1940–1945 is an essential companion volume to Bonhoeffer's better-known writings from the war years: *Ethics* (*DBWE* 6), *Fiction from Tegel Prison* (*DBWE* 7), and *Letters and Papers from Prison* (forthcoming as *DBWE* 8). *Fiction from Tegel Prison* contains an incomplete drama, a novel fragment, and a short story. Bonhoeffer admitted to Eberhard Bethge that these pieces of fiction contained a number of autobiographical elements.[83] Most of the correspondence and other documents from Bonhoeffer's two years in prison are included in *Letters and Papers from Prison*. The documents from the time of Bonhoeffer's imprisonment in *Conspiracy and Imprisonment* consist primarily of petitions, protocols, indictments, and defense materials related to the interrogations of Bonhoeffer, Dohnanyi, and the other conspirators. Even the letter from Dohnanyi to his wife and the letter from Constantin von Dietze to his wife focus on the interrogation process. The only exceptions are a letter from Bishop Bell to Archbishop Erling Eidem of Uppsala, Sweden, and Bonhoeffer's final words to Bishop Bell, conveyed by S. Payne Best. Bell's letter to Eidem was occasioned by the tragic death of Theodore Hume, a young Congregational pastor who had been sent to Europe to represent U.S. churches at the World Council of Churches secretariat. Killed when his airplane was shot down on a flight from London to Stockholm, Hume had been bearing a number of messages from Bell to Eidem concerning a proposed postarmistice conference of churches. Since Hume had not reached Eidem, Bell wanted to make sure Eidem received the messages concerning the conference.

Most of *Conspiracy and Imprisonment* consists of letters, essays, and other documents from the time of the closing of the Sigurdshof collective pastorate in March 1940 until Bonhoeffer's arrest on April 5, 1943. This was the period in which Bonhoeffer wrote *Ethics*, his unfinished attempt to write a "concrete Protestant ethics."[84] Thus, *Conspiracy and Imprisonment* serves

---

[81.] See 1/230.1.

[82.] See 1/230.2.

[83.] See *DBWE* 7:6.

[84.] See 1/228.2, p. 417. See also Bonhoeffer's explanation of the difference between an abstract ethic and a concrete ethic in "Ethics as Formation" (*DBWE* 6:99–100).

as a particularly important companion volume to the new *DBWE* edition of *Ethics*. A number of the essays that were in part 2 of the sixth German edition of *Ethics* (1963) are now included in *Conspiracy and Imprisonment*: "State and Church"; "'Personal' and 'Objective' Ethics"; "The Doctrine of the Primus Usus Legis according to the Confessional Writings and Their Critique"; and "What Does It Mean to Tell the Truth?" These essays overlap with the content of *Ethics* and shed new light on many of its arguments. Furthermore, Bonhoeffer's extensive correspondence and accompanying editorial commentary provide valuable insight into the historical context in which Bonhoeffer wrote *Ethics*.

In his introduction to the new *DBWE* edition of *Ethics*, Clifford Green identifies two impulses that motivated Bonhoeffer's writing of *Ethics*. The first was "the renewal of Christian life in Germany and Europe after the war." The second, arising from his position as a theologian and pastor in the conspiracy, was "to get rid of Hitler and National Socialism."[85] *Conspiracy and Imprisonment* provides further evidence of both impulses. Much of the evidence is implicit and must be gleaned. However, several documents in part 2 of *Conspiracy and Imprisonment* indicate how concretely Bonhoeffer was preparing for the overthrow of Hitler and Nazism, as well as for the future reordering of the church and the reconstruction of Germany following the war—especially his "Thoughts on William Paton's Book *The Church and the New Order*";[86] "Unfinished Draft of a Pulpit Pronouncement following the Overthrow";[87] and "Draft Proposal for a Reorganization of the Church after the 'End of the Church Struggle.'"[88] In these documents and elsewhere in this volume, we see Bonhoeffer's special concern for the public responsibilities of individual Christians and the church as a whole, both in extraordinary situations of crisis and in more ordinary times. Individual and corporate responsibility is a central theme of Bonhoeffer's *Ethics*;[89] it is echoed throughout *Conspiracy and Imprisonment* as well.

Bonhoeffer was also peripherally involved in the development of the Freiburg memorandum *(Freiburger Denkschrift)*, which articulated a number of the insights that appear in his *Ethics*.[90] In January 1943 the Freiburg circle, a group of distinguished experts from various fields, completed a document that laid out detailed proposals for the reorganization of Germany after

---

[85.] *DBWE* 6:10–11.

[86.] See 2/11.

[87.] See 2/15.

[88.] See 2/16.

[89.] See especially the two versions of "History and Good" in *DBWE* 6 (219–98).

[90.] For the text and a more complete account of the Freiburg memorandum, see Rübsam and Schadek, *Der "Freiburger Kreis."*

Hitler's removal from power. The Freiburg memorandum was developed to a large extent in response to proposals by William Paton and Bishop George Bell. In *The Church and the New Order,* Paton advocated that Confessing Church leaders be included in postwar talks. In *Christianity and World Order,* Bell issued a call for a postarmistice conference of European church leaders.[91] The Provisional Administration of the Confessing Church had asked Bonhoeffer to contact the Freiburg circle about the possibility of working together with the Confessing Church in their reflections about a post-Nazi Germany. Erik Wolf's diary entry of October 9, 1942, records that Bonhoeffer and Constantin von Dietze met with him late into the night for preliminary conversations in preparation for a November 17–18, 1942, meeting of the Freiburg circle for work on the memorandum.[92] *Conspiracy and Imprisonment* includes both Bonhoeffer's notes[93] and Dietze's notes[94] from those preliminary conversations. These notes indicate the areas that were to be addressed: economic questions, legal system, God and state, God and rights, church and state, education, and policies regarding the Jews. Bonhoeffer did not participate in the November 17–18 meeting. However, Dietze later recalled meeting with Bonhoeffer in his home, at Dibelius's home, and in a restaurant with Walter Bauer in early 1943 for discussions of a draft of the Freiburg memorandum.[95] The postarmistice conference never materialized in the form Bell envisioned, although some sections of the Freiburg memorandum were discussed at the founding meeting of the World Council of Churches in 1948.

Another key set of documents in *Conspiracy and Imprisonment* that sheds light on *Ethics* is the Bonhoeffer-Barth correspondence during the period of Bonhoeffer's three trips to Switzerland in 1941 and 1942. This correspondence was first translated into English by John Godsey.[96] It is newly translated here. One of the most significant discoveries from this correspondence is that Bonhoeffer had an opportunity, while he was working on his *Ethics,* to read the galleys of Barth's *Church Dogmatics* 2/2, which included Barth's discussion of "The Command of God." In turn, the final manuscript Bonhoeffer wrote for his *Ethics* during this period focused on "The Concrete Commandment and the Divine Mandates."[97]

[91.] See *DB-ER,* 774.

[92.] See 1/205.1, ed. note 1.

[93.] See 1/205.1.

[94.] See 1/205.2.

[95.] *DB-ER,* 775–76.

[96.] *Newsletter,* International Bonhoeffer Society, English Language Section, no. 22 (June 1982).

[97.] *DBWE* 6:388–408.

Traces of Normality

This volume documents Bonhoeffer's activities while under constant surveillance and censorship. It is all the more remarkable that Bonhoeffer continued to live with some semblance of normality. As Eberhard Bethge has observed, "for weeks at a time he worked in the peaceful surroundings of the Kieckow fields or the snow-covered slopes of Ettal. In terms of time alone, he had more periods of time for steady work than he had during the Finkenwalde years. And in Berlin not every meeting for quartet playing served conspiratorial ends; as in his youth, Dietrich Bonhoeffer accompanied his brother-in-law Rüdiger Schleicher in the violin sonatas of Mozart, Beethoven, and Brahms."[98]

From November 1940 through February 1941, Bonhoeffer lived at the Benedictine monastery in Ettal in Bavaria. The Ettal monastery became one of the three places (the others were the Kleist estates, Kieckow and Klein-Krössin, in Pomerania)[99] that Bonhoeffer had for reflection and study. At Christmas 1940 the monks read passages aloud from Bonhoeffer's *Discipleship*.[100] In the shadow of the beautiful snow-covered slopes, he worked on two of his manuscripts for the *Ethics*: "Ultimate and Penultimate Things"[101] and "Natural Life."[102] The people and the setting at Ettal provided a fitting context for work on a Protestant rediscovery and new appropriation of the concept of the natural.[103]

During this period Bonhoeffer's friendship with the widowed Ruth von Kleist-Retzow at Klein-Krössin took on added significance. An engaging woman with a strong concern for the renewal of the church, she eagerly read Barth's books and loved to discuss theological questions with Bonhoeffer. She had been a strong supporter of the Finkenwalde seminary and an ardent promoter of Bonhoeffer's interests. Beginning in the autumn of 1935 she and some of her grandchildren regularly attended worship services at Finkenwalde. Bonhoeffer spent many holidays at Klein-Krössin with Ruth

---

[98.] *DB-ER*, 705.

[99.] See *DB-ER*, 685.

[100.] *DB-ER*, 453.

[101.] *DBWE* 6:146–70.

[102.] *DBWE* 6:171–218.

[103.] In "Natural Life" Bonhoeffer explains that "the concept of the natural must be recovered from the gospel itself. We speak of the natural as distinct from the created, in order to include the fact of the fall into sin. We speak of the natural as distinct from the sinful in order to include the created. The natural is that which, after the fall, is directed toward the coming of Jesus Christ. The unnatural is that which, after the fall, closes itself off from the coming of Jesus Christ" (*DBWE* 6:173).

von Kleist-Retzow or at Kieckow with Hans-Jürgen von Kleist-Retzow, her son. In 1938, after Finkenwalde was closed, she persuaded Bonhoeffer to offer confirmation classes to three of her grandchildren, one of whom was Bonhoeffer's future fiancée, Maria von Wedemeyer.[104] Even after the grandchildren were confirmed, Bonhoeffer continued to be welcome at the Kleist-Retzow estates. The hospitality there proved especially helpful during the early war years, when he needed a quiet place to work on *Ethics*, and in the summer of 1942 Bonhoeffer renewed his acquaintance with Maria von Wedemeyer.

Conspiracy and Imprisonment brings out the human side of Bonhoeffer's life and work. We can glean numerous traces of normality. One of those traces is the friendship he maintained with Eberhard Bethge throughout this difficult time. This volume includes more than fifty letters to or from Bethge. Their closeness is illustrated by a moving passage Bonhoeffer wrote to his friend in early 1941: "To have a person who understands one both objectively and personally, and whom one experiences in both respects as a faithful helper and adviser—that is truly great deal. And you have always been both things for me."[105] We read with some amusement Bonhoeffer's exhortation to Bethge to make sure he is "eating well"[106] and his reminder that Bethge should not forget to make full use of Bonhoeffer's clothing ration for "woolen things" if he is called up into the military.[107] Bonhoeffer also cherished time at his parents' home in Berlin and maintained a regular correspondence with them when he was away; here his affection and appreciation for his parents shine through.

On January 13, 1943, less than three months prior to his arrest, he became engaged to Maria von Wedemeyer.[108] Their correspondence during the prison years is not included in *DBWE* 8 or 16, since it has already been published in *Love Letters from Cell 92: The Correspondence between Dietrich Bonhoeffer and Maria von Wedemeyer 1943–45*.[109] Nonetheless, the

---

[104.] *DB-ER*, 438–39.

[105.] See Bonhoeffer's letter of February 1, 1941, to Eberhard Bethge, 1/68.

[106.] See Bonhoeffer's letter of November 23, 1940, to Eberhard Bethge, 1/31.

[107.] See Bonhoeffer's letter of November 28, 1940, to Eberhard Bethge, 1/34.

[108.] In Bethge's biography of Bonhoeffer, January 17, 1943, is identified as the date of the engagement (*DB-ER*, 790). Since Wedemeyer accepted Bonhoeffer's proposal of marriage in writing on January 13, 1943, that date is now considered the day of the engagement; see the January 13 entry in appendix 2, p. 692. For more on the details of their engagement, see *Love Letters from Cell 92*, 329–47, and *DB-ER*, 787–90.

[109.] This volume also contains some correspondence and diary entries from the months leading up to and through their engagement, up until the time of Bonhoeffer's arrest; see *Love Letters from Cell 92*, 329–47.

present volume includes the first publication of ten early letters to Maria von Wedemeyer, written by Dietrich Bonhoeffer between October 31, 1942, and March 24, 1943.[110]

Bonhoeffer's Early Letters to Maria von Wedemeyer

These letters were written in the weeks just prior to and immediately following their engagement on January 13, 1943. The original German text of the letters will be published in the *Dietrich Bonhoeffer Jahrbuch.*

These letters form part of a larger collection of Bonhoeffer manuscripts that Maria von Wedemeyer, then a resident of the Boston area, donated to Houghton Library, Harvard University, in April 1966.[111] This collection includes the following writings from Bonhoeffer: (1) six letters to his parents between April and August 1943 that included information for Maria von Wedemeyer, published in *Letters and Papers from Prison;* (2) a letter of August 1942 to Maria von Wedemeyer's brother Max von Wedemeyer;[112] (3) a letter of May 5, 1943, to Hans von Dohnanyi, published in *Letters and Papers from Prison;* (4) twenty-seven letters to Maria von Wedemeyer, from July 30, 1943, to December 19, 1944, published in *Love Letters from Cell 92;* (5) the poems "The Past," "Jonah," "Powers of Good," and "The Death of Moses,"[113] and the reflection known as "The First Table of the Ten Commandments";[114] and (6) the ten letters to Maria von Wedemeyer published in this volume. There are no letters to Bonhoeffer from Maria von Wedemeyer or other papers written by her in the Houghton collection.

In September 1977, before her death two months later, Maria von Wedemeyer imposed the condition that these manuscripts might be consulted after her death or after twenty-five years, whichever would come later. Having

---

[110.] See 206a, 208a, 209a, 209b, 214a, 215a, 215b, 215c, 220a, and 220b. Published by permission of the Houghton Library, Harvard University; manuscript catalog number bMS Ger 161 (9) – (18). Any republication of these letters requires separate permission from Houghton Library. Scholars wishing to mention the originals should cite the Houghton manuscript catalog number. Literary rights to these letters are held by the Bonhoeffer estate. Transcription and editing of the German text was done by Hans Pfeifer. The translations were done by Lisa Dahill.

[111.] See Clifford Green and Hans Pfeifer, "The Bonhoeffer Papers at Houghton Library, Harvard University," *Newsletter,* International Bonhoeffer Society, English Language Section, no. 82 (Summer 2003): 6–7.

[112.] See 1/196.

[113.] Published in *Letters and Papers from Prison,* except for "The Death of Moses," which is partially published in Bonhoeffer, *Prayers from Prison,* and published in full in *The Prison Poems of Dietrich Bonhoeffer,* edited by Edwin Robertson.

[114.] Originally published in Godsey, *Preface to Bonhoeffer.*

contemplated publishing the correspondence with Bonhoeffer herself,[115] she gave copies of the manuscripts and other papers, including her own letters to Bonhoeffer, to her sister, Ruth-Alice von Bismarck. Bismarck collaborated with Ulrich Kabitz, and in 1992 the German edition of the correspondence was published[116] and eventually translated and published in Britain in 1994 as *Love Letters from Cell 92: Dietrich Bonhoeffer Maria von Wedemeyer 1943–45*. A slightly revised American edition was published in 1995.[117] As implied by its title, the book was confined to the correspondence with Bonhoeffer "during his imprisonment." That qualification and the year 1943 in the title made it possible to say of the volume that "the present compilation embraces the whole of the couple's correspondence and reproduces it unabridged."[118] Nonetheless, *Love Letters from Cell 92* did not include ten letters from Bonhoeffer and five letters from Maria von Wedemeyer from the early months of the courtship (October 1942 to March 1943), prior to Bonhoeffer's arrest. As these letters from Bonhoeffer reveal, there were initially some tensions among members of Maria von Wedemeyer's extended family about the relationship between Dietrich and Maria. As Maria von Wedemeyer reported, her mother wished them to observe a waiting period and to cease all correspondence and phone calls for a time. Maria von Wedemeyer later wrote that Bonhoeffer responded to the situation with "great sensitivity." However, she continued, "after our engagement Dietrich became less cautious. He had at first accepted a waiting period out of respect to my family, but soon he objected clearly, decisively, and repeatedly in letters and telephone calls to me. When we succeeded in changing the dictum, it was too late; he had been imprisoned."[119]

When the embargo on the Houghton manuscripts expired in 2002, plans were made to publish the unpublished Bonhoeffer letters. It was also hoped that the five letters to Bonhoeffer from Maria von Wedemeyer might be included in this volume. However, her family decided that, rather than publish these letters separately from the others, they would consider a new edition of *Brautbriefe Zelle 92* that contained all the letters. *Conspiracy and Imprisonment* therefore makes only Bonhoeffer's side of this early correspondence

---

[115.] In fact she quoted from them rather extensively in an article, "The Other Letters from Prison" (*Union Seminary Quarterly Review* 23, no.1: 23–29), which was then incorporated as an appendix in subsequent editions of *Letters and Papers from Prison*.

[116.] Bismarck and Kabitz, *Brautbriefe Zelle 92*.

[117.] The U.S. edition carried the subtitle *The Correspondence between Dietrich Bonhoeffer and Maria von Wedemeyer 1943–45*.

[118.] *Love Letters from Cell 92*, 13 and 15.

[119.] "The Other Letters from Prison," in *Letters and Papers from Prison*, 413.

available. These letters appear here for the first time with the permission of the Bonhoeffer estate, the Houghton Library, and by agreement between the publishers, Gütersloher Verlagshaus and Fortress Press.

Description and Organization of Material

Volumes 9 to 16 of the new English edition of the *Dietrich Bonhoeffer Works* organize his shorter writings in eight successive chronological time periods. Each volume is structured in three main parts: part 1, letters, journals, documents; part 2, essays, seminar papers, papers, lectures, compositions; and part 3, sermons, meditations, catechetical writings, exegetical writings. Within each part the documents are organized chronologically. The German editors of the *Dietrich Bonhoeffer Werke* have organized undated material according to the most likely date of composition.[120]

In *Conspiracy and Imprisonment* (vol. 16) the three-part structure becomes problematic, because during most of this period Bonhoeffer was banned from public speaking, including preaching, and from publishing. While we have a wealth of correspondence and other documents prior to and con-nected with his arrest,[121] and while a significant number of writings fit into part 2, there are only five documents in part 3. The only actual sermon is a funeral sermon for Hans-Friedrich von Kleist-Retzow, held at the Kieckow estate in August 1941. As the editors of the German edition of volume 16 have observed, "any assessment of Bonhoeffer's theological work during the last years of his life must be mindful that his silence as a preacher was in fact a coerced silence."[122]

The section headings for part 1 reflect key factors that shaped his life and work during this period: Bonhoeffer's work as a "theological adviser" for the Confessing Church; his travels on behalf of the conspiracy; the ban on his public speaking, including preaching, and the residency restrictions placed on him; temporary stays between travels; and his arrest and impris-onment. Eberhard Bethge has given the following approximate reconstruc-tion of the course of events in this time period:

> The months of the western offensive, April and May 1940, were spent in Berlin. From June to August he went to eastern Prussia three times on church business. In September and October he was in Klein-Krössin. From November 1940 to February 1941 he lived in the Ettal monastery. From 24 February to 24 March 1941 he undertook the first journey to

---

[120.] See *DBW* 16:9.

[121.] Most of the correspondence and documents from the prison years is included in *Letters and Papers from Prison*.

[122.] *DBW* 16:8.

Switzerland. He returned to Friedrichsbrunn at Easter; from May to August he commuted between Klein-Krössin, Berlin, and occasionally Munich. His second journey to Switzerland was from 28 August to 26 September 1941. In late October and during November he had pneumonia and stayed at his parents' home; December he spent convalescing in Kieckow. From January to April 1942 he was mainly in Berlin, spending Easter in Kieckow. From 10 to 18 April 1942 he went to Norway, and from 12 to 23 May 1942 to Switzerland for the third time. From 30 May to 2 June 1942 he was in Sweden. In June he visited Klein-Krössin, Munich, and Freiburg, leaving several times for Berlin in between these trips. From 26 June to 10 July he was in Italy. During the autumn and winter of 1942–1943 he left Berlin only for short spells in Munich, Klein-Krössin, Freiburg, Magdeburg, and Patzig—his prospective mother-in-law's estate.[123]

In general, Bonhoeffer's own letters are included in their entirety. Those of his correspondents are occasionally abbreviated; such omissions are indicated in the text by an ellipsis enclosed in brackets. The German editors chose not to include a number of significant documents from the period following Bonhoeffer's execution in Flossenbürg on April 9, 1945, including the first notice of his death in a telegram from Geneva, Bishop Bell's letter to Bonhoeffer's twin sister, Sabine Leibholz, and various protocols from the postwar trials of Manfred Roeder and Walter Huppenkothen. Ten newly discovered letters from this period (not originally published in *DBW* 16 [1996] but published in the supplemental volume to the German edition, *DBW* 17, *Register und Ergänzungen* [1999]) have been incorporated into *DBWE* 16. They are inserted in appropriate chronological order in part 1. Of particular interest are Paul Lehmann's letter of August 2, 1941, to Bonhoeffer[124] and Bonhoeffer's letter of September 20, 1941, responding to Lehmann.[125] Lehmann's letter offers a glimpse into American attitudes toward World War II and Nazi tyranny shortly before the United States entered the war. He also identified the "ecumenical spirit in the Church" as the most important religious development of that era and advocated a "world of political and economic democracy." In response Bonhoeffer predicted that in the future the world would be dominated by the United States, and he expressed his reservations that Germany would not be ready immediately for an Anglo-Saxon form of democratic government.

Although the documents in part 2 are organized chronologically, they fall into three categories. The first group of writings (2/1–2/8) addresses questions concerning the Confessing Church's proclamation and life in

---

[123.] *DB-ER*, 686.
[124.] See 1/116a.
[125.] See 1/126a.

Pomerania and eastern Prussia. A second group (2/9–2/14, 2/18, and 2/19) focuses on issues raised in his *Ethics*. A third group (2/15–2/17) includes documents relating to the anticipated overthrow of Hitler and the reorganization of the church after the coup.

Since Bonhoeffer was banned from public speaking, including preaching, and from presiding in any official capacity in public worship services, the German editors debated whether the three-part structure of the other series B volumes (9–15) should be preserved. As noted, the only sermon was a private one; and the meditations, devotional aids, and reflections on Exod. 20:2-11 could have been included in part 2. In the end they decided to preserve part 3 in this limited form to represent the continued importance of preaching and meditation to Bonhoeffer's theological work, while highlighting the severe restrictions that were placed on him. As the German editors write, "this man, who was no longer permitted to be a preacher, nonetheless kept his focus on preaching."[126]

Translation and Editorial Issues

The translation of the text of *Conspiracy and Imprisonment* seeks to preserve the tone and style of each literary form. An effort was made to emulate the phraseology and sentence structure of each document while rendering the document into readable English. This effort was complicated by the striking diversity of the literary genres included in this volume, which includes personal correspondence with family, friends, and colleagues; formal correspondence with ecclesial, military, and governmental officials; circular letters to Bonhoeffer's Finkenwalde seminarians; diary and notebook entries; calendar notes; memos and messages; discussion and presentation notes; guest-book entries; minutes of meetings; brief official documents such as file entries, a courier identification card, and application information; reports, statements, and petitions; legal documents such as indictments, interrogation reports, decrees, and defense briefs; a draft and outline for a lecture; notes for a Bible study; theological reflections for a newsletter article; theological position papers and essays; theological reflections on a book; a pulpit pronouncement for the aftermath of the coup; a proposal for the reorganization of the church; a draft of a church constitution; a thesis fragment; a memorial sermon; meditations and devotional aids; a biblical exposition; and even fictitious diary fragments and a "camouflage letter."

In translating certain government, military, and legal documents, translator Lisa Dahill attempted to make the English wording reflect the rather

---

[126.] *DBW* 16:8.

stilted bureaucratic language of the original documents. A good example is the report of the "Königsberg SD Regional Headquarters to the Reich Central Security Office."[127] Accordingly she retained some of the obfuscating characteristics of the German such as passive-voice constructions.

When the German edition of *Conspiracy and Imprisonment* was compiled, the editors preserved the peculiarities of Bonhoeffer's orthography and punctuation while correcting obvious mistakes. That which was underlined in original documents is italicized in the *DBW* 16 texts. Significant deletions and additions in the original manuscripts are cited in the editorial notes. The *DBWE* 16 edition follows the *DBW* 16 text in this regard. Documents written originally in English have been reproduced as they were written, complete with spelling and grammatical errors. In such documents the first editorial note indicates that the original is in English.

It was standard practice in German letters in Bonhoeffer's time to punctuate salutations with an exclamation point at the end. In translating these salutations we have used commas or colons, as is standard practice in letters in English. When Bonhoeffer himself wrote letters in English, he used standard English punctuation for the salutation.[128]

German abbreviations are given in the text in their original form; a translation and, if necessary, an explanation are provided in an editorial note on first occurrence of the abbreviation in a document. A list of frequently used abbreviations appears following the general editor's foreword.

The New Revised Standard Version (NRSV) of the Bible has been used to translate biblical passages, except where the Greek or the German differs significantly from the NRSV version; such cases are indicated in the editorial notes. Abbreviations of the books of the Bible conform to the *Chicago Manual of Style* (15th ed.).

The first seven volumes of the *Dietrich Bonhoeffer Works* English Edition, which contain Bonhoeffer's early theological writings, followed a policy of using inclusive, non-gendered language, even where the German indicates a masculine reference. Because the later volumes in this series, including the present one, comprise primarily historical documentation, we have followed the German more closely, even where this language may appear to contemporary readers to be gendered or exclusive. The present volume includes not only Bonhoeffer's theological writings but correspondence from other people, documents from the Church Struggle and the ecumenical movement, and documents from German church officials and Nazi officials. These are historical documents from an era in which inclusive

---

[127.] See 1/15.

[128.] See, for example, Bonhoeffer's letter of February 25, 1941, to Sabine Leibholz, 1/91.

language and thinking are rarely evident (and all the more striking when they are). Readers and scholars of historical works often encounter language and attitudes that would not be acceptable today, yet to suppress this alters something essential in the history. Document 2/15 of this volume, for example, is particularly striking because it reflects Bonhoeffer's Finkenwalde-based understanding of the ministry and the church. In this statement he is addressing the German Protestant church as a whole—but speaking to his colleagues throughout the church as "brothers"—speaking, in other words, as the founder, teacher, and pastor of the brotherhood he had founded at Finkenwalde. After the end of Nazism, Bonhoeffer and his closest friends hoped for a different kind of church, based on the Finkenwalde model.[129] In the midst of his resistance period and his reflections on a post-Nazi Germany, Bonhoeffer was trying to articulate the Finkenwalde sense of relationship for the larger church, and his language of the importance of "brotherhood" here is particularly moving.

The translation of certain historical and ecclesiological terms posed challenges for the translator. Bonhoeffer was a member of the German Evangelical Church, which was the central Protestant church in Germany and included Reformed, Lutheran, and United churches. "Evangelical" in this sense means something other than the common understanding of the term in the United States. In *DBWE* the institutional church and its governing offices are referred to using this official name; when Protestant is used in this book, however, it does refer to the German Evangelical Church and its members.

The translation of other terms, especially those peculiar to the Nazi era, was also challenging. As is standard in works on this period, the term "German Christian" refers exclusively to the Deutsche Christen, the German Protestant movement that embraced Nazi ideology and sought to change the institutional church, its theology, and its liturgies along ideological lines. Editorial footnotes explain language that had particular ideological nuances in Nazi Germany, such as *Volk* and *Reich*. In particular, the word *Volk* and its derivatives (e.g., *völkisch*) would have been used and understood differently after 1933. In such cases we have indicated the German in brackets following the translation, even where it appears that Bonhoeffer is using these words in their traditional sense. Similarly, some religious language is understood in post-Holocaust Christian theology as reflective of the anti-Judaism that permeated the Christianity of that era. In several passages Bonhoeffer uses *Pharisäer*, "Pharisee," or *pharisäisch*, "pharisaical," in a pejorative manner

---

[129.] See Barnett, *For the Soul of the People*, 276–78 and 289–90.

that is understood today to be anti-Judaic; this has been noted where it appears in the text.[130]

The word *Volksmission* posed a unique challenge, and we finally translated it contextually—that is, in different ways, depending on the context, to convey its meaning to English-speaking readers. Emerging in the early twentieth century, the original German *Volksmission* was an evangelization movement that swept both Catholic and Protestant churches. By the 1920s, however, the word had taken on nationalistic and even "Aryan" connotations, and during the 1930s the German Christians deliberately continued the *Volksmission* tradition as part of their vision for a Reich church.[131] At Finkenwalde and in his underground teaching, Bonhoeffer revived and practiced *Volksmission* within the Confessing Church in deliberate opposition to the German Christians, and his own conception of this activity was not so much traditional evangelization as the revival of the true Christian church itself— a church that would not succumb to ideological pressure. Hence, in many places we have translated this term as "church renewal." During this same period, however, Eberhard Bethge began to work for the Gossner Mission and was engaged in *Volksmission* for them. Bethge's work entailed more typical "missionary work" and evangelization—along Confessing Church lines, of course—and in these documents the word has been translated accordingly. Editorial notes explain the context of the variations in translation.

Supplementary Material

Appendix 1 is a map of Bonhoeffer's Germany locating many of the places where Bonhoeffer lived and worked during this period, with brief descriptions of his actions in each place. This map was originally published in a booklet, *Bonhoeffer: Fifty Years On*, published in 1994 by the British section of the International Bonhoeffer Society. It is reproduced here with the kind permission of the author, Hugh Searle. Appendix 2 provides a chronology of key events from 1940 to 1945 in the life and work of Bonhoeffer, in the German resistance against Hitler and the Nazis, in the Confessing Church, and in World War II. Appendix 3 is a list of the unpublished material from 1940 to 1945 that is cataloged in the *Nachlaß Dietrich Bonhoeffer* but not included in *Conspiracy and Imprisonment*. Appendix 4 provides a synopsis of texts published in *DBWE* 16 and in *Gesammelte Schriften*, the English edition of *Ethics* (Simon and Schuster, 1995) prior to *DBWE* 6, or *Letters and Papers from Prison*.

[130.] Cf. 1/145, 1/192, 1/202, 2/5, and 2/18.

[131.] See Ustorf, *Sailing on the Next Tide*.

The initial editorial note in each document identifies the specific archival source or private collection in which the original is located; a complete list of the archives consulted is included in the bibliography. The bibliography includes all books and articles cited in the editorial notes. For foreign works the title and publication information of the original publication is given first, followed by the title and publication information of the English translation if one exists. When no published English translation exists, a translation of the title has been provided.

Acknowledgments

We are thankful for the careful work of the German editors, Jørgen Glenthøj (†), Ulrich Kabitz, and Wolf Krötke, in compiling and editing *Konspiration und Haft: 1940–1945*, volume 16 of *Dietrich Bonhoeffer Werke*. This German edition provided a solid base for our preparation of the English edition, *Conspiracy and Imprisonment: 1940–1945*.

Conspiracy and Imprisonment is published in grateful memory of Timothy Lull (†), the late president of Pacific Lutheran Theological Seminary, whose sudden death on May 20, 2003, shocked us all. Lull was a creative and energetic theologian and church leader who readily acknowledged the impact Bonhoeffer's life and writings had on him. He was a strong supporter of the *DBWE* 16 translation project from its earliest stages. In 1997, serving as the dean of PLTS, Lull reached an agreement with the *DBWE* editorial board for PLTS to sponsor the English edition of volume 16. This sponsorship entailed: (1) providing a translator—Lisa Dahill; (2) providing one consultant—Everett Kalin; (3) offering significant financial and administrative support; (4) hiring the volume editor to teach an annual weeklong Bonhoeffer seminar; and (5) hosting a one-day theological conference at PLTS to celebrate the publication of *DBWE* 16. We appreciate the support of the entire PLTS community in bringing this project to a successful conclusion. We regret that Tim Lull is not alive to celebrate the completion of *Conspiracy and Imprisonment*.

From the beginning, the process of translating and editing *DBWE* 16 was a team effort. It was truly a blessing to work with this team. Lisa Dahill's gifts as a translator were readily apparent. During one of our team consultations, Martin Rumscheidt, a native German speaker, was deeply moved by one of the letters she had translated. He commented to her, "I did not think it was possible for a nonnative speaker to have such a feel for the German language." Ev Kalin, our PLTS consultant, went beyond the call of duty and read through the text line by line after the volume editor had done a first reading of the translation. Kalin's years of experience as a biblical translator as well as a translator of German were a valuable asset to us. Rumscheidt served as our *DBWE* editorial board consultant. As a native German speaker and an able translator, he was invaluable in helping us figure out how to translate some of the most difficult German terms and phrases. *DBWE* editorial board members Geffrey B. Kelly and Peter Frick assisted in the translation and review of Latin and Greek terms; Kelly also assisted us with material related to the Catholic tradition and contributed additional commentary to several editorial notes. G. Clarke Chapman, who over the years has assisted in the preparation of several *DBWE* volumes, prepared the text concordance appendix for this one.

Wayne Floyd, as general editor of *DBWE*, was especially attentive to consistent translation of terms, to accurate application of editorial guidelines, and to formatting issues. In editing translated text, one of my primary tasks was to identify translation and editorial issues on which the team needed to consult. Annual consultations were held at the American Academy of Religion. In addition, we gathered for a week in the summer of 1999 in Berkeley. In the mornings we taught a Bonhoeffer seminar on the "Renewal of Christianity" for the Graduate Theological Union summer session, and in the afternoons we consulted on *DBWE* 16 at PLTS. Then in the summer of 2001 we gathered in Tacoma for four days of consultation. Some of my best memories of this project come from the work we accomplished and the good times we shared during these West Coast consultations.

Douglas W. Stott provided a timely translation of much of the front and end matter of *DBWE* 16, including the German editors' afterword. This allowed Lisa Dahill to focus on translating parts 1, 2, and 3 of the text itself, as well as the new material from *DBW* 17 and Bonhoeffer's previously unpublished letters to Maria von Wedemeyer.

Hans Pfeifer, the liaison between the German and the English editorial board, participated in several of our consultations at the American Academy of Religion. In addition to doing the editorial work and commentary on all the letters inserted from *DBW* 17 (1/53a; 1/92a; 1/93a; 1/116a; 1/126a; 1/134a; 1/184a; 1/199a; 1/239a), as well as the letters to Maria von Wedemeyer, he was a valuable resource on translation issues and on theological and historical questions. Pfeifer reviewed the translation of part 1 and part 2, documents 1–12, and his comments sharpened the translation and enhanced the editorial notes. Christine Kasch reviewed the translation of the remaining documents in part 2, part 3, and the German editors' afterword. Her insights were much appreciated. She also served as the liaison for queries and correspondence with Wolf Krötke on some of the more difficult translation issues.

We benefited on numerous occasions from the expertise of Clifford Green, the editor of *Ethics*. The *Ethics* team struggled with the translation of a number of the same terms that appear in this volume. Because of the number of cross-references between our two volumes in the editorial notes, it was imperative that we carefully compare our work. We appreciated having Cliff in attendance at several of our volume 16 consultations. In preparing the manuscript of volume 16 for submission to the publisher, we were greatly assisted by having the newly published edition of *Ethics* in hand.

I served as the pastor of two different Trinity Lutheran churches while I was working on volume 16, one in McMinnville, Oregon, and the other in Tacoma, Washington. Both congregations were supportive and understanding of the necessary commitment of time and resources. Trinity in McMinnville made a substantial financial commitment to the project. Trinity in Tacoma gave me a very generous continuing education fund so that I could attend the *DBWE* editorial board meetings and hold consultations on volume 16 at the American Academy of Religion meeting each year, and it hosted the 2001 consultation of our translation team.

General editor Wayne Floyd's integral role in the volume 16 consultation process has already been noted. In the latter stages of editing our volume, Floyd completely reformatted the text from WordPerfect into Microsoft Word and did a line-by-line reading of the text. With his attention to detail and his concern for consistency and clarity, he identified a number of necessary revisions. The current general editors, Victoria Barnett and Barbara Wojhoski, took the final steps to prepare the manuscript for submission to Fortress Press. Barnett reviewed the entire text and the front and the back matter and made necessary revisions. She was effective in resolving glossary issues and in providing accurate historical information, both during the consultation process on volume 16 and in the final preparation of the manuscript. Wojhoski copyedited the manuscript and then worked closely with James Korsmo and others at Fortress Press to bring it to publication.

On a personal note, I want to express my deep appreciation to David Knutson (†), the college professor who first introduced me to the life and writings of Dietrich Bonhoeffer. He was my parishioner at Trinity in Tacoma. He died in November 2004 of complications from diabetes, which he had dealt with since he was a teenager. He continued to teach religion at Pacific Lutheran University for many years even after he was legally blind. He did not live to see the completion of *Conspiracy and Imprisonment;* but while he lived, he was one of the strongest supporters of my work on this volume.

Finally, thanks to my wife, Donna, and to my children, Isaac, Rachel, Matia, Hailey, Luke, and Mary. Daunting tasks do not seem quite so overwhelming when one is surrounded by people who love and care for you.

Mark S. Brocker
August 2005

PART 1
Letters and Documents

A. After the Dissolution of the Collective Pastorates. Berlin. March–May 1940

15

1. Eberhard Baumann to Friedrich Onnasch[1]

Stettin, March 12, 1940

Dear Brother Onnasch,

Just today I received the guide for the study of Article 7 of the Lutheran Formula of Concord, sent out to the brothers "as the Confessing Church's Lenten greeting" and "as a stimulus to theological work";[2] I had to ask for the document from others. It has filled me, as I reflect on the future of our Protestant church, with a sadness that I can describe only as deep despair or depression.

This "greeting" is no brotherly greeting for members of the Protestant-Reformed confession but a downright excommunication[3] and may hardly be called a guide to study or a stimulus to theological work in that it sharply and one-sidedly anticipates the results of such study.

This "greeting" is a scholasticism that is asserting solely to make known the Word of God (Christ) yet cannot bring itself humbly to hear the whole word of the scriptures,

---

[1.] LKA der Evangelischen Kirche in Westfalen, Bielefeld, Bestand 5,1, no. 522, fasc. 2; typewritten; cf. *NL,* A 60,1; carbon copy; previously published in *GS* 3:398–400. On the circumstances of its composition, see *DB-ER,* 570–72.

[2.] "Vom heiligen Abendmahl: Eine Anleitung zum Studium des VII. Artikels der lutherischen Konkordienformel" (*DBW* 15:548–53 [*GS* 3:393–98]). This essay was written in February 1940.

[3.] [This document was not, of course, a literal bull of excommunication. Baumann is claiming that it makes members of the Protestant-Reformed confession feel as if they have been, in effect, excommunicated.—MB]

giving us insight into the mystery of Holy Communion; rather, it fixates on wording that can have various meanings. The research of recent years and decades ought to have taught us how carefully one must study the whole scripture in order not to go astray. There would be much, much more to say about this in detail.

To mention but two examples: 1. Did Judas share in the body and blood of Jesus? As is well known, the Gospels report differently on this. And if so, did he physically partake of it, since it was, after all, the still-living Lord who handed it to him?

2. Like the Lutheran Church, the Reformed Church knows that the word creates the sacrament; and like the Reformed, the Lutheran Church (cf. Luther) knows that the word calls for faith (pure believing hearts). Whoever thinks to separate the word from faith—for both belong to the most personal realm and are correlates—reifies the treasure of grace [Gnadengut] (cf. the Catholic Church).

16

This "greeting" is a repristination of the Formula of Concord, setting it equal to the Holy Scriptures, without remembering how all too human, partisan, and political the circumstances of its emergence were, how it has found only partial acceptance even in the Lutheran churches, and how it has been named, not without some truth, the Formula Discordiae.[4]

This "greeting" thoughtlessly rips open the confessional division within the Confessing Church, the division that became evident as a faint tear even in the very hour of the church's birth at Barmen and was deliberately widened by the "intact" churches in their concern for their own continuing existence, leading up to the arduous though still cordial negotiations of the Halle synod.[5] It exacerbates this painful division right in the middle of the battle that the church of Jesus Christ as such is waging with all its spiritual power for its very existence and right to exist in the German fatherland. For confessionalism with all its narrowness and self-righteousness plainly is not from God but rather from Satan, no matter how blessedly the confessions themselves may function as a revelation of multiplicity in unity. Satan is disarming and destroying the church in battle (Mark 3:24-25).

This "greeting" is for me a painful confirmation that I made the right decision to step back from all participation in the Pomeranian Council of Brethren in order to spare it the accusations that would burden it in the "Lutheran" province of Pomerania. It has also brought one of our young Reformed brothers in the field to the conviction that there is no room for him in the Confessing Church of Pomerania.

[4.] "Formula of Discord" (rather than of unity).

[5.] This is a reference to the second meeting of the Fourth Confessing Synod of the Old Prussian Union in Halle (May 10–13, 1937), which ratified a declaration on the confessional question formulated jointly by Lutheran, United, and Reformed leaders, thereby taking the final step toward altar fellowship [the agreement among different churches that their members may share in Holy Communion—MB], which had been disputed until then.

Yet all the deeper is my humble thanks to the king of the passion, that he is so infinitely greater and richer in life and light than all human dogmatics for those who have recognized and embraced him as the bread of life in his death on the cross.

Besides, dear Brother Onnasch, I cannot believe that you personally truly stand by this document.

B.[aumann]

2. To Eberhard Baumann[1]

17

March 21, 1940

Dear Superintendent Baumann:

Your letter to Brother Onnasch has been directed to me, presumably with your consent. I am dismayed by your complete misunderstanding of my theological letter. This letter neither reflects my personal view of the Lord's Supper nor presents a general exegetical or systematic treatment; rather, it is a *rendering of the key ideas of Article 7 of the Formula of Concord*, which I do try hard to understand and which I love and treasure more and more the longer I work on it. As the heading should have made clear, this treatment of Article 7 was intended to guide pastors in their own study of the article. I can scarcely believe that you would consider it particularly promising for the future of the church if such objective work on significant dogmatic documents were stifled for whatever reason, resulting gradually in the complete cessation within the Confessing Church of reflection on the confessions. I might add that personally I depart from the Formula of Concord on several points and do so precisely because of the *Institutes'* thorough exegetical work.[2] Yet my task in these letters is not to lay out my personal theological convictions but rather to commend a portion of our confessions' dogmatic material for further thought. If you (and the young brother in the field, whom I believe I understand) wish to draw conclusions about the Confessing Church and its future in such a process, then this appears to me to derive more from liberal views than from confessionally Reformed ones, unless perhaps the whole thing has truly been a great misunderstanding. In any case, I have a clear conscience in terms of the church regarding the task that has fallen to me, and I do not consider it healthy to suppress our forefathers'[3]   18

[1.] LKA der Evangelischen Kirche in Westfalen, Bielefeld, Bestand 5,1, no. 522, fasc. 2; typewritten, probably from Berlin; cf. *NL*, A 60,1; previously published in *GS* 3:400–401.

[2.] See Bonhoeffer's notes, "Calvin, *Institutio* IV, Abendmahl," *NL*, A 54,11.

[3.] *Unserer Väter* ["Our forefathers'"—MB] is a handwritten insertion by Bonhoeffer.

serious theological utterances simply because they elicit divergent opinions. Only a thorough knowledge of the confessions themselves can in fact help us here.

When you say that confessionalism is "of Satan," and by that mean my letter, I puzzle over this almost Lutheran way of speaking yet must in all seriousness note that there exists a sort of confessional sensitivity that risks being unable to hear objective data objectively. I would welcome the day when a Reformed colleague were to provide us with a guide for studying the *Institutes'* doctrine of the Lord's Supper.

Wishing you a blessed Easter, I am

Sincerely and respectfully yours,
Bonhoeffer

3. To Ruth Roberta Stahlberg[1]

My dear lady,

Many thanks for your letter. I have delayed somewhat in answering it, because I wished to find a quiet afternoon, but also because I can respond only hesitantly to your thoughts and concerns and above all to your legitimate hopes. Under no circumstances would I wish to trot out a long list of handy counterarguments and by doing so appear to have actually answered you. That would be too glib. On the other hand, however, I cannot simply unconditionally agree with your letter without saying that in church affairs even the best claims do not ensure victory.

Thus I fear you will be disappointed at my response. For what you are actually urging is a drastic reformation of the church, and that is something

19

[1.] *NL,* A 60,4 (1); handwritten draft from Berlin likely datable to March 23, 1940 (see ed. note 3); previously published in *GS* 3:37–43. There are two extant versions, one shorter and incomplete, and the longer and complete one reproduced here. In contrast to most of Bonhoeffer's correspondence, both drafts reveal a good number of purely stylistic corrections. Editorial note 2 includes an additional quotation from the shorter version that is important to the sense of the letter. Ruth Roberta Heckscher (née Stahlberg), a granddaughter of Ruth von Kleist-Retzow, says regarding this letter, "It may have been 1940. He (earlier?) wrote me (at least) one other letter. I had published a discourse on Stifter in Gertrud Bäumer's monthly, *Die Frau* (October 1938), titled "Am Nachsommer gemessen" [Measured by *Indian Summer*—MB] (the title was the best thing about it). And he wrote to me, probably spurred on by my grandmother, of his objections to it, climaxing in the statement that 'it is not Christian.' It was humanistic blather. . . . All his critiques stayed with me a long time. In fact, even more than that" (conversation of the German editor with Ruth Roberta Heckscher, August 2, 1987). Cf. Pejsa, "Dietrich Bonhoeffer's Letter to an Unknown Woman," 3ff.

I truly cannot accomplish.[2] I would like to attempt to use your letter's ques-   20
tions to reflect on what we pastors, or what you as a layperson, actually can
do—not to reform the church but at least to avoid hindering and destroying that new thing that perhaps is emerging. I believe that we must limit our
task in this way from the outset. We are not the ones who reform the church,
but we are indeed very capable of blocking the way if God has decided to
renew it. For us it can only be a matter of making room, of creating space.
Reforming impulses can cause as much damage in the church as merely letting things go under the comfortable assumption that God alone will take
care of it all. This is very likely what you mean when you write that the way
forward lies "only in avoiding what is harmful." That which is original, genuine, and pure asserts itself by virtue of its own power. Of course, if one
truly takes these thoughts seriously, this implies that we cannot simply
approach the matter with whatever preconceived standards we may have,
however creative or widely accepted, nor cherish the hope that everything
would fall into place if we would only put these standards to use. Even the
best standards can be quite damaging to the true life of the church. The

---

[2.] In the shorter version, Bonhoeffer continued, "Yet right at the outset I must add
that something in me protests very powerfully against all longings for reformation. In the
past four hundred years and up to the most recent era, we have experienced them almost
without interruption in the most varied forms; and all of them have resulted—I must
add, thank God—in nothing. The one true Reformation sprang not from a so-called
longing for reformation but rather from a single, newly given biblical discovery that then
in and of itself—in Luther's case, of course, in opposition to any ecclesial desire for
renewal!—broke open the church and renewed it. Waiting for reformation has as little to
do with the Reformation itself as the Reform Councils with the Diets of Worms and Augsburg. Please allow me to put it even more clearly. The liveliest longings for reformation in
our church in the last four hundred years have always resembled the not particularly
respectful intention of fashionably dressing up one's elderly mother so as not to have to
be ashamed of her. I do not wish to dispute that there is also a true desire for renewal in
the church, but we easily distinguish between true and false by asking whether we are
more concerned about doing something new or about Jesus Christ. In the genuine desire
for a renewed church, one's own wishes and the demands that one is placing on the
church give way to the unselfconscious accommodation to the church as it actually is, to
love for it precisely in its brokenness, and to the orientation of one's entire thought and
action to the word of Christ alone and indeed within the concrete congregation. How I
wish the church to be is as unimportant as my thoughts about how I wish my mother to
be. The essential point is that it is my church and that I place myself entirely in its service
just as it is. I hope I am making myself clear. As willingly as we must hear and ponder the
pia desideria [pious wishes] that emerge from the church, so we must necessarily remain
down-to-earth and realize that the fulfillment of even numerous pia desideria will not
renew the church; rather, such renewal comes from an entirely different dimension and
claims us anew and quite differently, not wishing any longer but participating."

"harmful" thing that is to be avoided, as you note, is actually only what stands in the way of what is original, true—let me state it even more clearly—in the way of Christ himself. In the church, the good and beautiful is what serves Christ.

At this point I am not certain I am still in agreement with you. For it appears to me that you wish to know in advance from some other source what is beautiful and true, and only subsequently bring it to be appropriated by the church. Is this the reason you would become "terribly stubborn" if for the sake of Christ you were supposed to deny "the many possibilities given to a person in creation"? Even in the church you want to have and to cling to something else beyond and besides Christ himself, whom you nevertheless name as the personal Son of God. But this will not work. There is no room in the church for Christ *and* human creativity but, strictly speaking, only for Jesus Christ, and in Christ—but truly only in Christ!—for the earth's full glory insofar as it can serve Christ alone. Only when that aspect of our own creative possibilities that we ourselves consider lovely has in fact been denied for Christ's sake—that is, when we have let go of all our own measures for the sake of Christ, who is the standard of all standards—can that which is in a Christian sense beautiful, true, etc. emerge. And it will emerge only where Jesus Christ alone truly becomes the driving power of our creative activity. In reality everything beautiful, good, and true that we import into the church from outside hinders the breakthrough of what is beautiful, good, and true from God.

Last evening I listened again to the *St. Matthew Passion.*[3] What is "beautiful" about it? Precisely this: that all the music's own beauty in and for itself is sacrificed, is "denied" for the sake of Christ, that the music here only comes to itself through Jesus Christ and does not desire to be anything for itself but everything for Jesus Christ. Bach wrote Jesu Juva[4] or Soli Deo Gloria[5] above his works. That is its beauty. The "beauty" denied is the true and only possible beauty in the church of Christ. Whenever in the *St. Matthew Passion* the music begins to desire to be something in itself—I see this in a few of the arias (Heinrich Schütz is the only one in whom I have never noticed it!)—this is the point where it loses its authentic beauty. As long as we are discussing music, I must say, too, that I do not consider it quite true

21

[3.] According to Jutta Jochimsen, this is probably a reference to the performance by the Berlin Vocal Academy and the Berlin Philharmonic conducted by Fritz Stein on March 22, 1940, Good Friday, in the Berlin Garrison Church (information provided to the German editor by Jutta Jochimsen, August 25, 1988).

[4.] ["with Jesus' help"—MB]

[5.] ["To God alone be the glory."—MB]

that the church is not keeping up with the times in this area as well. Rather, I am convinced that the newest Protestant church music—I am thinking now of Distler and Pepping (but one could list many others as well)—has a distinct advantage in purely musical terms over other contemporary music and that even here it is precisely the "denial" of beauty in the strict union of music to the word of God that makes this achievement true and great. I 22 understand too little of the fine arts, likewise of poetry. Yet the fact cannot be disputed that there are beginnings there that distinguish themselves very significantly and favorably from the achievements of the late nineteenth century. Once again it is the powerful focus on the subject itself, on the word of God and Holy Scripture, which makes something appear "beautiful" or "ugly" to us.

Everyone knows today that the Protestant church—though not only the Protestant church—drew the scathing criticism of many intellectuals in the last century by its appalling aberrations in matters of taste. There is really no possible rejoinder to your angry listing of these; you are right in every case, and the list could be lengthened even more. So why is it that we nevertheless are compelled today to judge these things more leniently and with less self-certainty? From its very beginnings, the church has been made up of ordinary, unimpressive people. But is it not these same people, those who display "tasteless Christian decorations" [Haussegen in Brandmalerei] in their living rooms, who in the face of innumerable obstacles so movingly sacrifice their pennies for the cause of Jesus Christ, who support the Inner Mission institutions, who indeed stake their entire existence on the church of Christ? And, on the other hand, is it not those intellectuals who understand more about taste and such matters who have collapsed into such shocking inner turmoil that they are capable in only very rare cases of the simplest deeds of sacrificial love and prayerful action?

None of us may make accusations in these matters. We are all in the same boat. But the facts remain. In the face of this highly strange and surprising turn of events, isn't our judgment forced by necessity into distinguishing the essential from the nonessential? Is it not more essential to be a devoted and responsible Christian, regardless of one's petit-bourgeois household decorations, than to have the best of taste yet never to arrive at what is decisive? Is it not more essential to live and act and die a Christian, singing one's sentimental favorite hymns, than with artfully chosen hymns of the sixteenth century to shy away from the necessary decisions of contemporary Christian 23 existence? And finally the matter of pastoral emotionality [Pastorenpathos]: it is truly quite problematic. Even more problematic, however, are well-educated pastors who would never err in this direction but who delight their congregations with their own erudition rather than with the gospel of

Jesus Christ. You are speaking for the intellectuals. Are they not precisely those who need to be asked to look beyond nonessentials and to cling to what is essential? It is quite simply the case that ordinary people and not the well educated uphold the church; and from the point of view of the gospel, we have truly not the slightest cause to be dissatisfied with this or to desire better for ourselves. We might wish, of course, that the intellectuals would not stand off to the side, being repelled by this or that, but that they would come, participate, cooperate. There will indeed have to be the sacrifice of certain forms and traditions in all this, but perhaps this is necessary only in order that even more delightful and freer new forms may emerge.

I can see that this letter already is taking on impermissible proportions even before I begin to speak of the ideas in your letter that in fact most engaged me. You open up the whole problem of church language, and rightly so, in my opinion. Yet this is the point where I feel most awkward about answering you. In the Protestant church, the church of the proclamation of God's word, language is no trivial thing. I understand so well how it continually angers you that we articulate such tremendous and ultimate things,[6] which ordinarily a person can scarcely find words to frame, in such matter-of-fact and mundane ways. You are also quite correct to note that words like sin, grace, forgiveness, and so on have a very different sound, take on a very different weight, when they are spoken by someone who otherwise never speaks such words. The word emerging at last from a long silence carries more weight than the same word in the mouth of a nonstop talker. I also concede to you that there are certain words that we should not use at all because they are worn out. Many have often noted that there should be much less preaching in order to give the word even stronger emphasis.

But this is also clearly "tendentious," arbitrary, and untrue! We pastors experience countless times in providing pastoral care that a Bible passage from the mouth of a sick, poor, or lonely person means something quite different than if we ourselves say it. Thus we keep quiet often enough in order not to stand there like spiritual professionals in our ministry. Yet we know that we must speak and often dare not keep silent where we ourselves might like to. And now place yourself in our position, having to deal all day from morning to evening, "because of our calling," with the greatest words of the world, reading, studying, praying, teaching, baptizing, marrying, burying, preaching. We cannot be grateful enough when someone then tells us where we have done it wrong, where, perhaps by our own subjective involvement, we have fallen into empty verbalization. But above all we want to

---

[6.] Cf. "The Ultimate and the Penultimate Things," *DBWE* 6:146–70.

know how we can improve. A radical measure like excising the words "cross," "sin," "grace," etc. from our vocabulary does not help. First, "cross" cannot be replaced by "guillotine," because it was a cross on which Jesus died. Second, replacing something like "manger" with "feed trough" might initially be a good idea but after the third or fourth use would be just as hackneyed. Of course, there are words, especially one's favorite self-chosen and idiosyncratic words, that one can and should eliminate entirely; yet we must still speak in words. Whether the "everyday speech of the average intellectual" is the best, I do not know. It was certainly not Luther's language, in any case. I am quite opposed to the idea of seeking a particular style of speaking. This is a sure path into complacency. Of course, it does not help that Christianity is two thousand years old and has its own language. In my view, this simple language of the Bible should best be maintained (also because for daily use one desires "water and not juice," to echo your own words). But what matters is the depth from which they come and the context in which they stand.

And now in conclusion I must say something "spiritual": surely you know 25 the works of Bernanos?[7] When those pastors speak, their words carry weight. This is because they come not from some semantic reflection or observation but quite simply from daily personal intimacy with the crucified Jesus Christ. This is the depth from which a word must come if it is to carry weight. One could also say that what matters is that we daily orient ourselves to the image of the crucified Christ and allow ourselves to be called to conversion. When our words come directly, as it were, from the cross of Jesus Christ himself, when Christ is so present to us that it is he who is speaking our words, only then can we be released from the terrible danger of empty spiritual verbosity. But who among us lives in this kind of composure [Sammlung]?

So! I hope that I have not talked you to death but that you note in this letter the hope and expectation of receiving yet another response from you.

With many thanks for your letter, I am

Yours respectfully,
[Dietrich Bonhoeffer]

[7.] Bonhoeffer was apparently from an early age interested in the French writer Georges Bernanos (see *DB-ER,* 139–40). At the end of the 1920s, he read *Die Sonne Satans.* His library also contained the following (mostly in first editions of the German translation): *Der Abtrünnige; Johanna: Ketzerin und Heilige; Der heilige Dominikus; Tagebuch eines Landpfarrers.* On the latter, see *DB-ER,* 562–63. (Bonhoeffer considered this book "of fundamental importance on the subject of pastoral counseling" [*DB-ER,* 562].)

4. From Eberhard Baumann[1]

Stettin, March [?,] 1940

Dear Licentiate Bonhoeffer:

I was grateful to receive your friendly response of the twenty-first of this month indicating to me that my complaint about your theological letter had arisen from a complete misunderstanding. Needless to say, all sorts of conclusions that I drew in my protest to Brother Onnasch have thereby collapsed insofar as we are looking at the intention and not the possible effects of your letter.

As you can imagine, I keep asking myself how I could have come to such a misunderstanding. Was it due to the confessional oversensitivity that you assume of me or to the specific circumstances under which your letter appeared?

You are already aware that I am not alone in my position, which you have corrected. I will attempt in all brevity to sketch the accompanying circumstances that caused me such trouble.

First, there was the blending of quite disparate elements: this study guide and an Easter greeting; Article 7 of the Formula of Concord and the inner preparation for approaching the Lord's Table in Holy Week; dogmatic study and this intended spiritual immediacy.

Second, there was the choice of this particular object of study, which provoked the question: Why specifically the Formula of Concord and only this, without placing it within the broader context of other symbols of the Reformation era?

Third, there was the stimulus and guidance for study of this material solely through description of its content, without any actual guidelines as to methodological process. If the estimation of the academic ability of the younger generation is correct that such help is necessary, then methodological guidelines would seem to me to be essential.

Far be it from me to criticize the way you as a teacher of theology have chosen to proceed. But in order that you may understand me, I would ask you kindly to consider the following thoughts I would like to express.

Surely you cannot imagine that I would consider it particularly promising for the future of the church if objective work on significant church documents were suppressed, etc. I can assure you that pure objectivity has been my guiding star all my life. Thus I have not the slightest objection to all Protestant theologians, not just my Lutheran colleagues, immersing themselves in the study of the Lutheran symbols, just as all of us, not just the Reformed colleagues, should attend to the confessional documents of the Reformed church. For we all have a stake in the communion of the whole Protestant church. To be sure, my experience over a decade and a half on the

---

[1.] LKA der Evangelischen Kirche in Westfalen, Bielefeld, Bestand 5,1, no. 522, fasc. 2; typewritten; cf. *NL,* A 60,1; carbon copy; previously published in *GS* 3:401–3.

theological examination board has taught me that the Lutheran theologians of Pomerania generally do not consider actual study of the Reformed confessions to be necessary and thus from the outset view Reformed doctrine through confessional lenses.

Of course, what seems to me incomparably more important in all questions of the 27 teaching of the faith, however, is returning with ever greater commitment to the scriptures, because only deep immersion in them can heal the unhappy rift that has come down to us from the Reformation of the sixteenth century. I have been forced to observe repeatedly and with increasing sadness that even in the present crisis my Lutheran colleagues lack this commitment, since for them their Reformation has become the canon, the regula fidei,[2] requiring no revision.

The method to follow for any guided study of articles of faith seems to me to be one of comparing the Reformation writings on both sides in the light of Holy Scripture and returning from the reformers[3] to the scriptures, read by all of us as impartially as possible—in fact, best of all would be to begin the whole process from scripture.

My comment that confessionalism is from Satan could be attributed as easily to biblical diction as to Lutheran. As I have made explicitly clear, it refers to the development that I have followed with such sorrow from Barmen to Halle and beyond. I would value hearing from you whether you also see the great tempter and accuser in action here.

Finally, I warmly reciprocate your wishes for a blessed Easter and extend my own for your ministry; this Easter has seen me returning to full-time work after an extended illness.

Yours,
[Baumann]

5. Eberhard Bethge to Herbert von Bismarck[1]

Berlin

Honorable Mr. Secretary:

I am being advised to ask you to attempt as soon as possible to procure a response to my petition, at least preliminary information as to whether the request has any hope of success. Should this reply be in the negative, I would soon need to begin seek-

---

[2.] "rule of faith"

[3.] [In this context *Vätern* is more likely a reference to the reformers than to the patristic fathers.—MB]

[1.] *NL,* A 61,3 (2); handwritten draft, probably written shortly before May 12, 1940 (Pentecost). The Nachlaß also contains an earlier draft, first in Bonhoeffer's handwriting, then in Bethge's, from around April 1940. It concerns the attempt to revoke the conscription into military service that Bethge had already received.

28   ing a position as a driver. Following the advice given to me here, I am venturing to
urge you to look into my situation once again; I am extremely grateful and indebted
to you for your guidance in these matters up to this point.—Our trip planned for
this week had to be postponed unexpectedly, since my friend is still urgently needed
here for a few days.[2] Nevertheless, I hope by the end of next week to be able to
report to you in person the matters discussed here regarding my concern.[3] But in
any case it would be important to have received this other information by then.

We think often these days of your whole family, particularly those who are on the
front.[4] What a Pentecost this is for Christians on both sides!

With sincere thanks and warm wishes,
Your devoted E. B.

6. Finkenwalde Circular Letter[1]

Personal Letter[2]

Dear Brothers,

Today I must thank all of you collectively for the recent greetings and letters that I have received from you. Otherwise I shall be unable to work
through all my correspondence, and I do not want you to have to wait even
longer for my thanks. Every greeting and longer letter has given me pleasure and made it possible for me to focus again on each one of you. But you
must not think that I also wish to make claims on the small amount of free
29   time that you have and that you need for your families and yourselves. I can
clearly imagine that with all you are going through, you might sometimes
wish simply not to have to talk or write any more about it, particularly if you

---

[2.] This apparently refers to consultations in Canaris's office. See Bonhoeffer's note
of May 27, 1940, to the Schlawe recruiting station (1/9).

[3.] Bonhoeffer and Bethge did then in fact visit the Bismarcks in Lasbeck on May 19,
1940.

[4.] Two sons, Jürgen und Hans-Otto von Bismarck, were part of the German invasion
of France, which had begun on May 10, 1940.

[1.] *NL*, A 48,3; carbon copy of typewritten letter; notation at top in other handwriting
"May 1940"; previously published in *GS* 2:564–69. The Nachlaß also contains an attached
sheet with handwritten notes.

[2.] Since the June 30, 1937, decree of the Reich Ministry for Public Enlightenment
and Propaganda that all newsletters and mimeographs fell under the Editor Law, every
newsletter had to be signed by hand. [The Ministry for Public Enlightenment and Propaganda was Goebbels's office and was part of the Reich Ministry of Propaganda. Under the
April 1933 Editor Law, editors of all publications had to be Nazi Party members and members of the Reich Chamber of Literature. Hence Bonhoeffer's circular letters had to be
signed and mailed as personal letters.—MB]

are also writing home. I truly do not want to pressure you for letters. I often
feel ashamed when I receive a long letter from the front and think that the
one who has written me could surely use his sleep and rest for himself. That
I deeply rejoice at every greeting from a truly free hour goes without saying! I thank you for all your sacrifices of time and rest that you have made
in writing these letters.

Many of you wish to hear more of how it is going for us, so that we do
not lose touch. I understand that completely. Yet you must keep in mind
that in these times each of us is happy when he can do his work where he is,
and that we often lose sight of the big picture. As painful as this is, there is
also something good about it; it is a time of testing for each of us as to
whether we can faithfully do our work alone for a while. We still do not know
how it will all come out, but as far as I can see, I do not have the impression
that the whole endeavor is suffering by this. Whoever has learned by now
what this is all about will stand fast, even if he must stand alone for a time,
provided it is not too long. As you can imagine, the greatest difficulty cur
rently is the question of replacements.[3] Truly every conceivable possibility
is being attempted here. In some places it nearly overwhelms the brothers'
strength. Yet at those places where we run up so clearly against the limits of
our service, we should not let ourselves be worn out by scruples. This is
where prayer and faith step into the gap, and gratitude for what we still can
do. I would not find it right to burden individuals at home or on the front
with particular concerns. Most of you are bearing enough already. Each of
us must know how to fight his way through his tasks with God's word, and
while doing so he may be certain of the intercessions of the community and
the power of Jesus Christ.

Indeed, I think the time has come once again to say something about
the freedom of our Christian life and the grace of God. Quite a few of you
who are at the front write somewhat dejectedly about the difficulty of rec-   30
onciling an order for the Christian life[4] with the daily duty that claims
you completely. For many the time and leisure for reading scripture and for
prayer and intercession are simply not available. But beyond this there seems
to be a range of possibilities for holding the sort of conversations for which
we as Christians long, and for gaining a certain influence over the topics of
general conversation. Some write very pleased about this; others are quite
troubled. At present I do not know if it is entirely right when people keep

---

[3.] [It was difficult to find pastors to take the place of those who were serving on the
front lines.—MB]

[4.] The theme "Ordering of Life" was to be discussed at the upcoming Ninth Confessing Synod of the Evangelical Church of the Old Prussian Union in Leipzig on October
12–13, 1940. See also the calendar notations for June–July 1940; see 1/10, ed. note 27.

on writing to you that you on the front also are and must be "in the ministry."
Certainly none of us is ever released from the responsibility of being a Christian, and we dare not deny that we are pastors. But is this not something different from saying as a matter of course that even on the front you are "in the ministry"? In my opinion you are not, in fact, and cannot be. I am wary of an illusion that will become a rigid law for the serious-minded, one that will rub them raw and eventually cause them to founder. Perhaps you will reply that it is your ordination itself that lays such a law on you. I do not wish to go into the theological questions of ordination and its meaning for those who for various reasons cannot fulfill their office (thus, for example, in the case of a change of career). Opinions vary on this point. But one thing is certain: ordination is given to us for comfort and as a grace to make us certain in our ministry. It is not intended to torment us so that we despair of it, and in any case it is certainly not intended to do this to you now. It seems crucial to me to state this outright. In this matter we must protect ourselves carefully against fanatical ideas that may sound nice for a while but can become quite dangerous over time and can throw our faith into total confusion. When one of you writes in distress that he is only able to be a soldier among other soldiers and that in the process he tries to remain a
31   Christian but has no strength to do any more than this, I want to console him and all who live in this way. I can see no unfaithfulness to your ministry in that. One cannot as a soldier simply go on leading the life of a pastor, and one should not torment oneself internally about this. Naturally it is marvelous when duty allows the time one needs for the word of God. But generally you yourselves are not personally responsible for whether this is the case. Naturally it is heartening to be able to affect something and be of assistance in conversations. But clearly we alone are not to blame for the limits that we run up against in this regard. Naturally it would be good if we could gain some influence on certain expressions and conversations in our surroundings. But once again I do not think it is good or advisable to cultivate a sort of oversensitivity within ourselves that might actually make us weak and incapable of more energetic help. Those of us who have learned to discern the power and nature of the world and of our own particular evil in the cross of Jesus Christ and who, in that same cross, deeply trust in the unending love of God for this world will surely not be so very surprised and shocked by certain expressions of this worldliness. Thus, I hope you understand what I mean: we rejoice with all those for whom doors open and are grateful with them, but we also stand with those whose experience is different and do not wish for them to despair of their calling to ministry.

My dear brothers on the front, the chief difference between your existence and ours, we who still stand in the freedom of our ministry, consists in the fact that we may still engage ourselves in a place that, through our calling, we ourselves have freely chosen, whereas you now share the life of millions of people whose work and life commitment have never been free in this sense. The inner reorientation required here is probably the most difficult part of this for us and sometimes even makes it difficult to understand one another. Even apart from the whole Christian problematic, this profound change in our lives surely also necessitates a reordering of our life with the word of God. A different measure of the consciousness of being a Christian distinguishes your present existence from your past. Whereas those of us in the ministry are reminded of being a Christian constantly throughout the day, for you hours and whole days may go by without any moment for such recollections, just as is the case for most working people. If then, some morning or evening or at some unexpected hour, the moment for such recollection comes—and it will come—then it is often so overwhelming that we can hardly bear it; and we long that much more passionately for the sort of ongoing communion with the word of God that we had in ministry. And then it can also happen that we wrongly accuse ourselves of seeking a stable order of Christian life that we simply cannot have at this point. We do truly know that the ordering and consciousness of Christian existence are good and extremely helpful, but they are not everything. The sudden, hard collision of daily work and the word of God, as you surely often experience it at present, must at times simply replace such a regular ordering. We must not oppress ourselves. God knows your present life and finds a way to you even in the most strained and overburdened days, when you can no longer find the way to God.

But now let us all stop looking at and reflecting on our differing situations and work; instead, let us look together to the work of God, which does not stand still regardless of how we participate in it, to God's work in us, in the church, in the whole world. Let us look to God's grace, which has preserved us all to this day through many frightening and dark hours. Let us look to God's faithfulness, which has always kept its promises. God has begun all this with us and our church, and God will also bring it to the end that is good for each person. May the Lord Jesus Christ preserve us in his grace unto the end.

For the sake of the brothers on the front, the meditation texts[5] have been chosen this time in particularly close connection to the weekly verses and cover a longer span of time ahead. If for some reason any further distribution of texts should not occur, we always want to stay close to the weekly verses. Once again I would like to remind you of the small edition of the

[5.] See the May 22, 1936, Finkenwalde Guide to Scriptural Meditation (*DBW* 14: 945–50).

Stuttgart Jubilee Bible, whose notes regarding text and content can sometimes greatly facilitate the reading of especially the Old Testament, particularly when one does not have any other reference aids available.

My dear brothers at home! Perhaps you find that this letter has spoken
too little to you. But we cannot carry on our work without thinking unceasingly of our brothers on the front and holding them in our thoughts, and it
is surely the same for them. How suddenly everything could change for us
as well. Until then be joyful in your work and thankful for every new day in
which God allows you still to serve your congregations. Let us pray for one
another that we may rightly bear the responsibility laid on us and be faithful shepherds of the congregations. At Pentecost our church was founded
by the Holy Spirit. The Holy Spirit will also sustain it. May God, the Holy
Spirit, fill our hearts with new love for God's word, for the Lord's congregation, for all people.

God preserve you, your homes, and your congregations.

Regards from your
Dietrich Bonhoeffer

7. To Georg Eichholz[1]

May 20, 1940

Dear Brother Eichholz,

Only today am I responding to your newsletter. At the outset I would like to
let you know that in a worship service recently you gave great pleasure to
one of our conscripted brothers who happened to attend your church and
wrote quite happily of the sermon, intercessions, and offering intentions.
This pleased me greatly as well.

34   Now to the point: to be honest, I had my suspicions regarding your project
from the beginning. What are sermon meditations? I have never truly understood it, and this has not changed much in the meantime. I tend to see
partly exegesis, partly sermon outlines. And it seems to me that one can find
exegeses elsewhere, and there are already enough sermon series on the
Gospels and better than what we have delivered. We can also find better
theological reflections (see Vogel) or simply general marginal notations on
the text (see Asmussen) elsewhere. I fully include myself in this judgment.

Perhaps the whole thing is the attempt to allow the young generation of
theologians to speak about the old Gospels; and since a book of sermons is

---

[1.] Literary estate of Georg Eichholz; handwritten letter, probably from Berlin. Cf.
NL, A 60,2; previously published in *GS* 6:479–80. On the circumstances, see *DB-ER,* 667–68.

too demanding or too hackneyed, you do it in this somewhat more modern form? I think this could be the case. So my reservations about the whole endeavor still stand. But I must also concede that when I listen to the younger theologians, they are very thankful for this project, and not only those who lack confidence but also the others. Thus some sort of gap—perhaps in many cases simply a gap in the library—is doubtless being filled; and that fully justifies the work that has gone into it. What should be improved in the forthcoming volume I do not know. I do not see much that needs to be done, although I would consider it infinitely more important to treat the Old Testament lessons than the Epistles. I should also pass this on to you as the explicit wish of several young colleagues. Could you not still change this? This is truly a place where help is still needed.

This sort of thing would be my criticism—certainly less constructive than "destructive"—as you requested. We must speak sometime in person about all this. Perhaps you could invite all the participants to gather at some point. That would really be the best thing.

With my best wishes for your work, your
Dietrich Bonhoeffer

8. To Eberhard Baumann[1]

35

May 21, 1940

My dear and honored Consistory Councilor Baumann,

Please forgive me for not thanking you for your letter until today. I am delighted that extensive consensus has emerged in our views, and I may hope and pray that no personal discord remains from the original misunderstanding. Being at odds with you was particularly painful for me since in the past I have considered myself especially close to you theologically; this is why I deeply regret that you can no longer bring yourself to participate in the work of the Council of Brethren. But it is not my place to comment on this, since I have never belonged to the Council of Brethren, either in the past or presently. Perhaps you have heard that my primary field of work will no longer be in Pomerania. On the one hand, this saddens me after five years of work in the province; but, on the other hand, I realize that I have never been at home in Pomerania, from the outset until the present. What has caused this I do not wish to judge. But my work has always fulfilled me and

---

[1.] LKA der Evangelischen Kirche in Westfalen, Bielefeld, Bestand 5,1, no. 522, fasc. 2; typewritten letter with handwritten signature, from Berlin; cf. *NL*, A 60,1; previously published in *GS* 3:404.

made me happy, and now that it is coming to an end, I am particularly grateful for it.

With heartfelt wishes for your work and your personal health, my deeply honored colleague,

Yours always respectfully,
Dietrich Bonhoeffer

36 ### 9. Excerpt from File: To the Schlawe District Military Recruiting Station[1]

Since I will presumably still need to remain a few days in Berlin, I am requesting, following consultation with my military office here, that my service record be sent to the chief of staff for the Foreign Office of Military Intelligence in OKW.[2] Address: Colonel Oster, Foreign Office of Military Intelligence, OKW, Berlin W 35, Tirpitzufer 80. Schlawe should remain my official district military recruiting station.

[1.] Vojenský ústřední archiv, Prague, "Reichskriegsgericht," [War Court] file 9: "Sammlung von Anklagen und Urteilen—gKdos 1943" [Collection of Indictments and Judgments—Top Secret Military Documents 1943], VÚA-VHA, RKG (39), 2(I), Geh. Kdos.—rozsudky 1943–45; copy of an excerpt from the September 21, 1943, court-martial indictment against Bonhoeffer, which is reproduced in full in 1/230.2. This recently discovered document, containing quotations from Bonhoeffer's own writings to the Schlawe recruiting station, verifies that he was already working in some form with the "Canaris office" as of October 12, 1939. The excerpt reproduced here is from a document dated May 27, 1940, from Berlin. According to the indictment, Bonhoeffer was given a medical examination at the Schlawe recruiting station on June 5, 1940, and was classified KV (*kriegsverwendungsfähig*, "fit for wartime service"). [KV is equivalent to the U.S. Selective Service classification 1-A.—MB]

[2.] [Abbreviation for Oberkommando der Wehrmacht, "Armed Forces High Command."—MB]

B. Visitations in East Prussia. June–August 1940

37

10. Calendar Notes, June 5–July 26, 1940[1]

June 5: Schlawe conference[2]
    6: Block's[3] birthday
       Königsberg
    7: Meeting. Seckenburg (Daase)[4] 7:30.
       Elder (Bauer) worship service reading. Lay liturgy.[5] Sermon rec-
       ommendations. Funerals for teacher, parish pastor's wife [Pfarr-
       frau]. Instruction by organist (pastor's wife) [Pastorsfrau]. 100
       children.
       Evening worship service Full church. Intercessions. Offering.

[1.] *NL*, A 59, 4; handwritten entries in the pocket calendar titled "Agenda 1940." Items crossed out, as well as information gained from other sources, appear in square brackets.

[2.] From the time of the collective pastorates, Schlawe remained Bonhoeffer's official place of residence; on the other hand, he felt an obligation to fulfill various functions for the Pomeranian Council of Brethren. Thus, along with Heinrich Rendtorff, he was assigned the chair of a committee for meetings of clergy. According to statements in the indictment of September 21, 1943, on this date Bonhoeffer took the medical exam for military induction at the Schlawe District Military Recruiting Station (see 1/230.2).

[3.] Eduard Block, the superintendent of the Schlawe church district, had already personally assisted Bonhoeffer in decisive ways with the implementation of the collective pastorates. See *DB-ER*, 590–91.

[4.] This is the beginning of the actual visitation work, undertaken at times together with Bethge. This initially included places in the Niederung church district, in the vicinity of Tilsit, and the area near Kurischer Bay.

[5.] Shortly after the beginning of the war, in light of the many Confessing Church pastors conscripted into military service, the Council of Brethren of the Old Prussian Union had already provided the church elders of the orphaned congregations with a "lay liturgy" for their leadership as lectors.

8: 5:30 leave for Herdenau (Dumschat). Prepared questions

1) Young colleagues; 2) Baptismal *discipline* in the case of an unbelieving father; 3) *Karkeln*.[6] No access to the church due to intercessions[7]

38

9: *Sunday* worship (intercessions, offering) well attended.
C[hildren's]. w[orship]. Congregational meeting. Regarding the situation.

Karkeln. Women's circle. Sailing.

Kuckerneese (Pastor Potschka) Zippel as replacement (Musician[8]—neutral—hard to see through [undurchsichtig]).[9] *Women's circle* overflowing. Devotions.

Situation (Zippel not admitted). Parish pastor's wife conducts the women's circle.

10: 6:00 to Tilsit. Lenkitsch. Meeting
10–11 pastors and even more women.
Theolog. presentation. Good discussion. Situation.
(Council of Brethren should encourage reports on meetings!)
8:00 Holy Communion. Sermon. Church full. / Pract. results:
Not too rushed. Have enough time. Directions for pastoral visits.
Breaks. Sermon or *pastoral visit? Offerings?*
Lodging. Finances. Board. *Theolog.* society.[10]

11: Königsberg. Worked afternoon.

12: Co[uncil of] B[rethren] Meeting CC.[11] Meditation, Rom. 8:17ff.[12]

[6.] The fishing village of Karkeln, located on the banks of Kurisher Bay, had already won renown in the East Prussian Church Struggle when in 1936–37, despite police action, the entire population committed itself unanimously to the Confessing Church. See Linck, *Der Kirchenkampf in Ostpreussen,* 197 ff.

[7.] [This suggests that, despite strong popular support, the Confessing Church in Karkeln was under pressure either from local church authorities who were German Christians or from the Gestapo. Throughout the Church Struggle, Confessing groups wishing to hold services were sometimes barred from church buildings.—MB]

[8.] Uncertain reading.

[9.] [Throughout the Church Struggle, "neutral" church members and staff attempted to steer clear of the conflicts between the Confessing Church and German Christian church authorities. In the process they sometimes undermined the Confessing position, and Bonhoeffer and other radical Confessing Christians viewed them as a threat. Bonhoeffer's notes here indicate distrust and perhaps insecurity about where the local church musician stood on church politics.—MB]

[10.] This apparently refers to the Society for Protestant Theology founded in February 1940 by Ernst Wolf; see 1/81, ed. note 5.

[11.] ["CC" refers to the Confessing Church.—MB]

[12.] No corresponding draft is found in the Nachlaß.

13: Thurs. Schakendorf. Waldmann
    13:53 16:45 Brittanien 18:00
    Telep[hone]! Fornaçon
    Telegram 90 pf.
    Worship service 8:30 Mark 9:24.[13]
    Missionary. CC examination. (Heb. 9)[14]
14: Groß-Friedrichsdorf (Fornaçon)
    14:20–15:55 Brit[tanien]. 17:49 to Heinr[ichswalde].
    Worship 7:00 Rom. 6:3, 4[15] 46   39
    Songbook?
15: [crossed out: Heinrichswalde Fornaçon]
16: Sunday. Tilsit Reformed / [crossed out: "Lenkeningken"]
    Lenkweten[16] [crossed out: worship] Eberhard/women's circle/
    Ordination proceedings Thimme
    von Arnim[17]
    Worship. Reformed C[hurch]. Rom. 6:3-4.
    Kramp[18]
17: Mon. Memel / Meeting[19]
    Wiesner, Riedesel, Abromeit, Lay
    theologian meeting. Lay instruction.
18: Tues. Two pastorates
    Pokraken (Heidmann) Eb[erhard].
    Women's circle
    Argeningken (Pr. Braun). Poor congregation.
    Pers. visit.
19: Wed. Aulenbach (via Grünheide)

[13.] See on the same text the 1938 confirmation sermon (*DBW* 15:476–81 [*GS* 4: 441–47]).

[14.] See Bonhoeffer's April 1940 "Reflection on the Ascension," 2/2. [Again, "CC" refers to the Confessing Church.—MB]

[15.] Cf. *DBWE* 4:207 and *DBW* 14:348–50.

[16.] The correct spelling is "Lengwethen."

[17.] This apparently refers to Wilhelm von Arnim-Lützlow, a member of the Council of Brethren of the Old Prussian Union; it presumably has to do with contacts regarding exemption from military service.

[18.] The East Prussian writer Willy Kramp, who was just achieving public recognition for his novel *Die Fischer von Lissau* and was an active member of the East Prussian Confessing Church, had lived since 1939 with his brother Erich, a Confessing Church pastor, in Kaporn on the Fresh Bay; cf. 1/15, ed. note 14.

[19.] On the events of this day, see *DB-ER*, 681. Bonhoeffer and Bethge's June 17–18 stay at the parsonage of Schloßbach is confirmed by their entry in Pastor Paul Melzer's guest book; cf. *NL*, Anh. D 9.

Matern,[20] Stoldt
Worship, very well attended. 60 RM
(Stoldt ordination [...][21])

20: 1 h[our] visit to merchant Hellwig-Skaisgirren
    Lekszas. Worship Eb[erhard]? Faithful
    women's circle dissolved
    Königsberg.

21: Königsberg. Move. Becks[22]

40   Tragheimer Pulverstr[aße] 46

22: Danzig.

23: Sunday. Worship Grunow.[23] Baltic Sea. Student group.

24: Mon. Baltic Sea—Schlawe

25: Stettin Kleist[24]
    Berlin

26: Wed. Berlin

27: —

28: —

29: Köslin[25]

30: Sunday sermon Köslin Rom. 6:3-4
    Lay meeting.[26]
    Evening meeting.

July 1: Clergy meeting. Köslin
     Berlin

2: [Nowawes, Council of Brethren]

3: —

4: —

5: —

6: Students.

7: Sunday [crossed out: students] Königsberg.

[20.] Bonhoeffer and Bethge's June 19–20 stay is confirmed by their entry in the guest book of Pastor Gerhard Matern in Aulenbach/Insterburg.

[21.] Illegible.

[22.] See 1/12.

[23.] See 1/14.

[24.] Ibid.

[25.] Cf. Ruth von Kleist-Retzow's itinerary in her letter of June 13, 1940 (see 1/11).

[26.] The primary promoter of the Pomeranian "lay meetings" was Dr. August Knorr, a doctor at the Diaconal Hospital in Köslin; cf. Knorr, "Laienkonvente," *Junge Kirche* (1938): 899ff.; cf. also Lehndorff, *Die Insterburger Jahre,* 67ff. We find a clue to Bonhoeffer's personal exchange with Dr. Knorr in a book that he apparently borrowed during this weekend, Wach's *Das Problem des Todes in der Philosophie unserer Zeit,* which was found in Bonhoeffer's library after his death, inscribed with Dr. Knorr's name (*NL-Bibl.,* 7 A 90).

Mail. Ordering of eccl[esial] life[27]
Agricultural work?

8: Mon. [Blöstau] pastors' retreat[28]
[crossed out: Prot[estant] confession] Presentation.
Baptismal grace and baptismal discipline.[29]

9: Tues. pastors' retreat.
Presentation: Our Proclamation Today.[30]
Presentation: Confession for Protestants.[31]
Evening discussion

10: Wed. pastors' retreat. Bible study, Matt. 7:13ff.[32]
Discussion of the prophetic mission of the C[hurch][33]
Afternoon Königsberg 3.00 until 6.30 Council of Brethren theol.
discussion of church and ministry.[34]
Evening meeting with soldiers.

11: Thurs. work. Sermon on Matt. 7:13ff.
Presentation on death[35]
Presentation for Monday

12: Fri. work as above.

13: Sat. Blöstau[36]

41

[27.] Cf. the Finkenwalde circular letter of May 1940, 1/6, ed. note 4.

[28.] Arno Dumschat, conversation with German editor of *DBW* 16, August 16, 1988. Pastor Dumschat had entered the following in his professional calendar: "Retreat with Bonhoeffer in Blöstau" (the location of the East Prussian Confessing Church preachers' seminary, led until 1937 by Hans-Joachim Iwand).

[29.] Thematically the corresponding parts of Bonhoeffer's *Discipleship* come particularly close to this; see *DBWE* 4:205–12 and 269–75. Principle 6 on "The Power of the Keys and Congregational Discipline in the New Testament" from May 1937 is similar (*DBW* 14: 834–35; cf. also *DBW* 14:738–41).

[30.] Cf. "Draft of a Lecture on the Theme of 'Glory,' " 2/4, ed. note 1.

[31.] Cf. "Confession and the Lord's Supper" in *DBWE* 5:108–18; cf. also the 1936 lecture on confession as part of pastoral counseling, *DBW* 14:559–71.

[32.] Matt. 7:13-23 was the appointed preaching text for the following Sunday, on which Bonhoeffer then also preached in Blöstau. On the same text, see "The Great Separation" in *DBWE* 4:175–81. This corresponds in content to Pastor Arno Dumschat's recollections of this Bible study (Dumschat, conversation with the German editor, July 27, 1988).

[33.] This may be identical to the lecture mentioned in ed. note 30; cf. also ed. note 42.

[34.] See Anna Ohnesorge's notes on Bonhoeffer's remarks during this discussion of church and ministry: "Important that we bring ourselves to speak of the glory of the Gospel, and of the glory of the pastoral office!" (*DB-ER*, 683). [Anna Ohnesorge served on the Pomeranian Council of Brethren for Catechetical Questions.—MB]

[35.] Cf. the book title cited in ed. note 26.

[36.] On this momentous weekend with Königsberg students, which the police brought to an abrupt end, see the report, 1/15; see also Bonhoeffer's own September 15, 1940, written account to the Reich Central Security Office, 1/21.

14: Sunday sermon
15: Mon. Gumbinnen
16: —[Königsberg][37]
17: —
18: Enzuhnen. Dörr
19: Enzuhnen
42   20: Eberhard
21: Eidkau
22: —
23: [Königsberg, Danzig][38]
24: —
25: 10:42 to Marienburg
[crossed out: Marienwerder. Sporleder. Mühlengraben 5 tel: 2196]
26: [crossed out: Marienburg]

December 14:[39] Miss von Wessling [Königsberg] Hinterroßgarten 11.
22: *Word* and *deed* / defense of one's own interests
Power and truth
Glory of the word, of the office, of love (faith, hope, love)
Babylon.
Proclamation of Luke?
We wish to preach: [...][40]
[We wish] to act: mercy
We confess that [...][41]
Joy for the sake of the congregation, of our work, of unity[42]
24: Send *Discipleship* to Fornaçon
Dumschat
Waldmann
25: —
26: 13th supper 1.50
14th dinner 2.50
13–14th Britt[anien].—Schokau—Britt[anien] 2.40

[37.] See Bonhoeffer's letter of July 16, 1940, 1/14.

[38.] See Bonhoeffer's letter of July 23, 1940, 1/16, and its altered plan for the following days.

[39.] The entries beginning with December 14 clearly do not refer to these dates but are still connected to the East Prussian activities.

[40.] Illegible.

[41.] Illegible.

[42.] Cf. the "Draft of a Lecture on the Theme of 'Glory,'" in which these key terms recur in part, 2/4.

14th supper 1.50

Friedr.— [...]^[43] 0.60 Bus

15th supper 2 x 3.00   43

7/7 supper 1.50

7/8 dinner 2.50

7/10 supper 1.50

7/11 all meals including breakfast 6.00

7/12 [all means including breakfast] 6.00

7/12 Telegraph to Schlawe 3.75

[Telegraph to Schlawe] 2.25

30:   Offerings

      Schakendorf 6/13, 28.23

      Gr. Friedrichsdorf (Niederung) 6/14, 46.00

      [Final pages:]

      Legalization. Aryan paragraph, offerings. Recheck.

      nearly 90.

      Themes? GC literature^[44]

      Elbing. Küßner, Jeschke, Hecht. Bishop strong.

      Group.

      Pastors.

      Consistory Spiritual Administration

      Visitation reports

      Sermons

      Periodicals

      13.53 Heinrichswalde.

      Ortelsburg. Seckenburg (Daase)

      Herdenau Dumschat

      Lay meetings

      Bauer Kailuweit Gr. Friedrichsdorf

      Ch[urch] D[istrict], Niederung

      Visits. Bookstores.

      C[ouncil of] Br[ethren]. Königsberg Schützenstraße 2, 2, with
        Mrs. von Grot

      Office 33942^[45]

      Beckmann 44416

      Koschorke 31927

      [crossed out: appointment for 6/19, 21927]

[43.] Illegible.

[44.] [Literature from the German Christians.—MB]

[45.] [This number and those that follow are ostensibly telephone numbers.—MB]

44   Leidreiter 32165
          Koschorke 31927; Steinmetzstraße 27
          Civil tax annually 36 RM.
          Postal check 4239 Stettin
          Main municipal bank Schlawe
          Income tax account "supplement"
          (praenumerando)
          Income tax, 87.75
          (58.50 income tax
          29.25 war tax)
          (prae!) 400 (312.25)

11. Ruth von Kleist-Retzow to Dietrich Bonhoeffer and Eberhard Bethge[1]

June 13, 1940

Dear friends,

I wish to allow you to partake of this hour in which my heart is full of praise and thanksgiving for the merciful protection of Alla.[2]

My daughter[3] writes: "Just received word from Alla from the twelfth; yesterday, from the tenth. Today only, 'I am doing well.' He lay for twenty-four hours in the artillery fire of a 7.5 and a 10 cm. division, whose six batteries fired only on that bridge." She adds, "But after reading the letter I have the impression (from the tenth) that his nerves are giving out." No wonder. The only wonder, a great and indescribable wonder, is that he was not shot. "A thousand may fall at your side, ten thousand at your right hand, but it will not come near you"[4]—this line sings in my heart.— What may well take place in the soul of a man who experiences such a thing! Is it not perhaps worth the entire war? This is what we must pray. And also that we not question afterward whether we might see it, or whether it must remain quite hidden.

45   My thoughts are leaping about: I have reread Karl Barth, *Der Christ als Zeuge,* with such great joy.[5] It is God who is at work in you, enabling you both to will and to work for God's good pleasure.[6]—Only let us be still and allow God to work, particularly

---

[1.] *NL,* Anh. C 4 (2); typewritten copy from Eberhard Bethge.

[2.] Alla was Ruth von Kleist-Retzow's grandson, Alexander Stahlberg. On his war experiences, see Stahlberg, *Bounden Duty.*

[3.] Spes Stahlberg née Kleist-Retzow was married to the Stettin industrialist Walter Stahlberg.

[4.] Ps. 91:7.

[5.] Karl Barth, "The Christian as Witness," *The Student World* 27, no. 4 (1934).

[6.] Phil. 2:13.

toward the neighbor as well. And yet do everything that presents itself to us, in order to be an instrument in this place.

In these days I have received many painful notices from acquaintances of deaths on the front. A widow who lost her husband in the world war[7] had to surrender a son and a son-in-law in a single day. Two distant nephews, Winterfeld[8] and Batocki,[9] both particularly promising boys, have been killed. Jürgen Bismarck's[10] best friend, whom I knew and who occasionally wrote to me, married only six months, gave his life. And yet we know that there is some meaning in all this. Yes, "for faith one day is long enough."[11] For "God's goodness and mercies are new every morning."[12] This morning I am focusing completely on the prayer: let these six hours following the cease-fire pass graciously.

Dear Dietrich, I thank you for your kind letter from Tilsit. I very much look forward to seeing you again. Here again is my plan: I will be in Lasbeck (Gr. Sabow 34) from the twenty-eighth at five o'clock in the afternoon until the same time on the twenty-ninth.—Then I wish to travel via Kolberg—Belgard to Köslin, where I will arrive at 9:30 in the evening.[13]

I am looking forward to Bärbel and Klaus,[14] to their exuberance, and to the possibility of new connections to your family.

With greetings from my whole heart to both of you,
Your devoted RKR

Looking back on the death of his brother and his friend, Jürgen writes, "I do not wish to inquire after the Why. Fortunately I still know our New Year's song ('Das Jahr geht still zu Ende')[15] by heart."

Could this not also be an answer?

[7.] [She lost her husband in World War I.—MB]

[8.] Hans von Winterfeld, first lieutenant and company commander, was killed on May 15, 1940, near Reaucourt, France.

[9.] Otto von Batocki, first lieutenant, was killed on the Aisne on June 9, 1940.

[10.] Jürgen was the eldest son of Herbert von Bismarck of Lasbeck.

[11.] This sentence echoes the sentence "One day is long enough to preserve faith" from Bonhoeffer's April 9, 1938, confirmation homily in Kieckow (*DBW* 15: 476–81 [*GS* 4: 443]).

[12.] Lam. 3:23.

[13.] Cf. Bonhoeffer's calendar notes, 1/10, ed. note 25.

[14.] The Dohnanyi children were able to spend their July vacation with Ruth von Kleist-Retzow in Klein-Krössin.

[15.] ["The year draws quietly to a close," composed by Eleonore von Reuss and one of the most famous New Year's hymns in Germany. It reads in part, "Why is there such great suffering and such brief joy?"—MB] *Evangelisches Kirchengesangbuch*, 44.

46   **12. To His Parents**[1]

June 21, 1940

My dear Parents,

Today I sent off a package to you, dear Mama, with the request to have the laundry done right away. Also included is a birthday present for Klaus[2] (and for Bärbel, if she will also be celebrating her birthday), which I hope will arrive on time. I would like to come to Berlin for three or four days at the beginning of next week (with Eberhard). On the thirtieth we both have to preach again in Pomerania.

Today as I was looking for a home base in Königsberg, someone in the Council of Brethren told me that a Miss Becks wished to rent out a room. I went there and found your old school friend; she was very nice. At this point I also discovered that since the first day here we have been staying in your old house in Königsberg, where Christel was born, Rhesastraße 18. It is now a Protestant hostel. These two coincidences were quite delightful.

I like East Prussia very well, much better than Pomerania. The people seem more generous; Königsberg too seems like a city in which one can live well, in contrast to Stettin. But behind everything that we see, other experiences loom[3] that fill our thoughts unceasingly, even into our dreams.

It has been a long time since I heard from you. I had some canned fish sent to you from Tilsit. I hope you like it. It cost six marks but is not available in Berlin. Has the situation with Mrs. von Kleist and the Dohnanyis been resolved?[4] Hoping to see you soon,

Your grateful Dietrich

47   **13. From Herbert von Bismarck**[1]

Stettin, June 24, 1940

Dear Pastor Bonhoeffer:

My wife and I thank you with all our hearts for your kind and loving words.[2] You are right that no one can or should ever fill the hole. The pain of this "never again" is

---

[1.] *NL,* A 59,1 (1); handwritten card from Königsberg; previously published in *GS* 6: 476; partially published in *GS* 2:373.

[2.] The birthday of his nephew Klaus von Dohnanyi was June 23; that of Klaus's sister Barbara was the twenty-seventh.

[3.] He is alluding to the surrender of France on June 17, 1940. Bethge reports on the experience of this day with Bonhoeffer in the village of Memel (*DB-ER,* 681).

[4.] Cf. 1/11, ed. note 14.

[1.] *NL,* Anh. C 5 (5); handwritten letter. Cf. Bethge's letter of May 12, 1940, 1/5.

[2.] Bismarck's son Hans-Otto was killed in France. Bonhoeffer's letter not extant.

there and will remain. But we are permitted to experience that pain with faith in God's goodness in these events that are so incomprehensible to us. You probably recall our last conversation: Should God not also be able to lead our people into God's way again by means of a victory exceeding all historical measure? God can surely also do this; let us ask God to do so.[3]

I am very grateful that my wife is completely without bitterness. Only we are full of worry about Jürgen, because we have not heard from him since the ninth. Now we are waiting hourly for the cease-fire—and then for the news that he is alive!

With heartfelt greetings and thankfulness,
Your Bismarck

14. To Paula Bonhoeffer[1]

July 16, 1940

Dear Mama,

I am sending along a few stamps[2] that we cannot use. Miss Becks did leave me some sugar here, around half a pound, which should at some point perhaps be given back to her. Also I am sending a small package of laundry. I do not need it at the moment. From August 1 on, I am hoping to spend a few days with Mrs. von Kleist;[3] if I could then receive some things there, I would be very grateful to you. Since yesterday Eberhard is back in East Prussia as well. Tomorrow we are going to the Stallupöner region. Would you please send my mail on to Pastor Link now, at Löbenichtscher Kirchplatz 3, Königs- 48
berg? From the twenty-eighth on, I will be in Danzig, Neugarten 1, with Pastor Grunow, Diaconal House. Then with Mrs. von Kleist.

Unfortunately, my hair lotion recently came open in my suitcase and has once again ruined my jacket. This is so annoying. I hope I can still salvage it.

We are amazed at the calm in the world. But it can change at any time.[4]

Hopefully it is quieter than usual in your empty house.

Love to you all,
Your grateful Dietrich

[3.] On the mood during this period, see *DB-ER*, 681ff.

[1.] *NL*, A 59,1 (2); handwritten letter from Königsberg; previously published in *GS* 6:477.

[2.] [Food rationing stamps.—MB]

[3.] This plan was later changed because of the incidents in Blöstau; see Bonhoeffer's letter of July 23, 1940, 1/16.

[4.] At this time the preparations were under way for Operation Sea Lion, the planned amphibious invasion of England; these plans were abandoned in October 1940. On the other hand, in July 1940 Hitler gave the first directives to the Armed Forces High Command in preparation for an attack on the Soviet Union.

15. From the Königsberg SD Regional Headquarters to the Reich Central Security Office[1]

Königsberg (Prussia)[2]

Re: Activities of the Protestant Student Service[3] and the Confessing Church in East Prussia.

No file on record.

49   The Protestant Student Service held regular Bible studies on Tuesday and Friday of every week in this trimester. This office learned of such activity and commissioned a student to take part. According to this student's report, in addition to the aforementioned Bible studies, two retreats have taken place since the month of May. The third student retreat was planned for Saturday and Sunday, July 13 and 14, at Gut Blöstau, which was already familiar as the site of the private seminary of the Confessing Church under Licentiate *Iwand*. The agent of this office also participated in this retreat. He was invited by the acting student chaplain, *Koschorke*. The invitations were sent on hectographed cards to those individual students known to the student chaplain to be interested. At the instigation of the SD Regional Headquarters, three officials of the state police headquarters and a member of this office went to Blöstau on Sunday, July 14, in order to disband the retreat, which fell under the May 9 and June 21 edicts[4] of the SS high commander and the chief of German police.[5] In particular, the following was determined.

[1.] BA Potsdam, ZB 1, no. 193, pp. 4–13; typed, undated letter from the SD regional headquarters to the Reich Central Security Office on letterhead reading "SS National Security Service, Security Service Regional Headquarters, Königsberg (Prussia)," with the file number II B 31. It is marked: "Eh./Sz." The letter is addressed: "To the Reich Central Security Office—II B 31—Berlin." A stamp indicates that it was received on July 20, 1940, by the SS high commander at the SS Security Service Central Office no. 10125 and marked "Top Secret" and directed to the file numbered II B 3 on July 22, 1940. It bears the initials "Ku" (perhaps SS First Lieutenant Kunze). It is also bears the stamps "Certified Mail" and "Top Secret!" In the margin is the abbreviation "Wm" (in the handwriting of SS First Lieutenant Wilm). This document was previously published in the German newsletter of the Internationales Bonhoeffer Komitee, no. 36 (September 1991) with a detailed analysis by Christian Tilitzki and Johannes Tuchel. Within the Reich Central Security Office, Office II (Research on Opponents) was divided into four groups; Group II B (Philosophical Opponents) oversaw Department II B 3 (Political Churches), led by SS Major Albert Hartl.

[2.] No date is given; it was drafted and mailed around the same day as the attached report, July 17, 1940.

[3.] An apparent reference to the office of the student chaplain.

[4.] The edicts mentioned appear neither in the Reich Legal Gazette nor in the Command Gazette of the Chief of the Security Police and the SD or the General Collection of Edicts of the Reich Central Security Office. Wolfgang Sauer, however, provides evidence that the May 9 edict banned all confessional youth and Bible camps as well as all church retreats and rallies (Sauer, *Württemberg in der Zeit des Nationalsozialismus*, 447). See also Tilitzki and Tuchel, *IBG-Rundbrief*, no. 36, September 1991.

[5.] [Heinrich Himmler.—MB]

The entire event was led by the aforementioned *Koschorke*. Participants were:

Pastor Dietrich Bonnhöffer [*sic*],[6] born February 4, 1906, in Breslau, residing in Schluwe [*sic*]/Pomerania, Koppelstraße 9.

Pastor Bonnhöffer belonged to Niemöller's circle of friends and, by his own account to his own circle, was expelled for life from Berlin in 1937. He only seldom resides at his domicile and appears there only in order to foster the impression that he has actually set up his residence in Pomerania. In fact, however, he travels continually through the entire country and holds Confessing Church gatherings in individual congregations.

The current Lieutenant Hans *Kollmann*, born on February 21, 1912, in Graudenz, presently Königsberg, Third Battalion, Heavy Artillery Division 37.

Kollmann is also a theologian and in December of last year took his second exam before the consistory in Königsberg. He is not a member of the Confessing Church but judging by his theological orientation is thoroughly in their camp.

Theology student Siegfried *Baumdicker*, born April 6, 1921, in Allenstein.

Baumdicker is also not a member of the Confessing Church but clearly stands   50
completely under Koschorke's influence.

Agricultural student Paul *Laske*, born November 23, 1914, in Riga. Laske lives with Koschorke and is a regular participant in the Bible studies.

In addition to the informant, student Bracks (department of humanities),[7] several pastors' wives attended and also participated in most of the discussions. The same is true of *Bunke*, a lawyer living in Blöstau.[8]

According to Koschorke, thirty invitations to this retreat were mailed out. The meager turnout was attributed to the remarkably poor weather.

The exact course of the retreat can be seen from the enclosed report of Agent Bracks. The remarks threatening to state security about the treatment of Polish prisoners and the necessity for the Confessing Church to oppose the conception of work held by the National Socialist state could not be proven in the interrogation; similarly, the allegations in Bracks's report about collections being taken up to support imprisoned colleagues and the publication of Council of Brethren flyers remain unsubstantiated. No reproach was given because Agent Bracks has in no way seemed suspicious before now, and the hope of obtaining more specific information about the entire organization of the Confessing Church and its further activities appears still justified. The state police intervention in Blöstau has led to an actual increase in Koschorke's trust of Bracks, since Bracks was interrogated just like the rest of the participants and

---

[6.] Bonhoeffer's name is underlined by hand here and in all further references.

[7.] The word "informant" appears in the margin.

[8.] Dr. Adolf Bunke came from Glogau in Silesia and was a member there of the Silesian provincial Council of Brethren; in 1936 he was taken into "protective custody" and transferred to the concentration camp at Lichtenburg near Torgau. Eventually expelled from Silesia, he became legal adviser and finally head of the East Prussian Council of Brethren. The absence in this document of any knowledge of this background is striking.

revealed after the interrogation that he did not think much of it, since he was accustomed to such treatment from Memel.

Since Koschorke and Bonnhöffer spoke of not sending invitations openly anymore but only in envelopes, it is clear that more rallies and similar events are being planned despite the dissolution of this retreat and the ban on such activity.

The Protestant Student Service retreats are not the only things planned or carried out by the Confessing Church. A collaborator from the SD Headquarters has confirmed that such gatherings are also being planned by the Evangelical Agency for Young Women [...][9]

51 Regarding the activities of the above-mentioned Pastor *Bonnhöffer*, it is known that B[10] hopes to speak to Confessing Church gatherings in various East Prussian locations. On Monday, July 15, he was in Gumbinnen; and he plans to speak in Eydtkau on Sunday, July 21.[11] The district office in Tilsit was asked to monitor this gathering inconspicuously and report here on its outcome. Intervention by the state police does not appear to be called for at the moment since a larger circle of the Confessing Church can presumably be seized by continuing the investigations. Given the present situation, however, it would be appropriate to impose on Bonnhöffer a ban on public speaking in the entire country. Because Koschorke fully subscribes to the remarks of Bonnhöffer noted in the enclosed report, he also appears sufficiently incriminated to justify action against him.

The manor house and park in Blöstau are rented by the Evangelical Agency for Young Men for ca. one hundred reichsmarks per month, and all rooms are at the disposal of the Confessing Church for its events. It is clear that the Agency for Young Men was put forward only as a pretext to avert state police intervention.

On Saturday, July 14,[12] the poet and army psychologist Dr. *Kramp*, Caporn,[13] also took part in the retreat.[14] From conversation it emerged that he frequently leads "roundtable discussions" in a larger group, in which he discusses questions of Christian faith in an informal manner. The most recent roundtable discussion took place on the preceding Friday between him and a group of girls. It could not be ascertained where this discussion took place. It is possible, however, that the manor house in Caporn rented by Dr. Kramp may be the gathering place, since such meetings have taken place there in the past. It was unmistakable that Koschorke urgently desired to

---

[9.] There follow at this point unrelated findings about activities of the Evangelical Agency for Young Women and a confirmation retreat planned by Pastor Hildebrandt in Ponarth.

[10.] [Dietrich Bonhoeffer.—MB]

[11.] Cf. calendar entries for July 15 and 21, 1940, 1/10.

[12.] The actual date is July 13.

[13.] [The East Prussian writer Willy Kramp lived in Kaporn (Caporn) on the Fresh Bay; cf. 1/10, ed. note 18.—MB]

[14.] Cf. calendar entries, 1/10, ed. note 18.

communicate with Dr. Kramp–Caporn as soon as possible about the intervention of the state police. Obviously, Kramp had a similar meeting on Sunday or Monday whose disbanding was feared. Since, according to Agent Bracks, courses for theology students are still taking place somewhere, the suspicion remains that the disbanded seminary in Blöstau is being carried on somewhere else in another form. It remains to be determined whether the continuation of the seminary is connected with Dr. Kramp's meetings.

The investigations in the above matters are proceeding and will be reported in due course.

(signed) Gritschke
SS Major

Enclosure[15]   52

Königsberg (Prussia), July 15, 1940

Retreat of the Confessing Church at Gut Blöstau near Konradswalde

Beginning of the Retreat: Saturday, July 13, 1940.

The first event of the retreat was the coffee hour from around 3:30 until 4:15 p.m. During the coffee hour, the theme of the Polish prisoners was addressed. There Pastor Lic[entiate] *Bonnhöffer* stressed that imprisoned enemies cease being enemies as soon as they are disarmed, and that from a political standpoint it is therefore wrong that the state continues to make prisoners out to be enemies and officially depicts them as such. In the same way, the women and children of enemy nations are not enemies. Based on these considerations, the standpoint of the state is wrong from both a political and a Christian perspective. The following examples were provided: the interrogation of an NSV nurse[16] who had asked a landowner not to treat the prisoners so harshly but to deal kindly with them. Then a case was cited in which two pastors were interrogated because they had admitted Polish prisoners to a worship service. In the latter case the analysis was that this act of the state had prevented further work within the Christian church and was an attempt to convert the believers to a different point of view. In other words, they were prevented from coming to God.

Following the coffee hour, the interpretation of the Bible passage Matthew 19, verse 16 (Mark 10), "The Story of the Rich Young Man,"[17] was undertaken. This interpreta-

---

[15.] The following report was unmistakably prepared on the same typewriter and with the same style of writing as the above document.

[16.] [The Nationalsozialistische Volkswohlfahrt, "National Socialist Social Welfare Agency," was created in 1933 to replace the traditional state social service agencies.—MB]

[17.] See Bonhoeffer's letter of September 15, 1940, to the Reich Central Security Office, 1/21.

tion provided the point of departure for a later discussion on the theme "Creating a Christian Order of Life."[18] There the following conclusions were reached.

At the moment two orders among the people face each other. On the one side, the state's demand toward exerting all energies to secure life for the people and, on the other side, the ordering of the Christian community to submit to the command of Christ alone. If the state continues to force each individual to work on its own behalf, it thereby prevents the individual person who believes in God from achieving the highest insight on the Christian path. Currently work is a necessity. This means that the state has made a necessity into a virtue by setting up work as the most important consideration at present. For this reason, the Confessing Church must fight to ensure that the state allows the individual sufficient free time to live out the Christian faith.[19] Pastor *Bonnhöffer* cites here an example from Pomerania in which a clergy colleague poured out to him his distress because several farmers of his parish were working in their fields on Sunday rather than attending worship. Further, it is an important task of the Confessing Church to reach youth in particular, since especially now they are receiving an upbringing containing nothing at all of Christian ideals. Young people must be made aware that it is not work alone but the surpassing faith in Christ that makes them complete human beings.

I am not able to comment on what took place in the period from 7 to 10 p.m. (lights out) since at that time I was in Königsberg.[20]

Sunday, July 14, 1940

The Sunday program began with the worship service held from 9 to 11 a.m. Here it was discussed how only a small gate and narrow way lead to eternal life;[21] and only members of the Confessing Church traverse this narrow way, while the nation as a whole, all humanity, goes on the broad path that leads to damnation. At the close of the sermon, Pastor *Bonnhöffer* announced that the Sunday offering was designated for publication of Confessing Church writings and newsletters and for the support of colleagues who are in prison. While those gathered prepared for departure, the lawyer *Bunke,* who accompanied the songs and liturgy on a harmonium, brought out the offering collection box and placed it at the exit.[22] He later locked it back into a cupboard located in the same room.

[18.] Cf. calendar notes, 1/10, ed. note 27.

[19.] See Bonhoeffer's related exposition in *DBWE* 6:152 and 213–14.

[20.] Apparently the writer was reporting in at this time at his place of duty, thus triggering the actions of the following day; see the rest of this document.

[21.] Matt. 7:13-23 was the designated sermon text for this Sunday. See Bonhoeffer's letter of September 15, 1940, to the Reich Central Security Office (1/21, ed. note 4) and his calendar notes on July 10 and 11, 1940 (see 1/10).

[22.] [Under the 1937 Himmler decree, it was illegal for the Confessing Church to take up collections; thus, this information would have been considered significant for the Nazi police officials receiving this report.—MB]

Afterward Pastor *Koschorke,* a lieutenant, and the lawyer *Bunke* held a children's   54
worship service. During this period, Pastor *Bonnhöffer,* the theological student Siegfried
Baumdicker, the agriculture student *Laske,* and I held a conversation revisiting the question of the Polish prisoners, at which time Pastor *Bonnhöffer* made the same assertions he had previously. In addition he reported that in 1938 he had personally called
on the archbishop of Centerbury [*sic*] and explained some details of the customs of
the English high church. At this moment the conversation was interrupted as Pg.[23]
Ehemann appeared with a member of the Gestapo and broke up the retreat. Following
this the interrogations took place. During the period in which each person was being
interrogated, the others remained completely silent. Only occasionally were remarks
made to the effect that this breaking up of the retreat was ludicrous. The interrogation lasted until approximately 2 p.m. Afterward dinner was eaten. Between 2:30 and
3:30 there was discussion of the previous questioning. There the lawyer *Bunke*
declared that the questioning and dissolution were completely unjustified from a legal
perspective since an ordinance must first be made public; and because that had not
occurred, the Gestapo would have had the right only to forbid the gathering but not
to dissolve it. He further offered suggestions as to how one should behave during
interrogation, that one should bring up as many things as possible that could be interpreted ambiguously. In addition he described how every individual Security Service
office as well as each Gestapo office is directly subordinate to Berlin and that it is
therefore impossible for individual local officials to be in collusion together; every dissolution of a meeting, expulsion, etc., represents only a local matter, and therefore
there was absolutely no danger for the participants in this retreat. Pastor *Bonnhöffer*
explained further that though the "visit" was, of course, unpleasant and such events
would probably occur frequently, the other participants need not worry excessively,
since it was obvious that the primary purpose was to find grounds to pin something
on Pastor *Koschorke.*

    At 2:30 p.m.[24] a trip was made to a baron whose property was in Kuggen.[25]
During the stay there, hymns were sung, and in addition the theme "Death in Conversations"[26] was discussed. For Sunday afternoon a lecture by Pastor *Bonnhöffer* had   55
been scheduled, treating the theme "Death in Biblical Perspective."[27] But since further

---

[23.] ["Pg." is an abbreviation for *Parteigenosse* (party comrade), that is, a fellow member of the Nazi party.—MB]

[24.] [The time should perhaps read 3:30 p.m. In the preceeding paragraph Agent
Bracks reports that between 2:30 p.m. and 3:30 p.m. the retreat participants discussed the
interrogations that had just occurred.—MB]

[25.] The landowner was Baron Eberhard von Meerscheidt-Hüllessem. The East Prussian Council of Brethren was indebted to him at that point for providing his manor house
to lodge the preachers' seminary in Blöstau.

[26.] This is clearly a typographical error; the intended reading is "The topic of
'death' was discussed in conversations."

[27.] Cf. the calendar notes of July 11, 1940, 1/10.

work had been forbidden, there was agreement to the suggestion by the lawyer *Bunke* to treat the same theme in the form of conversations, because in his opinion only the lecture was forbidden and not conversations. In the course of the discussion, it was asserted that the conception of death as heroic greatness is false and only serves to make people unbelievers.[28] In contrast, the Christian conception of death as humanity's enemy is correct. The conversation at the baron's home lasted until 6 p.m. Then we returned, had supper in Blöstau, and at 8:13 p.m. departed for Königsberg. In the period between supper and the departure, Pastor *Bonnhöffer* described how he had been expelled from Berlin for life in 1937 and was presently staying in Pomerania—that is, he occasionally made an appearance there in order to foster the impression that he had actually established his new residence in Pomerania. In truth, however, he was traveling constantly throughout the entire country and holding Confessing Church gatherings in individual congregations. For the coming week a gathering in Gumbinnen had already been arranged for Monday and the following Sunday one in Eydtkau. This conversation, which for the most part took place between Pastor *Bonnhöffer* and Pastor *Koschorke,* revealed further that Pastor *Koschorke* knows very precise information about the entire Confessing Church organization in East Prussia; it gave the impression that he in large part controls the leadership of the East Prussian Confessing Church.

(signed) Heinz Bracks

16. To Paula Bonhoeffer[1]

July 23, 1940

Dear Mama,

I am sending you a baggage claim ticket and key for a suitcase that I have sent to Charlottenburg. Today I am going ahead to Danzig, then to Mrs. von Kleist, and on Monday or Tuesday will be in Berlin since I need to discuss something with Hans.[2] Would you please have my good summer suit

56

[28.] [This would have been considered a subversive statement in wartime Nazi Germany, which gloried the "heroic deaths" of its soldiers.—MB]

[1.] *NL,* A 59,1 (3); handwritten card from Königsberg; previously published in *GS* 6: 477; excerpt previously published in *GS* 2:374.

[2.] See 1/14, ed. note 3. At this point the East Prussian visitation trip was temporarily put on hold. The effects of the Blöstau police action, the ban on speaking, and the obligation to register with the police could be minimized by assignment to the Foreign Office of Military Intelligence within the Armed Forces High Command, in which Hans von Dohnanyi had been active since the beginning of the war. Thus there was another trip to East Prussia at the end of August. See *DB-ER,* 698–700.

sent to Klein-Krössin? I may need it there. I have heard nothing from you for a long time. Regards,

Your grateful Dietrich

17. To Hans-Werner Jensen[1]

August 17, 1940

Dear Brother Jensen,

I owe you many thanks for your letter, your book, and for the latest news of the birth of your first child. I rejoiced at all of it, since in fact every word from you is a great joy to me. We have had such cause for thanksgiving in recent days in thinking of you! There were surely also things that were hard or required sacrifice. But it is singular: in your company one hears and notices this side of life less often. Everything moves toward praise and thanks, and I am very glad of this.

I have only briefly paged through your book[2] but will soon be able to read it more closely in conjunction with some of my own work.[3] That will particularly allow me to think of you. I recently read Knak's appreciative review of the book.[4] I understand very well that you long for the ministry. But we too long for the return of our brothers on the front and pray fervently to God for it. "The harvest is plentiful . . ."[5] The activity of congregation members and pastors' wives in particular is often quite amazing.[6] It is indeed a time of preparation for coming days. At the moment all sorts of negotiations about the future shape of the church are in process.[7] It appears also

57

[1.] *NL*, A 60,4 (2); handwritten letter from Berlin; previously published in *GS* 2:586–87.

[2.] *Christliche und nichtchristliche Eheauffassung, dargestellt am Konfuzianismus.*

[3.] The reference is to Bonhoeffer's work on *Ethics.*

[4.] Bonhoeffer is probably thinking of the review by H. Maurer that appeared in *Evangelische Missionszeitschrift*, a journal of which Professor Knak was an editor.

[5.] Matt. 9:37.

[6.] [Almost half the German Protestant clergy and almost all the seminarians were mobilized as soldiers during the war. The Confessing Church was kept alive in many places by lay leadership and particularly by the leadership of women seminarians and pastors' wives (some of whom had theological degrees). See Barnett, *For the Soul of the People*, 166ff., and Thomas, *Women against Hitler*, esp. 51ff.—MB]

[7.] In the first half of June conversations took place between the Councils of Brethren of the Old Prussian Union and the Lutheran bishops at the Evangelical High Church Council in Stuttgart. A committee was appointed, consisting of Meiser, Wurm, Dibelius, Held (see Niemöller, *Die evangelische Kirche im Dritten Reich*, 152).

as if there were a greater unanimity here than previously. But if it should come to a meeting . . . ? It is a wonder that there are any Confessing Church congregations left. For this we must be daily grateful. I have just come from worship led by G. Dehn[8] on "The Widow's Mite" at the Friedenau Confessing Church congregation. As long as there are worship services like this, we need never despair of the future of the church in Germany.

I did some visitations in East Prussia and ran into the usual sort of clash but hope to be able to return this week. Brother Bethge will assume responsibility for the mission outreach office of the Gossner Mission.[9]

God protect your wife and child. May God protect you and bless every word and deed you can undertake to the divine glory.

In deep fellowship,

Yours truly,
Dietrich Bonhoeffer

[8.] [Günther Dehn.—MB]

[9.] See Bethge, *In Zitz gab es keine Juden* ("Drei Kriegsjahre bei der Gossner Mission"), 113–34. [In *DB-ER* Victoria Barnett translates *Volksmission* as "evangelical mission." In *DBWE* 16 we usually translate it as "renewal movement" but have tried throughout this volume to convey the meaning in the particular context of the work. Thus it is rendered "mission outreach" in this letter. The Gossner Mission (to which Bethge was assigned partly in an attempt to prevent his military conscription) was primarily a foreign missionary organization with the German Protestant church. While German churches had programs for *Volksmission* long before 1933, the German Christians imbued the word with decidedly nationalist and *völkisch* connotations. In contrast, Bonhoeffer viewed the goal of *Volksmission* as the revitalization of the life of "dead" congregations or parishes and stressed that such renewal work needed to focus on providing a clearer revelation of the gospel (see *DB-ER*, 542). Thus, Bonhoeffer and the Finkenwalde seminarians became extensively involved in such renewal work. (Bonhoeffer had early experience with this form of mission in Mexico and Bruay, France, with his friend Jean Lasserre.) According to Eberhard Bethge, "in June 1936 the entire seminary made its way to Belgard, a group of parishes in eastern Pomerania where four of the Finkenwalde brothers were serving six parishes." Four-person teams "spent the whole week in one village. During the day they split up to visit houses and attend children's classes and Bible discussions. For four days these activities were followed by an evening meeting in the church, where each of them spent ten minutes on the pulpit dealing with one particular aspect of the theme they had prepared" (*DB-ER*, 543). The Belgard experience led to renewal movement work for Bonhoeffer and the Finkenwalde seminarians in Pomerania, Saxony, and Brandenburg (see *DB-ER*, 545).—MB]

18. General Decree of the Reich Central Security Office[1]   58

Berlin, August 22, 1940

To: All State Police Headquarters[2]

Re: Protestant Pastor Dietrich Bonhoeffer, born February 4, 1906, in Breslau, resident of Schlawe/Pomerania, Koppelstraße 9

File: See above.[3]

Because of his activity subverting the people [volkszersetzenden Tätigkeit], I impose on Pastor Dietrich Bonhoeffer of Schlawe/Pomerania a ban on public speaking within the entire German Reich.

By commission (signed) Roth[4]
(Stamp)

19. To Eberhard Bethge[1]   59

August 26, 1940

Dear Eberhard,

Yesterday evening I arrived two hours late. In Dirschau we had to leave the train,[2] walk to the ferry, cross over, and go on to the next station, where

---

[1.] *NL*, A 61,2; typed copy from the file of the Düsseldorf State Police Headquarters on letterhead reading: "No. 40591 personal file of Dietrich Bonhoeffer/Reich Central Security Office IV A 4 b-776/40." Office IV (Gestapo) was divided into four groups: Group IV A (Opponents, Sabotage, and Security) was divided into four departments, including Department IV A 4 (Church Political Matters). See the September 20, 1940, general decree of the Düsseldorf Gestapo (reproduced in Bethge, Bethge, and Gremmels, *Dietrich Bonhoeffer: A Life in Pictures*, 183), which includes more precise directives: "Bonhoeffer, Dietrich, Protestant pastor, born February 4, 1906, in Breslau, resident of Schlawe (Pomerania), Koppelstr. 9, is forbidden to speak within Germany. Should Bonhoeffer move into your area or in some other way distinguish himself, submit a report. Any appearance is to be averted." According to the same document, a residency restriction and a ban on public speaking in the Reich were imposed on the Confessing Church pastors Helmut Gollwitzer, Friedrich Linz, Walter Kreck, and Superintendent Friedrich Onnasch. The document closes with a "Remark for Provincial Officers: Copies for Mayors Enclosed." Accordingly, the October 10, 1940, Gestapo newsletter, Magdeburg headquarters, no. 9/140, lists under "Surveillance" the names, among others, of Dietrich Bonhoeffer and Helmut Gollwitzer (BA Potsdam, Bestand ZB II, no. 4405 A. 20, p. 5; the reference is from Tilitzki and Tuchel, *IBG-Rundbrief*, no. 36 [1991]).

[2.] [After 1933 the state police were subsumed within the Gestapo.—MB]

[3.] See ed. note 1.

[4.] Erich Roth, state assistant attorney and SS first lieutenant, was the head of Department IV A 4.

[1.] *NL*, A 59,2 (1); handwritten letter from Königsberg; excerpt previously published in *GS* 2:374–75.

[2.] The bridge across the Vistula River was destroyed in the Polish campaign.

only half the necessary train cars were available, so that I then would have had to stand the rest of the trip had I not insisted that eight seats be made from each six in second class. I did this because a large number of very young people had climbed through the windows into the compartments, and as a result nearly all the older people, elderly women, officers, etc., were having to stand outside. Good manners are rapidly going out of circulation.

The Blocks send their warm greetings and regret your departure. They will also be writing soon to my parents regarding a young woman who may perhaps be a possibility for Christel von Dohnanyi. Please tell my parents as well that there is room in the Park Hotel here, a large room with bath for fourteen reichsmarks. They should simply telegraph here in advance (not telephone): Park Hotel, Königsberg, Pomerania. I think they will feel comfortable there. It is apparently not full in Masuren. That would then have to be arranged from here.—Early this morning I was at my workplace.[3] Unfortunately, the conditions are presently not right for my planned activity, which is highly regarded here. Perhaps there will be a change in a few weeks so that I may then begin my work. I am anticipating a phone call from there yet today. Otherwise I will probably return soon.

I think very much now of your birthday. I could not stand that you would receive nothing at all from me. So you will be receiving a package, and I hope you will find joy in it. It is the sixth birthday we will celebrate together, as it were—nearly a fifth of your life! That is something. I think back with gratitude on these past years and with confidence on those yet to come. While traveling and now here, I have had time to reflect on your future work[4] and everything new that awaits you. It is peculiar and in fact shameful how staying in Berlin repeatedly takes away my spiritual breath, so to speak. You probably know the feeling. This is why I would like to spend a few more days with you in Sigurdshof or somewhere else, simply in order to attend somewhat more to the spiritual aspects of the day; that is vital for us. Bible, hymnal, psalms slip so far away from us. And for this, of course, we have only ourselves to blame, though perhaps also our unregulated life and

---

[3.] This refers to the Königsberg military intelligence office, through which reports from border areas were to pass on their way to Dohnanyi/Oster. See Hans von Dohnanyi's letters to his wife, Christel, on August 7, 1940: "This noon Dietrich left for Klein-Krössin but will return in two or three days. The military intelligence office director from Königsberg is supposed to come to Berlin at that time, and they are to travel here together"; and on August 13, 1940: "Dietrich will come home tomorrow or the day after. He missed the Königsberg man, but that does not matter since they have great interest in the whole affair there; he will therefore be expected to go" (BA Berlin-Lichterfelde, Nachlaß Dohnanyi 8/1).

[4.] Cf. 1/17, ed. note 9.

work. Anyway, it would be lovely if we had a few more days together. God protect you in the new year and give you joy in your work.

Affectionately,
Your Dietrich

P.S. Tomorrow I am traveling to Eydtkuhnen.

C. Following the Ban on Public Speaking and the Requirement to Register. Berlin and Klein-Krössin. September–October 1940

20. To Georg Eichholz[1]

September 14, 1940

Dear Brother Eichholz,

I am eager to continue working with you, since my travels in East Prussia in recent months have succeeded in convincing me that the meditations have become a real help for preaching, especially for isolated colleagues.

I reiterate my request that the project move soon into the Old Testament texts! This is an area still quite bereft of theological, exegetical, and homiletical resources.—As for the timetable, I would ask that you not schedule me before Christmas.

Sincerely yours,
Dietrich Bonhoeffer

[1.] Literary estate of Georg Eichholz; handwritten letter, probably from Berlin. See *NL*, A 60,2; previously published in *GS* 6:480. On the circumstances, see 1/7.

21. To the Reich Central Security Office[1]

September 15, 1940

On September 9, 1940, the state police headquarters in Köslin notified me of the decree of the Reich Central Security Office IV A 4 b 776/40, which has forbidden me to speak publicly throughout the Reich.[2] The reason for this ban is stated as "activity subverting the people." I reject this charge. My entire outlook, my work as well as my background, make it inconceivable for me to allow myself to be identified with circles warranting the stigma of such a charge. I am proud to belong to a family that has rendered outstanding service to the German people and nation for generations. Among my ancestors are Field Marshal Count Kalckreuth[3] and the two great German artists of the same name, the Jena church historian Karl von Hase, renowned in the entire scholarly world of the past century, and the Cauer family of sculptors; my uncle is Major General Count von der Goltz, who freed the Baltics; his son, the state attorney Count Rüdiger von der Goltz, is my first cousin; Major General von Hase, who serves in active military duty, is my uncle; my father has been a full university professor of medicine in Berlin for nearly thirty years and serves to the present day in distinguished public offices; his ancestors lived for centuries as highly esteemed craftsmen and councilors of the then free state of Schwäbisch Hall, and even today their pictures hang proudly in the city church; my brothers and brothers-in-law serve in high government positions; and one of my brothers was killed in the world war. It has been the aspiration of these men and their families to serve the German nation and people at all times and to risk their lives for this service. In conscious affirmation of this spiritual legacy and moral position of my family, I cannot accept the charge of "activity subverting the people." Action corresponding to this charge is foreign to my very nature and is completely out of the question for me.

My personal work consists overwhelmingly of scholarly research. I have seldom appeared in public in the church and then only to give scholarly theological lectures. There has never before been any criticism from the state of any of my statements. I consider it my duty within the German Evangelical

62

[1.] *NL*, A 61,2 (3); draft sent from Berlin; previously published in *GS* 2:363–66. Addressed "To the Reich Central Security Office/Berlin SW 11/Prinz-Albrecht-Straße 8." On the circumstances, see the report of the SD Headquarters, Königsberg, 1/15.

[2.] In addition, a requirement to register with the police had been imposed, according to which Bonhoeffer had to report at regular intervals to the state police headquarters in Köslin, which was the police office for his place of residence, Schlawe.

[3.] [A field marshal is the equivalent of a five-star general.—MB]

Church to attend to quiet scholarly work and research of quality in order to do my part to uphold the reputation of German scholarship.

63   It has been communicated to me that "lectures" that I supposedly held at a "theological student retreat" have led to the ban on public speaking. I have the following to declare in this matter:

On the occasion of a stay in East Prussia, I was invited to lead a Bible study and give a lecture at a small gathering of Königsberg students of various disciplines. On July 13, 1940, three or four students arrived in Blöstau near Königsberg, in addition to a similar number of parishioners. In the afternoon I held a Bible study followed by a brief discussion on the gospel of the rich young man. I am attaching the outline of the Bible study to this report. On Sunday morning I led the worship service for the local Blöstau congregation and preached on the Sunday gospel.[4] Following the service, I was sitting privately with the handful of students for a moment when a larger number of Gestapo officials appeared and announced that we must disperse. We were alerted to a decree from the end of June 1940 that none of us knew of, since it had never been published, and which despite repeated requests was never presented to us; according to this decree, the ban on Christian youth retreats was now to apply also to "confessional events" with adults. One of the officials told me on his own initiative that I had nothing more to fear; it was simply a matter of carrying out the decree. Another official said that they would never have come had they realized there were only four or five people gathered here. This ended our time together. Which of those things I have reported could be held against me, I do not know. I know only that I dealt exclusively with religious and pastoral questions that have not the slightest to do with "activity subverting the people." Needless to say, I am available for any further details or consultation. I am also convinced that even a brief discussion would reveal that this represents some sort of misunderstanding and that the accusation of any less than politically irreproachable action on

64   my part cannot hold up. In such a conversation I would also be able to indicate the reasons for my activity in East Prussia. For when I preached in several congregations there, I did so as a service to pastors serving on the front, to give them the certainty and reassurance that their congregations were being provided for in their absence; I did it also as a service to the homeland congregations [Heimatgemeinden], that they not feel abandoned during their pastors' absence. The state police have never made the slightest accusation against me regarding even a single one of these sermons.

If I may, then, I hereby request to be invited to such a meeting, or at least to be informed as to whether the ban on speaking also prevents me from

---

[4.] Matt. 7:13-23.

presenting the results of my entirely nonpolitical scholarly activity in small gatherings—thus, for example, to speak on Luther's views on this or that question of Christian faith to twenty or thirty interested listeners. I cannot imagine that the ban on public speaking could be interpreted in this sense. I thus request to be allowed at least this sort of activity.

Heil Hitler!
Dietrich Bonhoeffer[5]

22. Willem A. Visser 't Hooft to George K. A. Bell[1]

CT 3/5 41 THOOFT CHAMPEL
ELT RP 3/5 BISHOP CHICHESTER STMARTINS VICARAGE BRIGHTON
DIETRICH WELL PLEASE NEWS OF HIS SISTERS FAMILY AND PASTORS
THOOFT 41 AVENUE DE CHAMPEL

23. To Eberhard Bethge[1]

65

Wednesday

Dear Eberhard,

Tomorrow when you come home from the meeting, you must have at least this greeting from me. In any case, you are presently leading a much more eventful and more productive life for the general cause than I am; only you

[5.] Bonhoeffer received no answer. See 1/107.

[1.] In possession of Sabine Leibholz; photocopy of a telegram with receipt stamp: "Brighton 153 CCC CRP 5 TH GENEVE 22 6 Oct 40 Sussex." Cited in German translation in Bell and Leibholz, *An der Schwelle*, 17. See also Bishop Bell's letter of October 7, 1940, to Gerhard Leibholz: "You and your wife will I know be happy to see this telegram from Dietrich, which arrived last night. I have replied: 'Sister husband and children all well Oxford stop pastors well though several away from home please give inquirer affectionate greetings reaffirming ecumenical faith and fellowship'" (Bell and Leibholz, *An der Schwelle*, 17). The telegram and Bell's message are in the original English. Regarding the address, during the war the seat of the bishop of Chichester was temporarily transferred to St. Martin's Vicarage, Brighton. The impetus for the above telegram may have been a meeting on August 5, 1940, of Hans Schönfeld with Hans von Dohnanyi and Bonhoeffer. See Hans von Dohnanyi's letter of August 8, 1940, to his wife (BA Berlin-Lichterfeld, Nachlaß Dohnanyi 8/1). Apparently Dr. Schönfeld also personally brought Bishop Bell's return telegram to Bonhoeffer's parents at their Marienburger Allee home; see Bethge's letter of January 20, 1941, to Dietrich Bonhoeffer, 1/59, ed. note 17.

[1.] *NL*, A 59,2 (2); handwritten letter from Klein-Krössin, October 9, 1940; previously published in *GS* 6:484–86.

must not let yourself be consumed and must preserve your own integrity as much as possible. I believe that a great deal of the exhaustion and sterility in our ranks is rooted in the lack of "selfless self-love."[2] Since this topic has no place in the official Protestant ethic, we arrogantly disregard it and become work obsessed, to the detriment of the individual and of the whole. It belongs, however, to that humanum for which we are redeemed. Thus may this be a timely word for you as well!

I rejoice here in daily morning prayer, which requires me to do some exegesis and during which, as well as while reading the Bible, I think of you and your work a great deal. Such well-organized days make work and prayer as well as my interactions with people easy for me and spare me the spiri-

66   tual, physical, and mental hardships resulting from disorder. Recently, however, a rough autumn storm[3] left me quite depressed, and it was not at all easy to regain my equilibrium. My work progresses. I am writing the outline of the whole thing;[4] for me this is always one of the greatest joys and trials. I will probably spend the rest of the week on it.

On Sunday we were in Kieckow.[5] We also discussed the church situation. There it became quite clear to me again that the struggle regarding the church government [Kirchenregiment] is actually the question necessarily emerging from church history regarding the possibility of a Protestant church for us. It is the question whether, following the separation from papal and worldly authority in the church, an ecclesial authority can be erected that is grounded in word and confession alone. If such an authority is not possible, then the final possibility of a Protestant church is gone; then there truly remains only a return to Rome or a state church or the way into isolation, into the "protest" of true Protestantism against false authorities. It is no accident but rather divine necessity that the question today has to do with the authority of true church government.[6]

My thoughts travel often to Sabine and to you these days. I experience a remarkable sense of closeness to each of you, in contrast to my thoughts of other people. When one has the feeling that others expect something of him and that one has fulfilled these expectations so poorly, then an awareness

---

[2.] Cited from Pieper, *Four Cardinal Virtues,* 149; cf. *LPP,* 287 (*DBW* 8:417). This key phrase also occurs in *Ethics* working note no. 50 from the fall of 1940 under the heading "Natural Life" (*ZE,* 56); see *DBWE* 6:125, ed. note 100.

[3.] ["Rough autumn storm" appears to refer to the German air assault going on at peak intensity over the English Channel and southern England in preparation for an invasion. Bonhoeffer would have been particularly depressed by it since his twin sister, Sabine, and her husband, Gerhard Leibholz, were living in England.—MB]

[4.] See *DBWE* 6:443.

[5.] Kieckow was the home of Hans-Jürgen von Kleist-Retzow.

[6.] See *DBWE* 6:124–25 and ed. note 100.

of guilt lodges itself in one's memory, as well as a simultaneous longing for forgiveness and for being able to help again.

In the next few days you will hopefully be receiving something from Mrs. Verges. I spoke to her as we were looking through the books. Also you still have a chest and five boxes there. I had them sent along to me. We can then unpack them together.

How are you doing financially? And in the air-raid shelter? In Köslin we had another alarm.

All my best to you! See you next week!

Regards,
Your faithful Dietrich

D. Stay at
Ettal Monastery.
November 1940–
February 1941

24. To Eberhard Bethge[1]

Dear Eberhard,

Arrived yesterday four hours late in Munich;[2] the whole day quite lively with many acquaintances. In all this I thought often of the gathering at your house! Did it go well?

Today a brief visit up here, where I am invited to come and stay. But this evening back to Munich for a few days to meet several people. Up here it is the loveliest winter. I hope you can come! More soon.

In haste,
Your Dietrich

All the best to you in Magdeburg!

[1.] *NL,* A 59,2 (3); handwritten card from Ettal postmarked: "Munich, 10–31–40"; previously published in *GS* 2:377. [Ettal is located in the rural district *(Landkreis)* Garmisch-Partenkirchen in Upper Bavaria.—MB]

[2.] In light of Bonhoeffer's police restrictions, Oster and Dohnanyi wanted to have him assigned as an agent to the Military Intelligence Office in Munich, where he also had to move his official residence. This was a preliminary approach to Military Intelligence officials, in particular Dr. Josef Müller. It was apparently through him that the contact with Ettal Monastery ("up here") was established right at the beginning of the stay.

25. To Eberhard Bethge[1]

November 4, 1940

Dear Eberhard,

You will have now returned from Magdeburg, and I hope that the work you had to do there[2] in my stead brought you much pleasure. Now you are probably hard at work preparing for the Bible week. It is too bad that we cannot prepare together once again.

At the moment I am attempting to gain a foothold, so to speak, in the circles that interest me; and I think this will be easier in this other confession[3] than among our own people; we'll see. In any case, it is already quite clear that the necessary connections are completely lacking here. I am presently visiting many people and discussing these things. Today there was an uproar in the Bishop's office [Ordinariat]: a ban on book displays in churches;[4] scheduling of premilitary training for Sunday mornings from 8 to 11 a.m.;[5] after an air-raid alarm no worship service before 10 a.m. and no ringing of bells before 1 p.m.[6] These three things have come all at once and have unleashed a considerable response, not to mention also a great deal of open criticism of the bishops.

68

My plans are now as follows: if tomorrow (Tuesday) I have not heard any news about my return to Berlin, I will call home that evening (please pass this along!), so that I will be able to plan further the use of my time here. Hopefully my visits today and tomorrow will provide some clarity.

In the evenings I often attend the theater. I saw *Ariadne* and *Othello*, and tonight I will go to a Bach concert.

[1.] *NL*, A 59,2 (4); handwritten letter with letterhead: "Park Hotel, Munich"; previously published in *GS* 2:377–78.

[2.] Bonhoeffer is referring to a gathering in Magdeburg of the brotherhood of vicars and assistant pastors in the Confessing Church province of Saxony.

[3.] [Bonhoeffer is referring to the Catholic Church; Ettal is a Benedictine monastery in southern Bavaria. His time at Ettal would bring him together with a number of Catholic opposition figures, including Josef Müller and Johannes Neuhäusler.—MB]

[4.] According to Ordinance no. 145 of the Reich Chamber of Literature, dated October 26, 1940, documents of all kinds could be displayed and sold only in commercial spaces.

[5.] The decree of the Reich Youth Leader of September 17, 1940, was communicated to the church authorities in writing by the Reich Ministry for Church Affairs.

[6.] These were directives of the Reich Ministry for Church Affairs, no. I 22416/40 II, dated October 25, 1940, and no. I 13086/40 II, dated October 29, 1940.

Guess what—in a side pocket of my briefcase I found two hundred marks. Shall we use it for our Christmas trip? Or shall I send you something very nice? Half of it is yours, in any case. More soon! Now I think I will go see my publisher;[7] later on the day is full. I am thinking of you and your work.

All the best to you!
Your faithful Dietrich

For now, write to me
    c/o Countess Kalckreuth[8]
    M.-Schwabing
    Unertlweg 1.

69   **26. To Eberhard Bethge**[1]

Wednesday

Dear Eberhard,

Warm greetings to you in the rush before my departure. I am still planning to travel by way of Jena tomorrow, in order to speak with St.[2] I have just finished the other letter and sent it to the address in Leipzig.[3] It ran long and has not been read over. Do with it as you wish. But—cave canem![4]—I think often of your work. It is surely wonderful, and I would very much like to listen in. Write soon! c/o the "Europäischer Hof" in Munich. God protect you!

Your Dietrich

[7.] Bonhoeffer's publisher was Albert Lempp, owner of the publishing house Chr. Kaiser Verlag.

[8.] Countess Christine von Kalckreuth was Bonhoeffer's aunt and, like her brother Johannes, lived in Munich.

[1.] *NL*, A 59,2 (5); handwritten letter from Berlin, November 13, 1940; previously published in *GS* 2:378 and *GS* 6:486.

[2.] "St." is an abbreviation for Staemmler. He was now chair of the Old Prussian Union Council of Brethren and was responsible for reworking Bonhoeffer's position and responsibilities in the church following the disbanding of the seminary and the breakdown of the East Prussian effort—a difficult task necessitating delicate handling, given the Military Intelligence and resistance interests.

[3.] Letter not extant.

[4.] "Beware of the dog!" Used figuratively: "Watch out!"

27. To Eberhard Bethge[1]

November 16, 1940

Dear Eberhard,

I am sitting in the train to Munich and have just realized with great disappointment that the train does not arrive at 8:30, as I had thought, but at 10:30. I can no longer read, so I am writing you an illegible letter. The visit to Staemmler was quite good. He spoke from the perspective of his conversation with you, in which you apparently presented my situation movingly and sympathetically, with the result that they all now have guilty consciences on my behalf. That wasn't my intention, of course, but it was very nice of you in any case to have set the ball rolling in this way! The decision, therefore, was that I continue as the director of the Confessing Church pastoral training center and remain available but until then take up my scholarly work, since they are greatly interested in that. He was very skeptical about a pastorate. He was not especially in favor of Bismarck.[2] So for now I am free, yet with the comforting awareness that this is what is wished for me. What shall I do now? If I am really free for five months at the very least, it is not very pleasant to live in a hotel. But what then? Rent a small apartment in the mountains? And have some of my books sent? The Rads have a small house for rent (heated) near the Chiemsee, thirty to forty marks monthly, furnished, several rooms. It is certainly tempting. Though also very lonely over the long term. I still have to await the military side of things.[3] And after all, it doesn't even have to be Bavaria. How lovely it would be if there were something we could do together! Can you think of anything? (Rad wants to visit me in December in Ettal.) When are you coming? You could visit Neuendettelsau[4] and afterward take a look into the Catholic renewal movement[5] and even travel to Austria. Talk this over with Lokies. Or should I write to him? As you wish!

St. was very nice personally. We also discussed Catholicism—very reasonable. Asmussen is said to have preached in an Una Sancta worship service![6]

70

[1.] *NL,* A 59,2 (6); handwritten letter; previously published in *GS* 2:379–81.

[2.] Bonhoeffer was briefly considered for this pastorate in the Altmark. [The Altmark is a historic region west of the Elbe River in the district of Magdeburg in what is now Saxony-Anhalt.—MB]

[3.] See 1/24, ed. note 2. [The reference is to Gerhard von Rad, Old Testament scholar and Confessing Church member.—MB]

[4.] Bonhoeffer is referring to the deaconess center and mission seminary in central Franconia.

[5.] [See 1/17, ed. note 9.—MB]

[6.] [The term *Una Sancta* refers specifically to the "high church" movement in German Lutheranism and to a variety of ecumenical activities among Protestants and Catholics

That's going too far for me. He has no steadfastness.—But the modesty, or even poverty, of St.'s life is just not quite right. It must sap his strength for work and surely also occasionally hinder his demeanor. On the other hand, it is impressive to see the head of the Confessing Church living like a member of the proletariat with his family. Nevertheless, I don't know if it should be that way.—I exchanged many reminiscences with von Rad. He is very lonely, and—even after eighteen years!—I liked him very much. He seemed to me to be quite clear on church matters.—St. asked whether you were

71   coming.[7] When I confirmed this, he said, quite relieved, "Oh, that is very good!" He too needs strengthening and help. On the other hand, you yourself have enough else to do! Remember my admonition about loving yourself!

One more word on the Catholic question: How did we Lutherans come together with the Reformed? Actually quite untheologically (for the theological formulation of Halle[8] is, of course, more of a determination of facts than a theological solution—which it by no means is!!); by two things: by the "guidance" of God (Union, Confessing Church),[9] and by the recognition of what is objectively given in the sacrament—Christ is more important than our thoughts about him and about his presence. Both are theologically questionable foundations, and yet the church made a decision for fellowship of the altar—that is, for church fellowship. It made a decision to recognize the Union as God's guidance; it made a decision to subordinate its thinking and doctrine of Christ to the objectivity of Christ's presence (even in the Reformed Lord's Supper). But it came to no sort of theological unity (apart from Halle!). Would not both of these things also be possible in relation to the Catholic Church: recognition of the "guidance" of God in recent years and recognition of the objectivity of the presence of Christ (for traditional Lutherans, even easier with Catholics than with Calvinists!). It seems to me as if churches unite not primarily theologically but rather

---

since 1918. Leaders on the Protestant side included Berlin pastors Friedrich Heiler and Friedrich Siegmund-Schultze. The most prominent leader on the Catholic side was Father Max Joseph Metzger, who was martyred by the Nazis in 1944. The rise of Adolf Hitler and the Nazis breathed new life into the Una Sancta movement, as many Catholics and Protestants recognized the need for Christians to cooperate in resisting National Socialism (*New Catholic Encyclopedia,* 2nd ed., s.v. "Una Sancta"). Pastor Hans Christian Asmussen was actively involved in the leadership committees of the Confessing Church. He served as the head of the theological section of the administrative committee of the Confessing Synod in Bad Oeynhausen. Bonhoeffer clearly has reservations about Asmussen preaching in a worship service associated with the Una Sancta movement, but the precise reason for those reservations is not made explicit.—MB]

[7.] See 1/25, ed. note 2.

[8.] See 1/1, ed. note 5.

[9.] ["Union" here probably refers to the Church of the Old Prussian Union.—MB]

through faith-based decisions, in the sense above. That is a dangerous sentence, I know! One could make anything of it! But isn't this how we have acted, practically speaking, in the Confessing Church? Of course, the guidance was more visible then. I am not suggesting all this could take place tomorrow or the next day, but I would like to keep my eyes open in this direction!

So now the train is shaking too much. Excuse the scrawl!

Thinking devotedly of you,
Your faithful Dietrich

Greet all our old friends in Jena! Write to me in Ettal via Oberau (Bavaria), Hotel Ludwig der Bayer.

28. To His Parents[1]   72

November 15,[2] 1940

My dear Parents,

I have just arrived in Munich, following my day in Jena. It passed quickly in visits with Staemmler and G. von Rad, who is now a professor there, so that unfortunately I had no chance to see anything of the city or of our relatives.[3] St. conveyed to me the council's desire that I proceed with academic work; he was pessimistic about a pastorate. Most of all, they want me to be freely available to them. I told him that I would like to be done with this nomadic existence soon. All the same, on this basis I am free at least until spring. Thus the best thing would be to plant myself somewhere a little more permanently. I will have to see whether the hotel in Ettal would do for this. The Rads have a little house near the Chiemsee for rent (thirty to forty marks monthly). But I still have to await the military side of things. I will not be able to make a decision before then.

Nevertheless, it is a comfort to me to know that I will be going about my academic work on behalf of the church rather than only on my own initiative.

Love,
Your grateful Dietrich

[1.] *NL*, A, 59,1 (6); handwritten card from Munich; previously published in *GS* 6:487.
[2.] The actual date is November 16.
[3.] He is referring to the descendants, living in Jena, of his great-grandfather Karl August von Hase.

29. To Eberhard Bethge[1]

November 18, 1940

Dear Eberhard,

I have been here since yesterday, was received most warmly; I eat in the refectory, sleep in the hotel, can use the library, have my own key to the cloister, and yesterday had a long and good conversation with the abbot.[2] In short, I have everything that one could desire. The only things missing are a desk and what in these nearly six years has become a matter of course, the exchange of my impressions with you. To supplement your invitation here further, I wanted to tell you that I have the best personal connections to the largest Catholic missionary society (Steyler Mission) (in Vienna) and that I have been cordially invited to visit there.[3] Surely that would justify a trip for you. I experience the people as open and responsive and so can imagine a fruitful conversation between you and them. I could bring you along without any difficulty; I can also easily find connections to the Catholic renewal movement.[4] Thus I think it is both interesting for you[5] and perhaps also expedient to make use of these connections. It is not certain how long I will be here to make this possible—so come in December! Tell Lokies that I consider it important to establish these connections now. Of course, being here would be interesting for you also. So I hope you will come! Let me know soon. Did you receive the mail from Leipzig? All the best!

Most affectionately,
Dietrich

[1.] *NL,* A 59,2 (7); handwritten card from Ettal; previously published in abbreviated form in *GS* 2:381–82.

[2.] Father Angelus Kupfer. For more details, see Koch, "Die Benediktinerabtei Ettal," 381–413.

[3.] Bonhoeffer's connections to the Steyler Mission cannot be clarified because of the lack of corresponding evidence at the St. Gabriel mission house in Vienna-Mödling. The Steyler mission did not have an office in Munich at the time.

[4.] Cf. 1/37, ed. note 8. [See also 1/17, ed. note 9.—MB]

[5.] ["You" is plural here.—MB]

73

30. To His Parents[1]

November 21, 1940

My dear Parents,

I am sending along the change of address form;[2] it seems to me, however, as if this were the form for permanent change of residence rather than for shorter absences!? I hope there has been no mix-up. You will presumably still need to sign it. Thanks very much.

Everything has progressed quite nicely here. I am a guest (which, of course, does not work well over the long term), live in the hotel, eat in the monastery, have access to the library, and receive whatever I need. This form   74
of life is naturally not foreign to me,[3] and I experience its regularity and silence as extremely beneficial for my work. It would certainly be a loss (and was indeed a loss in the Reformation!) if this form of communal life preserved for fifteen hundred years were destroyed, something those here consider entirely possible. I believe that infinitely many irritations that would otherwise necessarily arise in such a close and ongoing common life are precluded by the strict order and that this provides a very healthy foundation for the work. Some things are truly curious, such as how at dinner and supper various historical works are recited in the chant tone of the liturgy; sometimes when the subject matter is humorous, it is impossible to suppress a smile. Otherwise I consider recitation not at all a bad idea in such a large group. I had also introduced it at the seminary.—As time goes on, one becomes acquainted with all sorts of things in this way. Also the food is excellent.

Now I am waiting for Christel and the children.[4] I wanted to pick them up in Munich but have heard nothing regarding their arrival.

[1.] *NL,* A 59,1 (7); handwritten, from Ettal; previously published in *GS* 2:382.

[2.] [Germans had to register with the authorities in their place of residence or elsewhere if they were there for a prolonged stay. The change of address notification *(Abmeldung)* was a form to be completed so that one's registration with the local authorities was canceled.—MB]

[3.] He gained this familiarity through his glimpses into English monastic life as well as through the praxis of "life together" in Finkenwalde and in the collective pastorates.

[4.] Because of the increasing frequency of night air-raid alarms, the decision was made for Christine von Dohnanyi to bring her children, Barbara, Klaus, and Christoph, to Ettal to enroll them in school and also periodically to live there with them. Annemarie Koch and Lieselotte Diem, who were friends of the Dohnanyis, came with their children at the same time. On the day of their arrival, November 22, about one hundred school children evacuated from Hamburg also had to be accommodated at the monastery.

I received Block's letter.[5] — At the moment people are being called up in droves around here. What on earth for, in the winter?[6] Have you seen Eberhard? When will you be taking a break?

All my best,
Your grateful Dietrich

75 **31. To Eberhard Bethge**[1]

Sunday, November 23, 1940

Dear Eberhard,

I don't think I have ever received so much mail from you before! Thank you very much! And please continue sending these short greetings and updates. It means so much to know how your work is going. Despite everything, I rejoice that you are now coming so fully into your own and truly can do something that is necessary and that claims your whole being. In contrast, my own withdrawal strikes me as so useless, but it doesn't hurt to experience oneself as quite dispensable for a time. Of course, you are presently not at all dispensable and that provides its own — "penultimate"[2] — satisfaction for you. I have the impression that your report to Hans[3] was by no means ineffective — judging by Christel's response, in any case. It appears that they also consider it to be a very serious matter. Could you not find some connection to the Ministry of Labor, or is there no point to that? I sometimes think the whole thing, while certainly unavoidable, can also be a form of protection for the future. But truly, how incomparably easy and pleasant our way has been through even these past years, in comparison with all that has weighed on the others for years! What right would I have to quibble with my own circumstances, which for others would be the very foretaste of paradise! So please do not imagine that I am giving myself over to resignation

---

[5.] Letter not extant; it presumably had to do with the police notification of Bonhoeffer's move from Schlawe.

[6.] Preparations were being made for the war against the Soviet Union.

[1.] *NL,* A 59,2 (9); handwritten letter from Ettal; previously published in *GS* 6:488–90; excerpt previously published in *GS* 2:383–84.

[2.] This refers to "Ultimate and Penultimate Things," *DBWE* 6:146–70.

[3.] Hans von Dohnanyi's wife, Christine, had brought Bonhoeffer up to date immediately following her arrival regarding the latest efforts to extend Bethge's UK classification (UK = *unabkömmlich,* "reserved [deferred] occupation"). [A reserved occupation is a wartime classification for an indispensable civilian profession, and thus the person so classified cannot be spared for military service. —MB]

without restraint; I know clearly all that I have to be thankful for and repeat it to myself mornings and evenings.

I have just come from quite a wonderful mass. With the Schott[4] book in hand one can pray along with and readily affirm it. It is indeed not simply idol worship, even if the way the Mass proceeds from our sacrifice for God to God's sacrifice for us is difficult for me and seems to be going in the wrong direction. But I need to understand it better. I am still a guest there, after all. The ordered life is again very good for me, and I am amazed at the extent to which in the seminary we did similar things quite on our own. By the way, the abbot and several priests are presently reading *Life Together.* Then we will hold a discussion. The apparently characteristic Benedictine hospitality, which comes so naturally to them, the truly Christian deference shown to the stranger for Christ's sake, is almost embarrassing. You should really come visit sometime! It is a rich blessing.

I received a whole shipment of books from the Steyler Mission, which I will give you when it is convenient. There, too, one could surely hear and learn much that is important. Perhaps a trip there might still be arranged? Did you receive my parcel? I saved a sausage for you. Christel is bringing it to you at the end of the week. You need to make sure you're eating well!

Hans said something on the phone the other day about a call-up order that has subsequently been canceled again. That will surely be a blow to you. For how long is it? You ought to remind Hans sometime about your conversation with Oster last summer![5] Otherwise I will do so. That must surely not be lost sight of!

Otherwise I am doing well spiritually and physically. I am longing for the Lord's Supper. Recently I accidentally happened into a Lutheran service of confession in Munich. But the questions being asked were so dreadfully legalistic that I was quite glad not to be invited to Communion. That was not much better than the sacrifice of the Mass! And in Meiser's church to boot (a young man, Brodersen, from Schleswig-Holstein)![6]

Farewell for now, dear Eberhard! In the calm of this stay here I think often of our colleagues, and the Confessing Church, and of you and your work. Regards,

Your faithful Dietrich

[4.] Bonhoeffer sent Bethge a copy of the lay missal *(Missal for Sundays and Feast Days following the Larger Missal)*; cf. *NL-Bibl.*, 11.7.

[5.] See *DB-ER*, 698.

[6.] At that time the White Hall of the former St. Augustine Church (now a hunting museum) in Munich was temporarily serving as the worship space for the St. Matthew Church congregation to which the local vicar, Peter Brodersen from Flensburg, was assigned.

I was very pleased and amazed at Gerhard's decision.[7] Now of all times!— Today the pope has ordered a prayer for peace in the whole church.[8] Could we not also have prayed along with them? I did.

32. To Eberhard Bethge[1]

November 26, 1940

Dear Eberhard,

This morning's telegram[2] was a bolt from the blue. I am pondering all possibilities but am certain that you will find all conceivable counsel at home and will also realize again that you completely belong, as it were, and they are glad to help you.[3] That is a great comfort. If you think that I can help in any way, I will come immediately.

So tell me, how are you anyway?[4] You just recently had your condition again, and is the sudden lumbago or sciatica that you get so severely at times not perhaps related to this? Ask Papa about that sometime!—How is your flute? Have you joined an ensemble? Would that not be possible?

Mrs. Koch[5] was here until yesterday. Have you ever visited her husband? He is always very kind.—So, thus my feeble reflections. It is good to know that you can be with my parents and Hans.[6] He will know of some kind of help. So I am still somewhat optimistic. Yes, and if all else fails, then you must obey with good grace, but certainly—this is my view—not too hastily! But ultimately, when you do so, in a genuine fashion. You have always been better at that than I.

I have just spoken with Mama, and I hope to talk to you tomorrow. Can I do anything for you? Did you receive the parcel?

[7.] Former Finkenwalde seminarian Gerhard Vibrans had decided to get married; see 1/61.

[8.] On the peace prayer ordered by the pope for November 24, see *Acta Apostolicae edis*, 32, 394ff. The *Motu Proprio* is dated from October 27, 1940. [The phrase *motu proprio* means "on one's own accord." Thus, a *Motu Proprio* is a decree or edict of the pope in which he decides the provisions on his own accord in response to a question of doctrine or discipline (*The Catholic Encyclopedia*, online edition, s.v. "Motu Proprio").—MB] Cf. Faulhaber, *Akten*, 2:703.

[1.] *NL*, A 59,2 (10); handwritten letter from Ettal; previously published in *GS* 6:490–91.

[2.] This telegram informed Bethge of his call-up into the military.

[3.] [Bethge at the time was staying at the Bonhoeffer home in Berlin.—MB]

[4.] Bonhoeffer is alluding to possible ailments or conditions for certification of Bethge's unfitness for duty.

[5.] Mrs. Koch was the wife of the Berlin lawyer Dr. Hans Koch.

[6.] Hans von Dohnanyi.

Christel[7] sends her greetings to you; today the children went to school here for the first time. Yesterday we brought them to the rector, who tested them. They will have a great deal to learn here, but they liked it well today. The teachers are friendly. Greet my parents and especially Hans from me, and thank them from me for everything they are doing for you.

With my best wishes and thoughts of you and your work,

Your faithful Dietrich

33. To Eberhard Bethge[1]

November 27, 1940

Dear Eberhard,

I have just received your extensive letter, which gave me great pleasure. It is especially good of you that you found time to write in the midst of all the turmoil. This is just the sort of descriptive letter I like so much. I am not very good at it myself, however, so I mostly write in other ways.

Just now a telephone call came from Mama, kindling a new ray of hope. It would be marvelous; but I don't dare give in to it fully. I suggested also that Diestel and Lokies go together to K.[2] again. Perhaps Papa could prompt Diestel in this. But hopefully that would not be necessary. So I am now waiting without being able to do anything. I have wavered back and forth on whether I should just come on up. Then I thought: everything is moving along; you have your hands full already; we will see each other in three to four weeks at Christmas; the trip costs a great deal of money, which you would perhaps need more urgently later as a soldier—and then came Hansen's[3] order not to travel.[4] That decided it.—Should I write to Lokies about the trip? I will do it without delay but was just not certain from your letter whether you really wanted it. We must then make our Christmas plans soon. Possibly Friedrichsbrunn?[5] I would come to Berlin only if you have to be there as a soldier; but in that case certainly.

79

[7.] Christine von Dohnanyi.

[1.] *NL*, A 59,2 (11); handwritten letter from Ettal; previously published in *GS* 6:491–92; excerpt previously published in *GS* 2:384.

[2.] This may be an abbreviation for *Konsistorium*, the church consistory.

[3.] Hans von Dohnanyi.

[4.] Bonhoeffer was told by Dohnanyi not to travel because of preparations for the first Switzerland trip.

[5.] [In 1913 the Bonhoeffer family purchased a former forester's lodge at Friedrichsbrunn in the eastern Harz Mountains. It was a traditional gathering place for the family during holidays.—MB]

Have you called Walbaum?[6]

Today a possible title for my book occurred to me: "Preparing the Way and Arrival"[7] corresponding to the division of the book (into penultimate and ultimate things).[8] What do you think of that? But do not let yourself be distracted by such questions. You have enough else to think about. Could you not (in the best case!) take some vacation immediately following East Prussia? You would not need to call it that; but could you take a quiet week, which you need in any case, somewhere other than in Berlin and afterward celebrate Christmas? How would that be?

All for now. The mail is being collected. I will simply wait! All the best, however it may come out!

Your faithful Dietrich

34. To Eberhard Bethge[1]

November 28, 1940

Dear Eberhard,

Since I am still consigned to waiting, I would like at least to send you a daily greeting. If in the meantime it should have been decided that you must depart on Monday[2] (and from your silence I almost fear that this may be the case), then I want to be with you at least by letter. It seems quite unnatural to me not to be able to help you at all now. At the moment all sorts of external things are running through my head. You mustn't forget to make full use of your clothing ration for woolen things. I don't think you have much in wool, and you would surely need it. Of course, I can give you all sorts of things myself if you cannot find any more in Berlin. In Munich there is still much available. Otherwise, if I were you, I would buy another suit. You can have the money from me. I have saved a great deal this month. Also take cigarettes, etc., with you.

I am leaving now for Munich, where I will be doing some Christmas shopping for the brothers; then I am meeting Hans.[3]

80

[6.] Bethge's pocket calendar still contains Walbaum's Berlin address: "Alexandrinen 101, phone: 173172"; Walbaum is not identified otherwise.

[7.] [The possible title in German is *Wegbereitung und Einzug.*—MB]

[8.] Cf. *DBWE* 6:443.

[1.] *NL*, A 59,2 (13); handwritten letter from Ettal; previously published in *GS* 2:385.

[2.] Bonhoeffer surmised that Bethge had received an immediate call-up to active military service.

[3.] Hans von Dohnanyi came to Munich, among other reasons, for discussion of Bonhoeffer's forthcoming trip to Switzerland.

My work is progressing somewhat.—Today there was a great celebration here, the anniversary of the abbey's consecration, with speeches and a banquet. It was very nice. I need to be able to tell you about it in person soon. Christmas at the latest. Now I must pack. I am thinking of you with all my best wishes,

Your Dietrich

35. To Eberhard Bethge[1]

November 28, 1940

Dear Eberhard,

At the moment I was leaving the hotel, your card arrived with its joyful news.[2] Why on earth did you not telegraph? Just to save a few cents? I will send you my telephone number![3] Of course, I am extremely happy and am eager to hear more. Now you will be in Pomerania and East Prussia; do be sensible. Who in Finkenwalde actually invited you?[4] If you come with Fritz[5] to Mrs. Verges, could you check on the books: Kant (six volumes);[6] Doré picture Bible; Mirbt, *Quellen*;[7] Roman breviary, four leather volumes.[8] Has Winfried Kraus's shipment ever been paid (14.75)?[9] I don't know if I asked Mama to do this; in any case, I never sent it myself. Please do so! Perhaps via Mama's checking account. Did you call Walbaum? Also, I need more income. I am expecting the 5 RM, but Justus[10] will possibly need to advance it. There is no rush! I still have 150 RM coming to me from November. I spoke to Staemmler about these matters regarding my stipend. Have the taxes

81

[1.] *NL*, A, 59,2 (12); handwritten postcard from Ettal, postmarked "Munich, Nov. 28, 1940." Address: "Mr. Eberhard Bethge, Berlin-Dahlem, Rudeloffweg 27 [Burckhardthaus]"; previously published in *GS* 6:493. [As Victoria Barnett explains, the Burckhardthaus was a "small church college in Berlin that trained women for church work; although part of the official church, it served as a refuge for many of the illegal women theologians in the Confessing Church" (*For the Soul of the People,* 161). It also housed Bethge's office for the Gossner Mission.—MB]

[2.] The good news was Bethge's new UK (reserved occupation) classification; cf. 1/31, ed. note 3.

[3.] Cf. *DB-ER,* 327.

[4.] It was the small Confessing Church congregation there for a Bible study evening.

[5.] Friedrich Onnasch.

[6.] Kant, *Sämtliche Werke* (*NL-Bibl.,* 7 A 35).

[7.] See Mirbt, *Geschichte der katholischen Kirche* (*NL-Bibl.,* 6 B 29).

[8.] *Breviarium Romanum* (*NL-Bibl.,* 6 B 5).

[9.] [The cost for the shipment was 14.75 RM.—MB]

[10.] Friedrich Justus Perels.

been paid? So, now you have a whole pile of tasks again. Well, you really are indispensable![11] Good-bye! In deepest joy,

Your Dietrich

36. To Margret Onnasch[1]

Dear Mrs. Onnasch,

Would you please give this letter[2] to Eberhard? It is urgent. I can make no additional sense of the accompanying page. Eberhard knows about it. Is there anything else for me?—The letter from Y.[3] to the council seems quite gen-
82   eral to me and not very significant. These are really not new ideas. I have very little desire to comment on them, but I shall still consider it.—The letter to Eberhard is intentionally written in such a way as to be sent on to Lokies, perhaps personally by Justus.[4]

How are you doing? You will be glad to have Eberhard come! I hope to be with him for Christmas. He may go ahead and tell this to L., in case L. should want to rope him in. I may also come to the Harz Mountains. In January I will be traveling for a longer period.

L. should at some point go back to the Ruhrstraße[5] after consultation with Hymmen.[6] We think that is a good idea, to ensure that nothing is repeated.

I wish the three of you a joyous Advent week and wish I were there.

Regards to you all,
Your D. B.

If Eberhard yet wishes me to write specifically to L., he should let me know this right away! Please give this page to him also.

[11.] [Bonhoeffer is playing on the German word *unabkömmlich*, taken from the name for Bethge's *uk-Stellung*, "reserved occupation classification," for being indispensable to the church; thus he is busy, unable to get away; see 1/31, ed. note 3.—MB]

[1.] *NL*, A 60, 4 (6); handwritten letter from Ettal, undated; previously published in *GS* 6:493–94.

[2.] The letter, apparently passed on to Lokies, is not extant.

[3.] This refers to Count Paul Yorck von Wartenburg, a member since 1939 of the Council of Brethren of the Old Prussian Union. In the minutes of the Berlin Council of Brethren meeting of November 26, 1940, a "York memorandum" is mentioned (Niemöller, *Die evangelische Kirche im Dritten Reich*, 152). In this connection it is worth mentioning that Yorck's essay, "Das Bild des abendländischen Menschen" (The human being in western perspective), which was somewhat like a memorandum, was discussed in Helmuth von Moltke's Kreisau resistance circle; see Ringshausen, "Die Begründung des Staates und der Stellenwert der Kirchen," 207–8.

[4.] Friedrich Justus Perels.

[5.] The military recruiting station for that district was located on Ruhrstraße.

[6.] Johannes Hymmen was the vice president of the Berlin Consistory.

37. To Eberhard Bethge[1]

November 29, 1940

Dear Eberhard,

Since last evening I have been in Munich and among other things have done some Christmas shopping. Papa will be receiving *German Satirical and Polemical Writings*;[2] Mama some sugar I have saved; my godchildren by Jochen,[3] Albrecht,[4] and Winfried Krause the picture on the back of this card,[5] larger and framed (4.60 marks, not expensive at all, and beautiful). I thought of giving the same to the Blocks and Mrs. Martin,[6] to whom I always send something—this time perhaps you could do that for me. My siblings and the Dohnanyis will receive nothing this year. Shall we perhaps give Hans something together? Or do you want to give your own gift? I don't know what yet. Additionally, I bought one hundred postcards with the Altdorfer[7] that appears on the other card. This picture seems quite timely to me: Christmas amid the rubble. Something I would like to send is the Furche edition of Calvin's letters to the Huguenots! Very impressive.

Today I spoke with the man assigned here to the church renewal movement[8]—extremely interesting and actually worthwhile for you! Partly as at Finkenwalde but also some truly new ideas. I think you[9] need to know this! It is practiced here and in the cities, no less. I don't know whether you have any other connections to this. As soon as my trip is set, we will have to make the arrangements. You must tell Lokies this! I still don't know how

83

[1.] *NL*, A 59,2 (14); handwritten on the back of the two art postcards from Munich that are mentioned in this letter; previously published in abridged form in *GS* 2:386–87.

[2.] Reifferscheidt, *Deutsche Spott- und Streitschriften*.

[3.] Joachim Kanitz.

[4.] Albrecht Schönherr.

[5.] Stephan Lochner, *Birth of Christ*.

[6.] Martin Niemöller.

[7.] Albrecht Altdorfer, *Holy Night*. [Bonhoeffer bought one hundred postcards of the Altdorfer while in Munich; he referred to it again from prison in a letter to his parents from Advent 1942 (*LPP*, 152).—MB]

[8.] This was probably Father Simon Scherzl. "In Munich he was at that time the leading Redemptorist. In 1930 he put out a book titled *Compelle intrare*, in which he described in detail the methods of the house mission of that time. From around 1928–39, the Redemptorists had made a great effort with home visits in their mission efforts in large cities in order to reach inactive people" (communication from Father Josef Spielbauer to the German editors, March 24, 1987). Bethge had in fact received from Bonhoeffer the book mentioned; see 1/80, ed. note 14. Bernhard Ebermann's work, *Die Redemptoristen*, 518–19, serves also to confirm this. [On the church renewal movement, see also 1/17, ed. note 9.—MB]

[9.] [The plural form of "you" is used in the German text.—MB]

long you will now be free. But without a doubt it is a tremendous gift; in any case, I experience it this way very strongly, a real reprieve. What matters now is that we use it well so that when it is over we will know how good it was. We must each help one another in this. Now you can have your Advent and Christmas seasons for yourself and your work. I will miss the hymns very much, to say nothing of the preaching; for we had these even in the seminary. All the more do I rejoice for you that you can even be in Finkenwalde itself. One will be especially thankful for this. I wish you παρρησία joined with σωφροσύνη[10] and will be with you in my thoughts every day.

I find the mountain landscape difficult to tolerate physically. The insurmountable quality sometimes lies like a burden on my work as well. Does 84 "mountains" actually have anything to do with "to hide"?[11] At times I think this and also even experience it that way, though less frequently.

On Monday morning the Dohnanyis are coming to Berlin; they are bringing a sausage along for you—you will surely be able to use it by now. I hope it will still be good. They are also bringing pictures and books along. Perhaps you could wait to leave until four o'clock?

Farewell, and God protect you!

Your Dietrich

38. To His Parents[1]

November 29, 1940

My dear Parents,

Today I was in Munich, and tomorrow I am expecting Hans.[2]—Many thanks for your letter. I spoke with the publisher;[3] he holds the same view

---

[10.] The Greek word παρρησία means "boldness" (e.g., Acts 4:29). The Greek word σωφροσύνη means "temperance" or "prudence" (e.g., Acts 26:25; 1 Tim. 2:9 and 2:15).

[11.] [This passage is a play on the German words *Gebirge,* "mountains," and *bergen,* "to hide."—MB]

[1.] *NL,* A 59,1 (8); handwritten letter from Ettal; previously published in *GS* 6:494–95.

[2.] From Hans von Dohnanyi's letter of November 25, 1940, to his wife: "Provided nothing intervenes, I will be in Munich early on Saturday and have some things to do then regarding Dietrich's affairs; so I will probably arrive in Ettal in the afternoon" (BA Berlin-Lichterfeld, Nachlaß Dohnanyi 8/1). In fact he arrived on November 30; see 1/39.

[3.] Bonhoeffer was able to discuss with Albert Lempp the "request of November 21, 1940" to the Reich Chamber of Literature, mentioned in the letter of March 17, 1941; see 1/99, p. 181. On Lempp's advice, Bonhoeffer sought membership in the Chamber of Literature [this was compulsory for anyone who wanted to publish—MB] and the securing of a military exemption; see 1/100. This stemmed from a renewed reduction in confessional writings brought about by a document of March 8, 1940 (BA Koblenz 089), from

as you. I will write accordingly. Unfortunately, I don't have a proof of ancestry.[4] How does a person get one anyway? I am writing to Block today regarding the NSV.[5]

Thank you also very much for all your help to Eberhard. He wrote so gratefully about it; and without it, of course, everything would have gone differently. Needless to say, I am also extremely glad that he is free a little longer.—Even the fact that I can now be in Ettal was actually your idea, dear Mama. I have not forgotten that.   85

Today I did some Christmas shopping. This year I must primarily remember the wives of the brothers on the front. So my own siblings will be somewhat deprived. It has not yet been decided where I shall be for Christmas, especially since I may soon have to travel for a few weeks. Are you going to the Harz? I do not know yet what Eberhard is planning.

The children have adjusted well to their life up here, and they have been received warmly by their schoolmates as well. It is a nice environment.—I find the picture on this card lovely; Christmas comes even in the midst of rubble.

Best wishes to all! With my warm regards,

Your grateful Dietrich

39. To Eberhard Bethge[1]

1st Sunday in Advent

Dear Eberhard,

I wish you a joyful Advent season! May you find much joy in your work and in the Advent hymns!

Martin Bormann, the head of the party chancellery, to Max Amann, the president of the Reich Chamber of Literature; this document was followed by the July 17, 1940, ordinance of the Ministry Council for Reich Defense, regarding proof of membership in the Reich Chamber of Literature (*Reichsgesetzblatt* 1, 1940, 1, 1035–36; guidelines for implementation, ibid., 1038); cf. Brunotte, "Der kirchenpolitische Kurs der Deutschen Evangelischen Kirchenkanzlei von 1937 bis 1945," in Brunotte and Wolf, *Zur Geschichte des Kirchenkampfes*, 126–27.

[4.] At that time, for an application for membership in the Reich Chamber of Literature it was imperative to demonstrate "Aryan" descent through a "certificate of ancestry," or *Ahnenpaß*.

[5.] Bonhoeffer joined the Nationalsozialistische Volkswohlfahrt (NSV), or National Socialist Public Welfare Agency, in 1940. Cf. 1/230.2, p. 437.

[1.] *NL*, A 59,2 (15); handwritten letter from Ettal, December 1, 1940; previously published in *GS* 2:387–88.

Hans[2] came yesterday. I heard your whole saga from him. We think that the moral of the story is that we know too few people and the circle is becoming too small. Just before Wolfgang's illness,[3] I spoke to him quite extensively on this very point, and he wanted to get something under way relating to that. But he was probably not able to do so then. That is all the more reason why it must now be undertaken. We also owe it to Hans to listen to him on this point. Now, before Christmas I could be of some assistance to you in this direction. Afterward I myself will be traveling for some time.

86   Thus I suggest that you come here immediately after East Prussia (from the twentieth on will presumably be difficult!)[4] to rest for a few days, which you need, in any case, then visit a few people with me, not only for professional reasons in the narrow sense but also with the broader horizon in mind. Whether you must go home for Christmas is not for me to decide. If not, it would naturally be lovely if we were together. Yet we shall still be here as well, though that hinges on the larger trip. You must help Lokies to grasp the bigger picture here; we cannot always rely on only one pair of eyes.[5] I would thus expect you after the fifteenth. If that doesn't work, please let me know! It will perhaps be our last chance for a long time to come. I will then most likely be traveling to Sutz[6] and other places. All the best!

Your Dietrich

[2.] Hans von Dohnanyi.

[3.] This refers to Wolfgang Staemmler's imprisonment. He was arrested on November 16, 1940, because despite the ban on public speaking he had given a lecture.

[4.] Train service was restricted before Christmas to free up trains for soldiers coming home on leave.

[5.] [Bethge had begun working under Confessing Church pastor Hans Lokies, director of the Gossner Mission in Berlin. Bonhoeffer welcomed the assignment, since it kept Bethge out of the military. At the same time, Bonhoeffer's growing role in the resistance meant that he now relied more than ever on Bethge to supervise the underground collective pastorates in East Prussia, and as this letter shows, he also wanted Bethge to have contacts with the resistance people in Munich. Hence he did not want Lokies to place too many demands on Bethge.—MB]

[6.] Erwin Sutz, a friend of Bonhoeffer's since their time together as students in New York, was at that time a pastor in Rapperswil on Lake Zurich; as Bonhoeffer was indicating, the destination of his trip was Switzerland.

40. To Eberhard Bethge[1]

December 2, 1940

Dear Eberhard,

Here are a few random thoughts.[2] By the way, in giving such presentations it never matters so much that you rigidly hold to the formulation of the theme as that you tell people something that concerns and interests them. There you surely have enough from before!

Many thanks for your letter from Stettin. It reached me in just one day!—Today was [minus] 17 degrees.[3]

Are you traveling from Breslau to East Prussia? My parents are staying in Berlin for Christmas. We just phoned. But you and I could still go to the Harz anyway. Perhaps your mother could also come? Just an idea!?

You may give Papa the satirical writings;[4] I will think of something yet. Otherwise they would have been fun for Hans[5] as well. Whatever you think best. Good night. I am very tired!

Affectionately,
Your Dietrich

41. To Hans Meiser[1]

December 4, 1940

Esteemed Bishop Meiser:

Since I will be in Munich on Friday and Saturday of this week[2] because of military service,[3] I would be most grateful were I able to visit you at your convenience regarding a certain matter. I will take the liberty of telephoning

---

[1.] *NL*, A 59,2 (16); handwritten letter from Ettal; previously published in *GS* 6:497–98.

[2.] Cf. 2/7: "The Significance of Mission to Non-Christians for the Church Renewal Movement."

[3.] [Celsius.—MB]

[4.] Cf. 1/37, ed. note 2.

[5.] Hans von Dohnanyi.

[1.] LKA Nuremberg, Nachlaß Meiser, no. 240; handwritten letter with receipt stamp: "Bishop of the Evangelical Lutheran Church of Bavaria east of the Rhine (no. 1242), December 6, 1940." Cf. *NL*, A 60,5 (1).

[2.] The dates were December 6 and 7.

[3.] This was Bonhoeffer's way of defining his current status to people outside the circle of those who knew of his resistance work.

on Friday morning to inquire whether and when I might come.[4] With sincere deference to you, dear Bishop, I remain

Your very respectful
Dietrich Bonhoeffer

88   **42. To Eberhard Bethge**[1]

December 5, 1940

Dear Eberhard,

By now you will surely also have read that traveling will be difficult from the twentieth on.[2] So we must come to a decision now. I have just heard that at Christmas the sun no longer reaches Ettal, which is in a deep valley. So we may have to stay somewhere else. If you prefer Friedrichsbrunn,[3] let me know in time! In principle I have nothing against that, especially if not too many children are there. I am just now traveling to Munich to set various things in order. I am supposed to register there officially. As time goes on, there is so much to tell you and talk over with you that it is high time that we meet.

Justus[4] just wrote, quite excited about your staying: it would be a "fruitful and lively exchange" of the sort that rarely happens in Berlin. You see!

Forgive my writing in pencil. I forgot my fountain pen. Greet the Onnasches. With my best wishes and thoughts of your work,

Your Dietrich

[4.] Meiser wrote a note by hand on December 6, 1940: "Arranged for December 7, 1940, at 11:00 o'clock." Meiser's official diary includes this entry for December 7: "Pastor Dr. Bonhoeffer, Ettal (religious instruction of children in Berlin)." As a result of this conversation, Bishop Meiser dispatched his assistant at that time, Hermann Dietzfelbinger, to Ettal to hold worship services and confirmation instruction once every two weeks in the school chapel. "I met Bonhoeffer a few times in those months as well, in worship also" (Dietzfelbinger, *Veränderung und Beständigkeit*, 91ff.).

[1.] *NL,* A 59,2 (17); handwritten postcard addressed to Mrs. Margret Onnasch, Stettin, Pestalozzistraße 16; previously published in *GS* 2:388.

[2.] Because of the expected large number of soldiers on leave, civilian holiday traffic was being restricted.

[3.] Friedrichsbrunn in the Harz region had been the vacation site for the Bonhoeffer family since 1913.

[4.] Friedrich Justus Perels.

43. To Eberhard Bethge[1]

Ettal, 2nd Sunday in Advent

Dear Eberhard,

I wanted to send you a greeting for this Sunday, but I did not know where. So I hope you find this card waiting for you in East Prussia.

Yesterday when I returned I was overjoyed to find your letter and card of the fourth and fifth! Thank you so much! I am now looking forward to your coming. If for some reason it should not work out, just let me know in time. Then we can go together to the Harz. Hopefully you will still get a sleeping car or a couchette car.[2] Otherwise you will have to ride second class all night (bring a thermos!!) and then go right to sleep in Munich!

89

Please don't worry so much about the Christmas shopping! We can still do some shopping in Munich right away. Four days will surely be enough. So just put that worry aside. If possible, bring along the 150 marks still due me. But don't go to any trouble about this. It would just give us more freedom.

I wish you a nice time in East Prussia. The Catholic Advent seems somewhat strange to me. I am looking forward to Christmas with you. So keep me posted! It is snowing like crazy here. I have not yet used my snowshoes! So we will be together as before. God preserve you in all your work. Affectionate regards from

Your faithful Dietrich

The conversation between Gü. and Ke.[3] seems to have gone well.

[1.] *NL,* A 59,2 (18); handwritten postcard, December 8, 1940; previously published in *GS* 6:498–99.

[2.] [A sleeping car on a train has rooms with actual sleeping berths; a couchette car has seats that can be converted into sleeping berths.—MB]

[3.] The abbreviations refer to the Reich Minister for Church Affairs Hanns Kerrl, and Reich Minister of Justice Franz Gürtner, who had a son in the Ettal *Gymnasium* (high school). The conversation concerned the attempt to push through the possibility of UK classification for Confessing Church pastors, that is, their release from the required service decreed by the November 6, 1940, ordinance of the Reich Minister of Labor; see 1/31, ed. note 3. In this matter Hans von Dohnanyi benefited from his close contacts with the Gürtner household. In any case, he reported in a letter of the same day to his wife on a conversation with Gürtner. Cf. *DB-ER,* 690–91.

90   **44. To Paula Bonhoeffer**[1]

2nd Sunday in Advent

Dear Mama,

Here are ten of these cards as you wished. I am also sending them to the brothers in the field.—By now Walter[2] will have received all of them. I am asking him to send the Calvin.[3]—It was indeed too bad that Klaus[4] passed through Munich yesterday without stopping.—Ninne[5] has declared herself quite willing. Would you please send her a copy of *Life Together*? There are several upstairs in my room under the "Apostles."[6] In addition, if it were possible for you to send me another two copies of *Discipleship* and one of *Life Together* from upstairs, I would like to give them to the abbot here. Possibly also *Creation and Fall*. One more big favor, but please don't do it if it's too inconvenient for you. The pictures for my godchildren and for the Blocks will need to be sent on time. I had hoped that Eberhard would be able to do it. But now he is traveling. One picture is to go to Mrs. Niemöller; I have always sent her something for Christmas. Actually, it could be delivered in person when the opportunity presents itself. Many thanks!

Today it is snowing hard again. The children are outside. But they still do not look quite fully recovered. The work is no doubt strenuous and uncustomary.

Hopefully the Gü.-Ke. matter will develop favorably.[7] It looks that way.

Best wishes from
Your grateful Dietrich

[1.] *NL,* A 59,1 (9); handwritten postcard from Ettal, December 8, 1940; previously published in *GS* 6:499–500.

[2.] Walter Dreß was Bonhoeffer's brother-in-law, married to Dietrich's sister, Susanne.

[3.] This course of events can no longer be reconstructed. It is also an open question to what extent Bonhoeffer used certain Calvin passages in his composition of the *Ethics.* [Cf. the brief comment on parallels between Bonhoeffer and Calvin on civil government in *DBWE* 6:392–93, ed. note 16.—MB]

[4.] Klaus was Bonhoeffer's brother.

[5.] Ninne was Countess Christine von Kalckreuth. Bonhoeffer was able to declare her address as his official residence. In fact, now and then he stayed with her; otherwise, while in Munich he stayed at the European Inn, the Catholic hostel.

[6.] "Apostles" refers to Bonhoeffer's reproduction of the two panels (oil on lindenwood) by Albrecht Dürer from 1526, *The Four Apostles,* in the Alte Pinakothek, Munich.

[7.] See 1/43, ed. note 3.

45. To Eberhard Bethge[1]

91

December 10, 1940

Dear Eberhard,

Your letter and enclosures have just arrived. That is quite welcome news. My warm congratulations to you also on the definite appointment.[2] It must please you just a little, doesn't it? For me it is a source of both relief and pride. We need to discuss the matter concerning the chairman of the board. I am thinking of my acquaintance who writes to me more or less monthly.[3] We'll see.

Needless to say, I shall be delighted if you come down here. That was my original plan all along, and if it works for you, all the better. I shall, of course, pick you up in Munich. Perhaps we will stay there a little while to take care of a few things. It is possible that Gü.[4] will come around the same time as you in order to pick up his son. It would be very nice if you could also meet him then.

I am writing to Christel[5] regarding the skis. You must inquire once again as to how it gets worked out. I have not gone out skiing once; the days are too short. But there is a great deal of snow, and it is not cold at all. It would be nice if you had yours here.

From Chr. Kaiser I found out that I earned 764 RM in March and April 1939 (when we were away).[6] Do you remember whether we ever received it? Part of it was supposedly a check from the Bavarian Hypobank. I have no idea about this. Say, did we already give Mama the taxes for November

---

[1.] *NL*, A 59,2 (19); handwritten letter from Ettal; previously published in *GS* 6:500–501; excerpt previously published in *GS* 2:389.

[2.] Bethge had received an official call to the Gossner Mission; cf. Bethge, *In Zitz gab es keine Juden*, 115. [In September 1940, the Confessing Church curatorium appointed Bethge as inspector of missions for the Gossner Mission. The appointment removed Bethge from the immediate threat of conscription, and because Bethge's job would include contacts with foreign missions, Hans von Dohnanyi planned to create a subterfuge for Bethge (namely, that he should use his foreign church contacts for Military Intelligence) similar to the one he had created for Bonhoeffer. In July 1943, Bethge did indeed travel to Switzerland on Military Intelligence business, after the arrests of Bonhoeffer and Dohnanyi. See de Gruchy, *Daring Trusting Spirit*, 52–58.—MB]

[3.] Bethge surmises that Bonhoeffer was thinking here of Friedrich Justus Perels. His brother, Pastor Otto Perels, recalls: "Friedrich Justus told me at that time that he was called to the board of the Gossner Mission, but said nothing about the chair" (conversation with the German editor, October 12, 1989).

[4.] Franz Gürtner was the Reich Minister of Justice.

[5.] Christine von Dohnanyi.

[6.] This refers to royalties for *Discipleship* and *Life Together.*

(payable until December 5)? I seem to recall this clearly. But she had Hans[7] pay her for it again. I am afraid this is yet another misunderstanding. See if you can remember!

Please do not worry so much about the Christmas present for my parents. December 30 is Mama's birthday anyway. We can still find something for her together. Just give both of them the *Spott- und Streitschriften*.[8] I read some of them. They are quite nice and timely and will certainly please her. You can give Hans my copy here. I will then give him the first volume of Ricarda Huch.[9] We can discuss that further here. I think the flask will be very nice for your mother. Of course, you can give Mama something like that as well, but I think the book for both of them is almost nicer. They belong together. You do not still need to obtain pictures for Mrs. Block and Mrs. Martin.[10] They are already in Berlin, and I asked Mama to send them. How long is Christoph's[11] vacation? Do you want to have him perhaps come here later on? Or will you send him something nice? I still do not know what to get for Margret and Fritz.[12] Didn't you want to send your mother a little picture?

Do we want to go to Nuremberg on the way back? I am expecting around four hundred reichmarks from Kaiser. Many thanks for your effort in Altdamm![13] So you, rather than Fritz, will receive the bequeathed book!

There was an inquiry about me,[14] what I do here and why I am over there so often. They answered well and clearly. One gradually grows accustomed to everything.

Now I am thoroughly back into my work. May all continue to go as it has so far, and may things not unduly tax your energy! We will then try to have a genuinely restful time. I am looking forward to it.—I am now beginning the section on "Natural Life."[15] You are right: it is dangerous material but precisely for this reason so stimulating.

Farewell. God protect you! With my best wishes

Your faithful Dietrich

[7.] Hans von Dohnanyi.

[8.] [Reifferscheidt, *Deutsche Spott- und Streitschriften,* 1940. Cf. 1/37.—MB]

[9.] Presumably Bonhoeffer is referring to *Römisches Reich Deutscher Nation,* volume 1 of Huch's three-volume *Deutsche Geschichte.*

[10.] Bonhoeffer is referring to the wife of Martin Niemöller.

[11.] Christoph Bethge.

[12.] Margret and Fritz Onnasch.

[13.] Regarding the list of books, see 1/35.

[14.] The police had inquired about Bonhoeffer. On the Ettal surveillance measures of that time, see Koch, "Die Benedikterabtei Ettal," 52, and Neuhäusler, *Amboß und Hammer,* 111.

[15.] Cf. *DBWE* 6:171–218.

46. To Eberhard Bethge[1]   93

December 11, 1940

Dear Eberhard,

I have just received a letter from Papa in which he informed me that it was impossible to get a sleeping car for the eighteenth or nineteenth. Even though the chauffeur was sent at 8:30 a.m. the first possible day, people were already standing in line; moreover, the military grabbed up a lot of the tickets, etc. So your sacrifice will be even greater. I am truly sorry that after all these efforts you will still have to sit through the night, or would you rather ride second class during the day? It takes eleven hours; that may be less stressful, I would then pick you up on the evening of the nineteenth. If you bring along something nice to read (I just read Ibsen again with great excitement: *The Wild Duck, Nora, Ghosts,* ideal for the train!), then it may even be quite relaxing! Just be sure to bring a thermos of coffee along! There are two up in my room! And head to the station at least an hour beforehand! But if it should all become too much for you, then write to me and I will come somewhere else.

Yesterday was Christiane's[2] birthday! Christoph[3] is now sick in bed, and I am taking care of him. He is sleeping in my room at night. Today he is feeling better.

I am quite busy with Christmas letters to those on the front. There are ninety.[4]—Today it is snowing steadily again. I wonder how things look where you are. Last night we had fifteen minutes of air-raid alarm! Very exciting for the uninitiated.

All the best to you and lots of energy for these last days! As ever,

Your faithful Dietrich

47. Finkenwalde Circular Letter[1]   94

Dear Brothers,

When in 1914 the war shattered what is now called the "prewar period," it was experienced as a turning point without equal. A whole way of thinking

---

[1.] *NL,* A 59,2 (20); handwritten card from Ettal; previously published in *GS* 6:501–2; excerpt previously published in *GS* 2:389.

[2.] Christiane Leibholz.

[3.] Christoph von Dohnanyi.

[4.] See Finkenwalde circular letter, 1/47.

[1.] *NL,* A 48,3; carbon copy, only incompletely preserved, from Ettal, dated around the middle of December; previously published in *GS* 2:570–73. Cf. "Sermon Meditation

and of living was overturned, and something completely new moved into its place. This new thing brought by the world war did not, however, give way again after the "peace treaty" to the old life, to what existed before the war. The break in time remained; in fact, it was intensified and became even clearer in ever new phases. It is probably for this reason that we do not experience the present war, as we did in 1914, as a radical change of our life, but rather only as a newly sharpened clarifying of our existence in this world, whose quality we have been tasting in fundamental ways for years. Just as time-lapse photography makes visible, in an ever more compressed and penetrating form, movements that would otherwise not be thus grasped by our vision, so the war makes manifest in particularly drastic and unshrouded form that which for years has become ever more dreadfully clear to us as the essence of the "world." It is not war that first brings death, not war that first invents the pains and torments of human bodies and souls, not war that first unleashes lies, injustice, and violence. It is not war that first makes our existence so utterly precarious and renders human beings powerless, forcing them to watch their desires and plans being thwarted and destroyed by more "exalted powers." But war makes all of this, which existed already apart from it and before it, vast and unavoidable to us who would gladly prefer to overlook it all.

95   It is precisely here that war provides for us in a special way the possibility of authentic Christmas celebration. "The world was lost" is the insight from which it can first be grasped what it means that "Christ is born."[2] But we all shrink from this insight with every means at our disposal. For it is an unbearable insight. Confronted with it, we want to stick our heads into the sand: it's not so bad! We wish to escape to some isle of the blessed: my life at least is lovely and joyful and harmonious! How often the parsonage and pastoral life are just such isles of the blessed. And how often we Germans have made of Christmas just such an island onto which one can escape from the actual reality of life for a few days or at least a few hours. How utterly

---

on Isa. 9:6-7, Christmas 1940," 3/1. According to a July 12, 1940, decree of the Reich Ministry for Church Affairs and the Armed Forces High Command (I 25181/40), it was forbidden for civilians to send publications of all kinds, including duplicated circular letters, to members of the armed forces; therefore, Bethge and Bonhoeffer had switched to writing the Finkenwalde circular letters with carbon copies on the typewriter. Bonhoeffer entered the name of the addressee by hand at the beginning. At times the letters went out to nearly 150 recipients.

[2.] This is from the first verse of the hymn "Once Again My Heart Rejoices," by Paul Gerhardt, a favorite hymn writer of Bonhoeffer (*Lutheran Book of Worship,* no. 46 ["O du fröhliche," (*Evangelisches Gesangbuch für Brandenburg und Pommern,* 540, 1; *Evangelisches Kirchengesangbuch,* 408, 1)]).

our entire usual celebration of this feast, which we have decorated with all that is cozy and well loved and sweet and colorful, is oriented toward this "magic" that is supposed to carry us for a time into fairyland. Christmas—it is a "vacation from myself," a "vacation from life." Thus the authentic Christmas celebration, as it stands before us in the shepherds' approach to the manger, has been transformed into these days of outer and inner comfort; moreover, the message of God's love in the background may also then be quite useful in safeguarding these days as such.

In recent years this form of Christmas celebration—we may now ourselves confess the extent to which it has become ours in our parsonages as well— has become difficult for us. The "magic" has today entirely lost its power; it now fails to banish reality.[3] Our escape has backfired. The colorful haze, which once was truly able to deceive us for days and hours, has now come clear to us as deception and lies. The essence of the world has revealed itself. "The world was lost" is no longer a dogmatic proposition; it is manifestly the reality in which our actual life comes to pass. Yet for this reason we now also hear the ancient tidings with new meaning and new longing: "Behold, I bring you—those who live in darkness and the shadow of death—great joy! For to you is born today the Savior, Christ the Lord!" Now in the Christmas celebration we are pointed in a new way to precisely that which in the Bible also stands at the center: the simple reality of the gracious and merciful action that comes from God into this lost world. It is no longer fine, colorful pictures and images that matter to us, but out of the concrete reality of need, we thirst for the reality of abundant divine help. Whether God truly sent the One who holds the right and power of full, encompassing, conclusive salvation—that is the question we are asking. And the Christmas message is the full, glorious Yes in answer to this question. To hear this Yes in all simplicity and to speak it in all reality is our task, our blessed task, at Christmastime. From time immemorial, the world has always been full of a thousand demands, plans, appeals, and directives by which we seek to overcome the afflictions of the world, which become painfully evident to all of us sooner or later. Thanks be to God, we do not have to go on demanding, planning, and making appeals. We have only to hear and to speak of what is truly bestowed, apart from all our action and effort, as real and all-sufficient help from God.

96

[3.] The echo of Jochen Klepper's "Communion Hymn for Christmas," which Bonhoeffer doubtless knew from the volume published by Eckart in 1938 titled *Kyrie*, is unmistakable: "The celebration became too gaudy and cheerful, / as the world keeps your feast. / So make us better prepared for the night / in which your star appears in the sky" [Die Feier ward zu bunt und heiter, / mit der die Welt dein Fest begeht. / Mach uns doch für die Nacht bereiter, / in der dein Stern am Himmel steht] (*Kyrie*, 85).

It is true that we do not receive in this way any Christmas celebration other than that which the shepherds in Bethlehem had, even though we may draw into our Christmas the full riches of Jesus' cross, resurrection, and ascension. Like the shepherds, we remain those who believe. Like them we see the child in the manger, who does not claim to differ from other children, and we hear the message "as it was made known to them concerning this child." The world's night is just as dark for us as it could only have been for the shepherds then. Despite all the rich and blessed experience of all Christendom on earth, the fact that the rule of the world lies on this child's shoulder, that all power in heaven and on earth is given him, is as hard to see today as it was then and is still only to be heard and believed. So too our Christmas celebration does not lead us out of the needs and burdens of our life in the world, does not lead us straight to paradise. We, too, like the shepherds, must again turn back to the old relationships with all their pressures that wound us. Yet if we are given only the shepherds' Christmas celebration, if we are able only in this way to hear and believe, even so, the Savior is here! God's hand rests again on the world and will never let it go! Salvation is at hand! The night is far spent; the day is near at hand! The rule of the world has already been denied to the princes of this world and been laid on the shoulders of this child! Then it may be said of us as well as of those shepherds not only that "they returned again" to all the old bitter affliction but also that "they praised and rejoiced in God for all that they had heard and seen, as it had been told to them," in the midst of all personal anguish, in the midst of the world's night, in the midst of war…

97

48. Excerpt from File: Hans von Dohnanyi to the Schlawe District Military Recruiting Station[1]

Berlin, December 11, 1940

B.[2] has been commanded to military service in Munich; please carry out expeditious transfer to Munich WMA.[3]

[Hans von Dohnanyi]

[1.] BA Berlin-Lichterfelde, Nachlaß Dohnanyi 13/2–33,41; hectograph of an excerpt from the investigation files of the Reich wartime bar of September 1943. This excerpt (cf. 1/49) concerns the return of documents from a binder (Supporting Documents [*Beiakte*] 3 D1 Armed Forces High Command) that was seized upon von Dohnanyi's imprisonment.

[2.] [Dietrich Bonhoeffer.—MB]

[3.] [Wehrkreismeldeamt, "District Military Recruiting Station."—MB]

49. Excerpt from File: Hans von Dohnanyi to Munich Military Intelligence Office[1]

98

December 11, 1940

Please make note of the enclosed document to the Schlawe WMA[2] and hasten Bonhoeffer's UK classification[3] as soon as the Schlawe WMA has made note of the transfer to Munich.

[Hans von Dohnanyi]
Attachment:[4]

Dear Captain Schmidhuber:

Allow me to alert you to the fact that Lic.[5] Dietrich B. is traveling for a time; please direct any communications for him to me.

[Hans von Dohnanyi]

50. To Eberhard Bethge[1]

Dear Eberhard,

I hope that this greeting will still reach you before you move on. It has been snowing here for over forty-eight hours without a break, and snow banks are piling up even higher than those we saw last year —out of the ordinary

99

[1.] BA Berlin-Lichterfelde, Nachlaß Dohnanyi 13/2–33,41; hectograph. See 1/48, ed. note 1. Hans von Dohnanyi's correspondence with the Schlawe District Military Recruiting Station and the Munich Military Intelligence Office documents in part the complicated efforts to regulate Bonhoeffer's "military issues" and thereby to assure his stay in Munich (and Ettal); cf. *DBER*, 700–701. Along with Bonhoeffer's "camouflage letter" to Hans von Dohnanyi (see 1/221), antedated November 4, 1940, this correspondence would play a considerable role at the subsequent interrogations of Bonhoeffer, Dohnanyi, and Oster; cf. below, 1/229.2, ed. note 17.

[2.] [Wehrkreismeldeamt, "District Military Recruiting Station."—MB]

[3.] [For an explanation of the UK classification, see 1/31, ed. note 3.—MB]

[4.] A note appears at this point in the document: "Letter of November 26, 1940, to AST Munich, Attn.: Major Hundt; carbon copy of v[on] D[ohnanyi]'s letter of November 26, 1940, to Schm[idhuber]." Major Dr. Anton Hundt was the head of the Munich Military Intelligence Office. Consul and Captain Wilhelm Schmidhuber was assigned to the Department I/Air and simultaneously drawn into conspiracy work with Oster, Dohnanyi, Josef Müller, and Bonhoeffer.

[5.] ["Lic." is the abbreviation for "Licentiate."—MB]

[1.] *NL*, A 59,2 (21); handwritten letter-card [*Briefkarte*], December 13, 1940, from Ettal; previously published in *GS* 6:502–3; excerpt previously published in *GS* 2:390.

even here. Because of Christoph's[2] flu—I am completely responsible for his care—I do not get out much these days. Today he is doing better. My work has, of course, suffered as well. On the sixteenth I shall meet Hans[3] in Munich; whether I shall stay on for your arrival depends on exactly when you will be coming.

I now wish you a joyful conclusion to your demanding period of work. Do not rush around too much in Berlin. There are plenty of Christmas gifts here already. You also wanted to give *Adelheid* [4] away. It is in my room. If you already have something else for Aunt Lene,[5] it would be lovely for the Onnasches, from both of us. I do not know yet what might be right for Mrs. von Kleist-Retzow. I will have to look around in Munich some more. If necessary, simply a nice letter would do. I am sending Hans-Friedrich and Max[6] a small book (the short stories).

You are still entitled to a two-pound sausage from Christel.[7] Save it for January, if it will keep. I still have some provisions here. I am looking forward to seeing you again! All the best until then!

Your faithful Dietrich

Please send a telegram to Ettal as soon as you know when you will be arriving!

51. To His Parents[1]

December 22, 1940

Dear Parents,

I wish you a beautiful and peaceful Christmas celebration. I have just heard that the pope has appealed to the governments for a cease-fire during 100   Christmas.[2] Whether such a voice can be heard at all anymore remains to be seen. I doubt it.

[2.] Christoph von Dohnanyi.

[3.] Hans von Dohnanyi.

[4.] *Adelheid: Mutter der Königreiche* is a historical novel by Gertrud Bäumer.

[5.] Eberhard Bethge's aunt, Helene Bethge.

[6.] Hans-Friedrich von Kleist-Retzow and Max von Wedemeyer were Bonhoeffer's former confirmands.

[7.] Christine von Dohnanyi.

[1.] *NL*, A 59,1 (11); handwritten letter from Ettal; previously published in *GS* 6:504–5; excerpt previously published in *GS* 2:390.

[2.] *Allocutio*, or papal manifesto challenging the secular authorities, of December 24, 1940 (*Acta Apostolicae Sedis* [Rome] 32 [1940]: 5–13).

This year we will again be thinking primarily of Sabine, Gert,[3] and the children. I am quite convinced that there is still so much Christian spirit in their surroundings that, despite everything, they will celebrate a joyful day with many signs of friendship and love; and under the circumstances, those signs must be experienced as especially comforting and strengthening. For the children these must surely be impressions that will remain important their entire lives. Of course, we regret that we can do so little. But I always believe that where our hands are utterly tied[4] something better is at work and that it is good for us to recognize this. Those so far away will likely experience and receive it in this way, and so a certain peace may come over us in all these thoughts. It seems to me that precisely the Altdorfer picture that I recently sent conveys this meaning.[5]

Today Hans[6] is due in. Gürtner came yesterday noon. We spent the day together and discussed various things.[7] In the Kerrl matter he is quite optimistic; the only question is what Kerrl himself can actually do. This is now a somewhat urgent matter, for the reports of work call-ups are ever increasing.[8]

It is now wonderful weather for skiing here, and since Eberhard's arrival, I am also skiing again. Last night we had another alarm. But we slept.

My gifts to you this year are somewhat odd. The sugar for you, dear Mama, is saved from breakfasts here. You must now truly use it yourself. The thermometer for Papa is quite useful in winter and midsummer. We had one like it in Pomerania. But perhaps it is nevertheless too elaborate for you.

Before my trip to my friend Sutz (of which no one else need know),[9] I am hoping to make a quick trip to Berlin again. This is, however, not at all certain.

[3.] In 1938 Bonhoeffer's brother-in-law Gerhard Leibholz had immigrated with his family to England.

[4.] Cf. the verse "Suffering" in the poem "Stations on the Way to Freedom," *LPP*, 371 (*DBW* 8:570–73).

[5.] [See 1/37.—MB]

[6.] Hans von Dohnanyi.

[7.] Cf. Bethge, *In Zitz gab es keine Juden*, 127–28.

[8.] [The Confessing Church was increasingly burdened by the fact that most of its clergy and seminarians were now in the military. This meant that those not in the military were serving multiple parishes. The regime was now targeting them for wartime civilian duty, which would have made it impossible for many of them to continue their work for the church. Bonhoeffer hoped to persuade Kerrl and Gürtner to change government policy.—MB]

[9.] This trip to visit his friend Sutz was the first Swiss trip. [Bonhoeffer needed to keep the full scope of this trip a secret. It was his initial commission abroad as an agent of the Military Intelligence Office. He had been recruited to assist with conspiratorial activity against Hitler within that office. The hope was to utilize Bonhoeffer's ecumenical contacts

101   I thank you very much once again, dear Mama, for all the effort you have exerted with the packages for me. (By the way, did Mrs. Niemöller receive the picture?) Now after all this back and forth I hope you truly have some rest. With all my best wishes

Your grateful Dietrich

52. To Hans-Werner Jensen[1]

December 26, 1940

Dear Brother Jensen,

Finally the letter for which I had hoped so long has arrived; and above all, finally I have the military post address without which I was not able to write to you, since for months my letters to you have been returned. This was particularly painful for me when I wrote a Christmas greeting to all the colleagues and sent a small book. There was still a question mark by your name then. Now I am very happy to be back in touch with you, even if what you report is not pleasant. How sorry I am that I knew nothing this whole time of your stroke of bad luck and so could think of you only in general ways. Is your wife now actually in Aalen? And your son?

     Now I must tell you something of us. In the summer I was making visitations in East Prussia, in part together with Brother Bethge. In September, along with five other brothers of the Old Prussian Union Church (Superintendent Onnasch, Gollwitzer, Linz, Kreck, [. . .]),[2] I received the ban on public speaking and the requirement to register with the police, all of us with the scandalous accusation of "activity subverting the people." There was no possibility of response, no concrete charges were raised, always the same old tune! Oh well, in this matter we can have a very clear conscience, for we did nothing at all but proclaim the gospel of Jesus Christ the Lord. Nevertheless, outwardly this represents a decisive break. Since October I

102   have been in the thick of scholarly work and for this reason have withdrawn to Ettal, where I can use the monastery library; I have been most kindly

---

with foreign church leaders to communicate with the Allied leaders. As Eberhard Bethge explains, Bonhoeffer's primary tasks in Switzerland were "first, to restore communication with the churches; second, if possible, to give signs of new resistance activity; and third, to explore ideas about peace aims" (*DB-ER*, 727).—MB]

     [1.] *NL*, A 60,4 (3); typewritten copy by Hans-Werner Jensen of Bonhoeffer's handwritten letter from Ettal; previously published in *GS* 2:587–88.

     [2.] Ellipsis indicates illegible text; a September 20, 1940, decree circulated by the Düsseldorf Gestapo mentions only four other names in addition to Bonhoeffer's; cf. 1/18, ed. note 1.

received there. *Life Together* was read here, and I hear that yesterday, at the monastery Christmas celebration, part of *Discipleship* was read aloud. That is quite pleasing, is it not? I am doing well and have reason to be thankful for everything but really hope to return soon to the practical work of the Confessing Church. Brother Bethge is hard at work, which makes me happy for him. How lovely and important it would be to know you were also soon back in the parish. I can imagine what a sacrifice that is for you.

Now let us move confidently and thankfully into the new year and fully entrust ourselves anew to our Lord Jesus Christ, persevering in prayer for one another that our souls may remain healthy and find salvation anew each coming day.

God preserve you. With best wishes from your faithful

Dietrich Bonhoeffer

53. To Paula Bonhoeffer[1]

December 28, 1940

Dear Mama,

First I must thank you and Papa very much for the lovely Christmas things; I was delighted with everything, but especially that you sent me Walter's[2] magnifying glass. The dictionary will surely interest me greatly.[3] The handkerchiefs are very welcome, also the woolen piece. We had some lovely hours on Christmas Eve; after the gift giving we took the children along to the High Mass at the church. In the following days we were able to be outdoors in the snow a great deal. Needless to say, we are disturbed to think of Emmi[4] and would be grateful to hear frequently how she is doing.

Last year when we celebrated your birthday and came to the end of the year, we probably all thought that this year we would be decisively further along and would see more clearly. Now it is questionable at the very least whether this hope has come true. Hans[5] thinks so.[6] It almost seems to me as if we must come to terms with it over the long haul, to live more deeply out of the past and the present—and that means out of gratitude—than

103

[1.] *NL*, A 59,1 (12); handwritten letter from Ettal; previously published in *GS* 6:506–7; excerpt previously published in *GS* 2:391.

[2.] Bonhoeffer is referring to the magnifying glass that had belonged to his brother who was killed in World War I.

[3.] Bonhoeffer wanted a French dictionary for his time in Geneva, which he would visit on his trip to Switzerland.

[4.] Bonhoeffer's sister-in-law Emmi Bonhoeffer was sick with typhus.

[5.] Hans von Dohnanyi.

[6.] This refers to the hope of removing Hitler.

from any vision of the future.[7] On the other hand, one notices how strongly human life desires to live from the future, more than from anything else. It always involves a very conscious act, a conscious restriction, self-denial, to forbid oneself such thoughts and to be thankful and glad for what has been and still is. But it is still perhaps a blessing of this period that we can learn this, and that we then also learn to see somewhat more confidently, courageously, trustfully into the future. For it is indeed the case that things always look darker and more ominous beforehand than they are in reality, when they approach, and that worry does not clarify our vision. Dear Mama, you are living through this period with an intensity that is repeatedly so astonishing to us who are younger. Therefore, your birthday is probably the right day for all of us, who simply cannot imagine this time without you, to wish that in the new year, even if the veil of things to come has not yet lifted, we shall nevertheless be thankful for what we have in one another up to this hour and look together with great trust into the future. For we have not only one another, but we all have and know the one who has given us this time and also holds our future in hand.

I am being called away. We are invited out, so the letter is on its way. Eberhard drew our present for you. Wishing you a happy new year, dear Mama,

Your grateful Dietrich

17:126   **53a. To Erwin Schutz**[1]

January 2, [19]41

Dear Brother Schutz,[2]

It was truly a great surprise, an excitement without equal, when under the noses of several of my nephews and nieces[3] your package [was] opened
17:127   and a real live rabbit emerged. After reading your kind letter,[4] for which I am very grateful to you, and finding out the particulars and the various migrations of this splendid specimen, I am truly and deeply moved by your kindness. I can only thank you from the heart for the sacrifice you have

---

[7.] Cf. Bonhoeffer's November 18, 1943, letter to Eberhard Bethge (*LPP*, 129 [*DBW* 8:186–93]) and the poem "The Past" (*LPP*, 320–23 [*DBW* 8:468–71]).

[1.] Literary estate of Erwin Schutz: handwritten from Ettal; previously published in Krause, *Erwin Schutz, 1907–1942.* Page numbers in the margin refer to *DBW* 17.

[2.] Erwin Schutz, a pastor in Groß-Schlönwitz, had let Bonhoeffer and his collective vicariate use his parsonage until his wedding. On Schutz, see Krause, *Erwin Schutz.*

[3.] Cf. 1/30, ed. note 4, and Bethge, Bethge, and Gremmels, *Life in Pictures*, 186.

[4.] Letter not extant.

made and for the joy you have given to me and my family. I also most sincerely thank your wife, who would surely rather have prepared this roast herself for you! As a small token of this thanks, I am sending the books[5] off today, as well as a small package that will perhaps give you pleasure. How long have you been in Schlönwitz now?[6] I was very pleased that you are able to be among your beloved congregation. How I would love to attend your Sunday morning worship service once again and hear you preach. Those were lovely, peaceful months with you in Schlönwitz. That changes have taken place in your congregation in these times, that the flock is smaller, must not surprise or discourage you. We will have to move through a very deep valley, I believe much deeper than we can sense now, before we will be able to ascend the other side again. The main thing is that we let ourselves be led entirely and not resist and become impatient. Then it will all go right. For you and yours I wish God's help and presence in the new year. May your home and your word be a fountain of God's word, of truth and love in Jesus Christ, for your congregation.

In heartfelt communion, and with sincere thanks, I remain your faithful

Dietrich Bonhoeffer

54. From Eberhard Bethge[1] 104

Dear Dietrich,

Last night, when I got back here, I found the message to call your home, but it was already 10:15. So we were not able to talk anymore. But we should connect tonight, when I go to your house to see Father Johannes[2] and to wish Rüdiger[3] a happy birthday.

Now I would like to ask you a favor. Lokies is still immersed in the literature on the church renewal movement.[4] Yet he would need to include the Catholic side, as they have such significant things to say on the subject. If you will be going to the bishop's office sometime, could you inquire as to what they have, beyond what was

---

[5.] This apparently refers to Bonhoeffer's fulfillment of a request in Schutz's letter. It may have concerned copies of *Life Together,* which appeared in a fourth edition in 1940.

[6.] Schutz, who had been drafted into the military on January 28, 1940, had received home leave at this point.

[1.] *NL,* C 26; typewritten letter from Berlin, January 14, 1941. On the second page are Bonhoeffer's handwritten notes for his upcoming trip to Switzerland.

[2.] Fr. Johannes Albrecht, who had become acquainted with Bonhoeffer, was required as the "foreign minister" of his monastery to report not infrequently to higher officials in Berlin. See Koch, "Die Benediktinerabtei Ettal," 60ff.

[3.] Rüdiger Schleicher.

[4.] [Cf. 1/17, ed. note 9.—MB]

recently noted, that the prelate there might wish to send me?[5] I shall enclose a piece of stationery with my signature; perhaps you can have the letter typed on it there. I don't know the proper salutation. Otherwise, just let me know what it is, and I shall take care of it from here. Whatever you think. Lokies is feeling some urgency about it.

Now as to my noble mission. Please send the letter back to me. Then you simply must give my Breslau lecture a critical reading.[6] I am quite pleased that they have invited me to do it. In addition, East Prussia wants me to stay there a while to stimulate the catechetical work. But that must first be discussed. Are you traveling to Metten now?[7] From the eighteenth to the twenty-fourth I myself shall be in Lagendorf via Salzwedel near Henheik[8]/(Altmark) and from the twenty-fifth to the twenty-seventh in Kade.[9]

Your mother thinks she remembers the 1939 money from Lempp.[10] She also said that you have quite a nice sum accumulated there. But she has nothing in writing on this any longer.

105   The sermon on Sunday went quite well. But they sent me first to the wrong church, so that I arrived at the right one sopping wet and today have caught a cold. But I was nevertheless able to concentrate. Afternoon with Hans[11] and the evening with the Schleichers, to whom I brought some of my sugar and also paid for the telephone and Bene.[12] We played lovely music together, a new trio by Bach. I have arranged to get together with Harnack[13] next Friday.

The military business is going quite well to date. Lokies went again to Tempelhoferfeld[14] and was well received in light of what has gone on. The only thing missing was something in writing from that time; now he has been asked for a UK application[15]

[5.] See Bonhoeffer's letter of January 19, 1941, 1/58, ed. note 3.

[6.] According to Eberhard Bethge's recollection, this lecture was a reflection on the figures of individual disciples; cf. Bonhoeffer's reflections on "John the Evangelist" in his letter to Eberhard Bethge, June 18, 1942, 1/178, pp. 314–15.

[7.] This is the first reference to Bonhoeffer's interest in contact with the Benedictine monastery of Metten in Lower Bavaria. For more information, see Bonhoeffer's letter of January 17, 1941, 1/56, ed. note 2.

[8.] Bethge had been active as a vicar in Lagendorf in 1934–35; now he was invited to the *Volksmission* event there.

[9.] Kade was the residence of Eberhard Bethge's mother.

[10.] On the accounting of royalties from Chr. Kaiser Verlag, see Bonhoeffer's December 10, 1940, letter, 1/45, ed. note 6.

[11.] Hans von Dohnanyi.

[12.] Benedikt von Hase, Paula Bonhoeffer's youngest brother, received regular financial support from his siblings.

[13.] This refers to Ernst von Harnack, the son of the church historian Adolf von Harnack. Regarding these contacts, see 1/59, ed. note 6; cf. *DB-ER*, 623, and John, *Zweimal kam ich heim*, 58–59 et passim.

[14.] This was the district military recruiting station responsible for Bethge.

[15.] [For an explanation of the UK classification, see 1/31, ed. note 3.—MB]

from the registration office, which he is having completed today by the EOK[16] and is mailing in. So we shall hope for the best.

Thank you again for the things you sent on.

All for now. Just keep on working hard.

Affectionately yours,
Eberhard

Wolfgang's matter[17] has been postponed a second time to a new meeting. It appears to be becoming a more fundamental discussion of the obstacles all of you face. Perels thinks this is not good. The day before yesterday Licentiate Anna Paulsen also received a work order here.[18]

Schmidt[19]/Hotel Zur[ich]. / Shoes
G[isevius's][20] address, register here / Financial settlement[21]
Residence? Certificate of departure for trips
Hans: soap, ring, leather bag
Joachim[22]
Suitcase, dictionary
Ges.[23] tel. address   106
Cons[ul][24] remittance

[16.] [*Evangelischer Oberkirchenrat*, "Evangelical senior church official."—MB]

[17.] The imprisonment of Wolfgang Staemmler for political reasons preoccupied the Council of Brethren, which had reservations as to whether his name should be placed on the intercessory prayer list. [When people were arrested for "political" reasons, the Confessing Church did not place their names on the intercessory prayer lists that were circulated among congregations. This reflected the bias, widespread even in the Confessing Church, against antigovernment political activity. Thus, while Bonhoeffer's name did appear on the lists in 1939 because of the Gestapo ban on his public speaking, traveling, and publishing, his name did not appear on the lists after 1943, when he was arrested for his role in the conspiracy. For more on this, see Barnett, *For the Soul of the People*, 57–61.—MB]

[18.] Anna Paulsen was the head of Burckhardt House in Berlin-Dahlem. [As Victoria Barnett explains, Burckhardt House was a small church college "that trained women for church work; although part of the official church, it served as a refuge for many of the illegal women theologians in the Confessing Church" (*For the Soul of the People*, 161). Bethge's reference here means that, like most Confessing clergy during the war, Paulsen had been ordered to appear for civilian wartime duty.—MB]

[19.] Bonhoeffer's handwritten marginal notes begin here. Lore Schmid née Delbrück, Emmi Bonhoeffer's sister, lived in Herrliberg near Zurich.

[20.] Hans Bernd Gisevius, assigned since 1940 as vice consul of the German general consulate in Zurich, was at the same time envoy of the German Military Intelligence.

[21.] Uncertain reading.

[22.] This person is not identified.

[23.] [It is not clear to whom this abbreviation refers. It may refer to Hans Bernd Gisevius, mentioned above.—MB]

[24.] Wilhelm Schmidhuber; see 1/49, ed. note 4.

Joachim
Ick[radt][25] 32086
Schmidh[uber]. 26885

55. To Eberhard Bethge[1]

January 15, 1941

Dear Eberhard,

It was nice to talk to you again last night. I would, of course, already have answered your letter, for which I thank you very much, if I had not wanted to wait for the telephone conversation. The matter[2] must now be pursued with all vigor. This is surely not how the action in December was intended! And when the EO[3] finds out that people on the military side are already interested in the matter, they will certainly become more open. I would definitely hint at that. The main thing is that the whole affair not lose steam. You[4] also owe this to Hans,[5] etc. For the time being I am confident enough in your[6] activities that I have resolved not to worry prematurely.

I am back at work. The Kochs'[7] company is very nice. In contrast, the recently arrived Mrs. Lenz[8] appears to be a conceited silly goose. She criticizes everyone around her but gives the impression of being quite ordinary. Unfortunately, I am not alone in this opinion. Also the girl who is the same

107

[25.] Reserve Captain Heinz Ickradt, who belonged to the Munich Military Intelligence Office as head of the I/Air department, was a friend of Consul Schmidhuber and had already become acquainted with Bonhoeffer in Munich.

[1.] *NL*, A 59,2 (22); handwritten letter from Ettal; previously published in *GS* 6:507–9; excerpt previously published in *GS* 2:391–92.

[2.] This refers to the continuation of the measures, in this case a renewed initiative by the Berlin Consistory, to protect Confessing Church pastors from being drafted or conscripted into wartime civilian duty; cf. Bethge, *In Zitz gab es keine Juden*, 129–30.

[3.] The Evangelical High Council [*Evangelischer Oberkirchenrat*] was supposed to submit an application for [Bethge's] exemption from military service in order to sustain the domestic work of the Gossner Mission as a particular institution with connections to India, which was of interest to Military Intelligence. [This was intended to help Eberhard Bethge evade military duty, similar to Bonhoeffer's assignment to Military Intelligence.—MB]

[4.] [The German pronoun is plural, probably referring to Hans Lokies, head of the Gossner Mission, as well as to Bethge.—MB]

[5.] Hans von Dohnanyi.

[6.] [The German possessive pronoun is plural.—MB]

[7.] [Hans and Annemarie Koch.—MB]

[8.] Not otherwise identified.

age as Bärbel,[9] who was extolled as so marvelously Catholic and pious, in fact stands out from all the other children and is quite a Berliner. Miss von Rütz's task is not an easy one, and she accomplishes it quite exceptionally. She deserves to be assisted in every way. Our children are presently doing very well. Pass that on to Christel.[10] Yesterday I had a whole list of things I would have liked shipped here from Berlin, but the conversation was too short. Please tell Mama I need my ration card, wool socks, underwear, the good thin gray summer shirt; did you or Christel pack a woolen undershirt of mine? Please send the dictionaries, also the small Metoula's.[11] Also tell Mama that I myself had a vague memory of the 700 RM, but what about the 240? But if you would prefer, do not get involved in the whole affair. We don't want to worry Mama; it is not worth it.

I am eager for your letter. Is Christiane truly expecting us to visit soon?[12] I had that impression, but perhaps I was mistaken. How nice that you[13] got together with Johannes yesterday. But above all, how wonderful that you were here. I am still richly nourished by it. I piled such a great heap of requests and discussions on you. In retrospect I am sincerely sorry about this; you certainly have enough else to do.

Read Exod. 23:7 sometime.[14] So I will close for today and now write to Mrs. Martin on his birthday.[15] Thank you so much for everything and take care!

Affectionately yours,
Your faithful Dietrich

[9.] Barbara von Dohnanyi.

[10.] Christine von Dohnanyi.

[11.] A foreign phrase book, to help Bonhoeffer in Geneva circles.

[12.] "Christiane" stands for England; the question refers to the state of preparations for invasions. [Bonhoeffer probably based this code name on Christiane Leibholz, the daughter of Bonhoeffer's twin sister, Sabine, and her husband, Gerhard Leibholz; because of Gerhard's Jewish background, they had been compelled to immigrate to England in 1938.—MB]

[13.] [The German is plural.—MB]

[14.] "Keep far from a false charge, and do not kill the innocent and those in the right, for I shall not acquit the guilty." Cf. *DBWE* 6:195. Apparently Bonhoeffer was working at that very moment on this section of *Ethics,* clearly confronting the immediate euthanasia measures.

[15.] "Mrs. Martin" is the wife of Martin Niemöller.

108   **56. To Eberhard Bethge**[1]

January 17, 1941

Dear Eberhard,

By now this letterhead has become familiar to you. I am here again for a few days and leave today for two days in Metten.[2] Monday I will be back in Ettal.

This is simply meant as a greeting that you will find on arrival in Lagendorf, and a sign of my heartfelt gratitude for your work. How is the matter with Lokies proceeding?[3] You have now been away from Berlin for some time. Just make sure that everything necessary there happens! Later Hans will be traveling as well.[4] It is good that in case of his absence you also know O.[5] The date of my trip is again being postponed until Hans has been here. I am going right now to ask about my visa. Last night I was over at Müller's again. It was satisfying in every way. So now I must run. It is 9:30 a.m. The mind is not very productive in the morning either, it seems. All the more, best wishes,

Your Dietrich

109   **57. To Karl Friedrich Bonhoeffer**[1]

Dear Karl Friedrich,

Warm (if somewhat belated) greetings for your birthday, and best wishes to all of you in the new year.

[1.] *NL,* A 59,2 (23); handwritten letter from Munich, on hotel stationery "Hotel Europäischer Hof"; previously published in *GS* 2:392–93.

[2.] Bonhoeffer's contacts with the Benedictine monastery at Metten (Lower Bavaria) and its abbot, Corbinian Hofmeister, have been understated here and in the following letter. In truth, according to Josef Müller, Bonhoeffer probably was in Metten more than just this once. Additionally, according to Annie Oster's recollection, Bonhoeffer met with Abbot Hofmeister several times for hours in Müller's legal chambers. "His connection, or even bond, with my friend Dietrich Bonhoeffer became very close," wrote Müller in memory of the "Abbas" [*Abbas* refers to Hofmeister—MB]. See Müller, "Der Abbas," 3–4. Cf. further Benedikt Busch, "Die Abtei Metten im Dritten Reich."

[3.] See 1/55, ed. note 2.

[4.] Hans von Dohnanyi traveled to Rome, January 24–February 5, 1941.

[5.] This refers to Colonel Hans Oster; see 1/9.

[1.] *NL,* A 59,3 (2); handwritten postcard from Landshut, postmark: "17. 1. 41" [January 17, 1941—MB]; previously published in *GS* 6:509.

I am presently traveling to the Benedictine abbey of Metten, where I have many things to discuss concerning the question presently engaging me.[2] Next week I anticipate traveling to Switzerland for a few weeks. Afterward I will probably return briefly to Berlin. All the best to you all!

Your Dietrich

58. To Eberhard Bethge[1]

January 19, 1941

Dear Eberhard,

Many thanks for your second letter, which I have just received. Late last night we arrived by car back in Munich from Metten. It was too bad you weren't there. I brought back a goose, which I sent to Ursel[2] with the request that she preserve some for you and eat the rest with her family. So you will find something from Metten to greet you when you return.

Unfortunately, I simply have been unable to reach anyone in the bishop's office. I have now sent a letter to Neuhäusler[3] with the request to send you the materials[4] as soon as possible. The other person was Monsignor Stadler,[5] but I think that N[6] will take care of it more quickly. You can still write to Stadler yourself if you wish. I have no typewriter at my disposal here at the hotel, and I am going back to Ettal at three o'clock.

I am quite pleased about your invitation to lecture. Of course, they will want to become theologically acquainted with you at the same time on this

110

[2.] This question cannot now be ascertained; it could have been regarding the pressing problem of the euthanasia measures, which Bonhoeffer was dealing with at that time in his *Ethics*. The Mainkofen hospital located near the Metten monastery was affected by this (information provided to the German editor by Fr. Benedikt Busch, March 17, 1988).

[1.] *NL*, A 59,2 (24); three handwritten cards from Munich; previously published in *GS* 6:509–11; excerpt previously published in *GS* 2:393.

[2.] Ursula Schleicher.

[3.] Prelate Johannes Neuhäusler was Cardinal Faulhaber's representative on church-political matters. [On February 4, 1941, Neuhäusler was arrested. He was transferred to Sachsenhausen concentration camp on May 5, 1941, and then to Dachau on July 12, 1941. On April 24, 1945, he was freed.—MB] Bonhoeffer owed the contact with him to Dr. Josef Müller, who often delivered important materials and information to the Vatican for Neuhäusler. [See also Deutsch, *Conspiracy against Hitler*, 122–23 and 128.—MB]

[4.] In his letter of January 14, 1941, Bethge had requested literature on the Catholic *Volksmission* movement (see 1/54).

[5.] Monsignor Thomas Stadler was at the cathedral in Munich. A more precise connection can no longer be determined.

[6.] [Johannes Neuhäusler.—MB]

occasion. If you want me to look over the Breslau presentation,[7] you must send it at once or wait until my return (there really is time! and we will talk about it in Berlin). I am now not traveling until the twenty-seventh or twenty-eighth[8] and will thus arrive in Berlin at the end of February. Make sure that you will not be in East Prussia at that point! By then we will surely have a great deal to discuss. It would be nice to talk to you by phone again before my departure. But I don't know when I will need to be back in Munich. It is good that I know your schedule. Perhaps I will still give it a try.

What is up with the seeder [Sämaschine]?[9] If that works, then you should keep the silver bell since it just doesn't fit for Papa.—How do you like *The Last Puritan*?[10] The Reinhold Schneider[11] is very good.—Today you are preaching in your old congregation! How nice! God protect you! With my best wishes,

Your faithful Dietrich

I have just succeeded in reaching Neuhäusler after all. I went right to his home and received from him the crucial book,[12] which he had just acquired for himself, but from which he very generously allowed himself to be parted so that I could send it to you. It will go out in this same post. Bibliographic citations are in the book. I'm pleased that it worked out.

I am writing this over lunch at the place of our last two farewell meals in the Excelsior.

111   **59. From Eberhard Bethge**[1]

Lagendorf, January 20, 1941

Dear Dietrich,

When I consider that given the postal conditions in this place a letter may not get posted until Wednesday, I come to the conclusion that you ought to receive yet another

---

[7.] See 1/54, ed. note 6.

[8.] His destination was Switzerland.

[9.] [The circumstances underlying this remark can no longer be determined.—MB]

[10.] The novel by the American author and philosopher George Santayana. [Bonhoeffer was reading the German translation of the English original.—MB] On the influences of this reading, see the letters of January 20 and 25 as well as those of February 2 and 4, 1941, 1/59, p. 123; 1/62, p. 128; 1/69, p. 137; and 1/71, p. 140.

[11.] Schneider, *Macht und Gnade*. To see how his reading of this book influenced Bonhoeffer's *Ethics*, see *DBWE* 6:135, ed. note 39, and 265, ed. note 68.

[12.] Scherzl, *Compelle intrare*. Cf. 1/37, ed. note 8, and 1/80, ed. note 14.

[1.] *NL*, C 26; typewritten letter.

greeting. Yours arrived early today, according to which, however, you must have arrived back in Ettal already early this morning. Many thanks. There you will have received the short message about my UK classification[2] by now. It went entirely through this time without having to involve Hans at all.[3] The impetus he had provided earlier is apparently still having its effect. The red note[4] is even dated the fourteenth and had thus already been issued even before Hymmen's[5] application could have arrived there. It was thus still useful only as extra security for my file. Overall, Lokies did it by himself this time; and I was able to leave again in peace, since I sent back the summons for early February without hesitation. For a change my time in Berlin was not consumed at all by these things. Nevertheless, I still had practically not one moment of free time, because I constantly had to arrange all sorts of things. Still, on Friday evening I was at Ernst Harnack's.[6] All alone with him, which was very nice for conversation, looking through sheet music and records and actually making music. We played duets, or I accompanied him on the piano.

I arrived here right in the middle of a hectic day. On Saturday evening I went directly from the train to a village for Bible study, and then early on Sunday to another village for worship (John 2) and came here at ten. At three in the afternoon to a place seven kilometers away for Bible study, going by foot through the deepest snow and snowstorm without any aid. And that evening another Bible study in a location closer by. There are in fact ten villages here, small ones; yet all want to participate. Now it is going better and more calmly from day to day. On Saturday I shall be in Magdeburg and shall then probably stay in Kade until early Tuesday. Maybe I shall send along my Breslau lecture to you right away so that you can read it over before it is too late and you are perhaps on the road. But you must send it back to me beforehand, since otherwise I am in trouble for April. For the East Prussian visits I must now delve into the Hammelsbeck somewhat,[7] in order to get the picture there.

I am reading Santayana with great eagerness. It is only too bad that I cannot talk over the individual passages with you some. It is truly brilliant and remarkable. Actually a difficult book up to this point, don't you think?

I shall bring back all kinds of delightful things with me to Berlin. The congregations are quite well provided with pastoral leadership. Emmi[8] will be very pleased with my earnings. Did I tell you that I was together with Klaus[9] and the John brothers at

112

[2.] [For an explanation of the UK classification, see 1/31, ed. note 3.—MB]

[3.] Hans von Dohnanyi.

[4.] This refers to the district military recruiting station's document specifying the UK classification.

[5.] See 1/36, ed. note 6.

[6.] See Bethge's letter of January 14, 1941, 1/54, ed. note 13.

[7.] Hammelsbeck, *Der kirchliche Unterricht.*

[8.] Emmi Bonhoeffer.

[9.] Klaus Bonhoeffer.

Rüdiger's[10] in Berlin?[11] They were interested in various things. At dinner John suggested we talk later about the question of what the church demands in order to allow someone to be considered a Christian. The sonhood of Christ, etc. But unfortunately nothing came of it later because they had to leave.

Couldn't you come up with a convincing reason to bring Justus[12] down to where you are (charged to general expenses)? He would indeed like to come but does not know precisely how to justify it to the authorities. But perhaps you can do so? It would truly be a good thing if he were to come. I was with him briefly nearly every day, but we simply did not find the time, for instance, to straighten out the salary question. Please forgive that. But it was truly not possible because the examinations still had to be carried out.

All the best to you,
Your Eberhard

Please pass on my greetings to Father Johannes. I was unfortunately not able to get hold of him anymore in Berlin, since he was apparently too busy; and afterward I had to leave. He is supposed to take care of the pictures.[13] Also greet the children and Miss von Rütz. What is up with the skis? My brother was unfortunately away for so long that I was only able to give him instructions about the ski boots Saturday morning. He then wanted to send them right away. I hope they will arrive and that you can wear them with extra socks.[14]

I also phoned Renate[15] and left a message alerting her to the possibilities, perhaps

---

[10.] Rüdiger Schleicher.

[11.] These meetings, like those with Ernst von Harnack, had both a musical/social character and a conspiracy aspect. Otto John, a corporate lawyer for the German company Lufthansa in Berlin and since 1940 in frequent contact in Madrid and Lisbon with Iberia, the Spanish subsidiary company, was a friend of Klaus Bonhoeffer's and participated with him in planning for the coup. Since 1939 his younger brother, Hans John, also a lawyer, had been Rüdiger Schleicher's research assistant at the Institute for Aviation Law of the University of Berlin.

[12.] Friedrich Justus Perels, previously the legal adviser to the Confessing Church in Berlin, had officially resigned from this position on November 1, 1940, and had assumed the duties of the lawyer Dr. Holstein, who had been drafted into the military. In the case at hand, Perels hoped that through Bonhoeffer's trip he might get assistance for his uncle who was being interned in southern France. [The Perels family was affected by the Nazi racial laws; his uncle was interned in Gurs, a concentration camp for Jews and political prisoners.—MB] See Schreiber, *Friedrich Justus Perels,* 154–55.

[13.] These photographs had been taken during the 1940–41 Christmas vacation in Ettal.

[14.] The following section is handwritten.

[15.] Renate Schleicher.

with Christel.[16] She gives such good violin lessons. Christiane has sent a greeting via Schönfeld;[17] Christel will bring it to you.

60. To Eberhard Bethge[1]

January 20, 1941

Dear Eberhard,

Since our correspondence will be much restricted in coming weeks, it does not hurt if in this last week before my trip we write a little more frequently. Today your short letter arrived with its welcome news about your acquisition of the desired certificate.[2] How odd the steps were to get there! Since November a year ago! This may be a more important decision for your entire life than one can discern in the moment. As diverse as the motives in all such things may be, it is nevertheless certain that a person must take this path if it is possible and do so for very clear, objective reasons. And that is what is decisive. I believe that I am writing this because I myself was involved in this decision, and of course because every decision of far-reaching import calls forth the wish for some justification. In this sense I am thus very much at peace and now also truly very pleased.

Johannes has just come home and recounted with delight his visit to Marienburger Allee, where he met all of you. He was particularly inspired by Mama. He said he so much would have liked to come to tea with you that he also called you twice but unfortunately could not reach you. He would have liked very much to meet a few people through you but is intending another trip up soon. Then you must invite a couple of good people over, perhaps Böhm,[3] Willi,[4] Walter,[5] Lokies, in any case people who can discuss things other than theology and dogmatics (perhaps Otto?).[6] You could take him to Mrs. Martin[7] also.

114

[16.] Christine von Dohnanyi.

[17.] Hans Schönfeld apparently delivered Bishop Bell's response to the Geneva telegram of October 6, 1940; see 1/22.

[1.] *NL*, A 59,2 (25); handwritten letter from Ettal; previously published in *GS* 2:393–95.

[2.] [The red-colored certificate for Bethge's UK classification.—MB] See 1/59, ed. note 4.

[3.] Dr. Hans Böhm, Confessing Church district pastor in Berlin, was called in 1936 to the new Provisional Church Administration. [The Provisional Church Administration was the governing council of the Confessing Church.—MB]

[4.] Wilhelm Rott.

[5.] Walter Dreß.

[6.] Otto Dibelius.

[7.] Elsa Niemöller, the wife of Martin Niemöller.

Justus[8] has just announced he will be coming here on Friday. That pleases me greatly before my trip.

In my work I am just coming to the question of euthanasia.[9] The more I am able to write, the more the material engages me. I find Catholic ethics in many ways very instructive and more practical than ours. Up to now we have always dismissed it as "casuistry."[10] Today we are grateful for much — precisely on the topic of my present theme. I am already looking forward to the conversations of the next weeks and shall perhaps let you read some of it when I come to Berlin. In any case, it will be long!

In the meantime I have to write a shorter essay for Weckerling for the "spa ministry"[11] (!) on Exod. 15:26[12] in a volume to which Kramp,[13] Vogel,[14] etc., are also contributing.

These days it is thawing here. So I may remain in my room in peace and work. You really were able to experience the best weeks. That lovely time still carries me every day; and since it is philistine to wish things always to be so lovely, I am glad that it was as it was.

Now take care! I think daily of all the brothers in the parish and especially of you and your work.

God protect you! With warm wishes,

Your faithful Dietrich

Please also greet your mother and your aunt!

115   **61. From Eberhard Bethge**[1]

Dear Dietrich,

Many thanks for your letter of yesterday and for taking care of the book order so promptly. That was splendid. Today I just want to quickly send you Gerhard's[2] announcement,[3] as he requested, and his letter as well. It is legible and intelligible. It would be

---

[8.] Friedrich Justus Perels.

[9.] See *DBWE* 6:189–96.

[10.] Casuistry is the treatment of individual cases, sometimes approaching hair-splitting, in Catholic moral theology.

[11.] [The "spa ministry" *(Badermission)* was carried out among people who flocked to such places as Wiesbaden and Baden-Baden, where there are spas with hot springs that supposedly help certain physical conditions.—MB]

[12.] See "The Best Physician," 2/9.

[13.] Cf. 1/10, ed. note 18.

[14.] Heinrich Vogel.

[1.] *NL*, C 26; typewritten letter from Lagendorf, January 23 or 24, 1941.

[2.] Gerhard Vibrans.

[3.] Gerhard had announced his marriage to Elisabeth, née Trebesius.

very good if you were to read it despite its length. He is asking about a good medical book for his new circumstances in the future. What should a person recommend? It is surely important that something be suggested to him. It would have to be something like the Velde.[4]

A letter has arrived from East Prussia saying that they would like me as soon as possible. Not so close to Easter. It ought to be time for Erfurt again, but I have so far received no answer from there. Albrecht Schönherr[5] would like me to visit for four days from the eighth or the sixteenth of February, depending on the Erfurt arrangements. And then it is time again for East Prussia. How shall I do it? Next Tuesday Beckmann[6] will allegedly be in Berlin, and I am to meet with him and discuss matters. There, too, I still do not have any clarity. Perhaps it will yet come. On Saturday I shall be meeting in Magdeburg with Inge Koch,[7] Trebesius,[8] and H.-H. Zippel,[9] who, as I have just heard, is in the second phase of his leave. I shall talk to him regarding Maubeuge[10] and perhaps arrange something. I did the same thing in a letter to Gerhard. I don't know, however, where he presently is.[11]

Thank you very much for the greetings, the tangible ones, from Metten. Metten's character is different. And still more thanks for the provisions of goose. I shall conduct myself accordingly. I recently also brought Ursel[12] some of my sugar, which I have in abundance. I do notice, however, that I always need to bring some along on my trips.

The seeder[13] is being procured by my uncle in Magdeburg. I shall be inquiring about it now. We don't want any decision to be made yet about the bell!!

That's all for today! Every evening I am in a different village. I can get there only on foot, through snow, rain, and black ice. But everything is going quite well.

Affectionately yours,
Eberhard

Greet the Dohnanyis, Johannes, and the children warmly from me.

116

[4.] Velde, *Die vollkommene Ehe.*

[5.] Since 1937 Albrecht Schönherr had been pastor in Brüssow (Altmark) under the patronage of General Field Marshall August von Mackensen.

[6.] Pastor Leopold Beckmann; cf. 1/10, p. 57, where Bonhoeffer had noted Beckmann's telephone number.

[7.] Inge Koch was the head of the Brotherhood of Vicars and Assistant Pastors for the church province of Saxony.

[8.] Pastor Hulda Trebesius was on the staff of the Confessing Church office in Magdeburg.

[9.] Hans-Henning Zippel, staff person of the Council of Brethren in Magdeburg, was at that time a soldier in France.

[10.] Maubeuge was the residence of the French pastor Jean Lasserre, who was a friend of Bonhoeffer's dating to their mutual period of study in New York. On the circumstances here, see Jean Lasserre's letter of February 8, 1941, 1/73.

[11.] Bethge knew Vibrans was a soldier in occupied France but not exactly where.

[12.] Ursula Schleicher.

[13.] [See 1/58, ed. note 9.—MB]

62. To Eberhard Bethge[1]

January 25, 1941

Dear Eberhard,

I have two letters to thank you for! That was very nice of you! I just found them here, when I arrived from Munich with Christel.[2] Now at least this greeting to you shall be on its way today. I started a letter yesterday, but it got pushed aside with Justus's[3] arrival. He had to go back to Berlin today with a stiff neck rather than being able to drive around here as planned. I felt sorry for him. Otherwise his visit was nice. The only thing left is to calculate the additional payment. He wanted you to tell him my exact income. So you will have yet more work to do with this. Sorry! I shall read your essay[4] today and tomorrow. Then you will get it back. I am eager to dig in.

I shall not leave until February 3. Do plan, if at all possible, to be in Berlin in early and mid-March. I can also adjust this somewhat to your schedule. Then the matter of registration[5] will likely be taken care of.

I talked a long time with Justus about Catholicism. He will tell you about it. Nothing new. In March I would like to get a little further with this. If Albrecht Schönherr could postpone his date with you somewhat, I would gladly come over for a day or two, to hear you and to speak with A.[6]

117

I am pleased that you find Santayana interesting. Nothing special, but very clever and authentic. We shall have to talk it over sometime. I have sometimes recognized myself in Oliver. Do you understand that?

Yesterday I went with Justus to the opera, *Creatures of Prometheus,* by Beethoven, performed as a pantomime. I was not too excited about it. The Schiller film[7] that I recently saw, was terrible: pathetic, clichéd, phony, unreal, unhistorical, badly acted, kitsch! Go see it yourself. This is the way I imagined Schiller as a junior in high school.

How nice that you have something for Emmi.[8] Give my parents some of it too. They seem to need it. Many thanks for your heartwarming care!

[1.] *NL,* A 59,2 (26); handwritten letter from Ettal; previously published in *GS* 6:511–12; excerpt previously published in *GS* 2:395.

[2.] Christine von Dohnanyi.

[3.] Friedrich Justus Perels.

[4.] Cf. 1/58, p. 122, and 1/67, p. 134, concerning the Breslau lecture.

[5.] The requirement to register with the police was transferred from Köslin to Munich, and then the requirement for him to report regularly to the police was suspended by the Gestapo through the agency of the Military Intelligence Office. [Cf. *DB-ER,* 700–701.—MB].

[6.] Albrecht Schönherr.

[7.] *Friedrich Schiller,* directed by Herbert Maisch, with Heinrich George and Horst Caspar, was first screened in November 1940.

[8.] Emmi Bonhoeffer.

Tomorrow or the next day I shall be sending you a package with all sorts of things, including some surprises.—Regarding the bell, let's simply view the whole thing as decided! Enough!

How did your mother like the jewelry?—I shall write tomorrow or Monday when I have more leisure. This is just a quick note.

Greet your family and take care!

Always thinking of you and your work,

Your Dietrich

63. From Eberhard Bethge[1]

Kade, January 27, 1941

Dear Dietrich,

Last night you must have thought (and complained) that I had gone crazy. And rightly so. The effects of a week of peaceful village existence? I was completely unable to get to sleep because of it. It may be that we were not especially waiting for the conversation. When it didn't come, Aunt Lene and Mother and I entered into intense conversation about God and sin, which (as always here) demanded a great deal from me. And the phone call came in the middle of this. Aunt Lene had a huge laugh about it and afterward tried to comfort me. So please forgive me for causing you such a shock. You behaved quite appropriately.[2]

I am very pleased to be able to write you for another week. Also, thank you kindly for the letter that was waiting here for me. I spent Saturday in Magdeburg at Zippel's; he is again home on leave and sends you his warm regards. I. Koch[3] was also present and Hulda Trebesius—I heard more details about the factory situation.[4] I. Koch has nothing to do but must sit from 7 a.m. until 7 p.m. in darkness and poor air. She leaves in the morning in the dark, spends the entire day in the Central (Tel.), where the electric lights can never be turned off because of the pall cast by the Leuna haze,[5] and returns home again in the dark at night. They are now urgently requesting me to make myself available for visits, etc.

Are you not allowed to go over to the monastery anymore because of scarlet fever?

118

[1.] *NL*, C 26; handwritten letter.

[2.] Eberhard Bethge could not remember this incident.

[3.] [Ingeborg Koch.—MB]

[4.] A November 6, 1940, decree by the Reich Ministry of Labor established wartime work requirements that were applied above all to theologians and pastors of the Confessing Church.

[5.] The Leuna Works was a large chemical industry complex crucial to the war effort.

I am noticing very clearly here how I have moved into a certain alienation in my attitude toward matters in the extended family.[6] Yet one can only live in ways that can be sustained internally and outwardly.

Please give Johannes my best greetings; I received the news of his telephone calls here. Hopefully he will soon have the pictures ready.[7] I am eager to see them. Have a picture of Bärbel[8] made for me sometime. Let me know in plenty of time when he (Johannes) is coming.

When I was talking at Zippel's yesterday, Christmas came to mind for me quite vividly. The mail is being picked up.

All the best,
Your faithful Eberhard

The car insurance is paying for everything immediately!
Very respectable behavior on their part.

119   **64. To Eberhard Bethge**[1]

January 27, 1941

Dear Eberhard,

Unfortunately, in all the hurry yesterday I still forgot to give special congratulations to your mother, which I had expressly intended to do. But it was nice to talk to you, despite the fact that at times I could scarcely understand you. Nevertheless, we discussed what was most important. You will probably have noticed that at the end, at your personal revelation that was both pleasing and candid, I struggled—unfortunately in vain—for a suitable response.[2] Needless to say, I rejoice greatly at all your personal successes.

Now the clinic will also rejoice greatly if you come home. Emmi[3] weighed only seventy-eight pounds following her typhus, and her convalescence is particularly difficult. But you will surely do everything you can to help there, and I thank you deeply for that.

If I were in Lokies's position I would not allow you to go now for an extended period into that raw climate.[4] It would be simply too much if your

---

[6.] Cf. "Die neue Welt," in Bethge, *In Zitz gab es keine Juden*, 102–8.

[7.] Cf. 1/59, ed. note 13.

[8.] Barbara von Dohnanyi.

[1.] *NL*, A 59,2 (27); handwritten from Ettal; previously published in *GS* 6:512–14. It was previously published in *GS* 2:396 without the salutation and signature.

[2.] See 1/63, ed. note 2.

[3.] Emmi Bonhoeffer.

[4.] Bonhoeffer is referring to East Prussia, where in 1940 he was banned from public speaking, including preaching, and required to register with the police; cf. 1/21.

trachea and larynx were also to be as weakened as mine were that time.[5] I also do not consider Beckmann's[6] approach appropriate. One must eventually learn from experience, and you simply cannot afford to catch cold in this season. Let the others know this also, with my regards.

I am hoping to see you at the beginning of March in Berlin and perhaps also somewhere else? You must plan this! My parents will probably not be at home at that point. If it becomes too difficult at our house, I could possibly move in with you for a few days; then we could also play *The Art of the Fugue* again!

I read Gerhard's[7] letter with joy. Despite the unprepossessing facade he presents in so many ways, he is truly a fine, deep, and intelligent fellow; I like him very much. [...][8]

120

It pleases but hardly surprises me that you can write such intelligent and helpful letters in the midst of human difficulties. I believe that you have particular gifts of this nature from which I myself profit as well. That which you have to say in these sorts of human questions is generally simple and clear; and in complicated matters I am particularly grateful for that. [...][9] Please throw this part of the letter straight into the trash!

65. To Emil Brunner[1]

January 31, 1941

Dear Professor Brunner:

I would like to extend my sincere thanks for your great kindness in helping make possible a short visit to Switzerland for purposes of research. To date the visa has still not arrived, and at the Swiss consulate here I was advised to ask you again to request the police section that deals with aliens to process my application, which has been held up longer than usual there. Since for personal reasons I must be home at the beginning of March, my trip would

---

[5.] The illness metaphors here refer to impending Gestapo measures.

[6.] Pastor Leopold Beckmann; cf. 1/61.

[7.] Gerhard Vibrans.

[8.] Here a few sentences of a particularly intimate nature have been omitted.

[9.] Here another sentence has been omitted for the same reason.

[1.] Staatsarchiv Zürich, Nachlaß Brunner, W 55.5; handwritten from Munich with the heading: "Dietrich Bonhoeffer, presently at Munich 23, Unertlstraße 1, c/o Countess von Kalckreuth." There is no other known corroboration for this instance, according to which Bonhoeffer had earlier approached Professor Emil Brunner with the request for assistance in making his Swiss trip possible and had received a promise from him. Erwin Sutz was the most likely intermediary.

scarcely be worth taking given further delays in this matter. Also, my foreign currency would cease to be valid.

I very much hope to be able to see you and speak with you soon, and I am looking forward to it.

With my thanks once again for all the efforts that you are making on my behalf, and with best regards,

I remain yours very respectfully,
Dietrich Bonhoeffer

121   **66. To Eberhard Bethge**[1]

January 31, 1941

Dear Eberhard,

Once again I am using the occasion of a stay in Munich to write a word to you. By now you will have heard from me via Koch;[2] he claimed not to know you yet, which I didn't believe. But he has probably already invited you for a discussion.

Gürtner's death[3] hit us hard due to the presence of the boy,[4] who behaved extraordinarily bravely. I am very glad that we were still able to be with him when the news came. Hopefully the ice-cold walk didn't worsen his flu.[5] Of course, it is now completely uncertain what will result from the conversations he had undertaken. Perhaps Hans[6] can take the matter in hand? Hopefully I shall still see him here.

My visa has still not arrived; this is a maddening delay. The day before yesterday the constable visited me and notified me that the obligation to register has now been transferred to Munich, after I had just been promised

---

[1.] *NL,* A 59,2 (28); handwritten from Munich; previously published in *GS* 2:396–97.

[2.] Cf. Bonhoeffer's letter of November 26, 1940, 1/32, ed. note 5.

[3.] January 29, 1941, in Berlin.

[4.] [Gürtner's son.—MB]

[5.] [Through Hans von Dohnanyi, Bonhoeffer had persuaded Franz Gürtner, the Minister of Justice, to negotiate with Hanns Kerrl, the Minister of Religious Affairs, about the widespread military conscription of Confessing Church pastors as well as the mandatory wartime duty for civilian pastors; both measures were decimating the Confessing Church. Bonhoeffer wanted the same treatment and exemptions for Confessing Church pastors that other pastors were given. At Ettal toward the end of December 1940, Bonhoeffer had an opportunity to discuss this matter personally with Gürtner on a long walk in extremely cold weather. Gürtner was quite optimistic with Bonhoeffer that something could be done. However, after his untimely death a month later, the hope of dealing with this matter through official government channels waned. Cf. *DB-ER,* 690–91.—MB]

[6.] Hans von Dohnanyi.

by another office that it would be lifted altogether. So today I went there, and they will respond to me on Monday. Apparently their wires got crossed.

I am reading R. Schneider[7] with great pleasure. This is worth owning. I would very much like to give it to you. Please buy it for yourself! I shall not be able to do so now, and we can settle up in Berlin. And anyway, you have already paid for all sorts of things for me. I also do not think the Schneider book will be available long. It is selling very quickly. Last night I was at the Kalckreuths'[8] with several nice people. You would have enjoyed it as well. I talked particularly with Franz Königs's brother-in-law, who has been through a great deal;[9] I also had breakfast with him this morning.

To change the subject completely: sometimes there are weeks in which I read very little of the Bible. Something prevents me from doing so. Then one day I pick it up again, and suddenly everything is so much more powerful, and I can't let go of it at all. I do not have a clear conscience about this; there are also human analogies. But then I wonder whether perhaps even this aspect of being human is and shall be borne by the word of God. Or do you think—actually I think this myself!—that one should force himself? Or is that in fact not always good? We must talk about this sometime.

Farewell! I am hoping to find something from you in Ettal today. Thank you very much for your letter following the telephone call.[10] Truly I was frustrated only at my own lack of quick-wittedness; afterward I thought of all kinds of things I could have said. It was so obvious that you were revealing something so joyful to me, and I was actually afraid that you could have been angry with me. How is the clavichord?

Don't forget Aunt Ruth's birthday![11] Or mine either, please! All the best to you.

With warmest greetings,
Your faithful Dietrich

Quite unexpectedly, six priests have been drafted as of February 3: Simon, Athanas, Augustin, Willibald, Gregor, Albert.[12] This is a cruel blow to the school.

[7.] Reinhold Schneider. Cf. Bonhoeffer's letter of January 19, 1941, 1/58, ed. note 11.

[8.] Cf. Bonhoeffer's letter of November 4, 1940, 1/25, ed. note 8.

[9.] Franz Koenigs, banker and art collector in Amsterdam, married to a daughter of the painter Leopold von Kalckreuth, was temporarily imprisoned in the fall of 1940.

[10.] Cf. 1/63.

[11.] Ruth von Kleist-Retzow shared Bonhoeffer's February 4 birthday.

[12.] Simon Wellnhofer, Athanas Kalff, Augustin Kessler, Willibald Sedlmair, Gregor Rümmelein, Albert Kretzer.

67. From Eberhard Bethge[1]

February 1, 1941

Dear Dietrich,

It certainly does feel odd to me that I should wish you a happy birthday in writing. This is the first time since 1935—no, the first time ever. As a result I am at a complete loss for the right words. But even more there is no opportunity for me to arrange something fitting for you and structure the day suitably. Instead, you arranged something for me when I came home last night. More on that later.

So I offer my hearty congratulations and wish you a good and fruitful use of your powers, success in articulating your new insights,[2] good stimulating friends, and good coffee and tea in your new year. Along with all this I wish for myself frequent opportunities for us to get together. And finally I offer you a summary thanks—perhaps I can do this in writing—for your care and faithfulness, your kind work for me, availability in all personal and professional needs, intellectual and spiritual generosity and partnership, sharing of neckties and shoes, imagination and encouragement.

How shall I summarize? The secure feeling of knowing someone with whom counsel and solutions are to be found in all circumstances. Of course, you will think this is formulated much too broadly.

So how will you spend the fourth? Christel[3] did not yet know anything precise. Unfortunately, I was not able to see her again to give her something to bring along. That is highly unsatisfying. As a foretaste I am enclosing this small musical treatise[4] for you, which is truly interesting, though of course not at all adequate in resolving the problem. On the contrary, it opens new puzzles for me. According to this reasoning it would be understandable why Catholics perform Bach but not Schütz, but this cannot be the case either. The whole thing seems to me to be in need of critical theological assessment. The rest you will have to receive when you get here.

I haven't written to you for a long time. Two letters of yours have come in the meantime and then the package last evening. Say, you rascal: what a fabulous hat! I had not the slightest inkling. With a liner added, it will sit perfectly. You really chose well. And all the extra treats! So now I shall sort through my treasures with reckless abandon. Otherwise I would need a warehouse. And I also thank you very much for your help with my lecture.[5] I shall probably have to go ahead and give it on March 4 in Königsberg. By then I shall work it over quite carefully. It is now certain that I shall go to East Prussia around February 16–March 7. Without homiletic presentations by the

---

[1.] *NL*, C 26; handwritten from Berlin.
[2.] Bethge is referring to Bonhoeffer's work on his *Ethics*.
[3.] Christine von Dohnanyi.
[4.] Moser, *Heinrich Schütz*.
[5.] Cf. 1/62, ed. note 4.

Gossner Mission, the whole thing up there will come to an end; this is the reason I am coming. From February 9 to 12, I shall be with Albrecht.[6] This could not be rescheduled. We could perhaps still travel there ourselves.

Now I have again been interrupted. Koch[7] phoned, and I am to meet Justus.[8] This is how it goes every day. That is why you have heard nothing at all from me. On Wednesday I visited your parents and brought them flowers. Last evening at the Schleichers' we dined on the goose. Thank you again for that.

124

Gürtner's death affected me greatly, as it surely did you there as well. My mother is coming today to celebrate a birthday at the Busses'.[9] She will stay a few days and sleep at my house here. On Monday I shall visit Aunt Ruth briefly.[10] In short, it is almost more than I can manage. Nevertheless, I was at Harnack's on Thursday evening. I bought some more sheet music: lovely trios of Friedemann and Philipp Emanuel,[11] and Schubert's Müllerlieder variations,[12] originally written for flute but very difficult. I am truly happy that you are receiving a clean file.[13] Now surely you will not have any more difficulty with that. Many thanks for the letters you sent along.

So this letter must be off, and I as well. It is too bad that I was disturbed. Affectionately and devotedly yours, with all best wishes,

Your Eberhard

Gollwitzer has become engaged to a daughter of the actor Paul Bildt.[14]

[6.] Albrecht Schönherr.

[7.] Hans Koch.

[8.] Friedrich Justus Perels. This is an example of the conspiracy circle's communication being impeded by surveillance measures.

[9.] Margarete Busse was a sister of Bethge's mother.

[10.] Ruth von Kleist-Retzow.

[11.] Wilhelm Friedemann and Carl Philipp Emanuel were sons of J. S. Bach.

[12.] [*Die Müllerliedervariationen* is a set of variations composed by Franz Schubert. —MB]

[13.] [Bethge seems to be referring to the lifting of the requirement to register with the police. —MB]

[14.] Confessing Church pastor Helmut Gollwitzer had become acquainted with Eva Bildt in August 1940 at the home of the writer Jochen Klepper and soon thereafter became engaged to her. She had been educated at the Burckhardthaus and was the daughter of the actor Paul Bildt, who was a member of the Dahlem Confessing Church congregation. The public announcement of their engagement was quite a risk since she was "non-Aryan." During the final battles in Berlin in April 1945, Eva Bildt took her own life.

68. To Eberhard Bethge[1]

February 1, 1941

Dear Eberhard,

This year I am having to write you a birthday letter as well.[2] Since 1936 I have scarcely been able to imagine a birthday without you. What wonderful days we have had on the various February 4ths, in Finkenwalde, in Schlön-

125   witz, and Sigurdshof! In this respect it has gone undeservedly well for me in recent years. I always had the sustaining circle of colleagues around me that gave this day a certain spiritual character as well. And that the two of us could be connected for five years by work and friendship is, I believe, a rather extraordinary joy for a human life. To have a person who understands one both objectively and personally, and whom one experiences in both respects as a faithful helper and adviser—that is truly a great deal. And you have always been both things for me. You have also patiently withstood the severe tests of such a friendship, particularly with regard to my violent temper (which I too abhor in myself and of which you have fortunately repeatedly and openly reminded me), and have not allowed yourself to be made bitter by it. For this I must be particularly grateful to you. In countless questions you have decisively helped me by your greater clarity and simplicity of thought and judgment, and I know from experience that your prayer for me is a real power. So I wish for myself that in this new year all of this may continue to be so and increasingly more so, that by these things we may both be aided more and more in spirit as well. This is what I wanted to write to you today.

In gratitude and affection,
Your faithful Dietrich

69. From Eberhard Bethge[1]

February 2, 1941

Dear Dietrich,

When I found your letter here waiting for me and read it with joy, I also felt such pain at your expectation: "I am hoping to find something from you in Ettal." For there was nothing there for you. And yesterday as well, the letter I began for you in such leisure

---

[1.] *NL,* A 59,2 (29); handwritten from Ettal; previously published in *GS* 6:514–15; partially reproduced in *GS* 2:397.

[2.] This letter was written on the occasion of Bonhoeffer's own birthday on February 4.

[1.] *NL,* C 26; typewritten from Berlin.

had to be sent off in a rush, so that I forgot to include some things: the *Junge Kirche*[2] that your mother wanted me to send and the musical journal with two interesting small excerpts. Please do not throw them away.

Now I am attempting to see whether yet another letter may still arrive for you, in case the visa affair has still not worked or you still need to be with Hans.[3] It is terrible that your birthday has been so up in the air with these travel plans. So we have not been able to work around them, and the whole thing has come out wrong.

126

My mother is now here with me; she stayed here last night and was very surprised and pleased by my nice lovely apartment. I was quite proud. It truly is beautiful and cozy.

Yesterday I also had to go to the diocesan offices here, regarding a rumor about Martin;[4] Koch had requested this of me. It appears that you have sung my praises rather inordinately!! But that was nice. The rumor appears in fact to be false again. Tomorrow then I hope to see Aunt Ruth.[5] Tonight I shall phone. And next week I shall finally get to see Dieter Zimmermann.[6]

I was somewhat startled by your paragraph about Bible reading.[7] For here in Berlin, and indeed always, I far too often let myself be held back from it by all the "urgent" matters at hand. Normally I am ever more inclined to resist the utterly personal condemnation directed at me by the commandment, when I am sitting in worship and such. But it is still not right that for me the moments of proclamation, Bible study, etc., are the occasions for my greatest subjective joy in the faith. In the process, one is also addressing oneself, so to speak; but so be it!

Do you think the Schneider book[8] would be something for Aunt Ruth? Oh, that reminds me, you wrote once about Oliver[9] and your occasional feelings about him. Before you wrote that, I had been thinking the exact same thing. Particularly in the passages about the school and sports there: always being the best even in those things but without inner participation and satisfaction. Mother and Father, of course, do not concur at all. But otherwise I may understand this somewhat.

With regard to Gürtner, I always keep thinking of that walk we took. We kept looking at each other surreptitiously, with cold cheeks and ears: when will he ever finally turn around? In all that rush it was truly good that you had so insisted on my coming down. I shall also never forget how he sang along in such an unassuming way in our four-part singing.

[2.] [This was the periodical published by the Confessing Church.—MB]

[3.] Hans von Dohnanyi.

[4.] Bethge is referring to the rumor that while in the concentration camp Martin Niemöller had decided to convert to Catholicism.

[5.] Ruth von Kleist-Retzow.

[6.] Wolf-Dieter Zimmermann, former Finkenwalde seminarian, was at that time a Confessing Church pastor in Werder near Berlin.

[7.] [See 1/66.—MB]

[8.] See 1/58, ed. note 11.

[9.] See 1/58, ed. note 10.

127   Tomorrow is Lokies's birthday. I am giving him *Der grobe Brief.*[10] Mother sends her greetings and congratulations and thanks you for your regards.

Will this be the last extended letter?

[Signed] cordially in red (my mother wrote with my fountain pen),
Your Eberhard

Now do be careful with your health and your energy for work when you are there and greet Erwin[11] and other friends.

70. To Joachim Beckmann[1]

February 4, 1941

Dear Brother Beckmann,

Your request for the two sermons reached me only a few days ago. At the moment and in the next weeks I am so completely tied up with military trips that I cannot estimate a definite date when you will receive them. I shall get to work immediately and hope to be done in five weeks. Will that suit you?

Cordially,
Dietrich Bonhoeffer

128   ### 71. To Eberhard Bethge[1]

February 4, 1941

Dear Eberhard,

The day is over, and before I go to sleep I want to spend some time with you in this way, after we have just now had to content ourselves with a few minutes on the telephone. But it was wonderful to be able to exchange at least a word or two with each other. This made my memory of other birthdays especially vivid again and also my awareness that without a morning hymn

---

[10.] Reck-Malleczewen, *Der grobe Brief.*

[11.] Erwin Sutz.

[1.] Archiv der Evangelischen Kirche im Rheinland, Düsseldorf, reference files of Joachim Beckmann, *Kirchenkampf,* A 5; handwritten from Ettal. This letter is the only documentation of this surely already long-standing contact; cf. the sample sermon on Matt. 2: 13-23, written for *Meine Worte werden nicht vergehen,* a book of sermons edited by Joachim Beckmann and Friedrich Linz, pp. 42–46; see *DBW* 15:492–98 (*GS* 4:473–79). The publication envisioned here never ensued.

[1.] *NL,* A 59,2 (30); handwritten from Ettal; previously published in *GS* 2:398–400.

outside my door, as you have arranged for me over the course of years, and without morning and evening devotions together and personal intercession, a day like this is actually without meaning and substance. Everything else, all outward signs of love, need to appear in this light, or they lose their splendor. It is also not entirely easy to produce this backdrop for oneself alone, especially when a person is accustomed to having it otherwise. I miss Finkenwalde, Schlönwitz, Sigurdshof more and more. *Life Together*[2] was in many ways a swan song. Johannes was very dear and nice; quite unexpectedly he showed up to congratulate me with two cakes, a bottle of schnapps, and a gorgeous azalea. My parents wrote me birthday letters, which I was very pleased about, and sent me some nice things with much love. You wrote me a letter of great friendship, for which I especially thank you. When occasionally such things are actually expressed outright, one experiences it gratefully and pleasurably, especially when one can be so certain, as with you, that every word is meant just as it stands. By the way, our letters for today bear a remarkable resemblance to each other in their content. This is surely no coincidence and confirms that what the letters articulate is really so. Among other things, you wish me good stimulating friends. One can well wish such a thing for oneself, and it is a great gift today. And yet the human heart is created in such a way that we seek not the many but the one particular other and rest there. That is the challenge, the limit, and the treasure of authentic human relationship insofar as it touches the realm of individuality and is at the same time grounded fundamentally in faithfulness. There are individual relationships without faithfulness, and there is faithfulness without individual relationship. Each of these can be found in the many. But to find both (and this happens seldom enough!) one seeks the particular other, and blessed is the one "possessing that noble prize."[3]

129

You sent me such a charming book.[4] I have begun to read it with interest. I am indebted to you for H. Schütz and with him for a whole rich world. Gladly I would accompany you on "Eile mich, Gott, zu erretten,"[5] which I have been humming to myself again with the attached sheet music. And I

[2.] *Life Together* (*DBWE* 5) first appeared in 1939 as volume 61 of the series Theologische Existenz heute.

[3.] Bonhoeffer is referring to lines 13–16 of Friedrich von Schiller's poem "An die Freude" ("Ode to Joy"): "He, that noble prize possessing— / He that boasts a friend that's true, / He whom woman's love is blessing, / Let him join the chorus too!" Translation from the Project Gutenberg Titles by Friedrich Schiller: http://www.gutenberg.org/dirs/6/7/9/6795/6795-h/6795-h.htm. See also Bonhoeffer's remarks on friendship in *LPP*, 192–93 (*DBW* 8:290–92).

[4.] See Bethge's February 1, 1941, letter, 1/67, ed. note 4.

[5.] "Eile mich, Gott, zu erretten" (Hasten to save me, O God) comes from Heinrich Schütz, "Kleine Geistliche Konzerte," no. 1; cf. *LPP*, 171 (*DBW* 8:248).

believe it is no coincidence that Schütz came to me through none other than you. In any case, I find a significant connection perceptible there.

How far are you with Oliver?[6] The meaninglessness of his existence consists in the fact that he pours himself out for every conceivable thing without being convinced of the inner meaning of this outpouring, and that in so doing he does not become free for the authentic and utterly unique pouring out of his life. He knows, understands, desires, and is capable of all that is good, beautiful, and true; but everything is devoid of life and therefore irrelevant. In regard to God and human beings, he never risks everything and as a result eventually becomes lonely, even ridiculous. In its asperity it is a haunting book. Whether it is challenging is another question. We will have to talk about it again sometime.

Yesterday was Gürtner's funeral. Meiser preached (the Catholics had refused!). Much consternation here at the monastery. The abbot and Johannes came to the funeral at our request and from their own conviction as well! But please do not pass along this news to outsiders, I mean regarding the refusal. Afterward the abbot also went to Faulhaber, who appears to have aged considerably! (Unfortunately!) I am truly glad that you got a chance to meet Gürtner here.

You are concerned about your occasional silences. Please don't worry! First, you truly do write to me often! Second, you have so much to do that I really do understand! Third, it goes without saying that I rejoice at every little greeting you send.

I still do not have my visa. But now it must be coming soon. Yet this delay allows us to hear from each other one more time. I am looking forward to March 10, etc.

So, I shall need to close for today. It is late at night, and I am tired. Again, many thanks for everything.

Your ever faithful Dietrich

72. From Eberhard Bethge[1]

February 5, 1941

Dear Dietrich,

Well, your birthday was yesterday, and I was able to talk to you very briefly at least. Because of the presence of Hans-Christoph von Hase, it was not entirely according to plan, and there were a few too many people waiting to talk to you on the phone,[2]

[6.] See Bonhoeffer's letter of January 19, 1941, 1/58, ed. note 10.

[1.] *NL*, C 26; typewritten from Berlin.

[2.] [Bethge was at a gathering at the Bonhoeffers'.—MB]

but the actual goal was accomplished. The red wine your father bought was truly a good one. I had brought along a small piece of pound cake for your parents from my mother's birthday; even in the most peaceful times, it would have been considered excellent. Afterward I went on over to Klaus's[3] to talk to him just briefly and, of course, didn't get home until 1 o'clock, but then I found your letter waiting and thus as I went to bed, I was filled with the loveliest and liveliest birthday thoughts of you. It was already too late for other thoughts. But today it is somewhat earlier now and thus the right time for them. Thus I am taking a break... I have very little free time these days, and now I am preparing a sermon for Brüssow on 2 Corinthians 4:6. This evening the young women upstairs[4] invited me, along with a few men I hadn't met   131
before, over for music making; and we sang magnificently in four parts for two hours and then played some Bach arias with flutes. Now you will be envious of me! When you come, we truly must take some time for playing; I have wonderful new trio sonatas by Philipp Emanuel and Friedemann Bach.

Tomorrow I am finally going to see Dieter Zimmermann, who was surely almost angry at me by now, since he had invited me so often.

Gabriel–Halle[5] is in Dachau. The reason??? Rudi Klein[6] must now work twelve hours instead of eight because he is continuing to hold evening youth and Bible events. I saw Fritz[7] only very briefly in Stettin, but he didn't have anything in particular. Robert Zenke[8] had undergone reexamination and was then very unhappy when he came to Fritz's the same evening. He had wished thereby to create a home for himself but now wanted to write immediately to Böters[9] and regard the matter as invalid and revoked. He apparently did this, but no one is to know that it ever happened in the first place, thus perhaps not even you.

[3.] Klaus Bonhoeffer.

[4.] These young women were seminarians at Burckhardthaus, where Bethge had his official residence. [This was during his work for the Gossner Mission.—MB]

[5.] Walther Gabriel was a Confessing Church pastor in Halle. He was imprisoned on January 9, 1941, and was held in Dachau concentration camp from February 7, 1941, until 1943.

[6.] The reference is to Rudolf Kühn, Confessing Church pastor in Potsdam.

[7.] Fritz Onnasch.

[8.] Zenke, a former Finkenwalde seminarian from Pomerania, was a Confessing Church pastor in Berlin. "Reexamination" refers to the controversial act of "legalization"; see 1/151, ed. note 3. [Confessing Church candidates who became "legal" had to retake their ordination examinations before an official consistory committee; most of these committees included German Christian examiners. Bonhoeffer fought bitterly against legalization and urged his former students not to do it, but the temptation was strong due to the wartime circumstances. Most young clergy and seminarians were in the military. The widows and families of legal church clergy killed in action were guaranteed a pension; the families of illegal Confessing Church clergy were not.—MB]

[9.] Ernst Boeters was a consistory lawyer in Stettin.

Now I thank you very, very much for your letter and also for the pictures. To send me a birthday letter too was truly an inspired idea, and I am very grateful to you for it. I have now been wandering around for several days looking for a good Go[10] but can't even find a bad one. They are always "about to come in." So I will just have to prepare your birthday table[11] later on.

I brought Aunt Ruth[12] a half-pound of sugar, plus six carnations, plus a volume of Kierkegaard on "The Expectation of Eternity" (?).[13]

Now I want to go to bed right away. Hans[14] will surely bring more detailed news.

Yours truly,
Your Eberhard

Are you skiing again? With proper insole supports?

132 **73. Jean Lasserre to an Unknown Woman**[1]

February 8, 1941

Dear Madame,

I received your letter with great joy and would like to thank you for it immediately. Thank you for the news that you have passed along to me, which I would only have wished were more detailed! I hope that you and yours continue to be well.

During the invasion, my wife and our little Jean Claude remained in the north near Bruay, at her mother's and sister's. I rejoined them at the end of September after going through the entire campaign; I escaped without any injury. But one of my brothers and a brother-in-law were taken prisoners and are in Germany. In mid-October we were back in our parsonage; by God's grace it was spared. I have resumed my pastoral duties with more joy than ever before.—Our little Christiane was born last December 6, and we are infinitely grateful that we were reunited for that event. Everything is

---

[10.] "Go" is a Japanese board game.

[11.] [It is a German custom to decorate a table for the birthday person with flowers, wrapped gifts, treats, and so on.—MB]

[12.] Ruth von Kleist-Retzow.

[13.] Søren Kierkegaard, "The Expectancy of an Eternal Salvation," in *Eighteen Upbuilding Discourses,* 253–73. Bethge is probably referring to a German anthology of Kierkegaard's writings published at the time, Haecker's *Über die Geduld und die Erwartung des Ewigen.*

[14.] Hans von Dohnanyi.

[1.] *NL,* C 23; handwritten in French; letterhead: "Pasteur Jean Lasserre/9, Rue Henri Sculfort/Maubeuge (Nord)." It cannot be ascertained to whom this letter was addressed, how it came to arrive in the Marienburger Allee home, nor what had been undertaken from Bonhoeffer's side in regard to this contact; cf. on this Bethge's letter of January 23–24, 1941 (see 1/61, ed. note 10). Renate and Eberhard Bethge guess Paula Bonhoeffer to be the recipient. On Jean Lasserre himself, cf. *DB-ER,* 153–54.

going well, and so far we have not been overwhelmed by the difficulties facing us. On the contrary, in great joy we praise God for everything. The future remains uncertain, and we savor each new day given to us, as if it were the last that we have to proclaim freely the good news of salvation.

Please remember me warmly to your friend. I have often thought of him, even yesterday,[2] and am worried about him. Nothing can separate us from the communion of Jesus Christ.

With respectful greetings, I remain, yours truly,
Jean Lasserre

P.S. According to the latest news, now three months old, my friend Jehle[3] was interned in a camp in the free part of France—I know nothing else—nor anything of the others.

74. From Eberhard Bethge[1]   133

February 8, 1941

Dear Dietrich,

Before I travel to Albrecht's[2] tonight, another note that will still reach you. Later in the train I won't be able to write, since I shall then have to be going over my sermon. Many thanks for your letter from the evening of your birthday.[3] It is indeed true: we weren't together, but we put more into words this year.

I just want to jot down a couple of things here: the clavichord has now been registered as being with us on the trip.—With Oliver does Santayana in fact intend a

---

[2.] Lasserre may have been thinking of Bonhoeffer's birthday.

[3.] Herbert Jehle, research assistant in 1938–40 at the Free University of Brussels, had previously come into contact with Lasserre through Bonhoeffer in their common engagement in church peace work. [A Quaker activist and physicist, Jehle became acquainted with the family through Karl-Friedrich Bonhoeffer. Because of his interest in theology, he attended Dietrich Bonhoeffer's 1931 theology lectures in Berlin.—MB] In the course of the German occupation, he was imprisoned by the Gestapo and transferred to the Gurs concentration camp near Pau in southern France [Gurs was primarily for foreign-born Jews—MB]; in 1941 his emigration to the United States was made possible by ecumenical friends and academic colleagues; and by 1942 he was already able to resume his academic work at Harvard University. Jeanne Merle d'Aubigné describes an encounter with Jehle in the Gurs camp in Freudenberg, *Befreie die zum Tode geschleppt werden*, 86–87. See also Jehle's card of August 6, 1941, 1/117.

[1.] *NL*, C 26; typewritten from Berlin; the end was handwritten on the way to Brüssow. The date was written at the top of the page, and underneath it "Saturday" was presumably added later.

[2.] Albrecht Schönherr.

[3.] See Bonhoeffer's letter of February 4, 1941, 1/71.

more encompassing critique of the American situation? He is really such a form of negative modern Simplizissimus![4] I consider the narrative technique of alternation outstanding—recounting an incident directly and then frequently narrating the following incident in the thought and reflection of one of the characters, whereby the whole thing takes on a particular gripping appeal and a certain geniality regarding the things of the world. Various sentences are worthy of being lifted out for quotations. But one does not do that, of course.

Are you acquainted with Rieker?[5] Lokies has asked me to read it for the overview of literature on church renewal[6] and to give him my opinion. So before my train leaves I still have to go there. Much uniquely well observed, but dogmatically weak and intent on forcing doors that are already open.

Tomorrow I am preaching on 2 Corinthians 4:6. But I must say again that in sermon preparation it still feels very difficult for me to concentrate on clear logic, on formulations, and even on the perception of what is. The actual preaching of a clear sermon does give me joy. Then on Monday I have the young women and on Tuesday a Confessing Church gathering there. Wednesday back here and then Saturday to East Prussia.

Have you been skiing again? Or have you kept silent about that in order not to tantalize me too much? When I have my flute here and can pipe away a little every day apart from my duties, that means a great deal, and I look forward to it every morning. This is also a somewhat dangerous tendency with me, in that when I am working I catch myself thinking about how and when I can set aside a period for playing.

Last night I was over at your house and saw Hans.[7] He was somewhat laid low by a cold and such, and it was not possible to get much out of him or communicate much. But there has also been a great deal weighing on him in recent weeks. In contrast, some things in the south[—]Greece, Yugoslavia[8][—]were quite interesting indeed in connection with the events.

Please write me before you leave as to when I can expect you with some certainty here. That is important for me in East Prussia.

I bought the Schneider book[9] and eagerly paged through it a little. Dieter Zimmermann was also utterly enthusiastic.[10]

[4.] [The reference is to the famous German novel of the Baroque period *Simplicissimus Teusch*, by Johann Jakob Christoffel von Grimmelshausen. Bethge is comparing *The Last Puritan* to the title figure of Grimmelshausen's book. In Bonhoeffer's reply to this letter, he refers directly to Bethge's use of the term "Simplizissimus"; see 1/77, p. 149.—MB]

[5.] See Bethge's February 14, 1941, letter, 1/80, ed. note 13.

[6.] ["Church renewal" = *Volksmission*. See 1/17, ed. note 9.—MB]

[7.] Hans von Dohnanyi.

[8.] Bethge added the two country names by hand.

[9.] See 1/58, ed. note 11.

[10.] From this point on the letter is handwritten.

...So now I am sitting in the train to Stettin (second class) and quickly finishing the letter. Visits to Martin[11] these days were reassuring as to health and otherwise; he is said to have smiled at the rumors. His wife was in Münster (her father is extremely ill) and saw the bishop,[12] who with deep respect enjoined him to stay where he is. Now I wish you a good trip, with joy and profit in it.

Do people in Pomerania know anything at all about the rescinding?[13] That would be a good thing. Or only those in Munich? Greet the Dohnanyi children once more and above all Johannes, and thank you again for the lovely birthday arrangements.

Faithfully, your Eberhard

75. To Eberhard Bethge[1]

135

February 8, 1941

Dear Eberhard,

I would like to send all of you at least a note during your stay in Brüssow, in which I had hoped to take part, and at the same time to thank you at once for your last letter. While you are in Brüssow, I wish you much energy and concentration for your work as well as much joy and profit from your time together with Albrecht[2] and his wife.

The musical essays have interested me a great deal. Wouldn't we like to buy a viola da gamba for you after all? I would be much in favor of this. In addition, also practice the Müllerlieder variations;[3] I would very much like to play them with you! I happily read the book on Schütz–Bach[4] and found the individual expositions good and convincing, although some things are still unclear to me. What separates the portrayal of the spiritual content of something like tears (Peter) and a realistic reproduction or translation of the physical into the musical is not at all clear to me; I understand the essential difference but don't know whether it can be carried out so easily in practice.

[11.] Martin Niemöller. His wife apparently passed this information along.

[12.] Count Clemens August von Galen was at that time one of the most courageous figures of the resistance in the Catholic Church; copies of his blunt sermons circulated throughout the country.

[13.] This refers to the earlier requirement of registration with the police; cf. Bonhoeffer's letter of January 25, 1941, 1/62, ed. note 5.

[1.] *NL*, A 59,2 (32); handwritten from Ettal; previously published in *GS* 6:515–16; partially reproduced in *GS* 2:400–401.

[2.] Albrecht Schönherr.

[3.] [Cf. Bethge's letter of February 1, 1941, 1/67, ed. note 12.—MB]

[4.] Cf. Bethge's letter of February 1, 1941, 1/67, ed. note 4.

On Wednesday, N. in M.[5] suddenly became ill and went into the hospital. The diagnosis is still uncertain (might he have brought home a disease from the mission field?), and it is possible he may need specialized treatment.[6] I am extremely sorry about this. But of course everything conceivable is being done. How is Wolfgang doing?[7] What is happening with Gabriel?[8]

It was nice that you visited my parents on my birthday with cake and bananas! That surely gave them great pleasure. My trip is being delayed again for some time due to technical difficulties.[9] The news was initially negative. But it will be attempted again. So we will not be able to meet in Berlin before the middle of March. It has now been more than four weeks since you departed from here! Perhaps we could meet in Friedrichsbrunn the next time you travel to Saxony; I would like that very much. Think about it! For as long as I am employed in Munich, my registration situation is taken care of.

It is thawing again here. Also, I have developed a flourishing sniffle. So there is no skiing for me.

Have you bought Schneider[10] yet? If not, then I shall send it to you. I received an extra one here.

Greet Albrecht and his wife warmly and send along my thanks for his birthday wishes! Take care; I wish you much joy and all the best every day.

Your faithful Dietrich

[5.] Neuhäusler in Munich.

[6.] This is an example of the use of coded language in the letters. Here "hospital" means "prison"; "specialized treatment" means "concentration camp"; "mission field" means "relationships with enemy countries." The imprisonment occurred on February 4. After the occupation of Holland, a report from Munich was found in the Catholic press office in Breda in which Neuhäusler's name was mentioned several times. The list of names about whom he was interrogated in the Wittelsbach Palais (the Munich Gestapo headquarters) is remarkable: the Apostolic Nuncio [at that time, this would have been Archbishop Cesare Orsenigo—MB]; Fr. Johannes from Ettal; the lawyer Dr. Josef Müller in Munich; Abbot Corbinian Hofmeister, Metten; the publisher Bitter from Recklinghausen; Baron Franz von Reitzenstein, a journalist in Rome; Professor Schwarz, Budapest; Archbishop Cisar in Bucharest; General Abbot Noots in Rome; Dr. Michael Höck, editor of the Munich Catholic church newspaper; Dr. Josef Himmelreich, Munich; Prelate Eras, Rome; Ms. Thea Schneidhuber; the Una Sancta movement; Brother Paulus Metzger; Pastor Dietrich Bonhoeffer (cf. Neuhäusler, *Amboß und Hammer,* 154–55). After initial interrogation, Neuhäusler was brought on February 15 to Berlin, on May 24 to the Sachsenhausen concentration camp, and in July 1941, with Martin Niemöller, to the Dachau concentration camp.

[7.] Wolfgang Staemmler.

[8.] See Bethge's letter of February 5, 1941, 1/72, ed. note 5.

[9.] This refers to disagreements with the Military Intelligence official in Switzerland, Hans Bernd Gisevius; see 1/54, ed. note 20.

[10.] See 1/58, ed. note 11, and 1/74.

76. To Georg Eichholz[1]

Ettal, Upper Bavaria, February 9, 1941

Dear Brother Eichholz,

How good that your express letter reached me before my departure. I regret that because of my obligatory and nearly nonstop traveling, my mail repeatedly does not arrive or comes many weeks delayed. Now I am glad to know what is going on. Since in the next few days I shall be leaving for another month away (this is unfortunately not in my control), I would be very grateful to be reassigned to a later date. Would you then please let me know the pericopes and the deadline immediately at the address, Ettal, Upper Bavaria, Hotel Ludwig der Bayer, so that I can plan accordingly. I shall then answer as soon as I have received your letter. Hopefully it will work this time. With my best regards,

Your Dietrich Bonhoeffer

Did you actually ever receive my request to begin treating the Old Testament pericopes as soon as possible?

77. To Eberhard Bethge[1]

February 10, 1941

Dear Eberhard,

Your letter arrived yesterday, the one written before your departure to visit Albrecht.[2] Thank you very much! It is always a fresh joy to find a letter   from you in my mailbox. They also keep me up to date with the news!

Today I am traveling with Christel[3] to Munich for a day. I wish to speak with the consul again before my trip.[4] My official registration has been

---

[1.] Literary estate of Georg Eichholz; handwritten. Cf. *NL*, A 60,2; *GS* 6:481. Following some delay in this correspondence, Eichholz had sent an express letter on February 6, 1941, repeating his request that Bonhoeffer take over "the old church *[altkirchlich]* epistles for the second through fifth Sundays after Trinity" and suggesting to him April 20 as the deadline. "Should this letter not reach you in time, that is, if I have not heard an affirmative response from you by January [actually, February] 15, I shall have to ask you to work on a different set of pericopes" (*NL*, A 60,2).

[1.] *NL*, A, 59,2 (33); handwritten from Ettal; previously published in *GS* 6:517–19; partially reproduced in *GS* 2:401–2.

[2.] Albrecht Schönherr.

[3.] Christine von Dohnanyi.

[4.] Consul Schmidhuber himself went to Switzerland to take care of the problems raised in granting Bonhoeffer's visa; he did this by means of direct contact with the German vice consul in Zurich, Hans Bernd Gisevius.

transferred from Köslin to Munich and there rescinded, so Köslin has nothing more to do with it. Spring arrived here a few days ago. It is absolutely beautiful, but the skiing is over. Johannes keeps saying, "Since Bethge left, nothing more has come of it." He inquires about you constantly and sends his greetings. Now there are the marvelous, clear full-moon nights again that we so rejoiced in a month ago. I am sending along a few things for you with Christel, such as the fur hat that I just recently found. You will perhaps still need it in East Prussia.

Is Rieker the author of the works on the sovereign church government [das landesherrliche Kirchenregiment] in Luther? Holl engages him thoroughly (and negatively, in my view) in his book on Luther.[5] I have not read R.

Gerhard[6] wrote and requested lodging in Friedrichsbrunn[7] for his honeymoon. I am waiting for news about the date before I ask my parents. The heating question is the main difficulty as far as I know. Otherwise I would be happy if it works. I wrote him that. If it should conflict with my parents' stay there, Christel thought that her mother-in-law's apartment could be considered. Otherwise I would gladly give him something substantial as a contribution toward the honeymoon.

I am now working on the question of marriage (the right of free choice of one's spouse, marriage laws according to confessional or racial considerations [Rome, Nuremberg], sterilization, birth control).[8] In all these matters the Catholic moral code is in fact almost unbearably legalistic. I spoke a long time with the abbot and Johannes about this. They believe that the church's position on birth control is the main reason most men do not come to confession anymore. On this point the practice of confession seems to me truly to be extremely dangerous.[9] Without remorse nothing is absolved, of course; but what is the point of remorse whose untruth is demonstrated anew every three days? This engenders hypocrisy. The fact is that there exists no perception of the sinfulness of this action, and thus the whole thing makes no sense. I think that one must allow a great deal of freedom here. What do you actually think about this?

139

[5.] See Holl, "Luther und das landesherrliche Kirchenregiment," 326–80. This is the section discussing Karl Rieker, *Die rechtliche Stellung der evangelischen Kirche Deutschlands in ihrer geschichtlichen Entwicklung*. For an explanation of the person to whom Bethge had actually been referring, Otto Riecker, see his February 14, 1941, letter, 1/80, ed. note 13.

[6.] Gerhard Vibrans.

[7.] Friedrichsbrunn was the Bonhoeffer family vacation home.

[8.] Cf. *DBWE* 6:203–14. "Rome" refers to the regulations of Catholic moral theology, "Nuremberg" refers to the laws announced on September 15, 1935, at the Nuremberg Party Rally "to protect German blood and honor." Among other things, these laws forbade marriages between "Aryan" and "non-Aryan" partners.

[9.] Cf. on this *DBWE* 6:209–10.

I like your reflections on Oliver.[10] Ultrasimplistic? Perhaps. I am not sure yet. It is clearly a real tragedy.—How I wish I could hear you preach Sunday!—Don't let them pile nonstop appointments on you in East Prussia! Turn them down from the start. It is not worth damaging your work for such things. One must be more rigorous and self-directed than I was then and than you tend to be. This is necessary for the sake of your work!

Now take care of yourself, dear Eberhard! Work hard and with joy, and play your flute with a clear conscience! Thinking of you every day,

Your faithful Dietrich

78. From Eberhard Bethge[1]

Brüssow, February 11, 1941

Dear Dietrich,

So you can still receive letters. That is, of course, very nice. Nonetheless, I feel truly sorry for you with all the back-and-forth and uncertainty. I would only hope that this is not disturbing you too much in your work, but rather that these days can prove useful for it. Thank you very much for your letter here. Its news, of course, was not all good. In Gabriel's[2] case it most likely had to do with things he said in a sermon; I don't know yet what. He is, of course, not the most prudent.

Now I'm having a few lovely days here with Albrecht[3] and his family. I marvel at these three healthy, flawless children. In every way apparently healthy. Sermon went very well. Tonight another gathering. We also made music until my cheeks hurt. I asked Albrecht to come to Breslau with me in May (Exaudi week) for the renewal movement event,[4] which he is happy to do. When you come up to visit us, we want to go to the discussion of the work. We have planned it that way. They are already looking forward to it. You will also need to visit Aunt Ruth[5] sometime as well. When [I] went to see her again on Saturday, she was once again sick in bed with the flu (it began right on her birthday); she was enormously pleased about your letter and said to tell you that she cannot answer as long as she is in bed. Fritz and Margret[6] are doing well; they are expecting again in August! They also now have a telephone at last. Note the apocalyptic number: 3 666 2.[7]

140

[10.] See Bethge's letter of February 8, 1941, 1/74.

[1.] *NL,* C, 26; handwritten.
[2.] See Bethge's letter of February 5, 1941, 1/72, ed. note 5.
[3.] Albrecht Schönherr.
[4.] ["Renewal movement" = *Volksmission.* See 1/17, ed. note 9.—MB]
[5.] Ruth von Kleist-Retzow.
[6.] Fritz and Margret Onnasch.
[7.] See Rev. 13:18.

There is nothing new to report about Wolfgang.[8] In any case, I don't know anything new. Justus[9] recently slipped on the street and dislocated his shoulder. So he is presently somewhat hampered in his movements. Hopefully your sniffles will not develop into anything; the flu is everywhere these days.

I already bought the Schneider book![10] For me there is to be no thought of a favor—but for you there is! The Müllerlieder variations[11] are, I believe, among the most difficult things available in flute literature. But perhaps a few variations can be played? I also now have original Beethoven flute variations.

So now I must still prepare a bit for tonight. All of us send you our warmest greetings and wish you good progress in your work.

Your Eberhard

If you could, please ask Bärbel[12] to have another print of the music picture from Christmas[13] made. My mother, who by the way is still in Berlin, would very much like to have it!

141   Best wishes and many thanks for your greetings. These have been marvelous days with Eberhard here. Last night he spoke magnificently. We've been making inordinate amounts of music. Now we are looking forward to your visit. But not just for two hours!

Yours truly,
your Albrecht

Best regards from Hilde.[14]

79. From Karl Bonhoeffer[1]

Dear Dietrich,

Now that we have gradually overcome our flu, we are again thinking of traveling and wanted to ask you whether you know of a quiet place to stay in Oberammergau—a well-heated (i.e., with central heat) hotel or private residence with comfortable nearby

---

[8.] Wolfgang Staemmler.
[9.] Friedrich Justus Perels.
[10.] See 1/74.
[11.] [See 1/75, ed. note 3.—MB]
[12.] Barbara von Dohnanyi.
[13.] In Ettal; see Bethge, Bethge, and Gremmels, *Life in Pictures,* 186.
[14.] Hilde Schönherr, née Enterlein. Along with her husband, she had been part of Bonhoeffer's circle of students in Berlin.

[1.] *NL,* A 82,15; handwritten; postmarked "Berlin, February 13, 1941." Stamped: "via express mail."

options for eating—or whether you could find this out with the help of your friends there. Otherwise, even in Ettal, perhaps at the consulate or in the Benedictine monastery. Mama is leaning toward Oberammergau, where, since we don't walk much anymore, we would have coffee and even a movie theater if the occasion arises and yet would still be within reach of Ettal.

We were thinking of coming at the end of February. Will you still be in the country? Early this morning I received a phone call from a Swiss colleague who is presently here as a member of the exchange commission for the severely wounded; as is customary with the Swiss, he is a colonel. I commended you to him; in Zurich he is a highly regarded person and is perhaps useful, and thoroughly reliable. Dr. Brunner, proprietor of the Küsnacht sanatorium near Zurich.[2] In any case, he will prove to be friendly.

A number of army postal cards have been returned as undeliverable: Staude, Pfisterer, two from Emmerich.

Christel[3] brought such lovely things back for us from you: cards, candy, and the wonderful schnapps. Many thanks. I am writing an express letter. It will presumably not roust you out of bed at night but will perhaps nevertheless reach you somewhat more quickly. Since people are fleeing from the north to the south in dramatically increasing numbers,[4] it might be good to make the arrangements quickly.—The family news is by and large good; that is, the flu is presently not too severe at Suse's.[5] Emmi[6] is at home and is soon to leave for her convalescence.

142

Write us as quickly as you can as to whether and when you think you will have something for us.

Love from Mama and the rest of the household and neighbors,[7]

Your Father

February 13, 1941

80. From Eberhard Bethge[1]

February 14, 1941

Dear Dietrich,

Many thanks to you for your letter this morning. It was a great joy to me. Also for the enclosures. I am quite pleased and cheered by the letter from Heinz Fleischhack.[2] In

---

[2.] There is no record of a personal contact between Bonhoeffer and Dr. Theodor Brunner.

[3.] Christine von Dohnanyi.

[4.] This was because of the increasing Allied air attacks.

[5.] Susanne Dreß.

[6.] Emmi Bonhoeffer.

[7.] The Schleicher family lived next door.

[1.] *NL*, C 26; typed from Berlin.

[2.] Heinz Fleischhack was at that time a Confessing Church pastor in Eisleben.

Jena he seemed to me to be worn down by the cross fire of opinion among his circle of colleagues there and almost too severely burdened by this tension. Gerhard's[3] letter is nice but typical. Your parents are now going to Oberammergau. I just spoke with your mother and recommended this. Johannes or someone there will know of good lodgings. Tomorrow night I shall be going over to their house and will also hear from Christel[4] then.

Today at last I can present you "in spirit" with your real birthday present. I have finally found something that brings me pleasure to give you, and for the time being I am putting it in your cupboard upstairs: five nice sterling silver cordial cups—quite unpretentious. I hope they will appeal to you. They are unbreakable; and I received them without even having to trade in any silver,[5] which generally seems to cause great difficulties everywhere around here.

Your mother told me that the clavichord has also come in. I am to unpack it tomorrow. Now I am excited again! I thank you also for the flute blessing you gave me to free my conscience. Thus I am looking at a few of the Müllerlieder variations[6] more closely.

143   I am sending on some mail to you. Don't be surprised at the one from Aunt Ruth.[7] On both visits we had discussed the ever-popular topic of marriage; that is the explanation. But you will surely discern in the letter some of her frailty. Spring cannot come too quickly for her. But that will still be a while up here despite the beautiful weather we are presently having. I am now leaving early Monday.[8] I don't know the address yet. Koschorke's is M. Koschorke, Königsberg, Junkerstraße 53. You can always reach me there. I will be in Königsberg for two days for meetings primarily with Quittschau, and then I shall apparently be in the south. I don't know anything more detailed than that. I am enormously pleased that you are progressing from theme to theme, according to your letters. And it will surely be of great importance that you are not conducting the discussion with Catholicism alone in the ivory tower.[9] Regarding suicide,[10] I wanted to mention before—but forgot—that it is not condemned in and of itself in the Bible, but nevertheless is definitely the death of the godless

---

[3.] Gerhard Vibrans. See 1/77.

[4.] Christine von Dohnanyi.

[5.] [Because of the war, Bethge normally would have needed to exchange a measure of silver equivalent to the silver in these cordial cups.—MB]

[6.] [See 1/67, ed. note 12.—MB]

[7.] Ruth von Kleist-Retzow.

[8.] This refers to his renewal movement [*Volksmission*] trip to East Prussia. [See 1/17, ed. note 9.—MB]

[9.] [The German expression here is *vom grünen Tisch*. The point is that Bonhoeffer's discussion of the Catholic approach to ethical issues is based on his conversations with Catholics in Ettal and not just on theoretical reflection conducted in the privacy of his study.—MB]

[10.] Cf. *DBWE* 6:196–203.

(Saul). It would actually be good to speak to people about marriage.[11] This would surely be possible with Albrecht[12] and others.

To my knowledge, Rieker[13] is the author of a larger work on pietism and revival movements (also in the Anglo-Saxon countries), probably in Heidelberg. Also one must actually read Scherzl[14] *(Compelle intrare)*. This is praxis, utterly Catholic, and truly possible in this way only by means of celibacy, but nevertheless having much to teach.

Did I write you already that Margret[15] is expecting another child in August? Today Fritz[16] called my mother to ask a favor; the doctor has prescribed a full week of bed rest for Margret because of an irregularity. They have gone back to the same doctor!?

This evening I had Justus[17] over for supper. Tomorrow I shall be at Willi's[18] to "agitate" for O.[19] The day after tomorrow with Oskar Hammelsbeck. Now keep on being so wonderfully productive and receive my warmest greetings (also the children and above all Fr. Johannes).

Faithfully, your Eberhard

144

81. To Eberhard Bethge[1]

February 14, 1941

Dear Eberhard,

Now I am wishing you a good beginning and a good end to your stay up there. I shall particularly think of you in these days. You, too, will need—and will need to adhere to—a firm morning prayer time in such an unsettled

[11.] Cf. *DBWE* 6:203–12.

[12.] Albrecht Schönherr.

[13.] Apparently Eberhard Bethge had not meant the canon lawyer Karl Rieker but rather the Heidelberg pastor Dr. Otto Riecker. His dissertation, *Das evangelische Wort: Pneumatologie und Psychologie der evangelistischen Bewegung* (1935), was followed by the writings *Die Wiedererweckung der Kirche* (1937) and *Ruf zur Seelsorge* (1939).

[14.] See Bonhoeffer's letter of November 29, 1940, 1/37, ed. note 8.

[15.] Margret Onnasch.

[16.] Fritz Onnasch.

[17.] Friedrich Justus Perels.

[18.] Willi Rott.

[19.] According to Annie Rott, this refers to an initial contact on the part of the Provisional Church Administration of the German Evangelical Church with Colonel Oster in the Foreign Office/Military Intelligence, regarding emigration assistance for the "non-Aryan" colleague Charlotte Friedenthal (communication of January 1, 1988). See Wilhelm Rott's letter of October 1941 to Alphons Koechlin, 1/134.

[1.] *NL*, A 59,2 (33); handwritten from Ettal; previously published in *GS* 6:519–20; partially reproduced in *GS* 2:402–3.

life. This clarifies what one is to do and say throughout the day, and one becomes "self-directed" in daily decisions. That is what I especially wish for you during this week.

Many thanks for your letter from Brüssow.[2] How lovely it must have been! I like the idea of going back there with you. And then on to Stettin. I rejoice at Margret's good news.[3]

This time of waiting here is not wasted. In recent days I have been able to write very well again. But, of course, I would much prefer to have the trip behind me. Today Schmidhuber is going there and attempting to rectify the situation personally. Then I shall receive the news by telegram. I only hope that you are free awhile after this. But I can easily arrange myself around your schedule. But you must at least be in Berlin for a time. I am especially looking forward to music with you. How wonderful that you [have] learned to play the flute. That is a great enrichment of our relationship. I think that you will be the one who also learns the viola da gamba! I am too old for that; it would hardly be worth it anymore!

145   By the way, you are reimbursing yourself for restaurant meals there, aren't you? Otherwise it will be too much. Take care also that so many extra leaflets are not printed this time.[4]

Have you read the recent issue of *Verkündigung und Forschung?* It is quite interesting. Asmussen is taken to task rather severely, which is quite appropriate. You will surely also join the Society for Protestant Theology?[5] At least, if you think much of yourself! I have not yet done so but shall need to as well. If we don't do such things, who will? Then one receives the journal delivered free. The newly published poems by Adolf Schlatter on John the Baptist, among other things,[6] are something quite remarkable. I have been reading them with great joy.

[2.] See Bethge's letter of February 11, 1941, 1/78.

[3.] Margret Onnasch.

[4.] There were thirty invitations mailed out for the retreat in Blöstau, which was attended by only three students on July 13–14, 1940, during Bonhoeffer's trip through East Prussia; these invitations helped bring about the ban on speaking (cf. 1/15; 1/21; 1/107).

[5.] In 1940 the Gesellschaft für evangelische Theologie (Society for Protestant Theology) was founded at the initiative of Ernst Wolf in Berlin (board: Joachim Beckmann, Martin Fischer, Hans von Soden, and Ernst Wolf). To replace *Evangelische Theologie*, which was banned in 1938, their mouthpiece was the journal *Verkündigung und Forschung: Theologischer Jahresbericht*, edited by Günter Dehn, Gerhard von Rad, Heinrich Schlier, Edmund Schlink, and Ernst Wolf. Volume 1/2 (1940) included Edmund Schlink's review of Hans Asmussen's *Die Kirche und das Amt* and Otto Michel's review of Asmussen's *Die Bergpredigt*. Regarding subsequent events, see 1/147–49.

[6.] Adolf Schlatter, *Johannes der Täufer.*

Today we are enjoying beautiful weather. Frost, sun, but no snow. Perhaps I shall go out for a bit. I miss having a partner! You see, you simply must come back. Johannes and Müller check in almost daily, "What is that Bättge up to?" They always want me to greet you from them; it seems as if they think something of you—strange!

Now take care of yourself, greet all our acquaintances, Koschorke, Jänicke,[7] Kramp, Link, Beckmann, etc.

God preserve you. With my greetings,

Your faithful Dietrich

146

82. From Georg Eichholz[1]

Wuppertal-Barmen, February 14, 1941

Dear Brother Bonhoeffer,

Thank you for your letter. In accordance with your suggestion may I request that you work on the Old Church epistle pericopes for the sixteenth, seventeenth, eighteenth, and nineteenth Sundays after Trinity[2] and have the manuscript in my hands by June 1, 1941, at the latest? I very much hope that this arrangement will make it possible for you to contribute.

I have received and weighed your idea regarding the Old Testament pericopes[3]— but at this time such a task seems too difficult to me. If we had the paper,[4] such a volume could appear simultaneously in installments distributed over long intervals; but unfortunately that will not work either. I would be in your debt, however, if you were to let me know whom you would be thinking of as contributors to such a project.

With my best regards and the request of a prompt reply,

Your [G. Eichholz]

83. To Eberhard Bethge[1]

Dear Eberhard,

[7.] Johannes Jänicke was a pastor in the East Prussian Confessing Church in Palmnicken.

[1.] Literary estate of Georg Eichholz; carbon copy. Cf. *NL*, A 60,2. Previously published in *GS* 6:482; partially reproduced in *GS* 2:403–4. Regarding the circumstances, see Bonhoeffer's letter of February 9, 1941, 1/76.

[2.] Eph. 3:13-21; Eph. 4:1-4; 1 Cor. 1:4-9; Eph. 4:22-32.

[3.] See 1/7 and 1/20.

[4.] In 1941 the paper ration for church presses and theological writings was virtually eliminated.

[1.] *NL*, 59,2 (35); handwritten card from Ettal; its date, "February 15, 1941," was apparently added later in Eberhard Bethge's hand; previously published in *GS* 6:521–22.

It was a happy surprise to reach you at my parents' today! I was under the impression that you were leaving tomorrow; otherwise I would have written you again. So I shall attempt to reach you with an express letter. You will then also find something at Manfred's.[2]

147 Do you know whether my taxes have been taken care of for February? Might I ask you to clear this up before your departure if at all possible? Also, I would naturally love to know (partly in regard to the viola da gamba!) soon what I shall still receive as a further payment for my library. But I don't want to bother you with this now. There is time when you return.— Did I interrupt Mama this evening right in the middle of her work?[3] I am sorry about that. My primary work period is now actually in the afternoon. There I find plenty of leisure and very little disturbance.

Otherwise, I've been making quite good progress during the past few days. I have now finished dealing with the difficult questions of sterilization, birth control, etc.[4] I will now address the natural right to work, freedom, and thought. Sometimes I am startled and fear that, apart from the spirit, the σάρξ[5] is energetically engaged in this work.

Now take care of yourself. Don't worry about the clavichord. If it doesn't affect the tone, that is not so terrible. Should a bomb fall on it, it is gone anyway; and if no bomb falls, then we can still repair it later. Might Neupert perhaps do something through his Berlin firm? All the best for your trip! May God remain with you.

Your faithful Dietrich

This saying[6] actually surprises me! Even apart from all dogmatics, on a purely practical level, it never proceeds this way around but rather always just the opposite. If the heart of God is not opened to me in God's word, then I simply cannot lift my heart to God! Or do you experience it the other way around?

[2.] Manfred Koschorke.

[3.] Her "work" was listening to the news broadcasts transmitted in German by the BBC (British Broadcasting Corporation); these broadcasts reached many people even though severe action was taken against such listeners when others informed on them.

[4.] Cf. *DBWE* 6:203–14.

[5.] "Flesh."

[6.] On the back of the card was a saying by Angelus Silesius: "Human one, give God your heart; God will give you the divine heart in return. Oh, what a precious trade: you climb up; God comes down."

84. From Ruth von Kleist-Retzow[1]

148

Stettin, February 15, 1941

My dear Dietrich,

I admit I am still writing from a horizontal position—and so please excuse my handwriting; nevertheless, when I found out from Eberhard today that you are still in the country, I wanted to convey to you the thanks that I have carried in my heart since the fourth.[2] In these days of my illness your words have accompanied me often and filled me with thanksgiving. How God has blessed you! And me, that I have won your friendship! The foundation on which it rests is the only unchanging one on earth. That you do not begrudge this old person room in your young life is a great gift for me. Indeed, in the church age and youth are melted together. But God does not always grant such a gift. Yet that is the dearest and loveliest experience of my life, that what is arid did not remain so, but that something new always came along and brought with it precisely that which was needed: "You satisfy all the needs of life."[3]

I fully share your good wishes for our new year of life. If only one could do something to allow you to find a position where you could work effectively. Sometimes one would like to peer over the shoulder of almighty God; why does God allow gifts to lie fallow that would be so essential for the building of the divine reign? Does God want to show that God does not need us? Yet we go on thinking that we have to prop up the Almighty....

I almost envy you your imminent plans. What a reunion it will bring![4] Reimer[5] is severely criticizing the Schäble book[6] that brings me such joy. In his basic idea he may well be right, but he is always throwing out the baby with the bathwater. To be sure, I am convinced that in theology there can be growing insight, from one step to the next—thus by no means merely one step for building the reign of God among human beings. When I think of Venzke and Braun,[7] Schäble is a hundred times too great for them, let alone Calvin, Luther, Karl Barth, whom they could not wrap their minds around at all. Thus there must be stages in which people, even theologians, move forward. It is

149

[1.] Literary estate of Ruth von Kleist-Retzow; handwritten; published in Ruth von Wedemeyer's *In des Teufels Gasthaus,* 165ff.

[2.] This refers to their shared birthday on February 4.

[3.] This is the beginning of the twelfth stanza of Paul Gerhardt's hymn "Ich singe dir mit Herz und Mund" (*Evangelisches Gesangbuch für Brandenburg und Pommern,* 249; *Evangelisches Kirchengesangbuch,* 230).

[4.] Mrs. von Kleist-Retzow was presumably thinking of the fact that during his stay in Switzerland Bonhoeffer would be reunited with Karl Barth, whom she greatly esteemed.

[5.] Karl-Heinrich Reimer, pastor in nearby Naseband, Belgard church district.

[6.] Walter Schäble, *Evangelium im Durchbruch.*

[7.] The Confessing Church pastor Herbert Venske in Muttrin and the German Christian pastor Werner Braun in Gross-Tychow were two neighboring pastors.

probably not even so important which corner they stand on; the only thing that matters is that they not sit down to relax.

These days I have been reading *In der Finsternis wohnen die Adler*.[8] I followed along through two-thirds of the book with the greatest excitement and agreement. But then I countered it with a passionate No. It is a false theology of earned grace, justification from one's own capacity, self-deception. . . . Eberhard wrote me that you both approved of the book, but I think it was not very clear in his memory. Around fifteen years ago I got mixed up with so-called spiritualists; today I think of this with shame. Not that I would deny that world of souls and spirits; in fact I believe in its reality. But I believe that it is in reality forbidden to us. God wishes to protect us from it. God may use it, or permit it, now and then to frighten people. . . . But it has nothing to do with the divine plan of salvation. I do not doubt that these enormous effects in Scandinavia are historical. Is that proof that they are pleasing to God? The people lie there on the ground convulsing and screaming and work wonders. The Egyptian priests did that too. But we were not the ones who died for our salvation; Jesus did that alone. While I was reading the book, this rang constantly in my head: "*He* has done enough for us all" . . .[9]

But perhaps you do not perceive this the way I do and think that my judgment is wrong? We would probably have to talk about it in person. When shall we see each other again? Things are looking up with me again, because God wills it so. When I have a fever, I am always in an unspiritual mood and suffer with this. Only when it is over can I be thankful again. Eberhard writes that your book[10] is coming along well. A lovely thought. I am accompanying it in spirit.

Your mother also sent a birthday note. With such nice, embarrassing words. Should a person defend oneself against such overestimation? Yet one may still be grateful.

150   While Spes[11] was here to care for me, we spoke often of the lovely years of our "grandchildren hostel," and then she said repeatedly, "How nice that we went to Finkenwalde for worship! And the confirmation sessions!"[12] Truly, what a happy, innocent time that was!

[8.] Markusson, *In der Finsternis wohnen die Adler.* The book was also among Bonhoeffer's possessions; cf. *Love Letters from Cell 92*, 44.

[9.] "*Er* hat genug für uns all getan" is a paraphrase of a line from the first stanza of the hymn "Es ist das Heil uns kommen her" (*Evangelisches Kirchengesangbuch*, 242). In English the line reads: "Faith looks to Jesus Christ alone, who did for all the world atone" (*Lutheran Book of Worship*, 297, st. 1).

[10.] She is referring to his *Ethics*.

[11.] Spes was the daughter of Herbert von Bismarck in Lasbeck; Bonhoeffer had confirmed her. See *DB-ER*, 439–40.

[12.] Ruth von Kleist-Retzow had kept an apartment in Stettin to make it possible for her grandchildren to attend the high school [*Gymnasium*] there. She and her grandchildren attended worship services at the preachers' seminary in Finkenwalde that Bonhoeffer led from 1935 to 1937. In 1938, Bonhoeffer gave three of the grandchildren confirmation instruction. See *DB-ER*, 439.

Please greet the Dohnanyi children. I shall thank them myself soon. Yesterday I read all the Luther hymns one after another, and it made me so happy. What an effort! And now take care of yourself and may God's angels guide you on your trip.

As ever, yours,
Aunt R.

85. To Eberhard Bethge[1]

February 17, 1941

Dear Eberhard,

I am utterly at a loss for words in response to the birthday present that just arrived today! It is truly beyond all bounds, completely impermissible, and nevertheless a tremendous joy. The cordial cups are still sitting here on my desk, and I keep glancing at them in disbelief. Clearly you have spent months searching and eventually turned your whole wallet inside out to give this joy to me. It is incredible that you even came upon such cups. Now they are awaiting a worthy inauguration and the chance to use them with you! They are precious vessels intended for precious contents; I shall take good care of them and use them eagerly and often, and they will surely last well beyond my lifetime. How wonderful to have received them from you of all people! I shall drink the first glass to the constancy of our friendship. And so, my warmest thanks to you for this great gift!

On this day of your arrival in East Prussia I am especially thinking of you and your work. May it all go well! Wurm[2] wrote today, responding in a detailed and very personable way to my recent letter. I shall send you the letter as soon as I have showed it to Johannes.

What decisions will the next weeks bring? Take care of yourself! Many thanks again for everything, dear Eberhard!

As always, affectionately,
Your faithful Dietrich

Shall I send the birthday letters from our colleagues?

[1.] *NL*, A 59,2 (36); handwritten from Ettal; previously published in *GS* 6:522–23; partially reproduced in *GS* 2:404.

[2.] This contact with Theophil Wurm, bishop of the regional church in Württemberg, cannot be further illumined because there is no other direct or indirect evidence. Cf. Bonhoeffer's letter of February 19, 1941, 1/88, ed. note 5. Even the form of its transmission (probably through trusted intermediaries) is puzzling. Since as of February 9, 1941, Bishop Wurm was extremely ill with a lung infection, his letter must be attributed to an earlier date.

86. To Georg Eichholz[1]

February 17, 1941

Dear Brother Eichholz,

Many thanks for your letter. I am in agreement with your proposal and look forward to working on these texts, which are by no means simple ones.

While I also agree with you that work on the Old Testament pericopes would raise great difficulties,[2] I myself would infer from this that we must then take on this task since we expect it from every pastor Sunday after Sunday, or we must come to the practical realization that these texts will simply not be preached anymore. In my opinion, more help is needed here than anywhere else. If you need participants, I could probably give you a whole string of younger pastors who have not yet been called upon and who would not complete the task any worse than those who are called upon over and over again. Thus I very much hope that you will take this matter in hand.

With warm regards,
Your Dietrich Bonhoeffer

152   87. To George Eichholz[1]

Dear Brother Eichholz,

Unfortunately, I forgot yesterday to recommend Pastor Albrecht Schönherr, Brüssow, north of Prenzlau, Mark Brandenberg, to you (in case you need such a recommendation) to take my place for the meditations. I know from him that he would gladly do it, and I consider him suitable. He has worked on "Lutheran confessional doctrine and practice."[2] He is a young man, legally ordained just in time;[3] and his patron is the old Mackensen.[4] I have known him for many years, and it would please me to be replaced by him.

With my regards,
Your Dietrich Bonhoeffer

[1.] Literary estate of Georg Eicholz; handwritten from Ettal. Cf. *NL*, A 60,2; previously published in *GS* 6:482–83.

[2.] [Some German Christians wanted to eliminate all usage of the Old Testament because of its Jewish connection.—MB]

[1.] Literary estate of Georg Eichholz; handwritten from Ettal, February 18, 1941. Cf. *NL*, A 60,2; previously published in *GS* 6:483.

[2.] Albrecht Schönherr, *Lutherische Privatbeichte.*

[3.] [After the October 1934 Dahlem synod, the official church no longer recognized as legal any theology student who took ordination exams from a Confessing Church board

88. To Eberhard Bethge[1]

February 19, 1941

Dear Eberhard,

Now it appears that matters have progressed to the point that I can travel, presumably leaving from Munich on the twenty-third or twenty-fourth, for exactly four weeks. On the twenty-first I shall go to Munich and stay as usual at the Europäischer Hof. But at the moment you will have nothing urgent to convey to me, and I shall be bringing your good wishes and thoughts with me in any case. Then, on the way back I am thinking of coming through here and perhaps bringing my parents home to Berlin. I hope that you will pick us up in the Mercedes. I would be eager then to go with you to Friedrichsbrunn over Easter. Can you not arrange to have some sermon around Easter so that you could be in Friedrichsbrunn for a day or two? For by then there will be a great deal to tell and discuss. I am simply afraid, in Berlin there is again much unrest, and a few days there would suffice. I shall greet Erwin[2] and if possible also Lang[3] warmly from you.

Yesterday Mama disclosed to me that Aunt Hanna Goltz[4] has inoperable liver cancer and that the doctor gives her only four to six weeks. This will be very hard for Mama. It certainly makes one thoughtful. What would I do if I knew that in four to six weeks it would all be over? That is running through my head. I believe that I would try to teach theology again as before and to preach often.

Wurm also sent me his lecture with the request for my comments.[5] That is something else I must still do before the trip.—Although I am presently

153

(Barnett, *For the Soul of the People*, 66); this problem became particularly acute after the 1937 Himmler decree declared Confessing Church seminaries and examination boards illegal (ibid., 94–98).—MB]

[4.] See Bethge's letter of January 23–24, 1941, 1/61, ed. note 5.

[1.] *NL*, A 59,2 (37); handwritten from Ettal; previously published in *GS* 6:523–24; partially reproduced in *GS* 2:404–5.

[2.] Erwin Sutz.

[3.] Pastor Kurt Lang in Montreux stayed with Bethge in 1936 during the Chamby conference.

[4.] Countess Hanna von der Goltz, Paula Bonhoeffer's sister.

[5.] On this matter as well, there are no reliable points of reference; cf. 1/85, ed. note 2. Of the lectures that Bishop Wurm held between fall 1940 and the early part of 1941, only two manuscripts are found in his papers; one of these may be the one mentioned here. It is a congregational presentation for the Reformation Day on the "The Nonnegotiable Concern of the Reformation" (Landeskirchliches Archiv Stuttgart, Nachlaß Wurm D 1, vol. 3/2), held first in Stuttgart and Nuremberg and finally also on January 11, 1941, at St. Mark's Church in Munich. Bonhoeffer could have heard about this and reacted to it

being completely interrupted in my work, I nevertheless hope to return having gained considerable profit in that regard as well.

Now take care of yourself, dear Eberhard! I will try to write at least once more. I will think of you and your work every day.

With my best wishes,
Your faithful Dietrich

Now it will be the end of March before we see each other again, ten weeks! This often seems so absurd to me. The Müllerlieder variations[6] will simply go all the better!—My parents are set to arrive on March 3 at the Benedictine monastery. I shall perhaps then come back here to pick them up.—The cordial cups truly give me great pleasure!

Greetings to all! All the best,

D.

154   **89. To Eberhard Bethge**[1]

February 22, 1941

Dear Eberhard,

Today I made the necessary arrangements here. I leave the day after tomorrow. I shall then scarcely be able to write to you. All the letters home will include you also, and even those will be only the most urgent signs of life. So don't be surprised. Telling about it afterward will be all the more wonderful. I actually wanted to ask you to open my mail and take care of it. Now I shall request that it be held until you come back to Berlin. I shall forward it to Marienburger Allee.[2]—Many thanks for your letter from my room. It always gives me joy when you are there. It is wonderful that you were at the Schleichers' for music making! ... [3]

How nice that you had a conversation with my parents about the topic in question.[4] I do not think that anything moral can be said at all against suicide; it is a sin of unbelief; that is not, however, a moral disqualification.[5]

---

with a letter. It is possible that Wurm's distinctively differentiated depiction of the interconfessional situation interested him and also prompted him to pass it on to Fr. Johannes. Based on the dates involved, this chain of events is at least conceivable.

[6.] [See 1/75, ed. note 3.—MB]

[1.] *NL*, A 59,2 (38); handwritten from Ettal; previously published in *GS* 6:524–25; partially reproduced in *GS* 2:405–6.

[2.] [Bonhoeffer's parents lived at Marienburger Allee 43.—MB]

[3.] Here a few sentences of a particular intimate nature have been omitted.

[4.] See Bethge's letter of February 14, 1941, 1/80.

[5.] Cf. *DBWE* 6:198–99.

I don't think I wrote to you that at Gürtner's funeral the Regensburg "Domspatzen,"[6] which he himself belonged to, sang first "Ach Herr, lass Dein lieb Engelein...in Abraham's Schoß tragen" and then "O Haupt voll Blut,"[7] where the line "Yet, though despised and gory, I joy to call thee mine" came out quite movingly;[8] and at the end an unfamiliar sentence from Job 19. The family had chosen the hymns. This was the best part of the whole event. Of course, funerals always particularly exhaust me. The question of what has lasting existence in the face of death won't let me go. Regret over useless and perverse things especially overwhelm a person then, also the hope of leading a life that will more powerfully stand up to death. But we make a beginning and then we fall, an incessant up and down. Will this ever change?

Yesterday I saw the Bismarck film;[9] not bad at all. B.[10] reminds me ridiculously of Lasbeck.[11] I shall still write to Mrs. von K.[12] It is generous of you to be willing to take over my finances and to have done so in the past. Hopefully you will soon be free of all that!   155

I have heard nothing further from Gerhard![13] And now Friedrichsbrunn will probably be occupied by the children. If necessary, go ahead and send him fifty marks from me for his honeymoon!—The cordial cups will be inaugurated at my departure from Ettal. Everyone admires them and suspects that they are a wedding present; they expected great revelations from me. Unfortunately, I had to disappoint them.

Can you not arrange the visits set up with Inge Koch in such a way that Friedrichsbrunn becomes the base, and I come along here and there? That would be a magnificent idea! Make it happen. From the end of March to the middle of April! Or even a little later. I need to be back in Munich on March 24. Farewell! I shall write again briefly before my departure.

God preserve you!

As ever, Your faithful Dietrich

[6.] [*Domspatzen* means literally "cathedral sparrows." The reference is to the cathedral boys' choir in Regensburg.—MB]

[7.] ["Oh Lord, Let Your Dear Little Angels...Be Carried in the Bosom of Abraham" followed by the Bach cantata "O Sacred Head, Now Wounded."—MB]

[8.] [This is the last line of verse 1 (*The Lutheran Book of Worship*, nos. 116, 117).—MB]

[9.] This film premiered in December 1940, with Wolfgang Liebeneiner as director and Paul Hartmann in the role of Bismarck.

[10.] Bismarck.

[11.] Herbert von Bismarck.

[12.] Ruth von Kleist-Retzow.

[13.] Gerhard Vibrans.

90. To His Parents[1]

My dear Parents,

One more affectionate greeting before my departure, and let us hope for a nice reunion in Ettal in four weeks!—The room at the Europäischer Hof has been reserved for March 2/3.

I am having my mail sent to Marienburger Allee, where Eberhard will then look through it and take care of it all when he returns. The enclosed things are also for Eberhard.

156 I shall not write much in the next weeks, only an occasional sign of life. Thus there will be all the more to relate later. I shall, of course, write first to Anneliese[2] and if possible also send a telegram to Christiane.[3] I am very much looking forward to that and to the answer. I shall visit Dr. Brunner in Küßnacht[4] if possible. I do not have much hope of getting the shoes, since the same conditions apply there. One should, however, be able to get ration coupons easily in Berlin now. I shall of course try.

Have a good trip to Ettal and rest well! Love from

Your grateful Dietrich

[1.] *NL*, A 59,1 (13); handwritten postcard from Munich, February 23 or 24, 1941; previously published in *GS* 6:526.

[2.] See Bonhoeffer's letter of March 20, 1941, to Anneliese Schnurmann, 1/97.

[3.] "Christiane" was the code name for the Leibholz family in London.

[4.] See the letter of February 13, 1941, from Karl Bonhoeffer, 1/79, ed. note 2.

E. First Trip to Switzerland.
February 24–March 24, 1941

---

91. To Sabine Leibholz[1]

Zurich, February 25th 1941

My dear Sabine,

after a long time of unsuccessful attempts to find out your new address I have got it here from Lore.[2] You cannot imagine my joy to be able to write to you directly after this period of silence and after all you had to pass through during the last year. Our thoughts and more than that our prayers were with you every day. You and Gert and the children must know that, and certainly you are feeling the invisible stream of good wishes and loving thoughts that goes from us to you always. Karl and Paula[3] have only one wish, namely to see the day when they may meet and have you again. We hope that this day is not too far and even if one more year may pass, we feel sure that it cannot last much longer. It is so difficult for us to put ourselves into your position. But it is a great comfort to us to know that you have found the friends on whom you can rely. As far as I know from Max[4] you

---

[1.] *NL*, A 59,3 (3); typewritten, in original English, including errors; copy from Sabine Leibholz; previously published in *GS* 6:527–28. [It is interesting that Bonhoeffer writes to his sister in English. He may have done so to avoid problems with the British censors. Since England was at war with Germany, he may have thought it would draw less attention to the German background of his sister and her family and show that they were trying to fit into the English culture. On the experience of the Leibholz'es in England, see Sabine Leibholz-Bonhoeffer, *The Bonhoeffers: Portrait of a Family*, 89–159.—MB] Bonhoeffer's entry into Switzerland had been the previous day. During this first portion of his stay (February 24–March 1), he apparently found lodging at the Pestalozzi home; see his letter of June 10, 1941, to Gerty Pestalozzi, 1/112.

[2.] Lore Schmid née Delbrück, Emmi Bonhoeffer's sister.

[3.] Karl and Paula Bonhoeffer were their parents.

[4.] Max Delbrück, Emmi Bonhoeffer's brother.

are well again and the children are making good progress in school, Gert is doing research work. But, of course, you will be eager to know from your relations here. Karl's have just gone for a short holiday down south[5] to meet Barbara[6] and her brothers who have moved to the Alps and are enjoying the quietness of the mountains and a good school. Christel and Hans[7] are still living with their parents. Emmi was seriously ill with typhus which she caught on a trip to Italy with Klaus,[8] but she has recovered well and is now quite allright again. Her children will join Barbara very soon. Ursula[9] with her family is at home and is planning to move from there to her country house in the near future. I am still doing research work. Hans Walter[10] is busy with his matriculation. He will take up chemistry at the University next summer. There are no special news from Susi[11] and from Karl Friedrich.[12]

As you see I am in Zurich, where I will stay for 3 or 4 weeks. I met Lore Schmid, who sends you her best regards. Sutz has moved to Rapperswil, Kanton Zurich and would also be glad to have a word from you sometime. I am spending a beautiful holiday here with my friends. Gert's paper of 1939[13] has made a great impression on many people here. Now I will finish that letter and I hope that it will not take too long to reach you. I am longing for the day when we will meet again in unchanged fellowship and in the old spirit. I shall write to George[14] tomorrow. Give all my good wishes to Gert, to Marianne and Christiane, and to all friends.

Cordially Yours ever
Dietrich

[5.] This refers to the parents' vacation spent in Ettal.
[6.] Barbara von Dohnanyi.
[7.] Christine and Hans von Dohnanyi.
[8.] Emmi and Klaus Bonhoeffer.
[9.] Ursula Schleicher.
[10.] Hans Walter Schleicher.
[11.] Susanne Dreß.
[12.] Karl Friedrich Bonhoeffer.
[13.] This became the chapter "Germany, the West and the Possibility of New International Order: Report on Behalf of the Study Department of the Universal Christian Council for Life and Work (1940)," in Leibholz, *Politics and Law*, 154–73.
[14.] Bishop George K. A. Bell.

92. To George K. A. Bell[1]

My Lordbishop,

this is just to give you a sign of life after a long time of silence. My thoughts have been with you and with our fellowchristians in your country almost every day. It was most encouraging indeed to me to get your message in which you assure me of your unchanged christian fellowship.[2] You can   159
hardly imagine what comfort such a word means to us in these days. I need not assure you that we shall do everything to maintain that fellowship in faith and prayer.

I have to thank you for all you have done for me and for us. I shall never forget it. When will we meet again? God knows and we have to wait. But I cannot help hoping and praying that it will not last too long.

In deep gratitude and in the fellowship of Jesus Christ I remain
Yours ever Dietrich

Will you be good enough to give my love to Sabine[3] and her children? A letter would reach me through Pf.[4] Sutz, Rapperswil, Kt.[5] St. Gallen.

92a. To Paul Lehmann[1]   17:128

My dear Paul,

You will certainly be surprised to get a letter from me. But I must, of course, make use of the unusual opportunity of a short stay in Zürich to write to

---

[1.] *NL,* A 42,1 (32); typewritten, in original English, including errors; copy from Eberhard Bethge; from Zurich; previously published in *GS* 6:528–29.

[2.] See Bishop Bell's answer to Visser 't Hooft's telegram of October 6, 1940, 1/22, ed. note 1.

[3.] On March 14, 1941, Sabine Leibholz received the following telegram from Bishop Bell: "Dietrich staying Geneva this week sends love all well shall I send message = Chichester" (*NL,* A 42,1 [32]). On March 25, 1941, he wrote her: "... in response to Dietrich's telegram I have telegraphed and given him your greetings. And now I have already received a letter (see above) from him; I enclose a copy that will certainly give you joy. Do you know who Pastor Sutz is? I do not know if one may write to Dietrich directly, or if it would be better to write through Pastor Sutz; therefore I am writing first to Pastor Sutz himself and then shall see what else I can do" (Bell and Leibholz, *An der Schwelle,* 22).

[4.] ["Pf." is the abbreviation for *Pfarrer,* "pastor."—MB]

[5.] ["Kt." is the abbreviation for *Kanton,* "canton."—MB]

[1.] Princeton Theological Seminary Library, Paul Lehmann papers; handwritten in English from Zurich; first published in *DBW* 17:128–29; reproduced in original English,

you and to many friends abroad. It is just to give you a sign of life and to let you know that I am still well. I also wish to assure you of my unchanged friendship and sympathy, and of my deep appreciation of all you have done for me last year[2] when we met in New York. I shall never forget these hours. After the experiences of the passed[3] 1 1/2 year I am convinced that my decision of July 1939 to go home and to join my friends was right. I never doubted, as you know, the great difficulties we would have to pass through.[4] But even if you hear very little about us, be sure we are still there, we work and we hope. There is not the slightest change of mind in the essential questions. The ecumenic feeling is strong and still growing. Many sacrifices are[5] being brought by young and old people to keep up the good cause. But we realise, of course, that it must be extremely difficult for you not to loose[6] your confidence in us. Be patient, imagine the immense difficulties which will still be greater in this year, and do not give up praying for us. We need it.

Now I must ask a great favour from you. Please, by return of post, write a letter to me—a long one!—about your view of the situation and of the future, about the activities of the churches in the present crisis, shortly[7] about everything that is interesting to us in the present moment.[8] We know very little and we wish to know much. What do you think will be after the war, what will be the new social and political order? What rôle will the church play in that order? Sometimes I think that the word of the churches might become more important in coming decisions than it has ever been before. Sometimes I think, Christianity will only live after this time in a few people who have nothing to say. Please direct your letter to Erwin Sutz, Rapperswil, Kt. St. Gallen and do not mention my name. I saw Erwin today and he sends you his best regards. Before I go home in 4 weeks I shall see him again and I hope to find a letter from you there.

17:129

---

including errors. On Bonhoeffer's stay in Switzerland, see *DB-ER,* 726–30; see also the German editors' afterword of this volume, pp. 653–55. Page numbers in the margin refer to *DBW* 17.

[2.] Cf. *DBW* 15:239–40, as well as Paul Lehmann's own depiction in a letter to Reinhold Niebuhr on July 31, 1939 (*DBW* 15:256–57).

[3.] Bonhoeffer meant "past."

[4.] This refers to the numerous complications following the closing of the collective pastorates, as well as the conscription of young Confessing Church pastors into the military, but it also refers to the restrictions placed on Bonhoeffer by the ban on public speaking (including preaching) and the requirement to register with the police. [See 1/99; 1/104; 1/107; 1/188.—MB]

[5.] Illegible. Perhaps "were."

[6.] Bonhoeffer meant "lose."

[7.] [Bonhoeffer meant "in short."–MB]

[8.] See Lehmann's response on August 2, 1941, 1/116a, ed. note 1.

How is your work going on? How is Marion? What is Reinhold[9] doing. Please, remember me to him. Let me hear from you soon!

With all good wishes in unchangeable fellowship
Yours ever Dietrich

93. Nils Ehrenström: Calendar Notes, March 8–15, 1941[1]

[March]

8. 10–12.00. V. H.,[2] Freudenberg, Bonhoeffer
NE[3] with Bonhoeffer (HS apparently absent on a long trip again).[4]
10. Morning. V. H., Freudenberg, NE with Bonhoeffer: the work among Jewish refugees, ec.[5] studies.
afternoon: The same plus Guillon[6] re the situation in France. 160
11. 17–19.00. V. H., Bonhoeffer, Henriod, Guillon, NE: the situation in France and Switzerland; W. Alliance; peace aims.[7]
19.30–23.00. Supper at our home.

[9.] Reinhold Niebuhr.

[1.] *NL,* A 65,14; typewritten, in original English, including errors; previously published in *GS* 6:529–30. Regarding the circumstances, see *DB-ER,* 726–30, esp. 728–29; see also Boyens, *Kirchenkampf und Ökumene,* vol. 2, *1939–1945,* 171–79. In the preceding days, Bonhoeffer had visited Erwin Sutz in Rapperswil (March 2) and made arrangements for conversations with Karl Barth, Alphons Koechlin, and Friedrich Siegmund-Schultze in Basel (March 4–7).

[2.] Willem Visser 't Hooft.

[3.] Nils Ehrenström.

[4.] Hans Schönfeld was in Berlin and Belgrade, February 26–March 23, 1941.

[5.] [This is an abbreviation for "ecumenical."—MB]

[6.] Charles Guillon was a French ecumenist, the pastor and mayor of Le Chambon-sur-Lignon, and a leading member of the YMCA [Young Men's Christian Association] central office, in Geneva. Because of his double residence, he was the middleman for the aid missions between Geneva and the French groups of the Comité Inter-Mouvements auprès des Evacués (CIMADE) that reached even into the internment camps in the south of France. [CIMADE was a French Christian group that "helped camp inmates wherever they could." These rescue efforts continued until 1942, and then "they joined the French Resistance and worked to help Jews over the Swiss border" (Barnett, *For the Soul of the People,* 324 n. 72).—MB] "Chambon-sur-Lignon (in the Haute Loire) is perhaps the most famous of these Protestant centers, virtually an entire commune mobilized for rescue" (Marrus, "French Churches and the Persecution of Jews in France," 326). The French church president recalls, "Charles Guillon, who often visited me in Nîmes, reported to me on March 15, 1941, that Dietrich Bonhoeffer... had told him, 'our churches are for the collaboration and have thus betrayed the cause'" (Boegner, *Ein Leben für die Ökumene,* 183).

[7.] See Visser 't Hooft's March 12, 1941, letter to William Temple, 1/94. [Times here are given in European format. For example, "17–19.00" indicates 5–7 p.m.—MB]

12. 10–12.00. Bonhoeffer. V. H. NE: notes for a memo on Christian peace aims: his critique of our outline for the volume in Ecclesia Militans on "Verkündigung der Kirche im Krieg."[8]

    17.30–19. B. and NE: re studies on the social function of the Church, and on the changing RC[9]-Protestant relations in Germany.[10]

13. 14–16.30. B. and NE at V. H.'s home: debate on "Church and world" in relation to V. H.'s memo.[11]

    17–18. B. and NE: continued discussion on RC-Prot. problems.

    20–23. B. V. H., d'Espine, Courvoisier,[12] Leenhardt at Freudenberg's place.[13]

161 14. 17–18 at the office. B. and NE.

15. Lunch and afternoon, in Bellevue.

    A theol. colloquium on the ethical proclamation and action of the Church, internally and vis à vis the world, its legitimacy and its forms.[14]

    V. H., Freudenberg, d'Espine, Courvoisier, Leenhardt, Senarclens, NE and some others, around Bonhoeffer.

[8.] "The church's proclamation during the war." On September 27, 1940, Otto Salomon had announced to Visser 't Hooft the completion of a study on this theme suggested by Hans Schönfeld. On October 3, 1940, Visser 't Hooft reacted critically to his draft: "You have left all political opinions out of the picture entirely, probably intentionally. . . . It is in fact not permissible that we speak of 'The Church's Proclamation during the War' without mentioning the proclamation of men such as Barth, Niebuhr, or the archbishop of York, who are perhaps the most outspoken of those who have addressed the situation." This position may well have influenced the conversations with Bonhoeffer as well. It was not until July 5, 1941, that Salomon delivered his final draft, along with a letter of that date. This draft appeared in 1942 as no. 2 in the series Ecclesia Militans (Ecumenical Document Series), Department of Studies, WCC, Geneva.

[9.] ["RC" is the abbreviation for "Roman Catholic."—MB]

[10.] Cf. 1/27.

[11.] Visser 't Hooft was planning his "Entwurf eines einleitenden Memorandums" (Outline of an introductory memorandum); see ed. note 14.

[12.] The Geneva church historian Professor Jacques Courvoisier was also the president of the Ecumenical Commission on Prisoners of War.

[13.] Cf. the recollections of Adolf Freudenberg and Jacques Courvoisier in Zimmermann, *I Knew Dietrich Bonhoeffer,* 166–69 and 173–75.

[14.] The theme "Wie erfüllt die Kirche ihre ethische Aufgabe?" (How does the church fulfill its ethical task?) was one of a series of suggestions that Otto Salomon had sent to Visser 't Hooft on December 26, 1940, for the Ecclesia Militans series. This developed into the Department of Study's project on "Ethical Reality and the Function of the Church." On April 4, 1941, Visser 't Hooft sent Salomon "a list of the materials that [he would] use for the brochure on 'The Church's Speech to the World.'" In April 1941 he wrote the "Entwurf eines einleitenden Memorandums" (Archives of the World Council of Churches, Department of Studies, no. 1 G/41, and Visser 't Hooft archives, box 994.2.08). Cf. Boyens, *Kirchenkampf und Ökumene,* vol. 2, *1939–1945,* 172–73.

93a. To Gerty Pestalozzi[1]

March[2] 9, 1941

My dear lady,

Since I visited you, my plans have changed a bit,[3] and I will probably not be back in Zurich before next Saturday. I will phone as soon as I have returned.[4] Basel[5] was very nice. I am very happy about these days.

Yours with heartfelt thanks and devoted best wishes,
Dietrich Bonhoeffer

94. Willem A. Visser 't Hooft to William Temple[1]

March 12, 1941

Dear Archbishop,

I enclose some notes on the post-war settlement which are the result of a number of conversations with friends from different countries. I showed this draft to three of these friends and made certain changes on their suggestion. Thus in the present form it represents the common mind of four of us who belong to the four different

---

[1.] NL A addendum (not included in the Nachlaß index); handwritten card from Geneva; published in Röthlisberger-Pestalozzi, *Gerty Pestalozzi-Eidenbenz*, 313, and in *IBG-Rundbrief* 56 (July 1998). Page number in the margin refers to *DBW* 17.

[2.] In the version published by Esther Röthlisberger-Pestalozzi, this was erroneously interpreted to read "May."

[3.] Bonhoeffer had arrived in Geneva and had realized that he would need to stay there longer than he had earlier assumed.

[4.] At the end of his trip, March 19–20, 1941, Bonhoeffer returned one last time to the Pestalozzis'. A diary entry by Gerty Pestalozzi on April 9, 1941, provides a record of this visit: "The last sentences I read from *Macht und Gnade*, by Reinhold Schneider, are preying on my mind. This is what my thoughts are constantly revolving around, echoes of the conversations with Bonhoeffer: 'There is no hostility, no opposition, no division that love cannot and must not overcome. There is perhaps no more urgent task than this'" (Röthlisberger-Pestalozzi, *Gerty Pestalozzi-Eidenbenz*, 312; the reference is to Schneider, *Macht und Gnade*, 226); cf. 1/58 and Bonhoeffer's letter to Gerty Pestalozzi on June 10, 1941, 1/112.

[5.] This refers to his visit with Karl Barth.

[1.] WCC Archives, Geneva, General Correspondence, Temple; carbon copy from Geneva; Boyens, *Kirchenkampf und Ökumene*, vol. 2, *1939–1945*, 352–53. Letter is in the original English, including errors. Enclosed with the letter was the memorandum written by Visser 't Hooft titled "Some considerations concerning the post-war settlement" (Boyens, 2:353–55). Regarding the circumstances at the very time of Bonhoeffer's March 1941 visit, see Boyens, 2:202–4; see also Visser 't Hooft, *Memoirs*, 151–52, and von Klemperer, *German Resistance against Hitler*, 271–72.

categories—one of each side of the war, one from a neutral, and one from an ex-neutral occupied country.[2]

[...]

162   I have to add a point of considerable importance. By friends who belong to a group which I need not mention by name since you can guess who they are, the question is often raised:—What are the minimum-conditions on which peace would be possible? They consider the plans put forward at Malvern[3] and in some of your addresses as maximum-propositions, but would like to know what you and others consider to be the minimum-conditions of peace. The main point is really this:—Would their country have a chance of being offered acceptable terms if it would change its regime? Or would such a change of regime be used to crush their country altogether? This is a problem which is much discussed, and it is clear that a clear answer on this point may be of considerable importance for the decisions which this group may take. At present their fear is that it is too late for an action of this kind. If, however, they could be convinced that this is not the case, they might get busy again. This whole matter is, of course, very confidential. I should, however, be glad, you would keep Bill[4] and George Bell informed.

We have read with interest and admiration what you did at Malvern. Please keep us informed of any further developments along this line. We need all we can get to pass it on to the right people over here.[5]

I remain with my very cordial wishes, Yours ever,
W. A. Visser 't Hooft

[2.] "It is most probable—although I cannot say it with absolute certainty—that these four were Bonhoeffer, Ehrenström (my colleague from Sweden), Denzil Patrick (Scotland), and I" (Visser 't Hooft, *Memoirs*, 152).

[3.] Malvern was the site of a Church of England conference led by Archbishop Temple (January 7–10, 1941) at which ten points regarding a future peace order, inspired by the pope's Christmas address, were formulated. See also 1/170, ed. note 91, and 2/12, p. 535.

[4.] "Bill" is William Paton, who in 1940 had founded the Peace Aims Group, a working group for peace activities chaired by William Temple; for detailed information, see Jackson, *Red Tape and the Gospel*, 267–70.

[5.] Archbishop Temple responded on April 29, 1941: "I was immensely interested in your letter and especially in what you said about the discussion of prospects of people of varied types. It is very hard to say what would be the minimum conditions of peace put forward in this country, but I think that the main body of opinion would support the start of negotiations if the following conditions were fulfilled: (1) the disappearance of the Nazi regime; (2) the evacuation of all the occupied countries; (3) the cessation of that type of tyranny which is represented by the Gestapo" (cited in Visser 't Hooft, *Memoirs*, 152).

95. Willem A. Visser 't Hooft to George K. A. Bell[1]   163

March, 19, 1941

Dear Bishop,

Many thanks for your telegram[2] which has reached Dietrich just before he returned home. It will mean a great deal to him to have this message. He was a week with us and spent most of his time extracting ecumenical information from persons and documents. It is touching to see how hungry people like him are for news about their brothers in other countries, and it is good to know that he can take back so much which will encourage his friends at home.

On the other hand, we learned a lot from him. The picture which he gave is pretty black in respect to the exterior circumstances for the community which he represents. The pressure is greater than ever. But fortunately he could also tell us of many signs that their fundamental position has not changed at all and that they are as eager as ever for fellowship. Many of them have really the same reaction to all that has happened and is happening as you have or as I have. And this is remarkable after such a long period of isolation. I hope to send soon through Bill[3] some fuller notes on all that we learned through him about the situation.[4]

I can well understand that you are wondering about Martin,[5] for there have been all sorts of rumors about him. The truth is that the situation has not changed at all. He is still as courageous as ever and his health does not seem to give reason for anxiety. In the last autumn he had been concentrating on Roman Catholic literature, probably with the desire to find out why the Roman Catholic Church could keep a united Church while his own Church had been so hopelessly divided during the last years. At that time some of his friends were concerned about his passionate interest in this direction. This fact must have become known to others more recently, and so the story has been broadcasted by irresponsible people that he had gone over. As a

---

[1.] WCC Archives, Geneva, General Correspondence, Bell: carbon copy from Geneva; in original English, including errors; cf. *NL*, A 42,4 (15); previously published in *GS* 6:530–31.

[2.] See 1/92, ed. note 3.

[3.] William Paton.

[4.] See Visser 't Hooft, "Notes on the State of the Church in Europe," written in March 1941 on the basis of Bonhoeffer's reports, 1/98; cf. *DB-ER*, 729–30; Boyens, *Kirchenkampf und Ökumene*, vol. 2, *1939–1945*, 171–72 and 383.

[5.] This refers to Martin Niemöller. The ultimate clarification of rumors of Niemöller's conversion to the Catholic Church (see 1/69, ed. note 4) similarly came from Bonhoeffer; cf. Bethge's letter of February 8, 1941, 1/74.

164   matter of fact he seems to be much more balanced in his judgment of this matter than he was some months ago.

I remain with very good wishes for you personally and for all common friends,

Yours ever
Visser 't Hooft

96. To Charlotte von Kirschbaum[1]

March 19, 1941

My dear Miss von Kirschbaum,

I shall be able to leave Switzerland more easily tomorrow if I might hope to be able to read the *Dogmatics*[2] at home in the foreseeable future. Please have it shipped in the period shortly before Easter to: Superintendent's Residence, Schlawe Pomerania. Many cordial thanks for this!

It was quite magnificent in Basel. Only too short. Perhaps it would be better to wait until summer or late summer for the letter in question that we had discussed.[3] I assume that by that time the receptivity to hearing it will have become even greater.

Please give Professor Barth my best and warmest thanks. With kind regards from your respectful

Dietrich Bonhoeffer

165   ### 97. To Anneliese Schnurmann[1]

Zurich, March 20, 1941

Dear Anneliese,

Best wishes from a short vacation stay in Zurich! Especially from my parents and also to your siblings. My parents are very grateful to you (as we all are

---

[1.] Karl Barth-Archiv, Basel: handwritten, probably from Zurich.

[2.] This refers to volume 2/1 of Barth's *Church Dogmatics*. Cf. Bonhoeffer's letter to Barth, May 30, 1941, which confirms the volume's arrival (see 1/110).

[3.] It is not known what sort of letter had been considered.

[1.] *NL*, Anh. A 1; handwritten; address: "Dr. Strauß, Avenida Delphin, Moreira 4 (Leblon), Rio de Janeiro, Brazil." Stamped: "Opened by Examiner 56." Anneliese Schnurmann, a friend of Susanne Dreß, had emigrated to England as a consequence of the Nazi racial laws of 1933. Bonhoeffer assumed that she had in the meantime followed her twelve-year-older sister and her husband, the Berlin physician Dr. Moritz Straus, to Brazil; in hindsight, Ms. Schnurmann thinks this assumption was due to the fact that she herself had been raised by her sister after the early death of their parents, and that she thus belonged in every respect to the Straus family (communication with the German editors, October 11, 1991).

naturally!) for all that you have written us about Sabine.[2] We rejoice with you that you can now be with your family. So far everything is going well for us at home. Susi[3] has not yet gone to the mountains with her children. But it will surely become necessary. Our parents are suffering considerably under it all. It is really too much for elderly people! Things are about the same for me. Gert's[4] new address is Oxford, 100, Banbury Road. Might you not know of something nice for him in Brazil? The last few letters sounded rather depressed. Please keep your ears open as to whether a man like him might be needed somewhere. Apart from his scholarly field, he understands all sorts of things about the banking business. It would be such an incomparable relief. Of course, I know how difficult this is these days. But perhaps something will yet emerge. Also, I am to thank you from my parents for the magnificent coffee, which they enjoy greatly.

And now farewell! I sincerely wish you all good things and that you may quickly become settled and flourish there.

With my best wishes to you and your sister's family,

Your Dietrich

98. Willem A. Visser 't Hooft: Notes on the State of the Church in Europe[1]   166

Notes on the State of the Church in Europe

[...]

3. Germany

In Germany the Church Conflict continues. It is the common opinion of those concerned and of all well informed observers that there is no truth in the statements which have been published here and there that in view of the war situation the conflict is less acute. As the following facts show the Party is as active as ever in its anti-Christian propaganda and in narrowing the "vital space" of the Church.

The number of pastors in prison and concentration camps is not large (perhaps 5 to 10), but no fewer than 40 to 50 pastors are forbidden to preach or speak in public and many are also forbidden to leave their place of residence. A number of young pastors

---

[2.] Sabine Leibholz.

[3.] Susanne Dreß.

[4.] Gerhard Leibholz.

[1.] WCC Archives, Geneva; World Council of Churches, in process of formation (WCC ipof), box 14; hectograph; in original English, including errors. This excerpt is published in *GS* 6:531–34. As Visser 't Hooft wrote to Eberhard Bethge on June 5, 1961, this was a set of "'notes' that [he] sent to England at the end of March 1941. The section on Germany definitely reflects the conversations with Dietrich." Cf. *DB-ER*, 729–30; Boyens, *Kirchenkampf und Ökumene*, vol. 2, *1939–1945*, 171–72 and 383.

of the Confession Church[2] have been told that they must do "useful work" and have, therefore, been forced to work in offices.[3] When some of them tried to carry on their pastoral activities in their leisure-hours, they were given a 12 hour workday.[4] It is forbidden to send religious literature to the soldiers.[5] Pastors are not allowed to enter the evacuation camps in which large numbers of children of the big cities are brought together. In these same camps Christian Christmas hymns have been forbidden.

A document emanating from the Brown House[6] at Munich, the contents of which has become known through the indiscretion of a Party official, gives a clear idea of Nazi policy with regard to the Church. It contains thirteen points which are described as goals to be realized after the war, but which are in fact already being used as guiding principles in certain areas (especially the Posen area).[7] The most important of these points are: vigorous control of Church finance by the State; no religious instruction except in the church-building; the dissolution of church movements among youth; no membership of the church except by definite declaration and not under 21 years of age; no contact of regional churches with each other. The purpose is clear. It is to make the Church into an innocuous sect which is imprisoned in its churchbuilding and cannot exert any influence in public life.

In these circumstances it is all the more remarkable that the Confession Church still exists and carries on its work. Thus in Western Germany the Confession Church has recently ordained a group of 50 candidates. These pastors are not recognized by the "official" Church and have to be supported from unofficial collections in confessional parishes. This means a great effort of Christian solidarity (25 000 Marks per month are collected for this purpose in the Rhineland). It means also that there is now in Germany practically a free Church which is still vaguely connected with the official Church, but which is in fact living its own life under the direction of the brotherhood councils. The situation is, of course, better in Württemberg and Bavaria. There is now collaboration between the Confession Church (Niemöller's movement) and the Bishops of those two Churches.[8] Bishop Marahrens[9] is, however, considered by the Confession Church as having gone over to the side of the State Church.[10]

[2.] [Visser 't Hooft is referring to the "Confessing Church."—MB]

[3.] See Bethge's letter of January 27, 1941, 1/63, ed. note 4.

[4.] See Bethge's letter of February 5, 1941, 1/72.

[5.] See the December 1940 circular letter, 1/47, ed. note 1.

[6.] This refers to the Nazi Party headquarters.

[7.] This refers to the "Thirteen Points," a March 14, 1940, decree of Reich regional governor Arthur Greiser regarding the relationship of church and state in Warthegau (text in Wilhelm Niemöller, *Die evangelische Kirche im Dritten Reich*, 369–70). Cf. the corresponding passage in the draft of "Petition to the Armed Forces," 1/139, ed. note 4.

[8.] See Bonhoeffer's August 17, 1940, letter to Hans-Werner Jensen, 1/17, ed. note 7.

[9.] Bishop Marahrens was the Lutheran bishop of Hanover.

[10.] [The Lutheran churches of Württemberg, Bavaria, and Hanover were the three largest Lutheran regional churches in Germany. In the Church Struggle they were referred

But while the Confession Church is active, the regional brotherhood councils continue to function, and even small synods are still being held, it should not be thought that the Confession Church is a strong organization. The national organization (the old Provisional Church Government) has lost most of its leaders since these have been called up or are forbidden to travel and to speak, or are exiled from Berlin. Again the number of those who have been willing to accept the full consequences of Confessional Church policy is small. Many who are basically in sympathy with the Confession Church have made their peace with the official Church since they are afraid of the development toward a free Church and cling to the historical German idea of close relationship between Church and State.

This is one of the main reasons Martin Niemöller has become so interested in the study of Roman Catholicism. He is disappointed by the lack of consistency in his followers. His desire is for a Church which has its own independent existence over against the world and he is impressed by the Roman Church as a Church which is conscious of its own identity apart from the state and from secular society. Some   168
months ago there was some fear that this interest might lead him all the way to Rome. But in the meantime he has given to understand that he has no intention of going over.[11] The irresponsible newspaper reports which came with such emphasis that even his friends were impressed for a time, are now seen to be due to gossip about the concern felt by his associates in the early autumn of last year.

Religious literature is still being produced in considerable quantity, but in some cases permission for the printing of such literature is refused and general booksellers are not allowed to sell religious books.[12]

---

to as the "intact" churches, because their bishops were able to retain control of their churches, in contrast to regional churches, where German Christians seized the governance. Bishop Marahrens was opposed to German Christian ideology. However, as long as his church was not in danger of being taken over by the German Christians, he willingly supported many Nazi policies. Bishop Meiser of Bavaria pursued a strategy of nonconfrontation with the German Christians in an effort to keep his church intact. Bishop Wurm and the church of Württemberg collaborated most closely with the Confessing Church in Prussia, and during the war Wurm took a stand against the Nazis on the issue of the "mercy killing" of the mentally ill and physically disabled. Nonetheless, even Wurm hoped to work out a peaceful relationship with the state and resented radical elements in the Confessing Church that hindered that effort. See Barnett, *For the Soul of the People*, esp. 47–50.—MB]

[11.] See Bethge's letter of February 8, 1941, 1/74.

[12.] In the secret ministerial conference at his home on February 24, 1941, Goebbels gave consent to the resolution from the Ministerial Council for the Defense of the Reich: "Thirty thousand employees of the printing trade will shortly have to be released for the armaments industry. This entails the need for a considerable curtailment of printed matter in the entire Reich territory.... The Minister points out that here is a good opportunity to abolish and ban the entire Church press" (Boelcke, *Secret Conferences of Dr. Goebbels*, 120). On March 28, 1941, Goebbels informed the Reich Ministry for Church Affairs that he had decreed that the entire confessional press, with the exception of newspapers

Inside the Confession Church there is a certain difference of conviction with regard to the stand which the Church should take. There is, on the one hand, a group which believes that the Church should stick to what is called "the inner line," and concentrate exclusively on the building up of its own spiritual life. This tendency is often combined with a strongly apocalyptic note.[13] There is, however, another group which believes that the Church has also a prophetic and ethical function in relation to the world and that it must prepare for the moment when it can again fulfill that function.[14]

With regard to the attitude to the war, it is generally recognized among believing Christians that a victory of their own government will have the most fateful consequences for the Church in their own country as well as in other countries. On the other hand, they consider that a defeat of their country would probably mean its end as a nation. Thus many have come to believe that whatever the outcome of it all will be, it will be an evil thing for them. One hears, however, also voices which say that after all the suffering which their country has brought upon others they almost hope for an opportunity to pay the price by suffering themselves.[15]

169   Euthanasia continues.[16] Nobody knows how many people have been killed, but it is generally believed that the number is very large. There have been a number of courageous but ineffective protests, i.e., by Bishop Wurm, by Cardinal Faulhaber, and by some doctors. Bodelschwingh has refused to fill out the questionnaires which are used as a basis of selection, and so far no Bethel patients have been killed.

The youth situation is characterized by an increasing nihilism. National Socialist ideology seems to have a negative rather than a positive effect, for the official ideology is not taken seriously, and is in any case lacking in sufficient substance to give direction to the life of boys and girls. Now that large numbers of young people are in evacuation camps where they are completely cut off from influence of their homes, the grip of the state on youth becomes stronger and stronger. There are many stories about the terrible effects which this whole development has on sexual conditions. Thus it

---

appearing under official auspices, was to be suspended, effective immediately, until further notice (Boelcke, 120–21).

[13.] See "Thoughts on William Paton's Book _The Church and the New Order_," 2/11, 1. c.

[14.] See Nils Ehrenström's calendar notes for March 8–15, 1941, 1/93, ed. notes 8 and 14.

[15.] Cf. Visser 't Hooft, _Memoirs,_ 153: "We also spent an evening with Swiss friends in the apartment of Adolf Freudenberg. One of us asked Bonhoeffer: 'What do you pray for in the present situation?' He answered without hesitation: 'Since you ask me, I must say that I pray for the defeat of my country, for I believe that this is the only way in which it can pay for the suffering which it has caused in the world.'" Cf. Bell's diary notes of May 31, 1942, 1/170, p. 300.

[16.] The euthanasia actions were reduced early in 1941 and then officially eliminated by "order of the Führer" on August 28, 1941, although still carried on in more covert forms.

happens that when illegal children are born parents say simply, "The Führer desires this."[17] In an old Roman Catholic region like Tirol the influence exerted on youth is openly anti-Church, and boys are told to repeat in choir that the bishop is a racketeer and the Pope an arch-racketeer.[18]

[...]

[17.] Cf. *DBWE* 6:140.

[18.] Bonhoeffer likely received such information from the Munich Catholic Bishop's office; cf. Neuhäusler, *Kreuz und Hakenkreuz,* 1:270.

F. FOLLOWING THE BAN
ON WRITING.
BERLIN, KLEIN-KRÖSSIN, MUNICH.
APRIL–AUGUST 1941

99. From the Reich Chamber of Literature[1]

Berlin-Charlottenburg 2, March 17, 1941

With this notice, a fine in the amount of
30 (Thirty) Marks
is hereby levied against you, in accordance with paragraph 28, subparagraph 1, of the
First Regulation of the November 1, 1933, Reich Chamber of Culture Law (*RGBl.* I,
page 797).[2]
You have published the following works:

Discipleship, appearing in 1937 from Chr. Kaiser Publishers, Munich; *Year Together*,
appearing in 1938 from Chr. Kaiser Publishers, Munich;

Introduction to the Psalms, appearing in 1940 from MBK Publishers, Bad Salzuflen;

Contribution to the anthology *Sermon Letters* [*Predigtbriefe*], appearing in 1940
from G. Müller Publishers, Wuppertal.[3]

[1.] *NL*, A 61,4; typewritten; letterhead: "The President of the Reich Chamber of Literature II D 1-026055 mi."; addressed to "Pastor Dietrich Bonhoeffer, Schlawe/Pom. Koppelstr. 9"; stamped: "Registered"; previously published in *GS* 2:367–68. Bonhoeffer found this letter from the Reich Chamber of Literature in Munich awaiting him on his return from Switzerland and therefore decided to make a stop in Halle on the way home to Berlin, in order to consult with Professor Ernst Wolf as to appropriate further steps. On the events, see *DB-ER*, 730–31. [See Bonhoeffer's reply, 1/107.—MB]

[2.] [*RGBl.* is the abbreviation for *Reichsgesetzblatt*, "Reich legal gazette."—MB]

[3.] [As Bonhoeffer points out in his letter to the Reich Chamber of Literature of April 22, 1941 (see 1/107), the titles of three of the four works mentioned by the Chamber are inaccurate. *Year Together* is actually *Life Together*. *Introduction to the Psalms* is the subtitle

You have therefore taken an action that falls under the jurisdiction of my Chamber. According to paragraph 4, cited in connection with my official notice [Amtliche Bekanntmachung] no. 88 of April 1, 1937, revised November 11, 1938, regarding the registration of those engaged in literary activity with the Reich Chamber of Literature[4] (published in the *Völkischer Beobachter* of July 1, 1937; *Börsenblatt* no. 148/1937, 275/1938; *Der deutsche Schriftsteller*, volume 2, page 157, and volume 3, page 277), you were obligated to gain membership in my Chamber or to apply for exemption from membership.

Only as a result of my request of November 21, 1940, did you seek membership   171
or the procurement of an exemption from my Chamber.[5]

In order to preclude disciplinary measures, this fine is to be paid to the Reich Chamber of Literature, Berlin postal account no. 80915, within a week of your being served with this notice.

By order of: Ihde[6]

100. From the Reich Chamber of Literature[1]

Berlin-Charlottenburg 2, March 19, 1941

In accordance with paragraph 10 of the implementation order [Durchführungsverordnung] of the November 1, 1933, Reich Chamber of Culture Law (*RGBl.* I, page 797),[2] I hereby reject your application for admission to the Reich Chamber of Literature, Author Group, as well as for procurement of a certificate of exemption, due to lack of the requisite political reliability.

I have determined that on August 22, 1940, the state police imposed on you a ban on public speaking as a result of your activity subverting the people.

This fact sufficiently demonstrates the deficiency in reliability as noted in the sense of paragraph 10 above.

---

of *Prayerbook of the Bible.* Bonhoeffer contributed to a volume titled *Eine Predigthilfe* (A sermon aid), not *Predigtbriefe* (Sermon letters), that was published by E. Müller-Verlag (Publishers), not G. Müller Verlag. Bonhoeffer concluded that the Chamber officials must not have had the books in front of them when they levied the fines.—MB]

[4.] See Albert Lempp's letter to Bonhoeffer of April 1, 1941, 1/104.

[5.] See Bonhoeffer's letter to his parents on November 29, 1940, 1/38, ed. note 3.

[6.] Wilhelm Ihde had been acting director of the Reich Chamber of Literature since 1937. The writer Jochen Klepper also dealt with Ihde in 1937–38, after Klepper was allowed a certain flexibility following a broadly imposed ban on writing under the condition that he submit his manuscripts to the Chamber for examination prior to publication. [These restrictions were imposed because of Klepper's marriage to a Jewish woman.— MB] Cf. Riemschneider, *Der Fall Klepper,* 40 et passim.

[1.] *NL*, A 61,4; typewritten; letterhead: "The President of the Reich Chamber of Literature II D 1 026055 ini."; stamped: "Postal Delivery Certificate!" [Postzustellungsurkunde]; previously published in *GS* 2:368.

[2.] [*RGBl.* is an abbreviation for *Reichsgesetzblatt,* "Reich legal gazette."—MB]

On the basis of the present decision, you are forbidden every activity as a writer. In the case of a violation, the penal provisions set forth in paragraph 28 of the implementation order cited above would necessarily be initiated against you.

By order of: Ihde

172   **101. To Christine von Dohnanyi**[1]

March 24, 1941[2]

Dear Christel,

I have just heard from the consul[3] here that the children[4] are now not supposed to be traveling until Thursday after all. This at least resolves all the confusion! Your apparent understanding that I could also travel on Thursday was quite inexplicable to me. I had never said that. It would have made no sense for me either, since I had to come here[5] anyway this afternoon and have absolutely nothing I can do here for this day and a half; and in the process I would have been out a great deal of money, of which I have very little at the moment. Also, in Ettal the only accommodations were on Christoph's[6] sofa and thus not very enticing. So I considered the trip on Tuesday with the children to be the best thing and also no more expensive than the couchette car ticket and my round trip to Halle, even if I had taken the children with me into the hotel in Halle, which I suggested. I myself preferred to visit Wolf[7] in Halle on the way, since over Easter he will be here in Bavaria. I am sorry that has now not worked, but I did not think my suggestion was as bad as you apparently did. Perhaps the situation was muddied because of all the various partners in this conversation. I only wanted to take the safest route for the sake of the children. They will also be greatly disappointed now to have to remain in school two days longer. I shall arrive in Berlin on Wednesday or Thursday. That is perhaps also quite good, since the funeral[8] was only today.

[1.] *NL*, A 59,3 (5); handwritten, from Munich; previously published in *GS* 6:535–36.

[2.] The day of Bonhoeffer's return from Switzerland.

[3.] Consul Wilhelm Schmidhuber.

[4.] The Dohnanyi children, who at the time were in Ettal and would be traveling home to Berlin for Easter vacation.

[5.] Bonhoeffer had to go to the Munich Military Intelligence Office.

[6.] Christoph von Dohnanyi.

[7.] Bonhoeffer wanted to visit Professor Ernst Wolf because of the ban on writing he had just received and to report to Wolf from Karl Barth; cf. *DB-ER*, 730–31. Eberhard Bethge came to meet Bonhoeffer in Halle.

[8.] Countess Hanna von der Goltz had died on March 20, 1941.

Shortly before leaving I received a telegram from Sabine via George.[9]   173
Everything is going well. Earlier a detailed letter had arrived for Lore.[10] I
shall tell you about it when I get there. I wrote her two long letters. For her
sake I didn't want to write more frequently.

So, see you soon, and forgive the series of misunderstandings! My greetings
to all of you!

Your Dietrich

102. To Rudolf Weckerling[1]

March 29, 1941

Dear Brother Weckerling,

I have not heard a thing about my manuscript[2] since sending it off; not
even its arrival was confirmed for me. But now as of yesterday I have received
a ban on all forms of writing[3] and must now request that you return the
manuscript to me, since otherwise difficulties would ensue for both the
publisher and me. I cordially ask you to take care of this matter immediately.
I am very sorry.

With best regards and wishes,
Your Dietrich Bonhoeffer

103. To Walter Schmidt[1]   174

March 31, 1941

Dear Brother Schmidt,

When, after five months away, I returned at last to Berlin, I discovered a
tremendous and truly moving surprise from you: the Danzig Goldwasser.[2]

[9.] See Visser 't Hooft's letter to Bishop Bell on March 19, 1941, 1/95.

[10.] Lore Schmid; see Bonhoeffer's letter to Sabine Leibholz on February 25, 1941,
1/91, ed. note 2.

[1.] *NL*, A 60,4 (7); handwritten from Berlin; previously published in *GS* 6:536.

[2.] See Bonhoeffer's letter to Eberhard Bethge on January 20, 1941 (1/60, ed. note
12, and the essay "The Best Physician" (2/9).

[3.] This indicates that Bonhoeffer found the letter of March 19, 1941, from the Reich
Chamber of Literature (see 1/100) awaiting him upon his arrival in Berlin on March 28.

[1.] *NL*, A 60,4 (8); handwritten from Berlin; *GS* 6:537. The recipient, a participant in
the collective pastorates in Köslin in the summer of 1938, was at that time a pastor at Salz-
furth Chapel near Bitterfeld.

[2.] The name of a liqueur produced in Danzig.

I have gathered that this can be traced back to an extremely broad hint dropped by Eberhard Bethge. I truly do not know how he came up with it. But I can't deny that I am enjoying it enormously. So thank you very much and above all forgive me that this thanks is so late in coming. But, as I said, they kept the bottle here for me as a surprise. These sorts of greetings and kindnesses are naturally a sign of a meaningful relationship; and I rejoice in both: the sign and especially the relationship itself. I would very much like to see you and speak with you again.

It is good that you can still work. Only be sure to make full use of it. On the basis of the ban on public speaking, they have now also imposed on me a ban on writing, so there is very little left of my ministry. Then one thinks particularly of those times when it was still possible to work fully, and wonders whether many possibilities were left untapped, and rejoices for all those who can still carry on their work relatively unimpeded.

I think of you with joyful memories and in abiding fellowship [Gemeinschaft]. With thanks again for your remembering me and best wishes from

Your Dietrich Bonhoeffer

175   **104. From Albert Lempp**[1]

Munich, April 1, 1941

Dear Dr. Bonhoeffer:

I have received your letter of March 28[2] regarding the Reich Chamber of Literature and would like to let you know that a great number of theological authors have now received such penalties, not only those who publish here but also those with other publishers. The penalties are generally being handled in such a way that the amount fined is paid with reservations, but then the author protests the penalty to the Reich Chamber of Literature. This protest appeals to the Reich Chamber of Literature's official notice no. 88, paragraph 2, which reads, "Scholars who publish purely academic papers in their discipline do not fall under the jurisdiction of the Reich Chamber of Literature," and it appeals also to the statement of the Reich Minister of the Interior on November 14, 1934, based on this paragraph, which reads, "Officials, scholars, clergy, physicians, and attorneys are for this reason not included within the Reich Chamber of Literature when they write in the areas of their professional expertise." It is on the basis of these pronouncements that you then seek the rescinding of the penalty and repayment of the fine. I myself have not yet received any penalty, apparently because

---

[1.] *NL,* A 61,4; typewritten. See Bonhoeffer's letter to his parents on November 29, 1940, 1/38, ed. note 3.

[2.] Letter not extant.

the infractions of the various authors are collected first and then an overall infraction will be produced against me. Until now I have received a summons to respond to only two infractions [—] three more have just arrived[3] [—] which I did along the lines noted above.

You write that you simultaneously received a letter of March 19, 1941, that prohibited you from engaging in any writing. If this letter is also from the Reich Chamber of Literature, then I believe that you can protest it, since you are working not as a writer but as a scholar who does not fall under the Reich Chamber of Literature's jurisdiction, and request that they confirm with you explicitly that this interpretation of yours is correct. If, on the other hand, your letter comes from another source, such as from those who imposed on you the ban on public speaking, then the situation would be different; and I do not know whether you would be able to speak in any way against it.

When your situation is presented as an infraction to me, presumably very soon, then needless to say I shall testify as well on your behalf to the effect that these are scholarly books.

With best regards,
Your very respectful A. Lempp

105. From MBK Publishers[1]

176

Bad Salzuflen, April 2, 1941

Dear Pastor Bonhoeffer.

The Leipzig Reich Chamber of Literature has communicated with us in a letter of March 29, 1941, that with our publication of your volume *Prayerbook of the Bible*, we have violated the Chamber decree, since you are not a member of the Chamber nor have you requested a certification of exemption from it.

So that you may be informed about this correspondence, we are enclosing for you: 1) the decree as to Chamber membership, i.e., official notice no. 88; and 2) our return correspondence to the Chamber, dated today.[2] Regarding our publication of your volume, the situation appears to us to be quite clear; this is what we have articulated to the Chamber as well. Thus there has been no infraction committed here.

[3.] This inserted sentence fragment was handwritten.

[1.] *NL*, A 61,4; carbon copy. ["MBK" is the abbreviation for *Menschen begegnen — Bibel entdecken — Kirche gestalten*, "Encountering human beings — discovering the Bible — shaping the church." According to the contemporary MBK-Verlag Web site, MBK-Verlag is associated with the Evangelisches Jugend- und Missionswerk, "Protestant Office for Youth and Mission." This press originally published *Prayerbook of the Bible*; see DBW 5:11.—MB]

[2.] A carbon copy of this letter is found in *NL*, A 61,4.

You do not need to return either the carbon copy of the letter or the official notice to us.

Sincerely,
MBK Publishers, signed Elfriede Rättig

106. To His Parents[1]

April 22, 1941

My dear Parents,

As Eberhard conveyed to me, you had a tolerable trip and arrived safely at home. Hopefully, your relaxation will last for a while. It was quite lovely to spend a few quiet days with you up here. I haven't had that for a long time. I thank you very much for it.

177   In the past few days I have been working well again. For a break I chop a little wood. By the way, according to expert opinion—I asked some people— the wood should remain out in the open air; it will dry better there. So I shall stack it up and put a mark on the wall.[2] The coal still hasn't been delivered. But with the heat from the next room it's going well nevertheless.

So, as planned, I shall leave on Friday on the 10 a.m. train from Thale, change trains in Potsdam, and go on to Grunewald. If I could be picked up there, I would be very grateful. I have a great deal of luggage, and it is rather heavy. I have asked Eberhard to telephone you and let you know if he can do this.

Love to you and everyone,

Your grateful Dietrich

P.S. Perhaps Perels could then come on Friday with his wife. On Monday I shall be going to Pomerania for a few days.

107. To the Reich Chamber of Literature[1]

April 22, 1941

On March 27, 1941, I received by registered mail a decree from the Reich Chamber of Literature regarding a fine of thirty marks. At the same time, I

[1.] *NL*, A 59,1 (14); handwritten from Friedrichsbrunn; previously published in *GS* 6: 538; partially reproduced in *GS* 2:407.

[2.] Apparently some had been stolen.

[1.] *NL*, A 61,4 (6); handwritten draft from Friedrichsbrunn; address: "To the President of the Reich Chamber of Literature, Berlin-Charlottenburg"; previously published in *GS* 2:369–71. [Cf. 1/99.—MB]

was forbidden to work as a writer. I have paid the fine, although I cannot thereby acknowledge its legitimacy. I object to both the fine and the ban for the following reasons:

1. Official notice no. 88, par. 2, reads, "Scholars who publish purely academic papers in their discipline do not fall under the jurisdiction of the Reich Chamber of Literature." The statement of the minister of the interior on November 4, 1934, reads, "Officials, scholars, clergy, physicians, and attorneys are for this reason not included within the Reich Chamber of Literature when they conduct research in the areas of their professional expertise."[2] The sum of my publications consists of the results of my scholarly—dogmatic, ethical, and exegetical—research. Therefore, they do not fall under the jurisdiction of the Reich Chamber of Literature; and thus I have no right to apply to the Reich Chamber of Literature. It would otherwise be incomprehensible to me that I would be notified only in 1941 of my duty to apply regarding a publication dating from 1937.

2. As to the details of those works enumerated in your letter, I have the following to note: The 1937 book, *Discipleship,* is everywhere acknowledged in theological circles as a purely scholarly work (cf. the discussion in *Die Theologische Literaturzeitung* and elsewhere). The 1938 volume, *Life Together,* appeared in the scholarly series Theologische Existenz heute and is intended for theologians. The 1940 paper, *Prayerbook of the Bible: Introduction to the Psalms,* comprises only sixteen pages and therefore falls clearly within paragraph 3 of official notice no. 88 regarding documents of "negligible size," which do not require registration. The paper contains the results of scholarly work. The anthology *Predigthilfe* provides scholarly textual exegeses for sermons; these exegeses are not at all accessible to laypeople. Not one of my publications, therefore, justifies the imposition of this fine.

3. The enumeration of my writings for the purpose of the fine levied on me is so imprecise that I must assume the writings themselves were not even at hand. I never wrote a book titled *Year Together* but rather *Life Together.* The volume subtitled *Introduction to the Psalms* was missing its title, namely, *Prayerbook of the Bible.* There is no such anthology as *Sermon Letters* [*Predigtbriefe*]; I contributed to the volume titled *An Aid to Preaching* [*Eine Predigthilfe*] that appeared not with G. Müller Publishers but rather with E. Müller Publishers.

4. I object to your use of the ban on public speaking previously imposed on me to justify a ban on further publications. When the ban on public speaking was imposed, I defended myself with detailed written argumentation against the general accusations raised and to date have received neither

178

179

[2.] On both quotations, cf. 1/104. In the latter quotation Bonhoeffer mistakenly wrote "conduct research" rather than "write."

a response nor a rebuttal of my reasoning. Furthermore, anyone who is familiar with my theological writings will realize that they consist of purely innertheological discussions that have not the slightest to do with the rationale for the ban on public speaking.

During a stay in East Prussia in the summer of 1940, I was requested by a pastor in Königsberg to hold a Bible study and lecture at a small student gathering outside Königsberg.[3] I agreed and on July 13, 1940, met around six persons in Blöstau, among them three students and three members of the congregation. I held a Bible study on the story of the rich young man. The next morning I conducted the congregational worship service. In the afternoon a lecture on "The Problem of Death" was planned. After the worship service, when I was sitting with the students in informal conversation, several officials of the Gestapo arrived, dissolved the gathering, and interrogated those present. At this time we were alerted to an ordinance of April 26, 1940,[4] according to which the ban on religious youth events can be extended also to such adult events. None of us could have been aware of this ordinance, which had never been published. The Gestapo officials also expressed their surprise at the small number of attendees, and one of them said that they never would have come if they had known that. I personally was told that no further unpleasantness would ensue for me as a result of this matter, since I was participating in this event only by chance as a guest. A week later I received a ban on public speaking throughout the Reich because of activity subverting the people, and in the disclosure I learned that this gathering had furnished the cause for it. No specific accusations were made against me. I personally am convinced that the ban on public speaking had nothing to do with any particular utterances, but rather with the fact that during my stay in East Prussia I preached in several places in very well attended churches.[5]

180

108. To Hans-Werner Jensen[1]

Munich, May 14, 1941

Dear Brother Jensen!

Your April 24 letter was a great joy to me, since I glean from it that you are healthy again and had a nice time at home. As to your inquiry, I never

---

[3.] See the report of the SD Headquarters in Königsberg (1/15) and Bonhoeffer's letter to the Reich Central Security Office on September 15, 1940 (1/21).

[4.] See 1/15, ed. note 4.

[5.] The draft breaks off at this point.

[1.] *NL*, A 60,4 (4); typewritten copy of Hans-Werner Jensen; previously published in *GS* 2:588–89.

received your birthday letter; that could, however, be because during the time I was traveling (February–March) (I was with Karl Barth and others), my mail was being held and was inadvertently never delivered to me. In any case, I only recently received a letter from January that had been held for me.

I would be very glad if you could become an army chaplain. But it will not be easy. In Berlin things are recently quite unsettled again. They suddenly arrested, among others, Albertz, Dehn, Asmussen, Böhm, Vogel, Harder, and some women, because of the examinations.[2] Truly it is scarcely conceivable why now, of all times, congregations are being provoked and alarmed in such a way. But it can only help our cause. "A child of so many tears cannot go astray," it is said of Augustine;[3] and the same is surely true of the Confessing Church. Despite many mistakes and weaknesses, God's hand protects God's church. This is daily cause for amazement and thanks.

We now lay our future—personally and ecclesially and in all things—   181
entirely in God's hands again, doing our part gladly and letting God guide the whole.

Farewell, and God preserve you!

Yours faithfully,
Dietrich Bonhoeffer

109. From the Reich Chamber of Literature[1]

Berlin-Charlottenburg 2, May 22, 1941

Taking into consideration your counterproposal of April 22, 1941, to my decision of March 17, 1941, I hereby rescind the fine in the amount of thirty reichmarks in acknowledgment of the absence of guilt and authorize your reimbursement in this amount.

Your explanations are not, however, sufficient to induce me to rescind or revise my decision of March 19, 1941. The refusal to accept you into the Authors' Group of the Reich Chamber of Literature or to confer an exemption remains in force. This refusal has the effect of an official prohibition on writing for publication.

When in numeral 2 of my April 1, 1937, notice (revised November 21, 1938) on the registration with the Reich Chamber of Literature of those engaging in writing for publication, I decreed that whoever as a scholar publishes purely academic writings in his area of scholarly expertise does not fall within the jurisdiction of the Reich Chamber

---

[2.] In May 1941, the entire examination commission of the Council of Brethren of the Old Prussian Union was imprisoned; cf. *DB-ER*, 689.

[3.] Korpp, *Monika: Das Bild der Mutter in den Bekenntnissen Augustins*, 18. Bonhoeffer gave the book to Ruth von Kleist-Retzow; see 1/142.

[1.] *NL*, A 61,4 (7): typewritten; letterhead: "The President of the Reich Chamber of Literature I C 026055-VZ."; previously published in *GS* 2:372.

of Literature, I thereby had in mind the delimitation of areas of jurisdiction between the Reich Ministry for Science, Instruction, and Education and the Ministry for Public Enlightenment and Propaganda,[2] of which my Chamber is a part.

Accordingly, only those theologians who are occupants of chairs at state colleges and universities are exempted from membership in my Chamber—Authors' Group.

Furthermore, because of their overwhelming dogmatic allegiance, I cannot readily acknowledge clergy as scholars in this sense.

On behalf of the Reich Chamber of Literature, Ihde

182   **110. To Karl Barth**[1]

May 30, 1941

Dear Professor Barth,

Just now I have a suitable opportunity to give someone a letter to deliver to you personally;[2] and in this way I wish above all to thank you sincerely for providing me a copy of the *Dogmatics*.[3] It arrived safely, and I was overjoyed to receive it. I am now well along and take pleasure in it daily and am once more studying real theology.

The days I spent with you were especially delightful. The friends here hung on every word I was able to tell them, and they return your greetings with deep and unfailing loyalty. They all sorely envied me the hours I spent with you and yet were happy that at least one of us could speak with you again.

In Berlin many council members[4] are once again in the place where they have already spent several weeks and months; it has to do with the examinations.[5] Along with several others I have now also received a ban on doing any writing for publication. I now hope to be able to return to your area at

---

[2.] [The Ministry for Public Enlightenment and Propaganda was Goebbels's office, and it was part of the Reich Ministry of Propaganda.—MB]

[1.] *NL,* Anh. A 3 (1); handwritten from Berlin; Bethge, *Schweizer Korrespondenz,* 11; on the circumstances of the letter, see Bethge's comments, ibid., 22–24.

[2.] The letter was most likely delivered through Hans Schönfeld, who visited Holland and Berlin between May 25 and June 2, 1941.

[3.] See Bonhoeffer's letter of March 19, 1941, to Charlotte von Kirschbaum, 1/96, ed. note 2.

[4.] [The German word is *Brüder,* "brothers." However, *Brüder* here refers to members of the examination committee of the Old Prussian Union Council of Brethren, and in Bonhoeffer's letter to Hans-Werner Jensen on May 14, 1941 (see 1/108), he mentions a number of the *Brüder* by name who had been imprisoned on account of the examinations and notes that some women were among them. Thus, a more inclusive translation of *Brüder* would seem to be in order.—MB]

[5.] Bonhoeffer is referring to the imprisonment (mentioned in 1/108) of the members of the examination commission of the Old Prussian Union Council of Brethren.

the end of the summer for a few weeks to work and write there. Much encouraged by my trip, I have recently been making excellent progress in my work. Yet it is often difficult to concentrate, and soon I would very much like to be able to discuss with you, at some length, certain questions concerning my work. You will surely permit me to provide your name to the consulate as recommendation for a visa?

If you will greet the Vischers and Thurneysens when you have the opportunity, I would be most grateful. I cannot send any more letters with my friend. But I think of Basel with enormous gratitude. 183

With all good wishes for your work, in fellowship
Your Dietrich Bonhoeffer

111. To Richard Grunow[1]

June 4, 1941

Dear Richard,

It has taken more than three months for your book, *Wir fragen...*,[2] to reach me. During my trip it was repeatedly left unattended and incorrectly forwarded. So please now accept my sincere thanks for this token of remembrance and of the work we've done together. It truly always gives me a sense of some pride to see that some of those who "learned" from me are writing things of such proficiency; but more than that, a person simply rejoices in anyone who independently moves in the same direction as oneself. You had rather difficult texts, and I think that you succeeded in putting things simply, it truly proclaims Christ. I have actually only one objection, to question 2 on December 1.[3] There is no answer to this question! Thus it cannot be the point of the text. Rather, the point is the proclamation of the weakness and power of the Word of God—i.e., of the cross and resurrection. Your question is legalistic-pietistic.—Matt. 21:28ff. is somewhat too brief for me. In 1934, in a sermon in Augsburg,[4] Schlink gave a very nice reading of this story, which I particularly love. But that is beside the point. I rejoice greatly in what you have written.

How are you doing otherwise?

With all good wishes for your work, and in fellowship,
Your Dietrich

[1.] *NL*, A 60,4 (9); handwritten letter from Berlin; previously published in *GS* 2:589–90.

[2.] Bannach, *Wir fragen die Bibel: Die Bibellese in Frage und Antwort.*

[3.] This is in reference to the parable of the sower (Matt. 13:1-9, 18-23); Grunow's question 2 reads, "To which group of listeners do you think you belong?"

[4.] This was a morning prayer service; see Niemöller, *Die dritte Bekenntnissynode*, 266–68.

184   **112. To Gerty Pestalozzi**[1]

June 10, 1941

My dear lady,

Since the possibility of passing along a greeting to you has just arisen, I am seizing this opportunity with great joy in order—finally!—to thank you very cordially for all you did to make my days in Zurich so pleasant. From the conversations on the balcony to the evening activities, everything has remained most fresh and delightful in my memory. We shall have to continue the conversation about the ordering of Christian life[2] at some point! Incidentally, I hope very much that it can happen in the late summer; I would be very eager to come over again and shall make every effort from this end.

The wonderful coffee arrived recently, and I am not the only one it has delighted. Friends here were enormously pleased to receive your greetings. I had to tell many stories. Everything went fine at the border, by the way, although my neighbor had to hand over his second bar of chocolate.[3] Also many thanks again for your book on Portugal.[4] I took great pleasure in it.

For the past four weeks we have been deeply concerned about Günther.[5] We hope that he will survive it all well. He is not alone but with several friends.[6] Being together with him was always especially delightful. He is so devoted to you and your friends, and he is not the only one. There are many just like him. This is a great joy and will surely be heartening for you to hear as well.

185   This letter must be on its way! With heartfelt gratitude and regards to you and yours,

Your sincere and respectful Dietrich Bonhoeffer

[1.] *NL,* Anh. A 3 (2); handwritten letter from Berlin; Bethge, *Schweizer Korrespondenz,* 12 and Bethge's commentary on pages 24–25. Gerty Pestalozzi-Eidenbenz and her husband, the Zurich industrialist Rudolf Pestalozzi, were early members of Karl Barth's closer circle of friends. Apparently this letter was quickly passed on from Zurich to Basel, since it was found in the papers of Charlotte von Kirschbaum.

[2.] Cf. the May 1940 Finkenwalde circular letter, 1/6.

[3.] [Travelers were allowed to bring only one bar of chocolate into Germany.—MB]

[4.] The book *Fahrt nach Portugal,* published by Rudolf Pestalozzi and bearing the inscription, "A sign of mutual remembrance, Rudolf and Gerty Pestalozzi," was found in Bonhoeffer's library; see *NL-Bibl.,* 9:20.

[5.] Günther Dehn was imprisoned in Plötzensee with the other members of the Old Prussian Union Church examination commission.

[6.] [Twenty-three members of the examination commission were arrested and tried in December 1941; most of them, including Harder, spent months in prison. See Barnett, *For the Soul of the People,* 93–94.—MB]

I have just heard that this matter will in fact take quite a while after all. We must have a great deal of patience. Incidentally, you will surely permit me to say that you would give his wife much joy with some coffee. I have experienced that with the others as well. They are extremely grateful for the smallest things!

113. To George K. A. Bell[1]

12th June 1941

My dear Lord Bishop,

you can hardly imagine my immense joy when I received your letter.[2] When exchange of thoughts and views is not possible, the smallest sign and the shortest word of fellowship becomes a real and great comfort. I am at home again and my people share my joy about your words. Martin[3] is sound in health and faith and many of my friends are with him now. Our hope for the outcome of our cause is unchanged. We rejoice in the great fellowship in which we stand. I wish to thank you for [what you] are doing for my sister. It is so good to know that they will always have a wise and benevolent adviser. Please give her my love.

In sincere thankfulness, I remain as ever
Yours Dietrich

114. To His Parents[1]

186

My dear Parents,

For the past few days I have again been enjoying the tranquillity of country life. My work[2] is proceeding well, and I take intermittent breaks walking in the garden. I would very much wish a few such weeks for you as well. Mrs.

[1.] *NL*, A 42,1 (33); typewritten letter from Berlin; in original English, including errors; previously published in *GS* 6:538–39. The dating could possibly be from the seventeenth rather than the twelfth. The mention in Bishop Bell's letter of August 8, 1941, to Gerhard Leibholz that he had just received a letter from Bonhoeffer via Zurich demonstrates how long the conveyance of this letter took.

[2.] This letter, presumably conveyed through Erwin Sutz in Switzerland, is not known.

[3.] Martin Niemöller.

[1.] *NL*, A 59,1 (15); handwritten postcard from Klein-Krössin, end of June 1941; previously published in *GS* 6:539; partially reproduced in *GS* 2:407. From about June 25 until the middle of July, Bonhoeffer was a guest of Ruth von Kleist-Retzow in Klein-Krössin.

[2.] He was working on his *Ethics*.

von Kleist is writing to you today regarding a possibility at an inn near Polzin, from July 15 on. Would that suit you?[3] The food supply here is actually still at nearly prewar levels. It has been stormy for the past two days here and has fortunately cooled off considerably.

I also wanted to thank you now once more that I was able to stay with you for so long and especially also that Eberhard could be there too. Now it is surely very quiet at your house.

With my best wishes, your grateful
Dietrich

115. To His Parents[1]

Klein-Krössin, Saturday, June[2] 5, 1941

My dear Parents,

By now you will have received the letter from Mrs. von Kleist-Retzow. If you have now decided to come out to the estate, I could perhaps go by there on my return trip to speak to the people myself. I wanted to come to Berlin sometime around the end of next week to spend a few days there before I have to go to Munich.[3]—After raining a great deal in the past few days, it now appears to be becoming somewhat sunnier.—Ursel[4] should please write with the day of the children's arrival. They should also try to send their bicycles here via express freight!

Dear Mama, thank you very much for straightening up my room. I hope it did not exhaust you too much. Today I received the request from Christel[5] to look around for a maid for her. This will not be so easy.

To date there has been no word regarding the sons and grandsons of this household. Mrs. von Kleist's brother[6] in Kieckow has been killed in the war. Her other brother had died in the war with Poland. Needless to say, the war reports are being followed with the greatest interest, and some people are even beginning to be impatient that it is not yet all finished. That is, of course, extremely childish. Nevertheless, the people here have the

187

[3.] His parents did then vacation at Schloß Rosenhöh near Polzin in autumn 1941.

[1.] *NL*, A 59,1 (16); handwritten postcard; previously published in *GS* 6:539–40.
[2.] This should actually read "July."
[3.] This was in preparation for his second trip to Switzerland.
[4.] Ursula Schleicher.
[5.] Christine von Dohnanyi.
[6.] Gerhart von Diest, who died on the eastern front.

impression from everything they hear that the resistance is particularly tenacious.—Naturally, that disturbs them.

Looking forward to seeing you at the end of next week, if that suits you. With my best wishes,

Your grateful Dietrich

116. Wilhelm Jannasch to the Executive Committee of the Pastors' Emergency League[1]

To the Members of the Executive Committee:

On April 24, 1941, an application for salary compensation payment for Pastor Licentiate Bonhoeffer was presented to the Executive Committee. At that time, the Executive Committee came to the following resolution:

"Until 1933, Pastor Bonhoeffer was an assistant lecturer and as such received no fixed salary. *His entire situation is a concern of the Confessing Church—not of the Emergency League.*"

Pastor Scharf is now requesting that the Executive Committee examine the question once again. He mentions the following points for consideration of this matter:

Pastor Bonhoeffer has been a member since the founding assembly. He asserts that   188
he paid his dues in the initial period through Pastor Hildebrandt. (These dues payments have never been recorded as such with us in the administrative office. Perhaps he did not indicate the purpose of the money clearly enough or this indication was lost.)

Because of the missing dues payments in the meantime, and particularly to establish that this is a case of salary loss for which the Emergency League is responsible, Pastor Scharf asserts the following:

1. His contributions in Pomerania ceased because as the director of a seminary he received no salary of his own but rather lived with his seminarians from a monastic-style common purse. Most likely it is for this reason that the Pomeranian administrative office never reminded him to pay. He performed valuable services for the Confessing Church in Pomerania and always stood within the association of pastors of the Emergency League.

2. He has lost his ecclesial office through police intervention.

3. It is now impossible for him to receive a new position through the Confessing Church, because he has been banned from writing and speaking, has been forbidden to go to Berlin and Brandenburg, and is required to make each current place of residence known to the Gestapo. He is without ecclesial position and without any salary.

[1.] Evangelisches Zentralarchiv, Berlin, Bestand 50/700, page 199; typewritten letter. On the circumstances, see *DB-ER*, 701.

I have yet to attempt to ascertain the extent of the salary loss that Pastor Bonhoeffer has suffered. Pastor Scharf is in any case of the opinion that Pastor Bonhoeffer lost his office because of his support of the Confessing Church, making this a clear case for the Emergency League. Back payment of the dues could also be considered. In any case, Pastor Bonhoeffer for his part would be glad to pay the back dues.[2]

Berlin, July 30, 1941

[W. Jannasch]

17:130   **116a. From Paul Lehmann**[1]

1. For Dietrich Bonhoeffer

August 2, 1941

This is the beginning of August, and I have wanted since the end of February to set down my thoughts about the times through which we are passing. But the rapidly shifting events have a way of combining with the unexpected tasks of daily life to leave one with insufficient leisure and composure to formulate impressions that ought not to go unexpressed. Perhaps the most remote and yet unmistakable sign that we too are affected by the war[2] is the fact that letters abroad, even air mail, take more than four weeks. Who knows, therefore, when these thoughts will be read, or whether they will be related at all to this world, if they should happen to be read.

Another sign of our nearer participation in the life of a world at war is the historic departure from long established policy in the adoption of universal military training.[3]

[2.] On the further development of this matter, see Bonhoeffer's letter of November 23, 1941, to Wilhelm Jannasch, 1/138. The April 22, 1942, minutes of the Executive Committee read as follows: "It was determined that the Confessing Church—and not the Emergency League—is responsible for Pastor Bonhoeffer. The back payment made to him for the year 1941 was subsequently approved as a onetime payment. Since his loss of salary did not result from its being cut off by the church authorities, no ongoing loan can be made to him; rather, he is henceforth to be paid by the Confessing Church office, which has been his employer for some time."

[1.] Princeton Theological Seminary Library, Paul Lehmann papers; carbon copy of a typewritten manuscript written in English from Maine. First published in *DBW* 17:130–37. This text is the primary portion of a letter directed to Erwin Sutz on August 4, 1941; cf. Bonhoeffer's letter of September 20, 1941, 1/126a. That this letter was addressed to Sutz in response to Bonhoeffer's letter of February 28, 1941 (see 1/92a) can be clearly deduced from its correspondence to the requests expressed there. Page numbers in the margin refer to *DBW* 17.

[2.] In the United States the atmosphere was highly charged following Hitler's attack on the Soviet Union in June 1941.

[3.] Mandatory service in the United States armed forces, having first been introduced in 1863 during the Civil War and then again in 1917 during World War I, was

I shall never forget the day I went to register. It seems to me that this was a sign that we in America had come to the end of one way of life and were starting out upon another and uncertain one. Most of us, of course, could at first think only of the inconvenience of having to take a year out from civil life for military training and we were secretly troubled whether it would stop with a year. But the deeper meaning of this new order for us in America is that our democracy is not an isolationist democracy. If constitutional government survives here it will be because it survives in Europe and Asia. It was the passage of the conscription act[4] which brought home to this country the fact of our interdependence with the destinies of all men round the world. And this was a good thing.

The conscription act has done another thing for me. It has deepened and made concrete my sense of civic responsibility on a national scale. I think it is largely true of my generation that we were divided between jingoists and internationalists, i.e., between those whose nationalism was fanatic and intolerable and those who had no national feeling at all. I have not realized until now how much this lack of national feeling means that one's life and thoughts are suspended in mid-air. They have no solid roots and they are not knit into the fabric of history. I do not disguise the danger that this innocent sense of duty to one's country can be corrupted and become chauvinistic. But the alternative is not the complete absence of the sense for the meaning of the state. Many of us see this more clearly now that all national existence is threatened with chaos. I hope we have not awakened too late.

The conscription act has deepened and made 17:131

It is interesting to me to discover in this connection how much of my pacifism and socialism have been predicated upon this lack of appreciation of the ideal and the real function of government in the life of an individual. We believed too completely that bad government was the obstacle to the realization of our dreams and did not see clearly enough that the political problem is the perennial expression of the struggle between chaos and order in sinful human existence. In so far as our pacifism and socialism were directed at political and economic injustice at home, they were right. They are still right. But because they left out of account the international problem they became alternatively romantic and doctrinaire. The best proof of this is the current alignment of the socialist party with the republican party in opposition to the President's foreign policy. It is difficult to tell which is in a more pitiable state. The socialist party is virtually impotent, whereas the Republicans have been greatly embarrassed by Mr. Wilkie's ardent support of the President.[5] They must now look forward to the

---

employed in peacetime for the first time in September 1940 through the passage of the Selective Service Training Act (*Concise Columbia Encyclopedia,* 260).

[4.] The September 1940 Selective Service Training Act.

[5.] Wendell Willkie, who had run unsuccessfully as the Republican presidential candidate against Roosevelt in 1940, had more recently begun to support Roosevelt's foreign policy.

next campaign at which time they will have either to repudiate Mr. Willkie and be frankly oppositionist or lose the campaign from the start because they have no issue. Of course, they might take up a man like Lindbergh.[6] But then, that would be too much like Quisling.[7] Events would have to move terribly fast for that to become a political reality by 1944.

17:132

Politically we face now what seem to me to be the two most immediately pressing questions. One is the question whether the Western hemisphere should surrender Europe to the Nazi tyranny and prepare to fight its future out alone or whether we on this side of the Atlantic should make common cause with every effort to restrain the chaos of the new barbarism. There is still considerable appeasement sentiment in the country. But I think that on the whole the country will support the government in its determination to aid Britain[8] until the issue on the continent has been settled and the safety of the islands is assured. There is no doubt in my mind that in the end we should be ready to send even an expeditionary force. I say this even though I know very well that the country would not be ready for such a bold act tomorrow or even this year. The main direction of our politics is and will remain away from appeasement. Lindbergh is losing rather than gaining popular support. The attack on Russia has left him too obviously on the side of the attackers and has robbed him of all support except of the incorrigeable peace-at-any-price idealists and the behind-the-scenes-big-business fascists. The other question is whether we in the United States shall be able to undertake this war effort with sufficient protection of the rights of labor and minorities or whether we shall submerge these vital democratic elements beneath the all absorbing international problem. There are some encouraging signs that we shall succeed in a measure in preserving democratic forms. The President has skillfully avoided any sharply anti-labor policies and has his finger on the more fundamental danger to our national life from profiteers. He wants to regulate prices, and, at the moment at any rate, not wages. This is, in my judgement a sound step in the direction of social reconstruction. The attack on Russia has also helped here. Dissident elements who had taken the Moscow line after the pact of 1939[9] were making nuisance attempts upon our industrial war effort. These are now dying down if not disappearing altogether. The labor movement itself while not being as developed politically as

---

[6.] Charles Lindbergh was adulated by the Germans, particularly Göring, who was also the German minister of aviation. [Lindbergh was also known for his pro-Nazi sympathies. It is ironic that in the following month, on September 16, 1941, Lindberg was to make his infamous speech in Des Moines, Iowa, blaming the Jews for pushing the United States toward war. See Dinnerstein, *Anti-Semitism in America,* 129–30.—MB]

[7.] Vidkun Quisling was the leader of the Norwegian Nazi Party; his name became a synonym for collaboration and betrayal.

[8.] Here Lehmann is placing himself solidly behind President Roosevelt and the Lend-Lease Act passed in the spring of 1941, the goal of which was to support England in the war.

[9.] This refers to the German-Soviet nonaggression pact of August 27, 1939.

the British movement is showing signs of growth in statesmanship. This was evident recently when the head of the labor movement endorsed the President's occupation of a factory because labor's own prerogatives had been violated by outside influences. 17:133

I go into this little review of what is happening here because it bears directly upon my view of the future course of things. Everything depends, in my judgement, upon a British victory. But that victory cannot come too soon. If it did, then we should have a return to capitalist imperialism for economic power would remain where it has been for too many decades already. The trend at the moment in Britain is definitely toward a reconstructed social economy. The strain of the war is levelling the tremendous distance between rich and poor and the labor movement is exercising an increasing influence upon public policy. The most significant fact for the future in my judgement is that it is this rising influence of labor and the common sense of the British people—and not British toryism—which have insisted upon the continuance of the war and indeed upon the resistance which brought the war about in the first place. If the possibilities of social reconstruction that lie here can be encouraged and developed, then I see the direction of the future course of things. Some kind of socialized economy is inescapable and indispensable. The nucleus for it is there. If this tiny germ of hope cannot be brought to birth, then frankly, I think the future is very dark indeed.

Again the uncertain quantity is Russia. It is unlikely, I think, that the course of her domestic development can be left unchanged by the war. She is fighting now by the strength of the slavic love of the fatherland and not by the power of Stalinism. Is there a possibility here of a new understanding between the Russian and the British labor movement? Or will the result of the present battle be the occasion for the bolshevist triumph over Europe? It is too early yet to say. But if the latter happens, then, the only satisfaction that can come to us for our support of Britain is that we acted in terms of our responsibility to restrain tyranny. But God in his judgement has called us to endure the terror of yet another tyranny. From this distance, at any rate, the war on Russia seems to be the first major Nazi military mistake. It has outlined real possibilities of a Nazi defeat. Though no one could wish to predict the end of the war.

So much for the political aspect of things. What about the Church? In England, the Malvern conference[10] under the leadership of the Archbishop of York is a most heartening sign. This group has come out frankly for a socialized economy and for a peace which shall not in any way be vindictive but genuinely reconstructive. On this side of the Atlantic, I can say that I attended in early June the Western Hemisphere Ecumenical 17:134

[10.] [This refers to the Anglican conference at Malvern College, January 7–10, 1941, convened by William Temple, then archbishop of York, "to consider in the light of the Christian faith the crisis confronting civilization" (*Oxford Dictionary of the Christian Church*, 862). The resolutions of the conference were published in *Malvern 1941*.—MB] The Malvern document offered a ten-point peace plan "that included the Five Peace Points enunciated by the Pope in his Christmas address of 1939" (von Klemperer, *German Resistance*, 294). See also 1/94.

conference at Toronto.[11] It was heartening there to hear a resolution in support of the Malvern conference; to hear from Canadians and Americans the firm desire and resolve that there shall be no hatred of the German people and that the Churches shall continue to be places of refuge for all afflicted souls, where even enemies may meet and where prayers shall be said for enemies; and to note that the Churches, in marked contrast to the last war, were not being used as arms of the military or as recruiting stations. I think too that at Toronto the American delegates saw more clearly than before that the issue of participation or non-participation in the war threatened to divide the American Church rather hopelessly. And the[y] resolved there that this division should not occur. It will be easier for both groups, I think, to keep the unity of the household of faith.

Perhaps it is not too much to say, that the most important religious fact of this time is the ecumenical spirit in the Church. This spirit is doing two things: 1) keeping Christians sensitive to the fact that there is one Lord; 2) keeping Christians sensitive to the fact that all particular divisions between men—nation, and war, and hatred, and race—are transcended by the unity of the household of faith. Of course, I am troubled by the problem of the unity of faith. There is still too much liberalism in theology over here. I get very discouraged at times because there seems to be no way of getting across the barriers which spring from divergent presuppositions. One is either silent or talking past one another. And yet there are growing signs of understanding, particularly among students. I am encouraged too as I go about preaching how much people sense that the preaching of the last decades has no power[12] and how eager they are for the gospel of God's judgement and forgiveness. It is not at all unlikely that the war will deepen the understanding for this gospel.

17:135

So you see, I find it possible to continue to work. Sometimes the horizon of the future seems bright with hope, at other times, very dark. But the direction is clear and the resources are clear. We must have a world of political and economic democracy, i.e., one in which the goods of life are enjoyed by all the people, in which the basic securities—employment, old age, health—are provided, in which all nations shall have

---

[11.] [This refers to the North American Ecumenical Conference in Toronto, June 3–5, 1941. Its theme was the significance of the church for the present. In practical terms, however, it had to do with maintaining the unity of the churches in light of the diverse views on the war and in particular with American participation in the war. A further theme was the relationship of the German and Japanese churches to their governments; for instance, participants debated the question "whether the church in Germany, for example, has so far capitulated to the demands of the nazi regime as to sacrifice its unity with the church universal." A report appeared in the June 18, 1941, issue of the *Christian Century*, 798–800.—MB].

[12.] Cf. Bonhoeffer's report on his educational stay in New York in 1930–31, particularly the section titled "Church and Preaching" (*DBW* 10:271–77) and the essay "Protestantism without Reformation" (*DBW* 15, especially 455–60).

access to the resources of the earth.[13] That world can only be nourished and motivated by the Christian Church because its gospel of redemption and of responsibility
is alone capable of inspiring and sustaining that world. My daily prayer is for all those
who suffer and labor for the coming of that world, that that world may come in God's
good time and pleasure, and that I may be faithful in whatsoever suffering and agony
may yet befall me and all the children of men. 2 Cor. 3:2-11.

You are always in our prayers, in our thoughts, and in our hearts.

2. To Erwin Sutz

August 4, 1941

Dear Erwin;

[...] One of these days you will get a copy of my book.[14] It appeared a year ago in
April under the title "Forgiveness: Decisive Issue in Protestant Thought." The reviews
have been on the whole sympathetic but it is by no means a "best seller." It was, however, a great relief to have this work done. You know that I was working on it already
in Zuerich so that the time did drag out considerably. Of course, I had meanwhile also
to teach. In this connection, we have had a rather disappointing experience. Last year
in May, a call came to teach in Eden Seminary. Do you remember it? The Swiss one
parted company there with the French one and the German and the uncertain Olds-
mobile.[15] Well, we have followed the Swiss one too. After one year, we have parted   17:136
company with Eden Seminary and are going to teach for the next few years at *Wellesley
College, Wellesley, Massachusetts* I underline this not because it is particularly important
but in order that you may not forget our address.

My going to Eden was attended by a great deal of resentment in the faculty. This
resentment was both personal and theological. And while I must say that our life at
Eden this year was not marked by any personal disagreements, there was always an
undercurrent of uneasiness. I discovered then, in addition to this, that Eden is not
really a theological Seminary. It is not, that is, interested in theological scholarship and a
cultured ministry. It is a leadership training school, very good, perhaps, for lay workers,
but very bad for training ministers.[16] Then, in June this year, for the second time an

---

[13.] Cf. the passage from Roosevelt's New Year's speech on January 6, 1941; see
1/126a, ed. note 2.

[14.] This refers to Lehmann's dissertation; cf. Bonhoeffer's letter to Lehmann on
November 5, 1931 (*DBW* 17, 11/1/16a, ed. note 6).

[15.] This alludes to Bonhoeffer's trip to Mexico with Jean Lasserre in May and June
1931. Erwin Sutz had left the other two in St. Louis; see *DB-ER,* 152.

[16.] Eden Seminary, located near St. Louis, was a theological seminary for pastors of
the German Evangelical Synod of North America [and is now affiliated with the United
Church of Christ—MB]. This synod had taken over the confessional foundations of the

invitation came to teach in Wellesley. This is a girls' school and a college. I do not like either of these facts very much. But there is a very good department of Bible there and they have invited me because they want the kind of thoughts which I have emphasized there. The head of the department has collaborated with Erminie Huntress (do you remember her, that very strange, tomb-like girl at Union?) in translating Bultmann's *Jesus*.[17] Besides, the eastern seaboard is a much more stimulating place for theological development than the Mississippi river. So, although I regret very much that I shall

17:137   have to defer theological teaching, I am counting on the sympathetic environment and the leisure to enable me to study and work at theology and perhaps even to write some more. *Dei providentia et hominum confusione*,[18] we have decided to try it.

So you have seen Dietrich?[19] Did you ever get our card from New York?[20] It was good news to me that he is still at work and I am terribly sorry that I could not send the statement before now. Will you read it and dispose of it as you think best? You see, my theological lectures this year took so much of my time that I could not get sufficient hours together to write what I wanted to send to you. And then, as I have said, the mail takes such a long time. [...]

Marion joins me in ever[y] affectionate greeting and regard,

[Paul]

Old Prussian Union but was itself for all practical purposes nonconfessional. "The synod, like most frontier faiths, cared less about the fine points of dogmatic theology than about inner spirituality and practical results: conversions made, churches raised, welfare structures built" (Fox, *Reinhold Niebuhr,* 14). "Paul's statement... seems to me to be an accurate and restrained account from his viewpoint. He was after all an old 'Evangelical,' having a presidential father at Elmhurst (Timothy), where he taught after Union Graduate work from 1933–40.... But in spite of all that German-oriented semi-Barthianism, Lehmann's Eden teaching was stormy. My recollection from conversation... is that Lehmann was too successful as a young Eden teacher, having the students behind him in a kind of 'throw out the conservatives' youth movement which is normally not too successful in educational institutions.... I would observe that Eden has difficulty with systematic theology professors right up to date and Reinhold Niebuhr's repeated statements, that he was not a theologian, is part of that same Eden syndrome [Niebuhr had studied there himself].... Perhaps he [Lehmann] might have been able to make Eden a theological seminary, if he had been given a chance" (statement by Lowell H. Zuck, transmitted to the German editors of *DBW* 17 by Clifford Green on November 16, 1998).

[17.] Rudolf Bultmann, *Jesus.*

[18.] "By means of God's providence and human confusion."

[19.] See Bonhoeffer's mention of this meeting in his letter on February 28, 1941, 1/92a.

[20.] See *DBW* 15:215.

117. From Herbert Jehle[1]

My dear Dietrich,

Many warm greetings and best wishes from my trip, which will probably also lead me to Kalbfleisch, whom I met in Amsterdam in 1939.[2] It is a great joy to me that, thanks to the efforts of dear friends,[3] I shall be able to do scholarly work again in the near future (in astronomy or mathematics). It was a very great joy to hear from you indirectly,[4] and I hope that we shall see each other again at some point. It is very beautiful here in Seville and Cádiz; the cathedral and Alcazar[5] are astonishingly beautiful. I often think of you all; please give my warm greetings to your dear parents and siblings and to all our colleagues. God preserve all of you!

Your faithful Herbert

[1.] *NL*, C 25; handwritten picture postcard: Seville, Jesus del Gran poder. Sender: "Jehle H., Pension Armal, Fred Sánchez Bedoya 33, Seville." Postmark: "Seville 6 Ago 41." Address: "Pastor Lic. D. Bonhoeffer, Marienburger Allee 43 Berlin—[crossed out: "Eichkamp"—MB] Heerstraße Alemania." Overprint stamp: "Berlin–Charlottenburg" [handwritten: "9"—MB]. Round stamp: "Checked. Armed Forces High Command"; red postbox stamp: "3218" = number of the inspector responsible for Spain in the Munich office of the censor (information provided by Norbert Kanuupin on April 8, 1988). On the circumstances, see Jean Lasserre's letter of February 8, 1941, to an unknown woman; see 1/73, ed. note 3.

[2.] George Kalbfleisch, a student of Professor Paul Lehmann at Elmhurst College, was a U.S. youth delegate in 1939 to the World Conference of Christian Youth in Amsterdam and on that occasion also visited the collective pastorate at Groß-Schlönwitz. See *DBW* 15:205.

[3.] [Jehle was eventually released from Gurs and emigrated to the United States via Spain. His release was achieved primarily through the efforts of the World Christian Student Federation and the British Quakers, particularly Sir Arthur Eddington (information given to the editors of this English edition by Jehle's widow, Dietlinde Jehle, March 2004). See also Jeanne Merle D'Aubigné's chapters on Gurs in Fabre, *God's Underground*, 58–85, and her account of Jehle's rescue, 71–72.—MB] For a description of a similar journey that Friedrich Forell, a German pastor to refugees, undertook with the help of a complicated arrangement of ecumenical contacts, see Röhm and Thierfelder, "Ein langer Weg," 315–22.

[4.] In any case, Bonhoeffer's efforts in this regard had a certain measure of success, whether through his Geneva connections (see Nils Ehrenström's calendar notes, 1/93, ed. note 6) or thanks to the activities of Consul Schmidhuber (see 1/122, ed. note 9).

[5.] [An alcazar is a castle or fortress of the Spanish Moors. The Alcazar is the castle of the Moorish kings in Seville, but here the alcazars in both Seville and Cadiz are in view.—MB]

190   **118. Rüdiger Schleicher to Paula, Karl, and Dietrich Bonhoeffer**[1]

Tempelburg, August 14, 1941
Villa am See

Dear Parents, dear Dietrich,

If you have perhaps generally viewed the arrival of our letters with somewhat mixed feelings, because there have always been various requests in them, then let it be said at the outset: this letter is purely one of thanks and news. It is intended solely to report on our perfectly happy existence, devoid of requests—well, except for the weather and the war.

First, our most grateful thanks for all your packages; the flashlights, songbooks, HJ belt,[2] and everything else have arrived safely. Since the family is now all here, everything can be fully used; also with our six children in four rooms, we are now "master of our own house," so to speak. We have enough space even with bad weather and rejoice in our presence here. This has been especially true following our extraordinarily beautiful excursion or visit to Klein-Krössin on Tuesday and Wednesday. Ursel and I had stayed overnight and took the train there on Tuesday afternoon; Hans Walter followed on his bicycle on Wednesday morning. Mrs. von Kleist was so very kind; she showed us not only her own home and estate but also Kieckow, where we became acquainted with her son's family, such likable people—that is actually quite an understatement—who despite all the horrifying events[3] manifested a calm that was truly admirable. For me it was in fact the first time to have seen an East Elbian estate, and I can attest sincerely to Dietrich that I was quite taken with even these Pomeranian noble elite types. On the way back we had a four-hour stop in Neu-Stettin, an extremely pretty town, where we went shopping (actually finding shoes made out of leather patches for the children); and that evening we were all home again by 8:30. The children were looking very cheerful and radiant, which, given the excellent cuisine of Klein-Krössin, was no great wonder. And now here too they are still well provisioned, so the decrescendo from that fortissimo back to piano again in Berlin will not be so great. Yet the children also

191   like the marvelous lake so much that indeed on every level the transition has been satisfying.

But now above all, dear Dietrich, I must thank you sincerely for all this. For you were the one who prepared the ground for it; how unfortunate that we did not see you there in Klein-Krössin, where, of course, you are held in high esteem. I am looking forward to

---

[1.] *NL,* A 89 (1); handwritten letter. Bonhoeffer and Eberhard Bethge, along with Dorothea, Christine, and Renate Schleicher, had recently completed a two-week stay in Klein-Krössin.

[2.] *H. J.-Koppel;* this refers to a belt for their son's Hitler Youth uniform.

[3.] The family had received the news only shortly before this that their sons Hans-Friedrich and Jürgen-Christoph von Kleist-Retzow had been killed on the eastern front.

being able to discuss all this with you in person. If I have any general critical observation to make—as a Swabian and Naumannian,[4] of course—it is the question: Where in all this is the independent farmer? How can small farmers improve their lot in life here? In this great agricultural region the real villages in fact are missing; in any case, one would, of course, have to roam through it and get to know it with different eyes, if one simply doesn't want to parrot all one's (pre-)judgments. But that doesn't apply to the people I met here.

Many thanks for your letter and the boat key; we shall see how Hans Walter gets to Schlawe. If we had had it by yesterday, he would have been able to keep right on going. Today we have a marvelous wind and great crashing of waves in the lake, and we are going swimming. Ursel is the only one who will need to spend the day resting.

We wish you all the best, especially at night. Yours most sincerely and gratefully,

Rüdiger

119. Finkenwalde Circular Letter[1]

August 15, 1941

Dear Brother... [2]

Today I must inform you that our brothers Konrad Bojack, F. A. Preuß,[3] Ulrich Nithack, and Gerhard Schulze have been killed on the eastern front. Konrad Bojack was with us in the summer of 1935. He became a pastor in Lyck (East Prussia), where he leaves behind his wife and two small children With the earnestness and joy of his Christianity, his sermons emerging completely from the Word of God, and his love for the church, the ministry, and the congregation, he was a fine witness of Jesus Christ for us all. As a native of Silesia who chose to make his home in East Prussia, he had allowed the questions and needs of the German border region to grow dear to his heart. He proved his love for this new homeland as a faithful pastor

192

[4.] [As a representative of social liberalism and Christian responsibility, Friedrich Naumann was associated with the politics of the ordinary "person on the street"; as a native Swabian, Schleicher was familiar with the concerns of independent farmers.—MB]

[1.] *NL,* A 48,3; carbon copy from Berlin; previously published in *GS* 2:573–78.

[2.] On the copy sent to Werner Koch, the following note was handwritten: "Many thanks for your letter. Today I have just gotten up for the first time following a bout of pneumonia. Thus only this short greeting!" Bonhoeffer became ill at the end of October (see *DBER,* 746). Accordingly, this letter was probably first sent to some people in November 1941. [Bonhoeffer used the singular in the salutation and then added individual names by hand, since circular letters were no longer permitted. In the letter itself Bonhoeffer addresses the brothers in the plural.—MB]

[3.] [The reference is Adolf-Friedrich Preuß.—MB]

of his congregation. He found his mission and his congregation's salvation in the authentic preaching of Jesus Christ. He was killed on June 22 close to the East Prussian border. We grieve the loss of this quiet, honest brother. In this life he trusted in Word and sacrament. Now he may behold that in which he believed.

F. A. Preuß was with us at the same time as Konrad Bojack. He became a pastor in Landsberger Holländer in Neumark, where he leaves behind his wife and two small children. In him we had a brother who was always friendly and joyful, whose faith in Jesus Christ was secure, who attended faithfully to the office entrusted to him even under difficult conditions, and who served his congregation with great love and devotion. Now Christ has called him to his own heavenly congregation.

Ulrich Nithack was with us in the summer of 1938. No one who met him could have failed to experience his radiant happiness and inner confidence, rooted in his faith in Christ. His never-failing readiness to serve other members of the community and his thankfulness for the smallest things brought him the love of all the brothers. His pursuit of a personal life of sanctification through Jesus Christ emerged from a faith that was in the best sense childlike. For him, prayer was at the center. In a certitude that strengthened all of us, he saw his path and calling to be entirely within the Confessing Church, which he loved with all his heart. He gave himself completely to every task assigned to him. With his death some of that light of Jesus Christ, which we are given to glimpse here and there through one another, has gone out for us—but only so as to shine all the more brightly in the eternal sun of Jesus Christ.

Like Ulrich Nithack, Gerhard Schulze was with us in the summer of 1938. He came from a conflict-ridden congregational post in which he represented the concerns of the church bravely and clearly. With his lively, cheerful, winning manner he quickly found friends and community wherever he went. He desired to devote his life completely to the Confessing Church's struggle. God led him in a special way through depths and heights; he was allowed to experience the power of the grace of God in his life more powerfully than others. He wished to proceed in his future ministry from within this experience. His death affects many friends who accompanied him through his life. Yet a life so rich in grace fills us anew with the certainty that the mercy of God has no end.

In addition to these brothers, who through our common work were especially close to us, other brothers have also fallen: Hans-Otto Georgii, the brother of Wolf Georgii, who was with us in the winter of 1937–38 and whom we now particularly wish to remember; Martin Franke of Pomerania; Engelke from Brandenburg; Heyse from Sachsen; Nicolaus from the Rhineland. Some of you will still remember my confirmands Hans-Friedrich von Kleist-Retzow and his brother Jürgen Christoph from Stettin. They have both been killed on the eastern front.[4] His open New Testament was found next to Hans-Friedrich.

They have gone before us on the path that we shall all have to take at some point. In a particularly gracious way, God reminds those of you who are out on the front to remain prepared. And we are kept awake through unceasing thoughts of you. To be sure, God shall call you, and us, only at the hour that God has chosen. Until that hour, which lies in God's hand alone, we shall all be protected even in greatest danger; and from our gratitude for such protection ever new readiness surely arises for the final call.[5]

Who can comprehend how those whom God takes so early are chosen? Does not the early death of young Christians always appear to us as if God were plundering his own best instruments in a time in which they are most needed? Yet the Lord makes no mistakes. Might God need our brothers for some hidden service on our behalf in the heavenly world? We should put an end to our human thoughts, which always wish to know more than they can and cling to that which is certain. Whomever God calls home is someone God has loved. "For their souls were pleasing to the Lord, therefore he took them quickly from the midst of wickedness" (Wisdom of Solomon 3).[6]

We know, of course, that God and the devil are engaged in battle in the world and that the devil also has a say in death. In the face of death we cannot simply speak in some fatalistic way, "God wills it";[7] but we must juxtapose it with the other reality, "God does not will it." Death reveals that the world is not as it should be but that it stands in need of redemption. Christ alone is the conquering of death. Here the sharp antithesis between "God wills it" and "God does not will it" comes to a head and also finds its resolution. God accedes to that which God does not will, and from now on death

194

[4.] See Ruth von Kleist-Retzow's letter of August 24, 1941, to Eberhard Bethge, 1/120.

[5.] [Bonhoeffer's letters to the Finkenwalde members, including those who had become soldiers, are eloquent testimony to his continued sense of pastoral ministry to these young men, even as he himself moved into the resistance. As the German editors of this volume observe in their afterword (see pp. 647, 651, 673), contemporary readers will be struck by some phrases in these letters that seem to ignore the reality of what the German army was actually doing. Bonhoeffer's letters of this period to his students, as well his letters to the families of those who had lost someone in the war, should be understood from the perspective of his ministry, his deep affection for former students, and his grief for friends and colleagues who had died in the war. He was naturally also aware that his circular letters were read by Nazi censors. His criticism of the regime, including its atrocities, was expressed through his resistance.—MB]

[6.] This verse is actually Wisd. of Sol. 4:14.

[7.] Cf. the slogan of the Knights of the Holy Sepulcher in Jerusalem: *Deus lo vult.* Bonhoeffer makes note of this for his *Ethics*; see the "*Zettelnotizen,*" 120.

itself must therefore serve God. From now on, the "God wills it" encompasses even the "God does not will it." God wills the conquering of death through the death of Jesus Christ. Only in the cross and resurrection of Jesus Christ has death been drawn into God's power, and it must now serve God's own aims. It is not some fatalistic surrender but rather a living faith in Jesus Christ, who died and rose for us, that is able to cope profoundly with death.

In life with Jesus Christ, death as a general fate approaching us from without is confronted by death from within, one's own death, the free death of daily dying with Jesus Christ. Those who live with Christ die daily[8] to their own will. Christ in us gives us over to death so that he can live within us. Thus our inner dying grows to meet that death from without. Christians receive their own death in this way, and in this way our physical death very truly becomes not the end but rather the fulfillment of our life with Jesus Christ. Here we enter into community with the One who at his own death was able to say, "It is finished."[9]

Dear brothers, it may be that right now you have little time or inclination for such thoughts. There are times in which everything real is so bewildering and so distressing that any direct word seems to us to destroy the mystery of God, that we wish to speak and listen to others speak of the last things only obliquely. Everything we are able to say about our faith then appears so flat and empty in contrast to the reality we are actually experiencing, behind which we believe is an inexpressible mystery. For you out on the front this is scarcely different than for us at home; all that is spoken is scattered away as if in an instant, and nothing formulated corresponds to reality anymore. Something deeply authentic can reside here, as long as only one word, that is to say, the name of Jesus Christ, is not extinguished in us. This name abides as a word, the Word, around which all our words revolve. In this Word alone lies clarity and power. "When darkness round me gathers, Thy name and cross, still bright, Deep in my heart are sparkling, Like stars in blackest night."[10]

Let me close with a request. I know that some of you both on the front and at home are plagued with thoughts about your professional future.[11]

[8.] Cf. 1 Cor. 15:31, "I die every day!" This finds many echoes in *DBWE* 4; see the index to biblical passages in that volume.

[9.] John 19:30. Bonhoeffer had intended to give a talk on death in East Prussia in July 1940; see 1/10, ed. note 35, and 1/15, ed. note 27.

[10.] This is a citation of verse 3 of "Farewell I Gladly Bid Thee" (*Lutheran Hymnal*, no. 407 ["Valet will ich dir geben" (*Evangelisches Gesangbuch für Brandenburg und Pommern*, 312, 3; *Evangelisches Kirchengesangbuch*, 318, 3) —MB]).

[11.] The consistories were offering Confessing Church pastors serving on the front a "legal" position with reduced requirements or even none at all.

Lay these thoughts to rest for a while. Up to this point you have been allowed to provide a good witness to our church, that church for which our brothers are also suffering. Let us not obscure anything at this point. We need this little bit of earthly light, and we will come to need it even more. Who could possibly overlook that with this war we have been given a decisive break, which we are truly not able to reconcile with our thoughts. Thus let us wait in peace.

Every letter and sign of life from you, of course, gives me and many others with me heartfelt joy. I had received greetings from Brother Bojack and Brother Nithack immediately before their deployment, for which I am especially grateful today. Please let me know right away of any changes in your address. So often things come back as undeliverable —a book or a letter. That always gives me sorrow because then one more thread has been ripped away. At that point it is generally very difficult to get the correct address again.

I commend all of you to the One who can protect you day and night, who can give you power in your service, who will lead you and us all into his kingdom.

Greetings from your faithful
D. B.

120. Ruth von Kleist-Retzow to Eberhard Bethge[1]

196

Klein-Krössin, August 24, 1941

My very dear Eberhard,

Now your birthday is at hand, and I do not know whether my greeting will still reach you before the day is over. You will know even without words that my thoughts will seek you out with heartfelt love. I am also grateful from my heart for your friendship. May God reward you for it and preserve and protect your future life, which stretches before you in such impenetrable darkness. Dietrich wrote so beautifully and fittingly to the brothers.[2] It is surely very, very important that he keep doing this, for he has the gift of finding the right words for things one does not say every day. In such a difficult time it seems that expressions of comfort have become so hackneyed and must continue to be reborn if they are not to have a banal effect. Perhaps that is now D.'s only task. I worry about him somewhat at times, for to be without a profession in that way cannot be good. You have it better in that you are employed.

I am truly living as if in a dreamworld. The impact of this most recently experienced reality is still rather inconceivable.[3] We are living between heaven and earth.

[1.] Private papers of Eberhard Bethge; handwritten letter, partially published in *GS* 2: 408–9.

[2.] See the Finkenwalde circular letter, 1/119.

[3.] [She is referring to the deaths of two grandsons on the front.—MB]

And almost daily we hear of those who are newly fallen. Every piece of news rips the wound open again and places us once more before the questions Dietrich outlines in that letter: war, death, future. A new sense of being part of these horrible events has awakened in me. I understand that, at the news of Konstantin's[4] withdrawal, brought about by my nephew Tresckow,[5] my son telegraphed to Tresckow that he did not concur with this decision. Somehow one doesn't want to be excluded from the inexorable fate and guilt that has come upon us. And this is also, if I may say so, what makes me uncertain for the first time concerning your path and Dietrich's during these times. Do we not belong within this entanglement, and must we not employ our spiritual energies—without considering the cost—at the very places where the battle is fought? Would we not proceed on our way more confident of our goal if we did not evade this final contact? I do not know if you can understand what I am feeling. D. would most likely dismiss this thought entirely. It has probably taken root in me through the countless sympathy letters from our boys' friends and superiors and above all through their death,[6] with which I must wrestle. When I hear how bravely our children died, I tell myself that it was not only spiritual power that made this possible for them but also an instinct that drove them to risk their lives. Oh, I know we dare not then derive some new law from this, that the way things appear to me now must be how it is. In your case I am counting on your trust in me, and that you will not attach too much importance to my words.[7]

197

Something in me is still quite torn. When our news speaks of the "unimaginable losses" that we are inflicting on the enemies, I experience this like a knife to my soul.

We still have no news of Konstantin. On August 1 we telegraphed him of the death and burial of Hans-Friedrich. On the seventh the same thing for Jürgen Christoph. In the meantime the withdrawal action has taken place. On the seventeenth, Fabian[8] wrote that my son's telegraphed objection (which took five days to reach the army group) had arrived too late. Konstantin was already marching back. Since then we have been waiting daily for some sign of life from him. Oh, these days life itself consists almost

---

[4.] Konstantin von Kleist-Retzow, son of Hans-Jürgen von Kleist-Retzow in Kieckow.

[5.] Major General Henning von Tresckow, head of the general staff of the Center Army Group, which included one of the most active cells within the military resistance during these years. [The Center Army Group was at the front in Russia between the northern and southern army groups.—MB]

[6.] She is referring to the deaths of her grandsons Hans-Friedrich and Jürgen Christoph von Kleist-Retzow.

[7.] Two days later she added the following sentences: "My conscience plagues me that I expressed doubt about your path. How am I to know what is binding for you! Forgive me if I have prematurely expressed an opinion that essentially was not even an opinion but a feeling. Since then it has become questionable again even to me" (private papers of Eberhard Bethge, *GS* 2:409).

[8.] Fabian von Schlabrendorff, who in 1941 was first lieutenant (reserve) on the staff of Brigadier General von Tresckow, was married to one of her granddaughters, Luitgarde von Bismarck.

solely of waiting. I can almost imagine that he did not wish to leave that area without looking for the graves of his brothers. In that case it could be a long time before he comes. [...]

121. To Eberhard Bethge[1]   198

August 26, 1941

Dear Eberhard,

Now it looks as if I shall travel on from here on your birthday.[2] Things have been delayed a bit, since my express trunk has only just arrived (!). But now I shall have all that much more time and leisure to think of you on August 28, 1941. I shall think of so many lovely trips together, especially 1936[3] and 1939,[4] of horizons we discovered together in connection with these trips, of European hopes and tasks, of the mission of the church in the future—and all of this in the hope that you and I and many, many others who are of the same mind, that all of us may one day work together toward this future. What could I wish you for this new year but that you may be able to experience this, that you be able to work as circumstances allow, and that in your own personal life you can also make a plan for the future that at present is still denied to us? And I see how these wishes for you are, at the same time, my own wishes. It is impossible to imagine how it shall be a year from now. But I am very confident.

Perhaps at times we run the risk of forgetting, above and beyond these hopes, the One who alone can bring it to pass and who can also follow entirely different paths. Perhaps recently we have prayed too little. Then may God forgive us this and lead us back into prayer.

I have had good, long conversations with M.,[5] who sends his warm greetings and thinks very highly of you; among other things, we discussed the question of Protestant monasteries and orders. Fr. Johannes also asked often about you and sends his greetings. It was a very lovely reunion up there. Because of the trunk I was not able to go to Metten after all. I shall do it on the way back. Let Reimer give you the honey that he promised me and keep it entirely for yourself. The Dohnanyis received some from here. (If possible, I might want some of it.) By the way, Hans[6] also told me that he would   199

[1.] *NL*, A 59,2 (41); handwritten letter from Munich; previously published in *GS* 2: 411–12.

[2.] This refers to his second trip to Switzerland.

[3.] This refers to a trip to Switzerland and Italy.

[4.] In March and April 1939 they were in England.

[5.] Josef Müller.

[6.] Hans von Dohnanyi.

discuss your situation with a Mr. Olbricht in case of a recurrence of the problems from January of this year and April of last year.[7] This is only in case it again becomes urgent. I hope this will not happen.

I shall write once more before my trip. Have a wonderful birthday celebration! I wish I could be there! Greetings to your mother.

God preserve you in the new year.

Affectionately, Your faithful Dietrich

122. To Eberhard Bethge[1]

August 28, 1941

Dear Eberhard,

The evening of your birthday gives me the peace and quiet to write you once more before traveling further. I was almost about to go to the movies in your honor, but—as is usual—I am once again choosing a peaceful conversation with you over the dubious pleasures of film (although *The Case of the Holm Murder* does sound very promising!). So, if the weather is as nice for you as it was here, you will be celebrating your birthday together somewhere on the Havel. That gives me great joy. I have thought of you a great deal today. This morning I was greatly pleased by the beautiful watchword.[2] It

---

[7.] General Friedrich Olbricht, who after March 1940 was chief of the General Armed Forces Office and commander in chief of the reserve army, was involved in the plans for a military coup d'état.

[1.] *NL*, A 59,2 (42); handwritten letter from Munich; previously published in slightly abridged form in *GS* 2:412–14.

[2.] The watchword, or *Losung*, for August 28, 1941, was Ezek. 34:11: "For thus says the Lord God: I myself will search for my sheep, and will seek them out." The New Testament interpretative verse, or *Lehrtext*, was John 10:11: "I am the good shepherd. The good shepherd lays down his life for the sheep." [This watchword and New Testament interpretative verse were part of the *Daily Texts*, produced by the Moravian Church. Currently the *Daily Texts* are published in approximately forty languages and distributed worldwide. The basic format includes a daily Old Testament verse or watchword, chosen by lot from a specific collection of two thousand verses, and a New Testament interpretative verse, chosen to match the theme of the Old Testament watchword. The beginnings of the *Daily Texts* can be traced back to Nicolaus Ludwig Count von Zinzendorf, who provided a refuge known as Herrnhut for those fleeing religious persecution in Bohemia and Moravia. On May 3, 1728, Pastor Zinzendorf offered his congregation their first watchword. His intention was to provide a verse "new every morning" that would accompany a person through the day. His first compilation of the *Daily Texts* included 365 Old Testament verses. Eventually a New Testament verse was added for each day. Today a team of people representing the Moravian Church meets to select the texts for a complete year (*Daily Texts 2005*, Mt. Carmel Ministries edition, 236–37).—MB]

directs our gaze toward the future of the church, toward that which Christ has done for us, and finally also toward our own ministry. If we are to be "shepherds" of the congregation in the way Christ was, then that says significantly more than that we are to be preachers. All the terms for ministry in the New Testament (ἀπόστολος, διδάσκαλος, προφήτης, ποιμήν)[3] are origi- 200
nally terms for the ministry of Christ; they are used by Christ himself. Also the office of ministry assumes a likeness of form with Christ.[4] This is the high dignity of the ministry. How good it is to be reminded of this again. People need shepherds, Christ was the shepherd; like him and through him, we are to be shepherds for the people.[5] I myself am grateful to have rediscovered this passage. If only the ban that now hinders us in the free exercise of this ministry would soon be lifted; if only our thoughts could again belong undividedly to this work! By the way, wasn't the reading for the twenty-seventh[6] also beautiful? So I hope that throughout this year you will have enough from your readings!

This morning I still had to make travel preparations. At noon I ate a festive meal in your honor. By the way, this miserable guest-house feeding, which has sunk to new lows even here, has again made me aware of how dreadful you have it in Berlin. You must now make intentional use of Reimer. You can promise him coffee, perhaps even bring some along to him! He will be very happy about that! If anything should come of the side of bacon from Kieckow, I would also like to request a piece of it. Please tell Klaus[7] that when it arrives. Did you receive all the cards?[8] Please make full use of them. If you don't have them, please write to Friedrichsbrunn and ask there. How dull the good food in Switzerland will be for me, all alone. This noon Per.[9] called from Salzburg just to say good-bye; he also wanted to forward a bit of information to his uncle.

[3.] "Apostle," "teacher," "prophet," "shepherd."

[4.] On this point, see *DBWE* 6:93–96.

[5.] In the lecture he gave at Finkenwalde, "The Visible Church in the New Testament," in the section titled "The Sphere of Offices and Gifts" (*DBW* 14:452–60), Bonhoeffer only touched on the office of the shepherd; in his book *Discipleship*, under the "Office of Shepherd," his own thematic index directs the reader to *DBWE* 4:184–85.

[6.] The Old Testament reading for August 27, 1941, was Jer. 23:35: "Thus shall you say to one another, among yourselves, 'What has the LORD answered?' or 'What has the LORD spoken?'" The New Testament reading was Col. 4:2: "Devote yourselves to prayer, keeping alert in it with thanksgiving."

[7.] Klaus Bonhoeffer.

[8.] [Bonhoeffer is referring to the wartime ration cards that were needed to buy food. Bonhoeffer had sent his ration cards to Bethge, since he did not need them in Switzerland.—MB]

[9.] This refers to Friedrich Justus Perels, whose uncle Leopold Perels was being held in the Gurs concentration camp in southern France. Because Gurs was not under direct

201   By the way, I think that you really should go back to learning English. Who knows how you might yet need it?[10]

Have you spoken with Klaus regarding Mrs. Ebeling?[11] Please do so, so that it not be forgotten!! Does Renate[12] have her fountain pen? Have you paid the check to Limburg?

The news of Staude deeply disturbed me.[13] It is truly quite dreadful. When you write to his mother, please include a greeting from me and say that I am traveling and cannot write at this time myself.

I wish all of you, also Christoph,[14] all the best. Greet him and Gerhard[15] warmly! I shall make an effort not to worry when I hear of attacks on Berlin. At least be careful! Now farewell, dear Eberhard, I shall be back on September 25 or 26 at the latest.[16] I shall bring everyone your greetings! God preserve you!

Most affectionately, your faithful Dietrich

Practice, and find something new and lovely for the flute!
Greetings to your mother!

German control, ecumenical officials in Geneva and their contacts were able to visit the camp and (like Consul Schmidhuber) offer various forms of assistance. See Jean Lasserre's February 8, 1941, letter to an unknown woman, 1/73, ed. note 3; and Schreiber, *Friedrich Justus Perels*, 174–75.

[10.] This is likely a reference to the period following the coup.

[11.] According to Otto Dudzus, Gerhard Ebeling vaguely recalls that this reference concerned attempts to make it possible for his Swiss wife to visit her relations.

[12.] Renate Schleicher.

[13.] This refers to Joachim Staude, who was missing in action on the eastern front in the summer of 1941.

[14.] Christoph Bethge.

[15.] Gerhard Vibrans.

[16.] This refers to his return from his second trip to Switzerland.

G. Second Trip to
Switzerland.
August 29–September 26, 1941

123. Nils Ehrenström: Calendar Notes, September 3–10, 1941[1]

[September]

3. 20–23.30[2] Bonhoeffer at NE[3] home: on the whole German situation. Amazing news: the opposition plans to get rid of Hitler and the Nazi regime are getting increasingly crystallised.
4. morning. Bonhoeffer, VH,[4] NE discussing the theol. problems of "The Word of the Church for the World."[5] Afternoon. Group at V. H.'s to meet with Bonhoeffer on the German and on the general ec.[6] situation: Henriod, Courvoisier, de Saussure,[7] Guillon, etc.
5. Bonhoeffer leaves for Freudenberg's vacation place.[8] While here, he has again written memos to be forwarded by V. H. to Bell, Paton, etc.[9]

[1.] *NL*, A 65,14; typewritten notes; in original English, including errors; previously published in *GS* 6:541. On the circumstances, see *DB-ER*, 734–45, and Boyens, *Kirchenkampf und Ökumene*, vol. 2, *1939–1945*, 174ff.

[2.] [8:00–11:30 p.m.–MB]

[3.] Nils Ehrenström.

[4.] Willem Visser 't Hooft.

[5.] Cf. Ehrenström's March 8–15, 1941, calendar notes; see 1/93, ed. note 14.

[6.] [Abbreviation for "ecumenical."—MB]

[7.] Jean de Saussure.

[8.] Lake Champaix is a small mountain lake in Canton Valais, also known as the Matterhorn state; see Adolf Freudenberg's reminiscences in Zimmermann, *I Knew Dietrich Bonhoeffer*, 166–69.

[9.] See Bonhoeffer's "Thoughts on William Paton's Book *The Church and the New Order*" (2/11).

10. Bonhoeffer again in Geneva, before leaving for Basel next day.[10] 19:30–23[11] with us.

203   **124. Willem A. Visser 't Hooft to Hugh Martin**[1]

September 12, 1941

Dear Hugh,

Many thanks for sending Bill Paton's book.[2] It is being eagerly read by all who are in touch with us, not least by those whom it concerns in a very special manner. I enclose a Continental reaction. Will you pass this document on to Bill with the following message:

These comments on your book have been written by me in close collaboration with a friend who came to us and who is a good friend of George Bell. I hope you will circulate them to all who are interested and also send a copy to Pit Van Dusen.[3] You must accept my word for it that all that we say about the next steps and the urgency of the situation is not based upon wishful thinking on our part, but on actual developments in discussion with responsible persons in the country concerned. This is also why I hope that some of these considerations will be brought before responsible people in Britain. I must ask you not to publish the document as it is, but there is no reason why its substance cannot be used in the Christian News Letter. In that case, however, no clue should be given as to the authorship. We should, of course, appreciate some answer to this statement, and, if possible, in the near future.[4]

Very good greetings,

Yours ever

Visser 't Hooft

Enclosure[5]

[10.] Karl Barth's calendar states that Bonhoeffer was with him on August 31 in the morning and on September 19, most likely in the afternoon (communication from Hinrich Stoevesandt).

[11.] [7:30–11:00 p.m.—MB]

[1.] *NL*, A 65,1; typewritten letter; in original English, including errors; previously published in *GS* 1:361. Cf. Boyens, *Kirchenkampf und Ökumene*, vol. 2, *1939–1945*, 175–76, 206–7. At the time Hugh Martin was the head of SCM Press, London.

[2.] Paton, *Church and the New Order*; the first edition appeared in July 1941. On this, see Jackson, *Red Tape and the Gospel*, 253–58.

[3.] This refers to Henry Pitney van Dusen, who since 1936 had been professor of systematic theology at Union Theological Seminary in New York and was also a delegate to ecumenical conferences. Cf. also *GS* 1:355. For his reaction, see Boyens, *Kirchenkampf und Ökumene*, vol. 2, *1939–1945*, 176. See also Visser 't Hooft, *Memoirs*, 153–55, and von Klemperer, *German Resistance against Hitler*, 271–75.

[4.] On the reactions in England, see Boyens, *Kirchenkampf und Ökumene*, vol. 2, *1939–1945*, 207–8, and von Klemperer, *German Resistance*, 274–75.

[5.] See Visser 't Hooft, "The Church and the New Order in Europe" (2/12).

125. To the Leibholz Family[1]   204

19th of September 1941

My dears,

thank you ever so much for your cable which has just reached me. It is such
a joy to know that you are well and that I may expect a letter from you.[2]
My holiday is coming to an end now, but it has been an extremely satisfactory
time with my friends here. I am going home to my work with new strength
and hope. My parents will enjoy hearing from you. I hope to see them on
their return from the mountains in October. What will the winter bring us?
I do not think we shall have to suffer much here in Switzerland. But all our
neighbours will have to go through grave times, I suppose. May God grant
that all these terrible sufferings will make men mature for a better future. I,
personally, do believe it, and I am optimistic enough to hope that peace is
not so far off as it sometimes seems to be. For my part, I hope to find
sufficient time to finish a book on which I have been working for about a
year now.[3] But who may dare to make plans now for a long time? One
must take the day as God gives it. It is a great thing to learn to rely entirely
on God's will and help. I have received Gert's letter[4] and I am thankful to
have it. The more difficult it becomes to keep in close contact with one's
friends abroad the more one feels the inseparable fellowship with them.
Thoughts and prayers must make up for deeds and actual help now.

I shall try to find out if your brother's housekeeper knows anything more
about his death[5] and I shall let you know about it. The graves of your parents are being taken care of, you may be sure. Would you, please, let me
know the address of Annylisa,[6] if you have it? In one of your last letters you
mentioned a nice present for Charles, but since there are many Charles   205
whom I know I am not quite sure to whom you referred.[7] I have just written to George[8] and have asked him with regard of the stipend.[9] Do you

---

[1.] *NL*, A 59,3 (6); typewritten letter from Zurich; in original English, including
errors, property of Sabine Leibholz; previously published in *GS* 6:542–43.

[2.] Letter not extant.

[3.] This refers to his *Ethics*; see *DBWE* 6:458.

[4.] This letter from Gerhard Leibholz is not extant.

[5.] Hans Leibholz, the oldest brother of Gerhard Leibholz, had emigrated to Holland; he committed suicide when the German troops invaded.

[6.] This refers to Anneliese Schnurmann. See Bonhoeffer's letter to her on March
20, 1941, 1/97.

[7.] It is possible that this reference, presumably to Karl Bonhoeffer, was intentionally
made obscure.

[8.] Bishop George K. A. Bell.

[9.] A letter from Bonhoeffer from this period that mentions a stipend has not been

know anything about Francis?[10] Nobody here knows anything about him. I hope you have got the money from Heinz.[11] Perhaps he may be able to send you a little sometime. It is just a very small sign of unchanged fellowship and more symbolic than an actual help. Now let me finish this letter. I shall always be with you and so will my family. Give all my love to my Godchild[12] and to Christiane. God keep your hearts in courage and confidence as he may keep ours.

Much love from
Dietrich

126. To Charlotte von Kirschbaum[1]

September 20, 1941

My dear Miss von Kirschbaum,

I am quite enchanted at the suggestion.[2] That would truly be a wonderful solution exceeding all expectation! Whether Quervain's name is necessary and advisable would still have to be considered.[3] In any case, the relief agency[4] should certainly not be named. We thought that around ten copies could be sent to each of the people whose names you and Vogt have. We would then take care of the distribution. The booklet would then cross the border as an academic work. Certainly we would still be able to find a good title. If the individual essays could somehow take Christmas as their point of departure, it would possibly not even have to be mentioned in the title at all.

I shall still be here through early Wednesday.[5] Do accept my thanks,

206

---

found. Cf. his letter of June 1, 1942, to George K. A. Bell (see 1/175) on his plans to go to the United States.

[10.] This refers to Franz Hildebrandt, who had lived in England since 1937.

[11.] Sabine Leibholz can no longer remember this incident.

[12.] Marianne Leibholz.

[1.] *NL*, Anh. A 3 (3); handwritten letter from Zurich. See Bethge, *Schweizer Korrespondenz*, 13; on the circumstances, see Bethge's commentary, ibid., 25–27.

[2.] Cf. Charlotte von Kirschbaum's letter of September 22, 1941, to Paul Vogt, 1/128.

[3.] The Swiss theologian Alfred de Quervain, since 1935 a pastor in the Reformed congregation and at the same time a lecturer in the Confessing Church theological seminary in Elberfeld, had taken a position in 1938 as a pastor in Laufen (Canton Bern) and as a lecturer in Basel so that he and his "non-Aryan" wife could leave Germany.

[4.] [*Hilfswerk*. The reference is to the Swiss Relief Agency for the Confessing Church, which tried to aid the Confessing Church in its work; it also helped refugees from Nazi Germany. Karl Barth supported its efforts.–MB]

[5.] September 24, 1941.

and please let Karl Barth know once again how happy I am about the conversations with him.

Cordially and with best wishes,
Your Dietrich Bonhoeffer

My address in Schlawe is still valid.
    Schlawe/Pomerania
    Koppelstraße 9

126a. To Paul Lehmann[1]

17:137

20th Sept[ember 19]41

My dear Paul,

thank you ever so much for your letter which I got from Erwin a few days ago. It has been most interesting for me to read this account of your thoughts and experiences. But, of course, one ought to talk about it personally and to exchange views. The development that we believe is bound to come in the near future is world domination—if you will forgive me this expression—by America. The part England will play in the coming new world order seems rather uncertain. I, personally, do not believe as most people do that she will just become the "junior-partner" of U.S.A. and, moreover, I do not hope so. But at any rate the power of USA will be so overwhelming that hardly any country could represent a counterbalance. Now, you see, it is this idea that to a certain extent troubles us. You will not misunderstand me. USA domination is indeed one of the best solutions of the present crisis. But what is to become of Europe? What, for instance, of Germany? Nothing would be worse than to impose upon her any anglosaxon form of government—as much as I should like it. It simply would not work. The four liberties of your President[2] seem to indicate something in this direction. As far

17:138

[1.] Princeton Theological Seminary Library, Paul Lehmann papers; handwritten letter from Zurich; in original English, including errors. First publication in *DBW* 17:137–38. Cf. other documents connected with Bonhoeffer's second trip to Switzerland, August 28–September 26, 1/123–1/132. Page numbers in the margin refer to *DBW* 17.

[2.] In his New Year's address of January 6, 1941, President Roosevelt had said, among other things, "In the future days, which we seek to make secure, we look forward to a world founded upon four essential human freedoms. The first is freedom of speech and expression everywhere in the world. The second is freedom of every person to worship God in his own way everywhere in the world. The third is freedom from want, which translated into world terms, means economic understandings which will secure to every nation a healthy peacetime life for its inhabitants everywhere in the world. The fourth is freedom from fear—which, translated into world terms, means a worldwide reduction of

as I know Germany, it will just be impossible, for instance, to restore complete freedom of speech, of press, of association. That sort of thing would throw Germany right into the same abyss. I think we must try to find a Germany in which justice, lawfulness, freedom of the churches is being restored. I hope there will [be] something like an authoritarian "Rechtsstaat"[3] as the Germans call it. I[t] will need a long process of education before the people as a whole will be in the position to enjoy all the liberties it used to have. Well, we ought to talk it over as we did in July 1939.—What has become of your friend Kalbfleisch?[4] I hope he safely arrived in USA.—Give my greetings to Reinie,[5] please. I remember Pit[ney] v[an] D[usen][6] saying in 1939, if war broke out U.S.A. would take part in it within 2 months! How difficult it is to foretell the future!—I am thinking of you and of your wife with great joy and many beautiful remembrances. I am optimistic enough to hope that we shall meet again in a time not to[o] far off from now. With all good wishes

I remain

Yours ever
Dietrich

127. To Erwin Sutz[1]

September 21, 1941

Dear Brother Sutz,

Over the years I have written many a letter for the wedding of one of the brothers and preached many a wedding sermon. The chief characteristic of such occasions essentially rested in the fact that, in the face of these "last" times (I do not mean this to sound quite so apocalyptic), someone dares to take a step of such affirmation of the earth and its future. It was then always very clear to me that a person could take this step as a Christian truly only from within a very strong faith and on the basis of grace. For here in the

---

armaments to such a point and in such a thorough fashion that no nation will be in a posi-
tion to commit an act of physical aggression against any neighbor—anywhere in the world"
(*Congressional Record,* 1941, vol. 87, pt. 1). These freedoms were included in the Atlantic
Charter on August 14, 1941.

[3.] ["State governed by law."—MB]

[4.] George Kalbfleisch, Lehmann's student at Elmhurst College; cf. *DBW* 15:205 and
1/117.

[5.] Reinhold Niebuhr.

[6.] See *DBW* 15:228.

[1.] *NL,* A 29,4 (22); handwritten letter from Zurich; previously published in *GS* 1:50.

midst of the final destruction of all things, one desires to build; in the midst of a life lived from hour to hour and from day to day, one desires a future; in the midst of being driven out from the earth, one desires a bit of space; in the midst of widespread misery, one desires some happiness. And the overwhelming thing is that God says yes to this strange longing, that here God consents to our will,[2] whereas it is usually meant to be just the oppo-   207
site. Thus marriage becomes something quite new, powerful, marvelous—for us who wish to be Christians in Germany. And now I wonder whether for you here it is something quite different, something quieter, stiller, as it once was for us as well? Yet I can scarcely believe that. How difficult it surely is to understand one another! But let us leave that for now. With my whole heart I rejoice with you; I wish you that bit of future, space, and the happiness that God always desires to give us. I wish you that full measure of community that God still gives us in a period in which Christians are becoming lonely. I wish you the great gratitude that makes all the gifts of God most fully ours by offering them back to God.

It was a great joy to visit you and your father- and mother-in-law. Farewell—please greet your bride,[3] and be commended to God with all my heart!

Your faithful Dietrich Bonhoeffer

128. Charlotte von Kirschbaum to Paul Vogt[1]

[. . .] And now on another question: Pastor Bonhoeffer has discussed with us here the question of a Christmas booklet for the Confessing Church, and he has apparently already mentioned the plan to you. He considers it important that Karl Barth participate with a contribution—while the latter, for his part, wishes to endorse and contribute to the project only if the volume demonstrates a certain unity theologically. Given these viewpoints, the proposal was subsequently made that the three theologians who worked for years in Germany, namely, Wilhelm Vischer, Pastor de Quervain, and Karl Barth, would treat the three themes that Bonhoeffer described as the most relevant for this present time: history and eschatological expectation (W. Vischer),

---

[2.] Cf. Bonhoeffer's "A Wedding Sermon from a Prison Cell" (May 1943), *LPP*, 41–47.

[3.] This refers to Dora Vogt, who lived in the neighborhood of the Rapperswil parsonage. The wedding took place on September 23, 1941.

[1.] *NL*, Anh. A 3 (6); carbon copy of a letter from Basel, September 22, 1941; the portion of this letter reproduced here is published also in Bethge, *Schweizer Korrespondenz*, 26 (see Bethge's commentary, ibid., 26–27). Cf. also Bonhoeffer's letter of September 20, 1941, to Charlotte von Kirschbaum; see 1/126. Paul Vogt, a Zurich pastor, was head of the Swiss Relief Agency for the Confessing Church in Germany during the Second World War.

208 Christian responsibility (K. Barth), and the forgiveness of sins (Pf. de Quervain).[2] Thurneysen, who had also been approached, considers it better that the choice truly remain limited to those who have worked abroad, so that the "Basel crowd," as such, would not dominate.

What do you think about this? It would probably turn out to be a booklet of around sixty pages total, like *Und lobten Gott* a few years ago.[3] Of course the question of how it would then be shipped still remains open. When I inquired of the German customs and excise office whether the importing of books is still allowed, I received the reply that academic books and those intended solely for entertainment are still permitted. [...]

129. To Charlotte von Kirschbaum[1]

September 23, 1941

My dear Miss von Kirschbaum,

Unfortunately I was not able to reach Vogt again. But I let him know of the proposal.[2] I am pleased to be able to return home with this good news.

According to a comment he made rather offhandedly in a conversation, Siegmund-Schultze must have something else in mind after all.[3] I did not wish to question him further on it. Just to let you know.

Tomorrow I am returning home.

With my best wishes,
Your respectful Dietrich Bonhoeffer

[2.] All three themes find particular emphasis in Bonhoeffer's *Ethics*; see *DBWE* 6: 143–45, 146–70, 254–98.

[3.] Hinz, ed., ... *und lobten Gott: Zeugnisse evangelischer Pastoren und Laien—Der fürbittenden Gemeinde dargeboten.* This volume was banned in March 1939 by the German state police. [After 1933 the state police were subsumed within the Gestapo.—MB]

[1.] Karl Barth-Archiv, Basel; handwritten letter from Zurich.

[2.] Cf. Charlotte von Kirschbaum's letter of September 22, 1941, to Paul Vogt; see 1/128.

[3.] The context referred to here is not known. In any case, this letter verifies that Bonhoeffer apparently met with Friedrich Siegmund-Schultze at some point following September 13, 1941. On the full scope of the relationship between them, see Grotefeld, "Widerstand," chapter 7, in "Opposition gegen den Nationalsozialismus."

130. To Alfred de Quervain[1]

September 23, 1941

Dear Brother de Quervain,

How unfortunate that H.[2] did not work. Probably also too bureaucratic! Things will not be at all easy now, of course. I shall also speak with Wolf.[3] You may reach me at Schlawe/Pomerania, Koppelstraße 9.

I have fond memories of the evening at your home. With warmest greetings to you and your wife,

Yours, Dietrich Bonhoeffer

131. Entry in the Guest Book of Otto Salomon[1]

September 15–24, 1941
Ecclesiasticus 9:15[10][2]
Dietrich Bonhoeffer

132. To George K. A. Bell[1]

September 25th 1941

My dear Lordbishop,

may I thank you most sincerely for your letter[2] which has been a source of greatest joy to all of us, to my friends and to my family. Today I take once

---

[1.] *NL*, Anh. A 34; handwritten postcard, postmarked [Zurich-]Zollikon, September 24, 1941. Address: Pastor de Quervain, Laufen, Canton Berne.

[2.] It is possible that this refers to Licentiate Hermann Albert Hesse in Wuppertal-Elberfeld, in connection with de Quervain's earlier work at the seminary, or *theologische Hochschule*, there (communication from Anna de Quervain, February 26, 1988).

[3.] Professor Ernst Wolf in Halle.

[1.] Deutsches Literaturarchiv, Marbach, Nachlaß Otto Bruder [pseudonym for Otto Salomon]; handwritten; previously published in *GS* 6:542. See Otto Salomon's reminiscences in Zimmermann, *I Knew Dietrich Bonhoeffer*, 170–72.

[2.] "A new friend is like new wine; when it has aged, you can drink it with pleasure."

[1.] *NL*, A 42,1 (34); typewritten letter from Zurich; in original English, including errors; previously published in *GS* 6:543–44. Bishop Bell mentions an earlier letter from Bonhoeffer (or one passed on to him by Gerhard Leibholz) in his September 20, 1941, letter to Leibholz. There he writes, "I was very pleased to receive Dietrich's greeting. In and of itself it is a comfort. And its contents are additionally very reassuring." See Bell and Leibholz, *An der Schwelle*, 34–35. In an October 30, 1941, writing of Bishop Bell's, he mentions receiving the present letter as well as the Geneva commentary on Paton's book (see *An der Schwelle*, 35).

[2.] Letter not extant.

again the opportunity to write to you a little more in detail. First of all I must convey to you the kindest regards and most cordial thanks of Mrs. Martin.[3] She appreciated your greetings very much indeed and is personally quite well. Her husband is still in the same position, of course, but living in the south now.[4] He is feeling considerably better since he is enjoying the company of two colleagues. There is no reason to worry about his physical and spiritual state of health. In spite of increasing difficulties the work is continually going on, though it is not easy to fill the many gaps. The certainty of our ecumenical fellowship is growing and is a great comfort and encouragement. I have had the great pleasure and satisfaction to read your newest book[5] and I am sharing your hope for a strong stand of the churches after the war.

Sometime ago I got a letter from Sabine.[6] She expresses her thankfulness for all kindness that is being shown to her and her family in these hard times. I feel, however, that she is worrying a little about the future of her husband. I do not think that there is any particular reason for depression on her side. But I am sure that a good word from you would mean much to both, Sabine and her husband. I know that your time is filled up to the last minute, but I feel, I should just let you know that I am a little troubled about their inner balance. If you would be good enough to inform them of my letter to you and to encourage them a little I should be very thankful to you indeed.

Personally I am rather optimistic in hope for better days to be not too far off and I do not abandon the hope that in the coming year we may meet again. What a strange day will that be!

With all good wishes to you and to our friends I am in sincere thankfulness

Yours ever Dietrich

[3.] Martin Niemöller's wife.
[4.] Martin Niemöller was in the Dachau concentration camp along with Prelate Johannes Neuhäusler and Michael Höck.
[5.] *Christianity and the World Order*; cf. *DB-ER*, 735–37.
[6.] Sabine Leibholz.

H. BERLIN.
OCTOBER–NOVEMBER 1941

---

133. Deportation Reports

133.1 Report on the Mass Deportation of Jewish Citizens[1]

Over the course of the week of October 5–12, a number of Jewish families, who for the most part lived in Aryan houses,[2] received a letter from the

---

[1.] *NL,* A 65,2; typewritten report; previously published in *GS* 2:640–43. On the circumstances, see *DB-ER,* 745–47, 817–18; also see Winfried Meyer, *Unternehmen Sieben,* 7–11. [For the larger context of the deportations and the particular significance of this date, see Browning, *Origins of the Final Solution,* esp. 316. Around one thousand Jews in the first deportation from Berlin were taken to the Lodz ghetto. Eventually, sixty thousand Jews were deported from Berlin; almost all of them were killed in camps in the East.— MB]. This documentation of the deportations, which was preserved among Bonhoeffer's papers and was one of the first of this period, consists of two parts that do not fully agree, of which the first was put together on October 18, 1941, and the second on October 20. "The two reports written by Bonhoeffer and Perels were intended for Bonhoeffer's brother-in-law Hans von Dohnanyi. . . . Dohnanyi put copies of the reports into the collection of documentary evidence of Nazi crimes he was assembling and also forwarded copies to General Ludwig Beck, the leading personage of the German military opposition" (Meyer, 10–11). The prerequisite for the reports' rapid compilation was a network that had been created in 1938 by Martin Albertz and Heinrich Grüber and encompassed twenty-two outposts in twenty larger cities (see Ludwig, "Die Opfer unter dem Rad verbinden," 9; see also Barnett, *For the Soul of the People,* 144–46). One copy was presumably passed on to the WCC in Geneva via Hans Schönfeld, who was staying in Berlin at that time (see Boyens, *Kirchenkampf und Ökumene,* vol. 2, *1939–1945,* 328). The mass deportation began in Berlin on October 16, 1941. See also Schreiber, *Friedrich Justus Perels,* 168–72.

[2.] [It is difficult to know what information Bonhoeffer and Perels are trying to convey here. After 1939, Jewish real estate and other property was systematically expropriated *(Entjudung),* and a Reich law ordering Jews into segregated housing was passed in April 1939. This proved difficult to enforce, particularly in Berlin. Hence, the reference here to "Aryan houses" may simply indicate houses owned by "Aryans" where Jews were still living. It may also be to stress the distinction from the *Judenhäuser* that had been established by the April 1939 law.—MB]

Jewish Community[3] that their apartment "was scheduled to be vacated." They were quickly informed that they were not allowed to look for a new apartment, and they were given lists on which they were required to indicate their entire stock of furniture and clothing—except for "bare necessities"—and, apparently, their bank balances as well. An additional number of these letters was sent out again until October 18. Exact numbers are not known at this point. Persons of all ages are affected, even those who for months have been mobilized to work.

213   During the night of October 16, some of those affected were taken from their apartments, some even being taken from the night shift at Siemens. The people had between fifteen and ninety minutes to pack. Their treatment varied, including what they were permitted to take along. They were then gathered in the synagogue on Levetzow Street, which had already been emptied, and apparently stayed there until 4 p.m. on Saturday, October 18. According to the reports, around fifteen hundred of the letters mentioned above are said to have gone out to the first group, of whom not all have yet been deported. The criteria according to which the selection was made are not yet clear—for example, lodgers were affected but not the main tenant and vice versa. Following the deportation the apartments were sealed by the Gestapo.[4]

[3.] [Jüdische Gemeinde. The Jewish Community had lost its legal status in 1939; at the time of the deportations, it was a branch of the Reich Association of Jews in Germany (Reichsvereinigung der Juden in Deutschland). In this capacity it oversaw cultural, religious, and educational affairs. The Gestapo sent the deportation orders to affected individuals via the leaders of this organization.—MB]

[4.] This is confirmed by a letter from Superintendent Max Diestel to Johannes Hymmen, vice president of the Evangelical High Church Council, on October 20, 1941: "You are probably well aware that, as was reported, during the night on Thursday [the night of October 16, 1941] of last week, fifteen hundred Jews were brought by the police into the synagogue on Levetzow Street in Moabit in order to be deported the next day or one of the following days to the East.... Yesterday a flyer against the Jews was distributed through the block captains [low-level Nazis who served as local informants], which reads: 'Now you too will realize that every German who in any way supports a Jew out of false sentiment, even merely through friendly encounter, commits a betrayal of our people.' Among these Jews are numerous members of the Protestant congregations in our capital city of Berlin. Through baptism they have become the brothers and sisters of those who are children of God according to the will of Jesus Christ. As persons who have long since dissociated themselves internally from the Judaism being battled by the party and the state, they have their home in neither the ghetto nor the synagogue. Pastors are obliged by their ordination to intercede for their parishioners with their own honest witness and supportive love. What does the council [i.e., the Clerical Advisory Council] intend to do to avert this emergency?" (Evangelisches Zentralarchiv, Berlin, Bestand 50/110, 290).

We have heard of similar actions in other cities. It has been determined that on Tuesday, October 21, a transport is to leave the Rhineland (Cologne, Düsseldorf, Elberfeld) heading for Poland. It is said that in Berlin further transports are to leave on October 19 and 22 as well. In the Rhineland it was reported that fifty pounds of luggage, one hundred marks, and provisions for eight days were allowed to be brought along.[5]

In addition to this action that was taken by the Gestapo, there is an action by a division of Speer's department to have Jewish apartments vacated by a certain date. Those affected by this action do have the opportunity to seek new accommodations.

Even baptized Jews were affected by the deportation.

133.2 Report on the Evacuation of "Non-Aryans"

Report on the N.A. Evacuation

I. *Preparation:* Short written notifications were sent to the Jewish community by the housing office to the effect that one's apartment or room (in the case of lodgers) was scheduled to be vacated by "official decree." The recipients of this notification, some of whom received it by pneumatic post,[6] were required to go in person to the housing office (along with any lodgers) on the same or the following day; workers were required to take time off for this purpose. The questions asked mainly concerned family status, work conditions, and genealogy, above all that of the spouse. The notifications had to be brought along and turned in so that no one retained anything in writing. The people were forbidden from seeking another apartment or room.

The meaning and purpose of this measure were kept secret. Either immediately before or after these findings by the Jewish community, most of those affected received questionnaires regarding their assets, the contents of their apartments, clothing, linens (towels, bedding, table linens). All their property had to be declared; for clothing and linens this referred to whatever exceeded the "normal amount." As a guide an itemized list of these "normal requirements" was attached. (For a woman, for example, two dresses, two undershirts, three pair of underpants, six handkerchiefs, etc.). This questionnaire had to be filled out and returned within one day, or two at the latest.

[5.] See Visser 't Hooft's letter of October 29, 1941, to Carl Burckhardt at the International Red Cross (Boyens, *Kirchenkampf und Ökumene,* vol. 2, *1939–1945,* 331).

[6.] [Pneumatic mail is sent through tubes that run on a track or chute.–MB]

215   II. *Implementation:* Without any prior notification, the Berlin police or
Gestapo appeared during the night of October 16[7] in the apartments of
those who had been required to fill out the aforementioned lists, and they
brought those affected to the police station; from there they were transported
in groups to the synagogue on Levetzow Street. As far as can be determined,
the authorities entered the apartments between 8 p.m. and 12 a.m. The resi-
dents had only a short time to pack; the time limit ranged from one to four
hours.

They were allowed to bring along fifty kilograms of luggage. (Apparently
the "normal requirements.")

III. *Conjectures Regarding Destination, Number, and Selection:* To the extent that
any destinations have been mentioned in rumors, they are without exception places in the East. The Berlin non-Aryans were probably transported to
Lodz. According to not yet verified communications, the deportation ensued
on Saturday[8] in three stages: at 7 a.m., around 2 p.m., and around 7 p.m.

Overall, between four and five thousand people were to be deported
from Berlin alone. This first wave is said to have encompassed around fifteen
hundred.[9]

216   Those not removed were persons over seventy-five years of age, the sick,
and the very frail. In general, those who have been mobilized to work were
also spared. Families in which the work mobilization played a relatively
minor role were transported as well.

Those affected appear to be persons who have come into conflict with
legal or police regulations. But even the completely "blameless" were also

---

[7.] Thursday night and early Friday.

[8.] October 18 was the Jewish Sabbath.

[9.] In his November 11, 1941, "Notes on the Situation of the Churches in Europe,
No. 3" (WCC Archives, Geneva; document in original English), Visser 't Hooft is apparently relying on information from Berlin: "The persecution of the Jews has again come to
a new climax. In October fifteen thousand Jews have been deported to Poland from the
city of Berlin, and ten thousand from other places. It is, however, reported that the reaction of the people to the rule that all Jews have now to wear the Jewish star is one of
remarkable sympathy. It is significant that in several of the Protestant churches in Berlin
converted Jews wearing their stars are regularly taking part in the communion services."
On the connection between the Berlin information and Geneva activities, see Boyens,
Kirchenkampf und Ökumene, vol. 2, *1939–1945,* 114ff. A copy from Switzerland postmarked
October 22, 1941, with no return address ("presumably from Dr. Visser 't Hooft") and
addressed to William Paton, Edinburgh House, 2, Eaton Gate, London SW 1, was inter-
cepted by the censors on November 8, 1941. Copies of it were distributed to a series of
departments (London Public Record Office, Foreign Office 371/26/528 [C 07701]).

taken. Breaking of traffic laws (e.g., crossing the street on a red light, etc.) was also taken into account.

IV. *Outside Berlin* the action is said to have extended above all to the Rhine cities, such as Cologne, Düsseldorf, Mönchen-Gladbach, Rheydt, Bonn, etc. In addition, Vienna has been affected a second time.

V. *Continuation of the Evacuation:* Further waves are expected on Friday, October 24, i.e., during the night of October 23 and in addition during the night of October 28. It is to be assumed that these reports are accurate, since three transports of fifteen hundred people each from Berlin would correspond to the indication that between four and five thousand people total are to be deported from Berlin alone.

That the action is to be continued is proven by the fact that on the evening of October 17 and the morning of October 18 eviction notices and lists have arrived anew for families.

Since these newly affected families now already know what these communications mean, the desperation is unprecedented. Grave illnesses among those suffering heart disease, gallstones, etc., and the danger of suicide are the understandable results—also other impulsive actions such as senseless flight and the like. . . .

Privileged mixed marriages[10] have apparently remained entirely spared. We were also not able to ascertain any deportation of nonprivileged mixed   217
marriages. Nevertheless, Christian non-Aryans and observant Jews were affected in equal measure by this harsh measure and also those who were baptized immediately following their birth and whose parents were already Christians.

[10.] [A privileged mixed marriage was a marriage between an "Aryan" of high status and a "non-Aryan"; for a time, this status protected the "non-Aryan" spouse from deportation.—MB]

134. Wilhelm Rott to Alphons Koechlin[1]

Berlin, October 1941

Dear Dr. Koechlin:

On behalf of Superintendent Licentiate *Albertz*,[2] the chairman of the Provisional Administration of the German Evangelical Church who is imprisoned at this time, I am taking the liberty of expressing a request, as heartfelt as it is urgent, to you as the president of the Swiss Reformed Church and to this body itself.

This request concerns the bitter distress in which many of our non-Aryan brothers and sisters have found themselves for several weeks.[3] The events will be familiar to you. Since around the middle of October, authorities have begun to deport non-Aryans from Berlin and other cities to the East. The entire matter opens the Christian churches to questions and needs that we are almost helpless to face.

We know that your hands are also more or less bound. To receive the non-Aryan Christians who are in immediate danger into Switzerland seems impossible, given the stance of the immigration office and for other reasons. Professor Courvoisier of Geneva was recently obliged to confirm this again.[4] Nevertheless, a request was also passed along through him in relation to the following cases. Our question to you

218

[1.] *NL*, A 60,4 (10); typewritten copy of a letter from the WCC Archives, Geneva, written during the last week of October 1941; previously published in *GS* 6:545–47. Cf. *DB-ER*, 747–49, 817–18. "Since at this time B[onhoeffer] was still sick in bed, F. J. Perels conveyed the matter to Wilhelm Rott, on whom in the meantime the entire weight of the imprisoned VKL (Vorläufige Kirchenleitung, or Provisional Church Administration) had come to rest. He hoped that the VKL could urge the Swiss Church Federation to provide sponsorship for the threatened persons. Rott and Perels wrote a letter of appeal. . . . Rott directed the letter to Switzerland by way of Consul Schmidhuber" (Schreiber, *Friedrich Justus Perels*, 172 n. 46); cf. Oehme, *Märtyrer*, 248–49, where portions of this letter are also reproduced. On Schmidhuber's visit to Koechlin, see 1/226.2 and 1/228.1. "Rott's efforts aided by Bonhoeffer and Perels toward a Swiss immigration approval were not yet part of the Military Intelligence Foreign Office's 'Operation 7'" (Winfried Meyer, *Unternehmen Sieben*, 77 n. 345). At this time Rott could not have known that a "circular order of the Reich Central Office for Jewish Emigration" dated October 23, 1941, was on its way to the subordinate police stations: "The SS high commander and chief of the German police has decreed that the emigration of Jews is to be prohibited, effective immediately" (Winfried Meyer, *Unternehmen Sieben*, 81).

[2.] "Albertz was director of the section of the VL (Provisional Administration) concerned with the 'non-Aryan question'" (Schreiber, *Friedrich Justus Perels*, 94). As a member of the Old Prussian Union examination commission, he was imprisoned [see Barnett, *For the Soul of the People*, 93–94—MB]. Cf. Bonhoeffer's letter of May 14, 1941, to Hans-Werner Jensen; see 1/108, ed. note 2.

[3.] This refers to the mass deportations; see the deportation report (1/133).

[4.] Professor Courvoisier was among Bonhoeffer's dialogue partners during his visit to Geneva on September 4, 1941; see 1/123. It is also possible that the conversation mentioned here took place when Courvoisier visited Berlin around that time as chair of the World Council of Church's commission on prisoners of war.

today is whether, by means of an urgent introduction and an official action by the Swiss churches, a door could not perhaps be opened for a very few people or at least for the one single case we especially endorse.

The first and most urgent case is that of *Miss Charlotte Friedenthal*.[5] Born on December 1, 1892, in Breslau and baptized there as a child, daughter of the late Justice Friedenthal, Miss Friedenthal is a trained social worker. Since the beginning of 1934 she has worked in the service of the church; from January 1, 1934, to February 28, 1936, she was deputy director of the Protestant district welfare office of Berlin-Zehlendorf (chair, Pastor Niemöller). Beginning on March 2, 1936, she worked with the Provisional Administration and after October 1, 1937, was personal secretary to Superintendent Albertz, the Reformed member of the Provisional Administration. Her mother has recently died, and her siblings are in England. (Her sister is married to Dr. Ernst Brieger, MD, the former chief of staff of the Tuberculosis Clinic of Breslau-Herrnprotsch, and until 1933 the sole German member of the International Tuberculosis Committee. Her brother is the attorney Ernst Friedenthal, who like his brother-in-law was a decorated officer in the world war and the former director of the Deutsche Zentral-Bodenbank AG.) For the past two years or so, Miss Fr. has been registered for 219 emigration to the United States. However, no opportunity for this has materialized to date, and in addition she is so rooted in the church and in church work that up to this point the suggestion of emigration did not seem responsible to us. But to hold her here now would be quite irresponsible. Thus now the urgent request from Brother Albertz to take her into the Swiss church, where with all certainty she would prove to be a valuable, particularly well-informed, and collegial member.

Miss Friedenthal has a cousin in Switzerland, a married woman who is an MD; Dr. Dulivo's address is Place Chaudron 24, Lausanne.[6] This woman and her husband have repeatedly assured her of their readiness to assist her in the case of her immigration to Switzerland. Along with Mrs. Dulivo, Dr. Freudenberg, Avenue de Champel 41, Geneva, has been asked to assist her. It would certainly be possible to find a number of distinguished persons willing to take a personal interest in her case. Pastor Maas of Heidelberg, a close acquaintance and adviser of Miss Friedenthal for many

---

[5.] In a December 2, 1941, letter to Adolf Freudenberg, Charlotte von Kirschbaum wrote, "The matter stands as follows. Professor Barth has received the immigration permit for Miss Friedenthal from Dr. Rothmund, and accordingly the approval for her residence in the Basel city canton is provided here as well" (WCC Archives, Geneva, General Secretary). Heinrich Rothmund was the director of the Swiss Confederation Police Division and, most importantly, of the Bern immigration office. He had a decisive influence on Swiss immigration policy and on the stance of officials there with regard to those persecuted on political or racial grounds who were seeking refuge in Switzerland. See Häsler, *Lifeboat Is Full*, 41–46; Boyens, *Kirchenkampf und Ökumene*, vol. 2, *1939–1945*, 113, with notes 78 and 79.

[6.] The cousin's name is actually Catherine (formerly Käthe) Dolivo, née Meyer, a physician, married to Dr. Dimitri Dolivo, who came from Berlin and had resided since 1920 in Lausanne.

years, urgently and heartily underscores our request as well. Miss Friedenthal's address is Ehrenbergstraße 23, Dahlem.[7]

We would further like to commend to your ecclesiastical help and care Miss Inge Jacobsen[8] and Dr. Emil Zweig.[9]

Miss *Inge Jacobsen* was born in March 1915, the daughter of a Christian non-Aryan doctor, Kurfürstenstraße 99, Berlin W 62. She was trained in business and in particular worked with the congregation of Kaiser Wilhelm Memorial Church (Pastor Jacobi). After 1938 she was the secretary to Pastor Grüber, director of the Relief Agency for Protestant Non-Aryans. His incarceration made it impossible for him to keep his promise to assist Miss Jacobsen in emigrating if the situation worsened. Thus we wish to take up this mission on behalf of our brother, now unable to carry it out. Miss J. has an affidavit for the United States and could continue her emigration in that direction from Switzerland.

Dr. *Emil Zweig*, born May 25, 1883, is a national economist and was most recently active in banking, where he rose to a leading position. Before the world war, he spent five years in the United States and Canada and from that period retains good linguistic ability and connections that he could activate from Switzerland. For this purpose a relative has placed a two-thousand-dollar credit balance at his disposal at the Swiss Bank in Zurich, which would be available to him in Switzerland. In recent years Dr. Zweig has kept the books for the congregation of Bethlehem Reformed Church, Yorkstraße 4, Berlin SW 61 (Pastor Licentiate Nordmann), and has acquitted himself exceedingly well in this church work. In the final interview he made a positively youthful, flexible, and in every respect engaging impression. By the way, in his case as in both of the others, their Jewish extraction is barely if at all visible to the casual observer.[10] If the first case is particularly emphasized, this is because hers represents the most

220

[7.] See Winfried Meyer, *Unternehmen Sieben,* 70–82.

[8.] She also led Bible studies in the Dahlem congregation and was called "dear little Jöckli." Along with others, she participated "in short courses toward ordination as an elder, so that she could conduct baptisms, funerals, etc. 'there'. . . . I am quite concerned about Jöckli; she has no work now. But if she looks for work, she will attract attention. And her father is still an observant Jew" (Gertrud Staewen to Adolf Freudenberg, December 7, 1941). See Boyens, *Kirchenkampf und Ökumene,* vol. 2, *1939–1945,* 326–27. "All efforts to save her failed. Died in the concentration camp" (communication with Freudenberg, February 24, 1971); see Boyens, *Kirchenkampf und Ökumene,* vol. 2, *1939–1945,* 327 n. 4.

[9.] Alphons Koechlin wrote on November 10, 1941, to Adolf Freudenberg: "In response to your letter, I must report with sorrow that it was possible to obtain an immigration permit to Switzerland for Miss Friedenthal, but that this was no longer an option for the two other cases requested from Germany, Miss Jacobson and Zweig" (Winfried Meyer, *Unternehmen Sieben,* 80).

[10.] [After eight years under Nazism, there was widespread awareness of who "looked" Jewish or "Aryan"; those involved in a rescue (which often involved hiding people "in plain sight") would certainly have been aware of this factor because of the danger of being caught.—MB]

urgent church responsibility, given the lady's church position, and we do not wish to make our request unnecessarily burdensome by mentioning three at once. The situation of personal need is the same in this case and others. It would be very important and perhaps reduce the risk to them if those affected could quickly receive the news from Switzerland (by telegraph) that their immigration or transit visa was in process.

Given the special character of the cases depicted here, the resumption of the connection with someone like D. Thurneysen of Basel and Pastor Vogt of Zurich-Seebach would perhaps be worth considering. But we pray to God, who is a father to the forsaken, that GOD might show a way out of all this hopeless distress.

In the bonds of brotherly faith,
Your very devoted Wilhelm Rott

134a. Dr. Sch[...] to Charlotte von Kirschbaum[1]   17:139

Zurich, October 29, 1941

My dear Baroness,[2]

On behalf of Dr. Bonhoeffer and Dr. Rott, I am enclosing for you a copy of a letter directed to President Dr. Köchlin.[3] These gentlemen request that if possible you add your support to the petition as well. The danger for those affected is quite imminent;

[1.] Karl Barth-Archiv, Basel; handwritten letter; the name of the sender has not been deciphered (a name corresponding to the general impression of the sender's handwriting has not yet surfaced); published in *IBG-Rundbrief* 57 (November 1998): 10. Page number in the margin refers to *DBW* 17. The addressee, Charlotte von Kirschbaum, was Karl Barth's closest colleague; the letter was therefore indirectly intended for him as well. The sender is apparently an informant, himself located in Zurich, of the Munich Military Intelligence Office. Consul Schmidhuber had entrusted him with copies of the documents transmitted from Berlin to be passed on to Karl Barth, while Schmidhuber himself traveled on with the documents to Church President Koechlin in Bern. The preparations for Operation 7 were the background for this (still not fully clarified) course of events. Operation 7 was the plan that enabled fourteen German Jews, including Confessing Church member Charlotte Friedenthal, to reach Switzerland. It was planned out of Canaris's Office of Military Intelligence; Bonhoeffer and Wilhelm Rott were involved. Cf. *DB-ER*, 745–49; Winfried Meyer, *Unternehmen Sieben*, 75–80. See also 1/133.2; 1/134, ed. note 1; and 1/198, ed. note 2. "After having received these lines Barth on November 4 1941 wrote to the 'Fremdenpolizei Basel-Stadt' [immigration office in the city of Basel] and asked for a permit for Miss Friedenthal to stay in Basel. His application was successful" (Letter, written in English, from Hans-Anton Drewes, Karl Barth-Archiv, September 11, 1998).

[2.] In his letter of September 11, 1998, Drewes writes, "'Baroness' is most likely a masking expression to avoid the name of Barth's secretary Charlotte von [!] Kirschbaum."

[3.] Cf. Wilhelm Rott's letter of October 1941 to Alphons Koechlin, 1/134. [Dr. Koechlin was president of the Swiss Church Federation.—MB]

Miss Friedenthal in particular would be a personage of great potential value for the work of the church in this region.

Both gentlemen request that you please destroy this letter and its enclosure following your perusal of them. I request that you do the same with this letter as well.[4]

Yours in humble service,
Dr. Sch[. . .].

135. From Ruth von Kleist-Retzow[1]

Stettin, October 30, 1941

My dear Dietrich,

Are you able to read—or even listen to—letters yet? Not seeing you was very painful for me. The reason was even more distressing. Have you experienced, as I have, that being sick[2] does not provide for intellectual stimulation even though one would very much like to have such a nice expanse of time in which to engage in it? No, it is always a warning to us to "make the most of the time" when we are healthy.[3]

221

Although neither you nor the good Professor Gaedertz[4] was able to see me, the days in Berlin were nevertheless quite "well-rounded." It was absolutely lovely at the Schleichers'. What a cultured household! And I quite proudly imagine having some claim on the dear young ladies! I also went to Dahlem and heard truly satisfying news about M.[5] The situation is in fact really more bearable. He was even reported to say, "For the time being I do not wish anything different for myself. Not yet."

It appears that my dear Alla[6] is part of a new offensive. Where, I do not know yet. But this is a terrible ordeal.

Tomorrow evening Rau[7] wants to visit me. He was conscripted here into the regional shooters.[8] It truly gave me a turn to think of his weak constitution. I imagine

---

[4.] This request documents the security measure, apparently considered necessary even in neutral countries, of destroying written materials. The fact that it was not carried out in this case has allowed this document to become available to us.

[1.] Literary estate of Ruth von Kleist-Retzow, handwritten letter.

[2.] Bonhoeffer was sick with pneumonia and during this time was recuperating at his parents' home; see *DB-ER*, 746.

[3.] Eph. 5:16; Col. 4:5.

[4.] Alma Gaedertz was lecturer for ophthalmology at the University of Berlin.

[5.] Martin Niemöller.

[6.] Alexander Stahlberg.

[7.] Arthur Rau, a former Finkenwalde seminarian, had been serving as Confessing Church pastor in Prädikow, located in the Oberbarnim district.

[8.] [The regional shooters *(Landesschützen)* were a subdivision of the regional forces *(Landwehr)*, an auxiliary militia that included all men between thirty-five and forty-five years of age who were neither on active military duty nor in the reserves. Some volunteered;

it would be horrible for him. I have spoken to the Onnasches only by telephone so far. I simply could not leave the house because of cleaning and negotiations with the officials and food-rationing offices, etc. I was really gone too long. But now a spare room with two beds is always available to welcome special guests. The other guest room is occupied by my "nieces" Hülst and Lindenberg,[9] who are taking a secretarial course here.

Are you familiar with the short work by Thielicke, *Wo ist Gott?*[10] I think it could have a good effect, although I also find it too contrived and while reading it kept thinking that *you* would necessarily handle the question "Why is God silent in our time?" quite differently. What has happened to your letter to the brothers?[11]

An affectionate farewell to you, and do get better quickly and completely. It is reassuring to know that you have a robust nature. And I think that if you had made no progress in the meantime, Eberhard would surely have notified me?

Greet him and your poor weary mother.

Faithfully yours,
Ruth von Kleist-Retzow

136. To Christoph Bethge[1]   222

November 17, 1941

Dear Christoph,[2]

It was quite a tremendous surprise you gave me with the package for Eberhard. I had not even dared to hope of coming across this revered item[3] in the next ten years. Every winter this led to the same aggravation. Once you experienced it yourself. Hence you have now remedied this and thereby performed a great service not only to me but also to those around me, who have suffered under my frequent outbursts of rage because of poorly attached skis. In short, many thanks that you have made this possible! This was very nice of you! I am now racking my brains with Eberhard as to how I might be

---

in some cases men were conscripted. Regional shooters served as guards on bridges, in railroad stations, and in prisoner-of-war camps.—MB]

[9.] Marie-Luise von Hülst, daughter of the landowner Hülst of Rohrbeck/Neumark (adjacent to the Pätzig estate of the Wedemeyers), and Annelise Lindenberg, daughter of the retired parliamentary representative and estate owner Lindenberg of Kremlin, Soldin/Neumark district.

[10.] Thielicke, *Wo ist Gott?* 1940.

[11.] See Finkenwalde circular letter of November 22, 1941, 1/137.

[1.] *NL*, A 60,4 (11); typewritten copy of letter; previously published in *GS* 2:414–15.

[2.] At this point, Christoph Bethge was a radio operator at sea.

[3.] The item was a pair of ski boots.

able to give you some joy as well. If you could support me in this, that would naturally be the best thing. Thus, if you have some wish, please let me know. It would give me great pleasure to fulfill it for you.

I would much like to see you again and hear your stories. You are now finding your own way, and it is so very different from that which I myself experienced at your age. In this regard, I believe that a great deal depends on what a person experiences in his twenties or thereabouts and above all *how* one experiences this. In my case these were the years around 1926.[4] My studies came to an end; one was able to study and work in all freedom; one traveled and saw something of Europe. At that point Europe was very gradually recovering again from the poverty, the disruption, and the hate that the world war had brought upon it. Germany began to create a place for itself again in the world through work, scholarship, and intellectual accomplishments. The old prejudices of peoples against one another receded in the face of a renewed hope among western and central European peoples for a better, more fruitful life together in a spirit of peace. The best powers of the peoples strove to attain peace—which, to be sure, was heavily encumbered from the outset. One felt such a thing as a western and central European duty, even a mission, in the world. People worked and thought they knew why. They created circles of support that were conscious of being intellectually responsible. They discussed things passionately against and yet ultimately *with* one another.

I could go on and on, and you will understand that the heart is not indifferent to such remembrances. But I also understand that for you this world has gone under. You will say, "illusions, romanticism, dreams." You see other things and perhaps think that what you are now seeing and experiencing is the real world—just as we thought back then. Each will turn out to be as true and as false as the other.

Perhaps we can put it this way: *you*[5] today are claimed so completely by the present that you have little inclination, though perhaps also little energy, to think of the future, to plan; *we* were so strongly captivated by the future that we decisively misjudged the present in many ways. Now I think that in not too long a time both will be necessary in equal measure, those who see the present soberly and who nevertheless do not let go of the future— which also belongs to reality! To be irresponsible with regard to the future is nihilism; to be irresponsible with regard to the present is sentimentalism. We must overcome both; and no matter how diverse the backdrop of our experiences, we shall one day have to and be able to reunite in this task—

[4.] Cf. *DB-ER*, 45–96.
[5.] [Bonhoeffer uses the plural, *Ihr*, here.—MB]

which is also a highly personal one. It is my firm conviction and also my experience in conversation with many people that today they cannot look the present straight in the eye and at the same time have energy for future tasks unless they believe in the Creator—and the Redeemer.

It would be wonderful to speak about this sometime. Perhaps in the process we would discover that with very different words we are each speaking of the same thing and have the same goal in mind. Or perhaps not.

Enough of this. Farewell, Christoph. God preserve you, wherever you may be. With love and all good wishes,

Your Dietrich Bonhoeffer

137. Finkenwalde Circular Letter[1]

224

Dear Brother...[2]

Today I must let you know that our dear brothers Christoph Harhausen, Günther Christ, Wolfgang Krause (Anhalt),[3] and Johannes Staedler have now also fallen in Russia and that Joachim Staude has been missing since August. The brothers F. E. Schröter, H. D. Pompe, Winfried Krause, G. Seydel, G. Biesental are wounded. It causes me pain to write this to you. I suppose that God wills to tear especially great holes into the ranks of young pastors and thereby to lay upon us a particular burden. With our fallen brothers we are losing coworkers in the struggle for a church that is to belong solely to the Lord Jesus Christ. Every one of them had to go through especially difficult times in his congregation and experienced all the obstacles and blessings of faithful conduct in ministry. In just a few years God showed them what it means to be a shepherd of a congregation, and today we believe that God wished in this way to prepare them for an early death. The uncertainty about Joachim Staude is particularly difficult. Let us pray God's presence and timely help for this quiet brother, always kind and patient, firm in his faith. Christoph Harhausen repeatedly strengthened and gladdened us by his joyful confidence toward our church's situation, by the rectitude of his speaking and acting. Günther Christ proved himself faithful in many difficult congregational situations and was a good brother to us in his sturdy,

[1.] *NL*, A 48,3 (15); carbon copy of circular letter; previously published in *GS* 2:578–82. The date, "November 22, 1941," was added later in another hand.

[2.] [Bonhoeffer used the singular in the salutation and then added the individual names by hand, since circular letters were no longer permitted. In the letter itself he speaks to the brothers in the plural.—MB]

[3.] [Saxony-Anhalt, one of thirteen federal states in Germany; located southwest of Berlin.—MB]

cheerful way. Wolfgang Krause had come to us from his home province for ecclesial reasons. With his thoroughly upright and open nature he was utterly committed to the clarity of the church's situation and of the message of Jesus Christ. One could not spend time with Johannes Staedler without being touched by his great love of Jesus Christ and his congregation. His last message to his wife was, "Gloria and Hallelujah to our Lord and Savior Jesus Christ." Günther Christ leaves behind his fiancée. W. Krause and J. Staedler had married young. Our thoughts go to those whom death has now robbed of the greatest happiness of their earthly life, and let us also not forget the relatives of our fallen brothers Bojack, Preuß, Nithack, G. Schulze, Kahn, and Maaß.

It is the case that the passing of time, at least initially, makes the departure of a beloved human being ever more painful. On top of grief come the daily pangs of loss. The more silent the names of our fallen ones become all around us, the more loudly an inner voice names them to us from day to day. Who would not know the secret wish to trade places with them, to have stood in their place? How frequently we are pierced with horror when we think of the loneliness of their death. Why could we not offer them the final service of fellowship? Brother Heise, W. Schrader's brother-in-law, was able to die in the presence of a brother with the words, "I am consoled." But does Christ not have all power, with his holy and gracious presence, to compensate richly for the distance of one of his own from all human help? Did he not hear that which no human ear was able to hear any longer, that "I am consoled" also in the hearts of those who died alone, but with Him? A great number of young preachers of the Gospel have now departed. But the word that they preached here as the word of God is alive; it lives in the believing congregation; it is fruitful; it creates faith and bears fruit for the Last Day. The mouths of our brothers, closed on this earth, now and eternally laud and praise the name of the One who holds the kingdom,[4] Jesus Christ. "Now let all the heav'ns adore you, and saints and angels sing before you . . ."[5]

Each one of us is drawn into the actuality of this war on different levels. For the dimensions of this war are so incalculable. It is a different reality if

---

[4.] Cf. the last line of Martin Luther's hymn, "A Mighty Fortress Is Our God" (*Lutheran Book of Worship*, no. 228/229, verse 4 ["Ein' feste Burg ist unser Gott" (*Evangelisches Gesangbuch für Brandenburg und Pommern*, 90, 4; *Evangelisches Gesangbuch*, 201, 4)]), which reads: "The Kingdom's ours forever!"

[5.] This is the beginning of stanza 3 of Philipp Nicolai's hymn "Wake, Awake, for Night Is Flying" (*Lutheran Book of Worship*, no. 31 ["Wachet auf, ruft uns die Stimme" (*Evangelisches Gesangbuch für Brandenburg und Pommern*, 311, 3; *Evangelisches Gesangbuch*, 121, 3)]).

we experience the war fighting on the front line, whether as an officer or as 226
a simple soldier or a stretcher-bearer or a chaplain, or whether we are ordered
to some duty behind the front lines without the possibility of being particularly tested, stretched, distinguished, or whether we do our duty quietly at
home, or whether we were given to receive our place in some faraway country. To be sure, none of us is spared the hours in which our life seems meaningless to us and our time wasted, because we cannot share in the monstrous
experience of the war at the front lines. This also rings through some letters of brothers who are stationed behind the front in some sort of seem-
ingly inconsequential duty.[6]

But this points to a grave danger of which we must be aware. Danger,
experience, and testing in sufficient abundance are available for Christians
who know what their faith is about, in every moment, wherever they may
be. If God, in pure grace, has made it possible for even these unique and
sinister experiences to afford grace to our fighting, wounded, and dying
brothers on the front lines, then it would be irreverent in the face of this
miracle to crave such experiences for ourselves as well. For who knows how
well we would stand up? Who wishes to provoke God's miracle? But God
knows what can be demanded of us, and in God's own time it surely will be
demanded. For this hour let us prepare ourselves by accepting the measure
of danger and testing granted to us humbly and faithfully every day. Particularly in regard to our brothers on the front, I perceive it to be almost a robbery when others demand for themselves as well the indescribable reality
allotted to them. We should also ponder the fact that being human finally is
not about having this or that experience but rather about this: "to keep
God's word, to love kindness, and to walk humbly with your God."[7] We dare
not let wishes and fantasies trivialize for us the task given to us daily by God.
If one or another of you today is still called to "lead a quiet and peaceable
life in all godliness and dignity"[8] in the midst of the world's strife, thus in
the service of Jesus Christ, then that is also a miracle of God that also belongs 227
to the inconceivable dimensions of this war's actuality and that is full of
importance and promise for the world, for the war, and for the brothers on
the front. The letters from the front themselves confirm this over and over.
For those to whom it is given, it is one of the most solemn duties to preserve for the day of the brothers' homecoming that "quiet and peaceable
life" with God's word as the hearth fire that dare not be allowed to go out.
In both places what matters is one's entire faithfulness to the divine mission;

[6.] [See the Finkenwalde circular letter 1/119, ed. note 5; also see the German editors'
remarks in the afterword, 647, 651, and 673.—MB].

[7.] [Mic. 6:8. "To keep God's word" is rendered in the NRSV as "to do justice."—MB]

[8.] 1 Tim. 2:2.

and yet both at home and on the front we live not from our own faithfulness but rather always solely from the forgiveness of our sins. It has been so compelling for me to read in so many letters from the front how the Bible and even meditation accompany you into the shell craters. We thank you for this. For us it is a goad, comfort, disgrace, and help. Thank you for every word we hear from you, for every prayer for us. Let us move into the last days of the church year with open hearts and also become certain and glad again about the future of our church.

The letter was not sent out because for several weeks I was coping with pneumonia. Now Edgar Engler and Robert Zenke have also fallen. It is very, very sad. In their firm church stance both of these Pomeranian brothers were particularly important to the province. In every gathering one sensed how their heart belonged completely to the service of Jesus Christ and his church. They also knew themselves to be responsible in a special way for the community of brothers and served it faithfully. Uninhibited joyfulness and profound seriousness belonged to each. Those came from the same source, from faith in Jesus Christ. Now we know our brothers to be with the One whom they served here according to the divine calling. In the midst of all our sorrow let us rejoice in this.

God preserve you! Your faithful
D. Bonhoeffer

228   **138. To Wilhelm Jannasch**[1]

November 23, 1941

Dear Brother Jannasch,

I am pleased to have received a detailed bill from the PNB[2] office. I am hereby remitting 234 RM right away for the period of September 1939–November 1941. The remaining 192 from September 1937–39 will follow in the next month. For reasons of personal exoneration—but not excuse—I would like to say once again that until Easter 1940 my entire salary, with the exception of a few personal expenses, went into the common purse of my workplace at that time. I thank you that the matter is now straightened out.

My uncle[3] has written once again. An answer is not yet forthcoming.

[1.] *NL*, A 60,3: handwritten letter from Berlin; previously published in *MW* 5:219 and *GS* 6:548.

[2.] Pfarrernotbund, or Pastors' Emergency League, which Jannasch directed in Berlin at that time; cf. 1/116.

[3.] Major-General Paul von Hase, city commander of Berlin, was a brother of Bonhoeffer's mother, Paula Bonhoeffer, née von Hase.

But he was again extremely eager to help. I would think it a good thing if [you] looked up my two brothers-in-law regarding this matter[4] as soon as possible. There is indeed no time to lose.

Cordially yours,
Dietrich Bonhoeffer

139. Petition to the Armed Forces[1]

The hope of Protestant Christians that the antichurch measures would cease, at least for the length of the war, has been bitterly disappointed. Many thousands of Protestant clergy have taken up arms for the fatherland and have been highly decorated and mentioned by name in the reports from the front; a large percentage have been wounded or killed, and millions of faithful Protestant church people fight on all fronts. And yet at the same time, antichurch measures at home are taking on ever harsher forms. In congregations the impression is gradually emerging that the calamity of the war and the absence of the clergy are here being intentionally exploited by the party and the Gestapo to destroy the Protestant church even during the war itself. Sooner or later this must surely seriously compromise the necessary engagement of all powers in the war.[2]

A few examples of interventions into church life during the war:

[4.] The brothers-in-law are Hans von Dohnanyi and Rüdiger Schleicher. The matter in question is the UK classification of Jannasch's son Hans Peter, and it later played a role in the interrogations: senior military prosecutor Roeder wished to prove that Bonhoeffer had been involved in the evasion of military service; cf. 1/150 and 1/230.2 as well as *DB-ER*, 819; see also the draft of a letter to Manfred Roeder, 1/228.6. [For an explanation of the UK classification, see 1/31, ed. note 3.—MB]

[1.] *NL*, A 65,4; typewritten early draft; previously published in *GS* 2:428–32. According to a communication of Christine von Dohnanyi to Eberhard Bethge on February 11, 1957, this was a document for Admiral Canaris and Carl Goerdeler, intended to aid them in approaching generals responsive in this area. The author was Friedrich Justus Perels, advised by Bonhoeffer; cf. Schreiber, *Friedrich Justus Perels,* 171. In light of various conspicuous parallels, this document dates from the same period as Bishop Wurm's petition to Hitler as well as to Kerrl, the Reich minister for church affairs, in December 1941; cf. Schäfer, *Landesbischof D. Wurm und der nationalsozialistische Staat,* 275–79 and 279–86. Since documents of such importance were typically carbon-copied to other church offices and thus to the office of the Old Prussian Union Council of Brethren, Perels and Bonhoeffer may well have had access to them there.

[2.] Cf. Schäfer, *Landesbischof D. Wurm und der nationalsozialistische Staat,* 276–77. Cf. also Bonhoeffer's notes (file Z, page no. 1) in early 1943 on the same problem; see 1/224.1.

1. In Warthegau the attempt is being made to implement the church program of the so-called Thirteen Points, worked out in the Brown House[3] for the postwar period.[4] That is above all an attempt to shut the church completely out of public life by banning all forms of church offerings, all congregational youth work, all men's and women's work outside worship, as well as an attempt to impede every connection with the German home churches. The Protestant congregations of the liberated[5] Warthegau are engaging in fierce battle.

230 2. The printing of all sorts of congregational and worship folders, Christian calendars, monthly bulletins, etc., which are familiar to many pastors and millions of Protestant church members, has been forbidden in the entire Reich. The officially given rationale of the paper shortage is scarcely credible when at the same time party brochures are being newly published, as in Warthegau.[6] Because of the conscription of clergy, these congregational newsletters were the sole remaining possibility of the church's care for many rural congregations that cannot be reached by pastors any longer (as gasoline is not being made available to pastors). This lack will be experienced quite painfully, particularly in the upcoming Christmas season.

3. State police interventions, bans, and arrests are being carried out against Protestant laypeople who, because of the conscriptions, have made themselves available for presiding at Services of the Word[7] and children's services, confirmation instruction, etc., in congregations without pastors. In rural areas, where the church is often located far away, it is forbidden to hold a worship service in schools or in private homes.[8]

[3.] [The Brown House, *Das Braune Haus,* was the name of the headquarters of the Nazi Party in Munich.—MB]

[4.] Cf. Schäfer, *Landesbischof D. Wurm und der nationalsozialistische Staat,* 278. Cf. also the section on Germany, based on information from Bonhoeffer, in Visser 't Hooft's "Notes on the State of the Church in Europe," written at the end of March; see 1/98, ed. note 7. On the events in Warthegau, see Gürtler, *Nationalsozialismus und evangelische Kirche im Warthegau,* 47–51. In opposition to the "Thirteen Points" mentioned here, Bishop Wurm's later "Thirteen Statements regarding the Mission and Service of the Church" represented an appeal for the "act of unification"; see Thierfelder, *Das kirchliche Einigungswerk,* 62.

[5.] *Befreit.* This was the official language of the day.

[6.] See Schäfer, *Landesbischof D. Wurm und der nationalsozialistische Staat,* 277, 279.

[7.] [Services of the Word were conducted by laypeople. The Lord's Supper was not celebrated, and the sermon—written by a minister—was read by the conducting layperson.—MB]

[8.] This may refer to the situation in Warthegau. "Events of worship on private property were under the control of Gestapo authorization" (Meier, *Der evangelische Kirchenkampf,* 3:127).

4. Protestant chaplaincy is now forbidden even in church-run hospitals, except for cases where an individual patient wishes to call the pastor.[9]

5. The CVJM[10] house in Berlin and the youth home for committed Christianity in Woltersdorf have been confiscated without explanation.

6. A circle of high school students in Köslin who were continuing to hold their Bible study on their own following the pastor's conscription had their permission for this activity revoked by the school authorities; the two senior class students who led the studies were removed from the school; and the participants were demoted and penalized in the H.J.[11]

7. Expulsion and the ban on public speaking were imposed on the highly regarded superintendent in Köslin,[12] because he carried out the wishes of the congregational leadership in protesting the appointment of a national-church DC[13] as pastor of his church. At the same time, several bans on public speaking were imposed on leading clergy of the Protestant Confessing Church without providing any particular rationale.[14]

8. Since May 1941, almost all the leading pastors of the Confessing Church in the provinces of Berlin and Brandenburg have been in prison, because they took part in the theological examinations of young theologians of the Confessing Church.[15] The Gestapo was aware of the administration of these examinations for quite some time. Of the more than two thousand young theologians who have taken these exams in all provinces, at the moment more than fifteen hundred are in the military. They and their congregations are deeply concerned about the imprisonment of their theological instructors, who have otherwise in no way incriminated themselves. In one particular case the wife of one of the incarcerated pastors was told that release from prison was only possible if the pastor changed his profession, which in

231

[9.] Cf. Bishop Wurm's letter of May 30, 1941, to the Reich defense council (in Schäfer, *Landesbischof D. Wurm und der nationalsozialistische Staat,* 176).

[10.] [Christlicher Verein Junger Männer, or Young Men's Christian Association, was the German branch of the international YMCA.—MB]

[11.] The information in this paragraph relies on an extensive report compiled at that time by Pastor Karl Scheel, a copy of which is found in the papers of Birger Forell preserved by Glenthøj, published with commentary by Klän in *IBG-Rundbrief* 39 (1992): 23–37. [HJ is the abbreviation for Hitler Jugend, "Hitler Youth."—MB]

[12.] Friedrich Onnasch was the superintendent in Köslin. On September 12, 1940, he was banned from public speaking and expelled from Pomerania.

[13.] [Deutscher Christ, "German Christian.—MB]

[14.] Cf. the August 22, 1940, Circular Decree of the Reich Central Security Office; see 1/18.

[15.] [This refers to the imprisonment and trial of the twenty-three members and staff of the Confessing Church examination commission.—MB] See Bonhoeffer's letter of May 14, 1941, to Hans-Werner Jensen, 1/108.

fact is ever more frequently being demanded of pastors by the Gestapo. Another incarcerated pastor, who during his imprisonment was drafted for military service and was released by the judge for this purpose, was then arrested by the Gestapo all over again as he left the courtroom. At the order of the SS high commander,[16] almost all young Confessing Church clergy who have not been drafted were conscripted by the employment offices "in order thereby to supply them with some useful activity."[17]

The Gestapo's treatment of pastors at interrogations, etc., is now in general the same as that of criminals.

The imprisonment of the members of the so-called Christian Community,[18] who are known to be quiet and completely apolitical people, is most deeply deplored in the Protestant church as well.

232   9. A prominent layman of the Protestant church, whose son had been killed in the East, was forced to endure great abuse through an anonymous communication. He had announced the death of his son with the following words: "Fallen in faith in his Lord and Savior…" The communication speaks of "shame on the sanctimonious clan and their degenerate blood" that has denounced the son as a believer in an "obscure itinerant preacher."[19]

10. In Württemberg the state subsidies for the Protestant church were not paid in full, so that the pastors' salaries had to be reduced while the pastors were on the front.[20]

11. Nordland Publishers, which is responsible for the ideological indoctrination of the party, published seven hundred thousand copies of a book by Friedrich Schmidt, *Das Reich als Aufgabe*, which demands the break with all traditions, in particular the decisive destruction of the churches even during the war, since the inner conditions for victory could only be achieved in this way. The bishop of Württemberg protested publicly against this text.[21]

[16.] [Heinrich Himmler.—MB]

[17.] Cf. Bethge's letter of January 27, 1941, to Bonhoeffer; see 1/63, ed. note 4.

[18.] This refers to the Christian branch of the Rudolf Steiner anthroposophy movement, cofounded by Friedrich Rittelmeyer.

[19.] ["Preacher" is a reference to Jesus.—MB]

[20.] In a communication of April 3, 1941, the Württemberg Minister of Culture informed the Stuttgart senior church official of a war-driven reduction in state payments to the church of 1.9 million RM per year; see Schäfer, *Landesbischof D. Wurm und der nationalsozialistische Staat*, 225.

[21.] Friedrich Schmidt, head of the Reich central educational office, a former teacher, and a German Christian member of the Württemberg regional church assembly, proclaimed in his book, "The basis for the new Reich in accord with creation is the people [[*Volk*] as the God-ordained unity of human beings of the same blood. The National Socialist worldview sees in the people a conception of the creator God and in the German person a helpmate of God in the perfect completion of the world. It is in this life that Germans are to endure, and their fate is fulfilled here in this world.…The war will be more

12. The killing of so-called unworthy lives, which has now become better [233] known in the congregations and has claimed its victims from them, is viewed by Christians of all confessions[22] with the deepest alarm and with revulsion, especially in connection with the general abrogation of the Ten Commandments and any security of law and thus as a sign of the anti-Christian stance of leading authorities in the Reich.[23]

This enumeration could be continued at length. Yet none of these facts is kept secret either from congregations at home or from the pastors and parishioners at the front.

In view of the acute dangers, the Protestant church requests that the military effect the following, namely, that:

1. all antichurch measures be halted for the duration of the war.

2. imprisonments, expulsions, bans on speaking, etc. resulting from ecclesial and/or church-political grounds be rescinded.

3. help and protection at home be extended to the church for its responsible mission during the war.

Dietrich Bonhoeffer

---

successful and the other nations will adopt the National Socialist worldview more quickly, the more radically it is implemented in Germany in opposition to Christianity" (Hermelink, *Kirche im Kampf*, 504–5). Bishop Wurm spoke on this before the regional church assembly [*Landeskirchentag*] on September 9, 1941, saying: "If these views are predominant in the upper levels of the party, it cannot surprise us that events have taken the turn that we have now experienced in Württemberg, especially in our own body. It can be no surprise to us that gossip and rumors never cease to circulate that, once the victory is won, quite decisive measures will be undertaken against the church" (Schäfer, *Landesbischof D. Wurm und der nationalsozialistische Staat*, 261). For extensive citations translated into English, see Visser 't Hooft, *Notes on the Situation of the Church in Europe*, October 22, 1941, Geneva (Public Record Office, London, Foreign Office 371/26/528 [X 07701]).

[22.] See the sermon of Bishop Count Clemens August Graf von Galen of July 13, 1941: "By this example [Martin Niemöller], dear Christians, you see that it is not a confessional-Catholic matter" (Portmann, *Bischof Graf v. Galen spricht!* 50).

[23.] See Schäfer, *Landesbischof D. Wurm und der nationalsozialistische Staat*, concerning the protests that followed earlier petitions from 1940 against "so-called planned economic measures toward the purging of the mentally ill and feeble-minded" (279). The resemblance here to the third sermon of Bishop Count von Galen in the Münster Lambertikirche on August 3, 1941, is unmistakable (see Portmann, *Bischof Graf v. Galen spricht!* 66–76). See also Visser 't Hooft, *Notes on the Situation of the Church*, September 3, 1941, Geneva: "The situation had become that with the consent of the national leaders all ten commandments were being violated" (Public Record Office, London, Foreign Office 371/26/528 [C 07701]).

I. Kieckow.
December 1941

---

140. From Ruth von Kleist-Retzow[1]

Stettin, December 12, 1941

Dear Dietrich,

I still have five hundred sheets of typing paper and two hundred sheets of office paper [Kanzleipapier] ready for you, as well as one hundred envelopes[2] like those I use in writing to you. What would we like to do with them now? Should I send the package to Berlin? Or do you still need it in Kieckow?[3]

My son's illness is now one more impediment to all our plans (please give him the enclosed letter).[4] But I hear that you are practicing the piano diligently, which I hope gives you joy. I hope you feel better. I shall probably not be able to come to Krössin before the eighteenth, and I assume that you will not be needing me?

The death of my nephew Rohr[5] is yet another grievous blow to our family.... He is his parents' only son, and I am experiencing my poor sister's pain very deeply. What will yet befall us?

I would also like to say to you what a great and new joy it is to me to hear *Discipleship* read aloud. Most recently we heard and discussed the section on the extraordinary, including love of enemies, as well as those on (truthfulness) and the hidden

---

[1.] Literary estate of Ruth von Kleist-Retzow; handwritten letter; previously published in Ruth von Wedemeyer, *In des Teufels Gasthaus,* 167ff.

[2.] This is all presumably in reference to the sending of Finkenwalde circular letters.

[3.] At the time Bonhoeffer was staying at Kieckow to recuperate from pneumonia and work further on his *Ethics.*

[4.] Hans-Jürgen von Kleist-Retzow was ill with gallbladder problems and later had surgery at a Berlin clinic; cf. Ruth von Kleist-Retzow's letter of December 30, 1941, to Bonhoeffer (see 1/142).

[5.] Fritz Robert von Rohr, a son of her youngest sister, Ehrengard. He died in May 1941; both his parents were executed by the SS in April 1945.

righteousness,[6] which led to long and fruitful conversations. These are always periods of composure, which are extremely beneficial at this moment when all our nerves are palpably taut. It is remarkable how Mrs. Kübarth,[7] by virtue of her own teaching, shows glowing interest and genuine understanding of your arguments. And it is delightful when, after her occasional statement, "Well, I did not understand this at all," she won't rest until we arrive at an explanation. Once again I am finding that *Discipleship* is a book not that one "reads through" but rather *within* which one is allowed to read. Perhaps this is its greatest value. In all this I often have the impression that some things have not yet been articulated in full, that some links are missing, or however I might express this. To be sure, that's the reason you are continuing to write. Are you making any progress yet, or is it still not possible?

235

Yours with my warm regards,
RKR

Might you be willing to write Dr. Tielsch[8] a note of thanks? This would be a relief to me.

141. To Eberhard Bethge[1]

December 14, 1941

Dear Eberhard,

Greetings to you on this third Sunday of Advent. I hope to be back there on the fourth.[2] I shall probably come on the train that arrives at 3:45. But you may not come pick me up and disrupt your whole afternoon! I shall meet you later at home. We still have to practice the cantata.[3] How are the brethren doing?[4] We shall have much to discuss. Mr. von Kleist is still in bed with his gallbladder problem. Tomorrow I am going to Reimer's.[5] Mrs.

[6.] *DBWE* 4:128–52.

[7.] Not identified.

[8.] Dr. Tielsch was presumably the family's private physician.

[1.] *NL*, A 59,2 (43); handwritten postcard from Kieckow; postmark: "Belgard/Pom[erania], December 15, 1941"; previously published in *GS* 2:416.

[2.] The fourth Sunday in Advent.

[3.] The cantata by Heinrich Schütz for voices and instruments "Es ging ein Sämann aus zu säen seinen Samen" (The sower went out to sow his seed), which was to be performed in the family for Paula Bonhoeffer's birthday on December 30, 1941.

[4.] This refers to the imprisoned members of the Old Prussian Union examination commission. Cf. Bonhoeffer's letter of May 14, 1941, to Hans-Werner Jensen (see 1/108) and the "Petition to the Armed Forces" (see 1/139, p. 243–44). The trial of Albertz, Asmussen, Dehn, Niesel, and others ended on December 22, 1941, with varying sentences.

[5.] Pastor Karl-Heinrich Reimer.

von Kleist-Retzow is coming on the seventeenth. Is your mother going to Stettin? Write your sermon for the second in plenty of time.[6] If it doesn't work out any other way, you will have to come back from Kade on the first and return on the third. In short, we also need you urgently for the singing. Without you it won't work!

All the best! Yours most affectionately,

Dietrich

236   **142. From Ruth von Kleist-Retzow**[1]

Kieckow, December 30, 1941

Good, dear Dietrich,

I cannot bring the old year to a close without sending you a special greeting and thanks. Although I am not uneasy about my son's upcoming operation,[2] it is a tremendous relief to me to know that you are near him. Needless to say, it is a sacrifice for me not to be able to be near him myself in these days. Although I have long since given up my claims on him, he nevertheless is and remains my own child, who once lived with me in utter dependence. These are probably thoughts that are still totally foreign to you, but they were stirred up for me again by the book[3] you have given me. (I have not yet finished it, since in the past few days my eyes have repeatedly refused to function for me, and it has now reached the point that I must ration their use.) Monika traveled across the stormy seas to follow her son. . . . It is compelling to read how unimportant everything else was to her because she was so concerned about the salvation of her son's soul. But I also comprehend well that all interventions with the exception of intercessory prayer were insignificant. That is still the case today and yet can be learned only very gradually.

I thank you most especially for the good words that accompanied your gift. Do you know as well that with them you have granted me a right? The right not to have

---

[6.] This refers to the sermon on January 2, 1942, in the Confessing Church congregation in Gossner-Saal, where Jews who had converted to Christianity and wore the compulsory star of David were also allowed to meet; see Bethge, *In Zitz gab es keine Juden,* 120. A corresponding report is found in Birger Forell's papers; see "Petition to the Armed Forces," 1/139, ed. note 11.

[1.] Literary estate of Ruth von Kleist-Retzow; handwritten letter, previously published in Ruth von Wedemeyer, *In des Teufels Gasthaus,* 169ff.

[2.] The reference is to Hans-Jürgen von Kleist-Retzow; see Bonhoeffer's letter of December 14, 1941, to Eberhard Bethge, 1/141.

[3.] This refers to the volume published by Furche, *Monika: Das Bild der Mutter in den Bekenntnissen Augustins;* see Bonhoeffer's letter of May 14, 1941, to Hans-Werner Jensen, 1/108, ed. note 3.

to scrutinize all my words when something personal at times escapes from me.... I shall certainly not exploit this right, for then you could take it away from me again. But all this is related to the fact that despite your youth and my age you have a pastoral role in my life. It is of tremendous significance to know of a person whom one may ask for counsel when the end is ever more nearly approaching. So let us both thank God for bringing our meeting to pass and make use of its benefits as long as we still have them.

December 31. How eerie is the great stillness that has followed the storm.[4] What is going on? What will happen? Last evening Konstantin[5] and I were with the   237 "lonely one in the woods."[6] He did not know any more than we did, but he was quite shaken. May God remain close by us. Tonight I shall be leading the New Year's Eve[7] service in Krössin and in Kieckow. It is to be tuned to the keynote, "Do not be afraid—only believe." Perhaps God will grant that a ray of light may penetrate through my inadequate words. I would no longer dare to open my mouth if I did not know that I only wish to be the instrument God can choose if God wills.

On the third I want to travel with the children to Lasbeck for two days and land in Stettin on the fifth. Did you receive the laundry package intact? It was sent off before the holidays. Yes, it gives me pleasure when I can take care of something "motherly" for you along the way. How *caring* your entire family has been about my son! If you would like to write me once more with your impressions of my son's condition, I would be very grateful to you; tonight I shall inquire about what is new. He wrote to me with such peacefulness, and it is wonderful that he has taken so well to Professor Br..[8] "I love him with all my heart," he wrote me. Of course, I am glad that I can be here with the children and others. I am also getting to know the children so much better than otherwise. It seems to me that they are moving in a good direction.

Please greet your parents and especially all the Schleichers, who were so very considerate to me. I shall write as soon as I can. The only thing that concerns me is what happened to the bouquet of flowers that was meant to greet me but arrived when the door was closed.

Be commended to God in the New Year, with all worries and troubles. By the way, is the question of divorce ruled out?[9] Of course, it always becomes impossible when

---

[4.] [This passage refers to the total lack of news after the German army had come to a standstill because of great difficulties caused by the winter weather.—MB]

[5.] Konstantin von Kleist-Retzow.

[6.] This refers to the Confessing Church pastor Karl-Heinrich Reimer in Naseband.

[7.] In Germany, as in the United States, New Year's Eve is celebrated on December 31 as the close of the year.

[8.] Presumably Prof. Dr. Kurt Brandenburg, who was the head physician of Berlin's Virchow Hospital.

[9.] The circumstances to which this remark alludes are unknown.

one party does not consent. I experienced this that time with my daughter.[10] But do we have any idea what we are doing when we tamper with fate?—Oh, our poor soldiers. What will ever become of them?

Very faithfully,
Your R. K.

[10.] Spes Stahlberg, née von Kleist-Retzow.

J. BERLIN AND KLEIN-KRÖSSIN.
JANUARY–APRIL 1942

143. From Erwin Sander[1]

Russia, February 4, 1942

Dear Brother Bonhoeffer,

On January 7, 1942, I received your letter,[2] for which I am very grateful. Of those brothers whom you name as missing or fallen, I know Joachim Staude and Edgar Engler. Indeed, God has torn great holes in the ranks of our brothers. The fate of J. Staude is particularly difficult. Who knows whether he is still alive and under what conditions he is living?

Especially important for me was, among other things, your word that the brothers at home must and are allowed to keep the hearth fire burning until the day of our longed-for homecoming. What you were able to report about the brothers, who are accompanied by the Bible and meditation even into the shell craters, is testimony to the power of spiritual life. I lost my old Bible, given to me by my mother for my birthday twelve years ago, in the events of the second half of January,[3] along with my *Daily Texts* for 1941.[4] You will understand how greatly I regret this loss.

For the last week and a half we have been housed in one of the few villages with a church. That there is no minister here almost goes without saying. Russia is a truly distressing country. Here the war has cast traditional conceptions about the treatment of others to the winds. In mid-January a unit of our division had to shoot fifty prisoners in one day because we were on a march and were not able to take these prisoners

---

[1.] *NL,* C 25; handwritten letter. Lieutenant Sander had participated in the collective pastorate in Groß-Schlönwitz in the summer of 1938.

[2.] See Bonhoeffer's Finkenwalde circular letter of November 22, 1941, 1/137.

[3.] In January 1942, the Red Army had succeeded in breaking through the front in several places, forcing the German units into hasty retreat.

[4.] [For more on the *Daily Texts,* see 1/122, ed. note 2.—MB]

along. In partisan areas, children and women who are suspected of supplying partisans with provisions are disposed of with a shot through the base of the skull. These persons must be done away with in this manner because otherwise German soldiers would have to forfeit their lives.[5] At the end of December and the beginning of January, at a large lake, our soldiers had to wipe out hundreds of Bolshevist soldiers who were pig-headedly attacking in wave after wave, using machine guns, rifles, and howitzers. The battery that I have led since January 15, 1942, following the death of the previous battery leader, lost four dead in January. There are now seventeen in our battery who have fallen in battle. For the last week and a half we have been building up the defenses around the villages we are occupying. We fortified a cemetery from which we would have to defend ourselves in case of an attack. We cannot give special consideration to the civilian population's stores of provisions, which unfortunately consist more often than not only of potatoes (including seed potatoes), if we are in need of them. We have had to burn down many a village in the last three weeks out of military necessity. Here and there the Russian soldier was thus forced, despite the cold, to live in the woods. But we must marvel repeatedly at what Russians can or must endure.

239

Over against all these experiences stands the promise, "I have called you (faceless person [Massenmensch], slaughtered and shot like cattle) by your name; you are mine!" God says "you"[6] to each person. God has promised each one eternal life and resurrection of the body. And to us soldiers the promise comes from the Sermon on the Mount, "Blessed are the merciful, for they shall receive mercy."[7] The contradictions are enormous, for many, no doubt, unbearably great.[8]

Under different circumstances you come to know yourself from different angles. — But in all this it remains a marvelous comfort to know that Christ is present everywhere with his forgiving love.

I am always very pleased to receive letters and cards from others who believe in Christ. One experiences there a little of the church-community one has already lived without for so long. Thus I thank you especially for your letter.

[5.] [This troubling comment reveals a great deal both about the actual situation that these seminarians faced as German soldiers on the front as well as about their rationalizations for their behavior. Such comments were widespread throughout the German army; as this letter shows, even Bonhoeffer's former students were not immune to such rationalizations. — MB]

[6.] [The intimate form of address *Du*, "you," is used in the German text. — MB]

[7.] See Matt. 5:7.

[8.] [Again, a troubling passage that seems to turn to Christianity as a form of solace and of denial, but one that gives insight into the experiences of those on the front. — MB]

What are Brothers Bethge, Schutz, Buchmann, and Lynker doing?[9]—I am glad that you have recovered from pneumonia. I wish you all the best and God's power in your work.

Very sincerely,
Your Erwin Sander

My new field post number is 37 04 6C.

144. Finkenwalde Circular Letter[1]   240

Dear Brother... [2]

Our dear brothers Bruno Kerlin, Gerhard Vibrans, and Gerhard Lehne have been killed in action. With all the brothers who have gone before them they now sleep awaiting the great Easter Day of resurrection. We see the cross, and we believe in the resurrection; we see death, and we believe in eternal life; we experience sorrow and separation, but we believe in an eternal joy and community. In the cheerfulness of his faith, in the clarity of his being, in his brotherly readiness for service, Bruno Kerlin has been for us a witness of this Easter faith for whom we thank God. Gerhard Vibrans was hit by an aircraft bomb just as he was about to sing with his comrades from *Ein neues Lied*.[3] All who knew this single-hearted, selfless brother, in whom simplicity and maturity were joined in a way that elicited the trust of all kinds of people, know what we have lost with him. The interpretative verse for the day of his death (February 3), Rev. 1:14,[4] particularly moved me. The life of this brother stood beneath the "flame of fire" of the eyes of Christ; it was a reflection of this purifying fire. I shall never forget that he taught me the hymn of Claudius, "Ich danke Gott und freue mich,"[5] and through his

---

[9.] Schutz, Buchmann, and Lynker, like Sander, were participants in the collective pastorate of summer 1938.

[1.] *NL,* A 48,3; carbon copy, probably from Berlin, March 1, 1942 ("March 1" is indicated by Bonhoeffer himself in the next-to-last paragraph); previously published in *GS* 2:583–85.

[2.] [Bonhoeffer used the singular in the salutation and then added the individual names by hand, since circular letters were no longer permitted. In the letter itself he speaks to the brothers in the plural.—MB]

[3.] The songbook for Protestant youth, *Ein neues Lied* (2nd ed., 1933), was used at Finkenwalde.

[4.] "His head and his hair were white as white wool, white as snow; his eyes were like a flame of fire." [For more on the tradition of the *Daily Texts,* see 1/122, ed. note 2.—MB]

[5.] The lyrics of "Ich danke Gott und freue mich" ("I thank God and rejoice"; *Ein neues Lied,* 349/444) were written by Matthias Claudius, the melody by Johann Abraham Peter Schulz.

own life gave me a convincing interpretation of this hymn. Gerhard Lehne was a man of questioning, seeking, journeying, restlessness, of many-sided interests and experiences, and in this was marked by great candor and straightforward honesty. The goal that so deeply moved him shone through it all. He performed his service to the church in devoted faithfulness. Now

241 God has brought him at such a young age to rest and peace. We praise and thank God for the life and death of our brothers. Their death reminds us of the blessing that God once gave us through a common sharing of God's Word and table; we hear also the admonition to render faithfulness to one another as long as we are still able.

I have experienced the signs of such faithfulness in an overwhelming way in recent weeks. I can never express my gratitude for this in words. Throughout the entire month letters for my birthday arrived from those who perform difficult service in our homeland and also from the bitterest cold of Russia, some written in brief pauses in the midst of battle. How am I to return such faithfulness? I thank you from my heart. Let us hold fast to our prayer for one another. Who knows how much protection we owe by God's grace to the intercession of a brother?

It was a surprising experience for me that precisely in these recent weeks there has been an increase in the voices, both from the front and at home, requesting new assistance in meditation. I confess that I would not have dared on my own to try to talk you into this. I didn't want to add something more to the daily burdens you bear. So even today I desire nothing other than to say a few words about the precious gift given to us with meditation— and about one aspect that is particularly important for us today. For me the daily silent reflection on the word of God as it applies to me—even if only for a few minutes—tends to become the crystallization of all that brings inner and outer order to my life. With the interruption and dissolution of our previously ordered life that the present age has brought about—with the danger of losing our inner order through the profusion of events, through the all-consuming claims of work and service, through doubts and moral conflicts [Anfechtung], battle and unrest of all kinds—meditation gives our life something like constancy. It preserves the connection with our former life, from baptism through confirmation to ordination; it sustains us in the healing community of the congregation, of the brothers, of the spiritual home; it is a spark of the hearth fire that the congregations at home want to tend for you; it is a fountain of peace, of patience, and of joy; it is like a

242 magnet directing all the available powers for ordering our life toward its pole; it is like pure deep water in which the heavens with their clouds and sun are radiantly mirrored. But it also serves the Most High, in that it opens for God a space of discipline and quiet, of healing order and contentment. Do we not all have a deep longing, however unacknowledged, for such a gift?

Could it not become a healing power promoting renewal for us? For many reasons I consider it best if for the time being we stick to the old epistles[6] for our meditation. May God bless these hours for us.

Today, March 1, is the first day a warm spring sun has shone; the snow is dripping from the eaves, the air is clear, and the earth is beginning to appear again. Our thoughts are with you who in the past months have endured unimaginable things on the front and during the winter, wishing for you that the sun and warmth and earth will soon give you joy again. "He gives snow like wool; he scatters frost like ashes. He hurls down hail like crumbs—who can stand before his cold? He sends out his word, and melts them; he makes his wind blow, and the waters flow" (Psalm 147).[7] God will one day break even the winter and the night of evil and allow a spring of grace and joy to draw nigh. "Summer is right at hand, the winter is past, the tender little flowers spring up, the one who has begun this will also complete it" (Luther).[8]

In the confidence and community of this faith I commend you to God and to our Lord Jesus Christ.

Your faithful
Dietrich Bonhoeffer

145. To Karl Vibrans[1]   243

March 4, 1942

My very dear and esteemed Brother Vibrans,

In this season in which our thoughts are drawn to the passion of our Lord Jesus Christ, in which we attempt to bring under the cross of Jesus all the

---

[6.] [In Finkenwalde Bonhoeffer had introduced daily meditation to his seminarians and made it a point to have them meditate on biblical texts using the same text for a whole week (cf. *DB-ER*, 462–65, and *DBW* 14:947–49). The term "epistles" refers to the two biblical readings in Sunday worship services, one taken from the Gospels and the other taken from the Epistles. Luther had adopted the medieval Sunday readings for the Lutheran church. In 1896 at Eisenach the German Protestant synod accepted a new series of Sunday readings to be used alternatively. Since then Lutheran churches distinguish between "old" and "new" Sunday reading.— MB]

[7.] [Bonhoeffer is quoting verses 16 and 17 (in the NRSV translation verses 16–18).—MB]

[8.] Cf. verse 12 of "Eyn newes lied wyr heben an" in Luther, *Die deutschen geistlichen Lieder*, 11–12.

[1.] *NL*, A 60,4 (13); copy of typewritten letter, presumably from Berlin; previously published in *GS* 2:590–92. The recipient, Pastor Karl Vibrans in Ballenstedt (in the Harz region), was the father of the former Finkenwalde seminarian Gerhard Vibrans.

universal suffering that never releases its hold on us, God has sent enormous personal suffering to you and to us. The death of your dear son Gerhard has been a blow to me like no other sad news in this war to date. I believe that the pain and that particular feeling of emptiness that has followed in the wake of his death could scarcely be different if he were my own brother. Gerhard stood particularly close to my heart. I have become poorer by his death. How much more must this be true for you who knew him so much better, who thus know so much more deeply what you have lost with him. How inconceivably difficult Gerhard's death is for his young wife, how hard for his siblings and for Eberhard.[2] Ever since I got to know Gerhard—and I thank God that I did get to know him—I have known that he was a person like very few others; and the closer we grew to each other, the more I deferred to him. With his integrity, his love of the truth, his selflessness, his purity, he meant more to me personally than I can say and than he knew. Wherever he went, his combination of simplicity and maturity brought him the kind of trust found by very few others. He was strict in his demands on himself and yet never hypocritical;[3] he had a cheerful heart and yet knew all the needs and temptations, all the inner chaos of the human heart. I shall remain grateful to him the rest of my life for two things: for the manner in which he kept the Sabbath holy, and for how he taught me the Claudius hymn, "Ich danke Gott und freue mich."[4] Through him these two things have become a living part of my own life.

244

At the seminary Gerhard was a good brother to his companions. Not only his heart but also his hand belonged to anyone who needed it. In the process he was continually drawn to those who were especially in need of help. In chivalrous love he always stood with the weak and the difficult. Gerhard was always eager to learn, and yet in all things he remained himself. Thus what he said and did was always genuine. When, following the news of his death, I checked the watchword for February 3,[5] I shrank at first from its terrible severity. But then I realized that both the watchword and the

---

[2.] Eberhard Bethge. [Vibrans and Bethge were cousins. They were quite close; they began their theological training together, and both first met Bonhoeffer at the first Finken-walde session.—MB]

[3.] [Bonhoeffer uses the word *pharisäisch*; see the discussion of this in the editor's introduction, pp. 26–27.—MB]

[4.] See the March 1, 1944, Finkenwalde circular letter, 1/144.

[5.] The Old Testament watchword was Jer. 17:10: "I the LORD test the mind and search the heart, to give to all according to their ways, according to the fruit of their doings." The New Testament interpretative text was Rev. 1:14: "...his eyes were like a flame of fire."

interpretative text[6] could apply to him in particular. It was always a matter of utmost gravity to him that faith must bear fruit, that faith cannot be without works. He always had the Holy Judge before his eyes. One could sense from his very nature that the eyes of the one whose gaze is like flames of fire rested on him. It was this purifying, consuming, ennobling fire that was reflected in his love of the truth and in his unselfishness. Thus I am able to read even these words on the day of his death with great thankfulness and confidence.

Now we must all let go of that which we had with him. May we do so beneath the cross under which he himself lived and found grace, with our whole hearts, in great thankfulness, in wholehearted love of God. May we now let go of our worry for him. God has done for him all that is good; he is at peace. May we find this peace as well beneath the cross. God grant to us all and provide for us a joyous Easter celebration following this Lent.

With sincere respect, I wish to express to you and your wife, as Gerhard's father and mother, the thanks I can no longer say to Gerhard himself for that which he was for me and for our larger community of brothers, and I do this deeply moved by the remembrance of splendid hours spent together with Gerhard in your home.

245

In deep fellowship, your devoted brother
Dietrich Bonhoeffer

146. To Elisabeth Vibrans[1]

March 5, 1942

Dear Mrs. Vibrans,

How shall I express to you all that has moved me in these past days and how your grief fills me with deep sorrow and how I beseech God to help you now to truly bear and overcome all this? I do not wish to say anything now about what Gerhard's death means for me personally. With very feeble words I attempted to say what Gerhard was for me in the letter to your father- and mother-in-law. When I think of you, all personal sorrow disappears under the crushing load with which you have been burdened. Now the very first

---

[6.] This Old Testament watchword and New Testament interpretative text were part of the Moravian *Daily Texts*. For more on the tradition of the *Daily Texts*, see 1/122, ed. note 2.—MB]

[1.] *NL,* A 60,4 (14); copy of typewritten letter, presumably from Berlin; previously published in *GS* 3:44–45.

days of shock and bewilderment have passed. We grasp that it is really true that we shall never see Gerhard again, and the question emerges in us how we shall now come to terms with this loss, how we shall get over it. Yet already, when we ask this, we sense an inner resistance. We don't want to get over this grief at all; if we are not to have Gerhard alive any longer, then we wish to hold on to him at least in our grief. And yet we must not think this way. This is a rebellion against God's action. We must let go of Gerhard; we must overcome this great sorrow, however difficult it will be for us. Otherwise we would not be able to go on living without being alienated from God, from others, and ultimately from ourselves as well. But then the gift that God has given for a short time with Gerhard's life would in the end become a curse for us rather than a blessing. Even if life has now become void and empty for you, even if it will seem to you that your life has been destroyed—and who could not humanly grasp that?—nevertheless your life is also from God and has its goal in God alone, and if you forget yourself out of love for God, becoming utterly selfless and thereby live for God and those around you, then God alone can and desires to give your life meaning and abundance again. But that can only happen if you now truly and with your whole heart give yourself over to God and to his inscrutable will, if this terrible loss can evolve into willing and humble renunciation, if the angry revolt of your whole being can evolve into free self-denial, if you can become free and open out of love of God and for the sake of your fellow human beings. How deeply Gerhard's congregation will need a Christian example for the bearing of such pain in these war years, how deeply the congregation will thus perceive in you Gerhard's own nature and faith, how securely you will remain united with Gerhard precisely in such self-sacrificial love of God and others.

May God grant that, by the time you travel the difficult path into the Rosian parsonage and church,[2] you will have struggled through to the point where you have become one with God, with others, with yourself, and with Gerhard. God will grant this to you, and those who love you will help you in it.

In the fellowship of great sorrow, great thankfulness, and great hope,
    your devoted
Dietrich Bonhoeffer

[2.] Rosian is a one-parish village *(Pfarrdorf)* in the district of Magdeburg. [Vibrans had been pastor there since 1936.—MB]

246

147. From Ernst Wolf[1]

Halle, March 16, 1942

Dear Mr. Bonhöffer,

You are surely familiar with *Verkündigung und Forschung*.[2] Unfortunately, for the time being nothing has come of our hope to publish this annual for 1942 as well (around one-third has already gone to press), since two appeals from the publisher for access to available paper were refused on specifically war-related economic grounds. Now I intend to make a third appeal myself and am arming myself to this end with recommendations from various corners, even from the Conference of Deans[3] and the Clerical Advisory Council[4] (you see that I can also be unscrupulous in pursuit of this cause). In fact, it is the case that for many conscripted theologians and pastors, this annual is their only connection to their discipline. For this reason various consistories and regional church councils have taken it upon themselves to buy up larger batches and send them to their pastors. My question is this: is there an office of the OKW[5] responsible for attending to the professional connections of conscripted academicians, particularly younger scholars? And if so, could you please let me know how to contact them? An endorsement from them would, of course, be decisive. As mentioned, the paper is available, but its release is being refused.

In case you did not yet know, volume 2 of Vischer's *Christuszeugnis* has appeared;[6] and the A. Lempp publishing house in Munich[7] hoped to receive a limited number for distribution. The new work I've been doing on the side[8] has been up and running for some time. I do not know officially yet whether it is having any effect, but I believe

---

[1.] BA Koblenz, Nachlaß Ernst Wolf, vol. 37, *Verkündigung und Forschung,* carbon copy.

[2.] Cf. Bonhoeffer's letter of February 14, 1941, to Eberhard Bethge; see 1/81, ed. note 5.

[3.] The Conference of Deans of Theological Faculties.

[4.] Created on August 29, 1939, this body consisted of German Evangelical Church Chancellery director Dr. Friedrich Werner, the regional bishops D. August Marahrens (Hanover) and Walther Schultz (Mecklenburg), and the senior consistory officer Johannes Hymmen (Münster). See *Gesetzblatt* 18 (1939). According to a letter of April 7, 1942, to Pastor Walter Holsten, Marahrens turned down Wolf's request (BA Koblenz, Nachlaß Ernst Wolf; see ed. note 1). [*Geistlicher Vertrauensrat* is often translated as "Confidential Spiritual Council," a somewhat misleading term. In fact, it is an advisory body of church leaders whom Werner had invited to consult with him on church and political matters. See Helmreich, *German Churches under Hitler,* 235 and 304–6.—MB]

[5.] [Oberkommando der Wehrmacht, "Armed Forces High Command."—MB]

[6.] *Das Gesetz,* the first volume of Vischer's *Das Christuszeugnis des Alten Testaments,* was published in 1934; it was followed in 1942 by a volume on the early prophets.

[7.] After the Chr. Kaiser Verlag in Munich was banned, Albert Lempp led the publishing house in his own name.

[8.] Not identified.

I can infer this based on a communication conveyed by P. Holsten[9] from the Gossner House.

With sincere thanks and best wishes,
Your [E. Wolf]

248   **148. To Ernst Wolf**[1]

March 24, 1942

Dear Professor Wolf,

Following extensive investigation, we have located an office that desires to take an interest in the annual. Please have the last two volumes sent to the address of my brother-in-law, Reich judicial councilor Dr. von Dohnanyi, OKW, Tirpitzufer 80.[2] From there the matter will be handled further.

The recent[3] situation has been successfully resolved in the minds of the people here. That pleases me greatly. — I take great pleasure in the new Bultmann volume.[4] The intellectual honesty of his work never ceases to impress me. Apparently Dilschneider[5] recently disparaged you and Bultmann quite stupidly here at the Berlin pastors' meeting; and, as I was told, the meeting came within a hair's breadth of sending you a protest against Bultmann's theology! And from Berliners, of all people! I would like to know if any of them has actually worked through the commentary on John.[6]

[9.] Like Eberhard Bethge, Pastor Walter Holsten, at that time one of the editors of *Verkündigung und Forschung* responsible for literature on missions, worked at the Gossner Mission in Berlin.

[1.] BA Koblenz, Nachlaß Ernst Wolf, vol. 37, *Verkündigung und Forschung*; handwritten letter, probably from Berlin; partially reproduced in *GS* 3:45–46.

[2.] Accordingly, Ernst Wolf wrote on March 27, 1942, to Hans von Dohnanyi. In a letter to Albert Lempp of March 30, 1942, Wolf wrote, "Regarding *Verkündigung und Forschung*, Bonhoeffer has opened a way into the OKW [Oberkommando der Wehrmacht, "Armed Forces High Command"—MB] for me, one which is not entirely hopeless. Perhaps the annual will be declared to be of military importance, which in fact it is" (Archives of the Chr. Kaiser Verlag).

[3.] Cf. Bonhoeffer's letter to Manfred Roeder (see 1/228.6) and a portion of Bonhoeffer's letter to Hans von Dohnanyi (see 1/150). In March 1942, Bonhoeffer requested help for Wolf from Hans von Dohnanyi.

[4.] Bultmann's *New Testament and Mythology* triggered a decades-long discussion about the demythologization of New Testament concepts; cf. Eberhard Jüngel's introduction to the 1988 German edition.

[5.] Licentiate Otto Alexander Dilschneider was at that time a pastor in Berlin-Zehlendorf. Cf. Bonhoeffer's "Study on 'Personal' and 'Objective' Ethics"; see 2/13.

[6.] Bultmann, *Gospel of John*.

This arrogance, which flourishes here—under the influence of several blowhards, I think—is a real scandal for the Confessing Church.[7]

Could you please assist me in procuring Vischer's second volume?[8] I   249
wrote to Lempp but do not know whether that will suffice.

Sincerely and with best wishes,
Your Dietrich Bonhoeffer

149. From Ernst Wolf[1]

Halle, March 28, 1942

Dear Mr. Bonhöffer,

When I came home last night from the hospital,[2] my wife said there was a letter for me that I would be very glad to see. It was yours.[3] Thank you very much, both for the information regarding my personal matters and above all for the advice and assistance regarding *Verkündigung und Forschung*. I sent the 1941 annual report first thing today along with a cover letter to Mr. von D.;[4] and since I cannot surrender my last copy of the 1940 annual, which is totally out of print, I at least included a copy of its table of contents. And thank you most especially for your words about the Bultmann volume. You express precisely that which moved me to publish it. From the enclosed you will see that the Berlin meeting did in fact consider itself compelled to protest.[5]

[7.] Ernst Wolf wrote Albert Lempp from Halle on March 30, 1942: "The publication of volume 7 of the series [Bultmann, *Offenbarung und Heilsgeschehen,* which included the essay "New Testament and Mythology"; the series was Beiträge zur evangelischen Theologie.—MB] has won me lively approval from Bonhoeffer and Hammelsbeck and others but also a solemn protest from Asmussen in the name of the Berlin general meeting of Confessing Church pastors. The protest only strengthens me in my conviction, however, that it was right and good to print these lectures. When the occasion arises, I can submit the correspondence, which is not entirely pleasant, to you" (Archives of the Chr. Kaiser Verlag).

[8.] See Ernst Wolf's letter of March 16, 1942, to Dietrich Bonhoeffer, 1/147, ed. note 6.

[1.] BA Koblenz, Nachlaß Ernst Wolf, vol. 37, *Verkündigung und Forschung*; carbon copy of a letter.

[2.] Cf. Karl Barth's letter of May 12, 1942, to Otto Salomon; see 1/158. Ernst Wolf was in training in the army medical corps.

[3.] See Bonhoeffer's letter of March 24, 1942, to Ernst Wolf, 1/148.

[4.] Hans von Dohnanyi.

[5.] Cf. Ernst Wolf's letter of March 30, 1942, to Albert Lempp (see 1/148, ed. note 7) regarding Hans Asmussen's protest in the name of the Berlin general meeting of Confessing Church pastors. Cf. also Ernst Wolf's May 18, 1941, letter to Hans von Soden, regarding the invitation to Rudolf Bultmann to present a paper on his demythologizing agenda to the Gesellschaft für Evangelische Theologie, or Society for Protestant Theology,

A letter as disturbing as it is foolish, equipped with many a "theological error"
250   (particularly at the end), to which I am still putting off my reply so as to respond in proper measure.

That it is the theological con man Dilschneider, of all people, who lurks behind this actually makes the matter more bearable on one level. I have known this gentleman for quite a while. [...] Your reference to a certain arrogance is absolutely true in his case. Yet he seems to continue to fascinate people—this is presumably simply part of the arrogance. And most likely the advertising of his own books has angered him; the pastors' newsletter publicized them as "workbooks" for the pastor, in part with K. Heim's help (!). The book is very clearly considered to have a phenomenology of Christ reminiscent of Hegel and a tendency toward Sabellianism.[6]

I can only ask Asmussen to withdraw his letter and to reflect carefully on the necessity of theological error within a theological work consciously committed to the church. His own errors could fill an entire book, and yet no one wishes on that basis to forbid him so quickly to speak "intra muros"[7] (what a category!). To be sure, I would not have accepted his *Wiederum steht geschrieben*[8] for the Beiträge,[9] and I also prevented it at that point from appearing in Existenz.[10]

Today I am also sending you a small essay[11] that, only because it was designated for the von Soden Festschrift, ended up in *Theologische Blätter*, for which I have said I cannot write any longer because of the editor's political escapades.[12] It treats a topic

---

in Alpirsbach, June 4–6, 1941: "The danger of oversimplification in the church is very great indeed right now. It corresponds to the dismantling of academic rigor that is happening before our very eyes in the Institutum antijudaicum, since it has no connection with the church" (*Theologie und Kirche im Wirken Hans von Sodens,* document 27b, 279). ["Institutum antijudaicum" refers to the Institute for the Study and Eradication of Jewish Influence on German Religious Life, founded by the German Christians in 1939 and located in Eisenach. As its name suggests, it was founded to promote an "Aryanized" version of Christianity consistent with Nazi ideology. Its director was Walter Grundmann, professor of New Testament at the University of Jena. See Heschel, "When Jesus Was an Aryan," in Ericksen and Heschel, *Betrayal,* 68–89.—MB]

[6.] In the third century, Sabellius regarded Father, Son, and Holy Spirit as three manifestations of the one divine essence (modalism).

[7.] "Within the walls" means within the church, particularly the Confessing Church.

[8.] Hans Asmussen, *Wiederum steht geschrieben.*

[9.] [The series Beiträge zur evangelischen Theologie.—MB]

[10.] The series Theologische Existenz heute.

[11.] Ernst Wolf, "Communio Sanctorum: Erwägungen zum Problem der Romantisierung des Kirchenbegriffs," 1942. [No further publication information is available. This may have been a self-published essay.—MB]

[12.] [Hermann Strathmann, who became editor of *Theologische Blätter* in 1937, was an outspoken advocate of a *völkisch* church. See Gerlach, *And the Witnesses Were Silent,* 42.—MB]

that once engaged you and concerning which, to no small extent, I have both learned and found confirmation from your book.[13]

Again many thanks!

[E. Wolf]

150. Excerpt from File: To Hans von Dohnanyi[1]

251

Dear Hans.

1) Contains statements on Prof. Schniewind.[2]

2) Statements on the Jewish professor Perels,[3] in the Gurs evacuation camp in the Pyrenees, both of them are to be helped.[4]

3) Licentiate Niesel,[5] one of our most qualified and clear-headed people, is threatened with conscription. A date is not yet known; presently he is in Breslau, having been expelled from Berlin. At the moment there is nothing to be done, but I wanted at least to let you know of it.

4) —[6]

5) Jannesch's[7] son Hans Peter (long wounded, etc.) —you probably already know about this—has now been declared GV[8] again; and naturally his father[9] is making efforts to get him out of this again (he is now the

---

[13.] This refers to Bonhoeffer's dissertation *Sanctorum Communio*, which Wolf subsequently republished in 1954, see *DBWE* 1:5–6

[1.] Vojenský ústřední archiv, Prague, "Reichskriegsgericht," [War Court] file 9: "Sammlung von Anklagen und Urteilen—gKdos 1943" [Collection of Indictments and Judgments—Top Secret Military Documents 1943], VÚA-VHA, RKG (39), 2(I), Geh. Kdos.—rozsudky 1943–45; excerpt from the September 21, 1943, indictment against Bonhoeffer, reproduced in full in 1/230.2; hectograph. The section printed here is an excerpt from a letter from Bonhoeffer to Dohnanyi included in the indictment, putatively dating from March 1942. In this portion of the letter, points 3 and 5, which are of significance for the indictment, are cited word for word, whereas the remaining points are merely summarized. The indictment against Bonhoeffer referred to this letter excerpt on page 26 of the interrogation transcript and in "supplementary file red enclosure 2." On the context, see 1/230.2.

[2.] Julius Schniewind.

[3.] Leopold Perels.

[4.] See Schreiber, *Friedrich Justus Perels*, 174–75, and Winfried Meyer, *Unternehmen Sieben*, 120–21.

[5.] Wilhelm Niesel. Cf. Bonhoeffer's letter to Manfred Roeder, see 1/228.5, ed. notes 40 and 41.

[6.] It is possible that Ernst Wolf was mentioned at this point; see Bonhoeffer's letter to Manfred Roeder, 1/228.6, where Bonhoeffer mentions a "letter to my brother-in-law concerning Niesel, Wolf, and Jannasch"; cf. also *DB-ER*, 819.

[7.] The correct spelling is "Jannasch." Cf. Bonhoeffer's letter of November 23, 1941, to Wilhelm Jannasch, 1/138.

[8.] [*Garnisonsverwendungsfähig*, "fit for limited duty."—MB]

[9.] Wilhelm Jannasch.

only son, since his brother was killed). Do you see any possibility of doing something? I did not give him much hope. I only feel terribly sorry for the father, who has personally endured a great deal in recent times; and I am constantly pondering what could be done. Could we give someone in Poznan[10] a personal hint? I suppose it is very difficult.

252   6) Concerns an action to benefit two pastors' sons in Stettin who had been temporarily taken to a concentration camp because of activities endangering the state.

Forgive me for upending this vat of requests and needs over you, but by now you must be used to it. Many thanks for all your help.

Cordially, Dietrich

151. Finkenwalde Circular Letter[1]

Dear Brother...![2]

Permit me to answer all at once those letters with the same subject matter, namely, the question of legalization.[3] One of you writes as having been legalized, another as having recently refused legalization, yet another in the midst of pondering it. In all cases the questions are the same. I would like to attempt to clarify some basic points.

1. In times of uncertainty about the church's path, the following rule applies for us:

a) I should never make a decision out of uncertainty; that which already exists takes precedence over change, unless I discern with certainty the necessity of the change.

[10.] [Poznan is located in a region of Poland that had formerly been a part of Germany but became Polish after World War I. During World War II it was reoccupied by Germany; it has been Polish since 1945.—MB]

[1.] *NL*, A 48,3; handwritten, incomplete draft, undated, probably from April (although possibly also October) 1942; previously published in *GS* 2: 594–95.

[2.] [Bonhoeffer used the singular in the salutation and then added the individual names by hand, since circular letters were no longer permitted.—MB]

[3.] The consistories repeatedly offered a more or less unconditional "legalization" to the "illegal young brothers" who were in the field during the war to give them full rights to or within a pastorate. Because the Reich church constitution had the force of church law, they were all considered "illegal" since the church authorities dependent on the state, and thus also the corresponding government offices, did not recognize the examinations of the Confessing Church and the resulting right to become a civil servant as a pastor. In April 1942, the Old Prussian Union Council of Brethren again issued a statement refusing to endorse any exam administered by the consistory and refused to acknowledge any church government functions of the consistory. In the province of Saxony, the Council of Brethren conducted legalization proceedings from July until September. On the legalization debate, see 1/72, ed. note 8.

b) I should never act alone, first, because I need the counsel of the brothers; second, because they need me; third, because there are church rules 253 that I may not carelessly disregard.

c) I should never rush a decision or allow myself to be forced. If today a door is closed to me, God will open another if God wills it.

From this rule it becomes clear that our present wartime situation is particularly unsuited for attempting a far-reaching alteration of the church's way. Now more than ever I must wait for the word of my church leadership and have patience. Any decision that gives preference to those serving at home over against those brothers on the front is even more questionable.

2. The matter of the proper education of preachers of the gospel is worthy of our ultimate commitment. It remains a legitimate Protestant stance to renounce one's readiness for an established ministry or even for any exercise of the pastoral office at all and to serve Christ in another vocation, rather than submitting oneself to fraudulent spiritual leadership (for this is what is at stake with regard to the coming generation). It must be questioned whether the ultimate commitment, entailing such a renunciation, must be demanded of every single individual, when every attempt toward proper education is made impossible both practically and by law, and thus where martyrdom is the necessary result of any such attempt. To be sure, at the moment this is not yet certain, since no verdict has yet been rendered in the trial.[4] Under the present circumstances, we can no longer reject in principle that it is a Christian option to assume office and serve Christ as a pastor while renouncing every church government (for the recognition of a false church government is impossible!) and "maintaining one's personal theological convictions."[5] But this option must be seen as one burdened with heavy ecclesial and personal dangers and responsibilities.

3. What does it mean for a church to follow a straight path? Can what was true for the Dahlem synod be false today? Is our conscience bound to 254 Dahlem III/3?[6] The word of God alone is what makes our path straight, even if to our eyes it is crooked. God's word alone is true. Our conscience is bound to God's word alone.

[4.] See the discussion of the trial of the examination committee, 1/141, ed. note 4.

[5.] Thus reads the official offer of legalization for Confessing Church candidates.

[6.] "We challenge the Christian congregations, their pastors and elders, to accept no instructions from the present Reich church government and its officials and to withdraw from cooperation with those who wish to continue in obedience to this church government. We challenge them to adhere to the directives of the Confessing Synod of the German Evangelical Church and the organs it recognizes" (Wilhelm Niemöller, *Die zweite Bekenntnissynode*, 38).

K. Trip to Norway and Sweden. April 10–18, 1942

255 **152. To Eberhard Bethge**[1]

April 9, 1942

Dear Eberhard,

Just in case, you should know that it is my wish for you someday to receive my books, musical instruments, and pictures.

Affectionately,
Dietrich

153. Calendar Notes, April 10–18, 1942[1]

April

Friday, 10th	*10:35 leave from St.*[2] — *Saßnitz Hotel Victoria*
Saturday, 11th	*4 o'clock ferry to Trelleborg. Overnight in Malmö.*
Sunday, 12th	*8 a.m. departure. Oslo 12 a.m.*
Monday, 13th	*O[slo].*
Tuesday, 14th	*O[slo].*
Wednesday, 15th	*O[slo].*
Thursday, 16th	*Day for travel to Stockholm*
Friday, 17th	*Stockh[olm]. Evening to Malmö. Flight*
Saturday, 18th	*Flight 10 min[utes] to Cop[enhagen]. 4 o'clock to B[erlin].*

[1.] *NL*, A 82,21; handwritten note from Berlin, before Bonhoeffer embarked on the trip to Norway.

[1.] *NL*, A 82,21; Bonhoeffer's handwritten entries, italicized here; partially reproduced in Bethge, Bethge, and Gremmels, *Dietrich Bonhoeffer: A Life in Pictures,* 190. Cf. *DB-ER,* 754; see also Helmuth von Moltke's letters to Freya von Moltke, 1/154.

[2.] This refers to the Stettin station in Berlin.

154. From Helmuth von Moltke's Letters to Freya von Moltke[1] 256

Berlin, April 9, 1942

If my plans remain unchanged, I shall leave tomorrow morning, arrive in Oslo Saturday noon, and shall leave Tuesday morning for Stockholm. Wednesday night from Stockholm to Copenhagen and early Friday from Copenhagen to Berlin. [. . .]

On Friday morning, Dohnanyi and Bonhoeffer are coming to me at 8:15 and the flight departs at 10. [. . .][2]

Saßnitz, April 10, 1942

Now we've missed the ferry, and the next one presumably doesn't leave until early the day after tomorrow. It got stuck several times in the ice and thus does not keep to a schedule. [. . .] Now we are going to go eat and then to a movie! I let myself be talked into it, because I didn't want to disappoint the good Bonhoeffer. [. . .]

Grand Hotel Oslo, April 15, 1942

I've been here three days now and in all the commotion have not yet written.[. . .]

So on Saturday morning we woke up in Saßnitz, and since the day was tolerable, although also very hazy, we decided to take a walk. My primary reason for doing so was to clarify the game plan with Bonhoeffer, which seemed easier on a walk than in the hotel room. So we walked then from 9:00 till 1:30, around 6 km to the chalk cliffs of Stubbenkammer. [. . .] Apart from a woodsman, we encountered not a living soul, so 257 we had plenty of time to discuss everything. That also led to results that to this point at least have been satisfactory. When we got back to the hotel at 12:30, there was still no news of the ferry. [. . .] After learning this, we ate our lunch, and as we were sitting at table (!), the ferry appeared suddenly in the window, coming out of the fog. It was truly marvelous. So we rushed to the harbor, where we were told that the ship would depart two hours later, so we should hurry; they were still going to attempt to make the connection to Oslo in Trelleborg.

[1.] Excerpts from Moltke, *Letters to Freya*, 210–15; translations adapted by Lisa Dahill. These diary-like depictions of the trip to Norway augment Bonhoeffer's calendar notes; see 1/153. For more information, see *DB-ER*, 752–55.

[2.] In his essay "Der Kreisauer Kreis," Ger van Roon writes erroneously: "In April 1942, Moltke flew with Bonhoeffer to Oslo" (they flew together only on the segment from Malmö to Copenhagen to Berlin on the return trip), but he notes correctly: "to save the life of Bishop Berggrav" (Berggrav was the initiator of the Norwegian pastors' resistance). On the other hand, he writes misleadingly: "Both were known to the Gestapo" (*Geschichte in Wissenschaft und Unterricht* 39 [1988]: 147). Both Himmler and Martin Bormann intervened to rescue Berggrav in April 1942, Himmler with a telegram to Reich commissioner Terboven ("Why has Berggrav been arrested?") and Bormann with a telegram on April 15, 1942 ("Bishop Berggrav should be released immediately"). On April 13 the judicial proceedings against Berggrav were suspended, and on April 16 he was released from prison, although interned in his forest cottage. Cf. *MW* 5:262–64 (note).

In fact we left at 4:30. The ship was comfortable; our travel companions simply unpleasant and awful. [. . .]

Our train was scheduled to depart at 9:26 p.m., and at 9:00 Trelleborg came into view. But it took another two hours before we got in, because we got stuck in an ice barrier. And just as I was thinking that we would be stuck there forever, the enormous ice floes parted and made room for us, and ten minutes later we docked in Trelleborg. The train had already left. We got on an extra train[3] to Malmö and stayed overnight there in the Hotel Savoy. [. . .] At 12:15 a.m. did I ever go to sleep quickly, since our train was leaving at 8:00 the next morning.

[. . .] At 12:00 we were in Oslo, where Steltzer[4] picked us up from the train and brought us to the hotel, where I am being lodged in an enormous, sumptuous apartment, half salon and half bedroom, with bath, etc., on the Belle-Etage,[5] while my companion, as he is called here, is staying on the fourth floor. [. . .]

[April 17, 1942][6]

Monday morning at 9:30 the first official visit, and from there it continued without a break until 8:00 p.m. Finally at 8:30 we had our first visit with three topnotch Norwegian men,[7] where Steltzer, Bonhoeffer, and I were most sumptuously fed. [. . .] The conversation lasted until 1:30, which was actually a little long. That Monday evening was the high point of the visit. On Tuesday morning more official visits were on the agenda, and in the afternoon a consultation from 3:30 until 8:00 p.m. with one of the three

258

[3.] [This was a supplementary train, not listed in the schedule but added in emergency situations.—MB]

[4.] Theodor Steltzer, former parliamentary representative in Rendsburg, who since 1933 had been serving chiefly in church and ecumenical roles; he had been in contact with Moltke from work camps in Silesia. Their contact increased during the war and led to his active participation in the Kreisau circle. At that time Steltzer was stationed in Oslo as a lieutenant colonel, was the authorized transportation officer on the general staff of the armed forces commander for Norway, and had established connections between the German and the Norwegian resistance.

[5.] [The Belle-Etage was the first-class floor of the hotel.—MB]

[6.] This is a continuation of the letter of April 15, 1942, and was presumably written on April 17, 1942, in Stockholm.

[7.] These three men were probably Pastor Alex Johnson and Conrad Svendsen, and perhaps Professor Arvid Brodersen (whose connection to Steltzer remains obscure) or the painter Henrik Sørensen; cf. *DB-ER*, 752–55; *MW* 5:262–64; and Brodersen, *Fra et nomadeliv,* 192–93. In *Eivind Berggrav: God's Man of Suspense,* Alex Johnson recalls the encounter with Moltke as follows: "When I related that the pastors were threatened with having to leave their parishes if we could not rescind their resignations, he [Moltke] replied: 'Splendid. Just take your wife and children along, and travel the roads with a handcart. Hold a parish meeting every evening. I am sure that if Norway's one thousand pastors set out that way, the men in Berlin will understand fast enough how foolish this whole business is'" (167, note; trans. altered).

Norwegians from the previous evening with whom some details had to be worked out. B. was scheduled to meet with a different Norwegian. In the evening then I was alone with Steltzer. On Wednesday I first had to write a great deal. [...][8] At 10:30 I met with Falkenhorst's chief of staff[9] for concluding discussion, at 12:00 with the general; and at 1:00 I ate with the general and his staff. In the afternoon the concluding discussions continued; at 7:00 I was finished, and at 8:30 Bonhoeffer and I went to Steltzer's.

Today, early Thursday morning, we departed at seven o'clock for Stockholm and are now delayed at the border station.

[...] B. and I always took breakfast together in my suite, because we had the best opportunity there to coordinate our plans for the day with each other. Monday noon I ate with the head of the military intelligence office, Monday evening at Steltzer's, Tuesday noon with Falkenhorst's chief of staff, Tuesday evening at Steltzer's; Wednesday noon I ate with Falkenhorst; and Wednesday evening I didn't eat at all, because I was feeling too wretched and didn't want to demand even the work of digestion from my body.—With the exception of the meal with St. all of them were actually unsatisfying, because there was too little going on with the people. The best one was actually the chief of staff, a Colonel von Loßberg, but the general is truly a piece of work. He is incapable of listening, holds monologues, tells stupid stories, and is quite extraordinarily foolish. What a difference from Falkenhausen![10] At the meal I did nothing but commit minor violations of discipline, primarily to amuse Steltzer and the I c,[11] Major [Müller?], and that succeeded only too well, for [Müller?], who sat across   259 from F., couldn't keep a straight face at all. That at least was a pleasure. In terms of our work, I have the impression of success with regard to both the overt as well as the covert dimensions. I came to an agreement with all the soldiers involved—except for the general—regarding the contents and request of my report to Admiral Canaris; and needless to say this was very significant for me.[12]

[8.] Among other things, he wrote a detailed letter to Lionel Curtis in England.

[9.] General Nikolaus von Falkenhorst was commander in chief for Norway until 1944. [His chief of staff was Colonel Bernhard von Loßberg.—MB]

[10.] [The German DBW edition here incorrectly reads "Falkenhorst." General Alexander von Falkenhausen was commanding officer in Belgium and northern France; he was implicated in the July 20 attempt to assassinate Hitler.—MB]

[11.] ['I c' was the name for an army subdivision whose function was to collect and evaluate intelligence about the enemy. 'I c' can also refer to the chief of that subdivision.—MB]

[12.] Cf. MW 5:298, which contains the two reports of the Swedish general consul in Oslo, Claes Westring, dated April 14 and 22, 1942; cf. also van Roon, ed., Helmuth James Graf von Moltke, 286–87, on the visit of the German "commission."

Berlin, April 28, 1942

[. . .]This morning the opus[13] has made its way to Bonhoeffer, and tomorrow morning he will be returning with it. I hope I can then bid it farewell tomorrow in the course of the day. [. . .]

155. To Erling Eidem[1]

Aboard ship,[2] April 11, 1942

My dear and honored Archbishop Eidem:

While traveling through Sweden on my way to Norway,[3] I am very pleased to make use of this rare opportunity for a personal greeting as a sign of abiding and grateful fellowship. It has now been over six years since you extended to me and my seminary such unforgettable hospitality.[4] We shall never forget it. Terrible things have taken place in the meantime. But the more hopeless the ruptures in the world become, the more strongly Christians must maintain the bond of peace that unites them in Jesus Christ. Only in this way can the peoples someday find their way back to one another.[5]

I had the great pleasure of seeing Ehrenström more frequently in the past year and found myself to be in complete agreement with him in our

260

[13.] This refers to the summary report, signed by Moltke, which integrated Bonhoeffer's own reconnaissance. In the indictment against Hans von Dohnanyi it was argued that Bonhoeffer "did not submit even a single written report" on the trip in April 1942; see 1/229.2, p. 432.

[1.] Landsarkivet, Uppsala, Arkiv Erling Eidem; handwritten letter. See *NL*, A 60,4 (17); previously published in *MW* 5:297–98 and *GS* 6:550–52. On the circumstances, see *DB-ER*, 752–55, and *MW* 5:260–66 and 299–304.

[2.] This letter was written on the Saßnitz-Trelleborg Ferry; cf. Bonhoeffer's calendar notes (see 1/153).

[3.] Erling Eidem presumed that Bonhoeffer was under way as a soldier (as Bishop Bell reported to Gerhard Leibholz on June 20, 1942; see 1/184). Germany had forced neutral Sweden to allow German soldiers stationed in Norway to pass through Sweden in sealed railway cars when going on leave, a practice that was halted toward the end of the war. The Swedish general consul in Oslo, Claes Westring, let Eidem know only on April 22, 1942, that a German commission had arrived there. On April 25, 1942, further information was provided that the commission consisted of two men, neither of whom was a pastor.

[4.] See *DB-ER*, 506–17, and *MW* 5:156–65 and 170–91; see also his report on his trip to Sweden in *DBW* 14:142–43 et passim.

[5.] These sentences doubtlessly express the ecumenical dimension of Bonhoeffer's motivation for resistance activity; see Boyens, *Kirchenkampf und Ökumene*, vol. 1, *1933–1939*, 385–87, 395–406; vol. 2, *1939–1945*, 295–98.

judgment of the situation and the tasks.[6] It is very disturbing for us that our dear friend Forell[7] will be leaving Berlin. We have the feeling that this departure is coming too soon; he should have stayed at least one more year. Both Ehrenström and Forell will, by the way, be attempting to make a trip to Sweden possible for me. There would be many important matters to discuss. Perhaps from Malmö, before continuing on my winter trip to Oslo, I can still briefly visit one of the professors in Lund.[8] On the trip back in five or six days, I shall perhaps be coming through Stockholm.[9] It would be a very great joy to me to see you again, dear and honored archbishop. But that will probably hardly be possible this time. Thus I must simply pass along to you the greetings of all my friends and also my own in this manner. We know that particularly in recent months your responsibilities have become especially extensive and weighty and that many of the Nordic brothers and   261
sisters look to you. Thus we pray that God may give you for your ministry all divine power, aid, and love as a blessing for the entire Protestant church. It will please you to hear that our dear brother Martin Niemöller is doing comparatively well, considering the circumstances. He is now together with three Catholic clergy[10] and has in the meantime perceived with new certainty the proclamation of the pure gospel in the Reformation.—My former work has unfortunately come to an end. But all of this would need to be related in person.

In genuine fellowship and gratitude, I remain

yours very respectfully, Dietrich Bonhoeffer

[6.] Cf. Nils Ehrenström's calendar notes; see 1/93 and 1/123. Bonhoeffer probably had contact with him and Birger Forell in Berlin during Ehrenström's trip home to Sweden at the beginning of April 1941.

[7.] Birger Forell.

[8.] This probably refers to Anders Nygren.

[9.] Bonhoeffer stayed in Stockholm the evening of April 16 through the evening of the seventeenth. He visited the secretary of the Swedish Ecumenical Council, Pastor Arnold Werner. On April 16, Chaplain Clemens Harold Jones informed Archbishop Erling Eidem of Bishop George Bell's planned arrival in Sweden on May 11, 1942. After receiving this letter, Eidem telegraphed Bell on April 17: "British chaplain Stkhlm informs me to day about your coming Sweden middle may. Heartily welcome. Eidem." It is quite likely, though not proven, that Bonhoeffer was informed in Stockholm about Bell's trip to Sweden.

[10.] Niemöller was imprisoned in the Dachau concentration camp, along with Monsignor Johannes Neuhäusler, Munich priest Michael Höck, and Monsignor Nikolaus Jansen of the cathedral in Aachen. See 1/75, ed. note 6.

156. To Anders Nygren[1]

April 11, 1942

Dear Professor Nygren:

On this trip through Sweden to Norway, I gratefully recall that lovely time six years ago when I and my preachers' seminary enjoyed your hospitality— which unfortunately no longer exists.[2] I wish to use this brief moment to let you know that—despite all the terrible things that have taken place in the meantime—we stand unchanged in the same cause and the same struggle— which you must believe even though you seldom hear from us—and that we are more conscious than ever before of our communion with Christians of all lands. This is the only way to overcome these dreadful times.

In sincere admiration and gratitude, I remain yours very respectfully
Dietrich Bonhoeffer

157. To the Leibholz Family[1]

Stockholm, 17th of April 1942

My dears,

as you see I am here for a day or two on my way home from a short and interesting trip to the north. I went to see friends of mine upthere and inspite of all difficulties I had a very satisfactory time. I am just now enjoying a few hours of rest and a wonderful warm day in Stockholm. So I wish to send you all my love and all my best wishes for you and for the children. Not long ago I got your letter and the pictures of you and the children. You

---

[1.] Lunds Universitetsbibliotek, Arkiv Anders Nygren; handwritten letter, probably sent from Malmö following Bonhoeffer's arrival at the Hotel Savoy around 11:30 p.m.; cf. 1/154; the envelope, which is no longer extant, bore Swedish stamps; see the following statement by Nygren. Professor Nygren lived in Lund until the end of his life. In an undated, unaddressed handwritten statement, probably at the end of the 1960s, written in English from memory and not as an exact translation, he wrote, "Since this encounter [March 2, 1936], I heard only once more from Bonhoeffer. It was through a letter during the war. I do not know from where he had written it. It came with swedish stamps, and it was only a few lines and his name. He wrote, 'If you will now and in the future not hear much from us, you may know, that we keep always the same position as we did when we met in Sweden.' He held this position unto the bitter end."

[2.] Cf. *MW* 5:170–91. The visit on March 2, 1936, to Anders Nygren in Lund has only recently been documented by newly discovered letters in Nygren's papers; see *DBW* 14:130.

[1.] *NL*, A 59,3 (7); handwritten; in original English, including errors; previously published in *GS* 6:551–53. The letter was probably conveyed through Pastor Arnold Werner in Stockholm.

262

can hardly imagine what a joy it was for me and for my people. Marianne has such an open, good and most intelligent face. There can be no doubt that she will make her way and be a great joy and help for you. Christiane is such a lovely, friendly girl as she has always been. Sabine is looking very well again and showing us her kindest face inspite of all sorrows and difficulties she is having as we know. Unfortunately there was no picture of Gert. But we were most happy to hear that he is lecturing again. Now just a few words about my family. There are no important changes to report. Wolfgang has been extraordinarily successful recently in his job.[2] I saw him a few weeks ago with my parents. He is a clever boy and most efficient. His successes are really unique. Ursula is, of course, a little troubled about the future of her son.[3] But we are all doing our best to help her. The boy is still at home which is best for him. He is, by the way, a very reasonable fellow and listens to good advice. I am travelling a good deal besides I am writing a book.[4] My friend[5] is often with us, he has become a great flutist and his friendly good-humored nature is a source of joy to the family. He has a great friendship for you all. When I wrote to you last, I thought uncle Rudy[6] would not live much longer, but in January and February he recovered a little, though I am quite convinced only for a very short time. He is so weak, that I and my people do not believe that he can live longer than a few months.

I am still looking forward with good confidence to seeing you again in the near future. It cannot last long anymore, I think. Let us keep up our courage and hope for better days. God be with you all

Please, give my best regards to all friends. What about Mary's confirmation?[7]

Much love to all of you

Yours ever Dietrich

[2.] This refers to the jurist Dr. Wolfgang Grote, former assistant to Professor Gerhard Leibholz in Göttingen. Grote took care of Leibholz's financial concerns in Germany after the Leibholzes emigrated to England.

[3.] Ursula and Rüdiger Schleicher's son Hans-Walter had to reckon with conscription for military service.

[4.] This refers to his *Ethics*.

[5.] Eberhard Bethge.

[6.] "Uncle Rudy" was the family code word for Hitler's conduct of the war; cf. George Bell's letter of June 20, 1942, to Gerhard Leibholz (see 1/184). [Bonhoeffer used code words in his correspondence with relatives and friends. Bethge points out that there was an actual "Uncle Rudy," Count Rüdiger von der Goltz, a retired general and brother-in-law of Bonhoeffer's mother. Goltz lived near the Bonhoeffer home on Marienburger Allee (*DBER* 626). In this letter Bonhoeffer uses the code word to tell his sister and brother-in-law that he thinks the war will be over soon.—MB]

[7.] This refers to Marianne Leibholz, Bonhoeffer's godchild; cf. Sabine Leibholz-Bonhoeffer, *Bonhoeffers: Portrait of a Family*, 139–40.

L. Third Trip to Switzerland. May 12–26, 1942

158. Karl Barth to Otto Salomon[1]

Basel, May 12, 1942

Dear Mr. Salomon,

[...]

How does the world situation strike you? Since Adolf gave his last speech,[2] everything now seems much more agreeable to me; and after the Japanese were unable to land anywhere with their troop ships, I would like to assume that they were the ones who lost the great naval battle.[3]

I hear that Mr. Bonhoeffer is already in the country.[4] I knew of his coming from the police here, who inquired of me regarding clearance for his entry. Would you quietly suggest to him that he be most circumspect when discussing politics with

---

[1.] Deutsches Literaturarchiv, Marbach, Nachlaß Otto Bruder; typewritten letter. ["Otto Bruder" was Otto Salomon's pseudonym.—MB] During the war Salomon resided at Schloßbergstraße 18 II, Zurich-Zollikon. Bonhoeffer gives the address in his May 21, 1942, letter to the Leibholz family; see 1/165.

[2.] This refers to Hitler's speech to the Reichstag on April 26, 1942: "We have a mighty winter battle behind us. The hour will come in which the front will free itself again from its torpor, and then history will decide who has triumphed this winter" (Domarus, *Hitler: Reden*, 4:1875).

[3.] In the Java Sea naval battle of February 27–March 1, 1942, all the Allied naval forces involved were destroyed by the Japanese; Japan occupied the entire Dutch Indies and controlled vast regions of East Asia and the Pacific. During the Coral Sea naval battle of May 4–8, 1942, the Japanese aborted their planned landing at Port Moresby. The Allied counteroffensive did not get under way until August 1942.

[4.] Bonhoeffer may have arrived in Switzerland on May 11, 1942 (according to *DB-ER*, 755) or, as Barth's remark indicates, one or two days earlier; cf. Bonhoeffer's letter of May 13, 1942, to Karl Barth (see 1/160), in which he tells Barth that he has been in Zurich "for several days."

Swiss people? If I discern rightly, German public credibility has sunk considerably since he was last here.[5]

Today we received a letter from Prof. Wolf's wife indicating that her husband[6] has also now been conscripted to the medical corps and is being trained. Thus far it seems to agree with him. Hopefully the whole business will come crashing down before they also get around to sacrificing this important man to their idiotic purposes. From the same letter we became aware of the repercussions of the most recent Bultmann furor. It saddened me as well; but should the "pious Hans"[7] truly desire to burn him at the stake over this, I would most likely join the other side. Oh, if only our dear friends in the Confessing Church would leave all that and would finally begin to rack their brains, five minutes before midnight, whether there is anything, anything, they could do to deal with the inexorable coming disaster! The demythologized New Testament is truly only the dotting of an i, that is, in comparison with all that the Germans have done and daily continue to do in the occupied regions, stirring up a cloud of wrath. But I am afraid that all their eyes are still closed and behind them they are only dreaming, dreaming . . . [. . .]

And now please greet your wife and accept my best regards and, once again, my sincere thanks,

Yours, Karl Barth

265

159. To the Leibholz Family[1]

Zurich, 13th of May 1942[2]

My dears,

once again I have taken a short holiday to have a little rest and to see my friends here. This gives me a little time to write you a letter and to tell you something about my family. Yesterday I saw Lore[3] and read your last letters to her. It is such a comfort to know you are all well, according to circumstances. Your cable to my father's birthday was a great joy indeed. Charles[4] and his wife spent a few weeks' holiday in the south and had a good time there. They are thinking of you daily and heartily and asked me to give you

---

[5.] His last trip had been August 29–September 26, 1941.

[6.] Ernst Wolf.

[7.] Hans Asmussen; see 1/148, ed. note 7.

[1.] *NL*, A 59,3 (8); handwritten letter; in original English, including errors; previously published in *GS* 6:554–55.

[2.] "1942" was added in a different hand.

[3.] Lore Schmid, née Delbrück.

[4.] "Charles" is the code name for their father, Karl Bonhoeffer.

their greetings and best wishes. Aunt Elisabeth[5] just had a very nice letter from the old housekeeper[6] who also thinks of you with great love. At home everything is quite allright and the children always like to know about your children and are longing to see them again soon. Uncle Rudy[7] has recovered a little bit, but he is terribly nervous and full of anxieties with regard of his personal future that his family can hardly keep [him] much longer at home, but it is, of course, difficult to know what to do with him. It is so sad to see when a man gets physically and mentally weaker and weaker, a real burden to his family. But his illness is so grave that I believe he will not do much longer. Spring has come rather late this year which is rather awkward for the work in the gardens that we are doing with great passion. We are becoming more and more specialists for agriculture which is very good and necessary. John[8] and his family is enjoying his house at the lake. About Wolf's successes, I think, I wrote to you already.[9] I gave him your address which he already knew, but he is so busy that he is very seldom able to write letters. But we are glad to see his successes in his job.

Let me finish this letter for today. I hope to be able to write again soon. Let us keep up our courage till times become better, and I do not believe it will last long anymore. Give my special greetings to the girls.

Much love to you all

Yours ever Dietrich

160. To Karl Barth[1]

May 13, 1942

Dear Professor Barth,

I have been in Zurich for several days and since yesterday have been staying at the Pestalozzis'.[2] Now, armed with the galley proofs of your new *Dogmatics* volume,[3] which Mr. Frey[4] procured for me, I am departing for a leisurely

---

[5.] Elisabeth von Hase was Bonhoeffer's aunt.

[6.] This is a reference to the cook; cf. Sabine Leibholz-Bonhoeffer, *Bonhoeffers: Portrait of a Family*, 98–99.

[7.] See 1/157, ed. note 6.

[8.] "John" is the code name for Hans von Dohnanyi, who had recently moved to Sakrow near Potsdam.

[9.] Cf. Bonhoeffer's letter of April 17, 1942, to the Leibholz family; see 1/157.

[1.] *NL*, Anh. 3 (4); handwritten letter from Zurich; Bethge, *Schweizer Korrespondenz*, 14. On the context, see Bethge's commentary, ibid., 31–36. [See also *DB-ER*, 755–77.—MB]

[2.] Cf. 1/112, ed. note 1.

[3.] Barth, *Church Dogmatics* 2/2, *The Doctrine of God*; the preface is dated Pentecost 1942 (May 24).

[4.] Arthur Frey, owner of the Evangelischer Verlag, Zollikon.

week en route via Geneva to a guesthouse on Lake Geneva recommended to   267
me by the Pestalozzis. There I would like to attempt to work through at least
the second part of your volume,[5] in addition to reading a bit in Vischer's
second volume.[6] On the way back then I would be very eager to visit you.
In the meantime let me convey to you many greetings from those in Berlin
and particularly from your Pomeranian supporters,[7] who truly are doing
their work in great isolation and self-sufficiency and are awaiting your new
volume with great eagerness. But the likelihood of getting it through is
probably not very great. It was unfortunate that nothing ever came of the
proposed Christmas booklet.[8] The most recent theological happening for
us was the Bultmann volume, which gave rise to a fiery dispute between
Asmussen and Wolf and beyond.[9] Despite it all, I took great joy in the essays.
Asmussen is beside himself. More in person.[10]

   With best wishes and in the hope of seeing you soon,

In gratitude, your devoted
Dietrich Bonhoeffer

161. To Karl Barth[1]

May 17, 1942

Dear Professor Barth,

Please forgive me if what I am about to write is nonsense and not worth talking about. But I must nevertheless ask, because the matter keeps hounding
me incessantly. When, last week in Zurich, I first heard someone say that
you found my stay here "unsettling as to its objectives" [wegen der Aufträge

---

   [5.] Bonhoeffer is referring to "The Command of God," chapter 8 of *Church Dogmatics*
2/2:509–781.
   [6.] See 1/147, ed. note 6.
   [7.] [Bonhoeffer may be referring to former Finkenwaldian students now serving
either in the military or in congregations of the Confessing Church. In general there was
very little affinity among Pomeranian church people to Karl Barth. Cf. Bonhoeffer's letter
of May 17, 1942, to Karl Barth, 1/161.—MB]
   [8.] Cf. Charlotte von Kirschbaum's letter of September 22, 1941, to Paul Vogt, 1/128.
   [9.] Cf. Ernst Wolf's letter of March 28, 1942, to Bonhoeffer, see 1/149, ed. note 5.
   [10.] Eberhard Bethge comments, "The available materials unfortunately disclose not
a word as to how the conversation with Barth on this question [i.e., the Bultmann discus-
sion] proceeded" (Bethge, *Schweizer Korrespondenz*, 29). But see Barth's comments in his
letter of May 12, 1942, to Otto Salomon, 1/158.

   [1.] *NL*, Anh. 3 (5); handwritten letter from Geneva; previously published in Bethge,
Schweizer Korrespondenz, 14; an excerpt (up to "if mistrust arises [wenn Mißtrauen aufkommt]")
is reproduced in Bethge, Bethge, and Gremmels, *Dietrich Bonhoeffer: A Life in Pictures*, 191.

268   unheimlich], I simply laughed; when shortly thereafter I ran up against this
purported statement of yours a second time in Zurich, I thought it would
be best simply not to respond. Now I have heard the same thing twice here
in Geneva, and having pondered the matter a few days, I simply wish to let
you know of it. It is clear to me that in such tight circles there is a great deal
of idle gossip, and that it is quite possible this is some sort of overinflated
rumor. If this were not the case, however, then I would be at a complete loss
as to how to respond. In a time in which so much simply has to rest on personal trust,[2] *everything* is lost if mistrust arises. I can, of course, understand
that this curse of suspicion gradually afflicts us all, but it is difficult to bear
when for the first time it affects oneself personally. Yet it must also be terrible
for you—perhaps even worse than for me—to be compelled suddenly to
be suspicious. Our conversations must have been simply unbearable for you.
And I never perceived this and cannot imagine it, even in reflecting back on
them. I was actually so glad to be able to tell you everything in response to
your question in our last conversation.[3] I thought, now all of this is clear.

        I wish to add only that it would be unimaginably painful for me if the
result of the—very laborious—attempt to continue my relationship with you
were to be an inner separation, and why should I not also go ahead and tell
you that I believe that at least in the eastern part of Germany there are only

269   a few who have remained as loyal to you in countless conversations over
these years as I have attempted to do. On the other hand, I wish to spare
both of us the torment of a conversation laden with mistrust. In that case I
would rather not come at all, although in my Swiss trips I have looked forward to nothing more than to these visits with you. I had wished now also to
tell you even more and to pass on greetings. But after all of this, Basel has
now become somewhat "unsettling" to me in turn; and I don't know what is
right. Otherwise I would gladly have asked whether the Monday or Tuesday

---

[2.] Cf. the newsletter "The Church as an Ecumenical Community in Wartime" that
was distributed in April 1939 to the members of the temporary committee of the WCC,
which was in the process of formation: in these times it is important "to assume a steadfast
responsibility for the maintenance of relations to churches on all sides and to keep the
lines of communication between the various churches open by means of correspondence
or whenever possible through personal contact" (Boyens, *Kirchenkampf und Ökumene*, vol. 1,
1933–1939, 386).

[3.] According to a February 1955 communication from Karl Barth and Charlotte von
Kirschbaum to Jørgen Glenthøj, during the conversation in September 1941, Karl Barth
had directly asked Bonhoeffer, "Dear Bonhoeffer, I wish to ask you openly, 'Why are you
actually here in Switzerland?'" In response Bonhoeffer "spoke openly of the plans for
Hitler's removal and of the attempts to create a new government and to struggle for a
peace plan" (*MW* 2:185). Cf. 1/162, ed. note 8.

after Pentecost[4] might suit you. My visa expires on Thursday.[5] But please write me a word (preferably c/o the address of Otto Salomon). This is all quite dreadful for me in facing Thurneysen and Vischer as well.

May I let you know just once more that you truly have no need to mistrust me? And that this prospect, as bitter as it is for me, nevertheless even now sometimes simply causes me to laugh. But I need a word from you as to whether I should come.

Please forgive this long letter that interrupts you in your work and keeps me from reading your *Dogmatics*.

With sincerely respectful greetings, your grateful devoted
Dietrich Bonhoeffer

162. From Charlotte von Kirschbaum[1]

Basel, May 17,[2] 1942

Dear Mr. Bonhoeffer,

What a pickle to be in! Above all, please be assured that we too are laughing at this matter, although with tears in our eyes; for the fact that such tumult could arise is reason enough to be troubled and in its own way demands to be taken seriously as a "sign of the time." To state it clearly: Karl Barth has never mistrusted you for a second, or to be quite precise, when a *question* did arise as to how your trips were made possible, he posed this question to you immediately and directly.[3] If in these days, in response to an inquiry in this matter, he were to have *articulated* to his friends some such question as to how it is that you have such freedom (an inquiry that we field over and over), this can have been the only trace of reality within the statement, which now appears to be circulating widely, that your presence here is "unsettling as to its objectives." He himself has no recollection of speaking about this, and I have heard nothing of the sort. And when then in conversation with you the question was answered for him clearly, he has subsequently only affirmed your coming to all who

270

[4.] Monday, May 25, and Tuesday, May 26, 1942.

[5.] The Thursday after Pentecost 1942 was May 28, the last possible day to depart Switzerland. See 1/168, ed. note 1.

[1.] *NL*, Anh. 3 (6); carbon copy; Bethge, *Schweizer Korrespondenz*, 16–18. An excerpt is reproduced in Bethge, Bethge, and Gremmels, *Dietrich Bonhoeffer: A Life in Pictures*, 191.

[2.] This date is more likely May 18; cf. Bethge's commentary in Bethge, *Schweizer Korrespondenz*, 31. It is unlikely that a response would have been written on May 17, the same day as Bonhoeffer's letter, particularly since that was a Sunday. [Bonhoeffer's letter would not likely have been delivered on a Sunday.—MB]

[3.] Cf. 1/161, ed. note 3.

ask. The fact that this has been necessary again and again, and is still so, proves to you how anxious and suspicious people have become with "us" here.[4] A few weeks ago[5] the immigration officials inquired of Karl Barth as to whether he would vouch for your entry. He did so without hesitation, and as a result permission was granted.

You see, then, the matter is groundless. At one point a small ripple went through the closer circle of friends as well (Thurneysen, Vischer) at your freedom of movement, but after Karl spoke with you, the matter was completely cleared up; and when we told them both the other day that you were here, their response was one of quite unequivocal *joy*. Thus you may think of them as well without even the slightest murmur of distress.

The situation is more difficult with Karl Ludwig Schmidt, who was remarkably interested in your coming and accompanied this with suspicion [Argwohn] probably attributable to his own painful wounding at the hands of the Third Reich (expatriation). This suspicion is directed at the German nationals in Geneva, Dr. Schönfeld and Freudenberg,[6] as much as to you. No amount of persuasion has yet succeeded in dissuading him from raising extremely grave accusations—and unfortunately not only off 271 the record—the least of which is that you have been "manipulated." To date we have not made this known because we truly regarded it as a "case of individual pathology." Perhaps with a visit to him you could resolve the matter—he finds it hard to bear that you "passed him over" the last time!![7] This is by no means certain; the case is very complicated.

This would seem to be the situation. But I would very much like to add one more thing so that openness truly prevails on all levels. For Karl Barth there is in fact something "unsettling," and that is all the attempts to rescue Germany, by means of further "national" endeavors, from the immense predicament into which it has now been swept. This also includes the attempts that may be undertaken if necessary by the

---

[4.] This sentence echoes some of the political tensions in Switzerland, particularly following Hitler's victory over France. Against the powerful factions that more or less openly advocated joining the "new order," as well as those that promoted anxious conformity with political authorities, an [anti-Nazi] National Resistance Movement was begun by Hans Hausamann; Karl Barth and Arthur Frey were among its founders in September 1940. Cf. A. Meyer, *Anpassung oder Widerstand,* 191–208; and E. Busch, *Karl Barth,* 307–10.

[5.] If this phrase, "a few weeks ago," means not more than four weeks earlier, then the application for this trip's visa was probably submitted to the Swiss general consulate immediately following Bonhoeffer's return from Norway on April 18, 1942, without a corresponding notification of Barth in Basel. Already before his second trip to Switzerland, Bonhoeffer had named Karl Barth as sponsor; see Bonhoeffer's letter of May 30, 1941, to Karl Barth, 1/110.

[6.] [Freudenberg, of course, had to leave Nazi Germany because his wife was of Jewish descent.—MB]

[7.] Cf. Bonhoeffer's letter of May 20, 1942, to Charlotte von Kirschbaum, 1/163.

generals. He has, of course, intimated this to you already and is certainly prepared to speak with you about it. In this regard he has likely spoken openly here and there and has perhaps also mentioned your name in this connection occasionally, with the deep sigh, "Oh, if only people like . . . would also see that . . ."[8]

Dear Mr. Bonhoeffer, please do not take offense that I am the one writing to you. He is fervently at work on the series of lectures on creation, and you would have had to wait two days for his next free hour. That would not have been right.

We shall be *overjoyed* at your coming. The Monday after Pentecost is much more opportune; Tuesday would be free only after five o'clock. On Pentecost Sunday evening we are looking forward to a pleasurable evening with most delightful Mozart records,   272
to be shared with the very interesting Jesuit priest[9] with whom K. B. is now in ongoing conversation. If this too would entice you, then you would simply need to arrive sometime Sunday evening! There could surely be overnight accommodations arranged with the Thurneysens or the Vischers—unfortunately we no longer have a guest bed here.

We wish you restful days yet and send you our best regards.

Your L. von K.[10]

[8.] In a letter to Jørgen Glenthøj of September 12, 1956, Barth clarified the statements in *MW* 2:185: "In the information you [Glenthøj] communicate of our Basel conversations [in February 1955, *MW* 2] on page 185, some misunderstandings have apparently arisen: at that time Bonhoeffer did not speak to me of a regime, led by generals, that 'wished to *pull back*' the German troops 'to the 1939 borders' (this was apparently only *later* their intent [see 1/181, ed. note 9]) but rather of a regime that wished for the time being to *leave* them at the fronts and in the occupied regions and wished to negotiate with the Allies on this basis. And I recall clearly Bonhoeffer's definite bafflement when I said I considered it impossible that the Allies would agree to this. Further, though I was always certain that in Bonhoeffer I was not dealing with a 'nationalist,' I could give no rejoinder when asked (understandably, given the various double agents surfacing in Switzerland at that time) how it came about for him to travel in our country with a German passport (issued by the Secret Service!) and money for three weeks. This was what gave rise to my question.—But the main focus of that conversation with Bonhoeffer was the question you mention on page 191: would the new German government being planned take a conservative-authoritarian or a democratic form?" See *Evangelische Theologie* 26 (1966): 490 n. 58.

[9.] Hans Urs von Balthasar from Einsiedeln.

[10.] [Charlotte von Kirschbaum's nickname was "Lollo," hence the abbreviation "L."—MB]

163. To Charlotte von Kirschbaum[1]

May 20, 1942

My dear Miss von Kirschbaum,

I am very happy about your letter. Thanks be to God that it is as you write.

I am very sorry about K. L. Schmidt. I did not visit him the first time because he was deathly ill in the hospital; the second time I was in Basel only four hours; and after all, I have no particular connections to him from before. This time it will again be a short visit as well; that is to say, I am also to visit de Quervain[2] and would like to go there and stay over that Monday evening.[3] Thus I shall take a noon train to Basel and hope to spend the afternoon with you. My time is terribly budgeted, since I have found an unending amount to read and to work on. I have just read *This Above All,*[4] by Eric Knight, with the greatest pleasure. Are you familiar with it?

Again, many thanks. I am looking forward to Monday.

Sincerely,
Yours very respectfully, Dietrich Bonhoeffer

273   164. To Alfred de Quervain[1]

Geneva, May 20, 1942

Dear Brother de Quervain,

Many warm thanks for your letter. Of course I would be eager to come. As far as I can tell, the only possibility for me is Monday evening until early Tuesday morning.[2] Would that be suitable for you? There would be much to discuss.

Sincerely,
Your Dietrich Bonhoeffer

[1.] *NL,* Anh. A 3 (7); handwritten letter from Geneva; previously published in Bethge, *Schweizer Korrespondenz,* 18–19.

[2.] See Bonhoeffer's letter to Alfred de Quervain dated the same day, 1/164.

[3.] May 25, 1942, Pentecost Monday.

[4.] According to Bethge, *This Above All* is a "novel about England in 1940, the story of a skeptic concerning England's situation after Dunkirk and the overcoming of his doubt. It was written by Eric Knight, who was born in 1897 in Yorkshire and died in 1943 as an American major. On the basis of this first war novel, he is ranked on a level with Hemingway and Steinbeck" (Bethge, *Schweizer Korrespondenz,* 32–33).

[1.] Universitätsbibliothek Bern, Nachlaß Alfred de Quervain; handwritten.

[2.] May 25 and 26 (Pentecost Monday and Tuesday). This visit did not take place; see 1/167, ed. note 2. Bonhoeffer met de Quervain on the afternoon of May 25 at Karl Barth's

165. To the Leibholz Family[1]

Zürich, May 21st, 1942

My dears,

I have just received your letter from April 29th[2] and I wish to thank you by return of post, so to speak, for, once my holiday is over—which will be the case day after tomorrow[3]—my work starts again and it is difficult to find sufficient time for letters. It is always a joy that brightens the whole week and more than that to get your letters and to know that your are well. What a marvel that it is still possible to keep up personal contact over such a long distance in a time that separates so many friends and families all over the world. By the way, I am awfully sorry to say that your telegram for your brother's birthday[4] has apparently never arrived. Or did you perhaps confuse it with my father's birthday? For, we had a telegram then[5] and were most happy about it? But we must not demand too much, it is already a great thing to hear from one another from time to time. We also got your letter after Sabines birthday[6] and were so glad that the photo pictures of the children had reached you. We have to be thankful indeed for everything that has been left in order in this chaotic world of ours. You know that we are with you in our thoughts and prayers every day and we know the same of you. By the way, Sutz[7] is always very glad indeed to get letters from you, (Lore,[8] of course, too), so is Mrs. Weber[9] who has moved to Zürich-Zollikon, Schloßbergstraße 18. A few months ago I had a very friendly letter from George[10] which gave me much encouragement. I think he is one of the absolutely trustworthy and most sympathetic people. I am so glad about your friendship with him.

274

---

residence. Mrs. de Quervain believes she recalls that the visit did in fact take place, but she may be confusing this with a meeting in September 1941.

[1.] *NL*, A 59,3 (9b); handwritten letter; in original English, including errors; previously published in *GS* 6:555–58.

[2.] Letter not extant.

[3.] This indicates that until then Bonhoeffer had estimated May 23 as his date of departure.

[4.] This probably refers to Bonhoeffer's own birthday on February 4.

[5.] The telegram arrived on March 31, 1942; it is, however, not extant.

[6.] As Bonhoeffer's twin sister, Sabine, had the same birthday, February 4. This letter is also not extant.

[7.] Erwin Sutz in Rapperswil functioned as the primary courier of letters between Berlin and London.

[8.] Lore Schmid, née Delbrück.

[9.] Elfriede Salomon, née Weber, wife of Otto Salomon.

[10.] Regarding this letter from Bishop Bell, see 1/132, ed. note 2. The letter itself is not extant.

I have always been thinking during the last months, specially in the depth of winter how you were getting through the severe cold. I remember a very biting winter in England myself and I am, therefore, so happy that you got through the worst without illness. Now you are over the mountain in every respect, I think. I wonder when we will meet again, but I am quite convinced that it will be sooner than many people expect.

Now just a few words about the family. Charles had a very beautiful holiday with his wife[11] down south in the mountains. It was very necessary since he is working hard. But I think it is just his work which is keeping him healthy and strong. It is surprising the way they share all our interests. Suses little son[12] had broken his foot, so he is at home and will be there for quite a while. I am travelling a good deal and my work at home is going on. By the way, I saw Miss Schoch[13] recently. She told me that she has written to you three times and that she will write again soon. She is a very friendly person whom I like very much. We have talked much about you. She is working now in the office of the Ecumenical Council.

275

We are so very happy about all you write about your children. I hope Marianne will have a good time with your methodist minister.[14] It is so important that she finds her way to Christianity and the church. There are so many experiences and disappointments which make a way for nihilism and resignation for sensitive people. So it is good to learn early enough that suffering and God is not a contradiction but rather a necessary unity; for me the idea that God himself is suffering has always been one of the most convincing teachings of Christianity.[15] I think God is nearer to suffering than to happiness and to find God in this way gives peace and rest and a strong and courageous heart. I was moved so much about what you wrote me about the 90th psalm[16] and about the vers Marianne likes so much: wait unto the Lord . . . [17] How much would I like to speak with her about all that. Being my God-child she is particularly in my heart and in my prayers.

[11.] This refers to the Bonhoeffer parents.

[12.] Andreas was the youngest son of Susanne, née Bonhoeffer, and Walter Dreß.

[13.] She was employed in the Geneva office of the World Council of Churches and was similarly helpful in transmitting letters.

[14.] Frederick Reeves was the pastor of the Methodist church in Oxford and was particularly involved in caring for the refugee families there. Marianne Leibholz was confirmed by Herbert Kramm in St. Mary's Church in Oxford; cf. Sabine Leibholz-Bonhoeffer, *Bonhoeffers: Portrait of a Family*, 135.

[15.] Cf. Bonhoeffer's letter of September 13, 1942, to Ernst Wolf, 1/202.

[16.] The verse reads, "LORD, thou hast been our dwelling place in all generations" (King James Version). [The Leibholz family was in England and would have used the King James Version.—MB]

[17.] Ps. 27:14; the King James Version reads: "Wait on the LORD."

While I write this letter Lore[18] rings me up and tells me about a new letter from you. What a joy! I will take it home. I am so sorry that you were a little troubled about us because you have got no letter from us for a long time. Meanwhile you will have received my last two letters from April and May. Please, do not worry at all about us. We are all very well indeed and we all hope to see you in not too far a future. I congratulate you to your new house. So you will once again have a real family life. It will be a lot of work for you but I suppose a satisfactory one. I hope that my and Miss Schoch's last greetings which were still directed to your former address will be forwarded to you. If you meet Francis[19] give him my kindest regards, please.   276
I read his little book[20] with great joy. Will you also give my love to the friends in London and to Julius.[21] I just write a few lines to George.[22] So I will finish this letter and I really wish to express once more how happy we all feel whenever we hear from you, and once again, do never worry about us and I am sure the day is not far when we shall all meet again in unspeakable joy. God be with you and the children—and with all of us.

Much love from
Dietrich

166. To George K. A. Bell[1]

May 23rd, 1942

My Lordbishop,

let me, please, thank you for your very kind letter[2] which I received only now. It has been such an unspeakable joy to hear from you personally. I am so grateful to you for giving your time and encouragement to my brother-in-law. My only possibility to express my gratitude is to assure you that we are going on with our work in the same spirit and that we shall never forget what you have done for us. Mrs. Martin has been ill for a few weeks, so we have no news about her husband.[3] But last time I heard from him he was

---

[18.] See ed. note 8.

[19.] "Francis" refers to Franz Hildebrandt, who had been pastor since 1939 to the German refugees in Cambridge.

[20.] This may refer to Franz Hildebrandt's *Theologie für Refugées: Ein Kapitel Paul Gerhardt* or perhaps *And Other Pastors of My Flock: A German Tribute to the Bishop of Chichester.*

[21.] Julius Rieger was the pastor of St. George's Church, London.

[22.] See Bonhoeffer's letter of May 23, 1942, to George Bell, 1/166.

[1.] *NL*, A 42,1 (35); typewritten letter from Zurich; in original English, including errors; previously published in *GS* 6:558–59; see *DB-ER*, 757.

[2.] Letter not extant.

[3.] Else Niemöller was unable to visit her husband at the Dachau concentration camp during her illness.

said to be well physically and mentally. Since I know that Wednesday is your special day of intercession[4] I will meet you in prayers and my friends when I will tell it will do the same. Thank you so much for letting me know that. It means so much to us. As far as I can see the day is not so far when we might meet again not only in spirit. What a comfort to know that you will be there in that moment! May God give us strength for the days that will come. May God be with you and your work.

277

In sincere gratitude I am, my Lordbishop,

Yours ever
Dietrich

167. To Charlotte von Kirschbaum[1]

May 25, 1942

My dear Miss von Kirschbaum,

I forgot today[2] to say that Dr. Gisevius (Zurich, Nüschelerstraße 24, Muralto Apartments) is prepared to bring me books in Germany if an opportunity

---

[4.] Cf. Bonhoeffer's letter of June 1, 1942, to George Bell, 1/175.

[1.] *NL,* Anh. 3 (8); handwritten letter from Zurich; previously published in Bethge, *Schweizer Korrespondenz,* 19.

[2.] The reference is to Bonhoeffer's visit that day to Karl Barth. Jørgen Glenthøj's notes on this visit state that, according to Barth's desk calendar for the afternoon of May 25, 1942, Eduard Thurneysen and Alfred de Quervain were also present and they listened to the BBC news together. When they heard the report on Molotov's visit to London and the British-Soviet treaty, which was signed on May 26, 1942, with the mutual pledge not to secure a separate peace with Germany, Barth remembers Bonhoeffer crying out, "Now it's all over!" In a letter to Carl Zuckmayer on June 29, 1968, regarding Zuckmayer's plan to write a drama on the "dialogue of those doomed to death," Barth was moved to speak of this encounter with Bonhoeffer: "I still remember, as if it were yesterday, how the hints that Dietrich Bonhoeffer personally gave me about the venture [the conspiracy to remove Hitler], that is, about the conversations preceding it, gave me the impression of something hopelessly passé . . . for all my human sympathy for the fate of the participants . . . a dead end which did not seem to offer any light of promise for the future. Until I am better instructed, of course!" (Barth and Zuckmayer, *Late Friendship: The Letters of Karl Barth and Carl Zuckmayer,* 67; trans. altered). At this visit, which was Bonhoeffer's last encounter with Barth, the following dialogue ensued in Charlotte von Kirschbaum's presence (Bonhoeffer had just worked through Barth's *Church Dogmatics* 2/2 in a guest house on Lake Geneva; see Bonhoeffer's letter of May 13, 1942, to Karl Barth, 1/160): "Bonhoeffer asks, 'Do you believe that everything will come back? Will it be—like Lake Geneva?' Karl Barth: 'Yes, like Lake Geneva!'" (communication of Karl Barth and Charlotte von Kirschbaum to Jørgen Glenthøj, published in *MW* 2:198).

should arise.[3] Thus, if B., V., Th.[4] could somehow be brought here, this would provide a sure way of bringing these things safely across. Needless to say, I would see myself as a lending library for those interested as well. It would be simply marvelous if this were to be possible. The books would then simply need to be sent to Dr. G. Many thanks, then!

By the way, G. would like to visit B.[5] again. I told him, however, that B. is presently so immersed in his work that he should wait at least a couple of weeks. He was quite amenable to that.

Again, many thanks for everything!

Wishing all of you all the best,
Your respectful Dietrich Bonhoeffer

168. To Friedrich Siegmund-Schultze[1]

May 25, 1942

Dear Professor Siegmund-Schultze:

After I had purposely taken the earlier train from Basel in order to see you, it had to be this train that was delayed over thirty minutes shortly before Zurich! I have just now eaten, and it is already 9:30, so that my coming is no longer a possibility. I am very sorry. I was looking forward to telling you some more things and also hearing from you. I lost too much time during my stay in Geneva, which was somewhat too long, and then the day in Rapperswil.[2] This was a mistake I greatly regret. Who knows now when we shall

278

279

[3.] This indicates that Bonhoeffer had contact with Hans Bernd Gisevius, the Military Intelligence envoy in Zurich, during his time in Switzerland. [Gisevius was the source of most information about the German conspiracy for Allen Dulles, director of U.S. intelligence in Europe at the Office of Strategic Services in Geneva.—MB]

[4.] Bonhoeffer is referring to books by Barth, Vischer, and Thurneysen.

[5.] Karl Barth.

[1.] Evangelisches Zentralarchiv Berlin, 51/L V a/4; handwritten letter from Zurich, discovered by Stefan Grotefeld. The Thursday after Pentecost, May 28, 1942, was the last possible day for Bonhoeffer to depart from Switzerland; see Bonhoeffer's letter of May 17, 1942, to Karl Barth, 1/161. Bonhoeffer's "military passport no. II/1939/42," issued in Berlin, was supposed to be valid from May 27, 1942 (i.e., the day before his visa expired) until August 26, 1945; see 1/201.2. The question remains whether Bonhoeffer left Switzerland on the day after his visit to Karl Barth in Basel, i.e., on May 26, thus reaching Berlin via Munich on May 27 to begin preparing for his trip to Sweden, or whether he stayed until May 28. In the latter case, those in Berlin would have been preparing his trip to Sweden even before he returned from Switzerland. The first possibility—that Bonhoeffer set off for Munich on May 26, 1942—is the most probable.

[2.] Bonhoeffer visited Erwin Sutz in Rapperswil.

see each other again? Since I shall have to reckon with conscription in the near future,[3] a conversation with you would have been particularly important for me.

With all my heart I wish the best for you and for your work, and greet you with long-standing gratitude and respect.

Your very respectful
Dietrich Bonhoeffer

169. Entry in the Guest Book of Otto Salomon[1]

In a time of great decisions
May 1942
Ecclesiastes 7:15[2]
Dietrich Bonhoeffer

[3.] Bonhoeffer could not have known at that point that his UK classification had been renewed on May 15. [For an explanation of the UK classification, see 1/31, ed. note 3. Officially, Bonhoeffer was considered indispensable (UK) in his position in Military Intelligence and thus was exempt from being drafted to serve on the front lines.—MB]

[1.] Deutsches Literaturarchiv, Marbach, Nachlaß Otto Bruder; handwritten and undated; previously published in *GS* 6:554. Bonhoeffer stayed with Otto Salomon in Zurich-Zollikon May 21–26, 1942. "One afternoon, after he had fetched his *poste restante* ("general delivery") letters, we found him depressed. He said, 'Things are serious for me' and departed the same day" (Zimmerman and Smith, *I Knew Dietrich Bonhoeffer,* 172).

[2.] "In my vain life I have seen everything; there are righteous people who perish in their righteousness, and there are wicked people who prolong their life in their evil-doing."

M. Trip to Sweden, Berlin, Munich. June 1942

170. George K. A. Bell: Diary Notes, May 13–June 11, 1942[1]

280

Visit to Sweden

May 13 2.45 (Swedish time) arrived at Stockholm airport, after a pleasant flight, in a plane with Norwegian pilot | 2 crew, no other passengers [...]

[1.] LPL, London, George Bell Papers, vol. 276; handwritten notations in English in a seventy-four-page notebook. The first half of the diary (up to p. 31, referred to henceforth as "Diary Notes") records the various events of Bishop Bell's trip to Sweden; the excerpts reproduced here as text are taken from this portion. The latter sections contain, to begin with (up to p. 36), entries in the same style concerning meetings and conferences (including the "Peace Aims Group" in Balliol, Oxford) until mid-June 1942, which are partially assessed in Bell's diary notes of June 14–July 13, 1942 (see 1/186). The final section contains notes, composed of keywords and usually in incomplete sentences, to his diary entries. These notes, cited here according to the "Key Word," correspond in wording to the earlier sections and are probably to be regarded as his own notes. Bishop Bell obviously relied on them for the two accounts he published after the war: the 1945 essay, "The Background of the Hitler Plot," and his 1957 Göttingen lecture, "The Church and the Resistance Movement" (*GS* 1:390–98 and 399–413). On the context, see *DB-ER*, 755–63; *MW* 5:260–73; and von Klemperer, *German Resistance against Hitler*, 281–93. Since everything brought back from Sweden had to go through the censors, Bishop Bell had not yet received back his papers, including his "Diary Notes," by June 19, 1942 (see 1/181, ed. note 1). The "Diary Notes" were intended solely for his own use and are commensurately difficult to decipher and decode. The German editors of *DBW* 16 deciphered the shorthand used. The umlaut used in both German and Swedish, which Bell almost universally omitted, was added as needed. Where the interpretation of text is doubtful, a note follows to that effect. Passages of two or more words that do not permit clear reconstruction are indicated by {...}; omissions by [...]; and illegible text by <...>.

281

May 15: [. . .] After breakfast Westman and Professor Fridrichsen came in to tell me about Norwegians.[2] [. . .] Karl Hartenstein (with Bonhoeffer) should be invited to postarmistice conference.[3] They agreed generally with Leibholz's letter to Butler,[4] and importance of Peace Aims with alternatives to Nazi and Communism. Fridrichsen promises to send message from Leibholz to Bonhoeffer.[5] [. . .]

May 26: [. . .] Dinner to Yngve Brilioth, Carl and Mrs. Carl Söderblom at Staadts Hous-Restaurant.[6] Pleasant conversation. Ehrenström fetched me and took me on to meet S.[7] at Student House with Werner and his wife. Most interesting conversation. Gave me copies of Chaplains' sermons for English prisoners of war in Germany—circulated by Evangelische Hilfswerk[8] and Gerstenmaier. These sermons replaced sermons prepared by Lilje and others. Oecumenical movement and centre at

282

Geneva made work for prisoners of war of different countries possible.[9] Trusted[10]

[2.] This refers to Norwegian refugees in Sweden. Bishop Bell's notes furnish detailed information on the political and ecclesial situation in Norway, which was occupied by the German military, and above all on the resistance being carried out by Bishop Berggrav.

[3.] See 1/94, ed. notes 1, 3, and 4.

[4.] In this exhaustive letter of March 27, 1942, Gerhard Leibholz articulated his critical thoughts regarding the British political approach toward Germany to the warden of Nuffield College in Oxford, Harold Butler. Bishop Bell received a copy from him on April 2; see Bell and Leibholz, *An der Schwelle,* 49–53.

[5.] Apparently this was the means by which Bonhoeffer was intended to receive the letter in question—a sign of the importance ascribed to contact with him.

[6.] The Swedish word is *Stadshuset,* "city hall."

[7.] Hans Schönfeld; instead of his name, the initial "S." appears in the original here and in all further references. On Schönfeld's trip preparations, particularly the preceding conversations with Adam von Trott and Eugen Gerstenmaier, see *MW* 5:266–67. For his subsequent reflections, see "Notes on the Work and Fight of the Churches in Germany, March 1943" (Boyens, *Kirchenkampf und Ökumene,* vol. 2, *1939–1945,* 363–79, with critical commentary), a memorandum written by Schönfeld and Gerstenmaier together, which reached London and helped clarify many points (henceforth referred to as "Notes on the Work"). Regarding its sometimes noticeably optimistic tone, cf. William Paton's judgment that Schönfeld "somewhat exaggerates the more hopeful tendencies in Germany" (Boyens, *Kirchenkampf und Ökumene,* vol. 2, *1939–1945,* 417).

[8.] Das Evangelische Hilfswerk für Internierte und Gefangene (EHIG), "Protestant Aid Society for Internees and Prisoners," which had been founded at the beginning of November 1939 under the direction of the Church Foreign Office, but which considered itself primarily responsible for "service to German compatriots abroad," according to a statement of its managing director, Pastor Hans Helmut Peters; see Boyens, *Kirchenkampf und Ökumene,* vol. 2, *1939–1945,* 27–30.

[9.] Following groundwork laid by a September 4, 1939, memorandum by Willem A. Visser 't Hooft, Das Ökumenische Komitee für die Pastoration der Kriegsgefangenen (Ecumenical Committee for Pastoral Care of Prisoners of War) was able to take up its work in Geneva at the beginning of November 1939; see Boyens, *Kirchenkampf und Ökumene,* vol. 2, *1939–1945,* 27–30. This activity simultaneously served as a cover for Schönfeld's and Gerstenmaier's activities.

[10.] This may read instead "Printed."

by Foreign Office sympathizers and military dito.[11] Acted as protector of YMCA, Student movement etc. Easter pamphlet was prepared for interned.

Then spoke of an important movement inside Germany first of Evangelicals linking with Catholics—leaders trusted by confessionals. Bishop Wurm who intervened government together with Roman Catholic Bishop—von Preysing, and another (2 occasions)—Wurm taking initiative.[12] Fulda conference authorized Roman Catholic Bishops[13] for approaching government quietly, said what they stood for, and what was not tolerable. Pastoral letter of Roman Catholic Bishops demanding 3 human rights—*freedom, law, preaching and living Christian life.*[14] This whole action very important, Block of Christians very important.

Workers, tradeunionists met Schönfeld and Gerstenmaier to ask, "How will your churches face National Socialism?"[15] Clearly looking for unsubsidized church. (Dutch Roman Catholics and Protestants also uniting—not organised—Kraemer as leader.)[16]

[11.] Uncertain reading; cf. "Key Words," in Bell Papers, 47: "courageous group in F. O. [Foreign and Commonwealth Office] and Military."

[12.] Hans Schönfeld was directly in touch with Bishop Wurm and hence informed about Wurm's various initiatives; Wurm undertook several initiatives directed at state authorities after mid-1941. These included his December 9, 1941, memorandum directed to Hitler and his December 1941 letter to the Reich minister for church affairs; see also 1/139, ed. note 1.

[13.] On the part of the Catholic bishops, a corresponding memorandum was prepared in coordination with Bishop Wurm and given to the Reich Chancellery by Bishop Wienken at the same time as Bishop Wurm's memorandum on December 12, 1941; see *Akten deutscher Bischöfe*, 5:651–58.

[14.] The German Catholic bishops' pastoral letter of March 22, 1942, reads: "[The church] has the courage to speak the truth in its struggle for freedom of conscience, for human dignity, and for the freedom to exercise the rights with which God and nature have endowed human beings" (cited in Neuhäusler, *Kreuz und Hakenkreuz*, 2:68).

[15.] See ed. note 43.

[16.] Since the summer of 1940, Hans Schönfeld and his friend Paul Collmer (at that time the German adviser to the Dutch Ministry of Social Welfare) had paved the way for these contacts through many visits. In 1942 these contacts also proved useful to Adam von Trott and Helmut von Moltke (see Boyens, *Kirchenkampf und Ökumene*, vol. 2, *1939–1945*, 157–59, and Roon, *German Resistance to Hitler,* 206–8). In "Notes on the Work," we read that "[i]n Holland Christians from Germany were the first ones who have shown Church leaders like Prof. [Hendrik] Kraemer . . . how one can best mobilise the Christian forces effectively in a totalitarian situation" (371). In a letter of November 12, 1941, Willem A. Visser 't Hooft transmitted information from Prof. Kraemer (Leiden), Prof. Berkelbach van der Sprenkel (Utrecht), Prof. Paul Scholten (Amsterdam), Prof. Baron van Asbeck (Leiden), and Dr. C. L. Patijn, to Dutch minister president Pieter S. Gerbrandy in London. On January 14, 1942, Gerbrandy caustically replied that Visser 't Hooft's informants, the men named as leaders of the Dutch resistance, were too "lenient" toward Germany, because they had already been engaging in programmatic reflection about a postwar European confederation in which a reborn Germany would take its place. At the same time, he invited Visser 't Hooft to come to London. See Lipgens, *Documents on the History of European Integration,* 1:561–64 (no. 175).

283   Their points of attack on Nazis (1) their interference with education; (2) with law and
             order; (3) anti-semitism. Importance of building up of cells—training of elders: think-
             ing how Christian ethics can penetrate common life.[17] Confessional Church putting in
             foreground now Christian understanding of *law* and of *men* (against Nietzsche).[18]
                  Gradual development of Christian groups in military circles, in civil service, in
             worker's circles. Much thinking going on about preconditions of civilized life. To be
             ready for a chance—when it should appear. A chance seemed probable in December
             1941. Refusal of officers to go on in Russia. Preparation extensive. But no lead was
             given. General development of last winter opened their eyes. Hitler's principle that
             lawlessness is the law of his action never so clearly stated as in his last speech.[19]
             Movement for charter of Human Rights: much thinking on similar line in literature
             from USA and Britain—and how to incorporate freedom in economic structure.[20]
284   Economic cooperation between peoples of Europe one of strongest guarantees against
             power politics ({against what}[21] has frankly sufficed to prepare this war). Gen-
             eral plan for future Federation of European Nations with executive (in small coun-
             try?), delegating[22] special department to special rule or regulation,—e.g., Poland,
             Czechoslovakia, with common army under authority of Executive.[23] Many Germans

---

[17.] Cf. Nils Ehrenström's calendar notes of March 15, 1941 (see 1/93, ed. note 14).

[18.] This formulation is less in line with Confessing Church statements than with Kreisau reflections, to which Schönfeld naturally had particular connections (communication of Gerhard Ringshausen with the German editors of *DBW* 16, January 12, 1993).

[19.] This is a reference to Hitler's speech on April 26, 1942, before the German Reichstag: "I am asking...the German Reichstag for explicit confirmation that I have the legal right to compel everyone to fulfill his duties.... Likewise, I expect that the German justice system grasps that the nation does not exist for its sake, but it [the justice system] for the nation's—that is, that the world, which also includes Germany, shall not be allowed to go to ruin to uphold a formal process of law, but that Germany must live, regardless of how formal conceptions of justice may repeatedly contradict this" (Domarus, *Hitler,* 4:1874).

[20.] Cf. Paton, *Church and the New Order,* chap. 5, 40–54, and Bonhoeffer's "Thoughts on William Paton's Book *The Church and the New Order*" (see 2/11, ed. note 5). Economic questions were a theme of the Freiburg circle; see 1/205.1. The Freiburg circle anticipated that it would be able to influence peace arrangements by means of a memorandum during an extended truce.

[21.] Uncertain reading; perhaps "again this."

[22.] This reading is extremely uncertain. Perhaps it means that Poland and Czechoslovakia were to have a special status in relation to the European federation.

[23.] Cf. Bell's Göttingen lecture: "And he [Schönfeld] spoke of a plan for a federation of European nations with a European army under the authority of an executive which might have its headquarters in one of the smaller countries" (*GS* 1:402). Such thoughts are found in various memoranda of the German resistance, including a memo written by Adam von Trott for Lord Halifax (see 1/172, ed. note 7, and 1/180, ed. note 3; see also Graml, "Resistance Thinking on Foreign Policy," in Graml et al., *German Resistance to Hitler,* 39).

convinced they must sacrifice much of personal income to atone for damage in occupied territories.[24]

Point of special importance follows. People behind it are high officers in all key positions political, industrial, military. Likelihood of British victory not very great. Certainty of revolt against Hitler. In first stage revolt inside party—Himmler and SS to overthrow Hitler.[25] Army to take charge. Would England and America deal with such? Army necessary to take control of Germany. No confidence that England would do better than at Versailles.[26] Essential preliminary elimination of Hitler and Gestapo and gangsters of SS—withdrawal from occupied countries—with a [view to the territory's being taken over by a][27] *European* authority. Do not think Russia c[oul]d be kept away from harm unless German army retreated in haste. Has confidence that such army would be free from militarism, and that crimes were done by SS prohibited by army itself. Would government encourage such revolters to hope for negotiation[28]   285 if archgangsters removed? Alternative further chaos. Bolshevism—etc.[29] as war went on. [...]

May 29 [...] At 3.30 saw Schönfeld, Ehrenström and Werner again. More discussion of "opposition in Germany." Emphasized reality of *church* opposition. Success against Bormann's (Hess' successor) wishes to dissolve church into associations in society, Blau in Posen[30]—of Wurm and others against euthanasia in religious institutions.[31]

[24.] This thought is also expressed in the Göttingen lecture (*GS* 1:402).

[25.] "Outside Germany, for instance in the Spanish Ministry of Foreign Affairs or the British Secret Service, Himmler was long seen as the only German who could topple Hitler and shorten the war. Even among German resistance fighters there were those who believed themselves able to march in step with the SS chief a short distance against Hitler—until after the day of the coup itself. Dohnanyi belonged to these and maintained a connection to Himmler and above all to his chief adjutant [Karl] Wolf[f]" (Höhne, *Canaris,* 486). A more thorough treatment is provided in G. Ritter, *Carl Goerdeler,* 447–51.

[26.] Cf. 2/11, ed. note 8.

[27.] This section is indecipherable but has been amplified here according to Bell's Göttingen lecture (*GS* 1:403).

[28.] Cf. Göttingen lecture: "would the British encourage the leaders of such a revolution to hope for negotiations" (*GS* 1:403).

[29.] Ibid.: "with Bolshevism increasing."

[30.] The secret Bormann circular letter of June 9, 1941 (Zipfel, *Kirchenkampf in Deutschland,* 512–16), regarding the incompatibility of National Socialist and Christian world views, contains the statement, "The interest of the Reich lies not in the overcoming of ecclesial particularism but in its continuance and strengthening." The "Reichsgau Wartheland," a new territorial arrangement created by the Nazis on October 8, 1939, was never under the jurisdiction of the "Old Reich" legislation; people thought there would be no hindrances in Wartheland to introducing a model church ordinance that, once the war had been won, would also prove valid for the Old Reich itself. [After the conquest of Poland, the Reichsgau Wartheland was created in the regions occupied by Germany; the "Old Reich" (Altreich) referred to the German territories before Nazi expansion began

294 Conspiracy and Imprisonment: 1940–1945

Temple's article in Fortnightly[32] great shock to friends, justifying necessity of occupation on historical grounds. That found in "no other way than occupation, impartial, not taking advantage." Jews and Christians can help in this task job of Europe.[33] Temple
286   excluded possibility of another group of similar ideals to English-American coming into power.[34] Sign of this already.

Paton failed for understanding of far-reaching change. True a "church of prayer" but prayer as new kind of power, *not* resignation.[35] Fight for church as whole unit has been carried on as never before. In May 1941 Bormann's attempt with Hitler to deprive church of power of Church tax defeated by 3 cabinet ministers (including Schwerin Krosigk).[36] Fighting for integrity of church as whole a political fact. All other associations (trade unions <...> etc.) dissolved. Paton wrong about Euthanasia. Protestant
287   church in association with high officers did resist. Bishop Wurm always sent letters of protest to Reichsstellen. "If you invade our Protestant institutions our farmers will

---

with the Austrian *Anschluß.*—MB] Thus, the Warthegau would be set up, in the words of Reich regional governor Arthur Greiser, as a "parade ground of the National Socialist worldview" (in Gürtler, *Nationalsozialismus und evangelische Kirchen im Warthegau,* 39, ed. note 84). See also 1/139, ed. note 4. General Superintendent Paul Blau, who had led the Posen church district since 1911, stood up to the Nazi attacks on the church; cf. p. 295.

[31.] See the documentation in Hermelink, *Kirche im Kampf,* 512–36.

[32.] *The Fortnightly* (November 1941): 405–13.

[33.] "Key Words," Bell Papers, 55, reads: "Schönfeld. Temple's article criticising military group's suitability to govern. Occupation necessary: on historical grounds. Great shock to their group—(superiority attitude). Clue in last part of article 'no other way than occupation, impartial, not taking advantage . . . Jews and Christians can help in this great job of Europe.'" Hans Schönfeld and his friends in Germany did know of Temple's article in *The Fortnightly*; reference in this (imprecise) citation is probably being made to the sentences: "Hitler is the naked expression of that bad tradition in all its power and hideousness. Such history cannot be ignored. . . . Consequently we should on moral grounds by no means refuse, but rather welcome, the necessity on political grounds for a military occupation of Germany. It is the one and only possible method of bringing home to the soul of Germany the completeness of its failure. But this can be undertaken rightly, and without creating a resentment bound to result in another outbreak, if it is undertaken in a spirit of true justice and without any exploitation of the situation to the advantage of the victorious powers. We must establish order in Germany and security for Germany" (409, cf. 413).

[34.] "Key Words," Bell Papers, 55, reads similarly: "Temple excluded all possibility of another group coming into power with similar ideal to America and England."

[35.] Uncertain reading; see "Key Words," Bell Papers, 55: "Paton got wrong end of stick—church of prayer, yes, but as new kind of power—*not* resignation!"

[36.] Count Lutz Schwerin von Korsigk, Reich government finance minister from 1932 to 1945, belonged to the Dahlem Confessing Church congregation. The new ordinance being promoted by Bormann and Greiser (cf. ed. note 30), which was taken up at a departmental meeting of the Reich Ministry of the Interior on May 2, 1941, "aroused great resentment in several of the ministries in Berlin, whose hopes had been raised of regaining in the newly won territories some of their dwindling influence" (Conway, *Nazi Persecution of the Churches,* 313).

stand up against it,"[37] and formulated doctrinal statement, founded on Bible, dealing with this and underlying principle—said that 90% of parents instructed.[38] Lilje preached against [it] to 2000 people. A nation will be judged by God according to its behaviour to the people: Let a girl who wishes to know character of fiancé take him to bed [of] such sick person and see how he reacts.[39]

General Superintendent Blau's stand in Posen. Party's failure to dissolve church into simple associations by abolishing church collections, works etc. Blau's courageous stand triumphed and helped Roman Catholics. State tried to stop Good Friday services.[40] Churches fuller than ever. Attendance at the Easter larger than ever. Chief   288
Commander of district with deputation attended his 80th birthday.[41]

Further points. All the generals in opposition related to church.[42] All agreed

---

[37.] There is no such statement by Bishop Wurm in his writings to the Württemberg Reich regional governor Murr. However, the following passage in the "Notes on the Work" referring to Bishops Wurm and Galen is instructive: "If they have not been shot or put into prison it is because the Gestapo leaders had to face the fact that thousands of peasants and workers in Westphalia or Württemberg would have arisen against such action" (Boyens, *Kirchenkampf und Ökumene*, 2:366).

[38.] "Key Words," Bell Papers, 55, reads similarly, under Dr. Schönfeld's communications on May 29: "target be 90% of parents instructed." The nearest correspondence to this statement is found in a letter of late April or early May 1942 from the Württemberg church administration to the chancellery of the German Evangelical Church: "it is now time that the countless pleas and cries for help of the Christian sector of the population, who today still account for 95% of the German people be heard, and that, in accordance with the expressly articulated will of parents and guardians, . . . freedom of faith and conscience be restored at least to the extent that the Christian population, parents and children, be at liberty to attend their church service on Sunday" (Schäfer, ed., *Landesbischof D. Wurm und der nationalsozialistische Staat*, 94).

[39.] See "Key Words," Bell Papers, 55: "Lilje to 4000 people." The "Notes on the Work" reads: "During this springtime Dr. Lilje spoke every evening in one of the Ruhr district cities before 6000 people, simple workers and directors of factories, engineers and teachers" (in Boyens, *Kirchenkampf und Ökumene*, vol. 2, *1939–1945*, 368). At the request of Pastor Wilhelm Busch, Lilje spoke on biblical themes for seven nights at a church mission week in Essen in early May 1942. Since a church hall was the only room available for this, the number of listeners reported by Schönfeld is doubtlessly exaggerated. The last two sentences above are presumably quotes from Lilje's addresses.

[40.] On the circumstances, see Gürtler, *Nationalsozialismus und evangelische Kirchen im Warthegau*, 146–50.

[41.] See "Notes on the Work," which states: "When Dr. Blau became 80 years old the Church leaders from the Evangelical Protestant Church were refused to get visas for representatives who should bring their congratulations. When at the birthday reception the speaker announced that to their deep regret these representatives could not arrive in time he could say at the same time that the general of the German army present in this area with his whole staff gave the honour to Dr. Blau to come to this reception" (Boyens, *Kirchenkampf und Ökumene*, vol. 2, *1939–1945*, 367).

[42.] Cf. "Key Words," Bell Papers, 56: "People in highest command, cadres in Home army, cadres in business, civilians and workers—all related to church."

upon Christian basis of life. "What are the Church leaders saying?"[43] A Christian basis for government in their view essential. Significance of Dutch and Norwegian church—speak to both sides. Service by German people[44] probably Evangelical.[45] No longer capitalist ideas[46] of property.[47] How [answer][48] danger in Far East?[49] No request for colonies[50] in Hitler's speech.[51]—Göring: Now you are beginning to wake [—] opened our eyes.[52] Waffen SS SA {united} *not* supporting.[53]

289

May 29 Arrived Upsala 6.30 pm—met by Archbishop Eidem. Dinner: long talk. Archbishop had been approached by Heckel about linking Church of Sweden with German Church, but refused to do anything without Church of Norway and Denmark. This disappointed Heckel.[54] Told him of talks yesterday: much interested, and wondered what lay behind—thinks him sincere. Strongly for Wurm as churchman for conference.[55]

[43.] Cf. the similar question by labor unionists (see p. 291).

[44.] Cf. "Key Words," Bell Papers, 55: "Dutch Church significant. Norwegian Church ditto. Speaks to both sides ({reactionary with} many conflicts avoided). Service by German people to peoples of Europe."

[45.] Uncertain reading.

[46.] Uncertain reading; perhaps "view."

[47.] At this time there was such consideration both in Geneva and in the Kreisau circle then being formed by Adam von Trott and Count Friedrich von der Schulenburg. See Mommsen, "Social Views and Constitutional Plans of the Resistance," in Graml et al., *German Resistance to Hitler,* 79–86.

[48.] Uncertain reading; perhaps "view."

[49.] Temple's article states: "Power throughout this period should be British-American in the West and Russo-Chinese in the East" (*The Fortnightly,* 411).

[50.] Cf. "Key Words," Bell Papers, 56: "No request with regard to colonies." Cf. 1/172, section 3.

[51.] Cf. ed. note 19.

[52.] Cf. "Key Words," Bell Papers, 56: "Hitler's *speech.* Göring: 'Now you are beginning to wake.'" The words "opened our eyes" appear in the following line as a separate keyword. In the "Diary Notes" of May 26, 1941 (see p. 292), Bell writes: "General development of last winter opened their eyes."

[53.] One word is illegible; cf. "Key Words," Bell Papers, 57: "Waffen SS SA not supporting." Some members of the resistance movement, among them Hans von Dohnanyi, assessed the stance of the SA and the Waffen-SS (in contrast to the actual SS) as one that would take a wait-and-see attitude toward any coup.

[54.] With his Church Foreign Office, Bishop Heckel had aspired to a supremacy within European ecumenism that would parallel Hitler's triumph over France. Thus, on July 10, 1940, he wrote to the Ministry of Foreign Affairs: "By ecclesial means the hegemony of the Anglican influence in the churches must be broken and a new spiritual orientation toward the Reich implemented." With this in mind, Eugen Gerstenmaier traveled to Sweden in September, and Theodor Heckel at the end of November. It was then that Heckel was rebuffed in a conversation with Archbishop Eidem; see Boyens, *Kirchenkampf und Ökumene,* vol. 2, *1939–1945,* 83, 87–88.

[55.] See p. 290: "postarmistice conference."

[…]

May 31 To Sigtuna.[56] Met by Johansson. Björkquist took me over building before and after church. Lunch with Björkquists. Much talk. Norway and Holland show church not something in past—but a living reality and to do with future.[57] After tea D.[58] spoke messages for sister. Spoke of conversation already had; and named important 290 people.[59] General Oberst Beck, chief of General Staff before Czechoslovakian crisis 1938, age 60; trusted in Army, Christian, conservative, in touch with Trade Union leaders; General Oberst Hammerstein, Chief of General Staff before Beck—older, little more Prussian, convinced Christian; Goerdeler, ex Preiss Commissar, Lord Mayor of Leipzig, highly esteemed by civil service people—civil front leader; Leuschner, President of United Trade Unions (before dissolution); Kaiser, Catholic Trade Union leader. Also some people to be named, though not such clear Christian characters— Schacht (ambiguous) a seismograph of contemporary events—has withdrawn from all political events. Hopes to be minister of cabinet. Some others also ambiguous. If Beck and Goerdeler come up, worth trying. Organisation in every ministry, officers in all big 291 towns. Generals in command, and those near them in command of Home Front (Wehr-kreis[60] commanders), (Hitler always staying in his post in East Prussia—afraid—will

---

[56.] Sigtuna was the site of the Nordic Ecumenical Institute. On Bishop Bell's arrival at this location, see *MW* 5:269–71.

[57.] "Key Words," Bell Papers, 59, is similar: "Bjorq. Church a living reality—not the past as {time like} regarded, *but the future.*"

[58.] Beginning here and throughout, the abbreviation "D." stands for Dietrich [Bon-hoeffer]. Bonhoeffer is named here abruptly, without any mention of his obviously unex-pected appearance. In another place ("Key Words," Bell Papers, 38), Bishop Bell noted, "Two pastors quite unexpected / long associations / refusals [1941] / Peace feelers pos-sible. But those men extremely well known to me. Staunch anti-Nazis, one modest (Switzer-land), the other very strong / Independently.... Second pastor courier Gestapo." George Bell also wrote about this to Eivind Berggrav, November 8, 1956: "I never saw Helmut von Moltke. Bonhoeffer came over expressly, under cover of a message to Norway, so I was told, to meet me in Stockholm. He had heard through the German Press that I was in Sweden and got a visa to do some Foreign Office messenger work which took him to Nor-way and allowed him transit through Sweden.... I don't think Helmut von Moltke was mixed up in it at all, so far as I was concerned. One suggestion was that if the British Gov-ernment were effectively interested, some diplomat from Berlin, like Adam von Trott, might be sent to have conversations with a diplomat from England. I feel certain it was Adam von Trott who was involved" (Bell Papers, vol. 42).

[59.] On these lists of names, which appear in similar form in 1/181 and 1/187, cf. among others G. Ritter, *Carl Goerdeler,* 604–5. Giving these names involved an enormous risk that presupposed unconditional trust. The list of names, however, also served later toward constructing lists of persons who would be able to assume responsible positions in Germany after the war. Cf. Bell and Leibholz, *An der Schwelle,* 169 (September 4, 1944).

[60.] [It was and still is customary in Germany to partition the country into adminis-trative districts for military purposes, for example, draft registration, soldiers on reserve, transportation, supply lines, and so on. In such a military district, or *Wehrkreis,* the com-mand structure exercises significant power during wartime.—MB]

need a Regiment to get rid of him).[61] He suddenly cancelled visit to Smolensk.[62] Most of the Field Marschalls reliable—von Kluge (Christian) von Bock Küchler Witzleben (not so likely to come up in the front). I stressed importance of Act of repentance.[63] We are sorry. . . [64]

Schönfeld joined us later,[65] and Ehrenström, Dietrich, Manfred Björkquist, Harry Johansson and he and I,[66] joined in general conversation. Schönfeld said it was impossible to tell the number of those opposing. The point was that key positions were held by members of opposition and that key positions < . . . >[67] in Germany itself are of chief importance. The coup should be carried through in two or three days. All ministries contained such keymen on our side. One of the most important services was radio, and the wireless building would be occupied by Opposition. Close links with *State* Police. Keymen {are around}[68] in big factories, water, gas etc. I thought on

292

[61.] Units of the "Brandenburg" Regiment, directly subordinate to the Foreign Office of Military Intelligence of the Armed Forces High Command, were earmarked for a surprise raid on the Führer's headquarters. Later, in the spring of 1943, a special cavalry regiment *(Mitte)* was formed for the same purpose by Baron Georg von Boeselager from the Center Army Group (Heeresgruppe Mitte). See P. Hoffmann, *History of the German Resistance,* 275–77. [The Center Army Group was a group of German armies fighting in the middle of the eastern front. There was another army group to the north, the Heeresgruppe Nord, and one to the south, the Heeresgruppe Süd.—MB].

[62.] This probably refers to the plan to seize Hitler during a visit to the Smolensk headquarters. These plans could therefore have been conveyed to Bonhoeffer even before his trip to Sweden. Gerhard Ritter notes this plan as having been delayed until "late fall 1942," according to Goerdeler's statement to the Gestapo; see Ritter, *Carl Goerdeler,* 535, ed. note 14.

[63.] Bonhoeffer's declaration is implied by the subsequent three words. In "Resistance Thinking on Foreign Policy," Graml writes on the subject: "Those who were unable to grasp this idea and who, in fact, looked for 'foreign-policy solutions,' were not in a position to understand that they were rejecting the only attitude that held any prospect of success in foreign affairs. In an extreme situation the totally unpolitical thought may well be the genuinely political thought" (in Graml et al., *German Resistance to Hitler,* 52).

[64.] Within the "Key Words" (Bell Papers, no page number given), the sentence reads: "We are sorry, with this General's government." In another place it states: "Germany is guilty. We have to be punished. *Names.* Not worthy such solution. 'Oh! We have to be punished' some feel" ("Key Words," Bell Papers, 38).

[65.] On Hans Schönfeld's arrival in Sigtuna, see *MW* 5:270–71.

[66.] See the entry in Harry Johansson's guest book, reproduced in Bethge, Bethge, and Gremmels, *Life in Pictures,* 193. It is noteworthy that Schönfeld did not dare to enter his name. Even in neutral Sweden, one had to reckon with surveillance. A photograph of the entry (from the street side) of the Nordic Ecumenical Institute in Sigtuna is found in *Life in Pictures,* 192.

[67.] Illegible, perhaps a word crossed out.

[68.] Uncertain reading; perhaps something crossed out; it may read "armed" or "carried."

document giving background.[69] Opposition in existence some time—not only the 293
war has prepared the opportunity and it crystallized last autumn.[70] Some numbers
of auxiliary cadres—members of opposition know of plot of the A.[71] If leaders of
Allies feel themselves responsibility for fate of millions in occupied countries they will
consider very earnestly means of preventing great crimes against this [these?] people.
(Was attempt on Heydrich, who was designated as commissar (?) for France, part of

---

[69.] This may refer to a statement in "Key Words," Bell Papers, 62: "'t Hooft has document giving background." In *Streit und Friede,* Gerstenmaier writes: "There were several
difficulties with this memorandum. After the invasion of Russia, Hans von Haeften and
Adam von Trott came to the conclusion with me that the stormy advance in the Russian
winter of 1941/42 would come to a standstill and that the torturous second half of the war
for us was thereby beginning. Haeften in particular inferred from Hitler's character the
prediction that this second half would end in a scorched-earth policy. In contrast to the
more favorable expectations that Helmuth von Moltke placed in England's behavior,
Adam von Trott added gloomily that he was unable to set any great hopes on the Western,
English-American influence on the victorious Soviets. We believed that for this reason it
was high time now, at the zenith of German power, to approach the British government.
Following a concise analysis of the situation and of what was likely to happen, the political
conceptions held in common by the political resistance to Hitler in Germany were to be
outlined. The practical purpose of all of this was to receive a political statement from London that could promote an overthrow attempt by the critical German military. In the
conversation the three of us were quite unanimous. I was asked to prepare a written presentation. Adam von Trott was then to deliver the English version. We sat several evenings
together in my apartment at Goethestraße 12 over the drafts until we had agreed on every
comma and period. Shortly thereafter, Hans Schönfeld took them along to Geneva. But
before he passed them on to Visser 't Hooft, he allowed our friends at the German consulate in Geneva, Albrecht von Kessel and Gottfried von Nostitz, to inspect our memorandum. Hans Schönfeld reported to me later, somewhat hesitantly, that he had been
convinced by the two diplomats to edit this and that in our wording. I was never able to
see the final result of this editing with my own eyes. Nevertheless, Visser 't Hooft found it
so tolerable that he promised to bring it to the man in England. But he did not arrive in
London until the beginning of May 1942. Lying around for so long did our memorandum no good. In autumn 1941 we had miscalculated insofar as the turn in the Russian
campaign and thus in the Second World War came only a year later, that is, in the winter
of 1942/43, evident to a great extent in the defeat at Stalingrad. . . . A second communication made by Schönfeld during that visit to Berlin in May 1942 had become more important to me in the meantime. He reported that in a few days he would be flying to Stockholm
to meet Bishop Bell. He would report to him concerning our memorandum and also
give him information about who in Germany would be primarily responsible for convey-
ing the ideas set forth in this record."
    [70.] At the beginning of October 1941 the first connection between the conspiring
officers' circle in the Center Army Group and the Berlin center of the resistance (Beck,
Oster) was made by Fabian von Schlabrendorff; shortly thereafter the first verbal contacts
were made between these and the "newer circles" (Moltke, Trott, Count Yorck) (see Gaertringen and Reiss, *Die Hassell-Tagebücher,* 278 and 289–90. Cf. 1/181, ed. note 7).
    [71.] The context implies "Army"; otherwise, capitalization is used only for "Allies."

this movement?).[72] Allies remember Germany holds 1000 Miles of Russian territory. Stalin could be satisfied in the boundary question, if Allies by cooperation with Soviet government can give guarantee that peaceful cooperation will be possible with Germany (?). German high officers have been impressed by Soviet Russian elite and believed in possibility of understanding.[73] Germans in opposition hope Russia no longer imperialistic. What would help very much would be a statement by Christian leaders of Britain giving their demands for a new cooperation with Russia—a live church etc. Could this be made known through neutral channels ('t Hooft, e.g.).

294 Dietrich commented on Schönfelds views in following way.[74]

Christian conscience not quite at ease with Schönfeld's ideas. There must be punishment by God. We should not be worthy, of such a solution. We do not want to escape repentance. Our action to be such as will be understood as act of repentance and spoken out. Have been speaking to families whose anti-Nazi sons have been killed in Poland and ask why? He replied: our innocent ones suffer, as the innocent Poles suffer. Christians do not wish to escape repentance, or chaos if God wills to bring it on us. We must take this judgment as Christians.

[72.] On May 27, 1942, in Prague an attempt was made to assassinate Heydrich, the acting Reich protector of Bohemia and Moravia; he died on June 4. Apparently at this point the perpetrators were not yet known in Sweden. See Walter Schellenberg's reference to a conversation with Heydrich in spring of 1942: "He then touched on the problem of France and Belgium. His aim was to increase his own authority and organization by appointing supreme SS and police leaders there" (*Schellenberg Memoirs*, 331).

[73.] On the attempts at agreement with the Soviets, cf. Graml, "Resistance Thinking on Foreign Policy," in Graml et al., *German Resistance to Hitler*, 48–49. A March 19, 1942, telegram of the British embassy in Washington reported rumors of a German-Russian agreement. These rumors were circulating in Stockholm. The assessment of these rumors varied; the Swedes believed they were launched from the German side "to frighten Swedes into thinking that the Germans intended to abandon Finland to the mercies of Russia," in order to extort concessions from Sweden (Public Record Office, London, Foreign Office 371/32/906).

[74.] On these various perspectives, see Boveri, *Treason in the Twentieth Century*, 16. Klemens von Klemperer believes that Schönfeld's "statement" primarily conveyed the position of the Kreisau circle (the ethnographic principle) but also contained elements from Goerdeler (to resolve the question of colonies under an authentic system of mandates), while the ideas on the Russian problem can be traced more likely to Friedrich von der Schulenburg (*German Resistance against Hitler*, 284). It could be observed, though, that a great deal of this statement was already common ecumenical property in William Paton's *Church and the New Order.* This included, for example, the question of the colonies, which Bishop Bell, on the other hand, excluded in his memorandum. Schönfeld and parts of the German resistance movement still believed in a negotiated peace after Hitler's removal; thus they had not grasped that this position had become hopeless. Bonhoeffer attempted to secure a new basis of trust (especially with ecumenical circles in England). His divulgence of the leading names of the German resistance movement, which he was doubtless authorized to do, served this purpose and did so out of an awareness of the actual political situation.

We take this act as fact[75] of repentance; importance of *declaring* repentance (which I stressed). I also spoke of importance of Allied Armies occupying Berlin. Schönfeld agreed, but it would be a great help if they were to come—and to help; great difficulties certain to arise. Allied Armies valuable as mediators—keeping control. Their cooperation with German army against reactionary or hostile forces. It would make a great difference if they occupied for assistance, not as conquering army.[76] Very useful if neutral armies could be brought in—e.g. Swedish. Great danger will arise after armistice—vengeance—the churches in *Holland* are preparing a human wall against a terror; fear of 300,000 Dutch being killed in one night.[77] Similarly in *Norway* group of Berggrav in touch with German Army group as to situation which will arise when Nazi regime breaks down (Berggrav and Norwegian High Court President and Infantry German officer of rank of major).[78]   295

Would England favour Monarchy in Germany? {There is}[79] possible Prince Louis Ferdinand, the Crown Prince's eldest son died in heroic way. Hitler sent for other sons. Louis Ferdinand was fetched from USA where he had been working in Ford factory, as workman. He now lives on farm in East Prussia. Dietrich knows him,[80] he is Christian, and has outspoken social interests.

[75.] Uncertain reading, perhaps "We take this act as part." "Key Words," Bell Papers, 63, reads "*Must be understood as act of repentance; and spoken out.*"

[76.] Similarly, "Key Words," Bell Papers, 63, reads: "Cooperation against *reactions of polish government.* Bring in *neutral* armies. Occupying for assistance, not as conquering army." This hope for possibilities of a military cooperation is expressed in various memoranda of this period, for instance, by Adam von Trott and Carl Goerdeler. See Graml, "Resistance Thinking on Foreign Policy," in Graml et al., *German Resistance to Hitler,* 37–39; G. Ritter, *Carl Goerdeler,* 340; as well as in Archbishop William Temple's article that states "contingents from the German army could be used for part of the task" (*The Fortnightly,* November 1941, 406).

[77.] On November 12, 1941, Willem A. Visser 't Hooft had written to Dutch minister president Pieter S. Gerbrandy in London: "A blood-bath is imminent, and it will be extremely difficult to limit, let alone prevent it. It is therefore imperative that the government should warn again and again" (see ed. note 16). Bishop Bell's "Notebook," Bell Papers, records, following a conversation with Visser 't Hooft in London on May 5, 1942: "Visser 't Hooft. Important to be conscious of tragedy" (no page numbers given).

[78.] "High Court President" can only refer to Paal Berg; the German major is probably Theodor Steltzer, who belonged to the Kreisau circle. Following (the German editors') consultation with Norwegian scholars, Professor Torleiv Austad of Oslo has ascertained that the papers of Eivind Berggrav offer no traces of the formation of such a group. It is conceivable that prior to his imprisonment Berggrav formulated a plan (mentioned to Bishop Aulén?) that was not yet realized.

[79.] Uncertain reading. Cf. Bell's Göttingen lecture: "A possible monarch was Prince Louis Ferdinand" (*GS* 1:405–6).

[80.] Prince Louis Ferdinand himself remembers encounters with the Bonhoeffer family; see his book, *Die Geschichte meines Lebens,* 288ff. For the considerations during that period concerning a revived monarchy, see Mommsen, "Gesellschaftsbild und Verfassungspläne des deutschen Widerstandes," in *Der Nationalsozialismus und die deutsche*

Possible alternative representative for opposition to me e.g. Paton[81] is von Trott, friend of S. Cripps' son, working in freelance way in Foreign Office, age about 34—thoroughly reliable, Christian.[82]

296   Arranged form of communication as follows:[83]

The Bishop of Chichester and certain proposals.

On returning to England I shall report as soon as possible to the Foreign Office; and according to the attitude adopted I have arranged to send one of the following messages to *Harry Johansson, Sigtuna,* and signed by *Bell*

(1) If attitude is that nothing can be done—Reply

    Circumstances too uncertain

(2) If attitude is sympathetic but shows no special wish to pursue further—Reply

    Friendly Reception

(3) If attitude is that a conversation is desirable between someone from the other side and someone from our side at Stockholm—Reply

    Friendly Reception—Paton can come

(NB Paton covers any kind of person)

In the event the Reply being as in (3), Johansson from Sigtuna (or 't Hooft from World Council of Churches in Geneva) would answer giving date convenient for meeting in Stockholm, but the answer would state date a month later than the month really intended; so that e.g. July 30 would signify June 30 as real date of meeting.[84]

Gesellschaft, 124 and 126; G. Ritter, *Carl Goerdeler,* 308–11; Gaertringen and Reiss, *Die Hassell-Tagebücher,* 220 and 273; *DB-ER,* 762; as well as von Klemperer, who notes that despite the prince's friendship with Roosevelt, Roosevelt was dismissive (*German Resistance against Hitler,* 233–34). Cf. also Geoffrey Harrison's commentary, 1/187.1.

[81.] In the recommendations for communication "Paton" was assigned as a general code name that could refer to anyone (see ed. note 83).

[82.] Adam von Trott had not been mentioned previously in Bishop Bell's notes, although Bell knew of him through Trott's memorandum that Visser 't Hooft had recently delivered. Cf. von Klemperer, *German Resistance against Hitler,* 268–70; see also 1/186, ed. notes 15 and 13. The phrase "alternative representative for opposition to me" could mean that Adam von Trott was envisaged as a second discussion partner alongside Bonhoeffer. On this, cf. Lindgren, "Adam von Trotts Reisen nach Schweden," 274–83.

[83.] Attachment to "Diary Notes," Bell Papers, 31. Of the notes found there, we see in the "Diary Notes" a shorter version (p. 29) presumably jotted down the same day, as well as a more extensive version (p. 30a) that took shape a few days later, though still while Bell was in Sweden; this latter version is included here because of its significant content. In the left-hand upper margin of this reworked version, the word "copy" appears, presumably from Bell's own hand. Following these notes on communication, a further excerpt from the "Diary Notes" (p. 29) is included here specifying arrangements for further ecumenical contacts and illuminating the communication network at that time.

[84.] In "Key Words," Bell Papers, 65, the means of communication in this instance was described as follows: "Tele to B by Ehr, by Joh per Bag to Forell—given to B" [Telegram

The wording of Reply from Sigtuna or Geneva would be as follows:

(1) If someone connected with political circles could come to Stockholm for June 30 (e.g.)

Please send manuscript before July 30

or (2) If it is desired that conversation should be with churchman at Stockholm—

Please send manuscript before July 30   297

    emphasize religious aspect

In case of Sigtuna or Geneva replying as in (1) it would be understood that Foreign Office would instruct its representative to see the other man at Stockholm.

In case of Sigtuna or Geneva replying as in (2) it would be understood that some British churchman would meet some churchman from the other side at Stockholm.

If however the other side wished Dr. Ehrenström (from World Council of Churches at Geneva) to interview Foreign Office (and British churchman) in London at this stage for further investigation the Reply from Sigtuna or Geneva would be

    Please arrange to see Strong July 30

(July 30 would still mean June 30)

In this case Dr. Ehrenström would visit legation on way to London[85] and ask for visa and passage on aeroplane.

    3/6/42[86]

Ehrenström on Oecumenical Intercommunication 31/5/42[87]

    For Sigtuna *Harry Johansson*

Would like Paton and van Dusen documents,[88] and similar papers sent to Sigtuna automatically.

Valuable for passing on to Denmark, Norway, Finland (Swedish group of experts also considering such questions as federation of Scandinavia).

Similarly JHO[89] documents.

Documents could be graded. Some shown only to special group of 6 persons.

German opposition documents could also come to England, and other German military and economic papers in wartime, for comment by British and American groups.

All literature of similar kind we have.

---

to Bonhoeffer by Ehrenström, by Johansson with diplomatic mail to Forell—given to Bonhoeffer].

[85.] The shorter version expands this to read: "after seeing friends in Berlin."

[86.] This date clearly concludes the end of the preceding section; the next page (30b) begins with "June 4."

[87.] This returns to "Diary Notes," Bell Papers, 29.

[88.] [The reference is probably to Paton's *Church and the New Order* and Dusen's response to the book. For Dusen's response, see Boyens, *Kirchenkampf und Ökumene*, 2: 176.—MB]

[89.] Initials of Joseph Houldsworth Oldham, General Secretary of the International Missionary Council.

PEP[90]—MALVERN[91]—Chatham House etc.

298 Pay via Paton's Ecumenical M.[92]

Will send from Sigtuna information about Finland, Baltic States etc.

Could send messages to Denmark or Norway.

Pastor Söderberg[93] could receive Sigtuna, also if necessary from Paton, for Diplomatic Bag. [...][94]

On personal side Dietrich told me that his seminary was dissolved for second time in 1940. He had then gone through country visiting parishes for Brethren Councils. Gestapo forbid speaking and preaching at end of 1940. In 1941–2 he had worked on a Book on Ethics, and memos for Brethren's Council, and in evening political activity. There had been some danger after closing seminary of his being called up for military service. He had seen high officer in war office,[95] friend of Confessional Church who had told him "I'll try and keep you out of it"—and had secured him position as courier.

Wurm was very good now. He had had a good meeting with Confessional Church leaders,[96] and apologized for his attack on peace liturgy of Böhm[97] in Munich since 1938.[98] He said "it was the darkest hour in my life."

Meiser not strong—helped to better attitude by Böhm. *Marahrens* hopeless—had introduced Aryan clause into his congregations i.e. forbidden Jews with *star* to join in church worship. *Niemöller* in good health: with 3 Roman Catholic priests, in Dachau, each his own room—common sitting room.[99] Much discussion, but N's position as

---

[90.] PEP is an acronym for "Political and Economic Planning," an independent group of experts that had been working in London since the end of the 1920s. Cf. 2/12, ed. note 8.

[91.] "The Ten Points and the Conclusions of the Malvern Conference [January 1941] came to form the basis for the war and peace aims debate which ensued in Britain in the course of 1941" (von Klemperer, *German Resistance against Hitler,* 294). Cf. 2/12, ed. note 3.

[92.] "M." may be an abbreviation for "Movement." "Key Words," Bell Papers, 47, reads: "Paton made it possible for Germ. books to have [?] Germ. payers."

[93.] Söderberg was a Swedish pastor in London.

[94.] The section omitted here is the abbreviated version of "The Bishop of Chichester and certain proposals"; cf. ed. note 83.

[95.] This high officer was apparently Colonel Hans Oster.

[96.] Cf. 1/17, ed. note 7.

[97.] This refers to Hans Böhm, who may have known of Schönfeld's trip to Sweden. [See Roon, *Neuordnung im Widerstand,* 314 n. 10. This additional information in the German edition of Roon's book is not provided in the English translation, and Roon cites Anton Böhm as the source. It remains unclear, however, whether Roon is referring to Hans Böhm or (this is more likely) to Franz Böhm, who was a member of the Freiburg circle.—MB] On the prayer liturgy that emerged in the context of the Sudetenland crisis in September 1938 and the correspondence at that time between Bishop Bell and Hans Böhm, see Meier, *Der evangelische Kirchenkampf,* 3:53–55.

[98.] In the "Key Words," Bell Papers, the phrase "in Munich since 1938" is omitted.

[99.] Cf. 1/155, ed. note 10.

Protestant very clear. Mrs Niemöller ill with strenuous troubles. *von Thadden* in Belgium. *Grüber* not well.[100] *Asmussen* well, out of prison. *Albertz* and *Müller*[101] well. *Heckel* the same as ever, now critical of government—a regular seismograph (like Schacht).[102] 299
Many good pastors put in dangerous posts and killed on Russian front.

June 1 Johansson took me to Märsta for train to Stockholm. [...] At 3:30 Meeting with Free Church ministers [...] Before that again saw Dietrich gave me message for Leibholz[103] [...] Dinner with Mallets[104] quietly, long talk, and friendly about Sigtuna conversations.

June 4–9 Each day spent in Stockholm hoping for an aeroplane; but the weather was never right (want of clouds) till the night of Tuesday 9th when Swedish aeroplane took me and I arrived in Scotland (Aberdeen) June 10, catching train to London, and got to there about 11 on June 11.

171. Courier Identification Card from the Ministry of Foreign Affairs[1]

Courier Identification Card
No. 474

The bearer of this card,
Mr. *Bonhoeffer,*

[100.] Heinrich Grüber was in the Dachau concentration camp at that time as well.

[101.] Friedrich Müller of Dahlem.

[102.] Cf. Ulrich von Hassell's diary entry of July 13, 1941: "Bishop Heckel, once a truly obsequious coworker in all attempts to build bridges between the Protestant church and Nazism, recently visited me and showed utterly clear comprehension of the unmistakable will of the party to smash the churches" (Gaertringen and Reiss, *Die Hassell-Tagebücher,* 259).

[103.] See George Bell's separate notebook entry of June 1, 1942, 1/174.

[104.] Victor Mallet, British envoy in Stockholm and Bishop Bell's host there, was a friend of Sir Stafford Cripps.

[1.] *NL,* A 61,5 (1); a preprinted form, filled out by hand (the handwritten portions are italicized). The letterhead reads: "Ministry of Foreign Affairs." This form is reproduced in Bethge, Bethge, and Gremmels, *Life in Pictures,* 192. Gerhard Leibholz's September 11, 1944, communication to George Bell regarding the news of Adam von Trott's execution is revealing: "As you know, it was Adam von Trott who always made it possible for Dietrich to travel abroad and also to meet you in Sweden" (Bell and Leibholz, *An der Schwelle,* 170). See also Leibholz's letter of September 13, 1944, to Bell: "I also know that he was legation counselor for the Ministry of Foreign Affairs and that you mentioned his name upon your return from Sweden, when you spoke of Dietrich. On the radio it was reported that Trott had had contact with foreign agents in Sweden (most recently in 1943)" (Bell and Leibholz, *An der Schwelle,* 192).

is traveling to *Stockholm* on *May 30, 1942,* with official documents and baggage of the Foreign Ministry.

300   It is requested that the above-named person be granted whatever he needs to facilitate his trip and that protection and assistance be extended to him when necessary.

Berlin, *May 30, 1942*

Stephany[2]

This courier identification card and the courier baggage are to be submitted to the German Foreign Office in the destination city, which is to return the courier identification card to the courier dispatch of the Foreign Ministry.

172. Hans Schönfeld: Statement by a German Pastor[1]

Statement by a German Pastor at Stockholm
31st May 1942

I

The many opposition circles in Germany who had beforehand no real contact with each other have crystallized during the last winter into active opposition groups working now closely together as centres of a strong opposition movement to the whole Nazi regime on the European Continent.

There are three main groups of action preparing definitely to overthrow the Nazi regime and to bring about a complete change of power.

1. Essential parts of the leadership in the Army and in the central State administration.

(In the Army they include key men in the Highest Command (O.K.W.)[2] for the front troops, Navy and Air forces, as well as in the Central Command of the Home Military forces; also in the State administration the liaison men to the State Police forces largely in opposition to the Gestapo.)

[2.] Dr. Werner Stephany was first-rank consul and head of the courier department of the Foreign Ministry.

[1.] LPL, London, Bell Papers, vol. 42, handwritten with ink; in original English, including errors; previously published in *GS* 1:378–81. This draft reproduces key statements of Hans Schönfeld. This material was preserved by Bishop Bell in his "Diary Notes," Bell Papers (see 1/170), but at Bell's request Schönfeld put it in writing and transmitted it to Bell with a cover letter on June 1, 1942 (see 1/173). In *Streit und Friede,* Gerstenmaier writes: "In the draft he wrote down in Sweden as a memory aid for Bishop Bell, explaining the scope and character of the German resistance, Hans Schönfeld demonstrated a full grasp of the situation. In any case, he said more than we could document at that point, but he said almost nothing that did not later prove to be accurate" (141).

[2.] [Oberkommando der Wehrmacht, "Armed Forces High Command."—MB]

2. The leaders of the former Trade Unions and other active liaison men to large   301
parts of the workers.

(Through a network of key men systematically developed during the last six months
they control now key positions in the main industrial centres as well as in the big
cities like Berlin, Hamburg, Cologne, and throughout the whole country.)

3. The leaders of the Evangelical Churches (under Bishop Wurms)[3] and of the
Roman Catholic Church (the Fulda Bishop Conference) acting together as the great
corporations and as centres of resistance and reconstruction.

By their close cooperation these three key groups of action have formed the
strong opposition movement which, in the given situation, would have sufficient power
to overthrow the present regime because of their control over large masses now
having arms in their hands, and, as regards the workers, at their disposal.

II

The leaders of these key groups are now prepared to take the next chance for
elimination of Hitler, Himmler, Goering, Goebbels, Ley and Co., together with whom
the central leaders of the Gestapo, the S.S. and the S.A.[4] would be destroyed at the
same time, especially also in the occupied countries.

This change of power would not lead to the establishment of a military clique controlling the whole situation but to the coming into power of a government composed
by strong representatives of the three key groups who is[5] able and definitely prepared
to bring about a complete change of the present system of lawlessness and social
injustice.

Their program is determined by the following main aims:

1. A German nation governed by law and social justice with a large degree of
responsible self-administration through[6] the different main provinces.

2. Reconstruction of the economic order according to truly socialistic lines;[7]
instead of self-sufficient autarchy a close cooperation between free nations; their   302

[3.] This name should read "Wurm."

[4.] [Sturmabteilung, "Storm Troopers."—MB]

[5.] *GS* 1:379 has "are."

[6.] Bell's copy for Anthony Eden has a typographical error at this point, reading
"throught" (see 1/186, ed. note 6).

[7.] This corresponds to Adam von Trott's formulation in his April 1942 memorandum (Public Record Office, London, Foreign Office 371/30/912): "Application of modern socialist principles in all sectors of political and economic life." Trott's memorandum
was published (together with the Schönfeld document), with an introduction by Hans
Rothfels, as "Zwei außenpolitische Memoranden," *Vierteljahresheft für Zeitgeschichte* 15
(1967): 388–97. On Trott's memorandum, cf. 1/180, ed. note 3. Both the Trott and the
Schönfeld document are also reprinted in Roon, *German Resistance to Hitler,* 358–64.

economic interdependence becoming the strongest possible guarantee against self-reactionary European militarism.

3. A European Federation of free States or Nations including Great Britain which could cooperate in a close way with other federations of nations.

This federation of Free European Nations to which would belong a Free Polish and a Free Czech Nation[8] should have a common executive, under the authority of which a European Army should be created for the permanent ordering of European security.

The foundations [and] principles of national and social life within this Federation of Free European Nations should be orientated or reorientated towards the fundamental principles of Christian Faith and life.

III

The internal circumstances are becoming now peculiarly favourable to a coup d'état by the Army and the other combined forces of the Opposition. It would help and quicken this process toward the change of power along the lines mentioned above (see II) if the Allies would make it clear whether they are prepared for a European peace settlement along the lines indicated.

If otherwise the Allies insist on a fight to the finish the German opposition with the German Army is ready to go on with the war to the bitter end in spite of its wish to end the Nazi regime.

In the case of agreement for a European peace settlement as indicated, the Opposition Government would, after a coup d'état, withdraw gradually all its forces from the occupied and invaded countries.

It would announce at once that it would restitute the Jewish part of the population at once to a decent status, give back the stolen property, and cooperate with all other nations for a comprehensive solution of the Jewish problem.[9]

[8.] Adam von Trott's memorandum reads as follows on this point: "within the limits of their ethnographic frontiers." In this context he speaks of "a free Polish state and a free Czech state"; Schönfeld speaks of "nation" instead of "state."

[9.] Cf. Paton, *Church and the New Order,* 60–63 (chap. 6, about the Jews). In Adam von Trott's memorandum this is formulated as follows: "The new Germany would be willing to co-operate in any international solution of the Jewish problem" (see Rothfels, "Zwei außenpolitische Memoranden," 394). [This clearly problematic perspective—the assumption that there was indeed a "Jewish problem"—was also very much evident in the section of the Freiburg memorandum on the Jews that, on the one hand, advocated reparations for the Jews and, on the other hand, warned against allowing them full citizenship after the defeat of Nazism. This illustrates the extent to which anti-Semitism remained an influence, even within the German resistance. Note, too, the emphasis in this document on the importance of a "Christian" post-Nazi Europe. This was common in the resistance documents at

It would be prepared to take its full share in the common efforts for the rebuilding 303
of the areas destroyed or damaged by the war. It would declare itself at once dis-
interested in any further cooperation with the Japanese Government and its war aims,
being prepared, on the contrary to give[10] at disposal its war material for finishing the
war in the Far East.

It would be prepared to cooperate for a real solution of the Colonial problem
along the lines of a true mandate system in which all member nations of the European
Federation should participate together with the other nations or federations of nations
concerned.[11]

It is to be expected that representatives of the S.S. will offer the elimination of
Hitler in order to secure for themselves power and a negotiated peace.

It would be a real support for the start of the whole process towards the change
of power as indicated if they would be encouraged in any way to go on.

It would help the opposition leaders to mobilize and to lead all the other forces of
the Army and the nation against Himmler and the S.S. leaders against whom the bitterness and hatred is greater than against anyone else.

In regard to the Russian Problem.

1. The opposition groups have no aims to conquer or to get for Germany parts of
Russia as a colonial area.

2. They hope it may be in the future possible to cooperate in a really peaceful way
with Russia,[12] especially in the economic and cultural field.

3. But they are not convinced that the totalitarian methods of revolutionary brutal
warfare would be changed without very effective guarantees, even when the totalitarian regime in Central Europe would have been abolished.

---

the time and in the "think pieces" of people such as Paton, partly in reaction to what the
conspirators viewed as the moral bankruptcy of Nazism and Communism. International
church leaders believed that an explicit return to Christian values would be necessary to
weaken the ideological hold of Nazism. On this, see especially von Klemperer, *German
Resistance against Hitler,* 264–315. —MB]

[10.] *GS* 1:380 has "place."

[11.] In his "Memorandum of Conversations" (see 1/181, section II), Bishop Bell omitted this point. Adam von Trott's April 1942 memorandum does not refer to Japan and the
colonies either, but in 1941, Paton's *Church and the New Order,* 54–57, had already taken
this point seriously as an international problem.

[12.] In his "Memorandum of Conversations" (see 1/181, section II), Bishop Bell
comments on the hope expressed here, with a communication received verbally from
Schönfeld regarding the impression that the high Russian officers had made on German
officers.

4. They would regard the building up of an Orthodox Russian Church by the renewal of Christian faith in Russia as a real common basis which could further more than anything else the co-operation between Russian and the European Federation.

304   **173. Hans Schönfeld to George K. A. Bell**[1]

My Lord,

May I express once more my deep gratitude that you were prepared with such great kindness to give the opportunity for these meetings and to consider with such great understanding the grave questions concerned.

I cannot express in words what this fellowship you have shown for us, for myself and my fellow-Christians who were with us to us means with their thoughts and prayers. Whatever may come out of these discussions we will know that our brethren in your country will go on to work in the same direction for a real peace, and that they will perhaps fight for the preparation of such peace in the same way against all hatred and all totalitarianism as Dr. Oldham has stated it here and there in the "News Letters."[2] Would you kindly say also my deep gratitude and my warm regards to Mrs. Bell and to all the friends you will meet.

Many thanks once more for your kindness and your blessing, my Lord, and many wishes that our Lord may bless you and your work and grant us this mercy that our Churches and countries may again stand and work together in real peace and in His service.

With warm regards, ever yours
H.S.[3]

[1.] LPL, London, Bell Papers, vol. 42; handwritten letter from Stockholm, June 1, 1942; in original English, including errors. Reprinted in *MW* 5:305; partially reproduced in *GS* 1:408.

[2.] [*The Christian News-Letter* was a weekly (eventually biweekly) newspaper that Joseph Oldham established in 1939. It published reports and analyses of the war's events, and its goal was to offer an explicitly Christian and democratic perspective. It was widely read in Britain and in the ecumenical world. See Clements, *Faith on the Frontier,* 389–405.—MB]

[3.] Hans Schönfeld. The use of his name was presumably to be avoided; cf. 1/170, ed. note 65 (no entry of Hans Schönfeld's name in a guest book in Sweden).

174. George K. A. Bell: Notebook Entry[1]

Leibholz: Title of Book?[2] He is expatriated generally (not by particular decree).[3] But not his wife, i.e. her money + girls money is, not confiscated, but under state super-   305 vision. Encourage her to [...][4] for early conclusion. Does she wish to return after war? + think this best for children? if so B ready to do utmost for finding position! Hans[5] in high command, and very active in good sense.

BBC Sermons much valued. Hildebrandt's Rieger's both give joy. Services very welcome. Especially among country pastors. Would we have more. Especially Sunday or Saturday evenings—not mornings.[6]

175. To George K. A. Bell[1]

June 1st, 1942

My Lord Bishop,

Let me express my deep and sincere gratitude for the hours you have spent with me. It still seems to me like a dream to have seen you, to have spoken to you, to have heard your voice. I think these days will remain in my memory as some of the greatest of my life. This spirit of fellowship and of Christian brotherliness[2] will carry me through the darkest hours, and even if things

---

[1.] LPL, London, Bell Papers, vol. 277; handwritten in ink, entered into Bishop Bell's Stockholm notebook (referred to as "Notebook") on June 1, 1942; in original English, including errors. Cf. Bell's "Diary Notes" for June 1, 1942: "Dietrich gave me message for Leibholz" (see 1/170); previously published in *GS* 1:404, 408, and 522.

[2.] In January 1942 Leibholz had held a lecture series at the Chapter House, Oxford, which was to have been published under the title "Christianity, Politics, and Power" as *Christian News Letter Book No. 15* [this would have been part of Joseph Oldham's *Christian News-Letter* series; see 1/173, ed. note 2—MB]. It was later published in Leibholz, *Politics and Law*, 91–132. He pondered whether he should have the book appear under a pseudonym out of regard for his German relatives; cf. Bell and Leibholz, *An der Schwelle*, 48.

[3.] Cf. Bonhoeffer's letter of June 1, 1942, to the Leibholz family; see 1/176. Leibholz was forced to emigrate because of his "non-Aryan" ancestry.

[4.] An illegible word of three letters, more or less, appears here, perhaps "ask."

[5.] Hans von Dohnanyi.

[6.] Cf. George Bell's letter to Hugh Martin on July 9, 1942 (see 1/188).

[1.] LPL, London, Bell Papers, vol. 42; letter handwritten in ink, from Stockholm; in original English, including errors. See *NL*, A 42,1 (36); typewritten copy; previously published in *GS* 1:382.

[2.] Cf. Bonhoeffer's last words in Schönberg on April 8, 1945 (see 1/239). On what would have been Bonhoeffer's fiftieth birthday, Bishop Bell sent a "Reminiscence of Dietrich Bonhoeffer by the Bishop of Chichester, 2.1.1956 [January 2, 1956]" for the Evangelische Rundfunkkammer (Broadcasting Council of the Protestant Church) in Berlin. This

go worse than we hope and expect, the light of these few days will never extinguish in my heart. The impressions of these days were so overwhelming that I cannot express them in words. I feel ashamed when I think of all your goodness and at the time I feel full of hope for the future.

God be with you on your way home, in your work and always. I shall think of you on Wednesday.[3] Please pray for us. We need it.

Yours most gratefully,
Dietrich

306   **176. To the Leibholz Family**[1]

June 1st, 1942

My dears,

what an indescribable joy to have heard from you through George! It still seems to me like a miracle.[2] The most important thing to me has been that as far as he can see there is no real need for worrying about your future. He does not underestimate your difficulties and hardships, yet he will always prove a true friend, I am quite convinced. I was so glad that he took the same attitude with your cancelled plans to go to USA as I did when I wrote to you last autumn.[3] All he told me about your research work has been of the greatest interest to me and I am happy to know that he and his friends value your work very highly indeed and that your lectures[4] have found such a good reception.

You will have heard, of course, as we have here in Sweden, that all persons of non-aryan descent who are outside of Germany have been in

---

had been arranged by Wolf-Dieter Zimmermann. The last sentence here about the 1942 meeting in Sigtuna reads: "…and we pledged one another again in unfailing Christian brotherhood. I shall never forget him."

[3.] Cf. Bonhoeffer's reference to Wednesday as a "special day of intercession" in his letter of May 23, 1942, to George Bell (see 1/166).

[1.] *NL*, A 59,3 (10); typewritten copy of letter from Stockholm; in original English, including errors; previously published in *GS* 6:560–61.

[2.] Cf. Bishop Bell's letter of June 20, 1942, to Gerhard Leibholz (see 1/184) as well as Leibholz's letter of July 11, 1942, to the Bonhoeffer parents (see 1/190). Cf. also Leibholz's letter of June 21, 1942, to Bishop Bell: "A few days ago we received an additional letter from Dietrich in Stockholm, dated June 1. We are deeply moved by all the news and share with him his 'indescribable joy' that he has seen you. He writes that it still seems to him like a miracle; and you can surely imagine, Eminence, how eager we are to hear the whole story. It goes without saying that we will keep this news to ourselves and will not speak of it even to our mutual friends" (Bell and Leibholz, *An der Schwelle*, 57). See also *DB-ER*, 757–63.

[3.] Cf. Bonhoeffer's letter of September 19, 1941, to the Leibholz family (see 1/125).

[4.] See 1/174, ed. note 2.

general expatriated. As far as I can tell the future of your fatherland that is a good thing for you and will make your return only easier on that day for which we are all longing. So I hope, you do not worry about it.

My heart is full of thanks for these last days. George is one of the very great personalities I have met in my life. Please, give my love to the girls. I hope they will enjoy the summer. Many happy returns for Mary's[5] birthday. It is such a joy to know that she is such a sensible, unselfish and clever girl. God be with her and with all of you. My family is well. Charles and his wife will go to the countryside in the north to friends of mine for several weeks.[6] That will do them good.

Much love from
Dietrich

177. To Hans-Werner Jensen[1]

May 9, 1942

Dear Brother Jensen,

Many thanks for sending me the homily for the funeral of your child. I have just been able to read it, with very great joy. You have preached the entire gospel in a few words. I say in all sincerity that I cannot remember ever having read such a full proclamation that so placed me under the Word myself. I thank you very much for this. Your father's words held and moved me unusually. For all their differences, both homilies are alike in that the personal is not separated from the objective but rather is taken up into it. I will keep this text and continue to read it often. Warmest thanks to you for it. May that which you were able to say at the casket of your child sustain you and your wife in many hours of daily sorrow and remain certain forever. That is the most difficult thing and the most important.

As ever, regards from
Your Dietrich Bonhoeffer

E. Bethge, who also took such great joy in the text, earnestly requests that, if possible, a copy be sent to him also.

[5.] "Mary" is Marianne Leibholz.

[6.] This refers to a recuperative visit by the Bonhoeffer parents to the Kleist-Retzows in Pomerania.

[1.] *NL*, A 60,4 (5); typewritten copy. The letter must have been written following the funeral for the child, who died on June 3, 1942, and the reception of the texts of the two homilies mentioned in the letter. June 9, 1942, is the probable date.

308   **178. To Eberhard Bethge**[1]

On the train,[2] June 18, 1942

I am attempting to reflect on John.[3]

1. It does not seem accidental to me that it is impossible to visualize his personality and character very clearly—in contrast to Peter or James. John seems to have nothing of his own, none of his own colors or temperament. Everything vanishes on closer examination. And tellingly, he is characterized only by a purely passive description.

2. This, however, is asserted of him: he is "the disciple whom the Lord loved" (John 19:26)—yet in this Gospel his name is not mentioned even once! So fully effaced is his own personality. It does not read, "the disciple who loved the Lord"; even that would be too much of himself. John 20[4] actually clearly comes to terms with the fact that Peter loved the Lord more than any other disciple did. Thus of John it is only to be said that he, more than any other, had experienced the love of the Lord—or, more precisely, even that is not said, but only that the Lord loved him; there are no comparisons here, no rankings. The love of the Lord is enough. After the mother of the sons of Zebedee was so clearly rebuffed by Jesus with her question about rank in heaven and the place of her sons and was completely redirected toward her sons' communion of life and suffering with Jesus, perhaps every thought of this sort was silenced in John, if such thoughts ever in fact dwelt in him at all; for he was not the one who asked, but rather his mother. He does not aspire to anything but to be the disciple whom Jesus loved, to whom Jesus gave his friendship (this is analogous to how the Greek reads; somewhere, John 20:2), who reclined on Jesus' breast at table.

309   3. Thus John becomes a witness of the experienced love of Jesus, of the most intimate proximity and communion with him. He is not the confessor, not the man of strong faith, not the denier who is later received again, not the rock, not the one called to pasture the congregation of Jesus (John 20);[5] he has no story of his own like Peter, but he is the one sheltered in Jesus' love, the one entirely effaced in it. Thus in dying Jesus is able to commend him to his mother as her son in his place, and thus he gives Mary to

---

[1.] *NL*, A 59,2 (44); handwritten; previously published in *GS* 2:416–17 and *GS* 4:585–87.

[2.] This letter was written on the train from Berlin to Munich.

[3.] The essay that follows (with no heading) is titled "John the Evangelist"; the draft appears in *GS* 4:585–87. Bonhoeffer's proposal was intended for a series of religious renewal *(volksmissionarische)* evenings on biblical figures that Eberhard Bethge was to lead in Breslau on June 21–27, 1942.

[4.] [The reference should be to John 21, not John 20. In John 21 Peter asserts his love for the Lord three times.—MB]

[5.] [Once again, Bonhoeffer should be referring to John 21.—MB]

John as his mother. The one who is entirely taken up into Jesus takes Jesus' place; he sustains the love of Jesus for his mother. Mary and John—both have only taken, only received, have had nothing of their own, have lived from Jesus alone. And so too the Risen One at the very end (John 21) takes John with him; no one knows to what end. Peter's question is deflected by Jesus. Martyrdom is foretold for Peter, but John abides with Jesus and his form disappears in communion with Jesus. All that lingers is a rumor among the people: this disciple will not die.

4. He did die, presumably at a great age. His proclamation remained: "In this is love, not that we loved God but that [God] loved us" (1 John 4:10); "God is love" (1 John 4:16); "No one has greater love . . ." (John 15:13) (referring to Jesus!). "We love because he first loved us" (1 John 4:19). As an old man he is said to have repeated over and over: Little children, love one another.

I do not believe that he is the author of Revelation. Too different a world, too many words for him, too colorful, not sufficiently effaced by the love of Jesus. Or might this represent the connection to Luke 9:54?—"James and John . . . said, 'Lord, do you want us to command fire to come down from heaven and consume them, as Elijah did?' "[6] Just a thought. The characterization of the sons of Zebedee as "Sons of Thunder" (Mark 3:17) could also be a reference to this, but its meaning is too unclear.

5. Everything of our own is effaced and consumed: sin, virtues, unfaithfulness, and faithfulness. The redemptive love of Jesus is sealed through death and resurrection. It abides forever, and we abide in it. The all-encompassing nature of Jesus' love (John 3:16!) must become evident against every pietistic narrowing, and yet this is the very place where the utterly personal must also be expressed, that we too belong to those whom Jesus loved and loves and will love, that Jesus' love is not a private affair but is the center of the world.

6. To be content in Jesus' love—I would see that as the conclusion and significance of everything that is to be said about John. Maybe you can also take something out of *Einer muß wachen* (Manfred Hausmann) [7] for illustration. What does it mean to recline at the breast of Jesus (John 13:23)? To be sheltered in him, guarded by him, protected from temptation and fall, held, drawn into trust? To be allowed to question him (John 13!), to receive an answer, to lie at the heart of God? Jesus with wide-open eyes that behold suffering and evil, while the other person sleeps like a child?

I hope that these comments have been helpful for you. You have difficult work ahead of you, and I would like to be able to help you a little with it.

310

[6.] [The NRSV has the phrase "as Elijah did" in a footnote, but Bonhoeffer's German Bible had it in the text itself.—MB]

[7.] *Einer muß wachen*, by Manfred Hausmann, was a leaflet of reflections, the last of which focused on a medieval depiction of the disciple John resting at the breast of Jesus.

By the way, just a few thoughts on your recent sermon. In hindsight I have the impression that you are somewhat afraid of the "present-day relevance" [Gegenwartsbezogenheit] of the sermon. I understand this fear well, but I think you are far enough along that you need not fear it anymore. You will hardly ever get off track in this direction. You read a great deal, and it is good material, and you know more of the world than many others. Why should this not be placed in full freedom in the service of the cause? Why should the knowledge of human and universal problems not ring through from time to time? For listeners this brings richness insofar as they perceive that their questions are not simply overlooked, disregarded. After your sermon, it was interesting to note that the point of departure for the ensuing conversation was the part about the sermon series on this text thirty years ago; you remember. Thus you might be somewhat freer in this, I think.—The same is true with regard to the personal arena; there too we should not be too fearful of pietistic dangers. If we are sure of our ground, we need not

311 have these fears. Please understand me: I am not wanting your sermon to be more modern or more pietistic, but I wish to free you of unnecessary inhibitions in this direction. Truly you do not need them.

This trip is pleasant and beautiful. It has been a long time since I traveled through the many beautiful cities whose cathedrals are well known to me. It was a joy; I thought of many of our experiences together, and Germany's future has become important to me anew.

Farewell. God be with you and your work.

As ever, regards from
Your Dietrich

P.S. Please send the letter to Christoph.[8] By the way, it makes a bizarre impression when one walks through the train and sees barely two or three people reading a book—is this the great exhaustion, the great stupor, the image of the future?—the train is full of mostly young people.

179. To Christoph Bethge[1]

On the train to Munich, June 18, 1942

Dear Christoph,

A few days ago Eberhard told me that today is your birthday, and so I wanted to write you. This trip has created the first opportunity for the leisure necessary to write. As I am traveling through old cities and the summer countryside, with beautiful sunshine, I am now thinking of you, of your

---

[8.] See Bonhoeffer's letter of June 18, 1942, to Christoph Bethge (1/179).

[1.] *NL*, A 60,4 (18); typewritten; previously published in *GS* 2:417–19.

present life and your future. What shall I actually write to you? What sorts of thoughts and wishes can I have for you? In terms of years, you are half a generation younger than I am, but in terms of the swift passage of the times at least a generation away. You are experiencing and doing and thinking things that I have never experienced, done, or thought; you face dangers unknown to me. I am leading a life that scarcely resembles yours in any way and that must be foreign to you. And yet, precisely this trip through our beautiful country—the views of the cathedrals of Naumburg, Bamberg, Nuremberg, of the cultivated and sometimes so bare fields, the thought that all of this has been the field of labor and the joy of many, many generations—all this gives me confidence that here there is a common ground, a common task, a common hope, indeed something that transcends the gap between generations. When we ponder this, then our own short personal life becomes relatively insignificant; we begin to think about greater periods of time and greater tasks. Right now you belong to a community that in any case is actively living through one of the great turning points of history. You yourself can do hardly anything about the broad course of things; you probably often feel utterly unnecessary, out of place, bearing all sorts of personal worry and struggle. So what other wishes should I have for you today than that you learn not to take these small personal things, desires and hardships, too seriously, but rather to understand yourself in your place and within the possibilities given to you as a link in the long procession of these generations who have worked and lived for a beautiful, authentic and—devout Germany, and still do so? For in fact it is not true that you wouldn't be able to do anything at all for this—even if it is less your doing than your being that matters here. How tremendous the tasks will be someday, when the battle no longer needs to be directed to the outside, but when all energy can be applied to inner building up. For this we shall someday need not only achievements, capabilities, but above all authentic human beings. And if you only understand this present period of your life in such a way that God now desires to make of you the person whom God will later someday wish to use and put to work with all your capacities and gifts, then a great deal has been gained! And now it is surely important that we who feel incompletely utilized at present, incompletely engaged—and in this too we share a common experience—allow ourselves to be prepared by this time for a future one. It may serve us very well to be put aside for a time, not to be taken seriously. Through this we can learn humility and patience, but also faithfulness. And if in this time God wants to make devout men of us, whom God can someday use, then let us be very grateful to the Lord for this period.

Now may God preserve you in body and soul.

Yours in faithful remembrance,
D.B.

[312]

[313]

180. George K. A. Bell to Anthony Eden[1]

June 18th, 1942

Dear Mr. Eden,

I have just got back from Sweden with what seems to me very important confidential information about proposals from a big opposition movement in Germany. Two German Pastors,[2] both of them well known to me for 12 years or more (one of them an intimate friend) came expressly from Berlin to see me at Stockholm. The movement is backed by leaders of both the Protestant and Catholic Churches. They gave me pretty full particulars, and names of leading persons in the civil administration, in the labour movement and in the Army, who are involved. The credentials of these pastors are such that I am convinced of their integrity and the risks they have run.

I ought to say that I was staying at the British Legation, and told Mr. Mallet all about it. He thought the matter important enough to justify me in asking if I might see you and tell you personally what the pastors had told me. The information is a sequel to the memorandum you have already seen, brought from Geneva by Visser 't Hooft of the World Council of Churches, and having to do with von Trott.[3]

314   I have also today reported to Mr. Warner[4] on my visit to Sweden and given him some information as to the visit of the pastors. It is his suggestion that I am writing

---

[1.] LPL, London, Bell Papers, vol. 42; carbon copy; in original English, including errors; see *NL*, A 42,3 (14); typewritten copy; sender: "The Bishop's Lodging, 22 The Droveway, Hove"; previously published in *GS* 1:383–84.

[2.] Bonhoeffer and Hans Schönfeld.

[3.] Adam von Trott zu Solz. In Visser 't Hooft's *Memoirs,* he writes of Trott: "During 1941 and 1942 he came several times to Geneva. His visit in April 1942 was especially important. He had heard about my plan to visit Britain and this seemed to him an excellent opportunity to get in touch with his friends in Great Britain. Sir Stafford Cripps was now an influential member of the British government and so Adam gave me a memorandum to be handed to Sir Stafford" (156). In his Stockholm notes ("Key Words," Bell Papers, vol. 276, 62), Bell recalled that Schönfeld's May 31, 1942, statements about the German resistance movement included the sentence "'t Hooft has document giving background," made in Bonhoeffer's presence. He did not cite this sentence in his reports, but it echoes in the title of his 1945 report ("The Background of the Hitler Plot," *GS* 1:390–98); cf. 1/170, ed. note 69. Schönfeld was also apparently aware of Trott's memorandum. Visser 't Hooft continued, "One of the few who showed a more positive interest in the message of the German resistance was the Bishop of Chichester whom I met just before he undertook his journey to Stockholm. He did not know at that time that he would meet there Bonhoeffer and Schönfeld and receive from them the same SOS which I had heard from von Trott" (*Memoirs,* 158). "Adam came to see me soon after my return to Geneva. When I told him about the British reaction to his memorandum he was so deeply disappointed that he was near despair" (ibid.).

[4.] Christopher F. A. Warner, director of the Northern Department of the Foreign Office, conducted talks with Bishop Bell on May 8, 1942, (Foreign Minister Anthony Eden was not able to receive him) and June 18, 1942. On the latter conversation, see 1/183, ed. note 3.

direct to you, and I should be very grateful if you could receive me. I will bring my papers with me. I could come any time on Saturday, or from 3 p.m. onwards on Monday. From Tuesday to Friday I have some engagements which I cannot break in my diocese. I do not know whether you will be at West Dean this week end. If so, and if it suited you, I could easily come over after tea on the Sunday.

Yours very sincerely,
George Cicestr

181. George K. A. Bell: Memorandum of Conversations[1]

315

Memorandum of Conversations
and
Statement by a German Pastor[2]

I.

Two German Pastors[3] came from Berlin to see the Bishop of Chichester in Stockholm at the end of May, 1942. They arrived independently, one of them[4] only staying for 48 hours. The Bishop saw them both individually and together on four separate days. They are men very well known to the Bishop, and have collaborated with him for many years in connection with the oecumenical movement, the World Council of Churches, and in different stages of the German Church Struggle. One lives in

316

[1.] Public Record Office, London, Foreign Office 371/30/913 (C 6570/48/18, formerly C 6570/416/G) (C = Central Department [i.e., Central Europe], G = Germany); typewritten, dated June 19, 1942; in original English, including errors; copy in Bell Papers, vol. 42, 264–71. In Bell's heading, the *s* in "Conversations" has been added by hand. In the upper right-hand corner of the memorandum is a handwritten note: "left with S/S [Secretary of State] by the Bishop of Chichester on June 30th, 1942." Cf. 1/186, ed. note 6; cf. also Anthony Eden's letter of July 17, 1942, to George Bell (see 1/191). On the copy in the Foreign Office appears a note in red ink: "Highly Confidential. Secret"; stamps: "Enter Green" [i.e., to be filed with secret papers]; "Dated: June 30. Rcd [received]: July 1. C 6570 416/G." Attached is no. 139 (June 24, 1942) of *The Christian News-Letter* with Bishop Bell's report of his trip to Sweden highlighted; see Bell's diary notes of June 30, 1942: "left him [Eden] my Newsletter" (see 1/186). Published with small deviations in *GS* 1:372–77. On June 19, 1942, the same day as the date of this memorandum, Bell wrote to Mr. Williams: "I am very anxious to get my diary and my other papers and books from the Censor. If you can speed it up in any way I should be grateful. I have got into quite a number of tangles, I fear, through want of my diary" (Bell Papers, vol. 42, 146). Cf. 1/170, ed. note 1.

[2.] Schönfeld's "Statement" (see 1/172), which Bishop Bell had integrated into his report, was clipped together with this memorandum.

[3.] It is worth noting that the names of Bonhoeffer and Schönfeld are not mentioned in the Foreign Office files, which instead speak only of "two German Pastors."

[4.] This refers to Bonhoeffer. Cf. "Courier Identification, No. 474" (see 1/171).

Switzerland, but pays constant visits to Germany. The other lives in Berlin, and is one of the leaders of the Confessional Church; he has been forbidden by the Gestapo to preach or speak. Their purpose was:

A. To give information as to the strong, organized opposition movement inside Germany, which is making plans for the destruction of the whole Hitler regime (including Himmler, Goering, Goebbels, and the central leaders of the Gestapo, the S.S., and the S.A.),[5] and for the setting up of a new Government in Germany of

1. Representatives of certain strong anti-Nazi forces in the Army and central State Administration.
2. Former Trade Union leaders.
3. Representatives of the Protestant and Catholic Churches;
   pledged to the following policy:
   a) Renunciation of aggression.
   b) Immediate repeal of Nuremberg Laws, and co-operation in international settlement of Jewish problem.[6]
   c) Withdrawal by stages of the German forces from occupied and invaded countries.
   d) Withdrawal of support to Japan, and assistance of Allies in order to end the war in the Far East.
   e) Co-operation with the Allies in the rebuilding of areas destroyed and damaged by the war.

B. To ask whether the Allies, *on the assumption that the whole Hitler regime had been destroyed*, would be willing to negotiate with such an new German Government for a peace settlement, which would provide for:

1. The setting up of a system of law and social justice inside Germany, combined with a large degree of devolution in the different main provinces.

2. The establishment of economic interdependence between the different nations of Europe, both as just in itself, and as the strongest possible guarantee against militarism.

3. The establishment of a representative Federation of Free Nations or States, including a Free Polish and a Free Czech Nation.

4. The establishment of a European Army for the control of Europe, of which the German Army could form a part, under central authority.

II. *Character of the Opposition*

The opposition has been developing for some time, and had some existence before the war. The war gives it its chance, which it is now waiting to seize. The opposition

---

[5.] [SA is the abbreviation for Sturmabteilung, "Storm Troopers."—MB]
[6.] [Regarding "the Jewish problem," see 1/172, ed. note 9.—MB]

crystallized in the Autumn of 1941, and might have seized the opportunity in December 317
1941, with the refusal of many officers to go on fighting in Russia.[7] But no lead was
given. Hitler's last speech, openly claiming to be above all laws,[8] showed the German
people more and more clearly the complete anarchy of the regime. The opposition
has full confidence in the strength of the German Army, and is ready to go on with
the war to the bitter end if the Allies were to refuse to treat with a new Government
controlling a non-Hitlerite Germany, *after the overthrow of the whole Hitler regime;* but it
believes that to continue the war on the present or on a greater scale in such circumstances would be to condemn millions more to destruction, especially in the occupied countries.

It also believes that a fight to the finish would be suicidal for Europe. Hence its
desire first to destroy Hitler and his regime, and then to reach a peace settlement in
which all the nations of Europe shall be economically interdependent, shall be protected against aggression by the possession of an adequate European military force,
and shall be in some way federated. The opposition, while having some hesitations
with regard to Soviet Russia, has the hope (as a result of impressions made by some
of the high Russian officers on some of the German officers)[9] of the possibility of
reaching an understanding.

III. *Organization of the Opposition*

The opposition is based on members of the State Administration, the State police,
former Trade Union chiefs, and high officers in the Army. It has an organization in
every Ministry, military officers in all the big towns, Generals in command or holding high
office in key places very near the Generals. It has key men armed in the broadcasting

---

[7.] In December 1941, Hitler made himself the commander in chief of the army,
while Field Marshall von Brauchitsch was dismissed as being responsible for Hitler's bad
decisions. [A field marshal was the equivalent of a five-star general or commander of the
army.—MB] Following Brauchitsch, "four army commanders and several dozen division
and corps commanding officers" were relieved of duties. In this way the army's "moral
backbone was broken" (see G. Ritter, *Carl Goerdeler und die deutsche Widerstandsbewegung,*
345).

[8.] This refers to Hitler's speech on April 26, 1942, before the German Reichstag;
cf. 1/170, ed. note 19.

[9.] Bernd Martin writes, "Following earlier contact with agents of the German Military Intelligence Office in Stockholm, the Russian side offered a peace agreement to a
colleague of the Foreign Office on December 14, 1942, predicated on the 1939 borders. . . .
Since official foreign policy by Hitler's order had forbidden such exploratory talks with
the Russians, the German negotiator Kleist did not report in Berlin on this sensational
offer at 'Wilhelmstraße' [the location of the German foreign ministry—MB] but rather
let only Trott and Count Schulenburg, the former German envoy to Moscow, in on this
possibility of a separate peace" ("Das aussenpolitische Versagen des Widerstands," in
Schmädeke and Steinbach, *Der Widerstand gegen den Nationalsozialismus,* 1042).

318   centres, in the big factories, and in the main centres of water[10] and gas supply ser-
        vices. It is impossible to tell the numbers of the opposition. The point is that key posi-
        tions everywhere are held by members of the opposition, and that key positions in
        Germany itself are of chief importance.

        The following names were given as those of men who were deeply involved in the
        opposition movement:

        Generaloberst Beck
            Chief of General Staff before the Czecho-Slovak crisis in 1938. Aged 60.
        Generaloberst von Hammerstein
            Chief of General Staff before Beck.
        Goerdeler
            Ex-Preiss Commissar.[11] Lord Mayor of Leipzig. Civil Front leader.
        Leuschner
            Former President of the United Trade Unions.
        Kaiser
            Catholic Trade Union leader.

        All of the above are said to be strong Christian characters, and the most impor-
        tant of all are Beck and Goerdeler.

        Certain other persons of a less clear Christian character would be available, such
        as Schacht. Most of the Field Marshals are reliable,[12] especially Von Kluger, Von Bock,
        Kuchler[13] and possibly Witzleben. Whether a member of the opposition or not, was
        not stated, but the question was asked whether England would favour a monarchy in
        Germany, in which case Prince Lewis[14] Ferdinand was possible. He had been fetched
        from the United States by Hitler after the heroic death of the Crown Prince's eldest
        son. He had been working in a Ford factory as a workman, and now lives on a farm in
        East Prussia. He is a Christian, has outspoken social interests, and is known to one of
        the two German Pastors.[15] The leaders of the Protestant and Catholic Churches are
        also closely in touch with the whole opposition movement, particularly Bishop Wurms
        of Wurtenburg[16] (Protestant) and Bishop Von Preysing of Berlin, acting as the spokes-
319   man of the Catholic Bishops. (At the same time it should be said that included in
        the opposition are many who are not only filled with deep penitence for the crimes

        ---

        [10.] The reproduction of this draft in *GS* 1:374 erroneously reads "war" here; thus
        the translation printed in *GS* 1:491 also reads erroneously *Heeresbelieferung*, "army supply."
        [11.] The former mayor of Leipzig, Carl Goerdeler, had used his position as Reich
        commissar for price controls during the economic and financial crisis of 1931–32 and
        then again in 1934–35.
        [12.] A marginal note here reads, "to whom?"
        [13.] *GS* 1:375 reads correctly: "von Kluge, von Bock, Küchler."
        [14.] *GS* 1:375 reads correctly: "Louis."
        [15.] Refers to Bonhoeffer.
        [16.] *GS* 1:375 reads correctly: "Wurm of Württemberg."

committed in Germany's name, but even say "Christians do not wish to escape repentance, or chaos, if God wills to bring it upon us.")[17]

IV. *Action of the Opposition*

The opposition is aware of impending revolt inside the Nazi party, of Himmler and his followers[18] against Hitler. But while a successful coup by Himmler might be of service to the opposition, the complete elimination of Hitler and Himmler and the whole regime is indispensable. The plan of the opposition is the achievement of a purge as nearly simultaneous as possible on the Home front and in the occupied countries, after which a new Government would be set up. In the securing of a new Government, the opposition realizes the need of an effective police control throughout Germany and the occupied and invaded territories; and it appeared that the help of the Allied Armies as *assistants in the maintenance of order* would be both necessary and welcome, all the more if it were possible to associate with the Allied Armies the Army of a neutral power in the maintenance of order.

V. *Enquiries by the Opposition of the Allied Governments*

The above being the policy and plan of the opposition, the question arises as to what encouragement can be given to its leaders with a view to setting the whole process in motion and the facing of all the dangers involved. As examples of encouragement, such enquiries as the following are made:

(1) Would the Allied Governments be willing to treat with a new bona fide German Government, set up on the lines described in A of Section I above, for a peace of the character described in B of Section I above?

(The answer[19] to this might be *privately* given to a representative of the opposition through a neutral country.)

Could the Allies announce now *publicly* to the world in the clearest terms that   320 once Hitler and the whole regime were overthrown, they would be prepared to negotiate with a new German Government which renounced aggression and was

---

[17.] *GS* 1:375 reads differently: "if it is God's will to bring it upon me." Cf. Bonhoeffer's statement on May 31, 1942: "Christians do not wish to escape repentance, or chaos if God wills to bring it on us" (see 1/170, p. 300). Also cf. 1/170, ed. note 64.

[18.] A marginal note appears at this point: "cf. Max Hohenlohe in Madrid. GWH [Geoffrey W. Harrison]." Max Egon Prinz zu Hohenlohe-Langenburg, a landed noble in Bohemia, had used his connections to British politicians during the Sudeten crisis of 1938. He was also in contact with the Foreign Office of Military Intelligence and during the war undertook further peace negotiations in which he found himself in agreement with forces in the Foreign Office as well as in the Reich Central Security Office. See Martin, "Das aussenpolitische Versagen des Widerstands," in Schmädeke and Steinbach, *Der Widerstand gegen den Nationalsozialismus,* 1039, 1055.

[19.] On the arranged forms of communication, see 1/170, p. 302.

pledged to a policy of the character described in A of Section I above, with a view to a peace settlement of the character described in B of Section I above?

VI. *Means of Communication*

Arrangements have been made by which any reaction in important British quarters which the Bishop of Chichester might be able to obtain could be communicated through a neutral channel. The British Minister in Stockholm was fully informed at the time of the tenor of the conversations. On his advice the Bishop warned the two German pastors not only that the American and Russian and the other Allied Governments would necessarily be concerned, but that the Foreign Office might take the view that the situation was too uncertain to justify any expression of opinion on its part. On the other hand, if it were thought desirable to obtain further elucidation, a confidential meeting could be arranged at Stockholm between a German representative and a representative of the Foreign Office or other suitable person.[20]

19th June, 1942.

321   **182. To Winfried Maechler**[1]

Munich, June 20, 1942

Dear Winfried,

I recently received your card, which pleased me very much. Also your wife was so kind as to allow me to read several of your recent letters to her. I was especially impressed by what you write about your son's upbringing. It is so important that no mistakes be made now in this regard that later can no longer be corrected. I was very sorry to hear that you are no longer a medical orderly. I will now most especially think of you. It is hard for someone when every kind of choice is taken away. All we can do is adhere to God's decision. The news of Willi Brandenburg's death will also hit you hard. His last

---

[20.] In his 1957 Göttingen lecture, Bell stated: "It was suggested that should there be any wish on the part of the British Government for preliminary private discussion, Adam von Trott, a friend of Sir Stafford Cripp's son, would be a very suitable person" (*GS* 1: 406). Cf. 1/170, ed. note 82. Later in the Göttingen lecture he said, "Next day, June 1, I returned to Stockholm, staying at the British Legation. In the afternoon I saw Johansson, who told me that Björkquist refused to allow Sigtuna to be used for purposes of communication between Chichester and the Resistance movement, as inconsistent with Sweden's political neutrality. This meant that messages would have to be sent through Geneva" (*GS* 1:408). Cf. Bell's telegram to Visser 't Hooft on July 23, 1942; see 1/191, ed. note 1.

[1.] *NL*, A 60,4 (19); typewritten letter; previously published in *GS* 2:593. Maechler belonged to Bonhoeffer's student circle as early as 1932 and in 1935 came to the preachers' seminary at Finkenwalde; shortly thereafter he became a member of the House of Brethren as well. Cf. *DB-ER*, 208, 389, and 468.

words in the hospital where he lay for a day, having been shot in the abdomen, were, "Now I am entering into the world of God's righteousness." He died in faith. Just a few weeks before him Brother Wälde, who was his friend, was killed. You probably scarcely remember him. Brother Lohmann died at home of tuberculosis. What a great cloud of brethren has now gone on ahead of us . . .

Your faithful Dietrich

183. Foreign Office: Minutes of Proceedings, June 18–23, 1942[1]

Germany: Peace Moves.

Records a conversation with the Bishop of Chichester who had met in Sweden two anti-Nazi German Protestant clergymen. They spoke of a widespread anti-Nazi movement.

The Bishop wishes to tell the S[ecretary] of S[tate][2] for he considers the matter very important.[3]   322

Minutes.

It is difficult to comment on this till more is known about it.

I think It would be useful for the S/S to see the Bishop but, if he agrees to do so, he might perhaps take the opportunity to impress on Mr Bishop the great importance of secrecy in matters of this kind. The S/S might also explain to the Bishop our attitude towards peace-feelers.

Mr. Loxley   P. F. Hancock[4] 20 VI [June 20]
              P. N. L.[5] 23.6 [June 23]

[1.] Public Record Office, London, Foreign Office 371/30/912 (C 6185/48/18, earlier C 6185/416 and 610); handwritten; in original English, including errors; stamp: "F.O. Minute (Mr. Warner). Dated: June 18, 1942 Central [i.e., Department for Central Europe]." Peter Ludlow provides information about the procedures in the Foreign Office, London ("Pius XII, die britische Regierung und die deutsche Opposition im Winter 1939/40," 324–25).

[2.] The "Secretary of State" here is Anthony Eden, the British foreign minister.

[3.] Christopher F. A. Warner encouraged Bishop Bell to write directly to Anthony Eden; Warner, to whom Bell had turned at the recommendation of Stockholm envoy Victor Mallet, was head of the Foreign Office Northern Department [i.e., for Northern Europe]. See Bell's letter of June 18, 1942, to Anthony Eden, 1/180.

[4.] Patrick Francis Hancock was deputy secretary in the British Foreign Office Central Department.

[5.] Peter Noel Loxley was private secretary to the permanent undersecretary of state in the Foreign Office.

It is quite likely that this overture will be found to chime in with the move from von Trott via Mr. Visser 't Hooft[6] (see C 5428/G).[7]

It will be interesting to hear what the Bishop has to say and perhaps the S/S will agree to see him.

R. M. Makins[8] 21/6 [June 21]
W. Strang[9] 22/6 [June 22]

What would be interesting would be to see what any group of this kind can *do*. We are not going to negotiate with any Government in Germany that has not thoroughly purged its tent, and we must take some convincing of *that*. And we have got to be convinced *first*. (Total defeat and disarmament is probably the only possible condition.)

A. C.[10] June 22, 1942.

323   [The S/S has received a letter from the Bishop,[11] and is writing to suggest that he should come see him one day next week.[12]

HL 23. June][13]

184. George K. A. Bell to Gerhard Leibholz[1]

Hove, Sussex 20th June, 1942

My dear Leibholz,

Very many thanks for your letter and its welcome back. To my great surprise I saw Dietrich at the end of my stay. He had come over specially as a courier[2] with a 48

[6.] Cf. George Bell's letter to Anthony Eden on June 18, 1942: "The information is a sequel to the memorandum you have already seen, brought from Geneva by Visser 't Hooft of the World Council of Churches, and having to do with von Trott" (see 1/180).

[7.] Refers to minutes taken by Geoffrey Wedgwood Harrison, private secretary to the parliamentary undersecretary of state, Foreign Office, on June 6 and 12, 1942, with critical commentary pertaining to Visser 't Hooft and Adam von Trott.

[8.] Roger Mellor Makins was acting counselor to the Foreign Office.

[9.] William Strang was acting assistant undersecretary of state, Foreign Office.

[10.] As of January 1, 1938, Sir Alexander M. G. Cadogan was permanent undersecretary of state, Foreign Office.

[11.] This refers to Bell's letter to Anthony Eden on June 18, 1942; see 1/180.

[12.] This response is dated June 24, 1942 (Bell Papers, vol. 42): "My dear Lord Bishop, Thank you very much for your letter of June 18th. I should be very pleased to see you, but I am afraid that I cannot manage any of the days you suggest. I wonder whether it would be possible for you to come up to London one day next week."

[13.] The initials "HL" cannot be identified. The square brackets in the original probably indicate that this was not a public statement but rather an internal communication.

[1.] Literary estate of Gerhard Leibholz; typewritten; in original English, including errors; in the upper right-hand corner was handwritten the word "Private"; previously published in German translation in Bell and Leibholz, *An der Schwelle*, 56–57.

[2.] Cf. Bonhoeffer's courier identification; see 1/171.

hours visa in order to see me. We talked very much on very important matters. I told him your news, of which he was very glad. He was very well. He said that Hitler's health was unfortunately very good; the uncle[3] of whom he spoke in his letter was the war, not Hitler. His Seminary had been closed twice, and he had been forbidden by the Gestapo to preach or speak. He is at work now on a book[4] and in connection with the Brethren's Council and at nights on political work.

I told him about your book[5] and your question as to publishing it anonymously. He wanted to know what was its exact subject, and whether there were things in the contents of the book which in themselves might cause difficulties for relations. We might get a word about this when we meet at Cambridge. He asked me to say Hans[6] was very well and continuing his work on the right side.[7] Of course he sent his sister and you and the girls his warmest love. It was a real delight to see him, as you can imagine. His coming was entirely unexpected. I had heard of his passing through Sweden on his way to Norway before I arrived (also as a courier), but Archbishop Eidem thought he had gone through as a soldier,[8] and I could not find any way of communicating with him in any case. But he heard that I was in Stockholm, and so arrived.

Yours ever,

George Cicestr

184a. To Gustav Seydel[1]

17:140

June 23, 1942

Dear Brother Seydel,

Since I have been on official trips nearly nonstop in recent months,[2] I have been unable to write to you. It would not have been in time for your wedding in any case, since I did not receive your announcement until weeks

---

[3.] See 1/157, ed. note 6.

[4.] The manuscripts that would become Bonhoeffer's *Ethics*.

[5.] Cf. 1/174, ed. note 2.

[6.] Hans von Dohnanyi.

[7.] This refers to Dohnanyi's activity in the political resistance.

[8.] Cf. 1/155, ed. note 3.

[1.] Literary estate of Gustav Seydel; handwritten letter, presumably from Berlin; published in *IBG-Rundbrief* 54 (November 1997), with annotations by Otto Berendts. Page numbers in the margin refer to *DBW* 17.

[2.] During this period Bonhoeffer had completed in close succession the third trip to Switzerland, his important meeting with Bishop Bell in Sweden, an appointment in Freiburg im Breisgau, and two official trips to Munich. In between he had spent time at the home of Ruth von Kleist-Retzow. His experience of being together there with the young Maria von Wedemeyer may resonate in the following sentences. Cf. "The Third Stage: Information on the Coup, 1942," *DB-ER,* 752–80.

later. Now I would like to tell you how greatly I rejoice with you. What always delights me in news like this is the self-assured glimpse into the future and the confidence that there is a reason to look forward to the next day or the next year, the joyful grasping hold of happiness where God still gives it to us. This is—don't misunderstand me—a protest against all false, inauthentic apocalypticism that is becoming so widespread today,[3] and I hail it as a sign of authentic and healthy faith. As earthly human beings, we have to take account of an earthly future. For the sake of this future we must accept tasks, responsibilities, and joys and sorrows. We need not despise happiness simply because there is so much unhappiness. We should not arrogantly push away the kind hand of God because God's hand is otherwise so hard. I think it is more important to remind one another of this in these days than of many other things, and I received your wedding announcement gratefully as a fine testimony to this very thing. May God preserve you now in the happiness and joy God has given you. May God also prepare you through this divine kindness to bear again the divine hardship if necessary. God protect you and your wife. May God preserve you also for us and our church.

17:141

I think of you always with joy and am aware that I have learned many things from you; for this reason I am grateful to know you.

In heartfelt communion,
Your faithful Dietrich Bonhoeffer

185. To Eberhard Bethge[1]

On the train to Munich, June 25, 1942

Dear Eberhard,

Greetings from this train once again. I think of your work every day and would so love to know how it all went.[2] It was after all a considerable task, but now you will surely be able to make repeated use of it and continue to expand the material. I hope everything was fine and satisfying.

Do phone my parents on Monday in the evening, when you have taken care of your Berlin business. They would like it very much, and I would consider it very nice.—I will be flying out tomorrow and shall return with

---

[3.] Cf. Bonhoeffer's letter to Erwin Sutz on September 21, 1941, on the occasion of Sutz's wedding; see 1/127. Here the critique of the apocalyptic tendencies of that period was already present. Cf. also 2/11, p. 529.

[1.] *NL*, A 59,2 (45); handwritten; previously published in *GS* 6:567–69; partially reproduced in *GS* 2:419–21.

[2.] Cf. 1/178, ed. note 3.

Hans[3] on the tenth (not the ninth!). Where will you be then? I have written to Mrs. von Kleist and announced I shall visit on July 20. On the nineteenth you will be at Röhrich's,[4] right?

By the way, I do hope that Thude's brother-in-law gives himself sufficient time for his massage treatment.[5] That sort of thing will surely take until September. Christel should remind him of it as well; for I do not think it is as good and effective if Thude does it.

My recent activity, which has largely been in the worldly [weltlich] sector, gives me much to think about. I am amazed that I am living, and can live, for days without the Bible—I would then perceive it not as obedience but as autosuggestion if I were to force myself back to it. I understand that such autosuggestion could be and is a great help, but I fear that I would thereby falsify an authentic experience and in the end still not be experiencing authentic help. When I then open my Bible again, it is new and delightful to me as never before, and I only wish I could preach again. I know that I only need to open my own books to hear all that can be said against this. I do not wish to justify myself either, but I realize that I have had much richer times in the "spiritual" sense. But I sense how an opposition to all that is "religious" is growing in me. Often into an instinctive revulsion—which is surely not good either. I am not religious by nature. But I must constantly think of God, of Christ; authenticity, life, freedom, and mercy mean a great deal to me. It is only that the religious clothes they wear make me so uncomfortable. Do you understand? None of these are new thoughts and insights at all. Because I believe that I am on the verge of some kind of breakthrough, I am letting things take their own course and do not resist. This is the sense in which I also understand my present activity in the worldly sector. Please forgive these confessions; it is the fault of this long train ride. We really need to speak again about these things at leisure.

I have not written to Maria.[6] It is truly not time for that yet. If no further meetings are possible, the pleasant thought of a few highly charged minutes

325

[3.] Bonhoeffer traveled to Rome with Hans von Dohnanyi to make preparations in the Vatican for receiving word from the Allies, as had been arranged during the Sweden trip; see 1/189, ed. note 3; see also *DB-ER,* 770–71. [For the larger context, see von Klemperer, *German Resistance against Hitler,* 171–80.—MB]

[4.] Hans Röhrig, a Confessing Church pastor in Pomerania.

[5.] This appears to mean that Pastor Hans Lokies, director of the Gossner Mission, was to resume efforts for a military exemption for Eberhard Bethge.

[6.] This refers to the encounter with Maria von Wedemeyer at the beginning of June at the home of her grandmother, Ruth von Kleist-Retzow, in Klein-Krössin; on this, cf. *Love Letters from Cell 92,* 329–30. [During the early days of their courtship, Maria von Wedemeyer's family did not permit them to see or to write each other. See 1/208a and 1/209b.—MB]

will surely eventually dissolve into the realm of unfulfilled fantasies, a realm that in any case is already well populated. On the other side, I do not see how a meeting could be brought off that would be inconspicuous and not painful for her. Even Mrs. von Kleist cannot be expected to arrange this, at least not at my initiation; for I am in fact still not at all clear and decided about this.

Farewell! Get plenty of rest. My parents thought you were not looking particularly well. In your cupboard in the hall you will find two cans of sardines in oil. Eat them up, but do it alone; otherwise there is no point in bothering. The soup spoons are in the small leather case. Mama knows about it.

With love and all best wishes,
Your Dietrich

P.S. By the way, today is just like my experience a week ago when I rode the same train: in every car there is on average one person reading a book. Most people are dozing off alone, only half awake. Clearly almost all are people who are coming out of hectic activity. Then they have a couple of spare hours merely to brood dully to themselves, neither happily nor unhappily—it is like a more or less apathetic waiting for some sort of future after having personally done everything in one's own power; and yet neither submission nor rebellion nor defiance rests on their faces, but more a tired indifference. The personal inner life carries no weight any longer. Focusing on a book seems to belong to a past age. Dietrich

N. Trip to Italy.
June 26–July 10, 1942

---

186. George K. A. Bell: Diary Notes, June 14–July 13, 1942[1]

[...]

On returning home met Press conference at MOI[2] on June 14 good number present. Published Impression of visit in Christian Newsletter.[3] Saw Grubb[4] told him about conversations. Saw Warner at F.O.[5]

On June 30 saw Anthony Eden gave him full account of conversations and left memo with him.[6] He was much interested.—I had told them to strict silence as most likely, opinion in England tend to blame all Germans for tolerating Nazis so long. Eden pleased with my way of handling, excellent diplomacy.[7] He knew some of

---

[1.] LPL, London, Bell Papers, vol. 276; handwritten "Diary Notes," 31–33; in original English, including errors; see 1/170, ed. note 1.

[2.] Ministry of Information.

[3.] *The Christian News-Letter*, vol. 139 (June 24, 1942); reprinted in *MW* 5:306–9.

[4.] Kenneth B. Grubb, later Sir Kenneth, was the controller of the British Ministry of Information.

[5.] [Christopher F. A. Warner, head of the Northern Department of the Foreign Office.—MB]

[6.] Bishop Bell's appointments for Tuesday, June 30, 1942, included "Air Ministry" at 11:15 a.m. and "Eden" at 12:00 p.m. (see "Desk Diary," Bell Papers, vol. 325). The memorandum mentioned here is Bell's "Memorandum of Conversations" (see 1/181).

[7.] In a letter of April 29, 1942, before his trip to Sweden, Bell attempted in vain to meet with Eden, who noted skeptically: "Dept. This seems a strange choice. I thought he was a pacifist? AE [Anthony Eden] April 30." Christopher F. A. Warner, the head of the Northern Department, had met with Bell on May 8 in Eden's place; cf. 1/180, ed. note 4. After the trip to Sweden, the following message was received from the British envoy in Stockholm: "The following is an extract from a letter of June 4th from Mr. Victor Mallet to Mr. Warner about the Bishop of Chichester's visit. '[The Bishop of Chichester's visit] has been an outstanding success and his honest sincerity, simplicity and common sense have made a deep impression in many quarters not only ecclesiastical. It is no mean compliment when over 1000 go to hear a sermon in a foreign language at 11 o'clock on a Bank Holiday morning, and it is also somewhat unusual in most countries for a Rotary Club

328   the names mentioned. Peacefeelers had been put out in Turkey, and Madrid[8] (from
Sam Hoare). He must be scrupulously careful not to enter even the appearance of
negotiations with enemy—and be able to say that this was so both to Russians and
Americans. Would write to me of his considerations. Spoke gratefully of my visit to
Sweden: left him my Newsletter. Talked about Anglo Soviet Treaty—it has been a
struggle, to leave out Baltic States and Finland.[9]

Turkey also afraid of Russia. Molotov had been sensible in seeing difficulties. About
Germany he said that Germany had a "bug" which led it to try and conquer other
countries: and in having this bug it differed from other countries.
[...][10]

July 13. I then went on to see Stafford Cripps[11]—told him of Russia, Finland,
329   Esthonia, Boormann[12] etc. He was much less sweet than before my visit.[13] About
communist interfer[ence] in Baltic States to Bolshevism; spoke of revolution having
unpleasant consequences, but not so assuredly as when I last saw him. He said that
different accounts of the Bolshevist occupation came from different sources, one of
our ministers (in cabinet) having reported favourably (? Latvia) another unfavourably
(? Esthonia). Then I spoke of the S.+B.[14] visit from Berlin. To this he listened most
attentively; spoke enthusiastically of von Trott (? Adam) remembered had talk with
't Hooft to whom had said that 't Hooft might encourage von Trott to hope *on basis*

---

luncheon at which the guest of honour is a foreign Bishop to be attended by the Crown
Prince, the Commander in Chief of the Air Force and some of the leading business men
in the capital.' JSSC [= John Sebastian Somers Cocks] *28th July, 1942*" (Public Record
Office, London, Foreign Office 371/33/055-N 2604/79/42).

[8.] Regarding Max Hohenlohe in Madrid, see 1/181, ed. note 18. Regarding Otto
John's "peace feelers" in Madrid toward England and the United States in early 1942 (cf.
"Germany: Peace Moves," 1/187.1), see von Klemperer, *German Resistance against Hitler,*
349 n. 243. The Foreign Office found that Trott's memorandum of April 1942, chapter 4, §§
1, 2, 3, expressed viewpoints similar to those expressed by Otto John; see 1/172, ed. note 7.

[9.] In the negotiations about the signing of a Soviet-British pact at the end of May in
London, Churchill had refused to recognize the Soviet western border as it stood in June
1941. Since Stalin was ultimately prepared to forgo those territorial stipulations until the
peace talks following the war, the treaty was signed on May 26.

[10.] On July 10, 1942, Bell informed Gerhard Leibholz: "I have heard nothing from
Mr. Eden since my interview with him on June 30th. I hope that he is giving careful consideration to the matters I laid before him. I hope indeed that other members of the cabinet may also have been informed of what I told him.... I realize that one has to act fairly
quickly" (quoted in *DB-ER,* 763).

[11.] Bishop Bell sought Sir (Richard) Stafford Cripps out before the trip to Sweden
on May 5, 1942, particularly in order to be advised about Russia and the Baltics.

[12.] This presumably refers to Martin Bormann; cf. the citation of the secret Bormann circular letter of June 9, 1941 (see 1/170, ed. note 30).

[13.] On Tuesday, May 5, 1942, Bell had met with Stafford Cripps at 3:30 p.m. and
with Willem A. Visser 't Hooft at 4:30 p.m., at which time he may well have received Trott's
memorandum ("Desk Diary," Bell Papers, vol. 325).

[14.] Bell is referring to Hans Schönfeld and Bonhoeffer.

of defeat.[15] He thought that v. T. memo was too much based on fear of Russia over-running Germany—with general massacres. Cripps would not like his country to be overrun by Russia either and sympathised. But we must remember Russia was ally. At this saw how he agreed that Stalin had virtually (for a purpose) said that what he wanted was the departure of Hitler's troops from Russia, so agreement with Russia not impossible.[16] Cripps had felt there must be army of occupation in Berlin—it would feel as a {*safer*}[17] satisfaction of the desire for revenge. But Russia now {in danger}[18] and at that moment inopportune. One must choose the right moment for making announcement to help the opposition in Germany. I showed him S. document[19] which he read and was greatly impressed "far-reaching." He thought it also very important, and was glad I had been to Sweden, and had these communications, and promised to talk to Eden. He agreed that encouragement in any case could do no harm—and at best might do much good.

[. . .]

187. Foreign Office: Minutes of Proceedings, July 1–August 2, 1942[1]   330

187.1. On Peace Moves from Germany[2]

Germany: Peace Moves.

Irs. a memorandum of conversations with two German pastors who saw the Bishop of Chichester in Stockholm. They gave information concerning the anti-Nazi movements

---

[15.] Another reference to Adam von Trott's memorandum. While the Allies were already confident of military victory, and Bishop Bell foresaw the occupation of Berlin by Allied troops, Adam von Trott, along with many in the German resistance, still counted on the possibility of a cease-fire and a negotiated peace; thus in Sigtuna, Hans Schönfeld had considered the outcome of the war as still undecided. He wished to see an occupation not as a conquest but rather as support for an intact army in the face of unrest and chaotic developments. The politics of the Allies, as announced by Roosevelt and Churchill in the Atlantic Charter of August 14, 1941, aimed meanwhile toward the full demilitarization of Germany. The demand for "unconditional surrender" was first articulated on January 24, 1943, in Casablanca.

[16.] On this rumor, cf. 1/170, ed. note 73.

[17.] Uncertain reading; perhaps "easier" or "entire."

[18.] Uncertain reading; perhaps "a danger."

[19.] Schönfeld's "Statement by a German Pastor"; see 1/172.

[1.] Cf. the Foreign Office "Minutes of Proceedings"; see 1/183. The names of Bonhoeffer and Hans Schönfeld do not appear in Bishop Bell's memorandum and letters, in Anthony Eden's correspondence, or in the commentaries of the officials of the British Foreign Office. In contrast, the names of Trott, Visser 't Hooft, Otto John, and Prince Hohenlohe are mentioned repeatedly.

[2.] Public Record Office, London, Foreign Office 371/30/913 (C6570/48/18; earlier 416/G), 1942; handwritten; in original English, including errors. The document is marked as follows: "Dated June 30. Rcd: July 1"; "Last Paper: C 6565 (C 6185)"; "Action completed: JM July 17."

in Germany, and gave details of a peace settlement. Records a statement by one of the German Pastors on the problem.

Minutes.[3]

This document was communicated to the Secretary of State by the Bishop of Chichester on June, 30th. The Bishop of Chichester was anxious to send a reply of some sort to the German pastors. If this were not possible I understand that he had arranged some elaborate code message whereby he could let them know that they should expect no reply.

The document is the most elaborate and illuminating that we so far received. It gives a good many practical details of the alleged organisation and sets out very fully the purpose and policy of the organisation. There is no need at this stage to consider whether the proposed policy and peace settlement is satisfactory or not. The first question is to determine whether the movement is (a) genuine, and (b) likely to be effective.

The first thing to note is the obvious resemblance between the organisation described by the German pastors in Stockholm, Otto John[4] in Madrid, Visser 't Hooft as a result of his contact with the German Consulate-General at Geneva, and a "neutral interlocutor" quoted in C 6565/G.[5]

Fundamentally, I cannot help feeling that the elements of such a movement do exist. Visser 't Hooft, von Trott, and these two pastors have been known to, and are highly recommended by, influential persons in this country. Sir Stafford Cripps and the Bishop of Chichester *are men of the world*[6] and I should imagine that, if they vouch for these people personally their recommendations should be accepted.

On the other hand can it be a mere coincidence that within the past six weeks overtures from abroad have come to our knowledge from cities so far apart as Stockholm, Madrid, Zurich and Geneva? It is no doubt arguable that the movement, if they wished to contact people in this country, would try to do so through a number of different channels. But I must admit that the list of names which we have now received does not inspire confidence. Goerdeler and Beck and Hammerstein are old friends,[7]

331

[3.] The following handwritten comment appears at this point: "Secret letter C/9956 of July 7th."

[4.] See 1/186, ed. note 8.

[5.] It will be possible to identify the "neutral interlocutor" mentioned here only when C 6565—Public Record Office, London, Foreign Office 371/30/913 (C 6570): "Last Paper: C 6565 (C 6185)"—is released to the public. Public Record Office, London, Foreign Office 371/30/912 (C 6185); see the Foreign Office "Minutes of Proceedings," 1/183.

[6.] These words are underlined and noted with a question mark in the margin by Anthony Eden himself.

[7.] In George Bell's "Diary Notes," he comments on his meeting with Anthony Eden on June 30, 1942: "He knew some of the names mentioned" (see 1/186).

who have cropped up often in the past and have so far achieved nothing. Hammerstein has always been outspokenly Christian and anti-Nazi, and was on that account removed by the Nazis, although a good soldier, in 1934. Beck rather less so. Goerdeler has been mixed up in many of the feelers which have been put out and is known to have been on good terms with the High Command. (I have instituted inquiries about Leuschner and Kaiser.) My general impression is that these persons, though they have not so far achieved anything, are probably genuine anti-Nazi, and that if the German secret service wished to put up a plausible façade, these are just the names which they would be likely to pull out of the hat. Moreover, I find it rather suspicious that Louis Ferdinand should crop up again.

My conclusion is that the elements of an anti-Nazi movement comprising representatives from wide circles in Germany do exist, but that there are grounds though no specific evidence, for suspecting that it may be being made use of by the German secret police for purposes of their own, unknown to the movement.

Whether this view is accepted or not, I think it would be dangerous at the present turn of the war to give the Bishop of Chichester any message to send to the two pastors; but we can keep in mind as a channel against the time [—] e.g. in 3 or 4 months' time[8] [—] when it may be considered opportune to play a more active part in stimulating the opposition in Germany. Meanwhile I think it would be a mistake to allow the Bishop of Chichester even to let the pastors know that their message has passed on to H.M.G.[9]

G. W. Harrison, 2/7 [July 2]
Mr. Loxley,[10]
Mr. Bentinck[11] C. F. W.[12] 9/7 [July 9]

Northern Dept. E. O. C.[13] 9/7 [July 9]

I agree with Mr. Harrison. Some at least of these people are certainly genuine in their desire for a peace on Christian foundations. I should certainly be prepared myself to vouch for the good faith of one of the persons concerned whom I used to know well. This is, however, largely irrelevant since it is only too likely that the present German Government have some idea of what is going on and would use these people to their own advantage.

[8.] This was added in the margin.

[9.] His Majesty's Government.

[10.] See 1/183, ed. note 5.

[11.] Victor Frederick William Cavendish-Bentinck, acting counselor, Central Department of the Foreign Office. [The Central Department was responsible for Central Europe.—MB]

[12.] Christopher F. A. Warner.

[13.] Edward Osborne Coote, first secretary, Foreign Office.

There is also what seems to me the fundamental difficulty that this approach represents what might be termed the sincere and relatively high-minded Prussian school of thought. These people naturally look to a strong armed Germany continuing to exercise what must be a decisive influence in Europe. It is unfortunately the fact that any federal reorganisation of Europe which includes as one of its members a strong armed Germany must be a Europe dominated by Germany. The whole basis of this approach, although no doubt this is the most that can be expected from patriotic Germans, is entirely inconsistent with our own policy as set out in the Atlantic Charter, with our essential interests and with our obligations towards our allies.

It would, however, be useful to retain contact with and even give some encouragement to these elements in Germany as they represent what is probably at present the only disintegrating force there. The present moment, owing to our setbacks in the Mediterranean, is not auspicious for any anti-Hitler movement in Germany and the risks of sending any message back through the Bishop of Chichester seem to outweigh any immediate advantages.

F. K. Roberts[14] 3rd July, 1942

(action)[15]

See attached secret letter. P. N. Loxley 5/7 [July 5]
with which I entirely agree.
t.[16] can we discuss? Bentinck 9.VII. [July 9]

333   And I [agree]. Perhaps the S of S[17] will now write to the Bishop. He might perhaps say that we have gone into this very carefully, and without casting any reflection on the *bona fides* of his informants, we are satisfied that it would not be in the national interest for any reply whatever to be sent to them.

R. Makins[18] 10/7 [July 10]

I agree with what Mr. Roberts says in his second paragraph, and with the action proposed by Mr. Makins. The Bishop of Chichester and his like have learnt nothing from

---

[14.] Frank Kenyon Roberts, later Sir Frank Roberts, was first secretary, Foreign Office.
[15.] Uncertain reading.
[16.] This may be a reference to a name that has appeared earlier.
[17.] [The secretary of state (foreign minister) Anthony Eden.—MB]
[18.] [See 1/183, ed. note 8.—MB]

two German wars and are now busily in all innocence, trying to lay the foundations of a third.

W. Strang,[19] 10/7 [July 10]
O. G. Sargent[20] July 11
I agree.
AE[21] July 12
Dpt. herewith. G. W. H.[22] 14/VIII. [August 14]

187.2 On the Bishop of Chichester's Trip to Sweden[23]

Germany: Bishop of Chichester
Minutes.

It will be recalled that the Bishop of Chichester recently returned from Stockholm where he had met two German pastors who had given him information about an alleged anti-Nazi organisation in Germany.

I have reason to believe that the Bishop has been talking very freely about his conversations with these two pastors. He has certainly given the German section of the P.W.E.[24] material based on these conversations and Mr. Marshall[25] told me this morning that the Bishop had also spoken to F.R.P.S.[76] about it.

334

[19.] [See 1/183, ed. note 9.—MB]

[20.] Sir Orme Garton Sargent was deputy undersecretary of state, Foreign Office, as of September 11, 1939.

[21.] Anthony Eden.

[22.] Geoffrey W. Harrison.

[23.] Public Record Office, London, Foreign Office 371/30/913 (C 4659/48/18); in original English, including errors; handwritten entries in the Central Department of the Foreign Office, marked as follows: "F.O. Minute (Mr. Harrison). Dated: July 21. Rcd. Aug. 5. Secret."

[24.] The Political Warfare Executive was an office established in August 1941 and assigned to the Foreign Office; it was responsible, on the one hand, for analysis of enemy propaganda and, on the other hand, for Allied propaganda and subversion initiatives. According to F. H. Hinsley, the Political Warfare Executive ended up "as a triumvirat of the Foreign Secretary, the Minister of Information and the Minister of Economic Warfare" *(British Intelligence in the Second World War,* 2:7); see also Child, introduction to *Weekly Political Intelligence Summaries,* xx n. 3.

[25.] Thomas (Tom) H. Marshall was a professor at the London School of Economics; during the war he was head of the German division of the Foreign Research and Press Service (FRPS). From 1943 on, he had the same position in the Foreign Office Research Department (FORD).

[26.] The Foreign Research and Press Service was a section of the Royal Institute of International Affairs (Chatham House), with headquarters at Balliol College in Oxford. After 1939 it was headed by the historian Arnold Toynbee; at his initiative it was combined with the Political Intelligence Department (PID) in 1943 and was attached to the British

It will be recalled that Dr. Visser 't Hooft also gave gratuitous and widespread advertisement in this country to this alleged anti-Nazi organisation.

The considered view of the Foreign Office is that there certainly exist in Germany groups of people who are genuinely anti-Nazi but that it is almost inconceivable that representatives of these groups would be allowed to travel abroad and meet persons like the Bishop of Chichester without the knowledge of the German secret police. The deduction is that such representatives are either the conscious or probably unconscious tools of the German secret service. If they have been allowed to go abroad it is because the German authorities are satisfied that they can do no harm to Germany but may be able to do harm to us.

Just as the German refugees in the United States, however genuinely anti-Nazi, remain at heart pro-German and will almost certainly cause us unending trouble when it comes to peace-making, so I fear that these propagandists of the better Germany are sowing the seeds of similar embarrassment to H.M. Government. It is one thing to divide the Germans into two categories for purposes of political warfare; it is quite another to propagate the theory of a category of "decent Germans" who will be able to take over the task of Government on the expulsion of the Nazis and who will merit special treatment and consideration.

When individuals like Messrs. Alexander and Catchpool of Friends Service Committee[27] used to try to go to Switzerland and elsewhere to contact enemy nationals they were, if I remember rightly, refused exit permits. Cannot we have an arrangement whereby the Central Department of the Foreign Office are always consulted before exit permits are granted to people like the Bishop of Chichester, who presumably had to state the object of his visit before he was given an exit permit? It is very unsatisfactory having these unofficial and unblessed contacts with enemy nationals.

I think it has already been arranged with Passport Control Department that we should be consulted before persons connected with international organisations like Dr. Visser 't Hooft are allowed into this country. I should like to confirm this understanding.

G. W. Harrison
Passport Control Dept.   } 21st July, 1942
Passport and Permit Office } first for obs.

Foreign Office as the Foreign Office Research Department (FORD). See Child, introduction to *Weekly Intelligence Summaries*, 7–26.

[27.] The Friends Service Committee was an organization of British Quakers. After World War I, Corder Catchpool was a colleague of Friedrich Siegmund-Schultze in the latter's social ministry in Berlin and became the director of the Quaker mission there in 1933. He was temporarily imprisoned [by the Nazis]. Siegmund-Schultze was able to obtain his release with the help of German foreign minister Constantin von Neurath. With the British Foreign Office's consent, Horace Alexander had attempted to make contacts in Switzerland, including Siegmund-Schulze, for the purpose of peace overtures in early 1940. Cf. Grotefeld, "Opposition gegen den Nationalsozialismus und Schweizer Exil," 68–69 and 219–20.

I agree with Mr. Harrison. We should not necessarily wish to recommend the refusal of an exit permit in such cases. But we should like to have an opportunity of expressing an opinion.

F. K. Roberts 21/7 [July 21]

The Passport Control Dept. have a note to the effect that F.O. must be consulted before the grant of visas in these cases.

I. U. Cledney[28] 23/7 [July 23]

I attach (1) our papers about the visit of the Bishop of Chichester to Sweden, and (2) copy of the standing instruction to our staff regarding the procedure for consulting the Foreign Office before exit permits are granted.

Richard S. Gore[29] 24.7.42. [July 24, 1942]

(Sent to N. Dept.[30] by Passport Office)

It will be seen from Stockholm telegram No. 98 Empax of February 17th (in N 985/79/42–flag A) that the initiative for the Bishop of Chichester's visit to Sweden came from our Legation there. The Bishop went under the auspices of the Ministry of Information to deliver lectures. N 2604 shows that the Secretary of State had some qualms about the visit but that they were set at rest by Mr. Lawford,[31] who consulted Mr. Makins. The extract from a letter from Mr. Victor Mallet quoted in my minute of today on that same paper shows that the Bishop's visit was a great success from the Anglo-Swedish point of view, and Northern Department can only express regret if it should have proved an embarrassment to Central Department.

336

Please see also C 6185/416/G attached. I understand that C 6570/G,[32] which is in Central Department, also deals with this subject.

J. S. Somers Cocks[33] *28th July, 1942.*
E. O. Coote 28./7. [July 28]

[28.] This person is not further identified.

[29.] This person is not further identified.

[30.] The Northern Department of the Foreign Office was responsible for events in Sweden and thus also for Bishop Bell's stay there.

[31.] Valentine George Lawford was the second secretary in the Foreign Office, the assistant private secretary to Anthony Eden.

[32.] The words "conversations with pastors" are handwritten in the margin; see 1/181.

[33.] John Sebastian Somers Cocks served in the Northern Department of the Foreign Office; cf. 1/186, ed. note 7.

I don't think there is anything more we can do. In the Bishop's case there were clearly special circumstances, and we hope that the good he did in Sweden may outweigh any harm he may possibly do in this country.

G.W. Harrison, 29.VII. [July 29]
F. K. R.[34] 29.7. [July 29]

187.3. Answer to the Bishop of Chichester[35]

Germany: Bishop of Chichester's Contacts
Minutes.

337

There are at least four reasons why we cannot at present take a more encouraging line towards the Opposition in Germany: (1) it is, to all appearance, unorganized, (2) it is ineffective, (3) it may be being made use of by Himmler, (4) any encouragement would probably have a correspondingly discouraging effect on our Allies. But there seems no need to go unto detail in replying to the Bishop, who might thereby feel encouraged to enter into controversy.

Draft answer herewith.

G.W. Harrison 31/VII [July 31]
F. K. Roberts 31/7 [July 31]
W. Strang 1/8 [August 1]
AE Aug. 2.

188. George K. A. Bell to Hugh Martin[1]

9th July, 1942

Many thanks for your letter. I had an extremely useful visit to Sweden; while there I saw anti-Nazi Germans from Germany, as well as men of many other nationalities. So

---

[34.] Frank K. Roberts.

[35.] Document, include grammatical errors, is in the original English. Public Record Office, London, Foreign Office 371/30/913 (C 4425/48/18, formerly C 4425/416/G) Green [= Secret]; handwritten entries in the Central Department of the Foreign Office; marked as follows: "Bishop of Chichester to S. of S. Dated: July 25. Rcd Aug 4. Action completed: G. H. 14. 8. 42 [August 14, 1942]"—"Ref[erence]. to Foreign Office letter of July 17th (C 6570/416/G): Hopes that in the near future it will be possible for the S. of S. to make it plain that the British Government have no desire to enslave a Germany which has rid itself of Hitler and Himmler, etc. Is convinced that there is a large opposition in Germany, but it [i.e., the German opposition] greatly fears the treatment which H.M.G. may mete out." Cf. Anthony Eden's letter of July 17, 1942, to George Bell (see 1/191) and Bell's July 25, 1942, letter to Eden (see 1/193).

[1.] LPL, London, Bell Papers, vol. 87, 185; carbon copy; no letterhead; in original English, including errors.

far as the broadcasting to Germany was concerned, and the Protestant programmes, I was told most emphatically that great value was attached to the religious services which had been recently broadcast. Great gratitude was expressed for the sermons preached by Pastor Hildebrandt and Pastor Rieger, one I think on Whitsunday and the other on Easter Day. My informant, who came from Germany,[2] said that the more such services could be given the better. They are especially appreciated by the country Pastors, who are very lonely. I know that you are tied with regard to times, and that I explained to my friend. But if they had the choice, the time they would choose would be Sunday or Saturday evening—not mornings.

I gathered that direct propaganda did not make very much impression. It was these Protestant services that really gave such joy; this of course as a background to the very strong and growing opposition to the Nazi regime, of which I had many reports while in Sweden, some of them first-hand reports of what seemed to me the greatest importance from Germany itself. The opposition is strong, and in particular connected with the Catholic and Evangelical Churches. I know that the Catholic and Evangelical Churches have made two very important demarches to the Government, pointing out their objection to the Nazi regime on the ground of the denial of justice and freedom, and the obstacles put in the way of proclaiming the Christian Gospel and living the Christian life.[3] The opposition now emerging in Germany is different in scale from anything of the kind that was current a year ago. I gathered from my informant a very real sense of crisis, and of hope for the future. Therefore it would to my mind be a real blunder to cut down broadcasting which deals with the Churches as such at this particular juncture. I have seen Eden on the general matter of the opposition in Germany; he gave me a very kind reception and listened carefully to what I said. I am hoping to hear from him.

With regard to the broadcasts generally, so far as I could gather from conversations in Sweden, my impression is this: the more factual broadcasts are, the better. The ordinary nine o'clock news is the model. I found that propaganda as such was not particular welcome, and that facts were the best propaganda—anything which made it plain that life in England was going on in a thoroughfully direct and straightforward way. I could not get any actual criticisms of for example the broadcasts in Swedish. The Crown Princess told me that the broadcasts seemed quite good to her; but Professor Segerstedt was more critical, and said they might be better. I found that the Swedes were immensely interested in any information which could be given about social reconstruction and post-war plans. Anything which is happening now on social

338

[2.] Bonhoeffer's name is not mentioned; on the sermons, cf. 1/174.
[3.] Cf. 1/170, ed. notes 12 and 13.

reconstruction lines, and any evidence of changes in our social structure are all grist to the mill.

Yours very sincerely
[George Cicestr]

189. To the Leibholz Family[1]

9th of July 1942[2]

My dears,

from a short trip to this marvellous city which you like so much too and where I am together with my brother in law,[3] I wish to send you our heartiest greetings and wishes. My family is well. Charles and his wife[4] are finally taking their holidays on a farm of friends of mine. The children of my sisters will go there in August and September for their holidays and perhaps even a little longer and we hope they will have a quiet and wholesome time in the countryside. They are all longing to see you again soon and so are all of us. I had a most enjoyable time with George.[5] You will certainly have had a letter from him too.

I am still optimistic enough to believe that it will not last long till we meet again.

Excuse me for being so short today. My time is too limited. You know that I think of you every day. Give all my love to the children.

Much love to both of you from

Dietrich

[1.] *NL*, A 59,3 (11); typewritten letter; in original English, including errors; previously published in *GS* 6:561.

[2.] This letter was written from Rome.

[3.] Hans von Dohnanyi; see 1/185, ed. note 3. On the trip as a whole, see *DB-ER*, 770–71; cf. also Bonhoeffer's letter to Bishop Bell on August 28, 1942 (see 1/199), as well as his diary fragments from July 16, 1942 (see 1/223).

[4.] "Charles and his wife" refers to Bonhoeffer's parents.

[5.] Bonhoeffer is referring to his meeting with Bishop Bell in Sigtuna and Stockholm.

O. BERLIN, FREIBURG, MUNICH, KLEIN-KRÖSSIN, PÄTZIG. JULY 1942–MARCH 1943

190. Gerhard Leibholz to Karl and Paula Bonhoeffer[1]   340

July 11, 1942

My dears,

You can hardly imagine how delighted we were to receive your recent news of May and June.[2] Our joy was greatly compounded because we had heard nothing from you for so long and then found out that at least you are all well. For us it is one of the greatest inspirations to know that in this difficult time you are able to be together and all can pursue their work.

If we have one request it is this, that you all simply remain healthy and go on vacation often—as much as possible—so that when this war one day comes to an end we shall all be able to see one another again in good health.

We ourselves are well. We have no help, and Sabine miraculously takes care of the entire house (apart from the heating), including the garden. In this way we don't have any aggravation with personnel, and everything is cleaner and better, and Sabine wonders sometimes what our maids actually used to do. In all this she still has plenty of time for the children, reads, works in the garden, etc. We christened the house "Schlößchen zur Eisenbahn"[3] because the ticket seller for the local station used to live here. But it serves our needs; and once our travel plans were finally decided in the negative,[4] we were happy to be free of boardinghouse life, at least for the time being. The

---

[1.] *NL*, C 6; handwritten from Oxford, via air mail; envelope stamp by the British censor: "Opened by Examiner 2197"; address: "Pastor E. Sutz, Rapperswil, Kanton St. Gallen, Switzerland. From Professor G. Leibholz, 33 Beachcroft Road, Oxford."

[2.] This refers to Bonhoeffer's letters from Zurich and Stockholm; see 1/159, 1/165, and 1/176.

[3.] ["Little Castle by the Railroad."—MB]

[4.] For a brief period the Leibholz family had considered moving on to America.

children are still in school, and in three weeks their vacation will begin. They like going to school. Christiane plays the piano nicely, and Marianne is presently taking her exam. It lasts fourteen days, and I only know that I would not pass it. But if nothing "gets in the way," we think that she will pass it easily. At just fifteen, she is the youngest, in any case. Both help Sabine occasionally, and Marianne is already quite a support.

341   I saw George[5] recently, and you can imagine how his good news moved us deeply. His most recent trip impressed him greatly, and I very much hope that his efforts will lead to visible success, although many of his and our friends unfortunately do not possess the breadth of his judgment and will find it difficult to free themselves from erroneous prejudices. We see Gertrud[6] as well. Her children work partly in the garden, partly at the hospital. They both earn decent wages, so they are now the family's primary breadwinners. Her husband's situation is still unchanged. I have good news about Peter.[7] He works as his own foreman for twelve hours per day in a factory of which he is part owner. It is good that he has so quickly found something that suits him. With great joy we have heard repeatedly in the recent past from Geneva. We are very grateful for these kind greetings. In fact the steady income that we still receive is just sufficient to cover rent, heat, and school fees. But since even up to the present we don't need to buy much thanks to careful provisioning, and since we occasionally also receive things here or there and our reserves are not yet depleted, things have been going quite well so far. If nothing extraordinary happens, and the war doesn't last too much longer (we still have our more valuable things as our last reserves), we shall continue to manage somehow. In any case, the children (and also we ourselves) are keeping well nourished so far. My eyes are getting worse. I am afraid that this is part of my family inheritance. And Sabine is severely hampered[8] when she is alone (though she virtually never is). Actually, is there anything that can be done for this? She thinks it is perhaps also an inherited trait. Normally nothing bothers her. And Christiane's presence is enough. She already spoke to Dietrich about this some time ago.

Our rent is so high because we live in a furnished house. Under present conditions, when the cost of furnished homes has risen so high, that means we are paying around double the normal rate. But all of this does not keep us from being of good courage—as long as we know that you are doing [well].

Do please also greet Wolfgang.[9] I am glad that he too is in our house, and I am very grateful to him for everything he does. Perhaps he can assert that the general law does not apply at all to the concrete situation, since he continues to reside with

342

[5.] Bishop George K. A. Bell.

[6.] Gertrud Wedell, a cousin of Bonhoeffer, married Dr. Hans Wedell; the latter had been a lawyer in Düsseldorf. Classified as a "non-Aryan," he lost his position and after studying theology then became a pastor and emigrated to England. Cf. *DBW* 14:88.

[7.] Peter Leibholz, Gerhard's youngest brother, had emigrated to Melbourne.

[8.] "Hampered" is a euphemism here for depression.

[9.] Wolfgang Grote [who was managing the Leibholzes' affairs and house in Göttingen—MB].

Lina.[10] But perhaps this is still worth doing. It is wonderful that Hans[11] is doing so well and that he has made professional changes. We have also seen Franz.[12] Because of his strong formal talent, he has developed into a great "speaker."

My work is going somewhat better, although, of course, the changed external circumstances are taking their toll. But all of that dare not be any reason to complain, when so many people have so much more reason for complaint.

Lotte[13] will probably move to the Scharfs', since her work here is coming to an end. Well, I have now reported thoroughly on all our personal news. Sabine and the children are writing separately. May poor Uncle Rudi[14] soon depart this life, and may divine providence bestow on us in the not too distant future the hour in which we shall all see one another once again. Yours in this hope, with the most loving wishes from us all,

Gert

By the way, Giacometti and Dietrich Schindler (Zollikon),[15] two colleagues whom we visited often, live in Zurich. If you have time, they would surely be quite delighted to see you. I have not written them for some time, but I could also write to them (the telephone book would have the address), if it would be worthwhile.[16]

Too bad that the tele[gram] did not arrive on time for the birthday in February.[17]

191. Anthony Eden to George K. A. Bell[1] 343

Foreign Office, S.W. I
17th July, 1942

Dear Lord Bishop,

When you came to see me on June 30th, you were good enough to leave with me a memorandum of your conversations with two German pastors[2] whom you met in Stockholm at the end of May, together with the record of a statement by one of the pastors.[3]

[10.] "Good old Lina" was the housekeeper in the Göttingen house; the context referred to here is unknown.

[11.] Hans von Dohnanyi.

[12.] Franz Hildebrandt.

[13.] Charlotte Leubuscher; cf. *DBWE* 9:43, 46, 565.

[14.] "Uncle Rudi" is their code for the war; cf. 1/184.

[15.] Zacharias Giacometti and Dietrich Schindler were both legal scholars and professors at the Zurich university. [Schindler lived in Zollikon near Zurich.—MB]

[16.] These words are written in the margin of page 1.

[17.] These words are written in the margin of page 2. [February 4 was the birthday of Dietrich Bonhoeffer and his twin sister, Sabine Leibholz.—MB]

[1.] LPL, London, Bell Papers, vol. 42; typewritten letter; in original English, including errors; cf. *NL*, A 42,4 (5). Previously published in *GS* 1:384. Address: "The Right Reverend The Lord Bishop of Chichester." Note: "Personal and Private." Cf. Bishop Bell's telegram to Geneva on July 23, 1942, "Interest undoubted, but deeply regret no reply possible."

[2.] See 1/181.

[3.] See 1/172.

These interesting documents have now been given the most careful examination, and, without casting any reflection on the *bona fides* of your informants, I am satisfied that it would not be in the national interest for any reply whatever to be sent to them.[4] I realize that this decision may cause you some disappointment, but in view of the delicacy of the issues involved I feel that I must ask you to accept it, and I am sure that you will understand.[5]

Yours sincerely,
Anthony Eden

344   **192. To Winfried Krause**[1]

July 25, 1942

Dear Winfried,

What a strange coincidence: Fritz O.[2] was just here to see me and told me that you're sick; I complained that I knew nothing about it; and then your card arrived in the mail. Thank you very much for it. I want to respond right away, even if today it can only be brief. What kind of silly thing is it that you have come down with? Are you sure that you are getting proper medical care? Please, your wife should also drop me a line! These lymph problems are said to be so protracted. I am so sorry for all of you. Do you have a fever? Are you able to read? How are you being cared for? Would a person be able to brighten your day with some coffee or tea or something like that? I would very much like to know. How long have you been confined to bed? I would so much like to visit you. But at the moment I cannot yet foresee whether or when I am coming to your area. Please keep me up to date!

I recently saw Dehn,[3] quite emaciated, but otherwise unchanged, a great joy, actually a miracle.

[4.] "When Baron Bonde, a Swedish agent of Göring, offered his services as a mediator, all missions in neutral countries abroad were instructed, at the Prime Minister's [Churchill] initiative: 'Our attitude towards all such inquiries or suggestions should be henceforth absolute silence' " (Lothar Kettenacker, "Der nationalkonservative Widerstand aus angelsächsischer Sicht," 719; the Churchill citation is from the Public Record Office, London, Foreign Office 371/26/542/0610).

[5.] The draft of this letter prepared by "A.C. [= Alexander Cadogan] July 14/42" (Public Record Office, London, Foreign Office 371/30/913) was completed by Anthony Eden with the signature "AE July 15"; the addition "and I am sure that you will understand" is handwritten.

[1.] *NL*, A 60,4 (16); handwritten from Berlin; previously published in *GS* 6:569–71.
[2.] Fritz Onnasch.
[3.] Günther Dehn had been released from prison.

Now as to Bultmann:[4] I belong to those who welcomed his writing—not because I agree with it. I regret the twofold approach it takes (the arguments deriving from John 1:14 and from the radio should not be mixed together; I do consider even the latter to be a valid argument, but the distinction should be clearer)—in this regard perhaps I have remained Harnack's student to this day. To put it bluntly: Bultmann has let the cat out of the bag, not only for himself but for a great many people (the liberal cat out of the confessional bag), and in this I rejoice. He has dared to say what many repress in themselves (here I include myself) without having overcome it. He thereby has rendered a service to intellectual integrity and honesty. Many brothers oppose him with a hypocritical faith[5] that I find deadly. Now an account must be given. I would like to speak with Bultmann about this and open myself to the fresh air that comes from him. But then the window has to be shut again. Otherwise the susceptible will too easily catch a cold.

345

If you see Bultmann, please give him my greetings.... Tell him that I would like to see him, and how I see these things.

In the meantime, farewell; I shall write again soon. God preserve you.

Cordially and faithfully,
Your Dietrich

193. George K. A. Bell to Anthony Eden[1]

25th July, 1942

Dear Mr. Eden,

Many thanks for your letter of the 17th July. I am very glad that after most careful examination of the documents which I left with you, you feel that no reflection can be cast on the bona fides of the two German Pastors. I must of course bow to your decision that it is not in the national interest to make any reply to them personally. But I do greatly hope that it may be possible for you in the near future to make it plain in an emphatic and public way that the British Government (and the Allies) have no desire to enslave a Germany which has rid itself of Hitler and Himmler and their accomplices. I found much evidence on many sides in Sweden, in addition to my information from the two Pastors, of the existence of a sharp distinction between the Nazis as such and a very large body of other Germans. It is the drawing of this distinction

---

[4.] On Bultmann's *New Testament and Mythology*, cf. Bonhoeffer's letter to Ernst Wolf on March 24, 1942; see 1/148, ed. note 4.

[5.] [Bonhoeffer's word here is *Glaubenspharisäismus*; see the discussion of the use of this term in the editor's introduction, pp. 26–27.—MB]

[1.] Public Record Office, London, Foreign Office 3471/30/913 (C 4425/48/18); typewritten letter, probably from Hove; in original English, including errors. Cf. *NL*, A 42,3 (15); previously published in *GS* 1:384–86.

(with its consequences) by the Government in the most emphatic way which is so anxiously awaited by the opposition.

I have read your Nottingham speech with great attention and with much sympathy. I appreciate all you say about our resolution to continue to fight against the Dictator powers until they are all finally disarmed and rendered powerless to do further injury to mankind. I appreciate to the full your words about the recent atrocities, and your statement that these atrocities represent the policy of the German Government, and your declaration of a resolve to exact full and stern retribution. All these words are clearly intended to show the [consequences of the][2] determined British and Allied policy to have no truck with the Nazis. But if you could at some convenient opportunity make it plain that the infliction of stern retribution is not intended for those in Germany who are against the German Government, who repudiate the Nazi system and are filled with shame by the Nazi crimes, it would, I am sure, have a powerful and encouraging effect on the spirit of the opposition. I cannot get out of my mind the words which the Norwegian Minister used in a private conversation with me in Stockholm about the reality of the German opposition. The opposition, he said, hates Hitler but sees no hope held out by the Allies of any better treatment for the Anti-Nazis than for the Nazis. "It is either this (i.e., Hitler) or slavery. We hate this, but we prefer it to slavery." And I see that Goebbels has just been intensifying his propaganda on the German home front to the effect that the Allies are determined to destroy Germany. I do not believe that Lord Vansittart's policy[3] is the policy of the British Government. But so long as the British Government fails to repudiate it, or make it clear that those who are opposed to Hitler and Himmler will receive better treatment at our hands than Hitler and Himmler and their accomplices, it is not unnatural that the opposition in Germany should believe that the Vansittart policy holds the field.

Mr. Churchill said in his first speech as Prime Minister in the House of Commons on May 13th, 1940 that our policy was "to wage war against a monstrous tyranny never surpassed in the dark and lamentable catalogue of human crimes," and that our aim was "victory at all costs." If there are men in Germany also ready to wage war against the monstrous tyranny of the Nazis from within, is it right to discourage or ignore them? Can we afford to reject their aid in achieving our end? If we by our silence allow them to believe that there is no hope for any Germany, whether Hitlerite or anti-Hitlerite, that is what in effect we are doing.

I am Yours very truly,
George Cicestr

[marginal number: 346]

[2.] These words were crossed out by Bishop Bell in the original.

[3.] In stark contrast to Bishop Bell, Sir Robert Vansittart endorsed a sweeping anti-German course with no distinction between Hitler and the German population as a whole. Cf. 1/213. See *DB-ER*, 762 n. 231, as well as von Klemperer, *German Resistance against Hitler,* 243 and 288–89.

194. Anthony Eden to George K. A. Bell[1]

347

4th August, 1942

My dear Lord Bishop,

Thank you very much for your letter of July 25th about the German problem.

I am very conscious of the importance of what you say about not discouraging any elements of opposition in Germany to the Nazi régime. You will remember that in my speech at Edinburgh on May 8th I devoted quite a long passage to Germany and concluded by saying that if any section of the German people really wished to see a return to a German state based on respect for law and the rights of the individual, they must understand that no one would believe them until they had taken active steps to rid themselves of their present régime.

For the present I do not think that it would be advisable for me to go any further in a public statement. I realize the dangers and difficulties to which the opposition in Germany is exposed, but they have so far given little evidence of their existence and until they show that they are willing to follow the example of the oppressed peoples of Europe in running risks and taking active steps to oppose and overthrow the Nazi rule of terror I do not see how we can usefully expand the statements which have already been made by members of the Government about Germany. I think these statements have made it quite clear that we do not intend to deny to Germany a place in the future Europe, but that the longer the German people tolerate the Nazi régime the greater becomes their responsibility for the crimes which that régime is committing in their name.

Yours sincerely,
Anthony Eden

195. George K. A. Bell to Anthony Eden[1]

348

17th August, 1942

Dear Mr. Eden,

Very many thanks for your letter of August 4th about the German problem, which has been forwarded to me in Scotland.

[1.] *NL*, A 42,4 (17); typewritten copy; letter in original English, including the errors; previously published in *GS* 1:386–87; sender: "Foreign Office S.W. 1"; addressee: "The Right Reverend The Lord Bishop of Chichester"; marked "Confidential."

[1.] Public Record Office, London, Foreign Office 371/30/913 (C 8231/48/18, previously C 8231/416/G); handwritten; letter in original English, including the errors. Letterhead: "Private"— "as from: The Bishop's Lodging, 22 The Droveway, Hove, Sussex." Note written in red ink, above left: "I don't think this requires any more. AE Aug. 19"; note: "*Peace Moves: Bishop of Chichester.* Ref. to F.O. letter of Aug. 4 (C 4425/416/G): Appreciates the S. of S's views on the importance of not discouraging any elements of opposition in Germany to the Nazi regime. The pastors and their friends in Germany are fully alive to the responsibility of the German people for the crimes committed by the

I much appreciate what you say about your consciousness of the importance of not discouraging any elements of opposition in Germany to the Nazi regime, and your reference to the very important speech which you made in Edinburgh on May 8.

I also see the force of your point that the opposition in Germany should be ready to take similar risks to those taken by the oppressed peoples in Europe. The German opposition would probably reply that there is a difference, in view of the fact that the oppressed peoples have been promised deliverance by the Allies, and that Germany has not exactly been promised that. At the same time I fully see the point has got to be rubbed home that the opposition Germans themselves must do their part in opposing and overthrowing the Nazi rule, and thus prove their sincerity as opposition.[2]

Certainly the pastors and their friends in Germany are fully alive to the grave character of the responsibility borne by the German people for the crimes committed by the Nazis in their name. The hopes of a return to a German State based on respect for law and the rights of the individual, after the overthrow of the Nazis, and of a place for a reformed Germany in the future Europe, ought to be powerful factors in making the opposition declare itself more and more plainly.

Yours sincerely,
George Cicestr

349　　**196. To Maximilian von Wedemeyer**[1]

August 24, 1942

Dear Max,

You have lost your father. I believe I can sense what that means for you and am thinking of you very much. You are still very young to be without a father. But you have learned from him to honor the will of God in everything God gives and in everything God takes away. You have learned from him that a person's strength comes solely from being united with the will of God. You know that God loved your father and that God loves you and that it was your father's wish and prayer that you continue to love God, no matter what God sends you and requires of you. Dear Max, as heavy as your

---

Nazis in their name." Cf. Bell Papers, vol. 42, 290, handwritten draft with many corrections; vol. 42:291, typewritten copy. Cf. *NL*, A 42,3 (36); previously published in *GS* 1:387–88.

　　[2.] The words "and thus . . . opposition" are missing from the handwritten draft.

　　[1.] *NL*, A 60,4 (21); handwritten from Klein-Krössin; previously published in *GS* 6: 571–72. The recipient of this letter, Maximilian von Wedemeyer, who had been confirmed by Bonhoeffer in 1938, was at this time a lieutenant on the eastern front, where his father, Hans von Wedemeyer, captain of a cavalry regiment, had been killed at Stalingrad on August 22, 1942. At the end of October the Wedemeyer family learned that this eldest son, Max, had died as well, on October 26, 1942. When his personal effects were sent home by the army, this letter lay on top; cf. *Love Letters from Cell 92*, 53.

heart must be now, let that which your father by God's goodness planted in you now grow strong. Pray to God with your whole heart to help you preserve and prove what has been given you. You have your mother, your grandmother, your siblings, who will help you; but help them as well. How greatly they will need it. In such times one must struggle through a great deal for oneself alone. You will have had to learn out there how one sometimes must come to terms with something alone before God. It is often very difficult, but these are the most important hours of life. From this sort of solitude with God comes a great deal of strength for the community. Someone who had a father like yours has received from God a great grace and a great responsibility. Now may God be with you and close to you and grant that you might experience God's full strength and help; may God answer you and strengthen you when you call to God; may God preserve and sanctify you in body and soul, and pour out divine grace over you just as God did for your father.

Heartfelt wishes from your faithful
Dietrich Bonhoeffer

197. To Ruth von Wedemeyer[1]

August 25, 1942

My dear lady,

It was around seven years ago that your spouse sat in my Finkenwalde room to speak about the confirmation instruction that Max was to receive at that time. I have never forgotten that meeting. It accompanied me throughout the period of instruction. I knew that Max had already received and would continue to receive what was decisive from his parents' home. It was also clear to me what it means for a boy today to have a godly father who at the same time stands in the thick of life. When in the course of those years I then came to know almost all your children, I was often extremely impressed by the power of the blessing that emanates from a father who believes in Christ. This is essentially one and the same impression that has become so important to me in my encounters with your entire extended family, including the families of your respected mother and your siblings.[2] This blessing is, of course, not something purely spiritual, but something that works its way deep into earthly life. Under the right blessing, life becomes healthy,

---

[1.] This letter is in the possession of Ruth-Alice von Bismarck; handwritten from Klein-Krössin; previously published in *GS* 6:572–73.

[2.] Her mother was Ruth von Kleist-Retzow; her siblings were Hans Jürgen von Kleist-Retzow in Kieckow, Maria von Bismarck-Lasbeck, and Spes Stahlberg.

350

secure, expectant, active, precisely because it is lived out of the source of life, strength, joy, activity. The image of your spouse living from such a blessing and passing on such a blessing in a final act of responsibility stands today before my eyes, and I am grateful for it. That is what I so wish to tell you, my dear lady, in these difficult days. If human beings have passed on to loved ones and to many the blessing they have themselves received, then they have surely fulfilled the most important thing in life; then they have surely themselves become persons happy in God and have made others happy in God. But the blessing in which they lived remains over them as the light of God's countenance over them.

351

The spirit in which he lived will be the spirit in which you are now together with your children. The same seriousness with which he spoke to me that day about the Christian education of his son will now fill you in order to help your children toward a Christian grieving for their father; the same love for Word and sacrament that was given to him will unite you to one another and to the heavenly congregation; the same spirit of sacrifice and obedience toward the will of God will be what allows you quietly and thankfully to accept everything God has sent you. What praise of God this sort of Christian bearing of grief by a large family for the father called home to God can be! My thoughts are particularly with Max. How he must miss his father, especially now. And yet I am quite certain that he can no longer forget and lose what he has received from his father, that he is sheltered just as his father was and is.

God help you, my dear lady, through God's own Word and sacrament, to be comforted yourself and to comfort others.

With regards to you and all your loved ones, respectfully and
in devotion, yours,
Dietrich Bonhoeffer

198. To Alphons Koechlin[1]

August 26, 1942

Dear Dr. Koechlin:

May I hereby beg you for the great favor of receiving my brother-in-law, who is in Switzerland for a few days and will deliver this letter to you, and of

---

[1.] Archiv des Schweizer Evangelischen Kirchenbundes Bern, file 323.1 "Verfolgung der Kirchen" (Persecution of the Churches); typewritten from Berlin. Address: "Herrn Präsident D. A. Koechlin Basel." Cf. *DB-ER,* 747–49.

assisting him with your advice and aid in a situation that lies very close to   352
our hearts?[2] I would be extraordinarily grateful to you for this. Not much
is new to report from us. Thank God, Martin[3] is still doing well—the colleagues who are with him[4] unfortunately not so well. How lovely it would
be if you could visit us once again![5]

With deepest respect I remain
your very devoted, Dietrich Bonhoeffer

[2.] This refers to the decisive preparations for "Operation 7," which made possible the
emigration to Switzerland of a group of fourteen Jewish citizens from Berlin, camouflaged
as a deployment of Foreign Office of Military Intelligence agents. The first emigration
(Miss Friedenthal) began on September 4, 1942 (arriving in Basel on September 5); the
thirteen others arrived in Switzerland on September 30 (see W. Meyer, *Unternehmen Sieben,*
303–4 and 314). Bonhoeffer's role in Operation 7 later became the object of Roeder's initial interrogations (cf. 1/225.2, 1/226.1, and 1/227). The present document, discovered
by Hartmut Ludwig in Bern, verifies the central function that fell to Hans von Dohnanyi
and Alphons Koechlin in this operation as well as the mediatory role that Bonhoeffer
played. According to Meyer, Gisevius was with Koechlin on August 30 on behalf of
Dohnanyi (*Unternehmen Sieben,* 303). Hans von Dohnanyi arrived in Switzerland on August
28 at 9 p.m. and was back in Berlin on September 4. It cannot be ascertained whether he
in fact visited Koechlin personally; Koechlin's calendar contains no documentation of
such a visit. Bonhoeffer's recommendation letter for Dohnanyi did, however, come into
Koechlin's possession (cf. Smid, *Hans von Dohnanyi, Christine Bonhoeffer,* 301–2).
    [3.] Martin Niemöller.
    [4.] Niemöller's "colleagues" were the other Confessing Church pastors in the Dachau
concentration camp: Heinrich Grüber, Helmut Hesse (who died there on November 24,
1943), Ludwig Steil (who died there on January 17, 1945), Werner Sylten (who died on
August 26, 1942), and Ernst Wilm, among others. See Niemöller, *Kampf und Zeugnis der
Bekennenden Kirche,* 523, as well as Niemöller, *Die evangelische Kirche im Dritten Reich,* 387.
[Niemöller believed that Sylten had died in Dachau; in the meantime, it has become
clear that he was taken with a group of other prisoners who were in the Dachau infirmary
to Schloß Hartheim, a nearby "euthanasia" institution, and murdered. See Klee, *"Euthanasie"
im NS-Staat,* 338.—MB]
    [5.] See Bell and Leibholz, *An der Schwelle.* As representative of the Ecumenical Coun-
cil, Koechlin had been an observer of the Confessing Synod at Dahlem, October 19–20,
1934 (Bell and Leibholz, *An der Schwelle,* 164); his final time in Germany was as a member
of an ecumenical delegation April 20–22, 1938 (W. Meyer, *Unternehmen Sieben,* 304 and
318). [The Ecumenical Council was a forerunner of the World Council of Churches that
was to be established in 1948.—MB]

353   **199. To George K. A. Bell**[1]

August 28th, 1942

My Lordbishop,

I have just received a letter from my sister[2] in which she tells me that she has met you after your long journey. I am so glad to know that you have returned safely and that you have already seen my people. Since I wrote to you last not much has changed here. Things are going as I expected them to go. But the length of time is, of course, sometimes a little enervating. Still I am hopeful that the day might not be too far when the bad dream will be over and we shall meet again. The task before us will then be greater than ever before. But I hope we shall be prepared for it. I should be glad to hear from you soon. Wednesday has for many of my friends become the special day for ecumenical intercession.[3] Martin[4] and the other friends send you all their love and thanks. Would you be so good enough to give my love to my sister's family?

In sincere gratefulness, I am yours ever
Dietrich

17:141   **199a. To Wiltrud Schutz**[1]

September 4, 1942

My dear Mrs. Schutz,[2]

A few days ago I heard through Brother Onnasch of the death of your husband;[3] and now today the announcement has arrived and thus the confirmation that it is true that you have lost your dear husband, we a fine brother, and the congregations their faithful pastor. For me this news is one of the most difficult blows we have suffered during this war. Once again one of our best has been taken from us, for whose work in the congregations we

---

[1.] *NL*, A 42,1 (37); typewritten copy; letter in original English, including the errors; previously published in *GS* 1:389. This letter was taken to Switzerland by Hans von Dohnanyi and conveyed to England from there.

[2.] Sabine Leibholz; presumably Bonhoeffer is speaking of the letter from Gerhard Leibholz on July 11, 1942; see 1/190.

[3.] Cf. 1/166.

[4.] Martin Niemöller.

[1.] Literary estate of Erwin Schutz; handwritten from Berlin; previously published in M. Krause, *Erwin Schutz, 1907–1942.* Page numbers in the margin refer to *DBW* 17.

[2.] [The greeting in the German text is "Sehr verehrte Frau Pastor," which means literally "Most esteemed Mrs. Pastor." In a German letter one may address a woman formally with the professional title of her husband.—MB] Wiltrud Schutz was the widow of Pastor Erwin Schutz; cf. Bonhoeffer's letter to Erwin Schutz on January 2, 1941; see 1/53a.

[3.] Schutz was killed on August 2, 1942, at Leningrad; cf. also the obituary by Bonhoeffer in the Finkenwalde circular letter for the first Sunday of Advent 1942; see 1/212.

had all hoped so much, one of the few from whom other brothers drew strength for their ministries, one of the faithful on whose word and action one could rely. I recall today with grateful and happy remembrance the year and a half he made his house available for our work, during which time he became a good friend and brother to all the younger brothers, and throughout which he took upon himself many a sacrifice on our behalf. Countless times we heard him proclaim God's word in the simple, clear way that was his; we saw how friendly and sure he was with the children and how he stood by his parishioners in word and deed. I was very fond of your husband; his cheerful and calm spirit emerging from his confident faith was always a particular joy for me during the time we lived together. I believe I have some sense of what you have lost with him and how great your sorrow must be But his own spirit, his own faith gives you direction and help for this most difficult period of your life. In his life he wanted to go the way of obedience, and it would have been his greatest wish that his death not separate us from this way. Now we must obey and believe without understanding and seeing. God help you in this, dear Mrs. Schutz. With heartfelt sympathy,

17:142

Your devoted Dietrich Bonhoeffer

200. To Grete Lynker[1]

Berlin-Charlottenburg, September 7, 1942

Dear Mrs. Lynker,[2]

The news of your husband's[3] death has had a deep impact on me. Of the small circle of seven brothers to which your husband belonged back then in Schlönwitz, he is now the fourth who has been taken from us. I don't know whether you knew Brothers Nithack, Schulze, and Schutz, who have already preceded him in death. Now God has led these brothers so quickly to fulfillment, and all of them—and with them your dear husband, our good brother—are now permitted to praise and serve God in righteousness, innocence, and blessedness in the eternity of God of which we so often spoke together. We all loved your husband very much. His clear, joyful, and masculine character in which his faith was mirrored earned him the trust and love of all the brothers. I shall remain grateful to him for what he

354

[1.] *NL*, A 60,4 (20); handwritten; previously published in *GS* 6:574–75.

[2.] [The greeting in the German text is "Liebe Frau Pastor," which means literally "Dear Mrs. Pastor." In a German letter one may address a woman formally with the professional title of her husband. Grete Lynker was married to Pastor Rudolf Lynker, who died on the eastern front on July 21, 1942.—MB]

[3.] Rudolf Lynker had been a member of the collective pastorate in Groß-Schlönwitz in the summer of 1938; cf. *GS* 2:553, *DB-ER*, 615, and *DBW* 15:137 n. 1.

meant to his circle at that time; I shall not forget the earnestness and devotion of his cooperation in the seminary. When I later heard about him occasionally in East Prussia, I was glad to know that he was not in immediate danger. Then I didn't hear any more about him for a longer period. But when I thought of him, I was quite reassured in thinking of his secure faith. And as much as his death now causes me pain, as much as I know what we brothers and also the church have lost in him, as much hope as we set upon his ministry, yet even today I rejoice and remain certain that he lived and died in faith, that God has perfected him and has now given him all that had been promised to him in this life.

I believe I can sense what you have lost with your dear husband. Nevertheless, what still remains is perhaps the greatest gift you have received through him, namely, that you were able to participate in a life of faith in God's Word. The only thing he will ask today of God, before whose throne he has been called, is that you might be helped to continue in this life in faith without sight or understanding, so that you might remain united to him now as well as in eternity. May God help you in this; and by comforting you, may God give you strength to comfort many others as your husband also did in his life.

In the communion of our Christian faith and prayer,
your sincerely devoted
Dietrich Bonhoeffer

355   ## 201. Application for Travel Visa

201.1. Munich Military Intelligence Office to Munich Police Headquarters[1]

Munich, September 10, 1942

Schönfeldstraße 7
Enclosures: 1 passport
Re: Visa

[1.] *NL*, A 82,10; typewritten; address: "*An das Polizeipräsidium—Paßamt, z. Hd. Herrn Oberinspektor Grädler oViA* [=oder Vertreter im Amt], *München*" ("To the Police Headquarters Passport Office, att: Chief Inspector Grädler or Current Officeholder, Munich"). Sender and file number: "*Abwehrstelle im Wehrkreis VII, Az. Pf 2/III c*" ("Military Intelligence Office in Military District VII, file Pf 2/III c"). Beginning October 4, 1942, Bonhoeffer was in Munich preparing for a trip to the Balkans. This plan was later scrapped on the basis of warnings from SS Major General [a military ranking in the Waffen-SS—MB] Arthur Nebe, Criminal Director of the Reich Central Security Office.

Military Intelligence Office requests issuance of a visa for Dietrich *Bonhoeffer* for repeated travel to and return from Hungary, Bulgaria, Greece, Turkey, Croatia, Italy, for a period of three months.[2]

Ficht[3]

Bu.[4]

201.2. Visa Issued by Munich Police Headquarters[5]

Department II/1

I. Visa No. 1109/2055 for Hungary, Bulgaria, Greece, Turkey, Croatia, and Italy, for all border crossing points, valid from September 10–December 10, 1942, for repeated use. Exempt from fees.

    (Service passport no. II 1939/42 from Berlin Police Headquarters, valid from   356
May 27, 1942[6]–August 26, 1945, issued for domestic and foreign travel.)

II. To be added to the files at Dept. II/Zi[7] 110.

Munich, September 10, 1942
Police Headquarters
by order of

201.3. Munich Police Headquarters to Munich Military Intelligence Office[8]

Department II/1

   With 1 service passport
   to the
   Military Intelligence Office in Military District VII

   [2.] There is no way today to know the purposes and intentions of these travel plans. With respect to Italy, this might have been a follow-up on Bonhoeffer's and Dohnanyi's recently renewed contacts with the Vatican. With regard to Greece, which was occupied by the German army, Bonhoeffer might have been involved with a transnational ecumenical relief action that wanted to furnish the suffering population with grain shipments from Egypt. Visser 't Hooft in Geneva, the Vatican, English bishops, and even the Berlin Church Foreign Office were active in this effort. On September 24, 1942, Eugen Gerstenmaier reported from the Balkans to the German Ministry of Foreign Affairs: "The English are supposed to release the grain determined for Greece, which is ready in Alexandria, and in part already paid for" (Archiv des Auswärtigen Amtes, Bonn, Kult. Gen 2071). Bishop Bell's corresponding message to Erwin Sutz on December 3, 1942 (see 1/213) was presumably intended to reach Bonhoeffer.

   [3.] Lieutenant Colonel Nikolaus Ficht was the head of Military Intelligence Office VII in Munich.

   [4.] This person is not identified.

   [5.] This is a typewritten page glued to the back of 1/201.1.

   [6.] Cf. 1/168, ed. note 1.

   [7.] [Abbreviation for *Zimmer*, "room."—MB]

   [8.] This is typewritten, as in ed. note 1.

—file number Pf 2 III c—

in Munich

Schönfeldstr[aße] 7

returned with the note that, according to the General decree of the SS Commander and Chief of the German Police in the Reich Ministry of the Interior[9] of April 30, 1941, S II B 1 (new) 1079/41–485, until further notice exit visas for officials and employees of the Reich and its territories, as well as for all other persons who travel abroad in official capacities, will be issued exclusively by the Ministry of Foreign Affairs in Berlin, regardless of whether such travel is official or personal.

Munich, September 11, 1942

Chief of Police

by order of Hiller

202. To Ernst Wolf[1]

September 13, 1942

Dear Professor Wolf,

357

Many thanks for your letter! Your query regarding *Verkündigung und Forschung* embarrasses me in that, despite countless inquiries at the office to which my brother-in-law had turned before and which had made promises to him, it is simply impossible to receive definitive information. Personally I think that the people there have overestimated themselves and are now feeling uncomfortable, but in fact it appears that a decision has not yet been made. Nevertheless, given the severity of present regulations, I have very little hope left. Unfortunately, at the moment I cannot do a thing, since those responsible are on vacation. In short, it doesn't look good. The people are also so confused that they constantly forget half of what is said to them and let week after week go by, apparently functioning according to the motto that most things can be dealt with by ignoring them. In our case, however, that unfortunately won't work. As soon as the people are here again, I shall make a final attempt and get back to you promptly.

I am very sorry that Stählin[2] has fallen. I did not know him personally, but I took pleasure in his work. You as well have probably lost a great number

---

[9.] The German document reads: "lt. RdErl. D. RFSSuChdDTPol. Im RmdI," or "laut Runderlaß des Reichsführers SS und Chefs der Deutschen Polizei im Reichministerium des Inneren." The reference is to Heinrich Himmler.

[1.] BA Koblenz, Nachlaß Ernst Wolf, vol. 37, published in *Verkündigung und Forschung*; typewritten, presumably from Berlin.

[2.] Leonhard Stählin, who graduated with a theological licentiate in 1940 from Halle, had already volunteered in 1942 to participate in a *Freundesgabe* [a literary work written by

of students by now. There are now twenty-one from my seminary. The church is becoming very poor. Spiritually as well. Why does everything that is presently happening rob us so utterly of speech? And in addition the dreadful looking back toward the fleshpots of Egypt and the illusion of finding them at the consistory![3] I am only glad that all the attempts at legalization keep falling apart from above. How much better it is to stand outside quite disgraced than to take part in some aspect of it. I find it a tremendously liberating thought that Christ is not at all dulled to the suffering and sin in the world, as we are, but rather that he experienced and bore it all unceasingly.[4]

I have read the second main section of the new *Dogmatics*;[5] I've not yet had a chance to read the first. I am presently working on Vischer.[6] As I hear from Marburg, the Council of Brethren there is presently in the midst of deciding about the expulsion of Bultmann from the Confessing Church! These theological hypocrites,[7] so works-righteous! Were it actually to come to expulsion, the matter would have to go to the Conference of Regional Councils of Brethren. If the same thing happened here, I think I would have to have myself expelled as well, not because I agree with Bultmann, but because I consider the others' attitude by far more dangerous than Bultmann's.

Are you presently on leave? How will things now proceed for you?

With best regards, yours cordially,
Dietrich Bonhoeffer

Perhaps it is for the best after all that the Bultmann monograph[8] was the last one to appear. This keeps open the question that, particularly in the Confessing Church, was permitted and had to be asked. And along with it, the question of the self-understanding of the Confessing Church also remains open for the time being, and that is surely a good thing.

---

friends to honor someone on a special occasion—MB] that was planned by Oskar Hammelsbeck for Karl Jaspers's sixtieth birthday.

[3.] [Bonhoeffer is referring to the temptations that legalization continued to pose for the illegal Confessing Church clergy; see 1/72, ed. note 8, and 1/151, ed. note 3.—MB]

[4.] Cf. Bonhoeffer's letter of May 21, 1942, to the Leibholz family, 1/165.

[5.] Karl Barth's *Church Dogmatics* 2/2; cf. 1/160.

[6.] Vischer, *Das Christuszeugnis im Alten Testament*, vol. 2; cf. 1/147.

[7.] [Bonhoeffer's word here is *Pharisäer*; see the discussion of the use of this term in the editor's introduction, pp. 26–27.—MB]

[8.] See 1/148, ed. note 4.

203. To His Parents[1]

September 18, 1942

My dear Parents,

Many thanks for your letter of September 16. First I want to answer your questions: so far hay has not come at all.[2] No one from the billeting office[3] has been by again. In the meantime I have received confirmation from Munich that I need a "bedroom and work space," i.e., presumably two rooms. It appears that Lotte[4] has departed with Papa's letter.

With regard to nourishment we are managing fine. Christoph Bethge sent some things to Eberhard again, and I also received a package. For a few days we have both had the gastrointestinal bug that is going around here. We have not descended upon your provisions, although we did want to open a bottle of red wine. But the key was missing, so nothing came of it. Luckily we do not yet need the oil you offered us. But now we are feeling better, and soon we shall be able to eat everything again.

Klaus[5] came over the day before yesterday and looked in splendid condition. At the end of this next week I shall travel to Munich and make my two trips from there and shall thus be away around six weeks.[6] If no attacks are made on Berlin until after the next full moon, then we shall probably not need to reckon with them anymore.

I have just heard that you have set up a phone conversation for tonight. Then I can close for today.

Love from
Your grateful Dietrich

204. To Karl Bonhoeffer[1]

September 24, 1942

Dear Papa,

Many thanks for your letter! We are now sufficiently back in shape that we can eat everything and will hopefully not be needing the red wine anymore. In the meantime I was at the Kleists' for a day and a half. Mrs. von

---

[1.] *NL*, A 59,1 (17); handwritten from Berlin; previously published in *GS* 6:575–76; partially reproduced in *GS* 2:421.

[2.] [The circumstances underlying this remark can no longer be determined.—MB]

[3.] This concerned the military's need for space.

[4.] Lotte was a servant in the Bonhoeffer household.

[5.] Klaus Bonhoeffer.

[6.] These two trips did not materialize. See 1/201.1, ed. note 2.

[1.] *NL*, A 59,1 (18); handwritten from Berlin; previously published in *GS* 6:576; partially reproduced in *GS* 2:422.

Kleist[2] is no longer capable of reading. In addition, she recently had an attack of fever that quickly subsided, but I think it is possible that she will ask you whether you might perhaps be able to come by to advise her. A trip to Berlin is too onerous for her at this point.

Else's brother[3] has fallen at the Terek.[4] Stalingrad appears to be a dreadful battle. That is certainly very depressing for everyone and takes a terrible toll on the nerves. Presumably new forces of personnel and leadership are always needed there. 360

Here everything is back to normal, and so we shall book patients for Friday and Monday.

Love from
Your grateful Dietrich

205. Preparations for the Freiburg Memorandum
205.1 Discussion Notes[1]

Economic Questions: Eucken,[2] v. Dietze,[3] Bauer[4] (Karrenberg[5]
Law of the State[6]   Domestic   Decalogue[7]

[2.] Ruth von Kleist-Retzow.

[3.] Else was a former servant in the Bonhoeffer household.

[4.] [The Terek is a river in the Caucasus, where the German army launched a major offensive in the summer of 1942.—MB]

[1.] *NL,* A 65,11; Bonhoeffer's handwritten notes in pencil on paper (DIN A 5) for a meeting of the Freiburg memorandum circle on November 17–18, 1942; see *DB-ER,* 776. These notes have been deciphered by Eberhard Bethge and Ilse Tödt; Bonhoeffer's abbreviations have been spelled out in full. These notes probably date from a preparatory meeting with Professor Erik Wolf on October 9, 1942, in Freiburg im Breisgau; Constantin von Dietze also participated in this meeting (see 1/205.2). Erik Wolf's diary entry of October 9, 1942, reads: "5 p.m. CvDietze came for talks with Pr. Bonhoeffer until late at night" (Rübsam and Schadek, *Der 'Freiburger Kreis,'* 78). Bonhoeffer did not, however, participate in the conference that was planned. On the entire course of events, see *DB-ER,* 775–77; also G. Ritter, *Carl Goerdeler und die deutsche Widerstandsbewegung,* 513–14; and Thielicke, *In der Stunde Null,* 27–28. [The Freiburg memorandum was completed in January 1943. It was one of several "think pieces" offering proposals for the future shape of European society after the war and the end of Nazi rule. It was to be submitted to a proposed postarmistice conference in which European church leaders wanted to participate and for which Bishop Bell solicited the memorandum. This postarmistice conference was never convened in the proposed form, but the Freiburg memorandum was discussed at the 1948 founding conference of the World Council of Churches in Amsterdam.—MB]

[2.] Walter Eucken was a political economist in Freiburg im Breisgau.

[3.] Constantin von Dietze was also a political economist in Freiburg im Breisgau.

[4.] Walter Bauer was a political economist and manufacturer.

[5.] Friedrich Karrenberg was a theologian and political economist.

[6.] The word "state" replaces what may have been the original term: "common[wealth]."

[7.] Cf. *DBWE* 6:357–60; see also 1/218, ed. note 11.

God and State	Foreign	
	Europe	Asmussen,[8] Ritter[9]
	Luther...	
God and Rights:	Fundamental rights[10] and human rights	
	v. Simson[11] Böhm-Jena[12]	
361	Natural law Mensing[13]	
	Criminal law	
	State–Church Tu 17th–18th in the evenings[14]	
The Jews [15]		

[8.] This word is barely decipherable; "Asmussen" is presumed on the basis of comparison with 1/205.2. On Hans Asmussen's participation in preliminary conversations about the Freiburg memorandum, see 1/235, p. 459.

[9.] Gerhard Ritter was a historian in Freiburg im Breisgau.

[10.] The word "fundamental" replaces what was probably the original word here, "natural-."

[11.] Werner von Simson, a Berlin lawyer, was a professor of public law in Freiburg im Breisgau after 1968. He knew of no explanation why his name came to be included in this plan. At that time he had no relation of any sort with the Freiburger circle, and he lived in England during the war. In the 1930s he was, however, well acquainted with the Bonhoeffer family.

[12.] Franz Böhm, a professor of jurisprudence in Jena, was a participant in the meeting in November 1942 and one of the authors of appendix 1 (Legal System) of the Freiburg memorandum.

[13.] Carl Mensing, an attorney in Wuppertal, was a member of the constitutional committee of the Provisional Administration (1936) of the German Evangelical Church.

[14.] The date of the gathering in Freiburg, a meeting in which Bonhoeffer apparently originally wanted to take part.

[15.] Bishop Bell records in his "Memorandum of Conversations" the following notes from the conversations in Sweden with Hans Schönfeld and Bonhoeffer: "Immediate repeal of Nuremberg Laws, and co-operation in international settlement of Jewish problem" (see 1/181, section 1 A). In *The Church and the New Order,* William Paton writes: "The treatment of the Jews in any community is an excellent guide to the moral health of that community." According to Paton, the "Jewish problem" is "at least as much a Gentile problem as a Jewish problem. . . . But the Christian religion, while it has removed all limitations of race and nation from its promises, holds as its utmost 'arcanum' of faith that the very God became incarnate at a point in space and time, and offers as its central philosophical problem the revelation of the infinite in the peculiar. For this reason Christians should be on guard when anti-Semitism raises its ugly head. As Professor Macmurray once remarked to me: 'When you find anti-semitism you may be sure that the real fight is about Christianity'—paradox, but one that contains a vital truth" (62). Appendix 5 of the Freiburg memorandum contains "Proposals for a Solution to the Jewish Problem in Germany," written by Constantin von Dietze; see Thielicke, *In der Stunde Null,* 146–51 (for a critical perspective on this, see ibid., 21–23). Also see Christine-Ruth Müller, *Dietrich Bonhoeffers Kampf,* 275–76. [Many Christian leaders of that age shared Paton's sentiment that anti-Semitism targeted Christians because of Jesus' Jewishness. Unfortunately, in most cases this did not lead to any meaningful solidarity with the Jewish victims of Nazism. The

Education[16]

The church's proclamation to the world[17]   362
  Word of God and counsel[18]
Legal ground[19] Existence of the church in the world. Perels[20]

205.2. Constantin von Dietze: Discussion Notes[21]

Tuesday, November 17,[22] 12 p.m.
Nov. 18–19 Dibelius[23] privately
            Bonhoeffer Jannasch?[24]
            Böhm-Jena 3 x privately
            2–3 restaurants
Bonhoeffer: Neither original sin nor creation, but Christ[25]
Privately: 1. Evening of the 24th
             2. Stuttgart
Tuesday   1. The church's proclamation to the world Bonhoeffer
             2. Legal ground of the church in the world Pz[26]

Freiburg memorandum's section on the Jews was extremely problematic; there is no evidence that Bonhoeffer ever saw it. See the German editors' afterword, p. 663.—MB]

[16.] See 1/205.2, "Litt and Delekat." In the space beneath these words, a horizontal line appears.

[17.] Cf. 1/205.2, according to which Bonhoeffer himself was foreseen as the expert on this topic. On this theme, see Bonhoeffer's sketch, "On the Possibility of the Church's Message to the World," *DBWE* 6:352–62; cf. 1/93, ed. note 14, and 1/123.

[18.] Bonhoeffer writes in his *Ethics:* "The church has a *twofold approach* here: *on the one hand,* it must declare as reprehensible, by the authority of the word of God, such economic attitudes or systems that clearly hinder faith in Christ, thereby drawing a negative boundary. *On the other hand,* it will not be able to make its positive contribution to a new order on the authority of the word of God, but merely on the authority of responsible counsel by Christian experts. Both these tasks must be strictly distinguished" (*DBWE* 6:361).

[19.] These words are added in the margin.

[20.] Friedrich Justus Perels. In fact Perels did write this contribution to the memorandum's appendix, but his manuscript did not reach Freiburg; cf. *DB-ER,* 776, and Schreiber, *Friedrich Justus Perels,* 176–77.

[21.] Archiv für Christlich-Demokratische Politik, papers of Constantin von Dietze I-345–002; handwritten (shorthand) notebook entries, transcribed by Gertrud Lampe and Karl-ernst Ringer. The notes were taken at the same time as those by Bonhoeffer (see 1/205.1).

[22.] As with Bonhoeffer's notes, this note looks ahead to the larger meeting that was planned.

[23.] General Superintendent Otto Dibelius participated in the November 1942 meeting and contributed to appendix 2 (Church Politics) of the memorandum.

[24.] According to the available documents, Pastor Wilhelm Jannasch did not participate in any meeting and did not write any contribution.

[25.] See *DBWE* 6:154–55 and 278–79.

[26.] The abbreviation "Pz" could also be interpreted to refer to Johannes Popitz, but cf. "Perels" in 1/205.1.

Wednesday 3. Europe: Asmussen
Historical: Luther—Prussianism—N.S.[27]
363   December: Eyck, Bismarck volume 1.[28] Bonhoeffer. Erich Marcks[29]
Fundamental and human rights Mensing Atty. Barmen, Reformed jurist
Permanent working group on natural law[30]
Education: Litt[31] and Delekat[32]
   Bonhoeffer: W. Kurfürstenstraße 78 at Wätjen's[33]
   Grunewald Kunz Buntschuhstraße 4[34]
      Halensee-Friedrichruhe Train Station

206. To Hans-Walter Schleicher[1]

October 10, 1942

Dear Hans-Walter,

I have just heard that your induction order is set for next Thursday. Unfortunately I shall not be able to see you again before then. Therefore I wanted at least to write you briefly. We have recently spoken repeatedly of your becoming a soldier—sometimes jokingly but also seriously. Now that it has come to pass—so that it is no longer a matter of possibilities, reflections,
364   free decisions, but rather one of a given actuality, in the face of which there are no longer any more reflections and possibilities—suddenly many things look much different; and so the first thing I want to say to you is that I truly

---

[27.] ["N.S." is the abbreviation for *Nationalsozialismus,* "National Socialism."—MB]

[28.] Eyck, *Bismarck: Leben und Werk.*

[29.] Marcks, *Bismarck.*

[30.] This presumably refers to the "Freiburg council," a discussion group that had originated by the end of 1938; it had formed around professors Dietze and Ritter and included Catholic theologians as well. "The conversations, which took place in an atmosphere that seemed private to outsiders, revolved around questions of natural law, Christian ethics, the national economy, and—under the influence of increasing state coercion—the right of Christian resistance" (Kluge, "Der 'Freiburger Kreis,'" 27).

[31.] Theodor Litt was an educator and philosopher in Leipzig.

[32.] Friedrich Delekat, a religious educator in Dresden who was forced to retire in 1937, had been given a pastorate in Stuttgart by Bishop Wurm; he had been a friend of Constantin von Dietze since their work together at the Oxford World Church Conference in 1937. He wrote appendix 3 of the memorandum on education.

[33.] The address of Dr. Eduard Wätjen, a Berlin attorney related to Dietze; he was a member of the Foreign Office of Military Intelligence of the Armed Forces High Command and worked in the same office as Helmuth von Moltke.

[34.] The house of the Delbrück family, occupied by two daughters of the historian Hans Delbrück.

[1.] *NL,* A 59,3 (13): handwritten from Munich; previously published in *GS* 2:422–24.

rejoice for you that the period of uncertainty and waiting is now over and that you can now [have] inner calm about being where your comrades of the same age are too. That was probably the main thing that bothered you, and that will be the thing that will help you mentally even in difficult situations. Not to want to separate oneself from fate and from the need of other human beings, to want to have community with them—that is, of course, something quite different from simply wanting to take part, to come along. One should also probably beware of *wanting to have a shared experience* of the war and its horrors; for who, lightheartedly wishing such a thing for himself, really knows how he will respond in the decisive hour? But to be called, to participate in the community, contributing and bearing one's share, whatever that may be—that is, I believe, fairly firm ground on which to stand and to endure even difficult things. And if from time to time one recalls these things and is finally able to live completely from the awareness that this being called is ultimately not accidental, but is God's own way for our lives, then I think one can go very confidently into the unknown. Of course, life in the new community will then also be given very definite and inviolable boundaries, and one's inner reality collapses utterly if one crosses these boundaries out of false solidarity.

You are, of course, entering into your life as a soldier differently from most of your contemporaries. You have a foundation of values. You have received certain fundamental concepts of life. You know—perhaps partly still unconsciously, but that doesn't matter here—what treasures a good family life, good parents, right and truth, humanity and education, and tradition are. You yourself have been making music for years and in recent years have read many books, all of which has not simply washed over you without any effect. And finally, you also somehow know what the Bible, the Lord's Prayer, and church music are. Out of all this, however, you have received an image of Germany that can never be entirely lost to you, that will accompany you into the war, and for which you will stand up wherever you are and no matter who might confront you. Perhaps as a soldier you are freer for this than we others. But it is clear, and you yourself know it as well, that because of this you will face conflicts, not only with those who are coarse by nature, whose power will shock you in the next few weeks, but simply because you, precisely because you come from a family of this kind, are different from most other people, different even into the smallest externals. The important thing is thus only that one conceive the ways one has an edge on others (and you definitely do!) not as your due but as a gift, and that you place yourself entirely at others' disposal and truly like them, despite their different way of being.

We shall miss you very much, even though we hope that we shall still have you here quite often and for extended periods. But we shall rejoice with you in the thought that you are now happy to be able to be a soldier, and shall think of you often. You will surely have a lovely evening together on Wednesday. I very much wish I could be there.[2] Now farewell, may it go well for you, and may the days ahead be bright for you! And even if I am otherwise sparing with such words, now let me say to you today:

May God watch over you!

Yours,
Uncle Dietrich

Give your parents my warmest regards, especially also Christine.

206a. To Maria von Wedemeyer[1]

October 31, 1942

Dear Miss von Wedemeyer,

If I might be allowed to say only this to you,[2] I believe I have an inkling of what Max's[3] death means for you.

It can scarcely help to tell you I too share in this pain.

At such times it can only help us to cast ourselves upon the heart of God, not with words but truly and entirely. This requires many difficult hours,

---

[2.] Because the plan for a trip to the Balkans was abandoned (see 1/201, ed. note 1), Bonhoeffer returned to Berlin from Munich on October 14. Maria von Wedemeyer's diary entry on October 15, 1942, establishes that he did participate in the farewell evening at the Schleichers' (*Love Letters from Cell 92*, 331).

[1.] This is the first of the previously unpublished letters from Bonhoeffer to Maria von Wedemeyer written during 1942–43. The other letters appearing in this volume are 1/208a, 1/209a, 1/209b, 1/214a, 1/215a, 1/215b, 1/215c, 1/220a, and 1/220b. These letters are from the literary estate of Maria Weller (née von Wedemeyer), archives of the Houghton Library, Harvard University, Cambridge, Massachusetts ("Papers of Dietrich Bonhoeffer, 1942–1944," bMS Ger 161); handwritten. These letters are also published in the *Bonhoeffer Jahrbuch 2005*; grammar, spelling, and punctuation are unchanged in the German edition. The German editor of these letters, Hans Pfeifer, and the editors of this volume gratefully acknowledge permission to translate and publish these letters from Houghton Library, Harvard. Bracketed numbers indicate the page numbers in the archival manuscript. On a listing prepared by the archive and included with the estate, letter 1/206a is noted as no. 9. For the background on Bonhoeffer's engagement to Maria von Wedemeyer, see Bethge, *DB-ER*, 787–90, and Bismarck and Kabitz, *Love Letters from Cell 92*, 9–10.

[2.] [Here and throughout this letter, Bonhoeffer uses the formal *Sie* for "you." The informal *Du* does not commence until the fifth letter, in January 1943, in which he also shifts in salutation from "Miss von Wedemeyer" to "Maria"—MB]

[3.] Maria von Wedemeyer's brother Max was killed on October 26, 1942, on the eastern front. Bonhoeffer had confirmed him in 1938; cf. the confirmation homily in *DBW* 15:476–82. See also 1/212.

day and night, but when we have let go entirely into God—or better, when God has received us—then we are helped. "Weeping may linger for the night, but joy comes in the morning" (Psalm 30:5).There really is joy with God, with Christ! Do believe it.

But each person must walk this way alone—or rather, God draws each person onto it individually. Only prayers and the encouragement of others can accompany us along this way.

Yet with God we find communion with those who belong to God, the living and the dead.

May God work miracles in you, in those you love, in us all during these days, and strengthen us for the life and work to which we return for God's glory.

Please greet your grandmother in particular once more.

In heartfelt communion,
Your faithfully devoted Dietrich Bonhoeffer

207. To Max Diestel[1]

Munich, November 5, 1942

My dear, honored Superintendent Diestel,

Fortunately, I was able to get wind of your high festive day,[2] although you gave no hint of it when I saw you recently. I am so happy about this because now at last I have the opportunity I have been seeking for so long to give you a word of thanks after many years. I realize that I am indebted to you for the decisive initiatives in my external, professional, and personal life. You will surely be surprised by this powerful statement—please do not consider it mere birthday hyperbole! It was perhaps one single telephone call—namely, in December 1927—that set my entire thinking on a track from which it has not yet deviated and never will. At that time you asked on the telephone—I shall never forget the details of the situation—whether I would like to go to Barcelona as a vicar.[3] Just a few weeks later, I had my first encounter with a foreign German congregation and with ecumenical Christianity. I came back after a year, and two years passed during which I wrote my habilitation dissertation in Berlin. Then in May 1930 a second telephone call followed that first one. You offered me the Union Theological Seminary stipend for 1930–31. In August I traveled across the ocean and experienced a year there that has been of the greatest significance for me up to

---

[1.] *NL*, A 60,4 (22); handwritten; previously published in *GS* 6:577–79.
[2.] The occasion was Diestel's seventieth birthday.
[3.] See *DBW* 10.

the present day. Scarcely had I returned when you invited me—and perhaps this was the most decisive of all—to come with you to Cambridge.[4] Most likely you have forgotten all about these "interventions" in my life, since within the full scope of your work these were all, of course, extremely minor, secondary matters. But for me they were foundational for my entire life and its formation. Later I was able to be with you at numerous ecumenical conferences; there, just from your way of speaking and maneuvering, I learned to recognize and understand the full responsibility of the German church toward other churches. I was allowed to see the honor and love that you as a German churchman enjoyed from the representatives of all other churches and how you succeeded in connecting personal trust with professional responsibility.

367

In the many years that then passed without my seeing you often, I have never forgotten this; the wish to be able to express my thanks to you one day—and at times this works better in written form than orally—has always remained alive in me. Now today I am privileged to do so, and I must also request that you forgive that only today is this happening. Today I also recall that I was fortunate enough to discuss my first sermon with you in 1925—I was all of nineteen years old then—I gave it in Stahnsdorf; that you were one of those who heard my first and second exam sermons and gave me some kind words at that time; and finally that I have spent many lovely hours in your home—and as all of this comes so vividly to my mind again, I am full of great gratitude. And when I think that besides me you were able also to help many, many other young theologians in such decisive ways, then I think that even for you it must be some small satisfaction and joy to know this.

I have heard that precisely in these days you have once again been experiencing many trials.[5] But surely the experience of the community, love, and gratitude that is being shown and demonstrated to you anew in these same days will be more important and more powerful for you than all the hardships that now surround you. May God long sustain you for us, our church, your work, your family, and the ecumenical community.

In faithfulness and gratitude,
Your respectfully devoted Dietrich Bonhoeffer

[4.] The World Alliance for Promoting International Friendship through the Churches held a conference in Cambridge, September 1–5, 1931; cf. *DB-ER*, 189–90, 199–202.

[5.] Diestel had been interrogated by the Gestapo.

208. To Hans-Walter Schleicher[1]

November 7, 1942

Dear Hans-Walter,

Today just this short greeting along with the booklets, which you can per-haps read in a quiet five minutes. Are you already able to learn and speak a little French? That would certainly be a great benefit.[2]

This ugly November weather is probably not making your adjustment any easier. But I think that you are tougher in these things than we were at your age. By the way, if you were truly to have downright homesickness at some point—I am very well acquainted with this myself, it's no disgrace—then you must say to yourself that it is simply a real illness that strikes some and not others, that has its peak and its end and lasts two to three weeks at the most. Perhaps you don't have it at all; it is in any case something very different from just a little longing for home. It is truly a painful illness, something quite peculiar—but you can count on it passing just like a fever. Now take care of yourself, use the time as well as possible, and write when you need anything. With all my best wishes,

Your Uncle Dietrich

208a. To Maria von Wedemeyer[1]

November 13, 1942

Dear Miss von Wedemeyer,

Your letter has brought a salutary clarity into an unnecessarily confused sit-uation. With my whole heart I thank you for this, as well as for the courage with which you have taken the bull by the horns. You will surely understand that I was unable to find your mother's request entirely comprehensible;[2] what I did understand readily—because it corresponds to my own feel-ings—was simply the wish not to be worried and burdened by something else altogether in these difficult days and weeks. Whatever else may have

---

[1.] In the possession of Hans-Walter Schleicher; handwritten from Klein-Krössin; pre-viously published in *GS* 2:424–26.

[2.] Bonhoeffer may have worried that Schleicher might become a prisoner of war in France.

[1.] Literary estate of Maria Weller (née von Wedemeyer), letter no. 10. Publication by permission of the Houghton Library, Harvard University. See 1/206, ed. note 1.

[2.] Ruth von Wedemeyer, Maria's mother, had asked Bonhoeffer not to participate in the funeral for her son Max in order to allow no opportunity for conversation, inappro-priate to that occasion, regarding a possible engagement between Dietrich and Maria. At this point neither of the two had come to any resolution of this question, nor had they spoken to each other about it. See also 1/185.

spurred her request was not spelled out in the letter, and I had no right to inquire about it. That you knew nothing of her letter is, of course, important to me. But above all I was concerned at that point to allow your mother and all of you that rest and peace whose disturbance would have seemed to me a sin against the dead.—

You, as much as or perhaps even more than I, will perceive as a painful inner burden that things not suitable for discussion were brought out into the open. Let me say openly that I cannot easily quite come to terms with your grandmother's[3] behavior; I told her countless times that I did not wish to discuss such things, in fact that this[4] would do violence to all parties. I believed that it was because of her illness and age that she could not cherish silently in her heart what she believed she was witnessing. My conversations with her were often difficult to endure; she did not heed my request. I then interpreted your premature departure from Berlin within that context and was grieved by it. In the meantime I have come to peace with all this—I mean, with what concerns my relationship with your grandmother. The[5] signs of her impending[6] blindness have afflicted her spiritually as well, and she is in need of particular patience and love from those who owe her as much gratitude as I do. We must make great effort to bear no hard feelings toward her. Nevertheless, so long as she has not yet learned to keep silent about what moves her, and to let tranquillity slowly return to hearts stirred up, I do not quite see how a visit to Klein-Krössin on my part could be fruitful. It will be hard enough for me that things stand as they do; I hope that you understand and believe this. But only from a peaceful, free, healed heart can anything good and right take place; I have experienced that repeatedly in life, and I pray (forgive me for speaking thus) that God may give us this, soon and very soon, and that God may bring us back together with such hearts, soon and very soon.—

Can you understand all this? Might you experience it just as I do?— I hope so, in fact I cannot conceive of anything else. But how difficult this is for you too! I think I know and understand this completely; for otherwise when one is inwardly anxious it is so difficult to be still and wait on God; and yet that is the only healing. You must often feel very lonely these days; if I may, I would like to write you from time to time. And if you could let me

---

[3.] Maria von Wedemeyer's grandmother was Ruth von Kleist-Retzow. She had noticed the early attraction between Dietrich and Maria, wished to encourage it, and thus spoke about it in the family. On Bonhoeffer's friendship with Mrs. von Kleist-Retzow, cf. *DB-ER*, 438–39, and elsewhere; as well as Wedemeyer, *In des Teufels Gasthaus*, 159–71.

[4.] Handwriting unclear.

[5.] Handwriting unclear.

[6.] Beginning of a new page, numbered 2 at the top.

know how your grandmother is doing (I mean emotionally), I will be very grateful to you.

Please forgive me this letter, which says so clumsily what I am feeling. I realize that words intended to say personal things come only with tremendous difficulty to me; this is a great burden for those around me. Your grandmother has often enough reproached me severely for my aloofness; she herself is so completely[7] different, but people must of course accept and bear one another as they are. —

"The last few weeks here have been awful." There is infinitely much to experience and endure together; I cannot write all that to you. But there's scarcely half an hour without interruption, and even this letter must be written quickly.

I am writing your grandmother very briefly, urging her to silence and patience. I will write to your mother tomorrow, that she not get upset at whatever your grandmother may be writing; the thought of it horrifies me.[8]

I hope to see you soon and would be grateful to you, when you are able, for some word as to whether you have been able to understand my letter. Thank you again for your letter as well.

Affectionately yours and with many best wishes,
Dietrich Bonhoeffer

By the beginning[9] of December I hope to have my travels behind me, if everything doesn't suddenly change again.[10] But this next week I will still be here. How happy I would be to come for a brief visit.

209. To Waltraut Distler[1]

Berlin-Charlottenburg, November 15, 1942

My dear lady,

You do not know me, and unfortunately I did not know your husband personally. But I loved his music very much and have heard of his death; and thus I wanted to write to you, simply as one of the many strangers who have taken part deeply in your husband's life and death and now in your own sorrow as well.[2]

369

[7.] Beginning of a new page, numbered 3 at the top.
[8.] These two letters are not included in *DBWE* 16.
[9.] These sentences are written into the side margin.
[10.] Cf. *DB-ER*, 784.

[1.] *NL*, A 60,4 (23); handwritten; *GS* 6:579–80.
[2.] Hugo Distler took his own life on November 1, 1942, out of despair at the deportation of Jewish fellow citizens. Cf. Bonhoeffer's letter to Maria von Wedemeyer, 1/209a, also dated November 15.

The day before yesterday I heard the *Musikalische Exequien*,[3] which he himself wished to perform and which as things now stand lamented his death and comforted all those who are distressed about his death. When the choir sang of the repose of the dead from their labor and of the peace of the righteous who are in God's hand, it was like a plea of the living for the one who had died and like a blessing from this departed one for the living, a blessing that silences all self-accusation and orients our minds toward the ultimate. Whoever knows of your husband's life work and his death will henceforth be unable to think about the present and the future without reference to them. May the thought of that peace and repose, which he attained for himself even through such deep darkness and perhaps was able only in this way to claim, secure our hearts and challenge us already here on earth to aid those around us toward the peace and repose found solely in the cross and the Holy Scriptures.

Sincere condolences from your very devoted
Dietrich Bonhoeffer

209a. To Maria von Wedemeyer[1]

November 15, 1942

Dear Miss von Wedemeyer,

Now that I have pondered the whole thing again, I would like to write to your mother only if she has been newly troubled by questions from your grandmother; in any other case a letter from me would be no help at all,[2] but would only disturb her peace of mind. For the sake of God, who has given her such enormous pain and such enormous comfort, I do not wish to bother her but want to allow her the rest she needs and to which she has every right before God and others. Please let us not forget this for a single

---

[3.] [*Musikalische Exequien*, op. 7, by Heinrich Schütz, was written in 1636 in Dresden; it is subtitled *Begräbnismusik in drei Teilen*, "Funeral Music in Three Parts." The lines Bonhoeffer cites in the letter come from the final, third part of the piece, sung by choir 2. Interestingly, in that same piece choir 1 is singing, "Herr, nun lässest du deinen Diener im Frieden fahren" (Master, now you are dismissing your servant in peace), from the Song of Simeon from Luke 2:29, the text that underlies Martin Luther's hymn "I Leave, as You Have Promised, Lord" (*Lutheran Book of Worship*, 349). Verse 4 of that hymn is sung in part 1 of the *Musikalische Exequien*. Bonhoeffer cites this hymn in his Finkenwalde circular letter for the First Sunday in Advent 1942 written shortly hereafter (cf. 1/212).For more information, see Graulich and Horn, *Heinrich Schütz: Musikalische Exequien.*—MB]

[1.] Literary estate of Maria Weller (née von Wedemeyer); letter no. 11. Publication by permission of the Houghton Library, Harvard University. See 1/206a, ed. note 1.

[2.] Cf. the letter of November 13, 1942, 1/208a.

moment.—How could *you* forget it?—it is too holy. But if your grandmother has written, then I will write immediately. Will you please let me know this? Ought I express again that what I wrote you yesterday regarding my relationship to your grandmother, I wrote in great confidence of your love for your grandmother, and yet that for the sake of clarity and openness I nevertheless needed to write it?—

You will have read in the newspaper of Hugo Distler's sudden death. I considered him the most significant composer and church musician to have emerged for some time. Now I hear that he took his own life in his office at the cathedral, Bible and cross in hand, because he could not bear it any longer. He was thirty years old.[3] I am quite shaken by this. Why was no one able to help him? Indescribable pain for his wife and his children. One can no longer pass by such events if one wants to look with integrity into the present and the future.—

With affectionate greetings and wishes, also for your work.[4]

Yours,
Dietrich Bonhoeffer

209b. To Maria von Wedemeyer[1]

November 19, 1942

Dear Miss von Wedemeyer,

Your mother called me this morning and told me of your wish.[2] The telephone is a very inadequate means of communication, not least because I was unable to be alone during the conversation. Please forgive me if I have burdened you too greatly with my letters; I have not wished this but desired your peace of mind. It appears—this was how I was obliged to understand your mother—that at the moment we are unable to give this to each other. So I ask it of God for you and for us and will wait until God shows us our way. Only in peace with God, with others, and with ourselves will we hear and do God's will. In this we may have great confidence and need not become impatient or act rashly.

[3.] Cf. Bonhoeffer's letter to Waltraut Distler, 1/209.

[4.] Maria von Wedemeyer was to complete the second half of her year of service in Groß Tychow with the Kleist family.

[1.] Literary estate of Maria Weller (née von Wedemeyer), letter no. 12. Publication by permission of the Houghton Library, Harvard University. See 1/206a, ed. note 1.

[2.] After consulting with her daughter, Ruth von Wedemeyer had requested that Bonhoeffer temporarily cease writing to Maria. Cf. the letter to Bethge, November 27, 1942, 1/210.

Do not think I failed to understand that you do not want to respond and cannot and most likely also did not wish to receive this letter. But if the timing proves feasible for me to come again to Klein-Krössin[3] at some point in the not too distant future, your wishes would not forbid this? This is what I understand, in any case.

Please forget every word that hurt you and burdened you further beyond what has already been laid on you by God.

I have written to your mother that I needed to write you briefly once more. —

God protect you and us all.[4]

Sincerely yours,
Dietrich Bonhoeffer

210. To Eberhard Bethge[1]

November 27, 1942

Dear Eberhard,

In these past days I have very much missed the opportunity to talk things over with you. The days were so full and my thoughts so unsettled that I never got around to writing; also, I still haven't heard anything from you since your departure. From Tuesday through Wednesday noon I was at Mrs. von Wedemeyer's.[2] Contrary to my fears that the house would have an excessive spiritual tone, its style made a very pleasant impression. She herself was calm, friendly, and not overwrought, as I had feared. Gist of the discussion she requested: a year of total separation to enable Maria to find some peace. No fundamental objection to the whole thing, but given the enormity of the decision, etc. . . . My response: these days a year could just as well become five or ten and thus represented a postponement into the incalculable; that I understood and recognized her maternal authority over her daughter; but future circumstances themselves would show whether such a stipulation could be followed; I didn't think so and would have more to say about this at the proper time. Mrs. von Kleist's view (whom I informed at Mrs. von Wedemeyer's wish): indignation at this demand on her daughter's part; I must calm her lest she cause even more trouble. Maria herself (as far as I can tell from things her mother said): a certain hiatus (she probably

370

[3.] Ruth von Kleist-Retzow's home in retirement. Cf. *DB-ER*, 438–39.

[4.] Preceding this sentence the words "God is our peace" are crossed out.

[1.] *NL*, A 59,2 (46); handwritten from Berlin; partially reproduced in *GS* 2:425–26.

[2.] Cf. *Love Letters from Cell 92*, 335–36 and the newly published letters from Bonhoeffer to Maria von Wedemeyer in this volume: 1/206a, 1/208a, 1/209a, 1/209b.

still knows nothing about the period of time) would be beneficial for inner clarification and calm; but only a further encounter can bring about clarity in the decision.

I am not yet decided about my next move; for now I shall remain silent. At this point there is no hurry; first the storm must pass somewhat. I think that if I wanted to I could prevail. I can argue better than the others and could probably talk them into it. But that seems dreadful to me; it strikes me as evil, like an exploitation of the others' weakness. Through the loss of her husband, thus precisely in her weakness, Mrs. von Wedemeyer is stronger than if I would have had to deal with him. It would be wrong of me to give her the feeling of defenselessness now—that would be deplorable. But this makes my situation more difficult. By the way, when we were driving through the estate as we left Wednesday morning, she spoke of the economic situation of the estate, as that would extend to the daughters, etc.; she thought I should know about it. Well, we shall have a chance to talk about all this. Two nights ago the Schleichers spoke with our parents about your situation:[3] I was not present. Apparently they discussed a lengthy separation; I did not speak with Ursel; everywhere these same—old-fashioned—ideas hearkening back to past times. If it begins to look ominous for you that something foolish will be done, I shall in that case say something about my own situation; then for once they will consider your situation not only from Renate's perspective but also from your own. But for now I shall hold my peace. Otherwise everything is normal—i.e., Winfried[4] is doing very poorly at the moment, and it appears that he may not be able to recover at all. Yet Hans Chr.[5] and his wife are slowly continuing to do better. Your mother recently wanted to consult with John[6] about family matters, but he behaved somewhat brusquely, so nothing came of it. By the way, I have the impression that once more your mother is not doing very well at all; most likely her nerves are just about shot. Also, on the trip back I went by way of Stettin and had a nice afternoon with Fritz and Margret.[7] Toward the end of the week she will be traveling to Kade for fourteen days.

371

[3.] This refers to Eberhard Bethge's engagement to Renate Schleicher. [The family concerns arose from the fact that she was seventeen years old at the time; Bethge was thirty-three.—MB]

[4.] Winfried Maechler was a soldier on the eastern front. "Winfried" served as a code name for the war situation in the east.

[5.] Hans Christian von Hase was a military chaplain. "Hans Chr." served as a code name for the coup preparations in the army.

[6.] It is no longer possible to determine what events were being signified here by the code names "mother" and "John." Perhaps this refers to Goerdeler's attempt to interest Göring in his plans.

[7.] Fritz and Margret Onnasch.

So, that's all the news from home. I hope to hear from you soon. I am thinking very much of your work. With all best wishes,

Your Dietrich

211. To Eberhard Bethge[1]

1st Sunday in Advent, 1942[2]

Dear Eberhard,

It is midnight, the first Sunday in Advent. It was a lovely day. In the morning, devotions at the Schleichers' on the Magnificat, later some beautiful hymns. I am thinking of you and your work. In these past years we have generally celebrated Advent together. How beautiful the Advent music making in Sigurdshof still was!

Despite her best intentions, Mrs. von Kleist is causing a good deal of trouble with her endless telephoning.[3] What do you think about the year?[4] Today Mrs. von Kleist wrote me, among other things, that Maria was "relieved and happy" about it. Of course that preoccupies me. I am neither relieved nor happy.

Nothing new from the family. Hans is back; nothing significant has changed.[5] Sepp[6] is very pleased and happy again and hopes to be finished with his work in four weeks at the most. Unfortunately, Winfried[7] is not doing very well at all these days. Renate is working a great deal. Klaus comes by often. The idea of visiting Margret[8] on the way doesn't make sense, because she is in Kade. So you will probably come home here on the seventh. There will likely be some things to discuss, if my forced silence about personal matters has not become second nature by then. I have also considered whether—without my knowledge—you might like to write to Mrs. von

---

[1.] *NL,* A 59, 2 (47); handwritten from Berlin; partially reproduced in *GS* 2:426–27.

[2.] November 29, 1942.

[3.] Ruth von Kleist-Retzow was trying to bring about a more favorable resolution for the relationship between Bonhoeffer and her granddaughter Maria von Wedemeyer. [Ruth von Wedemeyer's reservations about the relationship concerned her daughter's youth (Maria was eighteen) and the age difference with Bonhoeffer, who was thirty-six.—MB]

[4.] One year was the period of separation demanded by Maria von Wedemeyer's mother; see Bonhoeffer's letter to Eberhard Bethge on November 27, 1942, 1/210.

[5.] This refers to Hans von Dohnanyi's trip to Rome and Switzerland, which elicited no positive response from the Allies.

[6.] "Sepp" was Josef Müller's nickname and was also a code name for the coup preparations.

[7.] "Winfried" was a code name for the military situation in the east; cf. 1/210, ed. note 4.

[8.] Margret Onnasch.

Wedemeyer sometime as a friend, very nice and sweet and clever, as you are able to be when you want. But this could also be later; perhaps that would be even better.

So, enough for today. Tomorrow I hope finally to begin writing again.[9]

Wishing you all that is good and beautiful, with love,
Your faithful Dietrich

212. Finkenwalde Circular Letter[1]

373

1st Sunday in Advent, 1942

Dear Brother... ,

At the beginning of a letter that in this solemn hour is meant to call you all to true joy, there necessarily stand the names of those brothers who have died since I last wrote to you: P. Wälde, W. Brandenburg, Hermann Schröder, R. Lynker, Erwin Schutz, K. Rhode, Alfred Viol, Kurt Onnasch, Fritz's second brother; in addition to them, and presumably known to many of you, Major von Wedemeyer and his oldest son, Max, my former confirmand.[2]

"Everlasting joy shall be upon their heads..."[3] We are glad for them; indeed, should we say that we sometimes secretly envy them? From early times the Christian church has considered acedia—the melancholy of the heart, or "resignation"—to be one of the mortal sins.[4] "Serve the Lord with joy"[5]—thus do the scriptures call out to us. For this our life has been given to us, and for this it has been preserved for us unto the present hour. This joy, which no one shall take from us, belongs not only to those who have been called home but also to us who are alive. We are one with them in this joy, but never in melancholy. How are we going to be able to help those who have become joyless and discouraged if we ourselves are not borne along by courage and joy? Nothing contrived or forced is intended here, but something bestowed and free. Joy abides with God, and it comes

---

[9.] Bonhoeffer wanted to work further on his *Ethics*.

[1.] *NL,* A 48,3; handwritten draft composed in Berlin, November 29, 1942; previously published in *GS* 2:596–98. [As in the other circular letters, Bonhoeffer mimeographed these and filled in the individual names of his recipients; this made them personal letters, thereby circumventing the Nazi restrictions on his writing.—MB]

[2.] The father and brother, respectively, of Bonhoeffer's fiancée, Maria von Wedemeyer; cf. 1/196, 1/197, and 1/206a.

[3.] Isa. 35:10.

[4.] [Bonhoeffer himself struggled with "acedia" for many years and was preoccupied with its theological meaning. See *DB-ER*, 39, 506, and 833.—MB]

[5.] Ps. 100:2. [NRSV: "Worship the Lord with gladness."—MB]

down from God and embraces spirit, soul, and body; and where this joy has seized a person, there it spreads, there it carries one away, there it bursts open closed doors. A sort of joy exists that knows nothing at all of the heart's pain, anguish, and dread; it does not last; it can only numb a person for the moment. The joy of God has gone through the poverty of the manger and the agony of the cross; that is why it is invincible, irrefutable. It does not deny the anguish, when it is there, but finds God in the midst of it, in fact precisely there; it does not deny grave sin but finds forgiveness precisely in this way; it looks death straight in the eye, but it finds life precisely within it. What matters is this joy that has overcome. It alone is credible; it alone helps and heals. The joy of our companions who have been called home is also the joy of those who have overcome—the Risen One bears the marks of the cross on his body. We still stand in daily overcoming; they have overcome for all time. God alone knows how far away or near at hand we stand to the final overcoming in which our own death may be made joy for us. "With peace and joy I now depart..."[6]

374

Some among us suffer greatly because they are internally deadening themselves against so much suffering, such as these war years bring in their wake. One person said to me recently, "I pray every day that I may not become numb." That is by all means a good prayer. And yet we must guard ourselves against confusing ourselves with Christ. Christ endured all suffering and all human guilt himself in full measure—indeed, this was what made him Christ, that he and he alone bore it all. But Christ was able to suffer along with others because he was simultaneously able to redeem from suffering. Out of his love and power to redeem people came his power to suffer with them. We are not called to take upon ourselves the suffering of all the world; by ourselves we are fundamentally not able to suffer with others at all, because we are not able to redeem. But the wish to suffer with them by one's own power will inevitably be crushed into resignation. We are called only to gaze full of joy at the One who in reality suffered with us and became the Redeemer. Full of joy, we are enabled to believe that there was and is One to whom no human suffering or sin is foreign and who in deepest love accomplished our redemption. Only in such joy in Christ the Redeemer shall we be preserved from hardening ourselves where human suffering encounters us, and from becoming resigned under the experience of suffering. Only to the extent we believe in Christ, to the extent we ... to Christ[7]

[6.] The first line of Martin Luther's hymn for the dying, based on Luke 2:19-32, "Mit Fried und Freud fahr ich dahin" (*Evangelisches Gesangbuch für Brandenburg und Pommern*, 304; *Evangelisches Kirchengesangbuch*, 310). ["I Leave, as You Have Promised, Lord" (*Lutheran Book of Worship*, 349) is a paraphrase of verse 1 of Luther's hymn for the dying.—MB]

[7.] The draft breaks off at this point.

213. George K. A. Bell to Erwin Sutz[1]

3rd December 1942

My dear Pastor,

I have been thinking much of you and your friends during these days, and I was glad to hear from Dietrich.[2] Next time you see him give him my love.

The last I heard from Visser 't Hooft in Geneva was about a proposal that the Church of England should make a gift to aid the Greek Church in its relief work in Greece. But I am afraid that the Government will not agree to money being collected and sent out for that purpose. I expect you will have heard from Visser 't Hooft that the Government were unwilling that anything definite should be said on other matters, though I greatly regret this.

I do not know how much reaches Switzerland about the policy very often connected with the name of Lord Vansittart.[3] While it is true that there are quite a number of private individuals who agree with him in this country, such personal opinions are opposed to this country's official policy towards the German people. I know that Mr. Eden attaches a great deal of importance to a speech which he made on May 21st,[4] in which he distinguished between the Nazis and the Germans; and it so happens

---

[1.] Sammlung Sutz, Herrliberg/Schweiz; typewritten letter, from Chichester; in original English, including errors; previously published in *GS* 6:563–64. In addition to the "By Air Mail" sticker and the British stamp reading "Opened Examiner 851," the envelope shows the following stamps in German: "Geöffnet" (Opened); "Oberkommando der Wehrmacht" (Armed Forces High Command); "Dienststelle Feldpost Nr." (Military Post Office No.) 24032 D-2," as well as the handwritten figures "385/57, 164/1/163." Similar notations appear on the letter itself: "164/1" and "385/54." Norbert Kannapin reports that "the mail from England, or from other countries, traveled to Switzerland by way of Portugal (Lisbon) and then France (Lyon). As we see in this case, all incoming and outgoing letters were examined by the German censors at Lyon. The handwritten figures have to do with inspection notes made there" (communication to the German editors of *DBW* 16 on June 7, 1994).

[2.] This refers to Bonhoeffer's letter to Bishop Bell on August 28, 1942; see 1/199. Regarding this letter, see Bell's letter to Gerhard Leibholz on December 4, 1942: "I am very pleased at the news from Dietrich. I wrote to Pastor Sutz. Also I wrote more extensively to Harry Johansson in Sigtuna [see 1/214] in the hope that this somehow reaches Dietrich. Fortunately I can report that Bishop Brilioth spent many hours with me in Chichester when he was here from Sweden, and I gave him extensive information about the important talks. I very much hope that he sees some of our friends in Sweden so that they find out what I have attempted" (Bell and Leibholz, *An der Schwelle*, 72). On December 9, 1942, Leibholz wrote to Bell: "In any case, I hope that Dietrich finds out what great efforts you are making here" (ibid., 73). [The original Bell–Leibholz correspondence in English is not available; the English here is a translation of the German versions of the letters in the Bell and Leibholz volume.—MB]

[3.] [Cf. Bell's letter of July 15, 1942, to Anthony Eden, 1/193 and 1/193, ed. note 3.—MB]

[4.] This is also the date given in 1/214, but it is given as "May 8th" in 1/194.

that there [was] some extremely plain broadcasting through the German News Service to this effect, by means of seven Questions and Answers, in the early days of July.[5] I was myself particularly glad to hear, though it was some time afterwards, that these Questions and Answers were broadcasted to the German people in the name of the British people and their Allies, at that particular time. Their general effect was that Hitler's downfall would save Germany from destruction, and that the co-operation of the German people to this end, difficult as it might be, would considerably shorten the war.

With all kindest greetings, in which Gerard[6] and his wife and children join,

Yours very sincerely
George Cicestr

214. George K. A. Bell to Harry Johansson[1]

Chichester, 3rd December 1942

My dear Mr. Johansson,

It has been a great disappointment not to have been able to write to you before now, for the reason that though I tried very hard in the summer to obtain the information which you sought during our talks at Sigtuna, it was not possible to obtain it.[2]

377   I was very glad of the chance of seeing Bishop Brilioth on his visit to England[3] which we all greatly enjoyed, and having a good spell with him at Chichester. I hope very much you or Ehrenström may be able to see him; he would tell you what has been in my mind, whom I was able to see, and what I was able or unable to do.

Accessibility to Switzerland is, I am afraid, much more difficult since the total occupation of France.[4] Indeed, I do not know whether Ehrenström is now able to get to

---

[5.] See 1/214, ed. note 7; see also *DB-ER*, 768.
[6.] Gerhard Leibholz.

[1.] *NL*, A 42,3 (18); typewritten letter; in original English, including errors; previously published in *GS* 6:564–66. This letter was actually intended for Bonhoeffer; see 1/213, ed. note 2.
[2.] This refers to the arrangement made in Sigtuna on May 31, 1942 (see 1/170). In a letter to W. A. Visser 't Hooft, London, on October 28, 1942, Bishop Bell wrote in an "Addendum": "I take the opportunity of writing on one or two other matters. It was a disappointment not to see Tracey [should read "Tracy"] Strong, but we could not meet when he was in England, as I was in Scotland. I heard from him, however, expressing the disappointment which you and your two co-Secretaries felt that I was not able to report a better response. I think I told you that I had talks not only with Mr. Eden and Sir Stafford Cripps, but also with Mr. Winant, who seemed to be more receptive. Strong said that little was possible while the present campaign in Russia is raging" (*GS* 6:563).
[3.] Bishop Brilioth was in England November 4–27, 1942; cf. *MW* 5:273–77.
[4.] In November 1942 German troops had invaded the previously unoccupied part of France.

Sweden, or whether any other friends from the World Council can travel at all outside Switzerland.

The whole situation in Europe is very complex; though recent events have certainly
given enormous encouragement to us and our Allies. I enclose a copy of a speech I
made in Convocation, which may be of interest to you, though it is now nearly two
months old.[5]

If you have an opportunity, I think you would find it very well worth while to look
up the text of Mr. Eden's speech of May 21st, 1942. He told me himself when I was in
touch with him (for I both saw him and corresponded with him in June and early July),
that he attached a good deal of importance to what he there said in distinguishing
Nazis from Germans. I am sure that this is the official attitude of the Government,
though I wish it could be underlined in a more vigorous way.

I have put down a Question, which I hope to be able to ask next week in the
House of Lords,[6] referring to a series of seven Questions and Answers broadcast on
the German News Service of the BBC in the first two weeks of July. The answers
were to such Question as: "Would Hitler's downfall mean the destruction of Germany?" and the answers were very satisfactory from the point of view of those who

378

[5.] See George Bell, "The Threat to Civilisation," in *Church and Humanity*, 79–85.

[6.] This question was submitted on November 29, 1942. On December 15, 1942, in a
personal conversation with Eden, Bishop Bell suggested arranging a debate about Stalin's
"order of the day" of November 6, 1942, a suggestion that Eden accepted. "I spoke to Mr.
Eden on Tuesday regarding the R.A.F. [Royal Air Force]-flyer [see the following note—
MB]. He said that he was now waging political warfare; the flyers were being distributed
according to a certain plan, and he had made it an absolute condition that their content
be mentioned neither in Parliament nor anywhere else. In his opinion a debate about the
content of a particular flyer would be most detrimental from the perspective of the war
effort in general. I responded that the clear distinction between the Hitler-Germany and
the other Germany was made for me in the answers to these questions, a distinction which
had not emerged anywhere as clearly in his own or the Prime Minister's public statements, and that I was not bound to the content of the flyer but would lay great store by a
declaration indicating that His Majesty's Government pursues this policy and is also prepared to let Germany know of it officially" (Bell and Leibholz, *An der Schwelle*, 78; translation
from the German in that volume). On December 20, 1942, Gerhard Leibholz commented
in response: "I had been thinking that Mr. Eden would request that you not broach this
whole matter and thus was afraid that all your good intentions would lead to nothing. It is
therefore gratifying to hear that Mr. Eden takes a favorable view of your question" (Bell
and Leibholz, *An der Schwelle*, 80; translation from the German in that volume). The
debate in the House of Lords was postponed repeatedly and did not take place until
March 10, 1943. The effect of Bishop Bell's speech on this day was that "Viscount Simon,
speaking as Lord Chancellor on behalf of the Government in the House of Lords, made
the following statement in replying to the debate: 'I now say in plain terms, on behalf of
His Majesty's Government, that we agree with Premier Stalin, first that the Hitlerite State
should be destroyed, and, secondly, that the whole German people is not (as Goebbels
has been trying to persuade them) thereby doomed to destruction'" (Bell, *Church and
Humanity*, 109).

distinguish between the Nazis and the Germans. For example, the two main questions and answers in this series are as follows:

"Does Hitler's defeat mean Germany's destruction?

No. Again and again the British Government declared, first in September 39, finally on the 21st May, 1942 that it has two aims: to destroy the Hitler Tyranny and after the war to enable all the peoples of Europe, *including Germany*, to reconstruct a state which would ensure to every individual impartial Justice, Freedom of Speech and of Association, and protection against unemployment and economic exploitation. Therefore Hitler's defeat does not mean the destruction of Germany, but on the contrary the salvation of Germany from the destruction.

Does England expect that German people will take part in the destruction of the Hitler regime?

England recognizes the difficult position of Germans of all classes who are opposed to Hitler. To these Germans we say: the United Nations will destroy Hitler's war machine. If the German people accelerate Hitler's downfall, that will mean the saving of millions of human lives. We know, that revolt against Hitler will involve sacrifices, but the scale of such sacrifices would only be a fraction of that which Hitler offers up every day in the vain effort to escape his own downfall. The roots of German militarism must be destroyed by the German people themselves. And the sooner the better. So long as the German people have not freed themselves of German militarism, so long will England and her Allies remain armed in order to prevent a third World War."

In another answer, to the question "What is the result of all this for Germany?" the answer is: "The real enemies of Germany are the warmongers. Germany could have peace tomorrow if she would free herself of Hitler and militarism—a peace in freedom and justice." You, I know, will appreciate the importance of these Questions and Answers. It was only recently that I heard of them, but they have now been published in summary form in an extremely powerful book about the home front in Germany, called *The other Germany* by Heinrich Fraenkel[7] which only appeared three or four weeks ago.

You will, I am sure, be interested to hear that Hodder and Stoughton have published a book which I am producing, consisting of certain important articles by Bishop Berggrav written in his periodical *Church and Culture*,[8] as given to me by bishop Aulén, together with documents bearing on the Norwegian Church conflict, and an appreciation of Bishop Berggrav by myself and a kind of linking up of the various articles and documents so as to give a clear picture of the Norwegian church conflict. The book will probably appear in the spring and will probably have the title *With God in*

[7.] Among other things, the Fraenkel volume included "Seven Questions and Answers," which were dropped as a leaflet over Germany at the beginning of July 1942 and broadcast by the BBC's German News Service July 3–7, 1942. Reprinted in Bell and Leibholz, *An der Schwelle*, 291–92.

[8.] The Norwegian title is *Kirke og Kultur.*

Darkness.[9] If you have anything you would care to send me on this subject, or indeed on any other subject, I shall be very happy to receive it.

Please give my kindest regards to your wife. I remember my visit to your house, as   380
well as to Sigtuna generally, with the greatest pleasure. Bishop Brilioth told me of the appointment of a successor to Bishop Björkquist. I do wish Sigtuna and all at it very good and prosperity.

Yours very sincerely
George Cicestr

214a. To Maria von Wedemeyer[1]

Sunday, January 17, 1943

Dear Maria,

The letter was under way for four days before just now—an hour ago—arriving here! In an hour the mail is being picked up again, so at least an initial greeting and thanks must go with it—even if the words I wish to say now have not yet emerged. May I simply say what is in my heart? I sense and am overwhelmed by the awareness that a gift without equal has been given me—after all the confusion of the past weeks I had no longer dared to hope—and now the unimaginably great and blissful thing is simply here, and my heart opens up and becomes quite wide and overflowing with thankfulness and shame and still cannot grasp it at all—this "Yes" that is to be decisive for our entire life.[2] If we were now able to talk in person with each other, there would be so infinitely much—yet fundamentally only always one and the same thing—to say! Is it possible that we will see each other soon?

[9.] According to a May 27, 1942, entry in Bishop Bell's diary, Bishop Aulén "proposed some recent (crisis) articles in periodical (Church and Culture) with copies of letters from B[erggrav] and Norwegian Bishops" ("Diary Notes," Bell Papers, 18); cf. 1/170, p. 301. The Norwegian edition, *Med Gud i mørke* (1941), contained no documents from the Norwegian church struggle, but only contributions by O. Moe, Eivind Berggrav, Leiv Aalen, O Hallesby, Kr. Ljostveit, Johannes Smemo, H. E. Wisløff, and Roald Fangen.

[1.] Literary estate of Maria Weller (née von Wedemeyer), letter no. 13. Publication by permission of the Houghton Library, Harvard University. See 1/206a, ed. note 1.

[2.] On January 13, 1943, Maria von Wedemeyer had written Bonhoeffer: "In these past few days I spoke with my mother and my uncle from Kieckow [Hans Jürgen von Kleist-Retzow, who was Maria von Wedemeyer's guardian]. Now I am allowed to write you, and I ask you to respond to this letter. It is so difficult for me to have to put in writing what even in person can scarcely be spoken. I wish to rebut every word that wants to be spoken here, because words are so clumsy and forceful with things that want to be said gently. But because I have experienced that you understand me so well, I now have the courage to write you, although I actually have no right at all to reply to a question you have not even asked me. Today I can say Yes to you from my entire, joyful heart."

And where? Without having to be afraid of others' words again? Or for one reason or another shall this still not happen? I think now it *must* happen.

And now I cannot speak any differently than I have often done in my own heart—I want to speak to you as a man speaks to the girl with whom he wants to go through life and who has given him her Yes—dear Maria, I thank you[3] for your word, for all that you have endured for me and for what you are and will be for me. Let us now be and become happy in each other. Whatever time and calm you need to compose yourself, as you write, you must have, in whatever form is good for you. You alone can know that. With your "Yes" I can now also wait peacefully; without the Yes it was difficult and would have become increasingly difficult; now it is easy since I know that you want this and need it. I wish in no way to push or frighten you,[4] I want to care for you and allow the dawning joy of our life to make you light and happy. I understand well that you wish to be entirely alone for a time yet—I have been alone long enough in my life to know the blessing (though, to be sure, also the dangers) of solitude. I understand and understood also throughout these past weeks—if not entirely without pain—that for you it cannot be easy to say Yes to me, and I will never forget that. And it is this, your Yes, which alone[5] can give me the courage as well no longer to say only No to myself. Say no more about the "false image" I could have of you. I want no "image," I want you, just as I beg you with my whole heart to want not an image of me but me myself; and you must know those are two different things. But let us not dwell now on the bad that lurks and has power in every person, but let us encounter each other in great, free forgiveness and love, let us take each other as we are—with thanks and boundless trust in God, who has led us to this point and who loves us.

This letter must be off immediately so that you will receive it tomorrow. God protect you and us both.

Your faithful Dietrich

I assume as a matter of course that I will say nothing to your grandmother before you wish it. I won't in fact be seeing her any time soon. Wouldn't you like to write it to her yourself from Hanover?[6]—I am not yet certain of the

---

[3.] [Here Bonhoeffer changes to informal *Du*. Note also the use of the salutation "Dear Maria."—MB]

[4.] Beginning of a new page.

[5.] Handwriting unclear.

[6.] Maria von Wedemeyer had applied to be a student nurse at the Magdalena Home in Hanover. Through this she hoped to avoid the Reich labor service *(Reichsarbeitsdienst),* which was compulsory for young men and women over the age of eighteen. In early April 1943 she was admitted.

dates of my trip,[7] but I can't imagine it will be much longer now. Then I will be gone four weeks. I will now be waiting eagerly for a letter from you.[8]

215. From Ruth von Kleist-Retzow[1]

January 21, 1943

My dear friend,

Once you have read through the enclosed letter[2] please forward it immediately. Does it not show how God acts toward people when God destines them to be divine instruments? After everything he suffered, there followed a month sick in bed and then the prospect of a return to the hell in the east.

I would very much like to talk to you, even if it were for a single evening in which you came here to me and stayed overnight. The thoughts that occupy me are very difficult. But when I look at Werner K's[3] life, our afflictions seem light to me. On the twenty-seventh all sorts of eager learners want to come. I attempt to keep the circle free of blowhards, who wish to impart their own wisdom. My only hope is that the evening might be *fruitful*. To have you there would be *lovely*, but I fear that you will not want to?—also probably takes a toll on your energy level.

My daughter is traveling to Raba[4] on the thirty-first; thus I can scarcely come to Berlin on the first, as I had planned. But I could come on the twenty-ninth for two days, if I could coordinate it with seeing you again. It would still be nicest and simplest if you were to come here. A telephone call will suffice. Please—if you were to come— try to bring along a train schedule for me. There is not one in all of Stettin.

Warmest greetings from,
Your faithful Ruth von Kleist-Retzow

[7.] This refers to Bonhoeffer's planned travels to the Balkans and Switzerland; he was arrested before they could take place. Cf. *DB-ER*, 784.

[8.] The preceding note was written in the side margin.

[1.] Nachlaß Ruth von Kleist-Retzow; handwritten, presumably from Stettin.

[2.] Letter not extant; see ed. note 3.

[3.] Presumably Werner Koch (cf. *DB-ER*, 541); thus the first paragraph of this letter may well refer to him as well. [Koch, who had been a member of the second Finkenwalde session, was imprisoned in Sachsenhausen and then did forced labor as a result of his role in publicizing the 1936 Confessing Church memorandum to Hitler; he was then drafted into the German military in 1939. See also *DBW* 14:100, ed. note 3, as well as 142–43, 265, 287, and 992.—MB]

[4.] This refers to Spes Stahlberg, who lived in Berlin, and her daughter Ruth Roberta, who at the time was married to the Breslau physician Helmut Ripke.

215a. To Maria von Wedemeyer[1]

January 23, 1943

Dear Maria,

Tomorrow it will be a week since I wrote. I thought I needed to wait for your response before I could write again. Now that today's mail has again brought nothing, I *must* write simply so that I myself can continue to wait peacefully. I am not trying to push you, truly—I would much rather wait much longer. If responding is so difficult, then I will wait until it has become easy and inwardly necessary and free. Anything else would be wrong-headed—and how could I ever forget that it has to be a miracle for response to be easy. Even now, nothing ought to be rushed and forced; indeed, time *must* pass before everything can become clear. In all this we are so fully at one.

But I needed to write this note as a sign [of life] if I wanted to free myself from burdensome thoughts and restore peace of mind.

There would be so much more to say. But I don't want to do so today but rather simply wait and lay everything, truly everything, into God's hand.

From my heart,
Dietrich

In my previous letter, too, I didn't want to rush or force anything; if it nonetheless sounded different, it was my own incapacity to combine my joy and my sober desire for plenty of time for inner confirmation into a single reality. I think that the unfolding of external events,[2] which, of course, extend deep into our personal life, will bring us depth and clarity for our personal decisions in coming months as well. At the moment it seems to me as if it were in fact God commanding us to wait until we are shown the way. We can only hold our breath at what is now taking place in the world, with God's guidance.—

D.

[1.] Literary estate of Maria Weller (née von Wedemeyer), letter no. 14. Publication by permission of the Houghton Library, Harvard University. See 1/206a, ed. note 1.

[2.] This refers to the German surrender at Stalingrad, which was imminent (February 2, 1943).

215b. To Maria von Wedemeyer[1]

Sunday evening, January 24,[2] 1943

My dear Maria,

Now the letter is here, your kind letter—I thank you for it and thank you anew each new time I read it, indeed to me it is almost as if I were experiencing now for the first time in my life what it means to be thankful to another person, what a profoundly transforming power gratitude can be— it is the Yes—this word so difficult and so marvelous, appearing so seldom among mortals—from which all this springs—may God from whom every Yes comes grant that we may speak this Yes always thus and always more and more to one another throughout our entire life.

From every word of your letter I have sensed with joyful certainty that it will be good between us. The life together, toward which through God's goodness we hope to move, is like a tree that must grow from deep roots,[3] silent and hidden, strong and free, no hothouse growth forced into quick bloom. That everything may be entirely honest, authentic, simple, free— that, I believe, is our shared desire and thus do I understand your insistence on being alone,[4] and thus do I say yes to it—even if I find it nearly impossible to believe that your letter today is to be the last word I hear from you for a long, long time, at your own behest. We will need to help each other a great deal from afar in this interval. Yes, you must know that I now quite simply need your help, and in writing this I find I can only be amazed at the truth of the creation story by which the man receives in the woman a "helper."[5] —

Dear Maria, you have now placed the next half year under a rule of silence. This is your desire, your first request of me, and what should be more natural for me than to grant it willingly? But I must say one thing: every rule persons place on themselves has limits and dangers—namely,

---

[1.] Literary estate of Maria Weller (née von Wedemeyer), letter no. 15. Publication by permission of the Houghton Library, Harvard University. See 1/206a, ed. note 1.

[2.] Handwriting unclear. The date can be deduced with certainty from Maria von Wedemeyer's letter.

[3.] This echoes the words of Psalm 1 and Jer. 17:8, texts Bonhoeffer may well have had in mind at this point.

[4.] On January 21, 1943, in a letter from Pätzig, the Wedemeyer family's home, Maria had written: "I did not believe you would be able to understand my insistence on being alone. But it is good that you understand it.—Imagine, now when we see each other again there will be no more being alone! Please don't make it hard for me to say this to you now by being sad. I would like neither to write letters nor receive any. I know exactly what I am asking with this. But you have my Yes, my true and whole-hearted Yes."

[5.] Gen. 2:20.

where it ceases to protect what is authentic and natural and instead threatens it. We have learned this repeatedly in recent years when God has shattered[6] our plans, thoughts, forms of life, that we considered good and necessary. God's speech can be stronger than our own rules. It is possible that in the time ahead events of such fundamental significance,[7] for our personal life as well, could take place; it would be unnatural and forced if we then were not able to speak with each other—at least by letter. It is true, is it not, that the upcoming months of silence are meant to be a help to us, not a yoke, and so this means that we listen solely for God's voice and obey it alone.

You know, personally I would have considered an occasional letter back and forth—how strange if at Easter or on your birthday I were not to write to you—not as an interruption of being alone but as its bearing fruit. But on this you have the last word, and I am happy to be able to fulfill your wish.

Might you now be able to understand if I have a very great request of you, which you would make me very happy by granting: can I have a picture of you? You are entirely right—your Yes is everything—but you yourself, or at the very least your picture, come with this Yes.

Do you by any chance read the *Daily Texts*.[8] They are very dear to me.—

And now farewell, dear Maria, let us commend ourselves to God that God may help us through the time ahead, may make you happy in your new work, may protect you and me and those we love.

Yours with much love and continual thoughts of you,
Dietrich

If your grandmother asks, I will tell her that I request she not oblige me to speak of these things, but that I am unafraid and confident. I don't see how I could behave otherwise toward her. Don't you agree?

215c. To Maria von Wedemeyer[1]

January 29,[2] 1943

Dear Maria,

I thank you for the picture and the letter—more than I can say.

Yours always,
Dietrich

[6.] Beginning of a new page.

[7.] This is a reference to the imminent attempt on Hitler's life.

[8.] The daily scriptural readings published by the Moravian church. [For more on the tradition of the *Daily Texts*, see 1/122, ed. note 2.—MB]

[1.] Literary estate of Maria Weller (née von Wedemeyer), letter no. 16. Publication by permission of the Houghton Library, Harvard University. See 1/206a, ed. note 1.

[2.] This letter was possibly written on January 30.

216. From Oskar Hammelsbeck[1]

381

Dear Brother Bonhoeffer,

The relevant Luther quotation should read:

"A Christian is a rare bird! Would to God that the majority of us were good, pious non-Christians [Heiden], who kept the natural law, not to mention the Christian law!"[2]

Cordially yours,
Hammelsbeck

February 4, 1943

217. From Ruth von Kleist-Retzow[1]

Lasbeck, February 5, 1943

My dear Dietrich,

I thank you for your kind birthday letter. Still more for your telephone call that evening. And for ensuring that I would be freed from that excruciating uncertainty. Perhaps that was the best action of your life in this affair.[2] Do you grasp that? I am still struggling greatly with the intention to keep silent, without being able to understand. And how happily I would have sent you the letter from M.[3] that gave me great pleasure. But since so many things have gone wrong in this matter, I dare not do so. You know the state of affairs as well, and there is nothing new to you in the letter.

Now my heart is so full that I would very much like to tell you many things. And yet I do not know enough to be allowed to do so. But she says, "I am happy and grateful," and I now repeat that silently all day and entreat God that everything may turn out not only well but very, very well. You know utterly without saying how I desire to

382

[1.] *NL*, C 24; typewritten card, from Berlin-Zehlendorf, addressed to Marienburger Allee 43, Berlin-Charlottenburg; published in Hammelsbeck, "In Discussion with Bonhoeffer," in Zimmermann and Smith, *I Knew Dietrich Bonhoeffer*, 186. Hammelsbeck comments, "This quotation referred to our discussions on natural law." This presumably refers to the discussion in the Freiburg circle; cf. 1/205.

[2.] This quotation comes from Luther's 1525 treatise, "Admonition to Peace: A Reply to the Twelve Articles of the Peasants in Swabia" (*LW* 46:29). The original Luther German reads: "O, der losen Christen. Lieben freunde, die Christen sind nicht so gemeyne, das so viel sollten auf einem hauffen sich versamlen. Es is eyn seltzamer Vogel umb eyn Christen, Wollt Gott, wyr weren das mehrer teyl gute fromme Heyden, die das natürlich recht hielten, ich schweyge des Christlichen" (WA 18:310, lines 31–36; Gerhard Ebeling provided the German editors with this reference).

[1.] Literary estate of Ruth von Kleist-Retzow; handwritten.

[2.] Cf. Bonhoeffer's letter to Eberhard Bethge on November 27, 1942; see 1/210; cf. also *Love Letters from Cell 92*, 334–41.

[3.] Maria von Wedemeyer.

receive you fully as a son, when the time comes. That it should still take so long is probably the decision of the mother and Hans-Jürgen,[4] I am *presuming*. Perhaps this is the right thing for M., so that she remains quite clear. And if it appears too long for her and you, then there will be means and ways to shorten it. What does time mean today anyway?

Is it really true that you will now visit me in March? Believe me, things will work out.

God protect you and us all. Konstantin[5] is in Tunis. But God's hand is over him there as well.

I am in Stettin after 6 p.m. every evening, and can always be reached there as dusk falls, if you wish to say anything more. Oh, I am happy.

Grandmother

218. Constantin von Dietze: Discussion Notes[1]

2/6–7

10 a.m. UdL 28[2]

Ritter[3]vD[4]

Bö[5] Jena

Pr[6]

De[7]

Bhf:[8] 1. Being founded on conscience is the mark of bygone theology.[9] Will not be accepted by the theologians of the Confessing Church.

383   2. For submission to an ecumenical conference, do not emphasize what is Lutheran so strongly, but rather our common understanding. Attempts at theological rationales

---

[4.] Hans-Jürgen von Kleist-Retzow.

[5.] Konstantin von Kleist-Retzow.

[1.] Archiv für Christlich-Demokratische Politik, Nachlaß of Constantin von Dietze, I-345–002; handwritten (shorthand) entry in his 1942 calendar for December 20; transcription by Gertrud Lampe and Karlernst Ringer; published in Rübsam and Schadek, *Der Freiburger Kreis*, 86. On November 17, Dietze had noted: "Dec. 19/20th Berlin." Nevertheless, the evidence is greater that this meeting took place in Berlin on February 6–7, 1943: "At the beginning of 1943, C. von Dietze managed several times to discuss with insiders a few sections of the memorandum, although today it is no longer possible to determine which ones, after they had been reworked editorially in Freiburg" (Kluge, "Der 'Freiburger Kreis,' " 28).

[2.] "Unter den Linden 28" was the address of the office of Dr. Walter Bauer, who participated in the preparation of the memorandum.

[3.] Gerhard Ritter.

[4.] Constantin von Dietze.

[5.] Franz Böhm.

[6.] Friedrich Justus Perels.

[7.] Friedrich Delekat.

[8.] Bonhoeffer.

[9.] Cf. *DBWE* 6:307–9; *LPP*, 4–5 (*DBW* 8:21–23).

overflow their bounds. Perhaps restrict to individual questions and formulate the general portions in such a way that they [contain] what all Christians acclaim.

P:[10] Commitments are very strongly subjective. Decalogue[11] must at least be referred to.

219. Eberhard Bethge to Renate Schleicher[1]

On the train, February 8, 1943

[...] We are now heading toward Nuremberg. The train was delayed because of brake problems and so we are now nearly an hour late. But we dined all the better (!). [...] In the Saale River valley it was already like spring. [...] Actually I wanted to write a great many things. But I am simply not doing it. Dietrich is having the same problem. He brought many interesting and far-reaching things along from his visit this morning.[2] [...] Now we are in Munich. Went for a short walk to dissipate our travel weariness. We didn't arrive until 11:15. But it was actually very nice. I got to hear more in depth again about Dietrich's work.[3] He read me a portion of it that he had just written. Lovely things occur to him, and on a completely different level I perceive some similarities to Grandpapa[4] in balance, acuteness of observation and of judgment. Now we have a very pleasant hotel room, a Catholic hotel, and are enjoying our rest. Dietrich is already asleep. [...]

220. Eberhard Bethge to Renate Schleicher[1]

384

[...] A few changes have emerged for us. Dietrich will not be traveling to Switzerland after all; yesterday he was urgently advised against it.[2] So he will come back to Berlin with me. I have given up on Aulendorf.[3] It would scarcely be possible at this point.

[10.] Friedrich Justus Perels.

[11.] Cf. *DBWE* 6:282 and 357–60; cf. also 1/205.1. On the dissent within the Freiburg circle between an ethic of conscience vs. the Decalogue, see Ringshausen, *Die Überwindung der Perversion des Rechts im Widerstand*, 5ff.

[1.] In the possession of Renate Bethge; handwritten on the train to Munich and completed in Munich; cf. *DB-ER*, 784.

[2.] Bethge is apparently referring to a visit to Canaris's office for final discussions regarding the planned trip to Switzerland.

[3.] His *Ethics*.

[4.] "Grandpapa" is Karl Bonhoeffer.

[1.] In the possession of Renate Bethge; handwritten from Munich, postmarked February 10, 1943.

[2.] This advice came on the basis of renewed warnings from Reich criminal police director Arthur Nebe of the Reich Central Security Office, who was part of the resistance; cf. *DB-ER*, 784.

[3.] This refers to an evangelization program *(volksmissionarische Veranstaltung)* being planned for Aulendorf. [See also 1/17, ed. note 9, and *DB-ER*, 542–45.—MB]

Now we are pondering whether to travel out to Metten monastery to supply ourselves with provisions or on up to Ettal. But then perhaps nothing at all will come of this. Yesterday there were a great many conversations. I did not get many books. In the evening we attended an Italian trio. [. . .] Afterward we went over to Müller's,[4] the lawyer, and got home very late. [. . .] Later we want to go out for a very nice meal with Ninne Kalckreuth and Hanne K.[5] and afterward drink some fine coffee at Ninne's and look at pictures and drawings of the elder Kalckreuth.[6]

The people here are all extraordinarily dejected and also agitated.[7] Perhaps we shall telephone to let your grandparents know of our arrival. Your grandmother wanted to have enough time for Dietrich's room. [. . .]

Wednesday evening, February 10, 1943

[. . .] Regarding the money matter, some possibilities have suddenly emerged so that I called Lokies and said he had to come down tomorrow for further discussions.[8] We expect him early tomorrow morning. Ettal or Metten will now be impossible. [. . .]

220a. To Maria von Wedemeyer[1]

Tuesday afternoon [March 9, 1943]

Dearest Maria,

My heart is still beating noticeably and everything in me has been turned upside down—from joy, from surprise—but also from shock that you were worried.[2] Look now, I'm always causing this sort of mess. If you were here

---

[4.] [Josef Müller.—MB]

[5.] Christine von Kalckreuth and her brother Johannes.

[6.] Bonhoeffer's great uncle, the painter Count Leopold von Kalckreuth.

[7.] These reactions ensued from the German defeat at Stalingrad, where on February 2, 1943, the remnant of the trapped Sixth Army had surrendered.

[8.] They needed to discuss business matters of the Gossner Mission. A message the following day reads, "Lokies has just arrived and now we must negotiate. If no further messages arrive, then we will be in Berlin tomorrow evening, although unfortunately not until 10 p.m., on the train for official personnel." [*DBW* 16 does not give the source of this quotation; it appears to come from a message from Bethge.—MB]

[1.] Literary estate of Maria Weller (née von Wedemeyer), letter no. 17. Publication by permission of the Houghton Library, Harvard University. See 1/206a, ed. note 1.

[2.] For several months the Munich Military Intelligence Office had been closely watched by the Reich Central Security Office because of suspected foreign currency irregularities. (This was as a result of Schmidhuber's arrest and interrogation; see 1/229, pp. 429–30, and the German editors' afterword, p. 663.) Bonhoeffer had been incriminated. As matters worsened, Bonhoeffer told Ruth von Kleist-Retzow, after which she immediately informed Maria von Wedemeyer. Maria had then telephoned Dietrich. See also *DB-ER*, 780–85.

and we could talk, then I would have told you what I wrongly said to your grandmother. No, you needn't worry a single moment, I myself am not at all worried,—but, of course, you know from the little we have discussed together that there are dangers not only outside but also here within, sometimes lesser, sometimes greater. What man today could possibly avoid them or cower before them? And what woman today must not bear this along with him even when the man would gladly take this burden from her? And what an indescribable happiness it is for the man when the woman he loves stands beside him, with him, brave and patient—and above all prayerful. Dear, kind Maria, it is no wild fantasy (to which I'm not inclined anyway) that your being with me in these past weeks has helped noticeably. But that I cause you grief truly gives me sorrow. So now be utterly at peace again and confident and happy—and think of me as before, and as I continually think of you.

Am I impatient? Perhaps it was not entirely true when I just now said to you that I'm not. I should have said I don't want to be; and I'm not when I think it would trouble you. So it is true after all: no, I am not impatient—I only think at times it would be nice to be able to say things to you and to listen to you.—

I thank you so much that you phoned. It was lovely anyway! Shouldn't it be so? Of course! And if again something quite unusual happens, then do phone again, and I will too. Ultimately we already belong to each other, don't we?

I promised to write only briefly. Thus I won't begin a new page. There would be no point anyway, for otherwise the pages would never end.—I will be traveling for several weeks to Rome. When will we do that together?!—No, you mustn't go into the labor service.[3] I don't like that at all! If it must be, then please write me; it will be forwarded to me.—Now may God preserve you, dearest Maria, may God preserve us both![4]

Yours with much love and remembrance,
Dietrich

[3.] The wartime civilian duty required by the Nazi regime.
[4.] The preceding paragraph appears as a marginal note in the original.

220b. To Maria von Wedemeyer[1]

March 24, 1943

Dearest Maria,

Yesterday following a phone call from Stettin I spent a couple of hours in the hospital with your grandmother.[2] She was feeling very low, and your aunt[3] is quite concerned—I found her better than I feared. But no one knows how it will go from here, and she herself is preparing for death. I am writing you this because she told me she is very much hoping for a letter from you. Unfortunately she is still tormented by memories of the difficulties of this past winter—which we ourselves have already left far behind us. In her many sleepless hours at night she cannot let go of her own thoughts and then she surely seeks kind words from loved ones to console her.

I had to write you this, didn't I?

Under no circumstances should she have the perception in which she is now living that she is "useless"; for one thing, it is factually untrue! And second, this sort of feeling undermines every desire to live. I know how much you love her and how you can help her. —

Farewell, dear, kind Maria, be thanked anew from my heart for your recent short letter! What has come of the labor service requirement? Let me know. I will now finally be traveling one of these days and remember you with much love.

Yours,
Dietrich

Is it really completely impossible for you to visit your grandmother sometime?

[1.] Literary estate of Maria Weller (née von Wedemeyer), letter no. 18. Publication by permission of the Houghton Library, Harvard University. See 1/206a, ed. note 1.

[2.] Ruth von Kleist-Retzow was in the hospital in Stettin following an eye operation.

[3.] This refers to Maria von Kleist-Retzow (née von Diest); cf. Ruth von Wedemeyer, *In des Teufels Gasthaus,* 222.

221. To Hans von Dohnanyi ("Camouflage Letter")[1]   385

Munich, November 4, 1940[2]

Dear Hans,

In our recent conversation about ecumenical questions you asked me whether I would not be prepared, if need be, to make available my experience abroad and relationships to people in public life in Europe and overseas, in order to participate in acquiring reliable information about other countries. I have been thinking this over.

Within the scope of the problems that interest you, the unique feature of ecumenical work lies in the fact that leading political figures of various   386 countries are interested in this movement, in which all the major churches of the world (apart from the church of Rome) are united. This means that in fact it ought not to be difficult to ascertain the viewpoints and judgments

---

[1.] *NL,* A 65,12; typewritten draft with many handwritten corrections and additions, which are here reproduced within the text in square brackets. This "camouflage letter," or *Turnbrief,* is a fictitious letter prepared as a precaution in the spring of 1943, when heightened alerts from SS Major General Arthur Nebe [who was also director of the Criminal Police] warned of an imminent Gestapo action. This action was triggered by incriminating statements by Consul Schmidhuber, against whom proceedings had been in motion since the end of May 1942 because of breaches of foreign exchange regulations. [This was the so-called *Depositenkasse* affair (*Depositenkasse,* "cash fund deposit," was the name the Gestapo gave their investigation of what they believed was a money-laundering circle), which led to the discovery of the Operation 7 rescue; see p. 663.—MB] Cf. Höhne, *Canaris,* 515. The letter was antedated to November 4, 1940, in order to coordinate it with Hans von Dohnanyi's correspondence with AST [Abwehrstelle, "Military Intelligence Office"] VII in Munich (cf. 1/49) and to document adequately Bonhoeffer's UK classification [see 1/31, ed. note 3—MB] for service in Military Intelligence. A ring binder confiscated at Hans von Dohnanyi's arrest (Adjunct Files III D I Armed Forces High Command) contained a photocopy of this letter, with a note attached to it: "Ge[nera]l. O[ster]. Nov. 11, 1940. Have Schm[id]h[uber] AST Munich take care of the rest" (excerpt from the findings of the Reich wartime bar, BA Berlin-Lichterfelde, Nachlaß Dohnanyi 13 II/33,41; cf. 1/229.2, p. 429). Because General Oster participated in this retroactive dating, we may infer that the fabrication of this letter had been discussed with him. Published in *MW* 5: 316–18; previously published in *GS* 6:581–86. On the circumstances, see *DB-ER,* 783–84.

[2.] According to the indictment, the letter was dated November 11, 1940, not November 4; cf. 1/230.2, p. 438. Whether the original of the camouflage letter was in fact dated November 11, 1940, in contrast to this draft, cannot be ascertained, since it was incinerated in a bomb attack on Berlin on the night of November 23, 1943; see Chowaniec, *Der "Fall Dohnanyi,"* 70. The dating was to create problems for both Hans von Dohnanyi and Bonhoeffer later during their interrogations, since in previous letters to the Schlawe recruiting station on October 12, 1939, and May 27, 1940 (see 1/9), Bonhoeffer had already referred to his commitment to Military Intelligence. In fact Bonhoeffer did stay in Munich on November 4, 1940 (see 1/25) but had already previously been in contact with the Military Intelligence Office there, in particular with Dr. Josef Müller (cf. 1/24).

of such figures through ecumenical relationships. Furthermore, I believe it to be altogether within the realm of possibility to enter even into new relationships in this way, which could perhaps be of significance for answering specialized questions.

It is impossible within the scope of this letter to give you even a remote overview of the diverse connections that exist between the ecumenical movement and leading men of politics, economics, education, and science. Yet I implore you to consider that, precisely in these past few years, the ecumenical movement has set an ever-increasing value on the participation of such men. This has had the successful result of making the most recent major conferences not so much talks among theologians as "lay" affairs at which significant representatives from all arenas of life, from every country, have addressed burning contemporary issues. The relationships extend beyond the circle of active participants well into the responsible political circles of today. If I might just mention a few names for you here as an example: in England Lord Lothian, Sir Stafford Cripps, the workers' leader R. Crossman, Lord Noel-Buxton,[3] Sir Walter Moberly (not to mention the representatives of the state and free churches who sit in the Upper and Lower Houses); in Sweden, for instance, the royal family is very closely tied to our cause through Prince Bernadotte and Mrs. Cedergren (the king's niece); in the United States, Roosevelt has repeatedly shown a lively interest in our cause. Thus from the diverse character of those named, you will perceive the encompassing scope of those who are ecumenically "open to conversation."

387   In order to refresh your memory as to the nature of my own personal ecumenical relationships, the following are some notes to that effect: I spent a year in Spain in the service of the church,[4] lived another year in New York on an academic grant,[5] and in 1939[6] was there again for scholarly lectures; in 1933–35 I was German pastor in London,[7] and both beforehand and afterward went to England very frequently; I have been repeatedly to France, including spending some months there[8] — the same in Italy; at the invitation of the archbishop of Uppsala, I took a trip with students through Sweden and Denmark;[9] I have participated numerous times in

[3.] Lord Noel Buxton, Bishop of Willesden, was the brother-in-law of the British Quaker Dorothy Buxton.

[4.] Bonhoeffer served as a vicar in Barcelona in 1928–29; see *DB-ER*, 97–123, and *DBW* 10:3–4 and 613–19.

[5.] In 1930–31 Bonhoeffer studied at Union Theological Seminary in New York; see *DB-ER*, 147–69, and *DBW* 10:6–7, 616, 625–27.

[6.] See *DB-ER*, 648–62, and *DBW* 15:175–240.

[7.] See *DB-ER*, 325–417, and *DBW* 13.

[8.] "Some months" is an exaggeration.

[9.] See *DB-ER*, 506–17, and *DBW* 14:142–43.

church conferences in the Balkans[10] and have often traveled to Switzerland for the same reason. The ecumenical conferences brought representatives of all churches together often more than once per year, and relationships of personal trust have emerged from them. For the past twelve years[11] I have been a member of leading bodies of the ecumenical movement. Up until shortly before the outbreak of the war, I attempted to maintain these connections and to work in the spirit of mutual understanding. [In regard to languages, I am fluent especially in English but also in Spanish; I would be able to polish my French and Italian quickly.]

Perhaps I might also give you the names of a number of influential and distinguished church leaders and laypeople[12] whom I know personally—   388
some of them very well—and with whom I can resume contact at any time:

USA: President H. S. Coffin [a man with endless ties to all circles], Prof. Reinhold Niebuhr (the leading young theologian of America [a leading socialist]), Prof. W. A. Brown (the leading [most distinguished] elder theologian), the presidents and secretaries of the Federal Council of Churches (representing all the churches in the United States), the leaders of the [extremely] influential [in the United States] and extensive [encompassing all circles] YMCA [Young Men's Christian Association], the mission societies [which have (illegible) their branches in every part of the world], the president of the largest Negro university, Howard College in Washington, and several younger leaders of the Negro movement there, the president and the secretaries of the ecumenical associations, several significant and influential preachers in New York.

Sweden: Archbishop Eidem, in whose house I spent several days [and through whom I became acquainted with many interesting figures, the lead-

---

[10.] We know only of Bonhoeffer's participation in the conferences in Čiernohorské Kúpele in July 1932 and in Sofia in September 1933.

[11.] This chronology is accurate only if Bonhoeffer is counting back from 1943. In 1931 Bonhoeffer was elected in Cambridge to become one of three international youth secretaries of the World Alliance for International Friendship through the Churches. This inadvertent mistake in dating was not detected, however, in the interrogations.

[12.] In putting together the following list, Bonhoeffer relied on his copy of the World Alliance's "Annual Report and Handbook 1932" (*NL-Bibl.,* 6A 1).On the flyleaf in the back the following pencil notes, which he apparently used in preparing this letter, appear in Bonhoeffer's handwriting: "Alivisatos—[illegible] c[hurch] law / Papamichael Prof. / Minister of Culture Balanos. Prof. / Sofia. Zankow rector / Cripps—labor [illegible] / *Romania* Antonescu Patriarchate / Connection of the Iron Front with the lower clergy / Intercommunion will fall into oblivion. 1938 / *Bulgaria*—positive toward Serbia, negative toward Greece / *Greece*—London [?], Liverpool [?] emphasis; *State churches; Germanos* [illegible] ecum. Patr. in *London.* / *Yugoslavia* Irené—Russian influence. Brother [illegible] President rich family / catechism [?] Visser 't Hooft / Yanitsch—Minister of Culture."

ing] bishops Runestam, Aulén, Tor Andre,[13] [(crossed out:) Prof. Brilioth],
Dr. M. Björkquist (founder of the large Christian *völkisch* educational center in Sigtuna),[14] Prince Bernadotte [brother of the king], Dr. Cedergren
[nephew of the king by marriage] (both in the Young Men's Christian Association). *Denmark:* almost the entire theological faculty in Copenhagen, the
bishop of Copenhagen, Pastor Sparring-Petersen (general secretary for ecumenical work). *Norway:* Bishop of Oslo, P. Klaveness–Bergen. *Hungary:* Bishop
Raffay–Budapest, Prof. de Boer[15] [lawyer]. *Yugoslavia:* Bishop Iriney[16] of
Novi Sad (the most influential and popular church leader there [brother of
the president of Parliament, from an old and most respected family]). *Roma-*
nia: Patriarch of Bucharest, Prof. Michescu. *Bulgaria:* Prof. Zankow (presently
389   rector [who just received an honorary doctorate from the University of
Berlin and is presently rector of the university] in Sophia), Archbishop
Stephan, Bishop Paissy. *Greece:* Prof. Alivisatos [lawyer and (crossed out:)
national economist at the University of Athens], Prof. Papamichael, Prof.
Balanos (former minister of culture). *Italy:* Dr. Cesare Gay, Prof. Comba.
Spain: (in addition to numerous personal acquaintances) Pastor Arenales,
Juan Fliedner. *France:* the president of the Protestant churches [of France],
Pastor M. Boegner, [the leaders of the ecumenical work] Pasteur Jézéquel,
Pasteur Toureille, [the eminent socialist] Prof. Ph. André,[17] [the national
economist] Prof. Lasserre, [the leading pastor among the younger clergy]
P. P. Mauris.[18] *England:* Archbishop of Canterbury, lord bishop of Chichester
[bishop and politician], Professors Garvie [London], Micklem [Oxford],
Baillie [Edinburgh], who are all well acquainted with Germany, Lord Dick-
inson [the former president of the ecumenical work]. Lord Noel-Buxton
[leading member of the Upper House], Lord Lothian (presently in the
United States), Sir W. Moberly [President...university...,[19] Dr. H. G.
Oldham (inspiration for the great Oxford church conference).

The presidents of the Methodist and Baptist church communities, the
Christian Student Association, the ecumenical associations, the Quakers,

---

[13.] [This name should read "Andrae."—MB]
[14.] [Bonhoeffer is referring to the Nordic Ecumenical Institute, founded by Bishop
Björkquist in 1940; the institute became a frequent setting for meetings between ecumenical leaders and European resistance figures. Bonhoeffer's description of it as a
"Christian *völkisch* educational center" was probably deliberate, since the purpose of this
camouflage letter was to mislead the Nazi officials who would read it. See also von Klemperer, *German Resistance against Hitler,* 298 n. 5.—MB]
[15.] [This name should read "de Boér."—MB]
[16.] [This name should read "Irenae."—MB]
[17.] This name should read André Philip.
[18.] Bonhoeffer intended to refer to Pierre Maury.
[19.] This is partially illegible.

C. F. Andrews (friend and biographer of Gandhi). In 1935[20] I was personally invited by Mahatma Gandhi and R. Tagore for an extended stay in India.

To those named above should be added a great number of professors and pastors whom I know well personally in almost all these countries.

Through my visits to foreign countries I have also established connections to the Catholic clergy; I could easily expand these by means of my connections to representatives of the presiding clergy in Germany.

In view of the fact that the church is inextricably entwined with the life of the people, particularly in the Anglo-Saxon, Scandinavian, and southern European countries, and is able to exercise a decisive influence on public opinion, the possibilities that present themselves here [for commissions] should [would] not be underestimated [hardly by you?]. According to all we know, the authority of the spiritual leadership has only increased in those countries that at present must perhaps accommodate themselves to certain restrictions in the political realm, so that the connection to such men ought to be particularly valuable.[21] The anti-German [In addition, the foreign] propaganda, which took advantage of the German Church Struggle and has sown a great deal of suspicion precisely in the church-oriented countries, could be opposed successfully [in this way conceivably be effectively countered].[22]

I am now in Munich for the time being and [would, of course, be prepared to place myself at your service in some form that seems suitable to you, perhaps from here or wherever you think best. I think that it would not be difficult, even under present circumstances, to resume the great majority of connections—if necessary in a neutral location abroad—and to make full use of them for German interests] could—if this were desired—make myself available to the office there, though if necessary could also, of course, come to Berlin to discuss further details.

The Kalckreuths very much regretted not having seen you both again.

Please give my best regards at home. Yours very truly,

Dietrich

390

[20.] See *DB-ER*, 406–9, and *DBW* 13:213–14.

[21.] The sentence that reads "According to all we know… particularly valuable" replaces the following sentences, which are crossed out with pencil: "Precisely in those regions where peoples have to make certain sacrifices in the political arena today (Scandinavia, Holland, Belgium), it is important that their inner trust in Germany be strengthened. The available church connections could also serve in this regard, whereas their cessation or rupture would necessarily have damaging effects."

[22.] The following sentence is crossed out: "I am convinced that I would be able to resume the great majority of connections, if necessary from a neutral site, even under present conditions, and to make full use of them for German interests."

391   **222. From the Indictment against Hans von Dohnanyi and Hans Oster: Reproduction of Excerpts from Letters**[1]

221.1 Hans von Dohnanyi to Wilhelm Schmidhuber

To follow up on our telephone conversation yesterday, I am transmitting to you a photocopy of a letter sent to me[2] that prompted Colonel Oster to direct the AST[3] Munich to classify the author of the letter UK[4] for Military Intelligence purposes based out of Munich.

I shall also enclose a copy of the order directed to the AST Munich.

222.2 Hans Oster to the Munich Military Intelligence Office

I request that the author of the enclosed letter, whose name can be ascertained through Consul Schmidhuber, Am Kosttor 1, Munich, be classified UK for Military Intelligence purposes and that the details be discussed with Consul Schmidhuber. Consul Schmidhuber is receiving a copy of this letter and is instructed to contact Major Hundt directly.

223. Fictitious Diary Fragments[1]

May 1942
Impressions of Switzerland. This time particularly unfavorable. I tend to react oddly to Switzerland. In general, when I am abroad, I warm up to the people over time; in
392   Switzerland alone has this never happened. The people irritate me most particularly in

---

[1.] Niedersächsisches Hauptstaatsarchiv, Hannover-Nebenlager Pattensen, Nds 721 Lüneburg Acc. 69/76; hectograph, excerpts dated November 26, 1940 (see 1/229.2, p. 429); published in Chowaniec, *Der "Fall Dohnanyi,"* 171. These excerpts and the following material (see 1/223) are fictitious, antedated texts from early 1943 [made in conjunction with Bonhoeffer's camouflage letter—MB].

[2.] Dohnanyi is referring to Bonhoeffer's "camouflage letter" (see 1/221).

[3.] [Abbreviation for Abwehrstelle, "Military Intelligence Office."—MB]

[4.] [See 1/31, ed. note 3.—MB]

[1.] *NL*, A 65,5; typewritten copy (the original is not available, and the sections marked by ellipses "[...]" can no longer be clarified), written around February/March 1943 to camouflage the purpose of earlier trips. This diary was prepared in case of a search of the Bonhoeffers' house, which seemed increasingly likely given Schmidhuber's arrest at the end of October 1942; cf. *DB-ER*, 781–82. Previously published in *GS* 6:635–37. On March 18, 1957, Eberhard Bethge sent these diary fragments to Bishop Bell with an accompanying letter [in English—MB], saying: "I enclose the pretended diary of 1942 which Dietrich wrote that the Gestapo should find it on his desk. They did" (Bell Papers, vol. 42). The fictitious diary fragments apparently played no role in the cases against Bonhoeffer, Hans von Dohnanyi, and Hans Oster.

their arrogance and self-righteousness. They consider themselves to be specially sin-gled out by the loving God because once again the storms seem to be passing them by. In all this they often make extremely presumptuous comments about Germany. Some of these people I will visit again only after the end of the war; by then they will surely have learned something. Overall it is easier in Geneva than in the German parts of Switzerland. Even the newspapers there show more understanding. All their wailing about food is ridiculous when people are still swimming in fat! The anxiety about los-ing anything is enormous—appalling bourgeoisie. At the same time they consider the Swissification [Verschweizerung] of the world to be the reign of God on earth. Time and again the magnificent landscape brings a respite from these unappetizing impres-sions. Y. T.[2] is personally very pleasant and reasonable, again and again, a good Chris-tian; in the same way Kö.,[3] presently the president of the church.

Saw a good film: *Good-by Mr. Lipps*,[4] somewhat sentimental but engaging on a human level. Fortunately, the weekly newsreels from Germany are always available.

June 1942

A weekend flight to Stockholm,[5] terrible storm. Magnificent city, very friendly, but at the same time reserved, at least initially. Great astonishment, then warming up. In [...] not everyone kind, but correct. Always very difficult without knowing the lan-guage. Waiters often act as if they understand no German and respond only when addressed in English. Food was good but skimpy and no comparison with before. In [...] welcomed very warmly. B.[6] wants to become bishop of Stockholm. Strong anti-Bolshevist sentiment everywhere; that provides a certain shared foundation.

In Stockholm's shops everything still available for purchase, but again no money.   393
Sweden's location between Norway and Finland: they sympathize with both by nature and tradition—this characterizes their inner conflict.

Wrote to Eidem,[7] was unable to see him due to brevity of time, but received a very friendly response.[8] His position in Sweden very strong; he maintains our faithful and long friendship. Theologically the German influence seems in recent times to have unfortunately diminished sharply in favor of the Anglo-Saxon.

[2.] This person is not identified.
[3.] Alphons Koechlin.
[4.] This should read *Goodbye, Mr. Chips*.
[5.] The date of this trip was May 30, 1942.
[6.] Manfred Björkquist.
[7.] Letter not extant.
[8.] Letter not extant.

July 16, 1942

Two weeks in Italy, Venice, and Rome.[9] It is good to see Italy again from time to time. Main impressions: the Laocoön[10]—did the head of Laocoön become some sort of model for later portrayals of Christ? The ancient "man of sorrows."[11] No one was able to inform me about this; will attempt to investigate it. Curious, until now the Laocoön never made any particular impression on me.[12] Great joy again at Gentile's Madonna, very unusual. Was [...] mentally ill? His Madonnas give this impression. Attempt to become better acquainted with Raphael's Stanzas;[13] but not very accessible for me; no immediate significance.[14] Unfortunately too little time. Good that most of the museums are closed, otherwise one would never get through.

Exhaustive visit to the catacombs! Many problems. Above all, why does the symbol of the cross appear only so late? Questions about some of the paintings. Splendidly well-informed guides. But much too little time for real research. Later, after the war! Am beginning to gain an understanding and feeling for the Baroque cupola paintings, the [...] the splendor serves solely this movement upward. In St. Peter's. Feast of Peter and Paul,[15] with a Sistine Madonna: o felix Roma.

The great heat did not leave enough energy after the work of the day for areas of personal interest. The food was adequate. Unfortunately a question of money again. The poor appear to be getting by, while those with property can afford everything. Why can these plutocratic conditions not be eradicated, even with good will? The Italians' lack of talent for organization does seem to play a significant role, however.

Personal impressions: very positive Z.,[16] old world war officer, very collected, clear, smart, and despite many years in Rome irreproachably German. Otherwise no surprises.

394

[9.] Very little is known about the actual events of this trip. It began on June 26 with the flight from Munich to Venice. Furthermore, it is known that Bonhoeffer was in Rome July 3–10 and that the flight back to Munich departed from there. The extent to which Bonhoeffer and Hans von Dohnanyi were continually or only intermittently accompanied by Josef Müller and Wilhelm Schmidhuber can no longer be ascertained.

[10.] [In Greek mythology Laocoön was a Trojan priest of Apollo who with his two sons was killed by two serpents for having warned his people against the Trojan horse. Bonhoeffer is referring to the marble statue in the Vatican Museums, Rome.—MB]

[11.] Cf. *LPP,* 194 (*DBW* 8:293).

[12.] [In the diary of Bonhoeffer's trip to Italy as a young man of eighteen, he indicated that the Laocoön actually made quite an impression on him: "When I saw the Laocoön there for the first time, a chill actually went through me. It is unbelievable. I spent a lot of time there.... Then I had to tear myself away" (DBWE 9:89 and ed. note 33).—MB]

[13.] [The Stanzas are frescoes by Raphael in the Vatican.—MB]

[14.] [The Stanzas did not impress him very much on his first trip to Italy either. See *DBWE* 9:102 and ed. note 94.—MB]

[15.] Actually, this feast is on July 29.

[16.] Dr. Ivo Zeiger, the rector of the Collegium Germanicum. In a secret message smuggled to his wife, Hans von Dohnanyi wrote, "Zeiger is a German officer" (BA Berlin-Lichterfelde, Nachlaß Dohnanyi 14 III/5).

I liked Venice better ten years ago. The main attraction of the evening was the ducal palace, an architectural wonder: the heavy edifice practically floats on the two highly tapered pillars. Now the wooden paneling is ruining absolutely everything, just as at S. Marco. An afternoon stroll through the city on Sunday and a trip through the Grand Canal, very charming. Unfortunately the weather was overall not ideal.

Personal impression of Schm.[17] massively rich, amusing bon vivant, exclusively economic interests, helpful, but nevertheless not entirely to be taken seriously in his efforts and his entire manner. Fundamentally quite unapproachable on religious questions, so that I actually have nothing at all in common with him. In Rome I found him rather unappealing because of his pomposity.

To fly over Italy in an airplane is a disappointment. Fog over the Alps. The Mussolini[18] is marvelously equipped, went swimming there with M.[19] Read Gregorovius, *Wanderjahre in Italien.*

[17.] This probably refers to Wilhelm Schmidhuber.
[18.] The Foro Mussolini, renamed the Foro Italico after 1945, is a modern sports facility on the north side of Rome.
[19.] This probably refers to Josef Müller.

P. Imprisonment in Berlin-Tegel Military Prison.
April 5, 1943–October 8, 1944

224. File Z[1]

224.1. Note No. 1[2]

1. Over 60% of the Protestant clergy have already been drafted; of those younger clergy belonging to the Confessing Church, over 90%, since there exists no institution, recognized by the state, with the right to access indispensable personnel.[3]

[1.] 1/224 documents the wording of the three notes, preserved only as duplicates, that played a fateful role in Hans von Dohnanyi's arrest on April 5, 1943 (see *DB-ER*, 786–87, and Chowaniec, *Der "Fall Dohnanyi,"* 43–48). They were found in a "portfolio Z (gray)"; "Z" stands for Zentralabteilung, the Central Department within the Foreign Office of Military Intelligence of the Armed Forces High Command.

[2.] BA Berlin-Lichterfelde, Nachlaß Dohnanyi 13 II/33,4; hectograph. In his interrogation on April 13, 1943, Hans von Dohnanyi stated: "Note no.1 is a handwritten note by my brother-in-law that I requested because of the unrest that had ensued from the judicial proceedings against the Rhineland pastors" (II/33,3). According to Günther van Norden, "at the state prosecutor's office in Düsseldorf proceedings had been pending since 1939 against Pastors Beckmann and Lutze and Licentiates Klugkist, Hesse, and Schlingensiepen, because of participation in the forbidden exams. . . . In 1942 there were further interrogations, as well as brief imprisonments of Confessing Church pastors in the Rhineland, because of various "crimes"; this did indeed lead to unrest among the congregations, but not to trials" (communication with the German editors of *DBW* 16 on January 2, 1993). As was the case with the "Petition to the Armed Forces" (see 1/139), the statements were originally aimed at conspiratorial efforts in military circles but were interpreted during the interrogations as elements of a military-political procurement of information. Regarding the relevant interrogations, see Chowaniec, *Der "Fall Dohnanyi,"* 70–71.

[3.] In contrast to the German Protestant Church, the Confessing Church was not recognized by the state. Therefore (heralding back to the legalization controversy), pastors

2. Ca. 15% of the Protestant clergy have been killed in action.

3. The new Compulsory Work Law explicitly excludes the clergy.[4]

4. Large areas of the Reich are already without the church's care, which the populace increasingly longs for; this is especially true in rural areas.

224.2 Note No. 2[5]

The peace tidings of 1941 received maximum attention throughout the world; in England they were used as the basis for the establishment of peace goals by all the Christian churches.[6] There are signs that the peace tidings of 1942 are receiving similar notice. Therefore, efforts are now under way in Rome to prepare the precise formulation of the content of the principles of both messages and their later practical usage in both domestic and international life. The person responsible for this effort is the rector of the Germanicum, Dr. *Zeiger,* a German and a world war officer, who oversees relations with Germany closely and of whose pro-German stance there can be no doubt. Zeiger spoke with me about this entire complex of problems and at that point posed the question whether it might not be possible to undertake corresponding efforts on the part of the Protestant churches in

---

and vicars who had not taken their exams and been ordained by the official church—i.e., those who were under the governance of the Councils of Brethren—were considered illegal. [The term *Bedarfsträger,* translated here by the phrase "institution . . . with the right to access indispensable personnel," refers to an institution authorized by the state to employ, even in a time of war, personnel indispensable, *unabkömmlich,* to the work of that institution. These indispensable personnel were thereby rendered exempt from being drafted for military service.—MB]

[4.] Cf. 1/63, ed. note 4. [This law regulated compulsory work in industrial production considered essential in times of war. Those who were called up for this kind of work were either exempted from military service or unable to serve.—MB]

[5.] BA Berlin-Lichterfelde, Nachlaß Dohnanyi 13 II/33,3; hectograph. According to Hans von Dohnanyi's statement at his interrogation on April 13, 1943, this note is related to the following one (note no. 3): "I had the mission from the admiral to attempt in my trips to obtain militarily or military-politically significant information from the Vatican. . . . I considered it very possible to win the interest of the Vatican and thereby the disclosure of its orientation by approaching it from the Protestant side. I spoke with O[ster] about this. It was to have been presented to Adm[iral] C[anaris]. To prepare for this presentation, I drew up rough drafts of prescribed phraseologies for the agent who was to approach the Vatican. 'O' represents the code name for Gen. O[ster]. The content of the phraseology was a reproduction of the entire complex of questions that I had discussed with B[onhoeffer]. . . . Content of note no. 2 was communicated to me orally by Müller" (ibid.).

[6.] Cf. Visser 't Hooft's letter to William Temple on March 12, 1941 (1/94); this refers to "the five points of Pope Pius XII," cited by British church leaders in their "Foundations of Peace" of December 21, 1940; see Boyens, *Kirchenkampf und Ökumene,* vol. 2, *1939–1945,* 356, 433.

Germany and to coordinate these with the efforts of the Vatican. That seemed to him to be all the more significant since the Protestant churches of England and America were already occupying themselves with these questions—and in fact doing so by drawing on the principles established by the pope.

397   **224.3. Note No. 3**[7]

For quite some time a small circle of leading clergy of the German Protestant Church has been engaged with the question of what contribution the Protestant church might be able to make after this war toward the creation of a just and lasting peace and toward the building up of a social order grounded on Christian foundations.[8] The intention is to set forth a series of programmatic points, to compile an extensive commentary on the issues they discuss, and to put together some explanatory flyers, based on the programmatic tenets and intended for a general audience, that could be made available to the public when the occasion arises. These tasks are already well under way. It is well known that the pope has set forth his peace goals in his last two Christmas messages and that the English and American (not to mention the Dutch, Norwegian, and French) Protestant churches are already working on these same questions very intensively. Because it would be of the utmost significance if at the proper time all Christian churches were to take a *unanimous* position on the questions of the shape of peace, and because—as far as that can be assessed today—agreement on all important points could well be reached, it seems extremely important and desirable that a German Protestant pastor be given the opportunity both to conduct deliberations in this matter with representatives of the Catholic

---

[7.] Niedersächsisches Hauptstaatsarchiv, Hanover, 721 Lüneburg Acc. 69/76; hectograph (excerpt from the indictment against Hans von Dohnanyi and Hans Oster; cf. 1/229.2, p. 433). At the April 13, 1943, interrogation, Hans von Dohnanyi said of this material: "The third piece of paper in file Z was written at the beginning of 1943. At that time Dr. Müller came to Berlin and reported on the religious efforts of the Vatican and the commentary on the Christmas message. In connection with that I discussed with D[ietrich] whether it might not be possible to provide an agent to the Vatican who would be able to earn trust by advancing arguments in whatever way we wished to lay them down beforehand" (BA Berlin-Lichterfelde, Nachlaß Dohnanyi 13 II/33,3). This text was apparently written by Bonhoeffer.

[8.] This clearly refers to the Freiburg circle memorandum; cf. *DB-ER*, 775–77. [Cf. the editors' discussion of the Freiburg memorandum, pp. 662–63.—MB]

Church in Rome and to become acquainted with the relevant activities of the   398
Protestant world churches in Geneva or Stockholm.[9] sgd. O.[10]

225. Proceedings of Interrogations of Hans von Dohnanyi

225.1. Interrogation on April 16, 1943[1]

[. . .] At the outbreak of the war, Dietrich Bonhoeffer found himself on a trip to
America from which he prematurely returned in order to be in Germany when war
broke out. He then made the attempt to join the military as a chaplain. This attempt
failed, and we discussed on several occasions that he also wanted to do his part for
the armed forces, although at that time he was not yet up for the draft (year of birth
1906). We then considered various options, and eventually one or the other of us
came up with the idea that an assignment in the intelligence service would be the
obvious thing, given the extensive international connections in the ecumenical sector
that my brother-in-law had. At my request, my brother-in-law wrote me a letter in
which he described these connections. As far as I recall, this letter was initialed by
then Colonel Oster, with an instruction that the rest be handled by the Munich AST[2]
(Schmidhuber). I believe that the decisive idea here was that Schmidhuber, who in his
role as Portuguese consul was often called on by Military Intelligence for procurement of passports, visas, etc., would be able to assist my brother-in-law in this regard
in acquiring the necessary papers and that at the same time my brother-in-law would
be able to support Schmidhuber in his work. As we well knew, Schmidhuber was
working a great deal with contacts of a not purely military character—as is, of
course, necessary for an agent of the intelligence service—and my brother-in-law was   399
able to refer and open to him significant connections for this work. As far as I recall,
I sent this letter to the head of the Military Intelligence Office in Munich and
requested that he take care of the rest with regard to the necessary formalities.
[. . .]

To my knowledge, Division Leader I was not involved. At the time I did not perceive in this any "evasion"; as far as I recall, this incident took place at the beginning of
1940. Presumably at the time I was under the impression that what this amounted to
was no more than a matter of referring a subagent to an agent, namely, Schmidhuber,
who was under the command of Military Intelligence I in Berlin. I believe that I also
wrote to Schmidhuber at the time something to the effect that he could get in touch

---

[9.] This refers to the ecumenical activities toward "peace aims" and preparations for
a "postarmistice conference." Cf. *MW* 5:283–88 and Boyens, *Kirchenkampf und Ökumene*,
vol. 2, *1939–1945*, 215.

[10.] Cf. ed. note 5 and 1/228.2, ed. note 12. At his first interrogations, Hans Oster
had initially asserted that this initial was not his but then corrected this statement.

[1.] BA Berlin-Lichterfelde, Nachlaß Dohnanyi 13 II/33, 4ff.; hectograph.

[2.] [Abbreviation for Abwehrstelle, "Military Intelligence Office."—MB]

with the head of the Military Intelligence Office about this matter and could learn all the details from him. Since at that point I was quite new to these formalities and had to concentrate in principle on quite different things, namely, the purely military-political aspect of Colonel Oster's activity, I was unaware of the difficulties in the command structure [Führungsverhältnisse] between the divisions with specific responsibilities [Sachabteilungen] and Department Z. I became aware of these only when on some occasion or another, probably as one of the difficulties emerged with Munich, Colonel Oster emphasized what he later repeated often, that Z[3] had no agents to command. [...]

To my knowledge B. was in Italy only once, in July 1942. Now B. was approaching a trip to Italy that was contingent on the question by what means he should make connection with Zeiger. In addition, B. had the assignment of placing his ecumenical ties at the disposal of Military Intelligence, which he had done in relation to Schmidhuber as well as Dr. Gisevius. Further, he had taken care of two special assignments from the admiral in Oslo and Stockholm.

It is surely possible that Bonhoeffer and I had discussed that the easing of state police restrictions through his assignment in Munich would be a pleasant side benefit of the recruitment.[4]

400   225.2. Interrogation on May 5, 1943[5]

[...] After file D I of the Armed Forces High Command up to letter B—Bonhoeffer correspondence—was presented to the accused, and in particular after it was presented that B. first approached him in writing on November 11, 1940,[6] for the purpose of being employed by Military Intelligence and that the Military Intelligence Office in Munich was first informed in a document of November 26, 1940, that B. was to be assigned to Schmidhuber as an agent, but, on the other hand, two letters of B., of October 12, 1939, and May 27, 1940,[7] are located in the files of the Munich recruiting-inspection office in which B. declares that he is active in a position of military service and in fact serving the chief of staff of the Foreign Office of Military Intelligence in the Armed Forces High Command; he explains:

O. had B. give him domestic policy information of general interest, and so, in response to direct questioning, I declare that the church-political internal questions

---

[3.] On the tasks of Department Z ["Z" stood for *Zentrale*, or Central] within the Foreign Office of Military Intelligence of the Armed Forces High Command, cf. Wilhelm Canaris's statements at the June 15, 1943, interrogation; see 1/227.

[4.] [This refers to the Gestapo bans (in January 1938 and August 1940) on Bonhoeffer's publishing, public speaking, and travel. See 1/18.—MB]

[5.] BA Berlin-Lichterfelde, Nachlaß Dohnanyi 13 II/33,14–15; hectograph.

[6.] Cf. the draft of the "camouflage letter" of November 4, 1940, 1/221.

[7.] These two letters have not been located, either in the Hauptstaatsarchiv (the National Archives) in Munich or in the Militärarchiv (the Military Archives) in Freiburg im Breisgau.

did not play a preponderant role nor any role at all in this, but instead merely general domestic policy information.[8]

To the question when and how often pieces of information had been given to O. from fall 1939 until fall 1940:

At that point B. had only a very loose relationship with the Foreign Office of Military Intelligence. To my knowledge, such information had not been given very often and had the sole purpose of informing the Chief of Staff about any personal briefings of the admiral.

Question:

Then how did B., in his official writings to the Armed Forces Regional Command, even come to speak of his military status if he had no relationship at all to Military Intelligence? For telling Colonel Oster something once in a while in a personal conversation certainly does not establish that he was in the military.

Answer: I remember that at one point I spoke with Colonel Oster about whether B. could appeal with the recruiting station to the relationship he had with the Foreign Office of Military Intelligence, and the colonel explicitly said that he could.

[…]

226. First Drafts of Letters by Dietrich Bonhoeffer for His Interrogations[1]

401

226.1. To Manfred Roeder[2]

June 10, 1943

Dear Senior Military Prosecutor Roeder:

Please permit me to add two further points to my interrogation today that occurred to me in subsequently thinking through the Friedenthal[3] affair:

[8.] See, for example, *DB-ER*, 696–98, in reference to Bonhoeffer's visitation trips to East Prussia.

[1.] These drafts and those in 1/228 comprise a bundle of twenty-one pages filled with drafts of letters addressed to the senior military prosecutor, Dr. Manfred Roeder, who headed the investigations against Hans von Dohnanyi and Bonhoeffer. The drafts encompass the time period of June 10–August 2, 1943, the phase of the final interrogations before their temporary cessation; after this Roeder prepared the indictment. Bonhoeffer's handwriting shows that he made an extraordinary effort to come up with appropriate formulations through numerous deletions, corrections, and insertions; the drafts reproduced here include only materially relevant variants. These letters served his own defense as well as the concealment of the ongoing conspiracy; accordingly, truthful material often appears within a fictionalized context. Cf. *DB-ER*, 813–17.

[2.] *NL*, A 83,2; handwritten in ink; previously published in *LPP*, 61. This is apparently the first draft of a letter. It reflects the interrogations, which focused on the events of "Operation 7"; on this, see *DB-ER*, 747–49, and Winfried Meyer, *Unternehmen Sieben*, 391–98.

[3.] Cf. Wilhelm Rott's letter to Alphons Koechlin in October 1941, 1/134.

1. The gentleman who conducted the negotiations with Miss Friedenthal was to my knowledge Dr. Arnold[4]; my brother-in-law told me this later at some occasion or other. In addition, as far as I know, my brother-in-law himself spoke with her.[5] 2. Over the course of the summer, Miss Friedenthal once sought me out briefly and asked me whether I thought that she could responsibly undertake the task entrusted to her. At that time I affirmed that. She was here speaking only of the fact of the task, not of its *content,* of which I even later never learned anything.[6]

402   I beg you to believe me that these two points truly only occurred to me later. In actuality it is often difficult for me to follow the tempo of your questioning, probably because I am not accustomed to it; but I truly have no interest in not presenting the entire affair in the way it took place. Ultimately, of course, I too am concerned with the earliest possible clarification. I very much hope that you will believe these statements from me.

With Heil Hitler! I remain your very respectful
Dietrich Bonhoeffer[7]

226.2 To Manfred Roeder[8]

the 12th[9]

Dear Senior Military Prosecutor Roeder:

Because of the danger that you could begin to doubt the credibility of my statements, I must offer you an addition today to my comments of two days ago on the Friedenthal affair. While pondering your questions as to whether I had become aware of anything about this complex matter before the spring of 1942, several significant points occurred to me today. I can only assure you that this slow recapitulation of the event does not derive from my malicious intent but probably from the fact that this affair never particularly involved me and therefore truly did not make a very lasting impression on me. Whether you wish to believe me regarding this is something I can no longer control.

What took place was the following. 1.) The inquiry by my brother-in-law took place in my view not in early 1942 but rather in the fall of 1941, if not

---

[4.] See *DB-ER*, 747 (and Meyer, *Unternehmen Sieben*) on the role of Arnold, a lawyer; there also exists a report he wrote later (BA Berlin-Lichterfelde, Nachlaß Dohnanyi 23/1).

[5.] In the margin is written: "I thought of Mrs. Alt. [?] because I knew that she knew and cherished Miss Friedenthal through her relatives."

[6.] This sentence is in the margin.

[7.] Alongside Bonhoeffer's signature is written in pencil: "no church assignment for Miss Fr."

[8.] *NL*, A 83,2; handwritten in pencil on the back of the previous text.

[9.] From the content, this dating can be expanded to read June 12, 1943.

earlier. I conclude this because my brother-in-law occasionally said to me that the matter lasted over a year.[10]

2.) At a time I simply can no longer reconstruct, as a result of a conver- 403
sation I had with him, Dr. Schmidhuber asked Köchlin to procure a Swiss
entrance visa for Miss Fr.[11] I believe that at that time Miss Fr. wanted to
emigrate. I believe I also recall that Schm. informed me at that point that
K. had taken care of the matter. Why Miss Friedenthal didn't actually emigrate at that time I do not know. Since I last visited Köchlin in[12] August/
September '41 and certainly never spoke with him personally about the
affair, I assume that Schm.'s trip[13] still took place in September '41. In fact
I do not know any longer whether Schm.'s—as previously discussed, he was
engaged with the matter later as well—inquiry to Köchlin took place in
connection with my brother-in-law's inquiry or whether I expressed this
inquiry to Köchlin at the request of Confessing Church circles, which is
also possible.[14] In any case, it seems to me as if, after the point at which I
became involved in her situation, Miss Fr. received instructions from the
Military Intelligence Office that she was to make herself available for this.

But I know that in Confessing Church circles people occasionally discussed that Miss Friedenthal wanted to emigrate to relatives. The letters to
K. and M.[15] given to my brother-in-law to take along doubtless served to
support the purpose of the action of the military department, as I have
already explained.

When Hans's inquiry?

Probably Lokies would remember?

227. Minutes of Proceedings of an Interrogation of Wilhelm Canaris[1]   404

[...] At the head of Department Z of the Foreign Office of Military Intelligence stands
the director of the Central Department, whose task it is to handle and to direct

---

[10.] The following insertion was crossed out: "At that time, I was ill with severe pneumonia from October until the beginning of January and did not, or could not, leave the
house; I also recollect that my brother-in-law directed this inquiry re: Miss Friedenthal to
me on a visit in my room."

[11.] Cf. Wilhelm Rott's letter to Alphons Koechlin in October 1941, 1/134.

[12.] The word "July" is crossed out.

[13.] Schmidhuber's trip to Switzerland.

[14.] The following is crossed out: "In this case it would have been a matter of rendering personal assistance."

[15.] "K. and M." are not identified (perhaps Alphons Koechlin and Josef Müller).

[1.] BA Berlin-Lichterfelde, Nachlaß Dohnanyi 13 II/33,17–18; hectograph. In the minutes of June 15, 1943, p. 174, Wilhelm Canaris came to the defense of both Bonhoeffer

authoritatively on my behalf the organization, personnel, and in part the legal affairs, administration, and finances. Z does not have immediate oversight over agents, although in two exceptional cases an immediate contact took place between Department Z and agents Bonhoeffer and Müller, since Dohnanyi's overlapping connections to Müller (because of his connections to circles in Rome), which were of benefit to the military and military-political information service, were to be and were utilized.

I was the one who gave the command that Military Intelligence I—Colonel Piekenbrock was to be informed of the resulting reports to the extent they were of a military nature.

[. . .]

I know nothing of an involvement by Bonhoeffer in 1939–40 in Military Intelligence in the sphere of domestic church affairs. Neither General Oster nor Dohnanyi ever presented anything regarding this to me. As to whether this was actually the case or not, I can say nothing at all, as was just explained. If a demand of this sort had been directed to me, I would have flatly refused it, since repeatedly, even in presentations to the individual gentlemen, I was explicit that our duties extended to the military and military-political sphere. A general domestic political overview was naturally of value for headquarters, just as, of course, for an officer in my position this sort of overview is essential. On the other hand, the supervision of agents employed in domestic affairs was most strictly forbidden. Neither Dohnanyi nor Oster could have had any doubt of this prohibition. Dohnanyi gave me no indication that state police measures were in effect against Bonhoeffer at the time of his involvement with Military Intelligence. I was informed neither of the ban on Bonhoeffer's speaking nor of the restrictions on his place of residence.[2] If this had been the case, it would have been no immediate reason to prohibit engaging Bonhoeffer for the purposes of Military Intelligence. I would, however, have arranged for contact to be made with the Gestapo in order to find a modus vivendi concerning him.

[. . .]

405

---

and Hans von Dohnanyi without sacrificing himself: "I was not aware that the state police had any restrictions on him. If this had come to my awareness, I would have still made use of him because of his particularly good connections. The pages found written by Dohnanyi were not familiar to me. I assume that he was gathering supporting material for conversations in the Vatican. Needless to say, given the atmosphere there, he had to keep himself informed and be forearmed for all possible questions."

[2.] The ban on living in Berlin was imposed on Bonhoeffer on January 11, 1938; the ban on speaking was imposed by the Reich Central Security Office on August 22, 1940 (see 1/18).

228. Further Drafts of Letters by Dietrich Bonhoeffer regarding His Interrogations

228.1 To Manfred Roeder[1]

The main point concerns the date[2] of my discussion with my brother-in-law. Perhaps you recall from the interrogation that my first reaction to the question of the date was, "in any case it was a long time ago." When I then hesitantly named early 1942 and you immediately confirmed this, I considered this information to have been correct. In the meantime, however, it has become clear to me that this date, which intuitively at once seemed too recent to me, had to be completely wrong. I deduce this from two things: my brother-in-law occasionally said to me that the execution of the entire action had taken over a year. I further remember that during my extended illness—that is, in the autumn of 1941—my brother-in-law told me on the occasion of a visit to my room that the Friedenthal matter was getting under way. Accordingly, the first discussion of this matter took place a considerable time before. I further recall now[3] that Dr. Schm. was at one point involved with the matter and that on one of his trips to Switzerland he asked Köchlin, to whom he wished to be introduced through me, for the procurement of an immigration visa for Miss Fr.[4]

406

[1.] *NL*, A 83,2a (middle of page 3); handwritten in pencil, undated; previously published in *LPP*, 61–64. This draft is found on a different page than 1/226 but unmistakably continues where 1/226.1 leaves off ("Op 7").

[2.] With a later dating Roeder wished to prove that Dohnanyi and Bonhoeffer had been sabotaging the deportation policies of the Reich. Therefore, Bonhoeffer had to furnish proof that this date occurred before the beginning of deportations in October 1941 in Berlin; cf. *DB-ER*, 817.

[3.] The following is crossed out: "that I once had a conversation with Dr. Schmidhuber about whether he would be able to request from K[öchlin] an immigration visa for Miss Fr. on the occasion of one of his trips to Switzerland. I am quite unable to reconstruct the place and time of this conversation, as well as whether my brother-in-law took part in it."

[4.] The following is crossed out: "Despite all efforts to reconstruct the details of this event, I nevertheless do not remember whether I or my brother-in-law spoke at that time with Schmidhuber, whether it... [illegible] in Berlin or in Munich.—I remembered a story Schmidhuber told according to which he was once in a camp for Jews in the Pyrenees while on a Military Intelligence mission; perhaps this is... [illegible]—I myself find it incomprehensible that despite the effort to reconstruct the details of this event, I am no longer able to bring the situation to mind, whether either I or... [illegible]—To what extent the request to Schmidh. was already connected to the plans of military headquarters, or whether it merely derives from my having heard that Miss Friedenthal wished to emigrate, I am not able to say with any certainty. In terms of time... [illegible]." On the concentration camp Gurs in the Pyrenees, where Herbert Jehle and Leopold Perels were interned, cf. Bonhoeffer's letter of August 28, 1941, to Eberhard Bethge (see 1/122, ed. note 9).

Despite all my efforts I can no longer piece together how this came about; the situation in which the matter was discussed with Schmidhuber, whether I or my brother-in-law discussed it, whether in Berlin or Munich or perhaps in writing—all this has simply slipped my mind. In my view there are only two possibilities: either this request to Schmidhuber was already connected to the plans of military headquarters—then it can be that not I but my brother-in-law spoke with Schm.; or it dates back to my having been informed that Miss Fr. wished to emigrate to Switzerland to be with relatives and my having thereupon discussed this question with Schm.[5] Only in the latter case it strikes me as very odd that I should have no recollection at all of having spoken personally with Schm. about this. In any case, either possibility must have taken place at around the same time, and I believe I recall that since I have been involved with her case, Miss Fr. had a directive from the Military Intelligence Office to be available for this. My brother-in-law would probably remember; I do not believe that Schm. was already informed at that point about the plans of Military Intelligence, because the entire matter was handled very secretively. Since on my second trip to Switzerland in August '41 I saw Köchlin for the last time[6] and I never spoke with Koechlin about this affair, I actually assume that Schm.'s trip took place after August '41. But it would also be conceivable that by chance in conversation with K. I never got around to talking about this affair. Later I found out in some way from Schm. that K. had made contact with Miss Fr. directly.

In any case, my intuitive recollection of the Fr. case is that it was connected entirely with the planned Military Intelligence action. I will not dispute for a moment that for me inwardly the charitable impulse of the church always played a role in this entire case.[7]

That my memory of the entire Friedenthal case is so imprecise is presumably because negotiations with Miss Fr. by K. as well as by Military Intelligence took place directly, so that in both cases I only served once as a go-between, and this in a matter that otherwise had very little to do with me, since as stated above I hardly knew Miss Fr. In addition, Miss Fr. probably was not considered to be a "Jew" but a "non-Aryan," since she, like Dr. Arnold, did not wear a star.[8]

[5.] The following is crossed out: "and needed a Swiss visa."

[6.] See *DB-ER*, 743. [Bonhoeffer actually met with Koechlin again in May 1942 regarding "Operation 7." Koechlin was the president of the Swiss Protestant Church Federation.—MB]

[7.] Note in the margin: "Gürs [The following is crossed out: "I am not trying to evade the responsibility... [illegible] communication that"]"; cf. ed. note 4.

[8.] The following is crossed out: "this needs to be altered in yesterday's letter." This note is found in the margin: "Also, in the visit to me mentioned in my letter on the tenth,

And now I would like to be allowed to ask you a question myself, honorable Senior Military Prosecutor Roeder, in which I beg you to pardon my complete lack of orientation in legal matters. I simply cannot understand why, e.g., you allow me to persist in an error like that about the timing of my discussion with my brother-in-law, through which, of course, the entire   408
sum of statements becomes imprecise and unclear, when this can serve no one. The accused is thereby only brought into the embarrassing situation of having to make later corrections and thus give the impression of having earlier wished to assert something untrue. I am in fact convinced that you have your reasons for this form of interrogation; at least for someone who has no intention of speaking any untruth, it is very distressing and subsequently oppressive. It may sound like a dumb apology, but you will know from your own experience better than I do that human memory functions in diverse ways and that some people simply require certain external memory aids in order to reconstruct a state of affairs precisely.[9] Without these one forgets everything, and that is a most unpleasant situation.

I regret having caused you trouble with this long letter but hope that now truly everything has been said that I know to say about these things.

To your question about the extent to which my brother-in-law contributed to my trips, I can recall with certainty only the following contributions: 1 x sleeping car surcharge Berlin-Munich, 1 x 2nd-class surcharge express train Munich-Ettal, 1 x trip Schlawe-Berlin winter '39–'40, 1 round-trip Ettal-Munich-Ettal (Gürtner's funeral).

228.2. To Manfred Roeder[10]

Please permit me once again to take some of your time in this way, primarily in order to have truly done everything I can toward the expeditious clarification of my case. I would like to attempt once again to comment on the question that is indeed very important to me of my exemption on   409
account of the Military Intelligence position. Perhaps in the calm of writing I will succeed better in articulating matters more clearly than in the interrogation, where I sometimes forget to say important things. Also I would like to append a few other points on this matter that have not been discussed so

---

Miss Fr. was not wearing a star, just like Dr. Arnold, so that she was not to be considered a Jew but as a non-Aryan." In contrast, cf. the portrayal in *DB-ER*, 749.

[9.] The following is crossed out: "In regard to the fundamental principles significant to me, I can rely very well on my memory; particular details, however, easily escape me."

[10.] *NL*, A 83,2a; handwritten in pencil, undated (on the chronological sequence, see ed. note 12, regarding Hans Oster); previously published in *LPP*, pp. 56–60. The interrogations preceding this letter appear to have been concerned with the circumstances of Bonhoeffer's exemption from military service by Military Intelligence.

far. Before I do this, I would like to tell you that I am grateful to you for laying the situation out for me so openly in the last interrogation.[11] The episode with the statement of General Oster's must, of course, have truly cast me for a while in quite a dreadful light in your eyes, and I am glad that has now been resolved.[12] Perhaps there are other similar matters unknown to me that still impede the clarification of the events surrounding my exemption[13] and thus incriminate me. I am the last person who would want to dispute that I might have made mistakes in an enterprise as foreign and new to me and in itself already so complex as Military Intelligence service. For this reason, honorable Senior Military Prosecutor, please understand that in light of my profession, but also given my relatives and on a purely personal level, everything depends on clarifying *whether* mistakes were truly made here and, if so, *who* made them.[14]

In your words the suspicion remains that my exemption was brought about in order to extricate me from the Gestapo, which in September '40 imposed on me a ban on speaking and an obligation to report.[15] If I understood you correctly, this is supported by 1. the chronological circumstances, 2. statements I made to Dibelius,[16] and 3. statements by my brother-in-law. I would like to address these in sequence.

First in general: If I had had the suspicion that, following their imposition of the ban on speaking and the obligation to report, the Gestapo wanted to impose further measures against me, and if I had wished to evade these, then of course the best move to accomplish this would have been not exemption at all but induction. But by no means did I have grounds to fear

410

[11.] Crossed out: "I am truly prepared to bear the consequences for any mistakes I have made."

[12.] In the interrogation minutes of April 12, 1942, Hans Oster first asserted that he had never seen the "papers" and also never used "O." as an abbreviation of his name. Only on June 17, 1943, did he revise his assertions and bring them into correspondence with those of Bonhoeffer and Dohnanyi; and in a later interrogation he was finally also prepared to acknowledge that he must have seen the files. With this clarification, the claim that it had to do with feigned materials, or *Spielmaterial,* and "prearranged phraseology," *Sprachregelung,* became more credible; cf. 1/224, ed. note 5. Thus this letter stems from the period following this clarification.

[13.] Crossed out: "in the fall of 1940."

[14.] Crossed out: "and whether I was at fault in them." In addition the following is crossed out: "That following the ban on speaking imposed on me in September 1940, the rationale for which I was privately never able to accept, I attempted to petition to have it lifted, and that I asked my brother-in-law to be of assistance to me in preparing this petition."

[15.] [Wherever Bonhoeffer was residing, he was ordered to report his movements to the State Police on a regular basis (*DB-ER* 698).—MB]

[16.] The extent to which Otto Dibelius was involved in the investigations can no longer be ascertained.

further Gestapo measures, *first*, because the measures already imposed appeared to me to be more in the wake of a more strongly preventative stance on the part of the Gestapo toward the entire Confessing Church—at almost the exact same time in very different places in the Old Prussian Union Church around six bans on speaking were issued with exactly the same rationale—than that I was able to understand them directed against me personally—not one "subversive" sermon or comment from a lecture was ever held against me by the Gestapo; *second,* in order to avoid all further grounds for dispute, I had withdrawn to the Bavarian Alps to work on an extensive scholarly project and as required had reported this to the State Police and in this case truly had nothing at all more to fear. Since it was conveyed to me through the church that people were interested in my appending to my book *Discipleship* the explication of a "concrete Protestant ethic,"[17] and since I have always worked primarily as an academic theologian, I was able to be content with my work at that time with regard to the church as well. Of course, I experienced the ban on preaching and lecturing as quite severe, but once my petition was denied I was not able to count on the ban being lifted anytime soon, which indeed has not occurred even to the present day. Thus from that time on my church activity remained confined to the aforementioned scholarly work, and I have remained strictly in compliance with my ban on speaking. I resolved at that time to move my entire library to Munich in order to live there full-time, but because of the lack of clarity about the length of the war and the timing of my induction, I kept delaying the extremely expensive and difficult implementation of this decision. Despite considerable inner reservations, I seized the possibility, opened to me by my brother-in-law, of entering into Military Intelligence service and utilizing my church connections, because it promised me the engagement in the war effort I had sought since the beginning of the war and in fact in my role as a theologian. I have asserted repeatedly that mobilization as a military chaplain,[18] which in the meantime has turned out to be impossible, would have been much preferable to me.[19] I am of the opinion, gained in the years of my activity in German congregations abroad, that for very many people the church is the final and most solid

411

[17.] On this, cf. *DBW* 6:7–8. [Cf. also *DBWE* 6.99–102.—MB]

[18.] Cf. Bonhoeffer's application of September 9, 1939 (*DBW* 15:262–63; *NL*, Anh. A 26).

[19.] Crossed out: "If you were to ask me why I wanted to be engaged precisely as a theologian . . . [illegible] As unpleasant as it is to point to one's own merits, I would nevertheless ask you in your assessment not to overlook what an enormous sacrifice of my work for the church was entailed for me [this replaces: "included for me"] in the relinquishment of all my ecumenical connections for military purposes."

support of German identity and that for this reason even in war the church has a very decisive task to fulfill in the field and at home.

Concerning 1: Now, the fact that my exemption for Military Intelligence took place several months following the ban on speaking meant for me personally—I do not dispute this—a great inner relief inasmuch as I saw in it the welcome opportunity to rehabilitate myself in the eyes of the state authorities, which meant a great deal to me in light of the injurious and in my view completely unjustified accusation that had been leveled against me. The awareness of being needed for a military post was therefore of great significance to me personally. I paid a great price for this possibility of rehabilitation and for my activity in the service of the Reich, namely, the sacrifice of all my ecumenical connections for military purposes. I can well believe that this idea of rehabilitation also played a certain role with my brother-in-law, who knows me well enough personally to realize that, given my whole inner attitude, the political reproach did not apply to me and to realize how I suffered under it. At the same time, as he recently stated, our good personal relationship was conducted very intentionally with the understanding that official and personal matters had to remain completely separate; at times this became pedantic.

I was and am not aware that, as you stated, my age group was called up in the fall of 1940 in Schlawe;[20] presumably it occurred following my stay there in September '40. I consider it quite improbable that my brother-in-law and General Oster might have known of it. But it also surprises me insofar as I know that a colleague my age from the Schlawe district, who was a sergeant and was classified KV,[21] was active in his congregation until well into '41; however, that may be because the head of the recruiting station there[22] had considerable understanding for the task of the church at home during the war and deferred this colleague awhile at the request of the superintendent.[23] Perhaps I may add that if for me it had merely been an issue of exemption for church work, this could surely have taken place in Schlawe at that time at the superintendent's request. But in January '41 I was given an exemption not in fact for church work but explicitly for service in Military Intelligence; and if external technical obstacles had not kept arising at the last minute, I would have indeed been almost without interruption on Military Intelligence trips and would scarcely have been able

---

[20.] Cf. the statements in the indictment against Bonhoeffer (see 1/230.2, p. 437), according to which he was summoned to the mustering in Schlawe on June 5, 1940, and was classified KV, that is, *kriegsverwendungsfähig,* "fit for wartime service." [Regarding the KV classification, see 1/9, ed. note 1.—MB]

[21.] [See ed. note 20.—MB]

[22.] Colonel Dieter von Kleist; cf. *DB-ER,* 634–35.

[23.] Friedrich Onnasch.

to touch my scholarly-ecclesial work anymore. I personally was, of course, unable in any way to imagine that there could be any possible objection to my exemption for Military Intelligence, since, as was explicitly attested to me, Admiral Canaris himself had desired and ordered this. To my occasional question whether difficulties might not arise for either Military Intelligence or for me because of my state police record, I was told[24] these things did not mean anything for military duty and, in addition, Military Intelligence works with all sorts of people who are useful to it. So I felt quite reassured.[25]

Concerning 2: As my entire family and colleagues can themselves attest, it was always difficult for me to report on my present activities when encountering these very colleagues, whom I largely avoided in all these past years for this reason. To the extent they, e.g., General Superintendent Dibelius, Superintendent Diestel, knew of my connections to my brother-in-law and questioned me, I always said to them— having arranged this with my brother-in-law—that I was acting by order of the OKW[26] in Munich and abroad and that this concerned church assignments, that the OKW is interested in ecumenical questions of the church.

Neither could Dibelius have *known*, but only could have deduced, that I was serving in Military Intelligence; quite intentionally I never told him. Toward him I always had to sustain the fiction that my activity was primarily on behalf of the church; apart from the absolute maintenance of secrecy, this was also the case for other pastors, among whom this sort of thing could have leaked out and could have harmed me personally. For this reason it was important to me that my exemption was interpreted this way in church circles. I simply had to tolerate that this meant a rather odd light was cast on me as well as on the military office in question. This is the reason Dibelius will surely have testified along those lines.

Concerning 3: Naturally I do not know what sorts of statements my brother-in-law made to third parties. But I do know, e.g., that he in no way wanted Schm[idhuber]. to find anything out about the military assignments I received directly from the admiral; he did not think much of Schm.'s

413

414

[24.] Crossed out: "we work with enemies, communists, Jews, why not with the Confessing Church."

[25.] There is an additional marginal notation at this point: "[crossed out: that the military commission meant for me a greater freedom of movement, namely, the possibility of trips abroad"] inquiries Military Intelligence occasionally etc.—Bethel trip.—proposals Canaris repeatedly asserted interest.—Position papers!—" Regarding the trip to Bethel, which is later mentioned in the indictment (see 1/230.2, p. 441), but for which there is no evidence in Bonhoeffer's correspondence, it may well be connected with the fact noted by Heinz Höhne (*Canaris,* 171) that a mentally handicapped daughter of Admiral Canaris was housed in one of the Bethel institutions (the reference was supplied by Peter Möser). The sort of position paper being referred to here is unclear.

[26.] [Oberkommando der Wehrmacht, "Armed Forces High Command."—MB]

discretion.[27] This extended to the point that his first reaction to the news that my name had become suspect in church circles in Switzerland[28] ran along the lines that Schm. had probably been indiscreet. Thus I consider it quite possible that Doh. did not tip his full hand to Schm. I myself certainly expressed my pleasure many times at the opportunities being given to me to cultivate my ecumenical connections. In the end it is no different than when, e.g., a student or a chemist is sent abroad and can work there in areas of personal interest and at the same time has certain assignments to fulfill.[29]

228.3. To Manfred Roeder[30]

And now finally one more word about my stays in Berlin. I had to be in Berlin repeatedly for the following official reasons:
    1. Before and after every trip.
    2. To prepare for certain trips that in part claimed more time (see below).
    3. Was explicitly told that I should make myself available to Admiral C[anaris] for special assignments, so I was asked numerous times for addresses, recommendations, and advice.

    As to particular details, let me add: The preparation for the planned Scandinavian trip in June '41 kept me in Berlin the entire period of April–July '41 because of discussions with the Swedish embassy chaplain, trips to the embassy, and addresses and suggestions I had to procure from[31] Protestant clergy. Immediately after these travel plans fell apart, I had to apply in Munich for my second visa to Switzerland, to which I departed in August. After my return the further trip to Paris and Spain was planned—I forgot to mention this recently—which became untenable because of the prolonged illness I contracted in Berlin. I was not ready to travel again until mid-January, early February '42. From March until July '42, with only short interruptions, I was on official trips that had to be prepared in Berlin as well. For the fall this travel activity was planned to resume to the Balkans and Switzerland. That fell apart when Schmidhuber disappeared.[32] Thus

415

[27.] [This distrust was justified. The information Schmidhuber gave his interrogators implicated Bonhoeffer, Dohnanyi, Müller, and Oster. See Meyer, *Unternehmen Sieben*, 375 and elsewhere.—MB]

[28.] Cf. Charlotte von Kirschbaum's letter to Bonhoeffer on May 17, 1942, 1/162.

[29.] Marginal notation: "exemption 39/40—Jan[uary] 4, 41—in Mil[itary] Int[elligence]. assign[ment]., I."

[30.] *NL*, A 83,2a (beginning at the top of page 14, marked with III); handwritten in ink, undated; previously published in *LPP*, 66–67. This draft is connected both chronologically and in terms of content with the previous one.

[31.] Crossed out: "Dibelius, Diestel."

[32.] Cf. *DB-ER*, 818; Schmidhuber was arrested at the end of October 1942.

at my brother-in-law's request I remained in Berlin until the situation had been clarified, since in Munich I would have had to sit around uselessly. At that time the situation was so unclear that every day I reckoned with being sent back to Munich and on trips. I myself repeatedly pressed to be able to travel again since this military inactivity became too extended for me. That nothing came of this had in no way to do with me. My stay in Berlin was always known to the military office responsible for me as well as to those involved with my residence in Munich. I was reachable within the hour, and for all practical purposes was always reached immediately even in urgent cases, both through urgent phoning by my landlady in Munich[33] as well as through the Berlin Military Intelligence Office.

My parents could testify how uneasy I felt in this situation of permanent uncertainty about my travel plans. Thus for my part there was not a single week since January '43 in which I was not told that in the next week I would   416 have to go to Munich and then travel, which was then called off again shortly thereafter; I was kept almost constantly on alert without knowing how long this situation would last.

I have previously mentioned the personal reasons for which I was glad to stay in Berlin, namely, my books, which I needed for my work, and my elderly parents, whom I did not like to leave alone unnecessarily, particularly in light of the alarms.

228.4. To Manfred Roeder[34]

Finally, just a couple of personal words on the case:[35]

For you there can certainly be nothing conclusive (but perhaps you will believe it of me personally, and in this hope I will express it) about the fact that it is very painful for me to see how my early conflicts with the Gestapo, which, I am deeply convinced, arose from conduct strictly confined to church affairs, have now led to my being considered capable of so serious a crime against the obvious duty of a German toward one's people [Volk] and Reich. I also can still not believe that this accusation has actually been made against me. If this were my attitude, would I then have found my bride, who herself has lost father and brother at the front, from within a

---

[33.] This refers to his aunt Countess Christine von Kalckreuth.

[34.] *NL,* A 83,2a (beginning at the top of page 16, marked with IV); handwritten in ink, undated; previously published in *LPP,* 60–61.

[35.] Crossed out: "1. if I had had the intention of evading military service, I would not have returned to Germany [insertion: 'where I had to reckon with immediate induction'] precisely because of the imminent outbreak of war, thereby breaking all the commitments I had made in America."

long-standing family of officers, all of whose fathers and sons have served in
the field as officers since the beginning of the war, many serving with the
highest decorations and making the ultimate blood sacrifice? Would I then,
immediately before the outbreak of the war, severing all the commitments I
had made in America, have returned to Germany, where, of course, I had
to reckon with my immediate induction? Would I then, immediately following the outbreak of the war, have volunteered as a military chaplain?
Anyone who wishes to become acquainted with my conception of the Chris-
417   tian obligation of duty toward the governing authorities should read my
exegesis of Romans 13 in my book *Discipleship*. The appeal to submit oneself
to the will and the demands of the governing authorities for the sake of
Christian conscience has probably seldom been expressed more strongly
than there. This is my personal conviction on these questions! I cannot judge
the extent to which such personal arguments have any legal significance,
but I also cannot imagine that one can simply ignore them?[36]

228.5. To Manfred Roeder[37]

Dear Senior Military Prosecutor Roeder:[38]

I am truly sorry to trouble you repeatedly in this way, but I dare not neglect
to tell you something that seems important to me, and so I beg you sincerely to excuse this claim on your time as well. Yesterday when you read to
me from my long-forgotten letter to my brother-in-law,[39] I myself was initially profoundly shocked by the word "threat" in connection with Niesel's
being drafted and did not understand how I could have arrived at this sort
of expression; and I must confess that this language, in and of itself, does
truly make a very unpleasant impression. On the other hand, I would like
to be allowed to state:[40]

[36.] Note on the page: "Schlawe induction autumn 1940? Why then not to me?
Exempted earlier? Thus not because of State Police [*Stapo*]."

[37.] *NL,* A 83,2a (page 10, upper half); handwritten in pencil, undated; previously
published in *LPP,* 64–66. A duplicate (omitted here) of the first portion of this letter (*NL,*
A 83,2a, page 13; handwritten with pencil and ink, undated) is on the rough draft of the
letter to his parents of June 24, 1943 (Thursday). Therefore, this letter was apparently
written following that date.

[38.] In the manuscript, the German salutation ("Sehr verehrter Herr Oberkriegs-
gerichtsrat") is abbreviated: "S. v. H. O.!"

[39.] See 1/150 and 1/230.2, pp. 442–43.

[40.] Crossed out: "that according to the sense of my brief note this 'threat' refers to
Niesel's absence 'threatening' the church with a considerable loss, and that this was . . .
[illegible] also merely a pointed, condensed reference to this. That in a comparable case
I . . . [illegible] to my brother-in-law, that a pastor might survive for service on behalf of
the church had its explanation in that I, due to."

1. If a man like Niesel[41] had politically recognized church authorities 418
over him, they would definitely have declared him exempt for purely ecclesiastical reasons.[42]

2. During a war, only a church inwardly strong in faith can fulfill its
difficult service to the homeland, which consists[43] in the summons to an
unswerving trust in God, to the inner power of resistance, to perseverance,
to steadfast confidence, and in personal pastoral care to those Germans
fighting in the homeland. In that case, however, the church needs some of
its powerful forces at home as well. It was intended as a service to the German people at war when—within the framework of given possibilities—I
advocated for a strong church. I believe that in this war, too, the German
people still long to a great extent for the service of the church, and I am
horrified and ashamed to see how inadequately and feebly we by and large
are equipped and how thereby the spiritual strength of our people is lost,
strength that the people so need in order to survive.[44]

No matter what one may think of the Confessing Church, the one thing
it cannot be accused of, without a complete misunderstanding, is that at
times "induction" is seen in it as something "threatening." The hundreds of
voluntary enlistments by young Confessing clergy and the enormous
sacrifices in their ranks surely speak clearly enough against this view. In
addition, I have spoken to scarcely a single Confessing Church pastor who
did not enthusiastically seize his induction as an inner liberation from the
onerous pressure of the political suspicion that weighs on the Confessing 419
Church and as a long sought opportunity to demonstrate his inner orientation and willingness for sacrifice now as a soldier, and Pastor Niemöller's
volunteering for military service at the very beginning of the war has not
failed to have an effect in the Confessing Church.[45] I may be permitted to

---

[41.] Pastor Wilhelm Niesel was at that time the pastoral training supervisor for the
Old Prussian Union Council of Brethren. [The directors of the five Confessing preachers'
seminaries, including Bonhoeffer in Finkenwalde, reported to Niesel.—MB]

[42.] Crossed out: "particularly since he was only GV [*garnisonsverwendungsfähig*, "fit
for limited duty"—MB] or AV [*arbeitsverwendungsfähig*, "fit for work"—MB], 2. during a
war a church [can] by no means fulfill its enormous task at home with older clergy alone."

[43.] Uncertain reading.

[44.] Crossed out: "Because I suffer under this failure of the church, I believe I must
serve it and thereby the German people in my sphere." On a new page the following
insertion appears: "Perels, Niesel, Jannasch, Wolf"; crossed out: "On the other hand, I
would like nevertheless to be allowed to say that the sense of what was meant was that
Niesel's induction 'threatened' the church with a considerable loss; thus the expression
'threatened with induction' is in fact only shorthand (clumsy, to be sure, but in a brief letter scarcely misleading) for 'his induction threatens to introduce great difficulties.'"

[45.] [Although imprisoned in the Sachsenhausen concentration camp, Martin
Niemöller attempted to volunteer for military service in 1939. In a 1981 interview, he

say all this as one who knows and is connected with the young generation of Confessing pastors as few other clergy are. Precisely because this is irrefutably the case and because we can have a very clear conscience about it, I believed it permissible and necessary in an urgent individual case—such as Niesel's— to advocate with a clear conscience that a pastor be spared for church service and the homeland, assuming that this could be justified from a military perspective, which I was not able to judge and for which reason I approached my brother-in-law. Two things guided me here:

I know that even religious persons can judge the church very differently, but especially in wartime no one dare desire to deny that the motive for another's conviction and action is love of the German people and the wish to serve them during the war as much as possible.[46]

Since the beginning of the war, in several long conversations with Reich Minister Gürtner,[47] whom I knew personally, I advocated for a settlement of the Church Struggle and cooperative work of the different forces within the Protestant church; along these lines I submitted proposals to Reich Minister Gürtner, which he discussed with Reich Church Minister Kerrl and which evoked interest and approval from the latter. In December '40 Dr. Gürtner explicitly told me on a walk of several hours in Ettal that he hoped to reach this goal and how he hoped to do so. His death a month later and the illness and death of Reich Minister Kerrl shattered this hope. It was an attempt to establish peace within the church during the war in order to release the most powerful forces for engagement in the war. For me even this failed attempt means that I may have the awareness of having done everything in my power for the smoothest and strongest possible engagement of the church in the war.[48]

Although this appears to relate only remotely to the subject, I very much wanted, however, to have said [it], simply so that you, honorable Senior Military Prosecutor, can evaluate my personal orientation to these questions.

420

---

stated that he was motivated by his patriotism, despite his antipathy to Nazism, as well as by the fact that two of his sons had been drafted. See Barnett, *For the Soul of the People,* 156–59.—MB]

[46.] Crossed out: "consists of helping with the test laid upon it. In addition, I assume that the letter to my brother-in-law was not written until around spring '42 or summer '42, since the Stettin students had in the meantime become soldiers following several months of detention in Stettin, and Niesel had presumably been in Breslau for some time, where he can have arrived only in January or February 1942 since, as I now believe I recall clearly, he was involved in the trial of the examination committee in December 1941."

[47.] See *DB-ER,* 690–91; cf. also, among other things, Bonhoeffer's letter to his parents on December 22, 1940, 1/51.

[48.] Crossed out: "in order to make the church strong for the engagement assigned to it in the war and simply to clear away any reservations about this."

228.6 To Manfred Roeder[49]

Dear Senior Military Prosecutor Roeder:

You have allowed me to write you once again, and I wish to do so today once more for the last time before the trial. In the three days that have passed since you notified me that I have been charged with something, I have attempted, on your advice, to think through the entire complex of questions very calmly once more. I do not wish to bother you with personal matters; I do not need to tell you what even the fact of an indictment for subversion of the war effort means for me professionally and personally and for my family; you know my professional and personal relationships   421 well enough for this. If the law requires an indictment, then it must be issued; I understand this. That I did not expect it may be attributable to my deficient knowledge of the text of the law as well as to the fact that I have felt—and, following renewed consideration of what you told me on Friday,[50] still continue to feel—innocent of the charge of subversion of the war effort.

The results of my reflections are, briefly, the following: my UK classification[51] for service in Military Intelligence is similar in nature to an induction into Military Intelligence. I would not, of course, have been able to take the intended Military Intelligence trips if I had served in Military Intelligence as an inductee; for in that case the camouflage absolutely necessary for my trips would have been lacking. In my view, however, those who considered my connections abroad so numerous and significant that they claimed me for this service bear exclusive responsibility that I fulfilled my military service with Military Intelligence and not with the armed forces in the first place; that is to say, Admiral Canaris must actually be the one to determine this, since he himself commanded my employment by Military Intelligence. As a matter of fact, my own personal conviction is that I was able to render the Reich greater service through the utilization of my connections abroad than in any other arena. You know, of course, honorable Senior Military Prosecutor, that I do not fully grasp the legal issues; but

[49.] *NL,* A 83,2a (pages 17–18); handwritten in ink; previously published in *LPP,* 67–69. According to a communication of Bonhoeffer to his parents on July 30, 1943 (*LPP,* 80 [*DBW* 8:120–21]), his final interrogation in the Reich War Court took place the same day; accordingly, this draft was written on August 2/3, 1943. The corresponding communication was made to Hans von Dohnanyi only on August 9, 1943, with Dr. Roeder's statement "that whereas my brother-in-law had 'recognized' that he was unable to contest the content of the files, this was still not yet the case with me" (BA Berlin-Lichterfelde, Nachlaß Dohnanyi 13 I; letter to Roeder of August 29, 1943).

[50.] This probably refers to Friday, July 25, 1943.

[51.] [Regarding the UK classification, see 1/31, ed. note 31.—MB]

nevertheless I cannot suppress the question whether there is not a policy according to which a person is to be engaged during a war in those places where he can accomplish the most for the Reich—a chemist is also allowed to stay in the laboratory if he commands special knowledge that others do not have. However that may now be, in any case these are the reasons for which—without the slightest doubt in the legitimacy [Rechtmäßigkeit] of my action—I worked for Military Intelligence. And I must assign the responsibility for this to those who gave my orders.[52]

422   Now, as for the letter to my brother-in-law concerning Niesel,[53] Wolf,[54] and Jannasch,[55] I understand at the very least that it can have a disconcerting effect if it is read apart from the personal relationship I had with my brother-in-law. For me this letter belongs to those numerous, purely personal conversations in which for many years I have told my brother-in-law about church matters and difficulties and occasionally asked him for advice. The letter was an instance of requesting personal advice as to whether there could be any help in these or those difficulties. In the case of Jannasch I recall even telling the father explicitly, when he came to me very upset, having lost his other son very recently, that I did not think anything could be done. Was it then truly forbidden for me to ask my brother-in-law personally once more about this? A quickly written personal letter, that is the context in which the phrase "threatened with induction . . ." is to be understood, a phrase certainly misleading and offensive to outsiders. My brother-in-law surely did not misunderstand it; one need only ask him how he construed the phrase; [. . .][56] was the difficulty "threatening" the church. To advocate for church matters with my brother-in-law would never have seemed inappropriate to me, especially since he was solely responsible for handling all the military possibilities; and in dealing with him it would never have occurred to me to harass him or expect something of him that he considered irresponsible. My brother-in-law will confirm for you at any point that these things had to do exclusively with communications and questions and that I never pressed him to do anything. For ultimately I always kept in mind the significance of the church for the war effort at home and thus felt justified in presenting these things to my brother-in-law in the first

---

[52.] On this previously agreed-on "strategy of pushing all responsibility for details onto those who gave the orders in the Military Intelligence Office, namely, Canaris, Oster, and Dohnanyi," see *DB-ER*, 812.

[53.] Cf. the draft letter 1/228.5.

[54.] Cf. Bonhoeffer's letter to Ernst Wolf on March 3, 1942, 1/148, ed. note 3.

[55.] Hans Peter Jannasch; see Bonhoeffer's letter to Wilhelm Jannasch on November 23, 1941, 1/138.

[56.] Illegible.

place, and my brother-in-law knew this and understood it well. But I do not wish to evade the responsibility that even in wartime I still was an advocate   423 for the church where that seemed right to me in general and in the interest of the church; and I believe confidently that even before the law I can answer and account for what I did. Perhaps you believe me that I have too much respect for the law to have wished to see it trivialized or twisted for the sake of my own person. I believe that, at least in this fundamental orientation, both accuser and accused are at one in my case.

May I finally add to this something that actually goes without saying, that if in fact my activity for Military Intelligence is no longer regarded as important I will immediately make myself available for another form of service. But I am not the one to decide about this.

229. Indictment Files against Hans von Dohnanyi and Hans Oster[1]

229.1. Indictment by the Reich War Court

Berlin-Charlottenburg 5, September 16, 1943

Indictment.

[...] The defendants, acting in concert in two independent offenses in Berlin and in other places,

I. both defendants as coprincipals:

    a) in 1939–40,

    b) in 1942–43,

are reasonably suspected of having undertaken to keep another person entirely or   424 partially from the fulfillment of military service, partly through means calculated toward deception, partly in other ways.

[...]

Regarding I a):

The defendants arranged for Pastor Dietrich *Bonhoeffer* in fall of 1939 and spring of 1940 to communicate untruthfully to the Armed Forces District Command in Schlawe that Bonhoeffer, who belonged to the 1906 cohort and was classified KV[2] and thus at all times had to reckon with his induction, was working on behalf of an

---

[1.] Niedersächsisches Hauptstaatsarchiv, Hanover, Nds 721, Lüneburg, Acc. 69/76; hectograph; published in Chowaniec, *Der "Fall Dohnanyi,"* 166–93. Letterhead and file reference read: "Reich War Court Criminal Trial Docket (Reich War Court Prosecutor) III 114/43"; note: "33 copies"; stamp: "Top-Secret Military Document." See Dohnanyi's memorandum of October 19, 1943: "Today—October 19—the indictment was disclosed to me by Senior War Court Counsel Hofmeister. Since it is a top-secret military document, it can be handed over only by means of special application. I submitted such an application according to protocol" (BA Berlin-Lichterfelde, Nachlaß Dohnanyi 13 I/16,1).

[2.] [Regarding the KV (*kriegsverwendungsfähig*) classification, see 1/9, ed. note 1.—MB]

office of the military, whereas in fact he was conducting a domestic intelligence service for the defendants in the area of church politics, which lay outside the officially assigned field of duties of the Foreign Office/Military Intelligence. In addition, they sought Bonhoeffer's eventual UK[3] classification in violation of HDv[4] 3/14 of November 11, 1940, which is to be regarded as binding in official matters.

[...]

The President of the Reich War Court   The Senior Reich Military Prosecutor
as Presiding Judge
    Bastian   Kraell
    Admiral

229.2. Indictment by the Senior Reich Military Prosecutor[5]

[...]

Deeds of the Accused.

I. a) UK classification of Pastor Dietrich *Bonhoeffer* in 1939–40.

Office responsible for UK classifications within the Foreign Office/Military Intelligence is the ZO[6] Department. Official in charge is Lieutenant Colonel *Greßler.*

Pursuant to HDv D 3/14 of November 11, 1940, this regulation applies to the OKW[7] and its departments. Pursuant to number 16, it is impermissible for departments of the armed forces to submit UK applications for those obligated to military service who are not among their personnel.

Pursuant to § 4 of D 3/14 2 c, UK classification in special cases occurs only through the OKW (AHA/AG/E).[8]

425   The UK applications are to be submitted by the department making application [Bedarfsstellen], subject to the regulations of the military district headquarters responsible for the place of permanent residence of the applicant. § 11 of HDv refers explicitly to the penal liability of offenses against UK regulations. Major General Oster, the immediate superior of defendant Bonhoeffer, testifies that he was introduced to the latter by Dohnanyi at the home of Ministry Counsel *Schleicher,* that Bonhoeffer was recruited into Military Intelligence in 1940 because he claimed to have had good connections to the ecumenical circles in Switzerland and Sweden. Oster says that as far

---

[3.] [Regarding the UK *(unabkömmlich)* classification, see 1/31, ed. note 3.—MB]

[4.] [*Heeresdienstvorschrift,* "army regulation."—MB]

[5.] Unabridged version found in Chowaniec, *Der "Fall Dohnanyi,"* 168–93; the excerpt reproduced here appears on pages 169–75.

[6.] [Abbreviation for Group O of the Central *(zentrale)* Department in the Foreign Office/Military Intelligence.—MB]

[7.] [Oberkommando der Wehrmacht, "Armed Forces High Command."—MB]

[8.] [Allgemeines Heeresamt/Abwehrgruppe/E, the "General Army Office/Military Intelligence Group/E."—MB]

as he knew Bonhoeffer's UK classification took place through the AHA of the OKW and proceeded through Z.[9] He says that he was aware only that Bonhoeffer had been banned from speaking for a time, and that further state police injunctions against Bonhoeffer were unknown to him.

Major General Oster explained further that Bonhoeffer's activity for Military Intelligence first began with the letter sent by Bonhoeffer on November 11, 1940,[10] to defendant v. Dohnanyi. He said that he himself made a note on the letter: "read by O., November 22, 1940"; and he added: "arrange for the rest with Schmidhuber, Munich AST."[11] These statements by Major General Oster were initially confirmed by v. Dohnanyi to the extent that his brother-in-law first became active for Military Intelligence on the basis of this letter.

In contrast, Bonhoeffer testifies that this presentation of the matter is incorrect. He asserts that he was active already since the end of 1939 in procuring domestic intelligence from the circles of the Confessing Church for v. Dohnanyi and Oster, that in the course of these assignments he undertook various trips, including ones to Cologne, Bethel, Saxony, and Pomerania. He says v. Dohnanyi gave him subsidies for these trips and that he does not know whether these derived from official sources or from Dohnanyi's own pocket. Once presented with this statement, Major General Oster then admitted that Bonhoeffer was enlisted for domestic intelligence gathering in 1939–40; Major General Oster and Special Officer v. Dohnanyi[12] must both have been aware that a UK classification was not to be granted for this intelligence gathering, which lay completely outside the assigned scope of the Foreign Office of Military Intelligence.

On May 27, 1940, when he had already received his medical examination notice from military district headquarters at Schlawe, Bonhoeffer wrote the following to the Schlawe WBK:[13] "Since I will presumably still need to remain a few days in Berlin, I am requesting, following consultation with my military section here, that my service record [Wehrpass] be sent to the chief of staff of the Foreign Office of Military Intelligence, Z OKW[14] Berlin W 35, Tirpitzufer 80."[15]

In his second interrogation on this matter on June 17, 1943, Major General Oster no longer denied that he gave Bonhoeffer instructions to write along these lines.

426

[9.] [Abbreviation for the Zentral, the Central Department in the Foreign Office of Military Intelligence.—MB]

[10.] The date of Bonhoeffer's camouflage letter, or *Tarnbrief,* to Hans von Dohnanyi is November 4, 1940; see 1/221.

[11.] Cf. 1/221, ed. note 1. ["AST" is the abbreviation for Abwehrstelle, "Military Intelligence Office."—MB]

[12.] [Special officers, or *Sonderführer,* were professionals (doctors, lawyers, meteorologists, etc.) who received the rank of officer when they joined the military and did special assignments.—MB]

[13.] [Wehrbezirkskommando, "Military District Headquarters."—MB]

[14.] [Central Department of the Armed Forces High Command.—MB]

[15.] Cf. 1/9.

Major General Oster's statement that, in view of Bonhoeffer's ecumenical connections and later use in Military Intelligence, he wanted at that time to safeguard Bonhoeffer is completely unbelievable since, according to Bonhoeffer's own portrayal of the situation, as well as that of defendant v. Dohnanyi, this matter was first discussed only in September 1940 and Bonhoeffer's letter of November 11, 1940, to defendant von Dohnanyi was composed only on the basis of this consultation.

At that point, defendant v. Dohnanyi wrote to Major Schmidhuber on November 26, 1940, as follows: "In reference to our telephone conversation the day before yesterday, I am transmitting to you the photocopy of a letter addressed to me[16] that has prompted Colonel Oster to direct the Munich AST to classify the writer of these lines UK for Military Intelligence purposes based out of Munich.

"I am also attaching a copy of the command directed to the Munich AST."[17]

On the same date Major General Oster decreed:

"I request that the writer of the enclosed letter, whose name can be procured through Consul Schmidhuber, Am Kosttor 1, Munich, be classified UK by Munich for Military Intelligence purposes, and that the details be discussed with Consul Schmidhuber. Consul Schmidhuber is receiving a copy of this document and is directed to contact Major Hundt forthwith."[18]

Both the defendant and Major General Oster knew at this point that Bonhoeffer was not yet a member of the Foreign Office of Military Intelligence and that this UK classification contradicted the directives of HDv D 3/14, since this sort of instruction was permitted to be issued only by the E Office of the AHA. According to Major General Oster's testimony, defendant von Dohnanyi also gave no indication at all to then Colonel Oster that a short time previously a residence restriction had been imposed on Bonhoeffer by the Gestapo in addition to the ban on speaking. The fact that, in defiance of the directives of HDv D 3/14 § 2, this UK classification was not effected through the military district headquarters responsible for Bonhoeffer's place of permanent residence can be deduced from Bonhoeffer's testimony and the statements of defendant v. Dohnanyi as well as the correspondence with the Schlawe Military District Headquarters and the Munich Military Intelligence Office. Bonhoeffer never had a residence in Munich. In order formally to establish a residence there at all, he registered with the police by giving the address of an aunt, Countess Kalkreuth; before the UK classification and even afterward he stayed there for mere hours at a time. Furthermore, v. Dohnanyi was aware of this; he himself had to characterize it as unusual that an agent of the Munich AST had no residence in Munich but resided in Berlin.

Major Schmidhuber attests that Captain Ickrath[19] expressed the view that Bonhoeffer was recruited into Military Intelligence solely for the purpose of removing

427

[16.] This refers to the "camouflage letter" (see 1/221).

[17.] See 1/222.1; cf. 1/49.

[18.] See 1/222.2.

[19.] [Heinrich Ickradt—MB]

him from the reach of the state police and that defendant v. Dohnanyi had conveyed this to him in conversation as well.

In reference to this, Gisevius, special officer in the Switzerland K.O.,[20] declares the following: In March 1943, on the occasion of Bonhoeffer's departure for Switzerland, he brought to v. Dohnanyi's attention in a friendly manner the question whether Bonhoeffer's UK classification was in any way justifiable. V. Dohnanyi defended it with a reference to Bonhoeffer's successful trip to Sweden.[21]

V. Dohnanyi asserts that at the time of his brother-in-law's recruitment into Military Intelligence there was no reason to mention state police measures against him, since the restriction of residence imposed on Bonhoeffer had already been mitigated to the extent that Bonhoeffer, with state police approval, was now being allowed to stay with his parents;[22] to this extent these measures had no decisive significance.

In contrast to this, Bonhoeffer admits that he spoke extensively with defendant v. Dohnanyi about the ban on speaking as well as the restriction of residence.

If the assertions of defendant v. Dohnanyi are to be believed, then Bonhoeffer must have kept silent about the fact that he was permitted to be in Berlin only for family visits. Given the close relationship between v. Dohnanyi and Bonhoeffer, however, this assumption cannot be sustained, especially since even chronologically the activity of both immediately followed the state police measures.

V. Dohnanyi concedes this only to the extent that he considers it possible that there was conversation about the fact that the mitigation of the state police measures would be a pleasant side effect of Bonhoeffer's enlistment in Munich.

428

Defendant v. Dohnanyi wants to justify his actions, which deviate from the official provisions of HDv D 3/14 and which are also irreconcilable with the official division of responsibilities [Dienstverteilung] in the Foreign Office of Military Intelligence, by initially pushing back the timing of Bonhoeffer's recruitment to the beginning of 1940. He says that at that time he had not yet been instructed in the chain of command and the tasks of the departments with specific responsibilities and was quite new at the formalities.

But this is not accurate. The incident took place in December 1940. At this time defendant v. Dohnanyi had already been in service for more than fifteen months; after examination of the facts already established, his assertion not to have known that the processing of UK classifications was outside his sphere of responsibility can only be regarded as an evasion.

[20.] [*Kriegsorganisation*, "war organization"; this abbreviation designated branch offices of the Foreign Office of Military Intelligence.—MB]

[21.] Dohnanyi made this statement on May 12, 1943 (BA Berlin-Lichterfelde, Nachlaß Dohnanyi 13 II/33,16).

[22.] Karl Bonhoeffer had achieved an easing of the Gestapo restrictions on his son, so that the ban on Dietrich's presence in Berlin applied only to official business and not to family visits.

Defendant v. Dohnanyi admits further that the enlistment of the agent took place without input from Departmental Chief I, who was solely responsible for deciding upon the advisability of an agent's enlistment.

Similarly, an examination of the reliability of agent Bonhoeffer before his recruitment never took place. Given the state police measures, there would have been cause to examine this. On this, Chief of Staff Admiral *Canaris* testified:"V. Dohnanyi gave me no indication that state police measures had been imposed on Bonhoeffer at the time of his involvement with Military Intelligence. I was informed neither of the ban on speaking nor of the restrictions on his place of residence."[23]

To be sure, these measures were in themselves not grounds for impeding this activity, but nevertheless, the chief of staff would have called for talks with state police in order to find a way of handling the situation.

Chief of Staff Admiral Canaris testifies further:"The gathering of intelligence about the domestic situation lay outside the assigned sphere of the Foreign Office of Military Intelligence and had been explicitly forbidden by me."[24] In any case, the intentional direction of agents exclusively engaged in this arena was forbidden.

The chief of staff had no knowledge of any activity of Bonhoeffer in 1939–40 in Military Intelligence in the arena of purely domestic church politics. That the direction of domestic agents was most strictly forbidden could have been in doubt neither to Major General Oster nor to defendant v. Dohnanyi following the unequivocal statement of Admiral Canaris. Major General Oster does not seriously challenge Bonhoeffer's assertion that the latter was active in 1939–40 in the purely domestic realm and was authorized by him (Oster) to insist in May 1940 that the Schlawe recruiting station send Bonhoeffer's service record to Major General Oster. He considers this authorization of Bonhoeffer to have been possible. However, all the defendants, not only Pastor Bonhoeffer but also defendants v. Dohnanyi and Major General Oster, agree that Bonhoeffer did not have *official* assignments with the Foreign Office of Military Intelligence at that time. The final point to note against the defendants is that agent Bonhoeffer did not make the otherwise universally required declaration of secrecy and that, counter to the usual official practices, the reports Bonhoeffer submitted are not found in the agent file. V. Dohnanyi disputes the allegation that he or General Oster gave Bonhoeffer assignments, with the exception of the assignments Bonhoeffer received to undertake official trips to Sweden and Norway on behalf of the chief of staff. On the latter trip, however, whose significance is underscored by the defendants, Bonhoeffer did not submit even a single written report. This report was compiled by Count Moltke. By contrast, files D I of the OKW reveal numerous reports by Bonhoeffer demonstrating that following his UK classification Bonhoeffer continued

429

[23.] See Canaris's statement of June 15, 1943, 1/227.

[24.] [This sentence was part of Canaris's statement on June 15, 1943, but it is not included in the sections of that statement printed in 1/227.—MB]

to be active in gathering domestic intelligence, a sphere that in itself, according to the assigned duties of the Foreign Office of Military Intelligence, lay beyond official activity.

On April 5, 1943, defendant v. Dohnanyi was arrested in his office by the investigative officer of the senior Reich military prosecutor. During the search, he attempted to conceal the contents of a file (Z gray)[25] that the investigative officer had laid among those documents already secured. Observed in this, he was ordered to put the papers back. Next he attempted to draw the attention of Major General Oster, who was also present, to these sheets of paper while the investigative officer was busy searching elsewhere. The two defendants arrived at an understanding with the result that Major General Oster, his face turned toward the investigative officer, extracted these same sheets with his left hand behind his back and slipped them under the hem of his civilian suit. This was observed by the criminal secretary Sonderegger and the investigative officer, who promptly took him to task and forced him to surrender the sheets.

Note no. 3 contains domestic church political intelligence from Pastor Bonhoeffer and the following written presentation, which was prepared by Bonhoeffer in agreement with defendant von Dohnanyi:

"*Copy!* 430

"For quite some time a small circle of leading clergy of the German Protestant Church has been engaged with the question of what contribution the Protestant church might be able to make after this war toward the creation of a just and lasting peace and toward the building up of a social order grounded on Christian foundations. The intention is to set forth a series of programmatic points, to compile an extensive commentary on the issues they discuss, and to put together some explanatory flyers, based on the programmatic tenets and intended for a general audience, that could be made available to the public when the occasion arises. These tasks are already well under way. It is well known that the pope has set forth his peace goals in his last two Christmas messages and that the English and American (not to mention the Dutch, Norwegian, and French) Protestant churches are already working on these same questions very intensively. Because it would be of the utmost significance if at the proper time all Christian churches were to take a *unanimous* position on the questions of the shape of peace, and because—as far as that can be assessed today—agreement on all important points could well be reached, it seems extremely important and desirable that a German Protestant pastor be given the opportunity both to conduct deliberations in this matter with representatives of the Catholic Church in Rome and to become acquainted with the relevant activities of the Protestant world churches in Geneva or Stockholm. sgd. O."[26]

[25.] [The file for the Central Department.—MB]

[26.] See 1/224.3 (note no. 3).

Defendant v. Dohnanyi asserts that these pages represent a "prearranged phraseology" discussed with codefendant Major General Oster for Bonhoeffer's work at the Vatican. He says that it was intended that Major General Oster allow Bonhoeffer to work at the Vatican, and for this reason the page was signed by the Major General with an O.

In contrast, defendant Major General Oster resolutely disputes that he saw the "prearranged phraseology" or the other attached papers and the radio message by the pope; in the same way he states with certainty that he had never had an extended discussion or in fact any discussion with the codefendant v. Dohnanyi about the content of file Z (gray). Codefendant Major General Oster also considers such a conversation impossible because no agents were directed by "Z," and the appointment of a particular agent for reconnaissance lay entirely outside the assigned duties of "Z."

431   Defendant Major General Oster justifies this by stating that the agents reported to Military Intelligence I or III in order to ensure that the I and III chiefs were informed of all relevant intelligence information.

The findings ascertained about Bonhoeffer's enlistment into AST VII cast considerable doubt on the accuracy of this justification on the part of defendant Major General Oster. Defendant Major General Oster asserts with conviction that no discussion took place between him, Müller, and von Dohnanyi about Bonhoeffer's mission to the Vatican. In contrast to defendant von Dohnanyi, defendant Major General Oster declares that the papers in file Z (gray) were not of an official nature.

V. Dohnanyi calls into question the representation of the matter by Major General Oster, who was confronted with all the details of v. Dohnanyi's statements and held fast to his assertions.

The credibility of the defendants is purely conditional, as has also been shown in other points during the course of the investigations.

From the general circumstances and in light of the close family relationship between defendants v. Dohnanyi and Bonhoeffer, it can be assumed that v. Dohnanyi was the more active participant in the measures to remove Bonhoeffer from induction into active military service by enlisting him as an agent, while the codefendant Major General Oster, informed of the basic plan, in part gave von Dohnanyi carte blanche and in part concealed, and occasionally himself even ordered, the measures that violated existing decrees.

At the very least, when they authorized Bonhoeffer to direct his letters of October 1939 and May 1940 to the military district headquarters, the defendants were aware that at times they would be using improper means to keep Bonhoeffer from military service. The training and military rank of both defendants permits no other interpretation of their behavior.

[. . .][27]

[27.] In the catalog of the accompanying files: "III—file D I of the OKW top-secret documents: contains documentation of Bonhoeffer's UK classification"; "IV—file A 1–3

230. Indictment Files against Dietrich Bonhoeffer   432

230.1. Indictment by the Reich War Court[1]

Berlin-Charlottenburg 5, September 21, 1943

Indictment.

This indictment is brought against Pastor Dietrich *Bonhoeffer*, born February 4, 1906, in Breslau, Protestant, single, no previous criminal record, provisionally held since April 5, 1943, in the Berlin-Tegel Military Detention Center.

---

volume 1 and 2 top-secret documents: church reports, etc., of Bonhoeffer's." According to the final report of the criminal proceedings against Manfred Roeder in 1951, these accompanying files were incinerated in the Reich War Court in the air strikes against Berlin on November 26–27, 1943 (Niedersächsisches Hauptstaatsarchiv, Hanover, 721 Lüneburg Acc. 69/76). Höhne writes: "[B]ut Lehmann had recalled him [Roeder] to Berlin at the end of November 1943 because his offices had been damaged in an air raid and the 'Depositenkasse' files destroyed by fire. The judge appointed to reconstruct the interrogation transcripts had invited Roeder to Torgau, the temporary quarters of the Reich War Court [Reichskriegsgericht], at the beginning of January. Roeder had assisted him there for three days before rejoining his air fleet [*Luftflotte*]" (*Canaris*, 536). [*Depositenkasse* was the Gestapo file name for the case against the Operation 7 conspirators and their allies in Military Intelligence. It refers to the Swiss bank account that Military Intelligence had established for 1) money that the conspirators would have readily available in the wake of a successful coup and 2) the cost of visas and living expenses in Switzerland for those rescued by Operation 7. The Gestapo first stumbled onto the Operation 7 plan by tracing the movement of money abroad; they initially thought they had uncovered a money-laundering ring in Military Intelligence, since several hundred thousand marks were involved. Under interrogation, Schmidhuber (the first person they caught as they traced the money) spoke of a *Depositenkasse*, hence the name. See Meyer, *Unternehmen Sieben*, 363–65; and von Klemperer, *German Resistance against Hitler*, 399 n. 39.—MB]

[1.] Vojenský ústřední archiv, Prague, "Reichskriegsgericht," [War Court] file 9: "Sammlung von Anklagen und Urteilen—gKdos 1943" [Collection of Indictments and Judgments—Top Secret Military Documents 1943], VÚA-VHA, RKG (39), 2(I), Geh. Kdos.— rozsudky 1943–45; hectograph; previously published in *IBG-Rundbrief* (International Bonhoeffer Society Newsletter), no. 35 (April 1991): 2–11. According to a February 7, 1991, communication from Dr. Tuchel at the Berlin Gedenkstätte Deutscher Widerstand (Memorial to the German Resistance), her colleague Norbert Haase discovered these documents. Letterhead and file number read: "Reich War Court Criminal Trial Docket III 114/ 43"; stamp: "Red List [handwritten: "30."]"—"Top-Secret Military Document"—"Prison-related." Notes: "28 copies"—"Oct. 20 " The Reich War Court decree had already been issued; it read: "*Notarized Copy*. Torgau, Ziethenkaserne, September 16, 1943. *Decree*. Attorney Dr. Kurt Wergin, Woyrschstraße 8, Berlin W 35, is authorized as counsel for Pastor Dietrich Bonhoeffer, in accordance with § 323, section 4 Military Criminal Ordinance, § 51 War Criminal Ordinance. Signed, the President of the Reich War Court as Supreme Judicial Authority, Admiral Bastian.—Senior Reich Military Prosecutor. Signed on his order by Dr. Lotter, Reich War Attorney. To Mr. Dietrich Bonhoeffer, presently c/o *Berlin-Tegel* Military

He is reasonably suspected in Berlin and in other places because of two separate actions:

a) of having undertaken in 1939–40 to evade for a time the fulfilling of military service through measures based on deceit;

b) of having undertaken in 1942 to keep others from fulfilling military service entirely, partially, or for a time, by other ways and means.

—Crime against § 5 Section 1 No. 3 KSSVO,[2] § 74 RStGB[3] —

433   a) In 1939 and 1940, in three letters to the Schlawe District Military Recruiting Station, the accused wrote that he was a member of a military department, although given the state of affairs and his awareness of all circumstances, he knew precisely that he was not a member of a military department. He did not retract this statement when he was classified in 1940 as KV.[4] From 1939 on, he was forced to reckon with his induction since he belonged to the 1906 cohort and was KV.

b) In March 1942 he attempted through his brother-in-law von Dohnanyi to secure a UK[5] classification for Licentiate Niesel, whose military induction was imminent, although he knew that the supervisors responsible for Niesel could not file a UK petition. At the time he attempted to remove the son of Pastor Jannasch, who was declared fit for limited duty, from a similar obligation to serve.

President of the Reich War Court   Senior Reich Military Prosecutor
as Supreme Judicial Authority
    Bastian   Dr. Kraell
    Admiral

230.2. Indictment by the Senior Reich Military Prosecutor[6]

Berlin-Charlottenburg 5, September 21, 1943

Indictment.

Personal Circumstances of the Accused.

Defendant Pastor Dietrich *Bonhoeffer* was born on February 4, 1906, in Breslau as the son of the Privy Counsel of Medicine Prof. Karl Bonhoeffer. He is single, with no criminal record. After passing his matriculation examination in 1923, he studied theology in Tübingen, Rome, and Berlin.

Detention Center, Seidelstraße 39. Notarized: Ladenig, Army Judicial Inspector." Stamp: "Reich War Court 18." See also Bonhoeffer's will ("In the Case of My Death") of September 20, 1943 (*LPP,* 112–13 [*DBW* 8:163–64]; *NL,* A 82,22).

[2.] Kriegssonderstrafsrechtsverordnung [Special War Criminal Ordinance—MB].

[3.] Reichsstrafgesetzbuch [Reich Criminal Code—MB].

[4.] [Regarding the KV (*kriegsverwendungsfähig*) classification, see 1/9, ed. note 1.—MB]

[5.] [Regarding the UK (*unabkömmlich*) classification, see 1/31, ed. note 3.—MB]

[6.] Letterhead and file number: "Chief Reich War Criminal Trial Docket (Reich War Court Prosecutor) III 114/43."

In 1927 he graduated from the University of Berlin, spent a subsequent year as vicar of the German congregation in Barcelona. After a one-year assistantship at the University of Berlin, the defendant received his postdoctoral degree[7] in 1930. Thereafter he spent one year in New York through the German academic exchange service. After serving in 1931–33 as docent on the Protestant theological faculty, he went to London from 1933 until 1935 to the German Protestant congregation there.

Having returned to Germany, he took over the preachers' seminary of the Con-   434
fessing Church in Finkenwalde. This was shut down by order of the Reich government. Thereafter the defendant served as a pastor in Schlawe, since his authorization to teach had been rescinded because of a trip to Sweden with the preachers' seminary that was taken without permission of the Reich Ministry of Education.

In 1938 the defendant was forbidden by the Gestapo to reside in Berlin because he took part in a gathering of pastors of the Confessing Church (Niemöller-oriented).

In 1939 the defendant spent time from May to August in England and the United States.

In 1940 the defendant held retreats for members of the Confessing Church in Königsberg and in Litkau,[8] the latter even after he was made aware in Königsberg that holding this sort of retreat outside the church was forbidden.

Following this he was banned from speaking by the Berlin Gestapo.

The defendant did not belong to the NSDAP[9] or its organizations. By his account, he joined the NSV[10] in 1940.

The defendant's military service record is as follows:

As a member of the '06 cohort, the defendant did not serve prior to the outbreak of the war; he was registered with the military recruiting station in Schlawe. No transfer of registration took place, even though the defendant had his actual residence in Berlin from 1938 on.

On June 5, 1940, the defendant had his medical examination for military service. The result of the examination revealed that he was KV. According to the Schlawe District Military Recruiting Station, members of this cohort found to be KV faced their induction at any time following the day of mobilization, unless they were classified UK.

On January 23, 1941, the Military Intelligence Office in Military District VII applied for a UK classification for Bonhoeffer, which was granted on February 7, 1941, until further notice. On September 9, 1941, the Munich Military District Headquarters I revoked his UK classification; however, upon request of the Military Intelligence Office,

---

[7.] [The *Habilitation*, which qualified Bonhoeffer to teach at a German university.—MB]

[8.] This should read "Eidkau"; see the calendar notes of July 21, 1940 (1/10).

[9.] [Nationalsozialistische Deutsche Arbeiterpartei, "National Socialist German Workers' Party."—MB]

[10.] Nationalsozialistische Volkswohlfahrt, "National Socialist People's Welfare," an organization to which every household had to contribute; cf. Bonhoeffer's letter of November 29, 1940, to his parents, 1/38.

his UK classification was extended indefinitely on October 30, 1941. Further exten-
sions of the UK classification took place on May 15, 1942. These UK classifications
took place by means of direct correspondence between the Military Intelligence
Office or the Foreign Office of Military Intelligence and the District Headquarters.

435   The defendant was last classified UK on March 31, 1943, at the request of the
office of the OKW/AHA[11] responsible for this sort of UK classification; teletype of
this office of March 27, 1943, 10801/43.

Details of the Offense:

The defendant belongs to the Confessing Church as a pastor. The union of the
Confessing Church is not officially recognized. UK classifications for clergy take place
with the cooperation of the Ministry for Church Affairs only for those clergy who
belong to the orientation within the Protestant Church that is recognized by the
state; the Confessing Church does not belong to this orientation.

The defendant provides the following portrayal of his activity as an agent within
the purview of the Foreign Office:

In August 1939 he returned from the United States because of the imminent
threat of war and voluntarily made himself available to the chief of military chaplains
for service as a pastor. When several months later he received news from the chief of
military chaplains that he could not be used, he reflected on whether he was now
obligated to make himself available for the war effort with his numerous ecumenical
connections. The defendant wrote to his brother-in-law Special Officer Hans von
Dohnanyi, now accused in another case. V. Dohnanyi had been conscripted into the
Central Department of the Foreign Office of Military Intelligence in August 1939
because of his personal connection to General Oster, chief of staff of this office; there
he handled the ZB[12] report. In this letter the defendant delineated his connections
for his brother-in-law in order to bring about his employment as an agent within the
Foreign Office of Military Intelligence. The letter dates from November 11, 1940.[13]
Some time later the defendant learned that his offer had been accepted on the basis
of a consultation by his brother-in-law with chief of staff Admiral Canaris. The defendant states this as having occurred around Christmas 1940.

Prior to compiling his petition for employment with Military Intelligence, the
defendant had many consultations with his brother-in-law v. Dohnanyi, during which
the ban on speaking and restrictions of residence imposed on the defendant were
also thoroughly discussed. These measures were imposed by the Gestapo, and their

---

[11.] [Oberkommando der Wehrmacht/Allgemeines Heeresamt, "Armed Forces
High Command/General Army Office."—MB]

[12.] [ZB stands for Z Büro, or Zentralabteilung, the department of the Office of Military Intelligence that handled foreign policy reports; Dohnanyi was the special officer
assigned to this department. See also below, 1/231, p. 449.—MB]

[13.] Cf. 1/221, ed. note 2.

abrogation was expressly refused in the summer of 1940. These discussions took place in September 1940.

In June 1940, the defendant had his medical examination for military service and was deemed to be KV by the Schlawe District Military Recruiting Station.

436

In these conversations it was also thoroughly discussed that the opportunity should remain open for the defendant to continue to advocate for the aims of the Confessing Church; here he himself took into account that he would be able to pursue his vocation alongside his activity for Military Intelligence.

Regarding the UK classification of the defendant, the chief of staff of the Foreign Office of Military Intelligence—Admiral Canaris—had to say that he found out about this UK classification as a result of the Sweden crisis[14] (May 1942)

General Oster and Special Officer von Dohnanyi reported that the outset of the defendant's activity on behalf of the Foreign Office of Military Intelligence can be found in the letter of November 11, 1940.

In contrast, the defendant wrote (among other things) on October 12, 1939, to the military recruiting station in Schlawe:

"In the meantime, I have been given an assignment by the Armed Forces High Command that I must carry out in Berlin. Colonel Oster (Armed Forces High Command, Tirpitzufer 80) today authorized me to let you know that he is prepared to explain in case of further inquiry. For this reason I will be living for the time being in Berlin with my father."

The defendant thereupon received the order to report to the appropriate military recruiting station in Berlin. This, however, did not occur. On May 24, 1940, the defendant conveyed to the military recruiting station:

"As always, when I am in Berlin on business, I live in my father's home. This time I was required to remain available in Berlin longer than was originally planned."

On May 27, 1940, the defendant wrote:

"Since I will presumably still need to remain a few days in Berlin, I am requesting, following consultation with my military department here, that my service record be sent to the chief of staff for the Foreign Office of Military Intelligence in the OKW. Address: Colonel Oster, Foreign Office of Military Intelligence, OKW, Berlin W 35, Tirpitzufer 80. Schlawe should remain my official military recruiting station."

This letter by the defendant came at the point when he must already have received the summons for his medical examination, which was slated for June 5, 1940.

The official files of the Military Intelligence Office, by contrast, show that the defendant first appeared on the scene on December 11, 1940, and that this is the date of the first official communication of the Foreign Office of Military Intelligence from which an official employment of the defendant can actually be inferred.

[14.] [The indictment incorrectly states *Schwedenkrise.*—MB] It should read *Schwedenreise,* "trip to Sweden."

437   Regarding the beginning of the employment of his brother-in-law, the defendant
Bonhoeffer, v. Dohnanyi made the following statements:

He knew that Department Z, to which he and Colonel Oster belonged, supervised
no agents. To his knowledge, Bonhoeffer's recruitment occurred at the beginning of
1940. The basis for his recruitment into AST[15] VII was Bonhoeffer's letter to him
about his ecumenical connections. Only after being confronted with Bonhoeffer's correspondence to the Schlawe District Military Recruiting Station did v. Dohnanyi admit
that in violation of orders Bonhoeffer was active as an agent in the domestic arena
from 1939 until December 1940, a relationship he describes as very loose.

Furthermore, v. Dohnanyi claims to have known nothing of the alleged trips by his
brother-in-law in 1939–1940; he claims not to remember having contributed any
monies for this purpose.

General Oster testifies on this as follows: Bonhoeffer was brought into Military
Intelligence sometime in 1940, because he claimed to have good connections with
ecumenical circles, particularly in Switzerland and Sweden. Concerning Bonhoeffer as
a person, he heard only that Bonhoeffer had been banned from speaking. Nothing
about a restriction on residence was communicated to him either by v. Dohnanyi or
by the defendant. In his interrogation on May 14, 1943, General Oster asserted with
conviction that official relations between the Foreign Office of Military Intelligence
and the defendant were ruled out prior to November 11, 1940 (the date of Bonhoeffer's
letter).

The UK classifications, even provisional UK classifications, and the establishing of
contact with the Military District Headquarters were not affairs of the Foreign Office
of Military Intelligence but of the E Office of the AHA.[16]

This office first became involved, however, in March 1943 on the occasion of Bonhoeffer's further UK classification.

This statement of General Oster's of May 14, 1943, was retracted by him on June
17, 1943, as inaccurate, and another depiction of the matter was given that similarly
can lay no claim to accuracy.

Admiral Canaris testified that he knew nothing of any activity by Bonhoeffer in the
domestic church-political arena, that the supervision of domestic agents was most
strictly forbidden; both v. Dohnanyi and Oster knew of this. He asserted that he was
never informed of any existing state police measures against Bonhoeffer, which at the
very least would have given him cause to consult with the state police before engaging
Bonhoeffer. Furthermore, he said that he was informed of Bonhoeffer's activity only in
1942, on the occasion of the trip to Sweden.

438   In opposition to otherwise standard official practices, the Chief of Military Intelligence I was *not* involved in Bonhoeffer's recruitment.

[15.] [Abbreviation for Abwehrstelle, "Military Intelligence Office."—MB]

[16.] [The E Office was a different subdivision of the Office of Military Intelligence
within the General Army Office. See 1/229.2, ed. note 11.—MB]

When confronted with these statements and pressed for explanation as to why under these circumstances the defendant had in the fall of 1939 and the spring of 1940 furnished the military recruiting station with letters about alleged military activity, and this at the very time (May 1940) when he had to reckon with his induction, the defendant gave the following account:

At the beginning of the war in 1939 he heard in some way from his brother-in-law or a military captain that a Christian periodical was to be published for the soldiers. He initially made himself available for this. But this fell through.

Nevertheless, the defendant communicated with the Schlawe District Military Recruiting Station on October 12 regarding an assignment with the Armed Forces High Command and thereby gave the impression that he was engaged in a military department.

In December 1939 the defendant claims to have received a commission to provide domestic policy reports regarding the situation in Pomerania and in Berlin. He claims then to have brought these reports and to have discussed them with v. Dohnanyi and Colonel Oster. For this reason he regarded himself an agent of the Military Intelligence Office.

Considering that v. Dohnanyi was aware of the state police measure imposed on the defendant prohibiting residence in Berlin, it appears implausible that a department such as the Foreign Office of Military Intelligence would have the defendant gather reports on the domestic political situation.

The defendant himself was aware that the gathering of intelligence in the domestic sector was a matter for the Gestapo as well as the SD.

The Prague Accord of May 1, 1942,[17] reestablished the respective jurisdictions of the individual departments. This ruling declares that since 1935 domestic intelligence belongs exclusively to the SD's sphere of responsibility. It has not been established against the defendant that he knew the exact delineation of spheres of responsibility between Military Intelligence and SD; however, he could not have regarded himself as participating in military service based on the assignments given to him by his brother-in-law v. Dohnanyi and Colonel Oster.

As the rationale for his letter of May 24, 1940, to the Schlawe District Military Recruiting Station, the defendant asserts that it is possible he took trips at that time for himself to Bethel,[18] to the Rhineland, and to Saxony, which "in accordance with the OKW agreement" he also used for his official concerns. He says that these official trips were never reimbursed by the office but that his brother-in-law occasionally contributed, since he himself never had any salary. He maintains that he did not know whether

439

[17.] The Prague Accord (das Prager Abkommen) refers to an agreement, negotiated by Heydrich and Canaris in Prague in April 1942, between the Reich Central Security Office and the Foreign Office of Military Intelligence, that demarcated their respective spheres of activity; see Höhne, *Canaris*, 470–71.

[18.] Cf. 1/228.2, ed. note 25.

these subsidies were given from personal or official funds and that the assistance he received from his brother-in-law up until his recruitment into AST VII extended to the occasional payment for a sleeping car and of the price differential between second- and third-class cars, since the defendant himself generally traveled third class.

This traveling on the part of the defendant came to an end because the Gestapo imposed on him the injunction to register his every location immediately. Immediately thereafter the discussions with his brother-in-law v. Dohnanyi regarding the defendant's recruitment into the Munich Military Intelligence Office took place.

In particular, the defendant attests to the following as the basis for his work in the domestic intelligence service of the Foreign Office of Military Intelligence:

In countless reports the defendant directs the attention of his supervisors Colonel Oster and v. Dohnanyi to alleged persecutions of the Confessing Church and its adherents. By the defendant's own account, the purpose of producing these reports was to bring these matters to the only official agency he knew was willing to advocate on the questions of the Confessing Church that interested him and also in his view was willing to assist in these questions.

For this reason he also obtained the numbers of inducted clergy of the legalized church and the Confessing Church, in order to make this material accessible to Oster and v. Dohnanyi and, as he himself admits, in order to ensure thereby that one of the few agencies of an official character that was open to the Confessing Church, namely, the military, was informed about the state of affairs, and in order to advocate for the concerns of the Confessing Church that he himself represented.

In all this, however, the defendant knew that the concerns he represented stood in contradiction to the church policies held by the German Reich government, represented by the Ministry for Church Affairs.

440 He knew both from his brother-in-law v. Dohnanyi that the latter was prepared to advocate for the interests of the Confessing Church, and from conversations with General Oster that he, too, had a sympathetic orientation to the interests of the Confessing Church, particularly since he conversed generally with v. Dohnanyi about all the problems afflicting the church.

The content of the following letter, presumably written by the defendant in March 1942 to Special Officer von Dohnanyi, is to be considered a result of this cooperation:

"Dear Hans,

1) Contains statements on Prof. Schniewind.

2) Statements on the Jewish professor Perels, in the Gurs evacuation camp in the Pyrenees, both of them are to be helped.[19]

3) Licentiate Niesel, one of our most qualified and clear-headed people, is threatened with conscription. A date is not yet known; presently he is in Breslau, having

---

[19.] See Schreiber, *Friedrich Justus Perels*, 174–75, and W. Meyer, *Unternehmen Sieben*, 120–21.

been expelled from Berlin. At the moment there is nothing to be done, but I wanted at least to let you know of it.

4) — [20]

5) Jannesch's[21] son Hans Peter (long wounded, etc.)—you probably already know about this—has now been declared GV[22] again; and naturally his father is making efforts to get him out of this again (he is now the only son, since his brother was killed). Do you see any possibility of doing something? I did not give him much hope. I only feel terribly sorry for the father, who has personally endured a great deal in recent times; and I am constantly pondering what could be done. Could we give someone in Poznan a personal hint? I suppose it is very difficult.

6) Concerns an action to benefit two pastors' sons in Stettin who had been temporarily taken to a concentration camp because of activities endangering the state.

Forgive me for upending this vat of requests and needs over you, but by now you must be used to it. Many thanks for all your help.

Cordially, Dietrich."[23]

Pastor Niesel is a personal acquaintance of the defendant and belongs, like him, to the Confessing Church. When the defendant heard of Niesel's imminent induction into the army, he wrote this letter. Since Niesel did not belong to a recognized church and thus no authorities were pleading his case, he wanted to retain Niesel in cooperation   441
with his brother-in-law v. Dohnanyi for church work, in order to secure his abilities for the work of the Confessing Church. This is the way in which his letter to his brother-in-law is to be understood and has also been discussed.[24]

With regard to the comments in the defendant's letter about Hans Peter Jannesch, this concerns the son of the Confessing pastor Jannesch, against whom state police measures were similarly imposed. As a result of this letter, v. Dohnanyi attempted to bring Hans Peter Jannesch into Military Intelligence. Neither the defendant nor his brother-in-law von Dohnanyi were able to explain the substantive grounds for these measures.

It is indicative of the inner orientation [Haltung] of the defendant that at the same time he attempted to have his brother-in-law von Dohnanyi use his official capacities to provide financial support, through Military Intelligence intervention, for a Jew evacuated[25] by the German government to Gurs in the Pyrenees.

[20.] [See 1/150, ed. note 6.—MB]

[21.] This should read "Jannasch." Cf. Bonhoeffer's letter of November 23, 1941, to the father, Wilhelm Jannasch, 1/138.

[22.] [*Garnisonsverwendungsfähig*, "fit for limited duty." —MB]

[23.] This letter to Dohnanyi is not in his papers and has been found only in the documents of indictment reprinted here. It has also been reprinted in this volume as a separate document; see 1/150.

[24.] Cf. 1/228.5 and 1/228.6.

[25.] [The description of the Gurs camp as an "evacuation" camp was, of course, a Nazi euphemism. The Gurs camp in southern France interned foreign-born Jews and

In addition, the defendant was aware that his brother-in-law v. Dohnanyi was most inclined to occupy himself with UK classifications; thus two cases of UK classifications, whose names he refused to provide, were known to the defendant.

These sorts of UK classifications should be permitted only under the terms of the HDv[26] of November 11, 1940, to which von Dohnanyi did not adhere, as the UK classification of the defendant also demonstrates.

Furthermore, the handling of UK classifications did not lie within the sphere of responsibility of Special Officer von Dohnanyi. UK classifications were to be handled rather by Lieutenant Colonel Greßler according to the duty roster of the Foreign Office of Military Intelligence (Department ZO).

Testimony of the Defendant and Its Legal Evaluation.

The defendant appeals to the fact that his UK classification was instigated by the Munich Military Intelligence Office as authorized by chief of staff Admiral Canaris.

This testimony is refuted by the statement of Admiral Canaris and by the December 11, 1940, letter of Special Officer v. Dohnanyi.

V. Dohnanyi appeals to having discussed the UK classification with Colonel Oster and, with Oster's approval, having authorized what followed with the Munich Military Intelligence Office.

Insofar as the defendant, cognizant of the possibilities for UK classification through his brother-in-law, proposed to the latter in the undated letter of about March 1942 that von Dohnanyi take responsibility for Niesel's UK classification, the defendant attests that he had the intention of retaining Niesel for the church work of the Confessing Church and securing his abilities for the work of the Confessing Church.

This testimony cannot excuse the defendant. Whoever undertakes, through means calculated to deceive or by other means, to keep himself or another entirely, partially, or temporarily from fulfillment of military service, subverts military power (§ 5 KSSVO[27] sec. 1 numeral 3).[28]

Through these two independent actions of subversion, the defendant has made himself guilty.

a) Through the false pretenses in his letters of October 12, 1939, and May 24 and

---

political prisoners such as Herbert Jehle (see 1/73, ed. note 3). Many were German Jews who were deported there directly from Germany or who had reached France but were rounded up after the German occupation began. Most of those interned in Gurs (though not Perels's uncle) were eventually deported to extermination camps in the east and died there.—MB]

[26.] [*Heeresdienstvorschrift,* "army regulation."—MB]

[27.] [Kriegssonderstrafrechtsverordnung, "Special War Criminal Ordinance."—MB]

[28.] "Subversion of military power is punishable by death: . . . 3. Whoever undertakes, by self-mutilation, by means calculated to deceive or by other means, to keep himself or another entirely, partially, or temporarily from fulfillment of military service."

27, 1940, he gave the Schlawe District Military Recruiting Station the impression that he was a member of a military department. In reality he was aware that he had no justification of any kind to refer to official residence in Berlin. On the contrary, he was allowed to remain in Berlin only for visits, and this with his father, since he otherwise was forbidden to reside there.

He speaks of his local military department in the letter of May 27, 1940, even though there was no military service relationship or any other sort of contractual relationship between him and the department of the OKW/Foreign Office of Military Intelligence.

The fact that not only General Oster but also Special Officer von Dohnanyi and the defendant asserted, up until the assertion was shown to be untrue, that the letter of November 12, 1940, provided the basis for the defendant's activity in Military Intelligence, makes clear that the defendant himself did not genuinely believe that his occasional domestic gathering of intelligence had official character. From the circumstances, especially since he himself was previously a civil servant, he was aware that this gathering of intelligence was of a purely private nature also from the perspective of Commander General Oster and Special Officer von Dohnanyi. The manner of reimbursement of travel costs testifies to this as well, since the defendant as a civil servant knows well that travel costs are duly refunded to him by any official department.

The cohort of the defendant '06 had to reckon with induction as early as 1939; the defendant himself, in late spring 1940, all the more since he had been classified as KV. If under these circumstances he wrote to the military recruiting station the letters of May 24/27 and adheres to their content, he is by false assertions making himself guilty of deceiving the Schlawe District Military Recruiting Station. At the very least, the defendant thereby undertook to keep himself temporarily from military service.

443

The defendant himself admits that he placed church concerns above the self-evident duty to serve in the military; this is revealed also in the following action.

b) The letter of the defendant to his brother-in-law dating to around March 1942 is the attempt, referring to the demands made on von Dohnanyi for the person of Licentiate Niesel as well as for the person of the son of Pastor Jannesch, by one and the same action to keep them from military service entirely or partially.

After the defendant admitted that he wished to obstruct the induction of Niesel in the interests of the work of the Confessing Church, he wishes to have the words "threatened with induction" understood to mean that the inductions threatened the church. Given the circumstances and the overall pattern, this very belated defense can only be characterized as strained and untrustworthy.

In this regard the defendant also appears to be guilty of subversion of military power according to § 5 sec. 1 no. 3 and therefore is to be sentenced for two independent acts of subversion of military power.

The defendant is to be regarded as an ardent member and defender of the Confessing Church. The Confessing Church stands in opposition to the Reich Minister for

Church Affairs. If the act cannot objectively be seen as less severe, the application of sec. 2 § KSSVO is not excluded on the basis of the person doing the act.[29]

Means of proof:

I. The defendant's own testimony.

II. *Witnesses:*

a) Major General Oster, Bayrische Straße, Berlin W;

b) Special Officer Hans von Dohnanyi, Military Detention Center, Lehrterstraße, Berlin NW 40.

III. *Documents:*

Files of the Military District Headquarters, page 39 d. A.;

Red file Bonhoeffer;

Red file with correspondence.

By order of

Dr. Roeder[30]

444   231. Hans von Dohnanyi to Christine von Dohnanyi[1]

Dietrich 1) is asserted to have said that we had discussed extensively his state police restrictions. Yet not in conjunction with his recruitment into Military Intelligence? When were these restrictions?

2) I said that it was possible that D. and I discussed that his recruitment in Munich was a pleasant side effect with regard to the easing of the restrictions.[2] I consider it possible that we had such a conversation. Easing in the sense that D. was of course subject to no restrictive measures in Munich, as also was the case in all the other places he was allowed to reside. But only a side effect, not the reason.

3) Dietrich is asserted to have said that he conducted a domestic intelligence service for me and Oster from within the circles of the Confessing Church. Can't be true! Surely it's only a matter of Oster's military-political assignments! Which assignments?

4) Dietrich is asserted to have said that I subsidized his trips on behalf of Oster from my own pocket or from official funds. I don't understand!

[29.] "In less severe cases penal servitude or prison may be imposed."

[30.] In the lower margin appears "La" (presumably "Ladenig").

[1.] BA Berlin-Lichterfelde, Nachlaß Dohnanyi 14 III C+D: typewritten copy, undated, from notes smuggled out of prison; they were prepared by Dohnanyi in accordance with the information in the indictment of September 16, 1943 (see 1/229.2). [The interrogators were constantly trying to entrap the different members of the conspiracy into contradicting or betraying one another. Family members shared the messages that were smuggled out with the others who were imprisoned so that they could attempt to coordinate their stories. See, for example, Dietze's comment to his wife (1/235) as well as *DB-ER*, 800 and 812.—MB]

[2.] Cf. also the interrogation transcript of April 16, 1943 (1/225.1).

5) How many letters did D. send to the Schlawe WMA?[3] Only the letter of May 27, 1940? He probably received the red slip in answer to this letter![4]

6) O. is asserted to have said that he got to know D. at the Schleichers'. Is that true? Most likely confusing this with the party we gave at your parents' home. But surely O. knew D. already before that? When was the party?

7) Question of the notes is now playing a role against O. after all (because of the attempt to hide them). There can surely be no doubt that O. was aware of the notes? Were surely discussed in his presence with Müller, Dietrich, and me?

8) Gisevius maintains that, on the occasion of D.'s last trip to Switzerland, he "called to my attention in a friendly way" that D.'s UK classification was scarcely justifiable!!! When was the Munich trip from which D. was called back at G.'s request? before March certainly? D. will equally well remember the reason G. gave for his objection (passport problems with Switzerland and suspicion against D. that he belonged to the German intelligence service).[5] As you know, he surely benefited a great deal from D.   445 and never expressed reservations as long as D. was able to be useful to him. How was D. useful to him? By the way, Oster renewed his UK classification on March 27 in consideration of his imminent trip to Rome. So Oster knew about the trip to Rome! And if G. was supposed to have contradicted this, Oster in any case overlooked this contradiction!

9) D.'s trip to Rome was supposed to have the purpose of his remaining an extended period in Rome as a listening post for Müller, in order to observe the peace efforts, and particularly in light of the participation of the Italian traitor clique![6]

Oster 1) apparently is mixing up getting to know Dietrich at the Schleichers' with the small party at our house, but already knew D. at that point?

2) is said to have admitted that Dietrich was enlisted for the domestic-political intelligence service! That cannot be true! It is strictly a matter of reports of a military-political nature of interest to Großcurth and for the most part also handed over to him! Which?

3) will also recall that Gisevius did not polemicize against D.'s UK classification. D. was, of course, often enough in Switzerland with G. Then Gisevius would have to have said something sooner. Furthermore, he called D. back from Munich because passport difficulties with Switzerland made travel appear impracticable, and supposedly because D. had attracted attention as a member of the German intelligence service (this is surely a lie: merely professional jealousy!).

[3.] [Wehrkreismeldeamt, "District Military Recruiting Station."—MB]

[4.] [This refers to the "red slip" regarding Bonhoeffer's military classification. Since Bonhoeffer was in fact classified KV after he sent his May 27, 1940, letter to the Schlawe WMA, Dohnanyi's comment suggests that the red slip refers to a KV classification (fit for service). See the explanation of this in the editor's introduction, p. 11.—MB]

[5.] Cf. Charlotte von Kirschbaum's letter to Bonhoeffer on May 17, 1942; see 1/162.

[6.] Cf. 1/224.2 (note no. 2).

4) Indictment characterizes as implausible Oster's assertion that the purpose of the message to the Schlawe WMA[7] was only to safeguard Dietrich, because according to Dietrich's and my statements D.'s ecumenical connections were first discussed only in September of '40. This is a misrepresentation. The conversations in fall of '40 served the purpose of authorizing Dietrich to outline his ecumenical connections as documentation for the files and the actual appointment. I was interrogated only about this, not about the '39/'40 period. Needless to say, Oster's statement about safeguarding D. is true. Oster naturally knew of D.'s ecumenical connections from the very beginning.

5) According to Oster's statements, I supposedly gave him no indication of D.'s restriction on residence;[8] I consider this to be unlikely. Will Oster nevertheless concede the possibility that I told him this? Particularly since he himself says that I notified him about the ban on public speaking.

6) The idea that Dietrich was to have been "removed"[9] from the reach of the Stapo[10] is, of course, rubbish. Why remove him at all? Then Dietrich would have been forced to enlist. As everyone knows, nonenlisted persons are subject to the Stapo's clutches. Example: Halem,[11] who himself by means of Military Intelligence intervention was not released. Besides, the Munich Stapo was informed and agreed to D.'s recruitment.

7) The indictment adduces there "can remain no doubt that I had to make discretionary decisions regarding whether and to what extent the Foreign Office/Military Intelligence advocated for a firm."[12] This is pure nonsense! On the contrary, Oster will confirm that I neither was responsible for decisions of this kind nor gave advice about them, but rather at most—and even this only since relatively recently—I had to present to him incoming letters that fell outside my purview, including their contents, whereby he made the actual substantive decisions himself. In any case—and this is the decisive thing—in July 1941, the time of the loan application through Hübener, I had a narrowly defined area of responsibility, namely, processing the incoming military and military-political reports.[13] Oster will confirm this! Canaris too must know it.

[7.] See 1/9.

[8.] In his interrogation on April 29, 1943, Hans Oster stated: "Before his recruitment I was aware that, like a great many pastors of the Confessing Church, B. had a provisional ban on public speaking. I knew nothing of a restriction on residence up to the present day. Otherwise I would have inquired with the Gestapo" (BA Berlin-Lichterfelde, Nachlaß Dohnanyi 13 III/33,31–32).

[9.] Cf. 1/229.1.

[10.] [The *Stapo* were the state police *(Staatspolizei)*. After 1933 the state police were subsumed within the Gestapo. —MB]

[11.] Nikolaus von Halem; cf. *DB-ER*, 623.

[12.] See the complete text of the indictment in Chowaniec, *Der "Fall Dohnanyi,"* 181.

[13.] Roeder wanted to convict Hans von Dohnanyi of using his office for personal gain because the latter had received a particularly advantageous loan from the head of a

8) The indictment adduces that I had "become acquainted with" Hübener "as the ZB official."[14] How was I supposed to have met H. as ZB? In fact I had no official points of contact with him at all. In my ZB activity [...][15]

     9) [...][16]

232. George K. A. Bell to Erling Eidem[1]   447

Chichester, 3rd November, 1943

My dear Erling,

I wrote you just before the Swedish aeroplane was struck down with Theodore Hume[2] as a passenger. His death is a tragic loss. I had given him many messages for you, especially about the proposed post-armistice conference; and it may be that the letter I wrote was in that aeroplane, and so may never reach you. At any rate, I am sending you this letter now in the hope that it will reach you and convey something of what Hume would have said so much better in personal talk.

The war is going in such a pace now that one feels it is of the utmost importance that we should be prepared for oecumenical Church action at any moment. Here the *Archbishop* of Canterbury is in full sympathy with the project of a conference of Churchleaders of the different countries. And from my talks in Sweden last year with our Pastor friend,[3] I cannot doubt that the leaders of the Confessional Church would be equally in sympathy.

Hamburg firm for the purchase of a house in Sakrow, near Potsdam (see Chowaniec, *Der "Fall Dohnanyi,"* 85–89, especially 89: "Thus the application of § 140 of the MStGB [Militärstrafgesetzbuch, "Military Penal Code"] failed in that there was no evidence of professional misconduct").

     [14.] Chowaniec, *Der "Fall Dohnanyi,"* 179. ["ZB" refers to the Z Büro, or Zentralabteilung, the department in the Office of Military Intelligence that was responsible for foreign policy reports. Hans von Dohnanyi was the special officer assigned to this office. See 1/230.2, ed. note 12.—MB]

     [15.] Illegible.

     [16.] Illegible.

     [1.] Landsarkivet, Uppsala, Arkiv Erling Eidem; typewritten; letter in original English, including errors; previously published in *MW* 5:315.

     [2.] Theodore (Ted) Hume, a young Congregationalist pastor, had just been sent to Europe as a representative of the American churches in the secretariat of the World Council of Churches and was to have begun his work in Sweden. His airplane was shot down on the flight from London to Stockholm; cf. Visser 't Hooft, *Memoirs,* 182. In the event of an occupation of Switzerland, the secretariat was to have continued its ecumenical work in Sweden.

     [3.] This clearly refers to Bonhoeffer.

Leiper, with whom I discussed the matter when he was in England, left no doubt about the sympathy of the American Churches. Though I do not know at first hand, I am sure that Kramer[4] of Holland would respond, and Koechlin in Basle.

The point that the Archbishop of Canterbury and I feel, and made clear to Hume in a conversation in which some Free Churchmen joined only a few days before Hume started, on his flight, was that this conference would have to be held on another initiative than that of the World Council, for the very reason that the World Council does not include the Germans, and their presence is indispensable. I jot down my own collection of the names that you and I talked over at Upsala last year: yourself, Berggrav, Fugelsen Damgaard,[5] Canterbury, Aubrey[6] (perhaps *vice* Paton), Otto Dibelius, Wurms,[7] Bonhoeffer, Niemoller, Boegner, Kramer, Koechlin, 't Hooft.[8] The Americans I expect are best reached by contact with Cavert[9] at the Federal Council, or Bishop Tucker,[10] who was, and I think still is, its President.

It is most desirable that the conference should in the main be composed of people who already know one another. But there must be some exceptions. I wonder whether Orientals could be gathered in, like Dornakal, and some from China or Japan? I do not know these, I am afraid. And there are others, including some from Sweden, whose presence would be of great value. I only put down these names as you know in an attempt to make a start in preparing for the conference.

My wife joins me in love to your wife and your daughter. I do hope you are better.[11]

Yours affectionately,
George Cicestr

[4.] Hendrik Kraemer was a Dutch ecumenist.

[5.] This should read Hans Fuglsang-Damgaard, bishop of Copenhagen.

[6.] Edwin Ewart Aubrey.

[7.] [A misspelling of Bishop Theophil Wurm's name.—MB]

[8.] Following a conversation with Visser 't Hooft on May 5, 1942, Bishop Bell wrote in his notebook: "Boegner favours small meeting of leaders all of whom knew one another. Temple, Boegner, Eidem, Bergg
rav, Fuglsang Damgaard, Koechlin, Kraemer, Bonhoeffer, Germanos, USA + Paton, Leiper, 't Hooft" (cf. 1/170, ed. note 77).

[9.] Samuel McCrea Cavert.

[10.] A. R. Tucker.

[11.] This sentence was added by hand.

233. Decree of the Senior Reich Military Prosecutor[1]   449

Torgau (Zieten Barracks), November 18,[2] 1943

Decree.

I. In the criminal case against Pastor Dietrich *Bonhoeffer*, presently in the Berlin Military Detention Center, Tegel branch, a date for trial before the Fourth Senate of the Reich War Court, Witzlebenstraße 4–10, Berlin-Charlottenburg 5, has been appointed: *Friday, December 17, 1943, at 9:30 a.m.*

—Estimated length: 1 to 2 days—

II. Attorney Dr. Kurt Wergin, Woyrschstraße 8, Berlin W 35, is authorized as counsel for the defendant, in accordance with § 323, sect. 4 MStGO,[3] § 51 KStVO.[4]

III. through VII. pp

By order of
signed, Dr. Speckhardt
Senior Reich Military Prosecutor

234. Kurt Peschke: Defense of Hans von Dohnanyi   450
234.1. Cover Letter[1]

Berlin, May 5, 1944

In the case against... we attach in the enclosure the final formulation of the defense brief and request that it take the place of the partial defense briefs previously submitted.

---

[1] Literary estate of Maria von Wedemeyer-Weller; typewritten; letterhead and file number: "The Senior Reich Military Prosecutor Criminal Trial List (Reich War Court Prosecutor) III 114/43"; addressed on the back: "Attention: Defendant Dietrich Bonhoeffer, presently held in Military Detention Center, *Berlin-Tegel*. Torgau, November 18, 1943 [handwritten:] Ladenig, Army Judicial Inspector, as Clerk of Court of this office"; stamp: "Reich War Court 18." Apparently Bonhoeffer gave this document to his fiancée during one of her visits around this time. Bonhoeffer wrote to Eberhard Bethge on November 23, 1943: "The date is 17 December. At last! Will I see the week? Can't Rüdiger [Schleicher] ring up Speckhardt in Torgau about your permission to visit? We must also take care to see that the Captain takes it here!" (*LPP*, 137 [*DBW* 8:200]). The attorney Dr. Kurt Wergin did not arrive to meet with Bonhoeffer until December 16, 1943 (*LPP*, 164 [*DBW* 8:238–39]). However, the case never came up for trial. Because of their overview of the situation from the outside, family and friends worked to ensure that Bonhoeffer's proceedings took place only in conjunction with Dohnanyi's, if at all, because they feared that the case would not remain confined to the relatively harmless points named in the indictment (*LPP*, 173 and 265, note 101 [*DBW* 8:251, ed. note 39]). On Bonhoeffer's reaction, see *LPP*, 173–75 (*DBW* 8:251–54) and *Love Letters from Cell 92*, 133–34, 140–41.

[2.] The "18" is written in by hand.

[3.] [Militärstrafgerichtsordnung, "Military Criminal Ordinance."—MB]

[4.] [Kriegsstrafrechtsverordnung, "War Criminal Law Ordinance."—MB]

[1.] Niedersächsisches Hauptstaatsarchiv, Hanover, Nds 721 Lüneburg, Acc. 69/76; typewritten; notes: "Registered"—"*Re: File number Criminal Trial Docket (Reich War Court*

The criticism of the lead investigator by the defendant has been reproduced in its original formulation, on the one hand, from the conviction that the defense is justified and obligated to bring to the attention of the court the views presented by the defendant in his own defense in their full scope, but, on the other hand, in order to restrict this disclosure to the documentary level as far as possible and to be able to refrain from discussing it in the trial itself as far as possible.

From the letter of the president of the Reich War Court, we have inferred that the discussion of these questions within the framework of the objective conclusion of this matter sought by all parties can be and is to be avoided if at all possible, and in the enclosed new formulation of the defense brief, we bear in mind this wish for a smooth settlement.

Heil Hitler!

signed, Count Dr. von der Goltz   signed, Dr. Kurt Peschke

    Counselor-at-Law   Attorney

451   **234.2 Defense Brief for Hans von Dohnanyi**[2]

[...]

B. *Regarding the Specific Cases in the Indictment.*

1. The Case of Bonhoeffer.[3]

The charges in the indictment are refuted on purely objective grounds by the content of the files and the information in the indictment itself.

The case can be divided chronologically into the period from the end of 1939 until around November 1940, during which Bonhoeffer, without being inducted as a Military Intelligence agent, was secured by General Oster with a view to his ecumenical connections and their later use in Military Intelligence, and the period after his actual UK[4] classification, during which he was active as a Military Intelligence agent.

Prosecutor Attorney) III 114/43"; sender: "Counselor-at-Law Count von der Goltz, Attorney and Notary, Am Sandwerder 7, Wannsee"—"Dr. Kurt Peschke, Attorney and Notary, Joachim-Friedrich-Straße 55, Berlin-Halensee"; addressee: "President of the Reich War Court, Presiding Judge, Zieten-Kaserne, *Torgau/Elbe.*" Previously published in Chowaniec, *Der "Fall Dohnanyi,"* 194 (see also 165 on the difficulties of the proceedings).

[2.] Niedersächsisches Hauptstaatsarchiv, Hanover, Nds 721 Lüneburg, Acc. 69/76; typewritten; unabridged reproduction of this version of the defense brief submitted on February 19, 1944, to the Reich War Court, found in Chowaniec, *Der "Fall Dohnanyi,"* 195–205. The following extract is from pp. 200–205. (According to the explicit wish of the Reich War Court, this brief still had to be "cleaned up" several times.)

[3.] Regarding the points here in Bonhoeffer's case, cf. the indictment against Hans von Dohnanyi; see 1/229.2.

[4.] [Regarding the UK classification, see 1/31, ed. note 3.—MB]

1.) The state of affairs for the time period from autumn 1939 until November 1940 is extremely straightforward: at the beginning of the war *Bonhoeffer* interrupted a trip to the United States in order to make himself available to the armed forces. During the time in question, he waited for his conscription by the military bishop to whom he had volunteered himself. This conscription, however, never came about. At that time, when—contrary to the assumption in the indictment—Bonhoeffer's age group had not yet been called up for the draft, the defendant and Bonhoeffer often spoke about his aspiration to work for the armed forces. Bonhoeffer discussed with the defendant things such as the question of publishing a Christian pamphlet for soldiers, for which he prepared a few drafts. The defendant, however, was more inclined toward the idea of deploying Bonhoeffer in the intelligence service of the armed forces, given his extensive ecumenical connections, which would be useful for espionage. These connections were known also to General *Oster*, whom Bonhoeffer had met shortly after the outbreak of the war. That Bonhoeffer's connections were known to the defendant, even long before the war's outbreak, requires no further proof. There remained no other choice than a "securing of Bonhoeffer" for Military Intelligence, since for the time being the military bishop's decision regarding Bonhoeffer's deployment had to be awaited. This securing—which after all in no way hindered the 452 preparation for military conscription, as Bonhoeffer was then mustered in due course in June 1940—ensued in such a way that Bonhoeffer was permitted to convey to the Schlawe District Military Recruiting Station the fact that he had assignments from the chief of staff of the Foreign Office–Military Intelligence and in case of any further inquiries to refer these to him. When in his letter of May 27, 1940 [5] Bonhoeffer speaks of his military department or in other ways spoke to the Schlawe District Military Recruiting Station regarding official duties, this accordingly agreed with the facts and was not contrary to the truth. It is incomprehensible how the indictment reached the conclusion that it was "undisputed" among all the defendants that Bonhoeffer had no official duties for the Foreign Office of Military Intelligence during the period from the end of 1939 until fall of 1940. On the contrary, for his part the defendant explicitly referred to the fact that General Oster allowed Bonhoeffer to appeal to his official relationship with Military Intelligence in dealing with the military recruiting station. For his own part, as the indictment itself reveals (page 6), Bonhoeffer regarded the chief of staff of the Foreign Office of Military Intelligence as his "military department," and it is therefore impossible that he failed to conceive of his duties as official ones. The same applies to General Oster, who according to what the indictment has determined (page 6) even instructed Bonhoeffer to refer to him as his (Bonhoeffer's) military department.

With regard to the official duties conferred on Bonhoeffer by General Oster in the period from autumn of 1939 until November 1940, the indictment attempts to

---

[5.] See 1/9.

view them in terms of the accusation of "organizing a domestic intelligence service" among the staff of Admiral *Canaris*. Repeatedly the defendant has emphasized to the lead investigator that this accusation requires first a clarification of concepts. No one wishes to dispute that General Oster sent Bonhoeffer on fact-finding missions within Germany and that these missions were also concerned with political matters. In no way, however, does this imply that this referred to an organized domestic intelligence service, as the indictment appears to construe it—i.e., to the gathering of information about the general domestic situation—which would lie "completely outside the sphere of responsibility of the Foreign Office of Military Intelligence" and which—like any intelligence service—would depend on agents being systematically and continuously sent on information missions and continuously reporting back. The defendant

453   attempted repeatedly—but unfortunately in vain—to elicit some awareness on the part of the lead investigator that General Oster, in his role as *chief of staff* (to be distinguished from his position as head of the Central Department), has the task of orienting the director regarding peripheral subjects as well. Among other things, this includes instructions about general questions of *military political* interest. *This* was the realm in which the tasks assigned to Bonhoeffer—which, by the way, were not frequent—lay. That demonstrates surely that the division corresponding to the present Military Affairs Department of the General Staff, which at that time was led by Lieutenant Colonel *Großcurth* o[f the] G[eneral Staff], took an interest in Bonhoeffer's reports and that these reports were distributed to Großcurth as well. There was a close working relationship [Arbeitsgemeinschaft] between Military Intelligence and Großcurth's division.

2.) The material justification for Bonhoeffer's UK classification is not seriously cast into doubt even by the indictment itself, and in light of Bonhoeffer's obviously extensive international connections, as described in his letter of November 11, 1940,[6] can in no way be disputed. This is manifest particularly in that the department head himself made clear how highly he valued this agent's activity and connections for the intelligence service by assigning Bonhoeffer personal information-gathering missions. If the lead investigator believes that the significance of these missions is to be doubted (indictment, page 9), the department head himself may have an opinion. In any case, on the basis of one of these trips Bonhoeffer was already able to report in June 1942 about prospects for an invasion by the Anglo-Saxon forces in the West African region.[7] When the indictment argues that Bonhoeffer did not even file a written report about his trip to Oslo, but that Count *Moltke* wrote the report, it would have been simple

---

[6.] See the "Camouflage Letter," 1/221.

[7.] A note written by Hans von Dohnanyi on October 19, 1943, reads: "The mission to Stockholm was far more important! Dietrich reported on this as well. D. was the first person who reported on the prospects for an invasion by the Anglo-Americans in the West African region" (BA Berlin-Lichterfelde, Nachlaß Dohnanyi 13 I/16,2); cf. Chowaniec, *Der "Fall Dohnanyi,"* 82, and note 335.

to clarify that Bonhoeffer's information-gathering had been incorporated into Moltke's report.[8]

The indictment's assumption that Bonhoeffer's transfer to Munich was intended for him to escape the state police[9] is utter nonsense. This is the case because, as is well known, nonconscripted (UK-classified, etc.) agents come under the jurisdiction of the state police; the only way for Bonhoeffer to escape the state police would have been precisely by his conscription as a soldier, not by his UK classification. Since it can hardly be assumed that this obvious consideration has eluded the lead investigator, there is much to be said for the conclusion that the indictment has raised this accusation—that Bonhoeffer is said to have escaped from the state police—irrespective of its extreme improbability.

454

In this connection, it is remarkable that the indictment appeals to the testimony of Schmidhuber without citing the location in the files where Schmidhuber's statement is to be found. Yet even Schmidhuber does not assert his own awareness of those alleged reasons for Bonhoeffer's recruitment into Military Intelligence, but instead for his part refers to Captain *Ickrath*,[10] to whom the defendant is said to have communicated "orally" that Bonhoeffer was to be removed from the reach of the state police and from whom he had heard this. If Ickrath had confirmed this statement by Schmidhuber, the indictment would hardly have let this go unmentioned. With regard to the conspicuous fact that the indictment does not refer to Ickrath's testimony, there are only two explanations: Either Ickrath was interrogated and did not confirm Schmidhuber's statements; in this case the indictment has omitted this exonerating circumstance. Or else Ickrath was not interrogated; then the lead investigator has omitted a hearing that would have been absolutely required for adequate clarification of this matter and, above all, before the indictment endorsed Schmidhuber's assertions.

The indictment indulges in the speculation that Bonhoeffer had to be "removed" in view of the measures imposed on him by the state police.[11] In the meantime, any deliberation as to how this could actually have been brought about is missing here. No one can be removed from a ban on public speaking. That is technically impossible. One can withdraw from a restriction on one's residence only by residing in the forbidden place. Yet by dint of Bonhoeffer being inducted as an agent in *Munich*, he acted in *accord* with the restriction on his residence in Berlin and not counter to it. By the transfer of his military intelligence activity to Munich, Bonhoeffer's compliance with

---

[8.] Cf. Helmuth von Moltke's letter of April 28, 1942 to Freya von Moltke; see 1/154, ed. note 12.

[9.] [After 1933 the state police *(Staatspolizei)* were subsumed within the Gestapo.—MB]

[10.] [Heinrich Ickradt.—MB]

[11.] Cf. 1/227, ed. note 2 (restriction on residence in Berlin and national ban on public speaking).

the state police measures was in fact made easier, and it goes without saying that this was a "pleasant side effect" of his recruitment in Munich. Whatever accusations the indictment wishes to educe from this and whatever may need to be "conceded" here

455 are mysteries. Bonhoeffer himself was far from wanting to evade the Gestapo. On the contrary, he conceived of his engagement with Military Intelligence as a welcome opportunity to rehabilitate himself with the Gestapo.

With regard to the defendant's communication with his superior concerning Bonhoeffer's state police measures, the lead investigator allowed the defendant to persist during the interrogations in the belief that he had made no mention at all of this state of affairs. In retrospect the defendant considered this to be possible because for him personally the injunctions did, in fact, appear to be meaningless as gauges of the personality of his brother-in-law and the latter's trustworthiness. At this point the indictment itself (page 6) reveals, according to General Oster's testimony, that the defendant had at least made Oster aware of the ban on public speaking. The defendant is unable to state with certainty today whether he informed General Oster of the mitigated restriction of residence. If, however, the defendant reported to General Oster about the ban on public speaking, which undoubtedly represents the more serious injunction—since as a result of being allowed to stay with his parents the restriction on residence was for all practical purposes scarcely noticeable for Bonhoeffer—there is a certain probability that the defendant also mentioned the restriction on residence.

Moreover, Bonhoeffer's induction as an agent of the Munich Military Intelligence Office was, as the lead investigator could easily have determined, discussed with the Munich state police, which conferred its explicit consent on this (January 1941).

The question whether and to what extent formal military regulations were adhered to in the process of Bonhoeffer being classified UK at the end of 1940 becomes irrelevant in light of the fact that Bonhoeffer's final UK classification at the end of March 1943 was in any case authorized once again by the AHA[12] and, independently of this, was also applied for and effected with the appropriate offices by the Munich AST.[13] Nevertheless, the following material is presented to address this question.

a) HDv[14] 3/14, which is cited by the indictment, corresponds to MDv[15] no. 124, volume 5, and to LDv[16] 3/14. It does not bear the date of November 11, 1940, but is dated July 10, 1941. It concerns the "Procedures of the Military in Regard to Noncontentious Litigation." Regulations concerning UK classification are not treated here.

b) If we base our views on the indictment, we see that the indictment is obliged to prove the assertion that General Oster and the defendant "knew" on November 26,

456 1940, they were acting contrary to the stipulations of HDv 3/14. This would have

---

[12.] [Allgemeines Heeresamt, "General Army Office."—MB]
[13.] [Abbreviation for Abwehrstelle, "Military Intelligence Office."—MB]
[14.] [Abbreviation for *Heeresdienstvorschrift,* "army regulation."—MB]
[15.] [Abbreviation for *Militärdienstvorschrift,* "military service regulation."—MB]
[16.] [Abbreviation for *Luftwaffendienstvorschrift,* "air force service regulation."—MB]

been difficult to prove. It is doubtful even whether HDv 3/14 ever appeared on General Oster's desk; surely it was never shown to the defendant since he had absolutely nothing to do with the questions treated there. Since, however, according to the information in the indictment, HDv 3/14 was dated November 11, 1940, it can be asserted with a high degree of probability that General Oster could hardly have become aware of it as soon as November 26, 1940. In any case the earlier discussions with Bonhoeffer and Bonhoeffer's letter of November 11, 1940, could in no case have taken account of HDv 3/14.

c) The indictment itself asserts that UK classifications in Military Intelligence were handled by ZO.[17] The lead investigator considers ZO the "responsible department" (page 14). There is, however, no such thing as this "responsible department ZO," as anyone in the office and on the organizational flow chart would have confirmed without question for the lead investigator. ZO is a group subordinated to the chief of staff as the head of the Z Department. Consequently General Oster is the immediate superior of Major *Greßler,* and it remained his responsibility to take care of the details of a UK classification. Thus it is incorrect when the indictment asserts that the handling of Bonhoeffer's UK classification was "incompatible with the division of labor in the Foreign Office of Military Intelligence." Moreover, the "handling" of Bonhoeffer's UK classification, as is clear from the indictment itself, took place not in Berlin but, as the regulations stipulate, through the Munich branch, which was also responsible, if need be, for imposing on Bonhoeffer the obligation to secrecy (indictment, page 9).

If it were correct that departments of the military are not allowed to submit UK applications for draftees who do not already belong to their ranks (indictment, page 5), then Military Intelligence would be placed in the impossible position of procuring UK classifications for draftees who are merely being considered as agents. This would mean the crippling of the entire work of Military Intelligence. The request for UK classifications for draftees by local Military Intelligence offices is obviously permissible and is one of the ordinary occurrences of daily affairs; the same is true of the instruction to the local Military Intelligence office to take care of this sort of UK classification. Such a command cannot be a concern of the OKW, as the indictment (page 7) assumes, since local Military Intelligence offices report not to the BDE[18] but to the OKW, Foreign Office of Military Intelligence.

In general, a UK classification granted by a local Military Intelligence office assumes 457 the formal establishment of a residence in its jurisdiction. Since, for technical reasons, Bonhoeffer was classified UK in Munich, the necessity of establishing a formal residence in Munich arose.

[17.] [Abbreviation for Group O of the Central *(zentrale)* Department in the Foreign Office/Military Intelligence.—MB]

[18.] Abbreviation for *Befehlshaber des Ersatzheeres* [commander of the Army Reserve—MB]; until July 1944 this was General Fromm.

The files available to the lead investigator (blue file cover) reveal that the relevant Department I was informed of the fact that Bonhoeffer had been transferred to the Munich Military Intelligence office as a subagent. These files were seized by the lead investigator but, as secondary files, were not located with the main files and as a result were not burned along with them.[19] Since the record must exist in the blue folder in two identical copies, we hereby request that one of these two copies be returned to the care of one of the signatory attorneys in order to facilitate the defense.

To conclude:

The arguments presented here demonstrate that nothing wrong has been done in the case at hand.—Since Bonhoeffer was engaged for Military Intelligence and has proved himself admirably, since his UK classification as an agent was justified, the prior action to safeguard him for military intelligence purposes also cannot be protested.

[19.] Cf. 1/229.2, ed. note 27; this refers to the fire in the Reich War Court Building during the major air raid on Berlin on November 26 and 27, 1943.

Q. Imprisonment in the Reich Central Security Office Prison, Prince-Albrecht Straße, Berlin, until Bonhoeffer's Execution in the Flossenbürg Concentration Camp, Upper Palatinate. October 8, 1944–April 9, 1945

235. Constantin von Dietze to His Wife[1]

[...] Then it was not until October 21 that I was questioned again. Schrey, who on October 6 and 9 had read me most of Goerdeler's statements from September 4, although he claimed he wasn't really allowed to do so (they take up about six type-written pages in my files), showed me the minutes from October 11. There Dr. Perels, an attorney for the Confessing Church administration in Dahlem, whom I knew well, asserted that in the winter of '42–'43 conversations took place in Berlin and Freiburg in which Bonhoeffer, I, Dibelius, Asmussen, Pastor Böhm of Zehlendorf, Goerdeler, Walter Bauer, and the Freiburg professors Ritter, Eucken, Wolf, and Lampe took part. How they must have tortured the poor man![2] We are said to have wanted to draw up for Goerdeler the theoretical underpinnings of a new state structure. We suppos-

---

[1.] Universitätsbibliothek Freiburg im Breisgau, 22, Nachlaß Constantin von Dietze; typewritten copy; previously published in *GS* 6:589. This is an excerpt from notes origi-nally made in shorthand on October 10, 1944, that were successfully smuggled out of the Ravensbrück concentration camp and passed on to Dietze's wife.

[2.] Cf. *DB-ER*, 775–77 and 907.

edly knew for certain that Goerdeler was making preparations for the overthrow. In actual fact these discussions were purely ecclesial and were serving to prepare for a possible ecumenical conference in the period after the war.[3] The names of the participants were accurate. Thereupon I stated the actual course of events in detail for the record. That was really the only chance I still had to do something for the others. At the end Schrey again asked a few questions concerning other persons, which gave my conscience a scare. But it passed by without incident, and none of this went into the minutes.

My dear wife, at our last meeting at the police station I promised you not to lie and not to say anything unnecessary. It has all turned out differently than we could have imagined at that point. I have not forgotten my promise. The first part of it is what has brought me the most difficulty here.[4]

[...]

459   **236. Indictment against Klaus Bonhoeffer, Rüdiger Schleicher, Hans John, Friedrich Justus Perels, and Hans Kloß**[1]

Indictment

Against

1.) chief corporate attorney Dr. Klaus *Bonhoeffer* of Berlin-Grunewald, born on January 5, 1901, in Breslau, married,

2.) former ministry counsel and honorary professor Dr. Rüdiger *Schleicher* of Berlin-Charlottenburg, born on January 14, 1895, in Stuttgart, married,

3.) former research assistant Dr. Hans *John* of Berlin-Dahlem, born on August 31, 1911, in Treysa, near Kassel, single,

4.) assistant judge Dr. Friedrich Justus *Perels*, of Berlin-Lichterfelde, born on November 13, 1910, in Berlin, Jewish crossbreed [Mischling], married,

5.) business employee Dr. Hans *Kloß* of Berlin, born on November 28, 1905, in Vienna, Jewish crossbreed, married,

all at the present time in custody pursuant with the arrest warrant issued by the investigative judge of the People's Court in Berlin on December 20, 1944.[2] I bring an indictment against the defendants on the grounds of the following actions:

[3.] See 1/205 and 1/218.

[4.] [Dietze's comments reflect the pressures that were being placed on them in interrogations and their efforts not to betray one another; see 1/231, ed. note 1.—MB]

[1.] *NL*, A 89,6 (3); hectograph; letterhead and file number: "The Senior Reich Attorney for the People's Court O J 57/44 s[ecret] R[eich] c[ase] I, Berlin December 20, 1944."

[2.] The arrest of Klaus Bonhoeffer took place on October 1, that of Rüdiger Schleicher on October 4, and that of F. J. Perels on October 5.

In 1943–1944 on German soil the defendants Dr. Bonhoeffer and Dr. Schleicher took part and agreed to cooperate in the operation to overthrow the National Socialist regime, through the elimination of the Führer by cowardly assassination or by another act of violence that included the possibility of his death, and to end the war through ignominious dealings with the enemies. This operation was conducted by the former Lord Mayor Dr. Goerdeler along with officers who had lost their nerve and with other enemies of the state.

The defendants Dr. John, Perels, and Dr. Kloß received credible knowledge of the plans of the conspiratorial clique to commit high treason in betraying their country yet nevertheless failed in their duty to inform the responsible authorities of these plans.

The defendants Dr. Bonhoeffer and Dr. Schleicher, as traitors to their country, have thereby placed themselves outside the community of the German people, as have the defendants Dr. John, Perels, and Dr. Kloß by disregarding their obligation to tell what they knew in this particularly grave matter.   460

There is thus sufficient evidence to accuse them of violation of § 5 no. 1 of the Decree of the Reich President for the Protection of People and State, dated February 28, 1933, StGB[3] 73.47.

[…]

II. The Defendants' Participation in the Crime.[4]

[…]

D. Perels.[5]

Around New Year's Day 1942, the defendant Perels first found out from an acquaintance, Pastor Dietrich Bonhoeffer, a brother of the defendant Dr. Bonhoeffer,[6] that a plan was being considered in military circles to alter the existing political conditions by force. In subsequent months Dietrich Bonhoeffer gave repeated further hints in this direction. Along the way he said that Goerdeler was involved in these plans and that the goal was to rob the Führer forcibly of his ruling power. Goerdeler's plan, according to Bonhoeffer, was that officers were to demand that the Führer relinquish power, in order then to take over leadership of the Reich. Bonhoeffer also informed Perels that he had the impression that for this operation Goerdeler was recruiting people with whom, together with the officers, he wished to make common cause. In the numerous conversations with Dietrich Bonhoeffer, Perels learned the names of other participants in this plan; in particular he learned that former General Beck and former Field Marshal von Witzleben, Dr. Popitz, and von Hassell were deeply

---

[3.] [Abbreviation for *Strafgesetzbuch*, "penal code."—MB]

[4.] The following section is limited to the material concerning F. J. Perels, because this is the only section mentioning Dietrich Bonhoeffer's role.

[5.] See Schreiber, *Friedrich Justus Perels*, 205–10; *DB-ER*, 907.

[6.] Klaus Bonhoeffer.

involved. Perels also had a few conversations with Dr. Popitz himself regarding ecclesial matters, where the latter personally expressed his disapproval of Goerdeler.

At some point in fall 1942 Perels initiated an acquaintance, Dr. Bauer, mentioned above, into these plans and told him that there was political activity in certain military circles. In a later conversation he told him that the former General Olbricht was playing a special role in these military circles.

At the end of 1942 and beginning of 1943 Perels took part several times in discussions in Berlin and Freiburg im Breisgau with college professors and Protestant theologians,[7] at which Goerdeler was also in attendance once, and which perhaps served the purpose of working out religious-philosophical foundations for building a non–National Socialist form of government.

[...]

I petition to hold the trial[8] of the defendants before the People's Court.

Lautz

237. Statements of Dietrich Bonhoeffer regarding Assertions by Bishop Bell on English Politics

237.1. The Chief of the Security Police and the SD to the Foreign Office[1]

Berlin SW 11, January 4, 1945

Regarding: Assertions of Lord Bishop *Bell* of Chichester in 1942 on English Politics.

The Protestant pastor Dietrich *Bonhoeffer*, imprisoned in connection with the events of July 20, 1944, previously a pastor of the German Protestant congregations in

---

[7.] Perels's actual presence at these conversations can only be confirmed for the meeting in Berlin on February 6–7, 1943; see 1/218. Like Bonhoeffer, he did not participate in the general meeting, November 17–19, 1942.

[8.] This took place on February 2, 1945; it concluded with the sentence of death against four of the five defendants, carried out in the night of April 22–23 against Klaus Bonhoeffer, Rüdiger Schleicher, Hans John, and F. J. Perels. [The fourth defendant, Hans Kloß, was sentenced to four years imprisonment (Leber with Brandt and Bracher, *Conscience in Revolt*, 214).—MB]

[1.] Auswärtiges Amt, Politisches Archiv, Berlin, Inland II/g 44, Lord Bishop of Chichester, 1945; typewritten; letterhead: "The Chief of the Security Police and the SD"; file number: "IV A 4 a -5/45 E. [= Fighting against opponents (Gestapa), Denominations/Jews Group, Diary—No. 5, 1945, isolated occurrence]"; address: "To the *Berlin* Foreign Office"; entry stamp: "Foreign Office Dom[estic] II B 57 rec[eived]. January 8, 1945"; stamped: "Secret"—"Placed on the desk of the Reich Foreign Minister"; marginal notations: "B [= Harro Brenner, Legation Counsel 1st Class in Reich Foreign Minister Office] II/1"—"Return to Inl[and] II," registered there anew: "Foreign Office Dom[estic] II B 108 g rec. January 12, 1945" (a few underlinings in pencil presumably assisted in presenting this material to Ribbentrop but could also derive from later use, for instance, at

London, met in May and June of 1942 in Sweden with Lord Bishop *Bell*, a previous   462
acquaintance of his. This meeting took place by order of former Admiral Canaris.
Regarding the content of the discussion with Bell, Bonhoeffer gave the following statements in an interrogation:[2]

Lord Bishop Bell, the most highly regarded and best known of the lord bishops of
the Church of England, a decisive leader in the ecumenical movement, is apparently a
man of balance and understanding, an outspoken friend of Germany. Therefore, in light
of the war situation, will not, as might have been expected, become the successor to
Lang, the Archbishop of Canterbury. Is said to have visited Germany often in earlier
years and become more closely acquainted with Rudolf *Hess*.[3] In the beginning he
attempted to come to terms with the German Protestant Reich Church under Müller
but then switched his allegiance to the Confessing Church and stood in solidarity
with Niemöller,[4] Dibelius, and Koch.

Purpose of Lord Bishop Bell's trip to Sweden at that point was supposedly to
gather information about Swedish-Soviet relations and about church activities in Scandinavia. Bell is said to have declared that before beginning this trip he spoke at length
with Eden and asked him what he should do if in Sweden peace feelers were
extended from any direction. Eden is said to have answered very gruffly that short of   463

---

the Nuremberg Trials). Previously published in *Akten zur deutschen auswärtigen Politik
1918–1945*, series E, vol. 8, no. 329; *Evangelische Theologie* 26 (1966): 462–63 (cf. 462–99);
MW 5:320–21; and *GS* 6:590–91. [The office that filed this report, Inland II, was a new
bureau that was opened within the Foreign Office in 1943. Its primary purpose was to
gather domestic intelligence and oversee Jewish affairs. Its director, Horst Wagner, reported
directly to Ribbentrop (Browning, *Final Solution and the German Foreign Office*, 176).—MB]

[2.] On the particular background of this record, see *DB-ER*, 902–5, and *MW* 5:293–
96. See also the statement by Detective Superintendent Sonderegger in his trial before
the Munich Regional Court II in August 1948: "Prepared a draft for me about the ecumenical movement, which he dictated into a machine. When he reckoned with the death
penalty, voluntarily gave statement about Copenhagen [*sic*] meeting" (*NL*, A 87,7). In a
letter to the president of the Munich Regional Court I on January 14, 1951, Sonderegger
further reported that "Dietrich Bonhöffer was successfully convicted by the working
group of Gov[ernment] Counsel Günther of preparing a high-treasonous undertaking
and of making contact with the British government through the bishop of Chichester,
Dr. Bell, at a meeting in Copenhagen [*sic*]. The purpose of his meeting with Dr. Bell was
betrayed to the Gestapo by Helmuth von Moltke, who accompanied Bonhöffer to Copenhagen, whereas Bonhöffer refused to make any statement on this subject before the Reich
War Court" (26 Munich 1, file no. Ks 21/50).

[3.] In a lecture in Usher Hall, Edinburgh, on December 2, 1941, Bishop Bell
reported, "Four years before the outbreak of war I was in the house of Rudolf Hess at
Munich" ("The Church and Humanity," 58)—on September 20, 1935 (*DB-ER*, 475).

[4.] A handwritten note in ink is added here: "in protective custody" (the highest level
of police measures apart from judicial sentence).

an English victory peace would not be discussed. In this matter Eden is believed to conform fully to Churchill.[5]

The stance of Stafford Cripps toward the problems of the war is supposedly entirely different from that of Eden. It is incorrect to assert, as some do, that he is a Bolshevist—on the contrary, he is a Christian socialist. Speaks with great concern about Russia's power, which in England is almost universally underestimated. Cripps is said to know the situation in Moscow intimately[6] and fears that the Soviets will march right up to the Brandenburg Gate and no power, even England, will be able to keep this from happening. Yet he believes the consequences for England of a Soviet victory are incalculable. Bell is said to have asserted that this view corresponds more closely to that of the English church than does Eden's.[7]

When questioned as to any possible U.S. intention of destroying or absorbing England, Lord Bishop Bell is said to have disputed this possibility with full conviction. America needs a strong England, and without its global empire England is not strong. Bell is said to have not wanted to entertain further thoughts about a union between the United States and England.

In the course of the discussion Bell also remarked about a visit by Lord Beaverbrook to Switzerland that had apparently taken place shortly beforehand. Beaverbrook is said to have met there with German industrialists[8] and to have discussed the possibilities for negotiating peace in such a way as to create a united front between the Western powers and Germany against Russia.

Kaltenbrunner

[5.] Cf. 1/180, 1/191, 1/193, 1/194, and 1/195 (documentation of the trip to Sweden as well as the correspondence following it between Bishop Bell and British Foreign Minister Anthony Eden). Before the trip Bishop Bell did not speak with Eden but did speak extensively with the head of the Northern Department of the Foreign Ministry, C. F. A. Warner, and also with Sir Stafford Cripps.

[6.] [Stafford Cripps served as the British ambassador in Moscow from 1940 to 1942.—MB]

[7.] Cf. 1/186, ed. note 11.

[8.] This event could not be traced. According to Bethge, Bonhoeffer mentioned "enough about Beaverbrook to make further inquiries desirable if not imperative; this in itself could slow down the interrogations and be a means of gaining time" (*DB-ER*, 904). Cf. also David Owen's letter to W. A. Visser 't Hooft on October 1, 1964: "I am afraid I know nothing at all about the reported discussions during wartime between Lord Beaverbrook and German industrialists concerning a common front between the Western powers and Germany against Russia. I find it very hard to believe that they took place at all, but I have no basis in fact for any judgment."

237.2. Notes for the Presentation by Inland II B to the Reich Foreign Minister[9]

Berlin, January 8, 1945

Presentation Notes

Regarding: Statement by Pastor Bonhoeffer about Peace Aims of English Personages. Bell

In the attached document of the 4th of this month, SS Lieutenant General Kaltenbrunner discloses that the Protestant pastor Bonhoeffer, imprisoned in connection with the events of July 20, met by order of former Admiral Canaris in May and June of 1942 with Lord Bishop Bell, an acquaintance of his, in Sweden. He reports the following as to the content of his conversation:

Lord Bishop Bell, the most highly regarded and best known of the bishops of the Church of England, is apparently a man of balance and understanding, an outspoken friend of Germany. He is said to have become more closely acquainted with Rudolf Hess in his previous visits to Germany. Before traveling to Sweden, Bell apparently spoke at length with Eden and asked him what he should do if in Sweden peace feelers were extended from any direction. Eden is said to have answered gruffly that short of an English victory peace would not be discussed. In this matter Eden is fully united with Churchill.

The stance of Cripps is supposedly entirely different; he speaks with great concern about Russia's power, which in England is almost universally underestimated. He fears that the Soviets will march right up to the Brandenburg Gate and no power, even England, will be able to keep this from happening. Yet he believes the consequences for England of a Soviet victory are incalculable. Bell is said to have asserted that this view corresponds more closely to that of the English church than does Eden's.

465

[9.] Auswärtiges Amt, Politisches Archiv, Berlin, Inland II/g 44 (like 1/237.1); typewritten in extra-large type as a copy for presentation, signed "Wagner"; attached was the document of January 4, 1945 (see 1/237.1); notes: "To be presented to the Reich Foreign Minister by way of the Secretary of State"—"carbon copy for RAM [Reich Foreign Minister]"—"Secretariat has o[riginal]"; marginal notes: "Return to Inl[and] II"—"RAM has presented orig[inal]"—"For det[ails] January 12 Bk [Bobrik]." A second typewritten copy in normal-sized type exists as well for ordinary use, signed "Bk [Bobrik] January 8" with the note, "pa [please add] original and expl[anation] March 2" and with the following further initials: "After exit[ing] Pol I: W[eber] January 8; Pol VI [illegible], Gr. [by Grundherr] January 10; Pol XI att[ention] [illegible]"; at the bottom left: "effective January 9 Bö [not identified]"–"Inl[an]d II B please pass this on to Stockholm emb[assy] as well. Gr[undherr] January 10." A third version with the same text, typewritten in normal font size, bears the note: "Decree of the Foreign Office—Inl. II B—to the German Embassy in Stockholm, Berlin, January 13, 1945"—"effective January 15, 1945 B[obri]k"—"by order of Bobrik." Regarding the work of the Inland II office, see 1/ 237.1, ed. note 1.

Lord Bishop Bell apparently disputes the possibility that the United States intends to destroy or absorb England. He maintains that America needs a strong England and that without its global empire England is not strong. Bell did not wish to entertain further thoughts about a union between the United States and England. Bell also remarked about a visit by Lord Beaverbrook to Switzerland that had apparently taken place shortly beforehand, in which the latter is said to have met there with German industrialists and to have discussed the possibilities for negotiating peace in such a way as to create a united front between the Western powers and Germany against Russia.

(Wagner)[10]

238. Indictment against Constantin von Dietze[1]

Berlin, April 9, 1945

Indictment

against [. . .]

2.) former university professor Constantin von Dietze, of Freiburg im Breisgau, Maria-Theresiastraße 13, born on August 9, 1891, in Gottesgnaden, Calbe an der Saale district, married, taken into temporary custody on September 8, 1944, both[2] detained pending trial pursuant to the arrest warrant issued on January 17, 1945 (8/45/556), by the investigative judge of the People's Court in Berlin, presently in solitary confinement in the detention center, Lehrter Straße 3, Berlin NW 40.

I bring an indictment against the defendants on the grounds of the following actions:

In 1942 until 1943 or 1944 the defendants took part in the preparations on German soil for a coup by the traitor Goerdeler and his backers by making proposals for

---

[10.] This document is signed by the group leader Horst Wagner, the presenting legation counsel in the Foreign Office, Group Inland II B.

[1.] Universitätsbibliothek, Freiburg im Breisgau, 22, Nachlaß Constantin von Dietze; typewritten; partially reproduced in *GS* 6:591–92. Envelope: "Case-No.: 2 L 85/45. People's Court, (1) Berlin W 9, Bellevuestraße 15. To former university professor Constantin von Dietze, presently in solitary confinement in Berlin NW 40. Served on April 20, 1945"—"Do not stamp—paid by government. Enclosed is a form for documentary evidence of the delivery. Simplified document service. To be forwarded within the German Reich"; letterhead and file number: "The Senior Reich Attorney of the People's Court O J 62.44 g–2 1 85/45"; notes: "Secret! 1. This is a state secret according to § 83, RStGB [Reich Penal Code], as formulated in the law of April 24, 1934 (*Reichsgesetzblatt* [Reich legal gazette], vol. 1, pages 341ff.). 2. Transmit only in sealed envelope; in the case of postal delivery use registered mail. Secret! 3. Recipient is responsible for secure safekeeping. Subject to arrest!" On the circumstances, cf. 1/205, 1/218, and 1/235.

[2.] This indictment also applied to Dr. Walter Bauer; cf. *DB-ER*, 907.

the economic, social, and cultural-political reorganization of the Reich. In all this they knew that the overthrow was to be triggered by an act of violence against the Führer. As traitors guilty of high treason, they have thereby placed themselves outside the community of the German people.

—Violation of § 80 sec. 2, § 83 sec. 2 and 3, no. 1, §§ 91b, 47.73 StGB[3]—

[...]

II. The Criminal Acts of the Defendants.

[...]

2. *von Dietze.*

[...]

b.) Furthermore, in the fall of 1942 or thereabouts, Pastor Dietrich Bonhoeffer, whom the defendant von Dietze had met in 1937 in Berlin-Dahlem at discussions among leading members of the Confessing Church,[4] discussions that served to prepare for the ecumenical conference in Oxford, which was then about to take place, approached the defendant on behalf of leading personages of the Confessing Church with the demand that he cooperate in putting together proposals that were to be presented to a planned ecumenical conference following the war. Bonhoeffer informed him that in Anglo-Saxon circles the intention existed "to impose a long, perhaps multiyear, time period between the end of military hostilities and the eventual declaration of peace." This interval would give such an ecumenical conference the possibility, "by means of appropriate statements, of gaining influence over the conditions for peace and the structures to be established within the individual nations."[5] Bonhoeffer's depiction made clear that the church authorities instigating these efforts were operating from the assumption that "the war could be ended by means of a peace compromise and a corresponding regime change." As von Dietze asserted, he and Bonhoeffer avoided articulating the question whether this change of regime in the Reich would be accomplished by legal means or through a coup d'état, since their concern was "as far as possible to steer clear of any political incrimination." In particular, every participant in the deliberations was, if need be, supposed "to be able to say with a clear conscience that no plans for a coup d'état or political overthrow were ever discussed." These statements by the defendant von Dietze bring to light that in any case he and Bonhoeffer reckoned with the possibility of a violent realization of the domestic changes, which would establish the precondition for their ecclesial and economic-political plans, and that they also consented to this sort of violent solution.

467

[3.] [Abbreviation for *Strafgesetzbuch*, "criminal code."—MB]

[4.] During the Dahlem conversations, April 12–14, 1937, Constantin von Dietze took shorthand notes (published in *GS* 6:431–32).

[5.] On this aspect of Bonhoeffer's conversations with Bishop Bell in May 1942, see *MW* 5:282–83, and Boyens, *Kirchenkampf und Ökumene*, vol. 2, *1939–1945*, 214–17.

Von Dietze assured Pastor Bonhoeffer of his cooperation and, in agreement with him, brought on board the Freiburg professors Ritter, Erik Wolf, Lampe, and Eucken, who shared his views in church matters. At the end of October or beginning of November 1942, at a conference in Berlin at which, besides Bonhoeffer, General Superintendent Dibelius, Pastors Asmussen and Böhm, and Assessor Perels, as well as most likely also von Dietze's codefendant Bauer, took part, he then made known the names of the Freiburg colleagues he had won over and arranged with his Berlin confreres to invite Goerdeler, as "a personage with political experience and knowledge," to the next gathering, which was to take place in Freiburg im Breisgau.

At the discussion in Freiburg, which was carried out shortly thereafter, and in which his codefendant Bauer also took part, von Dietze presented his thoughts concerning the future economic and social order, while Goerdeler developed his aforementioned conception of the reordering of domestic society. In two further gatherings in Berlin, which took place at some point in January or February of 1943, von Dietze discussed with his like-minded Berlin friends the proposals worked out in the meantime by him and his Freiburg colleagues; and they agreed on a few amplifications and corrections. Subsequently he informed Goerdeler, who did not participate in these further conversations, of what had ensued there. These gatherings with members of the Confessing Church came to an end after Dietrich Bonhoeffer was arrested in the spring of 1943.

c) Defendant von Dietze has conceded these facts of the case. As to the inner dimensions of his action, in his final interrogation he summarized by stating that the primary motivations of his behavior had always lain in his church convictions. He considered himself obligated to strive for an ordering of civil, economic, and social life corresponding to the divine commandments. Since he believed that any other ordering sooner or later doomed any people submitting to it, he himself also earnestly attempted to bring his ideas into realization. He perceived an opportunity for this in Goerdeler's efforts.

[…]

239. S. Payne Best to George K. A. Bell[1]

[…] "Will you give this message from me to the Bishop of Chichester, 'tell him that this is for me the end, but also the beginning—with him I believe in the principle of

---

[1.] LPL, London, Bell Papers, vol. 42; typewritten; in original English, including errors; excerpt from S. Payne Best's letter of October 13, 1953. Here Captain Best, who was transported together with Bonhoeffer up until their stay in the schoolhouse in Schönberg in the Bavarian forest, conveyed to the bishop the full text of Bonhoeffer's parting message as he was summoned for court martial in the Flossenbürg concentration camp on April 8, 1945. In a preceding letter to Bell on September 23, 1953, Best wrote: "I remember that the thought flashed through my mind, that perhaps the message was a

our Universal Christian brotherhood[2] which rises above all national hatreds[3] and that our victory is certain—tell him, too, that I have never forgotten his words at our last meeting.' He gave me this message twice in the same words, holding my hand firmly in his and speaking with emotional earnestness."

[...]

239a. Erwin Sutz to Paul Lehmann[1]

17:142

Rapperswil, June 6, 1945

My dear Paul,

I have made you wait nearly four years since your letter of August 1, 1941,[?] which was as affectionate as it was weighty. The letter arrived shortly before our wedding on September 23, so I was able to give it to our friend Dietrich Bonhoeffer to read as he was visiting us briefly at that time. And today, when Victory Day for Europe is already behind us and we can slowly begin to breathe again after all the horrible things that have taken place around Europe and around the borders of our fatherland—today I am obliged first of all to give you the sad news that Dietrich too has been killed amid all the dreadful murder. A week ago in Bern I met Prof. Karl Barth and heard from his own lips this horrific message, which has subsequently also been published in the ecumenical news. In April or early May, Dietrich was hanged along with his brother Klaus in a concentration camp near the Bohemian border, shortly before the arrival of the Americans.[3] Just imagine what he must have had to suffer

17:143

---

prearranged code which only you would understand." To this Bell responded on October 5, 1953: "You will see that the message was short; and it was not a pre-arranged code." On the background, see Best, *Venlo Incident,* 180, 191, 200; *DB-ER,* 921–28; and the publication of the Best/Bell correspondence in Glenthøj, "Zwei neue Zeugnisse," 99–111. Cf. Schminck-Gustavus, *Der "Prozess" gegen Dietrich Bonhoeffer,* 31.

[2.] After the outbreak of the war, George Bell wrote to Pastor Julius Rieger on September 6, 1939: "Nothing shall disturb our friendship—or brotherhood in Christ" (*GS* 6: 468). Cf. 1/175, ed. note 2.

[3.] In his 1957 Göttingen lecture Bishop Bell erroneously cited this as "interests" (*GS* 1:412).

[1.] Center of Theological Inquiry, Princeton, Paul Lehmann papers; typewritten with handwritten underlining, on stationery with the letterhead, "Evang. Pfarramt Rapperswil-Jona, Telephon 2 16 54" and "Rapperswil, den [space given for the date]"; addressed to "Rev. Paul Lehmann, Wellesley College, Wellesley, Massachusetts. U.S.A." First published in *DBW* 17:142–43. Page numbers in the margin refer to *DBW* 17.

[2.] Cf. Lehman's letter of August 4, 1941, to Erwin Sutz, which includes comments directed to Bonhoeffer on August 2, 1941; see 1/116a. Clearly there had been no contact between Sutz and Lehmann since then.

[3.] This imprecise version of events reflects the form in which this news first began to spread at that time. In fact Klaus Bonhoeffer had been killed together with Rüdiger Schleicher on April 23, 1945, in Berlin.

before then! He was one of the most capable and brave theologians of the Confessing Church and was in touch with the best elements of the resistance movement. And for us he was surely "The big one"[4] without whom that year at Union Seminary would have been quite unmemorable. Poor, dear Dietrich. He has entered church history as one of those martyrs of whom it is written, "If we have died with him, we will also live with him; if we endure, we will also reign with him!" (2 Tim. 2:11).

I have also been without any news of our dear "French one"[5] Jean Lasserre for years.[6] He was (or is) pastor in Maubeuge, where the war raced through in 1940. I have attempted to find word of him and his family through the Protestant Children's Aid in Geneva, but so far without success. But I hope that we will one day again be in touch with him.

We ourselves are healthy and well. For our entire people it is an inconceivable miracle that we who were occasionally (especially in 1941) most gravely threatened have been spared the events of the war and a German occupation with all its terror. A few times your bombers caused us damage, and sometimes the alarm sirens wailed day and night. But we were not forced to go to the cellar even once. We had exemplary order in the nation, and food supplies were always sufficient and good. The flock of refugees and internees grew from year to year. Our most important task in these years was to shelter as many people as possible from deportation and death. [...]

With sincerest wishes for your well-being and deeply heartfelt regards to you and your dear wife—also from my wife—I remain your "old little one,"[7]

Erwin Sutz

Your letter from 1941[8] is here next to me. I just read it again. The photos will surely give you both pleasure.

[4.] ["The big one" is in English in Sutz's letter.—MB]
[5.] ["French one" is in English in Sutz's letter.—MB]
[6.] Cf. Jean Lasserre's letter to an unknown woman on February 8, 1941; see 1/73.
[7.] ["Old little one" is in English in Sutz's letter.—MB]
[8.] This refers to the letter of August 4, 1941; see 1/116a.2.

PART 2
Essays and Notes

PART 2
ESSAYS AND NOTES

1. Reflection on Easter: Resurrection[1]

The resurrection of Jesus Christ is God's Yes to Christ and his work of expiation. The cross was the end, the death of the Son of God, curse and judgment on all flesh. If the cross had been the last word about Jesus, then the world would be lost in death and damnation without hope; then the world would have triumphed over God. But God, who alone accomplished salvation for us — "all this is from God" (2 Cor. 5:18) — raised Christ from the dead. That was the new beginning that followed the end as a miracle from on high — not, like spring, according to a fixed law, but out of the incomparable freedom and power of God, which shatters death. "Holy Scripture plainly says / That death is swallowed up by death" (Luther).[2] Thus did God vindicate Jesus Christ; the apostle goes so far as to say that the resurrection is the day of the begetting of the Son of God (Acts 13:33; Rom. 1:4). The Son receives back his eternal divine glory; the Father has the Son again. Thus Jesus is attested and glorified as the Christ of God, who he was from the beginning. Thus also Jesus Christ's vicarious representative work of expiation is recognized and accepted by God.[3] On the cross Jesus cried out in desolation and then

---

[1.] *NL,* A 62,4; hectograph, enclosed with the March 1940 monthly newsletter of the Pomeranian Council of Brethren of the Confessing Church to its pastors; previously published in *GS* 3:405–9. On page 3 of the hectograph these words appear: "Stettin, in March 1940 — We would not wish to deprive one another of this reflection on the resurrection that became available for us at the last minute and are sending it along as a further greeting for the Easter season; on behalf of the Council of Brethren, Guddas."

[2.] From verse 2 of the hymn, "Christ Jesus Lay in Death's Strong Bands" (*Lutheran Book of Worship,* no. 134 ["Christ lag in Todesbanden" (*Evangelisches Gesangbuch für Brandenburg und Pommern,* 57, 4; *Evangelisches Kirchengesangbuch,* 76, 4) —MB]).

[3.] Here Bonhoeffer takes up the so-called doctrine of satisfaction that asserts that through his vicarious sacrifice before God, Christ has "done enough" for our sins (cf. Schmid, *Doctrinal Theology of the Evangelical Lutheran Church,* 342–44).

commended himself into his Father's hands,[4] that God should act toward him and his work according to the divine pleasure. In the resurrection of Christ it has become certain that God has in fact said yes to the Son and his work. Thus we call upon the Risen One as the Son of God, the Lord and Savior.

472   *The resurrection of Jesus Christ is God's Yes to us.* Christ died for our sins; he was raised for our righteousness (Rom. 4:25). Christ's death was the death sentence upon us and our sins. If Christ had remained dead, this death sentence would still stand: "We would still be in our sins"[5] (1 Cor. 15:17). Because, however, Christ is risen from the dead, our sentence has been lifted, and we are risen with Christ (1 Cor. 15).[6] This is the case because we are in Jesus Christ by virtue of his assumption of our human nature in the incarnation;[7] what happens to him happens also to us, for we are assumed into him. This is not an empirical judgment but rather a judgment of God that is to be received by faith in God's Word.

The resurrection of Jesus Christ is God's Yes to the creature. What takes place here is not the destruction of life in the body but its new creation. The body of Jesus comes forth from the tomb, and the tomb is empty.[8] We are unable to grasp how it is possible and thinkable that the mortal and corruptible body is now present as the immortal, incorruptible, transfigured body.[9] The variety of the accounts reporting the encounter of the Risen One with the disciples demonstrates perhaps nothing so clearly as the fact that we are unable to construct an image of the new life in the body of the Risen One. We know that it is the same body—for the tomb is empty; and it is a new body—for the tomb is empty. We know that God has judged the first creation and has brought about a new creation in the likeness of the first. It is not a Christ-idea that lives on, but the bodily Christ. This is God's Yes to the new creature in the midst of the old. In the resurrection, we acknowledge that God has not given up on the earth but has personally won it back. God has given it a new future, a new promise. The very earth God created bore the Son of God and his cross, and on this earth the Risen One appeared to his own, and to this earth Christ will come again on the last day. Those who

473   affirm the resurrection of Christ in faith can no longer flee the world, nor

---

[4.] Cf. Mark 15:34; Luke 23:46.

[5.] [This phrase is in the second person, present tense, indicative in the NRSV.—MB]

[6.] Admittedly, 1 Cor. 15:20-23 speaks more of the *future* resurrection of all the dead.

[7.] For Bonhoeffer's understanding of the *assumptio carnis,* or "assumption of the flesh," see his "Reflection on the Ascension," 2/2.

[8.] Cf. Mark 16:5-6 par.

[9.] Cf. 1 Cor. 15:35-57.

can they still be enslaved by the world, for within the old creation they have perceived the new creation of God.

The resurrection of Jesus Christ calls for faith. Although the accounts transmit what occurred and was experienced here in otherwise inconsistent ways, they agree unanimously that the Risen One shows himself not to the world but only to his own (Acts 10:40-41). Jesus does not present himself to a neutral authority in order to allow the miracle of his resurrection to be attested before the world and thereby force it to acknowledge him. He desires to be believed, preached, and further believed. In a sense, the world sees only the negative—that is, the earthly imprint of the divine miracle. It sees the empty tomb and declares it (although in conscious self-deception!) to be the pious hoax of the disciples (Matt. 28:11ff.). It sees the joy and the proclamation of the disciples and calls them vision, an autosuggestion. The world sees the "signs," but it does not believe the miracle. Yet only where the miracle is believed do the signs become divine signs and aids to faith. For the world the empty tomb is an ambiguous historical fact; for the faithful it is the historical sign, necessarily following from and confirming the miracle of the resurrection, of the God who acts in history among human beings. There is no historical proof for the resurrection, but only a number of facts, in themselves highly peculiar and difficult for historians to interpret—e.g., the empty tomb (for if the tomb had not been empty, this strongest counterargument against the bodily resurrection would surely have become the foundation of anti-Christian polemic; yet this objection never confronts us, but on the contrary the empty tomb is confirmed even by opponents [Matt. 28:11]) — [e.g.,] the sudden shift in things two days after the crucifixion (a conscious hoax is ruled out psychologically by the entire previous and later behavior of the disciples and equally by the inconsistencies of the resurrection accounts! Self-deception through a visionary frame of mind is virtually excluded for the open-minded historian by the disciples' thoroughly disbelieving, skeptical initial rejection of the proclamation [Luke 23:11 et passim], as well as by the great number of appearances and their nature). It follows that the determinations of historians in this matter, which scientifically remain so puzzling, are dictated by the presuppositions of their worldview. Thus, however, these determinations lose interest and substance for faith that is grounded in God's action in history. For the world, then, there remains an insoluble riddle that can in no way compel faith in the resurrection of Jesus. For faith, however, this riddle is a sign of the reality that it already knows, an imprint of God acting in history. Research can neither prove nor refute the resurrection of Jesus, for it is a miracle of God. Yet faith, to which the Risen One reveals himself as the Living One, perceives precisely in the witness of the scriptures the historicity of the resurrection

474

as an action of God that in its awesomeness can express itself to science only as a riddle. Faith receives the certainty of the resurrection solely from the present witness of Christ. It finds its confirmation in the historical imprints of the miracle, as scripture records them.—It is the grace of Jesus Christ that he does not yet reveal himself visibly to the world; for in the very moment in which that were to occur, the end and with it the judgment of unbelief would be present. Thus the Risen One holds back from any visible self-vindication to the world. In his hidden glory he is with his community and allows himself to be proclaimed to all the world through the word, until at the Last Day he comes again for judgment, visible to all people.

475   ## 2. Reflection on the Ascension[1]

The Ascension of Jesus Christ.
A Reflection on Its Christological, Soteriological, and
Parenetical Meaning

A. Christologically.

1. The ascension of Jesus is the return of the Son of God to his origin. Jesus enters into the glory of the invisible God. He remains human forever. His human nature,[2] assumed within time, is taken up into eternity. It has passed over from the state of humiliation into the state of fulfilled exaltation.[3] The Lutheran fathers distinguished emphatically between incarnation and humiliation. They said: the "subject of humiliation"[4] is not the

---

[1.] *NL*, A 62,5; hectograph, enclosed with the April 1940 monthly newsletter of the Pomeranian Council of Brethren of the Confessing Church to its pastors; previously published in *GS* 3:409–15. See *DB-ER*, 668. On page 3 of the manuscript the following words appear: "Dear Brothers! We are sending you a reflection on the meaning of the Ascension of Jesus Christ. This comes with our best wishes and with the hope that it may be helpful to you in your sermon preparations. Stettin, Pölitzer Str. 17 The Council of Brethren of the Pomeranian Province; on behalf of the Council of Brethren, Guddas."

[2.] The Christology of early Protestant Orthodoxy, which Bonhoeffer briefly refers to here, understood the assumption of human nature in the personal unity with the divine nature of Jesus Christ as incarnation; cf. Heinrich Schmid's compendium from *The Doctrinal Theology of the Evangelical Lutheran Church*, 294–95.

[3.] Cf. Luther's doctrine of the "states of Christ," *de statibus Christi*, in Schmid, *Doctrinal Theology of the Evangelical Lutheran Church*, 376ff., esp. 379–80.

[4.] "Exinanitio dicitur de filio Dei ἐνσάρκῳ s(eu) Christo θεανθρώπῳ; incarnatio de filio Dei ἀσάρκῳ. . . . Subjectum quo est sola humanitas, sed in unione considerata" ("The humiliation is asserted of the incarnate Son of God or of the God-human Christ; but the incarnation is asserted of the not-yet-incarnate Son of God. . . . The subject [of the humiliation] is regarded as solely the humanity of Christ, yet in unity [with his divinity]") (Hollaz, *Examen theologicum acroamaticum*, 765 and 767; cf. Schmid, *Doctrinal Theology of*

logos asarkos[5] but rather the logos ensarkos,[6] i.e., the incarnate Son of God. They thereby gave the humanity created by God and assumed in   476
Christ honor and hope with God. The incarnate Son of God humbles himself and is exalted in the descent into hell,[7] resurrection, and ascension. The human nature of Jesus Christ, when freed from the state of humiliation, participates in an unveiled way in the attributes of the divine nature. What was real from the first instant of Christ's human being and yet remained hidden in the state of humiliation, namely, the permeation of his human nature with the attributes of his divine nature,[8] is revealed in the state of exaltation. The assumed humanity, the human being Jesus Christ, enters the eternity of the Father. In order, however, to protect against philosophical speculation that allows humanity and divinity to merge into each other, that is, in order to confront any mysticism of identification,[9] the Lutheran fathers teach that, while humanity belongs to the Son of God forever and the Son of God remains in the full communion of the triune God, the assumed humanity (i.e., Jesus Christ's human nature) is not itself assumed into the Trinity but rather remains eternally subject to it. For humanity can never become divinity;[10] otherwise God would cease to be the Creator, Reconciler, and Redeemer of humanity.

2. The ascension is the last of the Lord's Easter appearances.[11] By his resurrection, Jesus has bodily entered the transfigured world of God. There   477
is no difference in mode of being between the Risen One and the Ascended

---

the Evangelical Lutheran Church, 371–72, annotations 1 and 2). Cf. also Bonhoeffer's own 1933 lectures on Christology in *CC*, 96 (*DBW* 12:279–349 [*GS* 3:166–242]), as well as *DBWE* 4:213–16.

[5.] Greek: λόγος ἄσαρκος, "Word without flesh," the not-yet-incarnate Son of God.

[6.] Greek: λόγος ἔνσαρκος, "Word in the flesh," the incarnate Son of God.

[7.] According to Lutheran doctrine, in distinction from Reformed Christology, the exaltation of Jesus Christ begins with his descent into hell (see Schmid, *Doctrinal Theology of the Evangelical Lutheran Church*, 379–80).

[8.] Bonhoeffer is here representing Luther's doctrine of the *genus maiestaticum* of the *communicatio idiomatum*, i.e., that the royal attributes of the divine nature accrue to the human nature of Jesus Christ on the basis of its personal unity with the divine nature (cf. Schmid, *Doctrinal Theology of the Evangelical Lutheran Church*, 314–15). During his life on earth, Jesus renounced the *use* of these royal attributes and to that extent *hid* them (cf. Schmid, *Doctrinal Theology of the Evangelical Lutheran Church*, 377; cf. also Bonhoeffer's 1933 Christology lectures (*CC*, 91–93 [*DBW* 12:330–32; previously published in *GS* 3:224–25]).

[9.] In his 1933 lectures on Christology, Bonhoeffer adduces Hegel's philosophy and its theological appropriation as an example of this sort of speculative identification (*CC*, 91 [*DBW* 12:321–22.; *GS* 3:211–12]). The person of Jesus is the actualized "principle" of the idea "that the self developing in a truly *human* way arrives at the self-conscious actualization of essentially *divine* being" (Biedermann, *Christliche Dogmatik*, 254 and 234).

[10.] Cf. Schmid, *Doctrinal Theology of the Evangelical Lutheran Church*, 405–6.

[11.] Cf. Mark 16:9-20; Luke 24:50-53; Acts 1:4-12.

One, but only a difference in the mode of appearance. In the forty days,[12] Jesus reveals himself as the one who now abides in eternity, as the living, bodily Lord who has returned to the world of God. It is impossible to derive from John 20:17 a distinction between the life in the body of the Risen One and that of the Ascended One (for Jesus is here refuting only Mary's erroneous belief that she could have him back now in just the same way she had him before his crucifixion; he would thus not remain with her now but would return only following his ascension and remain with his own). Nor can we say that although Jesus was, to be sure, corporeally perceptible following his resurrection (Thomas!),[13] he was no longer so following his ascension; this would overlook his appearance to Saul.[14] That Jesus denies himself Mary's touch, that he allows his wounds to be probed by Thomas, that he appears to Saul in the radiance of glory, means solely that he wants to heal Mary from the error of a false love of Jesus, Thomas from the doubt that this was all a hallucination, and Saul from his unbelief in the living Christ. But Jesus is the same in the one instance as in the others. Paul places the appearance that manifested his call into the series of Easter appearances (1 Cor. 15:1ff.).[15] It is the same risen Christ who calls him to be among the witnesses of his resurrection (see also Acts 7:56; 18:9; 22:17).[16] Nevertheless, the forty days between Easter and Ascension are of decisive significance. They bring about the new calling and sending of the witnesses in service of the Risen One. The office of the proclamation of the gospel rests on those forty days. Scripture testifies to this with one voice (Mark 16:15ff.; Matt. 28: 18-19; John 20:22ff.; Acts 1:8, 10:42). Yet it is not for his own sake but for ours that Jesus remains those forty days with those who belong to him. Because for Jesus himself the ascension represents no change in his mode of being, Scripture is often able, therefore, to refer to the resurrection of Jesus as the decisive act of salvation without mention of the ascension (Rom.

478   1:3-4; Acts 10:41, 13:31, et passim; on the other hand, see Acts 2:33, 3:21, et passim). Seen from this perspective, the ascension of Jesus represents only the conclusion of his appearances on earth, although even in this regard Christ remains free in his action (Acts 9:5).

3. The ascension is the exaltation of Jesus to the right hand of God. The sign of being lifted up into the clouds signifies simply that from now on Jesus will be entirely in the world of God. This, however, permits no speculation

---

[12.] Cf. Acts 1:3.
[13.] Cf. John 20:24-29.
[14.] Cf. Acts 9:3-6; 22:6-11; 26:12-18.
[15.] 1 Cor. 15:8.
[16.] This should read "22:17-18."

whatsoever regarding the location in which he now lives. When scripture wishes to assert that Jesus is no longer in the world of human beings but in the world of God, it expresses this with the simple statement that Jesus has gone "into heaven" (Heb. 9:24; Eph. 1:20). When, however, scripture wishes to preclude any conceivable idea that tries to hold Jesus in the created world, then it says even more pointedly: he has ascended above all heavens; he has passed through the heavens; he has become higher than the heavens (Eph. 4:10; Heb. 4:14, 7:26). Sitting at the right hand of God, Jesus participates in God's reign over the world; like God, he is simultaneously far from the world and close to it. Every thought that wishes to imagine Jesus bound to a specific location for the sake of his life in the body[17] overlooks these biblical assertions. Even in Acts 3:21 nothing is said other than that Christ is now in heaven and has not yet returned, which, however, does not preclude the divine omnipresence of Jesus Christ, who sits at the right hand of God. Whoever asks how Jesus can participate in divine omnipresence despite his life in the body must equally ask how the spiritual body[18] of Jesus was able to eat and drink and be touched in the days of Easter. Nothing has been revealed to us other than that Jesus Christ has been raised in transfigured life in the body to the glory of the Father and participates in God's power, distance, and presence.

B. Soteriologically. 479

1. The ascension is the proclamation of Jesus as the Lord of the world and the head of the church-community.[19] It is the proof of the "great power" of God, who "seated [Jesus] at his right hand in the heavenly places, far above all rule and authority and power and dominion, and above every name that is named, not only in this age but also in the age to come" (Eph. 1:20).[20] Christ has assumed dominion over the world. Fate, authorities, and powers are in his hand. Matthew lacks an account of the ascension. In its place we find the last words of Jesus in Matt. 28:18: "All authority in heaven and on earth has been given to me.... remember, I am with you always, to the end of the age."[21] That itself is the ascension proclamation.

[17.] This is the traditional teaching of Reformed doctrine (cf. Heppe, *Reformed Dogmatics*, 500–503).

[18.] Cf. 1 Cor. 15:44.

[19.] [Throughout *DBWE* we have translated *Gemeinde* as "church-community" wherever Bonhoeffer seems to be describing a larger context than simply the individual congregation.—MB]

[20.] This should read "Eph. 1:19-21."

[21.] [Matt. 28:18, 20.—MB]

The miracle is attested; only the sign remains unmentioned. Now Christ exercises his royal office—this is how the church fathers refer to it[22]—in its full scope. The King of all the world is simultaneously the head of the church-community. The head is in heaven, the body on earth. The invisible head rules the visible body. In this way the heavenly Christ is in fact utterly present to the earth; he fills his church-community, and with it and through it he fills all in all (Eph. 1:23); for through the church-community he gradually permeates the entire world, which belongs to him, and fills it with his active presence. As the one who has moved into the depths of hell and the heights of heaven, as the one who has passed through all things with divine power and fulfills all things, he is now also able to give the church-community the divine gifts it needs (Eph. 4:8ff.); he gives it the offices, which with authority call the world to God and keep the faithful close to Christ. The Lord who has vanished to the far reaches of the transfigured world of God has in this way become all the nearer to the world and the church-community.

2. Christ entered into heaven in order to appear before the face of God for us (Heb. 9:24). This is the fulfillment of his priestly office.[23] Because he has borne all our sins on the cross, he can therefore now be our advocate (1 John 2:1); and therefore our prayers, which would otherwise echo in emptiness, can be brought through him before the Father and granted a hearing. Only in the name of Jesus are we able to pray. For Christ as the high priest has reconciled us with God and, interceding on our behalf, presents his sacrifice before God in eternity. The church fathers called this the intercessio Christi[24] (Rom. 8:34; John 14:16; Heb. 4:14) and intended this priestly action of the exalted Lord to apply not only to the faithful but also to unbelievers, "so that the fruit of his saving death might be bestowed on them as well" (Hollaz).[25]

3. In the same way Christ went into heaven he will one day return from heaven for judgment. Thus, in the exalted Lord we recognize the future judge for whom we must wait. He is yet hidden; that is his patience, for faith can yet find grace in him. When, however, he returns visibly, then the day of judgment is at hand.

[22.] Latin: *officium* or *munus regium*. The royal office of Christ applies within the *regnum potentiae*, "reign of power," to the entire world; within the *regnum gratiae*, "reign of grace," to the church; and within the *regnum gloriae*, "reign of glory," to the heavenly world (cf. Schmid, *Doctrinal Theology of the Evangelical Lutheran Church*, 370–71).

[23.] Latin: *officium* or *munus sacerdotale*, which consists of *satisfactio*, "satisfaction for sins," and *intercessio* (see ed. note 24).

[24.] "intercession of Christ."

[25.] Latin: "ut salutaris mortis suae fructus illis applicetur" (Hollaz, *Examen*, 749; cf. Schmid, *Doctrinal Theology of the Evangelical Lutheran Church*, 345).

C. Parenetically.

1. The ascension of Jesus calls us to faith, to confession, to worship. Because God raised Jesus and gave him heavenly glory, we have faith and hope in God (1 Peter 1:21). Because our high priest is not an earthly human being but rather the Son of God who has entered into heaven, we hold fast to the confession of him as our salvation (Heb. 4:14). Because Jesus is exalted in immeasurable ways above us, we worship him (Luke 24:52, apparatus).[26]

2. The ascension of Jesus has transposed us into the heavenly places (Eph. 2:6) and thereby orients our gaze toward heaven (Col. 3:1). Just as we died and were raised with Christ in his body (Col. 2:12), so we have also already moved with him into the heavenly world. This high, albeit unparalleled, statement in the Letter to the Ephesians teaches us to locate ourselves in and with the Lord who has gone to heaven, as those who by the power of the humanity he assumed are always with him. Where he is, we are also. We are already in heaven with Christ. Yet precisely for this reason we seek and long for what is above.[27] "They move on earth and live in heaven," we sing with the hymn.[28] That which is future is present, and the present already past. In this way we live in the power of Christ's ascension.

3. The ascension of Jesus places us between having and waiting. We have heaven, and therefore we wait for it. We have been transposed into the heavenly places, our citizenship is in heaven (Phil. 3:20); and therefore we plead for the Lord's return from heaven. Those who are waiting stay awake and make themselves ready for the day of rejoicing (Matt. 24:43ff. et passim). For the believing church-community, the final appearance of Jesus, however, will bring about its transfiguration into the glory of the Lord and raise it up into the dominion of heaven forever.

481

[26.] The words "they worshiped him," προσκυνήσαντες αὐτόν, appear only in the New Testament manuscripts D, it, and sy^s. The Nestle edition of the *Novum Testamentum Graece* that Bonhoeffer used followed manuscripts P75 and rell and marked the alternate readings only in the apparatus (cf. now, however, *Novum Testamentum Graece*, ed. K. Aland and B. Aland, 27th ed., at this verse).

[27.] Cf. Col. 3:1-2.

[28.] This line comes from stanza 5 of the hymn, "Es glänzet der Christen inwendiges Leben" (The Inner Life of Christians Shines) (*Evangelisches Gesangbuch für Brandenburg und Pommern*, 176; *Evangelisches Gesangbuch*, 265).

3. Sketch of a Bible Study on 1 Corinthians 3[1]

1 Cor. 3:23   Monthly Watchword, May 1940[2]

Detached from its context as a monthly watchword, this text intends to say the following to the church-community: *All things serve the church-community; the church-community serves Christ. The church-community is subject to no one in the world, because it is subject to Christ. The church-community is free in and of the world, because it belongs to Christ and obeys him.*

482   1. A tremendous promise[3] *for our church-communities that are so constrained, afflicted,* tyrannized, and muzzled; our view becomes quite encompassing. All fetters that the world wants to impose on the church-community and its work are burst as if they were not there at all; the prison doors swing open, the great church bureaucracy collapses like a house of cards. The church-community is freed. *All things are yours.* The entire world belongs to you and must serve you.

2. A tremendous promise for the church-community during a war, which it faces powerless and bewildered in every respect. Its work has to a great extent come to a halt; with pastors gone, each person in utter faithfulness, with fullest possible commitment, serves the command of the government [Obrigkeit] that hinders the gospel. With incomparable burdens, anxiety and worries about men, work, children, future[4] — *all things are yours.* Here the church-community grows far beyond all these things. Even the war . . . is yours, serves you!

3. A tremendous promise for the church that is[5] in a struggle.[6] God has given it many teachers, spiritual powers among laity and theologians. They are not all equal to one another; there are great and small, varying tasks, gifts; in various ways they testify to the same thing.— "All is yours"— not only one aspect but the entire richness of the proclamation of the word of God belongs to you.

[1.] *NL,* A 63,1; handwritten; previously published in *GS* 4:466–72. The manuscript has been folded many times and gives the impression of having been used often. From this we can conclude that Bonhoeffer held this Bible study many times during his East Prussian visitations in June and July 1940. Bonhoeffer's handwritten corrections or changes are often cursory and cannot be inserted directly into the text. For this reason changes are noted only in the editorial notes, in contrast to the usual practice in the *DBWE* volumes.

[2.] This is written on the first page of the manuscript in the upper left corner. The verse itself reads: "and you belong to Christ, and Christ belongs to God."

[3.] Penciled correction: "The liberating word."

[4.] Handwritten addition: "worries about life and death, what is present and what is to come."

[5.] Penciled marginal addition: "for the youth of the congregation who have to move out into the world—conflicts, decisions, human, political."

[6.] Penciled correction: "in a spiritual conflict."

All is yours! The "all" is what matters. If we make a choice, if we say that only a portion, a certain preacher, etc., belongs to us, then we are making ourselves dependent on that person. Only because *all things* belong to us are we free of every individual. All things are *yours*. The "yours" is what matters. We are told that it is for *us* and serves *us* and not the other way around, and that we are free. That ceases if we do not embrace the "*all*," if we devote ourselves to only a part. Every constriction is false; it enslaves. It has the consequence that not "everything is ours," but that we fall into dependence on an individual person, an institution, an idea, a piece of the world.

But you are Christ's. [7] Not "Christ is yours," but the other way around. With all that is ours, we belong to Christ. Because we belong to Christ, *all things* belong to us. If we belonged to ourselves or to a human person, then it would be different. This is gospel and law in one. [8] *Gospel:* for it is promised to us that we belong to Christ. *Law:* for it is in Christ that we find the only boundary of that which is ours, or actually, *how* it is ours. For in Christ truly all things are ours in the sense that they *serve* us, even evil; but not in the sense that we appropriate them for ourselves and how we use them. Because we are in Christ, all things belong to us, yet in such a way that they belong to Christ.

The church-community belongs to Jesus Christ alone, and for this reason all things belong to it. With this goal in mind, let us read chapter 3.   483

> "And so, brothers and sisters, I could not speak to you as spiritual people, but rather as people of the flesh, as infants in Christ. I fed you with milk, not solid food, for you were not ready for solid food. Even now you are still not ready, for you are still of the flesh. For as long as there is jealousy and quarreling among you, are you not of the flesh, and behaving according to human inclinations? For when one says, 'I belong to Paul,' and another, 'I belong to Apollos,' are you not merely human? What then is Apollos? What is Paul? Servants through whom you came to believe, as the Lord assigned to each. I planted, Apollos watered, but God gave the growth. So neither the one who plants nor the one who waters is anything, but only God who gives the growth. The one who plants and the one who waters have a common purpose, and each will receive wages according to the labor of each. For we are God's servants, working together; you are God's field, God's building. According to the grace of God given to me, like a skilled master builder I laid a foundation, and someone else is building on it. Each builder must choose with care how to build on it. *For no one can lay any foundation other than the one that has been laid; that foundation is Jesus Christ.* [9] Now if anyone builds on the foundation with gold, silver, precious stones, wood, hay, straw—the work of each builder will become   484

[7.] Penciled marginal addition: "*Ground* and *Boundary.*"
[8.] Bonhoeffer here is following Karl Barth's way of speaking in *Evangelium und Gesetz*.
[9.] [The italicized text was underlined by Bonhoeffer in the original.—MB]

visible, for the Day will disclose it, because it will be revealed with fire, and the fire will test what sort of work each has done. If what has been built on the foundation survives, the builder will receive a reward. If the work is burned up, the builder will suffer loss; the builder will be saved, but only as through fire.

"Do you not know that you are God's temple and that God's Spirit dwells in you? If anyone destroys God's temple, God will destroy that person. For God's temple is holy, and you are that temple.

"Do not deceive yourselves. If you think that you are wise in this age, you should become fools so that you may become wise. For the wisdom of this world is foolishness with God. For it is written, 'He catches the wise in their craftiness,'[10] and again, 'The Lord knows the thoughts of the wise, that they are futile.'[11] So let no one boast about human leaders. For all things are yours, whether Paul or Apollos or Cephas or the world or life or death or the present or the future—all belong to you, and you belong to Christ, and Christ belongs to God."[12]

Quarrels in Corinth since the founding of the congregation by Paul.[13] These had to do with perceptions and persons. Forming groups and parties. Veneration of some people and deprecation of others. 1:12: groups. *Paul's group:* the old people. The unadorned gospel of free grace in Jesus Christ.

Apollos's group: Acts 18:24ff.; Acts 19:1; 1 Cor. 16:12 (Apollos in Ephesus). Jew with Greek education, full of the Spirit and the gift of speech; perhaps in contrast to Paul, whose proclamation gave offense, more of the gift of accommodation without renunciation.

Peter's group: Jewish Christians who had immigrated from Asia Minor. Legalistic, conservative, strict, traditional.

485   *Christ's group:* unmediated appeal to Christ in contrast to the apostles. They want "only" Christ without the mediation of the messengers. They make Christ into a party, claim him for themselves alone. The most dangerous group! Still present in 2 Cor. 10:7, whereas we hear nothing further of the other groups. Particularly hypocritical,[14] malicious, divisive, dismissive of the others. They refuse to render obedience to Paul, themselves know best about everything.

[10.] [1 Cor. 3:19, where Paul is quoting Job 5:13.—MB]

[11.] [1 Cor. 3:20, where Paul is quoting Ps. 94:11.—MB]

[12.] [1 Cor. 3; the translation used here is the NRSV, but the paragraph breaks reflect Bonhoeffer's text.—MB]

[13.] Penciled addition: "Personality cults and human wisdom in the church-community."

[14.] [Here Bonhoeffer uses *pharisäisch*; see the discussion of the use of this term in the editor's introduction, pp. 26–27.—MB]

Verse 3, 4. Jealousy and conflict. With the portion each has from Christ everyone wants to be right against the others, accords the other no success, followers.[15] According to the flesh! This is new to the Greeks. To that point, religion and philosophy had been available only in schools and parties that recruited for themselves and fought against one another. This was the church-community of God in which the individual counted for nothing, only everyone together. "*I belong to Paul,*" etc.; this was how they expressed that. They gave themselves over to bondage, the service to another.

Verse 5. Paul answers, what is Paul, Apollos? Do you really want to belong to servants rather than to the Lord? *Both* are servants, without distinction in this regard. Different in what the Lord has given them. Difference is desired by Christ. Both of them do the same thing: bring others to faith! Enormous assertion.

Verse 6. Planting and watering are nothing without the miracle of growing life, which God alone accomplishes.

Verse 7. Rivalries, envy, mistrust could emerge between those who plant and those who water, in that all attend to the indispensability of their own work rather than to the indispensability of the work of the others. Even the church-community can set one against the other.

Verse 8. Paul says: They are *one* (ἕν)[16] and thereby set great store by the common work and purpose, that the church-community grow. In doing so the distinction is not erased. God will reward the work accordingly. There are different rewards with God. God looks at the work.

Verse 9. God's coworkers. The accent falls on "*God*"; to be sure, truly   486
coworkers focused on the salvation of the *other,* not "synergistic."[17] Thus we should all see one another[18] as those through whom God alone does what is God's. We stand in God's work; you are God's *field, building.* The power of the work comes from God alone; the goal is God's alone. Those who do their *own* work with their own goals are seeking their own honor and corrupt the church-community. The church-community is *God's* church-community, not "*mine.*"

Verse 10. The church-community is founded only once. Paul did that in Corinth; now he expects people neither to think that everything has already occurred nor to act as if the foundation still needs to be laid. What matters

---

[15.] Penciled addition: "They consider themselves 'spiritual'—'human'—there is supposed to be a difference!"

[16.] Penciled addition: "*One* and yet difference according to the work!"

[17.] Here "synergistic" means "working together" in the sense of active human participation in God's action of grace.

[18.] This is written in pencil in the margin.

is the *proper* building on the foundation that has been laid. Each one steps in to continue the work of the other, a long series. This is the task.

Verse 11. The foundation laid is Jesus Christ, not a Pauline system of doctrine. This foundation is not to be shaken. It is the only possible foundation. We are allowed to *take for granted* that it is laid. The church is indeed *Christ's* church, otherwise nothing. My personality, my theology, etc., may never become the foundation of the church. To build further—that is the limited task.

Verse 12, 13. Many build with good intentions and yet so differently. It depends on one thing: that the building is stable when it is tested by God. The test of fire. Building has been done wrongly when despite an outward appearance of success—the church is full, the youth are active—but nevertheless no lasting stability. In many ways our goals are still too external, too strongly oriented toward earthly success.—The test of fire does not take place in this time but at the end; only then will it come to light. Those who build can have *assurance* in regard to their work only if they have placed the church-community *solely* on the foundation that is Jesus Christ (like Paul confident of his work). If, therefore, the test of fire of the divine judgment is carried out already here, if everything human-fleshly is judged already here.

Verse 14, 15. In judgment we remain bound to our work, cannot separate ourselves from it (1 Tim. 4:16). We receive reward or punishment. To be sure, God is gracious. Those who stood in faith and worked wrongly can be saved,[19] in that they must share the pain of judgment that accrues to their work.

Verse 16, 17. In distinction from these persons are those who knowingly desire to corrupt the temple of God. Such persons perish on their own. The holy *temple of God—the church-community*.[20] If only we would ponder this continually. Corrupters of the church-community are those who wish to topple the foundation and lay a new foundation.

Verse 18, 19. Mostly this occurs through accumulated wisdom. A new doctrine or form of knowledge takes the place of Christ. Only one escape: to become a fool[21] in order to be truly wise; to dispense with one's own knowledge in order to preach Jesus Christ.

Verse 20. One's own wisdom is one's doom. People believe they can place themselves above Christ, and they perish at precisely this point. The Old Testament citations:[22] For God, one's own wisdom is a means to capture

---

[19.] Penciled addition: "saved through the fire, i.e., from a burning house."

[20.] Penciled addition: "'*you* are'—very concrete."

[21.] Penciled addition: "how?"

[22.] Job 5:12-13 is cited in verse 19; Ps. 94:11 in verse 20.

persons and destroy them; one's own wisdom destroys God's work; for it is nothing and leads human beings into nothingness.

Verse 21. Summary: No one should promote human praise in the church-community. They thereby deprive the church-community of what is best in it. This is to be said to the church-community and to its teachers! The church-community falls into dependence, bondage. It belongs to Paul or Apollos. Instead: you do not belong to another human being, but *all things are yours.* All of them, Paul, Apollos, etc., whose praise you promote, to whom you submit, they in fact belong to you; they are here for you, and otherwise for nothing. They want to bring Christ to you, lay the foundation on him; beyond that they are nothing; and if they want to be something, they are fools. They belong to you. Let us consider the differences: Paul, Apollos, Peter—Barth, Heim, Brunner—what are they? Nothing and nevertheless servants. No fanaticism, rigorism (theologies, hymns, liturgy, etc.) is valid in the church-community. The church-community, but also the teacher, must take this to heart! No exclusivity, divisions, ambition. We *belong to* the church-community, not the church-community to us![23]

In contrast: The *world.* Not only the work of the church but the entire   488
world serves the church-community. Without exception. We think, either *church/word of God or world.* Paul says, both belong to you. Joy and preservation. *Life or death.* We either bet on life, in which case we hate death and are enslaved to it. Or vice versa. Paul says, both belong to you. Task and redemption. *Present or future:* we cling either to the present or to the future! Paul says, both serve you, belong to you! Faith and sight.

All things, only where all things belong to you are you truly free of all things, do you use them rightly, and belong *to Christ alone. But you are Christ's.* That is the goal. Yet Christ in his turn does not belong to this or that party that calls itself "Christian," but he belongs *to God* (11:3). This precludes false pride, petty quarrels over opinions, once and for all. The church-community is united in its submission to God.

+Rom. 8:28 All things for good; 1 Cor. 10:33 all power, but it is beneficial . . . 6:12; 1 Cor. 13:7 love bears . . . all things; 1 Cor. 15:27 everything under his feet; 2 Cor. 6:10 possessing *everything*; Eph. 5:20 giving thanks . . . for everything; Phil. 4:13 I can do *all things* . . . v. 18 I . . . have more than enough; Titus 1:15 all things are pure.

[23.] Penciled addition: "a great treasure is dumped out."

4. Draft of a Lecture on the Theme of "Glory"[1]

I. On the Glory of the Word

The Word and the deed. In a world in which actions speak their own language so overwhelmingly, of what use is the word of the church anymore? Has it not become superfluous? Should not even we simply conform ourselves to these deeds and just go to work in place of all these words? Action is what is credible. Are we to complain about how actions originate in the world? That actions are taken in self-defense? That this is a case where the saying is quite valid: God helps those who help themselves? Are we anxiously to repeat the trite sermon that we can build great and lasting things in the world only with Christ? Many of us, members of the church-community and pastors, have joined in working on these actions, struggling with them; we all share in responsibility, have said our Yes to them as human beings living in the world. Now we have a share in the actions that drown out the word of the church. There is no further escape. We are in the thick of them. Surrounded by actions we ask for the *Word*; there is no longer any other way we can do so.

Actions carry their own emphasis. Wordlessly they transcend all that is weaker than they are. They leave it behind and trample it underfoot. Pedantic criticism and disparagements are crushed by the force of the deeds themselves. This is the immanent law of action. Only one thing is greater than the action: the one who provides it. Every action knows this itself; it is allowed and given. It is to praise the one who gave it. Whether it does so is determined by its relationship to the *word of God*. The word of God is present and is the one thing over which action has no power. The human powers that accompany the word may be negligible and feeble so that they are also shattered and destroyed. The word alone endures. It challenges every action and is not afraid, for it is eternal, invulnerable, and almighty. Its representatives may not be worthy of it; in that case they must be gone. But the word commands its own way wherever it pleases and chooses its own hearers however it pleases, for it is God's own word. The poverty of the word. The same God who permits and provides great actions, who visibly and yet incomprehensibly gives and takes, desires to rescue human beings for eternity, for eternal salvation. God remains mute in actions but is revealed to those whom God desires to save, to those who are meant to find God. This

---

[1.] *NL*, A 62,6; handwritten; previously published in *GS* 3:416–17. In Bonhoeffer's calendar notes for the visitation trips to East Prussia in June and July 1940, the entry dated December 22 contains these notes: "*Word and deed* / defense of one's own interests, Power and . . . Glory of the word, of the office, of love" (see 1/10). This may refer to the pastors' retreat on July 9, 1940, for which Bonhoeffer noted, "Presentation: Our Proclamation Today."

revelation takes place in the poverty of the word; for God desires to be *believed*. God does not wish to force recognition through miracles but desires to encounter the heart and lead it to free faith by means of the word.

a. The word as the source of faith in Christ 490
b. The word as the source of truth
c. The word as the source of justice
d. The word as the source of mercy
e. Sunday (word and work)
f. Praise and thanksgiving for the church of the word

II. On the glory of the pastoral office
III. On the glory of the cross (eschatologically)
IV. On the glory of service
V. On the glory of unity
VI. Gratitude
What should we preach?
What should we do?

5. Reflection: On Gratitude among Christians[1]

On Gratitude among Christians

Gratitude arises not from the inherent capacities of the human heart but only from the Word of God. Gratitude must therefore be learned and practiced.[2]

Jesus Christ—and everything established in him—is the first and last ground of all gratitude. He is the gift from heaven, which we were not able to procure for ourselves, in whom the love of God encounters us in the flesh. In Jesus Christ alone are we able to thank God (Rom. 7:25). In Jesus Christ God gives us everything.[3]

Gratitude seeks the giver above and beyond the gift. It arises from the love 491 that it receives. Only when it breaks through to God's love has it arrived at its goal. But then it will itself become a wellspring of love for God and others.

[1.] *NL*, A 62,7 a; handwritten (= A); previously published in *GS* 3:418–21. In addition, cf. *NL*, A 62,7 c; hectograph (= C). Text C is part of a July 26, 1940, hectographed newsletter of the Council of the Confessing Synod of Pomerania. It contains some variations from the handwritten version (text A) in style and content and was published there without mentioning Bonhoeffer's name. The notes point out places where text C differs in materially relevant ways from text A.

[2.] Added in text C: "Gratitude is not the free exuberance of the heart but service owed to God."

[3.] The biblical reference given in text C is Rom. 8:32.

Gratitude is humble enough to allow itself to be given something. The proud take only what they have coming. They refuse to receive a gift. They prefer a punishment they deserve over an undeserved kindness; they prefer to perish by their own power than to live by grace. They reject God's love, which makes the sun shine on the good and the evil. Those who are grateful know that they deserve nothing good, but they allow the kindness of God to reign in them and are humbled even more deeply by unearned goodness (Rom. 2:4).

For the grateful everything is a gift, for they know that there are for them absolutely no deserved possessions.[4] Therefore they do not differentiate[5] between what is deserved and undeserved, between what is earned and what is received, because in their eyes even what is earned is received; even what is deserved is gift.

In gratitude every gift is transformed into a thank offering back to God, from whom it came.[6]

That for which I can thank God is good. That for which I cannot thank God is evil. But the determination whether I can thank God for something is discerned on the basis of Jesus Christ and his word. Jesus Christ is the limit of gratitude.[7] Jesus Christ is also the fullness of gratitude; in him gratitude knows no bounds. It encompasses all the gifts of the created world. It embraces even pain and suffering. It penetrates the deepest darkness until it has found within it the love of God in Jesus Christ.[8] To be thankful means to say yes to all that God gives "at all times and for everything" (Eph. 5:20). Gratitude is even able to encompass past sin and to say yes to it, because in it God's grace is revealed—o felix culpa[9] (Rom. 6:17).

492   In gratitude I attain the right relationship to my past; in gratitude what is past becomes fruitful for the present. Without gratitude my past sinks into darkness and enigma, into nothingness. In order not to lose my past,[10] but

---

[4.] Text C has *Gutes* ("something good," "that which is good") [Text A has *Gut*, "property, possession."—MB].

[5.] Text C reads: "decide [*entscheidet*]."

[6.] The biblical reference given in text C is 1 Tim. 4:4.

[7.] A new paragraph begins here in text C.

[8.] Text C reads: "until it encounters in it the love of God in Jesus Christ."

[9.] "O happy fault." The Exsultet of the ancient church praises the sin of Adam and its guilt, because through it the coming of the Redeemer and his death were made necessary (cf. *Lexikon für Theologie und Kirche*, 3:318–19). [The Exsultet continues to be used even in modern Protestant Easter Vigil services, for example, in the Episcopal Church and some Lutheran churches in the United States and Canada, although, like many of the early church's texts, usually without the *o felix culpa* line.—MB]

[10.] Text C adds: "that God gave me."

rather to reclaim it completely, repentance must, however, also accompany gratitude. In gratitude and repentance my life[11] is gathered into unity.

Gratitude can persist only in conjunction with sincere penitence and devoted love toward those who have not received the undeserved gift bestowed on me. Without penitence and love my gratitude becomes an accursed and hypocritical[12] thanks.

It is the accursed thanks of hypocrites when I misuse the gift I received undeserved to extol myself before God and others (Luke 18:9ff.), when I merely discharge my thanks to God as quickly as possible in order to ransom myself from God, so that I may return forthwith to my usual self-glorification. Hypocritical thanks is the religious ceremony of ingratitude.

It is the accursed thanks of hypocrites when the rich see the table of the poor empty and leave it empty, while giving thanks for what is theirs as God's blessing.[13]

It is the accursed thanks of hypocrites when I do not pass on the love of God that I have experienced, and for which I give thanks, to the disadvantaged. This is blasphemy against the Creator of the poor[14] (Prov. 14:31).

The word of God accuses me until I translate my thanks for gifts I have received into a sincere changing of my ways and into active love. But then the word of God bestows on me a free conscience to give thanks in the midst of a wicked and suffering world.

Ten cry out in their fear and need, "Jesus, dear Master, have mercy!" But only one of the ten[15] returns after experiencing salvation and thanks Jesus, and this one is a Samaritan (Luke 17:11ff.). In danger and pain many—more than we imagine—cry to their "dear" God, but after their recovery this God is not nearly so "dear" any longer for nine of the ten. The healing is all they care about, not the healer [Heiland].[16] Jesus asks, "But the other nine, where are they?" Jesus seeks thanks not for his own sake, but for theirs.[17]

Ingratitude suffocates faith, obstructs[18] access to God. It is only to the

493

[11.] Text C reads: "... my present life with my past."

[12.] [Bonhoeffer here uses *Pharisäerdank*; see the discussion of the use of this term in the editor's introduction, pp. 26–27.—MB]

[13.] Text C reads: "... when the rich give thanks for the divine blessing of their full table and leave the table of the poor empty."

[14.] Text C reads: "... to the disadvantaged; for this is robbery of God's grace and contempt for my brother or sister."

[15.] Text C is missing "of the ten."

[16.] Text C reads: "Healing is present, the healer forgotten."

[17.] Text C reads: "for the sake of the nine."

[18.] Text C reads: "hardens [*verstockt*]."

one thankful Samaritan that Jesus says, "Your faith has made you well." Despite their recovery the ungrateful are not truly made well.

It is the original sin of the Gentiles that although they knew of God's existence they have not "given thanks to God as God" (Rom. 1:21). Where God is recognized as God, the first thing God seeks is the thanks of God's creatures.[19]

Ingratitude begins with forgetfulness, from forgetfulness flows indifference, from indifference discontent, from discontent despair, from despair blasphemy.[20]

God shows those who are grateful the way to salvation. Ask yourself whether it is not perhaps through ingratitude that your heart has become so sullen,[21] so sluggish, so tired, so despondent.[22] Offer thanks to God, and "to those who go the right way I will show the salvation of God" (Ps. 50:23).[23]

6. Lecture Outline: Theology and the Congregation[1]

Theology and the Congregation

1. With regard to our people's intellectual life as a whole, no aspect of mental labor is more despised than theology. Above and beyond the rejection of the Christian proclamation and the church, theology has fallen into contempt. In its past form it was seen as an irrelevant task that could be performed just as well by philosophy and ethics; in its present form it is seen as an absurd and obsolete theorizing, a throwback to a world that is over, a completely useless activity. The theology professor—once a tolerated, unnecessary figure, now an offensive one. Beyond the German cultural world, theology is scarcely more valued. In the Anglo-Saxon countries the interest in worship and Christian life so fully overshadows theology that it tends to be perceived as an intellectual (or specifically German) private interest that

494

[19.] Text C adds: "and their ingratitude will become a source of all sins."
[20.] Text C adds: "and open apostasy."
[21.] Text C adds: "so impatient."
[22.] Text C adds: "and despairing."
[23.] Text C adds: "Through gratitude you can once again rejoice in your God."

[1.] *NL*, A 62,8; handwritten; previously published in *GS* 3:421–25. The date of this draft is uncertain. Eberhard Bethge conjectures that it dates from 1940 and was intended for use in the Confessing Church of Pomerania. The many abbreviations that Bonhoeffer used in the actual manuscript are written out in full in this version. [In this outline, *Gemeinde* is translated "congregation"; nonetheless, Bonhoeffer's theologically richer concept of a church-community informs his thinking about the theological questions with which individual congregations wrestled.—MB]

is of no significance for Christendom.[2] In the Catholic world theology is a necessary and respected function of the church, but one that is without meaning for laypeople. Theology[3] and laypeople are deeply separated from each other. For the laity "simple faith" (fides implicita) [4] is enough. Only the theologian needs the exposition of confessions of faith, for the teaching office of the church belongs only to pastors and bishops. In this way the positive valuation of theology is confined to an infinitesimally small portion of humanity and Christendom. This is an extremely peculiar situation.

2. For Protestant congregations there are certain prejudices that make it more difficult for the congregation to have a proper relationship to theology. The *pietistic:* Theology is a matter of the head; what matters is the heart.[5] Thus theology divides, while the piety of the heart unites.

The *orthodox:* All preaching is instruction, theology, true theology = true   495 faith, the sum total of true propositions.[6] The *academic:* Theology is rigorous scholarship, study, university, not for the laity.

The *evangelization [volksmissionarisch] circles:* People are not mature enough for theological distinctions—first mission, then theology. The *ecclesiastical political:* Theology disrupts the political unity of the church. The *sectarian:* A particular theology is the whole truth of the gospel. / How the views overlap.

3. The *practical* necessities promoting a clear relationship between congregation and theology.

a) The congregation must be able to evaluate the doctrine being preached. The teaching office is given to the congregation, and the pastor exercises it on their behalf.[7] b) The instruction of youth. c) The building

---

[2.] The following three sentences were inserted by Bonhoeffer at the end of the section.

[3.] This probably reads "theologians."

[4.] "Implicit faith"; the *fides implicita simplicium* refers to the faith of the simple who cannot know everything "that the church believes" in detail or at the same depth, but who, in their more or less humble faith, also believe in the entire truth embraced by faith (cf. *Religion in Geschichte und Gegenwart,* 3rd ed., 2:936–37).

[5.] Cf., for instance, August Francke's statements in *Werke in Auswahl:* "In a *studiosi theologiae* one seeks first and foremost that one's heart be upright before God. . . . No one who perceives the nature of true Christianity locates that Christianity in knowing, theorizing, and chattering—nor in lofty speculations" (172, 173).

[6.] Here Bonhoeffer is thinking of the "orthodox" Lutheran teaching of the *articuli fidei,* "articles of faith," which were understood as didactic propositions able to encompass the entire content of revelation; cf. Schmid, *Doctrinal Theology of the Evangelical Lutheran Church,* 92–99.

[7.] Cf. Luther, "That a Christian Gathering or Congregation Has the Right and Power to Judge All Doctrine and to Call Teachers, and Install and Depose Them. Foundation and Proof from the Scriptures," 1523 (*LW* 39:305–14 [WA 11:408–16]).

up of the congregation (baptism, sacrament, confession, eucharistic discipline) according to the word of God. Repelling of the enemies of the church of Christ. d) To be able to be independent of the pastor. e) To be able to read and interpret the Bible independently. To come of age [Mündigwerden] in knowledge, milk (1 Corinthians 3; Hebrews 6).[8]

4. *Nature of the Congregation and Theology*

The *congregation* is gathered around Word and sacrament. A community of faith, worship, and life. It is built solely on the word of God.

Theology is submission to the coherent and well-ordered knowledge of the word of God in its context and in its particular form as guided by the confessions of the church. It serves the pure proclamation of the word in the congregation and the building up of the congregation in accord with the word of God.

The essence of the congregation is not to engage in theology, but to *believe* and *obey* the word of God. Yet because it has pleased God to reveal himself in the *spoken human word,* and because this word is vulnerable to falsification and poisoning through human thoughts and opinions, the congregation is thus in need of clarity regarding true and false proclamation; it needs a resource, a weapon, not an end in itself. In times of trouble the congregation is particularly called to such maturity. The *word of God* is the sole norm and rule[9] of all true Christian insight. A *confession* is an interpretation of and witness to the word of God for a certain time and danger and is subject to the word of God. *Theology* is the interpretation of the confession from particular viewpoints and the ongoing testing of the confession against the scriptures. *Faith* arises from the preaching of the word of God alone.[10] It does not need theology, but true preaching needs the confession and theology. Faith, which arises from preaching, in turn seeks its confirmation in scripture and the confessions and thus itself does theology.

5. The theology of the congregation and the theology of pastors. In principle no difference. Why academic study of theology? *1* Sign that the exploration of Holy Scripture takes a lifetime, *2* as a corrective to the theology of

---

[8.] 1 Cor. 3:2; Heb. 6:1-3. Cf., however, *DBWE* 6:397–99: "Holy Scripture" belongs to the "office of teaching." The appeal to Holy Scripture in reference to the "coming of age," or *Mündigkeit,* of the congregation is questionable. [This passage naturally calls to mind Bonhoeffer's discussion of this in his prison writings; see, for example, *DBW* 8: 511.—MB]

[9.] Cf. the "Formula of Concord," Epitome, Summary, 7: "Holy Scripture alone remains the only judge, rule, and guiding principle [Latin: "iudex, norma, et regula"], according to which, as the only touchstone, all teachings should and must be recognized and judged" (*Book of Concord,* 487).

[10.] Cf. Rom. 10:17.

the congregation. *Dangers* of the theology of the congregation: *1* too strongly oriented toward praxis (doctrine of the Trinity? Christology?). *2* Bias, because of a lack of perspective. Arbitrariness of interpretation. Lack of competence in original languages. These *dangers are at the same time assets:* practical orientation; the *simple* approach without raising too many problems that only hinder decision making. *Advantages of academic theology: 1* knowledge of the foundations (linguistic, historical); *2* perspective regarding the connections between scripture and dogmatics. *Concomitant dangers:* theoretical sermons and instruction; being able to find a reason for every decision. A mature member of the congregation can teach the pastor without that being a disgrace for the pastor (Acts 18:26). Theology of the congregation—Acts 17:11.

497

6. What significance do the *theological disciplines* have for the congregation? Isn't knowledge of the Bible sufficient? Why dogmatics? Church history, practical theology? What is the correlation? One cannot understand the Bible without knowledge of the basic doctrines of the church, i.e., dogmatics.[11] One cannot engage in dogmatics without study of the Bible. One cannot overlook that between us and the Bible there stands a *church* that has a history; not to leap over this like fanatics but to learn, "to have access to the records" in order to make one's own decision. Not biblicism! Contempt for the Holy Spirit and the church. Practical theology: the *present* body of the church as—in submission to the word of scripture, the confessions, history, and theology—it acts and should act *today.*

7. The *authority of theology* and its limits. Theology does not rule in the congregation but *serves.* The word of God *rules.* Thus, in addition to theology, other offices and gifts: *church leadership* (elders, bishops, presbytery), *diaconate* (charism of love). Theology as *corrective,* nothing more. Not a church of theologians but the *word* and the *congregation.*

8. Theological parties and the unity of the congregation. First Corinthians 1 and 3: "All belong to you."[12] No harm in difference as long as it does not lead to schism. Out of theological parties church-dividing conflicts can arise (liberals—German Christians),[13] and out of church-dividing conflicts

498

[11.] Note added in the margin of the manuscript, p. 2: "Old Testament and New Testament theology does not = dogmatics."

[12.] Cf. 1 Cor. 3:22 and 1 Cor. 1:30.

[13.] The "liberal theology," or "neo-Protestantism," that shaped Bonhoeffer through his teachers Adolf von Harnack and Reinhold Seeberg was the attempt to bring an ethically interpreted Christianity into contact with the modern and, above all, bourgeois world as an influential force. The German Christians could make use of nationalism, which was

academic differences can arise (Lutheran Reformation doctrine of the Lord's Supper?!)[14] in which conflicts not grounded in the gospel are exposed. Theology serves not to rip apart the congregation but rather to unite it, because it serves the truth of the word. Unity is found only in the truth.

7. Sketch for a Lecture by Eberhard Bethge: The Significance of Mission to Non-Christians for the Church Renewal Movement[1]

The Significance of Mission to Non-Christians for the Church Renewal Movement

I. Throughout the nineteen-hundred-year history of the church, the problems and the situation we face have become so complicated that one longs for the simple relationships of a young congregation, i.e., for the experiences in the mission field. Among us [it is] questionable 1) whether the church renewal movement should exist at all, since, after all, *the message has gone out and the decision has been reached*; there are those who oppose the church renewal movement, who see in the church renewal movement a human encroachment on the judgment of God. The sermon is available, that is enough. Those who don't want to listen are themselves at fault; there is a limit to our going after them. If God wants to reject them, we should not restrain God. Against this: are we not allowed to restrain precisely the judging God[2] and remind God of divine mercy? Abraham's intercession,[3]

499

---

also a factor here [i.e., in neo-Protestantism—MB], to support their claim that God is revealed in the law of the German people, or *Volk*, in fact, even in the "Führer." For this reason Karl Barth considered the German Christians the "most monstrous offspring of the neo-Protestant essence" ("Abschied von *Zwischen den Zeiten*," in *Anfänge der dialektischen Theologie*, 2:316). This demonstrates what results when other sources of revelation, such as ethics or "the German people," are claimed in addition to the revelation of God in Jesus Christ.

[14.] In the self-understanding of the churches themselves, however, the overcoming of the opposition between Lutheran and Reformed doctrines of the Lord's Supper was not yet reducible in 1940 to a mere academic difference!

[1.] *NL*, A 59,2; handwritten; previously published in *GS* 6:495–97. In a December 2, 1940, letter from Ettal to Eberhard Bethge, Bonhoeffer characterizes this draft as "random thoughts" *(Gedankensplitter)* for a lecture that Bethge was to present on the subject (see 1/40). For more information on experiences with the task of church renewal [*Volksmission*] in the Finkenwalde period, see *DB-ER*, 542–45. [See also the explanation of our translations of *Volksmission* in the editor's introduction.—MB]

[2.] Cf. *DBWE* 1:184–89.

[3.] Cf. Gen. 18:22-33.

Moses',[4] Paul's,[5] Jeremiah's[6] plea for their people. 2) Should we not be *engaging solely in the church renewal movement* and to this end remove the pastors from villages where only three to four people still go to church and place them in the service of evangelizing the people? 3) To what extent does the church itself, as a state church, as a worldly institution, as a connection between throne and altar, bear the blame for the alienation? To what extent must we say that the church of Jesus Christ has always been there and there is no excuse for the others? 4) What does *infant baptism* mean? *Grace or judgment?* In the church renewal movement do we take infant baptism for granted as a real action of God, or do we act as if we had to begin completely from scratch? What does falling away from baptism mean? Must we limit infant baptism? Or is that a limitation of the grace and omnipotence of God?[7]—All these questions confuse our thoughts about the church renewal movement. Therefore longing for the original conditions. Mission to non-Christians. Learn two things: 1) *Awakening* to faith, 2) *Building up of the church-community.*

II. *What do we learn for the church renewal movement from mission to non-Christians?*

1) *Awakening to faith.* Preaching about the *true God* and the *false gods.* Depriving the false gods and pagan culture of its power. Worshiping nature, ancestor worship, fear of demons—all this needed today as well! Preaching the *God of grace.* Preaching Christ. Preaching *repentance*—putting away the old life—very concrete (blood feuds, adultery, theft, etc.). Along with that always the result: *confession. Baptism* only following extensive probation. No use of slogans, but substantial, concrete, a real event. Being called out— ἐκκλησία[8]—discipleship.

2) *Building up the church-community. Becoming a Christian* means immediately beginning to win others. No private Christian existence but the new life itself compels to speak, *to confess.* Much courage, patience, wisdom, *struggle* for the faith. *Order* of *worship,* of *life.* The *authority* of the elders. The *discipline of repentance.* Joint preparation of sermons by the elders, but only one in charge.—Communal prayer.—*Maturity* [Mündigkeit] of the church-community. Gifts of love (Acts 2:42ff. is fulfilled here).—Acclaim.

500

[4.] Cf. Exod. 32:30-32.

[5.] Cf. Rom. 9:1-5; 10:1.

[6.] Cf. Jer. 14:7-9, 19-22.

[7.] On these questions, see "A Theological Position Paper on the Question of Baptism," 2/14.

[8.] "Church" or "church-community." The Greek word derives from roots meaning "to call forth."

III. Not an ideal church-community but Christus praesens![9] This is something we could learn, to take seriously the presence of the living Christ; from this all the rest flows. No law but rather Gospel. *In our joy over what is new, full of life, not despising the time-honored old form of our mother church! Not sprucing it up! But loving and honoring it.*—Mission to non-Christians and the church renewal movement a mutual give-and-take. Unity of Christendom.

8. Thesis Fragment: What Do We Learn from the Mission to Non-Christians?[1]

What Do We Learn from the Mission to Non-Christians?

1. Mission not out of pity for the "poor heathen," as if they were particularly sinful and lost. On the contrary: experience often demonstrates a high moral standard among the non-Christian peoples, even the primitive peoples. But they do not have *Christ.* Thus not primarily out of *pity,* but because Christ *must* be preached (1 Cor. 9:16) ἀνάγκη,[2] a command; thus *preaching as a charge.*

2. Word of God *is power,* victory, overcoming. It still works and bears fruit; it creates new life out of nothing.

501   3. The *life* (of the missionary) must be an "example" (1 Tim. 4:12). The right Christian life is a part of preaching. Otherwise everything can fall apart.

4. God is self-bound to the "cooperation" of human beings, preachers, etc., for the divine plan of salvation. Strange (1 Cor. 3:9). God needs our sacrifice, money, readiness—high honor.

5. Preaching is public, attack, battle between God and devil, dangerous. Dethroning of false gods, dominion of Christ.

6. Preaching is calling forth—ἐκκλησία[3]—out of the old connections to the *one* sole connection to Jesus Christ.

7. Faith means obedience to the word of God, repentance, and discipleship.

[9.] The "present Christ." On the conception that the present Christ is the church-community, cf. *DBWE* 1:184–89.

[1.] *NL,* A 63,8; handwritten [by Bonhoeffer for Bethge], probably written around the time of the December 2, 1940, letter from Ettal (see 1/40) and the sketch "The Significance of Mission to Non-Christians for the Church Renewal Movement" (see 2/7), with whose second section this fragment corresponds.

[2.] "Obligation"; see 1 Cor. 9:16.

[3.] See 2/7, ed. note 8.

8. Preaching brings about the confession of sins (personal confession) and church renewal.

9. Baptism only on the basis of faith.

10. Being Christian means confessing, promoting Christ from the start.

11. Christ places us into struggle.

12. Being Christian places us in the community. Worship! Order! Discipline! Practice of repentance.

13. Being Christian demands the maturity of the church-community.

14. The authority of the offices of the church-community.

15. Mission to non-Christians is both giving and receiving.

9. Essay: The Best Physician[1]

The Best Physician

In the midst of glorious creation, we see a paralyzed child being pushed in a wheelchair. For those who still have a heart that has not become completely numb toward their neighbor, it becomes clear at that very moment   502 that here something in our world is not right, that the world in which this image of torment and sorrow is possible is not the original creation of God. Here something that defies God has broken into the world. The world has fallen away from its origin; destructive powers have won power in it. Sickness exists only in a world that has become God-less. Because the world is sick in relation to God, there are human beings who are sick. Only a world that was completely sheltered again in God, a redeemed world, would be without sickness.

In the Bible we encounter a strange assertion: "yet even in his disease he did not seek the Lord, but sought help from physicians."[2] It refers to a devout man to whom the Bible otherwise accords high praise for his zeal on behalf of God. Yet, despite all his godliness, this man thought in one regard in a very modern way, namely, he strictly distinguished between matters of religion, in which one turns to God, and earthly matters, in which one seeks help in earthly places. Illnesses, especially bodily illness, are earthly concerns with earthly causes and earthly cures. Illnesses, therefore, are to

---

[1.] *NL*, A 63,5; typed carbon copy, January 1941; previously published in *GS* 3:426–30. See Bonhoeffer's January 20, 1941, letter from Ettal: "In the meantime I have to write a shorter essay for Weckerling for the 'spa ministry' [*Bädermission*] (!) on Exod. 15:26" (see 1/60, including ed. note 12). Beneath the heading the following keywords, which were subsequently crossed out, appear in brackets: "sickness and—God. What physician can help me (help the best)? The true physician or the like."

[2.] 2 Chron. 16:12.

be presented to the doctor but not to God. How would we dare burden God, the Lord of the world, with our trivial bodily maladies? God has other concerns.

This is thought to be quite reasonable and perhaps even quite religious. But it is wrong. Certainly illnesses have their earthly causes and earthly remedies, but this is far from the last or most important word regarding the nature of illness. Certainly those who are sick should go to the doctor and seek help there. But doing this alone means failing to do and to perceive the most important thing. Behind the worldly causes and cures are found the causes and cures for sickness that are not of this world. As long as we fail to see this, we live truly oblivious to our own sickness; we fail completely to discern its true face. Its curse and its blessing go unrecognized.

In a special way, sickness belongs to God. The Bible reproaches us not
503 for going to the doctor with our sickness but rather for not[3] going to God with it. It is no accident that Christ lived in striking proximity to the sick, that the blind, the lame, deaf-mutes, lepers, the mentally ill felt irresistibly drawn to him and sought his company.[4] Why didn't Christ send these people to the doctor? It was certainly not in order to harm the reputation of doctors or to make a display of his own skill or suggestive power. Instead, it was in order to make clear that God and sickness, Christ and the sick, belong very close to each other. Christ wants to be the true physician for the sick. "I am the LORD who heals you."[5] God says this and so does Christ. The Creator and Redeemer of the world offers himself to the sick as their physician. Do we want to leave this offer unexplored, after we have pursued so many inferior offers with more or less success?

For those who even merely glimpse the connection between God and sickness, who take the unexpected offer seriously, for them sickness can become a pointer to human sin, to the destruction of the community of creatures with the Creator. These are the otherworldly causes and depths of sickness. I am reminded of the sin of the world and of my own sin. My sickness need not be merely the result of or punishment for a certain sin for which I would indict myself—this may be the case, but it is not necessarily so. Yet every sickness prompts me to look into the depths of the world's sin and of my personal God-lessness. This glimpse, however, drives me to God. When I have looked into the abyss, I do not first plead for liberation from this or that suffering, but I come with the confession of my long-hidden guilt before the face of God. Bodily illness teaches me to recognize that my actual illness is rooted much more deeply, so deeply that no earthly physician can

---

[3.] Here the word "also" is crossed out.
[4.] Cf. Mark 8:22–23; 10:46; Matt. 15:30; Luke 17:12; Mark 5:8; Luke 8:29 et passim.
[5.] Exod. 15:26.

heal it, because my actual illness is—my sin. Not only my body, my nerves, my psyche [Gemüt] is sick but my entire being, my heart is sick, sick from unbelief, from anxiety, from the godlessness of my life. And which healthy person does not also suffer from this most hidden [heimlich] and simultaneously most unsettling [unheimlich] illness?   504

Now I know that I can only be helped if my entire being is whole, healthy, new. How can that happen? The answer is quite simple and nevertheless penetrates the utmost depths of our life: through genuine confession and divine forgiveness of all my sins. For some this may seem like a strange change of and solution to this question, but this would be true only for those who have not yet experienced the healing [Heilwerden] of the whole person through confession and forgiveness. What does confession mean? To open yourself to Jesus Christ with all your sins, weaknesses, vices, suffering, and, on the strength of his word, to give him your whole heart without the slightest reservation. This is no easy task, and it may seem more difficult to us than a dangerous operation. It will probably be the case that most of us need a companion to help us in this, one who will stand by us in this sort of life confession, whether it be the person serving as the pastor or some member of the church-community who knows more of Christ than I do. What does forgiveness mean? Obliteration of my entire unholy [heillos], bungled, wrecked past (of which perhaps only I am aware) through God's word of power and through the gift of a new joyful beginning of my life.

Who can give me this sort of new beginning? No one other than the crucified and living Jesus Christ alone, who experienced for himself what life devoid of God's saving power is like and, in the community of God, overcame it. He is the only physician who knows my deepest sickness, who himself bore it; he is the "Savior" who can heal heart, soul, and body.

But what does the forgiveness of sin have to do with physical health? More than most people realize. To be sure, it is a mysterious relationship. But can we not grasp at least that a good many physical ailments simply fall away when people's hearts are made free and glad again? Many times the body becomes sick solely because it has been left to itself, because it has   505
become its own lord. But now the body has again received its true Lord, who rules it. The body is no longer the lord. It has become only a tool, indeed, more than this: a "temple of the Holy Spirit."[6] There are many forms of suffering that are not visibly alleviated and cured by the received promise of forgiveness. But the hidden connection between forgiveness and physical recovery can also become visible in such a way that all medical concepts are blown apart and the doctors are faced with an enigma. One thing

---

[6.] Cf. 1 Cor. 6:19.

is certain: just as unbelief is a source of destruction and illness of body and soul, so faith is a source of all healing [Heilung] and recovery.

When Christ is called the physician of the sick, then the radiance of divine mercy falls on all those who are sick, no matter how miserable they may be. The sick belong to God; God desires to make divine salvation [Heil] real in them. Thus, in sick brothers and sisters we encounter the very mercy of God, who in Jesus Christ is the physician of the sick. The sick want healing. Christ gives them more: their salvation.

506   ## 10. A Theological Position Paper on State and Church[1]

State and Church

[1.] Previously published in English translation in Bonhoeffer, *Ethics* (New York: Macmillan, 1955), 332–53; and *Ethics* (New York: Simon & Schuster, 1995), 327–48. See *NL*, A 72,6. Bonhoeffer's original manuscript disappeared following publication of the first German edition of the *Ethics* (1949), in which it was printed in the appendix, along with several other pieces now found in the present volume; in the 6th German edition, it was printed as an appendix (pp. 353–75). Bonhoeffer's work on this draft can be gleaned from three pieces of paper that have been preserved containing key terms relating to this material and the sequence of the themes to be covered (*NL*, A 74, 43–45; see *ZE*, 78–81). Working note no. 45 provides a complete outline of the present text. The material found in *NL*, A 75,89, which contains notes on the question of the state's incursion into matters of "religion," presumably also belongs to Bonhoeffer's work on this text. At the time of Bonhoeffer's arrest, this latter material was found on his desk (see *ZE*, 107–8). The time period of the drafting of this text and its purpose have not yet been resolved (on what follows, cf. the afterword, pp. 669–71). Formal and substantive indicators seem to point to the period after April 1941; however, there are also grounds for a later dating. The assumption that this text was intended as a "position paper for the Reich Council of Brethren" (as W. Niemöller conjectures in *Die evangelische Kirche im Dritten Reich,* 372) is not proven. Seen formally, this text resembles the genre of those position papers that Bonhoeffer produced at others' request (see "Theological Position Paper on the Question of Baptism," 2/14, and "Theological Position Paper on the *Primus Usus Legis*," 2/18). In the text Bonhoeffer works out his understanding of "government" [*Obrigkeit*] "from above" [*von oben*], which was also to provide a political orientation for the construction of a new state in Germany following the overthrow of Hitler. [From the very beginning of his theological career with *Sanctorum Communio*, a dominant theme of Bonhoeffer's thought was the church's responsibility in the world. His early reflections on this, particularly its implications for the church's very identity, were the foundation for his later writings on church and state, including this essay. After 1933 he was concerned with the particular challenges that confronted the church under Nazism. His April 1933 essay "The Church and the Jewish Question" (*DBW* 12:349–58) situated the church's response to the early Nazi anti-Jewish policies within the larger issue of governmental legitimacy and the legitimate or illegitimate exercise of governmental power. Bonhoeffer's essay here echoes many of the arguments in the 1933 essay, where he grounded that legitimacy on how both church and government fulfill their respective purposes in God's creation, and he deliberately critiques the

1. Conceptual[2]

The concept of the state[3] is alien to the New Testament. It is of ancient pagan origin.[4] In the New Testament the concept of government[5] replaces it. State means an ordered commonwealth; government is the power that creates and upholds the order. In the concept of the state, those who govern and those who are governed are combined;[6] in the concept of government only those who govern are meant. The concept of the polis,[7] which is con-   507
stitutive for the concept of the state, has no necessary connection with the concept of exousia.[8] In the New Testament the polis is an eschatological

---

Lutheran interpretations by Althaus and others that viewed the Nazi state and the German *Volk* as unchanging and divinely ordained "orders of creation." These arguments are developed throughout his writings, including in his 1939 essay on "Protestantism without Reformation" (*DBW* 15:431–60; see especially the section on "Kirche und Staat," 445–52) and, of course, his *Ethics* (here, see especially "The Concrete Commandment and the Divine Mandates," *DBWE* 6:388–94).—MB]

[2.] With this conceptual differentiation between "state" *(Staat)* and "government" *(Obrigkeit),* Bonhoeffer indicates already in this section the essential intent of his reflection.

[3.] The Greek word is πολιτεία (see Eph. 2:12; Acts 22:28, in the sense of "citizenship"). For πολίτευμα, "commonwealth," see Phil. 3:20.

[4.] Cf. Strathmann's article on πόλις κτλ., in *Theological Dictionary of the New Testament,* 6:529–35.

[5.] The term used here, *Obrigkeit* (government), was Luther's translation of ἐξουσία, which in German essentially means "power" *(Macht)* or "authority" *(Vollmacht);* cf. Rom. 13:1a (where the Greek term appears in plural form), which Luther translates: "Jedermann sei untertan der Obrigkeit." [NRSV: "Let every person be subject to the governing authorities." In "State and Church" we have almost always translated *Obrigkeit* as "government." When Bonhoeffer uses *Obrigkeit,* most often he is referring to the concrete, earthly institution of government—that is, the concrete form that governing authority takes in the world. However, it should be noted that Bonhoeffer does not restrict *Obrigkeit* "to the earthly polis; it can reach beyond it (just as it is present also in the smallest form of community in the father–child, master–servant relationship)" (see p. 504). Translating *Obrigkeit* as "government" in most cases is consistent with its translation in *Ethics* (*DBWE* 6). In *Ethics* as well as in "State and Church," Bonhoeffer identifies *Obrigkeit* as one of the four mandates. The other three are marriage, work, and church. A mandate is a divinely commissioned task, which is performed with "authority" in an "office." For more on government as one of the four mandates, cf. pp. 518–21, 549–50; cf. also *DBWE* 6:68–75, 388–408.—MB]

[6.] Cf. Thesis 5 of the Barmen Declaration of 1934 regarding the state: the church "calls to mind . . . the responsibility of those who govern and the governed" (*Creeds of the Church,* 521).

[7.] πόλις, "city."

[8.] [ἐξουσία, "authority."—MB] Cf. ed. note 4; on working note no. 44 (*ZE,* 78), next to the question "political responsibility of Christians?" Bonhoeffer had further noted, "connection between ἐξουσία and πόλις"; on working note no. 45, which contains

concept,[9] the future city of God,[10] the new Jerusalem,[11] the divinely ruled heavenly commonwealth. Governing authority is not fundamentally restricted to the earthly polis; it can reach beyond it (as it is also present in the smallest form of community in the father-child, master-servant relationship).[12] Therefore, the concept of government includes no definitive form of commonwealth, no definitive form of the state.[13] Government is the power set in place by God to exercise worldly rule with divine authority. Government is the vicarious representative action of God on earth.[14] It can only be understood from above.[15] Government does not emerge from

508   the commonwealth; instead, it orders the commonwealth from above. If it

---

the final arrangement, the keywords πόλις and ἐξουσία are placed at the very top, next to the words "Differentiation between State and Government" (see *ZE*, 80).

[9.] Karl Barth puts this more precisely in "Church and State," in *Community, State, and Church*, where he says that the πολίτευμα, "commonwealth," or the πόλις, "city," of Christians (!) "should not be sought in the 'present age' but in that 'which is to come'; not on earth but in heaven" (122).

[10.] Cf. Heb. 11:10; 12:22; 13:14.

[11.] Cf. Rev. 21:2.

[12.] Cf. working note no. 44 (*ZE*, 79): "ἐξουσία—government, parents, the most diverse figures, 'masters.'" In his explanation of the fourth commandment in the *Large Catechism*, Martin Luther derived the phenomenon of "government" itself from the parent-child relationship: "For all other authority is derived and developed out of the authority [*Oberkeit*] of parents" (*Book of Concord*, 405).

[13.] Cf. Dehn: "The form of state as such . . . does not interest Paul" ("Engel und Obrigkeit," 97); cf. also Brunner: "[I]n itself there is no Christian and non-Christian form of the State; no form, in itself, is wholly good or wholly bad" (*Divine Imperative*, 465). Given the number of echoes that resonate in the following material, Bonhoeffer clearly had Brunner's book before him as he was writing this text. For Bonhoeffer's reflections in reference to Brunner's understanding of the state, see also his letter to Gerhard Leibholz on March 7, 1940 (*DBW* 15:296–300 [*GS* 3:33–36]).

[14.] Luther: "Parents and governing authorities" function "in God's stead" (*Large Catechism, Book of Concord*, 411). According to John Calvin, those who enact state power are *vicarii Dei*, "God's representatives" (*Institutes* 4.20.6); cf. Lütgert, *Ethik der Liebe* (which Bonhoeffer had worked through): "The government is entitled to demand from the people that respect which is due its position as God's representative on earth" (222). This idea of "vicarious representative action" *(Stellvertretung)* shapes Bonhoeffer's reflection in the *Ethics* manuscript "The Concrete Commandment and the Divine Mandates" (1995 Simon & Schuster ed., 281–87 [*DBWE* 6:388–94]).

[15.] On the terminology of "above" and "below," cf., on the one hand, Holl: "Because Luther derives the state, not from below, but exclusively from above, from God's plan of salvation, he insists on its distinct character as a state whose essence is authority [*Obrigkeitsstaat*]," (*Cultural Significance of the Reformation*, 51). On the other hand, it is characteristic of Bonhoeffer that, building on Karl Barth, he understands the redemptive act of God in Jesus Christ as an action "from above" (cf. *DBWE* 6:131, 354, 385); on the understanding of government "from above," cf. above all *DBWE* 6:120–21, 390–93).

were exegetically correct to view government as an angelic power,[16] even this would refer only to its place between God and the world. Theologically, only the concept of government, not of the state, is usable. Yet in concrete reflection we cannot avoid, of course, the concept of the state.

In the concept of the church, especially where its relation to government as well as to the state is to be clarified, we must differentiate between the pastoral office and the congregation or the Christians. The pastoral office is the power set in place by God to exercise spiritual rule with divine authority. It emerges not from the congregation but from God.[17] Whereas worldly and spiritual rule[18] are to be strictly distinguished, Christians are   509 still at the same time citizens; and citizens in turn, whether they are believers, are at the same time subject to the claim of Jesus Christ. Thus the relation of the pastoral office to government is different from the relation of Christians to government. This distinction needs to be kept in mind to avoid continual misunderstandings.

2. The Establishment of Government

A. *In Human Nature*

Classical antiquity, especially Aristotle, grounded the state in *human nature.*[19] The state is the highest perfection of the rational nature of the

---

[16.] This is the understanding of Dehn, "Engel und Obrigkeit," 90–109; Schmidt, "Das Gegenüber von Kirche und Staat in der Gemeinde des Neuen Testaments," 1–16; Barth, "Church and State," 115. In contrast is Kittel's understanding in "Das Urteil des Neuen Testaments über den Staat," 651–80. [Kittel was one of the theological apologists for Nazism; see Ericksen, *Theologians under Hitler,* esp. 61–66.—MB] Further, the Freiburg memorandum (cf. 1/205) speaks of the "powers" in Rom. 13:1 as "dark angelic powers" (Thielicke, *In der Stunde Null,* 65), but at this point is referring to their demonization.

[17.] Cf. Schlink's *Theology of the Lutheran Confessions,* cherished and recommended by Bonhoeffer: "The public ministry is not a creation of the congregation...but it is an immediate institution of God through the command and promise of Jesus Christ" (245). Cf. also in the *Ethics* manuscript "The Concrete Commandment and the Divine Mandates" Bonhoeffer's statement that "this office is directly instituted by Jesus Christ, and receives its legitimacy not through the will of the congregation, but through the will of Jesus Christ" (*DBWE* 6:397).

[18.] Cf. Luther, "Temporal Authority: To What Extent It Should Be Obeyed": "For this reason God has ordained two governments: the spiritual, by which the Holy Spirit produces Christians and righteous people under Christ; and the temporal, which restrains the un-Christian and wicked so that—no thanks to them—they are obliged to keep still and to maintain an outward peace" (*LW* 45:91 [WA 11:251, 15–17]); cf. also the Augsburg Confession 16 and 28/10–14 (*Book of Concord,* 48–50, 92–93). On the interpretation of this, cf. Diem, *Luthers Lehre von den zwei Reichen.*

[19.] Cf. Lütgert: "According to Aristotle, the state is a necessary order of the people, deriving from human nature" (*Ethik der Liebe,* 219). Cf. Aristotle: "From these considerations

human being; to serve the state is the highest purpose of human life.[20] All ethics is political ethics. Virtues are political virtues. This grounding of the state has been taken over in principle by Catholic theology. The state emerges out of human nature. The capacity of the human being to live in community as well as the relationship between the ruler and the ruled are part of creation. Within the natural-created dimension, the state fulfills the destiny of human nature; it is the "highest manifestation of the natural communal character of human existence" (Schilling, *Moraltheologie,* vol. 2, 609). This Aristotelian and Thomistic teaching is found in somewhat modified form in

510 Anglican theology.[21] But it has also penetrated into modern Lutheranism.[22] The connection between natural theology and incarnational theology among Anglicans[23] (a dubious connection, now clearly recognized by young Anglo-Catholics and corrected by a theologia crucis)[24] opens up the possibility of a peculiar natural-Christian grounding of the state. By way of Hegel[25]

---

it is evident that the polis belongs to the class of things that exist by nature, and that man is by nature an animal intended to live in a polis" (*Politics,* 1253a). Further details are provided by Düring (*Aristoteles,* 474–505).

[20.] Cf. Schilling, *Lehrbuch der Moraltheologie,* 2:612 (Bonhoeffer's copy of this work is notated "1940"): "The state is the perfect society or more precisely the proper association that is organized for the purpose of fulfilling the highest, natural purpose of humanity's temporal existence" (with reference to Thomas Aquinas, *Summa Theologiae* 1–2, q.9, a.2 [The article from the *Summa Theologiae,* titled "Whether to Be Immutable Belongs to God Alone," distinguishes between the unchangeable God and creaturely institutions that are changeable and thereby open to corruption. Information provided to the editors by Geffrey B. Kelly—MB]; also with reference to the ten books of Artistotle's *Nicomachean Ethics* and his discourse on "First Things" (In decem Libros ethicorum Aritotelis ad Nicomachum expositio, praemium) that deals with "the guidance of First Principles" ("De regimini principum," 4,1).

[21.] Cf. Demant, "Zum Staatsverständnis des Anglikanismus," 25–34.

[22.] "Modern Lutheranism" is Bonhoeffer's collective designation here for theologians who wished to understand the state both as an order given by God and as the result of a religious-moral development. In the 1930s this group included Althaus (*Staatsgedanke und Reich Gottes*), Brunstäd (*Deutschland und der Sozialismus*), and Hirsch (*Deutschlands Schicksal,* 3rd ed.). For an analysis of the concept of the state in modern Lutheranism published during this period, see Gerber, *Die Idee des Staates,* 1930. [For works in English on this topic, see also Ericksen, *Theologians under Hitler,* and Barnes, *Nazism, Liberalism, and Christianity.*—MB]

[23.] See, e.g., Gore, *Lux Mundi.* For Gore the incarnation was the "crown of the development" of humanity.

[24.] These include, e.g., V. A. Demant (see ed. note 21), D. M. MacKinnon, and T. S. Eliot (cf. Ramsey, *From Gore to Temple*; and Norman, *Church and Society in England 1770–1970,* esp. chaps. 7 and 8). Bonhoeffer also expressed appreciation for Reinhold Niebuhr's "strong emphasis on the cross" in his 1939 report "Protestantism without Reformation" (*DBW* 15:458 [*GS* 1:352]).

[25.] See ed. note 31.

and Romanticism[26] modern Lutheranism has taken up the natural concept of the state.[27] Here the state is the fulfillment not of the universal rational nature of humanity but of the creative will of God in the people. The state is essentially a people's state [Volksstaat]. The people fulfill a God-intended destiny in the people's state.[28] What matters here is not the content of that destiny in its particulars. The ancient classical concept of the state lives on in the forms of the rational state, the people's state, the cultural state, the social state,[29] and also finally and decisively the Christian state.[30] The

511

[26.] See ed. notes 27 and 108.

[27.] Brunner: "Modern Lutheranism is labeled with the name of the Reformation, but it actually contains the ideas of romantic Idealism" (*Divine Imperative,* 682). Cf. also Lütgert, *Ethik der Liebe,* 226. Cf. also the view of the Freiburg memorandum concerning the "extremely dubious and confusing role" that "modern" theologians have played with the assertion of "'historical' orders as expressions of the will of God" (Thielicke, *In der Stunde Null,* 57); here, to be sure, Brunner himself is placed alongside Althaus and Gogarten.

[28.] Althaus: "The state is a *state of the people* [*Volksstaat*]. . . . It serves . . . the creative will of God, who through it desires to make a people into that which it can and should be" (*Kirche und Staat,* 8). Cf. the connection of this idea with popular nationalism in Stapel, *Der christliche Staatsmann,* 246–48. According to Alfred D. Müller's *Ethik* (which Bonhoeffer worked through), Hitler's idea of the state is grounded in the idea of the "state of the people" (8). [Bonhoeffer here is critiquing the concept of the people's state *(Volksstaat)* and the Lutheran concepts (particularly the concept that the state and the ethnically defined *Volk* were fixed "orders of creation," or *Schöpfungsordnungen*) that Althaus and others used to defend it. Critiquing Althaus, Bonhoeffer stressed that the state was based not on orders of creation but rather on an "order of preservation" *(Erhaltungsordnung)* by which God, not human beings (or a collective *Volk*), preserves a world awaiting its redemption. In this essay Bonhoeffer's analysis of the state parallels his earlier thinking about the orders of preservation and of creation; see *DBWE* 3:12, ed. notes 37 and 38, 148–49. He contrasts the orders of preservation and of creation in section C, "From Christ."—MB]

[29.] These expressions of the understanding of the state are characteristic of the so-called liberal theology that preceded Bonhoeffer; cf., e.g., Herrmann: "The state is one of the highest products and an indispensable mediator of culture" (*Ethik,* 183); Haering: the state "is not to be merely a 'state governed by law' [*Rechtsstaat*], but also a 'cultural state'" (*Das christliche Leben,* 467); and Seeberg: the state is the "effectively organized social will of a people to an autonomous national existence" (*System der Ethik,* 227).

[30.] Cf., e.g., Rieker, who states that through the Reformation's overcoming of the medieval opposition between state and church, "Christ has only one body, namely, the Christian state" (*Die rechtliche Stellung der evangelischen Kirche Deutschlands,* 479). For this assertion, Rieker appeals to Rothe and others who in the perfected form of the state see the only all-encompassing organization of Christian society (Rothe, *Theologische Ethik,* 418–25). In watered-down forms, such conceptions are consistent also within liberalism; see, e.g., Haering, who says that it is "a high ideal, ever more fully to be realized, precisely of Protestant ethics that the state . . . is a Christian state—namely, inasmuch as it is influenced by the Spirit of the gospel on the way of freedom" (*Das christliche Leben,* 477). [These notions of a "Christian" state and a specifically Christian understanding of the state were often explicitly anti-Jewish and (even when this was not the original intent) fed into Nazi anti-Jewish propaganda. Heinrich von Treitschke, one of the earliest to promote the

state is the fulfillment of certain given realities contained in it; indeed, in the final honing of this teaching it becomes the actual subject of these realities—thus of the people, of the culture, of the economy, of religion. It is "the real God" (Hegel).[31] The understanding of the state as commonwealth is common to all these teachings; by that understanding the concept of government is obtained only in a difficult and roundabout way. Fundamentally, then, government also must be derived from human nature; and it is hence difficult to understand it at the same time as the coercive power that turns against the human being,[32] for it is precisely in coercive power that the authority of the state is essentially different from the voluntary superordination and subordination that exists in every community. Wherever the state is derived from created human nature, the concept of government is dissolved and reconstructed from below, even where one does not at all intend this. Where the state becomes the fulfillment of all spheres of human life and culture, it forfeits its true dignity, its specific authority as government.[33]

512

---

conception of Germany as a Christian culture and state, described Judaism in the nineteenth century as "alien" to that culture (see Barnett, *Bystanders*, 104–5), and this perspective was echoed by many in Bonhoeffer's time, even in the Confessing Church (see Gerlach, *And the Witnesses Were Silent*, esp. 9–87). Thus we find disturbing contradictions even in documents such as the 1942 Freiburg memorandum, which proposed detailed plans for a post-Nazi government that included the payment of reparations to the Jewish victims—while at the same time it spoke of the need to address "the Jewish problem" and opposed citizenship for Jews (Thielicke, *In der Stunde Null*, 146–51, esp. 151; see also 1/205.1, ed. note 15). Bonhoeffer's thinking, it should be noted, was different. While his reflections here and elsewhere about the ordering of society are indeed influenced by his Christology, he warned against any explicitly "Christian society," particularly one aligned with governmental power. See 2/18, section 11.—MB]

[31.] In *Philosophy of Right*, Hegel states: "In considering the Idea of the state, we must not have our eyes on particular states or on particular institutions. Instead, we must consider the Idea, this actual God, by itself" (*Hegel's Philosophy of Right*, 279, addition 152 to paragraph 258). This is also cited in Brunner, *Divine Imperative*, 685–86. Cf. Lütgert on Hegel: "The state is divine and for this reason legally almighty" (*Ethik der Liebe*, 226).

[32.] Althaus based the subordination of human beings to coercive power (*Zwangsgewalt*) on the recognition of its necessity (*Grundriß der Ethik*, 98–101).

[33.] Cf. working note no. 44: "The state's loss of authority when it becomes the subject of all culture and forms of community" (*ZE*, 78). Cf. Delekat: "The state *cannot* prescribe for people what is good and bad, right and wrong, true and false. If it attempts to do so, it undermines its own authority" (*Die Kirche Jesu Christi und der Staat*, 168), and Brunner, who says that the state cannot "draw all spheres of life under its control and . . . dominate them. To the extent in which it has done this it has lost real authority" (*Divine Imperative*, 444). In contrast, Heinz-Dietrich Wendland affirmed the Nazi state as a purely authoritarian state ("Staat und Reich," 186–88). In the Barmen Declaration (see ed. notes 6 and 73), Thesis 5 formulated the boundaries that must be set against the totalitarian state.

B. In Sin

Building on the thought of Augustine,[34] the Reformation overcame the ancient classical concept of the state. It establishes the state not as a commonwealth in the created nature of the human being (although certain hints in this direction appear among the Reformers);[35] instead, it establishes the state as government *in the fall.*[36] Sin made the divine institution of government necessary. By means of the sword given to it by God, government is to protect human beings from the chaos that sin causes. It is to punish the criminal and preserve life. Thereby government is established as a coercive power *and* as guardian of an external justice.[37] The Reformation takes both into account in the same way. Nevertheless, the development of thinking diverged along two paths. The first defined the concept of justice by means of the concept of coercive power and was led to the concept of the state governed by power [Machtstaat]. The second defined power by means of justice and arrived at the concept of the state governed by law [Rechtsstaat]. The first saw exousia[38] only where there was power; the second saw it only where there was law. Thereby both diminished the Reformation concept of exousia.[39] Yet it remained common to both that they

513

[34.] Augustine, *City of God* 14.28; cf. Duchrow, *Christenheit und Weltverantwortung*, 247–98, for interpretative material.

[35.] Ernst Troeltsch in particular pointed out such hints with his thesis of a relative natural law in Luther and Melanchthon (cf. in summary form his "Christian Natural Law"). In contrast, Karl Holl wrote: "Luther did not appeal to a natural law, which he might have derived from the biblical accounts of the original state and Adam's fall into sin or, somewhat more philosophically, from our innate rationality" (*Reconstruction of Morality*, 103).

[36.] Cf. Holl, *Reconstruction of Morality*, 132; Lütgert, *Ethik der Liebe*, 218–19; and Brunner, *Divine Imperative*, 681.

[37.] Cf. Holl, *Cultural Significance of the Reformation:* the state provides "coercive power" (53) for the "maintenance of peace and order" (48). [*Gerechtigkeit*, translated here as "justice," can also mean "righteousness" and is translated that way in much of Bonhoeffer's work. With few exceptions in this chapter, we have translated it as "justice" because Bonhoeffer is writing here about the means by which the state can achieve legal or political "righteousness," i.e., justice.—MB]

[38.] See ed. note 5.

[39.] On these alternatives, cf. Delekat, *Die Kirche Jesu Christi und der Staat:* "[E]ither the state, according to its nature, is power or it is law" (161). "A state governed by law" signifies then that the state as power "is to be overcome by means of law" (212). Yet the state's permeation of all spheres of life necessarily results in "democratically heightened Machiavellism" (175). The Freiburg memorandum (see ed. note 16) spoke of the "demonic nature of power" (45, 67) that inevitably takes hold in this sort of total state. On this, cf. also G. Ritter, *Corrupting Influence of Power*, and Meinecke, *Machiavellism*. Brunner characterizes the prevalence of power within the state as "positivism" and the prevalence of law as "idealism" (*Divine Imperative*, 442).

recognized the state not as the fulfillment of creaturely capacities but as an order of God established from above. The state is understood not from below—from the standpoint of the people, of the culture, etc.—but from above, that is, as government in the true sense. So in this way the original point of departure, both of the Reformation and of the Bible, was preserved. The state is thus not essentially a people's, cultural, etc. state. All these are merely possible, divinely permitted forms of the political commonwealth that can be replaced by an abundance of other forms yet unknown to us. In distinction from the forms of commonwealth permitted by God, government is established and ordained by God alone. People, culture, social nature, etc. are world. Government is order equipped with divine authority in the world.[40] Government is not itself world, but of God. In addition, the concept of the Christian state is from this perspective untenable, for the governmental character of the state is independent of the Christian character of persons in government.[41] Government exists also among non-Christians.

C. From the Standpoint of Christ

Especially from what has just been said, but also from the preceding discussion, it becomes clear that the establishment of the state in sin as well as in human nature leads to a concept of the state in itself and thus apart from its relation to Jesus Christ. Whether as an order of creation or an order of preservation, the state exists for itself, more or less independent of the revelation of God in Jesus Christ.[42] Despite all the advantages of the second grounding over the first, even here this conclusion cannot be avoided. But now the question arises: from what standpoint can I say something theologically tenable—in contrast to a general Christian philosophy—concerning paradise or the fall, if not *from the standpoint of Jesus Christ*? Through Jesus Christ and for Jesus Christ all things are created (John 1:3; 1 Cor. 8:6; Heb. 1:2) and in particular also "thrones or dominions or rulers or powers" (Col. 1:16). Only in Jesus Christ does all this actually have its existence (Col. 1:17). Yet he is the same one who is "the head of . . . the church" (Col. 1:18). Insofar as the government instituted by God is intended and not some kind of philosophical concept of government, it is therefore under no circumstances possible to speak theologically of government apart from Jesus Christ

---

[40.] In the *Ethics* manuscript "The Concrete Commandment and the Divine Mandates" (*DBWE* 6:389), the "conferring of divine authority" on an earthly institution [*Instanz*] is termed a "mandate" (cf. ed. note 85).

[41.] See Delekat: the "hope of the Christianization of the state is the great temptation to which the church dare never succumb" (*Die Kirche Jesu Christi und der Staat,* 319).

[42.] This was also Karl Barth's general critique of the Reformation doctrine of the state ("Church and State," 102–4).

nor, since he is indeed the head of his church, apart from the *church of Jesus Christ*. The true grounding of government is therefore Jesus Christ himself. The relation of Jesus Christ to government can be expressed in seven parts:

1. As the mediator of creation, "through whom" government is also created,[43] Jesus Christ is the only and necessary connection between government and the Creator; there is no immediate connection of government to   515 God; Christ is its mediator.

2. Like everything created, government also has "existence only in Jesus Christ,"[44] and hence its essence and being. If Jesus Christ did not exist, then nothing created would exist any longer; it would thus be destroyed in the wrath of God.

3. Along with everything created, government is oriented "toward Jesus Christ."[45] Its purpose is Jesus Christ himself. It is supposed to serve him.

4. Because Jesus Christ has all power in heaven and on earth (Matt. 28: 18), he is also the Lord of the government.

5. By the reconciliation on the cross Jesus Christ restored the relationship between government and God (Col. 1:20 τὰ πάντα).[46]

6. Beyond this connection to Jesus Christ, which government has in common with everything created, government stands also in a special relation to Jesus Christ:

a) Jesus Christ was crucified by permission of the government.

b) The government, which recognized and openly bore witness to the innocence of Jesus (John 18:38; cf. also the role of Lysias,[47] Felix,[48] Festus,[49] and Agrippa[50] in the legal proceedings against Paul), thereby manifested its true nature.[51]

c) The government that does not risk standing by its knowledge and judgment in exercising governmental power has abandoned its office under the pressure of the people. Therein lies no condemnation of the office as such, but only of the inadequate exercise of this office.

d) Jesus submitted to the government, yet reminded it that its power is not up to human discretion but is "given ... from above" (John 19:11).

e) Jesus thereby bore witness that the government in the proper or improper execution of its office, precisely because it is power from above,

---

[43.] Cf. Col. 1:16.
[44.] Cf. Col. 1:17 [NRSV: "in him all things hold together"—MB].
[45.] Cf. Col. 1:16.
[46.] "all things."
[47.] Cf. Acts 24:7, 22.
[48.] Cf. Acts 23:24, 26; 24:2-27; 25:14.
[49.] Cf. Acts 25:1—26:32.
[50.] Cf. Acts 25:13—26:32.
[51.] On this and the following points, cf. Karl Barth, "Church and State," 108–14.

516   can only serve him. Absolving him from guilt and yet handing him over to
       be crucified, the government necessarily bore witness that it stands in the
       service of Jesus Christ. Thus precisely through the cross Jesus reclaimed his
       dominion over government (Col. 2:15), and at the end of all things "every
       ruler, government, and power" will be "sublated"[52] (in a double sense)
       through him.
            7. As long as the earth exists, Jesus will always be at the same time the
       Lord of all government and the head of the church-community, without
       government and church-community ever becoming one. But in the end
       there will be a holy city (polis) without a temple, for God and the Lamb will
       themselves be the temple (Revelation 21), and the citizens of this city will be
       believers from the community of Jesus in all the world, and God and the
       Lamb will exercise dominion in this city. In the heavenly polis, state and
       church will be one.
            Only the grounding of government in Jesus Christ leads beyond ground-
       ings in natural law, which is where, finally, the groundings both in human
       nature and human sin end up. The grounding in human nature sees in the
       given realities of peoples, etc., the foundation of the state in natural law.
       Imperialism and revolution—that is, external and internal revolution—draw
       upon this to justify themselves.[53] To limit the concept of power by means
       of the concept of law, the grounding in sin must discern norms of natural
       law and through these will have a more strongly conservative orientation.[54]
       However, because the concept and the content of natural law are ambigu-
       ous (depending on whether it is obtained from various given realities or
       from various norms), it does not suffice as the grounding of the state. Nat-
       ural law can establish the tyrannical state [Gewaltstaat] as well as the state
       governed by law, the people's state [Volksstaat] as well as imperialism, democ-
517   racy as well as the dictatorship.[55] We secure firm ground under our feet

---

      [52.] [This standard translation of Hegel's term (*aufgehoben*, "sublated") means both
to overcome and to redeem.—MB] Cf. 1 Cor. 15:24.
      [53.] Cf. the Freiburg memorandum: "Natural law and historical law... provide only
an uncertain, flickering light, which historically has all too often become an illusion. That
cliché—historical authorities willed by God—has over and over been forced to conceal
horrifying abuses; in their honest conviction to strive for 'natural' or 'divine' law, all revo-
lutionaries from time immemorial have assaulted existing legal conditions" (Thielicke, *In
der Stunde Null*, 59).
      [54.] Cf. Quervain, *Die theologischen Voraussetzungen der Politik*, on "naturalistic conser-
vatism" (130–57); cf. also *DBWE* 6:376–77.
      [55.] For Bonhoeffer's refusal to ground ethics in "natural law," cf. his sketch in the
Ethics, "On the Possibility of the Church's Message to the World" (*DBWE* 6:352–62). On
the ambivalence of the groundings of the state in natural law, cf. also Quervain, *Volk und
Obrigkeit*.

only by the biblical grounding of government in Jesus Christ. If and to what extent then from this standpoint a new natural law can be found is a theological question that remains open.[56]

3. The Divine Character of Government
A. *In Its Being*

Government is given to us not as an idea or as a task but as reality, as "existing" (αἱ δὲ οὖσαι,[57] Rom. 13:1c). In its being it is a divine office. Persons in government are God's "liturgists," servants, vicarious representatives (Rom. 13:4). The being of government is independent of its having come into being. Even if the path of human beings to governmental office may again and again pass through guilt, even if guilt hangs on almost every crown (Shakespeare's royal dramas),[58] the being of government stands beyond its earthly origination; for government is an order of God not in its origination but in its being. Like everything that exists, government is also   518 in a certain sense beyond good and evil[59]—i.e., it has not only an office but also a historical being. Through an ethical failure it does not yet lose eo ipso its divine dignity. "My country, right or wrong, my country"[60] expresses this state of affairs. It is the historical relation of one entity to another, repeating itself in the relation of father to child, brother to brother, and master to servant, and in those cases becoming immediately obvious. There

---

[56.] On Bonhoeffer's own attempt to grasp "the natural" "in distinction from the creaturely, in order to incorporate the fact of the fall into sin," and "in distinction from the sinful, in order to incorporate the creaturely," see the *Ethics* manuscript begun at Ettal in December 1940, "Natural Life," in *DBWE* 6, esp. pp. 173–74.

[57.] NRSV: "and those authorities that exist"; cf. *DBWE* 4:240.

[58.] Bonhoeffer respected Reinhold Schneider's interpretations of Shakespeare, which he had read in 1941 in Schneider's book *Macht und Gnade* (cf. Bonhoeffer's letter to Bethge, 1/58: "Reinhold Schneider is very good"). In *Macht und Gnade,* Schneider writes about *Richard III:* "Guilt had long since clung to this crown"; yet as a "sign of ancient holy dignity," the crown itself has ordering and healing power (99). On "Cromwell and the Crown," he writes: "For the crown represents the holy insofar as the king has received it from God and . . . human beings may well violate it, but the crown itself remains inviolate" (111). In the *Ethics* manuscript "Guilt, Justification, Renewal," Bonhoeffer took up this idea: "It has often happened that the struggle for the crown begins with arbitrary force, and then the power inherent in the crown, the power of the divine institution of government, works gradually to scar over and heal" (*DBWE* 6:143). On this cf. also ed. note 107.

[59.] *Beyond Good and Evil* is the title of a book by Friedrich Nietzsche.

[60.] This phrase, in English in the original text, is the popular version of a toast given by the American naval officer Stephen Decatur in April 1816, in Norfolk, Virginia: "Our country! In her intercourse with foreign nations may she always be in the right; but our country right or wrong" (Mackenzie, *Life of Decatur,* chap. 14). Brunner cites this remark as well, in a different sense, in *Divine Imperative,* 460.

is no ethical isolation of the son from the father; on the basis of actual being, there is even a necessary sharing and acceptance of the guilt of the father or the brother. There is no glory in standing in the ruined city of one's birth, under the assumption that you yourself at least have not become guilty.[61] That is the self-glorification of the moralist over against history. The clearest expression for this dignity of government, which rests even in its historical being, is its power, the sword that it wields.[62] Even where government becomes guilty, ethically assailable, its power is from God. It has its existence only in Jesus Christ, and through the cross of Christ is reconciled with God.[63]

519   *B. In Its Task*

The being of government is connected with a divine task. Only in the fulfillment of its task is its being fulfilled. A complete apostasy from its task would call its being into question. However, by God's providence this complete apostasy is only possible as an eschatological event. There, under severe martyrdom, it leads to the church-community's complete separation from the government as the embodiment of the anti-Christ.[64] The task of government consists in serving the dominion of Christ on earth by worldly exercise of the power of the sword and of the law.[65] Government serves Christ inasmuch as it establishes and preserves an external righteousness by wielding the sword given to it, and it alone, in God's stead. In this it has not only the negative task[66] of punishing the wicked but also the positive task

---

[61.] This sentence may reflect Bonhoeffer's own experience of the bombing of Berlin, which began in November 1941 and grew to greater proportions with the engagement of high-speed English bombers beginning in January 1942. Cf. also the first and second versions of the *Ethics* manuscript "History and Good," which were written in the period from January through summer of 1942. There Bonhoeffer writes that Jesus "does not want to be considered the only perfect one at the expense of human beings, nor, as the only guiltless one, to look down on a humanity perishing under its guilt. He does not want some idea of a new human being to triumph over the wreckage of a defeated humanity" (*DBWE* 6:233; cf. *DBWE* 6:275).

[62.] This is an argument widespread in Lutheran theology. Cf. Gogarten, who wrote that the "peculiar nobility" of the state, "whose symbol from time immemorial is the sword, is manifest in that it... provides and protects political existence for human beings... precisely by means of that sword" (*Politische Ethik*, 217).

[63.] See section 2 C.

[64.] On this, cf. Schlier, "Vom Antichrist," 110–23.

[65.] Cf. Barth: the state "as such, belongs originally and ultimately to Jesus Christ" and is to "serve the Person and the Work of Jesus Christ" ("Church and State," 118).

[66.] The following portion of the sentence (until "positive task"), which appeared in the first German edition of the *Ethics*, was inadvertently omitted from the 6th German edition.

of commending the good as well as the godly (1 Peter 2:14!). It is thereby granted, on the one hand, legal power, and, on the other hand, the right to educate for the good—that is, for outward justice. To be sure, how it practices this right to educate is a question that can be dealt with only in connection with government's relationships to the other divine orders. The frequently addressed question—namely, of what the good, the outward justice that government is to cultivate, consists in—is easily answered if one stays focused on the grounding of government in Jesus Christ. In any case, this good cannot stand in contradiction to Jesus Christ. The good consists in the existence of space for the final goal—the service to Jesus Christ— within every action of government. This refers not to an action that is Christian but to an action that does not exclude Jesus Christ.[67] Government arrives at such an action when it takes the contents of the second table[68] as its measure in any given historical situation and decision. But how does government become aware of these contents? First of all, from the preaching of the church. In the case of a godless government, however, a providential correspondence[69] exists between the contents of the second table and the law inherent in historical life itself.[70] The failure to observe the second table destroys the very life that government is supposed to protect. Thus the task of protecting life, rightly understood, leads inherently to the upholding of the second table. Is the state, then, grounded after all in natural law? No, for here we are speaking only about the government that does not understand itself and nevertheless can arrive providentially at the same decisive insights for its task that are revealed in Jesus Christ to the government that understands itself rightly. Thus, suffice it to say that here natural law is grounded in Jesus Christ.

520

Thus the task of government, whether or not it knows its true grounding, consists in establishing, by the power of the sword, an outward justice in which life is preserved and in this way remains open for Christ.

Does the government's task also include upholding the first table, i.e., the decision for the God and Father of Jesus Christ? We want to deal with this

---

[67.] Cf. Barth, "Church and State," 118–19; on this, cf. also Bonhoeffer's thoughts regarding William Paton's book in point 4 of "The Church and the New Order in Europe": "A worldly order that abides within the Decalogue will be open for Christ." It "is, to be sure, not 'Christian,' but it is a legitimate earthly order according to God's will" (see 2/11).

[68.] [Bonhoeffer is referring to the second table of the Decalogue.—MB]

[69.] By this Bonhoeffer means a correspondence brought about by God's providence.

[70.] Cf. Bonhoeffer's comments in "Church and World I" on the retrieval of ethical and humanistic values for the church when it is threatened with destruction (*DBWE* 6: 339–41); cf. also point 4 of his "Thoughts on William Paton" (see 2/11). On the theological basis for all this, cf. Bonhoeffer's reflections on the openness of the "natural" for Christ (*DBWE* 6:171–78).

question in the section on government and church and here say only this: the knowledge of Jesus Christ belongs to the destiny of all human beings, including those with governmental authority. To the task of government as such, however, belongs the praise and protection of the godly (1 Peter 2:14), independent of the personal faith of the governmental authorities. Indeed, only in the protection of the godly does government fulfill its true task of serving Christ.

521   The task of government to serve Christ is at the same time its inescapable destiny. It serves Christ, whether knowingly or unknowingly, indeed, whether it is faithful or unfaithful to its task. It must serve him, whether it wants to or not. If it desires not to, it serves the witness to the name of Christ through the suffering of the church-community. So close and inseparable is the relation of government to Christ. One way or another it cannot escape its task of serving Christ. It serves him by its existence.[71]

C. In Its Claim

The claim that government has on the basis of its power and its task is the claim of God and binds the conscience.[72] Government demands obedience "because of conscience" (Rom. 13:5), which can also be interpreted as "for the Lord's sake" (1 Peter 2:13). Such obedience is combined with respect (Rom. 13:7; 1 Peter 2:17). In the performance of the governmental task the demand for obedience is unconditional, qualitatively total, extending to conscience and bodily life.[73] Faith, conscience, and bodily life are bound in obedience to the divine task of government. Uncertainty can emerge only where the content and the scope of the task of government become questionable. The Christian is not obliged and not able to prove in every single case the right of the governmental demand. The duty of Chris-
522   tians to obey binds them up to the point where the government forces them

---

[71.] This is also Barth's conclusion in "Church and State," 110–14.

[72.] The binding of the conscience by God is the decisive criterion of the Freiburg memorandum; see its subtitle: ". . . for the self-reflection of the Christian conscience." Cf., however, Delekat: "Only in the church is it possible to render the obedience due to the state without, however, thereby becoming bound *in conscience* to the state" (*Die Kirche Jesu Christi und der Staat,* 174).

[73.] The delimitation against the "total state" in the Barmen Declaration (cf. *Creeds of the Church,* 521) is directed against the commandeering of "*all of* existence" by the state (cf. Delekat, *Die Kirche Jesu Christi und der Staat,* 175). "Qualitatively total" can therefore only mean that the state claims "the entire life of the people within the boundaries set by God" (cf. Hans Asmussen's paper on Thesis 5 of the Barmen Declaration, *Die Barmer Theologische Erklärung,* 55). On Bonhoeffer's personal stance regarding "the duty of obedience to the government" according to Romans 13, cf. 1/228.4, which also contains a reference to the ongoing validity for him of his reflections in *Discipleship* (*DBWE* 4:240–44).

into direct violation of the divine commandment, thus until government overtly acts contrary to its divine task and thereby forfeits its divine claim. When in doubt, obedience is demanded, for the Christian does not bear the governmental responsibility. But if government oversteps its task at some point—e.g., by making itself lord over the faith of the church-community— then at this point it is indeed to be disobeyed for the sake of conscience and for the sake of the Lord.[74] Yet it is not permissible to draw the sweeping conclusion from this offense that this government now has no further claim to obedience in any or even all other demands. Disobedience can only be a concrete decision in the individual case.[75] Generalizations lead to an apocalyptic demonization of government. Even an anti-Christian government remains in a certain respect still government.[76] It would therefore not be permissible to refuse to pay taxes to a government that was persecuting the church. Conversely, the act of obedience to government in its state functions—paying taxes, taking oaths, serving in the military[77]— is always a proof that this government is still not understood apocalyptically. An apocalyptic understanding of a concrete government would have to entail total disobedience; for in that case every single act of obedience is manifestly connected with a denial of Christ (Rev. 13:7). Because in all decisions of the state the historical entanglement in the guilt of the past is incalculably large, it is for the most part not possible to judge the legitimacy of a single decision. Here the venture of responsibility[78] must be risked. But

523

[74.] This corresponds to Luther's position in the question of the duty of obeying governmental authorities; cf., e.g., "Temporal Authority: To What Extent It Should Be Obeyed," 1523 (*LW* 45:75–129 [WA 11:245–81]) and "Whether Soldiers, Too, Can Be Saved," 1526 (*LW* 46:87–137 [WA 19:623–62]). [This also echoes Bonhoeffer's conclusion in "The Church and the Jewish Question" that Christians, when government does not exercise its power in legitimate ways, may be compelled to stop the wheel (*DBW* 12:353).—MB]

[75.] This is also Schlink's position in *Theology of the Lutheran Confessions:* "Here the possibility of concrete disobedience is mentioned, not of disobedience in principle" (264).

[76.] Cf. Dehn: "The same government that is fundamentally from God can *in concreto* be the enemy of God and of the church-community" (*Engel und Obrigkeit,* 108).

[77.] Barth includes the same list in "Church and State," 141–43. On the issue of oaths, cf. Glenthøj, "Die Eideskrise," 377–94. In the case of Bonhoeffer's own conscription into Hitler's army, he himself had wanted to refuse the draft (cf. C. Strohm, *Theologische Ethik im Kampf,* 333–34 n. 26).

[78.] Cf. the significance in Bonhoeffer's *Ethics* of the category of "venture" *(Wagnis),* which increases with his participation in the conspiracy against Hitler (*DBWE* 6:248, 257, 274, et passim). Cf. also "After Ten Years": "Only now are the Germans beginning to discover the meaning of free responsibility. It depends on a God who demands responsible action in a bold venture of faith, and who promises forgiveness and consolation to the one who becomes a sinner in that venture" (*LPP,* 6 [*DBW* 8:24], trans. altered; cf. also *LPP,* 174 and 370–71 [*DBW* 8:253 and 570–72]). The category of the venture must remain strictly connected to God in Jesus Christ and to his commandment. Cf., in contrast, the

the responsibility for such a venture on the part of government can in concreto (i.e., apart from the general shared responsibility of individuals for political action) be borne only by the government. Even where the guilt of government is blatantly obvious, the guilt that gave rise to this guilt may not be disregarded. The refusal to obey within a specific historical political decision of the government, as well as this decision itself, can only be a venture of one's own responsibility. A historical decision cannot be completely incorporated into ethical concepts. There is one thing left: the venture of action.[79] That holds true for the government as well as for subjects.

4. Government and the Divine Orders in the World[80]

524   Government has the divine task of preserving the world with its God-given orders in reference to Christ. It alone bears the sword for that purpose. Every person is obligated to obey it.[81] But with its task and its claim it always presupposes the created world. Government keeps what is created in its order but cannot itself produce life; it is not creative. However, within the world it governs it discovers two orders through which God the Creator

---

way it is used as a motto for the "national-socialist revolution" by Emanuel Hirsch, who appealed to Søren Kierkegaard: "The confidence with which one ventures [*wagen*] provides superhuman powers" (Hirsch, *Die gegenwärtige geistige Lage,* epigraph and introduction).

[79.] This is one of the few places in Bonhoeffer's written work from the time of his participation in the conspiracy against Hitler that provides a glimpse of his own personal view of this participation.

[80.] Bonhoeffer here takes up the theme of the "orders of creation," which since the mid-1920s had been the theological crystallization point of the conflicting understandings of the state. In the June 1934 Ansbach memorandum [*Ansbacher Ratschlag*], with which leading Lutheran theologians such as Werner Elert and Paul Althaus turned against the Barmen Declaration, the duty of all persons through "the natural orders... such as family, people [*Volk*], race (i.e., blood relationship)," of which government is one, becomes the basis for the grateful affirmation of the "national-socialist state order." [The first Ansbach memorandum was published in the early years of the Reformation by Lutheran theologians in the region of Franconia.—MB] Throughout this period, Bonhoeffer clearly distanced himself from this interpretation of the "orders" (on this cf. C. Strohm, *Theologische Ethik im Kampf,* 87–147). [See also ed. note 1.—MB] But he did not let the matter rest, as his 1932–33 debates with Friedrich Gogarten's *Politische Ethik* and Emil Brunner's *Divine Imperative* reveal; Bonhoeffer's rejoinders are found in *DBW* 12:162–68 and 173–78 (*GS* 5:321–30 and 335–40), as well as in his March 7, 1940, letter to Gerhard Leibholz (*DBW* 15:296–300; *GS* 3:33–36). In his work in the *Ethics,* however, the concept of the "mandate" (i.e., the divine task or commission) replaced that of the "order"; on this, cf. also ed. note 85.

[81.] Bonhoeffer lifted portions of the following text verbatim, but also with characteristic changes, for his *Ethics* chapter titled "Christ, Reality, and Good"; see *DBWE* 6:70–73. This refers to a passage that Bonhoeffer subsequently (in the second half of 1941, according to the hypothesis of the German editors of *DBW* 6) inserted into the chapter conceived in 1940; see *DBWE* 6:65, ed. note 67, and 68–69, ed. note 75.

exercises creative power and upon [which] it is therefore by nature dependent: *marriage* and *work*.[82] We find both in the Bible, already in paradise,[83] attesting that they belong to God's creation, which exists through and toward Jesus Christ. Even after the fall, i.e., in the form in which alone we know them, both still remain divine orders of discipline and grace,[84] because God desires to be revealed even to the fallen world as the Creator, and 525 because God allows the world to exist in Christ and makes the world Christ's own. Marriage and work exist from the beginning under an appointed divine mandate[85] that must be performed in faithful obedience to God.

[82.] Cf. *DBWE* 6:72: "In the world that it rules, government finds already existing these two mandates through which God the Creator exercises creative power and upon which government must rely. Government itself cannot produce life or values. It is not creative. Government maintains what is created in the order that was given to the creation by God's commission." Here Bonhoeffer has replaced "two orders" with "two mandates." He does not insert the bracketed "which" missing in the manuscript of this text (the editors of both *DBW* 6 and *DBW* 16 have inserted it). He also reverses the order of "marriage" and "work" (cf. *DBWE* 6:68–69, ed. note 75). In the remaining places where Bonhoeffer speaks of the "mandates," however, "marriage" and "family" again take their place before "labor" and "culture," respectively; cf. *DBWE* 6:296, 380, 388); cf. "'Personal' and 'Objective' Ethics," 2/13.

[83.] Cf. Gen. 1:22, 28; *DBWE* 6:70–71.

[84.] Cf. *DBWE* 6:70. "After the fall, work remains a mandate of divine discipline and grace." Bonhoeffer understands the orders, therefore, in the duality of the preserving work of the Creator against sin and of the "Redeemer" (like Brunner, *Divine Imperative*, 122–31); cf. also Bonhoeffer's letter to Leibholz on March 7, 1940 (*DBW* 15:297; *GS* 3:35).

[85.] The term "mandate" is derived from the Vulgate Latin translation, *mandatum*, of the Greek term ἐντολή, "commandment," e.g., John 13:34. Whether Bonhoeffer came up with his doctrine of the four mandates (marriage, work, government, church) from the usage of the mandate concept developed in this text must remain an open question, so long as the dating of the entire text is insufficiently clear. In any case, the linguistic usage in the material inserted into "Christ, Reality, and Good" has shifted in such a way that Bonhoeffer there speaks of marriage, work, government, and church as mandates, not simply of marriage, work, government, and church each standing "under" a certain mandate; cf. *DBWE* 6:68–69, including ed. note 75. Yet Bonhoeffer does not wish here to defend a certain quality of being of marriage, work, government, and church. He speaks "of divine mandates rather than divine orders, because thereby their character as divinely imposed tasks [*Auftrag*], as opposed to determinate forms of being becomes clearer" (ibid.). This remains the case in the final version of the doctrine of mandates from the beginning of 1943 ("The Concrete Commandment and the Divine Mandates," *DBWE* 6:388–94). What matters is the divine "authorizing, legitimizing, and sanctioning" of the "orders," not "the static element of order" (*DBWE* 6:393). In fact, this consideration is the decisive one here as well. In addition, the doctrine of the mandates represents a new interpretation of the traditional doctrine of the three estates; on this, cf. "'Personal' and 'Objective' Ethics," 2/13, ed. note 52. From the point of view of the tradition, what is unusual is the use of the concept of mandates with these "estates" or "orders." In distinction from "law," this concept brings to expression the *concreteness* of the divine command. In this sense it was surely

For this reason marriage and work have their own origin in God that is not established by government but is to be acknowledged by it. Through marriage bodily life is propagated, and human beings are procreated for the glorification and service of Jesus Christ. Yet that means marriage encom-
526 passes not only the place of procreation but also that of raising children to obey Jesus Christ. For the child its parents are God's representatives as the child's procreators and educators. Through work a world of values is created for the glorification and service of Jesus Christ.[86] As in marriage, work is not divine creation out of nothing; rather it is the production of something new on the basis of the first creation—in marriage of new life, in work of new values.[87] Work hereby encompasses the whole realm from agriculture, through trade and industry, to science and art (cf. Gen. 4:17ff.).[88] Thus, for the sake of Jesus Christ a special right preserves marriage and with it the family and preserves work and with it economic life, culture, science, and art. That means government possesses for this realm only regulative but not constitutive significance. Marriage is contracted not by government but before government. Economic life, science, and art are not cultivated by government itself, but they are subject to its supervision and, within certain limits (not to be further specified here), to its control. But at no time does government become the subject of these spheres of work. Where it extends its authority beyond its own task, it will in the long run forfeit its true authority in these matters.[89]

known to Bonhoeffer from the confessional writings and their interpretation. The concept of mandate is found in the doctrine of "good works" (cf. Luthardt, *Kompendium der theologischen Ethik,* 192), of the pastoral office (cf. Vilmar, *Dogmatik,* 275–76), and not least of the sacraments (the Augsburg Confession 8 and 28/23 [*Book of Concord,* 42–43 and 94–95]). On the question of the origin of the concept, cf. also *DBWE* 6:68–69, ed. note 75.

[86.] Cf. *DBWE* 6:71: "Through marriage human beings are procreated for the glory and service of Jesus Christ and the enlarging of Christ's kingdom. This means that marriage is the place where children not only are born but also are educated into obedience to Jesus Christ. As their procreators and educators, parents are commissioned by God to be representatives [*Stellvertreter*] of God for the children. Just as in work new values are created, so in marriage new persons are created to serve Jesus Christ."

[87.] Since in "Christ, Reality, and Good" Bonhoeffer deals with marriage and work separately, this passage is already anticipated in *DBWE* 6:70.

[88.] Cf. *DBWE* 6: 71.

[89.] Cf. *DBWE* 6:72: "Thus, marriage is not made by government, but is affirmed by government. The great spheres of work are not themselves undertaken by government, but they are subject to its supervision and within certain limits—later to be described—to governmental direction. Government should never seek to become the agent of these areas of work, for this would seriously endanger their divine mandate along with its own." The alteration of the phrase in parentheses verifies that "State and Church" was conceived as a self-contained work.

The order of the people is distinguished from the order of marriage and the order of work. According to scripture its origin lies neither in paradise 527 nor in an explicit divine mandate.[90] On the one hand (according to Genesis 10), the people [das Volk] is a natural consequence of the spread of the generations upon the earth. On the other hand (Genesis 11), it is a divine order that allows humanity to live in its disintegration and mutual misunderstanding, thereby reminding it that its unity lies not in its own absolute power but in God alone—i.e., in the Creator and Redeemer. But in scripture there is no special task of God for the people. Whereas marriage and work are divine offices, the people is historical reality that in a particular way points to the divine reality of the *one* people of God, to the church. Scripture provides no reference to the relationship of people and government; it does not call for a people's state; it knows of the possibility that various peoples can be unified under one government. It knows that the people grows from below, but that government is established from above.

5. Government and Church

Government is established for the sake of Christ. It serves Christ, and thereby it also serves his church. The reign of Christ over all government certainly in no way implies the reign of the church over government. But the same Lord whom government serves is the head of the church-community, the Lord of the church. Government's service to Christ consists in the exercise of its task to secure an outward justice by the power of the sword. In this respect it provides an indirect service to the church-community, which can only thus live a "quiet and peaceable life" (1 Tim. 2:2). By its service to Christ, government is essentially connected with the church. Where it properly fulfills its task, the church-community can live in peace; for government and church-community serve the same Lord.

A. *The Claim of Government on the Church* 528

The claim of government to obedience and respect extends to the church as well. With regard to the pastoral office, of course, government can insist only that this office not interfere with the worldly office[91] but fulfill its own task, in which indeed the admonition to obey the government is included.

[90.] Bonhoeffer is thus speaking here of an "order" of God without a mandate. By this he is distancing himself from the idea that the reality of a people in its history is to be heard as a "law of God" (as in Stapel, *Der christliche Staatsmann*, 174–76, along with many "Lutheran" theologians building on his work).

[91.] See Augsburg Confession 28/12–13 (*Book of Concord*, 92–93): the spiritual power should not "invade an alien office."

The government has no power over this task itself, as it is exercised in the pastorate and in the office of church administration. Insofar as the pastoral office is a publicly practiced office, government is entitled to oversee that everything happens in good order—i.e., in accordance with outward justice. Only in this respect does it also have a say in how the office is staffed and configured. The pastoral office itself is not subordinate to government. Nevertheless, government has full claim to the obedience of members of the Christian community. It does not thereby position itself as a second authority alongside the authority of Christ; rather its own authority is only a form of the authority of Christ. In obedience to government the Christian obeys Christ. The Christian as citizen does not cease to be a Christian, but serves Christ in a different way. In this way the content of the legitimate governmental claim is already sufficiently determined as well. It can never lead the Christian against Christ; rather it helps Christians serve Christ in the world. In this way the person in government becomes for the Christian a servant of God.[92]

B. The Claim of the Church on Government

The church has the task of calling the whole world to submit to the reign of Jesus Christ. It bears witness for government to their common Lord. It calls government officials to belief in Jesus Christ for the sake of their own salvation. It knows that in obedience to Jesus Christ the task of government

529   is properly executed. Its goal is not that government enact Christian politics, Christian laws, etc., but rather that it be genuine government in the sense of its particular task. The church is what first leads government to an understanding of itself. For the sake of the common Lord, it lays claim to the hearing of government, the safeguarding of public Christian proclamation against acts of violence and blasphemy, the safeguarding of church order against arbitrary encroachment, and the safeguarding of Christian life in obedience to Jesus Christ. The church can never abandon this claim. It must let it be publicly heard as long as government itself claims to recognize the church. Where, of course, government explicitly or actually stands against the church, the time can come when the church, while not relinquishing its claim, nevertheless no longer wastes its words.[93] It knows very well that government, whether it performs its task properly or improperly, must always only serve its Lord and thereby the church as well. The government that refuses to safeguard the church thereby places the church all the more conspicuously

---

[92.] Note the shift toward "personal" language about the government.

[93.] Cf. *DBWE* 4:43–44 where Bonhoeffer states that "cheap grace" means grace as "bargain-basement goods" *(Schleuderware)*. [Again, this echoes his perspective in the 1933 essay, "The Church and the Jewish Question," *DBW* 12:351–53.—MB]

under the protection of its Lord. Government that reviles its Lord bears witness thereby all the more resoundingly to the power of this Lord, who is praised in the church's martyrdoms.[94]

C. The Ecclesial Responsibility of Government[95]

The responsibility of government corresponds to the claim of the church. Here a reply needs to be given to the question of the government's stance in relation to the First Commandment. Must government come to a religious decision, or is its task religious neutrality?[96] Is government responsible for the cultivation of true Christian worship, and does it have the right   530
to prohibit other worship? Certainly government officials should also come to faith in Jesus Christ. However, the governmental office remains independent from religious decision. It is, nevertheless, the responsibility of the governmental office to safeguard, indeed to praise, the devout—i.e., to support the cultivation of religion. A government that overlooks this responsibility uproots true obedience and thus its own authority (France 1905).[97] The governmental office as such thereby remains religiously neutral and only inquires after its own task. It can, therefore, never become the subject of the founding of a new religion without dissolving itself. It safeguards any worship that does not undermine the governmental office. It makes sure that no antagonism that would endanger national order arises out of the diversity of forms of worship. It achieves this, however, not by suppression of worship, but by a clear observance of its own governmental task. It will then become clear that true Christian worship does not endanger this task

---

[94.] Cf. Cullmann: "The fact that Christ reigns is shown forth in the suffering of the Church. ... The suffering of the Church refers back to the conquest of the invisible powers that has already taken place and it points forward to their final defeat" ("Kingship of Christ and the Church in the New Testament," 134).

[95.] [For other examples of Bonhoeffer's thinking on this topic and the church-state relationship in general, see also his essay "Protestantism without Reformation," *DBW* 15, esp. pp. 445–52.—MB]

[96.] The phrases "religious neutrality," "religious decision," as well as "cultivation of religion" (see further discussion in this paragraph) derive from the discussion about the liberal understanding of the state and appear to point to Bonhoeffer's speaking here within a general legal conception of the state, using terminology that is theologically uncharacteristic for him.

[97.] In France the separation of church and state was introduced in 1905. [The 1905 Combes law and its doctrine of *laïcité* were the French state's attempt to combat Catholic clericalism and abuses of power.—MB] Cf. Lienhard, "Frankreich 3/2"; and Bauberot, "Secularism and French Religious Liberty," 459–60. Cf. also the Freiburg memorandum, according to which the result of the "culture war" in France was the utter "dissolving of state Christendom" and the "displacement of the church into a sort of insular existence as a private club" (43).

but instead continually constitutes it anew. If persons in government are Christian, then they must know that Christian proclamation occurs not by the sword but by the word. The sentence "Cuius regio, eius religio"[98] was possible only under very particular political circumstances, namely, the agreement of the sovereigns to take in any who were expelled. As a principle it is incompatible with the governmental office. But if there should be a particular state of church crisis, then it would lie within the responsibility of Christians in government to make their power available at the request of the church to restore healthy conditions. That does not, however, mean that the government as such takes over functions of church governance. What is exclusively at stake is the restoration of proper order, in which the pastoral office can be practiced rightly and in which government and church can fulfill their respective tasks.[99] Government will maintain its commitment to the First Commandment by being government in the proper way, also exercising its governmental responsibility toward the church. But it does not have the office of confessing and proclaiming faith in Jesus Christ.

531

D. The Political Responsibility of the Church

If political responsibility is exclusively understood to mean governmental responsibility, then clearly only government has to bear this responsibility. However, if with this concept life in the polis is meant quite generally, then in a manifold sense we can speak of a political responsibility of the church as a response to the claim of government on the church. We distinguish here once more between the responsibility of the pastoral office and the responsibility of Christians. Part of the church's role as guardian is to call sin by name and to warn human beings of sin; for "Righteousness exalts a nation [that is, temporally and eternally], but sin is a reproach to any people [that is, a temporal and eternal reproach]" (Prov. 14:34). If the church did not do that, then it would itself become implicated with the blood of the ungodly (Ezek. 3:17ff.). This warning against sin extends quite publicly to the church-community, and those who will not hear it bring judgment upon themselves. Thus, the purpose of the preacher is not to

---

[98.] "To whom a region [belongs, i.e., its ruler], his religion [becomes that of all subjects]" states the legal standard following the Peace of Augsburg, 1555.

[99.] On Bonhoeffer's conceptions of the government's functions in the reconstitution of the church following the overthrow, see his draft "End of the Church Struggle" (2/16) and the corresponding constitutional provisions by Friedrich J. Perels (2/17). In addition, cf. the material in *NL*, A 75,89: "Tolerance and relig. persecution—state not indifferent to religion, state intervention possible and correct under certain conditions" (*ZE*, 107).

improve the world but to call it to faith in Jesus Christ, to bear witness to the reconciliation through him and his reign. The theme of proclamation is not the depravity of the world but the grace of Jesus Christ. It is the respon-   532
sibility of the pastoral office to take seriously the proclamation of the kingly reign of Christ[100] and through direct, respectful speech to make government aware of its failures and mistakes that necessarily threaten its governmental office. If the word of the church is in principle not accepted, then all that is left to it is enough political responsibility to establish and preserve at least among its own members the order of outward justice no longer present in the polis, thereby serving the government in its own way.

Is there a political responsibility of the *individual Christian?* Individual Christians can certainly not be held responsible for the government's actions, nor dare they make themselves responsible for them. But on the basis of their faith and love of neighbor, they are responsible for their own vocation and personal sphere of living, however large or small it is. Wherever this responsibility is faithfully exercised, it has efficacy for the polis as a whole. According to scripture there is no right to revolution,[101] but there is a responsibility for all individuals to safeguard the purity of their offices and tasks in the polis. And thus in a genuine sense individuals serve government with their responsibility. No one, [not] even government itself, can take this responsibility from the people or forbid it from being a part of their lives in sanctification, for it derives from obedience to the Lord of the church and of government.

E. Conclusions

The various connections between government and church do not allow for the regulation of the relationship on the basis of a principle; neither the   533
separation of state and church nor the state church form is in itself a solution of the problem. Nothing is more dangerous than drawing generalized theoretical conclusions from isolated experiences. The programmatic endorsement of the church's withdrawal from the world, from the connections with the state that still exist, under the impression of living in an apocalyptic time, is, in this sort of generality, only a somewhat nostalgic historical-philosophical

---

[100.] This terminology is not characteristic of Bonhoeffer; however, cf. Cullmann, "Kingship of Christ and the Church in the New Testament," esp. 132–34; Obendiek, *Die Obrigkeit*, 45ff.

[101.] The rejection of the right to revolution is a consequence of the refusal to ground the state from below (cf. Dehn, *Engel und Obrigkeit*, 105). On Bonhoeffer's understanding of revolution "in the light of the Nazi seizure of power," cf. C. Strohm, *Theologische Ethik im Kampf*, 90–103.

interpretation of the times that, were it truly taken seriously, would necessarily lead to the most radical implications of Revelation 13.[102] By the same token, the vision and planning of a state church or church of the people [volkskirchlich] can likewise originate out of the philosophy of history. No constitutional form[103] can give suitable expression to proximity and distance in the relationship of government and church. Government and church are bound, and bound together, by the same Lord. Government and church are distinguished from each other in their task. Government and church have the same sphere of action, human beings. None of these relations may be isolated and in this way supply the ground for a certain constitutional form (thus, for example, arranged as state church, free church, church of the people);[104] what matters is giving concrete room in every given form for the relationship actually established by God and entrusting the way it develops to the Lord over government and church.

6. The Form of the State and Church

In the doctrine of the state deriving from the Reformation as well as from Catholicism, the question concerning the form of the state is always

---

[102.] The implication is that the state is the "beast rising out of the sea" (cf. Rev. 13:1) and that Christians must suffer martyrdom.

[103.] In the first German edition of *Ethics* (274) and the sixth German edition of *Ethics* (373), "constitutional reform" appeared here, presumably erroneously.

[104.] [In the introduction to *Sanctorum Communio,* Clifford Green explains: "*Volkskirche* literally means 'church of the people,' and that is what we finally decided was the best translation. The term derives from Schleiermacher's time when the word *Volk* referred to the people in distinction from the ruling princes. In a *Volkskirche* the emphasis is on *inclusivity,* rather than nationality, ethnicity, or connection to government. In Germany, both Protestant churches (whether Lutheran, Reformed, or Union) and Roman Catholic churches understand themselves as *Volkskirchen.* While the German *Freikirchen* (free churches) such as the Baptists require a definite act of commitment (e.g., baptism as an adult), membership in the *Volkskirche* is virtually automatic by birth; children of parents whose names are on the roll of a *Volkskirche,* however tenuous their connection to the church, will also be baptized into membership of the *Volkskirche.* People are included unless they take a definite step to exclude themselves by having their names removed from the roll." Furthermore, Green notes that the "phrase 'established church,' used to describe the Church of England, is not a good description of *Volkskirche,* notwithstanding the church tax collected by the German government, theological education within state-funded universities, and military chaplains funded by the government. For one thing, England has only one established church, Germany several *Volkskirchen.*" Finally, the translation "national church," which Neville Horton Smith utilizes in "State and Church" in *Ethics* (1995 Simon and Schuster edition), "is misleading—although the policy of the National Socialists was certainly to imbue the churches with a nationalistic spirit," and the German Christians, of course, certainly had a nazified understanding of *Volkskirche* (*DBWE* 1:18).—MB]

secondary.[105] As long as the government fulfills its task, the form under which it does so is not essential, at least for the church. But it is justified to ask which form of the state offers the best guarantee for the fulfillment of the government's task and therefore ought to be supported by the church. No form of the state is as such an absolute guarantee of a proper performance of the office of government. Only concrete obedience to the divine task justifies a form of the state. Nevertheless, some general guiding principles can be formulated to identify the forms of the state that offer relatively advantageous conditions for proper governmental action and thereby for a proper relationship between state and church; and precisely these relative differences can be of great import in practice.

I. The relatively best[106] form of the state will be that in which it is most clear that government is from above, from God, and in which its divine origin shines through most brightly.[107] A properly understood divine right[108] of government in its glory and in its responsibility belongs to the essence of

534

535

[105.] Cf. Schilling, *Lehrbuch der Moraltheologie,* 2:615, and Brunner, *Divine Imperative,* 465–68, among others.

[106.] Cf. Martensen, *Die christliche Ethik,* vol. 2 (owned by Bonhoeffer): "Without doubt, the English constitution has been relatively the best [!] over the course of years for the English people" (225–26).

[107.] In working note no. 45, Bonhoeffer writes. "Where the divine origin shines through" (*ZE,* 81). This is reminiscent of expressions and formulations about "kingdom" and the "crown" in Schneider's *Macht und Gnade,* e.g., "Das Schicksal Friedrich Wilhelms IV": "only the gleam of an otherworldly mystery draping the crown before his eyes bestowed on it the highest power" (19) and "King Richard III": "For him the crown . . . had . . . taken on a mysterious gleam" (99).

[108.] Cf. also "Das Schicksal Friedrich Wilhelms IV" in Schneider, *Macht und Gnade:* "For him kingship was the immediated commission of God. . . . The unshakable conviction of the distinction between above and below—that is, the knowledge indispensable in a king that not all are by the grace of God—finds its reflection in the decisive religious experience" (20). With the formulation of "a rightly understood divine right," Bonhoeffer sets himself apart from Brunner's polemic against a "false divine right" (Brunner, *Divine Imperative,* 447). Brunner was thinking of that view of divine right that was cultivated under Hegel's influence within "Christian Romanticism" (e.g., Stahl, *Rechts- und Staatslehre;* or Rothe, *Theologische Ethik*). Bonhoeffer was surely familiar with Vilmar's conception of the divine right of government, e.g., in "Von Gottes Gnaden" and "Obrigkeit" (cf. the presentation of Wollenweber, *Theologie und Politik bei A. F. C. Vilmar,* 94–95). The fact that in speaking of "divine right" Bonhoeffer was also thinking of the constitutional monarchy and its resulting form of state can be inferred from the closeness of his argumentation to that of Martensen, *Die christliche Ethik,* 2:224–26. Cf. Martensen's statements that Christianity has taught us "that the state is a divine order and that the source of perfect power and of sovereignty is to be sought in God. And the view that the government as the organ for the exercise of power is *'by the grace of God'* is grounded on this truth" (ibid., 220) and that "[i]n accordance with divine order, the direction of government should be downward *from above*" (ibid., 222). On the conception of the constitutional monarchy as the relatively best form of the state (in distinction from the rest of Western royalty, the Belgian kings called themselves "de grâce du peuple").[109]

II. The relatively best form of the state will see its power not compromised but sustained and secured

a) by a strict maintenance of outward justice,

b) by the right, grounded in God, of the family and of work,

c) by the proclamation of the gospel of Jesus Christ.[110]

III. The relatively best form of the state will express its solidarity with its subjects not through a restriction of its divinely bestowed authority but through just action and true speech that joins it and its subjects in mutual trust.[111] Here it will become apparent that what is best for government will also be best for the relationship of government and church.

536　**11. Thoughts on William Paton's Book *The Church and the New Order*[1]**

The Church and the New Order in Europe

1. Any serious consideration by Christians regarding the future is under the following provisos:

---

that was weighed by the resistance centered on Goerdeler, cf. G. Ritter, *Carl Goerdeler und die deutsche Widerstandsbewegung*, 289–93, and appendix 4, 567–68; cf. also *DB-ER*, 772.

[109.] "By the grace of the people"; to make sense within the context of this paragraph, this sentence must therefore read: "only [!] the Belgian kings called themselves..." The Belgian constitution of 1831, which was enacted "in the name of the nation" and drastically restricted the power of the king, legitimated the king clearly "from below"; cf. Diedrich, *Die Belgier, ihre Könige und die Deutschen*, 42ff. For Bonhoeffer, however, "Western royalty" is legitimated "from above"; cf. also the *Ethics* manuscript "Heritage and Decay," *DBWE* 6:120 and 131.

[110.] On this, cf. working note no. 45: "...which sees its power not compromised but guaranteed by justice" (*ZE*, 81); cf. the similar statement in Oettingen, *Die christliche Sittenlehre*, 294.

[111.] Working note no. 45 states: "Solidarity with the people through justice" (*ZE*, 81); cf. "Zu den Anekdoten von Friedrich dem Großen," in Schneider, *Macht und Gnade*, which speaks of "solidarity with the people" grounded in the highest virtue of the king: the "sense of justice" (71).

[1.] *NL*, A 65,1 a; typewritten copy; published in Visser 't Hooft, *Zeugnis eines Boten*, 8–10; previously published in *GS* 1: 356–60. The text assembled by Jørgen Glenthøj relies on the original in the possession of Visser 't Hooft, an incomplete copy (pages 1 and 4) supplemented by the material reprinted in *Zeugnis eines Boten*. Bonhoeffer's draft dates from his stay at Lake Champaix, September 5–9, 1941. From there he took it to Geneva for further conversations with the World Council of Churches staff; cf. Nils Ehrenström's calendar notes from September 3–10, 1941, 1/123. On the events surrounding Paton's book *The Church and the New Order*, published in July 1941 (see 1/124, ed. note 2), and the common

a) the conditio Jacobea (James 4:15) [2] —i.e., taking seriously the fact that the future rests entirely in God's hand.

b) "Today's trouble is enough for today" (Matt. 6:34) —i.e., faith in Christ must be won anew and tested in life each day.

c) The consideration of the future dare not become a flight into fantasy   537 but must be a concrete service to the neighbor.

It is evident that these three provisos underlie Paton's book, and so we may welcome it as a serious and responsible Christian witness. It is no coincidence that a book like this does not come out of Germany today. The absolute insecurity of human existence there leads nearly everywhere, even among Christians, to the total abandonment of any thought of the future, which in turn results in a strongly apocalyptic stance. [3] Under the impression that judgment day is at hand, attention to the historical future is easily lost. In turn, the German reader of Paton's book might miss the total absence of an eschatological perspective.

2. Why peace aims? [4]

In addition to the convincing arguments enumerated by Paton, Germany's internal political situation constitutes a further important argument. It may be that consideration of the internal political situation in Germany is

---

initiative of Bonhoeffer and Visser 't Hooft (see 2/11 and 2/12), see Visser 't Hooft's letter to George Bell on October 15, 1956 (LPL, London, Bell Papers, vol. 42): "Dietrich wrote first a German draft on Paton's book. We discussed this draft and I prepared a fuller English statement (using his draft) which Dietrich read and approved. My sentence in the letter to Hugh Martin [September 12, 1941, see 1/124] concerning 'actual developments in discussion with responsible persons in the country concerned' refers to what Dietrich had told me in those days about the work, plans and attitude of the resistance groups in Germany. This became specially clear in the last two pages of the 1941 memorandum. What we say there is obviously based on actual reactions in anti-nazi resistance circles in Germany. That is also why I asked in my letter for an answer in the near future. Dietrich came to Geneva with a double purpose: to maintain the ecumenical links and conversation as well as to try to find out for the resistance group in Germany what peace terms might be expected.—I do not believe that there was a close connection between Trott and Dietrich. As far as I know they belonged to different groups of the resistance though they of course had the same purpose and the same general outlook. In those days we found often that the people who came to us on behalf of the resistance movement knew very little about each other. This was inevitable under the circumstances." Cf. *DB-ER,* 739–45; *MW* 2:186–94; Boyens, *Kirchenkampf und Ökumene,* vol. 2, *1939–1945,* 175–77; and von Klemperer, *German Resistance against Hitler,* 272–75.

[2.] In the NRSV this verse reads: "Instead you ought to say, 'If the Lord wishes, we will live and do this or that.'"

[3.] Cf. 1/98. Oddly, Klemens von Klemperer, despite knowledge of this text, speaks of Bonhoeffer's "apocalyptic theology" (*German Resistance against Hitler,* 273).

[4.] Bonhoeffer and later Visser 't Hooft (see 2/12) refer directly to Paton's chapter titles, here of chapter 1, "Why Peace Aims?" For further titles, see 2/12, ed. note 4.

not possible in the official formulation of the peace aims; nevertheless, we must be clear that the demand for the unilateral disarmament of Germany, recently emphasized particularly strongly by English radio propaganda, is having an adverse effect on the internal political situation. Since, in terms of sheer power, only the military is capable of removing the present regime (any worker revolt would lead to a bloody suppression by the SS), one must take this into consideration when broadcasting these peace aims to Germany.[5] The little that to date has reached Germany concerning the great church discussion of the new order has made a very favorable and powerful impression in important political opposition circles. Why is English radio propaganda silent about this in its broadcasts to Germany?

3. The chaos of ethical concepts[6] in Germany derives not so much from publicly declared hostility to Christian ethics—this is instead clarifying and to that extent to be welcomed; the deepest reason for the ethical confusion has much more to do with the fact that the greatest injustice, as it is embodied in the National Socialist regime, was able to clothe itself in the garb of relative historical and social justice. The railroad car of Compiègne[7] is nothing less than the symbol for how evil feeds on pseudojustice. For those who do not see through the demonic nature of evil manifesting itself in the form of justice, this becomes the poisonous source of all ethical disintegration. That it has been possible for Hitler to make himself the executor of a relative historical justice derives not least from England's willingness since 1933 to extend to Hitler all those concessions it denied the Weimar Republic.[8] Thereby England—certainly strengthened by the loyalty of broad church circles in Germany toward Hitler—took the side of Hitler against his domestic opposition. Thus both from without and from within, Hitler

---

[5.] Cf. George Bell's "Diary Notes" of May 26, 1942, 1/170.

[6.] Cf. *DBWE* 6:375–76 ("ethical chaos").

[7.] On November 11, 1918, in a railroad car in the Compiègne/Oise forest, the German delegation was presented with the terms of surrender for their signature. Pointedly, on June 22, 1940, Hitler compelled the French delegation to sign the truce in that same railroad car. [Bonhoeffer's point here is that the Versailles Treaty, symbolized by the "railroad car of Compiègne," was widely perceived by Germans as a grave injustice. Hitler capitalized on this sentiment and claimed that Nazism would redress this historical injustice and restore German pride; this was certainly one reason for his widespread support among the German population. For Bonhoeffer's own reaction to the Versailles Treaty, see his letter of May 20, 1919, to his parents, *DBWE* 9:29, as well as the talk he gave as a student in the United States in 1930, "Vortrag zum Thema 'Krieg'" (Lecture on the Topic "War"), *DBW* 10:381–88, esp. 382.—MB]

[8.] This refers to the revision of the Versailles Treaty, which was a topic of discussion during Bonhoeffer's stay in the United States in 1930–31 as well as at ecumenical conferences of that period; cf. *DBW* 10:382–83.

received moral support for his claim to be the God-given executor of historical justice, and only a small remnant was able to perceive, precisely here, Satan in the form of the angel of light.[9]

4. [. . .][10] The foundation of a new world order can be sought in the will of God revealed in Jesus Christ. Because the world holds together only "in Christ" and "for Christ" (Colossians 1),[11] any consideration of humanity "in itself" or the world and its order "in itself" is an abstraction.[12] By the will of God, everything stands in relation to Christ, whether it realizes this or not. In the Ten Commandments, God has revealed the boundaries that can never be crossed if Christ is to be in the world. The Decalogue is composed negatively. The positive forms are brought forth by living history and find themselves limited and critiqued by the Decalogue.[13] A worldly order that abides within the Decalogue will be open for Christ—i.e., for the church's proclamation and for life according to his word. Such an order is, to be sure, not "Christian," but it is a legitimate earthly order according to God's will. What matters is the establishment of such an order. Until recently this order was threatened by liberal anarchy in all spheres of life. Today it is threatened by the omnipotence of the state (it could next be threatened by economic omnipotence).[14] This omnipotence of the state must be broken in the name of a legitimate order that submits to the command of God.[15]

The Anglo-Saxon world today conceives of its struggle against the omnipotence of the state in terms of the concept of freedom. It understands by this the protection of God-given human rights in the face of every violation. Germans perceive the omnipotence of the state more as the arbitrary dissolution of all authentic bonds (family, friendship, home, people, government, humanity, scholarship, work, etc.), and they fight against the omnipotence of the state for the establishment of authentic bonds.[16] In regard to the

539

540

[9.] "Even Satan disguises himself as an angel of light" (2 Cor. 11:14); cf. *DBWE* 6:77; "After Ten Years," *LPP,* 1–17 (*DBW* 8:19–39).

[10.] For the text that is missing here, see the additional material in 2/12, section 4.

[11.] Cf. Col. 1:16-17; cf. also 2/10, section 2 C.

[12.] Cf. *DBWE* 6:253 et passim.

[13.] Cf. *DBW* 6:358–60.

[14.] Cf. *DBWE* 6:361 regarding "economic systems that hinder faith" (*Glauben-hindernde Wirtschaftsgestalten*). Also see "Notes for a Book": "What protects us against the menace of [technical] organization?" (*LPP,* 380 [*DBW* 8:557], trans. altered).

[15.] See "Der *Führer* und der Einzelne in der jungen Generation," February 1, 1933 (*DBW* 12:259 [*GS* 2:37–38]): The "individuality of a person standing before God and submitting to an ultimate authority is destroyed when the authority of the leader [*Führer*] or the office is seen as ultimate authority."

[16.] Cf. *DBWE* 6:367.

matter itself, both sides have the same concern, namely, the restoration of an authentic worldly order under God's command. The forms of expression differ according to their varying historical and intellectual backgrounds. The concept of freedom is highly valued in German intellectual history as well (idealism). But it requires further definition. Being free *from* something is experienced only in being free *for* something.[17] Being free solely in order to be free, however, leads to anarchy.

Biblically, freedom means being free for service to God and to one's neighbor, being free for obedience to the commands of God. This presupposes being free from every internal and external pressure that hinders us in this service. Being free means, therefore, not the dissolution of all authority but living within the authorities and bonds ordered and *limited* by God's word.

The question of individual freedoms—such as freedom of speech, freedom of the press, freedom of assembly, etc.—can be addressed only within this overarching context. The important question is the extent to which these freedoms are necessary and suited for fostering and securing freedom to live according to the commands of God. That is, freedom is in the first place not an *individual* right but a *responsibility*; freedom is not in the first place oriented toward the individual but toward the neighbor. [...][18]

5. [...][19] The concrete political results of these reflections are now clear. What matters is whether a state order in Germany is realized that acknowledges its responsibility to the commands of God.

That will become evident in the total removal of the Nazi system, including and especially the Gestapo; in the restoration of the sovereignty of equal rights for all; in a press that serves the truth; in the restoration of the freedom of the church to proclaim the word of God in command and gospel to all the world. The entire question is whether people in England and America will be prepared to negotiate with a government that is formed on this basis, even if it initially does not appear to be democratic in the Anglo-Saxon sense of the word. Such a government could establish itself at once.[20] Much would depend on whether it could count on the immediate support of the Allies. [...][21]

541

6. [...][22] contradicts the actual power relationships, as long as the Soviet Union is undefeated. It is not pan-Germanism but rather pan-Slavism that is

---

[17.] Cf. *DBWE* 3:67.

[18.] For the text that is missing here, see additional material, 2/12, section 4.

[19.] For the text that is missing here, see additional material, 2/12, section 4.

[20.] Cf. George Bell's "Diary Notes," May 31, 1942, 1/170.

[21.] For the text that is missing here, see additional material, 2/12, section 5.

[22.] For the text that is missing here, see additional material, 2/12, section 6.

the coming danger.[23] Since a new Germany completely of its own accord will have the desire to disarm—even for economic reasons—the continuing insistence on this as a primary demand is not very shrewd, especially at the present time.

12. Willem A. Visser 't Hooft: On William Paton's Book *The Church and the New Order*[1]

The Church and the New Order in Europe

The following reflections about the problem of the post-war order in Europe represent the thinking of two Continental Christians from two nations which are on opposite sides in this war. They have read William Paton's "The Church and the New Order" with deep interest and desire to express their admiration and gratitude for this fine witness rendered in a truly ecumenical spirit. They have also studied the recent issues of the Christian News Letters[2] which deal with post-war problems.   542

I. Some basic considerations
The insecurity of life and the tremendous upheavals have made Continental Christians acutely conscious of the fact that the future is in God's hands and that no human planning, however intelligent and however well intentioned, can make men masters of their own fate. There is, therefore, in Continental Churches today a strongly apocalyptic trend. This trend may lead to an attitude of pure otherworldliness, but it may also have the more salutary effect of making us realise that the Kingdom of God has its own history which does not depend upon political events, and that the life of the Church has its own God-given laws which are different from those which govern the life of the world. We are, therefore, glad that Paton emphasises so strongly that the life of the Church does not depend upon victory in the war.

[23.] [The German resistance circles with which Bonhoeffer was connected, particularly the July 20 conspiracy, worried greatly about the threat of Soviet expansion into German territories in the wake of a German defeat. This was a consistent theme in their communications with Western diplomats, and the conspirators consistently urged the Western governments to ally themselves with the German resistance against the Soviets. See, for example, von Klemperer, *German Resistance against Hitler,* 334–35.—MB]

[1.] *NL,* A 65,1 b; typewritten; document in original English, including the errors; previously published in *GS* 1:362–71. On page 1, upper left: "Copy: not to be published. August 1941." However, this text can have been written only after September 10, 1941. On the circumstances, see the references given in 2/11, ed. note 1. On this, Visser 't Hooft wrote: "Bonhoeffer wrote a first draft in German and I used that draft to produce a document in English which would express our common convictions" (*Memoirs,* 153). [The title of Paton's book was *The Church and the New Order;* "The Church and the New Order in Europe" was the title of the responses written by Bonhoeffer and Visser 't Hooft.—MB]

[2.] A periodical published by Joseph Oldham that was widely circulated during the war.

But this does not mean that Continental Christians are indifferent as to the problem of the post-war order. Many who had previously considered that the Church has nothing to do with such secular problems have come to see in these last years that the Church is truly the salt of the earth and that the discarding of God's commandments means death for nations as well as individuals.

There is very especially a new recognition of the implications of the New Testament faith: that Christ is the King to whom all powers are subjected. Because the world is created "unto Him" (Col. 1:16), we dare not consider it as a domain which lives by itself quite apart from God's plan.

The commandments of God indicate the limits which dare not be transgressed, if Christ is to be Lord. And the Church is to remind the world of these limits. For a long time it has not exercised this ministry, but more recently it has again begun to do so, as in different countries it has taken a strong stand against the violation of God's commandments in political life.

543   Now the task of the Church in relation to the "new order" is to be seen in the light of this ministry. The Church cannot and should not elaborate detailed plans of post-war reconstruction, but it should remind the nations of the abiding commandments and realities which must be taken seriously if the new order is to be a true order, and if we are to avoid another judgement of God such as this present war.

We are deeply grateful that there has grown up a community of Christians of different nations which can undertake this task as a common task. We have good reason to hope that that community will come out of this war as an even more united body than it was before the war. Those who are conscious of their membership in this fellowship are as yet a small group, but they are nevertheless not unimportant, because they are practically the only international community which remains united in spite of war and conflict.

2. Why Peace Aims?

We agree with Paton as to the urgency of a clear statement of peace aims. But, as far as the Continent is concerned, we would say that this is especially necessary in view of the situation in *Germany*. The occupied countries have become sufficiently aware of the true character of the National-Socialist régime and are acutely conscious of the fact that their future depends on a British victory. There is, therefore, remarkably little criticism of the British blockade in these countries. But the situation in Germany is entirely different. In that country the attitude of the considerable groups who are against the régime, but who are at the same time good patriots, depends on the answer which is given to the question: how will Germany be treated if it loses the war? A positive statement of peace aims may have a very strong influence in strengthening the hands of this group. It is clear that recent events have created a psychological situation in which they have an opportunity such as they have not had since 1933. There is, therefore, reason to give great prominence to this aspect of the whole question.

Now it is clear that the very strong emphasis on the military disarmament of Germany in recent statements (and in the radio) has had an unfavorable effect on this development. The only group which can take action against the régime is the army (revolutionary action from other quarters would be suppressed by the SS). Now the opposition groups in the army are not likely to act unless they have reason to believe that there is a prospect of a more or less tolerable peace. In these circumstances statements about the future (and very especially the propaganda by radio) should at least give the opposition in Germany some basis of action. 544

We understand that the disarmament of Germany will have to be demanded. But it should certainly not be mentioned as the main peace aim, as is being done too often. It should rather be mentioned as part of a much wider programme, which would include the giving of a certain amount of political and economic security to a disarmed Germany, and the acceptance by all nations of a certain supra-national control of their armaments. In any case, far wider use should be made in all propaganda (especially the broadcasts to Germany) of all that is being thought out in the realm of economic reconstruction and social change. Such documents as the Malvern report[3] have made a deep impression in opposition circles in Germany. Why does the B.B.C. say so little about these things?

3. "The Chaos behind the War"[4]

There is an important point which Paton has not mentioned in his description of the chaos behind the war. The deepest reason for the moral confusion in Germany and to some extent in Europe as a whole is not merely the opposition against Christian ethical convictions (for this by itself might have created clear fronts rather than "chaos"), but rather the ability of National-Socialism to present its injustice as true justice. The railway wagon of Compiègne is as it were the symbol of this masking of injustice.[5] There was just enough relative justice in some of Germany's claims to make it possible for Hitler to present himself as a prophet who came to re-establish 545

[3.] This refers to the report on the conference on "Christianity and Social Order" in Malvern, January 1941. This conference was called by William Temple, at that time archbishop of York, to articulate the church's duties in regard to the tasks of rebuilding after the war; cf. 1/170, ed. note 91. [The conference on "The Life of the Church and the Order of Society" was called to consider a postwar "ordering of a new society, and how Christian thought can be shaped to play a leading part in the reconstruction" (*Malvern, 1941*, ix; this volume contains the papers presented there).—MB]

[4.] This is a chapter heading in Paton's book; cf. 2/11, ed. note 4. The chapters are titled as follows: II. The Chaos behind the War; III. Guiding Principles; IV. The Ideal and the Next Steps; V. Britain, America and the Future; VI. Some Special Problems: Colonies, India, the Jews, Religious Freedom; VII. The Church: Human Worth and Freedom; VIII. The Church: Law and Understanding; IX. The Church: Forgiveness and Power.

[5.] [See 2/11, ed. note 7.—MB]

justice. This is the main source of the present moral confusion. And it should not be forgotten that by making concessions to Hitler which had been refused to his predecessors, the statesmen of other nations became the supporters of Hitler against the opposition groups in Germany.[6] In this way it is explicable that it has become increasingly difficult for the German nation to understand the true character of the régime, and that relatively few have remained unshaken in their conviction that it represented Satan masquerading as an Angel of Light.

4. *"Guiding Principles"*

We consider it very important that Paton seeks the basis of the new order not in any particular form of government, but in certain fundamental principles concerning the life of the state and of society. For it must be said with great emphasis that in a number of European countries an immediate return to full-fledged democracy and parliamentarism would create even greater disorder than that which obtained before the era of authoritarianism. In those countries (Germany, France, Italy) where all centres of political creativeness and order have been discredited or destroyed there will for a considerable time to come be a need of strong centralised authority. Democracy can only grow in a soil which has been prepared by a long spiritual tradition. Such a tradition still exists in the smaller nations (Scandinavia, Holland, Switzerland), but not in most other nations of Europe.[7]

But this does not mean that we must continue to accept forms of state-absolutism. The minimum which must be required of every state and which must be guaranteed *internationally* (we now know that political régimes are not merely the affair of the nation concerned!), is that the state shall be limited by *law*, that is to say it shall recognise certain binding obligations to its citizens and to other states.

The Anglo-Saxon world summarises the struggle against the omnipotence of the State in the word "freedom." And Paton gives us a charter of human "rights and liberties" which are to provide the norm of action by the state. But these expressions must, as Paton indicates, "be translated into terms which relate them more closely to the life of other peoples." For freedom is too negative a word to be used in a situation where *all* order has been destroyed. And liberties are not enough when men seek first of all for some minimum of security. These words remind too much of the old liberalism which because of its failures is itself largely responsible for the development toward state-absolutism.

This is partly a quarrel of words, for the realities which lie behind such expressions as "civil and religious liberties," "freedom of speech" or "equality of all before

---

[6.] [See 2/11, ed. note 8.—MB]

[7.] Cf. Visser 't Hooft: "I added to Bonhoeffer's draft the point that democracy still had real roots in the smaller countries of Europe, but that this was not the case in some of the larger countries" (*Memoirs*, 153–54).

546

the law" must certainly be safeguarded in the new order. But it is also much more than a matter of words. For the whole orientation of the post-war states will depend on this ideological question. Now we believe that the conception of order limited by law and responsibility, an order which is not an aim in itself, but which recognises commandments which transcend the state, has more spiritual substance and solidity than the emphasis on the rights of the individual men.

Thus it is certainly true—as Paton indicates—that in a country like Germany it will be impossible to introduce all the various forms of democratic liberties. But it will be possible in that [country], as in other countries, to do away with all forms of National-Socialist terrorism, to make law once more the impartial arbiter, not only between citizens, but also between the citizens and the state, and to give full freedom to the Church. If then safeguards are formulated concerning the régimes of countries which have been totalitarian (will Russia be included among these?), they should be couched not so much in terms of individual rights, but in terms of norms which the state must recognise in all its actions.

5. "The Ideal and the Next Steps" 547

We agree wholeheartedly with the conception of international order which is given in Paton's chapter on the ideal and the next steps. We are especially glad, that he makes it clear that this order cannot be a mere restoration of the pre-war political and economic system. For it has become very clear on the Continent (and is understood by many who did not understand this a few years ago) that there must come drastic changes in these two domains. In the political domain there must be effective limitations of national sovereignty. In the economic domain there must be limitation of economic individualism, in other words, planning for economic security of the masses.

But, as Paton says, "the ultimate settlement is bound to be influenced profoundly by the nature of the temporary measures which are taken in the interim period, and upon the proper shaping of those measures the future may depend." Now we do not believe that Paton's book throws yet sufficient light on this problem. And we do not believe that the solution of this problem which is presented in the Christian News Letter of August 20 (Dr. Oldham's summary of a P.E.P.[8] report, which he considers to be "entirely right" in its approach to the problem) is adequate.

We do not deny that Great Britain has the right to demand safeguards against a return of National-Socialism in one form or another, and that it may therefore have to take far-reaching military measures against Germany. But we feel that for the sake of the future these unavoidable measures must be counterbalanced by a positive policy. Now it is recognized in Europe and America that this time there must not be a repetition

---

[8.] Political and Economic Planning (PEP) was a socioeconomic research organization based in London that was founded in 1930 at the time of the world economic crisis.

of the economic clauses of the Versailles treaty, and that is indeed an important insight. But that is not enough. There remains the question as to how Germany may find its way back to a system of government which is acceptable to the Germans and also be an orderly member of the family of nations. Now this question is not answered by the total occupation of Germany (though such occupation may prove necessary). On the contrary, the total disarmament and the occupation of Germany will make it exceptionally difficult, if not impossible, to create a new German government. Would a government which accepted such conditions not be regarded as a mere Quisling[9] affair? Would not those groups which are definitely anti-Nazi feel that even Hitler was better than this complete collapse of German integrity? Would this not lead to an even wilder form of German nationalism?

The question which must then be faced is whether it is not possible to offer such terms of peace to Germany that a new government composed of non-Nazi German leaders who are ready for international collaboration may not be discredited from the outset in the eyes of their own people. Or to put it the other way round: the question must be faced whether a German government which makes a complete break with Hitler and all he stands for, can hope to get such terms of peace that it has some chance to survive. If such a government would be formed, if it would make a genuine peace offer (evacuation of *all* occupied territories, ousting of all Nazi leaders, willingness to disarm), and if then this offer would be rejected—there is a danger that Germans of all sections and groups would be thrown into the nationalist opposition, and that for a very long time to come no German government worthy of that name can be formed.[10]

It is clear that the answering of this question is a matter of urgency, since the attitude of opposition groups in Germany depends upon the answer given. Realism demands that the world should be safeguarded against a return of National-Socialism, but realism demands also that we should safeguard the world against a repetition of the psychological process which has taken place in Germany between 1918 and 1933. We believe that it is possible to find men in Germany who have shown by their attitude during these last years that they are not infected with National-Socialist ideas, and who can be counted upon as loyal collaborators in a European community of

---

[9.] Beginning in May 1940, Vidkun Quisling, the founder and leader of the Norwegian Nasjonal Samling, cooperated with Hitler's Reich commissioner Josef Terboven; Quisling's name became a general term for collaborators in occupied countries.

[10.] Visser 't Hooft writes: "Bonhoeffer had written in his draft that such an anti-nazi government might be formed suddenly. But I omitted that phrase and he did not object. I had found that to announce again and again that Hitler might be overthrown at any moment made it more, not less, difficult to take the warnings of the resistance seriously. For you could not say at the same time: 'The attitude of the opposition groups in Germany will depend on the answer which they will get from the Allied governments' and: 'The opposition is ready to act in any case'" (*Memoirs*, 154).

nations. And we believe that they should be given a chance for the sake not only of Germany, but of Europe as a whole.

6. *The Russian Problem*[11]

It is understandable that in the present situation the problem of the relation of Russia to the future international order is not being treated as thoroughly as the problem of Germany. There is so much uncertainty as to the forces which are at work in Russia today and as to the effect which the war will have upon them, that it is almost impossible to visualise just what its place will be. But as Christians we dare not let ourselves be carried away by momentary reactions. Even though we may consider the British-Russian alliance[12] a justifiable and unavoidable political decision, we must not minimise the danger which Russia still represents for all what we hold dear. Unless the war calls forth very fundamental changes in the structure of the Russian state, Bolshevism may well become a tremendous menace to all countries which have been betting on the wrong horse and which will find their Fascist system discredited by a German defeat. This is then another very strong confirmation of the necessity for authoritarian, though non-Fascist, régimes in the post-war era, and also of the necessity of strengthening the hands of those non-Nazi elements in Germany which would be able to form a new government in that country. There is, furthermore, the very difficult question as to whether the Baltic States, the Bukowina, Karelia, Bessarabia,[13] shall go back to a Russia which recognises civil and religious liberties just as little as do the Nazis.

[11.] [See 2/11, ed. note 23.—MB]

[12.] In the British-Soviet Treaty of July 12, 1941 (the "mutual-assistance treaty"), both partners pledged "to offer each other help and support of every kind in the present war against Hitler-Germany" (Gruchmann, *Der Zweite Weltkrieg*, 141–42).

[13.] In the negotiations in Moscow on November 8, 1941, with British foreign minister Anthony Eden, Stalin unsuccessfully demanded British recognition of these Soviet annexations. The question was deferred to the later peace negotiations, which never took place.

13. A Study on "Personal" and "Objective" Ethics[1]

"Personal" and "Objective" [Sach] Ethics[2]

1. In his *Ethics,* Dilschneider formulated a statement that enjoys widespread acclaim today, particularly in so-called Lutheran circles:[3] "Protestant ethics has to do with the personhood of the human being and solely with this personhood. All other things of this world remain untouched by this Protestant ethos.[4] *Ethically the things of the world do not enter into the realm governed by ethical imperatives*" (page 87).[5] These assertions are intended to prove that

---

[1.] *NL,* A 72,5; handwritten; previously published in *Ethics* (Macmillan paperback ed.), 320–31; and *Ethics* (New York: Simon & Schuster, 1995), 316–26. This short essay cannot be dated with any certainty. The purpose for which it was written is unknown. The manuscript is written in an exceptionally clear hand (for Bonhoeffer's texts) in German script on DIN A 5–format paper. Presumably it was written for a lecture or for use by a third party. The type of paper used points to the summer of 1942; Bonhoeffer used this type of paper from the time of writing the second version of the *Ethics* manuscript "History and Good," *DBWE* 6:246–98. The terms "objective" [*sachlich*] and "personal" that appear in this manuscript (cf. *DBWE* 6:292) are the terms by which Bonhoeffer engages a thesis of Otto Dilschneider's book *Die evangelische Tat.* Cf. also *DBWE* 6:333 and the relevant note page *NL,* A 73,15 (*ZE,* 111), on which the keywords "'objective'—'personal'?" appear.

[2.] [To capture the meaning of *Sache* and its cognates, we have employed a variety of translations according to the specific context. *Sache* can have a number of meanings, including thing, object, affair, matter, business, concern, circumstance, fact, point, issue, case, cause, event, and subject. The translation of "*Sach"Ethos* in the title of this essay has proven to be a particularly difficult case. "Objective Ethics," while not an ideal translation, emphasizes the "objective" as distinct from the personal, subjective, and individual. "Objective" points to worldly orders and conditions better than the word "real," the translation of *Sach* in old editions of Bonhoeffer's *Ethics* (where the essay was printed in an appendix) prior to the new edition of *Ethics* in the Dietrich Bonhoeffer Works.

In this essay Bonhoeffer seeks to refute Dilschneider's thesis: "Protestant ethics has to do with the personhood of the human being and solely with this personhood" (see ed. note 34). If Protestant ethics is characterized by a personal ethos—that is, an ethos focusing on the personhood of the human being and solely on this personhood—then presumably they are not characterized by a '*Sach*' ethos—that is, an ethos focusing on all the things of this world—that is, worldly orders and conditions. The term *Sach* points to the "objectivity" of these worldly orders and conditions.—MB.]

[3.] Bonhoeffer is thinking here of those interpretations of the so-called two kingdoms doctrine, which attribute an "autonomous system of laws," or *Eigengesetzlichkeit,* to the "worldly orders." Cf. ed. note 34.

[4.] Here the following sentence of Dilschneider's has been omitted: "This world as creation, that is, as an objective worldly [*sachweltlich*] whole, and all the things of this world that bear a purely objective worldly character are ethically utterly untouched."

[5.] Bonhoeffer's emphasis. Dilschneider's sentence reads in its entirety: "The things of this world neither enter ethically into the realm governed by ethical imperatives, nor can they themselves serve as a resource from which ethical imperatives may be gleaned" (*Die evangelische Tat*).

Christian ethics does indeed have to do with the Christian businessman, Christian statesman, etc., but not with economics, politics, etc.[6] *To clarify:* The distinction between Personalethos and Realethos[7] is not identical to that between "individual" and "social" ethics[8]—on the contrary, Dilschneider recognizes that the Christian also has social worldly duties; equally, the rejection of the "Realethos" in no way implies a rejection of every concrete ethics in favor of a formal ethics; rather, within the Personalethos itself one speaks very concretely. In order to refute Dilschneider's thesis, therefore, it is not sufficient to refer either to the biblical commandments concerning community life or to the concreteness of the biblical ethic. Instead, it is a question—to be precise—of whether *in the realm of Christian ethics it is possible to make statements about worldly orders and conditions, thus, e.g., about state, economy, science,* i.e., whether Christian ethics has an interest in worldly orders and conditions, or whether these things of the world are in fact "ethically neutral," i.e., do not fall "in the realm governed by ethical imperatives." In other words, is it the sole task of the church to exercise love within the given worldly orders, i.e., to animate them as far as possible with a new way of thinking, to compensate for hardships, to care for the victims of these orders, and to establish *within* the *church-community* its own new order; or does the church have a mission in regard to the given worldly orders themselves, in the sense of correction, improvement, that is, of working toward a new worldly order? I.e, is the church merely to pick up the victims,[9] or must the church take hold[10] of the spokes of the wheel itself?

551

2. *The New Testament.*

A.) Liberal theology (especially Tröltsch,[11] Naumann) understood the original gospel as a "purely religious" power transforming individuals and their way of thinking, but at the same time indifferent to and separated

---

[6.] See Dilschneider, *Die evangelische Tat,* 89.

[7.] [The German terms *Personalethos* and *Realethos,* including the capitalization of the first letter, have been retained to avoid misleading translations such as "a real ethos" or "the real ethos." *Realethos* is used here as a synonym for *"Sach"Ethos.* See ed. note 2.—MB]

[8.] See Dilschneider, *Die evangelische Tat: "The Protestant ethos is a Personalethos, and not a Real ethos"* (88).

[9.] Crossed out: "of the worldly orders."

[10.] Here "take hold" *(greifen)* replaces "fall" *(fallen);* cf. Bonhoeffer's 1933 essay "The Church and the Jewish Question," in which he writes that "[t]he church has an unconditional obligation to the victims of any ordering of society" and beyond this, has the possibility "not just to bind up the wounds of the victims beneath the wheel, but to throw oneself between the spokes of the wheel itself" (*DBW* 12:353 [*GS* 2:48]; translation from the forthcoming *DBWE* 12).

[11.] [Ernst Troeltsch.—MB]

552   from worldly orders and conditions.[12] It appealed thereby, on the one
      hand, to the emphasis on the "infinite value of the human soul,"[13] and, on
      the other hand, to the gospel's supposed indifference regarding, for
      instance, slavery[14] or the political order.[15] This omission in the New Tes-
      tament gospel led Naumann to assert that he could be a Christian in only 5
      or 10 percent of his life, namely, to the extent he had nothing to do with
      worldly orders.[16] In contrast to liberal theology, the religious socialist the-
      ologians appealed to the social-revolutionary character of Jesus' words
      about the poor and the rich, about justice and peace and the dawning
      Reign of God on earth.[17] In the gospel of Jesus they saw the world-
      transforming power κατ᾽ ἐξοχήν.[18] "God and the soul" and "the Reign
      of God on earth"—these were the competing slogans.[19] We have recog-
      nized these alternatives as inauthentic, the form of the question as false.
      For both have read past the center of the New Testament, namely, the *per-
      son of Jesus Christ as the salvation of the world.* The ethical question is resolved in
553   the question of Christ, and the question of the gospel's relation to worldly

---

[12.] Cf. Troeltsch: "The message of Jesus is obviously *purely religious.* . . . The message
of Jesus is not a programme of social reform. It is rather the summons to prepare for the
coming of the Kingdom of God; this preparation, however, is to take place quietly within
the framework of the present world-order" (*Social Teaching of the Christian Churches,* 50,
61). Cf. also Naumann, *Briefe über die Religion,* 566–632, where he writes: "To be religious
means to gain a state of soul like that present with overwhelming force in Jesus. . . . The
utter rejection of political viewpoints is his [i.e., Jesus'] greatness" (601, 615). Cf. also Bonhoeffer's allusion to Troeltsch's concepts and reference to Naumann's in "History and
Good [1]," *DBWE* 6:236–37.
      [13.] Cf. Harnack: "In the combination of these ideas—God the Father, Providence,
the position of men as God's children, the infinite value of the human soul—the whole
Gospel is expressed" (*What Is Christianity?* 68).
      [14.] Cf. Troeltsch: slavery is "merely part of the general law of property and of the
order of the State, which Christianity accepted and did not try to alter" (*Social Teaching of
the Christian Churches,* 132).
      [15.] Cf. Naumann: "Early Christianity placed no value on the preservation of state,
law, organization, production. It simply does not reflect on the conditions for the existence of human society" (*Briefe,* 614). Cf. also Troeltsch, *Social Teaching of the Christian
Churches,* 61 and 146–47, and Harnack, *Mission and Expansion of Christianity,* 173–76.
      [16.] This reference cannot be located.
      [17.] Cf., e.g., Ragaz: "The Reign of God for the earth—this is the message of the
Bible. Nothing else is contained there. . . . The Reign of God . . . means *a new reality,* as real
as Switzerland or the British Empire" ("Christentum und Sozialismus," in *Von Christus zu
Marx,* 153–54). Cf. also Kutter, *They Must,* especially 180–92.
      [18.] "par excellence."
      [19.] See the differentiation of these alternatives, e.g., in Naumann (cf. I. Engel,
Gottesverständnis und sozialpolitisches Handeln).

orders can be answered only from the New Testament answer to the question of Christ.

a. All created things are through and for Christ and exist only in Christ (Col. 1:16), i.e., there is nothing that would stand outside the relation to Christ, neither persons nor things; indeed, only in relation to Christ do created things have their being, not only human beings but also state, economy, science, nature, etc.

b. In Christ "everything" (Col. 1:18) [20] is reconciled with God; the *world* (2 Cor. 5:19) is reconciled with God; *all things* "are gathered up in one head"—ἀνακεφαλαίωσις[21] (Eph. 1:10). Nothing is excluded. In Christ God loved "the world" (John 3:16).

c. The church-community of Jesus Christ is the place in which Christ is believed in and obeyed as the salvation of[22] the whole world. Thus, from its beginning and by virtue of its very nature, the church-community stands in a place of responsibility for the world that God in Christ has loved. Wherever the church-community does not perceive this responsibility, it ceases to be a church-community of Christ.

d. Christ as the salvation of the world means the dominion of Christ over persons and things. Here the dominion of Christ means something different for individual persons than it does, e.g., for the state, economics, etc. It is only through the dominion of Christ that all things—the human being, the state, the economy, etc.—first arrive at their true being. But all these things belong together and may not be arbitrarily torn apart.

e. Because all created things exist for the sake of Christ and on the strength of Christ, they therefore stand under the commandment and claim of Christ. For the sake of Christ and on the strength of Christ there exist and should exist worldly order in state, family, economy. For the sake of Christ the worldly order stands under the commandment of God. Here one should note that this is not a matter of a "Christian state" or "Christian economy," but rather of the just state, the just economy as a worldly order for the sake of Christ.[23] Thus there is a Christian responsibility for the worldly orders, and there are assertions within a Christian ethic that refer to this responsibility.

554

[20.] This should read "Col. 1:17"; on this and what follows, cf. "Christ, Reality, and Good" (*DBWE* 6:54–55) and "State and Church" (see 2/10).

[21.] This Greek word refers to the "gathering up of all things" in the sense of completion, or *Vollendung*.

[22.] The phrase "Christ...as the salvation of" replaces "Christ...in his dominion and his love for."

[23.] Cf. "State and Church," 2/10; cf. also "The Doctrine of the *Primus Usus Legis*," 2/18.

B.) *How does the New Testament concretely articulate this responsibility of the church-community for the world?*

a. What is decisive is that there is interest in the conditions of the world only in connection with the *entire proclamation of Christ.* A proclamation to the world without witness to Christ, i.e., without the sole foundation for such proclamation, is unthinkable for the New Testament. Thus the church-community's decisive responsibility for the world is always the proclamation of Christ. In the service of this proclamation of Christ, however, Paul appeals to Roman law; he bears witness before the Gentile authorities to his purity and righteousness (Acts 16; 24:14ff.; 25:9; 26:1).

b. But why does the New Testament not fight against slavery? The most far-reaching conclusions have been drawn from this single fact, disregarding all that is fundamentally said in the New Testament. The usual argumentation using the expectation of the imminent return of Jesus[24] is not convincing: either the fact of Christ's dominion over all realms of life was to be taken seriously, in which case the expectation of the imminent end could only lead to efforts to implement it all the more quickly (see Luke 12:45) to prepare the way for the coming of Christ; or it was not to be taken seriously at all, and certainly even less as the coming of the Lord was delayed. Since, however, the New Testament asserts that there can be no doubt as to the seriousness of Christ's claim over all creation, the following simple explanations remain: Paul did not consider the form of slavery at that time to be an institution that stood in contradiction to God's commandment. Sources 555 can be cited that testify to the relative mildness of slavery at that time.[25] But above all Paul could observe that slavery in itself did not prevent the slave from living as a Christian.[26] A worldly institution that permitted room for the community of Jesus Christ and for life according to the commandments of God was in itself not objectionable; it was to be improved from within. It may have been similar with the political and economic situation, whereas one must realize that the Roman Empire demonstrated a certain stability and legal security during this very period. We note further that the

---

[24.] Cf. Witte, "Sklaverei und Christentum," 576–81; Troeltsch, *Social Teachings of the Christian Churches,* 132–34; Lohmeyer, *Soziale Fragen im Urchristentum,* 106. Cf. Bonhoeffer's discussion of the problem of slavery in *Ethics* (*DBWE* 6:160–65).

[25.] "Even before Christianity gained influence, the situation of slaves in the Greco-Roman world was ... significantly improved" (Witte, "Sklaverei und Christentum," 577); cf. Troeltsch, *Social Teachings of the Christian Churches,* 132–33. [Here and in the other notes in this section about slavery, the German editors have cited works (and perspectives) that would have been likely influences on Bonhoeffer.—MB]

[26.] See, e.g., 1 Cor. 7:21-22; Col. 4:1 (Eph. 6:5).

apostle only much later encounters the form of slavery in the western part of the empire that was in some cases very much more severe, and that he could have taken a position on these questions only in the context of his proclamation of Christ. It appears, however, that he did not do [so] even in Rome, as we can deduce from the church's position after Paul. Yet more important than all these possible explanations is the following: there are distinctly different ways for the church-community to carry out its responsibility toward the world; it will act one way in a mission situation, differently in the situation of state recognition of the church, differently again in times of persecution. The mission church-community that is a minority will first have to pave its way by concentrating fully on the preaching of Christ as a call to the congregation in order to find some way to share its work for the world responsibly. For the church recognized by the state and for Christians with worldly offices and responsibility, the testimony to God's commandments regarding politics, economy, etc., is part of the proclamation of Christ. The more Christians (as in the situation described in Revelation 13) are not those responsible for the injustice of the world but are in fact themselves those who suffer injustice, the more their responsibility for the world will prove valid solely in the obedient suffering and earnest discipline of the church-community. But even in the catacombs[27] the church-community will never be relieved of the universality of its mission. In each case, it will have to be the church-community's own decision how it will fulfill this mission in light of the times.—Even the New Testament knows of political and economic forms that in and of themselves contradict God's commandment (Revelation 13). Shortly thereafter, military[28] and official service[29] in the Roman Empire become questionable.

556

[27.] The catacombs were burial sites, both above and below ground, used in Rome and other places in antiquity during the second through fifth centuries C.E. According to legend, Christians were said to have fled there in times of persecution. "Congregation in the catacombs" was a metaphor used often during the Church Struggle in Germany for the persecuted Confessing Church parishes. Cf. the striking similarity of this passage to the following citation from "The Doctrine of the *Primus Usus Legis*": "The more the situation of Revelation 13 emerges through proclamation and the more Christians are not those who share responsibility for the injustice of the world but are themselves those who suffer injustice, the more the worldly responsibility laid on them by the primus usus will prove valid by obedient suffering and earnest discipline in the congregation. But even the congregation in the catacombs never has the universality of its mission taken from it" (see 2/18, p. 597); cf. above, "State and Church," 2/10.

[28.] See Harnack, *Mission and Expansion of Christianity*, 1:308, as well as 2:52–64.

[29.] See Harnack, *Mission and Expansion of Christianity*, 1:307.

3. The Confessional Writings.

In the confessional writings the interest of the church of Christ in worldly orders is established in the doctrine of the primus usus legis.[30] We note here that the primus usus is possible only in the unity of the entire law and [the] entire proclamation.[31] The primus usus and justitia civilis[32] exist only for the sake of Christ. Where the primus usus threatens to be divorced from this unity, it becomes an abstract natural law without any foundations. The best example is Luther's Large Catechism, in which the unity is preserved.[33] With the primus usus the church testifies that it does not abandon the world to itself but calls it to come under the dominion of Christ, i.e., the primus usus is concerned not with the Christian within the worldly orders, but with the worldly orders themselves according to God's will—not with Christianizing them [Verchristlichung] or making them more like the

557　　church [Verkirchlichung], i.e., the abrogation of the "relative" autonomy[34] of worldly orders, but with their genuine worldliness,[35] "naturalness"[36] in obedience to God's Word. Thus precisely in their genuine worldliness, worldly orders stand under the dominion of Christ. This and nothing else is their "autonomy"—"autonomous," that is, not with respect to the law of Christ, but with respect to earthly heteronomies.

4. Critical Reflections on Dilschneider's Theses.

a. The isolation of the person from the world of things is idealistic,[37] not Christian. Christ releases the person not from the world of *things* but from the world of *sin*; those are two different things. There are no objects "in themselves" that would not be related to the person. There is no realm of objects that would stand in principle outside the realm of persons and thereby outside the reach of divine commandments. This is true not only for historical realities but even for the realm of nature—of course, this distinction itself is questionable biblically!—nature stands under the commandment,

---

[30.] This term refers to "the first use of the law"; see also "The Doctrine of the Primus Usus Legis," 2/18.

[31.] See, e.g., the Apology of the Augsburg Confession IV/8, 130, 34 (*Book of Concord,* 121, 141, 125–26).

[32.] "civil righteousness."

[33.] Cf. in particular Luther's exposition of the Decalogue in the Large Catechism, *Book of Concord,* 386–431.

[34.] On Bonhoeffer's understanding of autonomy, cf. *DBWE* 6:56, 114, 230, 237, 264, 340, 362 [here also: relative autonomy], 400–401, 402). On the tradition of the use of this concept in dialogue about "worldly legalities" for political ethics, see Huber, *Folgen christlicher Freiheit,* 53–70.

[35.] On this concept, cf. *DBWE* 6:228 and 400–401.

[36.] For Bonhoeffer's understanding of the "natural," see *DBWE* 6:173–75.

[37.] Cf. *DBWE* 6:220 ("private realization of ethical ideals").

revealed to us in the Word, of fruitfulness, growth, praise of God (Psalm 148), and subservience to human beings. Biblically, then, there is no separation of a world of objects, untouched by God's commandments, from the world of persons.—

b. At the root of the assertion that the world of things is untouched by God's commandment lies a false understanding of the doctrine of adiaphora.[38] The existence of adiaphora, in fact, implies not the ethical neutrality of the world of things but much more its divine purpose of serving   558 the freedom of humanity. *Nothing* is an adiaphoron *in principle,* but rather the adiaphoric character of a thing is *solely* a statement of *faith,*[39] thus in fact not a quality of the "object in itself," independent of the person, but rather the expression for a certain relation of the person to the object. A doctrine stating that some things are in principle adiaphora is antinomian.[40]

c. The separation of the objective world [Sachwelt]—how far does this separation actually extend? Does it not reach into the very midst of the church-community itself?—Based on God's commandments it means the proclamation of the autonomy of the objective world. This means the sacrifice of Christ's dominion over a sphere of life[41] and therefore antinomianism.

d. The biblical distinction between church-community and worldly order must replace the untheological conceptual schema of person and object.

5. Systematic Reflections on Possible Assertions of Christian Ethics regarding Worldly Orders.

a. All possible statements regarding worldly orders are grounded in Jesus Christ and must for this reason refer to him as the origin, essence, and goal of all creation. The dominion of Christ is what makes all these assertions possible and gives them meaning.

b. In the proclamation of Christ's dominion over the worldly orders, these orders fall *neither* under a *foreign dominion*—"He came to what was his

---

[38.] "Adiaphora" refers to indifferent matters "neither commanded nor forbidden by God" ("Formula of Concord, Solid Declaration X/2," *Book of Concord,* 635). Concerning the dispute on adiaphora in the time of the Reformation, cf. the "Formula of Concord, Solid Declaration X," *Book of Concord,* 635–40, and the Epitome X, *Book of Concord,* 515–16.

[39.] "Formula of Concord, Solid Declaration X/14," *Book of Concord,* 638.

[40.] According to Luther's understanding, the antinomians (i.e., those opposed to the law) denied that the law applied to believers. Cf. Luther's theses written to Johann Agricola, WA 39/1:342–43, and his theses in the disputations with the antinomians, WA 39/1:334–584. Cf. also the "Formula of Concord, Epitome V," *Book of Concord,* 500–501, and the "Solid Declaration V," *Book of Concord,* 581–86.

[41.] Cf. the repudiation by Thesis 2 of the Barmen Declaration: "We repudiate the false teaching that there are areas of our life in which we belong not to Jesus Christ but [to] another lord" (*Creeds of the Church,* 520).

own,"[42] "*in* him all things hold together"[43]—i.e., not under a clerical, humanitarian, rational, natural law, or Jewish law—but rather under the dominion of Christ they arrive at their own nature and come under the law innate to their created being;[44] *nor* do they fall under the arbitrariness of a so-called *autonomy* that in the end is only lawlessness—ἀνομία[45]—or sin, *but rather* within the world created, loved, and reconciled by God in Christ they obtain their own essential, particular, appropriate place. Thus, under the dominion of Christ they receive their own law and their own freedom.

c. The Decalogue is the law of life revealed by God for all living things standing under Christ's dominion.[46] It is the liberation from foreign dominion and from arbitrary autonomy. It reveals itself to believers as the law of the Creator and the Redeemer. The Decalogue is the framework[47] within which a free obedience becomes possible in worldly life. It liberates for free life under the dominion of Christ.

d. For the worldly orders the dominion of Christ and the Decalogue do *not* mean subjection to a human ideal of "natural law" or to the church— this is said in opposition to medieval-Thomistic doctrine[48]—but rather *liberation for genuine worldliness,* for the state to be the state, etc. For the worldly orders, therefore, the dominion of Christ and the Decalogue do not mean in the first place the conversion of the statesman, the businessman,[49] or the abolition of state harshness and gracelessness in favor of a falsely understood attempt to Christianize the state[50] that itself wants to be a kind of church. The dominion of Christ (i.e., the dominion of grace) is taken seriously precisely in the preservation of strict justice, of the office of the sword, and of the mercilessness of the state order (i.e., of genuine worldliness). The incarnation of God (i.e., the incarnation of love) would be misunderstood if one did not also want to understand the worldly orders of

---

[42.] John 1:11.

[43.] Col. 1:17.

[44.] In "History and Good [2]," Bonhoeffer speaks of the "law of being," or *Wesensgesetz,* of things; see *DBWE* 6:271.

[45.] "lawlessness."

[46.] See "Formula of Concord, Epitome V/3," *Book of Concord,* 500, and the "Formula of Concord, Solid Declaration V/17," *Book of Concord,* 584: the law is strictly speaking a divinely revealed teaching, "legem esse proprie doctrinam divinitus revelatam."

[47.] Karl Barth speaks this way as well (*Church Dogmatics,* 2/2:685–86).

[48.] According to the principle that grace presupposes and completes nature (Thomas Aquinas, *Summa Theologiae* 1–1, q.8, a.2: "gratia supponit naturam et perfecit eam"), the actual intent of "natural law," whose norms humans can discern by reason, is the "new law" of Christ proclaimed by the church (on this point, see Kluxen, *Philosophische Ethik bei Thomas von Aquin*).

[49.] This counters Dilschneider, *Die evangelische Tat,* 133ff. et passim.

[50.] Ibid.; see also p. 543.

the strict justice, punishment, and wrath of God as the fulfillment of this incarnate love, if one did not see the commandment of the Sermon on the Mount preserved in genuine state action. The spirit and goal of Christ's dominion is not to Christianize the worldly order or turn it into a church but to liberate it for genuine worldliness.

e. The liberation of the worldly orders under the dominion of Christ becomes concrete not through the conversion of the Christian statesman, etc., but through the concrete encounter of the worldly orders with the church of Jesus Christ, with its proclamation and its life. Inasmuch as the worldly orders allow this church of Jesus Christ to exist, give it space,[51] and accept that it proclaims Christ's dominion, they themselves find their genuine worldliness grounded in Christ, their own law grounded in Christ. The stance toward the church of Jesus Christ will always be the measure of genuine worldliness—unhindered by any ideological, foreign law and by any arbitrary autonomy. A false stance toward the church will always result in a failure of genuine worldliness, worldly orders, the state, etc., and vice versa.

f. Concerning the relationship of worldly orders with one another and with the church, in my view the Lutheran doctrine of the three estates (oeconomicus, politicus, hierarchicus) [52]—whose decisive characteristic and enduring significance [is] its ranking of these estates *alongside* one another rather than in any sort of hierarchical arrangement, i.e., the preservation of the worldly order from imposed ecclesial control and vice versa!—must be replaced by a *doctrine*—created from the Bible—*of the four divine mandates*[53] *(marriage and family, work, government, and church).* The mandates are divine *in that* they have a concrete divine mission, grounded and testified to in revelation, and a divine promise. Amid the change in all historical orders, these mandates abide until the end of the world. Their justification is not simply their historical existence—in this they are distinguished from orders such

561

[51.] On the problematic nature of conceptions of "space" [*Raum*], cf. "Christ, Reality, and Good," *DBWE* 6:61–64; on the terminology here, cf. "State and Church," 2/10, p. 514.

[52.] "The estate of those in economic life" [*Wirtschaftsstand*]; "the estate of those in political life" [*politischer Stand*]; and "the estate of those in holy orders" [*heiliger Stand*]. The popular German terms would be *Nährstand* ("those who feed us"), *Wehrstand* ("those who defend us"), and *Lehrstand* ("those who teach us"). On the so-called *ordo triplex hierarchicus,* cf. Schmid, *Doctrinal Theology of the Evangelical Lutheran Church,* 604–23; and see "State and Church," 2/10, esp. ed. note 85. [The term "estate" is the translation of *Stand* in Schmid's *Doctrinal Theology of the Evangelical Lutheran Church.* It refers to a station or position or role or office or status in the community. In the Lutheran tradition the term "orders" has also been used.—MB]

[53.] Cf. Bonhoeffer's understanding of the mandates in "State and Church," 2/10, ed. note 85; cf. also *DBWE* 6:68–75, 296–97, 380, 388–408.

as people [Volk], race, class,[54] the masses, society, nation, fatherland, Reich, etc.—but instead, positively, a divine mandate to preserve the world for the sake of Christ and upon Christ.—In this it is surely no coincidence that these very mandates seem to have their prototype in the heavenly world: *marriage* = Christ and church-community;[55] *family:* God the Father of Jesus Christ[56] and Christ as brother to all human beings;[57] *work* = the creative service of God and Christ toward the world[58] and of human beings toward God;[59] *government* = dominion of Christ in eternity;[60] city— πόλις—of God.[61]

g. A word of the church to the worldly orders will, therefore, need to place these divine mandates in their respective concrete form under the dominion of Christ and under the Decalogue, thus not placing them under a foreign law but liberating them for concrete, genuine service in the world. This word will speak of the divine mandates of the worldly order in such a way that the dominion of Christ is maintained *over them* and the divine mandate of the Christian church *alongside them.* It cannot relieve the worldly orders of their responsible decision and service, but it can refer them to that place where they themselves can then make responsible decisions and act.

562   *h.* The observation that the worldly orders can perform their service even without encountering the word of the church of Jesus Christ (the Turks for Luther) [62] is, *first of all,* accurate only to a limited extent—genuine worldliness is possible only through liberation by Christ; otherwise, foreign laws, ideologies, idols are in control. *Second,* the very limited accuracy of this observation can only be a confirmation—thankfully accepted—of the truth revealed to it. This, however, cannot lead the church to the view that this is alone sufficient, but much more to the proclamation of the dominion of Christ as the full truth within all partial truths. Therefore, by means of the recognition that worldly order is possible here and there even without *audibly received* preaching—although never without the *presence [Dasein]*

[54.] Cf. *NL,* A 75,115, the working note that was lying on Bonhoeffer's desk at the time of his arrest: "*Why these four* [mandates] *in particular?* Why not people, class, race?" (*ZE,* 140).

[55.] Cf. Eph. 5:21-35.

[56.] Cf. John 1:14, 18; Rom. 15:6.

[57.] Cf. Matt. 12:49; Rom. 8:29; Heb. 2:11.

[58.] Cf. Gen. 1 and 2; Col. 1:15-18.

[59.] Cf. Rom. 13:6; 1 Cor. 4:1.

[60.] Cf. Rev. 11:15; 21:2.

[61.] "city." Cf. "State and Church," 2/10, p. 504.

[62.] Cf. Luther, "On the War against the Turks," 1529 (*LW* 46:155–205 [WA 30/2: 107–48]); "Eine Heerpredigt wider den Türken" (An Army Sermon against the Turks), 1529 (WA 30/2:160–97); cf. Mau, "Luthers Stellung zu den Türken," 647–62.

of Jesus Christ—the church can be led not to dispense with Christ but rather to make full proclamation of the grace of Christ's dominion. The unknown God is preached only as the known—because revealed—God.[63]

14. A Theological Position Paper on the Question of Baptism[1]   563

Co-report on the "Reflection on the Question of Baptism" in Reference to the Question of Infant Baptism

A. *The Testimony of Holy Scripture.*

The practice of infant baptism cannot be directly proven in the New Testament (NT), to be sure, but can nevertheless be seen as probable there. In

---

[63.] Cf. Acts 17:23; here Bonhoeffer is alluding to Luther's distinction between the hidden God, *deus absconditus,* and the revealed, proclaimed God, *deus revelatus, praedicatus*; see Luther, "The Bondage of the Will," 1525 (*LW* 33:140 [WA 18:685]). To be sure, Bonhoeffer refers to this theme in such a way that the hiddenness of God is a dimension of God's revelation.

[1.] *NL,* A 64,2; typewritten carbon copy; reprinted in *Unterwegs* 6 (1948): 3–13, and in *GS* 3:432–54. In 1942 Confessing Church pastor Arnold Hitzer from Rehhof (Marienwerder district, East Prussia) distributed a document he had written with the title "Comments on the Question of Baptism with Particular Consideration of Infant Baptism" (*NL,* A 64,1; carbon copy; referred to below as Hitzer, "Question of Baptism." Page numbers given are from the copy in the *Nachlaß*). In this document the theological justification for infant baptism was characterized as "false doctrine" (33). He claimed it could not be substantiated on the basis of the New Testament (17–18) and in the Lutheran confessional writings is contradictory to the doctrine of justification and the Protestant understanding of the sacrament (34). For these reasons Hitzer called for a "believer's baptism," or *Glaubenstaufe* (41 et passim)—that is, a baptism that presupposes the hearing of the proclamation of the Gospel and a "free decision" (38) on the part of the baptismal candidate. He recommended rebaptism since "faithful laity and pastors . . . cannot regard their own infant baptism as a valid baptism" (44). As a result the East Prussian Council of Brethren asked Julius Schniewind and Bonhoeffer for position papers on Hitzer's work and on October 7, 1942, conducted a conversation with Hitzer on the basis of these position papers (cf. Johannes Jänicke's letter of September 23, 1942, and Hitzer's "Reflection on the Question of Baptism following the Marienburg Conversation," December 21, 1942). [There is no copy of Hitzer's "Reflection" in Bonhoeffer's literary estate, nor does it appear to have been published anywhere.] Hitzer insisted on his viewpoints and after the war became active in the free Pentecostal church in Germany, or Freie Christengemeinde. [*Christengemeinde* usually refers to congregations in the anthroposophical movement, but Hitzer was actually part of the Elim movement, a Pentecostal and revivalist group of individual congregations that called themselves *Christengemeinden,* "congregations of Christ."— MB] Part of Bonhoeffer's "co-report" reproduced here follows the outline of Hitzer's work. Bonhoeffer does not engage all of Hitzer's arguments but instead concentrates on statements that appear questionable to him and highlights points of view that to his mind Hitzer has neglected. On Bonhoeffer's understanding of infant baptism, see also *DBWE* 1:240–42; *DBWE* 2:159–61; *DBWE* 4:207–12.

any case, its presence and justification can be disputed neither on exegetical nor on theological grounds.

I. *Exegetical.*

Matt. 28:19. The coordination of βαπτίζοντες[2] with μαθητεύσατε[3] is, of course, linguistically possible but by no means necessary.[4] The old reading, βαπτίσαντες,[5] which according to Bengel's rule[6] cannot simply be disregarded, would preclude any such coordination. We must keep open the possible interpretations that "baptizing" and "teaching" fulfill the μαθητεύειν,[7] as well as that baptizing here precedes teaching. The αὐτούς[8] might mean that a smaller selection of the nations is referred to; further conclusions cannot be drawn from this word. To understand μαθητεύειν exclusively as evangelization through preaching is not sufficiently established linguistically.

Mark 10:15. In the present context, a possible translation of the words ὡς παιδίον is "*as* a child"; indeed, according to J. Jeremias (*Hat die älteste Christenheit die Kindertaufe geübt?* 25ff.), this is the most likely translation.[9]

Mark 10:14. Jesus promises the Reign of God to the children. The term τοιούτων[10] does not mean that the promise refers to those who in their

---

[2.] This Greek term is the plural of the present participle of βαπτίζειν, "to baptize."

[3.] "make disciples."

[4.] Hitzer had written: "The old translation of Luther is to be retained: 'Instruct all people *and* baptize them in the name of the Father, etc., *and* teach them to keep, etc.' It should not be translated, '*by* baptizing them'" (Hitzer, "Question of Baptism," 2).

[5.] This is the plural of the aorist participle of βαπτίζειν; this reading is attested in manuscripts B and D (cf. Nestle-Aland, *Novum Testamentum Graece,* on this passage).

[6.] In *Novum Testamentum Graece,* 379, § 10, Bengel asserts: "Proclivi scriptioni praestat ardua" (the more difficult reading is preferred over the easier reading).

[7.] Infinitive form: "to make disciples."

[8.] "them" (accusative plural). Hitzer had written: "and baptize *them* . . . does not refer to the 'nations' in the original Greek text . . . , since here a masculine pronoun . . . is being used." It is "not the nations or non-Christians as such who are to be baptized and thereby made disciples" ("Question of Baptism," 2).

[9.] Jeremias substantiates this with the observation that in the New Testament the term ὡς, "as," is often used "as the introduction of a characteristic" (*Hat die älteste Christenheit die Kindertaufe geübt?* 27). [Because the English translation of Jeremias's book contains material that Jeremias himself added, and the corresponding passages in the English edition are not precise translations of the passages from the German edition, all translations and page citations here are from the German edition.—MB] In contrast, Hitzer translates Mark 10:15: "Whoever does not receive the kingdom of God *like* a little child . . . cannot enter the kingdom of God."

[10.] Genitive plural of τοιοῦτος, "such as these."

frame of mind resemble children,[11] but rather that the promise does not belong only to these children brought here to Jesus but to all who are like them, thus to all children, analogous to the beatitude given the poor, cf. Lohmeyer, *Markuskommentar,* pages 202ff.[12]

565

Acts 16:40 says not that the "brothers and sisters" belong to Lydia's house but at the most that they gathered there.[13]

Acts 16:15, 33; 18:8; 1 Cor. 1:16; Acts 11:15 speak of the baptism of an "entire household"—see the terms ἅπαντες, ὅλως, πᾶς.[14]—Leaving aside the improbability of the assumption that these households were devoid of small children, it is impossible to exclude the "children" of these households in principle since in fact those children already grown were also counted among the "children." So the only question remaining is that of their age. Nowhere is there any mention that small children did not count as part of the "household" or that they were to be excluded from the baptism. Besides, in light of the conception of the household within which an indivisible whole is understood, this idea is improbable (cf. also Matt. 10:13).

Col. 2:11. Baptism as περιτομὴ τοῦ Χριστοῦ[15] would be an inappropriate designation if there were no infant baptism, since circumcision occurred on the eighth day after birth.[16] It can in no way be asserted from scripture that the circumcision of children was based in their *natural* inclusion within

---

[11.] This statement counters Hitzer, who wrote: "We should pay attention to the fact that what appears in the Greek is τῶν τοιούτων = *such as these,* not τούτων = *these.* That is to say, Jesus does not grant the kingdom of heaven to children as such..., but rather Jesus sees in the trustful, unselfconscious, and humble manner of children an *image* through which he makes clear to adults the frame of mind one must have to approach God" ("Question of Baptism," 1).

[12.] Lohmeyer, *Das Evangelium des Markus:* "He promises and grants the kingdom of God not to these children but to children in general, just as... not to certain poor people but to the poor in general" (203); cf. Matt. 5:3.

[13.] This sentence counters Hitzer, who wrote: "Although this reads, Lydia was baptized 'and her household,' nothing in this passage justifies the assumption that small children were baptized here as well. On the contrary, verse 40 speaks of *the brothers* in Lydia's house" ("Question of Baptism," 7).

[14.] "All," "entire," "every"; cf. Jeremias: "[B]eginning at what age were children baptized also when their parents converted? An initial answer can already be found in the observation that the terms ὅλος οἶκος (the entire household), πᾶς ὁ οἶκος (the entire household), οἱ αὐτοῦ ἅπαντες (all his own people) can stand in for οἶκος (house, household)" (*Hat die älteste Christenheit die Kindertaufe geübt?* 15).

[15.] "Circumcision of Christ."

[16.] Cf. Jeremias: "At the conversion to Judaism of a Gentile household, circumcision... is performed on all male members of the household, *even on infants more than eight days old*" (*Hat die älteste Christenheit die Kindertaufe geübt?* 15).

566   the Israelite community of the *people* [*Volks*gemeinschaft];[17] it has much more to do with the sign of the divine covenant that encompasses fathers and children. It is only for this reason that Paul can refer to baptism as περιτομὴ τοῦ Χριστοῦ, indeed, that circumcision can play such a great role in the NT's theological disputations in the first place.

Acts 2:38[18] ... "for you, for your children." In light of the imminent expectation of the end, "children" is intended to refer not to the coming generations but to the sons and daughters of those being addressed here;[19] cf. 2:17. The eschatological character of baptism as deliverance from the final judgment (2:40) makes a differentiation in the ages of the children improbable.[20]

Statements about Children in General.
John is filled with the Holy Spirit in his mother's womb (Luke 1:15); at the encounter with the pregnant Mary "the child leaped in [Elizabeth's] womb" (Luke 1:41). The newborn Jesus is the Savior and Lord of the world (Luke 2:10 and 2:30-31). Children are brought to Jesus (Mark 10:13, the same expression, by the way, as with healing miracles 7:32, 8:22,[21] thus with events of eschatological significance). The strong expressions, "the disciples spoke sternly to them," "rebuked them," cf. Mark 8:33;[22] Jesus "was indignant," cf. Mark 7:34; the call of Jesus "to let" the children "come to him," cf. Matt. 11:28; not to "hinder" them, his taking them into his arms, cf. Mark 9:36 and Luke 2:28 (thus this refers to very small children) — in the face of the longed-for blessing signify an event of eschatological substance (cf. Lohmeyer, loc. cit.).[23] The Reign of God belongs to the children (Mark 10:13-14); in Luke 18:15 we find in place of παιδία (child between the ages of eight days and twelve years) the term βρέφη (infants). There was no question of Jesus
567   baptizing children, since the baptism with the Holy Spirit became possible

---

[17.] Hitzer does not assert this. In correspondence with Rom. 4:11, he understands baptism as the "*seal* of the righteousness of faith" ("Question of Baptism," 16). But he makes no reference to the connection between Christian baptism and the Jewish baptism of proselytes, on which Jeremias places decisive weight.

[18.] Bonhoeffer's manuscript should instead read 2:39.

[19.] Cf. Jeremias: "The τέκνα [children] are therefore not the coming generations but the sons and daughters of the listeners" (*Hat die älteste Christenheit die Kindertaufe geübt?* 16).

[20.] The "restriction" to "older children" is "most unlikely, because the deliverance from the final judgment (2:40, cf. 2:21), a deliverance conveyed by baptism, precludes an age limit" (ibid.).

[21.] The Greek term is προσφέρειν, "to bring near."

[22.] Cf. also Mark 10:13-16.

[23.] Lohmeyer: "He therefore speaks in word and gesture ... the eschatological Lord who himself both is and brings this kingdom of God" (*Das Evangelium des Markus*, 206).

only after Jesus' resurrection and ascension, and John's baptism was super-seded by the presence of Christ.—In Matt. 18:2-3[24] the disciples are given the example of a child, not in its frame of mind but in its being. The receiv-ing of a child amounts to the receiving of Christ (Mark 9:37). Children cry in the temple, "Hosanna to the Son of David," and in this Jesus sees the fulfillment of Ps. 8:3 (Matt. 21:15-14). Here as well the eschatological char-acter of the event is clear. Nowhere in the NT are children slighted in regard to salvation, the in-breaking reign of God; on the contrary, that kind of attempt by the disciples (!) runs up against the "indignation"—i.e., the out-rage—of Jesus. Jesus' acceptance of children, like that of the blind, lame, poor, signifies an eschatological event of salvation. It occurs, therefore, pre-cisely not on the basis of some sort of natural, psychologically understood innocence of children—a thoroughly modern idea[25]—but rather as the miracle of God, who humbles the lofty and raises up the lowly.[26] The "inno-cence" of children is a gift of Christ but never a natural state by means of which the gifts of Christ—such as baptism, for instance—become super-fluous. The eschatological character of Jesus' acceptance of children calls instead for their baptism by the church.

Statements about Children in the Christian Church-Community.
In Eph. 6:1 and Col. 3:20, children are addressed under the obvious pre-supposition that they belong to the church-community—ἐν κυρίῳ.[27] (At the very least it remains questionable whether 1 John 3:12 and 14[28] do not belong in this category as well.) There is no reference elsewhere in the NT to unbaptized people belonging to the church-community. Yet there is also no mention that children should be baptized at a certain age; there is no exhortation along these lines to parents or children, which is most easily explained by the obvious presupposition of infant baptism. In any case, the argumentum e silentio[29] can be applied more strongly in favor of infant baptism than against it. First Cor. 7:14 implies infant baptism more readily

568

[24.] In the manuscript this citation reads "18:1."

[25.] Cf. Jeremias: "[T]hat a child is dependent on being accepted, is especially ready to receive, is a modern notion and not a commonplace one in the ancient world" (*Hat die älteste Christenheit die Kindertaufe geübt?* 26); cf. also Lohmeyer, *Das Evangelium des Markus,* 203.

[26.] Cf. Luke 1:52.

[27.] "in the Lord."

[28.] [Correct: 1 John 2:12 and 14.—MB]

[29.] "Conclusion drawn from silence," i.e., an inference from a particular subject matter not being mentioned. Because infant baptism is not mentioned in the New Testa-ment, "an *argumentum e silentio* advises that it is unknown there" (Jeremias, *Hat die älteste Christenheit die Kindertaufe geübt?* 3). Bonhoeffer uses the argument as follows: that infant baptism is not mentioned because it was taken for granted.

than not. If one views baptism as an act not of forgiveness of sins but of "sealing" for the last judgment,[30] the conception that baptism is in fact superfluous because of the "holiness" of children[31] is an impossible idea (apart from the fact that in the NT a gift of God's grace is never "superfluous"; otherwise even baptism might possibly be "superfluous" for faith). It is more the case that the holiness of children can serve as the very condition for baptism, that is, precisely as the suspension of the question of their maturity. The reference to Jewish laws for proselytes, according to which children born after their parents' conversion do not need to be baptized, because they are born in "holiness,"[32] is logically limited by the fact that even these children were circumcised. Christian baptism, however, is περιτομὴ τοῦ Χριστοῦ. The idea that children born before their parents' conversion needed to be baptized, whereas children born to Christian parents were not baptized, leads to the improbable and groundless conception of baptized and unbaptized persons existing as members of the Christian church-community.

569 II. *Theological Considerations.*
Baptism and Faith in the NT.

If infant baptism can be neither asserted nor disputed on purely exegetical grounds, perhaps a theological overview of other biblical statements will lead to further clarity.

1. *In the NT, baptism and faith are indissolubly connected.* As a result, the objective character of each is to be much more strongly emphasized than occurs in Hitzer's Observation.[33] Baptism is the actual consummated transfer of the human being into the church-community of the end times and incorporation into the body of Christ by means of a physical action instituted by Christ. Within it occur the washing away of sin,[34] being born again,[35] dying and rising with Christ, conformation with the image of

---

[30.] Cf. Jeremias: "[J]ust like John's baptism, Christian baptism possesses an eschatological character...; it bestows not only release from sin [*Entsündigung*] but makes a person a member of the body of Christ and is an eschatological seal. And these are gifts that even the 'innocent' child does *not* possess" (*Hat die älteste Christenheit die Kindertaufe geübt?* 18).

[31.] In the "Question of Baptism," 11, Hitzer appeals to this passage from Luther: "In the same way children are also holy, even though they are neither baptized nor Christians. They are not holy in themselves...but are holy to you" (*LW* 28:35 [*WA* 12/122:16ff.]). Hitzer gleans from this only that in referring to the "holiness" of children Paul does not refer to their being baptized.

[32.] Cf. Jeremias, *Hat die älteste Christenheit die Kindertaufe geübt?* 21.

[33.] Following the arrangement of Hitzer's work, Bonhoeffer is referring here to a section titled "Observation." [See ed. note 1.—MB]

[34.] Cf. Acts 22:16; 1 Cor. 6:11.

[35.] Cf. Titus 3:5.

Christ,[36] reception of the Holy Spirit,[37] sealing within the eschatological church-community for the day of judgment.[38] All of this occurs as Christ's own action toward his church (Eph. 5:26) apart from any cooperation and activity on the part of the person. Wherever the salvific gifts of baptism are referred to, hardly any attention is directed to the individual recipient or the personal "conditions" attached to receiving baptism; rather, the entire weight falls on the power inherent within the sacrament in its performance instituted by Christ, a power dependent on no human conditions, and on the entire church-community, the body of Christ, to whom this sacrament belongs. Indeed, in spite of all embarrassed interpretative attempts to evade it, 1 Cor. 15:29 speaks of a baptism on behalf of the dead (presumably Christians who had died unbaptized), a practice that Paul not only refuses to condemn but even uses as an argument against those who deny the resurrection of the dead. If baptism really is "being born again," resurrection from the dead (cf. also Eph. 5:14 in addition to Rom. 6:4), why shouldn't such a conception of baptism not lead to that sort of practice as an extreme expression of the power of the sacrament, albeit one not accepted by the church? The Pauline research of recent years has taught us to recognize this realism in Paul's thinking ever more clearly and has made impossible any reinterpretation into the "spiritual-moral" realm.[39]

570

Now, of course, it can escape no one that baptism is brought constantly into the closest connection with faith (in addition to the passages named earlier, cf. esp. Rom. 6:8 and 11; Col. 2:12b; Gal. 3:26ff.); and although it is never explicitly asserted that only believers may be baptized, the connection between baptism and faith is an unarticulated presupposition whenever baptisms occur. Now, to be sure, the concept of faith requires clarification in a certain dimension from the very outset. In the "Observation" the predominant definition of faith as "personal faith,"[40] as "personal decision for Jesus,"[41] as "free decision of the individual,"[42] gives the biblical concept an almost imperceptible twist that is foreign to it and necessarily has dubious consequences. At the very least it must be kept in mind that for

---

[36.] Cf. Rom. 6:4-5; cf. also *DBWE* 4:285, in the chapter "The Image of Christ."

[37.] Cf. Acts 2:38.

[38.] Cf. Eph. 4:30.

[39.] Cf., e.g., Schweitzer, *Mysticism of Paul the Apostle,* 286–87; on the discussion of vicarious baptism prior to 1942, see Oepke's entry, βάπτω, in *Theological Dictionary of the New Testament,* 1:542, and the overview of the research found in Rissi, *Die Taufe für die Toten,* 32–37, 47–50.

[40.] See Hitzer, "Question of Baptism," 15, 16, 29, 33.

[41.] See Hitzer, "Question of Baptism": "personal decision of faith" (32); "personal decision" (38); "to truly make a decision for Jesus" (43).

[42.] See Hitzer, "Question of Baptism," 38.

Paul the formulation "my faith" or "I believe" never occurs (cf. the limitation of the "I believe" in Mark 9:24; according to Nestle, Acts 8:37 is a later, poorly attested addition!),[43] that the noun "faith" [Glaube] is much more frequent in Paul than the verb "to believe" [glauben] (in Gal., e.g., 15 to 2; cf. Lohmeyer, *Grundlagen der paulinischen Theologie*, 115ff.),[44] that even "we believe" or "you [plural] believe" is relatively infrequent compared to the absolute use of the noun and the important modifier πίστις Χριστοῦ.[45] The formulations "faith came" and "faith was revealed"[46] (Gal. 3:23, 25)[47] are particularly striking. Faith is therefore first of all to be conceived objectively as revelation, event, grace, gift of God or Christ, through which the self [das Ich] is entirely superseded—"I . . . , no longer I" (Gal. 2:20!).[48]— In faith we receive a share in an event in which God alone and wholly is the one acting, as Father, Son, and Holy Spirit (cf. 1 Cor. 12:3; Rom. 8:15, 26-27). Only because "faith came," "was revealed," do *we* believe as a church-community; and only when this is recognized may it be said, with the reservation of Mark 9:24,[49] I believe, yet even then always in such a way that one's gaze rests at no time on one's own self but instead on the content of faith. It becomes clear even from this point that the concept of faith underlying the "Observation" places the accent in an unbiblical way on the "personal," on the self, on one's free decision; and it thereby considerably encumbers the problem of baptism and faith from the outset.

2. In reference to baptism the human person is purely passive. There is no self-baptism; but even the phrase "have oneself baptized," which occurs so strikingly often in the "Reflection,"[50] occurs in the NT only one single time

---

[43.] Cf. Nestle-Aland, *Novum Testamentum Graece*, on this passage.

[44.] See Lohmeyer, *Das Evangelium des Markus*, 115 n. 4.

[45.] "Faith in Christ," *Genetivus obiectivus*; cf. Phil. 3:9 as well as Rom. 3:26; Gal. 2:16; 3:22.

[46.] [NRSV: "faith has come."—MB]

[47.] Cf. Lohmeyer: "The concept of faith is conceived here first of all in its purely metaphysical determinacy and objectivity. For this reason it can read that 'faith came,' or even more clearly that it 'was revealed'" (*Das Evangelium des Markus*, 116).

[48.] [The German term *aufheben*, "to supersede," does not seem to be used in this instance in a technical Hegelian sense, as is often the case in Bonhoeffer's writings. Rather, the more literal "to supersede" is used here, meaning "to take the place of; replace or succeed" or "to cause to be set aside or displaced." In Gal. 2:20 Paul affirms that "it is no longer I who live, but it is Christ who lives in me." Christ, therefore, supersedes the self, that is, causes the self to be set aside and then takes the place of it.—MB]

[49.] "I believe; help my unbelief!"

[50.] This expression occurs in Hitzer, "Question of Baptism," 38 (as a quote from Acts 2:41, which in addition to Acts 22:16 should be mentioned above) and 43; see Bonhoeffer's quotation from Hitzer in section C 5, p. 569.

(Acts 22:16); the passive is used everywhere else. The person *is* baptized. The faith that receives baptism—and only in faith can baptism be received—can in no way be understood as an active cooperation in baptism; it is pure reception and only real in the very act of reception. For this reason faith is not an independent precondition that could be separated from the reception of baptism. Without faith there is no salvation, no community with Christ. But faith does not create salvation, does not create the sacrament; rather, it receives them. The human being is also or rather precisely in faith purely passive in the face of salvation; indeed, faith is nothing short of the theological terminus that characterizes pure human passivity in the reception of salvation.[51] This is the reason justification by grace alone is the same as justification by faith alone. "There is no trace of the view that the essence of faith for Paul or anywhere in the NT is self-surrender to God and Christ" (Cremer, *Biblisch-theologisches Wörterbuch*, 9th edition, page 844).

572

3. Since faith always springs from the Word of God (Rom. 10:17), it can be portrayed psychologically only as a conscious, comprehending hearing of and responding to the Word of God. Confession of faith and decision of faith are—necessary—expressions, forms of faith, but they are not identical with faith itself. There are confessions of Christ and personal decisions for Christ that cannot stand before Christ (Matt. 7:21; Luke 9:57ff.; Matt. 26:33ff.). The essence of faith—independent of our psychological faculty of imagination [Vorstellungsvermögen]! Faith is in fact not a psychological concept but a theological one!—is not conscious comprehending, responding, deciding [Sichentscheiden], but the pure reception of salvation as it is revealed to us in Christ as the Word of God. The NT does not reflect further on the psychological possibilities of this reception. The NT has no interest in what is of great interest in the "Reflection." Only in allusions does it speak of possibilities of receiving salvation, which in any case do not issue in personal confession of faith and personal decision of faith. In Matt. 9:2, Jesus promises forgiveness of sins to the paralytic on account of the faith of those who carried him (even if αὐτῶν[52] were to refer *also* to the paralytic, which is hardly possible linguistically, it is noteworthy that it does not read αὐτοῦ;[53] cf. the healing miracles that result from the faith and intercession of others, esp. Mark 9:23; Matt. 8:13!). First Cor. 7:14 speaks of a sanctification[54] of the unbelieving spouse by the believing one, a sanctification

---

[51.] Cremer, *Biblisch-theologisches Wörterbuch*, 844.

[52.] "their" [faith].

[53.] "his" [faith].

[54.] In the manuscript Bonhoeffer inadvertently wrote "healing," *Heilung*, instead of "sanctification," *Heiligung*. [NRSV: "made holy."—MB]

not conditioned by personal faith. First Cor. 15:29 belongs in a special way in this context (see above),[55] likewise the promise of salvation to the infants (Luke 18:15), the praise and thanks of Jesus for the revelation of God to

573   the "immature" (cf. also Luke 9:49-50, where in connection with the acceptance of children John reports in the name of the disciples that they stopped someone from performing miracles in Jesus' name because he was not following Jesus—the same thing is apparently taking place in this lack of discipleship [Nichtnachfolgen] as with the children, namely, not consciously making a decision—to which Jesus answers, "Do not stop him," cf. Luke 18:16; "for whoever is not against us is for us").[56] Finally, thinking about people in corporate terms in the NT (cf. Matt. 10:13 and the words about the cities in Matt. 11:20)[57] belongs here as well. From all these passages emerges no more, but also no less, than the warrant for the question whether it is permissible to withhold baptism from children born to believing parents on the grounds that they lack the psychological preconditions for a personal confession and decision.

4. The NT speaks explicitly only of the baptism of believers. Proclamation, repentance, faith, baptism is the sequence attested repeatedly. By baptism the person who has come to faith is incorporated into the body of Christ. The praxis of the NT thus solves the essential connection of baptism and faith concretely through the predominant practice of adult baptism. This corresponds to the mission situation. Yet, as we have seen, it would be false to understand the essential unity of baptism and faith *exclusively* as the temporal succession of personal confession of faith and baptism. Baptism takes place only where there is faith. In the mission situation this means the conscious confession of faith by adults; since, however, according to its nature even the confession of faith (which, by the way, is not passed on with certainty anywhere in scripture) must not be understood as a work, a psychological process, the question remains open whether faith as pure reception could not also be the vicarious [stellvertretend] faith of the church-community for its children and/or the faith of the young [unmündig] children of the church-community themselves. In this case, of course, we must constantly keep in mind that people are never baptized "in" their own faith; thus chil-

574   dren are also not baptized "in" the faith of the church-community or their own faith but solely in the name of Jesus Christ. The New Testament practice

---

[55.] See section A II 1, p. 557, where Bonhoeffer discusses the baptism of the dead.

[56.] [NRSV: "Do not stop him; for whoever is not against you is for you" (Luke 9:50)—MB]

[57.] Cf. Bonhoeffer's understanding of the "collective person" in *DBWE* 1:284, there appealing also to Matt. 11:21ff.; cf. also Robinson, "The New Hebrew Conception of Corporate Personality."

of the believer's baptism of adults can be understood theologically as merely one possible solution for the relationship of baptism and faith, alongside which the possibility of infant baptism cannot be ruled out. In any case, the *refusal* of infant baptism cannot be grounded in the New Testament; this is true precisely because of the conception of faith in the doctrine of justification. If we add to this insight, gained from the concept of faith, the baptismal command and promise of Jesus as a sacramental reality, and in addition come to the realization that every human being is born in sin and stands in need of rebirth, then the theoretical possibility of infant baptism becomes a concrete hope rooted in faith and a confidence, in light of which the church-community believes itself no longer permitted to withhold baptism from its children.

B. *On the Teaching of the Lutheran Confessional Writings.*

1. The grounding of baptism is the baptismal command of Christ.[58] This is universal. The gift of baptism is (summarized in the decisive concept of) rebirth.[59] The efficacy of baptism rests on the command and promise of Christ.[60] Baptism calls for faith as God's gift of grace.[61] What does this mean in regard to infant baptism? How is infant baptism received in faith? Answer: through the faith of infants and through the faith of the church-community. 575

2. Child's faith: The primary objection is directed against its psychological impossibility.[62] Against this the following can be said:

[58.] Cf. Smalcald Articles III/5 (*Book of Concord*, 319–20); Small Catechism, "The Sacrament of Holy Baptism," 1–4 (*Book of Concord*, 359); Large Catechism IV/3–9 (*Book of Concord*, 457). In his specification of the fundamental assertions on baptism of *The Book of Concord*, Bonhoeffer is following Schlink, *Theology of the Lutheran Confessions*, in this case, 145–48.

[59.] Cf., e.g., Augsburg Confession II/2 (*Book of Concord*, 37–38); Small Catechism, "The Sacrament of Holy Baptism," 10 (*Book of Concord*, 359–60); and Small Catechism, "Baptismal Booklet," 13 (*Book of Concord*, 373); et passim. Cf. Schlink, *Theology of the Lutheran Confessions*, 148–51.

[60.] Cf. Small Catechism, "The Sacrament of Holy Baptism," 10 (*Book of Concord*, 359); Large Catechism IV/14–18 (*Book of Concord*, 458) et passim.

[61.] Cf. the important passage in the Large Catechism IV/33–36 (*Book of Concord*, 460–61), on which Hitzer ("Question of Baptism," 23) places considerable weight: "[F]aith alone makes the person worthy to receive the saving, divine water profitably. Because such blessings are offered and promised in the words that accompany the water, they cannot be received unless we believe them from the heart. Without faith baptism is of no use, although in itself it is an infinite, divine treasure." Cf. on this Schlink, *Theology of the Lutheran Confessions*, 151–55.

[62.] This objection does play a role for Hitzer in that faith presupposes proclamation, and proclamation presupposes people's hearing and understanding (see "Question of Baptism," 28). His primary objection, however, is directed against Luther's declaration in

a) It is psychologically no less impossible to speak of the sin of infants, as the doctrine of original sin does. Sin and faith are not psychological acts but real relationships to God.

b) Unlike the pietistic concept of faith, the Reformation concept is defined not psychologically but theologically. "Such faith, such 'clinging'[63] and 'grasping' [Ergreifen], is so completely a reception of grace that every psychological description of this process must be eliminated. Nor can the act of reception be bound to psychological presuppositions" (Schlink, *Theology of the Lutheran Confessions,* page 152).

c) The later Lutheran differentiation between fides directa and reflexiva, immediata and mediata,[64] exists for a theologically good reason, and protects against any psychologizing and law-oriented distortions of the concept of faith.

d) Luther does not make an autonomous theologumenon[65] out of a child's faith; rather he contradicts the false reasoning that attempts to assert its impossibility.[66]

576   3. The faith of godparents:[67] the primary objection is directed against the impossibility of vicarious representative [stellvertretend] faith.[68] On this the following can be said:

---

the Large Catechism that in justifying infant baptism "we do not put the main emphasis on whether the person baptized believes or not" (IV/52; *Book of Concord,* 463). By this means, the faith of infants is also relativized for the argument. Luther continues in the Large Catechism: "even if infants did not believe—which, however, is not the case . . . still the baptism would be valid" (IV/55; *Book of Concord,* 463); cf. Hitzer, "Question of Baptism," 30–32. On the understanding of infant faith itself, see Large Catechism: "We bring the child with the intent and hope that it may believe, and we pray God to grant it faith" (IV/57; *Book of Concord,* 464).

[63.] [The term "clinging," *Hangen,* is being used in the sense of "hanging on to every word someone says."—MB]

[64.] Cf. Schmid, *Doctrinal Theology of the Evangelical Lutheran Church,* 421–22 n. 15; cf. also Bonhoeffer's appeal to the distinction between *fides directa,* "direct faith," and *fides reflexa,* "reflexive faith" in *DBWE* 2:158–61.

[65.] [Defined by the *Oxford English Dictionary* as "a theological statement or utterance reflecting personal opinion as opposed to defined dogma."—MB]

[66.] On Luther's view of a child's faith, cf. Brinkel, *Die Lehre Luthers von der fides infantium,* 1958. [See also Strohl, "Child in Luther's Theology," which includes a section on infant baptism.—MB]

[67.] [The Lutheran Church speaks of "sponsors" for baptism; we have used "godparents" for the term *Paten* throughout this essay.—MB]

[68.] Cf. Hitzer in reference to the baptismal questions posed directly to the child in the "Baptismal Booklet," 18–31, in Luther's Small Catechism (*Book of Concord,* 374–75): the "entire absurdity of infant baptism is now reflected here: because the questions, which contradict the sense of the baptism, presuppose a baptismal candidate capable of making decisions, the infant to be baptized obviously cannot answer these questions itself; and the godparents do so on its behalf. . . . This makes no sense at all!" ("Question of Baptism," 32).

a) The faith of the church-community always precedes the faith of the individual;[69] this is so in the double sense that the church-community administers baptism by faith in the command and promise of Christ and that it receives baptism in a faith that intercedes for the child to be baptized.

b) In intercession the faith of the church-community claims Christ's word for the child and is certain that God hears its prayers.[70]

c) The faith of the church-community baptizes the child not on the strength of the church-community's faith or the child's faith but on the strength of the word of Christ.[71]

d) The faith of the church-community bears the children through intercession and Christian instruction on the basis of the baptism that has taken place.[72]

e) The church-community cannot see any better into the hearts of adults, whom it receives in faith as members through baptism on the basis of their confession, than it can see into the hearts of children.

f) The faith of the church-community is not a work that it performs in place of the child; instead, it is pleading for, hoping for, and receiving the promises of Christ on behalf of the child—all of this brought about by the word of Christ.

g) The utilization of the Gospel text Mark 10:13ff. for infant baptism[73] relies on the promise to children that it includes about the kingdom of heaven. On what basis would we want to be allowed to deny baptism to those to whom the kingdom of heaven belongs?

h) The argument of the confessional writings does not so much aim   577
toward positive dogmatic proof of the necessity of infant baptism as it disputes the right to refuse infant baptism. "Vicarious representative" faith is meant to become an independent theologumenon no more than is a child's faith; rather the faith of the church-community, within which it dares to baptize children on account of Christ's promise, is not refuted; nor is it repudiated in biblicistic legalism as a heresy [Irrglaube].[74]

[69.] Schlink writes: "The faith of the church always precedes the faith of the individual" (*Theology of the Lutheran Confessions*, 153).

[70.] Cf. Luther's Small Catechism, "Baptismal Booklet," 3–9 (*Book of Concord*, 372–73); Schlink, *Theology of the Lutheran Confessions*, 153.

[71.] Cf. Large Catechism IV/52–63 (*Book of Concord*, 463–64).

[72.] Schlink states that the assertions of the confessional writings about infant baptism "obligate the congregation to offer up the most sincere intercession for every baptized child and to provide faithful instruction for those baptized, that they may in faith make use of their baptism" (*Theology of the Lutheran Confessions*, 154).

[73.] This occurs only in Luther's Small Catechism, "Baptismal Booklet," 16 (*Book of Concord*, 374).

[74.] Hitzer calls the doctrine of infant baptism a "false teaching," or *Irrlehre* ("Question

i) On the relation between a child's faith and the godparents' faith, let us note that the confessional writings name both alongside each other.[75] Here the emphasis falls decisively on the godparents' faith, without which there can be no infant baptism. Here as well the faith of the church-community bears the faith of the individual. The unarticulated faith of the child is confessed publicly by the godparents.

k)[76] In the end a child's faith and the godparents' faith are only an expression for that objectivity of faith that was spoken of in the New Testament context. Because "*faith* came," "*faith* was revealed," people can, where this event has taken place, be baptized in faith and receive baptism in faith.

4. In strict terms, the theological reflection must therefore confine itself to opening the possibility of infant baptism. The doctrine of infant baptism is a borderline doctrine on which nothing further can be built systematically yet which as such has its own justification. This internal limitation of theologically feasible assertions about infant baptism is crossed (even in the confessional writings) where an independent doctrine is advocated about the necessity of infant baptism for salvation and about the damnation of children who die unbaptized.[77] Even in those places where it is applied to individual aspects of the reality of revelation, the concept of the necessity for salvation leads, of itself, to an intolerable rending of the entirety of salvation and a legalistic understanding of these particular dimensions. The biblical question is not what *must* necessarily take place for salvation but rather what *may* take place. But in the light of salvation, who would want to decline doing something that was permitted? The question of the salvation of those who have died can never be answered directly, even when we consider the baptized. It makes sense and is justified only in that, repeatedly, it refers the individual and the church-community entirely to God's grace — that is, to Christ, his word, and his sacrament. The casuistic thinking that has developed around the question of the necessity of baptism for salvation makes

578

---

of Baptism," 33); and he calls the appeal to Christ's command for this doctrine and practice "misuse of the command," or *Befehlsmißbrauch* (ibid., 32).

[75.] In the Large Catechism the faith of godparents is mentioned only implicitly; thus here Bonhoeffer is probably thinking of the inseparability of a child's faith and godparents' faith, presupposed by the baptismal questions in the Small Catechism, "Baptismal Booklet," 18–31 (*Book of Concord*, 374–75).

[76.] [No item "j" occurs in the German original.—MB]

[77.] Cf., however, the repudiation of the doctrine that children can be saved without baptism in the Latin text of the Augsburg Confession IX (*Book of Concord*, 43) and in the Apology of the Augsburg Confession IX (*Book of Concord*, 183–84). Hitzer sees the actual error of the Reformation doctrine of baptism not only in the doctrine of the necessity for salvation of infant baptism but also in the doctrine of baptism in general ("Question of Baptism," 24ff.).

baptism into a human work. It is equally false to declare infant baptism "unnecessary" for the salvation of children and to appeal glibly to the grace of God that "is greater than baptism,"[78] an appeal of which scripture contains not one word. In this context we must refute the charge that the confessional writings tie the grace of God too strongly to baptism, thereby granting baptism an independent stature alongside Christ.[79] The authors of the confessional writings did not need to explicitly assert the fact that we are made holy not by faith in baptism but by faith in Christ. The confessional writings, however, correctly attest that God was pleased to "bind" God's grace to Christ—that is, to Word and sacrament—and that there has been no grace of God revealed to us apart from Word and sacrament; and the God who is supposedly "greater" than this grace, according to our own thoughts and wishes, is not the God of the Bible. Instead of longing for this sort of "greater" God, of whom surely we can know nothing, we should praise   579 and utterly abide by the gracious nearness of God as it is given to us in the bond to Word and sacrament.

5. The confessional writings rightly resist the fanatics who forbid infant baptism;[80] rather, on the basis of scripture and its "key," the doctrine of justification, they open the way for infant baptism. But above all, they repudiate as fanatical arrogance the idea that the baptism performed by the church in faith in the word of Christ and in his name is no baptism.[81] The *validity* of baptism rests solely on the command and promise of Jesus Christ. The *benefit* of baptism depends on the faith that receives it. For this reason the opponents of infant baptism may never question its validity but at the most its benefit.

6. The confessional writings do not provide any further information about the chronological relationship of baptism and faith. They are content with having established their essential mutual unity. While adult baptism places faith chronologically prior to baptism, infant baptism leaves the question open. To be sure, the faith of the church-community precedes the baptism, but the child's initial faith as well as its later, conscious faith are effects of baptism. The faith of the church-community today is impossible to imagine without the institution of baptism that preceded it. On the other hand,

---

[78.] Cf. Hitzer: "God is greater than baptism and will not allow any of God's own to be lost, even when they die unbaptized as infants or small children" ("Question of Baptism," 18).

[79.] Cf. Hitzer: By the doctrine of the necessity of baptism for salvation, "baptism receives an equal status with the redemptive work of Jesus Christ, indeed an independence over against him, that is irreconcilable with the unity and exclusivity of Jesus Christ" ("Question of Baptism," 26).

[80.] Cf. Augsburg Confession IX (*Book of Concord,* 42–43).

[81.] Cf. Large Catechism IV/55–59 (*Book of Concord,* 463–64).

those in the first church-community were already believers when they were baptized. Finally, however, the institution of baptism by Christ precedes the faith of the church-community as established at Pentecost. Thus, in the end (unless some arbitrarily chosen time period, such as, for instance, the baptism of the first church-community, is detached from the overall context) the question of the chronological relationship of baptism and faith comes down to the question of the chronological relationship of word and sacrament. But this question can no longer be theologically decided, since in Jesus Christ Word and sacrament are one. Even John 1:1 can no longer be separated from John 1:14. The argument that Christ first preached and only at the end of his life instituted the sacraments overlooks the fact that

580   the bodily presence of the preaching Christ was itself already a sacrament and that the institution of the sacraments before his departure can only be understood as ensuring his ongoing bodily presence. Thus the question of the chronological relationship of Word and sacrament, of faith and baptism, cannot be solved theologically but only pedagogically-psychologically-practically. It is certainly inadmissible—in this the "Observation" is correct—to deduce the necessity of infant baptism from, e.g., the dogmatic concept of gratia praeveniens,[82] to treat infant baptism as an illustration of a dogmatic proposition.[83] Of course, it is equally impermissible to deduce the repudiation of infant baptism from some concept of the church-community. All that determines the truth or falsity of infant baptism are the biblical assertions about baptism that are opened by the key of the Holy Scripture, the message of justification by grace and faith alone. Yet if from this perspective infant baptism can be regarded as permissible, then subsequently the concept of, e.g., gratia praeveniens can rightly be cited as an illustration of infant baptism.

C. *Baptism and Church-Community.*

1. Just as in the mission situation the relationship of baptism and faith is resolved in the predominance of adult baptisms, in the situation of the church of the people this relationship is resolved predominantly in infant

---

[82.] "Prevenient grace"; in the Catholic doctrine of justification, this concept refers to the graced preparation of the person by God (with the cooperation of that person) to receive justifying grace (see Decree no. 1525 in "Tridentinisches Konzil, decretum de iustificatione" (Council of Trent, Decree on Justification), chapter 5, in Denzinger and Schönmetzer, *Church Teaches.* In contrast, in the Lutheran baptismal theology, particularly of the nineteenth and twentieth centuries, the term refers to the grace of justification that precludes all human action. Cf. Kaftan: "Infant baptism" brings "to expression" that "grace is a prior phenomenon that desires and gives salvation to individuals before all their own desire and action" (*Dogmatik,* 638).

[83.] Cf. Hitzer: "[B]aptism was not instituted by Christ for the purpose of illustrating this theological idea [of gratia praeveniens]" ("Question of Baptism," 37).

baptism. Both possibilities are given in the freedom and responsibility of the church-community and will indeed be practiced according to the spiritual state of the church-community, according to the faith of the church-community, and according to its situation in the world. The misuse of 581 baptism occurs just as much in places where infant baptism is practiced amid neglect of its strict relation to the faith of the church-community as in places where the faith of adults becomes a work on which the validity of the baptism is said to rest. Infant baptism always threatens to separate baptism from faith, just as adult baptism always threatens to destroy the baptismal grace founded in Christ's word alone. A misuse of infant baptism of the sort one can unmistakably observe in our church's past will therefore necessarily lead the church-community to an appropriate limitation of its practice and to a new appreciation of adult baptism.

2. In times of the church's secularization,[84] the utter repudiation of infant baptism and the demand for the baptism and rebaptism of believers have been raised repeatedly as a battle cry for the renewal of the church as well as for the formation of a pure church-community of believers separated from the world. Never has this rallying cry renewed the church. Instead, it has led to innumerable splinter groups that in part led their own life on the periphery of the church and in part themselves returned again to infant baptism in the next generation. This observation is not a theological argument; it belongs, however, to the records of church history, which must be pondered by every responsible Christian who deals with these questions.

3. The historically speculative assertion that, along with the end in our time of the Constantinian epoch of church history, infant baptism, as a specific aspect of that epoch, had to fall away as well[85] rests on the error that infant baptism was first introduced under Constantine. On the contrary, it is certain that Irenaeus, Tertullian, Hippolytus, and Origen (who traces it back to apostolic tradition) take infant baptism for granted as general prac- 582 tice.[86] The Synod of Carthage of 251 gave advice regarding the question whether baptism should occur on the third or the eighth day following

---

[84.] Cf. Hitzer: "[T]he church today, in contrast to the earliest Christianity, finds itself in a situation of a terrible secularization, in the unhealthy, impossible, and guilt-ridden situation that many belong to the church who do *not* belong to it *at all*, indeed, that *most* of those who belong to it are not believers at all but are rather unbelieving, apathetic, hypocritical" ("Question of Baptism," 36).

[85.] Hitzer does not raise this assertion.

[86.] Here Bonhoeffer is referring to citations in Jeremias: "It is *Irenaeus* who (adversus Haereses II, 32, 2 Harvey) wrote: omnes enim venit semetipsum salvare: omnes inquam qui renascuntur in Deum, *infantes* et parvulos et pueros et iuvenes et seniores" (He comes, namely, so that through him he might save all: all I say who were born again through him in God: infants and small children and children and youth and adults). "*Tertullian,* in his

birth.[87] The mark of the Constantinian epoch is not that the Christian church-community baptized its children, but that baptism as such became a qualification for civic life; the problematic development lay not in infant baptism, but rather in this secular qualification of baptism. These should be clearly differentiated.

4. In a secularized church the longing for a pure, authentic, true, church-community of believers, separated from the world and prepared for bat-
583 tle,[88] is very understandable; yet it is full of dangers: too easily an ideal church-community replaces the real church-community of God; too easily the pure church-community is understood as an achievement to be enacted by human beings; too easily Jesus' parables of the weeds among the wheat[89] and of the fish net[90] are overlooked; too easily it is forgotten that God loved the *world*[91] and desires that *everyone* be saved;[92] too easily a fallacious, legalistic biblicism displaces responsible theological reflection. The separa-tion of the church-community from the world, the purity, readiness for battle, truthfulness of the church-community—these are not goals to be pursued directly in themselves but fruits that spontaneously follow an authentic

---

work De baptismo (18), indeed personally challenges the appropriateness of infant bap-tism," but "his comments suggest that he objects to a *widely used* practice." "*Hippolytus* also presupposes the practice of infant baptism 'as an indisputable rule,' when he writes in the church order likely established around 218 [chapter 46]: et primo baptizate infantes; omnes qui pro se loqui possunt, loquantur; *qui vero loqui non possunt,* pro eis parentes loquantur vel alius ad familiam pertinens" (And first of all, baptize the children; all of those who can speak for themselves ought to speak; for those who cannot speak, the parents or others who belong to the family ought to speak). "*Origen,* in his commentary on Romans 5:9, identifies infant baptism as a church practice *going back to the apostles:* "ecclesia ab Apostolis traditionem suscepit, etiam parvulis baptismum dare" (The church, beginning with the tradition of the apostles, baptized small children) (*Hat die älteste Christenheit die Kindertaufe geübt?* 18–21).

[87.] Cf. Jeremias: "How established a practice infant baptism was in North Africa is shown by a synod in 251 (or 253) in Carthage that deliberated over whether baptism was to be delayed until the eighth day after birth or whether it was to follow immediately on the second or third day" (*Hat die älteste Christenheit die Kindertaufe geübt?* 20).

[88.] Cf. Bonhoeffer's own view of the church-community in *Discipleship:* "The sanctification of the church-community consists in its being separated by God from that which is unholy, from sin.... [I]ts sanctification will manifest itself *in a clear separation from the world.* Its sanctification will, *second,* prove itself through *conduct* that is *worthy* of God's realm of holiness. And, *third,* its sanctification will be *hidden in waiting* for the day of Jesus Christ" (*DBWE* 4:261).

[89.] Cf. Matt. 13:24-30, 36-43.

[90.] Cf. Matt. 13:47-50.

[91.] Cf. John 3:16.

[92.] Cf. 1 Tim. 2:4.

proclamation of the Gospel.[93] Luther's Reformation came not from the attempt to realize a better, perhaps "original Christian" [urchristlich] ideal of church-community, but rather from the new recognition of the gospel from Holy Scripture. It can only be a matter of orientation to the gospel today, not of the reestablishment of the original Christian church-community. Authentic church renewal will always be distinguished from fanaticism in that the former always takes its departure from the central and certain teachings of scripture. Now it is, of course, incontrovertible that the proper administration of the sacrament of baptism is a central requirement of scripture; however, following all that has already been said, the repudiation of infant baptism can certainly not be characterized as a central and certain teaching of Holy Scripture. Where, however, human thoughts— even the best, purest, and most pious—are made the point of departure for efforts at church renewal, there the church's cause, which rests solely on the clear and certain word of God, is threatened, especially if human thoughts repudiating the faith of the church pass themselves off as divine truth.

5. Particularly dubious in the given "Special Reflections on Baptism and Church-Community"[94] are the following formulations: page 39: "Those who do not wish to step entirely over to Christ's side, to confess this and give expression to it by[95] having themselves baptized, should remain outside! . . . Here a clear, full decision is required. Here the air becomes pure. This truthfulness makes the message credible and the witness of the church attractive to youth."

584

Here we find a rigorism and idealism—definitely attractive to youth— that all too directly identifies personal decisiveness with faith (see above),[96] that quenches the dimly burning wick and breaks the bruised reed.[97] The statement on page 38 that, subjectively regarded, one's belonging to the community of Jesus Christ rests on the free decision of the individual, on the capacity to act voluntarily [Freiwilligkeit], corresponds to this.[98] Here, too, "free decision" is inserted in place of "faith" and thereby a dangerous

---

[93.] Cf. also Hitzer: "We do not mean that believer's baptism is a recipe for 'church reformers,' in order to wish to do this now in this way. . . . We know that renewal can only come through the Holy Spirit alone. . . . We cannot 'do' anything" ("Question of Baptism," 39).

[94.] See Hitzer, "Question of Baptism," 35ff.

[95.] Bonhoeffer incorrectly used *durch*, "by," instead of *mit*, "with," in this quotation.

[96.] Section A II 1.

[97.] Cf. Isa. 42:3.

[98.] See Hitzer: "It is a path into *freedom* where, subjectively speaking, one's belonging to the community of Jesus Christ rests on the free decision of the individual, on the capacity to act voluntarily, and not on religious coercion" ("Question of Baptism," 38).

distortion of the biblical concept of faith is undertaken (see above).[99] The introduction of the unbiblical concept of "believer's baptism"[100] and the striking, oft repeated use of the reflexive form "have oneself baptized" also correspond to this terminological and thereby at the same time objectively [sachlich] significant conceptual shift. All of this points in the same direction, toward a psychological-activist thinking deviating from the Bible. "Decision for Christ"—itself an [un]biblical[101] term—is the activist perversion of the passive character of faith. Decision for Christ places the human person in the center of view. "Faith" is entirely oriented upon its object, upon Christ. On page 37 infant baptism is characterized as an infringement not only of the freedom of the human being (where does *that* conception of freedom come from? from idealism[102] and liberal theology,[103] not from the Bible), but also of God in God's election by grace.[104] This denies the universality of the salvific will of God as it is attested in scripture; the grace of God is separated from the means of grace (as we already observed above in another place),[105] and the church-community and world move clearly away from each other as those chosen and damned from all eternity. What then, however, do we do with John 3:16? The same relationship of church-community and world that presented itself earlier on the psychological level as "personal decision" and "indecisiveness" repeats itself here on the basis of an abstract doctrine of double predestination[106] and a corresponding

585

[99.] Section A II 1.

[100.] Cf. Hitzer, "Question of Baptism," 37, 39, 41. This concept means: "faith without baptism is as unthinkable as baptism without faith. Baptism can and may be offered only to believers" (ibid., 14).

[101.] In the manuscript Bonhoeffer erroneously wrote "biblical."

[102.] Bonhoeffer is here certainly thinking of the understanding of freedom as *autonomy,* as found in Kant. On the various expressions of this concept of freedom within "idealist" philosophy, see Spaemann's article, "Freiheit," 1091–94.

[103.] See, e.g., Herrmann, *Systematic Theology:* "If, then, we can possess real life only in free dependence upon God, we see that the origin of this life lies unquestionably in our own free act" (91–92); cf. also Herrmann, *Ethik:* "The unconditional demand" determines "us in our innermost depths only... when that which it prescribes for us is an expression of our own perception. If we do not say it to ourselves, then no other, neither God nor human being, can say to us what the unconditional demand requires" (35).

[104.] See Hitzer: infant baptism infringes "in a much more impossible way on the freedom and majesty of the grace of God... [than on the freedom of the child],... for God alone elects, calls, gives faith. No human being may prescribe to God's unfathomable mercy and salvific decree the way through humanity, not even in regard to one's own children" ("Question of Baptism," 37).

[105.] See section B 4.

[106.] According to one form of Reformed doctrine, God has determined from all eternity some people for damnation and others for eternal life; cf. Heppe, *Reformed*

freedom of God from God's own means of grace, i.e., from God's revelation. In both cases the true relationship of church-community and world, which unfolds only in faith in the revelation of God in the world and encompasses both John 3:16 and 1 John 2:17, is missed and brought into a false, one-dimensional formulation. This may be more impressive, more attractive; but it makes the church of God into an ideal of the pious.

6. The abolition of infant baptism is not an effective means of confronting the secularization of the church, because even "believer's baptism" does not secure against severe relapses; indeed, experience has shown that it is precisely the special emphasis on personal conversion experiences that frequently leads to fanatical derailments and setbacks.

7. What is required of the Christian church-community today is not the   586 abolition of infant baptism but a correct Protestant baptismal discipline. Since infant baptism, where it is performed in faith (see above),[107] thus within the believing community, cannot be disallowed on the basis of scripture but may be gratefully adopted as a special gift of God's grace to the believing community, the correct Protestant baptismal discipline will have to direct its attention to the question of whether believing godparents and parents as members of the church-community bring their child to baptism. In the first place, positively, this discipline will take baptismal instruction for the church-community, godparents, and parents more seriously than previously; it will testify to the particular grace of infant baptism that dares not be thrown away like a cut-rate good;[108] it will warn of the misuse of baptism and, if necessary, will refuse infant baptism in places where in its clear judgment baptism is being sought apart from faith. Yet in its refusal it will be guided not by some sort of rigorism but by God's love for the world and for his church-community.

8. How does the church respond to Christians who say they must refuse infant baptism in its entirety for reasons of faith? a) The church has no right on the basis of Holy Scripture to discipline believing members of the church-community who do not have their children baptized. b) The same is true in regard to pastors who take this stance relative to their own children.

Dogmatics, 150–62. [This form of double predestination was not the main emphasis of Calvin, however, and certainly not of a Reformed theologian such as Barth.—MB]

[107.] See section C 1.

[108.] [*Verschleudern* could be adequately translated as "to squander" or "to throw away carelessly." The words "like a cut-rate good" have been added here to make the connection, which is clear in the German text but not in the English translation, to Bonhoeffer's reference to "cut-rate sacrament," *verschleudertes Sakrament,* in his discussion of cheap grace in *Discipleship* (*DBWE* 4:43).—MB]

In both cases the church will perceive a practical indication of the seriousness of baptismal grace. c) The church cannot, however, allow its pastors to deny baptism to believing Christians who desire it for their children, because this denial cannot be justified from scripture. d) The church cannot allow its pastors to proclaim a doctrine, counter to scripture, about the impermissibility of infant baptism, whereas it cannot bar them from recommending adult baptism on biblical grounds. e) But under no circumstances can the church permit rebaptism, i.e., the declaration of the invalidity of the baptism performed by the church of Christ in faith in the word of Christ from time immemorial. In doctrine and practice rebaptism destroys the unity and the community of the church in that it views all those baptized as children as unbaptized, i.e., as not belonging to the body of Christ. This is where the dangerous aspect of the "Observation" lies, to which the church can say only No. Those who are rebaptized divorce themselves not only from the world but also from the church of Jesus Christ.

587

15. Unfinished Draft of a Pulpit Pronouncement following the Coup[1]

God has not forgotten his church. In his unfathomable mercy God calls his unfaithful and tormented servants to repentance, to renewal of life according to his holy will. At the same time, God sets us before an unprecedented task.

In the midst of a Christendom enmeshed in guilt beyond all measure, the word of the forgiveness of all sins through Jesus Christ and the call to a new life in obedience to God's holy commands shall be allowed to go forth once again.

Therefore we call all who hold office in the church and all members of the community of Jesus Christ to come under this word as it is given to us in its entire fullness.

We call to proclamation. Proclaim and hear in all places the comfort of God's love in Jesus Christ, the love that forgives sin. Proclaim and hear in all places God's salutary commands to lead a new life. Come together to worship as often as possible.

We call to personal confession. For long years, oppressive guilt has made our hearts callous and numb. Christ has given his church-community the power to forgive sins in his name. In personal confession we are allowed in a special way to become sure of our liberation from sin and reconciliation

---

[1.] *NL,* A 65,8; handwritten; Eberhard Bethge suspects this was drafted around the end of 1942; previously published in *GS* 2:438–40.

with God. You pastors, tell your parishioners of this way to grace, this offer 588
of God, largely forgotten today; seek out for yourselves the fellowship of
confession and absolution; and give your parishioners the opportunity to
receive the grace of personal confession and forgiveness of sins.

We call to the holy sacrament of the Lord's Supper. Receive in it communion in bodily form with Jesus Christ, the Reconciler and Lord. Receive
also in bodily form eternal communion with one another as members of
the body of Christ, as brothers and sisters before our brother and Lord
Jesus Christ.

We call to the communion of Christian love and Christian discipline. Help
one another to manage and to get back to faith and obedience, show those
who err or have fallen the way to repentance and forgiveness, and model
this way for them. Only in repentance and conversion can we be helped.

We call you to prayer [. . .][2]

Open your churches for silent prayer. Let the bells ring for morning and
evening prayer.[3]

To the Pastors and Officeholders in the Church[4]

We call you to a new order for your life. We have suffered long enough
with each wanting to go his own way and separating himself from his brother.
That was the spirit not of Christ but of willfulness, of indolence, of defiance.
This spirit has done great damage to our proclamation far and wide. No
pastor today can do justice to his ministry alone. He needs his brothers. We
call you to faithful daily observation of set times for prayer, set times for
meditation on scripture and for studying it. We ask you to call on the help
of mutual conversation and personal confession; and we lay upon each one,
as a holy duty of office, to make yourselves available to one another for this
service. We ask you to come together to prepare your sermons with prayer
and to help one another find the right words. Gather in trust and brotherly
respect around those over you in the church; pray for them and help them
in every way to fulfill their difficult office faithfully. May all who serve the 589
church-community of Jesus Christ in any kind of office come together for
prayer, counsel, and conversation in new trust and fellowship.

Be guardians of the pure and unadulterated gospel, and guard yourselves against false doctrine and division.

[2.] In the manuscript space is left here for further reflections.

[3.] This was written into the margin of page 2 of the manuscript.

[4.] [Although he is addressing the entire German church here, Bonhoeffer's language throughout this document, particularly in this passage, is strongly evocative of his
Finkenwalde period, particularly in the way he emphasizes the need for community, fellowship, prayer, and repentance between "brothers."—MB]

To the Church-Community.

Listen to the word of the sermon, make use of confession, receive the sacrament. Make plenty of room for the love of Jesus Christ, resist hatred and revenge, and testify through word and life to the lordship of Jesus Christ. Let your homes be governed by Christ's Spirit. Gather around your pastors, pray for them, and help them as you are able.

We call on the Confessing Church congregations to continue fulfilling their service to the entire church-community as before.

16. Draft Proposal for a Reorganization of the Church after the "End of the Church Struggle"[1]

1. Reparation for the Injustice Done to the Protestant Church.
2. Autonomy of the Church.

590 A reorganization of the German Protestant church and a restoration of the relationship between state and church are possible only if the Church Struggle is successfully settled. To that end the following points need to be considered.

1. The Church Struggle arose when the National Socialist state attempted to bring the Protestant church into line. The Church Struggle was therefore not fundamentally directed against National Socialism but against every encroachment of the state into the life of the church.[2] It will last until these encroachments completely cease.

[1.] *NL*, A 65,7; typewritten copy (following a handwritten draft); previously published in *GS* 2:433–37. The draft presumably emerged in connection with Goerdeler's constitutional plans for the period following the overthrow that was planned in 1942 (cf. *DB-ER*, 772). As Christine von Dohnanyi recalled these events (*NL*, A 65,7 b; letter to Eberhard Bethge on February 11, 1957), the impetus for this text came from Hans von Dohnanyi. He planned to pass the document on to Canaris, who was to "use it, on the one hand, with Keitel, and, on the other hand,... [to give it] via Goerdeler to Falkenhausen and one other person whom I have forgotten." Bonhoeffer wrote the text in coordination with F. J. Perels (cf. 2/17, which is Perels's draft for a church constitution following the overthrow). Until shortly before his arrest, Bonhoeffer continued to make corrections in this text. During the Gestapo search of the Bonhoeffer house on the day of his arrest on April 5, 1943, a copy of the final draft fell into the hands of the lead interrogator, Manfred Roeder.

[2.] Hans Asmussen made this point explicitly in his lecture providing a theological declaration regarding the present situation of the German Evangelical Church (at the Confessing Synod in Barmen, May 29–31, 1934): We "are protesting not as members of the people [Volk] against the most recent history of the people, not as citizens against the new state, not as subordinates against the authorities" (Asmussen, "Vortrag über die Theologische Erklärung zur gegenwärtigen Lage der Deutschen Evangelischen Kirche" [Lecture on the theological declaration concerning the current situation of the German Evangelical

2. In the course of the Church Struggle, since 1934, the Confessing Church has established through "emergency law"[3] some organs of church administration, loyal to the confessions, which have been recognized as ecclesially legitimate by synods operating in accord with the confessions.[4] Councils of Brethren and Confessing synods are the only ecclesial organs that, despite every conceivable form of persecution, arrest, and obstacles, have survived through the years,[5] while the organs of the official German Christian church fell away in rapid decline; the Reich bishop,[6] German Christian bishops,[7] Clerical Ministry,[8] state commissioners,[9] church committees,[10]   591

Church], in Burgsmüller and Weth, *Die Barmer Theologische Erklärung,* 48; cf. also 41–46 regarding resistance to the state interference that had been legitimized by the German Christians).

[3.] [See Victoria Barnett's explanation of "emergency law"*(Notrecht)* in the Confessing Church *(For the Soul of the People,* esp. 65–66).—MB]

[4.] Cf. the resolutions of the Dahlem Confessing Synod on October 19–20, 1934 (*Bekenntnisse 1934,* 157–62), and Wilhelm Niemöller, "Von der Dahlemer Synode bis zur Gründung der ersten Vorläufigen Kirchenleitung," in *Wort und Tat,* 120–45.

[5.] These administrative organs existed in the Evangelical Church of the Old Prussian Union until 1945, while the Confessing synods of the German Evangelical Church met for the last time in February 1936, and the Reich Council of Brethren ceased its work in March 1938 (see W. Niemöller, *Die evangelische Kirche im Dritten Reich,* 134–36, and Niesel, *Kirche unter dem Wort*).

[6.] Reich Bishop Ludwig Müller. Müller's authority was removed on October 3, 1935, after the creation of the Reich Church Committee by Minister of Church Affairs Hans Kerrl, but he was never formally relieved of his office and continued to draw a salary, although he had no function.

[7.] On September 5, 1933, the Old Prussian General Synod (see *DB-ER,* 306–7) passed a resolution implementing the "church law regarding the establishment of the office of regional bishops and bishoprics" to restructure the Evangelical Church of the Old Prussian Union. In place of the general superintendents in the individual provincial churches, ten bishoprics were formed, each with a German Christian bishop. In the "intact" regional churches, outside the Old Prussian Union, there was no installation of German Christian bishops (see Scholder, *Churches and the Third Reich,* 1:471–73).

[8.] "Spiritual Ministry," or Geistliches Ministerium, was the name of the German Evangelical Church administration under the leadership of Reich Bishop Müller, according to the constitution of the German Evangelical Church of July 11, 1933, article 7, section 4. It existed only until the end of 1934 (see Gauger, *Chronik der Kirchenwirren,* 424, 462).

[9.] The Prussian minister of culture, Bernhard Rust, appointed August Jäger as state commissar for the Evangelical Church of the Old Prussian Union as of June 24, 1933. Jäger appointed deputy commissars for all the Old Prussian provincial churches to implement the German Christians' seizure of power in the Old Prussian Union as a whole (see Scholder, *Churches and the Third Reich,* 1:357–58). These deputy commissars remained in power until July 14, 1933. See also 2/17, ed. note 17.

[10.] With the September 24, 1935, "Law Securing the DEK [Deutsche Evangelische Kirche, "German Evangelical Church"]," Reich Minister for Church Affairs Hanns Kerrl introduced the "pacification" of the German Evangelical Church through the formation

consistories,[11] etc. were brought down one after another by the resistance of the Confessing Church. By its ecclesial legitimation and by the fearless struggle for the confession of the church, the organs of the Confessing Church have established an authority that is not easily shaken. They will hold their office until a church administration loyal to the confessions exists once more. The majority of young theologians stands determined behind the church administration operating in accord with the confessions.

3. The official church organs (consistory, EOK,[12] financial department),[13] with their anticonfessional actions, have been able to keep themselves in office only by the abuse of state power. They inevitably collapse in the same moment when the power of the state is no longer available to them. No spiritual powers of any kind stand behind them.[14]

4. An end to the Church Struggle is possible only in full agreement with the organs of the Confessing Church; they are backed by all those congregations and pastors true to the confessions who are ready for engagement and willing to sacrifice. It has become apparent that it is not possible to break this resistance by force. But it will cease at the very moment a church administration true to the confessions is again ensured. Such a church

---

of a Reich Church Committee and several regional and provincial church committees. These existed until August 1937 (see W. Niemöller, *Die evangelische Kirche im Dritten Reich*, 168–76).

[11.] Following the rescinding of the Reich Church Committee, the Reich minister for church affairs, Hanns Kerrl, decreed on March 20, 1937, that from then on the juridical leaders of the German Evangelical Church Chancellery and/or of the consistories were to assume the ongoing administrative duties. To allow for the jurists' supplementing of this administration, the Clerical Advisory Council (Geistlicher Vertrauensrat) was formed in August 1939 (see Melzel, *Der geistliche Vertrauensrat*, 1991).

[12.] Abbreviation for Evangelischer Oberkirchenrat, "High Evangelical Church Council." See Elliger, *Die Evangelische Kirche der Union*, 138ff. In October 1942 the Old Prussian Council of Brethren prepared a memorandum, "On Legitimate Church Order," for the reorganization of the Evangelical Church of the Old Prussian Union. This memorandum planned to do away with consistories and the High Evangelical Church Council.

[13.] With the March 11, 1935, Prussian "Law Regarding the Administration of Assets in the Protestant Regional Churches," financial departments were formed for the High Evangelical Church Council as well as for the consistories under it and several regional church offices. These financial departments were to ensure that financial resources were withheld from the Confessing Church. The June 25, 1937, executive order implementing the "Law Securing the DEK" extended the Prussian law to the entire church in Germany (see the chapter "Die Entwicklung der staatlichen Finanzaufsicht," in Brunotte, *Bekenntnis und Kirchenverfassung*, 55ff.).

[14.] A supplementary sheet with two further points that were meant to be inserted at this point had been lost by the time volume *GS 2* went to press in 1959. This copy reflects the original numbering.

592

administration can be established only with the assent of the Confessing Church organs.

5. Only very minimal resistance is to be expected from the German Christian side (National Church Union).[15] It would be eliminated if the possibility of a free religious union[16] were presented to the Thuringian German Christians, with the obligation that they refrain from political involvement and from disturbing the unity of the church. In that case only an infinitesimally small group would split off. If no state force is used against it, then this group is condemned before long to final dissolution.

6. The unity of the DEK,[17] broken by the leadership of the German Christians, could be reestablished by the recognition of an administration operating in accordance with the confessions. The special interests of the regional churches, still rooted in certain traditional historical and confessional scruples, would certainly be overcome in the near future by means of a strong church leadership. 593

7. As the new church is reorganized, the reactionary circles associated with the former general superintendent[18] and the official church bureaucracy must not under any circumstances be given new leadership responsibilities. For state and church that would be a regressive solution to the church question. A solution that is intended truly to place the relationship of church and state on new ground must have recourse to the young generation of pastors and laypersons who were tested in the Church Struggle.[19] The following specific measures would be taken immediately:

[15.] Various groups of radical German Christians had come together in June 1937 in the "National Church Movement of German Christians." When they were forced to drop the term "Movement," in accordance with the April 7, 1937, law protecting the terminology of the National Socialist German Workers' Party, they then called themselves "German Christians (National Church Union)." See Meier, *Die Deutschen Christen,* 219–26 and 258. [The National Church Union was essentially the Thuringian branch of the German Christians. See Bergen, *Twisted Cross,* 102–7. Thuringia remained a center of German Christian activity until the very end of the Nazi regime, and it was the location of the most radical sector of that movement. See also ed. note 16.—MB]

[16.] On the particular character of the Thuringian German Christians, see Meier, *Die Deutschen Christen,* 2–198.

[17.] [Abbreviation for Deutsche Evangelische Kirche, "German Evangelical Church.—MB]

[18.] Here Bonhoeffer is warning against a restoration of the order of the Evangelical Church of the Old Prussian Union prior to 1933. He is afraid that such a step backward would undercut the Confessing Church administration, which was composed of councils of brethren and synods. General Superintendent Otto Dibelius set the precedent in Berlin-Brandenburg after 1945 by binding the rebuilding of the church to "the existing legal structures." As Dibelius himself acknowledged, "This was the last thing my young friends of the Confessing Church desired" (*In the Service of the Lord,* 172).

[19.] See the three-volume work by Wolfgang Scherffig, *Junge Theologen im "Dritten Reich."*

1. A declaration of the state that it is willing to lift the limitations on the freedom of the church that have existed since 1933 and to grant it in proclamation and order an autonomy corresponding to its nature.[20]

2. The release of the pastors who for the sake of their confessional stance have been in a KZ[21] or in prison,[22] the lifting of the police bans, bans on public speaking, deportations, and bans on residence. Lifting of the bans on the church press.[23]

594   3. The measures for church government (education, examinations, ordination, installations of pastors, and so on) undertaken thus far by church administrations operating in accord with the confessions shall be formally recognized.

4. In the interest of Christian instruction, the church shall be granted once again the possibility of working freely with the youth. Hindrances to the charitable work of the church shall be lifted.[24]

5. All church leaders who came into office by means of National Socialism shall be removed from office.[25] To this number belong . . . [26]

6. A provisional church administration (Council of the DEK) shall be appointed for the DEK[27] The chair of the currently existing provisional administration of the DEK, who is simultaneously chair of the Old Prussian Union Council,[28] shall appoint the leaders of the regional churches in order to let them participate in the selection of the provisional church administration.

For the APU[29] . . .

a) For the church province of the APU

[20.] Cf. section II of Perels's draft, 2/17.

[21.] [Abbreviation for *Konzentrationslager,* "concentration camp."—MB]

[22.] Examples include Martin Niemöller, Heinrich Grüber, Werner Sylten, Martin Albertz, and Günther Dehn (cf. Niesel, *Kirche unter dem Wort,* 245ff.).

[23.] Cf. section III § 1 of Perels's draft, 2/17. As of June 1, 1941, nearly the entire church press was forced to cease its publications (cf. W. Niemöller, *Die evangelische Kirche im Dritten Reich,* 288).

[24.] See Kaiser, *Sozialer Protestantismus,* 279ff., and Strohm and Thierfelder, *Diakonie im "Dritten Reich."*

[25.] Cf. section IV, § 7 in Perels's draft, 2/17.

[26.] These names were not filled out.

[27.] Cf. section IV, § 1 and § 3 in Perels's draft, 2/17.

[28.] Pastor Friedrich (Fritz) Müller, Berlin-Dahlem, occupied this dual role from 1936 to 1939. Then Martin Albertz assumed the chair of the Provisional Administration; when Albertz was imprisoned, Hans Böhm took his place. The leadership of the Confessing Church Synod was first handled by Wolfgang Staemmler and, after 1941, by Martin Burgwitz. Martin Niemöller, despite being confined in a concentration camp at the time, was elected in October 1943 as the chair of the Old Prussian Union Council of Brethren.

[29.] [Abbreviation for (Evangelische Kirche der) Altpreußischen Union, "(Evangelical Church of the) Old Prussian Union."—MB]

b) Pomerania.

c) Westphalia.

The church administrations of the regional churches shall be established in agreement with the regional organs of the Confessing Church located there.

7. The financial departments of the DEK and of the regional churches shall be eliminated. Their authority shall pass over to the church administrations.[30]

8. All church administrations, guided solely by the church confessions, shall be empowered to undo laws, decrees, and orders that were enacted after July 23, 1933 (the church election carried out under pressure from the state).[31]

9. The church administrations of the DEK and of the regional churches, together with the synods, shall have six months to prepare a new election of church bodies (congregational council, provincial synod, regional synod, and a Reich synod) and to work out a new church constitution.

10. The national church bodies shall be *The Council of the DEK,* as the administrative and representative body of the DEK; *the Reich Synod,* as the highest representative body of the Protestant congregations; the *Federal Church Council* (as the representative body of the regional church administrations).

11. In agreement with the Council of the DEK, personnel changes shall be made at the Church Foreign Office,[32] which has lost the trust of the foreign churches and the majority of Germans living abroad.

12. The DC[33] members of the consolidated national church shall be allowed to form a free-church religious community, provided that they refrain from political activity and from any new threats to the unity of the church.[34]

595

[30.] [These departments were established by church chancellery director Friedrich Werner in February 1935. In March 1935 the Reich government passed a law requiring that all staff members in these financial departments be appointed by the Reich minister for church affairs, thereby making them state bodies. The finance departments became a primary means by which the government exerted pressure on the churches, particularly the Confessing Church. See Helmreich, *The German Churches under Hitler,* 184–85, 212, and 235.—MB]

[31.] For a list of all the Confessing Church actions throughout this period, see W. Niemöller, *Die evangelische Kirche im Dritten Reich,* 53–64.

[32.] Cf. section 4 § 4 of Perels's draft, 2/17. Theodor Heckel had been the head of the Church Foreign Office since February 1934. In August 1945 Martin Niemöller took over this office.

[33.] [Abbreviation for *Deutsche Christen,* "German Christians."—MB]

[34.] [Bonhoeffer's recommended postwar solution for the problem of German Christian radicalism—that they form a separate church—would have removed them

13. The Reich Church Ministry shall be eliminated. The tasks of the Reich Church Ministry shall be delegated to the Reich Ministry of the Interior.[35]

14. In the interest of a fundamental clarification of the relationship of church and state, the state shall seek a settlement concerning financial arrangements, because time and again they encumber the relationship between state and church.

15. The theological faculties that since 1933 have been to a large extent destroyed and robbed of their academic standing shall be reorganized, with the assistance of the church administrations, as centers of education for the emerging generation of pastors.

596   **17. Friedrich Justus Perels: Draft of a Church Constitution following the Coup**[1]

I.
VO[2] concerning the Jurisdiction of the National Government in Church Affairs.

§ 1   The tasks of national jurisdiction for church affairs shall be transferred to the National Ministry of the Interior.

§ 2   In the National Ministry of the Interior, church affairs shall be handled by a National Commissioner for Church Affairs. For the National Commissioner for Church Affairs I designate . . . [3]

§ 3   The Reich Ministry for Church Affairs shall be eliminated.

---

entirely from the German Protestant Church and given them the same voluntary status in Germany as other small free churches, such as the Methodists. This idea was not realized. After 1945 former German Christians remained part of the German Protestant Church and many of them retained church positions. See Bergen, *Twisted Cross,* 206–30, and Barnett, *For the Soul of the People,* 250–51.—MB]

[35.] Cf. section I §§ 1–3 of Perels's draft, 2/17.

[1.] *NL,* A 65,6; notes handwritten in pencil by Friedrich Perels, discovered in Bonhoeffer's copy of Emil Brunner's book, *Man in Revolt,* along with two addenda. Addendum A presents names for the provisional church administration in the Old Prussian Union and its church provinces (this includes a penciled note by Bonhoeffer regarding the appointment of the Old Prussian Union administration by the provincial administrations); it must have been written before September 20, 1942, the day Friedrich Müller of Dahlem died, since Müller is earmarked as a member of the provisional church administration of the Old Prussian Union. Addendum B contains an inventory of the collective resources as of March 31, 1942. The internal connections to Bonhoeffer's own draft for measures following "the end of the Church Struggle" (see 2/16) are so obvious that Perels's notes are reproduced here in full. On the cooperation between Perels and Bonhoeffer, cf. Schreiber, *Friedrich Justus Perels,* 165ff.

[2.] Abbreviation for *Verordnung,* "decree."

[3.] A space is left here for a name to be entered.

II.
Law concerning the Freedom of the[4] Christian Faith.

The state declares the Christian faith to be the most important moral and ethical foundation of its regulations. Accordingly, it shall allow the Christian churches the full practice of their faith in public. It shall revoke all measures that hinder the public practice of the Christian faith. 597

The churches shall practice their life of faith with full autonomy.[5]

III.
Initial Implementation—VO[6] as to the Law concerning the Freedom of the Christian Faith.

§ 1 Police measures that hinder the practice of the Christian faith shall be revoked.[7]

In particular, all preventive arrests, as well as other state police measures imposed for religious reasons, shall be revoked.[8]

Those affected or their families are to pass on petitions to the appropriate state police officials without delay.

IV.
Law concerning Religious Freedom for the German Evangelical Churches.

The state shall return to the Protestant church its full religious and confessional freedom. The church shall administer and represent itself in connection with its foundations of faith. The church itself is therefore responsible for the restoration of the order of the church.

For the implementation of this goal I appoint church administrations composed of such men who are legitimated by the church through an existing appointment to ecclesial administration by the Confessing Church or by a regional church loyal to the confessions.[9]

§ 1 The administration and representation of the German Evangelical Church[10] shall rest in the hands of the following committee:

[4.] The preceding text replaces "Freedom of Religion for the."

[5.] Cf. no. 1 of the specific measures to be taken immediately in "Proposal for a Reorganization of the Church," 2/16.

[6.] [See ed. note 2.—MB]

[7.] Cf. no. 1 of the specific measures to be taken immediately, 2/16.

[8.] This replaces "§ 2 Clergy and lay members of the Christian churches presently under preventive arrest shall be immediately released."

[9.] Cf. no. 5 of the specific measures to be taken immediately, 2/16.

[10.] Cf. no. 6 of the specific measures to be taken immediately, 2/16.

1) Pastor Niemöller, DD, as chair

598   2) Regional Church Bishop D. Wurm as permanent representative

3)

4)

5)

The committee shall make decisions by majority vote.

The National Chancellery and the Finance Department of the DEK[11] shall be placed under this committee.[12]

§ 2 The administration of the DEK shall be advised by the Conference of Regional Church Leaders that is to be developed. The Conference of Regional Church Leaders shall have no right to veto decisions of the church administration.

§ 3 The provisional church administration of the DEK shall convene the Confessing Synod of the German Evangelical Church as soon as possible and submit its laws and regulations for approval.[13]

§ 4 For the administration of the Church Foreign Office, after the removal of the previous leader[14] from office, a commission shall be appointed composed of:

D. Lilje[15]

Lic.[16] Bonhoeffer

. . . .

§ 5 For the regional churches the following is specified:

The church administrations of the regional churches in Baden, Bavaria, Braun-schweig, Hamburg, Hanover, Lutheran Hanover, Reformed Lippe, Ostmark (?), Warthegau, Württemberg shall remain in their offices.

Existing church agencies and financial departments shall be placed under the church administration.

599   For the remaining regional churches as well as for the Old Prussian church provinces, provisional church administrations shall be set up.[17] They shall be responsible

---

[11.] [Abbreviation for Deutsche Evangelische Kirche, "German Evangelical Church.—MB]

[12.] Cf. no. 7 of the specific measures to be taken immediately, 2/16.

[13.] Cf. nos. 9 and 10 of the specific measures to be taken immediately, 2/16.

[14.] This refers to Bishop Theodor Heckel; on Bonhoeffer's experiences with Heckel, cf. especially *DB-ER*, 344–54, 510–12.

[15.] As former vice president of the World Student Christian Federation and as general secretary of the Lutheran World Conference in the Confessing Church, Hanns Lilje could draw on extensive ecumenical experience.

[16.] [Abbreviation for "Licentiate."—MB]

[17.] [The intent behind these recommendations about which church administrations were to be retained and which removed was to undo the damage that the July 1933 church elections had done to many regional churches. The state appointment of church commissar August Jäger to oversee the churches in the Old Prussian Union had wrought

for all ecclesial and spiritual leadership and the representation of the regional churches until the reshaping of the church's conditions. The church agencies and financial departments shall be under the church administrations.

The church administration shall make decisions by majority vote.

The composition of the provisional church administrations is made known in the attachment.

In the region of the Evangelical Church of the Old Prussian Union, the Confessing Synod of the Evangelical Church of the APU[18] shall be recognized as the highest church organ. Additional laws and regulations for which the general synod was previously responsible shall be submitted to it for ratification.

In the church provinces the Confessing synods shall be recognized as the highest church organs of the church province.[19] Where a Confessing synod does not exist, it shall be established at once by the provisional church administration.

§ 6 In the region of the Evangelical Church of the APU, the high consistory of the Evangelical Church shall henceforth bear the name "The Council of the Evangelical Church of the APU," the consistories the name "The Council of the Church Province..." The name of the church province shall follow.

§ 7 The provisional church administrations of the DEK and in the regional churches shall have the autonomous right to appoint officials in church ministries. They shall dismiss any officials and employees of church ministries, without introducing disciplinary proceedings, if these were German Christians or have otherwise acted in a detrimental way toward the church and its mission.[20]

§ 8 Measures that have been introduced or declared and not implemented against Confessing Church pastors for church-political reasons shall be annulled

§ 9 Concluding Clause

In consultation with the Conference of Regional Church Leaders of the Confessing Synod of the DEK, the Church Commission of the DEK should promptly submit proposals for the new order of the DEK and its regional churches.

600

---

havoc within those churches as well. The Confessing Church was strongest and most organized in the Old Prussian Union; hence Perels's suggestions (below) were that authority in those churches simply be transferred to the existing Confessing Church bodies.—MB]

[18.] [Abbreviation for Altpreußische Union, "Old Prussian Union."—MB]

[19.] [This refers specifically to the Old Prussian Union churches. The eight member churches of the Old Prussian Union were divided into *Provinzen* that corresponded to the provinces of Prussia; elsewhere in Germany the churches were divided into *Landeskirchen*, or regional churches.—MB]

[20.] [This did not happen after 1945. See 2/16, ed. note 34.—MB]

18. A Theological Position Paper on the *Primus Usus Legis* [1]

The Doctrine of the Primus Usus Legis according to the Confessional Writings and Their Critique.

1. The *concept of the usus legis* is found in the headings to the section of the FC de tertio usu legis, translated "Concerning the Third Use of the Law,"[2] and also in the Solida declar[atio] VI/1[3] in the Latin text; in the German text instead of the concept of *usus* we find that of the "benefit" of the law.[4] In the Epitome we read that the law of God "has been given to people for three reasons"[5] (corresponding to the Smalc[ald] Art[icles], "Concerning the Law," page 311.[6] From this we infer that the question regarding the

601

[1.] *NL*, A 72,4; handwritten; previously published in English translation in Bonhoeffer, *Ethics* (New York: Macmillan, 1955), 303–19; and *Ethics* (New York: Simon & Schuster, 1995), 299–315. This study is a paper written for a committee appointed by the Tenth Old Prussian Confessing Synod in November 1941 for the purpose of preparing a presentation on "The Meaning of the Signs of the Times." As the first reports of the deportation of the Jews were becoming known, the Council of Brethren charged this committee with producing a draft statement on the Fifth Commandment ["Thou shalt not kill" in the Lutheran Bible—MB]. This presupposed the fundamental question of the preaching of the law (on this see *DB-ER*, 709). At the first full meeting of this committee in Magdeburg on August 10, 1942, Bonhoeffer took on the task of putting together a paper on the problem of the *primus usus legis*. He presented the text reprinted here in Magdeburg on March 15, 1943, at the second meeting of the committee (cf. *DB-ER*, 709–10). The text here is reproduced according to Ilse Tödt's deciphering of the manuscript. Bonhoeffer used the two-volume edition of the Lutheran confessional writings (*Die Bekenntnisschriften der evangelisch-lutherischen Kirche*, Göttingen, 1930). [In the present text, the page and paragraph enumerations and the abbreviations for individual texts follow the 2000 Fortress Press edition of *The Book of Concord*. The following abbreviations are used below by Bonhoeffer: CA=Confessio Augustana (Augsburg Confession); AC=Apology of the Augsburg Confession; SA = Smalcald Articles; LC = Large Catechism; FC = Formula of Concord, which consists of two parts: Ep = Epitome; SDec = Solid Declaration; and NT = New Testament. References to the confessional writings in the editorial notes are not abbreviated. The term *primus usus legis* means "first use of the law."—MB]

[2.] Epitome VI/1 (*Book of Concord*, 502).

[3.] *Book of Concord*, 587.

[4.] The German heading reads *Vom dritten Brauch des Gesetzes Gottes*, "On the Third Use of the Law of God." Later on, the German text translates the Latin *usus* with *nützet*, "is useful," or "benefits."

[5.] *Book of Concord*, 502. It appears that Bonhoeffer has translated from the Latin here: "legem Dei propter tres causas hominibus datam esse."

[6.] *Book of Concord*, 311–12, titled "Concerning the Law." Luther does not use the conceptuality of the "three uses." In fact, this section speaks only of the *usus politicus* and the *usus theologicus*. On the question whether Luther implicitly taught the *tertius usus legis*, cf. the references from the Weimarer Ausgabe collected in the *Bekenntnisschriften der evangelisch-lutherischen Kirche*, 435 n. 4. See also Schlink, *Theology of the Lutheran Confessions*, 121–22 n. 8.

subject of the usus, namely, whether it is God or the preacher, is, of course, not explicitly determined but nevertheless is to be answered with the sense that the subject is God. Epit. 7[7] also supports this: "Therefore, for both the repentant and the unrepentant, for the reborn and those not reborn, the law is and remains one single law, the unchangeable will of God. In terms of obedience there is a difference only in that those people who are not yet reborn do what the law demands unwillingly, because they are coerced (as is also the case with the reborn with respect to the flesh). Believers, however, do without coercion, with a willing spirit, insofar as they are born anew, what no threat of the law could ever force from them." Accordingly, the concept of the usus legis dare not mislead us into thinking primarily of different forms of preaching—that is, forms of using the law on the part of preachers—under different circumstances; but rather it has to do first with different effects of the one single law. In reference to their subject, these effects are to be understood equally as the free working of God on the human being and as belief and unbelief on the part of the person, so that the subject of the use of the law must be seen to be not the preacher but God, and then in addition, if so desired, the hearer of the sermon, the human being.[8]   602
Since, however, this question is not explicitly clarified in the confessional writings, dangerous ambiguities arise in the course of its delineation.[9] Because of its decisive importance for the entire preaching of the law, the question of the subject of the usus had to be answered from the FC. If, that is, the preacher or the church were the subject of the three usus, then there would be a preaching of the law for the world that would be significantly different from that for the congregation. The one would contain the demand of a civil-political-rational righteousness of works that would be cut off from the demand of the obedience of faith toward the triune God. The other would contain only an admonition to those who believe in Christ. But if God is the subject of the three usus, then there is *one* preaching of the law, which achieves different effects among unbelievers and believers. The preacher as

---

[Cf. the discussion of the third use of the law in the Formula of Concord; see Epitome VI (*Book of Concord,* 502–3) and Solid Declaration VI (*Book of Concord,* 587–91).—MB]

[7.] This should read: Epitome VI/6 (*Book of Concord,* 503).

[8.] Cf. Schlink: "It is God who uses the law in a threefold manner, either leaving and confirming a man in the delusion of civil righteousness, or leading others to fear and despair, or, in the case of believers, terrifying and gladdening them, bludgeoning or gently leading them." "Neither the person who hears the preaching of the law nor the preacher of the law himself can control in what use and to what benefit the law operates in him and through him" (*Theology of the Lutheran Confessions,* 122).

[9.] The following words are crossed out in the manuscript: "and the question must be asked whether the concept of the usus is well chosen."

the subject of the usus would know of an isolated preaching of works;[10] God as subject of the usus, by the preaching of the *one* law,[11] works different effects in believers and unbelievers. Because the concept of the usus leaves this decisive preliminary question unresolved, its usefulness ought to be questioned (cf. below 12.).

2. The law of God is "a divine teaching in which the righteous, unchanging will of God revealed how human beings were created in their nature, thoughts, words, and deeds to be pleasing and acceptable to God. This law also threatens those who transgress it with God's wrath and temporal and eternal punishments" (SDec V/17).[12] The law is "the commandments of the Decalogue, wherever they appear in the Scriptures" (AC IV/6).[13] The proper office of the law is "reproving sin and teaching good works" (duplex usus?)[14] (SDec V/18).[15] The primus usus legis effects the establishment of a disciplina externa et honestas (SDec V/1) through threats and promises.[16] The secundus usus[17] effects the recognition of sin.[18] The tertius usus[19] serves the converted as a guiding principle[20] of their action and as chastisement of the flesh still alive even in them.[21] The conception that the distinction between the three usus has to do with a chronological sequence of proclamation or with two groups of persons to be differentiated from one another in principle (unbelievers and believers)[22] is at least not ruled out in the confessional writings, but in actual fact it cannot be sustained. The

603

[10.] The words "of works" replace "(of the second table)" in the manuscript.

[11.] The words "of the *one* law" replace "of both tables" in the manuscript.

[12.] *Book of Concord,* 584.

[13.] *Book of Concord,* 121. Bonhoeffer translated this line from the Latin edition: "Decalogi praecepta, ubicunque illa in scripturis leguntur."

[14.] "double use."

[15.] *Book of Concord,* 584.

[16.] The Latin *disciplina externa et honestas* is translated "external discipline and respectability" (*Book of Concord,* 587); "threat and terror... promise and offer" are found in "Concerning the Law," Smalcald Articles III/2 (*Book of Concord,* 311). See Bonhoeffer's point 5.

[17.] "second use."

[18.] Solid Declaration VI/2 (*Book of Concord,* 587).

[19.] ["third use."—MB]

[20.] Solid Declaration VI/3 (*Book of Concord,* 587).

[21.] Epitome VI/4 and VI/7 (*Book of Concord,* 502–3); Solid Declaration VI/8–9 (*Book of Concord,* 588–89); Solid Declaration VI/18 (*The Book of Concord,* 590). Cf. Schlink, *Theology of the Lutheran Confessions,* 119–21.

[22.] Cf. the distinction made in early Protestant dogmatics between the law's preservation of the unregenerated in external discipline and the regenerated, by contrast, both outwardly as well as inwardly—i.e., spiritually; cf. Schmid, *Doctrinal Theology of the Evangelical Lutheran Church,* 510.

externa disciplina still applies to believers, as do the threat and chastisement of the law to the extent a believer is still flesh ("For the old creature, like a stubborn, recalcitrant donkey, is also still a part of them, and it needs to be forced into obedience to Christ not only through the law's teaching, admonition, compulsion, and threat but also often with the cudgel of punishments and tribulations," SDec VI/24);[23] believers also still require the recognition of sin through the law. In addition, the primus usus itself contains the entire contents of the law,[24] namely, the Decalogue in both tables, just as it also already contains threat and promise. The uncertainty as to whether the usus paedagogicus[25] is to be accorded an independent significance, whether it, as a fourth usus, is to be placed between the politicus and elenchticus,[26] and the fact that the Smalc. Art. know of only a twofold usus legis (primus and secundus)[27] make it clear that the differences between the usus legis must be understood not in chronological terms—and that means not with reference to groups of people that are different in principle—but instead with respect to their content. The primus usus defines the content of the law in reference to the establishment of certain external works; the secundus usus defines the relationship of the law to the person, in that the individual is led to the recognition of opposition to the law and of their condemnation; the tertius usus defines the law as a gracious help from God for doing the works commanded. The primus usus is the law as preaching about works; the secundus is the law as preaching about the recognition of sin; the tertius is the law as preaching about the fulfillment of the law. The proclamation of the law always contains all three elements. It works in different ways, depending on God's will and who the hearer is, bringing about the performance of external works, repentance, new obedience. Yet where the differentiation of the three usus misleads us, so that we understand these as distinctions of chronological sequence or of different preaching methods to address groups of persons thought to be different from one another in principle, the unity of the law of God is broken, and we face the question of the theological justification of the usus doctrine (see below 12.) in addition to the question treated under 1.) of the usefulness of the usus concept.

604

[23.] *Book of Concord,* 591.

[24.] Cf. Schlink, *Theology of the Lutheran Confessions,* 78 and 75–76.

[25.] "pedagogical use," i.e., the function of the law as a disciplinarian, or *Zuchtmeister,* for the sake of Christ; cf. Gal. 3:24.

[26.] Cf. the fourfold use of the law as *usus politicus, elenchticus, paedagogicus* as well as *didacticus* in Schmid, *Doctrinal Theology of the Evangelical Lutheran Church,* 510.

[27.] Smalcald Articles III/2 (*Book of Concord,* 311–12) does not explicitly refer to a twofold use. Cf. ed. note 6.

3. The primus [usus] is not treated consistently in the confessional writings.[28] It does not receive any separate attention.[29] We encounter its substance, with positive emphasis, in the polemic against the doctrine of monastic perfection,[30] against the Catholic Church's claim to worldly rule,[31] against the Enthusiasts, and in the doctrine of worldly rule;[32] with negative emphasis, in the doctrine of justification by faith and the critique of righteousness of works [Werkgerechtigkeit] connected with this in the doctrine of free will;[33] we encounter it in neutral systematic form in the debate regarding the tertius usus legis.[34] The confessional writings are interested in the primus usus only in its relation to the gospel.

4. Definition: The primus usus legis is used "to maintain external discipline and respectability against dissolute, disobedient people."[35] We shall now investigate the content, purpose, means of implementation, preacher, and hearer of the primus usus.

5. The *content* of the primus usus legis is the entire Decalogue with respect to the works it requires, combined with the threat and promise it contains. "Here we maintain that the law was given by God, in the first place, to curb sin by means of the threat and terror of punishment and also by means of the promise and offer of grace and favor" (Smalc. Art., "Concerning the Law").[36] In terms of its content, the entire law is contained within the primus usus legis (AC IV/8).[37] The idea that the second table of the law

---

[28.] The following text is crossed out in the manuscript: "Yet what is said about the justitia civilis, about natural law, about natural knowledge of God, about free will, and about worldly rule applies to it." In the margin of the text the following words appear, also crossed out: "law and gospel alongside one another."

[29.] The following text is crossed out in the manuscript: "Where its necessity is emphasized, this takes place only in order immediately to speak of its abrogation [Aufhebung] in the gospel."

[30.] Cf., e.g., Augsburg Confession XX and XXVII (*Book of Concord*, 52–57 and 80–91); Apology of the Augsburg Confession XVI (*The Book of Concord*, 231–33).

[31.] Cf., e.g., Augsburg Confession XVII (*Book of Concord*, 48–51); Apology of the Augsburg Confession XVI and XXVIII (*Book of Concord*, 231–33 and 289–94).

[32.] Cf. Apology of the Augsburg Confession XVI (*Book of Concord*, 231–33, especially the section against Karlstadt).

[33.] Cf. Augsburg Confession XVIII (*Book of Concord*, 50–53); Apology of the Augsburg Confession IV/40–44 (*Book of Concord*, 126–27); Epitome III/8–11 (Negative Theses) and IV/16 (*Book of Concord*, 497 and 499); Solid Declaration III/37–41 and IV/37 (*Book of Concord*, 568–69 and 580); cf. also Schlink, *Theology of the Lutheran Confessions*, 89–90.

[34.] Cf. Epitome VI/1 (*Book of Concord*, 502); Solid Declaration VI/1–25 (*Book of Concord*, 587–91).

[35.] Solid Declaration VI/1 (*Book of Concord*, 587).

[36.] Smalcald Articles III/2 (*Book of Concord*, 311).

[37.] *Book of Concord*, 121.

might be preached without the first is found nowhere in the confessional writings. On the contrary, such a division is criticized sharply throughout.[38] Nevertheless, the first table already contains the indication that even the second table cannot be fulfilled by works alone, thus overcoming the primus usus (AC IV/8, 35, 130).[39] The law, however, is not only contained in the Decalogue but permeates the entire NT.[40] "What could be a more sobering and terrifying demonstration and proclamation of the wrath of God against sin than the suffering and death of Christ, his Son? But as long as these things all proclaim God's wrath and terrify the human being, it is still not the proclamation of the gospel or of Christ, in the strict sense. It is instead the proclamation of Moses and the law *to the unrepentant"* (SDec V/ 12).[41] Although the confessional writings do not assert this, and perhaps do not even intend it (they are able even to speak of a "sermon" without Christ—sine mentione Christi [SDec V/10],[42] which can only be a reference to the primus usus), the preceding requires the conclusion that proclamation of the teaching and cross of Christ belongs also to the primus usus legis as preaching of the law. Yet insofar as the cross is always also proclamation of the gospel and, seen from this perspective, proclamation of the gospel is already contained even in the Decalogue, in the First Commandment, the primus usus legis can never be preached in abstract detachment from the gospel. Despite this, its proper nature is to require the works of the law that serve external discipline and respectability. By threatening punishment and by attracting people with the (earthly) blessings promised by God for an honorable life, the works of the law are compelled out of people's

606

[38.] For opposition to such division, cf. Apology of the Augsburg Confession IV/34 (*Book of Concord*, 125–26). On the unity of both tables, cf., e.g., Apology of the Augsburg Confession IV/8 and 130–31 (*Book of Concord*, 121 and 141).

[39.] *The Book of Concord*, 121, 126, 141.

[40.] [In the historical context in which he wrote, Bonhoeffer's comments in this document about the centrality of the law were a radical message that would not have been missed by his colleagues in the Confessing Church. The Institute for the Research and Removal of Jewish Influence on the Religious Life of the German People had been established in 1939, and by 1941 several regional churches had agreed to the segregation of "non-Aryan Christians" through the establishment of separate congregations. In their sermons and theological writings, pastors and theologians of that era pointedly attacked "the law" and "legalism" as Judaic influences. In contrast, here Bonhoeffer is discussing the continued validity and centrality of the law of Moses in Christianity. For a more thorough discussion of this aspect of Bonhoeffer's thought, see Christine-Ruth Müller, *Dietrich Bonhoeffers Kampf*, 213–22.—MB]

[41.] *Book of Concord*, 583–84. In his copy of the confessional writings, Bonhoeffer notes in the margin, next to these quoted lines, "the cross of Christ as law!" and at the top of the next page, "if law out of the cross of Christ, why then still law?"

[42.] "without mentioning Christ" (*Book of Concord*, 583).

fear or longing for happiness.[43] This is where the exclusive orientation of the primus usus legis to bringing about *works*, that is, certain *conditions*, is expressed. From this perspective the "natural law innate to human hearts" can now also be characterized as the content of the lex[44] in its primus usus; this natural law "is in agreement with the Law of Moses or the Ten (!) Commandments" (AC IV/7).[45] In all this the possibility of a lex naturae[46] deviating from the Decalogue and thereby introducing a conflict is not even considered; in any case, the sole standard is always the Decalogue.[47]

607 It is therefore the will *of God*, not of human beings, that takes effect in the primus usus as well as in the lex naturae. The organ through which the lex naturae comes into play is the ratio.[48] Standing opposed to it are the demonic powers, evil impulses, and the devil, which are mightier than the ratio, so that even despite "valiant effort" the ratio only seldom prevails (AC XVIII/71–72).[49] This makes clear that not every human urge can pass itself off as natural law. The Decalogue remains the final criterion. "God truly demands and desires this sort of outwardly honorable life, and for the sake of God's commands one would have to perform the same good works that are prescribed in the Ten (!) Commandments" (AC IV/22).[50]

6. The *purpose of the primus usus* is the establishment of the iustitia civilis or rationis, carnis[51] (AC IV/22–24, XVIII/70).[52] It consists of an honorable life in accord with the Decalogue in its first and second tables (to talk about

---

[43.] Cf. Solid Declaration V/17 (*Book of Concord*, 584); Smalcald Articles III/2 (*Book of Concord*, 311–12); cf. also Apology of the Augsburg Confession IV/24 (*Book of Concord*, 124); Solid Declaration IV/8–9 (*Book of Concord*, 575–76).

[44.] "law."

[45.] Cf. *Book of Concord*, 121. [The English edition of *The Book of Concord* at this place does not have wording similar to Bonhoeffer's. The editorial note in the German edition quotes the text of the Apology with which Bonhoeffer is working: "the natural law, which agrees with the Law of Moses, or the Ten Commandments, [is] innate in the hearts of all people."—MB]

[46.] "natural law."

[47.] See, e.g., Apology of the Augsburg Confession IV/7 (*Book of Concord*, 121); cf. Schlink, *Theology of the Lutheran Confessions*, 49–50.

[48.] "reason." On *ratio*, cf. Schlink, *Theology of the Lutheran Confessions*, 51–52 and 240.

[49.] The new numbering is Apology of the Augsburg Confession XVIII/5 (*Book of Concord*, 234). [Nothing at this place in the English edition of *The Book of Concord* corresponds to the words Bonhoeffer is quoting from the German text: *heftigen Bemühens*, "valiant effort."—MB]

[50.] Cf. *Book of Concord*, 124 [which once again does not have a translation based on the words Bonhoeffer is quoting—MB].

[51.] "civil righteousness" or "the righteousness of reason, of the flesh."

[52.] *Book of Concord*, 124. The new numbering is Apology of the Augsburg Confession XVIII/4 (*Book of Concord*, 233–34).

God, to display outward acts of worship and holy behavior, to honor one's parents, to refrain from stealing, AC XVIII/70).[53] This lies "to some extent" within the ability of free will[54] and of reason, although it is only rarely actualized (AC XVIII/72).[55] It is rightfully praised by humans and by God; "we willingly give this righteousness of reason the praises it deserves, for our corrupt nature has no greater good than this, . . . God even honors it with temporal rewards" (AC IV/24).[56] This means that all worldly life is subject to the Decalogue insofar as works are concerned. God desires the iustitia civilis from all people, even from Christians. This is said against the Enthusiasts, "who teach that Christian perfection means physically leaving house and home, spouse and child" (CA XVI/4)[57] and who thus wish to make the gospel into a new law for the world. By contrast, the truth is that the gospel "teaches an internal, eternal reality and righteousness of the heart, not an external, temporal one" (see above),[58] that the gospel does not provide new laws regarding civil life (CA XVI/55).[59] This statement about the gospel thus necessarily assumes the proclamation of the Decalogue for the establishment of iustitia civilis. Without this connection, such an assertion would itself be Enthusiastic [schwärmerisch]. The confessional writings therefore assert that, in regard to the content of the law,[60] the Decalogue contains the full teaching and the gospel contributes nothing additional.

608

7. As a *means for the implementation of the primus usus* legis, and thus for the establishment of iustitia civilis, "God provides law, regulates political authority, provides learned wise people who serve the government" (AC IV/22).[61]

[53.] [The new numbering is Apology of the Augsburg Confession XVIII/4 (*Book of Concord*, 233–34).—MB]

[54.] "It can to some extent produce civil righteousness or the righteousness of works. It can talk about God and offer God acts of worship with external works; it can obey rulers and parents. By choosing an external work it can keep back the hand from murder, adultery, and theft," The Apology of the Augsburg Confession XVIII/4 (*Book of Concord*, 233–34).

[55.] The new number is Apology of the Augsburg Confession XVIII/6: "[F]ew [human beings] lead an honorable life in accordance with natural reason" (trans. Mark Brocker; cf. *Book of Concord*, 234). Cf. Schlink, *Theology of the Lutheran Confessions*, 77.

[56.] *Book of Concord*, 124.

[57.] *Book of Concord*, 48.

[58.] Bonhoeffer is referring to the Augsburg Confession XVI/4–5 (*Book of Concord*, 48ff.).

[59.] The new numbering is Apology of the Augsburg Confession XVI/3 (*Book of Concord*, 231).

[60.] The words "in regard to the content of the law" replace "insofar as the content of the law, thus of works, is concerned."

[61.] [Translation by Lisa Dahill.—MB] Cf. *Book of Concord*, 124.

Thus the government is placed under the law of God and in the service of God. The law of the Decalogue preached by the church is implemented by the government by means of force. The sword is given to the government for this purpose. To be sure, the confessional writings presuppose that reason will dictate to the government the same law as the Decalogue; thus they do not reckon with the possibility of an opposition in principle between the lex naturae and the Decalogue.[62] Yet this does not signify a double grounding of government in natural law and revealed law; instead, it is only because both have been declared to be identical[63] (see above, section 5) that natural law, reason, can be given as the basis for governmental action. Natural law can never claim divine authority against the Decalogue. Although, or rather because, the government has its origin in God's law as proclaimed by the church and serves it, it has its own worth over against the church that proclaims the gospel. It has this worth, not in a freedom from God's law or the Decalogue that is grounded in its own law, but in the[64] obedience with which it brings about the implementation of God's law by means of its action. Insofar as it does God's will in this way, punishing evil and rewarding good,[65] it glorifies its divine office, it has a claim to obedience, and rulers may have a clean conscience (AC XVI/65).[66] The confessional writings laud the Protestant doctrine, which has restored to government its own worth over against the Roman human statutes.[67] In this way, the doctrine of the iustitia civilis serves polemically to free and honor natural, worldly life under the Decalogue over against the Roman doctrine of the perfection of monastic life. Yet when a natural law asserts itself against the law of God in the Decalogue, when the power of government no longer wishes to serve the Decalogue (a case that the confessional writings do not consider), this perverted nature and reason cannot in that case lay claim to their own divine law; instead, they must be placed under the law of God by means of proclamation. For the confessional writings the "natural" is determined solely by the Decalogue.[68]

609

[62.] Cf. Schlink, *Theology of the Lutheran Confessions*, 263–64.

[63.] Cf. Schlink, *Theology of the Lutheran Confessions*, 240–41.

[64.] The words, "from . . . the" replace the following phrase in the manuscript: "as revealed in the Decalogue, but in their."

[65.] Cf. Rom. 13:2-4.

[66.] The new numbering is Apology of the Augsburg Confession XVI/13 (*Book of Concord*, 232–33).

[67.] Cf. Schlink, *Theology of the Lutheran Confessions*, 71; Augsburg Confession XX/1–39 (*Book of Concord*, 52–57); Apology of the Augsburg Confession XVI/13 and XXVII/17–20 (*Book of Concord*, 232–33 and 280).

[68.] On Bonhoeffer's understanding of the "natural," see *DBWE* 6:171–78.

8. The one proclaiming the primus usus legis is primarily the church, sec-ondarily the government, head of the family, and master. The church pro-claims the primus usus by preaching the entire law in all three usus, thus indirectly; the government proclaims the primus usus directly. The church proclaims the primus usus in the service of the gospel; the government pro-claims it as an end in itself. The Decalogue belongs in the church *and* in city hall.[69]

9. Hearers of the primus usus legis are the "unbelievers, the unruly, and   610
the disobedient."[70] Thus it is *people,* not orders as such, who are being addressed. The orders belong instead, according to the confessional writ-ings, more on the side of those doing the proclaiming. For the confessional writings there is no theological problem about *whether* to preach to unbeliev-ers or about *what* to preach to them. Even the practical problem of reach-ing the unbelievers is assumed [to be solved]: some are reached by the church, others by the government. Although the confessional writings pre-sumably understand unbelievers to refer to a certain group of persons, this conception founders insofar as, according to the confessions, even Chris-tians themselves are still in the flesh and for this reason are in need of the primus usus legis just as fully as are unbelievers (cf. the New Testament vice lists).[71] Conversely, the unruly, the non-Christians, also stand under the call of the gospel and fall under the proclamation of the law for the sake of the gospel. There is no proclamation *solely* for unbelievers, but only the sort that applies to unbelievers *as well.* A clear division into two groups of persons is theologically inappropriate. Although the confessional writings do not explicitly preclude this understanding, it nevertheless cannot be rec-onciled with their theological assertions.

10. *The primus usus and the gospel.*
    a) The primus usus stands in tension with the gospel because it demands a righteousness of works and thereby makes people presumptuous (Smalc.

[69.] This is a reference to the antinomian thesis attributed to Johann Agricola: "Deca-logus ["The Decalogue"] belongs in city hall, not in the pulpit" ("Against the Antino-minians," *LW* 47:99–119 [WA 39/1:344, 30]). On the antinomian controversy, cf. Martin Brecht, *Martin Luther,* 3:158–60. On Bonhoeffer's own repudiation of antinomianism, cf. "'Personal' and 'Objective' Ethics," 2/13, ed. note 40.

[70.] The quotation reads: "The law has been given . . . that through it external disci-pline may be maintained against the unruly and the disobedient" (Epitome VI/1 [*Book of Concord,* 502]); Bonhoeffer himself adds "unbelievers." Cf. also the Solid Declaration VI/1 (*Book of Concord,* 587).

[71.] Cf. Rom. 1:24-32; Gal. 5:19-21, et passim, cf. also *DBWE* 4:263–66.

Art., "Concerning the Law"; SDec V/10).[72] For this reason the iustitia civilis is sin and hypocrisy before the gospel (AC II/34, IV/35).[73] "'Whatever does not proceed from faith is sin.' For a person must be acceptable to God beforehand . . . , before that person's works are at all pleasing to him" (SDec IV/8).[74] The primus usus legis is "sublated" [aufgehoben][75] (in the double sense of the word) by the gospel. It is broken and fulfilled. In following Jesus, the Sabbath is desecrated,[76] father and mother are deserted,[77] and God is obeyed more than are human beings;[78] yet precisely in following him the sanctification of the feast day,[79] the honoring of parents, and worldly obedience in faith are all the more truly fulfilled.[80]

b) *The primus usus legis* is *related* to the gospel: 1.) through this use of the law arises the worldly order, which according to God's will preserves the world from disorder and arbitrariness;[81] 2.) within this order human beings receive from God all good gifts of earthly life and are able to do good works through faith in the gospel. In the confessional writings this idea, that worldly orders are there for the sake of Christian life flowing from faith in the gospel, takes precedence over the conception that the orders[82] serve as the presupposition for deliverance by the gospel. 3.) The government, which protects these orders, is concerned with the maintenance of the Christian proclamation—"God the Lord demands this of *all* kings and princes . . ." (AC XXI/44)[83]—and, as God's order, is itself "preserved and defended by God against the devil" (AC VIII/50).[84] 4.) Within the iustitia civilis, following the First Commandment means going to church, listening to the

---

[72.] *Book of Concord,* 311–12: This sort of presumption comes about because some people imagine that they "can and do keep the law by their own powers" (*Book of Concord,* 583).

[73.] *Book of Concord,* 117, 126.

[74.] *Book of Concord,* 575, citing Rom. 14:23.

[75.] [When Bonhoeffer uses *aufheben* in a technical Hegelian sense, it is often translated "to sublate," which means that the "thesis" (here the *primus usus legis*) is both negated by and fulfilled in a new synthesis (here the gospel).—MB]

[76.] Mark 2:23-28 and parallels; Mark 3:1-6 and parallels.

[77.] Matt. 10:37 and parallels; Mark 3:31-35 and parallels.

[78.] Acts 5:29, cited in the Augsburg Confession XVI (*Book of Concord,* 50). Cf. Schlink, *Theology of the Lutheran Confessions,* 263–64.

[79.] Exod. 20:8-11; this corresponds to the third commandment in the Lutheran enumeration.

[80.] Honoring parents and worldly obedience both correspond to the Fourth Commandment, Exod. 20:12; see the Large Catechism (*Book of Concord,* 400–410). Cf. *DBWE* 6: 296–97.

[81.] Cf. Schlink, *Theology of the Lutheran Confessions,* 228–29 and 237–38.

[82.] The following is crossed out in the manuscript: "of preservation."

[83.] *Book of Concord,* 244–45 [trans. altered].

[84.] *Book of Concord,* 183.

sermon,[85] listening to the gospel, and thinking about it to a certain extent;[86] here one is not to "wait until God pours his gifts into them from heaven without means" (SDec II/53, 46, 24).[87] The access to this "means," to the sermon, is the closest possible connection and sharpest distinction between primus usus and gospel. To be sure, within the primus usus this obedience remains external worship and sin.[88] Yet precisely this itself becomes the "prerequisite" for faith in the gospel, even as it is simultaneously its most extreme contradiction. 5.) The gospel instructs us in gratitude for every worldly order in which it is found. It does not allow us to expect anything good from disorder. But it also calls us to the knowledge of Jesus Christ, through whom, for whom, and for whose sake all things are created.[89]

    c) *The primus usus legis cannot be separated from the proclamation of the gospel.* Because this use of the law applies to unbelievers and believers (Ep VI/6,[90] SDec VI/9),[91] because it is not a method of proclamation, but instead a dimension of the "one unchanging will of God,"[92] it cannot be separated from the other two usus. There is no Christian preaching of works without preaching the recognition of sin and the fulfillment of the law. Yet the law cannot be preached without the gospel. To be sure, the confessional writings see law and gospel proclaimed differently in individual words of scripture ("In some places it communicates the law. In other places it communicates the promise concerning Christ..." AC/5).[93] Nevertheless, at the same time they perceive law and gospel bound together always, from the Decalogue to the preaching of the cross; and they teach that from the beginning both proclamations have existed "alongside each other"—that is, not sequentially (SDec V/23).[94] Thus, in the final analysis it is not the preacher but

612

    [85.] Cf. Solid Declaration II/53 (*Book of Concord,* 554).

    [86.] Solid Declaration II/24 (*Book of Concord,* 549); here Bonhoeffer is drawing directly from the text.

    [87.] [*Book of Concord,* 554, 553, 448–49.—MB] The preceding quotation is from the Solid Declaration II/46 (*Book of Concord,* 553).

    [88.] Cf. Augsburg Confession XVIII (*Book of Concord,* 50–53); Apology of the Augsburg Confession IV/130–31 and XVIII/7 (*Book of Concord,* 141 and 234).

    [89.] Cf. 1 Cor. 8:6; John 1:3; Heb. 1:2.

    [90.] *Book of Concord,* 503.

    [91.] *Book of Concord,* 588–89.

    [92.] Cf. Solid Declaration VI/3: "according to the eternal and unchanging will of God" (*Book of Concord,* 587).

    [93.] *Book of Concord,* 121.

    [94.] *Book of Concord,* 585. [Again, Bonhoeffer's thinking here differs radically from that of his contemporaries, who sought to detach the law (as a "Jewish influence") from the gospel. Moreover, Bonhoeffer's point here, that the relationship between law and gospel is not sequential, but that they coexist as equals, would seem to argue against the Christian supersessionist view in which Christianity "replaces" Judaism. See also ed.

God alone who distinguishes law and gospel.[95] Wherever the primus usus is isolated, it turns into moralistic preaching and ceases to be God's living word. It is clericalism and hypocrisy[96] to preach only works to a person or a group of persons and to be satisfied with their external fulfillment, while withholding the entire proclamation of the law and gospel. The cleric who spouts moralism can engender only hypocrites [Heuchler]. The interpretation of the Decalogue in the Large Catechism[97] is the best practical instruction in the right preaching of the primus usus.

613

d) *The primus usus has its origin and goal in the gospel.* Because the gospel is to be preached to all people, because Jesus Christ became human and died for the sins of all people, because he procured salvation for his enemies, the Christian proclamation is directed to all people with the call to faith. For this reason it has no *independent* interest in the establishment of a certain civic order.[98] It calls for civic order, because it calls to faith. Because God in Christ loved human beings and the world, order should exist among human beings and in the world as well. Because human beings belong to God in grace, they should also obey God in works. Because a congregation is present, justice, peace,[99] order should and can be present. Faith remains the prerequisite and origin of all works. Only from this perspective, however, is the gospel now also the goal of the primus usus. God desires external order not just because the gospel is present but in order that it may be present. Understood in this way, the primus usus has a "pedagogical" character on account of Christ (AC IV/22).[100] Thus the sequence "gospel and law" as well as that of "law and gospel" has its own validity.[101] In the confessional

---

note 40. At the same time, however, note Bonhoeffer's pejorative use of "Pharisaism" later in the essay; see the discussion of the use of this term in the editor's introduction, pp. 26–27.—MB]

[95.] See Martin Luther: "Non est homo, qui vivit in terris, qui sciat discernere inter legem et evangelium [The human being living on earth is not the one who knows how to distinguish between law and gospel]. I would have thought I knew this because I have written so long and voluminously on the subject, but when it comes down to getting it right, I see clearly that my attempt falls far, really far from the target. Therefore God alone should and must be the holiest authority" (WA TR 2, 3,20, no. 1234).

[96.] [Here Bonhoeffer uses *Pharisäismus*; see the discussion of the use of this term in the editor's introduction, pp. 26–27.—MB]

[97.] *Book of Concord,* 386–431.

[98.] Cf. Schlink, *Theology of the Lutheran Confessions,* 247–48 and 226–27.

[99.] Cf. Barmen Thesis 5: according to divine "arrangement," the state is "to provide for justice and peace" (*Creeds of the Church,* 521).

[100.] *Book of Concord:* "The law was our disciplinarian (Gal. 3:24)" (124).

[101.] Here Bonhoeffer is referring to the debate sparked by Karl Barth's statement: "I should like . . . to call attention to the fact that I shall not speak about 'Law and Gospel' but about '*Gospel and Law.*' The traditional order, 'Law and Gospel,' has a perfect right in

writings the second order is predominant. In both sequences, however, the gospel is the "proper" word of God.[102]

e) *Primus usus and congregation.* In the primus usus unbelievers are   614
addressed on the basis of their being called into the congregation. Apart from this calling, the church has no authority for the proclamation of the law. This assertion is not articulated by the confessional writings but is a necessary conclusion from the preceding material.

f) *Primus usus and the reign of Christ.* The confessional writings address the biblical teaching of the lordship of Jesus Christ over all earthly rulers and powers[103] exclusively in the article on Christology, but not in connection with the doctrine of worldly orders.[104]

11. *Some conclusions and questions.*

a. The proclamation of the primus usus extends as far as that of the gospel; it is therefore unlimited according to God's will. But it encounters a concrete internal limit in human unbelief and disobedience, an external limit in the power of a government to oppose the proclamation, to hinder it, and to deprive those who proclaim it of all worldly responsibility. As long as Christians stand in worldly responsibility, the orientation provided by the primus usus is part of their confession of Christ. The more the situation of Revelation 13 emerges through proclamation and the more Christians are not those who share responsibility for the injustice of the world but are themselves those who suffer injustice, the more the worldly responsibility laid on them by the primus usus will prove valid by obedient suffering and earnest discipline in the congregation. But even the congregation in the catacombs[105] never has the universality of its mission taken from it. In preaching law and gospel, it professes this mission and thereby keeps alive its responsibility for the world. The congregation can never content itself with cultivating its own life; to do so means denying its Lord. Even in places where it can still preserve the iustitia civilis only among its own members, because its word is not received by the world, it does this in service to the   615
world and as part of its universal mission. Its experience will be that the world is in trouble and that the reign of Christ is not of this world,[106] but precisely

---

its place.... It must not, however, define the structure of the whole teaching to be outlined here" ("Gospel and Law," in *Community, State, and Church*, 71); see p. 96 for Barth's defense of the sequence "law and gospel."

[102.] Cf. Schlink, *Theology of the Lutheran Confessions*, 136–40.

[103.] Cf. 1 Cor. 15:24; Eph. 1:21; Col. 2:10, 15; 1 Peter 3:22; Luke 1:52.

[104.] Cf. the Augsburg Confession III (*Book of Concord*, 38–39).

[105.] Cf. 2/13, ed. note 27.

[106.] 1 John 5:19; John 18:36; cited in the Augsburg Confession XXVIII (*Book of Concord*, 92).

here it will be reminded of its mission to the world. Otherwise it would become a religious club.[107] The mission of the congregation is not limited in principle. It will have to make its own decision in each case about how it implements this mission in light of the signs of the time. To understand itself too directly within the situation of Revelation 13 will always be a grave danger for the congregation and the full scope of its mission. Apocalyptic proclamation can be a flight from the primus usus legis.[108] The congregation will neither compensate for the weakness of the word of God with religious fanaticism[109] nor confuse its own frailty with the weakness of the word.

b. In contrast to the other usus, in the confessional writings the primus usus is not given any explicit biblical grounding. Does this mean that it is unbiblical? 1. The Bible knows of no preaching of the primus usus detached from the gospel. 2. The Bible knows of no difference *in principle* between preaching to unbelievers and believers in the sense of a division between primus usus legis and gospel. 3. The Bible teaches, however, that the proclamation and the conduct of the congregation occur in responsibility for the world. There is absolutely no evasion of this responsibility; for God loved the world[110] and desires that all people be helped.[111] 4. The Bible's position regarding the orders of the world occurs primarily in concrete instructions to the congregation (Romans 13. Philemon. Tables of household duties.[112] Vice lists). There is, however, also direct preaching to the governing authorities (Paul before Felix: about the resurrection of the dead, about faith in Christ, about righteousness, chastity, and future judgment Acts 24:14ff.; before Festus: reference to the political right of protection against arbitrariness 25:9ff.; before Agrippa 26:1ff.; John before Herod Matt. 14:4). In each case the issue is one of concrete obedience[113] to the One to whom all power in heaven and on earth has been given.[114]

c. The silence within the confessional writings as to the form of the proclamation of the primus usus—whether it is [confined to] sermon and instruction, that is, whether it may be directed to those who govern only through addressing the congregation, or also through direct public or private

616

[107.] Cf. "State and Church," 2/10.

[108.] Cf. "Thoughts on William Paton's Book," 2/11, point 1.

[109.] Cf. *DBWE* 6:344: "Isolated from each other, however, the exclusive claim leads to fanaticism and sectarianism, the all-encompassing claim to the secularization and capitulation of the church."

[110.] Cf. John 3:16.

[111.] [NRSV: "saved."—MB] Cf. 1 Tim. 2:4.

[112.] Cf., e.g., Eph. 5:22—6:9; Col. 3:8—4:1.

[113.] Cf. Schlink: "God is feared and loved only in concrete obedience to his concrete commandments" (*Theology of the Lutheran Confessions*, 112).

[114.] Cf. Matt. 28:18.

speaking to persons in government, whether it must contain the explicit reference to the gospel each and every time, whether it consists of directly naming concrete sin or the general proclamation of the law, whether it consists in the form of protest, warning, or request—this silence gives proclaimers who face these questions freedom for a concrete, responsible decision to the extent that their awareness of the subject they are pursuing and of the status in which they find themselves (as preachers, heads of households, rulers) is grounded in faith. In fact, there is concrete evidence from the Reformation period for all these possibilities.[115]

d. The primus usus legis is just as far removed from moralistic preaching (which perceives its actual task as taking a position on events of the day, thereby attributing to worldly orders a significance in their own right and understanding the gospel only as a means to an end) as from the sermon that is "religious" in principle (which separates the gospel from a person's life in the world).[116] Both forms of preaching are determined thematically and are thus an arbitrary curtailment and denial of the living Word of God that places us into concrete worldly responsibility. Instead of the false juxtaposition of political and religious themes, the true distinction and connection of law and gospel is to take its place in the sermon. A relatively sure sign of the false theme is the polemical apologetics that dominate these kinds of sermons; even the greatest religious or "prophetic" emphasis cannot conceal that the world and the human being, and not the Word of God, are the standard of proclamation. But with this false theme, the listener is deprived of both the claim and the comfort of Jesus Christ.   617

e. The primus usus signifies the interest on the part of Christian proclamation in the content of the law. It excludes a purely formal definition of the law. It refers not to the responsible person in a conflict of duties[117] but to the realization of certain conditions; not to the Christian within the worldly order but to the form of the worldly order according to the will of God.[118] In the realm of the iustitia civilis there is a possible and necessary cooperation between Christians and non-Christians in clarifying certain

---

[115.] Cf., e.g., Luther, "Temporal Authority: To What Extent It Should Be Obeyed, 1523" (*LW* 45:79–129 [WA 11:245–81]).

[116.] In the manuscript "person" replaces "Christian."

[117.] Cf. "The Structure of Responsible Life," *DBWE* 6:257–89.

[118.] Cf. *DBWE* 6:163–66, 258–59 (regarding the establishment of certain "conditions"). A line in the manuscript used to transpose the words "It refers," or *ist in ihr gemeint,* was understood by Eberhard Bethge as intending to strike them out, making the sentence grammatically incomplete. Therefore, in the 6th German edition of the *Ethics,* utilizing a passage from "'Personal' and 'Real' Ethics" [the previous translation being cited here used "Ethos"], *Ethics* (Simon & Schuster, 1995), 321 (*Ethik,* 6th ed., 347), Bethge completed the sentence: "it is not concerned with the christianization of worldly institutions or with

subjects and in advancing concrete tasks. Because of their fundamentally different foundations, the results emerging from this cooperation have the character not of the proclamation of the word of God but of responsible deliberation or demand on the basis of human perception.[119] This distinction must be preserved under all circumstances. Cooperation can be desired and promoted by both worldly and spiritual rule. Whether cooperation among Christians of different denominations in matters of the iustitia civilis can lead beyond this to common ecclesial proclamation depends on the unanimity of interpretation of the word of God in faith in Jesus Christ. While the concrete form taken within the proclamation relates primarily to the punishment of concrete sins, in the realm of responsible deliberation and demand this concreteness can and must arrive at positive results.

618

12. *Critique of the usus doctrine* as found in the confessional writings.

a. The concept of the usus is misleading in respect to its subject.

b. The relation of the primus usus to unbelievers threatens to lead to a splintering of the unity of the law and of the wholeness of the proclamation.

c. The differentiation of the three usus ultimately lacks clarity. The primus usus itself contains an element of preaching that calls for repentance (the "threat"), just as the secundus and tertius usus contain an element of the primus usus. This lack of clarity is grounded in the distinction between groups of people that is connected with the usus doctrine and in an understanding of the usus, which has not been fully avoided, as different methods of proclamation.

d. The relationship of the preaching of the primus usus and natural law is not clear. In its present form, the doctrine of the primus usus can provide the impetus for a false theology of the orders.[120]

e. A renewal of the usus doctrine would need either to portray the one law in its threefold form as preaching works, preaching recognition of sin, and preaching the fulfillment of the law (by Christ and faith), avoiding

---

their incorporation in the Church, but with their genuine worldliness, their 'naturalness' in obedience to God's word" (*Ethics* [Simon & Schuster, 1995], 312 [*Ethik*, 6th ed., 338]).

[119.] Cf. Bonhoeffer's phrase "on the authority of responsible counsel" ("On the Possibility of the Word of the Church to the World," *DBWE* 6:361).

[120.] *Theologie der Ordnungen* is the title of a 1935 monograph by Paul Althaus. According to Althaus, "orders" are "means of ongoing divine creation" (13) and can, therefore, in their own right, even independently of the preaching of the law and the gospel, be recognized within the historical "destiny" of a people as "orders of creation" (cf. 29–39). On a scrap of paper with notes for this report Bonhoeffer writes, among other things, "*A Theology of the Orders*," as well as the keywords for the three usus from point 2 that are taken up once again in paragraph e, "works, recognition, fulfillment... transformation!" (*NL*, A 73,14; see *ZE*, 108).

distinctions made by the hearer; or (and) to treat the validity and effect of the entire law of God (in its threefold form) as a systematically separate question. More precisely, this is a question of its *validity* in the twofold perspective applying to unbelievers and believers and of its *effect* in the fourfold perspective as righteousness of works, discipline leading to Christ, despair, and gracious instruction. The vacillation of Lutheran dogmatics between duplex, triplex, and quadruplex usus legis[121] can be explained by the mixing up of all these questions, the question of form being triple, the question of validity double, the question of effect quadruple. Every attempt to absorb one question within another necessarily leads to confusion. The concept of the usus, however, harbors the danger of such confusion within itself

619

19. Fragment of an Essay: What Does It Mean to Tell the Truth?[1]

From the moment in our lives in which we become capable of speech, we are taught that our words must be true. What does this mean? What does "telling the truth" mean?[2] Who requires this of us?

[121.] "double, triple, or quadruple use of the law"; cf. Schmid, *Doctrinal Theology of the Evangelical Lutheran Church*, 508–20.

[1.] *NL*, A 72,8; handwritten; previously published in English in Bonhoeffer, *Ethics* (New York: Macmillan, 1955), 363–72; and *Ethics* (New York: Simon & Schuster, 1995), 358–67); see also the notes from Tegel prison, *NL*, A 75,122. In his letters from Tegel prison (cf. *LPP* [*DBW* 8]), Bonhoeffer reports several times on his work on this essay: a) on November 18, 1943: "Incidentally, I have written an essay on 'What does "telling the truth" mean?'" (*LPP*, 130 [*DBW* 8:189]; trans. altered); b) on December 5, 1943: "Also, 'telling the truth' (about which I wrote an essay) means, to my mind, to say how something is in reality, i.e., respect for secrecy, for trust, for concealment" (*LPP*, 158–59 [*DBW* 8:229]; trans. altered); c) on December 15, 1943: "I am writing again on my essay, 'What does "telling the truth" mean?'" (*LPP*, 163 [*DBW* 8:238]; trans. altered). Presumably the essay reached the manuscript form in which it appears here by the time of this final report about it. Bonhoeffer doubtless began it under the impact of the interrogations and the urgent accompanying constraint to conceal the truth (see the drafts of letters to Manfred Roeder, 1/226, and 1/228). The double sheet of paper (*NL*, A 75,122, *ZE*, 143–46) whose first page bears the title "The Eighth Commandment" demonstrates, however, that Bonhoeffer planned a fundamental ethical reflection on the problem, going far beyond this original impetus. The topics that Bonhoeffer noted on the four pages of the double sheet of paper are by no means all treated in this essay fragment.

[2.] In the archival copy, on the second page of the rough draft of his Morning Prayer for Prisoners, written in Tegel prison for Christmas 1943 (see *LPP*, 139–41 [*DBW* 8:204–8]), the following words are crossed out: "I. [= Bonhoeffer's enumeration on this page] From that point in our life in which we are capable of creating coherent words and sentences, we are taught that our words must be true. This is the same period in which we are told about Santa Claus [*Knecht Ruprecht*] and the Easter bunny and in which Grimm's fairy tales are the air we breathe. What does it mean that our words must be true? What does 'telling the truth' mean? It means to say how something is in reality."

620   It is clear that initially it is our parents who order our relationship with them by demanding truthfulness;[3] and accordingly this demand is also related and limited initially—in the sense our parents intend it—to this closest circle of the family. We note further that the relationship expressed in this demand cannot simply be reversed. The truthfulness of the child toward parents is by its very nature something different from that of parents toward their child. While the life of the small child lies open to the parents and the child's word is to reveal all that is hidden and secret, the same cannot be true of the reverse relationship. In regard to truthfulness, therefore, the parents' claim on the child is something different from that of the child on the parents.

From this we can see immediately that "telling the truth" means different things, depending on where one finds oneself. The relevant relationships must be taken into account. The question must be asked whether and in what way a person is justified in demanding truthful speech from another. Just as language between parents and children is different, in accord with who they are, from that between husband and wife, between friend and friend, between teacher and student, between governing authority and subject, between enemy and enemy, so too is the truth contained in this language different.

The objection that arises immediately, however, that persons owe truthful speech not to this or that person but to God alone, is correct as long as we do not thereby disregard that even God is not a general principle but is
621   the Living One who has placed me in a life that is fully alive and within this life demands my service. Those who say "God" are not allowed simply to cross out the given world in which I live; otherwise they would be speaking not of the God who in Jesus Christ came into the world but rather of some sort of metaphysical idol.[4] This is precisely the point, namely, how I bring into effect in my concrete life, with its manifold relationships, the truthful speech I owe to God. The truthfulness of our words that we owe to God

---

[3.] Cf. *DBWE* 4:128–31 on Matt. 4:33-37, under the heading "Truthfulness."

[4.] This sentence, which picks up Karl Barth's polemical use of language, refers not only to the image of God in the Greek doctrine but to every "absolutised image of man" "posited by human invention" (*Church Dogmatics* 2/2:24), which, in distinction from the "mystery of the living and life-giving God," is "the mystery of an enthroned but lifeless idol" (ibid., 2/2:31). This also corresponds to Bonhoeffer's questions in his letter to Eberhard Bethge on December 5, 1943: "Why is it that in the Old Testament [people] tell lies vigorously and often to the glory of God (I've now collected the passages), kill, deceive, rob, divorce, and even fornicate (see the genealogy of Jesus), doubt, blaspheme, and curse, whereas in the New Testament there is nothing of all this?" (*LPP,* 157 [*DBW* 8:227]). Cf. the compilation of Bible passages in *NL,* A 75, 122 (*ZE,* 143): Genesis 3; 13; 18:15; 22; 27; 31; 34; 37; 44; Exod. 1:1, 19-20; 3:18.

must take on concrete form in the world. Our word should be truthful not in principle but concretely. A truthfulness that is not concrete is not truthful at all before God.

"Telling the truth" is therefore not a matter only of one's intention [Gesinnung][5] but also of accurate perception and of serious consideration of the real circumstances. The more diverse the life circumstances of people are, the more responsibility they have and the more difficult it is "to tell the truth." The child, who stands in only one life relationship, namely, that with his or her parents, does not yet have anything to ponder and weigh. But already the next circle of life in which the child is placed, namely, school, brings the first difficulties. Pedagogically it is therefore of the greatest importance that in some way—not to be discussed here—the parents clarify the differences of these circles of life to their child and make his or her responsibilities understandable.

Telling the truth must therefore be learned. This sounds repellent to   622
those who believe that one's character alone must suffice, and that if this is blameless all the rest is child's play. Since it is the case, however, that the ethical cannot be detached from reality, the ever-greater capacity to perceive reality is a necessary component of ethical action.[6] But with reference to the issue we are discussing, action consists in speaking. *What is real is to be expressed in words.* This is what truthful speech consists of. Yet this assertion unavoidably contains the question of the "how" of language. What matters is the "right word" for any given circumstance. To discover this is a matter of long, earnest, and continual effort that is based in experience and the perception of reality. In order to say how something is real—i.e., to speak truthfully—one's gaze and thought must be oriented toward how the real is in God, and through God, and toward God.[7]

It is superficial to limit the problem of truthful speech to individual cases of conflict. Every word I speak stands under the stipulation that it be true; quite apart from the truthfulness of its content, the relationship it expresses between me and another person is already true or untrue. I can fawn over a person, or I can be overbearing, or I can dissimulate without expressing any

---

[5.] Cf. a similar viewpoint in Nohl, *Die sittlichen Grunderfahrungen,* which argues that what is "ethical" is not solely a matter of one's "intention" or "moral orientation," *Gesinnung.* "It must associate with reality and 'prove itself' there" (84–85). In working on his *Ethics,* Bonhoeffer had familiarized himself with Nohl's book.

[6.] Cf. Bonhoeffer's remarks on "accordance with reality" in "History and Good [1]," *DBWE* 6:222–24, and in *DBWE* 6:261–64 et passim.

[7.] Cf. *DBWE* 6:48: "All things appear as in a distorted mirror if they are not seen and recognized in God. All that is—so to speak—given, all laws and norms, are abstractions, as long as God is not known in faith to be the ultimate reality."

material falsehood, and my word is nevertheless untrue because I am destroying and undermining the reality of the relationship between husband and wife, or supervisor and subordinate, etc. The single word is always a portion of an entire reality that seeks expression in the word. Depending on the person to whom I am speaking, the person who is questioning me, or what I am discussing, my word, if it seeks to be truthful, must vary. A truthful word is not an entity constant in itself but is as lively as life itself. Where this word 623 detaches itself from life and from the relationship to the concrete other person,[8] where "the truth is told" without regard for the person to whom it is said, there it has only the appearance of truth but not its essence.[9]

The cynic is the one who, claiming to "tell the truth" in all places and at all times and to every person in the same way, only puts on display a dead idolatrous image of the truth. By putting a halo on his own head for being a zealot for the truth[10] who can take no account of human weaknesses, he destroys the living truth between persons. He violates shame,[11] desecrates the mystery, breaks trust,[12] betrays the community in which he lives, and smiles arrogantly over the havoc he has wrought and over the human weakness that "can't bear the truth." He says that the truth is destructive and demands its victims, and he feels like a god over the feeble creatures and does not realize that he is serving Satan.

There is such a thing as Satan's truth.[13] Its nature is to deny everything real under the guise of the truth. It feeds on hatred against the real, against the world created and loved by God. It gives the impression of carrying out God's judgment on the fall of the real into sin. But God's truth judges what is created out of love; Satan's truth judges what is created out of envy and

---

[8.] Cf. the sheet contained in *NL*, A 75, 122: "Eighth Commandment has to do not with the subject matter but with the neighbor" (*ZE*, 144).

[9.] Bonhoeffer's reflections here touch on Heidegger's thoughts on the nature of the truth. Truth is originally grounded not in sentences but in "being in the world"; the words participate in the "openness" that comes from being in the world (see Heidegger, *Being and Time*, 256–73). From a letter from his father, Karl Bonhoeffer, dated July 11, 1943 (*LPP*, 75 [*DBW* 8:112]), we know that Bonhoeffer had wrestled with Heidegger while in Tegel prison.

[10.] On the "tyrannical despiser of humanity," see *DBWE* 6:84–87; cf. Bonhoeffer's own reflections on this text on December 5 and 15, 1943 (*LPP*, 158–59 and 163 [*DBW* 8: 228 and 238]); finally, cf. *NL*, A 75, 122: "Only the *cynic* is entirely 'truthful'" (*ZE*, 145).

[11.] On shame as a "sign of disunion" and as a seeking after "covering," see *DBWE* 6: 303–7; in Bonhoeffer's letter to Eberhard Bethge on December 5, 1943, we read: "God is the one who made clothes for them" (*LPP*, 158 [*DBW* 8:228]; trans. altered).

[12.] See *NL*, A 75, 122: "Mystery, silence. Intimacy—trust" (*ZE*, 145). [The German words *Vertraulichkeit*, "intimacy," and *Vertrauen*, "trust," have the same root.—MB]

[13.] *Satanswahrheit*. The 6th German edition of *Ethics* erroneously printed *Satansweisheit*, "Satan's wisdom."

hatred. God's truth became flesh in the world and is alive in the real; Satan's   624
truth is the death of all that is real.[14]

The concept of the living truth is dangerous and arouses the suspicion
that the truth can and may be adapted to the given situation, so that the
concept of truth utterly dissolves, and falsehood and truth draw indistin-
guishably close to each other. Also, what was said about the necessary discernment of the real could be misunderstood in such a way that the measure
of truth I am willing to say to the other person is determined by a calculat-
ing or pedagogical attitude toward him or her. It is important to keep this
danger in mind. The only possible way to counteract it, however, is through
attentive discernment of the relevant contents and limits that the real itself
specifies for one's utterance in order to make it a truthful one. Yet the dangers inherent in the concept of living truth must never cause a person to
forsake this concept in favor of the formal, cynical conception of truth.

Let me try to illustrate this. Every word lives and has its home within a
certain radius. The word spoken in the family is different from the word
spoken at the office or in public. The word born in the warmth of personal
relationship freezes in the cold air of public exposure. The word of command appropriate to a civil service position would break the bonds of trust
in the family if spoken there. Every word should have and retain its own
place. As a result of the increasing profligacy of public discourse in newspapers and the radio, the nature and limits of different words are no longer
clearly perceived; in fact, what is distinctive about a personal word, for
example, is nearly destroyed. Chatter has replaced authentic words. Words
no longer have any weight. There is too much talking. Yet when the limits
of different words blur together, when words become rootless, homeless,
then what is said loses hold of the truth; indeed, at that point lying almost   625
inevitably emerges. When the various orders of life no longer respect one
another, then words become untrue. For example, a teacher asks a child in
front of the class whether it is true that the child's father often comes home
drunk. This is true, but the child denies it. The teacher's question brings
the child into a situation that he or she does not yet have the maturity to
handle. To be sure, the child perceives that this question is an unjustified
invasion into the order of the family and must be warded off. What takes
place in the family is not something that should be made known to the class.
The family has its own secret[15] that it must keep. The teacher disregards

---

[14.] Cf. the keywords given in *NL,* A 75,122: "John 8 [:44] Genesis 3 the lie and
Satan—Christ truth" (*ZE,* 145). On Gen. 3:1-3, see *DBWE* 3:103–10.

[15.] Cf. Bonhoeffer's letter to Eberhard Bethge on December 5, 1943: "since the fall
there must be reticence and secrecy." "In my opinion the greatness of Stifter lies in his refusal
to force his way into a person's inner life . . . Inquisitiveness is alien to him" (*LPP,* 158).

the reality of this order. In responding, the child would have to find a way to observe equally the orders of the family and those of the school. The child cannot do this yet; he or she lacks the experience, the discernment, and the capacity for appropriate expression. In flatly saying no to the teacher's question, the response becomes untrue, to be sure; at the same time, however, it expresses the truth that the family is an order sui generis where the teacher was not justified to intrude. Of course, one could call the child's answer a lie; all the same, this lie contains more truth—i.e., it corresponds more closely to the truth—than if the child had revealed the father's weakness before the class. The child acted rightly according to the measure of the child's perception. Yet it is the teacher alone who is guilty of the lie. By rebuking the questioner, an experienced person in the child's situation would also have been able to avoid a formal untruth in responding and thereby would have been able to find the "right word" in the situation. Lies on the part of children and inexperienced persons in general[16] can frequently be traced back to their being placed in situations that they cannot

626   fully fathom. For this reason it is questionable whether it makes sense to generalize and extend the concept of lying (which is and ought to be understood as something downright reprehensible) in such a way that it coincides with the concept of a formally untrue statement. Indeed, all of this demonstrates how difficult it is to say what lying really is.

The usual definition, according to which the conscious contradiction between thought and speech is a lie, is completely inadequate.[17] For instance, this definition includes the most harmless April Fool's joke. The concept of the "jocose lie"[18] rooted in Catholic moral theology removes from the lie its decisive characteristics of gravity and malice (just as, in the other direction, it removes from the joke its decisive characteristics of innocent play and freedom), and for this reason it is most infelicitous. The joke has nothing at all to do with the lie and must not be reduced with it to a common denominator. If one then asserts that a lie is the conscious deception of others to their harm, this also would include, e.g., the necessary deception of the enemy in war or in analogous situations (of course, Kant declared that he was too proud ever to tell an untruth, yet at the same time he was compelled to extend this assertion ad absurdum by declaring that

---

[16.] Cf. *NL*, sheet A 75,122: "Why do uneducated and inarticulate [*wortungewandt*] persons lie?" (*ZE*, 145).

[17.] Cf. Schilling: "And yet, strictly speaking," Augustine considers "only the contradiction between thought and statement to be the actual essence of lying" (*Lehrbuch der Moraltheologie*, 2:333). Schilling's book was available to Bonhoeffer in prison.

[18.] Cf. Schilling: "[T]he jocose lie [*Scherzlüge*] and the officious lie [*Dienstlüge*]" are told "for the benefit of the other. According to their nature, *jocose lies* and *officious lies* are venial sins"—that is, "not opposed to the love of God or of neighbor" (*Lehrbuch der Moraltheologie*, 2:336).

he would feel obliged to reveal truthful information on the whereabouts of a friend seeking refuge with him to a criminal in pursuit of the friend).[19] If one characterizes this sort of behavior as a lie, then lying receives a moral consecration and justification that contradicts its meaning in every respect. This leads initially to the conclusion that lying is not to be defined formally by the contradiction between thought and speech. This contradiction is not even a necessary component of lying. In this respect speech that is thoroughly correct and incontestable is nevertheless a lie, such as if a notorious liar once tells "the truth" to throw people off,[20] or if a known ambiguity lurks beneath the appearance of correctness, or the decisive truth remains intentionally hidden. Hence, a deliberate silence can be a lie, even though, on the other hand, it certainly need not be one.

627

These reflections lead to the recognition that the essence of lying is found much deeper than in the contradiction between thought and speech. We could say that the person who stands behind what is said makes it into a lie or the truth. Yet even this is not adequate; for a lie is something objective and must be determined accordingly. Jesus identifies Satan as the "father of lies."[21] Lying is first of all the denial of God as God has been revealed to the world. "Who is the liar but the one who denies that Jesus is the Christ?"[22] Lying is a contradiction of the word of God as it was spoken in Christ and in which creation rests. Consequently, lying is the negation, denial, and deliberate and willful destruction of reality as it is created by God and exists in God to the extent that it takes place through words and silence. Our word in union with the word of God is intended to express what is real, as it is in God, and our silence is to be a sign of the boundary drawn around the word by what is real, as it is in God.

In the effort to articulate the real, we encounter it not as a unified whole but in a condition of disruption and self-contradiction, requiring reconciliation and healing. We find ourselves embedded in various orders of the real, all at the same time, and our word that strives for the reconciliation and healing of the real is nevertheless continually drawn back into the existing disunion and into contradiction. It can only fulfill its purpose of expressing the real, as it is in God, by drawing into itself the existing contradiction as well as the context of the real. The human word, if it is to be true, may not deny the fall into sin any more than the creative and reconciling word of

628

[19.] See Kant, "On a Supposed Right to Lie from Altruistic Motives," in *Critique of Practical Reason and Other Writings in Moral Philosophy,* 346–50. Bonhoeffer refers to this writing in *DBWE* 6:279–80.

[20.] See *DBWE* 6:77: "It is worse to be evil than to do evil. It is worse when a liar tells the truth than when a lover of truth lies."

[21.] John 8:44.

[22.] 1 John 2:22.

God by which all division is overcome.[23] Cynics want to make their word true by always expressing the particular thing they think they understand without regard for reality as a whole. Precisely in this way they utterly destroy the real, and their word becomes untrue, even if it maintains the superficial appearance of correctness. "That which is, is far off, and deep, very deep; who can find it out?" (Eccl. 7:24).

How does my word become true? 1) By recognizing who calls on me to speak and what authorizes me to speak; 2) by recognizing the place in which I stand; 3) by putting the subject I am speaking about into this context.

These considerations tacitly depend on an earlier assumption, that speaking itself stands under certain conditions, that it does not accompany the natural course of one's life in a perpetual flow but has its own place, time, and mission, and therewith its limits.

1. Who or what authorizes or calls on me to speak? Whoever speaks without authorization or without being called upon is a windbag. Because what matters in respect to every word is the double relation to the other person and to a subject matter; this relation must be discernible in every word. An unconnected word is hollow; it contains no truth. This is an essential difference between thought and speech. Thought in itself has no necessary connection to the other person, but only to the subject matter. The claim that you are also allowed to say what you are thinking does not in itself authorize you to do so. Speaking includes the authorization and call given by the other person. Example: in my thoughts I can consider another person to be stupid, ugly, incompetent, corrupt, or alternatively to be clever or full of character; but it is something quite different whether I am justified in speaking this, what causes me to do so, and to whom I express it. Undoubtedly, a justification for speaking emerges from an office that has been bestowed on me. Parents can scold or praise their child, but in contrast the child is justified in doing neither toward his or her parents. A similar relation exists between teacher and students, although the rights of the teacher in regard to the child are more limited than those of the father. Thus the teacher, in criticizing or praising the student, is necessarily confined to certain particular mistakes or accomplishments, while, e.g., broad judgments as to character fall not to the teacher but to the parents. The justification for speech always lies within the boundaries of the concrete office that I fill. If these boundaries are crossed, the word becomes intrusive, arrogant, and, whether scolding or praising, harmful. There are persons who feel themselves called to "tell the truth," as they put it, to everyone who crosses their path.[24]

629

[23.] Cf. "God's Love and the Disintegration of the World," *DBWE* 6:309.

[24.] The manuscript breaks off at this point; points 2 and 3 are not developed.

PART 3
Sermons and Meditations

PART 3
Sermons and Meditations

---

1. Sermon Meditation on Isaiah 9:6-7, Christmas 1940[1] 633

Isaiah 9:6-7

[For a child has been born for us, a son given to us; authority rests upon his shoulders; and he is named Wonderful Counselor, Mighty God, Everlasting Father, Prince of Peace. His authority shall grow continually, and there shall be endless peace for the throne of David and his kingdom. He will establish and uphold it with justice and with righteousness from this time onward and forevermore. The zeal of the LORD of hosts will do this.]

In the midst of calamitous words and signs announcing imminent doom, divine wrath, and terrifying punishment to the apostate people: 1) the birth of the child; 2) his name—inexpressible; 3) his office.[2]

In the midst of the people's deepest guilt and distress, a voice speaks gently and mysteriously, yet full of blessing and assurance, of redemption through the birth of a divine child. There still remain seven hundred years until the time of fulfillment, yet the prophet is so deeply immersed in God's thoughts and decrees that he speaks of what is to come as if he has already seen it. He speaks of the redemptive hour as if he has already stood in adoration before Jesus' manger. "For a child has been born for us." What will take place someday is already real and certain in God's eyes, and this will be the salvation not only of generations to come but also of the prophet who

---

[1.] *NL*, A 63,4; handwritten; previously published in *GS* 4:570–77. For approximate dating, note the similarities in Bonhoeffer's Finkenwalde circular letter of December 1940 (see 1/47). Bonhoeffer's original text contained numerous abbreviations, which were spelled out by the German editors of *DBW* 16.

[2.] This paragraph before the beginning of the actual text appears to be Bonhoeffer's own clarification before he began the sermon.

sees it coming and of his own generation, indeed, of all generations on earth. "For a child has been born *for us.*" No human spirit can speak in this way by its own power. When we do not know what will take place in the next year, how are we to comprehend that someone gazes ahead over centuries? And the times were no more transparent then than they are now. Only the Spirit of God, who encompasses the beginning and the end of the world,

634   can reveal to a chosen person the mystery of the future in a way that compels prophecy to strengthen believers and to warn unbelievers. This voice of the individual, echoing softly through the centuries, here and there coming together with another isolated prophetic voice, is finally taken up into the nocturnal adoration of the shepherds[3] and into the full jubilation of the church-community that trusts in Christ: "for a child has been born for us."

This text speaks of the birth of a child, not the revolutionary deed of a strongman, or the breathtaking discovery of a sage, or the pious deed of a saint. It truly goes beyond anything our minds can grasp: The birth of a child is to bring about the great transformation of all things, is to bring salvation and redemption to all of humanity. That for which kings and statesmen, philosophers and artists, founders of religion and teachers of morals exert themselves in vain now takes place through a newborn child. As if to shame the most powerful human efforts and achievements, a child is placed in the center of world history. A child born of humans, a son given by God. This is the mystery of the redemption of the world; all that is past and all that is to come is encompassed here. The unending mercy of the almighty God comes to us, comes down to us in the form of a child, the Son of God. That this child, this son, is born *for us,* that this human child, this divine son belongs *to me,* that I know him, have him, love him, that I am his and he is mine—on this my life now depends. A child has our lives in his hand.

How do we wish to encounter this child? Have our hands, through the daily work they accomplish, become too hard, too proud, to be folded in adoration at the sight of this child? And our heads that have had to think so many difficult thoughts, solve so many difficult problems—do we hold them too high to be able to still bow in humility before the miracle of this child? Can we for once entirely forget all our efforts, accomplishments, and self-aggrandizements in order to worship like children with the shepherds[4]

635   and the sages from the east[5] before the divine child in the manger? Can we thus, with elderly Simeon,[6] take the child in our arms and in that moment

---

[3.] Cf. Luke 2:15-17.
[4.] Cf. Luke 2:8.
[5.] Cf. Matt. 2:1, 11.
[6.] Cf. Luke 2:25, 28.

perceive the fulfillment of our entire lives?[7] It is truly a strange sight when a strong, proud man kneels before this child, when with simplicity of heart he finds and honors him as his Savior. And most likely many in our old, clever, experienced, self-assured world shake their heads and even laugh with contempt when they hear the faithful Christian cry of salvation, "For a child has been born for us, a son given to us."

"Authority rests upon his shoulders."[8] Authority over all the world is to rest on the weak shoulders of this newborn child! One thing we know: in any case these shoulders will have to bear the entire weight of the world. Along with the cross, all the sin and need of this world will be loaded onto these shoulders. But the authority will consist in this, that the one bearing this load does not collapse but rather brings it to its goal. The authority that lies on the shoulders of the child in the manger consists in patiently bearing human beings and their guilt. Yet this bearing begins in the manger, begins in the place where the eternal Word of God took on human flesh and bore it. In the very lowliness and weakness of the child the authority over all the world has its origin. As a sign of authority over the house, the key used to be hung over the householder's shoulders. That meant that the householder had the power to open and close the door, to choose whom to allow in or to turn away. This is also the manner of authority of the one who bore the cross on his shoulders. He opens in that he forgives sins, and he closes in that he casts out the proud.[9] That is the authority of this child, that he accepts and bears the humble, the lowly, the sinners, and yet defeats and rejects the proud, the arrogant, the righteous.[10]

Who is this child, whom prophets foretell and at whose birth heaven and earth rejoice? Only with a stammer can one utter his name, can one

---

[7.] The words beginning with "and in that moment" to the end of the sentence are added in the margin.

[8.] [The German biblical text quoted by Bonhoeffer uses the term *Herrschaft*, "lordship." We have followed the NRSV use of the term "authority" in the biblical text, but readers should keep in mind that *Herrschaft* has the connotation of "dominion" or "ruling authority." Translating *Herrschaft* as "authority" in this meditation works as long as this connotation is kept in mind.—MB]

[9.] [Since this meditation was written during Advent in the Benedictine monastery at Ettal, we note the connection between the image of the key used here and the "Key of David" celebrated in the "O Antiphons" of Advent. The antiphon for December 20 is based on Isa. 22:22: "I will place on his shoulder the key of the house of David; he shall open, and no one shall shut; he shall shut, and no one shall open." Although it cannot be proven, it is very possible that Bonhoeffer heard these antiphons during vespers at the monastery, and that the connection he makes here between the Coming One and the power to open and close derives, even if unconsciously, from that liturgical image.—MB]

[10.] Cf. Luke 1:51-52.

636   attempt to paraphrase all that is contained in this name. Words pile up and
       pour out tumultuously when one is pressed to say who this child is. Indeed,
       strange and otherwise unheard-of verbal constructions arise where the name
       of this child is to be brought to human lips: "Wonder-Counselor," "God-
       Might," "Everlasting-Father," "Peace-Prince."[11] Every one of these words
       with its unending depth, and all of them together, are straining to express
       only one single name: Jesus.

       "Wonder-Counselor" is the name of this child. In him the wonder of all
       wonders has taken place; the birth of the Savior child springs from God's
       eternal counsel. In the form of a human child God gave us God's Son, God
       became human, the Word became flesh.[12] That is the wonder of the love
       of God for us, and it is the unfathomable, wise counsel that this love wins
       and saves us. Yet because this child is God's own Wonder-Counselor, he
       himself is also a source of all wonders and of all counsel. For those who per-
       ceive in Jesus the wonder of the Son of God, every one of his words and
       deeds becomes a wonder; they find in him ultimate, most profound, most
       helpful counsel. Indeed, before the child can open his lips, he is full of
       wonders and full of counsel. Go to the child in the manger, believe him to
       be the Son of God, and you will find in him wonders beyond wonder, coun-
       sel beyond counsel.

       "God-Might"[13] is the name of this child. The child in the manger is
       none other than God. Nothing greater can be said: God became a child. In
       Mary's child, Jesus, dwells almighty God. Pause here a moment! Do not
       speak, do not analyze further. Grow still before this Word. God has become
       a child![14] Here the child is poor like us, miserable and helpless like us, a
       human being of flesh and blood like us, our brother. And yet he is God; yet
       he is might. Where is the divinity, where is the might of this child? In the
       divine love by which he becomes like us. His misery in the manger is his
       might. In the power of love he overcomes the chasm between God and
       humanity, he overcomes sin and death, he forgives sin and raises from
       death. Kneel down before this wretched manger, before this child of poor

       ----

       [11.] [Isa. 9:6. The translations more familiar to English ears are "Wonderful Coun-
       selor" (Wunder-Rat), "Mighty God" (Gott-Kraft), "Everlasting Father" (Ewig-Vater), and
       "Prince of Peace" (Friede-Fürst). We have translated them more closely here to emphasize
       Bonhoeffer's point about strange verbal constructions; the standard NRSV translations do
       not necessarily reflect why Bonhoeffer makes so much of the "stammering" nature of
       these "piled-up" words.—MB]

       [12.] Cf. John 1:14.

       [13.] [The Luther Bible actually has *Gott-Held* (God-Hero) rather than *Gott-Kraft*
       here.—MB]

       [14.] This sentence is added in the margin.

parents, and repeat in faith the stammering words of the prophet: "God- 637
Might!"—and he will become your God and your strength.

"Everlasting-Father"—how can this be the name of the child? Only in
that the everlasting fatherly love of God is revealed in this child and that
the child desires nothing else but to bring the love of the Father to earth.
Thus the Son is one with the Father and whoever sees the Son sees the
Father.[15] This child does not want to be anything in himself, not a child
prodigy in the human sense, but rather an obedient child of his heavenly
Father. Born within time, he brings eternity with him to earth; as the Son of
God he brings to us all the love of the Father in heaven. Go there, seek and
find the heavenly Father in the manger, the one who here has become even
your own dear father.

"Peace-Prince"—where God comes in love to human beings, becomes
united with them, there peace is secured between God and human being,
and between human being and human being. If you are fearful of the
wrath of God, go to the child in the manger, and let the peace of God be
given to you here. If you have fallen into strife and hatred with your
brother, come and see how God has become our brother out of sheer love
and desires to reconcile us with one another. In the world violence reigns;
this child is the Prince of Peace. Where he is, peace reigns.

"Wonder-Counselor, God-Might, Everlasting-Father, Peace-Prince"—this
is how we speak at the manger in Bethlehem, this is how our words become
a jumble at the sight of the divine child, this is how we attempt to put into
words all that lies ordained for us in the one name, Jesus. Yet these words
are in fact nothing other than a wordless silence of adoration before the
inexpressible,[16] the presence of God in the form of a human child.

We have heard of the birth and the name of the divine child. Now let us
hear finally also of his kingdom.

Verse 7. The authority of this poor child will be great. It will encompass
the entire earth, and all generations until the end of time will be obliged,
consciously or unconsciously, to serve it. It will be an authority over human 638
hearts, yet even thrones and great kingdoms will thrive or founder on this
power. The secret, invisible authority of the divine child over human hearts
is more firmly grounded than the visible power and splendor of human
lords. Ultimately, all authority on earth will be obliged to serve only the
authority of Jesus Christ over humankind. Through all opposition, this
authority will only keep growing greater and more firm.

[15.] [Cf. John 10:30 and 14:9.—MB]

[16.] Cf. the beginning of Bonhoeffer's Christology lectures at Berlin University in the
summer semester of 1933; see *CC,* 27 (*DBW* 12:280 [*GS* 3:167]).

With the birth of Jesus the great reign of peace has dawned. Is it not a miracle that peace also reigns in those places where Jesus is truly Lord over human beings? That there are Christians all over the earth among whom peace exists in the midst of the world? Only where people do not let Jesus reign, where human obstinacy, pride, hatred, and greed are allowed to have full play without impediment, can there be no peace. Jesus does not desire to set up his reign of peace through force, but where people willingly submit to him, let him reign over them; he gives them his wonderful peace. If today Christian peoples [Völker] are again torn apart in war and hatred, indeed, if even the Christian churches cannot find their way to one another, this is the fault not of Jesus Christ but of human beings who will not let Jesus Christ reign. This does not, however, invalidate the promise that "there shall be endless peace" where the divine child reigns over us.

"For the throne of David and his kingdom"—this is where Jesus Christ reigns. It is no longer a worldly throne and kingdom as it once was but a spiritual throne and kingdom. Where are Jesus' throne and kingdom? They are where he himself is present, reigns, and governs with his word and sacrament, in the church, in the congregation.

Jesus governs his kingdom "with justice and with righteousness." His judgment does not spare the community of the faithful—no, it is precisely here that he exercises his strictest judgment, and the church-community proves itself to be his in that it does not withdraw from this judgment but submits to it. Only where Jesus judges sin can he bestow new righteousness. His kingdom is to be a kingdom of righteousness, not of self-righteousness but of divine righteousness, which can be established only by means of the judgment of sin. The strength of this kingdom will be that it rests on justice and righteousness. The longevity of this kingdom will be that injustice never goes unpunished in it.

639

A kingdom of peace and righteousness, humanity's unfulfilled desire, has dawned with the birth of the divine child. We are called into this kingdom. We can find it, within the church, in the community of the faithful, when we receive the word and sacrament of the Lord Jesus Christ and submit to his authority, when we recognize the child in the manger as our Savior and Redeemer and let him bestow on us a new life grounded in love. This kingdom will last "from this time onward"—that means beginning with the birth of Jesus—"and forevermore." Who guarantees that it will not be shattered and destroyed in the storms of world history, along with all other kingdoms?

"The zeal of the LORD of hosts will do this." The holy zeal of God for this divine kingdom guarantees that this kingdom will remain for eternity and will reach its final fulfillment despite all human guilt, all resistance. It will not depend on whether we participate. God brings his plans to fruition with or despite us. But God desires for us to be with him. Not for God's own sake but for our sake. God with us—Immanuel—Jesus—that is the mystery of this Holy Night. But we cry out with joy: "For a child has been born for us, a son given to us." I believe that Jesus Christ—a true human being, born of the Virgin Mary, and true God, begotten of the Father in eternity— is my Lord.[17]

2. Funeral Liturgy and Homily on Proverbs 23:26 for Hans-Friedrich von Kleist-Retzow, Kieckow, August 3, 1941[1]

640

A reading from Hans-Friedrich's baptismal verse, John 8:12: "I am the light of the world. Whoever follows me will never walk in darkness but will have the light of life."

Hymn 486,[2] verses 1–3, 7–9:

The day expires; / My soul desires / And pants to see that day.
When the vexing cares of earth / Shall be done away.

The night is here; / O! be Thou near, / Christ, make it light within;
Drive away from out my heart / All the night of sin.

The sunbeams pale, / And flee and fail; / O uncreated Sun!
Let Thy light now shine on us, / Then our joy were won.

When shall the sway / Of night and day / Cease to rule man thus?
When that brightest day of days / Once shall dawn on us.

Ah! never then / Her light again / Jerusalem shall miss,
For the Lamb shall be her Light, / Filling her with bliss.

O were I there! / Where all the air / With lovely sounds is ringing;
Where the saints Thee Holy Lord, / Evermore are singing!

[17.] Martin Luther, Second Article of Faith, Small Catechism, *Book of Concord*, 355.

[1.] *NL*, A 63,6 a: handwritten (*NL*, A 63,6 b: typewritten copy); *NL*, A 63,6 c: type-written carbon copy with liturgy; previously published (without the liturgy) in *GS* 4: 578–83. At the initiative of his grandmother, Ruth von Kleist-Retzow, Hans-Friedrich von Kleist-Retzow attended Bonhoeffer's confirmation class and was confirmed by him on April 9, 1938, in Kieckow (see *DB-ER*, 439). He was killed in July 1941 on the eastern front. See also Bonhoeffer's Finkenwalde circular letter of August 15, 1941 (1/119), and Ruth von Kleist-Retzow's letter to Eberhard Bethge on August 24, 1941 (1/120). The funeral ser-vice took place "around 8:00 p.m." Because its readings and hymns together with the homily form a cohesive whole, they are reproduced here as well.

[2.] *Evangelisches Gesangbuch für Brandenburg und Pommern*, 486 is a hymn setting of Rev. 21:23 by Johann Anastasius Freylinghausen. The English translation here is by Cather-ine Winkworth in *Lyra Germanica*, 173–75.

641   Lord Jesus, Thou / My rest art now, / O help me that I come,
           Radiant with Thy light to shine / In Thy glorious home!

A reading from the Wisdom of Solomon 3:1-3, 9; 4:7, 10, 14; 5:15, 16a: "But
the souls of the righteous are in the hand of God, and no torment will ever
touch them. In the eyes of the foolish they seemed to have died, and their
departure was thought to be a disaster, and their going from us to be their
destruction; but they are at peace. [3:9:] Those who trust in him will understand truth, and the faithful will abide with him in love, because grace and
mercy are upon his holy ones, and he watches over his elect. [4:7:] But the
righteous, though they die early, will be at rest. [4:10:] There were some
who pleased God and were loved by him, and while living among sinners
were taken up. [4:14:] For their souls were pleasing to the Lord, therefore he
took them quickly from the midst of wickedness. [5:15:] But the righteous
live forever, and their reward is with the Lord; the Most High takes care of
them. Therefore they will receive a glorious crown and a beautiful diadem
from the hand of the Lord."

Hymn 316,[3] verse 1:

   O my soul, rejoice, be merry, / And forget all doubts and fears.
   Be assured that Christ, thy master / Calls thee from this vale of tears.
   And thy pain and heavy grief / In his arms shall find relief.
   Joy which eye can picture never / Will in heav'n be found forever.

A reading from John 6:35, 37-39: "Jesus said to them, 'I am the bread of life.
Whoever comes to me will never be hungry, and whoever believes in me will
never be thirsty. [...] Everything that the Father gives me will come to me,
and anyone who comes to me I will never drive away; for I have come down
from heaven, not to do my own will, but the will of him who sent me. And
this is the will of him who sent me, that I should lose nothing of all that he
has given me, but raise it up on the last day."

642   Hymn 316, verse 8:

   O my soul, rejoice, be merry, / And forget all doubts and fears.
   Be assured that Christ, thy master / Calls thee from this vale of tears.
   His great joy and liberty / Shall you have eternally,
   Share with angels jubilation / Ever triumph with creation.

[3.] *Awake My Heart*, 56–57 (*Evangelisches Gesangbuch für Brandenburg und Pommern*,
316, 1, based on Rev. 21:4; *Evangelisches Kirchengesangbuch*, 319, 1). Translation is from
Awake My Heart: Bach Chorale Collection and Settings for the Eucharist, edited by Klaus Hofmann, English-language edition prepared by Len Lythgoe (Stuttgart: Carus, 2000),
reprinted by permission of the publisher.

A reading of a hymn by Paul Gerhardt, 322:[4]

Thou'rt mine, yes, still thou art mine own!
Who tells me thou art lost?
But yet thou art not yet mine alone,
I own that He who cross'd
My hopes, hath greatest right in thee;
Yea, though he ask and take from me
Thee, O my Son, my heart's delight,
My wish, my thought, by day and night.

Ah might I wish, ah might I choose,
Then thou, my Star, shouldst live,
And gladly for thy sake I'd lose
All else that life can give.
Oh fain I'd say: Abide with me,
The sunshine of my house to be,
No other joy but this I crave,
To love thee, darling, to my grave!

Thus saith my heart, and means it well.
God meaneth better still;
My love is more than words can tell.
His love is greater still;
I am a father, He the Head
And Crown of fathers, whence is shed
The life and love from which have sprung
All blessed ties in old and young.

I long for thee, my son, my own,
And He who once hath given
Will have thee now beside His throne,
To live with Him in heaven.
I cry, Alas! my light, my child!
But God hath welcome on him smiled,   643
And said: "My child, I keep thee near,
For there is naught but gladness here."

O blessed word, oh deep decree,
More holy than we think!
With God no grief or woe can be,
No bitter cup to drink.
No sickening hopes, no want or care,
No hurt can ever reach him there;

[4.] [*Lyra Germanica,* 300–303 (*Evangelisches Gesangbuch für Brandenburg und Pommern,* 322, written by Paul Gerhardt on the death of one of his sons).—MB]

Yes, in that Father's shelter'd home
I know that sorrow cannot come.

How many a child of promise bright
Ere now hath gone astray,
By ill example taught to slight
And quit Christ's holy way.
O fearful the reward is then,
The wrath of God, the scorn of men!
The bitterest tears by mortal shed
Are his who mourns a child misled.

But now I need not fear for thee,
Where thou art, all is well;
For thou thy Father's face doth see,
With Jesus thou dost dwell!
Yes, cloudless joys around him shine,
His heart shall never ache like mine.
He sees the radiant armies glow
That keep and guide us here below.

O that I could but watch afar,
And hearken but awhile,
To that sweet song that hath no jar,
And see his heavenly smile,
As he doth praise the holy God,
Who made him pure for that abode!
In tears of joy full well I know
This burden'd heart would overflow.

644   Then be it as my Father wills,
I will not weep for thee;
Thou livest, joy thy spirit fills,
Pure sunshine thou dost see,
The sunshine of eternal rest:
Abide, my child, where thou art blest;
I with our friends will onward fare,
And, when God wills, shall find thee there.

Hymn 76:[5]

To God the Holy Spirit let us pray
Most of all for faith upon our way,

[5.] The hymn "To God the Holy Spirit Let Us Pray" is based on 1 Cor. 12:3. Verse 1 was written in the thirteenth century (*Lutheran Book of Worship,* no. 317 ["Nun bitten wir," (*Evangelisches Gesangbuch für Brandenburg und Pommern,* 76, 1; *Evangelisches Kirchengesangbuch,* 99, 1)]).

That he may defend us when life is ending
And from exile home we are wending.
Lord, have mercy!

Homily on Hans-Friedrich's Confirmation Verse, Proverbs 23:26: "My child,[6] give me your heart, and let your eyes delight in my ways."[7]

We have gathered here in order to remember Hans-Friedrich together before God once more, to reflect on what God has done for him, to trace in our thoughts once again the way in which God has led him and called him home, and finally—if God's grace permits—to be able ourselves to return to our daily work, our earthly duties, with our faith strengthened, our hearts made secure, bound together with one another even more closely in love.

"My child, give me your heart, and let your eyes delight in my ways." A little more than three years ago Hans-Friedrich received this confirmation verse at the altar of this church, and today we are permitted to place his entire life, from baptism through death, beneath this verse, to see it held together in this verse.

In the face of his death it becomes significant to us all over again, in a whole new way, that Hans-Friedrich received holy baptism. At that time God's own hand was laid on Hans-Friedrich's life. God called the newborn child to eternal life, and those who brought him to baptism received God's call in faith and gave their child over to God. "My child, give me your heart"—God was the one who performed what the very young child did not understand. God took his heart, purified it, and sanctified it in the sacrament of baptism so that he would be able to belong to God and serve God eternally. "My child"—God received Hans-Friedrich as God's child. God became his dear father. God furnished a place for this child in God's own house. Now the basis of this life had been laid for all time and its eternal goal established. In Holy Baptism God did this for Hans-Friedrich and for each one of us. Let us be grateful for it.

During his childhood, through many witnesses and particularly through his parents, Hans-Friedrich was told repeatedly and in different ways about the events of his baptism. Hans-Friedrich was able to grow up in a home in which God's word was intended to govern life. He was allowed to experience by word and example what a power and a help Christian faith is in life. We say this with humble thanks to God, who so kindly led Hans-Friedrich, and

645

[6.] [The German biblical text uses *Sohn* here, which would normally be translated as "son." Since the NRSV uses "child" in Prov. 23:26, we translate *Sohn* throughout this homily as "child."—MB]

[7.] [NRSV alternative reading.—MB]

with the request that God remain close to this home and keep his word and fill many homes with his Spirit as a blessing to parents and children.

Then came the years in which what God had established in the child pressed toward a conscious decision. By the grace of God it came, the turning to a conscious faith that is decisive for every life. Hans-Friedrich became a conscious Christian. Let us not imagine that such a young person would be unable to realize what that means. God creates the miracle of faith in young and old, and in faith neither has an advantage over the other. In those years God saw to it that Hans-Friedrich, along with his cousins, came to live at his grandmother's home; and God granted to this house that it would become a decisive help for Hans-Friedrich. Hans-Friedrich and two of his cousins took confirmation instruction together. At their confirmation the verse that we have heard was addressed to him: "My child, give me your heart, and let your eyes delight in my ways." It was like a request by the almighty God and Father to God's dear child. "Give me your heart": that means, give me yourself, just as you are; do not hold anything back from me; give me all your thoughts, your desires, your soul, and your body; give me everything; give me your heart, for it belongs to God. "My child" was what God called him. It was no longer the underage child but rather the maturing young man, who was striding toward all the joys and dangers of life, and who now by a free decision and from a willing heart was to answer this call: Yes, my Father. By the grace of God, Hans-Friedrich gave his heart to God. He sincerely wanted this and struggled with himself over it. It was God's goodness that soon thereafter gave Hans-Friedrich a circle of boys his own age, with whom—bound together by their confession of Jesus Christ the Lord—he strove for a true Christian life. Here Hans-Friedrich experienced the full joy and the great power of an authentic Christian community. With the full devotion of his being, Hans-Friedrich served this circle and until the end remained gratefully and faithfully bound to it.

Let us remember that it is always a divine miracle when a person becomes a Christian, but it is an incomparably great miracle when a young man today becomes a conscious Christian. This means that he perceives God above as his Creator and Lord, from whom he receives everything and on whom he remains entirely dependent, that he allows God's commands to apply to him and strives to obey them, that he knows himself to need the forgiveness of sins, and that he recognizes the power and the love of the Redeemer. When a person becomes a Christian, this means that he gives his heart, which by nature attaches itself to so many unimportant things, to God and his Redeemer, always with the recognition, "I can't do this on my own, so take thou my heart to yourself and keep it safe with you." Hans-Friedrich became a Christian in an age in which it cost something to confess himself as a Christian and to live as a Christian. He did not balk at that. Perhaps it even spurred him on all the more. "My child, give me your heart." The child recognized the voice of his Father.

Through all this Hans-Friedrich remained open toward life and the world and its joys and tasks. God gave him open eyes, an alert heart, and a healthy understanding for real life. He followed the conversations having to do with the destiny and future of *his* native country [Vaterland] with the most concentrated interest. Then came the war, and Hans-Friedrich became a soldier. He conceived of his military service as a test of his life to that point, as the trial of his being before others and before God. He considered this capacity to stand in the hour of trial not as something to be taken for granted, given to him by nature, but as something that had to be bestowed on him from above, as grace. Most likely he also worried about whether it would be given to him, and precisely this was what strengthened him. He marched out full of joy. "In any case it will be lovely," he wrote shortly before going into action. In heavy battle, in the bravest trial he passed the final test; he gave his life. He gave it for his native country in the truest sense of the word, for the land his fathers had served with their power, their weapons, their conscience, their faith.

Beside him was found his open New Testament. In this way, for the last time, God had said to him, "My child, give me your heart." Now it was the final hour. Give me your life. Come home, my child, to your Father.

> I say in agony, My light has vanished!
> God says in love, Welcome, dear child,
> I want to have you close to me
> and refresh you richly forever. (Paul Gerhardt)[8]

The image of Hans-Friedrich continues to be present with us as the image of a young Christian who was a brave soldier, a good son and brother, a faithful friend to his friends. In this life his heart was with God. Thus in eternity it will also be with God.

But now we listen to his confirmation verse once more and let it apply to us: "My child, give me your heart, and let your eyes delight in my ways." It is the fatherly heart of God, as it has been revealed in Jesus Christ, that today longs for our hearts. The heart of God, which in Jesus Christ was attacked, suffered, and bled for us, draws our heart to itself. Give me your heart; give me everything, all your thoughts, your wishes, your shattered hopes, as well as all your doubt. Be my child. Be still with your father. If you give me your heart, it will be bound to Hans-Friedrich for eternity. "Let your eyes delight

647

648

[8.] *Evangelisches Gesangbuch für Brandenburg und Pommern,* 322, the second half of verse 4; Bonhoeffer slightly altered the text. Translation here by Lisa Dahill.

in my ways." Even if we do not understand why God has taken Hans-Friedrich from us, nevertheless we know that a way that leads to God is a good way, and so let us delight in the way by which God has drawn Hans-Friedrich to God's own heart. So let us also delight in the ways by which God has led us to this point and will still lead us; for we know and believe firmly that our way too can end only in that place where Hans-Friedrich's way reached its goal and its fulfillment, with God the Father of Jesus Christ. Amen.

Hymn 312,[9] verses 3 and 5:

> When darkness round me gathers, / Thy name and cross, still bright,
> Deep in my heart are sparkling / Like stars in blackest night.
> O heart, this image cherish: / The Christ on Calvary,
> How patiently He suffered / And shed His blood for me!

> Lord, write my name, I pray Thee, / Now in the Book of Life
> And with all true believers / Take me where joys are rife.
> There let me bloom and flourish, / Thy perfect freedom prove,
> And tell, as I adore Thee, / How faithful was Thy love.

Prayer[10] and Lord's Prayer.

649 Hymn 314:[11]

> For me to live is Jesus, / To die is gain for me;
> Then, when-so-e'er He pleases, / I meet death willingly.

Benediction.

[9.] "Farewell I Gladly Bid Thee," *Lutheran Hymnal,* no. 407 ("Valet will ich dir geben," *Evangelisches Gesangbuch für Brandenburg und Pommern,* 312, a hymn setting of Acts 7:55, by Valerius Herberger; *Evangelisches Kirchengesangbuch,* 318).

[10.] The actual prayer is not extant; all that remains, on the last page of the hand-written text, is a section of crossed-out material apparently intended for use in this prayer. It reads: ". . . have revealed yourself to us. We thank you that you allow your love to shine on us this evening. We praise your holy name for all you have done for Hans-Friedrich, that you were with him from the beginning until the hour of his death. We thank you for all you have given us and others through Hans-Friedrich. We thank you that you have redeemed Hans-Friedrich for eternal life with you. / Be with his brothers. Protect them according to your will. Help them to overcome their grief through faith in you. Their life rests in your hand."

[11.] "For Me to Live Is Jesus," *Lutheran Hymnal,* no. 597 (*Evangelisches Gesangbuch für Brandenburg und Pommern,* 314; this is a seven-verse hymn setting of Phil. 1:21, originally written before 1608; *Evangelisches Kirchengesangbuch,* 316).

3. Recommended Devotions on Jeremiah 16:21 and Ephesians 1:22-23, Berlin, October 1941[1]

Jeremiah 16:21
["Therefore I am surely going to teach them, this time I am going to teach them my power and my might, and they shall know that my name is the LORD."]

1. There is a last resort by which God leads his people (Israel), who have repeatedly misused and resisted God's grace and have toyed with it, to lead them to the recognition of God's authority: namely, the *powerful* angry strike of God's hand.

a. Once the friendly and admonishing *word* no longer does any good, *action* follows: God's hand strikes.

b. Following the "teaching" and glad "tidings" through the sermon and sacraments comes the terrifying new teaching of the *angry hand* and *might* of God. War, crises, imprisonment, distress of all kinds—this is the "alien" teaching of God, the "alien" proclamation and self-revelation of God.

c. Why? Because God's people have been worshiping other lords and gods as idols and do not [want to] acknowledge that God's name alone is "the Lord."

2. What we are experiencing today is this teaching, this proclamation of God. It is the last resort by which God desires to help us recognize that God alone is the Lord.

a. Precisely today we are in danger of looking at many other forces instead of toward God. Yet the *word* of God says to us: here the one before whom the mightiest powers crumble, before whom what is exalted is brought low and what is lowly exalted, wants to be acknowledged as the only Lord. In all that occurs today, recognize the angry call of God, who is nevertheless so merciful; recognize God's judgment upon us. God alone is the Lord. Humble yourselves before God!

b. God's angry judgment is a *dark* revelation. Few people recognize it. In this way, precisely in angry judgment, God's election takes place. Some perceive God in the final hour; others harden their hearts.

650

[1.] *NL,* A 63,7 a; handwritten, with the notation "Devotions for the Mission Festival in Ohlau, October 1941"; cf. *NL,* A 63,7 b; two different typewritten copies (the editorial comments in square brackets point to differences between the two); previously published in *GS* 4:583–84 and *GS* 5:582–83. Jer. 16:21 was the Old Testament watchword, *Losung,* and Eph. 1:22-23 was the New Testament interpretative verse, *Lehrtext,* chosen for October 20, 1941, in the Moravian *Daily Texts.* These reflections were intended to provide a basis for devotions that Eberhard Bethge was to hold in Ohlau, Silesia. This page was enclosed with a letter from Bonhoeffer to Bethge, presumably mailed from Berlin.

c. In God's anger at you, recognize that God *loves* you; God wants to be your Lord again! Last chance.

Gospel in judgment.

Ephesians 1:22-23
["And he[2] has put all things under his[3] feet and has made him the head over all things for the church, which is his body, the fullness of him who fills all in all."]

1. The miracle: God's wrath struck God's own being—in Jesus Christ. Jesus became our Lord in that he bore God's wrath.
2. We who submit to the wrath of God are God's church; and we have one Lord who has chosen and called us, Jesus the head of the church.
3. The world belongs to this Lord. He fills everything. We in him.

651   ## 4. Devotional Aids for the Moravian *Daily Texts*

4.1 *Daily Text* Meditation for Pentecost 1944[1]

For the Days of Pentecost. *Daily Texts* for May 28–30, 1944.

Isaiah 57:18
["Because I have seen their ways, I will heal them; I will lead them and repay them with comfort."][2]

Galatians 4:6
["And because you are children, God has sent the Spirit of his Son into our hearts, crying, 'Abba! Father!'"]

Healing, leading, comforting—this is God's action on Pentecost. God sees our ways; it is grace when he does so; God can also let us go along our ways without noticing them. But God has seen our ways—and saw us wounded, astray, frightened.

[2.] [God.—MB]
[3.] [Christ's.—MB]

[1.] *NL,* A 66,2, pages 1–4; handwritten in Bonhoeffer's roman script from Tegel prison; enclosed with a letter to Renate and Eberhard Bethge on May 24, 1944: "I've been trying to write you a few words on the readings [*Losungen*]—in fact, I was at it today while the alert was on, and so they are rather inadequate, and not as well thought out as I could wish" (*LPP,* 308 [*DBW* 8:448]); meditation previously published in *GS* 4:588–92.

[2.] [NRSV; translation altered to reflect the causal relationships that are more clearly indicated in the German biblical text. Bonhoeffer picks up on this causal aspect in his meditation on this verse.—MB]

Now God is there to heal us. God touches the wounds that the past has inflicted on us; and they heal, they no longer hurt, they cannot harm our soul anymore. Memories no longer torment us; all pain dissolves into nothing, into oblivion, as in the presence of someone beloved. God is closer to us than what is past.

God wants to lead us. Not all human ways are under God's guidance; we can often go long distances on our own paths; on them we are at the mercy of chance, whether it brings happiness or unhappiness. Our own ways always circle around back to ourselves. But when God leads our way, then it leads to him. God's ways lead to God. God leads us through happiness or unhappiness—always only to God. By this we recognize God's ways.

God wants to comfort us. God comforts only when there is reason enough for it, when people are at their wit's end, when the meaninglessness of life terrifies them. The world as it is in reality always makes us fearful.[3] But those who are comforted see and have more than the world; they have life with God. When God comforts, nothing is destroyed, lost, meaningless.   652

"I healed; I led; I comforted—because I have seen their ways"—has God not done this innumerable times in our life? Has God not often led those who belong to him through great distress and danger?

How does God heal, lead, comfort? Solely by putting a voice within us that says, prays, calls, cries, "dear Father!"[4] That is the Holy Spirit. That is Pentecost.

Psalm 94:12-13a
["Happy are those whom you discipline, O LORD, and whom you teach out of your law, that they may have patience in days of trouble."][5]
Galatians 5:22-23a
["... the fruit of the Spirit is love, joy, peace, patience, kindness, generosity, faithfulness, gentleness, and self-control."][6]

"Having patience in days of trouble"—this has been the focus recently of nearly our entire inner concentration. How do we accomplish it? By submitting to God's blows and God's law and saying, Happy are those who experience this! This is what those who call God "dear Father" must say. Those whom God disciplines through difficult life experiences, through war and

---

[3.] Cf. John 16:33b.
[4.] [NRSV omits "dear" before "Father."—MB]
[5.] [Ps. 94:12 is quoted from the NRSV; Ps. 94:13a has been translated from the German biblical text.—MB]
[6.] In Bonhoeffer's meditation Bible this verse is underlined three times.

deprivation, learn that they can insist on nothing from God; so they wait patiently and humbly until God again turns toward them kindly, and they know that this hour is coming. Those on whom God lays the law in its full severity perceive in their failure their shared guilt in the failure of all human beings, and they practice patience in obedience and demand nothing, but wait and pray. In bearing discipline and in obeying God's law, we know that God is teaching us, and we recognize the hand of the dear Father and say, Happy are those who experience this.

653   There is a danger for us today that patience appears as the sole and most important Christian stance, and that we thereby severely curtail the riches of God. In the midst of times of discipline, the entire fullness of the Holy Spirit wants to unfold and to ripen, and we should give it full space within us for the sake of God, for the sake of others, and for our own sake. The entire world of God, the dear Father, wants to be born in us, to grow and ripen. Love—where only suspicion and hostility reign; joy—instead of bitterness and pain; peace—amid internal and external strife; patience—where impatience threatens to overwhelm us; kindness—where only raw and hard words seem to make any difference; goodness—where understanding and empathy seem like weaknesses; faith, meaning here faithfulness[7]—where long separations and enormous changes in all relationships seek to rock the foundations of even what is most stable; gentleness—where recklessness and selfishness seem to be the only ways to reach one's goal; self-control—where short-term pleasures seem to be the only reasonable option and all bonds are about to dissolve.

Is all this a fanciful illusion? Is it impossible? It would be, were it not the fruit, growing entirely by its own power, of the Spirit to whom we have entrusted ourselves and who intends to bring all this about in us while we, astonished and adoring, let the Spirit work.

Genesis 39:23
["... the LORD was with (Joseph); and whatever he did, the LORD made it prosper."]

1 John 3:24
["All who obey (Jesus') commandments abide in him, and he abides in them. And by this we know that he abides in us, by the Spirit that he has given us."]

God blesses some of his children with happiness, allowing everything they touch to succeed. God is with them, gives them the goodwill of others, success and recognition in their deeds; indeed, God gives them great power

---

[7.] In the Luther German translation printed in his Nestle Greek-German New Testament, Bonhoeffer crossed out *Glaube,* "faith," and wrote in the word *Treue,* "faithfulness," another translation of the Greek word πίστις.

over others and brings his work to fulfillment through them. Of course, for the most part even they must go through times of suffering and testing, but even if people attempt to do evil things against them, God always allows it to turn out for the best for them. God blesses others among his children with suffering to the point of martyrdom. God makes alliances with happiness and unhappiness in order to lead people on his way and toward his goal. The way is keeping the commandments of God, and the goal is that we abide in God and God abides in us. Happiness and unhappiness reach their fulfillment in the blessedness of this goal: we in God, God in us. And the way to this goal, walking in the commandments of God, is itself the beginning of this blessedness. How do we discern that—through happiness or unhappiness—we are moving toward this blessedness? In that an irresistible love for this way and for this goal has been stirred up in us, even if we often fall down along the way and are in danger of missing the goal. This love comes from God. It is the Holy Spirit, whom God has given us. "May the Holy Spirit also remain above us / with its manifold gifts. / May the Spirit comfort and strengthen us in distress / and lead us back home to God. / Lord, have mercy."[8]

4.2 *Daily Text* Meditation for June 7 and 8, 1944[9]

[*Daily Texts* for] *June 7 and 8.*
Psalm 54:4
"But surely[, God is] my helper; the Lord is the upholder of my soul."[10]

1 Thessalonians 5:23
"...may your [spirit and] soul and body be kept sound and blameless [at the coming] of our Lord Jesus Christ."

The Bible first speaks of "helping" [Beistehen] at the creation of Eve: "I will make you a helper [Beistand] as your partner," God says to Adam.[11] Perhaps

---

[8.] This stanza comes from the pilgrimage hymn "In Gottes Namen fahren wir" (In the name of God we travel), *Ein neues Lied,* 406.

[9.] *NL,* A 66,2, pp. 5–10; handwritten in Bonhoeffer's roman script from Tegel prison; enclosed with a letter to Eberhard Bethge on June 2, 1944 (*LPP,* 315 [*DBW* 8:459–61]); previously published in *GS* 4:592–96. Until the end of the war, the manuscript was buried, and the text is obliterated in places. Additions appear in square brackets.

[10.] [In the NRSV the last word is "life." Later in this meditation, Bonhoeffer will make a point of how "soul" here means "life."—MB]

[11.] Cf. Gen. 2:18 (Luther Bible: *Gehilfin,* "helper") and *DBWE* 3:95–99 (*Beistand,* "helper"). [The NRSV has this verse in the third person; Bonhoeffer has it in the second person, which we have kept. *Beistehen* means "to assist or support"; *Beistand* means "support";

655   in favorable times this term may seem to us too modest to encompass what marriage is. Much later in the Bible, namely, in Jesus' farewell discourses, we see this term "helper" referring to the one Jesus will send to those remaining on earth following his ascension: "I will ask the Father, and he will give you another Advocate—literally: Helper—to be with you forever."[12] Here that first word from the creation story is fulfilled in an immeasurably sublime way. You are my helper for body, soul, and spirit; you comfort my body, my soul, my spirit—this is what people, whom God has created for one another as male and female, say to each other. Even though they are only earthly creatures, they do for one another divine work. It is in fact God who takes up this work and completes it through the Holy Spirit.—That this assistance is truly the essence of marriage is something we see most clearly once it appears as though we must do without it. We would gladly do without everything else—joy, pleasure, happiness—if we can only help[13] one another. Nothing is more painful for us than to be forced to leave the other person to face dangers[, duties], decisions, difficult situations alone, to be [un]able to help the other [with them]; this is what makes every separation [in marriage] so difficult. In such situations the Psalm's word applies to you[: "surely,] the Lord is my helper." This is how people speak to one another, how they comfort the other person and themselves. They point to all that God has done for them in the past; they point to the God who was faithful and remains faithful, who has never left them without help in dangers and difficulties and never will. Can we comfort one another in any better way, can we help one another any better than to say confidently and securely to one another: Don't worry about me, I am taken care of! Don't be afraid, I am not left alone! Look and see, God is helping me! Take heart, and then my heart is also consoled! Wherever I may be, God stands by me and helps me.[14] And God does this to preserve my soul—actually this

656   means "my life." "The Lord upholds my soul." With our worries, preoccupations, and efforts, we do not preserve our life even one single day, but the Lord who governs all the world and sets all things upon their courses, who can

---

here we have followed the NRSV wording. But cf. *DBWE* 3:94, ed. note 2, as well as ed. note 13 below.—MB]

    [12.] John 14:16. [The Luther Bible uses *Tröster* where the NRSV uses "Advocate." *Tröster* is commonly translated as "Comforter" or "Paraclete." The phrase "literally: Helper" is inserted into the NRSV citation here where Bonhoeffer inserted it into the Luther Bible text.—MB]

    [13.] [The term *beistehen* has connotations of remaining close by one another, a comforting proximity or solidarity, that are not necessarily suggested by "helper."—MB]

    [14.] [In this sentence Bonhoeffer makes *beistehen*, "to stand by" or "to support," parallel to *helfen*, "to help."—MB]

avert all dangers, who "has thousands of ways to rescue us from death"[15]—this is the one who alone upholds my life. "For [God] will command his angels concerning you to guard you in all your ways."[16] Look at this reality—let us reassure one another in this way—and not at all those other things that upset and oppress us. Surely God is my helper and the upholder of my soul.

Do we [then, in that case, finally] cease to give aid to one another? By no means[. We] can in no way help one another in truth if God is not our helper. By ceaselessly reminding one another of this, we are one another's helper. Is that unrealistic? No, if with full trust and great confidence of faith we commend one another to the God who helps us and comfort one another with that, then even in times of separation this itself is our help, a comfort for the body, for the soul, and for the spirit. In body, soul, and spirit we remain securely together and in this way also fulfill the word of creation: I will create for you a helper.

What is the goal of all this? The day of Jesus Christ, the day of his coming. For his sake God has given us our marriage; for his sake we help one another; for his sake God helps us and upholds us. For his sake God preserves our body, soul, and spirit—"blameless," which means so that we can stand fast before God with body, soul, and spirit in eternity. Together, whether close by or separated, we move toward this ultimate goal. Along the way we help one another and commend one another to the one who alone can uphold us and who for all eternity will [transfigure] our body, soul, and spirit into a new, eternal life. Then—ashamed and grateful—[we shall] say, Surely God is [my] helper. Amen.

Psalm 34:19   657
"Many are the afflictions of the righteous; but the LORD rescues them from them all."

1 Peter 3:9
"Do not repay evil for evil or abuse for abuse; but, on the contrary, repay with a blessing. It is for this that you were called—that you might inherit a blessing."

The righteous suffer from the world; the unrighteous do not. The righteous suffer from things that others take for granted and consider essential.

[15.] Cf. verse 5 of the hymn "Du meine Seele, singe" (Sing, O my soul) by Paul Gerhardt: "God knows thousands of ways to deliver us from death" (*Evangelisches Gesangbuch für Brandenburg und Pommern*, 248; *Evangelisches Kirchengesangbuch*, 197).

[16.] Ps. 91:11, cited in Matt. 4:6.

The righteous suffer from unrighteousness, from the meaninglessness and perversion of world events; they suffer from the destruction of the divine orders of marriage and the family. They suffer from this not only because these things represent for them a deprivation but also because they recognize in them something ungodly. The world says: that is just how it is; it will always be that way and must be so. The righteous say: it should not be that way; it is against God. This is the chief hallmark by which the righteous can be recognized, that they suffer in this way. To some extent they bring into the world God's own way of perceiving things; that is why they suffer just as God suffers at the hands of the world.—"But the Lord rescues them"[17]— God's help is not found in all human suffering. But in the suffering of the righteous God's help is always present, because the righteous suffer with God. God is always there. The righteous know that God allows them to suffer in this way [so that] they learn to love God for God's own sake. In suffering the righteous find God. That is their help. If you find God in your separation, you are finding help.—The response of the righteous to the suffering that the world inflicts on them is: to bless. That was God's response to the world that nailed Christ to the cross: blessing. God does not repay evil for evil, and thus the righteous should not do so either. No judgment, no abuse, but blessing. The world would have no hope if this were not the case. The world lives by the blessing of God and of the righteous and thus has a future. Blessing means laying one's hand on something and saying: Despite everything, you belong to God. This is what we do with the world that inflicts such suffering on us. We do not abandon it; we do not repudiate, despise, or condemn it. Instead we call it back to God, we give it hope, we lay our hand on it and say: may God's blessing come upon you, may God renew you; be blessed, world created by God, you who belong to your Creator and Redeemer. We have received God's blessing in happiness and in suffering. Yet those who have been blessed can do nothing but pass on this blessing; indeed, they must be a blessing wherever they are. The world can [be] renewed only by the impossible, [and] the impossible is the blessing of God.

When Jesus ascended into heaven ["lifting] up his hands, he blessed"[18] those who belonged to him. We now in this hour hear him speaking to us, "The LORD bless you and keep you; the LORD make his face to shine upon you, and be gracious to you; the LORD lift up his countenance upon you, and give you peace."[19] Amen.

658

[17.] [While the NRSV translation uses "rescues," the German text here reads *hilft*, "helps," and Bonhoeffer's reflections follow this meaning more closely.—MB.]

[18.] Luke 24:50.

[19.] Num. 6:24-26.

Dear Eberhard and Renate, These words flowed onto paper when, thinking of you, I meditated on the daily texts for the days that await you. They are merely thrown together in haste and not formulated in advance and are intended only to accompany you in your own reading of the texts and if possible to help a little. I take courage to send them to you because you, Eberhard, said that you both had been cheered by the Pentecost reflections. Now farewell, be fully confident, and hope along with me that we may see one another again soon! Your Dietrich.

5. Exposition on the First Table of the Ten Words of God[1]

First Commandment

Amid thunderclaps, lightning, thick clouds, mountains shaking, and powerful trumpet blasts,[2] God proclaims the Ten Commandments to his servant Moses on Mount Sinai. They are not the result of extended reflection on human life and its orders by astute and experienced men; rather, they are God's word of revelation, beneath which the earth shakes and the elements are thrown into turmoil. The Ten Commandments come into the world not as general worldly wisdom offered to any thinking person, but instead as a holy event that even the people of God under threat of death dare not approach,[3] as God's revelation in the isolation of a smoking volcanic peak. It is not Moses but God who gives them; it is not Moses but God who writes them with his finger on stone tables, as the Bible emphatically and repeatedly makes clear.[4] "And [God] added no more" (Deut. 5:22), meaning that these were the only words that God himself wrote; in them the entire will of God is contained. This distinguishing of the Ten Commandments from all the other words of God is shown most clearly by the preservation of the two tables in the ark of the covenant within the Holy of Holies. The Ten Commandments belong in the sanctuary; here, in the place of God's gracious presence in the world, one must seek them and from here they continually go forth into the world (Isa. 2:3).

659

Throughout history people have reflected on the fundamental orders of their life, and it is an exceedingly remarkable fact that the results of nearly

---

[1.] *NL*, A 66,3; handwritten in Bonhoeffer's careful roman script (photocopied from the estate of Maria von Wedemeyer-Weller) in Tegel prison, June or July 1944; first published in Bonhoeffer, *Dein Reich Komme*, 21–36; previously published in *GS* 4:597–612. [In his title, Bonhoeffer deliberately speaks of the "Ten Words" instead of the "Ten Commandments"; for his reasoning behind this, see pp. 634–35.—MB]

[2.] Exod. 20:18.

[3.] Exod. 19:12.

[4.] Cf. Exod. 31:18 ("two tables . . . of stone . . . written with the finger of God"), and references to Exod. 32:15-16; Deut. 4:13; 5:22; 9:10; 10:4.

all such reflections overwhelmingly correspond with one another and with the Ten Commandments. Whenever the conditions of human life descend into disorder through powerful external or internal crises and upheavals, those persons who are able to hold on to clarity and discretion in their thoughts and judgments recognize that without fear of God, without reverence for parents, without protection of life, marriage, property, and dignity—however these good things may be configured—no human life in community is possible. To recognize these laws of life, people do not need to be Christian but need only to follow their experience and their common sense. Christians rejoice at the common ground they find with other human beings in such important matters. They are prepared to work together with them whenever they are struggling for the realization of shared goals. They are not surprised that people throughout the ages have arrived at perceptions about life that broadly correspond to the Ten Commandments; for

660 the Giver of the Commandments is, of course, the Creator and Sustainer of life. For all this, however, the Christian never forgets the decisive difference between these laws of life and the command of God. There reason speaks; here God speaks. Human reason says in advance to those who transgress the laws of life that life itself will take its revenge by bringing about, after initial apparent success, their undoing and unhappiness. God, on the other hand, does not speak of life and its successes and failures; rather, God speaks of God's own self. God's first word in the Ten Commandments is "I." Human beings are confronted with this "I," not with some sort of general law—not with "one should do this or that," but with the living God. In every word of the Ten Commandments, God speaks fundamentally of God's self, and this is their main point. That is why they are God's revelation. It is not a law but God we are obeying in the Ten Commandments, and our failure when we break them comes not from disobeying a law but from disobeying God. Transgressors face not merely disorder and failure but the wrath of God. It is not merely unwise to disregard God's command; it is sin, and the wages of sin are death. This is the reason the New Testament calls the Ten Commandments "living words"(Acts 7:38).[5]

Perhaps we would do better to speak, with the Bible, of "the ten words" of God (Deut. 4:13) instead of the "Ten Commandments." Then we would not so easily confuse them with human laws; then we would not so easily push aside the first words, "I am the LORD, your God"[6] as a mere preamble with no apparent relation or correspondence to the commandments at all. But in

---

[5.] [NRSV: "living oracles." The German phrase is *lebendige Worte.*—MB]

[6.] Exod. 20:2: "I am the LORD your God, who brought you out of the land of Egypt, out of the house of slavery."

reality precisely these first words are the most important of all, the key to the Ten Commandments; they show us what eternally distinguishes God's command from human laws. In these "ten words" God is speaking as truly of God's grace as of God's command. They are not an entity cut off from God that we could in some way designate as God's will; instead, the entire, living God is revealed in them as the one who God is. This is the main point.

The Ten Commandments as we know them are an abbreviation of their biblical wording. What is the justification for such deviation from the Bible in so decisive a passage? The universal Christian church hears the Ten Commandments differently from the people of Israel. Whatever corresponds to the situation of Israel as a political people is not binding on the Christian church, which is a spiritual people within all peoples. Thus, set free by faith in the God of the commandments, the church has dared to allow a spiritually interpreted translation to take the place of a literal translation of the biblical wording.

"I am the LORD, your God." When God says I, this is revelation. God could also let the world take its course and say nothing about it. Why should God feel obliged to speak of God's self? When God says "I," this is grace. When God says "I," God thereby says all there is to say, the first and the last. When God says "I," that means, "Prepare to meet your God!" (Amos 4:12c).

"I am the LORD." Not *a* Lord, but *the* Lord! With these words God claims all dominion for himself alone. Every right to command and all obedience belong to God and God alone. By testifying that it is God who is Lord, God frees us from all human servitude. There is and we have only *one* Lord, and "no one can serve two masters."[7] We serve God alone and no human being. Even when we carry out the commands of earthly lords, in reality we are serving God alone. It is a tremendous mistake on the part of many Christians to think that for our earthly life God has placed us in submission to many other lords besides God, and that our life now stands in unceasing conflict between the commands of these earthly lords and this commandment. We have only one Lord whom we obey; God's commands are clear and do not plunge us into conflicts.[8] To be sure, God has given to parents and governing authorities the right and power to command us on earth. But all earthly authority is grounded in God's authority alone and finds therein its full power and honor, [otherwise][9] it has usurped authority and

661

662

[7.] Matt. 6:24.

[8.] Cf. *DBWE* 6:385–86 et passim on "conflict." In the last period Bonhoeffer devoted to his work before his arrest on April 5, 1943, he was planning expositions for his *Ethics* on "the concrete commandment of God and the law" (*DBWE* 6:387).

[9.] The manuscript erroneously reads *sondern*, "rather."

has no claim to obedience. Because we obey God's commandment alone, we also obey our parents and authority.[10] Our obedience toward God obliges us to obedience toward parents and authority. But not all obedience toward parents and authority is automatically obedience toward God. Our obedience is never owed to human beings, but only to God. "Whatever your task, put yourselves into it, as done for the Lord and not for your masters"[11] (Col. 3:23). "You were bought with a price; do not become slaves of human masters"[12] (1 Cor. 7:23). Obedience to God alone is the foundation of our freedom.

God, the Lord, has not only the sole right to command but also the sole power to put God's commandment into effect. All means are God's to command. Those who set themselves up as lords beside God are sure to fall. Those who disregard God's commandment are sure to die. Those, however, who serve and rely on God alone—God protects and sustains them and knows how to do good to them, now and forever.

"Your God."[13] God is speaking to his chosen people, to the church-community who hears him in faith. For them the Lord, the inaccessibly distant and powerful one, is simultaneously the close, present, and merciful one. "For what other great nation has a god so near to it as the LORD our God is whenever we call to him?" (Deut. 4:7).[14] No stranger, no tyrant, no blind fate shall impose unbearable burdens on us, crushing us, but God, the Lord, the one who chose, created, and loved us, who knows us, wishes to be close to us, for us, and with us. God gives us the commandments so that we can be and remain close to God, for God, and with God. God is revealed to be our Lord and helper by making known to us God's commandment. "[God] has not dealt thus with any other nation" (Ps. 147:20). God is so great that the smallest details are not too small for God, and God is so fully the Lord that he comes close by our side as helper. When God is with us, then his commandments are not burdensome; and God's law is our delight [Trost] (Ps. 119:92)—his yoke easy, his burden light.[15] "I run

663

[10.] [*Obrigkeit*; in most of this volume we have translated this term as "government." Here, however, Bonhoeffer seems to be speaking of authority in a more general sense.—MB]

[11.] [The Luther Bible uses the phrase *nicht den Menschen*, "not for human beings."—MB]

[12.] [The Luther Bible uses the phrase *nicht der Menschen Knechte*, "not the slaves of human beings."—MB]

[13.] [The German here is "Dein Gott," i.e., both singular and familiar.—MB]

[14.] Deut. 4:7 is marked in Bonhoeffer's Bible, with markings also next to verses 6, 8-9, and 2; above chapter 4 appears in Bonhoeffer's roman script, "*Law and History*."

[15.] Matt. 11:30.

the way of your commandments, for you delight my heart" (Ps. 119:32).[16] In the ark of the covenant, which is the throne of the gracious presence of God, both tables lie enclosed, encompassed, and enveloped by the grace of God. Those who would speak of the Ten Commandments must seek them in the ark of the covenant, and so they must speak of the grace of God at the same time. Those who would proclaim the Ten Commandments must at the same time proclaim God's free grace.

"You shall have no other gods besides me."[17] The words "You shall not," which then follow ten times, are simply the explication of God's preceding self-disclosure. What it means for our life, that God is the Lord and is our God, is explained to us in ten short sentences. This connection becomes clearest if we insert a "therefore" in front of each of these sentences. "I am the Lord your God; therefore you shall not . . ." It is out of loving-kindness that God wishes by such commandments to protect us from errors and transgressions and shows us the boundaries within which we can live in God's community.

"You shall have no other gods besides me."[18] This is by no means self-evident. In every era highly cultured peoples have known of a heaven of the gods, and it was a mark of the greatness and dignity of a god not jealously to dispute the place of another god in the pious hearts of the people. The human virtues of broad-mindedness and tolerance were attributed to the gods as well. God, however, does not tolerate any other god; God wants to be the only God. God wants to do and be everything for people; this is why God wants to be the only one they worship. Nothing has a place beside God; beneath God is the entire creation. God wishes to be the only God, because God is the only God.

At issue here is not that we could worship other gods in the place of God, but instead that [we][19] could believe that we are able to place anything *beside* God. There are Christians who say that, side by side with their   664
faith in God, which they would never give up, the world, the state, work, the family, science, art, and nature also have their rightful claim. God says that

---

[16.] Like many verses in Psalm 119 (see *DBW* 15:499–537 [*GS* 4:505–43]), this verse in Bonhoeffer's Bible is marked and underlined. Above *tröstest*, "(you) delight," Bonhoeffer has written in roman script "expand." [NRSV: "you enlarge my understanding."—MB]

[17.] Exod. 20:3. [NRSV: "You shall have no other gods before me." The preposition "besides" is listed as a marginal reading for "before." It more accurately translates *neben*, the preposition in the Bible used by Bonhoeffer.—MB]

[18.] The formulation in Luther's Small Catechism reads, "You shall have no other gods"; the addition of the words *neben mir*, "besides me," appears in the Nuremberg editions of 1531 and 1558 (*Book of Concord*, 351; cf. esp. note 27); see ed. note 17.

[19.] This word was inadvertently omitted from the manuscript.

nothing, not one thing at all, has any claim beside God—only under God. Anything we place beside God is an idol. We are now accustomed to saying our gods are money, sensuality, honor,[20] other people, ourselves. It would be more accurate if we were to characterize power, success, the development of strength as our gods. But as a matter of fact, human beings in their weakness have always hung their hearts on all these things, and none of those things mentioned here is what the First Commandment actually refers to when it speaks of "other gods." For us the world is stripped of idols; we no longer worship anything. We have experienced the fragility and futility of all things, all people, and ourselves too clearly to be able still to deify them. Our very being has gone too far off track still to be capable of having idols and worshiping them. If we still have an idol, it is perhaps nothingness, extinction, meaninglessness. Thus the First Commandment calls us to the one true God, the almighty, just, and merciful one who rescues us from falling prey to nothingness[21] and sustains us in God's own church-community.

665   There were eras in which the secular authorities punished the denial of God and idolatry most severely. Even though this occurred with the intent to preserve the community from temptation and disorder, nevertheless God was not served by it; for, first, God desires to be worshiped in freedom; second, according to God's plan the powers of temptation must serve the purpose of preserving and strengthening believers; but third, the open denial of God in us is more promising than a hypocritical confession extorted by force. Secular authorities should confer external protection for faith in the God of all Ten Commandments, but disputation with unbelief should be left solely up to the power of the word of God.

It is not always easy to determine the boundaries at which participation in a state-mandated action becomes idolatry. The ancient Christians refused to contribute a bit of incense to the sacrifice used in the Roman emperor cult, and thus they suffered martyrs' deaths. The three men in the book of

---

[20.] See Bonhoeffer's letter from Tegel prison to Eberhard Bethge on June 27, 1944: "I'm at present writing an exposition of the first three commandments. I find the first particularly difficult. The usual interpretation of idolatry as 'wealth, sensuality, and pride' seems to me quite unbiblical. That is a piece of moralizing. Idols are *worshiped,* and idolatry implies that people still worship something. But we don't worship anything now, not even idols. In that respect we're truly nihilists" (*LPP,* 336 [*DBW* 8:499], trans. altered).

[21.] Cf. working note *NL,* A 86,3 (which Bonhoeffer may have had with him in prison), which contains references to many of these terms. For instance, its title "Decay," *Verfall,* uses the same German stem as the verb in this sentence, "to fall," *verfallen*; and it also includes the phrases "*nothingness—the end*" and "life's emptiness of meaning" (see *ZE,* 82). This material was worked into the section of the *Ethics* manuscript titled "Heritage and Decay" (*DBWE* 6:127–31).

Daniel (chap. 3) refused to bend the knee, as commanded by the king, before the golden statue that was to represent the power of the king and his realm. On the other hand, the prophet Elisha explicitly allows the Syrian commander Naaman, in accompanying his king to the idol's temple, to bow down (2 Kings 5:18).[22] The majority of Christians in Japan have recently declared that participation in the state emperor cult is allowable.[23] In all decisions of this kind we are to keep the following points in mind: 1. Does the required participation in state activities of this kind involve the wor-   666 ship of other gods? Then Christians have a clear duty to refuse. 2. If there are doubts as to whether it is a religious or a political activity, the decision will depend on whether participation in it will cause scandal to the community of Christ and to the world, that is, whether the slightest appearance of a denial of Jesus Christ is aroused. If, according to the shared judgment of Christians, this is not the case, then nothing stands in the way of participation. If it is the case, however, then here as well participation must be refused.

The Lutheran Church has incorporated the second biblical commandment, the one forbidding images,[24] into the first. What is forbidden to the church is not the representation of God with images. After all, God assumed human form in Jesus Christ and was allowed to be seen by human eyes.

[22.] Cf. the working note *ZE*, 14b (*NL*, A 73,7) where Bonhoeffer has written, "Permission of foreign cult for Naaman!"

[23.] In 1941, under state pressure, nearly all Protestant churches in Japan came together in the United Church of Christ in Japan (Kyodan). At the beginning of the thanksgiving worship service for the formation of Kyodan, which took place June 24–25, 1941, all participants had to bow in the direction of the emperor's palace and pledge allegiance to the emperor. It was asserted that Shinto is actually not a religion but the "authentic Japanese form of life" and therefore in no way contradicted the Christian faith. The first president of Kyodan himself performed the rituals of the state/Shinto at the central shrine in Ise. He also forced the Christians in Korea, for instance, to obey the command of the Japanese government and to bow before the Shinto shrine; many Korean Christians resisted this to the death. Repeatedly, and even for a time after the end of the war, the president directed all Kyodan congregations to make a vow of obedience to the emperor. Eberhard Bethge, who at that time was working for the Gossner Mission, had informed Bonhoeffer of the events in Japan. The World Council of Churches being formed in Geneva had been thoroughly informed about the worship service at the formation of Kyodan (the German editors thank Hiroshi Murakami for this information).

[24.] Exod. 20:4: "You shall not make for yourself an idol, whether in the form of anything that is in heaven above, or that is on the earth beneath, or that is in the water under the earth." In the margin next to this verse in Bonhoeffer's Bible, a "2" is penciled, the numeration used in the Reformed tradition. Bonhoeffer emphasizes that this is the "biblical numbering" in the confirmation curriculum he presented on October 20, 1936, in Finkenwalde; see *DBW* 14:792.

What is forbidden is only the worship and honoring of images as if a divine power dwelt within them. The same prohibition forbids the superstitious honoring of amulets, protective images, etc., as if they had a special power in preserving us from misfortune.

"Hear, O Israel: 'The LORD is our God, the LORD alone. You shall love the LORD your God with all your heart, and with all your soul, and with all your might'" (Deut. 6:4-5). Jesus Christ has taught us to pray to this our God with full confidence, "Our Father, you who are in heaven."[25]

Second Commandment

"You shall not make wrongful use of the name of the LORD your God, for the LORD will not acquit anyone who misuses his name."[26]

667 For us "God" is not a general concept by which we designate the highest, holiest, mightiest thing imaginable, but instead "God" is a name. It is something very different when non-Christians say "God" than when we to whom the living God has spoken say "God." For us God is our God, the Lord, the Living One. "God" is a name, and this name is the greatest treasure we possess; for in it we have not something we have thought up on our own but God's entire being itself, in God's revelation. If we are allowed to say "God," this is solely because God has given himself in inconceivable grace to be known by us. When we say God, we at the same time always hear God speaking to us, calling and comforting us, commanding us; we perceive God acting in us, creating, judging, renewing. "We give thanks to you, O God; ... your name is near" (Ps. 75:1). "The name of the LORD is a strong tower; the righteous run into it and are safe" (Prov. 18:10). The word "God" is nothing at all; the name "God" is everything.

In many ways people today perceive that God is not only a word but also a name. For this reason they like to avoid saying "God" and instead say "the Divine," "Destiny," "Providence," "Nature," "the Almighty." To them "God" always sounds almost like a confession. They do not want that. They want the word but not the name; for the name entails an obligation.

The Second Commandment calls us to keep the name of God holy. Actually, the only ones who can violate the Second Commandment are those who know the name of God. The word "God" is no more and no less than other human words, and those who misuse it dishonor only themselves and their own thoughts. But those who know the name of God and misuse it dishonor and desecrate God.

[25.] This formulation follows Matt. 6:9 in Luther's Small Catechism (*Book of Concord*, 356).

[26.] Exod. 20:7.

The Second Commandment speaks not of blasphemy against the name of God but of its misuse, just as the First Commandment spoke not of the denial of God but of having other gods besides God. Not blasphemy but misuse is the danger for believers.

We who know the name of God misuse it when we speak it as if it were merely a word, as if in this name God himself were not always speaking to us. There is a misuse of the name of God for evil and for good. The misuse for evil is, to be sure, hard to imagine among Christians; and yet it does occur. If we mention and appeal to the name of God in order consciously to make something godless and wicked seem devout and good before the world, if we ask God to bless something evil, if we mention the name of God in a context that brings disgrace to God, then we are misusing it for evil. In that case we know well that God would always and only speak against this thing for which we are claiming God, but because God's name has power, even before the world, we appeal to it. The misuse of the name of God for good is more dangerous, because it is more difficult to discern. It happens when we Christians let the name of God slip so matter-of-factly, so often, so glibly, and with such familiarity from our lips that we violate the holiness and the miracle of God's revelation. It is a misuse when for every human question and need we instantly have at hand the word "God" or a Bible passage, as if it were the most obvious thing in the world that God responds to all human questions and is always immediately ready to help in every difficulty. It is a misuse when we make God a stopgap in our discomfort.[27] It is a misuse when we want to silence authentic scientific or artistic efforts simply with the word "God." It is a misuse when we give what is holy to the dogs.[28] It is a misuse to speak of God without being aware of his living presence in God's name. It is a misuse when we speak as if we had God at our disposal at all times and as if we were privy to God's own counsel. We misuse the name of God in all these ways by making it into an empty human word and insipid chatter, and we thereby desecrate it more than all blasphemers are capable of doing.

The Israelites dealt with the danger of such misuse of God's name through the prohibition against speaking this name aloud at all. We have much to learn from the reverence that is manifest in this rule. It is certainly better not to speak the name of God than to debase it into a human word. Yet we have the holy task and the high honor to testify to God before one another and the world. This occurs when we speak the name of God only in such a

668

669

[27.] [In a letter on May 29, 1944, Bonhoeffer explains in more detail why God is no "stopgap" for human beings (*LPP,* 311–12 [*DBW* 8:454–55]).—MB]

[28.] See Matt. 7:6.

way that in it the word of the living, present, righteous, and gracious God himself is testified to. This can take place only when we pray daily as Jesus Christ has taught us, "Hallowed be your name."[29]

The secular governing authorities of the West have always made public blasphemy a punishable offense. They have thereby made clear that they are called to protect faith in God and the worship of God from slander and defamation. But they themselves were never able to succeed in suppressing the spiritual movements from which, as rightly or wrongly understood off-shoots, such defamations arise; nor can this ever be their task. The church is not helped by the suppression of spiritual movements by force. The church only lays claim to the freedom of its proclamation and life, and it trusts the rightly confessed name of God to gain acceptance for itself and earn respect.

Is it a misuse to name God's name in an oath? As for the content of Christians' speech, there is no difference whether it is made under oath and whether it uses the so-called religious or nonreligious form of oath. Their Yes is Yes; their No is No, and whatever solemn declaration they add makes no difference at all. Among Christians there are no oaths, but only Yes and No.[30] Solely for the sake of other persons and for the sake of the deceit that reigns in the world, they may make their word—to be sure, no more truthful than it would otherwise be, but nevertheless—more believable by making use of the form of oath required by the state. Yet it does not matter for them whether this form mentions the name of God. For Christians the oath represents only the external ratification of that which is self-evident in any case, namely, that their word is spoken before God.

670   *Third Commandment*
"You are to hallow the day of rest."[31]

We find it nearly inconceivable that this commandment is as worthy as the prohibition against idol worship or the prohibition against killing, that the transgressor of this commandment is no less guilty than those who revile their parents or than thieves, adulterers, and slanderers. On workdays our life is lived at work and among people. The day of rest [Feiertag] seems to us to be a lovely and pleasant concession, but the idea that the gravity of a commandment of God backs it up has now become alien to us.

God commands us to observe the day of rest. God commands that we rest on and hallow the day of rest.

[29.] Matt. 6:9.

[30.] [Cf. Matt. 5:33-37.—MB]

[31.] This is Luther's formulation in the Small Catechism (*Book of Concord*, 352); cf. Exod. 20:8, which reads, "Remember the sabbath day, and keep it holy."

The Decalogue contains not a commandment to work but a commandment to rest from work. This is the opposite of what we usually think. Work is something taken for granted in the Third Commandment; but God knows that the work people do takes on such power over them that they cannot let it go, that they expect everything from their work and forget God in the process. Thus God commands that they rest from their labors. Work is not what sustains a person; God alone is. A person lives not from work but solely from God.[32] "Unless the LORD builds the house, those who build it labor in vain. Unless the LORD guards the city, the guard keeps watch in vain . . . for [the Lord] provides for his beloved during sleep"[33] (Ps. 127[:1-2]), says the Bible against all who make their work into their religion. A day of resting [Feiertagsruhe] is the visible sign that a person lives from the grace of God and not from works.

Outer and inner rest are to rule the day of rest. In our homes all work that is not necessary for life should cease; and the Decalogue explicitly includes servants and strangers, indeed, even livestock, in these commandments.[34] We are to seek not mindless diversion but rest and composure. Because this is not easy, because inactivity is much more likely to lead to bored laziness or exhausting distractions and amusements, such rest has to be explicitly commanded.[35] It takes effort to keep this commandment.

Actually resting is the indispensable precondition for hallowing the day of rest. Human beings who have been reduced to machines and have been exhausted need rest so that their thoughts can clear, their feelings be purified, and their desires be oriented anew.

The hallowing of the day of rest is the content of that day's rest. Hallowing the day of rest takes place through the proclamation of the word of God in worship and through hearing this word willingly and reverently. The desecration of the day of rest begins with the decay of Christian proclamation. It is thus primarily the fault of the church and in particular of those who hold office in the church. For this reason, the renewal of hallowing the day of rest begins with the renewal of preaching.

671

[32.] See *DBWE* 4:166 on Matt. 6:25-26: "Jesus dissolves the connection between work and food, which is conceived in terms of cause and effect apart from God."

[33.] [NRSV alternative translation used for last part of this quotation, since it corresponds more closely to Bonhoeffer's Bible.—MB]

[34.] Exod. 20:10. Cf. in Bonhoeffer's fragment of a novel: "If today weren't Sunday, they would have the horses and the coach brought out and would drive to the station. But unfortunately that wasn't possible now," since "the animals were resting today from their week's labors" (*DBWE* 7:178).

[35.] Cf. at the beginning of the fragment of a novel, regarding "the kindest of God's Ten Commandments": with Sunday rest "you had to force people to rediscover their happiness after they had so carelessly thrown it away" (*DBWE* 7:72).

Jesus broke through the Jewish laws about Sabbath rest. He did it so that the Sabbath could truly be hallowed.[36] The Sabbath is hallowed not by means of what human beings do or do not do, but by means of the action of Jesus Christ for human salvation. For this reason the ancient Christians replaced the Sabbath with the day of Jesus Christ's resurrection and called this the day of the Lord. That explains why Luther rightly renders the Third Commandment not with a literal translation of the Hebrew word Sabbath, but with the spiritually interpreted word "day of rest" [Feiertag]. Our Sunday is the day on which we allow Jesus Christ to act toward us and all people.

672   To be sure, this ought to occur every day; but on Sunday we rest from our work so that it might take place in a special way.

The goal of hallowing Sunday is the Sunday rest. God wants to lead God's people to God's own rest, to relax from the earthly workday. "Rejoice, my heart, you shall be / Freed from this earth's dark mis'ry / And from the daily work of sin."[37] Freed from imperfect human effort, the people of God are to gaze on the completed pure work of God and to participate in it. As a reflection and promise of this eternal rest with the Creator and Redeemer of the world, the Christian who keeps Sunday holy is permitted to experience Sunday rest.

Before the world's eyes, Sunday is the evidence that the life of the children of God proceeds from God's grace and that all people are called into God's kingdom. And so we pray, "May your kingdom come!"[38]

[36.] Cf. *DBWE* 6:278: Jesus "broke the law of the Sabbath in order to sanctify it, out of love for God and human beings."

[37.] This is the end of the fifth stanza of the hymn "Now All the Woods Are Sleeping," by Paul Gerhardt (*Lutheran Book of Worship*, no. 276; *Evangelisches Gesangbuch für Brandenburg und Pommern*, 280; *Evangelisches Kirchengesangbuch*, 361 ["*der Sünden Arbeit*"]). [This hymn in the *Lutheran Book of Worship* has only four stanzas, and the fifth stanza included here in Bonhoeffer's text is not one of them. The image of the "daily work of sin" seems to refer to the drudgery of our daily work because our "first parents" fell into sin; see Gen. 3:17.—MB]

[38.] Cf. Matt. 6:10 and Luther's Small Catechism (*Book of Concord*, 356). On the margin of Bonhoeffer's letter to Eberhard Bethge from Tegel on August 3, 1944, is a postscript: "The paper on the first three commandments seems to have been serviceable, which I am happy about" (*DBW* 8:556).

JØRGEN GLENTHØJ†, ULRICH KABITZ,
AND WOLF KRÖTKE

EDITORS' AFTERWORD
TO THE GERMAN EDITION

THIS VOLUME'S COLLECTION OF Bonhoeffer's correspondence and writings
from the years 1940–45 (part 1) falls into clearly delineated categories. First
we encounter the "illegal"[1] Bonhoeffer, who is trying to make the most of
the limited possibilities still offered by the weakened Confessing Church.
Then the Military Intelligence agent emerges, who exploits his role on
behalf of the forces of the church resistance and the conspiratorial political
resistance. Finally there is the prisoner, who even within the confines of his
cell and in interrogations continues to fight for survival—to the very end,
in the hope that after the war he will be able to participate in the new
beginning of the church and society.

In parts 2 and 3 of this volume, we clearly see the alternation between
attempting new initiatives and breaking them off, which corresponds to
what happened in the period leading up to Bonhoeffer's arrest in April
1943. The Reich ban on public speaking issued against him in August 1940
and the ban on publication imposed by the Reich Chamber of Literature
shortly thereafter explain the relative dearth of materials in part 3, even
though preaching was particularly important to Bonhoeffer.

The editors were astonished at how clear a picture the materials presented
here offer of the full and varied life Bonhoeffer led up until his arrest. On the
other hand, in the course of our work on this volume, we continually found
ourselves confronted with the problem that often in these materials only
the tip of the iceberg was visible. Particularly during this time period there
are all sorts of activities involving family, friends,[2] the church, and politics

---

[1.] During the period covered by this volume, "illegals" included all institutions and
officials who continued to be active in the Confessing Church without authorization by
the "legal" consistories and despite the prohibitions issued by the latter.

[2.] See in this regard Eberhard Bethge, "Bonhoeffer's Theology of Friendship," in
Friendship and Resistance, 80–105.

674   for which our explanatory footnotes do not provide adequate background and contextual information. The following two sections offer some supplementary information, in regard, first, to Bonhoeffer's correspondence and then to the theological materials. For the rest we refer the reader to Eberhard Bethge's classic biography *Dietrich Bonhoeffer,* which repeatedly provided support and guidance for us and which has proven to be undiminished in its scholarly reliability.

I

If the closing of the Confessing Church seminary in Finkenwalde at the end of September 1937, along with the transition to the collective pastorates in East Pomerania, was already a step into uncharted territory, that applied even more to the situation that presented itself when this illegal pastoral training was ended in March 1940 with the closing of Sigurdshof. Any possibility of continuing this training of young theologians was eliminated, partly because of police bans and partly in view of the fact that most young men were called up into military service.

The possibility of Bonhoeffer himself sooner or later receiving an induction order doubtless overshadowed the first weeks of spring 1940, which he and Bethge spent mostly in Berlin. The question is the extent to which Bonhoeffer himself could have expected that he would be spared for at least a certain period because of his semiofficial contacts with Colonel Hans Oster in the Foreign Office of Military Intelligence of the Armed Forces High Command since autumn 1939. In any event, he found it necessary to send a letter about this matter to the military recruiting office in Schlawe.[3] In this way it appeared that he did not have to worry about doing "violence to his Christian conviction" if he "would take up arms 'here and now.' "[4]

675   Of course, some of Bonhoeffer's activities were still connected with Pomerania. At the beginning of December 1939 the Pomeranian Council of Brethren appointed Bonhoeffer and Heinrich Rendtorff to head a commission for clergy working groups [Kommission für Konventsarbeit]. There was apparently also an agreement concerning regular contributions to the newsletters of the Pomeranian Council of Brethren in the form of "theological supplements," which also could have involved tedious discussions, as the correspondence with consistory official Baumann shows.[5] On the other hand, Bonhoeffer retained his personal relationships and contacts with the

---

[3.] See the excerpt of Bonhoeffer's letter of May 27, 1940, to the Schlawe District Military Recruiting Office, 1/9.

[4.] See Bonhoeffer's letter of March 25, 1939, to Bishop Bell, *DBW* 15:160 (*GS* 1:465).

[5.] See 1/1, 1/2, 1/4, and 1/8.

Pomeranian estates, especially with Ruth von Kleist-Retzow in Klein-Krössin, at whose behest Bonhoeffer in that period wrote the important letter to her granddaughter Ruth Roberta Stahlberg.[6]

Transitions

The following correspondence gives an inkling of the enormous strain that accompanied Bonhoeffer's continuing efforts to maintain at least a certain latitude for his own initiatives and activities in the face of the prevailing restrictions and increasing measures directed against the church. However, some events are not mentioned at all, including a meeting with Colonel Oster on March 24, 1940, or, shortly thereafter, the visit of pastors Friedrich von Bodelschwingh and Paul Braune in the Marienburger Allee on April 7 to discuss with Bonhoeffer's father possibilities for countering the increasing use of euthanasia.[7]

Ongoing political and military developments such as the invasion of Denmark and Norway and even more so the campaign in France, which began on May 10, provide more than merely the distant backdrop to all these events, since precisely the victories accompanying this "blitzkrieg" enduringly influenced other events as well. Such is reflected in Bethge's description of how he and Bonhoeffer, while in Memel on June 17, reacted to the special announcement of the capitulation of France as well as in Bonhoeffer's statement: "We shall have to run risks for very different things now."[8] We are aware of how such events influenced Bonhoeffer's *Ethics*.[9] We must certainly also note reflections of peculiar hopes in letters from Ruth von Kleist-Retzow and Herbert von Bismarck from this period: "[S]hould God not also be able to lead our people into God's way again by means of a victory exceeding all historical measure? God can surely also do this; let us ask God to do so."[10]

In his biography Bethge quite justifiably understands Bonhoeffer's remark in Memel, mentioned above, within the larger context in which Bonhoeffer

676

[6.] See Bonhoeffer's letter of March 23, 1940, to Ruth Roberta Stahlberg, 1/3. This letter was first published in *GS* 3:37–43, which identified it only as "To an Unknown Woman."

[7.] Cf. in this regard Christine-Ruth Müller, *Dietrich Bonhoeffers Kampf*, 291–92, and Winfried Meyer, *Unternehmen Sieben*, 30–31 et passim, which particularly assesses the assistance provided by Hans von Dohnanyi. For a thorough assessment of the role played by Karl and Dietrich Bonhoeffer, cf. Gerrens, "Medizinisches Ethos und theologische Ethik."

[8.] See *DBER*, 681.

[9.] *DBWE* 6:89–90 ("*idolizing success*"), written in 1940; cf. *DBWE* 6:138–45, on the church's confession of guilt and the "scarring over" of guilt in the history of nations (*Völker*), written in 1941.

[10.] See Herbert von Bismarck's letter of June 24, 1940, to Dietrich Bonhoeffer, 1/13. Cf. the corrective in *DBWE* 6:143–44, together with ed. notes 42 and 43.

now began to lead what amounted to a "double life."[11] Bonhoeffer continued his previous existence as a man of the Confessing Church; now, however, he was also a participant in the political conspiracy against Hitler's regime, an identity manifested concretely in his increasing contact with the circle around Colonel Oster and Hans von Dohnanyi in Canaris's office. In March 1940, after Josef Müller's reconnaissance in the Vatican involving what is known as the "X-report,"[12] Bonhoeffer doubtless caught wind of this circle's feverish efforts to win the military leadership over to the idea of overthrowing Hitler. After Hitler's victory in the West, the conspirators had to resist their own sense of resignation and instead move on to new possibilities under even more difficult conditions. Later we will discuss how Bonhoeffer became actively involved in this.

677

First we must consider the familiar course of Bonhoeffer's work for the Old Prussian Council of Brethren, with the additional new assignment to conduct visitations among the East Prussian congregations of the Confessing Church. The materials preserved from this period, extending from early June to late August, show him in dialogue with various colleagues and church elders, at work on sermons and Bible studies in the congregations being visited, and participating in weekend retreats.[13] One such retreat, which took place in Blöstau with a handful of students, had enormous and far-reaching consequences for Bonhoeffer. The police intervention in this instance[14] resulted in what amounted to a crippling penalty for Bonhoeffer: because of "subversive activity" he was banned from public speaking throughout the Reich and required to report his movements regularly to the police at his registered place of residence, Schlawe in East Pomerania. Bonhoeffer sought to counter this severe turn of events, which once again narrowed his options, by switching to the other track in his "double life." With the aid of his brother-in-law Dohnanyi, he now bound himself even more closely to Military Intelligence. Accordingly, the final visitation trip in East Prussia served a double purpose: to fulfill the commission of the Council of Brethren to Confessing Church congregations that to some extent had been orphaned; and at the same time, to carry out a commission from Canaris's office to gather information about "Red Army" troop concentrations across

---

[11.] See *DB-ER*, 681.

[12.] The "X-report" was Josef Müller's summary of information about peace feelers and the Allies' willingness to negotiate after Hitler's fall, based on his meetings at the Vatican with the British envoy; cf. *DB-ER*, 673–74.

[13.] See the calendar notes, 1/10.

[14.] The recently discovered July 17, 1940, report from the SD Regional Headquarters in Königsberg to the Reich Central Security Office (see 1/15) reveals that this intervention was prompted by a student acting as a spy for the SD.

the border. In contrast to his preceding activities, which are profusely documented, there are no corresponding materials from Bonhoeffer's own hand for this final stage, doubtless an indication that the experiences in Blöstau also prompted him to exercise increased caution.

As one looks back on the period of these visitations, the following emerges: the themes and tone of the available materials from his appearances there seem more closely related to Finkenwalde and the collective pastorates than to any particular interest in a book on "ethics." Bonhoeffer still seems completely focused on his pastoral concerns for his church colleagues and on encouraging and strengthening their resolve in this difficult situation.   678

We are not certain when Bonhoeffer actually began his work on the *Ethics* manuscripts. The material in the present volume offers no evidence that the first phase of such work began in the spring[15] and summer[16] of 1940. One reason is probably that Bethge, with whom Bonhoeffer would have corresponded about this, was almost always in Berlin or traveling with Bonhoeffer during this period. Not until Bethge was physically separated from his friend through his duties for the Gossner Mission did Bonhoeffer write to him, on October 9, 1940, from Pomerania: "My work progresses. I am writing the outline of the whole thing."[17] This letter constitutes the first evidence of Bonhoeffer's work on the *Ethics*, work for which he had temporarily withdrawn to Klein-Krössin.

In Ettal

Several factors prompted Bonhoeffer to spend three months in upper Bavaria during 1940–41. On the one hand, after receiving the commission from Provost Staemmler on behalf of the Old Prussian Council of Brethren, it gave him the opportunity to continue the work he had begun on his *Ethics* in a suitable, secluded setting.[18] On the other hand, it permitted his relationship with the Military Intelligence Office to come into effect. Even though Bonhoeffer's written offer to make himself and his ecumenical contacts available was composed only after the fact, in the form of a "camouflage letter,"[19] this particular characterization certainly must have played a role

---

[15.] However, a letter to the Leibholz family on March 7, 1940 (*DBW* 15:296–300 [*GS* 1:35]) does suggest that Bonhoeffer was reflecting on the basic problems of Christian ethics; cf. *DBWE* 6:414–15.

[16.] Cf. *DBWE* 6:420–21.

[17.] See Bonhoeffer's letter of October 9, 1940, to Eberhard Bethge, 1/23.

[18.] See Bonhoeffer's letter of November 16, 1940, to Eberhard Bethge (1/27) and Bonhoeffer's letter of November 16, 1940, to his parents (1/28).

[19.] See 1/221.

679   in the conversations he had with Dohnanyi and Colonel Oster that ultimately led to an arrangement with Military Intelligence Office VII in Munich, for that office already had a corresponding middleman on the Catholic side in the person of the lawyer Josef Müller, who handled the important contacts with the Vatican. The two men had already become acquainted in Berlin through Dohnanyi. On Bonhoeffer's first Munich trip, Müller had secured Bonhoeffer a room in the Park Hotel, near his own law office,[20] and then introduced him in the Benedictine monastery at Ettal, where he was graciously given the accommodations he desired for work on his *Ethics*.[21]

This arrangement had the significant side effect of extricating him from the complications in Pomerania that had been caused by the obligation to report his movements to the police as well as from his dependence on the military recruiting office in Schlawe. The messages Dohnanyi sent on December 11, 1940,[22] illuminate this aspect of Bonhoeffer's stay in upper Bavaria and indicate the extent to which these measures allowed and ensured Bonhoeffer's continued existence as a private citizen.

The materials from Bonhoeffer's time in Ettal are extraordinarily fertile, particularly because so much of his correspondence with Eberhard Bethge from this period has been preserved. Even this plethora of communications, however, reveals only fragments of Bonhoeffer's various activities. Ettal was by no means an isolated locale where he could pursue his scholarly work undistracted. Quite the contrary, one subsequently marvels how significant parts of *Ethics* could have been produced here while Bonhoeffer was simultaneously engaged in wholly unrelated activities and, moreover, was without a typewriter and utterly dependent on his own resourcefulness.

The first such activity involved family demands, since Christine von Dohnanyi and her children arrived a mere five days after Bonhoeffer's own

680   arrival. Together with a hundred schoolchildren from Hamburg, they had to be accommodated here to escape the bombing raids at home and were enrolled in the secondary school [Gymnasium]. This situation naturally brought with it certain obligations for Bonhoeffer to look after the new arrivals—even to the point of taking his godson, Christoph von Dohnanyi, into his own room to care for him when the latter got the flu.

Clearly Bonhoeffer was constantly concerned about the welfare of friends and family in Berlin. In particular, he was preoccupied with Bethge's fate and was especially concerned with where things stood with Bethge's new

---

[20.] During his later trips to Munich, Bonhoeffer stayed at a Catholic hostel, the Europäischer Hof, across from the main train station.

[21.] See Bonhoeffer's letter of November 18, 1940, to Eberhard Bethge, 1/29. Bonhoeffer stayed at the nearby Hotel Ludwig der Bayer.

[22.] See 1/48 and 1/49.

activities on behalf of the Gossner Mission and with his exemption from military service.[23] Bethge, in turn, provided Bonhoeffer with information about the Berlin Council of Brethren, for which Friedrich Justus Perels doubtless represented the primary contact.

One unusually powerful thread in the overall fabric of Bonhoeffer's correspondence was his continued contacts with the over one hundred former seminarians, contacts he faithfully maintained up until his arrest. With few exceptions these seminarians were now soldiers scattered across the various battlefronts. In frank and open letters, they related to him how it felt to be caught between their sometimes barbaric military activity and the spiritual practices learned in Finkenwalde. During his Christmas preparations in Munich, he was able to purchase a hundred postcards depicting Albrecht Altdorfer's painting of Christ's birth amid ruins, as a Christmas greeting to send to them, and in Ettal he took the time to compose a meditative pastoral Christmas letter for the brothers.[24]

We know very little about the Munich address that Bonhoeffer was able to register as his permanent address with the police and to which he also had some of his mail sent. The house, located on Unertlstraße in Schwabing, belonged to his aunt Countess Christine von Kalckreuth, a painter and graphic artist, who gladly opened her home to young relatives attending the university in Munich and to her artist friends. During his stays there, Bonhoeffer also met her brother Johannes, a highly regarded music critic.[25]   681

The material in this volume also demonstrates the singular importance of the network of Bavarian Catholic contacts to whom Josef Müller quickly introduced Bonhoeffer. Crucial focal points include the Ettal monastery itself, the bishop's office in Munich, Müller's own law office there, and the Benedictine monastery in Metten on the Danube. Lines of communication also emerge with the headquarters of the Steyler Mission in Vienna and the Vatican in Rome.

Recalling the early impressions Bonhoeffer acquired in Rome as a student in 1924, one is again struck by how adroitly Bonhoeffer accommodates himself with mind and heart to these new surroundings. Conversations with the Ettal abbot, Angelus Kupfer, and the monastery's "foreign minister," Father Johannes Albrecht, were valuable not just for dialogue on his immediate work on ethical issues, but even more so because of the possibilities

---

[23.] Here Bethge's importance in information gathering was of some consequence for the "Canaris office" in light of his contacts to the International Missionary Council in Switzerland.

[24.] See 1/47.

[25.] According to Eberhard Bethge's recollection (personal communication, April 1, 1994).

they suggested for productive future dialogue between Catholics and Protestants, particularly since both were having to withstand persecution by the ruling political system.[26] Noteworthy in this regard are Bonhoeffer's reflections on how previously separated churches could in more recent years come to establish a closer relationship through an acknowledgment of God's "guidance,"[27] and the fact that in his later conversations in Geneva Bonhoeffer apparently expressed such thoughts openly.[28]

682   To a certain extent, Bonhoeffer used his contacts in the appropriate Munich circles to familiarize Bethge, who had just assumed a new office himself, with the new methods for church renewal of the Redemptorists and the Steyler Mission. On the other hand, Monsignor Johannes Neuhäusler in the Munich bishop's office was an especially important dialogue partner for Bonhoeffer, since he gathered information significant for church policy and sent it along to the Vatican by means of reliable couriers such as Josef Müller. A copy of Bonhoeffer's report on his Swedish journey in June 1942[29] was taken to Rome by way of Dr. Müller's law office. Bonhoeffer allegedly also had several intensive conversations in that office with the Metten abbot, Corbinian Hofmeister.[30]

What evidence does Bonhoeffer's *Ethics* provide of the likely atmosphere of such encounters? His letters provide little information in this regard. Clearly there is a common perception of how the National Socialists' policy toward the churches was becoming increasingly harsh; new restrictions were constantly imposed under the subterfuge of war-related measures.[31] We do know that Bonhoeffer's experience in the monastery confirmed for him the model of the Finkenwalde seminary community.[32]

Bonhoeffer sensed that there would be an opportunity "to throw oneself between the spokes of the wheel" when he met with Reich Justice Minister

---

[26.] Eberhard Bethge recalls that during his stay in Ettal around Christmas 1940, Bonhoeffer also had a lengthy conversation with the Jesuit Rupert Mayer, who had been arrested several times and was placed under house arrest by the Gestapo in August 1940 because of his courageous sermons (personal communication on February 14, 1987).

[27.] See Bonhoeffer's letter of November 16, 1940, to Eberhard Bethge, 1/27.

[28.] See Nils Ehrenström's calendar notes from March 12, 1941, 1/93. See also Allen Dulles in his 1947 book *Germany's Underground*, 118: "Catholics and Protestants met secretly in the monastery of Ettal and found common ground in their resistance to the Nazi paganism." From late 1942 Dulles worked for the U.S. Office of Strategic Services in Bern; the question of his source for this early information remains open.

[29.] Cf. 1/170, pp. 297–305.

[30.] Communication from Mrs. Annie Oster, Josef Müller's former secretary, on March 10, 1987.

[31.] See, for example, Bonhoeffer's letter of November 4, 1940, to Eberhard Bethge, 1/25.

[32.] Josef Müller, "Der Abbas."

Dr. Franz Gürtner, who visited his son in Ettal at Christmas 1940. Bonhoeffer's hope that Gürtner, together with Reich Minister of Church Affairs Hanns Kerrl, might be able to counter the massive military conscription of Confessing Church pastors were dashed by Dr. Gürtner's death shortly thereafter.[33]

Switzerland   683

Traveling to foreign countries was nothing new for the former ecumenical youth secretary. What was new was the war, which made journeys even to neutral countries virtually impossible, and the role Bonhoeffer now assumed as an agent for German Military Intelligence and his simultaneous role as a secret agent for the resistance group around General Beck and Colonel Oster, a role that provoked some irritation among those who had known Bonhoeffer the theologian and Confessing Church pastor earlier.

The material in the present volume allows us to plot on the Swiss map with some degree of accuracy the various places that were significant for Bonhoeffer. In Zurich he was received by Hans Bernd Gisevius, vice-consul in the German Consulate and at the same time envoy of the "Canaris office"; he had once been close to Martin Niemöller and was now not entirely free of jealousy toward the newcomer in the service of "Military Intelligence."[34] There, too, Bonhoeffer found his first lodging in the house of the manufacturer Rudolf Pestalozzi and his wife, who belonged to Karl Barth's circle of friends.[35] Nothing suggests that he sought out the systematic theologian Emil Brunner, although Bonhoeffer had earlier been concerned with obtaining Brunner's recommendation for a visa for the first Swiss journey[36] and had thoroughly and critically dealt with Brunner's work *The Divine Imperative* as an ethical blueprint.[37] Bonhoeffer's contacts in Zurich also included

---

[33.] See Bonhoeffer's letter of January 31, 1941, to Eberhard Bethge, 1/66.

[34.] Cf. in this regard Christine von Dohnanyi: "In order to maintain complete control in Switzerland, Gis[evius] really did . . . constantly try to obstruct the trips my brother wanted to take for ecumenical reasons. After my husband's arrest (quite apart from the 'idiotic' defamation), Gisevius spread the rumor that my husband had engaged in family politics when he brought my brother into the Military Intelligence Office and was now paying for it. Gisevius also tried to get Dr. Müller away from this circle by explaining to him that he, Dr. Müller, was working with the wrong people. He alleged that Dietrich was not a representative of the Protestant church and that Karl Barth rejected Dietrich entirely" (in a unpublished letter to Paul Schulze zur Wiesche, May 28, 1946, cited in Smid, *Hans von Dohnanyi, Christine Bonhoeffer,* 7).

[35.] See Bonhoeffer's letter of June 10, 1941, to Gerty Pestalozzi, 1/112.

[36.] See Bonhoeffer's letter of January 31, 1941, to Emil Brunner, 1/65.

[37.] Cf., e.g., Bonhoeffer's lecture "Besprechung und Diskussion systematisch-theologischer Neuerscheinungen" (Review and discussion of new publications in systematic theology) at Berlin University in the winter semester 1932/33, in *DBW* 12:153–78 (*GS* 5:302–40).

684   the addresses of two German émigrés: Professor Friedrich Siegmund-Schultze drew on his own network of contacts for conspiratorial purposes;[38] and Otto Salomon, Bonhoeffer's former editor at the Christian Kaiser publishing house, offered his hospitality during subsequent visits. In nearby Rapperswil, Bonhoeffer had a reunion with a friend from his time in New York, Erwin Sutz, who had become the "mailbox" for Bonhoeffer's correspondence to and from England. The social ethicist Alfred de Quervain, who had settled in Laufen, Canton Bern, was of interest to Bonhoeffer with regard to the work on *Ethics*.

Basel and Geneva, however, are clearly the focal points of Bonhoeffer's Swiss encounters. Bonhoeffer recalls his first visit with Karl Barth this way: "The days I spent with you were especially delightful."[39] Regarding the content of their conversations there during the second Swiss journey, the concise outline of a book (which was never written) provides a glimpse at how thoroughly the two men discussed the questions of "theological existence today." They had taken up the themes that Bonhoeffer had set forth as the "most relevant for this present time," namely, "history and eschatological expectation," "Christian responsibility," and the "forgiveness of sins," and they were prepared to carry this discussion further.[40]

Although various motifs in the *Ethics* already resonate here, the third Swiss journey in May 1942 yielded even more direct points of contact with Bonhoeffer's plans, since the new volume 2/2 of Barth's *Church Dogmatics*, with its ethical section "The Commandment of God," had been completed.[41]

685   Hence, along with current church and political events, central theological questions must have guided their conversations.

Nonetheless, this essential contact was not without its own burdens. Their correspondence before the third meeting in Basel reveals that Bonhoeffer, quite to his dismay, found himself embroiled in a crisis. Shortly after his entry into Switzerland, he must have heard about Barth's warning that "he be most circumspect when discussing politics with Swiss people."[42] Even more ominous was the suggestion, frequently mentioned by others,

---

[38.] Stefan Grotefeld has thoroughly investigated these particular contacts, of which Bonhoeffer himself was hardly aware, and also cites Siegmund-Schultze's later recollections; the errors in these recollections confirm this lack of direct exchange (Grotefeld, "Opposition gegen den Nationalsozialismus und Schweizer Exil," 233–34).

[39.] See Bonhoeffer's letter of May 30, 1941, to Karl Barth, 1/110. Regarding this and the following discussion, see Eberhard Bethge's illuminating commentary in Bethge, *Schweizer Korrespondenz*, 22–36.

[40.] See Charlotte von Kirschbaum's letter of September 22, 1941, to Paul Vogt, 1/128.

[41.] See Bonhoeffer's letter of May 13, 1942, to Karl Barth, 1/160.

[42.] See Barth's letter of May 12, 1942, to Otto Salomon, 1/158.

that Barth actually found Bonhoeffer's stay somewhat "unsettling as to its objectives." Bonhoeffer's letter of May 17, 1942, shows how distressed he was by the situation: "In a time in which so much simply has to rest on personal trust, *everything* is lost if mistrust arises. I can, of course, understand that this curse of suspicion gradually afflicts us all, but it is difficult to bear when for the first time it affects one personally."[43] This vexing situation was quickly alleviated, but the incident allows us to sense the unpleasant side of these unusual opportunities to travel. At the same time, however, the experiential background of the following statements becomes clear: "We know that it is most reprehensible to sow and encourage mistrust, and that our duty is rather to foster and strengthen confidence wherever we can. Trust will always be one of the greatest, rarest, and happiest blessings of our life in community, though it can emerge only on the dark background of a necessary mistrust."[44]

The material in this volume provides impressive information about Bonhoeffer's visits with the small staff of the incipient World Council of Churches in Geneva. The material is noteworthy for showing how much attention was paid to the German guest, who found a splendid dialogue partner in the young general secretary, the Dutch theologian Willem A. Visser 't Hooft.

Deciphering the succinct calendar notes of Bonhoeffer's Swedish colleague Nils Ehrenström[45] so that they yield a cogent overview requires what virtually amounts to detective work. Certain keywords reveal the scope of the topics they discussed together as well as the intellectual proximity of their thoughts and perspectives. Bonhoeffer's work on his *Ethics* was on virtually the same wavelength as the concepts of the study section in Geneva that was dealing with questions of the "ethical reality and function of the church" and with the "proclamation of the church in war."

686

The expression "peace aims,"[46] however, conceals the most far-reaching initiative on an ecumenical foundation that was undertaken from Geneva in close contact with a similar English study group. These discussions focused on ideas about the church's political responsibility in regard to peace aims and the reconstruction after the war. Those ideas also bring us to a high point in this volume, where a brief retrospective might be helpful before focusing on some of the subsequent important stages in Bonhoeffer's traces as they can be discerned in our documents.

[43.] See 1/161.
[44.] "After Ten Years," *LPP,* 12 (*DBW* 8:31).
[45.] See March 8–15, 1941, 1/93.
[46.] See 1/93, ed. note 7.

Renewed Commission

In the spring of 1941, when Bonhoeffer managed to get to Geneva for the first time since the outbreak of the war, he did much more than merely reestablish his earlier ecumenical contacts. He made contact with the international headquarters and at the same time resumed his role as youth secretary, a role in which he had served since 1931. Hence what Visser 't Hooft said in his newsletter of March 15, 1939, "The Church and the Ecumenical Community in Times of War," about a common task certainly applied to Bonhoeffer during this period: "In times of war the ecumenical task of the church involves the following obligations: 1. the task of prayer and genuine proclamation; 2. the task of maintaining Christian relationships with churches in all countries; and 3. the task of preparing for a just peace." Regarding the third point, ongoing efforts were called for "to determine with Christians on the enemy side which peace conditions are more likely to create a lasting peace rather than further poisoning international relations," and practical steps are suggested, such as the creation "of advisory boards or study groups among the Christian laity for this purpose."[47] Other studies have examined how, step by step, this goal became reality, for example, with the July 1939 Geneva peace study, the Christmas 1940 proclamation by English bishops, the January 1941 Malvern conference, and William Paton's subsequent establishment of a "Peace Aims Group," as well as various activities in the United States and Sweden.[48]

And it is important for us to recognize that the date on which Bonhoeffer joined in on such strategic planning was the first step on the way to the full integration of the various aspects of his involvement with the ecumenical movement, the Confessing Church, and the political resistance.

The importance Bonhoeffer's friends in Geneva attached to his information and views is attested by the confidential information service through which Visser 't Hooft communicated with a small circle within the World Council of Churches and which, immediately after Bonhoeffer's first visit, was able to include a whole range of precise information from Germany.[49] Six months later Bonhoeffer and Visser 't Hooft jointly issued a kind of conceptual response to William Paton's program, "The Church and the New Order in Europe,"[50] thereby also providing Bonhoeffer his first contact with the British Peace Aims Group.

687

[47.] See Boyens, *Kirchenkampf und Ökumene*, 1:385ff.

[48.] See *DB-ER*, 735–43 et passim; Boyens, *Kirchenkampf und Ökumene*, 2:171–79 et passim; von Klemperer, *German Resistance*, 264–312.

[49.] See, e.g., Visser 't Hooft, "Notes on the State of the Church in Europe," from the end of March 1941, 1/98.

[50.] See 2/11 and 2/12.

Silent Witnesses of Evil Deeds 688

We must see Bonhoeffer's efforts at rescuing persecuted "non-Aryans" as embedded in this simultaneously ecumenical and conspiratorial engagement. Deeply personal experiences, including the emigration of siblings, relatives, and friends, doubtless helped prompt these efforts. We can sense the context behind terse key phrases from his initial conversations in Geneva, the aid network established by Adolf Freudenberg on behalf of persecuted and interned persons and in which the young members of the French CIMADE [Comité Inter-Mouvements auprès des Evacués] played an inestimable part.[51]

It is thus quite understandable that in the autumn of 1941 Bonhoeffer's recently renewed Swiss contacts led to an early dissemination of information to his ecumenical friends concerning initial deportation measures[52] and, among those members of the Berlin congregation threatened, generated a certain measure of hope that they might be helped to emigrate.[53] Such preliminary work did indeed pave the way for "Operation 7," that risky undertaking carried out by Dohnanyi, contacts in the "Canaris office," and Swiss partners, which involved smuggling a group of fourteen (rather than seven) "non-Aryans" past the Gestapo at the Swiss border at Basel, under the pretext that they were secret agents for Military Intelligence.[54]

Subsequent scholars have debated whether those at the center of the conspiracy should have taken such a risk,[55] since precisely this action did indeed prove to be the undoing of its initiators through a series of fateful developments. Bonhoeffer's defense letters to the lead investigator, Dr. 689 Roeder, during his imprisonment show the role that Operation 7 played in the interrogations.[56]

However, there is no doubt that both Dohnanyi and Bonhoeffer felt that what they were able to do in this regard was too little rather than too much. The motto of 1933, "Open your mouth for the dumb,"[57] is countered at the end of 1942 by the admission, "We have been silent witnesses of evil deeds."[58]

[51.] See 1/93, ed. note 6; Boyens, *Kirchenkampf und Ökumene,* 2:40–49 et passim; Visser 't Hooft, *Memoirs,* 132–33; Freudenberg, *Befreie die zum Tode geschleppt werden.* The former Finkenwalde seminarian Wolfgang Büsing was similarly active in England; at the end of 1938, Bishop Bell had entrusted him with caring for "non-Aryan" Christian émigrés (see *DB-ER,* 639–40).

[52.] See 1/133.

[53.] See Wilhelm Rott's letter of October 1941 to Alphons Koechlin, 1/134.

[54.] See the thorough portrayal of this rescue in Winfried Meyer, *Unternehmen Sieben.*

[55.] Ibid., 457–58.

[56.] June 1943; see 1/226, and 1/228.1.

[57.] See *DB-ER,* 273.

[58.] "After Ten Years," in *LPP,* 16 (*DBW* 8:38).

Relations to Colleagues

The defined Geneva task to "maintain Christian relations with churches in all countries" gave a plausible explanation for the journeys to Norway, Sweden, and Italy that Bonhoeffer undertook in 1942 at the behest of Military Intelligence.

Helmuth von Moltke's diary-like letters[59] provide some information about Bonhoeffer's participation in the trip to Oslo as well as about their respective roles in the meetings there with the heads of the German occupation troops and with representatives of the political and the church resistance. Theodor Steltzer, one of Moltke's friends stationed there as a transport officer, had established the requisite contacts and provided the necessary information. The urgent occasion was the conflict between the Norwegian state church and the Quisling government; shortly before, on Easter Sunday, April 5, 1942, this conflict had reached crisis proportions with the official strike of all bishops and pastors and with the arrest of the leading bishop, Eivind Berggrav.[60] Nothing more specific is known about Bonhoeffer's meetings except the laconic remark made by Bishop Berggrav later that "Bonhoeffer seems to have made a strong impression."[61]

690   Little is known about Bonhoeffer's trip to Italy in the summer of 1942 with Dohnanyi and Josef Müller. Bonhoeffer's own diary feigns a tone of loyalty to the regime and suggests that there were meetings in the Vatican[62] at which a conversation with the rector of the Collegium Germanicum, Ivo Zeiger, apparently followed up on trains of thought from Ettal. Josef Müller recalls that "after a while, an animated discussion began about whether it might be possible to pick up on the pre-Reformation period in the development of the two churches; for without a doubt both sides—Catholic and Protestant alike—after serious study have ascertained that the present time has gone beyond what the reformers actually intended."[63]

In this way Rome also became a new locus of fellowship and was able to awaken additional hopes for the future; at the same time, however, one waited in vain here for news from England.[64]

[59.] April 1942; see 1/154.

[60.] See Boyens, *Kirchenkampf und Ökumene*, 2:159–64; *MW* 5:262ff.; cf. 1/154, ed. note 2.

[61.] *MW* 5:263.

[62.] See 1/223; cf. also a similar reference on December 15, 1943 (*LPP*, 164 [*DBW* 8: 238]) with regard to Bonhoeffer's friend Eberhard Bethge, who was stationed near Rome.

[63.] J. Müller, *Bis zur letzten Konsequenz*, 241–42.

[64.] As agreed in Sweden, Bonhoeffer and Schönfeld were awaiting the results of Bishop Bell's exploratory talks with Foreign Minister Eden (cf. 1/170, pp. 302–4).

The Journey to Sweden

The historical significance of Bonhoeffer's and Hans Schönfeld's meeting with Bishop Bell in Sweden at the end of May and the beginning of April 1942 has long been acknowledged.[65] Accordingly, we have endeavored to document this event, together with its general background, more thoroughly than has hitherto been the case. Jørgen Glenthøj returned from his research in London with enough relevant material to write a book of his own. We limit ourselves here to selected material illuminating the main features of the preparations and consequences and highlighting Bishop Bell's previously unpublished diary notes from those days.[66] Indispensable supplemental　691 information was found in Bell's correspondence with Foreign Minister Anthony Eden as well as in the internal protocol notes of advisers in the British Foreign Office.[67]

In this material we have something akin to a case study in how efforts toward "peace aims" in reality could deepen into a crisis and become entangled in political complications. Because detailed analyses have been presented or can be anticipated elsewhere, we shall draw attention only to the following three points.

1. The background to these meetings includes the fact that various parties in London had already gone through a considerable number of such "peace feelers."[68] The most promising of such encounters, at least relatively speaking, had occurred some two years earlier when conversations initiated by Josef Müller with the British emissary to the Vatican had resulted in considerable progress.[69] Hitler's western offensive and the fall of Dunkirk brought these conversations to a disappointing end and predisposed Churchill's war cabinet to be even more distrustful of subsequent peace feelers, particularly since there were no signs of any opposition movement in Germany that was capable of taking action. Additional barriers emerged when the English fundamentally refused to enter into any negotiations without the participation of its allies and then finally with the Allies' demand for unconditional surrender. Moreover, papers from the British Foreign Office

---

[65.] See *DB-ER*, 757–63; Boyens, *Kirchenkampf und Ökumene*, 2:212; G. Ritter, *Carl Goerdeler*, 242–43; Hoffmann, *History of the German Resistance*, 218–20.

[66.] See 1/170.

[67.] See 1/183 and 1/187.

[68.] See 1/187.1; cf. Kettenacker, "Der nationalkonservative Widerstand in angelsächsischer Sicht," 718–23.

[69.] See Ludlow, "Pius XII, die britische Regierung und die deutsche Opposition im Winter 1939/40"; Hoffmann, *History of the German Resistance*, 159–62; J. Müller, *Bis zur letzten Konsequenz*, 130–38; Deutsch, *Conspiracy against Hitler*, 121–48.

reveal how someone like Trott was viewed suspiciously by the Allies as a "Nazi propagandist" despite his obvious sympathies for England.[70]

Hence both sides in the Sigtuna and Stockholm meetings knew what kind of difficulties they faced and that they were risking their own reputations on behalf of these efforts.

692   2. This model of ecumenical action also reveals the internal difficulties involved in harmonizing an ecclesiastical point of departure with political engagement. Even as excellent a peace representative as Paton found it difficult to accept Bonhoeffer's response to his book *The Church and the New Order*.[71] Among English church leaders, almost no one had followed developments in Germany as closely as Bishop Bell, for whom Bonhoeffer's brother-in-law Gerhard Leibholz, a constitutional lawyer who had emigrated to England, served as a trusted adviser from his new home in Oxford. Swedish friends found themselves repeatedly wondering whether, given their country's official position of neutrality, they could get involved in the prearranged courier mission.[72] It would require a separate chapter to examine all the differences that Bishop Bell's notes reveal between the two German representatives on this trip. Schönfeld's position was clearly characterized by a consciousness of military strength—Stalingrad had not yet occurred.[73] By contrast, Bonhoeffer's remark about the list of names of resistance leaders he had just handed over, "We are sorry, with this General's government," compels us to ask the extent to which he was acting as the courier of his Berlin informants or more in his personal role, namely, in critical loyalty to his fellow conspirators.[74]

3. Notwithstanding such questionable aspects, this undertaking does in any case surprise us with the obvious courage with which an extensive network of conspiratorial contacts was established. There can be no doubt that the basis already established by previous ecumenical work was enlisted to an extreme degree on behalf of clearly political ends. The same applies to Visser 't Hooft, who kept up even more comprehensive and complicated

---

[70.] This was the judgment of the U.S. chargé d'affaires in Sweden in a telegram to his government on June 26, 1944; see Boyens, *Kirchenkampf und Ökumene,* 2:197.

[71.] See *DB-ER,* 741–42.

[72.] See 1/181, ed. note 20.

[73.] See 1/170, pp. 298–300. Hedva Ben-Israel illustrates how this tendency can be observed in the foreign policy memoranda of many of the resistance groups until the Stalingrad crisis. Ben-Israel, "Im Widerstreit der Ziele," 735–38, 746–48.

[74.] A study of Bonhoeffer's closeness to or distance from related participants in the resistance such as Count Moltke, Adam von Trott, Eugen Gerstenmaier, and Hans Schönfeld remains to be done.

contacts from his office in Geneva.[75] Here as well as there, and without   693
question particularly for Bonhoeffer, this constituted a "responsible action
in a bold venture of faith"[76] in which Christians would have to engage for
the sake of a just peace.

The Engagement

When Bonhoeffer returned to Berlin from Sweden on June 2, 1942, he
had reached the high point of his activity in the service of the conspiracy.
At the same time, however, he must have received word of the serious threat
raised by the arrest of two members of the Munich office of Military Intelligence on charges of currency violations. The danger was that during interrogation they might reveal what they had learned about Dohnanyi's and
Bonhoeffer's foreign contacts and about their real intentions.[77] We must
keep these events in mind in our discussion of the special turn Bonhoeffer's life took at this juncture, namely, his engagement.

In a fortunate turn of fate, the literary estate of Maria von Wedemeyer-
Weller was opened, and the *Love Letters* were published during the course of
our own editorial work.[78] That material complements and clarifies various
individual letters in our volume that only occasionally allude to the relationship between Bonhoeffer and the secondary-school graduate [Abiturientin]
with whom he became reacquainted in early June 1942 as well as to their
difficult engagement.[79] The impression is that Bonhoeffer did not reveal
details of his present activities even to his fiancée. She nonetheless did hear
him remark in a conversation that there must be people who "could best   694
serve the Fatherland by operating on the internal front, perhaps even by
working against the regime."[80] A remark such as this initially struck her
quite hard, since her own father had recently been killed at Stalingrad, and
her brother, whom Bonhoeffer had confirmed, was just then with a combat
unit in Russia; indeed, barely three weeks later she learned that he, too, had
been killed.

The *Love Letters* provide hitherto missing information concerning the
last six months before his arrest, especially regarding the foreign journeys

---

[75.] See Visser 't Hooft, *Memoirs*, specifically the chapter "The Swiss Road," 136–49;
Heideking, "Die 'Schweizer Straßen' des europäischen Widerstands," 159ff.

[76.] "After Ten Years," *LPP*, 6 (*DBW* 8:24).

[77.] See in this regard the detailed presentation in Winfried Meyer, *Unternehmen Sieben*,
368–75.

[78.] Bismarck and Kabitz, *Love Letters from Cell 92*.

[79.] See 1/185, 1/210, 1/211, and 1/217.

[80.] *Love Letters from Cell 92*, 332.

he planned but was unable to undertake.[81] Hence we must use these letters to provide details about the terribly tense intervening periods when, for example, Bonhoeffer disregards Maria's mother's request that he not contact her and instead writes his fiancée on January 24, 1943, that "the immediate future may hold events of such elemental importance, to our private lives as well, that it would be forced and unnatural for us to be unable to communicate."[82] One can piece together an approximate picture of what he might have envisioned, namely, the disastrous situation on the eastern front—with the imminent fall of Stalingrad and the retreat from the Caucasus—accompanied by the secret hope that Hitler might be toppled by an assassination being planned by Maria's relatives Henning von Tresckow and Fabian von Schlabrendorff, among others.[83] But who at that time could have imagined that barely two months later his expectation was to become a reality for both of them in a completely different, horrific way, and that they would face an even longer, immeasurably more difficult test?

The Freiburg Memorandum

The motivation for the Freiburg memorandum must have emerged from conversations with Bishop Bell. Bell had raised the question whether, commensurate with the already extant "Peace Aims" study groups in England and the United States, a similarly qualified group might not also be formed in Germany to contribute a memorandum to a postwar conference of the World Council of Churches. The results of this suggestion have long become part of the history of the ecumenical movement and of the German resistance.[84] Closer examination shows that later reference to this working group of Freiburg professors as the "Bonhoeffer circle"[85] misconstrues Bonhoeffer's relationship to the group. Bonhoeffer did indeed provide the impulse for such a group during a visit in Freiburg and conveyed the explicit commission for such from the Provisional Church Administration; and as demonstrated in detail more recently, in October 1942 he discussed the disposition of the entire document with Constantin von Dietze and Erik

[81.] Ibid., 335, 342, 345. Bonhoeffer's letter of March 9, 1943, confirms that he was still planning to take a trip "to Rome for several weeks." [See also 1/220a.—MB]

[82.] Ibid., 342.

[83.] Hoffmann, *History of the German Resistance*, 280–89.

[84.] See *DB-ER*, 775–77; G. Ritter, *Carl Goerdeler*, 513–14; Boyens, *Kirchenkampf und Ökumene*, 2:216–17.

[85.] So Blumenberg-Lampe, *Das wirtschaftspolitische Programm*, 21, 29–30; similarly the subtitle "Die Denkschrift des Freiburger 'Bonhoeffer Kreises'" (The memorandum of the Freiburg "Bonhoeffer Circle"), in *In der Stunde Null*.

Wolf.[86] Bonhoeffer did not, however, participate in any subsequent meetings or work in this circle, for which Dietze provided the primary leadership. Dietze's notes about a final meeting in Berlin on February 6–7, 1943, that is, at a time when the memorandum itself was virtually finished, are revealing. Key phrases in those notes suggest that there was still a fundamental difference of opinion; Bonhoeffer and Perels emphasized their own position of "Decalogue ethics" over against those, such as Gerhard Ritter, who advocated an "ethics of conscience."[87]

We do not have to discuss here the extent to which the Freiburg memorandum, which was actually presented at the conference of World Council of Churches in Amsterdam in 1948, was of use as a building block for a new, democratic social order or, like many other such documents generated by opposition circles, was still captive to authoritarian models.[88] In any event, the respect due these Freiburg professors is unquestioned, particularly since several of them, including Dietze, fell into the hands of the Gestapo in the autumn of 1944 because of this activity. Of course, Bonhoeffer's name was bound to come up during their interrogations.[89]

Documents from the Period of Imprisonment

We have already mentioned the threat to which Dohnanyi and Bonhoeffer saw themselves exposed since the summer of 1942 and the Munich currency affair.[90] The *Depositenkasse* case, conducted by the relentless Air Force judge Manfred Roeder, had also aroused the interest of the Reich Central Security Office, since this case offered it an opportunity to gain influence in the central office of Military Intelligence, an office it had long regarded with suspicion.

Several documents represent precautionary measures faked and predated during the autumn of 1942: Bonhoeffer's "camouflage letter" to his

---

[86.] See 1/205.

[87.] See 1/218.

[88.] In his introduction to the materials included in *In der Stunde Null,* Helmut Thielicke draws several critical conclusions in this regard, especially with respect to section 5, "Suggestions for Solving the Jewish Question in Germany," a section written by Constantin von Dietze and doubtless unknown to Bonhoeffer (*In der Stunde Null,* 14–23). See also Nübel, "Bonhoeffer und die Denkschrift des 'Freiburger Kreises,'" 42–52; von Klemperer, *German Resistance against Hitler,* 50–51; Mommsen, "Social Views and Constitutional Plans of the Resistance," in Graml et al., *German Resistance to Hitler,* 112; Dipper, "Der 20. Juli und die 'Judenfrage,'" 70.

[89.] See 1/238.

[90.] See p. 657.

brother-in-law Dohnanyi; several diary entries from stays in Switzerland, Sweden, and Italy; and official orders from Oster and Dohnanyi.[91]

The events leading to the arrests of April 5, 1943, have been presented frequently in detail (sometimes erroneously).[92] There is no reason to gloss over any of these events. Despite previous warnings, some confusion arose when the Gestapo came to search Dohnanyi's office. Oster's hasty attempt to conceal three notes was noticed. Those notes immediately became incriminating evidence, and all involved Bonhoeffer.[93] The trial documents in Dohnanyi's literary estate, augmented by drafts of Bonhoeffer's letters to Roeder that were to be used in his defense, enable us to present here an appropriate selection of materials.[94] We learn the extent to which the interrogations, which concentrated initially on these "notes," focused on Bonhoeffer's function as a secret agent in Military Intelligence.

These interrogation protocols directly involve statements by Dohnanyi, Oster, and Canaris, and only indirectly those of Bonhoeffer; they provide an unvarnished picture of the initial situation, with all the numerous contradictory statements that could only incriminate Bonhoeffer. Only gradually through secret messages could a certain measure of consistency be established for later statements. Moreover, high officials such as Dr. Sack and Dr. Lehmann in the Reich War Court did what they could to defuse the proceedings and, ultimately, to cause the trial preparations to "fizzle out" in order to save the accused from even more serious consequences.[95]

We scored a significant success when the complete indictment against Bonhoeffer was discovered in the Archive for Military History in Prague and made accessible to us.[96] It and the complementary materials from the

697

[91.] See 1/221 and 1/222.

[92.] *DB-ER*, 785–87; Höhne, *Canaris*, 515–18; Hoffmann, *History of the German Resistance*, 293–94; W. Meyer, *Unternehmen Sieben*, 383–84; Chowaniec, *Der "Fall Dohnanyi,"* 42–48.

[93.] See 1/223.

[94.] See 1/226 and 1/228.

[95.] There is disturbing proof for these circumstances, namely, the statement made by Wilhelm Canaris under the intensified interrogations in the Reich Central Security Office after the "discovery of the Zossen files" on September 22, 1944: "Admiral Canaris has stated that Judge General [*Generalrichter*] Sack was closely acquainted with General Major Oster and was also on good terms with Special Officer Dohnanyi. He (Canaris) stated that he was quite concerned with the Dohnanyi case. His opinion is that these proceedings were in effect actually directed against the Foreign Office of Military Intelligence. For Sack, the Dohnanyi case represented the first intrusion of the SS into the Armed Forces. Canaris, whose statements followed the exact same line of thought, said that Sack was doubtless concerned with preventing the Dohnanyi trial from proceeding further" (Ernst Kaltenbrunner to Martin Bormann, October 18, 1944, *Spiegelbild einer Verschwörung*, 460).

[96.] See 1/230.

Dohnanyi files provide a detailed overview of the various aspects of the investigation as well as information regarding some events that were previ-   698
ously unknown.[97]

Seen as a whole, this material acquaints the reader with the merciless background that is at best only indirectly visible in *Letters and Papers from Prison* and *Love Letters from Cell 92*. A correct reading of these materials, however, requires that the reader keep in mind that here, too, camouflage was used constantly to shield as long as possible the progress of the conspiracy and the freedom of movement still enjoyed by contacts on the outside but also to fight to the bitter end for the conspirators' own survival.

Victims in the Immediate Circle

The decisive turning point, caused by the failed assassination attempt at Hitler's headquarters on July 20, 1944, and the subsequent prosecution of the "national traitors," is reflected in the present collection by an abrupt decrease in relevant documents. The "Special July 20 Commission" in the Reich Central Security Office disregarded and went beyond the investigative methods of the Reich War Court. Those who had landed in the Gestapo's prisons were now subject to the ruthlessness characterizing this organization, and family members of prisoners now often had trouble ascertaining whether their loved ones were even alive.

The scant written materials preserved from this period[98] deserve all the more attention insofar as they do occasionally provide a glimpse of the otherwise strictly shielded events. Of all those in Bonhoeffer's circle who were indeed ensnared in this net, only a few actually enter our field of vision. The first is Constantin von Dietze, whose communications to his wife were smuggled out of the Ravensbrück concentration camp.[99] These communications, together with the indictment against him issued by the People's   699
Court,[100] throw light on both the condition and the tortures to which the four members of the Freiburg circle were subject after their arrest.[101] Quite

---

[97.] See, for example, the documentation regarding early contacts with Colonel Oster and the "Canaris office" as well as trips to Bethel, the Rhineland, and Saxony at their behest.

[98.] These materials include the reports of Kaltenbrunner, director of the Reich Central Security Office, to Hitler's chancellery secretary, Martin Bormann, on October 12, November 2 and 29, and December 9, 1944, reports based on statements made by Klaus Bonhoeffer and Rüdiger Schleicher during the preceding interrogations (*Spiegelbild einer Verschwörung*, 440–44, 480, 508, 514, and 520).

[99.] See 1/235.

[100.] See 1/238.

[101.] Constantin von Dietze and Adolf Lampe were arrested on September 8, Walter Bauer on October 15, and Gerhard Ritter on November 1, 1944.

apart from the fact that, except for a few meager notes, this material represents the earliest authentic information we have regarding the development of the Freiburg memorandum, it also reveals the enormous stress these colleagues suffered when under interrogation they were blackmailed into mutually incriminating one another.

The other indictment from the People's Court, issued against Klaus Bonhoeffer, Hans John, Hans Kloß, Friedrich Justus Perels, and Rüdiger Schleicher,[102] resulted on February 2, 1945, in a death sentence for all except Kloß. We do not know whether Dietrich Bonhoeffer learned of this sentence, since at this very time he was being transported to Buchenwald. When these four were executed on April 23, both Dietrich Bonhoeffer and Hans von Dohnanyi had already been dead for two weeks. Hence in the final month of the war, Bonhoeffer's parents lost two sons and two sons-in-law.

Last Thoughts to Bishop Bell

Commensurate with a more profound context, two pieces of writing are included in the concluding section of our collection. In these pieces Bonhoeffer used an intermediary for communication and yet still used his own words. Both documents, each in its own way, bear witness to his special relationship with the bishop of Chichester.

The first document is the report by Kaltenbrunner, the director of the Reich Central Security Office, to the Foreign Ministry about Bonhoeffer's
700   statements concerning the possibility of international contacts with English politicians, at the center of which Bishop Bell appears.[103] Much suggests that this report reflects a momentary change in focus among the SS leadership, since at the time, at the eleventh hour and without regard for Hitler, its central leadership was seeking Swedish contacts through which they might offer themselves as dialogue partners to England for peace negotiations.[104] These circumstances may also have influenced the interrogations of the prisoners from the "Canaris office," and Bonhoeffer used this opportunity, probably in the style of his "official" travel reports of that period, to play his former role in secret, high-level negotiations as a trump card. It was doubtless also of some significance that the duties of Military Intelligence were now assigned to the Reich Central Security Office. Even though circumstances quickly changed again, and Bonhoeffer remained in prison, this

---

[102.] See 1/236. Hans John had already been arrested on August 18, Klaus Bonhoeffer on October 1, Rüdiger Schleicher on October 4, Friedrich Justus Perels on October 5, and Hans Kloß on October 7, 1944. Eberhard Bethge was then arrested on October 30, 1944.

[103.] See 1/237.

[104.] With regard to Goerdeler, Gerhard Ritter draws similar conclusions (*Carl Goerdeler*, 446–51).

document does throw light on the otherwise largely obscure course of the interrogations in the Reich Central Security Office and shows us Bonhoeffer one last time, engaging his entire energies in a high-stakes political game.

In the case of the second document, we make an exception in drawing on a later writing.[105] The English secret service officer Payne Best was with Bonhoeffer in the group of prisoners that was housed in the special barracks at the Buchenwald concentration camp and then transported to Schönberg in the Bavarian forest. Best published his recollections of these events in 1950 in his book *The Venlo Incident* and also referred to them in personal letters to Bishop Bell. Because the details of these last days have been presented elsewhere,[106] there is no need to repeat them here. Because no contemporaneous documents have been preserved regarding these final events, we have preferred to conclude with no more than this brief farewell.

This farewell, delivered to Bishop Bell after the end of the war, shows   701
how even in this final period Bonhoeffer endeavored to fulfill his mission on behalf of ecumenical unity during a time of war and sealed its enduring validity.

II

Theological Focus

His hectic travel life, existence under the conditions of the conspiracy, and the use of his remaining "free time" for work on the *Ethics* did not leave Bonhoeffer much opportunity for additional theological projects. Hence one cannot view the small pieces he managed to produce after the closing of the collective pastorates in March 1940 as polished examples of his theological work. They were prompted largely by demands made on him from time to time and were obviously composed under considerable time constraints. Furthermore, Bonhoeffer wrote without access to scholarly aids and relying on his own memory. During this period, he often wrote in fragments and key phrases.

Yet despite the limitations that his life circumstances imposed on his theological work, these pieces bear witness to a remarkable manifestation of spiritual and mental concentration. Bonhoeffer's constant struggle for theological precision and his clear distinction between what is true and what is false is evident at every point and challenges the reader to engage in similar reflections. There actually is no readily accessible text here. Bonhoeffer's

---

[105.] See 1/239; cf. J. Glenthøj, "Zwei neue Zeugnisse," 99–106, with corresponding documentation involving the correspondence between S. Payne Best and Bishop Bell.

[106.] *DB-ER*, 917–28; Best, *Venlo Incident*, 190–200; J. Müller, *Bis zur letzten Konsequenz*, 240–58.

determination to take the risk of articulating his own judgments and of pro-
voking objections is evident even in the fragmentary documents and those
characterized by key phrases. All these texts bear the imprint of Bonhoeffer's
confidence in the capabilities of a theology that is fully conscious of its subject matter, and precisely this characteristic elevates them above their ties to
any specific context.

It would thus be a mistake to think that these writings represent something that was not all that important to Bonhoeffer himself, not least because
most of them resulted from commissions given to Bonhoeffer by the Confessing Church, on whose behalf he speaks as a teacher. Moreover, every
reflection on a biblical text or on some topic—such as that on sickness in
the rather unusual essay for the spa ministry [Bädermission]—becomes for
Bonhoeffer a conscious path to the center of faith and of the church, a
path that he follows with characteristic intensity. That is especially true when
the Confessing Church in Pomerania and East Prussia engaged him in matters involving practices in church-communities. In Bonhoeffer's reflections
for the monthly newsletters of the Pomeranian Council of Brethren, in the
outline for a Bible study, and even in his sermon meditations, we are directed
exclusively to the reality of Jesus Christ as the source of all life in the church-
community. Bonhoeffer was not at all shy about enlisting the aid of the dogmatic tradition and in particular of the confessional writings. His reflections
on the resurrection and ascension of Jesus Christ, for example, are virtually
cast in the form of doctrinal statements. Bonhoeffer had as little patience
with dogmatic ignorance in the ministry of the Confessing Church as he
did with unfocused biblical exegesis that talked about everything but Jesus
Christ. Everything the church-community is and does acquires its freedom
and its value from this center, and virtually everything Bonhoeffer had to
say points ultimately in that direction. His goal was to teach people to discover the riches that this center unleashes.

Hence one should not be surprised at the decisiveness with which he
opposed, in a position paper solicited by the East Prussian Council of
Brethren of the Confessing Church in 1942, the doctrine of "believer's baptism" and thus the creation of a "pure" church-community that turns itself
away from the world. He was concerned with the freedom of the church-
community in the world, a freedom that Jesus Christ makes possible. In
Arnold Hitzer, a resolute Confessing Church pastor banned from Silesia
and sentenced to prison several times, Bonhoeffer saw the danger of a
legalistic isolation of the church-community from the world. Although Bonhoeffer shared Hitzer's concern with overcoming the indecisiveness and
inaction characterizing Christian existence, he felt that a rejection of infant
baptism and the demand for rebaptism were the wrong way to go about
inculcating the relevancy and binding nature of Jesus Christ for the life of

Christians. The exegetical and historical arguments for and against the prac-   703
tice of infant baptism are still being disputed; in this respect Bonhoeffer's
critical analysis of Hitzer's position can be seen as an early indication of
some of the problems that after the war shifted into a broader ecclesial consciousness in Barth's understanding of baptism.[107] However, by emphasizing
that the baptismal practice of the church-community must be developed in
a way that opens up the community's access to the world instead of blocking it, Bonhoeffer gives this debate a distinctive shape. But that shape is
undoubtedly connected with the insight set forth in his work on his *Ethics,*
that the concentration on Jesus Christ leads precisely to the recognition of
the "breadth of Christ's lordship."[108] Inasmuch as Bonhoeffer stresses the
freedom of a congregation, while recognizing its responsibility to the church-
community as a whole, to entertain different forms of baptismal practice,
he accentuates that at its innermost, essential core, the church-community
is in fact moved by precisely that which establishes its responsibility in the
world, namely, by the entirety of Christ's reality itself, and not only by the
human reception of an aspect of that reality.

Government

With the exception of Bonhoeffer's rejoinder to Paton's *Church and the
New Order* and his reflections on "State and Church" and "'Personal' and
'Objective' Ethics" and on the *primus usus legis,* his shorter texts make few
direct references to the material in his *Ethics.* All those writings, however,
revolve around a single theme, namely, the understanding of worldly orders
and thus of government. The various attempts to develop a doctrine of the
mandates of God show what is at stake for Bonhoeffer in this issue. The
replacement of the term "order" with the term "mandate" in the addendum
to "Christ, Reality, and Good," after April 1941 seems to represent the earliest evidence for the use of this terminology in his *Ethics* manuscripts.[109]   704
Bonhoeffer's goal is to avoid the traditionally static nature of the notion of
the orders and instead ground the structures of marriage (family), work
(culture), government, and church[110] in the inviolable commission of Jesus
Christ and inculcate the mutually limiting character of these mandates.
With respect to the three pieces related to this topic in the present volume,

[107.] Cf. Barth, "The Teaching of the Church regarding Baptism," in *Church Dogmatics* 4/4

[108.] Cf. "Church and World I," *DBWE* 6:344.

[109.] Cf. *DBWE* 6:67–69. The editors' afterword" in *DBWE* 6:426–28 delineates Bonhoeffer's discussion of the mandates within the *Ethics* manuscripts.

[110.] Despite being recast in "Christ, Reality, and Good" (cf. *DBWE* 6:68, ed. note
75), this schema is essentially carried through.

one does notice that in the position paper on the *primus usus legis* Bonhoeffer avoids the term "mandate" even though what is at issue for him here is present. As the *Ethics* manuscript "The Concrete Commandment and the Divine Mandates"[111] demonstrates, however, this by no means implies that Bonhoeffer had abandoned his plan to work out a doctrine of the mandates. The avoidance of his own terminology here merely suggests that his thoughts on this subject had not sufficiently matured.[112] The announcement of a precise "doctrine of the four divine mandates" in "'Personal' and 'Objective' Ethics"[113] shows that he was still planning to explicate such a doctrine of mandates. This work was especially influenced by the dispute with Otto Dilschneider and strongly articulates a point of view that is not delineated as clearly in the other passages of the *Ethics* dealing with the mandates or in the reflections on "State and Church," namely, the emphasis on the worldliness of the mandates of marriage, of work, and especially of government. Bonhoeffer is emphasizing here that no religious claims can be made on the basis of these mandates that affect the church's spiritual task. This point of view, together with the emphasis on the mutually limit-

705   ing character of the mandates, is directed against the tendency of the totalitarian state to subject to its power all realms of life in society. Particularly in the face of the power and violence of the National Socialist state, this point was important to Bonhoeffer.

On the other hand, his dissociation from a falsely understood Christianization of the state also leaves several questions open. His understanding, as articulated in "State and Church," of the establishment of the existence of government "from above" in contrast to a state established "from below" closely resembles the traditional concept of a "Christian state."[114] His advocacy of the form of state entailing a "properly understood divine right" of government[115] also essentially derives strictly from the notion that those authorized to fulfill the mandates as "God's vicarious representatives" are ascribed a position of the "above" in the world in contrast to the "subjects below." Clearly, such a state or such government can more likely be conceived in the sense of a constitutional monarchy than in the sense of a democracy, even if Bonhoeffer underscores the relative nature of the form

---

[111.] Cf. *DBWE* 6:388–408.

[112.] Pangritz ("Zur Neuausgabe von Bonhoeffers 'Ethik,'" 31) and Bethge ("Bonhoeffer's Theology of Friendship," in Bethge, *Friendship and Resistance*, 92–95 and 97) both draw attention to an otherwise unnoticed relativization of the doctrine of mandates in *Ethics* that Bonhoeffer himself had undertaken in Tegel in his letter of January 23, 1944, (*LPP*, 192–93 [*DBW* 8:290–92]) with regard to a sociological understanding of friendship.

[113.] See 2/13, point f in section 5.

[114.] Cf. 2/10, section 2 A.

[115.] See 2/10, section 6 I.

of the state. The abuse of power in a state constituted "from below," as exemplified in the National Socialist seizure of power, prompted members of the resistance against Hitler to consider seriously similar authoritarian models of the state. Bonhoeffer's own dissociation from "revolution"[116] and the "chaotic forces"[117] "from below" shows that he, too, was speaking from the context of having experienced this destruction of the true authority of the state. His considerable praise of Reinhold Schneider's book *Macht und Gnade*[118] and the incorporation of Schneider's terminology in the legitimation of the "crown" "from above" show that Bonhoeffer's own inclination in this situation was not in the direction of a democratic establishment of the state, though Karl Barth's essay "Church and State" might have suggested such to him.

The Future   706

In his reflections on William Paton's book *The Church and the New Order,* Bonhoeffer sought to advocate in the ecumenical movement, and that means among the Allies as well, this conception of the state that "initially does not" appear "to be democratic in the Anglo-Saxon sense of the word."[119] In addition to the theological arguments, an important role is played by references to the specifically German political experience with the Weimar Republic, on the one hand, and to the criminal self-idolization of the "Führer," on the other. Bonhoeffer insists that government must be understood on the basis neither of abstract individual freedom nor of abstract arrogated authority, but from the perspective of earthly authority "ordered and limited by God's word." This basic view admittedly allows considerable latitude for the means of constituting an actual state, so that we cannot reduce it to any one possibility merely by referring to the singular statement about the "properly understood divine right" of government. Because Bonhoeffer never got so far as to address the question of government in his final *Ethics* manuscript, it is difficult to say how binding this conception was, even for him. In any case, with its strict emphasis on the distinction between "above" and "below," the starting point for the final *Ethics* manuscript, "The Concrete Commandment and the Divine Mandates," does concur with the argumentation in his reflections on "State and Church."

Unfortunately, we know very little about the concrete political models that were discussed by Bonhoeffer and his dialogue partners. However,

---

[116.] See 2/10, section 2 C.

[117.] Cf. *DBWE* 6:392 and *DBWE* 7:35–36.

[118.] See Bonhoeffer's letters of January 19 and 31, 1941, to Eberhard Bethge (1/58 and 1/66).

[119.] 2/11, point 5.

Bonhoeffer's 1942 request that the Freiburg circle prepare a statement on the "political form of the community" for the future is surely related to his appreciation of the intentions he found in the first memorandum, "Church and World."[120] Though there is some new material in the present volume, much still remains obscure with regard to the various attempts at mutual

707   understanding between Berlin and Freiburg.[121] Notwithstanding the status acquired by "conscience" in the second Freiburg memorandum in the establishment of a proper political form of the community, it is nonetheless evident that at least the orientation of the political models articulated there concurs with those of Bonhoeffer. That applies both to the call for the true authority of the state[122] and to the critical view of democratic forms of the state.[123] Despite the lack of preference for any specific form of the state,[124] this concurrence also applies to the emphasis on the personal accountability of those in government to God's commission,[125] so that the emergence of a "new class of politically insightful and morally reliable representatives"[126] appears as the "ideal goal of creative politics in the future." This applies especially to the notion that, alongside the idea of justice, the best guarantee of the legitimacy of government is to ensure the free development of the church and its proclamation.[127]

It is certainly not unrelated to this complex of ideas when Friedrich Justus Perels remarks in his draft for a "Church Constitution after the Overthrow" that "the state declares the Christian faith to be the most important moral and ethical foundation of its regulations."[128] Ludwig Beck, former chief of the general staff of the army, was trying to establish the basic outlines for a new form of the state after the coup. Members of the circle around him asked Perels and Bonhoeffer to produce these outlines. The materials presented here clearly show the extent to which the two authors agreed. Perels concentrated more on presenting a draft of a proper, legally formulated constitution, while Bonhoeffer[129] assembled individual points

708   in his text. The general inclination of both drafts is clear: the state is to provide for the reestablishment of church independence, while the church is to reorganize itself on the foundation of the Confessing Church and its

---

[120.] Cf. Schwabe and Reichhardt, *Gerhard Ritter,* 635–36.
[121.] Cf. Schreiber, *Friedrich Justus Perels,* 176.
[122.] See Thielicke, *In der Stunde Null,* 76.
[123.] Ibid., 74–75.
[124.] Ibid., 73.
[125.] Ibid., 67.
[126.] Ibid., 74.
[127.] Ibid., 64ff.
[128.] See 2/17, under II.
[129.] See 2/16.

constitutional principles and especially under the leadership of the Councils of Brethren. The idea was to implement a thorough reorganization of the church, a new beginning, on the basis of the Confessing Church's experiences, and not—as was actually the case later—on a resurrection of pre-1933 church structures. For Bonhoeffer himself, a position was envisioned on a committee replacing the present Church Foreign Office, showing once more how much importance for the future of the German Protestant church he attached to the ecumenical contacts that he utilized in such a unique way on behalf of the resistance.

These plans, formulated in 1942, only became known long after 1945. Together with his draft for an anticipated pulpit pronouncement after the overthrow,[130] they illustrate his hope for a church that would live totally from its spiritual commission; they also illustrate his determination to do whatever was in his own power to make that hope a reality. The Bonhoeffer we encounter during the period from 1940 to 1943 could not envision any theology that did not have to insist on the realization of the revealed truth. For us today the form he chose to concretize such reality is sometimes alien; this is the case, for example, with his positive theological and pastoral assessment of dying for one's native country in his funeral sermon for Hans-Friedrich von Kleist-Retzow.[131] Sometimes because of our own limited knowledge of witnesses from that time, we cannot discern precisely where he was heading; such is the case with respect to the form of the state he was seeking. Often Bonhoeffer also intentionally spoke in a veiled fashion so as not to endanger either himself or others. In any event, everywhere one can sense that he was concerned with truth as concretely manifested in experiential reality, not with an abstraction above reality.

It is appropriate, therefore, that we were able to add to the theological works in this volume the fragment written in Tegel prison on the question   709
"What does it mean to tell the truth?" This fragment illuminates once more both Bonhoeffer's path and his theological work during the time of the conspiracy. It shows how aware Bonhoeffer was of what it means to bring God's inviolable truth to bear as the situation requires, with personal responsibility and proper attention to the issue at hand, within the turmoil of this sinful world.

The conclusion to the present volume appropriately includes two pieces that were also composed in Tegel, namely, the devotional aids for the *Daily Texts* for Pentecost 1944 and the fragment composed shortly thereafter, a reflection on the first table of the "Ten Words of God." Both pieces empha-

---

[130.] See 2/15.
[131.] See 3/2.

size once more the proximity of this material to the prison letters published in *Letters and Papers from Prison*. On the other hand, and this is what is most significant for us today, the "counterpoint" of the "whole" comes to expression here amid all the fragments, "an example of a way of life which has its genesis in the creative tension of prayer and faithfulness to the earth."[132]

"The world lives by the blessing of God and of the righteous and thus has a future. Blessing means laying one's hand on something and saying: Despite everything, you belong to God. This is what we do with the world that inflicts such suffering on us. We do not abandon it; we do not repudiate, despise, or condemn it. Instead we call it back to God, we give it hope, we lay our hand on it and say: May God's blessing come upon you, may God renew you; be blessed, world created by God, you who belong to your Creator and Redeemer."[133]

[132.] Moltmann, *Church in the Power of the Spirit,* 284.
[133.] See p. 632.

APPENDICES

APPENDIX 1.

Map of Bonhoeffer's Germany

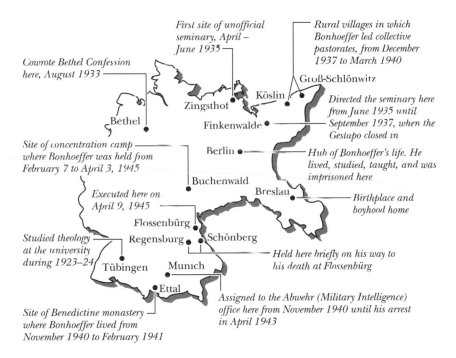

First site of unofficial seminary, April – June 1935

Rural villages in which Bonhoeffer led collective pastorates, from December 1937 to March 1940

Cowrote Bethel Confession here, August 1933

Groß-Schlönwitz

Zingsthof

Köslin

Directed the seminary here from June 1935 until September 1937, when the Gestapo closed in

Bethel

Finkenwalde

Site of concentration camp where Bonhoeffer was held from February 7 to April 3, 1945

Berlin

Hub of Bonhoeffer's life. He lived, studied, taught, and was imprisoned here

Buchenwald

Breslau

Executed here on April 9, 1945

Birthplace and boyhood home

Flossenbürg

Studied theology at the university during 1923–24

Regensburg

Schönberg

Tübingen

Munich

Held here briefly on his way to his death at Flossenbürg

Ettal

Site of Benedictine monastery where Bonhoeffer lived from November 1940 to February 1941

Assigned to the Abwehr (Military Intelligence) office here from November 1940 until his arrest in April 1943

Appendix 2.
Chronology of *Conspiracy* and *Imprisonment: 1940–1945*

1940

March 15 (Fri.)	Conclusion of the final course in the collective pastorate in Sigurdshof. Return to Berlin.
March 18 (Mon.)	Gestapo closes down Sigurdshof.
March 19 (Tues.)	Ludwig Beck, Hans Oster, Ulrich von Hassel, and Hans von Dohnanyi meet to discuss the "X-report."
March 22 (Fri.)	Attends Bach's *St. Matthew's Passion* at the Garnisonkirche in Berlin.
March 24 (Sun.)	Meeting with Oster.
April–May	Generally in Berlin.
April 9 (Tues.)	German invasion of Denmark and Norway.
Beginning of May	With Eberhard Bethge in Friedrichsbrunn.
May 7 (Tues.)	Paul Braune and Friedrich von Bodelschwingh seek Karl Bonhoeffer's advice and assistance in opposing the "euthanasia" measures.
May 9 (Thurs.)	Braune meets with Dohnanyi. Oster communicates to Dutch military attaché Sas the final invasion date of May 10.
May 10 (Fri.)	Invasion of Holland, Belgium, Luxembourg, and France.
May 19 (Sun.)	At the home of Herbert von Bismarck in Lasbeck.
June 4 (Tues.)	Fall of Dunkirk.
June 5 (Wed.)	Clergy meeting in Schlawe. Physical for military service.

June 6 (Thurs.)	Beginning of the first visitation journey with Bethge to East Prussia.
June 8 (Sat.)	Herdenau, Karkeln; theme: baptism. Italy enters the war.
June 10 (Mon.)	Tilsit, clergy meeting.
June 12 (Wed.)	Königsberg, clergy meeting. Meditation on Rom. 8:17ff.
June 13 (Thurs.)	Schakendorf, Brittanien, sermon on Mark 9:24.
June 14 (Fri.)	Paris taken without a fight.
June 17 (Mon.)	Memel. Surrender of the French armed forces.
June 21 (Fri.)	Königsberg. In the forest near Compiègne, presentation of the German conditions for the cease-fire requested by France.
June 22 (Sat.)	Danzig, student meeting at the home of Richard Grunow. Conclusion of the cease-fire between Germany and France.
June 25 (Tues.)	Return to Berlin.
June 29–30 (Sat.–Sun.)	In Köslin, lay meeting with Dr. Knorr.
July 1 (Mon.)	Köslin, clergy meeting. Return to Berlin.
July 2 (Tues.)	Session of the Council of Brethren in Nowawes. Bonhoeffer makes remarks concerning the political situation.
July 7 (Sun.)	Second visitation journey to East Prussia. Königsberg. Theme: "The Order of Church Life."
July 8–10	Königsberg, pastors' retreat. Themes: "Protestant Confession," "Baptismal Grace and Baptismal Discipline," "Our Preaching Today," "The Prophetic Task of the Church," "Church and the Office of Ministry." Bible study on Matt. 7:13ff.
July 8–12	Hans Schönfeld in Berlin.
July 8–15	Nils Ehrenström in Berlin.
July 8–9 (Mon.–Tues.)	Talks between the Council of Brethren and the southern German regional churches in Stuttgart.
July 11 (Thurs.)	In Stettin for a session of the Council of Brethren. Bonhoeffer gives a report on present circumstances.
July 13–14 (Sat.–Sun.)	Weekend retreat in Blöstau. Dispersed by the Königsberg Gestapo.
July 15 (Mon.)	Gumbinnen. Presentation on the topic of death.
July 17 (Wed.)	Königsberg; date in Bonhoeffer's copy of Nicolai Hartmann's *Ethik* indicates he bought the copy

714

		here. Journey continues into the area around Stallupönen.
	July 19 (Fri.)	Letter from Bishop Wurm to Reich Minister Frick regarding the euthanasia measures.
	July 20 (Sat.)	Report from the Königsberg SD headquarters about the weekend conference in Blöstau arrives at the Reich Central Security Office.
	July 23 (Tues.)	Danzig. "Today I am going ahead to Danzig, then to Mrs. von Kleist, and on Monday or Tuesday will be in Berlin."
	July 29 (Mon.)	Return to Berlin. Discussion with Dohnanyi.
715	August 1 (Thurs.)	In Berlin instead of in Klein-Krössin as planned.
	August 5 (Mon.)	With Dohnanyi and Schönfeld in Potsdam.
	August 6 (Tues.)	Discussion with Dohnanyi about the draft of a law to be presented to the Reich Minister of Justice.
	August 7 (Wed.)	At the home of Ruth von Kleist-Retzow in Klein-Krössin.
	August 13 (Tues.)	Return to Berlin with Bethge. Sometime "in August" meeting of Oster, Hans Bernd Gisevius, Dohnanyi, Bonhoeffer, and Bethge at the house on Marienburger Allee.
	August 18 (Sun.)	Attends Günther Dehn's worship service in Berlin-Friedenau.
	August 22 (Thurs.)	Reich Central Security Office issues a ban on public speaking against Bonhoeffer and others on the grounds of subversive activity.
	August 25 (Sun.)	Third visitation journey to East Prussia, via Dirschau to Königsberg.
	August 26 (Mon.)	Contact made with the Königsberg branch office of Military Intelligence.
	September 2 (Mon.)	Bethge begins work at the Gossner Mission Society in Berlin.
	September 4 (Wed.)	Bonhoeffer required to register at his official place of residence in Schlawe. Receives UK classification through Canaris's office.
	September 15 (Sun.)	Berlin. Letter of protest to the Reich Central Security Office.
	September 16 (Mon.)	Beginning of work on *Ethics* in seclusion at Klein-Krössin until about October 20
	September 24 (Tues.)	Dohnanyi flies to Rome.
	September 27 (Fri.)	Tripartite Pact between Germany, Italy, and Japan.

October 9 (Wed.)	In Klein-Krössin. To Bethge: "My work progresses; I am writing the outline of the whole thing. . . . I will probably spend the rest of the week on it."
October 20 (Sun.)	Back in Berlin. Sets up his library at home.
October 22 (Tues.)	Beginning of the deportations of Jewish citizens from southwest Germany to Gurs in southern France.
October 28 (Mon.)	Failed Italian invasion of Greece.
October 30 (Wed.)	To Munich. Assignment to the Munich head-quarters of the Military Intelligence Office.
October 31 (Thurs.)	Visit to the Ettal monastery.
November 4 (Mon.)	Still in Munich. Plans to return to Berlin.
November 15 (Fri.)	In Jena. Wolfgang Staemmler (Old Prussian Union Council of Brethren) "conveyed to me the council's desire that I proceed with academic work." Reunion with Gerhard von Rad.
November 16 (Sat.)	From Jena to Munich. Staemmler arrested.
November 17 (Sun.)	Guest at the Benedictine abbey Ettal until February 1941 (lodgings in the Hotel Ludwig der Bayer). First conversation with the abbot Angelus Kupfer.
November 22 (Fri.)	Arrival of Christine von Dohnanyi with her children in Ettal.
November 24 (Sun.)	Adam von Trott in Geneva.
November 27 (Wed.)	To Bethge: "Today a possible title for my book occurred to me: 'Preparing the Way and Entering In' corresponding to the division of the book (into penultimate and ultimate things)."
no date (November)	Letter to Margret Onnasch in which Bonhoeffer mentions among other things a memorandum of Paul Graf Yorck von Wartenburg.
November 28–29 (Thurs.–Fri.)	In Munich. Visits the Chr. Kaiser publishing company.
December 7 (Sat.)	Munich. Visits Bishop Meiser.
December 8 (Sun.)	Again in Ettal. Bonhoeffer mentions initial contact between Reich Minister of Justice Gürtner and Reich Minister for Church Affairs Kerrl.
December 9 (Mon.)	Ettal. To Bethge: "I am now beginning the section on 'Natural Life.'"
December 13 (Fri.)	Bonhoeffer takes care of Christoph von Dohnanyi, who is sick with the flu.

716

December 16–19	In Munich. Bethge arrives.
December 21 (Sat.)	In Ettal. Conversation with Gürtner. Announcement of the Ten Peace Points of British church leaders.
December 22 (Sun.)	Dohnanyi expected in Ettal.
December 24 (Tues.)	In Ettal, attends Christmas Eve midnight service. On one of these days Father Rupert Mayer meets with Bonhoeffer and Bethge.
December 28 (Sat.)	Letter to his mother. During the evening, music making in the monastery.

717 appears in the left margin beside December 22 (Sun.).

1941

January 7–10	In England, Malvern Conference; confirmation of the Ten Peace Points.
January 14 (Tues.)	Father Johannes in Berlin. UK classification comes through.
January 15 (Wed.)	To Bethge from Ettal: "I am back at work.... Read Exod. 23:7 sometime" (in view of the acute euthanasia measures).
January 17 (Fri.)	Trip to Metten monastery by car; postcard from Landshut.
January 18 (Sat.)	Return to Munich. Visit with Prelate Neuhäusler.
January 19 (Sun.)	Letter from Munich that mentions the books *The Last Puritan*, by George Santayana, and *Macht und Gnade*, by Reinhold Schneider.
January 20 (Mon.)	To Bethge from Ettal: "In my work I am just coming to the question of euthanasia."
January 24 (Fri.)	Dohnanyi on an official trip to Italy.
January 24–25 (Fri.–Sat.)	In Munich.
January 29 (Wed.)	Gürtner dies.
January 30–31 (Thurs.–Fri.)	In Munich at the Kalckreuth home.
January 31 (Fri.)	In Munich. Breakfast with Franz Koenigs. "Registration of residency" transferred from Schlawe to Munich.
February 4 (Tues.)	Neuhäusler arrested.
February 8 (Sat.)	In Munich for Gürtner's funeral. Phone call from Christine von Kalckreuth in Ettal: Gestapo had asked her about Bonhoeffer. Swiss visa temporarily refused.

February 10 (Mon.)	Letter from Ettal: "I am now working on the question of marriage."
February 14 (Fri.)	Letter from Ettal: "In recent days I have been able to write very well again." Consul Schmidhuber travels to Switzerland to resolve the visa problem.
February 15 (Sat.)	Letter from Ettal: "I have now finished dealing with the difficult questions of sterilization, birth control, etc. I will now address the natural right to work, freedom, and thought."
February 16 (Sun.)	Bethge in East Prussia until March 7.
February 17 (Mon.)	Ettal. Mail from Bishop Wurm.
February 19 (Wed.)	Ettal. Notes on "the right to work."
February 24 (Mon.)	Leaves Munich on first trip to Switzerland.
February 25 (Tues.)	In Zurich. Letters to the Leibholz family and Bishop Bell. Meeting with Lore Schmid, Erwin Sutz, and others. Stays with the Pestalozzis.
February 26 (Wed.)	Schönfeld travels to Berlin and Belgrade until March 23.
End of February	Meeting of Oster, Dohnanyi, Hassell, and Baron Alexander von Falkenhausen in Berlin.
March 2 (Sun.)	In Rapperswil, at the Sutz home.
March 4 (Tues.)	In Basel, at Karl Barth's home in the evening.
March 5 (Wed.)	In Basel, at Alphons Koechlin's home in the evening.
March 6 (Thurs.)	In Basel, visits Barth in the morning.
March 7 (Fri.)	Basel, visits Barth in the morning, also meetings with Friedrich Siegmund-Schultze and Koechlin.
March 8–13	Hans and Christine von Dohnanyi on vacation in Italy.
March 8–15	In Geneva, examines ecumenical publications; conversations with Willem A. Visser 't Hooft, Nils Ehrenström, Adolf Freudenberg, Charles Guillon, Henry Louis Henriod, Henri d'Espine, Jacques Courvoisier, Frantz Leenhardt, Jacques de Senarclens.
March 18–19 (Tues.–Wed.)	Trott in Geneva, visits Visser 't Hooft.
March 19 (Wed.)	Letter from Visser 't Hooft to Bishop Bell. Reich Chamber of Literature issues a ban on Bonhoeffer printing and publication.

718

March 20 (Thurs.)	Visits the Pestalozzis in Geneva. Conversation on the "order of Christian life."
March 24 (Mon.)	Back in Munich from Switzerland. With Schmidhuber. Funeral of Countess Hannah von der Goltz in Berlin.
March 26 (Wed.)	Visits Ernst Wolf in Halle for advice regarding the ban on publication. Bethge travels to Halle to meet Bonhoeffer.
719 March 27 (Thurs.)	In Berlin "after being away for five months."
April 1 (Tues.)	In Ettal. Letter from Albert Lempp.
April 6 (Sun.)	German attack on Greece and Yugoslavia.
April 8 (Tues.)	Easter vacation with his parents in Friedrichsbrunn.
Middle of April	In Klein-Krössin.
April 22 (Tues.)	Again in Friedrichsbrunn. "In the past few days I have been working well again." Letter of protest to the Reich Chamber of Literature.
April 25 (Fri.)	Again in Berlin. Invites Perels and his wife for the afternoon.
April 28 (Mon.)	Travels "to Pomerania for a few days," Klein-Krössin.
May 6 (Tues.)	Members of the Berlin examination commission arrested.
May 14 (Wed.)	In Munich. Letter to Hans-Werner Jensen.
May 22 (Thurs.)	In Berlin, visits Dr. Koch with Dohnanyi.
May 25 (Sun.)	In Berlin, visits Dr. Koch again with Dohnanyi in order to meet Arthur Nebe. Horst Thurmann taken to a concentration camp.
May 30 (Fri.)	Letter, presumably from Berlin, thanking Barth for sending *Church Dogmatics* 2/1. "Much encouraged by my trip, I have recently been making excellent progress in my work."
June 1 (Sun.)	Pentecost. Order issued by the Reich Chamber of Literature shuts down church presses.
June 1–4	Dohnanyi in Ettal.
June 7–19	Dohnanyi in Italy on official business.
June 10 (Tues.)	In Berlin, letter to Gerty Pestalozzi.
June 11 (Wed.)	Trott visits Visser 't Hooft in Geneva.
June 22 (Sun.)	German troops invade the Soviet Union. Bonhoeffer hears Bethge preach in Potsdam.

June 28 (Sat.)	Order issued regarding civilian war duty for pastors.
June 29 (Sun.)	In Klein-Krössin. "My work is proceeding well."
July 5 (Sat.)	Letter from Klein-Krössin. "I wanted to come to Berlin sometime around the end of next week to spend a few days there before I have to go to Munich."
July 6 (Sun.)	Martin Bormann issues secret order regarding future church politics.
July 7–11	Hans and Christine von Dohnanyi on vacation with Schmidhuber in Venice.
July 12 (Sat.)	In transit to Berlin. Conclusion of the British-Soviet alliance treaty in Moscow.
July 15 (Tues.)	To Munich.
August 1 (Fri.)	News that Hans-Friedrich von Kleist-Retzow has been killed in action in Russia.
August 3 (Sun.)	Memorial service in Kieckow.
August 5 (Tues.)	With Bethge in Klein-Krössin.
August 7 (Thurs.)	Jürgen-Christoph von Kleist-Retzow killed in action in Russia.
August 19 (Tues.)	Dohnanyi and Oster converse with Hassell.
August 20 (Wed.)	In Berlin. Discussion with the Pastors' Emergency League regarding salary.
August 25–28	In Munich and Ettal, conversations with Josef Müller and others. Perels telephones from Salzburg.
August 29 (Fri.)	Second journey to Switzerland.
August 30 (Sun.)	Visits Barth and Koechlin in Basel.
September 1 (Mon.)	Jews ordered to wear the yellow star of David and use Jewish first names (goes into effect September 19, 1941).
September 2 (Tues.)	Bishop Wurm speaks before the regional church conference and openly criticizes National Socialist church politics.
September 3 (Wed.)	Visits Ehrenström in Geneva during the evening.
September 4 (Thurs.)	In Geneva, conversations with Visser 't Hooft, Ehrenström, Freudenberg, Courvoisier, Henriod, Jean de Saussure, and others.
September 5–8	Stays at Freudenberg's vacation home on Lake Champaix in Valais to work on a memorandum

720

	concerning William Paton's book *The Church and the New Order.*
September 10 (Wed.)	Visits Ehrenström in Geneva during the evening. Moltke meets Dohnanyi and Justus Delbrück in Berlin.
September 13 (Sat.)	Orders issued by Reich regional governor Greiser regarding "religious assemblies and religious associations in the Reich district of Wartheland."
September 15–24	In Zurich, guest of Otto Salomon.
September 19 (Fri.)	Visits Barth in Basel. Among other things plans for a Christmas volume for the Confessing Church. Letter from Zurich to Sabine Leibholz: "I hope to find sufficient time to finish a book on which I have been working for about a year now."
September 19–20 (Fri.–Sat.)	Ehrenström in Berlin.
September 21 (Sun.)	Letter to Sutz regarding the latter's wedding.
September 22 (Mon.)	Charlotte von Kirschbaum reports to Paul Vogt about three themes that Bonhoeffer described as the currently most pressing, including suggestions for authors: history and the expectation of the end (Wilhelm Vischer), Christian responsibility (Barth), the forgiveness of sins (Alfred de Quervain).
September 24 (Wed.)	Fifteen governments of the Allied countries (including the Soviet Union) declare their support for the goals of the Atlantic Charter.
September 25 (Thurs.)	In Zurich, letter to Bishop Bell, whose book *Christianity and World Order* Bonhoeffer had read.
September 26 (Fri.)	Returns from Switzerland, probably to Berlin. In Berlin, Moltke meets Ludwig von Guttenberg and once again Dohnanyi, who "finally has delivered his text, 'On the Justification of the Oath to Hitler and the Right to Resistance.'"
September 26 (Fri.)	Hans and Christine von Dohnanyi on an official trip to Italy until October 7.
September 29 (Mon.)	Ehrenström in Berlin until October 2.
End of September	Fabian von Schlabrendorff has his first conversation with Oster.
October 10 (Fri.)	In Munich. Letter to Hans-Walter Schleicher. After returning to Berlin, Bonhoeffer comes down with

721

	the flu and then pneumonia and is taken care of by Bethge.
October 15 (Wed.)	Moltke meets Oster and Dohnanyi.
October 16 (Thurs.)	Mass deportations of Jewish citizens from Berlin, Cologne, Düsseldorf, Mönchen-Gladbach, Rheydt, Bonn, and Vienna.
October 18–20 (Sat.–Sun.)	Perels and Bonhoeffer prepare two reports about the deportation measures to pass on to the Armed Forces
October 23 (Wed.)	Order issued by the SS high commander and chief of the German Police immediately prohibiting the emigration of Jews. "Evacuation measures" [e.g., deportations] remain unaffected by this order.
End of October	After discussions with Bonhoeffer, Willy Rott writes to Koechlin requesting help in rescuing Charlotte Friedenthal, Inge Jacobsen, and Emil Zweig from being deported.
November 2 (Sun.)	Gerhard Ebeling and Erich Klapproth visit Bonhoeffer at the Marienburger Allee home.
November 8–9 (Sat.–Sun.)	Confessing Church synod in Hamburg; synodal commission chooses Bonhoeffer (in absentia) to prepare an explanation of the Fifth Commandment *(primus usus legis)*.
November 16 (Sun.)	Moltke meets Oster and Dohnanyi to arrange a meeting with Beck on November 22 and another with the general chief of staff Halder.
November 17 (Mon.)	Berlin, letter to Christoph Bethge.
November 24 (Mon.)	Schönfeld in Berlin until December 8.
December	In Kieckow for recuperation.
December 7 (Sun.)	Japanese sea and air attack on Pearl Harbor.
December 8 (Mon.)	Anthony Eden in Moscow. Stalin demands the Curzon line [as the postwar Soviet-Polish border] as well as annexation of East Prussia to Poland.
December 9–10 (Tues.–Wed.)	Memoranda presented by Protestant church leaders (Wurm) and Catholic bishops' conference to the Reich Chancellery protesting National Socialist church politics.
December 11 (Thurs.)	Germany and Italy declare war on the United States.

The "722" appears in the right margin beside the October 18–20 entry.

December 12 (Fri.)	Ruth von Kleist-Retzow is able to obtain for Bonhoeffer "five hundred sheets of typing paper and two hundred sheets of office paper." Verdict in the trial of the Confessing Church examination commission announced.
December 14 (Sun.)	Reich Minister for Church Affairs Kerrl dies in Paris.
December 16 (Tues.)	German offensive bogs down outside Moscow.
December 18 (Thurs.)	Trott visits Visser 't Hooft in Geneva.
December 19 (Fri.)	Field Marshal von Brauchitsch dismissed. Hitler becomes commander in chief of the army.
December 21 (Sun.)	Return to Berlin.
December 30 (Tues.)	Paula Bonhoeffer's sixty-fifth birthday.
December 31 (Wed.)	Attends Bach's *Musical Offering* at the Berlin Vocal Academy.

723 is a marginal note beside December 18.

1942

January 14 (Wed.)	End of the Arcadia Conference between Roosevelt and Churchill. Formation of a "Combined Chiefs of Staff Committee" (headquartered in Washington).
January 19 (Mon.)	In Berlin, music making with the Schleichers.
January 20 (Tues.)	Wannsee Conference meets to coordinate measures for the "final solution of the Jewish question."
January 23 (Fri.)	In Berlin. Meeting between Moltke, Guttenberg, Delbrück, as well as Bonhoeffer and his brother Klaus at the "Venetia."
February 1 (Sun.)	Reich Commissar Terboven installs a government in Norway headed by Prime Minister Quisling.
February 14 (Sat.)	Oster and Dohnanyi meet with Hassell. Increased surveillance by the Gestapo noticeable.
February 23 (Mon.)	Stalin's "Order of the Day": "Hitlers come and go; the German people, the German state will remain."
March	Heavy air attacks begin on German cities. Hans and Christine von Dohnanyi in Italy.
March 24 (Tues.)	Letter to Ernst Wolf regarding Bultmann's demythologization thesis.
March 28 (Sat.)	Oster and Dohnanyi meet with Hassell.
March 31 (Tues.)	Spends nine days with Bethge in Klein-Krössin, then travels on to Kieckow.

April 4 (Sat.)	Visit with Pastor Reimer in Naseband.	
April 5 (Sun.)	Easter in Kieckow. After the public reading of "Kirkens Grunn," all Norwegian pastors resign from office.	
April 8 (Wed.)	Dohnanyi summoned back to Berlin.	724
April 9 (Thurs.)	Gives first version of his will to Bethge.	
April 10 (Fri.)	Embarks for Norway with Moltke, by train to Saßnitz.	
April 11 (Sat.)	Stays on the isle of Rügen. By ferry to Trelleborg. While in transit, writes a letter to Archbishop Eidem. Stays overnight in Malmö.	
April 12 (Sun.)	To Oslo.	
April 13–15	Discussions in Oslo.	
April 16 (Thurs.)	To Stockholm. Archbishop Eidem informed about Bishop Bell's coming trip to Sweden.	
April 17 (Fri.)	In Stockholm. Visits Pastor Werner. Letter to the Leibholz family in Oxford.	
April 18 (Sat.)	In Copenhagen. Conversation with Pastor Sparring-Petersen. Flight back to Berlin.	
ca. April 25 (Sat.)	Trott visits Visser 't Hooft in Geneva; delivers to him a memorandum to the British government that he has composed together with Hans-Bernd von Haeften and Eugen Gerstenmaier.	
April 27 (Mon.)	Visser 't Hooft departs Geneva for London.	
April 28 (Tues.)	In Berlin. Bonhoeffer receives Moltke's official report of their journey for review.	
May 1 (Fri.)	Heydrich and Canaris conclude their "Prague Agreement" mutually limiting their functions. Telegram from Bishop Bell to Visser 't Hooft: "Visiting Sweden for three weeks commencing May 11."	
May 5 (Tues.)	Meeting between Visser 't Hooft and Bishop Bell in London. Delivery of the memorandum to Sir Stafford Cripps.	
May 8 (Fri.)	Bishop Bell received by G. W. Harrison in the British Foreign Office.	
May 11 (Mon.)	Beginnings of Bonhoeffer's third Swiss journey. Arrives in Zurich and stays at the Pestalozzis'.	
May 13 (Wed.)	In Zurich. Letter to Barth: "Now, armed with the galley-proofs of your new *Dogmatics* volume, . . . I am departing for a leisurely week . . . to a guest-	725

	house on Lake Geneva recommended to me by the Pestalozzis." Bishop Bell departs by plane for Sweden.
May 15 (Fri.)	UK classification renewed. Bishop Bell meets with Archbishop Eidem.
May 18 (Mon.)	Schönfeld departs Geneva for Berlin.
May 20 (Wed.)	In Geneva. Letter to Charlotte von Kirschbaum and to de Quervain. Investigations begin in Munich against Schmidhuber and Heinz Ickradt on suspicion of currency violations.
May 21 (Thurs.)	In Zurich. Letter to the Leibholz family.
May 22–25	First meeting of the Kreisau circle.
May 25 (Mon.)	Visits Barth in Basel. That evening, letter to Siegmund-Schultze from Zurich.
May 26 (Tues.)	Return to Berlin. First meeting between Schönfeld and Bishop Bell in Stockholm. Molotov signs the British-Soviet alliance treaty in London. Rejection of any separate peace.
May 27 (Wed.)	In Berlin. Preparations for trip to Sweden. Official passport issued dated May 27, 1942. Assassination of Heydrich in Prague.
May 29 (Fri.)	Second meeting between Schönfeld and Bishop Bell in Stockholm.
May 30 (Sat.)	Flight to Stockholm. Schönfeld meets Bishop Bell in Uppsala.
May 31 (Sun.)	From Stockholm to Sigtuna. Conversation between Bishop Bell, Schönfeld, and Bonhoeffer.
June 1 (Mon.)	In Stockholm. Second conversation with Bishop Bell. Schönfeld delivers his "Statement."
June 2 (Tues.)	Return flight to Berlin together with Schönfeld.
Beginning of June	Prepares a memorandum with Perels concerning immediate steps to be taken in the church after the war.
June 7 (Sun.)	Attends Bethge's sermon in Berlin-Friedenau.
June 8 (Mon.)	In Klein-Krössin to continue work on *Ethics*. Renews acquaintance there with Maria von Wedemeyer.
726 June 9 (Tues.)	Bishop Bell's return flight to England.
June 12 (Fri.)	Schönfeld again in Geneva; Visser 't Hooft returns there on June 14.

June 16 (Tues.)	Probably with the Freiburg circle to plan its memorandum.
June 19 (Fri.)	Bishop Bell finishes his "Memorandum of Conversations" and delivers it the next day to the British Foreign Office.
June 20 (Sat.)	In Munich. Letter to Winfried Maechler.
June 21 (Sun.)	In Berlin for three days of discussions with Dohnanyi.
June 21–27	Bethge in Breslau for mission renewal evenings.
June 24 (Wed.)	Moltke meets with Bishop Wurm.
June 25 (Thurs.)	In transit by train to Munich. To Bethge: "But I sense how an opposition to all that is 'religious' is growing in me.... Because I believe that I am on the verge of some kind of breakthrough, I am letting things take their own course and do not resist"; mention of Maria von Wedemeyer.
June 26 (Fri.)	Flight to Venice with Dohnanyi.
June 30 (Tues.)	Bishop Bell meets with Eden.
July 3–10	Stays in Rome. Visits include those to Father Leiber and Rector Zeiger.
July 10 (Fri.)	Return to Berlin.
July 13 (Mon.)	Bishop Bell meets with Cripps.
July 15–17	English "Peace Aims Group" in Oxford.
July 17 (Fri.)	Eden gives negative answer to Bishop Bell.
July 19 (Sun.)	Moltke meets again with Bishop Wurm.
July 20 (Mon.)	Expected in Klein-Krössin, but still in Berlin.
July 23 (Thurs.)	Bishop Bell's telegram to Visser 't Hooft: "Interest undoubted, but deeply regret no reply possible."
July 30 (Thurs.)	Bishop Bell reports to the American ambassador Winant.
August 2 (Sun.)	In Berlin, Joachim Kanitz visits.
August 3 (Mon.)	In Berlin; Bethge "spoke with Dietrich about problems with his work."
August 7 (Fri.)	Bonhoeffer and Bethge visit the Dohnanyis in Sakrow.
August 9 (Sun.)	In Berlin. House music with the Schleichers, Otto John as guest.
August 10 (Mon.)	In Magdeburg, first meeting with the synodal commission on the topic of the *primus usus legis*.

727

August 11 (Tues.)	In Berlin, with Goerdeler and Bethge at the "Fürstenhof."
August 18–25	In Klein-Krössin.
August 22 (Sun.)	Hans von Wedemeyer killed in action at Stalingrad.
August 26 (Wed.)	Again in Berlin.
ca. August 28–30	Dohnanyi in Switzerland, conveys Bonhoeffer's letter of August 28 to Bishop Bell and on August 30 writes to the Leibholz family from Vitznau on Lake Lucerne.
September 1 (Tues.)	In Klein-Krössin.
September 3 (Thurs.)	Again in Berlin (until September 21).
September 5 (Sat.)	Charlotte Friedenthal (via "Operation 7") can travel to Switzerland.
September 10 (Thurs.)	Munich office of Military Intelligence applies for Bonhoeffer's travel visa to the Balkans, Italy, and Switzerland.
September 12 (Sat.)	Hans and Christine von Dohnanyi on vacation in Rome and Capri until October 10.
September 16 (Wed.)	Moltke flies to Oslo and Stockholm.
September 18–28	Trott in Sweden.
September 22 (Tues.)	In Klein-Krössin for a day and a half.
September 24 (Thurs.)	Again in Berlin.
September 30 (Wed.)	"Operation 7" group travels to Switzerland.
October 2 (Fri.)	Visits Ruth von Kleist-Retzow at the Berlin Franciscan hospital (eye operation); meets once again with Maria von Wedemeyer.
October 3 (Sat.)	By military train to Munich (until October 14).
October 9 (Fri.)	Meeting in Freiburg with Erik Wolf and Constantin von Dietze regarding the memorandum.
October 10 (Sat.)	Again in Munich.
October 14 (Wed.)	Urgent warnings, journey canceled; return to Berlin.
October 15 (Thurs.)	Meets again with Maria von Wedemeyer when Hans-Walter Schleicher departs after being called up for military service.

728	October 16–18	Second meeting of the Kreisau circle.
	October 16–20	Dohnanyi breaks off his trip to Budapest because of warnings.
	October 18 (Sun.)	Morning devotions on Eph. 5:15-21 at the Franciscan hospital with grandmother Kleist and Maria von Wedemeyer.

October 26 (Mon.)	In Berlin. Preparation of faked documents. Maria von Wedemeyer's brother Maximilian killed in action on the eastern front.
October 28 (Wed.)	Moltke meets with Bishop Preysing.
October 31 (Sat.)	Schmidhuber arrested in Meran.
November 1 (Sun.)	During a worship service in Stuttgart Bishop Wurm reads his "Thirteen Points" about the unification of the German Evangelical Church. Composer Hugo Distler commits suicide in the Berlin cathedral.
November 5 (Thurs.)	In Munich. Letter to Max Diestel.
November 7 (Sat.)	In Klein-Krössin.
November 8 (Sun.)	Allied landing in northern Africa.
November 11 (Wed.)	German troops occupy southern France.
November 13 (Fri.)	In Berlin. Performance of the *Musikalische Exequien* by Heinrich Schütz. Letter to Maria von Wedemeyer: "'The last few weeks here have been awful' . . . there's scarcely half an hour without interruption. . . . By the beginning of December I hope to have my travels behind me, if everything doesn't suddenly change again."
November 14 (Sat.)	Moltke tries in vain to get the Armed Forces High Command to veto the deportation of Jews.
November 17–18 (Tues. Wed.)	Meeting of the Freiburg circle (without Bonhoeffer) regarding the memorandum. Dohnanyi speaks with Senior Military Prosecutor Roeder regarding the Schmidhuber case.
November 19 (Thurs.)	In Berlin. Mrs. von Wedemeyer forbids further letters to Maria von Wedemeyer.
November 24–25 (Tues.–Wed.)	Spends two days in Pätzig with Mrs. von Wedemeyer. German Sixth Army surrounded by Russian troops at Stalingrad.
November 25 (Wed.)	Visits Fritz and Margret Onnasch in Stettin.
November 26 (Thurs.)	Again in Berlin.
November 27 (Fri.)	Dohnanyi in transit to Rome and Switzerland. 729
November 28 (Sat.)	Advent service at the Schleicher home.
November 29 (Sun.)	First Sunday in Advent. Dohnanyi back from Switzerland. Two meetings in November at the homes of Klaus Bonhoeffer and the Schleichers with Prince Louis Ferdinand, Goerdeler, Jakob Kaiser, Wilhelm Leuschner, and Bonhoeffer.

December 2 (Wed.)	In Berlin.
December 3 (Thurs.)	Bishop Bell writes to Sutz and Harry Johansson.
December 11 (Fri.)	The writer Jochen Klepper commits suicide with his Jewish wife and daughter.
December 12–13 (Sat.–Sun.)	Visits Ernst Wolf in Halle with Oskar Hammelsbeck and Hans Böhm. Attends performance of Bach's Mass in B Minor. Pastoral letter issued by the Catholic bishops regarding rights violations.
December 15 (Tues.)	Bishop Bell meets with Eden.
December 20 (Sun.)	Fourth Sunday in Advent. Eberhard Bethge and Renate Schleicher become engaged at the Marienburger Allee home. Hassell converses with the "young" Kreisau members.
December 22 (Tues.)	Members of the "Rote Kapelle" resistance group executed.
December 24 (Thurs.)	"After Ten Years" presented to family and friends for Christmas.
December 31 (Thurs.)	New Year's Eve with the Dohnanyis in Sakrow.

1943

Beginning of January	German troops retreat from the Caucasus. Ernst Kaltenbrunner appointed head of the Reich Central Security Office.
January 3 (Sun.)	Perels composes his will.
January 13 (Wed.)	Maria von Wedemeyer in Pätzig, accepts in writing Bonhoeffer's marriage proposal; henceforth this date is considered the date of engagement. Nevertheless, the waiting period remains in effect.
January 14 (Thurs.)	Casablanca conference (until January 25). Allied demand for unconditional surrender.
January 17 (Sun.)	In Berlin. Answers Maria von Wedemeyer's letter. "I am not yet certain of the dates of my trip, but I can't imagine it will be much longer now. Then I will be gone four weeks."
January 22 (Fri.)	Hassell meets with Oster and Guttenberg.
January 23 (Sat.)	In Berlin. Letter to Maria von Wedemeyer: "We are holding our breath" in light of world events.
End of January	Freiburg memorandum finished.
February 2 (Tues.)	Fighting ends in Stalingrad.
February 6–7 (Sat.–Sun.)	In Berlin. Meeting with Walter Bauer about the Freiburg memorandum.

730

February 8 (Mon.)	To Munich by train with Bethge. "I got to hear more in depth again about Dietrich's work. He read me a portion of it that he had just written."
February 9 (Tues.)	Visits Josef Müller in Munich. Preparations for the trip to Switzerland. Josef Müller travels to Rome.
February 10 (Wed.)	Strongly advised by people in Berlin to cancel the journey. Visits Christine von Kalckreuth.
February 11 (Thurs.)	In Munich; meets with Hans Lokics.
February 12 (Fri.)	Returns to Berlin.
February 18 (Thurs.)	Goebbels proclaims "total war" at the Berlin Sport Palace. Hans and Sophie Scholl arrested in Munich (executed on February 22).
March 9 (Tues.)	In Berlin, worried phone call from Maria von Wedemeyer. The answer: "From what little we have discussed, you know that there is danger not only outside, but here inside as well, sometimes less, sometimes more. I will be traveling for several weeks to Rome."
March 10 (Wed.)	Bishop Bell speaks in the House of Lords.
March 13 (Sat.)	Summons from Munich for military examination. Schlabrendorff's assassination attempt fails.
March 15 (Mon.)	In Magdeburg, presentation at the second session of the synodal commission *(primus usus legis)*.
March 21 (Sun.)	"Heroes' Memorial Day"; Colonel Gersdorff's assassination attempt at the Berlin armory fails.
March 23 (Tues.)	Visit to Ruth von Kleist-Retzow at the Stettin hospital.
March 26 (Fri.)	Maria von Wedemeyer from Hanover: "In the next few days I . . . really am going to begin serving as a nurse." Goerdeler's memorandum to the generals regarding the necessity for a coup.
March 31 (Wed.)	In Berlin, Karl Bonhoeffer's seventy-fifth birthday.
Beginning of April	Maria von Wedemeyer begins training as a nurse at the Magdalena Home in Hanover.
April 5 (Mon.)	Bonhoeffer arrested by military authorities with cooperation of Gestapo. Taken to the Tegel Military Detention Center. Hans and Christine von Dohnanyi, Josef Müller, and his secretary, Annie Haser, are arrested the same day. Oster placed under house arrest.

731

April 12 (Mon.)	First interrogation of Dohnanyi (and probably also of Bonhoeffer) and Oster, who denies knowledge of the "notes" and any commission for Bonhoeffer. German Africa Corps surrenders in North Africa.
April 14 (Wed.)	First letter to his parents.
April 17 (Sat.)	Bonhoeffer moved to a larger cell.
April 19 (Mon.)	Warsaw ghetto uprising (crushed on May 16).
April 23 (Fri.)	Good Friday. Dohnanyi sends a letter to Bonhoeffer in which he accepts total responsibility. Maria von Wedemeyer celebrates her nineteenth birthday.
April 30 (Fri.)	Christine von Dohnanyi released from custody.
May 4 (Tues.)	Letter to his parents: "I read, learn, work"; particularly enjoying Jeremias Gotthelf.
May 13 (Thurs.)	Roeder confiscates defense documents in Dohnanyi's cell.
May 15 (Sat.)	Eberhard Bethge marries Renate née Schleicher. Letter to his parents: "I'm now trying my hand at a little study on 'The feeling of time'"; finds Adalbert Stifter "wonderfully clear and simple."
May 23 (Sun.)	First permission for parents to visit. Maria von Wedemeyer and her mother visit Bonhoeffer's parents.
732 June 10 (Thurs.)	First draft of Bonhoeffer's letters to Roeder between interrogations about "Operation 7."
June 12–14	Third meeting of the Kreisau circle.
June 14 (Mon.)	Whit Monday. To his parents: "My study on 'The feeling of time' is practically finished."
June 15 (Tues.)	Canaris interrogated. Maria von Wedemeyer on sick leave in Berlin.
June 17 (Thurs.)	Renewed interrogation of Oster, who revises his earlier statements, with negative implications for Bonhoeffer.
June 24 (Thurs.)	Visitation privileges for Maria von Wedemeyer.
July 3 (Sat.)	To his parents: "During the past week I've done a good deal of quiet work, and have read some good books."
July 8–10	Bethge visits Barth and Visser 't Hooft in Switzerland.

July 10 (Sat.)	Allied troops land in Sicily.
July 23 (Fri.)	Field Marshal Keitel orders that the case against Dohnanyi and Bonhoeffer no longer be prosecuted with the charge of high treason.
July 25 (Sun.)	Coup in Italy, Mussolini arrested. To his parents: "In my reading I'm now living entirely in the nineteenth century."
July 30 (Fri.)	Roeder informs Bonhoeffer that the interrogations are temporarily completed; indictment being prepared; writing privileges expanded. To Maria von Wedemeyer: "I'm allowed to write every four days, so I'll alternate between you and my parents." Concludes drama fragment and begins novel fragment.
August 1 (Sun.)	Final letter to Roeder: defends himself against various charges.
August 3 (Tues.)	To his parents: "I'm expecting more information any day" regarding his defense. Heavy air raids on Berlin.
August 8 (Wed.)	Heavy bombardment of Hamburg and Berlin.
August 9 (Mon.)	Only now is Dohnanyi informed of the conclusion of the investigation and indictment. Maria von Wedemeyer returns home to Pätzig.
August 17 (Tues.)	Rüdiger von der Goltz authorized as defense attorney. Because of increasing air raids, essential sections of the Reich War Court are transferred to Torgau.
August 23 (Mon.)	Roeder presents the report of his investigation.
September 3 (Fri.)	Heavy air raid; Bonhoeffer transferred to a lower story of the prison.
September 13 (Mon.)	Maria von Wedemeyer goes to Klein-Reetz for a week to recuperate.
September 15 (Wed.)	Bethge in a Spandau barracks for basic training.
September 16 (Thurs.)	Indictment issued against Dohnanyi and Oster. Dr. Wergin authorized as defense attorney for Bonhoeffer.
September 20 (Mon.)	Bonhoeffer composes new will.
September 21 (Tues.)	Indictment issued against Bonhoeffer.
September 25 (Sat.)	Maria von Wedemeyer attends memorial service for Frieder von Hülst in Rohrbeck. Dr. Langbehn arrested.

733

October 1 (Fri.)	Moltke in Copenhagen to warn against the planned mass deportation of Danish Jews. Thanks to the initiative of the German navy attaché Duckwitz, ca. seven thousand Danish Jews are smuggled to Sweden.
October 3 (Sun.)	Danish bishops read pastoral letter in the churches regarding the persecution of Jews.
October 16–19	Confessing Church synod in Breslau adopts an "Exegesis of the Fifth Commandment" (to which Bonhoeffer contributed) and a corresponding "Declaration to the Congregations."
October 17 (Sun.)	Karl Bonhoeffer writes to the president of the Reich War Court requesting Bonhoeffer's release from prison.
October 22 (Fri.)	Renate Bethge visits her husband, who is stationed in Lissa.
October 26 (Tues.)	Maria von Wedemeyer in Kniephof.
October 27 (Wed.)	Trott in Sweden (until November 13).
November 11 (Thurs.)	Latmiral transferred to Tegel.
November 18 (Thurs.)	Bethge on leave in Berlin. First letters to him smuggled out of Tegel. Reich War Court orders a trial date of December 17.
November 23 (Tues.)	Bonhoeffer makes yet another will after heavy air raids. Composes "Prayers for Fellow Prisoners."
November 26 (Fri.)	Air raids on the nearby Borsig factory. Dohnanyi, whose cell has been hit by an incendiary bomb, is taken to the Charité hospital with a brain embolism. Reich War Court severely damaged by air raid; trial documents destroyed by the fire. Bonhoeffer's parents, Bethge, and Maria von Wedemeyer visit Tegel together.
November 28 (Sun.)	Bonhoeffer composes a report about his experiences during air raids. End of November: Reich War Court orders Roeder for three days to reconstruct the trial documents.
December 1 (Wed.)	Maria von Wedemeyer in Klein-Krössin for a week.
December 3 (Fri.)	Dohnanyi's defense attorneys prepare a defense brief for him (first draft).
December 5 (Sun.)	In Bonhoeffer's letter to Bethge allusion to new theological themes; probably also finishes the novel fragment.

734

December 13 (Mon.)	Christmas letter to Maria von Wedemeyer.
December 15 (Wed.)	Works on the essay "What Does It Mean to Tell the Truth?"
December 16 (Thurs.)	Attorney Dr. Wergin visits Bonhoeffer; as a precaution trial date to be postponed as long as possible.
December 23 (Thurs.)	Bethge on leave in Berlin with visitation privileges in Tegel.
December 25 (Sat.)	To Bethge: "In addition, your visit prompted me to write a little piece . . . , and it has given me new courage and desire to do the larger work."

1944

January 1 (Sat.)	Roeder transferred to Air District 4 as chief judge in Lemberg. Reich Judicial Councilor Kutzner appointed to continue the proceedings against Oster, Dohnanyi, and Bonhoeffer.
January 4 (Tues.)	Red Army reaches the former eastern border of Poland.
January 5 (Wed.)	Maria von Wedemeyer in Tegel on her way to Altenburg, where she is to fill in for a teacher.
January 8 (Sat.)	Bethge in transit through Berlin on the way to his unit in Italy.
January 14 (Fri.)	To his parents: "I'm finding it a little easier to concentrate, and I'm enjoying Dilthey very much."
January 15 (Sat.)	Bethge writes from Rignano near Rome, where his field unit is headquartered.
January 19 (Wed.)	Solf resistance circle and Moltke arrested.
January 22 (Sat.)	Dohnanyi taken to the prison infirmary in Buch from the Charité hospital.
January 23 (Sun.)	Allies land near Nettuno.
January 27–28 (Thurs.–Fri.)	Heavy air raids on Berlin. Sergeant "Engel" killed.
February 3 (Thurs.)	Dietrich Bethge born.
February 10 (Thurs.)	Professor de Crinis declares Dohnanyi fit for interrogation.
February 11 (Fri.)	Hitler orders Canaris dismissed from office and the entire intelligence service placed under the SS high commander.
February 12 (Sat.)	To Bethge: "I've been in bed for a few days with slight influenza, but I'm up again; that's a good

735

		thing, because in about a week's time I shall need to have all my wits about me." Reich War Court sentences Schmidhuber to four years in the penitentiary, Ickradt to two years in prison.
	February 16 (Wed.)	Maria von Wedemeyer in Pätzig.
	February 19 (Sat.)	Attorney Dr. Wergin in Tegel; Dohnanyi's illness prompts postponement of the trial again.
	February 20 (Sun.)	Maria von Wedemeyer in Tegel in transit to Bundorf, where she will work as a teacher with the Truchseß family. Admiral Canaris under house arrest in Burg Lauenstein.
	March 1 (Wed.)	To Bethge: "I am entering this new month with great hopes" (regarding his coming trial).
	March 4 (Sat.)	Trial against Josef Müller ends with acquittal; remains in prison.
	March 6 (Mon.)	First daylight air raids on Berlin.
	March 9 (Thurs.)	To Bethge: trial date probably in May.
736	March 14 (Tues.)	Beginning of a new stage of interrogation (until May).
	March 25 (Sat.)	Bonhoeffer's parents visit in Pätzig (until April 4).
	Beginning of April	"Report on Prison Life after One Year in Tegel," composed for Berlin City Commandant Hase.
	April 4 (Tues.)	Beginning of the Berneuchen Easter week in Bundorf.
	April 11 (Tues.)	To Bethge: "I've been told that I had better not, for the time being, expect any change in my status."
	April 22 (Sat.)	To Bethge: "After a rather long unproductive period, I feel in better form for work now that spring is coming."
	April 26 (Wed.)	Writes his parents that he has absorbed "a radically new kind of life."
	April 30 (Sun.)	First theological letter to Bethge raising the question of "religionless Christianity."
	May 3–4 (Wed.–Thurs.)	On his interrogations in the Reich War Court, "extremely satisfactory results."
	May 5 (Fri.)	Dr. Peschke submits the final version of Dohnanyi's defense brief. Second theological letter to Bethge regarding the "reinterpretation of biblical concepts."
	May 7 (Sun.)	Heavy daytime air attacks on Berlin.

May 9 (Tues.)	To Bethge: "My own opinion is that the next few weeks will bring great and surprising events."
May 16 (Tues.)	Bethge on leave in Berlin.
May 21 (Sun.)	Dietrich Bethge's baptism, at which Bonhoeffer's "Thoughts on the Day of the Baptism" are read. Maria von Wedemeyer attends and then visits Bonhoeffer in Tegel.
May 23–24 (Tues.–Wed.)	Allied offensive in Italy.
May 24 (Wcd.)	To Bethge, expressing how impressed he is by Carl Friedrich von Weizsäcker's *Weltbild der Physik* [*World View of Physics*]; Bonhoeffer hopes "to learn a great deal from it for my own work."
May 26 (Fri.)	Consideration about securing a military chaplaincy for Bethge by approaching Military Bishop Dohrmann through Hans-Bernd von Haeften.
May 29 (Mon.)	Letter smuggled out to Maria von Wedemeyer. In a letter to Bethge, thoughts about God not being a "stopgap."

In June	Dohnanyi contracts diphtheria. Investigation temporarily halted.	737
June 3 (Sat.)	Bethge still on leave in Berlin. Bonhoeffer's parents in Pätzig.	
June 4–5 (Sun.–Mon.)	Julius Leber and Adolf Reichwein arrested. Rome in Allied control.	
June 5 (Mon.)	Illegal visiting privileges for Bethge. On the same day, Bonhoeffer writes Bethge about his attempts to write poetry; theme: the past.	
June 6 (Tues.)	Allied invasion of Normandy.	
June 8 (Thurs.)	To Bethge: continuation of theological discussion: Christ and the world come of age.	
June 13 (Tues.)	First V-1 launches against England.	
June 16 (Fri.)	Bethge writes from Munich, again in transit to Italy.	
June 17 (Sat.)	Response to Maria von Wedemeyer's communication that for the time being she no longer intends to come to Berlin.	
June 22 (Thurs.)	Red Army offensive against the Center Army Group.	
June 27 (Tues.)	To Bethge: work on an explanation of the first three commandments.	

June 30 (Fri.)	General Paul von Hase taken to Tegel prison. Letter to Bethge about the "world come of age."
Beginning of July	Dr. Kutzner requests that Keitel halt the legal proceedings. Bethge with his unit near Florence.
July 8 (Sat.)	Writes Bethge that the heat makes him feel "as if I were in an oven." Encloses the poems "Who Am I?" and "Christians and Pagans." Composes "Happiness and Unhappiness" and "Night Voices in Tegel."
July 18 (Tues.)	To Bethge: sharing in God's suffering in the world.
July 20 (Thurs.)	Stauffenberg's assassination attempt in Hitler's headquarters. Failed coup. Count Stauffenberg, Beck, Friedrich Olbricht, Werner von Haeften, and Albrecht Mertz von Quirnheim shot to death that evening.
July 21 (Fri.)	Reich Central Security Office forms "Special July 20 Commission." Oster and von Hase arrested. To Bethge: "I'm still discovering right up to this moment that it is only by living completely in this world that one learns to have faith." Includes the poem "Stations on the Road to Freedom."
July 23 (Sun.)	Canaris arrested.
July 25 (Tues.)	Himmler appointed commander of the Reserve Army. Bonhoeffer reflects on renewed heavy air raids.
July 27 (Thurs.)	To Bethge regarding the question of "unconscious Christianity."
August 3 (Thurs.)	Sends "Outline for a Book" to Bethge.
August 10 (Thurs.)	To Bethge: "Maria is coming to my parents permanently, as an assistant receptionist."
August 12 (Sat.)	Goerdeler arrested.
August 14 (Mon.)	Writes Bethge to wish him happy birthday and includes the poem "The Friend."
August 18 (Fri.)	Schlabrendorff in Reich Central Security Office prison; Hans John and Perels arrested.
August 22 (Tues.)	Dohnanyi taken to Sachsenhausen concentration camp.
August 23 (Wed.)	Maria von Wedemeyer in Tegel, "so fresh and steadfast and at the same time tranquil in a way I've rarely seen."
August 25 (Fri.)	Paris under Allied control; de Gaulle's return.

738

September 8 (Fri.)	Constantin von Dietze and Adolf Lampe arrested.
After September 8	Interrogations of Canaris, Oster, and Alexander von Pfuhlstein at the Reich Central Security Office.
September 9 (Sat.)	Beginning of V-2 launches against England.
September 22 (Fri.)	Gestapo criminal investigator Sonderegger discovers Dohnanyi's secret archive in the Armed Forces High Command outpost in Zossen.
September 25 (Mon.)	Conscription of all men between the ages of sixteen and sixty for service in the "German Volkssturm."
September 27 (Wed.)	Josef Müller in the Reich Central Security Office prison.
September 29 (Fri.)	Bethge receives the poem "The Death of Moses."
September 30 (Sat.)	Deta von Hase, widow of the executed city commandant, finds refuge in the Schleicher home.
October 1 (Sun.)	Klaus Bonhoeffer arrested. Dietrich Bonhoeffer then abandons his plan to escape.
October 4 (Wed.)	Rüdiger Schleicher arrested.
October 5 (Thurs.)	Perels arrested. Letter to Maria von Wedemeyer with the poem "Jonah." Huppenkothen visits Dohnanyi in Sachsenhausen.
October 8 (Sun.)	Bonhoeffer transferred to the prison at the Reich Central Security Office, first in cell 19, later cell 24.
October 15 (Sun.)	Walter Bauer arrested.
October 18 (Wed.)	Bethge's unit near Mantua.
October 21 (Sat.)	Aachen becomes first large German city to be occupied by the Americans.
October 28 (Sat.)	Near Mantua, Bethge learns of his own imminent arrest and destroys Bonhoeffer's recent letters.
October 30 (Mon.)	Bethge taken to the Lehrter Straße prison.
November 1 (Wed.)	Gerhard Ritter arrested. Bonhoeffer's renewed interrogations, "in a word: repulsive." That same week Himmler orders a halt to the gassings in Auschwitz.
December 16 (Sat.)	Beginning of the Ardennes offensive.
December 19 (Tues.)	Christmas letter to Maria von Wedemeyer with the poem "Powers of Good."
December 20 (Wed.)	Indictment issued against Klaus Bonhoeffer, Rüdiger Schleicher, Friedrich Justus Perels, and others.

739

December 22 (Fri.)	Maria von Wedemeyer's letter to Hedwig von Truchseß relates that both Hans Jürgen von Kleist-Retzow and Dietrich von Truchseß are in Berlin prisons.
December 28 (Thurs.)	Birthday letter to his mother.

1945

January 4 (Thurs.)	Kaltenbrunner reports to the Ministry of Foreign Affairs on Bonhoeffer's statements about Bishop Bell and English politics.
January 12 (Fri.)	Beginning of major Soviet offensive.
January 17 (Wed.)	Last letter: to his parents regarding the people's sacrifice. Thanks for Maria von Wedemeyer's Christmas letter.
January 24 (Wed.)	Moltke executed.
January 29 (Mon.)	The "Children's Trek"[1] leaves Pätzig with Maria von Wedemeyer as leader.
January 31 (Wed.)	Pätzig taken by Red Guards; Ruth von Wedemeyer flees west to relatives in Oberbehme.

740

February 1 (Thurs.)	Dohnanyi taken to the Reich Central Security Office prison.
February 2 (Fri.)	Goerdeler executed. People's Court, presided over by Roland Freisler, sentences Klaus Bonhoeffer, Rüdiger Schleicher, Friedrich Perels, and Hans John to death.
February 3 (Sat.)	Heaviest air attacks on Berlin. Freisler is killed in the attacks.
February 4–12	Yalta Conference of the "Big Three": decision to divide Germany into four occupation zones.
February 7 (Wed.)	Prisoner transport from the Reich Central Security Office prison to the Buchenwald concentration camp. Bonhoeffer in cell no. 1. Canaris taken to Flossenbürg.
February 13 (Tues.)	Maria von Wedemeyer in Berlin with Bonhoeffer's parents; adjuntant's office of the Armed Forces

---

[1.] [As the Russian army approached, several million Germans in the eastern regions, many of them women and children, began to flee on foot; Maria von Wedemeyer led one such "trek."—MB]

	High Command issues her a pass to travel toward Bundorf.
February 14–15 (Wed.–Thurs.)	Dresden destroyed by air attacks.
February 19 (Mon.)	Maria von Wedemeyer writes to her mother from Flossenbürg while searching unsuccessfully for her fiancé. Himmler meets secretly with Count Bernadotte.
February 24 (Sat.)	Payne Best and General von Rabenau arrive in Buchenwald; Rabenau shares cell with Bonhoeffer.
March 8 (Thurs.)	Dohnanyi sends a secret message: "They have everything."
March 10 (Sat.)	Allies take Cologne and Koblenz. In mid-March Dohnanyi transferred to the state police hospital.
March 16 (Fri.)	Schlabrendorff acquitted in his trial; remains in custody.
April 3 (Tues.)	Bonhoeffer transported from Buchenwald concentration camp during Easter week.
April 4 (Wed.)	Interim stop in Regensburg; kept in custody there with imprisoned relatives of conspirators.
April 5 (Thurs.)	During the "midday meeting" at Hitler's headquarters, Hitler orders the executions of the conspirators after additional Zossen files discovered. Prisoners transported from Regensburg toward the Bavarian forest. Dohnanyi taken back to Sachsenhausen.
April 6 (Fri.)	Early morning arrival at the schoolhouse in Schönberg. Huppenkothen goes to Sachsenhausen for Dohnanyi's court-martial.
April 8 (Sun.)	Morning service in the Schönberg schoolhouse. Best receives the farewell greeting for Bishop Bell before the continued transport to Flossenbürg, where a court-martial is held.
April 9 (Mon.)	Early morning executions of the Military Intelligence group: Bonhoeffer, Canaris, Ludwig Gehre, Oster, Karl Sack, and Theodor Strünck; Dohnanyi executed in Sachsenhausen.
April 20 (Fri.)	Indictment against Dietze.

741

April 22–23 (Sun.–Mon.)	Klaus Bonhoeffer, Rüdiger Schleicher, Hans John, Friedrich Perels, and others executed by firing squad during the night at the Lehrter train station.
April 25 (Wed.)	Bethge released from custody with others.
April 28 (Sat.)	First Red Army soldiers arrive at the Marienburger Allee home.
April 30 (Mon.)	Hitler commits suicide in the bunker of the Reich Chancellery.
May 2 (Wed.)	German troops surrender in Berlin.
May 7 (Mon.)	German Armed Forces surrender in Reims (repeated on May 9 in Berlin).
May 30 (Wed.)	From Geneva, Freudenberg telegraphs news of Bonhoeffer's death to London. Maria von Wedemeyer learns of it in June, Bonhoeffer's parents in Berlin only at the end of June through Gisevius's visit and the BBC broadcast of the London memorial service.

Appendix 3.
Unpublished Material from Bonhoeffer's Literary Estate
1940–1945

I. Letters and Documents

Addressee or content	Date	NL reference
To Herbert von Bismarck, Berlin	April 1940	A 61,3 (1)
To Paula Bonhoeffer, Klein-Krössin	October 8, 1940	A 59,1 (4)
To Eberhard Bethge, Ettal	November 21, 1940	A 59,2 (8)
To Georg Eichholz, Ettal	November 25, 1940	A 60,2
To Georg Eichholz, Ettal	December 3, 1940	A 60,2
To Paula Bonhoeffer, Ettal	December 15, 1940	A 59,1 (10)
To Eberhard Bethge, Ettal	February (?), 1941	A 59,2 (32)
To Georg Eichholz, Ettal	February 4, 1941	A 60,2
To Eberhard Bethge, Ettal	February 23, 1941	A 59,2 (39)
To Eberhard Bethge, Ettal	February 24, 1941	A 59,2 (40)
To his parents	June 1 (?), 1941	A 59,1 (15)
To Calise Forell	Beginning of 1942	A 59,1 (12)
To Wiltrud Schutz, Berlin-Charlottenburg	September 4, 1942	In possession of Wiltrud Schutz

Note for newsletter May 1940 (1/6)	A 48,3 (12)
Note concerning police action in Blöstau (1/15)	A 61,2 (2a)
Note concerning drafts of letters to Dr. Roeder (1/226 and 1/228)	A 3,1

II. Drafts and Papers

743   **III. Sermons and Meditations**

No additional material

Regarding the notes for various documents that are cited in this list, see *Zettelnotizen für eine "Ethik"* (Bonhoeffer's notes for a work on *Ethics,* a supplementary volume to *DBW* 6), edited by Ilse Tödt (Gütersloh, 1993), which contains the complete text and detailed commentary.

Appendix 4.
Texts Published in *DBWE* 16 and in *Gesammelte Schriften, Ethics* (1995), or *Letters and Papers from Prison*

2:396–97	132–33	2:596–98	377–78
2:397	136	2:640–43	225–29
2:398–400	138–140		
2:400–401	145–46	3:37–43	36–41
2:401–2	147–49	3:44–45	257–58
2:402–3	153–55	3:45–46	260–61
2:403–4	155	3:398–400	33–35
2:404	159	3:400–401	35–36
2:404–5	161–62	3:401–3	42–43
2:405–6	162–63	3:404	49–50
2:407	186	3:405–9	473–76
2:407	193–94	3:409–15	476–81
2:408–9	209–11	3:416–17	488–89
2:411–12	211–12	3:418–21	489–92
2:412–14	212–14	3:421–25	492–96
2:414–15	235–37	3:426–30	499–502
2:416	247–48	3:432–54	551–72
2:416–17	314–16		
2:417–19	316–17	4:466–72	482–87
2:419–21	328–30	4:570–77	611–17
2:421	360	4:578–83	617–24
2:422	360–61	4:583–84	625–26
2:422–24	364–66	4:585–87	314–16
2:424–25	369	4:588–96	626–33
2:425–26	374–76	4:597–612	633–44
2:426–27	376–77		
2:428–32	241–45	6:476	60
2:433–37	574–80	6:477	61
2:438–40	572–74	6:477	68–69
2:564–69	44–48	6:479–80	48–49
2:570–73	105–8	6:480	74
2:573–78	205–9	6:481	147
2:578–82	237–40	6:482	155
2:583–85	253–55	6:482–83	160
2:586–87	69–70	6:483	160–61
2587–88	112–13	6:484–86	77–79
2:588–89	188–89	6:486	82
2:589–90	191	6:487	85
2:590–92	255–57	6:488–90	88–90
2:593	324–25	6:490–91	90–91
2:594–95	264–65	6:491–92	91–92

6:493	93–94	6:543–44	223–24
6:493–94	94	6:545–47	230–33
6:494–95	96–97	6:548	240–41
6:495–97	496–98	6:550–51	270–71
6:497–98	99	6:551–53	272–73
6:498–99	101	6:554	288
6:499–500	102	6:554–55	275–76
6:500–501	103–4	6:555–58	283–85
6:501–2	105	6:558–59	285–86
6:502–3	109–10	6:560–61	312–13
6:504–5	110–12	6:561	342
6:506–7	113–14	6:563–64	379–80
6:507–9	118–19	6:564–66	380–83
6:509	120–21	6:567–69	328–30
6:509–11	121–22	6:569–71	346–47
6:511–12	128–29	6:571–72	350–51
6:512–14	130–31	6:572–73	351–52
6:514–15	136	6:574–75	355–56
6:515–16	145–46	6:575–76	360
6:517–19	147–49	6:576	360–61
6:519–20	153–55	6:577–79	367–68
6:521–22	155–56	6:579–80	371–72
6:522–23	159	6:581–86	395–99
6:523–24	161–62	6:591–92	466–68
6:524–25	162–63	6:635–37	400–403
6:526	164		
6:527–28	165–66	*E* (1995)	
6:528–29	167	299–315	584–601
6:529–30	169–70	316–26	540–51
6:530–31	173–74	327–48	502–28
6:531–34	175–79	358–67	601–8
6:535–36	182–83		
6:536	183	*LPP*	
6:537	183–84	56–60	415–20
6:538	186	60–61	421–22
6:538	193	61	409–10
6:539	193–94	61–64	413–15
6:539–40	194–95	64–66	422–24
6:541	215–16	66–67	420–21
6:542	223	67–69	425–27
6:542–43	217–18		

BIBLIOGRAPHY

1. Archival Sources and Private Collections

Dietrich Bonhoeffer's papers and personal library, as well as correspondence from others and relevant material in other archives, have been cataloged in the *Nachlaß Dietrich Bonhoeffer* volume compiled by Dietrich Meyer and Eberhard Bethge. All such citations in *DBWE* are indicated by *NL*, followed by the corresponding reference code within that published index. Not all this material is part of the actual Bonhoeffer Nachlaß in the Staatsbibliothek in Berlin; footnote citations of *NL* material from other archives also give the numbering from the respective archive. All the material listed in the Meyer and Bethge catalog, however, has been included on microfiches at the Bundesarchiv in Koblenz and in the Bonhoeffer collection at Burke Library, Union Theological Seminary, New York.

Archiv Chr. Kaiser Verlag, Gütersloh
    Korrespondenz mit Ernst Wolf
Archiv der Evangelischen Kirche im Rheinland, Düsseldorf
    Handakten Joachim Beckmann: Kirchenkampf
Archiv des Schweizer Evangelischen Kirchenbundes, Bern
    Akte 323, 1 "Verfolgung der Kirche"
Archiv für Christlich-Demokratische Politik der Konrad-Adenauer-Stiftung
    e.V., Sankt Augustin
    Nachlaß Constantin von Dietze
Archives of the World Council of Churches, Geneva (WCC Archives)
    Archiv Nils Ehrenström
    General Correspondence
    Willem Visser 't Hooft Papers
    World Council of Churches, in process of formation (WCC ipof)

Auswärtiges Amt/Politisches Archiv, Berlin (formerly in Bonn)
Inland II
Kult. Gen.
Bundesarchiv Berlin-Lichterfelde (BA Berlin-Lichterfelde)
Nachlaß Hans und Christine von Dohnanyi
Bd. 13 I, 13 II, 14 III
Bundesarchiv Koblenz (BA Koblenz)
Nachlaß Ernst Wolf
Reichskanzlei
Bundesarchiv/Militärarchiv, Freiburg im Breisgau
Bundesarchiv, Potsdam (BA Potsdam)
Bestand ZB I
Center of Theological Inquiry, Princeton University, Princeton, New
Jersey
Paul Lehmann Papers
Deutsches Literaturarchiv, Marbach
Nachlaß Otto Bruder
Evangelisches Zentralarchiv, Berlin
Bestand 50: Kirchenkampf Archiv
Bestand 626: Nachlaß Siegmund-Schultze
Foreign and Commonwealth Office, London
FO 371/30913: Correspondence Bell/Eden
FO 371/30913: Minutes: Germany, Peace Moves
Houghton Library, Harvard University, Cambridge, Massachusetts
Papers of Dietrich Bonhoeffer, 1942–44, bMS Ger 161
Karl Barth-Archiv, Basel
Korrespondenz mit Dietrich Bonhoeffer und Paul Vogt
Nachlaß Charlotte von Kirschbaum
Lambeth Palace Library, London (LPL)
George Bell Papers
Landeskirchliches Archiv der Evangelischen Kirche in Westfalen, Bielefeld
(LKA der Evangelischen Kirche in Westfalen)
Bestand 5,1: Archiv Wilhelm Niemöller
Korrespondenz Bonhoeffer/Baumann
Landeskirchliches Archiv der Evangelisch-Lutherischen Kirche in Bayern,
Nuremberg (LKA Nuremberg)
Korrespondenz Bonhoeffer/Meiser 1941
Nachlaß Hans Meiser
Landeskirchliches Archiv Stuttgart (LKA Stuttgart)
Nachlaß Landesbischof Theophil Wurm
Landsarkivet, Uppsala
Arkiv Erling Eidem

Lunds Universitetsbibliotek
    Arkiv Anders Nygren
Niedersächsisches Hauptstaatsarchiv, Hannover-Nebenlager Pattensen (HA
    Nds 721 Lüneburg)
    Akten zum Verfahren der Staatsanwaltschaft Lüneburg gegen Dr. Man-
    fred Roeder
Princeton Theological Seminary Library, Special Collections, Princeton,
    New Jersey
    Paul Lehmann Papers
Public Record Office, London
    FO 371/30912: FO Minutes
    FO 371/32906: Possible Russo-German-Peace
    FO 371/33055: British lecture tours in Sweden. Visit of the Bishop of
    Chichester
Staatsarchiv Zürich
    Nachlaß Emil Brunner
Staatsbibliothek zu Berlin
    Nachlaß Dietrich Bonhoeffer (Nachlaß 299)
Universitätsbibliothek Bern
    Nachlaß Alfred de Quervain
Universitätsbibliothek, Freiburg im Breisgau
    Nachlaß Constantin von Dietze
Vojenský ústřední archiv, Prague (Archive for Military History)
    Akten Reichskriegsgericht 1943

Private Collections (locations at the time of German *DBW* publication)
Eberhard und Renate Bethge, Wachtberg
    Personal correspondence 1943
    Correspondence with Ruth von Kleist-Retzow
Ruth-Alice von Bismarck, Hamburg
    Literary estate of Maria von Wedemeyer-Weller
    Literary estate of Ruth von Wedemeyer
Ehrentraut Bohren, the widow of Georg Eichholz, Heidelberg
    Literary estate of Georg Eichholz
Jørgen Glenthøj, Åbyhoj, Denmark
    Partial literary estate of Birger Forell
Konstantin von Kleist-Retzow, Rinteln
    Literary estate of Ruth von Kleist-Retzow
Sabine Leibholz, Göttingen
    Literary estate of Gerhard Leibholz
Hans-Walter Schleicher, Oberried
    Correspondence with Dietrich Bonhoeffer

2. Literature Used by Bonhoeffer

Bannach, Horst, ed. *Wir fragen die Bibel: Die Bibellese in Frage und Antwort* (We ask the Bible: Reading the Bible in question and answer). Berlin, 1940.

Barth, Karl. *Der Christ als Zeuge.* Theologische Existenz heute 12. Munich: Chr. Kaiser, 1934. Translated as "The Christian as Witness," *The Student World* 27, no. 4 (1934).

———. *Die Kirchliche Dogmatik* 2/1. Zollikon-Zurich: Verlag der Evangelischen Buchhandlung, 1942. Translated by Geoffrey William Bromiley and Thomas Forsyth Torrance as *Church Dogmatics* 2/1 (Edinburgh: T & T Clark, 1957).

———. *Rechtfertigung und Recht.* 1st ed. Theologische Studien 1. Zollikon-Zurich: Verlag der Evangelischen Buchhandlung, 1938. Translated by G. Ronald Howe as "Church and State," in Karl Barth, *Community, State, and Church,* edited by Will Herberg, 101–48 (1960; reprint, Gloucester, Mass.: Peter Smith, 1968).

Bäumer, Gertrud. *Adelheid: Mutter der Königreiche* (Adelheid: Mother of the kingdoms). Tübingen: R. Wunderlich, 1936.

Beckmann, Joachim, and Friedrich Linz. *Meine Worte werden nicht vergehen* (My words will not pass away). Gütersloh: C. Bertelsmann, 1940.

Die Bekenntnisschriften der evangelisch-lutherischen Kirche. Edited by Der Deutsche Evangelische Kirchenausschuss in the commemoration year of the Augsburg Confession (1530). 2 vols. Göttingen: Vandenhoeck & Ruprecht, 1930. *NL-Bibl.* 2 C 3, Bd. 2. Translated by Charles Arand, Eric Gritsch, Robert Kolb, William Russell, James Schaaf, Jane Strohl, and Timothy J. Wengert as *The Book of Concord: The Confessions of the Evangelical Lutheran Church,* edited by Robert Kolb and Timothy J. Wengert (Minneapolis: Fortress Press, 2000).

Die Bekenntnisse und grundsätzlichen Äußerungen zur Kirchenfrage (The confessions and fundamental statements concerning the question of the church). Vol. 2: *Das Jahr 1934* (The year 1934). Edited by Kurt Dietrich Schmidt. Göttingen: Vandenhoeck & Ruprecht, 1934. *NL-Bibl.* 2 C 4, 2b.

Bell, George K. A. *Christianity and World Order.* London, 1940.

Bengel, Johann Albrecht. *Gnomon Novi Testamenti.* German translation by C. F. Werner. Tübingen, 1942. Translated by Charleton T. Lewis and Marvin R. Vincent as *New Testament Word Studies,* 2 vols. (reprint of 1864 edition, Grand Rapids, Mich.: Kregel, 1971).

Bernanos, Georges. *Der Abtrünnige.* Hellerau: J. Hegner, 1929. *NL-Bibl.* 8 C 2. German translation from French original, *L'imposture* (Paris: Plon, 1927). Translated from the French original by J. C. Whitehouse as *The Imposter* (Lincoln: University of Nebraska Press, 1999).

————. *Der heilige Dominikus* (Saint Dominic). Leipzig, 1935. *NL-Bibl.* 8 C 3. German translation from French original, *Saint Dominique* (Paris: La Tour d'Ivoire, 1928).

————. *Johanna: Ketzerin und Heilige.* Leipzig, 1934. *NL-Bibl.* 8 C 4. German translation from French original, *Jeanne: Relapse et Sainte* (Paris: Plon, 1934). Translated from French original by R. Batchelor as *Sanctity Will Out: An Essay on St. Joan* (New York: Sheed & Ward, 1947).

————. *Tagebuch eines Landpfarrers.* Vienna: Thomas Verlag Jakob Hegner, 1936. *NL-Bibl.* 8 C 5. German translation from French original, *Journal d'un curé de campagne* (Paris: Plon, 1936). Translated from the French original by Pamela Morris as *The Diary of a Country Priest* (1937; New York: Macmillan, 1962).

————. *Unter der Sonne Satans.* Hellerau: J. Hegner 1927. German translation from French original, *Sous le soleil de Satan* (Paris: Plon-Nourrit et cie, 1926). Translated from the French original by J. C. Whitehouse as *Under Satan's Sun* (Lincoln: University of Nebraska Press, 2001).

The Book of Concord. See *Die Bekenntnisschriften der evangelisch-lutherischen Kirche.*

Breviarium Romanum ex decreto SS. concilii Tridentini restitutum (The Roman breviary restored in accordance with the decree of the most holy Council of Trent). Ratisbonae: Augustae Taurinorum, 1898. *NL-Bibl.* 6 B 5.

Brunner, Emil. *Das Gebot und die Ordnungen: Entwurf einer protestantisch-theologischen Ethik.* Tübingen: Mohr (Paul Siebeck), 1932. *NL-Bibl.* 4, 6. Translated by Olive Wyon as *The Divine Imperative* (Philadelphia: Westminster Press, 1947).

————. *Der Mensch im Widerspruch: Die christliche Lehre vom wahren und vom wirklichen Menschen.* Berlin: Furche Verlag, 1937. Translated by Olive Wyon as *Man in Revolt: A Christian Anthropology* (Philadelphia: Westminster Press, 1947).

Bultmann, Rudolf. *Das Evangelium des Johannes.* Kritisch-exegetischer Kommentar über das Neue Testament, 10th ed. Göttingen: Vandenhoeck & Ruprecht, 1941. Translated by G. R. Beasley-Murray from the 1964 printing as *The Gospel of John* (Philadelphia: Westminster Press, 1971).

————. *Jesus.* Tübingen: J. C. B. Mohr (Paul Siebeck), 1926.

————. "Neues Testament und Mythologie." In *Offenbarung und Heilsgeschehen,* Beiträge zur Evangelischen Theologie, vol. 7, 27–69. Munich: A. Lempp, 1941. Translated by Reginald H. Fuller as "New Testament and Mythology," in *Kerygma and Myth,* rev. ed., 1–44 (Harper Torchbook edition; New York: Harper & Row, 1961).

Calvin, John. *Institutio IV.* Munich, 1926. Translated by Ford Lewis Battles as *Institutes of the Christian Religion,* vols. 20–21 of *The Library of Christian Classics,* edited by John T. McNeill (Philadelphia: Westminster Press, 1960).

Cremer, Hermann. *Biblisch-theologisches Wörterbuch der neutestamentlichen Gräcität.* Edited by J. Kögel. 9th ed. Gotha, 1902. Translated from the second German edition by William Urwick as *Biblico-theological Lexicon of New Testament Greek,* 3rd ed. (Edinburgh: T & T Clark, 1883; New York: Charles Scribner's Sons, 1895).

Diem, Hermann. *Luthers Lehre von den zwei Reichen: Untersucht von seinem Verständnis der Bergpredigt aus. Ein Beitrag zum Problem, "Gesetz und Evangelium"* (Luther's doctrine of the two kingdoms: Examined on the basis of his understanding of the Sermon on the Mount. A contribution to the problem of "law and gospel"). Munich: Chr. Kaiser Verlag, 1938.

Dilschneider, Otto Alexander. *Die evangelische Tat: Grundlagen und Grundzüge der evangelischen Ethik* (The evangelical act: Foundations and concepts of an evangelical ethics). Gütersloh: Verlag C. Bertelsmann, 1940. *NL-Bibl.* 4 9.

Evangelisches Gesangbuch für Brandenburg und Pommern (Protestant hymnbook for Brandenburg and Pomerania). Berlin: Provinzialkirchenräte von Brandenburg und Pommern, 1931.

Gogarten, Friedrich. *Politische Ethik: Versuch einer Grundlegung* (Political ethics: Toward a foundation). Jena: Diederichs, 1932. *NL-Bibl.* 4 14.

Gregorovius, Ferdinand. *Wanderjahre in Italien* (Travels in Italy). Dresden: W. Jess, 1925.

Haering, Theodor. *Das christliche Leben: Ethik* (The Christian life: Ethics). 3rd ed. Stuttgart: Stuttgarter Vereinsbuchdruckerei, 1914. *NL-Bibl.* 4 16.

Harleß, G. C. Adolf. *Christliche Ethik.* 3rd ed. Stuttgart, 1893. Translated by A. W. Morrison as *System of Christian Ethics,* revised by William Findley (Edinburgh: T & T Clark, 1868).

Harnack, Adolf von. *Die Mission und Ausbreitung des Christentums in den ersten drei Jahrhunderten.* 4th ed. Leipzig: J. C. Hinrichs, 1924. *NL-Bibl.* 2 C 1, 11. Translated from the second German edition by James Moffat as *The Mission and Expansion of Christianity in the First Three Centuries,* edited by James Moffat, 2 vols. (Gloucester, Mass.: Peter Smith, 1972).

———. *Das Wesen des Christentums: Sechzehn Vorlesungen vor Studierenden aller Facultäten im Wintersemester, 1899/1900 an der Universität Berlin gehalten.* Leipzig: J. C. Hinrichs, 1926. *NL-Bibl.* 3 B 30. Translated by Thomas Bailey Saunders as *What Is Christianity?* with an introduction by Rudolf Bultmann (Philadelphia: Fortress Press, 1986).

Hausmann, Manfred. *Einer muß wachen: Sechs Versuche* (One must stand watch: Six attempts). Berlin: S. Fischer, 1941.

Hildebrandt, Franz. *And Other Pastors of My Flock: A German Tribute to the Bishop of Chichester.* Cambridge: Printed for subscribers at the University Press, 1942.

————. *Theologie für Refugées: Ein Kapitel Paul Gerhardt* (Theology for refugees: A chapter on Paul Gerhardt). London: Finsbury, 1940.

Hitzer, Arnold. "Anmerkungen zur Tauffrage unter besonderer Berücksichtigung der Kindertaufe" (Comments on the question of baptism with particular consideration of infant baptism). *NL* A 64,1.

Holl, Karl. "Die Kulturbedeutung der Reformation." In *Gesammelte Aufsätze zur Kirchengeschichte,* vol. 1: *Luther,* 359–413. Tübingen: J. C. B. Mohr, 1921. Translated by Karl Hertz, Barbara Hertz, and John H. Lichtblau as *The Cultural Significance of the Reformation,* with an introduction by Wilhelm Pauck (New York: Meridian Books, 1959).

————. "Luther und das landesherrliche Kirchenregiment" (Luther and sovereign church rule). In *Gesammelte Aufsätze zur Kirchengeschichte,* vol. 1: *Luther,* 326–80. Tübingen: J. C. B. Mohr, 1921.

————. "Der Neubau der Sittlichkeit." In *Gesammelte Aufsätze zur Kirchengeschichte* (Collected essays on church history), vol. 1: *Luther,* 131–244. Tübingen: J. C. B. Mohr, 1921. Translated by Fred W. Meuser and Walter R. Wietzke as *The Reconstruction of Morality,* edited by James Luther Adams and Walter F. Bense (Minneapolis: Augsburg, 1979).

Huch, Ricarda. *Deutsche Geschichte* (German history). Vol. 1: *Römisches Reich Deutscher Nation* (Roman empire of the German nation). Berlin: Atlantis Verlag, 1934.

Jensen, Hans-Werner. *Christliche und nicht christliche Eheauffassung, dargestellt am Konfuzianismus: Eine missionswissenschaftliche Untersuchung* (Christian and non-Christian concepts of marriage, described in respect to Confucianism: An investigation with a focus on mission). Gütersloh, 1939.

Jeremias, Joachim. *Hat die älteste Christenheit die Kindertaufe geübt?* Göttingen: Vandenhoeck & Ruprecht, 1938. Translated by David Cairns as *Infant Baptism in the First Four Centuries* (Philadelphia: Westminster Press, 1960).

Kant, Immanuel. *Sämtliche Werke.* 6 vols. Leipzig: Insel Verlag, 1921–24. *NL-Bibl.* 7 A 35. Translated as *The Cambridge Edition of the Works of Immanuel Kant,* edited by Paul Guyer and Allen W. Wood (Cambridge: Cambridge University Press, 1992–).

————. "Über ein vermeintliches Recht aus Menschenliebe zu lügen." (It is not clear what edition Bonhoeffer used. The edition cited in this volume is found in *Rechtslehre: Schriften zur Rechtsphilosophie,* 342–46. Berlin, 1988.) Edited and translated by Lewis White Beck as "On a Supposed Right to Lie from Altruistic Motives," in *Critique of Practical Reason and Other Writings in Moral Philosophy,* 346–50 (Chicago: University of Chicago Press, 1949).

Kaftan, Julius. *Dogmatik* (Dogmatics). 6th ed. Tübingen: J. C. B. Mohr, 1909. *NL-Bibl.* 3 B 48.

Klepper, Jochen. *Kyrie: Geistliche Lieder* (Kyrie: Spiritual songs). Berlin: Eckart Verlag, 1938.

Knight, Eric. *This Above All*. New York: Grosset & Dunlap, 1942.

Korpp, Heinrich, ed. *Monika: Das Bild der Mutter in den Bekenntnissen Augustins* (Monika: Portrait of the mother in Augustine's confessions). No. 75. Berlin: Furche-Bücherei, 1941.

Lohmeyer, Ernst. *Das Evangelium des Markus* (The gospel of Mark). 10th ed. Kritisch-exegetischer Kommentar über das Neue Testament, part 1, vol. 2. 10th ed. Göttingen: Vandenhoeck & Ruprecht, 1937.

———. *Soziale Fragen im Urchristentum* (Social questions in early Christianity). Leipzig: Quelle & Meyer, 1921.

Lütgert, Wilhelm. *Ethik der Liebe* (Ethics of love). Beiträge zur Förderung christlicher Theologie, series 2, vol. 39. Gütersloh: C. Bertelsmann, 1938. *NL-Bibl.* 4 24.

———. *Die Religion des deutschen Idealismus und ihr Ende* (The religion of German idealism and its end). Vol. 1: *Die religiöse Krisis des deutschen Idealismus* (The religious crisis of German idealism). 2nd ed. Gütersloh: C. Bertelsmann, 1923.

Luthardt, Christoph Ernst. *Kompendium der theologischen Ethik* (Compendium of theological ethics). 3rd ed. Leipzig, 1898.

Luther, Martin. *Werke: Kritische Gesamtausgabe.* Weimar: H. Böhlau, 1883–. Translated as *Luther's Works,* 55 vols., vols. 1–30 edited by Jaroslav Pelikan, vols. 31–55 edited by Helmut Lehmann, complete works on CD-ROM (Minneapolis: Fortress Press; St. Louis: Concordia, 2002).

Martensen, Hans Lassen. *Die christliche Ethik: Spezieller Teil.* 4th ed. Berlin, 1888. *NL-Bibl.* 4 29. Translated by William Affleck as *Christian Ethics: Special Part* (Edinburgh: T & T Clark, 1890–99).

Maurer, H. "Rezension zu Hans Werner-Jensen: Christliche und nicht-christliche Eheauffassung, dargestellt am Konfuzianismus" (Review of Hans Werner-Jensen: Christian and non-Christian concepts of marriage, described in respect to Confucianism). *Evangelische Missionszeitschrift* 1 (1940): 222–23. *NL-Bibl.* 7 B 10.

Meinecke, Friedrich. *Die Idee der Staatsräson in der neueren Geschichte.* 3rd ed. Munich, 1929. *NL-Bibl.* 2 A 15. Translated by Douglas Scott as *Machiavellism: The Doctrine of Raison d'état and Its Place in Modern History,* with a general introduction by W. Stark (1957; New Brunswick, N.J.: Transaction, 1998).

Michel, Otto. "Rezension zu Hans Asmussen: Die Kirche und das Amt" (Review of Hans Asmussen: The church and the ministry). *Verkündigung und Forschung* 1/2 (1940): 75ff.

Mirbt, Carl. *Geschichte der katholischen Kirche: Von der Mitte des 18. Jahrhunderts bis zum vatikanischen Konzil* (History of the Catholic Church: From the mid-eighteenth century to the Vatican Council). Berlin: G. J. Göschen, 1913. *NL-Bibl.* 6 B 29.

Moser, Hans Joachim. *Heinrich Schütz: Sein Leben und Werk.* Kassel: Bärenreiter Verlag, 1936. Translated from the second revised edition by Carl F. Pfatteicher as *Heinrich Schütz: His Life and Work* (St. Louis: Concordia, 1959).

Müller, Alfred Dedo. *Ethik: Der evangelische Weg der Verwirklichung des Guten* (Ethics: The Protestant way of realizing the good). Berlin: A. Töpelmann, 1937. *NL-Bibl.* 4 32.

Naumann, Friedrich. *Briefe über Religion* (Letters on religion). With an afterword "Nach 13 Jahren." 7th ed. Berlin: Georg Reimer, 1917. *NL-Bibl.* 7 14.

Ein neues Lied: Ein Liederbuch für die deutsche evangelische Jugend (A new song: A songbook for German Protestant youth). Berlin: Reichsverband weiblicher Jugend, 1933.

Nohl, Hermann. *Die sittlichen Grunderfahrungen: Eine Einführung in Ethik* (The fundamental moral experiences: An introduction to ethics). Frankfurt am Main: G. Schulte-Bulmke, 1939. *NL-Bibl.* 4 34.

Oettingen, Alexander von. *Die christliche Sittenlehre: Deduktive Entwicklung der Gesetze christlichen Heilslebens im Organismus der Menschheit* (Christian moral teaching: Deductive development of the laws of the Christian life of salvation in the human organism). Vol. 2 of *Die Moralstatistik und die christliche Sittenlehre: Versuch einer Socialethik auf empirischer Grundlage.* Erlangen: Deichert, 1868–73.

Paton, William. *The Church and the New Order.* London: SCM Press, 1941.

Pestalozzi, Rudolf, and Gerty Pestalozzi. *Fahrt nach Portugal* (Trip to Portugal). Zurich: Fretz & Wasmuth Verlag, 1934. *NL-Bibl.* 9 20.

Pieper, Josef. *Zucht und Maß: Über die vierte Kardinaltugend.* Munich: Kösel, 1939. *NL-Bibl.* 4 37. Translated by Daniel F. Coogan, Lawrence Lynch, Richard Wilson, and Clara Wilson as *The Four Cardinal Virtues: Prudence, Justice, Fortitude, Temperance* (New York: Harcourt, Brace, & World, 1965).

Reck-Malleczewen, Friedrich, ed. *Der grobe Brief von Martin Luther bis Ludwig Thoma* (The coarse letter [in history] from Martin Luther up to Ludwig Thoma). Berlin: Schützen Verlag, 1940.

Rieker, Karl. *Die rechtliche Stellung der evangelischen Kirche Deutschlands in ihrer geschichtlichen Entwicklung* (The legal status of the German Protestant Church in its historical development). Leipzig: C. L. Hirschfeld, 1893.

Ritter, Gerhard. *Machtstaat und Utopie: Vom Streit um die Dämonie der Macht seit Machiavelli und Morus.* 2nd ed. Munich, 1941. Translated by F. W. Pick as *The Corrupting Influence of Power,* with a foreword by G. P. Gooch (reprint, Westport, Conn.: Hyperion Press, 1979).

Rothe, Richard. *Theologische Ethik* (Theological ethics). 2nd ed. 5 vols. Wittenberg: Zimmerman, 1867–71. *NL-Bibl.* 4 41.

Santayana, George. *Der letzte Puritaner.* Berlin, 1936. German translation from English original, *The Last Puritan,* 1st Scribner/Macmillan Hudson River edition (1936; New York: Macmillan, 1989).

Schilling, Otto. *Lehrbuch der Moraltheologie* (Textbook of moral theology). 2 vols. Munich: Hueber Verlag, 1928. *NL-Bibl.* 6 41.

Schlatter, Adolf. *Johannes der Täufer* (John the Baptist). Stuttgart: Calwer, 1939.

Schlink, Edmund. "Rezension zu Hans Asmussen, Die Bergpredigt, Göttingen, 1939" (Review of Hans Asmussen's *Die Bergpredigt* [The Sermon on the Mount], Göttingen, 1939). *Verkündigung und Forschung* 1/2 (1940): 19–28.

———. *Die Theologie der lutherischen Bekenntnisschriften.* Munich: Chr. Kaiser Verlag, 1940. Translated by Paul F. Koehneke and Herber J. A. Bouman as *Theology of the Lutheran Confessions* (Philadelphia: Muhlenberg, 1961).

Schmid, Heinrich. *Die Dogmatik der evangelisch-lutherischen Kirche dargestellt und aus den Quellen belegt.* 7th ed. Gütersloh, 1893. *NL-Bibl.* 3 B 65. Translated from German and Latin by Charles A. Hay and Henry E. Jacobs as *The Doctrinal Theology of the Evangelical Lutheran Church,* 3rd ed., revised. (Minneapolis: Augsburg, 1899).

Schneider, Reinhold. *Macht und Gnade: Bilder und Werte der Geschichte* (Power and grace: Pictures and values from history). Leipzig: Insel Verlag, 1940.

Schönherr, Albrecht. *Lutherische Privatbeichte* (Lutheran private confession). Göttingen: Vandenhoeck & Ruprecht, 1938. *NL-Bibl.* 5 D 17.

Schweitzer, Albert. *Die Mystik des Apostels Paulus.* Tübingen: J. C. B. Mohr, 1930. *NL-Bibl.* 7 C 16. Translated by William Montgomery as *The Mysticism of Paul the Apostle,* with a prefatory note by F. C. Burkitt (1931; New York: Seabury Press, 1968).

Seeberg, Reinhold. *System der Ethik* (System of ethics). 2nd ed. Leipzig: A. Deichert, 1920. *NL-Bibl.* 4 46.

Stahl, Friedrich Julius. *Rechts- und Staatslehre auf der Grundlage christlicher Weltanschauung* (Jurisprudence and political science on the foundation of a Christian worldview). Heidelberg: Mohr, 1846. *NL-Bibl.* 7 C 16.

Stapel, Wilhelm. *Der christliche Staatsmann: Eine Theologie des Nationalismus* (The Christian statesman: A theology of nationalism). Hamburg: Hanseatische Verlagsanstalt, 1932. *NL-Bibl.* 4 49a.

Steinmeyer, Franz Karl Ludwig. *Der homiletische Gebrauch der evangelischen altkirchlichen Perikopen* (The homiletical use of orthodox Protestant pericopes). Leipzig: A. Deichert'sche Verlagsbuchhandlung, 1902.

Troeltsch, Ernst. *Die Soziallehren der christlichen Kirchen und Gruppen.* Vol. 1, first half of *Gesammelte Schriften.* Tübingen: Mohr, 1912. Translated by Olive Wyon as *The Social Teachings of the Christian Churches,* with a foreword by James Luther Adams, 2 vols. (reprint, Louisville: Westminster/John Knox, 1992).

Vilmar, August Friedrich Christian. *Dogmatik: Akademische Vorlesungen* (Dogmatics: Academic lectures). Pts. 1–2. Edited by K. W. Pierit. Gütersloh: C. Bertelsmann, 1874. *NL-Bibl.* 3 B 71.

Vischer, Wilhelm. *Das Christuszeugnis des Alten Testaments.* Munich: Chr. Kaiser, 1934. Translated from the third German edition by A. B. Crabtree as *The Witness of the Old Testament to Christ* (London: Lutterworth Press, 1949).

3. Literature Mentioned by Bonhoeffer's Correspondents

Asmussen, Hans. *Wiederum steht geschrieben!* (Again it is written!). Munich: Chr. Kaiser Verlag, 1939.

The Christian News-Letter. Periodical published by the Council on the Christian Faith and the Common Life, Great Britain.

Eyck, Erich. *Bismarck: Leben und Werk.* 3 vols. Erlenbach-Zurich: E. Rentsch, 1941–44. Translated as *Bismarck and the German Empire,* a summary of the three-volume work (New York: Norton, 1968).

Fraenkel, Heinrich. *The Other Germany.* London: Drummond, 1942.

Grimmelshausen, Johann Jakob Christoffel von. *Der abenteuerliche Simplicissimus.* 1669. 2nd rev. ed. Paderborn: Ferdinand Schöningh, 1980. Translated with an introduction by Mike Mitchell as *Simplicissimus* (Sawtry, Cambs., UK: Dedalus, 1999).

Hammelsbeck, Oskar. *Der kirchliche Unterricht: Aufgabe, Umfang, Einheit* (Church instruction: Task, scope, unity). Munich, 1939

———. "Mit Bonhoeffer im Gespräch." In Zimmermann, *Begegnungen mit Dietrich Bonhoeffer,* 157–68. Translated as "In Discussion with Bonhoeffer," in Zimmermann and Smith, *I Knew Dietrich Bonhoeffer,* 179–88.

Hinz, Paul, ed. *. . . und lobten Gott: Zeugnisse evangelischer Pastoren und Laien— der fürbittenden Gemeinde dargeboten* (. . . And they praised God: Testimonies of Protestant pastors and laypeople—presented to the interceding congregation). Stettin: Fischer & Schmidt, 1938.

Kierkegaard, Søren. *Über die Geduld und die Erwartung des Ewigen (Religiöse Reden).* Translated by Theodore Haecker. Leipzig: Verlag Jakob Hegner, 1938. Edited and translated with introduction and notes by Howard V. Hong and Edna H. Hong as *Eighteen Upbuilding Discourses,* Kierkegaard's Writings, vol. 5 (Princeton, N.J.: Princeton University Press, 1990).

Luther, Martin. "Ermahnung zum Frieden auf die zwölf Artikel der Bauernschaft in Schwaben." In *WA* 18:291–334. Translated as "Admonition to Peace: A Reply to the Twelve Articles of the Peasants in Swabia. Be

peaceful in response to the twelve articles of the peasantry in Swabia," in
  LW 46:17–43.

Marcks, Erich. *Bismarck: Eine Biographie* (Bismarck: A biography). 2 vols.
  Stuttgart: Cotta, 1915.

Markusson, Andreas. *In der Finsternis wohnen die Adler* (The eagles live in
  darkness). Translated by Konstantin Reichardt. 3rd ed. Göttingen: Vandenhoeck & Ruprecht, 1962.

Riecker, Otto. *Das evangelistische Wort: Pneumatologie und Psychologie der evangelistischen Bewegung* (The evangelistic word: The doctrine of the Holy
  Spirit and psychology of the evangelistic movement). Gütersloh: C. Bertelsmann, 1935.

Schäble, Walter. *Evangelium im Durchbruch: Geist und Gestalt* (The gospel
  comes to the fore: Spirit and form). Wuppertal-Barmen, 1940.

Scherzl, Simon. *Compelle intrare* (Compel them to enter). Munich, 1937.

Thielicke, Helmut. *Wo ist Gott?: Aus einem Briefwechsel* (Where is God?: From
  an exchange of letters). Göttingen: Vandenhoeck & Ruprecht, 1940.

Velde, Theodor Hendrik van de. *Die vollkommene Ehe* (The consummated
  marriage). 1926.

Wolf, Ernst. *Communio Sanctorum: Erwägungen zum Problem der Romantisierung
  des Kirchenbegriffs* (The communion of saints: Considerations on the problem of the romanticization of the concept of church). 1942. (No further
  publication information is available. This may have been a self-published
  essay.)

4. Literature Consulted by the Editors

Acta Apostolicae Sedis (Rome) 32 (1940): 5–13.

Akten deutscher Bischöfe über die Lage der Kirche, 1933–1945 (Documents of
  German bishops concerning the situation of the church, 1933–1945).
  Edited by Bernhard Stasiewski and Ludwig Volk. 6 vols. Mainz: Matthias-
  Grünewald-Verlag, 1968–85.

Akten zur deutschen auswärtigen Politik 1918–1945. Series E, vol. 8. Göttingen:
  Vandenhoeck & Ruprecht, 1950–. Translated as *Documents on German For-
  eign Policy 1918–1945, from the Archives of the German Foreign Ministry.*
  Washington, D.C.: U.S. Government Printing Office, 1949–.

Althaus, Paul. *Grundriß der Ethik.* Erlangen: R. Merkel, 1933. Translated by
  Arthur B. Little as *An Outline of Ethics,* new rev. ed. (self-published, 1936).

———. *Kirche und Staat nach lutherischer Lehre* (Church and state in Lutheran
  teaching). Theologia militans. Vol. 4. Leipzig: A. Deichert, 1933.

———. *Staatsgedanke und Reich Gottes* (The concept of the state and the kingdom of God). Schriften zur politischen Bildung, series 9, no. 1. Langen-
  salza: H. Beyer, 1931.

―――. *Theologie der Ordnungen* (Theology of the orders). Gütersloh: C. Bertelsmann, 1935.

Aquinas, Thomas. *Summa theologiae.* Cura et studio P. Caramello cum textu ex recensione Leonina. Edited by Petrus Caramello with the text of the Leonina edition. Vols. 1–4. Turin: Marietta, 1952–56.

Aristotle. *Politik.* Philosophische Bibliothek, vol. 7. Hamburg: F. Meiner, 1958. Translated, with an introduction, notes, and appendixes, by Ernest Barker as *The Politics of Aristotle* (New York: Oxford University Press, 1958).

Asmussen, Hans Christian. *Die Bergpredigt: Eine Auslegung von Matthias Kapitel 5–7* (The Sermon on the Mount: An exegesis of Matthew 5–7). Göttingen: Vandenhoeck & Ruprecht, 1939.

―――. *Die Kirche und das Amt* (The church and the ministry). Munich: Chr. Kaiser, 1939.

Augustine. *De civitate Dei: Der Gottesstaat.* Translated into German by C. J. Perl. 2 vols. Paderborn: Schöningh, 1979. Translated by Henry Bettenson as *The City of God*, with an introduction by John O'Meara (New York: Penguin Books, 1984).

Austad, Torleiv. "Der Widerstand der Kirche gegen den nationalsozialistischen Staat in Norwegen" (The resistance of the church against the National Socialist state in Norway). *Kirchliche Zeitgeschichte* 1, no. 1 (1988): 79–94.

Ball-Kaduri, Kurt Jakob. "Berlin Is 'Purged' of Jews: The Jews in Berlin." *Yad Vashem Studies on the European Jewish Catastrophe and Resistance* 5 (1963): 271–316.

Barnes, Kenneth C. *Nazism, Liberalism, and Christianity: Protestant Social Thought in Germany and Great Britain 1925–1937.* Louisville: University of Kentucky Press, 1991.

Barnett, Victoria. *Bystanders: Conscience and Complicity during the Holocaust.* Westport, Conn.: Greenwood Press, 1999.

―――. *For the Soul of the People.* New York: Oxford University Press, 1992.

Barteczko-Schwedler, Bärbel, and Hanns-Uve Schwedler. *Wegmarken: Einschnitte und Wendepunkte in der 150-jährigen Geschichte der Gossner-Mission (1836–1986)* (Signs along the way: Decisive events and turning points in the 150-year history of the Gossner Mission). Berlin: Gossner-Mission, 1986.

Barth, Karl. "Abschied von *Zwischen den Zeiten*" (Departure from *Zwischen den Zeiten*). In part 2 of *Anfänge der dialektischen Theologie* (Beginnings of dialectical theology), edited by Jürgen Moltmann, Theologische Bücherei 17: Systematische Theologie, 313–32. Munich: Chr. Kaiser, 1963.

―――. *Evangelium und Gesetz.* Theologische Existenz heute 32. Munich: Chr. Kaiser Verlag, 1935. Translated as "Gospel and Law," in *Community, State, and Church*, by Karl Barth, 71–100 (Gloucester, Mass.: Peter Smith, 1968).

————. *Die Kirchliche Dogmatik.* 4 vols. Munich: Chr. Kaiser; Zurich: Evangelischer Verlag, 1932–67. Translated by G. T. Thomson as *Church Dogmatics,* edited by G. W. Bromiley and T. F. Torrance, 4 vols. (Edinburgh: T & T Clark, 1956–77).

————. *Späte Freundschaft.* See Zuckmayer.

Baubérot, Jean. "Secularism and French Religious Liberty: A Sociological and Historical View." *Brigham Young University Law Review* 2 (2003): 451–65.

Bell, George K. A. *The Church and Humanity 1939–1946.* London: Longmans; New York: Green, 1946.

Bell, G. K. A., and Gerhard Leibholz. *An der Schwelle zum gespaltenen Europa: Der Briefwechsel zwischen George Bell und Gerhard Leibholz 1939–1951* (On the brink of divided Europe: The correspondence between George Bell and Gerhard Leibholz 1939–1951). Edited by Eberhard Bethge and Ronald Jaspers. 1st ed. Stuttgart: Kreuz Verlag, 1974.

Ben-Israel, Hedva. "Im Widerstreit der Ziele: Die britische Reaktion auf den deutschen Widerstand" (Amid the conflict of goals: The British reaction to the German resistance). In Schmädeke and Steinbach, *Der Widerstand gegen den Nationalsozialismus,* 732–50.

Bergen, Doris. *Twisted Cross: The German Christian Movement in the Third Reich.* Chapel Hill: University of North Carolina Press, 1996.

Bertheau, Carl. "Kirchenjahr." In *Realenzyklopädie für protestantische Theologie und Kirche,* 3rd ed., 393–98. Leipzig, 1901.

Best, S. Payne. *The Venlo Incident.* London: Hutchinson, 1950.

Bethge, Eberhard. *Dietrich Bonhoeffer: Theologe—Christ—Zeitgenosse: Eine Biographie.* Munich: Chr. Kaiser Verlag, 1967. Translated by Eric Mosbacher, Peter Ross, Betty Ross, Frank Clarke, and William Glen-Doepel as *Dietrich Bonhoeffer: A Biography,* under the editorship of Edwin Robertson, revised and edited by Victoria Barnett, based on the seventh German edition (1st Fortress Press ed., Minneapolis: Fortress Press, 2000).

————. "Der Freund: Dietrich Bonhoeffer und seine theologische Konzeption von Freundschaft" (The friend: Dietrich Bonhoeffer and his theological conception of friendship). In Gremmels and Huber, *Theologie und Freundschaft,* 29–50. English translation in Bethge, *Friendship and Resistance,* 80–105.

————. *Friendship and Resistance: Essays on Dietrich Bonhoeffer.* Grand Rapids, Mich.: Wm. B. Eerdmans, 1995.

————. "Gegen den Strom der Zeit: Aus einem Briefwechsel zwischen dem Lordbishop of Chichester und Gerhard Leibholz während der Kriegsjahre" (Against the currents of the times: From an exchange of letters between the lord bishop of Chichester and Gerhard Leibholz during the war years). In Bracher and Leibholz, *Die moderne Demokratie und ihr Recht: Modern Constitutionalism and Democracy,* 1:1–14.

————. *In Zitz gab es keine Juden: Erinnerungen aus meinen ersten vierzig Jahren* (There were no Jews in Zitz: Memories of my first forty years). Munich: Chr. Kaiser, 1989.

————. "Mein Freund" (My friend). In Gremmels and Huber, *Theologie und Freundschaft*, 13–28.

————. *Schweizer Korrespondenz 1941/42: Im Gespräch mit Karl Barth.* Theologische Existenz Heute 214. Munich: Chr. Kaiser, 1982. Translated by John D. Godsey as "More Bonhoeffer-Barth Correspondence," *Newsletter,* International Bonhoeffer Society, English Language Section, no. 22 (June 1982): 1–9.

Bethge, Eberhard, Renate Bethge, and Christian Gremmels, eds. *Dietrich Bonhoeffer: Sein Leben in Bildern und Texten.* Munich: Chr. Kaiser, 1989. Translated by John Bowden as *Dietrich Bonhoeffer: A Life in Pictures* (Philadelphia: Fortress Press, 1986).

Biedermann, Alois Emanuel. *Christliche Dogmatik* (Christian dogmatics). 2 vols. Berlin: Reimer, 1884–85.

Bielenberg, Christabel. *Als ich Deutsche war, 1934–1945: Eine Engländerin erzählt.* Munich: Biederstein, 1969. German translation from the English original, *The Past Is Myself* (London: Chatto & Windus, 1968).

Bismarck, Ruth Alice, and Ulrich Kabitz, eds. *Brautbriefe Zelle 92: Dietrich Bonhoeffer-Maria von Wedemeyer, 1943–1945.* Munich: C. H. Beck'sche Verlagsbuchhandlung, 1992. Translated by John Brownjohn as *Love Letters from Cell 92. The Correspondence between Dietrich Bonhoeffer and Maria von Wedemeyer, 1943–1945,* with a postscript by Eberhard Bethge (London: HarperCollins, 1994; Nashville: Abingdon Press, 1995).

Blumenberg-Lampe, Christine. *Das wirtschaftspolitische Programm der "Freiburger Kreise." Entwurf einer freiheitlich-sozialen Nachkriegswirtschaft: Nationalökonomen gegen den Nationalsozialismus* (The politico-economic program of the "Freiburg groups." Proposal for a free social postwar economy: National economists against National Socialism). Volkswirtschaftliche Schriften, no. 208. Berlin: Duncker & Humblot, 1973.

Boegner, Marc. *Ein Leben für die Ökumene: Erinnerungen und Ausblicke.* Stuttgart: J. Knecht, 1970. German translation by Herbert Schaad from the French original, *L'Exigence oecuménique: Souvenirs et perspectives* (Paris: A. Michel, 1968). Translated by René Hague, with an introduction by W. A. Visser 't Hooft as *The Long Road to Unity: Memories and Anticipations* (London: Collins, 1970).

Boelcke, Willi A., ed. *Wollt Ihr den totalen Krieg?: Die geheimen Goebbels-Konferenzen 1939–1943.* 1967. Munich: Deutscher Taschenbuch Verlag, 1969. Translated by Ewald Osers as *The Secret Conferences of Dr. Goebbels: The Nazi Propaganda War, 1939–1943,* 1st ed. (New York: E. P. Dutton, 1970).

Bonhoeffer, Dietrich. *Dietrich Bonhoeffer Werke.* 17 vols. Edited by Eberhard Bethge et al. Munich: Chr. Kaiser/Gütersloher Verlagshaus, 1986–99. Translated as *Dietrich Bonhoeffer Works,* Victoria J. Barnett, Wayne Whitson Floyd Jr., and Barbara Wojhoski, general editors. 17 vols. (Minneapolis: Fortress Press, 1996–).

Vol. 1: *Sanctorum Communio: Eine dogmatische Untersuchung zur Soziologie der Kirche.* Edited by Joachim von Soosten. Munich: Chr. Kaiser Verlag, 1986. Translated by Reinhard Krauss and Nancy Lukens as *Sanctorum Communio: A Theological Study of the Sociology of the Church,* edited by Clifford J. Green (Minneapolis: Fortress Press, 1998).

Vol. 2: *Akt und Sein: Transzendentalphilosophie und Ontologie in der systematischen Theologie.* Edited by Hans-Richard Reuter. Munich: Chr. Kaiser Verlag, 1988. Translated by Martin Rumscheidt as *Act and Being: Transcendental Philosophy and Ontology in Systematic Theology,* edited by Wayne Whitson Floyd Jr. (Minneapolis: Fortress Press, 1996).

Vol. 3: *Schöpfung und Fall: Theologische Auslegung von Genesis 1–3.* Edited by Martin Rüter and Ilse Tödt. Munich: Chr. Kaiser Verlag, 1989. Translated by Douglas Stephen Bax as *Creation and Fall: A Theological Exposition of Genesis 1–3,* edited by John W. de Gruchy (Minneapolis: Fortress Press, 1996).

Vol. 4: *Nachfolge.* Edited by Martin Kuske and Ilse Tödt. Munich: Chr. Kaiser Verlag, 1989; 2nd ed., Gütersloh: Chr. Kaiser/Gütersloher Verlagshaus, 1994. Translated by Barbara Green and Reinhard Krauss as *Discipleship,* edited by Geffrey B. Kelly and John D. Godsey (Minneapolis: Fortress Press, 2001).

Vol. 5: *Gemeinsames Leben: Das Gebetbuch der Bibel.* Edited by Gerhard Ludwig Müller and Albrecht Schönherr. Munich: Chr. Kaiser Verlag, 1987. Translated by Daniel W. Bloesch and James H. Burtness as *Life Together* and *Prayerbook of the Bible,* edited by Geffrey B. Kelly (Minneapolis: Fortress Press, 1996).

Vol. 6: *Ethik.* Edited by Ilse Tödt, Heinz Eduard Tödt, Ernst Feil, and Clifford Green. Munich: Chr. Kaiser Verlag, 1992; 2nd ed., Gütersloh: Chr. Kaiser/Gütersloher Verlagshaus, 1998. Translated by Reinhard Krauss and Charles West, with Douglas W. Stott, as *Ethics,* edited by Clifford J. Green (Minneapolis: Fortress Press, 2004).

Vol. 7: *Fragmente aus Tegel.* Edited by Renate Bethge and Ilse Tödt. Gütersloh: Chr. Kaiser/Gütersloher Verlagshaus, 1994. Translated by Nancy Lukens as *Fiction from Tegel Prison,* edited by Clifford J. Green (Minneapolis: Fortress Press, 2000).

Vol. 8: *Widerstand und Ergebung* (Resistance and submission). Edited by Christian Gremmels, Eberhard Bethge, and Renate Bethge, with Ilse Tödt. Gütersloh: Chr. Kaiser/Gütersloher Verlagshaus, 1998.

Vol. 9: *Jugend und Studium: 1918–1927.* Edited by Hans Pfeifer, with Clifford Green and Jürgen Kaltenborn. Munich: Chr. Kaiser Verlag, 1986. Translated by Mary Nebelsick, with the assistance of Douglas W. Stott, as *The Young Bonhoeffer: 1918–1927*, edited by Paul Matheny, Clifford J. Green, and Marshall Johnson (Minneapolis: Fortress Press, 2001).

Vol. 10: *Barcelona, Berlin, Amerika: 1928–1931* (Barcelona, Berlin, New York: 1928–1931). Edited by Reinhard and Hans Christoph von Hase, with Holger Roggelin and Matthias Wünsche. Munich: Chr. Kaiser Verlag, 1991.

Vol. 11: *Ökumene, Universität, Pfarramt: 1931–1932* (Ecumenical, academic, and pastoral work: 1931–1932). Edited by Eberhard Amelung and Christoph Strohm. Gütersloh: Chr. Kaiser Verlagshaus, 1994.

Vol. 12: *Berlin: 1932–1933.* Edited by Carsten Nicolaisen and Ernst-Albert Scharffenorth. Gütersloh: Chr. Kaiser/Gütersloher Verlagshaus, 1997.

Vol. 13: *London: 1933–1935.* Edited by Hans Goedeking, Martin Heimbucher, and Hans-Walter Schleicher. Gütersloh: Chr. Kaiser/Gütersloher Verlagshaus, 1994.

Vol. 14: *Illegale Theologenausbildung: Finkenwalde 1935–1937* (Theological education at Finkenwalde: 1935–1937). Edited by Otto Dudzus and Jürgen Henkys, with Sabine Bobert-Stützel, Dirk Schulz, and Ilse Tödt. Gütersloh: Chr. Kaiser/Gütersloher Verlagshaus, 1996.

Vol. 15: *Illegale Theologenausbildung: Sammelvikariate: 1937–1940* (Theological education underground: 1937–1940). Edited by Dirk Schulz. Gütersloh: Chr. Kaiser/Gütersloher Verlagshaus, 1998.

Vol. 16: *Konspiration und Haft: 1940–1945* (Conspiracy and imprisonment: 1940–1945). Edited by Jørgen Glenthøj, Ulrich Kabitz, and Wolf Krötke. Gütersloh: Chr. Kaiser Gütersloher Verlagshaus, 1996

Vol. 17: *Register und Ergänzungen* (Index and supplements). Edited by Herbert Anzinger and Hans Pfeifer, assisted by Waltraud Anzinger and Ilse Tödt. Gütersloh: Chr. Kaiser/Gütersloher Verlagshaus, 1999.

―――. *Akt und Sein: Tranzendentalphilosophie und Ontologie in der systematischen Theologie.* Beiträge zur Förderung christlicher Theologie 34. Gütersloh: C. Bertelsmann, 1931.

―――. *Akt und Sein: Tranzendentalphilosophie und Ontologie in der systematischen Theologie.* Edited by Ernst Wolf. Theologische Bücherei 5. Munich: Chr. Kaiser, 1956; 4th ed., 1976. Translated by Bernard Noble as *Act and Being*, with an introduction by Ernst Wolf (New York: Octagon Books, 1983).

―――. *Christ the Center.* New translation by Edwin H. Robertson. San Francisco: Harper & Row, 1978.

―――. *Dein Reich Komme: Das Gebet der Gemeinde um Gottes Reich auf Erden; Die erste Tafel: Eine Auslegung der ersten drei Gebote* (Thy kingdom come: The congregation's prayer for God's kingdom on earth; The first table:

An exegesis of the first three commandments). Hamburg: Furche-Verlag, 1957.

————. *Ethik.* Arranged and edited by Eberhard Bethge, 1949, restructured 1963. 6th ed. Munich: Chr. Kaiser Verlag, 1985 (11th printing). Translated by Neville Horton Smith as *Ethics* (New York: Macmillan, 1955, paperback edition, 1965; New York: Simon & Schuster, 1995).

————. *Fragmente aus Tegel: Drama und Roman.* Edited by Eberhard Bethge and Renate Bethge. Munich: Chr. Kaiser, 1978. Translated by Ursula Hoffmann as *Fiction from Prison: Gathering up the Past* (Philadelphia: Fortress Press, 1981).

————. *Gemeinsames Leben.* 1939; Munich: Chr. Kaiser, 1986. Translated by John W. Doberstein as *Life Together* (1954; London: SCM Press, 1986).

————. *Gesammelte Schriften* (Collected works). Edited by Eberhard Bethge. 6 vols. Munich: Chr. Kaiser, 1958–74.

————. *Nachfolge.* Munich: Chr. Kaiser, 1937, 1940. Reprint, 1961; reprinted with an afterword by Eberhard Bethge, 1985. Translated by Reginald H. Fuller as *The Cost of Discipleship,* with a foreword by Bishop George K. A. Bell of Chichester and a memoir by Gerhard Leibholz (London: SCM, 1948); with a preface by Reinhold Niebuhr (New York: Macmillan, 1949). (Both the 1948 and the 1949 editions were abridged.) Second unabridged edition with translation revised by Irmgard Booth (London: SCM, 1959; New York: Macmillan, 1960; paperback ed. [with different pagination], New York: Macmillan, 1963; London: SCM, 1964; first Touchstone ed., New York: Simon & Schuster, 1995).

————. *No Rusty Swords: Letters, Lectures, and Notes, 1928–1936.* Translated by Edwin H. Robertson and John Bowden. London: Collins; New York: Harper & Row, 1965.

————. *Prayers from Prison: Prayers and Poems.* Interpreted by Johann Christoph Hampe. Philadelphia: Fortress Press, 1978.

————. *Predigten—Auslegungen—Meditationen* (Sermons, interpretations, meditations). 2 vols. Vol. 1: *1925–1935.* Vol. 2: *1935–1945.* Edited by Otto Dudzus. Munich: Chr. Kaiser, 1984, 1985.

————. *The Prison Poems of Dietrich Bonhoeffer.* Translated and with a commentary by Edwin Robertson. Guilford, Surrey, UK: Eagle, 1998.

————. *Sanctorum Communio: Eine dogmatische Untersuchung zur Soziologie der Kirche* (The community of saints: A theological study of the sociology of the church). 26th Stück der neuen Studien zur Geschichte der Theologie und der Kirche. Edited by Reinhold Seeberg. Berlin: Trowitzsch, 1930.

————. *Sanctorum Communio: Eine dogmatische Untersuchung zur Soziologie der Kirche.* Edited by Ernst Wolf. New ed. Theologische Bücherei 3. Munich: Chr. Kaiser, 1954. Translated by R. Gregor Smith from the third German edition as *Sanctorum Communio* (London: William Collins Sons & Co.,

Ltd., 1963). Published in the United States as *The Community of Saints* (New York: Harper & Row, 1963).

———. *Schöpfung und Fall: Eine theologische Auslegung von Genesis 1–3.* 5th ed. Munich: Chr. Kaiser, 1968. Translated by John C. Fletcher and Kathleen Downham as *Creation and Fall/Temptation* (New York: Macmillan, 1959).

———. *Widerstand und Ergebung: Briefe und Aufzeichnungen aus der Haft.* Edited by Eberhard Bethge. Munich: Chr. Kaiser, 1951; expanded ed., 1970, 1985. Translated by Reginald H. Fuller as *Letters and Papers from Prison,* edited by Eberhard Bethge, translation revised by Frank Clarke et al., additional material translated by John Bowden for the enlarged edition published in London (London: SCM, 1971; New York: Macmillan, 1972; New York: Simon & Schuster, 1997).

———. *Zettelnotizen für eine "Ethik"* (Working notes for an "Ethics"). Edited by Ilse Tödt. Supplementary volume to *Ethik, DBW* 6. Gütersloh: Chr. Kaiser, 1993.

Bonhoeffer Gedenkheft (Bonhoeffer commemorative volume). Edited by Eberhard Bethge. Berlin: Haus & Schule, 1947.

Bösch, Hermann. *Heeresrichter Dr. Karl Sack im Widerstand: Eine historisch-politische Studie* (Army judge Dr. Karl Sack in the resistance: A historical-political study). Munich: G. Müller, 1967.

Boveri, Margret. *Der Verrat im 20. Jahrhundert.* Vol. 2: *Für und gegen die Nation: Das unsichtbare Geschehen.* Rowohlts deutsche Enzyklopädie 24. Hamburg: Rowohlt, 1956. Translated by Jonathon Steinberg as *Treason in the Twentieth Century,* 1st American ed. (1961; New York: Putnam, 1963; London. Macdonald, 1961).

Boyens, Armin. *Kirchenkampf und Ökumene: Darstellung und Dokumentation* (Church Struggle and ecumene: Description and documentation). Vol. 1: *1933–1939.* Vol. 2: *1939–1945.* Munich: Chr. Kaiser, 1969, 1973.

Bracher, Karl Dietrich, and Gerhard Leibholz, eds. *Die moderne Demokratie und ihr Recht: Modern Constitutionalism and Democracy. Festschrift für Gerhard Leibholz zum 65. Geburtstag* (The modern democracy and its authority: Modern constitutionalism and democracy. Festschrift for Gerhard Leibholz on his 65th birthday). Tübingen: Mohr, 1966.

Brecht, Martin. *Martin Luther.* Vol. 3: *Die Erhaltung der Kirche: 1532–1546.* Stuttgart: Calwer, 1987. Translated by James L. Schaaf as *Martin Luther,* vol. 3: *The Preservation of the Church: 1532–1546,* 1st English-language ed. (Minneapolis: Fortress Press, 1993).

Brinkel, Karl. *Die Lehre Luthers von der fides infantium bei der Kindertaufe* (Luther's teaching on the *fides infantium* in infant baptism). Berlin: Evangelische Verlagsanstalt, 1958.

Brodersen, Arvid. *Fra et nomadeliv: Erindringer* (Memoirs from the life of a nomad). Oslo: Gyldendal, 1952.

Broszat, Martin. *Der Staat Hitlers: Grundlegung und Entwicklung seiner inneren Verfassung.* Weltgeschichte des 20. Jahrhunderts, vol. 9. Munich: Deutscher Taschenbuch Verlag, 1969. Translated by John W. Hiden as *The Hitler State: The Foundation and Development of the Internal Structure of the Third Reich* (London: Longman, 1981).

Browning, Christopher R. *The Final Solution and the German Foreign Office.* New York: Holmes & Meier, 1978.

―――. *The Origins of the Final Solution: The Evolution of Nazi Jewish Policy, September 1939–March 1942.* With contributions by Jürgen Matthäus. Lincoln: University of Nebraska Press; Jerusalem: Yad Vashem, 2004.

Brunotte, Heinz. *Bekenntnis und Kirchenverfassung: Aufsätze zur kirchlichen Zeitgeschichte* (Confession and church polity: Essays on contemporary church history). 1st ed. Arbeiten zur kirchlichen Zeitgeschichte, series B, no. 3. Göttingen: Vandenhoeck & Ruprecht, 1977.

Brunotte, Heinz, and Ernst Wolf, eds. *Zur Geschichte des Kirchenkampfes: Gesammelte Aufsätze* (On the history of the Church Struggle: Collected essays). Arbeiten zur Geschichte des Kirchenkampfes, vol. 15. Göttingen: Vandenhoeck & Ruprecht, 1965.

Brunstäd, Friedrich. *Deutschland und der Sozialismus* (Germany and socialism). 2nd ed. Berlin: O. Elsner, 1927.

Burgsmüller, Alfred, and Rudolf Weth. *Die Barmer theologische Erklärung: Einführung und Dokumentation* (The Theological Declaration of Barmen: Introduction and documentation). Edited and with a foreword by Eduard Lohse. 2nd ed. Neukirchen-Vluyn: Neukirchener Verlag, 1984.

Busch, Benedikt. "Die Abtei Metten im Dritten Reich" (The Metten Abbey in the Third Reich). In *Das Bistum Regensburg im Dritten Reich* (The bishopric of Regensburg in the Third Reich), edited by Georg Schwaiger and Paul Mai, 333–62. Regensburg: Verlag des Vereins für Regensburger Bistumsgeschichte, 1981.

Busch, Eberhard. *Karl Barths Lebenslauf: Nach seinen Briefen und autobiographischen Texten.* Munich: Chr. Kaiser, 1975. Translated by John Bowden as *Karl Barth: His Life from Letters and Autobiographical Text* (Grand Rapids, Mich.: Wm. B. Eerdmans, 1994).

Calvin, John. *Opera selecta* (Selected works). Edited by Peter Barth and Wilhelm Niesel. 5 vols. Munich: Chr. Kaiser, 1926–36.

Child, Clifton. Introduction to *Weekly Political Intelligence Summaries.* Edited by Political Intelligence Department, Foreign Office, Great Britain. Millwood, N.Y.: Kraus, 1983.

Chowaniec, Elisabeth. *Der "Fall Dohnanyi": Widerstand, Militärjustiz, SS-Willkür* (The "Dohnanyi case": Resistance, military justice, SS arbitrariness). Schriftenreihe der Vierteljahreshefte für Zeitgeschichte, vol. 62. Munich: R. Oldenbourg, 1991.

The Christian Century 58, no. 25.

Clements, Keith. *Faith on the Frontier: A Life of J. H. Oldham.* Edinburgh: T & T Clark and World Council of Churches Publications, 1999.

The Concise Columbia Encyclopedia. 3rd ed. New York: Columbia University Press, 1994.

Conway, John. *Die nationalsozialistische Kirchenpolitik, 1933–1945: Ihre Ziele, Widersprüche und Fehlschläge.* Munich: Chr. Kaiser, 1969. German translation by Carsten Nicolaisen from English original, *The Nazi Persecution of the Churches, 1939–1945* (New York: Basic Books, 1968).

The Creeds of the Church. Edited by John H. Leith. 3rd ed. Atlanta: John Knox Press, 1982.

Cullmann, Oscar. *Königsherrschaft Christi und Kirche im Neuen Testament.* Theologische Studien, Heft 10. Zollikon-Zurich: Evangelischer Verlag, 1946. Translated as "The Kingship of Christ and the Church in the New Testament," in *The Early Church: Studies in Early Christian History and Theology,* abridged ed., 101–37 (1956; Philadelphia: Westminster Press, 1900).

Daily Texts. Mt. Carmel edition. Bethlehem, Pa.: Interprovincial Board of Publications and Communications, Moravian Church.

de Gruchy, John. *Daring Trusting Spirit: Bonhoeffer's Friend Eberhard Bethge.* Minneapolis: Fortress Press, 2005.

Dehn, Günther. "Engel und Obrigkeit: Ein Beitrag zum Verständnis von Römer 13:1-7" (Angels and authority: A contribution to the understanding of Romans 13:1-7). In *Theologische Aufsätze: Karl Barth zum 50. Geburtstag* (Theological essays: Karl Barth on his 50th birthday), 90–109. Munich: Chr. Kaiser, 1936.

Delekat, Friedrich. *Die Kirche Jesu Christi und der Staat* (The church of Jesus Christ and the state). Furche Studien 8. Berlin: Furche Verlag, 1933.

Demant, Vigo A. "Zum Staatsverständnis des Anglikanismus" (On the understanding of the state in Anglicanism). In *Die Kirche und das Staatsproblem in der Gegenwart* (The church and the problem of the state in the present), edited by Paul Althaus, Emil Brunner, and Vigo Demant, 2nd enlarged ed., 25–44. Geneva: Furche Verlag, 1935.

Denzinger, Heinrich, and Adolf Schönmetzer, eds. *Enchiridion symbolorum definitium et declarationum de rebus fidei et morum.* Freiburg im Breisgau: Herder, 1973. Translated by John Clarkson as *The Church Teaches: Documents of the Church in English Translation,* edited by Heinrich Denzinger (Rockford, Ill.: Tan Books, 1973).

Deutsch, Harold C. *The Conspiracy against Hitler in the Twilight War.* Minneapolis: University of Minnesota Press, 1968.

Dibelius, Otto. *Ein Christ ist immer im Dienst.* 2nd ed. Stuttgart: Kreuz Verlag, 1963. Translated by Mary Ilford as *In the Service of the Lord,* 1st ed. (New York: Holt, Rinehart & Winston, 1964; London: Faber & Faber, 1965).

Diedrich, Karlheinz. *Die Belgier, ihre Könige und die Deutschen: Geschichte zweier Nachbarn seit 1830* (The Belgians, their kings, and the Germans: History of two neighbors since 1830). Düsseldorf: Droste, 1989.

Dietzfelbinger, Hermann. *Veränderung und Beständigkeit: Erinnerungen* (Change and permanence: Remembrances). 2nd ed. Munich: Claudius, 1985.

Dinnerstein, Leonard. *Antisemitism in America.* New York: Oxford University Press, 1994.

Dipper, Christoph. "Der 20. Juli und die 'Judenfrage'" (July 20 and the "Jewish question"). *Die Zeit,* 1 July 1994, 70.

Domarus, Max, ed. *Hitler: Reden und Proklamationen, 1932–1945.* Vol. 4. Munich: Süddeutscher Verlag, 1965. Volumes 1–3 translated by Mary Fran Gilbert as *Hitler: Speeches and Proclamations* (Wauconda, Ill.: Bolchazy-Carducci; London: Tauris, 1970–).

Duchrow, Ulrich. *Christenheit und Weltverantwortung: Traditionsgeschichte und systematische Struktur der Zweireichlehre* (Christendom and world responsibility: Tradition history and the systematic structure of the two-kingdoms doctrine). Forschungen und Berichte der Evangelischen Studiengemeinschaft 25. Stuttgart: E. Klett, 1970.

Dulles, Allen Welsh. *Verschwörung in Deutschland.* Translated by Wolfgang von Eckhardt. Zurich: Europa, 1948. German translation from English original, *Germany's Underground* (New York: Macmillan, 1947).

Düring, Ingemar. *Aristoteles: Darstellung und Interpretation seines Denkens* (Aristotle: Presentation and interpretation of his thought). Heidelberg: Winter, 1966.

Ebermann, Bernhard. "Die Redemptoristen" (The Redemptorists). In vol. 2 of Schwaiger, *Das Erzbistum München und Freising in der Zeit der nationalsozialistischen Herrschaft,* 518ff.

Eichholz, Georg, ed. *Herr, tue meine Lippen auf* (Lord, open my lips). Vol. 1. 6th ed. Wuppertal: E. Müller, 1962.

Elliger, Walter. *Die evangelische Kirche der Union* (The Protestant church of the Union). Witten: Luther Verlag, 1967.

Engel, Huberta, ed. *Deutscher Widerstand—Demokratie heute: Kirche, Kreisauer Kreis, Ethik, Militär und Gewerkschaften* (German resistance—democracy today: Church, Kreisauer circle, ethics, military, and labor unions). Bonn: Bouvier, 1992.

Engel, Ingrid. *Gottesverständnis und sozialpolitisches Handeln: Eine Untersuchung zu Friedrich Naumann* (The understanding of God and social-political action: An inquiry into Friedrich Naumann). Göttingen: Vandenhoeck & Ruprecht, 1972.

Ericksen, Robert. *Theologians under Hitler: Gerhard Kittel, Paul Althaus, and Emanuel Hirsch.* New Haven, Conn.: Yale University Press, 1985.

Ericksen, Robert, and Susannah Heschel, eds. *Betrayal: German Churches and the Holocaust.* Minneapolis: Fortress Press, 1999.

Fabre, Emile, ed. *God's Underground.* Collected by Jeanne Merle d'Aubigné and Violette Mouchon. Edited by Emile C. Fabre. Translated by William and Patricia Nottingham from the French original, *Les Clandestines de Dieu.* St. Louis: Bethany Press, 1970.

Faulhaber, Kardinal Michael. *Akten* (Documents). Revised by Ludwig Volk. Vol. 2: *1935–1945.* Veröffentlichungen der Kommission für Zeitgeschichte A 26. Mainz: Matthias-Grünewald-Verlag, 1978.

Feil, Ernst. *Die Theologie Dietrich Bonhoeffers: Hermeneutik, Christologie, Weltverständnis.* 2nd rev. ed. Munich: Chr. Kaiser, 1991. Translated by Martin Rumscheidt as *The Theology of Dietrich Bonhoeffer* (Philadelphia: Fortress Press, 1985).

Fließ, Dorothee. "Geschichte einer Rettung" (Story of a rescue). In *20. Juli 1944: Annäherung an einen geschichtlichten Augenblick* (July 20, 1944: Approach to a historical moment), edited by Rüdiger von Voß and Günter Neske, 69–87. Pfullingen: Neske, 1984.

Foerster, Erich. *Unsinn und Sinn des "Christlichen Staates"* (Nonsense and sense of the "Christian state"). Giessen: A. Töpelmann, 1932.

The Fortnightly. Periodical published in London by H. Marshall & Son, 1934–1954.

Fox, Richard W. *Reinhold Niebuhr: A Biography.* New York: Panthcon Books, 1985.

Francke, August Hermann. *Werke in Auswahl* (Selected works). Edited by Erhard Peschke. Berlin: Luther Verlag, 1968.

Freudenberg, Adolf, ed. *Rettet die zum Tode geschleppt werden: Ökumene durch geschlossene Grenzen 1939–1945* (Free those being taken to their deaths: Ecumene through closed borders 1939–1945). Munich: Chr. Kaiser, 1985.

Gaertringen, Friedrich Freiherr Hiller von, and Klaus Peter Reiss, eds. *Die Hassell-Tagebücher 1938–1944: Ulrich von Hassells Aufzeichnungen vom Andern Deutschland* (The Hassell diaries 1938–1944: Ulrich von Hassell's notes from the other Germany). Berlin: Siedler, 1989.

Gauger, Joachim. *Chronik der Kirchenwirren* (Chronicle of the confusion in the church). Periodical published under the title "Gotthard Briefe." Vol. 3. Elberfeld, 1934–35.

Gerber, Hans. *Die Idee des Staates in der neueren evangelisch-theologischen Ethik* (The idea of the state in contemporary Protestant theological ethics). Berlin: Junker & Dünnhaupt, 1930.

Gerlach, Wolfgang. *And the Witnesses Were Silent: The Confessing Church and the Jews.* Translated and edited by Victoria J. Barnett. Lincoln: University of Nebraska Press, 2000.

Gerrens, Uwe. "Medizinisches Ethos und theologische Ethik: Die Position von Karl Bonhoeffer und Dietrich Bonhoeffer in den Auseinandersetzungen um Zwangssterilisation und Euthanasie im Nationalsozialismus" (Medical ethos and theological ethics: The position of Karl Bonhoeffer and Dietrich Bonhoeffer in the dispute over compulsory sterilization and euthanasia in National Socialism). Diss., Heidelberg, 1994.

Gerstenmaier, Eugen. *Streit und Friede hat seine Zeit: Ein Lebensbericht* (There is a time for conflict and peace: Report of a life). Frankfurt am Main: Propyläen, 1981.

Glenthøj, Jørgen Johannes. "Die Eideskrise in der Bekennenden Kirche 1938 und Dietrich Bonhoeffer" (The oath crisis in the Confessing Church in 1938 and Dietrich Bonhoeffer). *Zeitschrift für Kirchengeschichte* (Stuttgart) 96, no. 3 (1985): 377–94.

————. "Zwei neue Zeugnisse von der Ermordung Dietrich Bonhoeffers" (Two new accounts of the murder of Dietrich Bonhoeffer). In Mayer and Zimmerling, *Dietrich Bonhoeffer, Mensch hinter Mauern*, 99–111.

Godsey, John D., ed. *Preface to Bonhoeffer: The Man and Two of His Shorter Writings*. Philadelphia: Fortress, 1965.

Gore, Charles, ed. *Lux mundi: A Series of Studies in the Religion of Incarnation*. London: J. Lovell, 1889.

Graml, Hermann, Hans Mommsen, Hans-Joachim Reichhardt, and Ernst Wolf. *Der deutsche Widerstand gegen Hitler: Vier historisch-kritische Studien*. Edited by Walter Schmitthenner and Hans Burckheim. Cologne: Kiepenheuer & Witsch, 1966. Translated by Peter Ross and Betty Ross as *The German Resistance to Hitler*, with an introduction by F. L. Carsten (Berkeley: University of California Press, 1970).

————. "Der Fall Oster" (The Oster case). *Vierteljahreshefte für Zeitgeschichte* 14 (1966): 26–39.

Graulich, Günter, and Paul Horn. *Heinrich Schütz: Musikalische Exequien* (Heinrich Schütz: Musical exequies). Kassel: Bärenreiter, 1961.

Gremmels, Christian, and Wolfgang Huber, eds. *Theologie und Freundschaft* (Theology and friendship). Gütersloh: Chr. Kaiser Verlag, 1994.

Grotefeld, Stefan. "Opposition gegen den Nationalsozialismus und Schweizer Exil: Friedrich Siegmund-Schultze, ein deutscher Ökumeniker und christlicher Pazifist" (Opposition against National Socialism and exile in Switzerland: Friedrich Siegmund-Schultze, a German ecumenist and Christian pacifist). Diss., Heidelberg, 1993.

Grüber, Heinrich. *Erinnerungen aus sieben Jahrzehnten* (Remembrances from seven decades). Cologne: Kiepenheuer & Witsch, 1968.

Gruchmann, Lothar. *Der Zweite Weltkrieg: Kriegführung und Politik* (The Second World War: Warfare and politics). Deutscher Taschenbuch Verlag-Weltgeschichte, vol. 10. Munich: Deutscher Taschenbuch Verlag, 1967.

Gürtler, Paul. *Nationalsozialismus und Evangelische Kirche im Warthegau: Trennung von Staat und Kirche im nationalsozialistischen Weltanschauungsstaat* (National Socialism and the Protestant church in Warthegau: Separation of state and church in the National Socialist ideological state). Arbeiten zur Geschichte des Kirchenkampfes 2. Göttingen: Vandenhoeck & Ruprecht, 1958.

Haase, Norbert. "Aus der Praxis des Reichskriegsgerichts: Neue Dokumente zur Militärgerichtsbarkeit im Zweiten Weltkrieg" (From the experience of the Reich War Court: New documents on military jurisdiction in the Second World War). *Vierteljahreshefte für Zeitgeschichte* 39 (1991): 379–411.

Haeften, Barbara von. *Aus unserem Leben 1944–1950* (From our lives 1944–1950). Tutzing: private publication, 1974.

Hasler, Alfred A. *Das Boot ist voll: Die Schweiz und die Flüchtlinge 1933–1945*. Zurich: Fretz & Wasmuth, 1967. Translated by Charles Lam Markmann as *The Lifeboat Is Full: Switzerland and the Refugees, 1933–1945* (New York: Funk & Wagnalls, 1969).

Hauschild, Wolf-Dieter. "Geist" (Spirit). In *Theologische Realenzyklopädie*, 12: 196–217. Berlin: W. de Gruyter, 1984.

Hegel, Georg Wilhelm Friedrich. *Grundlinien der Philosophie des Rechts oder Naturrecht und Staatswissenschaft im Grundrisse*. Werke vol. 7. Frankfurt: Suhrkamp, 1970. Translated with notes by T. M. Knox as *Hegel's Philosophy of Right* (Oxford: Clarendon Press, 1958).

Heidegger, Martin. *Sein und Zeit*. 9th ed. Tübingen: M. Niemeyer, 1960. Translated by John Macquarrie and Edward Robinson as *Being and Time* (San Francisco: Harper & Row, 1962).

Heideking, Jürgen. "Die 'Schweizer Straßen' des europäischen Widerstands" (The "Swiss Roads" of the European resistance). In Schulz, *Geheimdienste und Widerstandsbewegungen im Zweiten Weltkrieg*, 143–87.

Helmreich, Ernst Christian. *The German Churches under Hitler: Background, Struggle, and Epilogue*. Detroit: Wayne State University Press, 1979.

Heppe, Heinrich. *Die Dogmatik der evangelisch-reformierten Kirche, dargestellt und aus den Quellen belegt*. Edited by Ernst Bizer. Neukirchen: Moers, 1935. Translated by G. T. Thomson as *Reformed Dogmatics: Set Out and Illustrated from the Sources*, revised and edited by Ernst Bizer (London: Allen & Unwin, 1950; reprint, Grand Rapids, Mich.: Baker Book House, 1978).

Hermelink, Heinrich. *Kirche im Kampf: Dokumente des Widerstands und des Aufbaus in der evangelischen Kirche in Deutschland 1933–1945* (The Church Struggle: Documents of the resistance and development in the Protestant church in Germany 1933–1945). Tübingen: R. Wunderlich, 1950.

Herrmann, Wilhelm. *Dogmatik*. Gotha: F. A. Perthes, 1925. Translated by Nathaniel Micklem and Kenneth Saunders as *Systematic Theology* (New York: Macmillan; London: G. Allen & Unwin, 1927).

————. *Ethik.* 2nd ed. Tübingen: J. C. B. Mohr, 1901.

Hettler, Friedrich Hermann. *Josef Müller ("Ochsensepp"): Mann des Widerstandes und erster CSU-Vorsitzender* (Josef Müller ["Ochsensepp"]: Man of the resistance and first chair of the Christian Social Union political party). Miscellanea Bavarica Monacensia, vol. 155. Munich: Stadtarchiv München—Kommissionsverlag UNI-Druck, 1991.

Hinsley, F. H. *British Intelligence in the Second World War.* Vol. 2. London: H.M.S.O., 1981.

Hirsch, Emanuel. *Deutschlands Schicksal: Staat, Volk und Menschheit im Lichte einer ethischen Weltsicht* (Germany's destiny: State, people, and humanity in light of an ethical worldview). 3rd ed. Göttingen: Vandenhoeck & Ruprecht, 1925.

————. *Die gegenwärtige geistige Lage im Spiegel philosophischer und theologischer Besinnung* (The current spiritual situation in the mirror of philosophical and theological reflection). Göttingen: Vandenhoeck & Ruprecht, 1934.

Hoffmann, Peter. *Widerstand-Staatsstreich-Attentat: Der Kampf der Opposition gegen Hitler.* 2nd revised and enlarged ed. Frankfurt am Main: Ullstein, 1970. Translated by Richard Barry as *The History of the German Resistance, 1933–1945* (Cambridge, Mass.: MIT Press, 1977).

Hofmann, Klaus, ed. *Awake My Heart: Bach Chorale Collection and Settings for the Eucharist.* English-language edition prepared by Len Lythgoe. Stuttgart: Carus Verlag, 2000.

Höhne, Heinz. *Canaris: Patriot im Zwielicht.* Special ed. Munich: Bertelsmann, 1984. Translated by J. Maxwell Brownjohn as *Canaris: Hitler's Master Spy.* 1st Cooper Square Press ed. (1979; New York: Cooper Square Press, 1999).

Hollaz, David. *Examen theologicum acromaticum universam theologiam theticopolemicam complectens.* Leipzig, 1763.

Huber, Wolfgang. *Folgen christlicher Freiheit: Ethik und Theorie der Kirche im Horizont der Barmer Theologischen Erklärung* (Consequences of Christian freedom: The ethics and theory of the church in the horizon of the Barmen Declaration). Neukirchener Beiträge zur systematischen Theologie 4. Neukirchen-Vluyn: Neukirchener Verlag, 1983.

Internationales Bonhoeffer Forum: Forschung und Praxis (International Bonhoeffer forum: Research and practice). Edited by Eberhard Bethge, Hans-Jürgen Degen, Ernst Feil, Hans Pfeifer, Ferdinand Schlingensiepen, and Heinz-Eduard Tödt. Vols. 1–5. Munich, 1976–83.

Jackson, Eleanor M. *Red Tape and the Gospel: A Study of the Significance of the Ecumenical Missionary Struggle of William Paton.* Birmingham, UK: Published for the Paton family by Phlogiston Pub. in association with the Selly Oak Colleges, 1980.

John, Otto. *Zweimal kam ich heim: Vom Verschwörer zum Schützer der Verfassung.* Düsseldorf: Econ Verlag, 1969. Translated by Richard Barry as *Twice through the Lines: The Autobiography of Otto John* (New York: Harper & Row, 1972).

Johnson, Alex. *Eivind Berggrav, Spenningens Mann.* Oslo: Land og Kirke, 1959. Translated by Kjell Jordheim with Harriet L. Overholt as *Eivind Berggrav: God's Man of Suspense* (Minneapolis: Augsburg, 1960).

Kaiser, Jochen-Christoph. *Sozialer Protestantismus im 20. Jahrhundert: Studien zur Geschichte der Inneren Mission 1918–1945* (Social Protestantism in the 20th century: Studies in the history of the Inner Mission 1918–1945). Munich: R. Oldenbourg, 1989.

Kalckreuth, Johannes. *Wesen und Werk meines Vaters: Lebensbild des Malers Leopold Graf von Kalckreuth* (The character and work of my father: Portrait of the painter Leopold Graf von Kalckreuth). Hamburg: Christians, 1967.

Kettenacker, Lothar. "Der nationalkonservative Widerstand aus angelsächsischer Sicht" (The Anglo-Saxon view of the national conservative resistance). In Schmädeke and Steinbach, *Der Widerstand gegen den Nationalsozialismus,* 712–31.

Kittel, Gerhard. "Das Urteil des Neuen Testamentes über den Staat" (The view of the New Testament on the state). *Zeitschrift für Systematische Theologie* 14 (1937): 651–80.

Klän, Werner. "Ein Kirchenkampf. Bericht aus Pommern: Mutmaßungen über seinen Verfasser und die Adressaten" (A church struggle. Report from Pomerania: Conjectures about its author and addressees). *Internationales Bonhoeffer Komitee—Rundbrief* 39 (July 1992): 20–37.

Klee, Ernst. *"Euthanasie" im NS-Staat: Die "Vernichtung lebensunwerten Lebens"* ("Euthanasia" in the National Socialist state: The "annihilation of life unworthy of life"). Frankfurt am Main: Fischer Taschenbuch Verlag, 1985.

Klemperer, Klemens von. See von Klemperer.

Kluge, Ulrich. "Der 'Freiburger Kreis' 1938–1945: Personen, Strukturen und Ziele kirchlich-akademischen Widerstandsverhaltens gegen den Nationalsozialismus" (The "Freiburg circle" 1938–1945: Persons, structures, and aims of church-academic resistance against National Socialism). *Freiburger Universitätsblätter* 27 (1988): 19–40.

Kluxen, Wolfgang. *Philosophische Ethik bei Thomas von Aquin* (Philosophical ethics of Thomas Aquinas). Mainz: Matthias-Grünewald Verlag, 1974.

Knorr, August. "Laienkonvente" (Lay conferences). *Junge Kirche* (1938): 899ff.

Koch, Laurentius. "Die Benediktinerabtei Ettal" (The Ettal Benedictine abbey). In vol. 2 of Schwaiger, *Das Erzbistum München und Freising in der Zeit der nationalsozialistischen Herrschaft,* 381–413.

Koschorke, Manfred, ed. *Geschichte der Bekennenden Kirche in Ostpreußen 1933–1945: Allein das Wort hat's getan* (History of the Confessing Church in East Prussia 1933–1945: The Word alone did it). Göttingen: Vandenhoeck & Ruprecht, 1976.

Kramp, Willy. *Die Fischer von Lissau* (The fishermen of Lissau). Berlin: Hans von Hugo, 1939.

Krause, Gerhard. "Bonhoeffer." In *Theologische Realenzyklopädie*, 7:55–66. Berlin: W. de Gruyter, 1981.

Krause, Martin. *Erwin Schutz, 1907–1942: Ein Landpfarrer in Hinterpommern* (Erwin Schutz, 1907–1942: A country pastor in Eastern Pomerania). Bonn: self-published, 1999.

Kutter, Hermann. *Sie müssen: Ein offenes Wort an die christliche Gesellschaft.* Jena: Eugen Diederichs, 1910. Translated as *They Must; or, God and the Social Democracy. A Frank Word to Christian Men and Women,* edited by Rufus W. Weeks (Chicago: Co-operative Printing, 1908).

Leber, Annedore, with Willy Brandt and Karl Dietrich Bracher. *Das Gewissen steht auf* (The conscience stands up). Frankfurt am Main: Büchergilde Gutenberg, 1960. Translated by Thomas S. McClymont as *The Conscience in Revolt: Portraits of the German Resistance 1933–1945* (Mainz: Hase & Koehler, 1994).

Lehndorff, Hans Graf von. *Die Insterburger Jahre: Mein Weg zur Bekennenden Kirche* (The Insterburg years: My path to the Confessing Church). Munich: Biederstein Verlag, 1969.

Leibholz, Gerhard. *Politics and Law.* Leiden: A. W. Sythoff, 1965.

Leibholz-Bonhoeffer, Sabine. *Vergangen, erlebt, überwunden: Schicksale der Familie Bonhoeffer.* Wuppertal: Kiefel, 1968. Translated as *The Bonhoeffers: Portrait of a Family,* based on the first English edition published by Sidgwick & Johnson, London, 1971 (Chicago: Covenant Publications, 1994).

Lexikon für Theologie und Kirche (Lexicon for theology and church). Edited by Michael Buchberger, Josef Höfer, and Karl Rahner. 10 vols. Freiburg: Herder Verlag, 1957–65.

Lienhard, Marcus. "Frankreich" (France), 3/2. In *Theologische Realenzyklopädie*, 11:373–85. Berlin: W. de Gruyter, 1983.

Linck, Hugo. *Der Kirchenkampf in Ostpreußen 1933–1945: Geschichte und Dokumentation* (The Church Struggle in East Prussia 1933–1945). Munich: Gräfe & Unzer, 1968.

Lindgren, Hendrik. "Adam von Trotts Reisen nach Schweden" (Adam von Trott's trips to Sweden). *Vierteljahreshefte für Zeitgeschichte* 18 (1970): 274–83.

Lipgens, Walter. *Documents on the History of European Integration.* Vol. 1: *Continental Plans for European Union, 1939–1945.* Berlin: W. de Gruyter, 1985.

Louis Ferdinand, Prince of Prussia. *Die Geschichte meines Lebens* (The story of my life). Göttingen: Göttinger Verlagsanstalt, 1968.

Ludlow, Peter. "Pius XII, die britische Regierung und die deutsche Opposition im Winter 1939/40" (Pius XII, the British government, and the German opposition in the winter of 1939–40). *Vierteljahreshefte für Zeitgeschichte* 22 (1974): 299–341.

Ludwig, Hartmut. "Die Opfer unter dem Rad verbinden: Vor- und Entstehungsgeschichte, Arbeit und Mitarbeiter des 'Büro Pfarrer Grüber'" (To bandage the victim under the wheel: Origins and the history of its founding, the work and staff of the "office of Pastor Grüber"). Diss. Habilitation, Berlin (GDR), 1988.

Luther, Martin. *Die deutschen geistlichen Lieder* (German religious hymns). Edited by Gerhard Hahn. Tübingen: Niemeyer, 1967.

———. *Studienausgabe* (Textbook edition). Edited by Hans-Ulrich Delius in cooperation with Helmar Junghans, Reinhold Pietz, Joachim Rogge, and Günther Wartenberg. Vols. 1–4. Berlin: Evangelische Verlagsanstalt, 1979–86.

———. *Werke: Kritische Gesamtausgabe* (Weimarer Ausgabe = WA). 58 vols. Weimar: H. Böhlau, 1883ff. Translated as *Luther's Works*, vols. 1–30 edited by Jaroslav Pelikan, vols. 31–55 edited by Helmut Lehmann, complete works on CD-ROM (Minneapolis: Fortress Press; St. Louis: Concordia, 2002).

Lutheran Book of Worship. Minneapolis: Augsburg; Philadelphia: Board of Publication of the Lutheran Church in America, 1978.

The Lutheran Hymnal. St. Louis: Concordia, 1941.

Lyra Germanica: Hymns for the Sundays and Chief Festivals of the Christian Year. Translated from the original German by Catherine Winkworth. London: George Newnes; New York: Charles Scribner's Sons, 1855.

MacDonogh, Giles. *A Good German: Adam von Trott zu Solz.* London: Quartet Books, 1989.

Mackenzie, Alexander Slidell. *Life of Stephen Decatur, a Commodore in the Navy of the United States.* Edited by Jared Sparks. Library of American Biography, vol. 11. 2nd series. Boston: C. C. Little & J. Brown, 1846.

Malvern, 1941: The Life of the Church and the Order of Society, Being the Proceedings of the Archbishop of York's Conference. London: Longmans, Green, 1941.

Marrus, Michael R. "Die französischen Kirchen und die Judenverfolgung 1940–1944." *Vierteljahreshefte für Zeitgeschichte* 31 (1983): 483–505. Translated as "French Churches and the Persecution of Jews in France, 1940–1944," in *Judaism and Christianity under the Impact of National Socialism,* edited by Otto Dov Kulka and Paul R. Mendes-Flohr, 305–26 (Jerusalem: Historical Society of Israel, 1987).

Martin, Bernd. "Das aussenpolitische Versagen des Widerstands (The foreign-policy failures of the resistance)." In Schmädeke and Steinbach, *Der Widerstand gegenden Nationalsozialismus,* 1037–61.

Matheson, Peter, ed. *The Third Reich and the Christian Churches*. Edinburgh: T & T Clark, 1981.

Mau, Rudolf. "Luthers Stellung zu den Türken" (Luther's position on the Turks). In vol. 1 of *Leben und Werk Martin Luthers von 1526–1546: Festgabe zu seinem 500. Geburtstag* (The life and work of Martin Luther from 1526 to 1546: Commemorative volume on the occasion of his 500th birthday), edited by H. Junghans, 2nd ed., 647–62. Berlin: Evangelische Verlagsanstalt, 1985.

Mayer, Rainer, and Peter Zimmerling, eds. *Dietrich Bonhoeffer, Mensch hinter Mauern: Theologie und Spiritualität in den Gefängnisjahren* (Dietrich Bonhoeffer, person behind walls: Theology and spirituality in the prison years). Giessen: Brunnen Verlag, 1993.

Meier, Kurt. *Die Deutschen Christen* (The German Christians). Halle: Max Niemeyer, 1965.

———. *Der Evangelische Kirchenkampf: Gesamtdarstellung in drei Bänden* (The Protestant Church Struggle: Portrayal in three volumes). Halle (Saale): Niemeyer, 1976–.

Melzer, Karl-Heinrich. *Der geistliche Vertrauensrat: Geistliche Leitung für die Deutsche Evangelische Kirche im Zweiten Weltkrieg?* (The confidential council: Spiritual guidance for the German Protestant church in the Second World War?) Arbeiten zur kirchlichen Zeitgeschichte, series B, no. 17. Göttingen, 1991.

Messerschmidt, Manfred. "Verschwörer in Uniform: Der militärische Widerstand gegen Hitler und sein Regime" (Conspirators in uniform: The military resistance against Hitler and his regime). In *Widerstand und Exil 1933–1945* (Resistance and exile 1933–1945), edited by Richard Albrecht and Otto Romberg, 134–44. Frankfurt am Main: Campus, 1986.

Meyer, Alice. *Anpassung oder Widerstand: Die Schweiz zur Zeit des deutschen Nationalsozialismus* (Accommodation or resistance: Switzerland during the time of German National Socialism). Frauenfeld: Verlag Huber, 1966.

Meyer, Dietrich, and Eberhard Bethge, eds. *Nachlaß Dietrich Bonhoeffer: Ein Verzeichnis. Archiv—Sammlung—Bibliothek* (Dietrich Bonhoeffer's literary estate: A bibliographical catalog. Archive, collection, library). Munich: Chr. Kaiser Verlag, 1987.

Meyer, Winfried. *Unternehmen Sieben: Eine Rettungsaktion für vom Holocaust Bedrohte aus dem Amt Ausland/Abwehr im Oberkommando der Wehrmacht* (Operation seven: A rescue action on behalf of those threatened by the Holocaust conducted by the Foreign Office of Military Intelligence in the Armed Forces High Command). Frankfurt am Main: Verlag Anton Hain, 1993.

Moltke, Helmuth James von. *Briefe an Freya 1939–1945*. Edited by Beate Ruhm von Oppen. Munich: Beck, 1988. Edited and translated by Beate Ruhm von Oppen as *Letters to Freya: 1939–1945* (New York: Knopf, 1990).

Moltmann, Jürgen. *Kirche in der Kraft des Geistes.* Munich: Chr. Kaiser, 1975. Translated by Margaret Kohl as *The Church in the Power of the Spirit* (Minneapolis: Fortress Press, 1993).

Mommsen, Hans. *Alternatives to Hitler: German Resistance under the Third Reich.* Translated and annotated by Angus McGeoch. Introduction by Jeremy Noakes. Princeton, N.J.: Princeton University Press, 2003.

————. *Der Nationalsozialismus und die deutsche Gesellschaft: Ausgewählte Aufsätze.* Reinbek: Rowohlt, 1991.

Müller, Christine-Ruth. *Dietrich Bonhoeffers Kampf gegen die nationalsozialistische Verfolgung und Vernichtung der Juden* (Dietrich Bonhoeffer's fight against the National Socialist persecution and annihilation of the Jews). Heidelberger Untersuchungen zu Widerstand, Judenverfolgung und Kirchenkampf im Dritten Reich, vol. 5. Munich: Chr. Kaiser, 1990.

Müller, Josef. "Der Abbas" (The abbot). *Alt und Jung Metten* 34 (1967): 3–8.

————. *Bis zur letzten Konsequenz: Ein Leben für Frieden und Freiheit* (To the bitter end: A life for peace and freedom). Munich: Süddeutscher Verlag, 1975.

Müller, Klaus-Jürgen. *Armee, Politik und Gesellschaft in Deutschland 1933–1945: Studien zum Verhältnis von Armee und NS-System.* Paderborn: Schöningh, 1986. Translated as *The Army, Politics, and Society in Germany, 1933–1945: Studies in the Army's Relation to Nazism* (New York: St. Martin's Press, 1987).

Mündige Welt (The world come of age). Vols. 1–4. Edited by Eberhard Bethge. Munich: Chr. Kaiser Verlag, 1955–63.

    Vol. 1: *Dem Andenken Dietrich Bonhoeffers — Vorträge und Briefe* (In remembrance of Dietrich Bonhoeffer — Lectures and letters). 1955.

    Vol. 2. Part 1: *Weißensee.* Part 2: *Verschiedenes* (Various items). 1956.

    Vol. 3: *Weißensee.* 1959.

    Vol. 4. Part 1: *Weißensee.* 1961. Part 2: *Verschiedenes* (Various items). 1963.

Mündige Welt (The world come of age). Vol. 5: *Dokumentation zur Bonhoeffer-Forschung 1928–1945* (Documents on Bonhoeffer research, 1928–1945). Edited by Jørgen Glenthøj. Munich: Chr. Kaiser Verlag, 1969.

Neuhäusler, Johannes. *Amboß und Hammer: Erlebnisse im Kirchenkampf des Dritten Reiches* (Anvil and hammer: Experiences in the Church Struggle of the Third Reich). Munich: Manz, 1967.

————. *Kreuz und Hakenkreuz: Der Kampf des Nationalsozialismus gegen die katholische Kirche und der kirchliche Widerstand* (Cross and swastika: National Socialism's fight against the Catholic Church and the church resistance). Munich: Katholische Kirche Bayerns, 1946.

Niemöller, Wilhelm, ed. *Die dritte Bekenntnissynode der Deutschen Evangelischen Kirche zu Augsburg: Text, Dokumente, Berichte* (The third Confessing Church synod of the German Evangelical Church at Augsburg: Text, documents, reports). Arbeiten zur Geschichte des Kirchenkampfes 20. Göttingen: Vandenhoeck & Ruprecht, 1969.

———. *Die evangelische Kirche im Dritten Reich: Handbuch des Kirchenkampfes* (The Protestant church in the Third Reich: Handbook of the Church Struggle). Bielefeld: L. Bechauf, 1956.

———. *Kampf und Zeugnis der Bekennenden Kirche* (The struggle and witness of the Confessing Church). Bielefeld: L. Bechauf, 1948.

———. *Wort und Tat im Kirchenkampf* (Word and deed in the Church Struggle). Munich: Chr. Kaiser, 1969.

———, ed. *Die zweite Bekenntnissynode der Deutschen Evangelischen Kirche zu Dahlem: Text, Dokumente, Berichte* (The second Confessing Church synod of the German Evangelical Church at Dahlem: Text, documents, reports). Göttingen: Vandenhoeck & Ruprecht, 1958.

Niesel, Wilhelm. *Kirche unter dem Wort: Der Kampf der Bekennenden Kirche der altpreußischen Union 1933–1945* (Church under the Word: The struggle of the Confessing Church of the Old Prussian Union 1933–1945). Arbeiten zur Geschichte des Kirchenkampfes. Supplemental series 11. Göttingen: Vandenhoeck & Ruprecht, 1978.

Nietzsche, Friedrich. *Jenseits von Gut und Böse: Vorspiel einer Philosophie der Zukunft*. Vol. 6/2 of *Nietzsches Werke*, edited by G. Colli and G. Montinari. Berlin: W. de Gruyter, 1968. Translated and edited by Marion Faber as *Beyond Good and Evil: Prelude to a Philosophy of the Future*, with an introduction by Robert C. Holub, Oxford World's Classics (Oxford: Oxford University Press, 1998).

Norman, Edward Robert. *Church and Society in England 1770–1970: A Historical Study*. Oxford: Clarendon Press, 1976.

Nübel, Hans Ulrich. "Bonhoeffer und die Denkschrift des 'Freiburger Kreises'" (Bonhoeffer and the memorandum of the "Freiburg Circle"). *Freiburger Universitätsblätter* 101 (December 1988): 41–52.

Obendiek, Harmannus. *Die Obrigkeit nach dem Bekenntnis der reformierten Kirche* (The government according to the confession of the Reformed church). Munich: Chr. Kaiser, 1936.

Oehme, Werner. *Märtyrer der evangelischen Christenheit 1933–1945* (Martyrs of Protestant Christendom 1933–1945). Berlin: Evangelische Verlagsanstalt, 1979.

Oepke, Albrecht. "βάπτω." In *Theologisches Wörterbuch zum Neuen Testament*, 1:527–44. Stuttgart: W. Kohlhammer, 1933. Translated as "βάπτω" (to dip) in *Theological Dictionary of the New Testament*, 1:529–46 (Grand Rapids, Mich.: Wm. B. Eerdmans, 1964).

Overesch, Manfred, and Friedrich Wilhelm Saal. *Chronik deutscher Zeitgeschichte: Politik-Wirtschaft-Kultur* (Chronicle of German contemporary history: Politics-economics-culture). Vol. 2, part 2: *Das dritte Reich, 1939–*

1945 (The Third Reich, 1939–1945). In collaboration with Wolfgang Herda and Artelt Jork. Düsseldorf: Droste, 1982.

The Oxford Dictionary of the Christian Church. Edited by F. L. Cross. 3rd ed. Edited by E. A. Livingstone. Oxford: Oxford University Press, 1997.

Pangritz, Andreas. "Zur Neuausgabe von Bonhoeffers 'Ethik'" (On the new edition of Bonhoeffer's *Ethics*). *Weißenseer Blätter* 5 (1992): 25–31, 49.

Patrologiae cursus completus (Complete Patrologia). Edited by Jacques-Paul Migne. Vol. 35. Reprint, Ridgewood, N.J.: Gregg Press, 1965.

Pejsa, Jane. "Dietrich Bonhoeffer's Letter to an Unknown Woman." *Newsletter,* International Bonhoeffer Society, English Language Section, no. 52 (1993): 3ff.

―――. *Matriarch of Conspiracy: Ruth von Kleist 1867–1945.* Minneapolis: Kenwood, 1991.

Portmann, Heinrich. *Bischof Graf von Galen spricht! Ein apostolischer Kampf und sein Widerhall* (Bishop Graf von Galen speaks: An apostolic struggle and its reverberation). Freiburg im Breisgau: Herder, 1946.

Quervain, Alfred de. *Die theologischen Voraussetzungen der Politik: Grundlinien einer politischen Theologie* (The theological prerequisites of politics: Foundations of a political theology). Berlin: Furche Verlag, 1931.

―――. *Volk und Obrigkeit, eine Gabe Gottes* (People and government, a gift of God). Frankfurt am Main: Bruderrat der Evangelischen Kirche der Altpreußischen Union, 1937.

Ragaz, Leonard. *Von Christus zu Marx—von Marx zu Christus* (From Christ to Marx—from Marx to Christ). Hamburg: Furche, 1972.

Ramsey, Arthur Michael. *An Era in Anglican Theology, from Gore to Temple: The Development of Anglican Theology between "Lux Mundi" and the Second World War, 1889–1939.* London: Longmans; New York: Scribner, 1960.

Die Religion in Geschichte und Gegenwart (Religion in history and the present). 5 vols. Tübingen: Mohr, 1909–13; 3rd newly revised ed., 1957–65.

Riecker, Otto. *Ruf zur Seelsorge* (A call to pastoral care). Leipzig: L. Klotz, 1939.

―――. *Die Wiedererweckung der Kirche* (The reawakening of the church). Leipzig: Leopold Klotz Verlag, 1937.

Rieker, Karl. *Die rechtliche Stellung der evangelischen Kirche Deutschlands* (The legal status of the Protestant church of Germany). Leipzig: C. L. Hirschfeld, 1893.

Riemschneider, Ernst G. *Der Fall Klepper: Eine Dokumentation* (The Klepper case: A documentation). Stuttgart: Deutsche Verlagsanstalt, 1975.

Ringshausen, Gerhard. "Die Begründung des Staates und der Stellenwert der Kirche" (The establishment of the state and the status of the church). In Huberta Engel, *Deutscher Widerstand—Demokratie heute,* 203–44.

―――. "Die Überwindung der Perversion des Rechts im Widerstand" (The overcoming of the perversion of law in the resistance). Manuscript. 1993.

Rissi, Mathias. *Die Taufe für die Toten: Ein Beitrag zur paulinischen Tauflehre* (Baptism for the dead: A contribution to the Pauline teaching on baptism). Abhandlungen zur Theologie des Alten und Neuen Testaments 42. Zurich: Zwingli Verlag, 1962.

Ritter, Adolf Martin. "Arianismus" (Arianism). In *Theologische Realenzyklopädie*, 3:692–719. Berlin: W. de Gruyter, 1978.

Ritter, Gerhard. *Carl Goerdeler und die deutsche Widerstandsbewegung.* Paperback ed. Munich: Deutscher Taschenbuch Verlag, 1964. Translated by R. T. Clark as *The German Resistance: Carl Goerdeler's Struggle against Tyranny,* abridged ed. (1958; reprint, Freeport, N.Y.: Books for Libraries Press, 1970).

Robinson, Henry Wheeler. "The New Hebrew Conception of Corporate Personality." *Beihefte zur Zeitschrift für alttestamentliche Wissenschaft* 66 (1936): 49–62.

Röhm, Everhard, and Jörg Thierfelder. "Ein langer Weg von Breslau nach New York: Der Flüchtlingsseelsorger Friedrich Forell" (A long way from Breslau to New York: Friedrich Forell—pastor to refugees). In . . . *und über Barmen hinaus, Studien zur kirchlichen Zeitgeschichte: Festschrift für Carsten Nicolaisen* (. . . Beyond Barmen, studies on contemporary church history: Festschrift for Carsten Nicolaisen), edited by Joachim Mehlhausen, 315–22. Göttingen: Vandenhoeck & Ruprecht, 1995.

Roon, Ger van, ed. *Helmuth James Graf von Moltke, Völkerrecht im Dienste der Menschen: Dokumente* (Helmuth James Graf von Moltke, international law in the service of human beings: Documents). Berlin: Siedler Verlag, 1986.

———. "Der Kreisauer Kreis" (The Kreisau circle). *Geschichte in Wissenschaft und Unterricht* 39 (1988): 142–54.

———. *Neuordnung im Widerstand: Der Kreisauer Kreis innerhalb der deutschen Widerstandsbewegung.* Munich: R. Oldenbourg, 1967. Translated by Peter Ludlow as *German Resistance to Hitler: Count von Moltke and the Kreisau Circle.* London: Van Nostrand Reinhold, 1971.

Rothfels, Hans. "Zwei außenpolitische Memoranden der deutschen Opposition" (Two foreign affairs memoranda of the German opposition). *Vierteljahreshefte für Zeitgeschichte* 15 (1957): 388–97.

Röthlisberger-Pestalozzi, Esther, ed. *Gerty Pestalozzi-Eidenbenz.* Aarau, 1993.

Rübsam, Dagmar, and Hans Schadek, eds. *Der "Freiburger Kreis": Widerstand und Nachkriegsplanung 1933–1945* (The Freiburg circle: Resistance and planning for after the war 1933–1945). Freiburg im Breisgau: Verlag Stadtarchiv, 1990.

Rürup, Reinhard. *Topography of Terror: Gestapo, SS and Reichssicherheitshauptamt on the "Prinz-Albrecht-Terrain"—A Documentation.* Translated from the German edition by Werner T. Angress, based on the 7th revised and enlarged German edition. 1st English edition. Berlin: Verlag Willmuth Arenhövel, 1989.

Sauer, Wolfgang. *Württemberg in der Zeit des Nationalsozialismus* (Württemberg in the era of National Socialism). Ulm: Süddeutsche Verlagsgesellschaft, 1975.

Schäfer, Gerhard, ed. *Landesbischof D. Wurm und der nationalsozialistische Staat 1940–1945: Eine Dokumentation* (Regional Bishop Dr. Wurm and the National Socialist state 1940–1945: A documentation). Stuttgart: Calwer Verlag, 1968.

Schellenberg, Walter. *Aufzeichnungen: Die Memoiren des letzten Geheimdienstchefs unter Hitler.* Wiesbaden: Limes, 1956. Translated by Louis Hagen as *The Labyrinth: Memoirs* (UK title: *The Schellenberg Memoirs*), with an introduction by Alan Bullock (New York: Harper & Row, 1956).

Scherffig, Wolfgang. *Junge Theologen im "Dritten Reich": Dokumente, Briefe, Erfahrungen* (Young theologians in the "Third Reich": Documents, letters, experiences). Vol. 1: *1933–1945: Es begann mit einem Nein!* (1933–1945: It began with a No!). Neukirchen-Vluyn: Neukirchener, 1989.

Scheurig, Bodo, ed. *Deutscher Widerstand 1938 bis 1944: Fortschritt oder Reaktion?* (German resistance 1938–1944: Step forward or reaction?). Munich: Deutscher Taschenbuch Verlag, 1969.

Schlier, Heinrich. "Vom Antichrist: Zum 13. Kapitel der Offenbarung Johannes" (On the Antichrist: Concerning chapter 13 of the Revelation of John). In *Theologische Aufsätze: Karl Barth zum 50. Geburtstag* (Theological essays: Karl Barth on the occasion of his 50th birthday), 110–23. Munich: Chr. Kaiser, 1936.

Schmädeke, Jürgen, and Peter Steinbach, eds. *Der Widerstand gegen den Nationalsozialismus: Die deutsche Gesellschaft und der Widerstand gegen Hitler* (The resistance against National Socialism: German society and the resistance against Hitler). Munich: R. Piper, 1985.

Schmidt, Karl-Ludwig. "Das Gegenüber von Kirche und Staat in der Gemeinde des Neuen Testaments" (The juxtaposition of church and state in the church community of the New Testament). *Theologische Blätter* 16 (1937): 1–16.

Schminck-Gustavus, Christoph U. *Der "Prozeß" gegen Dietrich Bonhoeffer und die Freilassung seiner Mörder* (The "trial" of Dietrich Bonhoeffer and the release of his murderers). Dietz Taschenbuch 67. Bonn: Dietz, 1995.

Schmitthenner, Walter, and Hans Buchheim, eds. *Der deutsche Widerstand gegen Hitler: Vier historisch-kritische Studien.* Cologne: Kiepenheuer & Witsch, 1966. Translated by Peter Ross and Betty Ross as *The German Resistance to Hitler,* with an introduction by F. L. Carsten (London: Batsford, 1970).

Scholder, Klaus. *Die Kirchen und das Dritte Reich.* Vol. 1. Frankfurt am Main: Ullstein, 1977. Translated by John Bowden as *The Churches and the Third Reich,* 1st Fortress Press ed. (Philadelphia: Fortress Press, 1988).

————. *A Requiem for Hitler and Other New Perspectives on the German Church Struggle.* Translated by John Bowden. Philadelphia: Trinity Press International, 1989.

Schreiber, Matthias. *Friedrich Justus Perels: Ein Weg vom Rechtskampf der Bekennenden Kirche in den politischen Widerstand* (Friedrich Justus Perels: A path from the legal battle of the Confessing Church into the political resistance). Heidelberger Untersuchungen zu Widerstand, Judenverfolgung und Kirchenkampf im Dritten Reich, vol. 3. Munich: Chr. Kaiser, 1989.

Schulz, Gerhard, ed. *Geheimdienste und Widerstandsbewegungen im Zweiten Weltkrieg* (Secret services and resistance movements in the Second World War). Göttingen: Vandenhoeck & Ruprecht, 1982.

Schwabe, Klaus, and Rolf Reichhardt, eds. *Gerhard Ritter: Ein politischer Historiker in seinen Briefen* (Gerhard Ritter: A political historian in his letters). Schriften des Bundesarchiv 33. Boppard am Rhein: Boldt, 1984.

Schwaiger, Georg, ed. *Das Erzbistum München und Freising in der Zeit der nationalsozialistischen Herrschaft* (The archbishopric of Munich and Freising in the era of National Socialist rule). Munich: Schnell & Steiner, 1984.

Smid, Marikje. *Hans von Dohnanyi, Christine Bonhoeffer: Eine Ehe im Widerstand gegen Hitler* (Hans von Dohnanyi, Christine Bonhoeffer: A marriage in the resistance against Hitler). Gütersloh: Gütersloher Verlagshaus, 2002.

Spaemann, Robert. "Freiheit" (Freedom). In *Historisches Wörterbuch der Philosophie* (Historical dictionary of philosophy), 2:1064–98. Basel: Schwabe, 1972.

Spiegelbild einer Verschwörung: Die Kaltenbrunner-Berichte an Bormann und Hitler über das Attentat vom 20. Juli 1944: Geheime Dokumente aus dem ehemaligen Reichssicherheitshauptamt (Mirror image of a conspiracy: The Kaltenbrunner reports to Bormann and Hitler concerning the attempted assassination of July 20, 1944: Secret documents from the former Reich Central Security Office). Edited by Archiv Peter für Historische und Zeitgeschichtliche Dokumentation. Stuttgart: Seewald Verlag, 1961.

Stahlberg, Alexander. *Die verdammte Pflicht: Erinnerungen 1932 bis 1945.* Berlin: Ullstein, 1987. Translated by Patricia Crampton as *Bounden Duty: The Memoirs of a German Officer, 1932–1945,* 1st English-language ed. (London: Brassey's, 1970; distributed in North America by Macmillan).

Stein, Albert. *Zur Geschichte des Kirchenkampfes: Gesammelte Aufsätze 2* (History of the Church Struggle: Collected essays 2). Göttingen: Vandenhoeck & Ruprecht, 1971.

Strathmann, Hermann. "πόλις." In *Theologisches Wörterbuch zum Neuen Testament*, 6:516–35. Stuttgart: W. Kohlhammer, 1959. Translated as "πόλις" (city), in *Theological Dictionary of the New Testament*, 6:516–35 (Grand Rapids, Mich.: Wm. B. Eerdmans, 1968).

Strohl, Jane. "The Child in Luther's Theology." In *The Child in Christian Thought*, edited by Marcia J. Bunge, 134–59. Grand Rapids, Mich.: Wm. B. Eerdmans, 2001.

Strohm, Christoph. *Theologische Ethik im Kampf gegen den Nationalsozialismus: Der Weg Dietrich Bonhoeffers mit den Juristen Hans von Dohnanyi und Gerhard Leibholz in den Widerstand* (Theological ethics in the struggle against National Socialism: Dietrich Bonhoeffer's path with the lawyers Hans von Dohnanyi and Gerhard Leibholz into the resistance). Heidelberger Untersuchungen zu Widerstand, Judenverfolgung und Kirchenkampf im Dritten Reich, vol. 1. Munich: Chr. Kaiser, 1989.

Strohm, Theodor, and Jörg Thierfelder, eds. *Diakonie im "Dritten Reich". Neuere Ergebnisse zeitgeschichtlicher Forschung* (Church social work during the "Third Reich": New findings in contemporary historical research). Veröffentlichungen des Diakoniewissenschaftlichen Instituts an der Universität Heidelberg. Heidelberg: Heidelberger Verlagsanstalt, 1990.

Sykes, Christopher. *Adam von Trott: Eine deutsche Tragödie*. Translated from the original English by K. H. Abshagen. Düsseldorf: E. Diederichs, 1969. Originally published as *Tormented Loyalty: The Story of a German Aristocrat Who Defied Hitler* (1968; New York: Harper & Row, 1969).

Thielicke, Helmut, ed. *In der Stunde Null: Die Denkschrift des Freiburger "Bonhoeffer-Kreises." Politische Gemeinschaftsordnung: Ein Versuch zur Selbstbesinnung des christlichen Gewissens in den politischen Nöten unserer Zeit* (In the zero hour: The memorandum of the Freiburg "Bonhoeffer circle." The political ordering of society: An attempted self-reflection of the Christian conscience in the political crisis of our age). With an afterword by Philipp von Bismarck. Tübingen: Mohr, 1979.

Thierfelder, Jörg. *Das kirchliche Einigungswerk des württembergischen Landesbischofs Theophil Wurm* (The unifying church work of the Württemberg regional bishop Theophil Wurm). Arbeiten zur kirchlichen Zeitgeschichte, series B, no. 1. Göttingen: Vandenhoeck & Ruprecht, 1975.

Tilitzki, Christian, and Johannes Tuchel. "Zur Vorgeschichte von Reichsredeverbot und polizeilicher Meldepflicht für Dietrich Bonhoeffer" (Preliminary history of the Reich ban on public speaking and the police requirement to register for Dietrich Bonhoeffer). *IBG-Rundbrief* 36 (September 1991): 15–20. (Newsletter, International Bonhoeffer Society, German Section.)

Troeltsch, Ernst. "Christian Natural Law." In *Religion in History*, translated by James Luther Adams and Walter E. Bense, with an introduction by James Luther Adams, 159–67. Minneapolis: Fortress Press, 1991.

———. "Naturrecht" (Natural law). In *Religion in Geschichte und Gegenwart* (Religion in history and the present), 4:697–704. Tübingen: J. C. B. Mohr (Siebeck), 1913.

Tuchel, Johannes, and Reinhold Schattenfroh. *Zentrale des Terrors: Prinz-Albrecht-Straße 8, Hauptquartier der Gestapo* (Headquarters of terror: Prinz-Albrecht-Straße 8, headquarters of the Gestapo). Berlin: Siedler, 1987.

Ustorf, Werner. *Sailing on the Next Tide: Missions, Missiology, and the Third Reich.* Studies in the Intercultural History of Christianity, 125. Frankfurt-am-Main: Peter Lang, 2000.

Die Verkündigung der Kirche im Krieg. Ecclesia Militans (Oekumenische Dokumentenreihe, Heft 2). Translated as *The Church Speaks to the World: Abridged Document in Oecumenical Study Program Series "Ecclesia Militans."* Geneva: World Council of Churches, 1942.

Verkündigung und Forschung: Theologischer Jahresbericht. Annual periodical. Munich: Chr. Kaiser, 1940–.

Vilmar, August Friedrich Christian. *Dogmatik* (Dogmatics). Edited after the author's death by K. W. Fiderit. Unaltered reprint of 1st ed. 2 vols. Gütersloh: C. Bertelsmann, 1937.

———. *Die Lehre vom geistlichen Amt* (Teaching on the pastoral office). Marburg: N. G. Elwert'sche Universitätsbuchhandlung, 1870.

———. "Obrigkeit" (Government). In *Zur neuesten Culturgeschichte Deutschlands* (On the most recent cultural history of Germany), 3:311–24. Frankfurt: Heyder & Zimmer, 1867.

———. "Von Gottes Gnaden" (On the grace of God). 1848. In *Zur neuesten Culturgeschichte Deutschlands* (Most recent cultural history of Germany), 1:6–14. Frankfurt: Heyder & Zimmer, 1858.

Visser 't Hooft, Willem A. *Die Welt war meine Gemeinde: Autobiographie.* Munich: Piper, 1972. Published in English as *Memoirs* (London: SCM Press; Philadelphia: Westminster Press, 1973).

———. *Das Zeugnis eines Boten: Zum Gedächtnis von Dietrich Bonhoeffer* (The witness of a messenger: In memory of Dietrich Bonhoeffer). Geneva: Oekumenische Kommission für die Pastoration der Kriegsgefangenen, 1945.

von Klemperer, Klemens. *German Resistance against Hitler: The Search for Allies Abroad, 1938–1945.* New York: Clarendon Press; Oxford: Oxford University Press, 1992. Translated into German as *Die verlassenen Verschwörer: Der deutsche Widerstand auf der Suche nach Verbündeten 1938–1945* (Berlin: Siedler, 1994).

———. "Naturrecht und der deutsche Widerstand gegen den Nationalsozialismus" (Natural law and the German resistance against National Socialism). *Vierteljahreshefte für Zeitgeschichte* 40 (1992): 323–37.

Wach, Joachim. *Das Problem des Todes in der Philosophie unserer Zeit.* Tübingen: J. C. B. Mohr (Paul Siebeck), 1934. Translated as "The Problem of Death in Modern Philosophy," in *Understanding and Believing: Essays by Joachim Wach.* 1st ed. New York: Harper & Row, 1968.

Wagner, Walter. *Der Volksgerichtshof im nationalsozialstischen Staat* (The People's Court in the National Socialist state). Quellen und Darstellungen zur Zeitgeschichte (Sources and presentations for contemporary history), vol. 16/3. Munich: Deutsche Verlagsanstalt, 1974.

Walle, Heinrich, ed. *Aufstand des Gewissens: Militärischer Widerstand gegen Hitler und das NS-Regime: Katalog zur Wanderausstellung* (Revolt of conscience: Military resistance against Hitler and the Nazi regime: Catalog of the touring exhibition). 2nd rev. ed. Herford: E. S. Mittler, 1985.

Wedemeyer, Ruth von. *In des Teufels Gasthaus: Eine preußische Familie 1918– 1945* (In the inn of the devil: A Prussian family 1918–1945). Edited by Peter von Wedemeyer and Peter Zimmerling. Moers: Brendow, 1993.

Wendland, Heinz-Dietrich. "Staat und Reich" (State and Reich). In *Die Nation vor Gott: Zur Botschaft der Kirche im Dritten Reich* (The nation before God: The message of the church in the Third Reich), edited by Walter Künneth and Helmuth Schreiner, 176–204. Berlin: Wichern Verlag, 1934.

Wind, Renate. *Dietrich Bonhoeffer: A Spoke in the Wheel.* Translated by John Bowden. Grand Rapids, Mich.: Wm. B. Eerdmans, 1992. Originally published under the title *Dem Rad in die Speichen fallen.* Weinheim: Beltz Verlag, 1999.

Winterhager, Wilhelm Ernst, ed. *Der Kreisauer Kreis—Porträt einer Widerstandsgruppe: Begleitband zu einer Ausstellung der Stiftung Preußischer Kulturbesitz* (The Kreisau circle—portrait of a resistance group: Accompanying volume to an exhibition of the Foundation for Prussian Culture). Mainz: Verlag Hase & Koehler, 1985.

Witte, Johannes. "Sklaverei und Christentum" (Slavery and Christianity). In *Religion in Geschichte und Gegenwart* (Religion in history and the present), 2nd ed., 5:576–81. Tübingen: J. C. B. Mohr (Siebeck), 1913.

Wollenweber, Martha. *Theologie und Politik bei A. F. C. Vilmar* (Theology and politics in A. F. C. Vilmar). Forschungen zur Geschichte und Lehre des Protestantismus, vol. 1. Munich: Kaiser, 1930.

Yorck von Wartenburg, Paul Graf. "Das Bild des abendländischen Menschen" (The image of the Western human being). Manuscript. 1940.

Zimmermann, Wolf-Dieter, ed. *Begegnungen mit Dietrich Bonhoeffer: Ein Almanach.* 4th enlarged ed. Munich: Chr. Kaiser, 1969. Translated from the 1st German edition by Käthe Gregor Smith as *I Knew Dietrich Bonhoeffer,* edited by Wolf-Deiter Zimmerman and Ronald Gregor Smith (London: Collins; New York: Harper & Row, 1966).

Zipfel, Friedrich. *Kirchenkampf in Deutschland 1933–1945: Religionsverfolgung und Selbstbehauptung der Kirchen in der nationalsozialistischen Zeit* (The

Church Struggle in Germany 1933–1945: Religious persecution and the self-assertion of the churches during the National Socialist era). Veröffentlichungen der Historischen Kommission zu Berlin 11. Berlin: de Gruyter, 1965.

Zuckmayer, Carl, and Karl Barth. *Späte Freundschaft in Briefen.* Edited by Hinrich Stoevesandt. 2nd ed. Zurich: Theologischer Verlag, 1978 (c1977). Translated by Geoffrey Bromiley as *A Late Friendship: The Letters of Karl Barth and Carl Zuckmayer,* with a preface by Hinrich Stoevesandt (Grand Rapids, Mich.: Wm. B. Eerdmans, 1982).

INDEX OF NAMES

757

Beck, Ludwig (1880–1944): career military officer; during World War I, general staff officer; 1933–35, head of the General Army Office; 1935–38, chief of the Army General Staff; August 1938, resigned after the Sudeten crisis, dismissed as colonel-general; shortly thereafter began participating as a central figure in the military resistance against Hitler; was designated to be the head of state after Hitler's removal; July 20, 1944, forced to commit suicide after the aborted coup attempt—225, 297, 299, 322, 334, 335, 461, 653, 672, 676, 685, 700

Beckmann, Joachim (1901–86): 1928, pastor, Westphalian Church Women's Association, Soest; 1932, secretary, Protestant Men's Services, Westphalia; June 1933, founder of the Rhineland Pastors' Brotherhood; 1934, head of the theological office of the Confessing Church in the Rhineland; until 1945, member of the Rhineland, Prussian, and Reich councils of brethren; 1945, member of the Rhineland Church administration and lecturer at the seminary in Wuppertal; 1951, professor there; 1958–71, president of the Evangelical Church of the Rhineland—138, 154, 155, 404

Beckmann, Leopold (1886–1946): Confessing Church pastor at the Ponarth church in Königsberg; 1938, placed on leave by the consistory, after which time he held worship services in the Löbenichts community hall; 1942, head of the East Prussian Council of Brethren; 1945, remained in Königsberg after Germany's surrender; 1946, presumably murdered—57, 127, 131

Becks, Miss: school friend of Paula Bonhoeffer in Königsberg; 1940, Dietrich Bonhoeffer stayed with her briefly— 54, 60, 61

Beethoven, Ludwig van (1770–1827): German composer—18, 128, 150

Bell, George Kennedy Allen (1883–1958): 1914–24, residential chaplain with the archbishop of Canterbury, assigned particularly to international relations; 1925, coauthored the statement of the Stockholm Church Conference; 1929–57, bishop of Chichester; 1932, head of the British section and executive committee of the Ecumenical Council for Life and Work; 1933, first contact with Bonhoeffer; 1934, head of the Ecumenical Council for Life and Work; 1937, member of the House of Lords; 1942, met with Bonhoeffer and Hans Schönfeld in Sweden to learn about German resistance plans; struggled to gain support from the British and U.S. governments for the German resistance; 1948, chair of the central and executive committee of the World Council of Churches; 1954, honorary president of the World Council of Churches; married to Henrietta Millicant, née Livingstone— 10, 12, 13, 15, 17, 77, 125, 166, 167, 172, 173, 178, 193, 215–18, 223, 270, 271, 283, 285, 286, 289–307, 309–12, 318, 319, 324–27, 331–40, 342, 344, 345, 347–50, 353, 354, 357, 361, 362, 379–83, 398, 400, 449, 450, 462–69, 529, 530, 532, 646, 657–60, 662, 666, 667, 681, 684, 687–90, 692, 693, 702, 703

Bell, Henrietta Millicant Grace, née Livingstone: wife of George K. A. Bell—310

Ben Israel, Hedva: Israeli-born historian; specialist on World War II and nationalism—660

Bengel, Johann Albrecht (1687–1752): Württemberg theologian—552

Bentinck: see Cavendish Bentinck, Victor Frederick William

Biedermann, Alois Emanuel (1819–85): Swiss Reformed theologian; professor of systematic theology and dogmatics, Zurich—477

Biesental, Günter (1913–43): from Berlin-Charlottenburg; 1938–39, participated in the collective pastorate in Köslin; ordination and ministry in Fürstenwalde; November 22, 1941, wounded on the eastern front; 1943, killed in action—237

Bildt, Eva: daughter of the Berlin actor Paul Bildt; educated in the seminar of the Burckhardt House; engaged to Pastor Helmut Gollwitzer; 1945, committed suicide during the final battles in Berlin—135

Bildt, Paul (1885–1957): Berlin actor; member of the Confessing Church in Dahlem—135

Bismarck, Hans-Otto von (1919–40): son of Herbert von Bismarck of Lasbeck; killed in action in the campaign in France—44, 60

Bismarck, Herbert von (1884–1955): estate owner in Lasbeck, district of Regenwalde; grand-nephew of Reich chancellor Otto von Bismarck; husband of Maria, née von Kleist-Retzow; 1918–31, regional representative, Regenwalde district; 1930–33, member of the national parliament (representing the German National People's Party); end of 1932, state secretary in the Prussian Ministry of the Interior; 1945, cofounder and first speaker of the Association of Pomeranians—43, 44, 59, 60, 61, 158, 163, 647, 676

Bismarck, Jürgen Philipp Robert Karl Herbert von: son of Herbert von Bismarck; businessman—44, 59

Bismarck, Luitgarde von: granddaughter of Ruth von Kleist-Retzow and wife of resistance figure Fabian von Schlabrendorff—210

Bismarck, Maria von, née von Kleist-Retzow (1893–1979): wife of Herbert von Bismarck—351

Bismarck, Otto Edward Leopold von (1815–98): Prussian statesman; 1871–90, chancellor of the (second) German Empire—163, 364

Bismarck, Ruth-Alice von, née von Wedemeyer: daughter of Hans and Ruth von Wedemeyer, sister of Maria von Wedemeyer—21, 351, 366, 661

Bismarck, Spes von: see Pompe, Spes

Bitter, Wilhelm (1886–1964): owner of the Paulus publishing company, Recklinghausen; prior to 1933, member (Center Party) of the national Parliament; after 1933, reprimanded as a Catholic publisher, traveled as a secret agent for the Catholic bishops' conference; 1938, Johannes Neuhäusler distributed his brochure "How can I raise my child in the Christian faith?"; together with Dr. Josef Himmelreich, prepared a Catholic memorandum addressed to Hitler—146

Björkquist, Manfred (1884–1985): Swedish theologian and ecumenist; 1910, director of the adult evening school, Hampness; founder of the Young Church Movement in Sweden; 1917, director of the Sigtuna Foundation; 1942–54, bishop of Stockholm; from 1943, court chaplain—297, 298, 324, 383, 398, 401

Blau, Paul (1861–1944): 1911, general superintendent, Posen; after 1918, spiritual head of the (German-speaking) United Evangelical Church in Poland—293–95

Bormann, Martin (1900–1945): agriculturist; 1933, chief of staff in the office of the deputy to the "Führer"; 1941, head of the party chancellery; 1943, secretary to the Führer; 1944, appointed Reich minister; April 1945, disappeared during the final battles in Berlin—97, 267, 293, 294, 332, 664, 665, 683

Boveri, Margret (1900–1975): German journalist; author of works on the German resistance and the Germans' experience under Hitler—300

Boyens, Armin: German Protestant minister, church historian, and ecumenist—169–71, 173, 175, 215, 216, 225, 227, 228, 231, 232, 270, 278, 290, 291, 295, 296, 303, 405, 407, 467, 529, 656–60, 662, 729

Bracher, Dorothea Sabine Julie, née Schleicher: daughter of Rüdiger and Ursula Schleicher; May 3, 1951, married the historian Karl Dietrich Bracher—204, 342

Bracks, Heinz: 1940, student in the humanities, Königsberg; secret agent for the SD in Königsberg—63, 65, 67, 68

Brandenburg, Kurt: head physician, Virchow Hospital, Berlin—249

Brandenburg, Willi Max Hermann (1909–42): from Berlin; 1932–33, among the circle of students around Bonhoeffer; 1934, participated in the Fanø youth conference; 1936–37, participated in the fourth Finkenwalde session; 1938, ordained; ministry in Pätzig/Neudamm (Neumark); 1942, killed in action on the eastern front—324, 377

Brauchitsch, Walter von (1881–1948): career military officer; 1938–41, commander in chief of the army; 1940, general field marshal; December 1941, dismissed by Hitler—12, 321, 686

Braun, Hermann: 1933, pastor, Argenbruck (formerly Neu-Argeningken) near Tilsit; 1937, Confessing Church district pastor, represented Tilsit in the East Prussian Council of Brethren; June 18, 1940, Dietrich Bonhoeffer visited him—53

Braun, Werner: from 1939, pastor, Greater Tychow, Pomerania; member of the German Christians—157

Braune, Paul Gerhard (1887–1954): 1922, pastor and head of Hoffnungstal (later called the Lobetal Institutes); 1932, also vice president of the executive committee of the Inner Mission; 1938, author of a memorandum "The Plight of Non-Aryan Christians"; July 1940, author of a memorandum opposing the euthanasia measures; August–November 1940, imprisoned as a result; 1945, president of the Inner Mission in eastern Germany and member of the Berlin-Brandenburg church administration—647, 676

Brecht, Martin: German scholar of Luther—593

Brenner, Harro: legation officer of the first class in the office of the Reich foreign minister—462

Brieger, Ernst: Berlin physician; married Käthe, née Friedenthal; emigrated to England as a "non-Aryan"—231

Brilioth, Yngve (1891–1959): Swedish theologian and ecumenist; 1920, participated in the first Conference for Faith and Order; 1925, professor of practical theology and 1928, cathedral provost in Lund; 1937, bishop of Vasjö; 1950–58, archbishop of Uppsala; 1947–56, chair of Faith and Order; member of

Dehn, Günther Karl (1882–1970): until 1930, pastor in Berlin; 1931–33, professor of practical theology, Halle; 1933, dismissed as a socialist and pacifist ("Dehn affair"); 1933, assistant to the Berlin Council of Brethren and Confessing Church; 1936–41, lecturer at the seminary in Berlin; 1941, arrested and convicted in the collective trial against the examination board of the Old Prussian Union Council of Brethren; 1942–45, parish curate, Ravensburg; 1946–53, professor of practical theology, Bonn — 70, 154, 189, 192, 247, 346, 504, 505, 517, 525, 578, 678

Delbrück, Justus (1902–45): son of the historian Hans Delbrück; childhood friend of the Bonhoeffer children; after studying law, was employed in various governmental offices; from 1940, worked in the Canaris office and was part of the conspiracy with Oster, Dohnanyi, and Klaus Bonhoeffer; August 1944, arrested; April 1945, released but picked up by the Soviets two weeks later; October 1945, contracted diphtheria and died in an internment camp in Niederlausitz — 364, 684, 686

Delbrück, Max (1906–71): son of the historian Hans Delbrück; professor of biophysics; 1937, California Institute of Technology; 1940, Vanderbilt University; 1969, Nobel Prize for medicine — 165

Delekat, Friedrich (1892–1970): 1925–29, academic head of the Religious Pedagogical Institute, Berlin; 1929, professor for religious studies, technical college, Dresden; 1937, forced retirement; 1946–60, professor of systematic theology, philosophy, and pedagogy, Mainz — 363, 364, 390, 508–10, 516

Demant, Vigo Auguste (1893–1983): English Anglican canon and historian of the Anglican church — 506

Deutsch, Harold C.: U.S. historian of the German resistance — 121

Dibelius, Otto (1880–1967): German pastor and church leader; 1921, High Church official and member of the Consistory; 1925, general superintendent of the Old Prussian province of Mark Brandenburg (Kurmark); June 1933, placed on forced leave by German Christian church authorities; 1945–66, bishop of Berlin-Brandenburg; 1949–61, chair of the national council of the Evangelical Church of Germany — 9, 17, 69, 125, 363, 416, 419, 420, 450, 459, 463, 468, 577

Dickinson, Willoughby Hyett, Lord of Painswick (1859–1943): British parliamentarian and ecumenist; founder and first president of the World Alliance for Promoting International Friendship through the Churches — 398

Diedrich, Karlheinz: author of work on Belgian-German relations — 528

Diem, Hermann (1900–1975): German theologian; 1934–50, pastor, Ebersbach, and leader of the Württemberg Ecclesiastical-Theological Society, which had ties to the Confessing Church; 1950, teaching appointment; 1957, professor of church law and organization, Tübingen — 505

Diem, Liselotte: wife of Carl Diem; 1936, Carl Diem was the secretary-general of the preparation committee of the Olympic Games in Berlin and director of the International Olympic Institute — 87

Diest, Gerhart von (1909–41): brother of Maria von Kleist-Retzow; killed in action on the eastern front — 194

Francke, August Hermann (1663–1727): German pietist and educator—493

Franke, Martin: young theologian from Pomerania; 1941, killed in action on the eastern front; August 15, 1941, mentioned in the Finkenwalde newsletter—206

Freisler, Roland (1894–1945): lawyer and judge under the Nazi regime; 1932, Prussian member of regional Parliament (representing the NSDAP); 1934, state secretary in the Reich Ministry of Justice; 1942, president of the People's Court; February 3, 1945, killed during an air raid on Berlin—702

Freudenberg, Adolf (1894–1977): German diplomat and pastor; 1922–35, in the Foreign Ministry, ultimately as legation officer; 1933, dismissed because of his wife's Jewish ancestry; studied Protestant theology and was ordained by the Confessing Church in Berlin-Dahlem; 1939, emigrated to England, where he became secretary for refugee relief in the provisional World Council of Churches in London and Geneva; during the war, contacts with Bonhoeffer during the latter's visits to Switzerland; 1947, pastor in the refugee settlement Heilsberg/Bad Vilbel near Frankfurt am Main—143, 169, 170, 178, 215, 231, 232, 280, 657, 681, 683, 704

Frey, Arthur (1897–1955): head of the Evangelical Press Service in Switzerland and owner of the Zollikon publishing house near Zurich—276, 280

Freylinghausen, Johann Anastasius (1670–1739): German pietist and hymnist—617

Frick, Peter: professor of New Testament, University of Waterloo; translator for *DBWE* 15—29

Frick, Wilhelm (1877–1946): Nazi government official; 1933–43, Reich Interior Minister; 1943–45, Reich protector of Bohemia and Moravia; 1946, executed after the Nuremberg trials—678

Fridrichsen, Anton Johnson (1888–1953): Swedish theologian; 1928, professor of New Testament, Uppsala—290

Friedenthal, Charlotte (1892–1973): daughter of a Berlin bank director; trained as a social worker; 1935–36, acting director of the Evangelical Welfare Office, Berlin-Zehlendorf; from 1935, employed by the Provisional Church Administration; from October 1937, personal secretary to Berlin church superintendent Martin Albertz; from 1939, registered for emigration to the United States; September 4, 1942, left Germany for Switzerland as part of the "Operation 7" rescue; after the war, again active in church work in Berlin—14, 153, 231–34, 353, 409–11, 413, 414, 685, 690

Friedenthal, Ernst: brother of Charlotte Friedenthal—231

Fromm, Friedrich (1888–1945): career military officer; 1939–44, ultimately colonel-general and commander in chief of the reserve army; after July 20, 1944, arrested despite speaking out against the Stauffenberg group; executed after being convicted by the People's Court—457

Fuglsang-Damgaard, Hans (1890–1975): Danish theologian; 1934–60, bishop of Copenhagen and primate of the Danish church—398, 450

Gabriel, Walther (1887–1983): from 1923, pastor, St. Laurentius Church, Halle/Saale; 1933, member of the Pastors' Emergency League; 1934, chair of the district Council of Brethren; Inner Mission representative in the Confessing Church; 1941–43, in Dachau concentration camp; 1962, retired—141, 146, 149

Gaedertz, Alma: 1931, assistant lecturer (unpaid) in ophthalmology, university in Berlin—234

Galen, Clemens August Count von (1878–1946): German Catholic priest; 1906, priest, Berlin; 1919, head of the Berlin Apprentice Labor Association; 1929, priest, St. Lamberti Church, Münster; after 1933, bishop of Münster; became known for his pastoral letters and sermons against National Socialist ideology and outspoken opposition to the euthanasia measures; 1946, cardinal—9, 145, 245, 295

Gandhi, Mohandas Karamchand (Mahatma) (1869–1948): Indian statesman and philosopher—399

Garvie, Alfred Ernest (1861–1945): British pastor and church leader; 1903, professor of religious philosophy, London; 1920, head of the Congregational Union; 1924, president of the Free Church Federal Council—398

Gauger, Joachim: author of work on the German Church Struggle—575

Gaulle, Charles de (1890–1970): initially career military officer; 1940, brigadier general and commander of a tank division; after France's surrender, leader of the French resistance from London; 1945, minister president; 1958–69, state president—700

Gay, Cesare: Italian attorney and ecumenist; represented the Waldensians on the World Alliance executive committee; spring 1943, Dietrich Bonhoeffer mentions him in the "camouflage letter"—398

Gehre, Ludwig (1895–1945): lawyer; initially manager in the construction industry; 1939, drafted into military service in the Military Intelligence Office III; member of the inner circle of the Oster and Dohnanyi resistance group; January 1944, escaped capture; November 1944, arrested after a suicide attempt; April 9, 1945, executed in the Flossenbürg concentration camp—703

Gentile da Fabriano (Niccolo di Giovanni di Massio) (ca. 1375–1427): Italian painter—402

George, Heinrich (1893–1945): German stage and film actor—128

Georgii, Hans-Otto (1911–41): from Berlin; 1936, assistant at the castle church *(Schloßkirche),* Altlandsberg; 1937, Buckow; 1937–38, participated in the collective pastorate; June 26, 1941, killed in action on the eastern front—206

Georgii, Wolfgang (1913–44): from Berlin; 1937–38, participated in the collective pastorate; 1939, assistant pastor, Confessing congregations, Havelberg and Stöbritz, district of Calau; 1944, missing in action at the Narew River—206

Gerber, Hans: author of works on state philosophy and Luther—506

Gerbrandy, Pieter S.: professor; minister president of the Dutch exile government in London—291, 301

Gerhardt, Paul (1607–76): German theologian and hymnist—106, 157, 285, 619, 623, 631, 644

Germanos, Lukas Panteleimon (1872–1951): Orthodox archbishop based in London; president of the Orthodox section of Life and Work; member of the World Council of Churches—397, 450

Gerrens, Uwe: German pastor and theologian; author of publications on Karl Bonhoeffer and Dietrich Bonhoeffer in relation to the Reichstag fire, forced sterilization, and "euthanasia"—647

Gersdorff, Rudolf-Christoph Baron von (1905–80): Silesian career military officer, ultimately general-major; 1941, military intelligence officer with the general staff of the Center Army Group on the eastern front; member of Major General von Treskow's resistance group there; March 1943, volunteered to carry out an assassination attempt against Hitler; 1944, chief of the general staff of an army in the west—693

Gerstenmaier, Eugen (1906–86): 1936–44, official in Bishop Theodor Heckel's Church Foreign Office; 1939–40, special assignments in the information section of the Ministry of Foreign Affairs; 1942, became member of the Kreisau circle through contact with Helmut von Moltke; July 24, 1944, arrested and sentenced by the People's Court to seven years' imprisonment; April 14, 1945, liberated from the Bayreuth penitentiary; 1945–51, head of the relief organization of the Evangelical Church of Germany, Stuttgart; 1949–69, member of German Parliament (representing the CDU) in Bonn; 1954–69, president of the German Parliament—9, 290, 291, 296, 299, 306, 357, 660, 687

Giacometti, Zacharias (1893–1970): professor of international law, University of Zurich—345

Gisevius, Hans Bernd (1904–74): from 1933, government official in the Prussian Ministry of the Interior; from 1939, special officer in the Military Intelligence Office; 1941, vice-consul and local representative of the Military Intelligence Office, German consulate, Zurich; on July 20, 1944, in Berlin; January 1945, fled to Switzerland; after the war, publicist—117, 146, 147, 286, 287, 353, 408, 431, 447, 653, 678, 704

Glenthøj, Jørgen Johannes (1922–96): Danish theologian; during World War II, member of the Danish resistance; studied theology after the war; 1949, ordination and assistant pastor at the Esajaskirke, Copenhagen; 1951, pastor, Hassing-Villerslev; 1964, Borum-Lynbby; 1966–73, taught at the theological seminary, Xrhus, 1974–82, on the congregational faculty, 1983–84, on the department of theology there; 1980–86, member, executive committee, theological commission of the World Evangelical Fellowship; 1990, retired; author of numerous works on church history, the Church Struggle, and Dietrich Bonhoeffer—2, 28, 243, 278, 281, 286, 469, 517, 528, 645, 659, 667

Godsey, John D.: U.S. professor of systematic theology; author of works on Bonhoeffer, including the first published monograph on Bonhoeffer's theology; coeditor of *DBWE* 4—17, 20

Goebbels, Joseph (1897–1945): National Socialist politician and publicist; 1933–45, Reich Minister of Public Information and Propaganda; 1945, committed suicide—177, 307, 320, 348, 381, 693

Goerdeler, Carl Friedrich (1884–1945): lawyer and government official; 1920–30, vice-mayor of Königsberg; 1930–37, mayor of Leipzig; 1931–32 and 1934–35, Reich Commissar of Price Controls; spring 1937, resigned in protest over the removal of the Mendelssohn-Bartholdy monument in Leipzig; 1937–39, foreign trips for the Krupp and Bosch companies; from 1939, leading figure,

worked in the administration of the secretariat of the Pomeranian provincial Council of Brethren, Stettin—473, 476

Guillon, Charles François (1883–1965): French Reformed pastor and ecumenist; from 1921, in the French border town Le Chambon-sur-Lignon; from 1931, also mayor there; from 1927, reporting member in the central office of the YMCA in Geneva; in close contact with the Swiss refugee aid organization and the French Cimade (a resistance organization that also helped prisoners); March and September 1941, took part in discussions with Dietrich Bonhoeffer in Geneva—169, 215, 681

Günther: government counselor and SS major in the Reich Central Security Office; member of the "July 20 special commission"—463

Gürtler, Paul: author of study on the German Church Struggle—242, 294, 295

Gürtner, Franz (1881–1941): lawyer; 1922, Bavarian Minister of Justice; member of the German National People's Party and representative of the (German National) Bavarian Middle Party; 1932–41, Reich Minster of Justice—101, 103, 111, 132, 135, 137, 140, 163, 415, 424, 653, 679, 680

Gustav, Adolf, crown prince of Sweden (1882–1973): married Louise née Mount-batten (1889–1965); from 1950, King Gustav VI Adolf of Sweden—332

Guttenberg, Baron Karl Ludwig von and zu (1902–45): estate owner, Salzburg near Neustadt/Saale; editor of the White Papers *(Weiße Blätter);* September 1939, colleague of Hans von Dohnanyi in the section ZB of the Military Intelligence Office; 1943, transferred for his own protection to Agram, on the staff of General Glaise von Horstenau, the general in charge of Croatia; after July 20, 1944, arrested; April 23/24, 1945, shot to death by the SS—684, 686, 692

Haase, Norbert: German military historian—435

Haeften, Hans-Bernd von (1905–44): confirmed with Bonhoeffer; from 1933, member of the Confessing Church; 1933, joined the Foreign Ministry; embassy officer, Copenhagen, Vienna, and Bucharest; 1940, reporting legation officer in the cultural section of the Foreign Ministry, Berlin; from 1941, active member of the Kreisau circle; after July 20, 1944, arrested; August 15, 1944, executed in Plötzensee—299, 687, 699

Haeften, Werner von (1908–44): brother of Hans-Bernd von Haeften; corporate attorney with a Hamburg bank; stationed on the eastern front as a first lieutenant; after receiving a serious wound, became adjutant for Count von Stauffenberg with the commander of the reserve army; July 20, 1944, shot to death with Stauffenberg in the courtyard on Bendlerstraße—700

Halder, Franz (1884–1972): career military officer; 1940, general; 1938–42, chief of the general staff in the Army High Command; 1942, dismissed by Hitler; after July 20, 1944, imprisoned in a concentration camp; 1945, liberated from Dachau concentration camp—685

Halem, Nikolaus von (1905–44): businessman; 1938, left legal service and entered business; February 1942, arrested on suspicion of conspiratorial contacts; October 9, 1944, executed—448

Halifax, Lord Edward (1881–1959): British statesman; 1938–40, foreign minister; ambassador to the United States—292

Hallesby, Ole (1879–1961): member of Norwegian confessional movement—383

Hammelsbeck, Oskar (1899–1975): religious educator and theologian; 1927, director of the adult education center, Saarbrücken; 1937, dismissed for political reasons; 1937, head of the catechetical seminar of the Confessing Church, Berlin, and consultant on religious education in the Council of the Old Prussian Confessing Church; 1942–43, worked with Dietrich Bonhoeffer on the "*primus usus legis*" committee of the Old Prussian Council of Brethren; 1944, ordination and pastor, Falkenhagen (Lippe); 1946–59, professor and rector of the Pedagogical Academy, Wuppertal; also lecturer at the Wuppertal seminary; chair of the Association for Education and Instruction in the Council of the Evangelical Church of Germany; advocate of the unity of a person's lifelong "religious instruction"—9, 123, 153, 261, 359, 389, 692

Hammerstein-Equord, Baron Kurt von (1878–1943): career military officer; general; 1930–34, chief of the army command staff; 1939, commander in chief of the army section A in the West; participated in plans for a military coup—297, 322, 334, 335

Hancock, Sir Patrick Francis (1914–74): British diplomat; from January 1942, second secretary in the Central Department of the British Foreign Office—325

Harder, Günther Heinrich Reinhold (1902–72): pastor, Fehrbellin; 1933, cofounder of the Pastors' Emergency League; 1936–72, lecturer and professor of New Testament at the Confessing seminary, Berlin; 1941, convicted in collective trial against the examination board of the Old Prussian Union Council of Brethren; 1942–43, together with Dietrich Bonhoeffer on the "*primus usus legis*" committee of the Old Prussian Council of Brethren—189, 192

Harhausen, Christoph Rudolf Constantin (1909–41): 1935, vicar, Dahme/Mark; 1935–36, participated in the second Finkenwalde session; afterward, Confessing Church pastor, Guben; August 26, 1941, killed in action on the eastern front—237

Häring, Theodor (1848–1928): 1895, professor of systematic theology in Tübingen—507

Harnack, Adolf von (1851–1930): after 1888, professor of church history, Berlin; 1911, cofounder and first president of the Kaiser Wilhelm Society for the Advancement of the Sciences; neighbor and friend of the Bonhoeffer family; influenced Dietrich Bonhoeffer's theological development—116, 347, 495, 542, 545

Harnack, Wolf Alexander Oskar Ernst von (1888–1945): lawyer; son of Adolf von Harnack; 1919, joined the Social Democratic Party; government president of Merseburg; 1933, dismissed; worked as a textile representative; ultimately worked in registration of the graves of famous persons in Berlin cemeteries; contacts with Beck, Goerdeler, Leber, and Klaus Bonhoeffer; after July 20, 1944, arrested; March 5, 1945, executed—116, 123, 124, 135

Harrison, Geoffrey Wedgwood (1908–90): private secretary in Parliament; undersecretary of state, British Foreign Office—302, 323, 326, 335, 337–40, 687

Hartenstein, Karl (1894–1952): Württemberg theologian; 1926, director, Basel Mission Society; 1941, seminary preacher and prelate, Stuttgart; 1948, member, Council of the Evangelical Church of Germany—290

Hartl, Albert: 1933, Catholic religious educator; 1934, as a relative of Himmler, received research position in the central SS headquarters; SS major and leader of the Group IV B (ideological and racial opponents), Reich Central Security Office; 1941–42, head of an SD strike force, Kiev; after 1945, interned in the Hammelburg prison camp—62

Hartmann, Nicolai (1882–1950): German philosopher and professor in Berlin and Göttingen—677

Hartmann, Paul (1889–1977): German stage and film actor—163

Hase, Benedikt Karl August von (Uncle Bubi) (1890–1979): son of Karl Alfred and Klara von Hase; painter, artisan, etcher; youngest brother of Paula Bonhoeffer; 1914–19, French prisoner of war; afterward, required psychiatric care and was supported financially by his siblings—116

Hase, Elisabeth von (1872–1945): Bonhoeffer's aunt; daughter of Karl Alfred and Klara von Hase; missing after the February 1941 bombing of Dresden—276

Hase, Hans Christoph von: Bonhoeffer's cousin; son of Hans and Ada von Hase; from 1930, Dietrich Bonhoeffer's successor as academic assistant to Wilhelm Lütgert; 1933–34, fellowship, Union Theological Seminary, New York; 1934–45, military chaplain; postwar, parish pastor; 1957, director, central office of the Diaconical Welfare and Social Agency of the Evangelical Church of Germany, Stuttgart—140, 375

Hase, Karl August von (1800–1890): professor of church history, Jena; father of Karl Alfred von Hase—75, 85

Hase, Margarete (Deta) von, née von Funck (1898–1968): wife of major general Paul von Hase—701

Hase, Paul (Karl Paul Immanuel) von (1885–1944): career military officer; cousin of Paula Bonhoeffer; 1940, major general and military commander of Berlin; 1944, general; July 20, 1944, participated in the attempted coup; August 8, 1944, executed in Plötzensee—75, 240, 698, 700

Haser, Annie: see Oster, Annie

Häsler, Alfred A.: Swiss Protestant official who worked with refugees—231

Hassell, Ulrich von (1881–1944): government official and diplomat; 1932, German ambassador, Rome; 1938, ambassador for special duty; with Goerdeler, leading participant in the civilian resistance; July 29, 1944, arrested; September 8, 1944, executed—299, 302, 305, 461, 681, 683, 686, 692

Hausamann, Hans: officer in the news service of the Swiss army; September 1940, initiated the founding of the "national resistance action"—280

Hausmann, Manfred (1898–1986): writer—315

Hecht, Siegfried: 1931, pastor, Dorschhymmen (East Prussia); member of the Thuringian German Christians—57

Heckel, Theodor (1894–1967): pastor and church official; 1928, high consistory officer, German Evangelical Church Federation office, Berlin; 1934–45, bishop and director of the Church Foreign Office of the German Evangelical Church,

Himmelreich, Josef: press adviser for the Reich governor of Bavaria, Munich; made multiple attempts to influence Catholic circles; editor of the journal *Der Rufer* (The calling voice); after the war, lived by the Lake of Thun in Switzerland—146

Himmler, Heinrich (1900–1945): agriculturist and National Socialist politician; 1929–45, *Reichsführer* of the SS; 1933, head of the political police in Bavaria and the other German states; 1935, chief of the German police; 1943, Reich Interior Minister; 1944–45, commander of the reserve army; May 23, 1945, committed suicide—4, 62, 66, 160, 244, 267, 293, 307, 309, 320, 323, 340, 347, 348, 358, 700, 701, 703

Hinsley, Arthur (1865–1943): Catholic archbishop of Westminster; cardinal—337

Hippolytus (ca. 170–236): ecclesiastical writer—567, 568

Hirsch, Emanuel (1888–1972): German Protestant theologian and professor of church history and systematic theology; National Socialist sympathizer, supporting member of the SS, and preeminent theological adviser to the German Christians—506, 518

Hitler, Adolf (1889–1945): National Socialist politician; 1933–45, Reich chancellor; 1938, became commander in chief of the armed forces; 1941, also commander in chief of the army; April 30, 1945, committed suicide in Berlin— 1–3, 5, 6, 8–10, 12–14, 16, 17, 24, 27, 61, 69, 77, 84, 111, 113, 121, 171, 196, 204, 215, 216, 241, 243, 259, 269, 273, 274, 278, 280, 286, 289, 291–94, 296– 302, 304, 307, 309, 318, 320–23, 327, 329, 332, 333, 336, 340, 347, 348, 380–82, 385, 388, 398, 410, 435, 452, 502, 505–7, 517, 518, 529, 530, 533, 535, 536, 538, 539, 579, 648, 659, 662, 663, 665, 666, 671, 684, 686, 697, 700, 703, 704

Hitzer, Arnold (1902–77): Confessing Church pastor; 1930–40, Rösnitz, district of Leobschütz/Silesia; 1937, expelled from Silesia; 1937–38, in prison; 1940, pastor, Rehhof/West Prussia; 1941–42, wrote his "Notes concerning Baptism"; December 1941, drafted into military service in Marienwerder; 1944–48, British prisoner of war; from 1949, head of the free *Christengemeinde* (anthroposophical congregation), Kiel; 1960–77, Munich—551–54, 556–58, 561–67, 569, 570, 668, 669

Hoare, Sir Samuel (1880–1959): British statesman; 1938–40, Minister of Aviation; ambassador in Madrid—332

Höck, Michael: Catholic pastor and publicist; editor in chief of the Munich Catholic church newspaper; after the newspaper was banned, he was a pastor at St. Benno in Munich; May 23, 1941, arrested; initially sent to the Sachsenhausen concentration camp, from July 1941, in Dachau with Neuhäusler and Niemöller; April 5, 1945, liberated; after the war, prelate and regent at the priests' seminary in Freising, Upper Bavaria—146, 224, 271

Hoffmann, Peter: German-born historian, professor of history (emeritus), McGill University, expert on the German resistance—298, 659, 662, 664

Hofmann, Klaus: director, Johann-Sebastian-Bach-Institut, Göttingen—618

Hofmeister: military prosecutor with the military high court—428

Hofmeister, Alexander Corbinian (1891–1966): abbot of the Benedictine monastery, Metten, Lower Bavaria; already an acquaintance of Josef Müller before the war; traveled with Müller to various neighboring countries and to Rome on church business; during the war, Müller introduced him to the Military Intelligence Office; April 1943, arrested and sent to the Dachau concentration camp; April 1945, liberated—120, 146, 427, 652

Hohenlohe-Langenburg, Prince Max Egon zu (1897–1969): Sudeten German noble; 1938, involved in contacts between Konrad Henlein and Lord Runciman; secret agent of the Military Intelligence Office, also close to the SS leadership and to the Foreign Ministry—323, 332, 333

Höhne, Heinz: biographer of Canaris—293, 395, 419, 435, 441, 664

Holl, Karl (1866–1926): German Protestant theologian, professor of church history, and Luther scholar—148, 504, 509

Hollaz (Hollatz), David (1648–1713): Lutheran dogmatician and pastor—476, 480

Holstein, Horst (1894–1945): Berlin lawyer and notary; had a law office in Berlin-Kohlhasenbrück; church elder, Trinity Church, Berlin; delegate to several Confessing Church synods; 1936, member of the constitutional committee of the Provisional Church Administration; defense attorney for Confessing Church members at several civil and criminal trials—124

Holsten, Walter (1908–82): 1932, pastor, Hanover regional church; worked with the Gossner Mission Society, Berlin; 1947, professor of religious studies and mission studies, Mainz—259, 260

Hübener, Otto: businessman; co-owner of the insurance firm Jauch & Hübener in Hamburg; during the war, had special contact with Colonel Oster and Hans von Dohnanyi; his loan to Dohnanyi for the construction of Dohnanyi's house in Sacrow was investigated by the military high court—448, 449

Huber, Wolfgang: German theologian and Bonhoeffer scholar; after 1990, chair of the editorial board of the *Dietrich Bonhoeffer Werke;* after 1994, bishop of Berlin-Brandenburg; after 2003, chair of the national Council of the Evangelical Church of Germany—546

Huch, Ricarda (1864–1947): German writer and literary scholar—104

Hülst, Friedrich (Frieder) von (1922–43): brother of Marie Luise von Hülst; September 1943, killed in action; September 25, 1943, Maria von Wedemeyer describes the memorial service in a letter—695

Hülst, Marie-Luise von (1921–84): daughter of the estate owner Hülst in Rohrbeck (Neumark); acquaintance of the Wedemeyer family in Pätzig; 1941, lived with Ruth von Kleist-Retzow in Stettin; after the war, lived in Essen, married name Schlemmer—235

Hume, Theodore: Congregational pastor from the United States; sent to Europe to work for the World Council of Churches; autumn 1944, killed when his plane was shot down by the German Luftwaffe on its flight from London to Stockholm—15, 449, 450

Hundt, Anton Adolf: career military officer; 1940–42, major and head of the Military Intelligence Office VII in Munich; 1943, colonel—109, 400, 430

Huppenkothen, Walter: governmental attorney; 1933, joined the SS, ultimately attaining the rank of unit leader; 1944, director; group leader, section IV E in the Reich Central Security Office; after the reorganization, sectional leader in section IV A 3; leading member of the "July 20 special commission"; from February 12, 1945, deputy leader of Group IV A; initiated the summary courts in the concentration camps Sachsenhausen (April 6, 1945) and Flossenbürg (April 8, 1945)—23, 701, 703

Hymmen, Johannes (1878–1951): 1926, church official, Münster; 1932, senior church official on the Evangelical Central Council, Münster; 1940–45, member of the Confidential Spiritual Council of the German Evangelical Church; vice president of the Evangelical High Church Council; 1946, retired—94, 123, 226, 259

Ibsen, Henrik (1828–1906): Norwegian poet and dramatist—105

Ickradt (Ickrath in 1/229 and 1/234), Heinrich Wilhelm (1897–1954): businessman; secretary in the Portuguese consulate, Munich; captain in the reserves; assigned to the Munich Military Intelligence Office VII as head of the office I/Aviation; acquainted with Wilhelm Schmidhuber; 1942, implicated and arrested with Schmidhuber in the *Depositenkasse* case (Gestapo file name for the currency violations that led to the arrest and interrogation of Hans von Dohnanyi, Dietrich Bonhoeffer, and others)—118, 430, 455, 688, 698

Ihde, Wilhelm: publicist; 1937, secretary, Reich Chamber of Literature; SS lieutenant—181, 182, 190

Irenaei: from 1919, Orthodox bishop of Novi Sad, Yugoslavia; secretary of the Yugoslavian branch of the World Alliance for Promoting International Friendship through the Churches; spring 1943, mentioned in Dietrich Bonhoeffer's "camouflage letter" as the "most influential and popular church leader there"—397, 398

Irenaeus of Lyon (ca. 125–202): Greek prelate and bishop of Lyon; known for his writings against Gnosticism—567

Iwand, Hans-Joachim (1899–1960): 1935–37, director of the preachers' seminary of the Confessing Church of the Old Prussian Union, Blöstau, East Prussia; 1937, after this seminary was closed, pastor in Dortmund; 1945, professor of systematic theology, Göttingen; 1952, Bonn—55, 62

Jackson, Eleanor M.: historian of the ecumenical movement—172, 216

Jacobi, Gerhard (1891–1971): 1930–54, pastor, Kaiser Wilhelm Memorial Church, Berlin; 1934–39, head of the Confessing Synod, Berlin; 1934, member of the Old Prussian Union and the Reich Council of Brethren; repeatedly imprisoned; 1941, acquitted in the collective trial against the examination board of the Old Prussian Union Council of Brethren; 1946, superintendent, Berlin (West) Sprengel I; 1954–67, bishop of Oldenburg—232

Jacobsen, Inge (1915–42): daughter of a "non-Aryan" Berlin physician; business training; employed by the Kaiser Wilhelm Memorial Church; 1938, secretary in the "Grüber office"; 1941, unable to emigrate to the United States, although she had an affidavit; eventually died in a concentration camp—232, 685

Jäger, August (1887–1949): state commissioner for all Protestant Prussian regional churches; April–October 1934, member and legal administrator of the Clerical Ministry (Geistliches Ministerium) for the Reich Church government;

Kölln-Land; July 18, 1943, as a senior officer cadet, killed in action near Orel—685

Klaveness, Frederik: Norwegian pastor; 1898, hospital chaplain, Bergen; until 1936, also senior pastor there; spring 1943, mentioned by Dietrich Bonhoeffer in the "camouflage letter"—398

Kleist, Dieter (Dennis) von (1893–1971): career military officer (ultimately colonel) and estate owner in Wendisch Tychow (Pomerania); 1933, commander of the military district Stolp, also garrison senior officer; March 1945, dispatched as commandant to the defense of Stolp—418

Kleist-Retzow, Hans-Friedrich von (1923–41): son of Hans Jürgen and Maria von Kleist; April 1938, confirmed by Dietrich Bonhoeffer in Kieckow; July 1941, killed in action as senior officer cadet on the eastern front—110, 204, 206, 207, 210, 617, 619, 621–24, 673, 683

Kleist-Retzow, Hans Jürgen von (1887–1969): estate owner in Kieckow/Pomerania; son of Ruth von Kleist-Retzow; husband of Maria, née von Diest; Dietrich Bonhoeffer often stayed at his home; after July 20, 1944, arrested; 1945, taken to the Soviet Union as prisoner of war; after return to Germany, secretary, Association of Evangelical Congregations in Pomerania in Lippstadt; from 1954, in Bremen-Kattenesch, where he was the client for whom the newly founded Thomas community was built—78, 210, 246, 248, 351, 390, 702

Kleist-Retzow, Jürgen Christoph von (1921–41): son of Hans Jürgen von Kleist; August 5, 1941, killed in action as a lieutenant in a rifle regiment on the eastern front—204, 207, 210, 683

Kleist-Retzow, Konstantin von: son of Hans Jürgen and Maria von Kleist-Retzow; 1936, confirmed by Martin Niemöller; after military service and being a prisoner of war, studied theology; 1951, missionary, South Africa; 1965, pastor, Kirchweye near Bremen; 1974, Hämelchenburg—210, 249, 390

Kleist-Retzow, Maria von (Mieze), née von Diest (1893–1965): wife of the estate owner Hans-Jürgen von Kleist-Retzow—204

Kleist-Retzow, Ruth von, née Countess von Zedlitz-Trützschler (1867–1945): grandmother of Maria von Wedemeyer; married Jürgen von Kleist; after 1897, following her husband's death, she owned the estate of Klein-Krössin near Kieckow; from 1935, attended the Confessing Church services in Finkenwalde; supporter of Dietrich Bonhoeffer—18, 19, 36, 54, 58–61, 68, 110, 133, 135, 137, 142, 149, 152, 157, 158, 189, 193, 204, 207, 209, 210, 234, 235, 246–48, 327, 329, 351, 360, 361, 370, 376, 384, 385, 389, 392, 394, 617, 647, 678, 686, 690, 693

Klepper, Jochen (1903–42): German poet and author, representative of the Christian historical novel, author of spiritual songs; took his own life along with his Jewish wife and her daughter—107, 135, 181, 692

Kloß, Hans: Viennese businessman; initially employed by the Austrian Aviation-AG; from 1933, worked in management of German Lufthansa; had professional as well as conspiratorial contact with Klaus Bonhoeffer; October 7, 1944, arrested; after February 2, 1945, following his trial before the People's Court, transferred to the Brandenburg prison—460, 461, 666

Kluge, Hans Günther von (1882–1944): career military officer; 1941, general field marshal, leader of the Army Group Center in Russia; 1944, commander in chief in the West; after July 20, 1944, deposed by Hitler; August 19, 1944, committed suicide—298, 322

Kluge, Ulrich: author of work on the Freiburg circle—364, 390

Klugkist-Hesse, Hermann: Confessing Church pastor of the Reformed church in Elberfeld; part of the leadership of the Coetus Reformed Preachers in the Rhineland—104

Kluxen, Wolfgang: philosopher, author of works on Thomas Aquinas—548

Knak, Siegfried (1875–1955): 1921–49, director, Berlin Mission Society; 1933, deputy head of the German Missionary Council; from 1950, professor of mission studies at the seminary, Berlin and at the University of Halle—69

Knight, Eric (1897–1943): British writer—282

Knorr, August (1900–1958): physician; 1932–45, head of the internal section of the Deaconess Hospital in Köslin, Pomerania; extremely active there on behalf of the Confessing Church; 1947, head of the Evangelical Academy, Tutzing, Upper Bavaria; 1950, director of the Palmenwald spa, Freudenstadt—54, 677

Knutson, David (1937–2004): professor of religion, Pacific Lutheran University—30

Koch, Annemarie: wife of the lawyer Hans Koch—87, 90, 118

Koch, Hans (1893–1945): lawyer; 1927, attorney-at-law; 1933, notary, Berlin; member of the Confessing Church; 1938, defense attorney, with Horst Holstein and W. Hahn, in the Martin Niemöller trial; because he also had Jewish clients, temporarily held in a concentration camp; conspiratorial contact with Canaris, Oster, and Dohnanyi; in the event of a successful coup, Goerdeler had designated him as head of the German Supreme Court; January 21, 1945, arrested; April 24, 1945, executed—90, 118, 132, 135, 137, 682

Koch, Ingeborg (Inge) (1914–76): from Merseburg; Confessing Church theological student in the church province of Saxony; married to Confessing pastor Hans Zippel; 1939–40, ministry, Merseburg; after Zippel was drafted into the military, she led the brotherhood of assistant pastors and vicars of the province of Saxony; 1943, Zippel was killed in action; after the war, married name Anz—127, 129, 163

Koch, Karl (1876–1951): 1904, pastor, Westphalia; 1934–43, president of the Old Prussian and Confessing Synods of the German Evangelical Church; 1945–49, president of the Westphalian regional church—463

Koch, Laurentius: author of works on Ettal—86, 104, 115

Koch, Werner (1910–94): from Wiesbaden; 1935–36, participated in the second Finkenwalde session; 1936, assistant pastor, Barmen; November 1936, arrested for having forwarded to foreign recipients the memorandum of the provisional church administration to Hitler; 1937–38, in Sachsenhausen concentration camp; 1939, drafted into military service as a translator; 1947, pastor, Berlin; 1952, Espelkamp; 1958, Netphen/Sieg; 1969, retired—205, 385

Koechlin, Alphons (1885–1965): Swiss theologian and ecumenist; 1926, vice president of the World Alliance of the YMCA; 1933, president of the Basel Church

wounded; 1937, forbidden to preach and speak publicly; 1937–38, after trial and conviction, inmate in Stadelheim and Sachsenhausen; 1940–45, interned in the Ettal monastery; 1987, beatified—652, 680

Meerscheidt-Hüllesem, Eberhard Sigismund Wolfgang Baron von (1870–1943): estate owner in Kuggen near Königsberg/East Prussia; retired major; royal Prussian chamberlain; member of the synodal committee of the East Prussian Confessing Church; put the neighboring estate house Blöstau at the disposal of the East Prussian Council of Brethren for use as a preachers' seminary; July 1940, hosted a student retreat led by Pastor Koschorke and Dietrich Bonhoeffer—67

Meier, Kurt: German historian of the churches during the Nazi era, particularly the German Christians—242, 304, 577

Meinecke, Friedrich (1862–1954): German historian; 1914–28, professor in Berlin; 1947, first rector of the Free University in Berlin-Dahlem—509

Meiser, Hans (1881–1956): from Nuremberg; 1928, high church official, Munich; 1933–55, first bishop of Bavaria; 1934, member of the Reich Council of Brethren and, in 1936, of the Lutheran Council, becoming its chair in 1938; 1949–55, senior bishop of the United Evangelical Lutheran Church of Germany; 1945–54, member of the council of the Evangelical Church of Germany, of the executive committee of the Lutheran World Federation, and of the executive committee of the World Council of Churches—69, 89, 99, 100, 140, 177, 304, 679

Melzel, Karl-Heinrich: author of work on the Spiritual Confidential Council of the Confessing Church—576

Melzer, Paul (1892–1970): after 1930, pastor in Schloßbach (formerly Pillupönen), Ebenrode (formerly Stallupönen) district, East Prussia; June 17–18, 1940, visited by Bonhoeffer—53

Mensing, Karl (1876–1953): lawyer in Wuppertal-Elberfeld; 1934, member of the council of the Rhineland Confessing Synod; 1936, member of a constitutional committee of the Provisional Church Administration; 1945, Rhineland delegate to the church conference in Treysa; member of the legal committee of the General Synod of the Evangelical Church of Germany established there—362, 364

Mertz von Quirnheim, Albrecht Ritter (1905–44): career military officer; acquainted with Count von Stauffenberg from their training years together at the War Academy; ultimately colonel on the general staff and chief of staff, General Army Office; July 20, 1944, participated in the coup attempt; shot to death on the same day, as was Stauffenberg, in the Bendlerstraße headquarters—700

Metzger, Paulus (formerly Max Josef) (1887–1944): Catholic priest from the Black Forest; 1917, cofounder and head of the Peace Alliance of German Catholics; 1921, first German at the International Peace Congress in Paris; 1938, founder of the Una Sancta movement; June 29, 1943, arrested; April 17, 1944, executed in Brandenburg—84, 146

Meyer, Alice—280

Müller, Christine Ruth: German theologian, scholar of Bonhoeffer's attitudes toward the Jews—362, 647

Müller, Friedrich (Fritz) (sometimes referred to as Müller-Dahlem) (1889–1942): from 1933, pastor, Berlin-Dahlem; cofounder of the Pastors' Emergency League; member of the council of the Evangelical Church of the Old Prussian Union, of the Reich Council of Brethren, and, from 1936, chair of the second Provisional Church Administration of the Confessing Church; 1939, dismissed from office; military service; September 20, 1942, killed in action at Leningrad—305, 578, 580

Müller, Josef (nickname Ochsensepp) (1898–1979): Catholic attorney in Munich; during the 1930s, active as legal adviser and attorney for Catholic institutions; in this capacity, became acquainted with later partners in the resistance such as Prelate Neuhäusler, the abbots of Ettal and Metten, and with various persons in the Vatican; 1939, reserve first lieutenant in the Military Intelligence Office VII in Munich; from October 1939, visited the Vatican several times with Bonhoeffer to extend resistance peace feelers to the British government; from 1940, maintained contacts on behalf of the resistance with the Vatican and the Allies; April 5, 1943, arrested; April 1945, liberated by U.S. forces; after the war, cofounder of the Bavarian Christian Social Union (CSU) political party; 1947–52, deputy Bavarian minister president and minister of justice—14, 80, 81, 109, 120, 121, 146, 155, 211, 376, 392, 395, 402, 403, 405, 406, 411, 412, 419, 434, 447, 648, 650–53, 658, 659, 667, 683, 693, 698, 701

Müller, Ludwig (1863–1945): German pastor; from 1914, military chaplain; 1926, military district chaplain, Königsberg; 1931, joined NSDAP; 1932, leader of the German Christians in East Prussia; 1933, appointed by Hitler as adviser on church issues; 1934, installed as Reich bishop; 1935, authority withdrawn by the Reich Church Committee; July 1945, committed suicide—463, 575

Müller, Major: major in the general staff of the military commander in Norway; mentioned in a letter from Helmuth von Moltke to Freya von Moltke—269

Murakami, Hiroshi—639

Murr, Wilhelm (1888–1945): businessman and National Socialist politician; 1928, regional Nazi party leader; 1933, Reich governor of Württemberg; 1939, Reich defense commissar for military district V (Stuttgart); 1945, committed suicide—295

Mussolini, Benito (1883–1945): Italian head of government and leader *(Duce)* of the Fascist Party; 1945, shot to death by partisans at Lake Garda—403, 695

Naaman: biblical character—639

Naumann, Friedrich (1860–1919): German pastor, theologian, and politician; representative of modern social liberalism advocating Christian responsibility and social justice—205, 541, 542

Nebe, Arthur (1894–1945): government lawyer; 1933, criminal and governmental adviser, Berlin police headquarters; 1937, Reich director of the criminal investigation department; 1940, general major of the police and SS lieutenant general; at the same time, in contact with Canaris, Oster, and Gisevius; January 16, 1945, arrested for his resistance contacts; March 21, 1945, executed—356, 391, 395, 682

Neuhäusler, Johannes (1888–1971): Catholic priest; 1932, appointed cathedral capitulary by Cardinal Faulhaber; shortly thereafter, as prelate, appointed to be Faulhaber's political adviser; had various secret contacts in resistance, including with Dr. Josef Müller and the Vatican; February 4, 1941, arrested; May 24, 1941, taken to Sachsenhausen concentration camp; July 12, 1941, to Dachau; April 24, 1945, released; 1947, suffragan bishop; 1955, cathedral provost of Munich—81, 104, 121, 122, 146, 179, 224, 271, 291, 652, 680

Neurath, Constantin Baron von (1873–1956): German statesman; 1932–38, Reich foreign minister; 1939–43, Reich protector of Bohemia and Moravia; 1946, sentenced at the end of the Nuremberg trials to fifteen years in prison; 1954, released from prison—338

Nicolai, Philipp (1566–1608): German theologian and hymnist—238

Nicolaus: young theologian from the Rhineland; August 15, 1941, announcement of his death at the front in the Finkenwalde newsletter—206

Niebuhr, Reinhold (1892–1971): U.S. theologian and social ethicist; 1930–31, one of Bonhoeffer's professors at Union Theological Seminary, New York—1, 168–70, 202, 220, 397, 506

Niemöller, Else, née Bremer: wife of Martin Niemöller—95, 102, 104, 112, 119, 125, 145, 224, 285, 305

Niemöller, Martin (1892–1984): World War I naval officer and submarine captain; 1919–24, studied theology, though also member of the Freikorps (a paramilitary group of World War I veterans); after 1931, pastor, Berlin-Dahlem; May 1933, cofounder of the Young Reformation movement; September 1933, cofounder of the Pastors' Emergency League; 1937, arrested; 1938, acquitted, but taken to the Sachsenhausen concentration camp as "Hitler's personal prisoner," then to Dachau (until 1945); 1945, member of the advisory council of the Evangelical Church of Germany and head of the Church Foreign Office; 1947–64, president of the Protestant Church in Hesse-Nassau—63, 95, 137, 145, 146, 173, 176, 177, 193, 224, 231, 234, 245, 271, 304, 353, 354, 423, 437, 450, 463, 578, 579, 582, 653

Niemöller, Wilhelm (1898–1983): brother of Martin Niemöller; Confessing Church pastor and member of the Westphalian Council of Brethren—69, 94, 176, 191, 353, 265, 502, 575, 576, 578, 579

Niesel, Wilhelm (1903–88): Reformed theologian from Berlin, leading member of the Confessing Church of the Old Prussian Union; 1930, pastor, Wuppertal-Elberfeld and academic inspector at the preachers' seminary there; 1934–45, member of the Council of Brethren of the Old Prussian Union, responsible for seminary education; 1935, lecturer in systematic theology at the seminary in Berlin; arrested several times by the Gestapo; 1941, convicted in the collective trial against the examination board of the Old Prussian Union Council of Brethren; 1945–72, member of the advisory council of the Evangelical Church of Germany; 1946, pastor in Schöller and professor at the seminary in Wuppertal; 1946–73, president and moderator of the Reformed World Alliance; 1947–63, member of the executive committee of the World Council of Churches; 1964–70, president of the Reformed World Federation—247, 263, 422–24, 426, 436, 442–45, 575, 578

Mission Council (founded 1921); 1934–38, chair of the Research Commission of Life and Work (Universal Christian Council for Life and Work); 1939, editor of the Christian *News Letter;* 1942–47, head of the Christian Frontier Council—303, 310, 311, 398, 533, 537

Onnasch, Friedrich (1881–1945): father of Friedrich Onnasch (Fritz); 1922, pastor at St. Mary's and superintendent, Köslin; member of the Pomeranian Council of Brethren; from December 1937, Bonhoeffer's collective pastorate met in his home; September 1940, Reich prohibition against speaking in public (at the same time as Bonhoeffer) and travel restrictions for the province of Pomerania; February 17, 1945, shot to death by Russian soldiers in Berlinchen—33–35, 42, 71, 112, 243

Onnasch, Friedrich (Fritz) (1911–45): son of superintendent Friedrich Onnasch; 1935, participated in the first Zingst/Finkenwalde session; Confessing Church pastor, Stettin; 1937–39, academic inspector in Finkenwalde (until its closure in September 1937), then in the collective pastorate in Köslin; 1945, like his father, shot to death in Köslin by Russian soldiers—93, 100, 104, 110, 141, 149, 153, 235, 346, 354, 375, 377, 418, 691

Onnasch, Kurt (1917–42): brother of Fritz Onnasch; studied theology in Marburg; 1942, killed in action on the eastern front—377

Onnasch, Margret, née Bethge; sister of Eberhard Bethge; September 17, 1939, married Friedrich (Fritz) Onnasch; second marriage to Gottfried Grude, pastor in Magdeburg—94, 100, 104, 110, 149, 153, 154, 375, 376, 679, 691

Origen (ca. 185–254): Alexandrian biblical critic, exegete, theologian, and spiritual writer—567, 568

Orsenigo, Cesare (1873–1946): 1930–45, apostolic nuncio with the German Reich government in Berlin—146

Oster, Annie, née Hauer: secretary in Josef Müller's Munich law office; later married Hans Oster's son Achim—120, 652, 693

Oster, Hans (1887–1945): career military officer; 1929, major in the Sixth Division, Münster; winter 1932–33, discharged; from October 1933, civilian employee in the Military Intelligence Office; 1935, reactivated as a lieutenant colonel by Admiral Canaris; 1938, during the Fritsch affair, beginning of resistance contacts with Ludwig Beck, Hans von Dohnanyi, Bonhoeffer, and others; September 1938, chief of section Z (Central Section) in the Military Intelligence Office; December 1942, major general; April 16, 1943, dismissed from service after Hans von Dohnanyi's arrest and transferred to the Führer reserves; July 21, 1944, arrested; April 9, 1945, executed in Flossenbürg—11–14, 50, 72, 80, 89, 109, 120, 153, 299, 304, 395, 400, 406–9, 412, 415, 416, 418, 419, 426–30, 432–34, 438–42, 444–48, 452–54, 456, 457, 646–48, 650, 653, 664, 665, 676, 678, 681, 683–86, 692–95, 697, 700, 701, 703

Owen, David (Lord): prominent British Social Democrat politician—464

Pacelli, Eugenio: see Pius XII

Paissy: see Raikov, Alexander

Pangritz, Andreas: German professor of systematic theology; author of numerous publications on Bonhoeffer and Barth—670

Church membership; February 9, 1945, killed with a refugee transport on the torpedoed *Steuben*—152

Rabenau, Friedrich von (1884–1945): artillery general; 1939–43, head of the army archives; after July 20, 1944, arrested; April 12, 1945, executed in Flossenbürg—703

Rad, Gerhard von (1901–71): Old Testament scholar from Nuremburg; acquainted with Dietrich Bonhoeffer from their youth; 1934, professor of Old Testament, Jena; 1945, Göttingen; 1949, Heidelberg—83–85, 154, 679

Raffay, Sándor (1866–1947): Hungarian theologian and ecumenist; 1896, professor, Preßburg; 1908, pastor, Budapest; 1918, bishop of the Montan district; 1945, retired—398

Ragaz, Leonhard (1868–1945): Swiss professor of religion and social activist—542

Raikov, Alexander (1888–1973): Bulgarian Orthodox theologian and ecumenist; initially a lecturer at the theological seminary in Sofia; 1923, archimandrite ("Father Paissy") and suffragan bishop in the church administration; 1930, elected metropolitan of Vratsa; 1925, participated in the conference of Life and Work in Stockholm, 1930 at the Lambeth Conference, and in various other activities of the World Alliance for Promoting International Friendship through the Churches—398

Ramsey, Arthur Michael: British theologian; 1961, archbishop of Canterbury—506

Raphael (Raffaelo Santi) (1483–1529): Italian Renaissance painter—402

Rättig, Elfriede: senior employee in the MBK publishing house in Bad Salzuflen—186

Rau, Oskar Richard Arthur (1910–67): from Berlin-Charlottenburg; 1936–37, participated in the fourth Finkenwalde session; 1938, assistant pastor, Berlin-Charlottenburg; 1939, pastor, Reetz; 1942, Prädikow, district of Oberbarnim; 1945, Berlin-Spandau; 1965, retired—234

Reeves, Frederick: pastor of the Methodist church in Oxford—284

Reichwein, Adolf (1898–1944): educator; participated as a personal adviser on pedagogical reform to the Reich minister of culture; 1930, professor, pedagogical college, Halle; after 1933, dismissed and employed as a village schoolteacher; July 4, 1944, arrested as a member of the Kreisau circle; October 20, 1944, executed—699

Reimer, Karl-Heinrich (1904–90): from 1930, pastor in Naseband, district of Belgard/Pomerania; Confessing Church member—157, 211, 213, 247, 249, 687

Reitzenstein, Franz Baron von: Catholic journalist in Rome—146

Rendtorff, Heinrich (1888–1960): 1926, professor of practical theology and New Testament, Kiel; 1930–33, bishop of Mecklenburg-Schwerin and honorary professor, Rostock; 1934, dismissed from office; 1934–45, pastor, Stettin-Braunsfelde; 1934, member of the Pomeranian Council of Brethren; 1945, professor, Kiel; 1956, retired—51, 646

Rhode, Kurt (1908–42): Confessing Church theologian from Pomerania; 1935–36, participated in the second Finkenwalde session; pastor, Treblin, Pomerania; 1942, killed in action on the eastern front—377

Thurneysen, Eduard (1888–1977): Swiss Reformed theologian; 1914, pastor, Leutwil; 1920–27, in Bruggen near St. Gallen; 1927, at the Basel cathedral; 1927, private lecturer, then 1939, professor of practical theology, Basel; since 1913, friend of Karl Barth; coeditor of *Zwischen den Zeiten,* then of *Theologische Existenz heute*—191, 222, 233, 279–81, 286, 287

Tielsch, Dr.: presumably the family doctor of the Kleist-Retzow family in Kieckow; not otherwise identified—247

Tilitzki, Christian: author of work on legal philosophy during Weimar era—62, 71

Tödt, Ilse (b. 1930): German scholar of anthropology and indigenous religion; since 1961, at the Protestant Institute for Interdisciplinary Research (FEST), Heidelberg; editor of many volumes of the *Dietrich Bonhoeffer Werke,* including *DBW* 6; since 1992, member of the *DBW* editorial board—361, 584

Toureille, Pierre C. (1900–1976): French Reformed pastor, theologian, and ecumenist; 1931–39, with Bonhoeffer, one of the youth secretaries of the World Alliance for Promoting International Friendship through the Churches (for Romance Europe, Poland, and Czechoslovakia); participated in numerous ecumenical conferences; 1940, appointed to lead ministry to Protestant foreign refugees in France and North Africa; member of the resistance in France and in Czechoslovakia; 1945, foreign pastor, Breslau; 1947, doctorate, Breslau, pastor and lecturer, United States; 1955, missionary in the Belgian Congo; 1966–74, European secretary of the Leprosy Mission in Morges (Switzerland)—398

Toynbee, Arnold Joseph (1886–1975): British historian and historical philosopher; professor, London University; director of studies, Royal Institute of International Affairs (Chatham House); 1939, director of the Foreign Research and Press Service; 1943, responsible for merging the latter with the Political Intelligence Department (PID) in the form of the Foreign Office Research Department (FORD); also a member of the English Peace Aims Groups founded by William Paton in 1940—337

Trebesius, Hulda (1907–80): from Halle; 1934, member of the Brotherhood of Assistant Pastors and Vicars of the Province of Saxony, Confessing Church; 1936, ordination in the provincial Saxon Confessing Church; commissioned with church women's groups; 1940, compulsory national service labor in a factory; 1948, pastor, Uchtspringe; 1972, retired—127, 129

Treitschke, Heinrich von (1834–96): German historian, known for his nationalism, anti-Semitism, and glorification of war—507

Tresckow, Henning von (1901–44): nephew of Ruth von Kleist-Retzow; career military officer; 1941, major general in the staff of the Army Group Center; 1943, chief of staff of the Second Army; heavily involved in the military resistance movement; July 21, 1944, committed suicide after the failed assassination attempt against Hitler—210, 662

Troeltsch, Ernst (1865–1923): German Protestant theologian, philosopher, and historian—509, 541, 542, 544

Trott zu Solz, Adam von (1909–44): German diplomat; 1931–33, Rhodes scholar

INDEX OF SUBJECTS

Editors and Translators

Mark S. Brocker (Ph.D., University of Chicago Divinity School) is lead pastor of St. Andrew Lutheran Church in Beaverton, Oregon. In addition to serving as pastor of churches in Tacoma, Washington, McMinnville, Oregon, and in Illinois, he has served on several synod councils of the Evangelical Lutheran Church of North America. He has taught courses on Bonhoeffer, theology, and ethics at Northwest House of Theological Studies in Salem, Oregon, and at Pacific Lutheran Theological Seminary in Berkeley, California. His dissertation is titled "The Community of God, Jesus Christ, and Responsibility: The Responsible Person and the Responsible Community in the Ethics of Dietrich Bonhoeffer." He was one of the founding members of the editorial board of the *Dietrich Bonhoeffer Works*, English edition.

Lisa E. Dahill (Ph.D., Graduate Theological Union) is assistant professor of worship and Christian spirituality at Trinity Lutheran Seminary, Columbus, Ohio. She is cochair of the Bonhoeffer: Theology and Social Analysis Group of the American Academy of Religion and was a member of the Carnegie Foundation team that wrote *Educating Clergy: Teaching Practices and Pastoral Imagination* (Jossey-Bass, 2005). Her scholarly interests include Bonhoeffer's spirituality, discernment, Lutheran hymnody, and the spiritual formation of clergy. She recently published *Truly Present: Practicing Prayer in the Liturgy* (Augsburg Fortress Worship Matters Series, 2005).

Wayne Whitson Floyd Jr. (Ph.D., Emory University) served from 1993 to 2004 as general editor and project director of the *Dietrich Bonhoeffer Works*, English edition. He is now the director of the Center for Christian Formation at the Cathedral College of Washington National Cathedral, Washington, D.C. Previously he was canon theologian and director of the Anglican Center for Theology and Spirituality in the Episcopal Diocese of Southern Virginia; visiting professor and director of the Dietrich Bonhoeffer Center at the

Lutheran Theological Seminary in Philadelphia; full-time visiting faculty member of the religion department of Dickinson College; canon theologian for the Episcopal Cathedral of St. Stephen in Harrisburg, Pennsylvania; dean of the School of Christian Studies of the Episcopal Diocese of Central Pennsylvania; and a faculty member of St. Luke's School of Theology (Sewanee) of the University of the South. He is the author of *The Wisdom and Witness of Dietrich Bonhoeffer* (Fortress Press, 2000) and *Theology and the Dialectics of Otherness: On Reading Bonhoeffer and Adorno* (University Press of America, 1988); he coauthored the *Bonhoeffer Bibliography: Primary Sources and Secondary Literature in English* (American Theological Library Association, 1992); and he coedited *Theology and the Practice of Responsibility: Essays on Dietrich Bonhoeffer* (Trinity Press International, 1995). His articles on Bonhoeffer have appeared in *Union Seminary Quarterly Review, The Lutheran, Modern Theology, Religious Studies Review, Dialog, The Christian Century,* and numerous anthologies.

Douglas W. Stott (Ph.D., Northwestern University) is a freelance editor and translator in Atlanta. A graduate of Davidson College, Northwestern University, and Emory's Candler School of Theology (M.T.S.), he also studied in Germany at the Philipps University in Marburg and at the University of Stuttgart. He held a teaching position at Davidson College in North Carolina, including serving as director of the year-abroad program and self-instructional language program. He is the translator of several volumes of the *Theological Dictionary of the Old Testament* and the *Exegetical Dictionary of the New Testament;* commentaries on Leviticus and Amos for the Old Testament Library; *DBWE* 10, *Barcelona, Berlin, New York: 1928–1931* (forthcoming) and *DBWE* 14, *Theological Education at Finkenwalde: 1935–1937* (forthcoming); F. W. J. Schelling's *Philosophy of Art;* and numerous theological works and scholarly articles by Claus Westermann, Jürgen Moltmann, Otto Kaiser, Dorothée Sölle, Wolfhart Pannenberg, Walther Zimmerli, and others.